The Middle East and North Africa in World Politics

A Documentary Record

The Middle East and North Africa in World Politics
A Documentary Record

Volume 1 European Expansion, 1535–1914
Volume 2 British-French Supremacy, 1914–1945
Volume 3 British-French Withdrawal and Soviet-American Rivalry, 1945–1975

Related Work:

Islamic Russia in World Politics: The Caucasus and Central Asia
A Documentary Record

Compiled and Edited by J. C. Hurewitz and Oles M. Smolansky

THE MIDDLE EAST AND NORTH AFRICA IN WORLD POLITICS

A DOCUMENTARY RECORD

Second Edition, Revised and Enlarged

Volume 1 European Expansion, 1535-1914

Compiled, Translated, and Edited by

J. C. Hurewitz

New Haven and London, Yale University Press, 1975

Copyright © 1956, 1975 by J. C. Hurewitz
First edition published July 1956 by D. Van Nostrand Company, Inc.,
under the title *Diplomacy in the Near and Middle East*
Reprinted March 1958
Reprinted 1972 by Octagon Books

Library of Congress catalog card number: 74-83525
International standard book number: 0-300-01294-2

Designed by John O. C. McCrillis
and set in Times Roman type.
Printed in the United States of America by
The Murray Printing Co., Forge Village, Massachusetts.

Published in Great Britain, Europe, and Africa by
Yale University Press, Ltd., London.
Distributed in Latin America by Kaiman & Polon,
Inc., New York City; in Australasia and Southeast
Asia by John Wiley & Sons Australasia Pty. Ltd.,
Sydney; in India by UBS Publishers' Distributors Pvt.,
Ltd., Delhi; in Japan by John Weatherhill, Inc., Tokyo.

FOR BARBARA

whose interest in the Middle East

has grown over the years

Contents

Doc. No.

Doc. No.

Doc. No.

Doc. No.

Doc. No.

Preface

The first edition of this work, which appeared in two volumes under the title *Diplomacy in the Near and Middle East,* encompassed non-Soviet southwest Asia to the eastern frontiers of Iran plus Egypt and Sudan in adjacent northeast Africa. The present edition adds the rest of North Africa and Afghanistan and will consist of three volumes, taking into account the international and regional realities that preceded and followed the pervasive Western European imperial presence. Had my concern been primarily cultural, I should also have treated the Caucasus and Central Asia. Since these two regions are still integrated into the Russian Empire, they require separate consideration, and I plan to include them eventually in a related volume.

Before the nineteenth century the Ottoman Empire embraced much of what is today labeled the Middle East and North Africa, with the exception chiefly of Morocco in the west and Persia and Afghanistan in the east. Although the Barbary Garrisons of North Africa—as the provinces of Tripoli, Tunis, and Algiers were known—became quasi-sovereign in the seventeenth and eighteenth centuries, they nevertheless did not sever their ties to the Sublime Porte. The wider compass of the present edition is designed, among other purposes, to encourage the comparative study of international and regional politics and their interplay in an historical context. It also conforms to the evolving internal and external perceptions of the region. In dealing with it, the concerned outside powers are commonly motivated by comprehensive strategic, political, and economic interests. Of greater significance, all the countries of North Africa and most of those of the Middle East are Arab and view themselves as belonging to a regional community of states. Indeed, as each has won its independence after World War II, it has joined the Arab League, created in 1945 to coordinate the members' foreign policies. The Arab states, moreover, form part of a bigger yet more deeply fractured Islamic world. This edition should provide an opportunity for scholars to redirect their customary focus from segments of an area that comprises contiguous Islamic sovereignties—with Cyprus, Israel, and Lebanon as the exceptions—to the area as a whole.

The materials on North Africa and on Afghanistan, representing a third of the total, are entirely new. Almost all the documents in the first edition have been retained. The notable exception, largely because of length, is Curzon's 1899 analysis of British policy and interests in Persia and the Persian Gulf. On the original area there are a number of new entries, most of them appearing in print or in English translation or both for the first time. These include: the secret articles of the treaty of Küçük Kaynarca (1774); the Russian-Ottoman convention at al-'Arish for the evacuation of French troops from Egypt (1800); the authentic text of the renewed Russian-Ottoman secret treaty of defensive alliance (1805); the Ottoman and British reports on the severance of British-Ottoman diplomatic relations (1807); the Russian-Ottoman treaty of peace at Bucharest (1812); the Nesselrode interpretation in 1838 of the treaty of Hünkâr İskelesi (1833); the Reuter and Falkenhagen draft railroad concessions in Persia (1872, 1874); the Reuter concession for the Imperial Bank of Persia (1889); the statement of British policy on Persia (1902); the problem of Russia, Constantinople, and the Straits as assessed by the British Committee of Imperial Defense (1903); and the British-Ottoman exchange of notes and agreement on an administrative separating line, confirming the continued attachment of Sinai to Egypt (1906). Furthermore, the Hatt-ı Şerif of Gülhane (1839) has been freshly translated from the Turkish. The introductory comments on many documents have been modified to reflect the findings of new research completed after the appearance of the first edition.

The history of international politics in the Middle East and North Africa in modern times is essentially concerned with the rise and fall of Western European imperialism in the region and with the regional effects of this rise and fall. The subject might seem, at first sight, to be one that has been more amply examined than most others. But such appearances are deceiving. The state of the discipline is deplorable, even a quarter century after the start in the United States of area studies on the Islamic world. Still, the condition is understandable, in view of the research concentration of area specialists on the region's internal political, social, and economic transformation. Far less systematic research attention, relatively, has been paid to intellectual and cultural developments, and least of all to the interplay of international, regional, and domestic politics in its historical setting.

The literature on the diplomatic history of the Middle East and North Africa is massive, but many of the works may be classified as special pleading, commonly in the form of memoirs and biographies. But even the worthwhile monographs relate mainly to particular international disputes and problems. There is no recent inclusive, systematic study by an area expert with an interest in international politics. The present edition, like the first, remains experimental. It is not, and I do not claim it to be, an exhaustive collection. In preparing the work, I have favored the selection of those documents that would provide insights into cross-regional comparisons of international issues, modes of dealing with them, and the creation of durable arrangements for their management.

One such theme is the evolution of the capitulatory regimes in the Ottoman Empire, Persia, and Morocco, the differences among them, and the uses to which the concerned extraregional powers put them. The capitulations received a great deal of scholarly attention in the nineteenth century and the first quarter of the twentieth; but this was overwhelmingly legal inquiry, with little or no reference to the social, economic, and political contexts. Even more neglectful than the international lawyers have been the economic historians; the transformation of European commerce with the Middle East and North Africa from the monopolistic practices of a mercantilist world to the free trade of an industrializing Europe and finally to the protectionism of rival expanding European empires has been given little more than spasmodic attention. The interaction of the European privateers and the Barbary corsairs in the sixteenth and seventeenth centuries and the later encouragement of North African piracy by the maritime powers until its suppression after the Napoleonic wars seems so far to have attracted more popularizers than social scientists. While not strictly an international issue, continuous unilateral European diplomacy in the Middle East and North Africa placed the regional states at a growing disadvantage. The origins and development of this practice and the progressive adoption of diplomatic reciprocity with Europe in the nineteenth century by the surviving sovereign and semisovereign Islamic states still await monographic investigation.

The time has come also for a fresh interpretation of the imperial competition preceding and attending the European expansion into the Middle East and North Africa, the contrasting imperial styles, and the lingering ambiguities arising in those cases in which the imperial powers did not annex the territories outright, as Britain in Egypt and the Persian Gulf, and France in Tunisia and Morocco. In particular, Britain's sustained imperial rivalry in the nineteenth and early twentieth centuries with France along the southern and eastern coasts of the Mediterranean and with Russia along the tsarist southward-moving frontier goes begging for systematic treatment. So, too, does a comparison of the internationalization of the Ottoman and Moroccan questions by European conference diplomacy between 1840 and 1880 and the later undoing of the multilateral arrangements, as the interested imperial powers sought to compose their differences through meshing bilateral agreements. Systematic evaluation of the European imposition on the Islamic states of such an alien concept as territorial sovereignty and the fixed boundaries that it entailed between the *dar al-islam* and the *dar al-harb* and even within the dar al-islam itself would help clarify many present as well as past interstate disputes in the Middle East and North Africa. No less timely would be a comparative study of the interplay of world, regional, and domestic politics in the internationalization of strategic waterways—the Turkish Straits and the Suez Canal—and the plan for the internationalization of Tangier on the southern bank of the Straits of Gibraltar. The documents in the present volume inform all these themes, as they do also the European scramble, starting early in the seventeenth century, for such concessions as pearl fisheries, river navigation, telegraphs, banks, railroads, and oil.

In a book of this complexity which draws upon materials on a region that today includes more than a score of independent states, among which four official languages (Arabic, Turkish, Persian, and Hebrew) are used and to these the interested extra-regional powers add five others (English, French, German, Russian, and Spanish), there are bound to be problems with transliteration from the regional and European languages into English. Inconsistencies are inescapable, since I have used translated documents wherever available in reasonably clear English. In my own translations and in the introductory comments I have tried to apply uniform rules of transliteration. North Africa, however, gave me special trouble because of the widespread acceptance of French transliterations. In a number of early translations and in the introductory comments prepared at about the same time, I did aim at standardizing the spelling of place and personal names by applying to the Arab West the rules I followed for such names in the Arab East, a practice I abandoned once I found it impossible to locate in every instance the original Arabic spelling for authentication. In transliterations from the Arabic and the Hebrew, the only diacritical mark retained is that for the letter *'ayn* (Arabic) and *'ayin* (Hebrew), which have no English equivalent. This letter is commonly rendered into English by an inverted apostrophe ('). The same word with the same meaning may be spelled differently in Arabic, Persian, and Turkish. For example, *firman,* the Arabic for "decree," becomes *farman* in Persian and *ferman* in Turkish; *dawlah,* the Arabic for "state," becomes *dawlat* in Persian and *devlet* in Turkish.

The introductory comments are not intended to tell the story in elaborate detail. They merely sketch the importance of each document, call attention at times to related papers that were not reproduced, and suggest books and articles to which the reader may turn for further guidance. The bibliographical entries are limited to works in English and Western European languages. They include monographs and general literature and, less frequently, articles in scholarly journals. On first mention in the earlier edition I provided complete title references to the pertinent literature. In this work, where full entries are listed in a detailed bibliography, only the author's last name and a short title are used, except in instances where the bibliography contains works by two or more authors with the same last name or where I furnish the author's first initial for the reader's convenience.

Many English translations selected for this volume were prepared by the Foreign Office in London or the Department of State in Washington and are reference or working but not official translations. With few exceptions documents have been reproduced in full, omitting only preambles, ratification clauses, signatures, and sections on geographic districts outside the Middle East and North Africa. In some cases (e.g., Docs. 52 and 68), because they possessed an historical value of their own, I have reproduced secret clauses that the signatories dropped in the ratification exchange. Ellipsis marks indicate excisions in the body of documents but are not always used at the beginning and the end to signify omission of preambles, ratification provisions, and signatures.

In introductory notes and in documents that I translated, foreign words with initial capitals are never italicized. Lowercase foreign words are italicized on first mention in each document but not thereafter. In documents reproducing English texts I have not tampered with capitalization or with transliteration or obvious grammatical and punctuation errors in the original instruments. I have, however, always shortened "article" to "art." when it is employed as a title, and in rare instances I have replaced the accompanying written numerals with Arabic numerals. To save space, I have omitted redundant titles in a few places (such as Docs. 61 and 150) from articles of treaties and other instruments, but only after ascertaining that the sense of the original was not in the least impaired. Hyphenated dates are used for Russian documents, since the tsarist regime stuck to the Julian or old-style calendar. To assist the reader, the Russian and the Western (Gregorian or new-style) dates (e.g., 7/18 September 1739 or 23 December 1798/3 January 1799) are mentioned. When cross-references call the reader's attention to other instruments, only the document number is given.

J.C.H.

Columbia University
29 November 1974

Acknowledgments

In the preparation of the present work I have become greatly indebted to many foundations, persons, and institutions. Preeminent among my sponsors has been the Ford Foundation. From it I received a travel grant for research at the Public Record Office and the India Office Library and Records in London and, indirectly, secretarial and other support through the School of International Affairs and the Middle East Institute at Columbia University under their grants from the foundation for the encouragement of research in international affairs. This project has also benefited from earlier fellowships: from the Guggenheim Foundation, which enabled me to collect source materials in Istanbul, Cairo, Tehran, London, and Paris; from the Rockefeller Foundation, which furnished me the opportunity to use these materials for analyzing the evolution of Ottoman diplomatic practice and for an assessment of Russia and the Turkish Straits; and from the Center for Advanced Study in the Behavioral Sciences in Stanford, California, which provided me a year's release from academic responsibilities to enlarge my geographic concerns to include North Africa, Afghanistan, the Caucasus, and Central Asia.

For unfailing encouragement in the execution of this project, I am especially grateful to Andrew W. Cordier, former director of the School of International Affairs of Columbia University, and the late Philip E. Mosely, former associate dean of international affairs, and to Charles P. Issawi and John S. Badeau, former directors of the Middle East Institute at Columbia. To Halil Inalcik I owe special thanks for generous help in the translation of documents 49 and 83 and for recurrent advice on Ottoman history, and to Cengis Orhanlu for invaluable assistance in the search for pertinent documents at the Turkish State Archives in Istanbul. I am obligated for counsel and other favors to Ahmad Abu Hakima, Alexandre Bennigsen, Noel Blakiston, L. Carl Brown, Hélène Carrère d'Encausse, Harold W. Glidden, Frank Ralph Golino, John B. Kelly, Ercümend Kuran, Roger Le Tourneau, Bernard Lewis, Henry Allen Moe, Thomas A. Naff, Robert O. Paxton, Shabtai Rosenne, Stanford J. Shaw, Thomas D. Scott, Ralph W. Tyler, and Wayne A. Wilcox.

For assistance with the assessment of materials on North Africa, I wish to thank Joan E. Spero. Sylvia Kowitt Crosbie, Oles M. Smolansky, and Joan C. Wilson were particularly helpful with translations; Miss Wilson also bore the brunt of the typing and retyping of the comments, the translations, and the bibliography, always in good cheer and with meticulous care. I am most appreciative to Warren J. Haas, the university librarian at Columbia, for allowing me special borrowing privileges in connection with the project and to Marc Brandriss, Shahram Chubin, Robert Mortimer, and Peter Todd for the leg work at the libraries and the attendant photocopying.

Jeffrey R. Ede, the keeper of the Public Record Office in London, and Stanley C. Sutton, the former director, and Joan C. Lancaster, the present director of the India Office Library and Records in the same city, and their staffs have laid me deeply in their debt for many courtesies, especially in the search for elusive materials. Materials in this volume from the Public Record Office (Docs. 49, 52, 73, 97, 121, 124, 126, 128, 140, 155, and 161), from the India Office Library and Records (Docs. 53, 66, 89, 102, 109, and 131), and from Her Majesty's Stationery Office publications (Docs. 11, 14, 16, 20, 21, 27, 29, 32, 45, 58, 61, 63, 72, 80–82, 84–88, 94, 97, 100, 105–07, 111–12, 114, 116, 124, 127–30, 132–33, 135, 137, 143–44, 146–48, 150, 155, 160, 162–64, 169–70, and 182–83) appear by permission of the Controller of Her Majesty's Stationery Office.

The quality of this work was substantially enhanced by Deborah E. Bell's efficient supervision of the concerned members of the staff and her management of the accounts, by Elizabeth W. Kodama's superlative copy editing, and by Marian N. Ash's persistent support of the project at the Yale University Press. To Herbert Johnson I am most grateful for brilliant advice on redesigning the revised edition, so as to make the comments and the documents more readable and to give a long book the appearance of a shorter one.

In a work of revision, an author remains indebted to all persons and institutions contributing to the preparation of the first edition. Much of the worth of this work, in its revision as in the first edition, I owe to them, even though their names are not repeated here, and to the many others whom I may have failed to mention then or now. The deficiencies are wholly my own.

1. DRAFT TREATY OF AMITY AND COMMERCE: THE OTTOMAN EMPIRE AND FRANCE
February 1535

[U.S., 67th Cong., 1st sess., Senate, doc. 34, pp. 94–96]

Continuous reciprocal diplomacy, an invention of Europe, traced back to the Italian city-states of the fifteenth century. The practice spread through the Continent in the sixteenth century and came of age with the peace of Westphalia in 1648. Until the nineteenth century, official European dealings with the Middle East were based on a form of unilateralism under which the concerned European states accredited permanent diplomatic or consular missions to sovereign and quasi-sovereign Islamic states which did not seek reciprocity, since their commerce with Europe was conducted almost wholly at home. For the handling of special problems, most commonly the negotiation of armistice or peace, the Islamic rulers sent ad hoc embassies to Europe. The Ottoman Empire, which became the first Muslim state to experiment with reciprocity, did not do so until the close of the eighteenth century; it was not until the mid-1830s that it created viable diplomatic machinery for resident missions abroad. Thereafter, other sovereign and quasi-sovereign Muslim states progressively adopted the practice. The most highly developed system of unilateral continuous diplomacy came into being in the Ottoman Empire, which began receiving permanent missions from Europe almost from the very start of the institution. In part this was attributable to the power, influence, and stability of the Ottoman state, which embraced a solid chunk of the Continent and therefore could not be ignored by the rising national states of Europe. In part, also, it was attributable to the durability of the Ottoman dynasty, for treaty commitments made to the European states became cumulative. This applied in particular to the capitulations, a class of commercial treaties which Western powers concluded with Middle East and Asian states and under which Western nationals enjoyed extraterritorial privileges. European residents were thus subject to the laws of home governments and immune from those of host governments. In the sixteenth century Ottoman merchants imported from south and east Asia spices, jewels, silks, and other wares for which the European demand was brisk. But apparently they made little, if any, effort to organize trade within Europe itself. European merchants instead came to Ottoman commercial centers in the eastern Mediterranean to purchase these items as well as goods originating in the Ottoman Empire, exporting them to Europe in European vessels. In treaties with European powers even as early as the sixteenth century, the sultans acquired elements of reciprocity, but the correspondent benefits related to other than exterritorial rights for Ottoman subjects. Despite Ottoman efforts to eliminate the marked inequality, after the mid-nineteenth century—following the progressive adoption of European legal codes—the capitulations continued to govern commercial relations between the empire and Western countries until the abrogation of the treaties by the Ottoman government on 1 October 1914. In 1352, at the time of the initial Ottoman conquest of territory on the Continent, the sultan granted a capitulation to Genoa, the first European power to obtain such privileges. As Ottoman possessions in Europe later expanded, Venice and Florence received comparable rights. France was the first of the maritime states of Western Europe to seek capitulatory privileges from the Otto-man Empire. Sultan Süleyman I (1520–66) never confirmed the following draft instrument, sometimes dated 1536 by retrospective application of the Gregorian calendar, since February was the penultimate month of the year in the prevailing Julian calendar. The Ottoman negotiator, Grand Vezir Ibrahim Paşa, was executed in mid-March 1535 for reasons unrelated to the commercial negotiations with France. The unratified instrument is nevertheless valuable because it reveals the scope of the privileges that France sought in its commerce with the expanding Islamic state. It should be noted that France was prepared to grant (art. 15) "In the dominions of the King reciprocal rights . . . to the subjects of the Grand Signior." Süleyman, who had reconfirmed pre-Ottoman French capitulatory privileges in Egypt, later permitted France to enjoy these privileges in his entire empire. France had to wait until 18 October 1569, however, for its first negotiated capitulation from the Ottoman govern-ment (French text in de Testa, *Recueil des traités*, 1: 91–96). Until the instrument of 28 May 1740, which Sultan Mahmud I (1730–54) granted in perpetuity in gratitude for the fruitful mediation of the French ambassador, the Marquis de Villeneuve, at Belgrade in the summer of 1739 (Doc. 24), the capitulations were renewable and renewed (July 1581, February 1597, 20 May 1604, and 5 June 1673) upon the accession of new sultans. Hurewitz, "Ottoman Diplomacy and the European State System"; Inalcik, "The Ottoman Empire," in Wansbrough et al., "Imtiyazat," EI², 3: 1179–89; Wansbrough, "Safe Conduct in Muslim Chauncery Practice"; Lewis, "Elçi" EI², 2: 694; Khadduri and Liebesny, *Law in the Middle East*, vol. 1, chap. 13 (Liebesny); Sousa, *Capitulatory Regime of Turkey*; Mears, *Modern Turkey*, chap. 19 (written by G.B. Ravndal); P. Brown, *Foreigners in Turkey*; Charrière, *Négociations de la France dans le Levant*, vol. 1; Pélissié du Raussas, *Le régime des capitulations dans l'empire ottoman*, vol. 1; Noradounghian, *Recueil d'actes internationaux de l'empire ottoman*; Hauterive and Cussy, *Recueil des traités de commerce de la France*, pt. 1, 2: 424–529 (texts of French capitulations); Zeller, "Une légende qui a la vie dure"; Saint-Priest, *Mémoires sur l'ambassade de France en Turquie*, pp. 179–268, 345–537 (biographical sketches of French ambassadors to the Ottoman Empire between 1535 and 1792 and French capitulations); on French trade with the Ottoman Empire, which in this period the Chamber of Commerce of Marseille conducted as a monopoly, see Masson, *Histoire du commerce français dans le Levant au XVIIᵉ siècle* and *Histoire du commerce français dans le Levant au XVIIIᵉ siècle;* Charles-Roux, *Les échelles de Syrie et de Palestine.*

Be it known to everybody that in the year of Jesus Christ one thousand five hundred and thirty-five, in the month of February, and of Mohammed 941, in the moon of Chaban, Sire Jean de la Forest, privy coun-cilor, and ambassador of the most excellent and most powerful prince Francis, by the grace of God most Christian King of France, accredited to the most powerful and invincible Grand Signior, Sultan Sulei-man, Emperor of the Turks, and having

discussed with the powerful and magnifi-cent Signior Ibrahim, Serasker of the Sul-tan, the calamities and disadvantages which are caused by war, and, on the other hand, the good, quiet, and tranquillity derived from peace; and knowing how good it is to prefer the one (peace) to the other (war), each of them guaranteeing the above-men-tioned monarchs, their superiors, they have negotiated and agreed upon the following chapters and conventions in the name and on the honor of the said monarchies which are the protectors of their component States and the benefactors of their subjects:

I. They have negotiated, made, and concluded a valid and sure peace and sincere concord in the name of the above Grand Signior and King of France during their lives and for the kingdoms, dominions, provinces, castles, cities, ports, harbors, seas, islands, and all other places they hold and possess at present or may possess in the future, so that all subjects and tributaries of said sovereigns who wish may freely and safely, with their belongings and men, navigate on armed or unarmed ships, travel on land, reside, remain in and return to the ports, cities, and all other places in their respective countries for their trade, and the like shall be done for their merchandise.

II. Likewise, the said subjects and tributaries of the said monarchs shall, respectively be able to buy, sell, exchange, move, and transport by sea and land from one country to the other all kinds of merchandise not prohibited, by paying only the ordinary customs and ancient dues and taxes, to wit, the Turks, in the dominions of the King, shall pay the same as Frenchmen, and the said Frenchmen in the dominions of the Grand Signior shall pay the same as the Turks, without being obliged to pay any other new tribute, impost, or storage due.

III. Likewise, whenever the King shall send to Constantinople or Pera or other places of this Empire a bailiff—just as at present he has a consul at Alexandria—the said bailiff and consul shall be received and maintained in proper authority so that each one of them may in his locality, and without being hindered by any judge, cadi, soubashi, or other, according to his faith and law, hear, judge, and determine all causes, suits, and differences, both civil and criminal, which might arise between merchants and other subjects of the King. Only in case the orders of the said bailiffs and consuls should not be obeyed and that in order to have them executed they should appeal to the soubashi or other officer of the Grand Signior, the said soubashis or other officers shall lend them the necessary aid and compulsory power. But the cadi or other officers of the Grand Signior may not try any difference between the merchants and subjects of the King, even if the said merchants should request it, and if perchance the said cadis should hear a case their judgment shall be null and void.

IV. Likewise, in a civil case against Turks, tributaries, or other subjects of the Grand Signior, the merchants and subjects of the King can not be summoned, molested, or tried unless the said Turks, tributaries, and subjects of the Grand Signior produce a writing from the hand of the opponent, or a "heudjet" (document) from the cadi, bailiff, or consul, outside of which writing or heudjet no other testimony of a Turk, tributary, or other person shall be valid nor received in any part of the States and dominions of the Grand Signior, and the cadis, soubashis, or other persons may not hear or try the said subjects of the King without the presence of their dragoman.

V. Likewise, in criminal cases the said merchants and other subjects of the King may not be called before the cadi or other officers of the Grand Signior by Turks, tributaries, or others, and said cadis may not try them, but must immediately refer them to the Sublime Porte (the official residence of the Grand Vizier) and in the absence of the Porte, to the principal lieutenant of the Grand Signior, where the testimony of the subject of the King and of the tributary of the Grand Signior shall be valid one against the other.

VI. Likewise, as regards religion, it has been expressly promised, concluded, and agreed that the said merchants, their agents, and servants, and all other subjects of the King shall never be molested nor tried by the cadis, sandjak-beys, or soubashis, or any person but the Sublime Porte only, and they can not be made or regarded as Turks (Mohammedans) unless they themselves desire it and profess it openly and without violence. They shall have the right to practice their own religion.

VII. Likewise, when one or more subjects of the King, having made a contract with a subject of the Grand Signior, taken merchandise, or incurred debts, afterwards depart from the State of the Grand Signior without giving satisfaction, [neither] the bailiff, consul, relatives, factor, nor any other subject of the King shall for this reason be in any way coerced or molested, nor shall the King be held responsible. Only His Majesty shall cause full justice to be done to the plaintiff as regards the person and goods of the debtor if they be found within his Kingdom and dominions.

VIII. Likewise, the said merchants, their agents, and servants, and other subjects of the King, their ships, boats, or other equipments, artillery, ammunition, and mariners shall not be seized, coerced, or used by the Grand Signior or other person against their pleasure and desire for any service or duty either on sea or land.

IX. Likewise, all merchants and subjects of the King in all parts of the Empire of the Grand Signior shall be allowed to freely dispose of their property by testament, and having died either a natural or violent death, all their effects—money as well as other goods—shall be distributed according to the testament; if they die intestate, the effects shall be turned over to the heir or his representative by and with the authority of the bailiff or consul at places where there may be one or the other, and where there is neither bailiff nor consul the said effects shall be protected by the cadi of the locality under authority of the Grand Signior, having first of all made an inventory in the presence of witnesses; but where said bailiff or consul are present no cadi, beitulmaldji, or other person shall take possession of the effects, and if they should be in the hands of one of them and the bailiff or consul should demand them [here a line is apparently missing in the text] they must at once and without contradiction be entirely turned over to the said bailiff or consul or their representative, to be later handed to whom they belong.

X. Likewise as soon as the present treaty shall have been ratified by the Grand Signior and the King, all persons and subjects shall be set free and liberated who may, respectively, be bought slaves, prisoners of war, or otherwise detained, both in the hands of the said sovereigns or of their subjects, galleys, ships, and all other places and countries owing allegiance to the said sovereigns, on the demand and statement of the ambassador, bailiff, or consul of the King, or persons delegated by them; and if any of the said slaves should have changed his faith and religion he shall nevertheless be free. And, especially, henceforth reciprocal-ly neither the Grand Signior nor the King, their captains, soldiers, tributary subjects, or mercenaries, shall or may in any manner, on sea or land, take, buy, sell, or detain as a slave any prisoner of war. But if a pirate or other person of the country of one of the said sovereigns should attempt to capture or destroy the goods or persons owing allegiance to the other sovereign, the sovereign of the country where the malefactor is found must and should be obliged to punish him as a disturber of the peace and to make an example to others, and also to return to the injured party whatever may be found to have been taken from him by the malefactor. If the said malefactor should escape without being caught and punished at once, he shall be banished from his country with his accomplices, and all their goods shall be confiscated by the sovereign, who shall also cause the malefactor and his companions to be punished if they should ever be in his power; and out of the said confiscation shall be paid the damages, and the injured party shall to that end have recourse to the protectors of the present peace, who shall be the Serasker on the part of the Sultan, and the "grand-maître" of France on the part of the King.

XI. Likewise when the navies of the said Grand Signior and King, respectively, meet vessels of the subjects of the other, they shall be obliged to lower the sails and hoist the flags of their ruler, in order to be recognized thereby and not be detained or otherwise molested by said navy or any unit thereof; but if any wrong or damage be inflicted upon them, the ruler to whom the navy belongs shall be obliged to make immediate reparation. When private ships of the subjects of said rulers meet they shall each hoist the flag of its ruler, salute each other by firing one gun, and reply truthfully when asked who they are. But after having spoken and recognized each other one shall not forcibly enter or visit the other, nor hinder it under any pretext whatsoever.

XII. Likewise when a vessel belonging to subjects of the King arrives, by accident or otherwise, in the ports or on the coasts of the Grand Signior, it shall receive food and other necessaries against a reasonable payment, without being obliged to discharge and pay duties, and it shall be allowed to go wherever it pleases; and having come to

Constantinople, it shall be ready to leave after having obtained and paid for the heudjet (permit) of the emin (official), and having been searched and visited by the said emin, they must not be visited at any other place, except the castles of the straits of Gallipoli, without, however, paying anything there or elsewhere, in the name of the Grand Signior or his officers, for the departure.

XIII. Likewise if any ship belonging to the subjects of one of the said sovereigns should, by accident or otherwise, suffer shipwreck within the dominions and the jurisdiction of the other sovereign all persons escaping from such danger shall remain free and be allowed to collect all their belongings; if all should have died in the shipwreck the goods which shall have been saved shall be consigned to the said bailiff, or consul, or their representative, to be returned to whom they may belong; and the captain gerneral of the sea, the sandjak-bey, soubashi, cadi, or other officer or subject of the Grand Signior shall not, under penalty of punishment, take or claim anything, and they must give facilities and assistance to those who shall be charged with the recovery of the goods.

XIV. Likewise if a subject of the Grand Signior should lose a slave who has escaped, such subject, claiming that the slave had lived and served on a ship or in a house of a subject of the King, can not force the subject of the King to do anything but search his ship or house, and if the slave should be found there, the person who received him should be duly punished by his bailiff or consul and the slave retunred to his master.

If the slave was neither in their ship nor in their house, said subjects of the King shall not and can not be molested in this connection.

XV. No subject of the King who shall not have resided for 10 full continuous years in the dominions of the Grand Signior shall or can be forced to pay tribute, Kharadj, Avari, Khassabiye, nor to guard neighboring land, storehouses of the Grand Signior, work in an arsenal, nor perform any other forced service. In the dominions of the King reciprocal rights shall be granted to the subjects of the Grand Signior.

The King of France has proposed that His Holiness the Pope, the King of England, his brother and perpetual ally, and the King of Scotland should be entitled to adhere to his treaty of peace, if they please, on condition that when desirous of doing so they shall within eight months from date send their ratifications to the Grand Signior and obtain his.

XVI. Likewise the Grand Signior and the King of France shall within six months exchange the confirmation of the present treaty in valid and due form, with the promise to observe it, and the order to all their lieutenants, judges, officers, and subjects to observe it without bad faith and in all its points; and in order that nobody should plead ignorance, this treaty, after the confirmations have been exchanged, shall be published at Constantinople, Alexandria, Marseille, Narbonne, and other principal cities and ports of the jurisdiction, kingdoms, and states of the said sovereigns.

2. TRADING PRIVILEGES TO ANTHONY JENKINSON BY SULTAN SÜLEYMAN I
1553

[Morgan and Coote, *Early Voyages and Travels to Russia and Persia*, 1: 5–6]

English ships began to make their way to Ottoman ports in the first half of the sixteenth century, but no factories (permanent merchant colonies) were established yet. Anthony Jenkinson, an enterprising English merchant, procured for himself and for accredited representatives—in an audience at Aleppo with Sultan Süleyman I (1520–66), who was then preparing for battle against Persia—freedom to trade throughout the Ottoman Empire on the same basis as the French and the Venetians. Jenkinson and his associates were allowed to bring their wares to Ottoman ports on English bottoms, but once within the area of Ottoman jurisdiction they were to travel and traffic under the French flag. No advantage was taken of the sultan's grant, and organized English commerce with the Ottoman Empire did not begin until three decades later. Foster, *England's Quest of Eastern Trade*, chap. 2; Horniker, "William Harborne."

Sultan Solyman, etc., to all Viceroyes, Saniaques, Caditz, and other our Justicers, Officers, and Subiects of *Tripolis* in *Syria, Constantinople, Alexandria* in *Egypt*, and of all other Townes and Cities vnder our Dominion and iurisdiction: we will and commaund you, that when you shall see *Anthony Ienkinson*, bearer of these present letters, marchant of London in England, or his factor, or any other, bearing the said letters for him, arriue in our ports and hauens, with his shippe or shippes, or other vessels whatsoeuer, that you suffer him to lade or vnlade his marchandise wheresoeuer it shal seeme good vnto him, traffiking for him selfe in all our countries and dominions, without hindring or any way disturbing of him, his shippe, his people, or marchandise, and without enforcing him to pay any other custome or tol whatsoeuer, in any sorte, or to any persons whatsoeuer they be, saue only our ordinary duties, contayned in our custome houses, which when he hath paide, we will that he be franke, and free, as well for himselfe, as for his people, marchandise, shippe, or shippes, and all other vessels whatsoeuer, and in so doing that he may trafficke, bargaine, sell, and buy, lade, and vnlade, in all out foresaide Countries, landes, and dominions, in like sorte and with the like liberties and priuiledges as the Frenchmen and Venetians vse, and inioy, and more if it be possible, without the hinderance or impeachment of any man. And furthermore, we charge and commaunde all Viceroyes and Consuls of the French nation, and of the Venetians, and all other Consuls resident in our Countreys, in what port or prouince soeuer they be, not to constraine,

or cause to constraine by them, or the sayde Ministers and Officers whatsoeuer they be, the saide *Anthony Ienkinson*, or his factor, or his seruants, or deputies, or his marchandise, to pay any kinde of consullage, or other right whatsoeuer, or to intermeddle or hinder his affaires, and not to molest nor trouble him any manner of way, because our will and pleasure is, that he shall not pay in all our Countries, any other then our ordinarie custome. And in case any man hinder and impeach him aboue and besides these our present letters, we charge you most expressly to defende and assist him against the sayde Consuls; and if they will not obey our present commaundement, that you aduertise vs thereof, that we may take such order for the same, that others may take example thereby. Moreouer, wee commaunde all our Captaines of our Gallies, and their Lieutenants, be they Foystes[1] or other vessels, that when they shall finde the sayde *Ienkinson*, or his factor, his shippe or shippes, with his seruants, and marchandise, that they hurt him not, neyther in bodie nor goods, but that rather they assist and defend him against all such as seeke to doe him wrong, and that they ayde and helpe him with victuals, according to his want, and that whosoeuer shall see these presents, obey the same, as they will auoide the penaltie in doing the contrarie: Made in *Aleppo* of *Syria*, the yeere 961. of our holy Prophet *Mahomet*, in the yeere of Jesus 1553, signed with the scepter and signet of the Grand *Signior*, with his owne proper hande.

1. Foist, a vessel with oars, smaller than a galley.

3. GRANT OF COMMERCIAL PRIVILEGES TO THE (ENGLISH) MUSCOVY COMPANY BY SHAH TAHMASP OF PERSIA 1566–1568

[Morgan and Coote, *Early Voyages and Travels to Russia and Persia*, 2: 403–04, 418–20]

The Muscovy Company, as a by-product of the search for the Northeast Passage, launched English commerce with Persia in a series of six trading expeditions via Russia between 1562 and 1581. The attraction of Persia to English merchants lay in its silk, produced in the provinces along the southern Caspian shores, and in transit rights for possible commerce with "India, or other countryes thereunto adjoyning." The Muscovy Company, with whom Anthony Jenkinson was associated, received from Shah Tahmasp (1524–76) a *farman* (royal decree), granting commercial privileges to Englishmen, including freedom of transit and exemption from customs and tolls. The shah amplified the rights two years later. Because of attendant hazards, the attempts to open up trade with Persia by way of Russia were abandoned after 1581. Willan, *Early History of the Russia Company*; Foster, *England's Quest of Eastern Trade*, chaps. 2–3; Morgan and Coote, op. cit.; Curzon, *Persia and the Persian Question*, 2: 532–36; Vaughn, "English Trading Expeditions in Asia."

1. Decree of 1566

1. It is granted that you shall pay no manner of Customes or tolles any kind of wayes now, nor in time comming vnto his heires after him; and that all English marchants, such as you shall appoint nowe and hereafter, shall and may passe and repasse into all places of his dominions and other Countreyes adioyning in the trade of marchandise, to buy and sell and manner of commodities, with all manner of persons.

2. Item, that in all places where any of our Marchants shall haue their resort or abiding, his chiefe Gouernours, Rulers, and Iustices shall take heede vnto vs, being our aide and defence against all euill persons, punishing those that shall doe vs any wrong.

3. Item, that for all such debts as shall be owing by any manner of person, iustice shall be done on the partie, and we paid at the day.

4. Item, that no manner of person, of whatsoeuer estate or degree they be of, shall be so hardie as to take any kind of wares, or any guifts, without any leaue and good will.

5. Item, if by chance medley any of our Marchants or seruants, as God forbid should kill any of his subiects, that no part of your goods shall be touched or medled withall, neither any partie but the offendour, and true iustice to be ministred; and being any of vs, not to suffer without the Princes knowledge and aduise.

6. Item, that all such debts as are nowe owing, or hereafter shall be, are to be paide vnto any of vs, in the absence of the other, be the partie dead or aliue.

7. Item, that no person returne any kinde of wares backe againe being once bought or solde.

8. Item, that when God shall send your goods to shoare, presently his people shall helpe vs a land with them. . . .[1]

2. Decree of 1568

10. Item, that the merchants haue free libertie, as in their first priuiledge, to goe into *Gillan* and all other places of his dominions, now or hereafter when occasion shall be giuen.

11. Item, if by misfortune any of their ships should breake or fall upon any part of his dominions on the seacoast, his subiects to helpe with all speed to save the

---

1. Article 9 was not reproduced by Morgan and Coote.

goods, and to be deliuered to any of the said merchaunts that lieuth; or otherwise to be kept in safetie vntil any of them come to demaund them.

12. Item, if any of the said merchants depart this life in any citie or towne, or on the high way, his gouernours there to see their goods safely kept, and to bee deliuered to any other of them that shall demaund them.

13. Item, the said merchants to take such camell men as they themselves will, being countrey people, and that no *Kissell Bash* doe let or hinder them. And the said owners of the camels to bee bound to answere them such goods as they shall receiue at their hands, and the camell men to stand to the losses of their camels or horses.

14. Item more, that the said carriers do demaund no more of them then [sic] their agreement was to pay them.

15. Item more, if they be at a price with any carriers and haue giuen earnest, the Camel men to see they keepe their promise.

16. Item, if any of the said merchants be in feare to trauell, to give them one or more to goe with them and see them in safetie with their goods to the place they will goe vnto.

17. Item, in all places, to say in all cities, townes, or villages on the high way, his subiects to giue them honest roume and vitails for their money.

18. Item, the sayd merchants may, in any place where they shall thinke best, build or buy any house or houses to their owne vses. And no person to molest or trouble them, and to stand in any Carauan where they will or shall think good.

4. TREATY OF COMMERCE: THE OTTOMAN EMPIRE AND ENGLAND
June 1580

(Ratified, Istanbul, 3 May 1583; renewed and expanded, 1603)
[Hakluyt, *Principal Navigations*, 5: 183–89]

Until late in the sixteenth century English merchants in the Ottoman Empire were required to conduct business under the French flag, even though Anthony Jenkinson had obtained special privileges in 1553 (Doc. 2). Not until the late 1570s, when a number of London merchants became interested in forming a chartered company with a monopoly of English-Ottoman commerce, were efforts made to acquire capitulatory privileges for England equal to those of France. The negotiation in 1577–80 of the first capitulatory treaty between the two governments produced loud cries at the Ottoman court from France, which resented the prospective loss of its preferential position. Rawlinson, "Embassy of William Harborne to Constantinople"; Horniker, "William Harborne"; Wood, *History of the Levant Company*, chap .1; Read, *Walsingham and the Policy of Queen Elizabeth*, 3: 225–30, 326–32; *Calendar of State Papers, Venetian, 1581–91*, introd., pp. xxix–xlvi; Pears, "Spanish Armada and the Ottoman Porte."

1 Our Imperiall commandement and pleasure is, that the people and subjects of the same Queene, may safely and securely come to our princely dominions, with their goods and marchandise, and ladings, and other commodities by sea, in great and smal vessels, and by land with their carriages and cattels, and that no man shall hurt them, but they may buy and sell without any hinderance, and observe the customes and orders of their owne countrey.

2 Item, if the aforesaid people and mar-

chants shalbe at anytime in the course of their journeis [sic] and dealings by any meanes taken, they shall be delivered and inlarged, without any excuse or cavillation.

3 Item, if their ships purpose to arive in any of our ports and havens, it shalbe lawfull for them so to do in peace, and from thence againe to depart, without any let or impediment.

4 Item, if it shall happen that any of their ships in tempestuous weather shall bee in danger of losse and perishing, and thereupon shall stand in need of our helpe, we will, and commaund that our men and ships be ready to helpe and succour them.

5 Item, if they shalbe willing to buy any victuals for their money, no person shall withstande them, but they shall buy the same without any disturbance to the contrary.

6 Item, if by any casualtie their shippes shall bee driven on shoare in perill of shipwracke, our Begs [governors] and Judges, and other our Subjects shall succour them, and such wares, and goods of theirs as shall bee recovered from the losse, shall bee restored to them, and no man shall wrong them.

7 Item, if the people of the aforesayd Queene, their interpreters and marchants, shall for trafique sake, either by lande or Sea repaire to our dominions paying our lawfull toll and custome, they shall have quiet passage, and none of our Captaines or governours of the Sea, and shippes, nor any kinde of persons, shall either in their bodies, or in their goods and cattels, any way molest them.

8 Item, if any Englishman shall grow in debt, and so owe money to any other man, and thereupon doth absent himselfe that he can not be found, let no man be arrested or apprehended for any other mans debt, except he be the surety.

9 Item, if any Englishman shall make his will and testament to whom soever by the same hee shall give his goods, the partie shall have them accordingly, and if hee die intestate, hee to whom the Consull or governour of the societie shall say the goods of the dead are to bee given, hee shall have the same.

10 Item, if the Englishmen or the marchants and interpreters of any places under the jurisdiction of England shall happen in the buying and selling of wares, by promises or otherwise to come in controversie, let them go to the Judge, and cause the matter to be entred into a booke, and if they wil, let them also take letters of the Judge testifying the same, that men may see the booke and letters, whatsoever thing shall happen, and that according to the tenour thereof the matter in controversie and in doubt may be ended: but if such things be neither entred in booke, nor yet the persons have taken letters of the Judge, yet he shall admit no false witnesse, but shall execute the Law according to justice, and shall not suffer them to be abused.

11 Item, if any man shall say, that these being Christians have spoken any thing to the derogation of our holy faith and religion, and have slandered the same, in this matter as in all others, let no false witnesses in any case be admitted.

12 Item, if any one of them shall commit any great crime, and flying thereupon cannot bee found, let no man be arrested, or detained for another mans fact, except he be his suretie.

13 Item, if any slave shall be found to be an Englishman, and their Consull or governour shall sue for his libertie, let the same slave be diligently examined, and if hee be found in deed to be English, let him be discharged and restored to the Englishmen.

14 Item, if any Englishman shall come hither either to dwel or trafique, whether hee be married or unmarried, he shall pay no polle or head money.

15 Item, if either in Alexandria, Damasco, Samos, Tunis, Tripolis in ye west, the port townes of Ægypt, or in any other places, they purpose to choose to themselves Consuls or governours, let them doe so, and if they will alter them at any time, and in the roome of the former Consuls place others, let them do so also, and no man shall restraine them.

16 Item, if their interpreter shalbe at any time absent, being occupied in other serious matters, let the thing then in question bee stayed and differred till his comming, and in the meane time no man shall trouble them.

17 Item, if any variance or controversie shall arise among the Englishmen, and thereupon they shall appeale to their Con-

suls or governours, let no man molest them, but let them freely doe so, that the controversie begunne may be finished according to their owne customes.

18 Item, if after the time and date of this privilege, any pirats or other free governours of ships trading the Sea shall take any Englishman, and shall make sale of him, either beyonde the Sea, or on this side of the Sea, the matter shalbe examined according to justice, and if the partie shalbe found to be English, and shall receive the holy religion, then let him freely be discharged, but if he will still remaine a Christian, let him then be restored to the Englishmen, and the buyers shall demaund their money againe of them who solde the man.

19 Item, if the ships of warre of our Imperiall highnesse shal at any time goe forth to Sea, and shall finde any English ships laden with marchandise, no man shall hinder them, but rather shall use them friendly, and doe them no wrong, even as wee have given and granted articles, and privileges to the French, Venetians, and other Kings and princes our confederats, so also wee have given the like to the English: and countrary to this our divine lawe

and privilege, let no man presume to doe any thing.

20 Item, if either their great or small ships shall in the course of their voyage, or in any place to which they come, bee stayed or arrested, let no man continue the same arrest, but rather helpe and assist them.

21 Item, if any theeves and robbers shall by force take away any of their ships, and marchandise, let the same theeves and robbers be sought, and searched for with all diligence, and let them be punished most severely.

22 Last of all the Beglerbegs [governors general], and Zanziacbegs, our Captaines, our slaves and servants of Captaines using the sea, and our Judges, customers and governours of ships called Reiz, and free Reiz, all these, according to the tenor of this privilege and articles, shalbe bound to doe accordingly: and, as long as the Queene of England on her part shall duely keepe and observe this league and holy peace, expressed in this privilege, we also for our Imperial part, do charge and commaund the same so long to be straightly kept and observed.

5. FIRST CHARTER OF THE (ENGLISH) LEVANT COMPANY
11 September 1581

[Hakluyt, *Principal Navigations*, 5: 192–202]

The creation of the Levant Company in 1581 inaugurated English commerce with the Ottoman Empire on a sustained basis. For more than two centuries thereafter, all English consular and diplomatic officials in the sultan's domains were employees of the company. Thus, by extension, the company was charged with supervising the execution of the English capitulations. Despite the monopoly, the company's commercial fortunes fluctuated in its long history, being exceeded in the mid-seventeenth century by those of Dutch merchants and throughout most of the eighteenth by those of the French, the latter representing the Chamber of Commerce of Marseilles. By the time the Levant Company forged far ahead of its closest competitors in the early nineteenth century, laissez-faire principles had come to dominate English foreign trade, so the company was finally dissolved by act of Parliament in 1825 (Doc. 63). Of the later renewals of the Levant Company's charter, that of 14 December 1605 was the most significant, since it survived with only slight modifications until the company's demise in 1825. The full text of the 1605 instrument appears in Epstein, *Early History of the Levant Company*, pp. 153–210. Wood, *History of the Levant Company*; Foster, *Travels of John Sanderson*; Rosedale, *Queen Elizabeth and the Levant Company* (documents); Horniker, "Anglo-French Rivalry in the Levant"; Rowland, *England and Turkey*; Rawlinson, "Embassy of William Harborne to Constantinople"; Scott, *English, Scottish and Irish Joint-Stock Companies*, 2: 83–88.

Elizabeth by the grace of God Queene of England, France and Ireland, defender of the faith, &c. To all our Officers, ministers, and Subjects, and to all other people as well within this our Realme of England, as else where under our obeysance, jurisdiction, or otherwise, unto whom these our letters shall be seene, shewed or read, greeting. Where are welbeloved Subjects Edward Osborne Alderman of our Citie of London, and Richard Staper of our sayde City Marchant, have by great adventure and industrie, with their great costes and charges, by the space of sundry late yeeres, travailed, and caused travaile to bee taken, as well by secret and good means, as by dangerous ways and passages both by lande and Sea, to finde out and set open a trade of Marchandize and trafique into the Lands, Islands, dominions, and territories of the great Turke, commonly called the Grand Signior, not heretofore in the memory of any man nowe living knowen to be commonly used and frequented by way of marchandise, by any of the Marchants or any Subjects of us, or our progenitours; and also have by their like good meanes and industrie, and great charges procured of the sayde Grand Signior (in our name,) amitie, safetie, and freedome, for trade and trafique of Marchandise to bee used, and continued by our Subjects within his sayde Dominions, whereby there is good and apparant hope and likelyhoode both that many good offices may bee done for the peace of Christendome, and reliefe of many Christians that bee or may happen to bee in thraldome or necessitie under the sayde Grand Signior, his vassals or Subjects, and also good and profitable vent and utterance may be had of the commondities of our Realme, and sundry other great benefites to the advancement of our honour, and dignitie Royall, the increase of the revenues of our Crowne, and generall wealth of our Realme: Knowe ye, that hereupon wee greatly tendering the wealth of our people,

and the incouragement of our Subjects in their good enterprises for the advancement of the Common weale, have of our speciall grace, certaine knowledge and meere motion, given and graunted, and by these presents for us, our heires and successours, doe give and graunt unto our sayd trustie, and welbeloved Subjects Edward Osborne, and unto Thomas Smith of London Esquier, Richard Staper, and William Garret of London Marchants, their executors, and administrators, and to the executours and administratours of them, and of every of them, that they, and every of them, and such other person and persons Englishmen borne, not exceeding the number of twelve, as they the sayde Edward, and Richard shall appoint, nominate, or admit to be parteners, adventurers, or doers with them the sayde Edward, Thomas, Richard and William, in their societie by themselves, their servants, Factours or deputies, and to such others as shall bee nominated according to the tenour of these our letters Patents, shall and may during the terme of seven yeeres from the date of these Patents, freely trade, trafique, and use feates of Marchandise into, and from the dominions of the sayde Grand Signior, and every of them, in such order, and maner, forme, liberties and condition to all intents and purposes as shalbe betweene them limitted and agreed, and not otherwise, without any molestation, impeachment, or disturbance, any Lawe, statute, usage, diversitie of religion or faith, or other cause or matter whatsoever to the countrary notwithstanding.

And that it shalbe lawful to the said Edward and Richard their executors and administrators, (during the said terme) to appoint or admit to be parteners and adventurers with them the sayde Edward, Thomas, Richard and William. such persons not exceeding the number of twelve (as afore is said) to trafique and use the said trade & feate of marchandise according to our saide graunt. And that all and every such person and persons, as shall hereafter fortune to bee appointed or admitted as parteners in the said trade or trafique according to these our letters patents, shall and may from the time of such appointment or admittance, have and enjoy the freedome and libertie of the said trade and trafique, during the residue of the said terme of seven yeeres, according to such limitation and agreement as is aforesaide, and that it shall and may be lawfull to and for the saide Edward, Thomas, Richard and William, their executours and administratours, servants, factours and deputies, and all such as shall be so appointed, nominated or admitted to bee partener or adventurers in the saide trade, or so many of them as can and will, to assemble themselves for or about any the matters, causes, affaires or businesse of the saide trade in any place or places for the same convenient, from time to time during the said terme of 7. yeres, within our dominions or elsewhere, and to make, ordeine, and constitute reasonble lawes and ordinances, for the good government of the said Company, and for the better advencement and continuance of the said trade and trafique, not being contrary or repugnant to the lawes, estatutes or customes of our Realme, and the same lawes or ordinances so made to put in use, and execute accordingly, and at their pleasures to revoke the same lawes and ordinances, or any of them, as occasion shall require.

And in consideration that the said Edward Osborne hath bene the principall setter foorth and doer in the opening, & putting in ure of the said trade, we do therfore especially ordeine, constitute, and provide by these patents, that the saide Edward Osborne shall be governour of all such as by vertue of these our letters patents, shall be parteners, adventurers, or trafiquers in the said trade, during the said terme of seven yeeres, if hee so long live: And that if the said Edward shall happen to decease during the saide terme, the saide Richard Staper then living, then the sayd Richard Staper shall likewise be governour during the residue of the said terme (if he so long live) and that if the said Edward and Richard shall both happen to decease during the said terme, then the partners or

adventurers for the time being, or the greatest part of them, shall from time to time as necessitie shall require, choose and elect a governour of the said Company.

Provided alwayes, that if there shall happen any great or urgent occasion to remoove or displace any person that shall be governour of the saide fellowship, that then it shall, and may be lawfull for us, our heires and successours, to remoove, and displace every such governour, and to place another of the said fellowship in the same office, during such time as such person should have enjoyed the same, according to this our graunt, if there had bene no cause to the contrary.

And we further for us, our heires, and successors, of our especiall grace, certaine knowledge, and meere motion, do graunt to the said Edward Osborne, Thomas Smith, Richard Staper, and William Garret, their executors and administrators, that nothing shall bee done to be of force or validitie touching the sayde trade or trafique, or the exercise thereof, without or against the consent of the said Edward, during such time as hee shall bee Governour as afore is saide. And after that time without the consent of the Governour for the time being, and the more part of the said Company.

And further, wee of our more ample and abundant grace, meere motion and certaine knowledge, have graunted, and by these patents for us, our heires and successors, doe graunt to the saide Edward, Thomas, Richard and William, their executors and administrators, that they, the saide Edward, Thomas, Richard and William, their executors and administrators, and the said person and persons by them the said Edward and Richard to be nominated, or appointed as afore is said, together, with such two other persons, as wee our heires or successors from time to time during the sayd term shall nominate, shall have the whole trade and trafique, and the whole entire onely libertie, use and privilege of trading, and trafiquing, and using feate of marchandise, into, and from the said dominions of the said Grand Signior, and every of them. And when there shall be no such persons so nominated or appointed by us, our heires or successors, that than the said Edward Osborne. Thomas Smith, Richard Staper, and William Garret, their executors and administrators, and such persons by them so to be appointed, shall have the saide whole trade and trafique, and the whole entire, and onely libertie, use, and privilege of trading and trafiquing aforesaid. And that they the said Edward, Thomas, Richard and William, their executors & administrators, and also al such as shal so be nominated or appointed to be partners or adventurers in the said trade, according to such agreement as is abovesaid, and every of them, their servants, factors and deputies, shal have ful and free authoritie, libertie, facultie, licence and power to trade and trafique into and from all and every the saide dominions of the saide Grand Signior, and into, and from all places where, by occasion of the said trade, they shall happen to arrive or come, whether they be Christians, Turkes, Gentiles or other, and into, and from all Seas, rivers, ports, regions, territories, dominions, coastes and places with their ships, barks, pinnesses and other vessels, and with such mariners and men, as they will lead with them or send for the said trade, as they shall thinke good at their owne proper cost and expenses, any law, statute, usage, or matter whatsoever to the contrary notwithstanding. And that it shalbe lawful for the said Edward, Thomas, Richard and William, and to the persons aforesaid, and to and for the mariners and seamen to bee used and employed in the said trade and voyage to set and place in the tops of their ships and other vessels the armes of England with the red crosse over the same, as heretofore they have used the red crosse, any matter or thing to the contrary notwithstanding.

And we of our further royal favor, and of our especiall grace, certaine knowledge and meere motion have graunted, and by these presents doe graunt to the said Edward Osburne, Thomas Smith, Richard Staper, and William Garret, their executors and administrators by these present, that the said lands, territories, and dominions of the said Grand Signior, or any of them, shall not be visited, frequented, nor haunted by way of marchandise by any other our subjects during the said terme, contrary to the true meaning of these patents.

And by vertue of our high prerogative royall (which wee will not have argued or

brought in question) we straightly charge and commaund, and prohibite for us, our heires, and successours, all our subjects (of what degree or qualitie soever they be) that none of them directly, or indirectly, do visite, haunt, frequent or trade, trafique, or adventure by way of marchandise into, or from any of the Dominions of the sayde Grand Signior, or other places abovesayde by water or by lande (other then the said Edward, Thomas, Richard and William, their executours or administrators, or such as shalbe admitted, and nominated as is aforesaide) without expresse licence, agreement, and consent of the said Governour, and company or the more part of them, whereof the said Governour always to be one, upon paine of our high indignation, and of forfeiture and losse, as well as of the ship and shippes, with the furniture thereof, as also of the goods, marchandizes, and things whatsoever they be of those our Subjects which shall attempt, or presume to saile, trafique, or adventure, to or from any the dominions, or places abovesaid, contrary to the prohibition aforesaid: the one halfe of the same forfeiture to be to the use of us, our heires & successors, and the other halfe to the use of the said Edward, Thomas, Richard and William, and the said companie, and further to suffer imprisonment during our pleasure, and such other punishment as to us, for so high contempt, shal seeme meete and convenient.

And further of our grace speciall, certaine knowledge, and meere motion we have condescended and graunted, and by these patents for us our heires and successors, doe condescend and grant to the said Edward, Thomas, Richard & William, their executors and administrators, that we our heires & successors during the said terme, will not grant liberty, licence or power to any person or persons whatsoever, contrary to the tenor of these our letters patents, to saile, passe, trade, or trafique into or from the said dominions of the said Grand Signior or any of them, without the consent of the said Edward, Thomas, Richard & William, and such as shalbe named or appointed as afore is said, or the most of them. And that if at any time hereafter during the said terme, ye said Edward, Thomas, Richard and William, or the survivors of them, shal admit or nominate any of our subjects to be partners & adventurers in the said trade to the number of 12. or under as afore is said, that then we our heires and successors at the instance and petition of the said Edward, Thomas, Richard and William, or the survivors of them in our Chauncerie to be made, and upon the sight of these presents, will grant and make to the said Edward, Thomas, Richard and William, or to the survivors of them, and to such persons as so shall be nominated or appointed by their speciall names, surnames, & additions as is aforesaid, new letters patents under the great seale of England in due forme of law with like agreement, clauses, prohibitions, provisoes and articles (mutatis mutandis) as in these our letters patents are conteined, for, and during the residue of the said terme of seven yeres then remaining unexpired. And that the sight of these presents shalbe sufficient warrant to the Lord Chancellour, or Lord keeper of the great seale for the time being, for the making sealing and passing of such new letters patents, without further writ or warrant for the same to be required, had, or obtained.

And the said Edward Osburne, Thomas Smith, and Richard Staper, and William Garret and such others as shalbe so nominated and appointed, as is aforesaid, to be of their trade or companie, shall yeerely during 6. of the last yeres of the said 7. yeres, lade out of this our Realme, and bring home yeerely, for, and in the feate and trade of marchandizing aforesaid, so much goods and marchandizes, as the custome, and subsidie inwards and outwards, shall amount in the whole to the summe of 500. li. yeerely. So that the said Edward Osborne, Thomas Smith, Richard Staper, and William Garret and the said persons so to be nominated as is aforesaid, or any of them, or their ship or shippes be not barred, stayed, restrained or let by any reasonable occasion from the sayde trade or trafique, and so that the said ship or ships do not perish by any misfortune, or bee spoyled by the way in their voyage.

And further, the said Edward Osborne, Thomas Smith, Richard Staper, and William Garret, and such others as shall be appointed as aforesaide to be of their saide trade or Company, shall give notice unto the Lord Admirall of England, or to some of the principall officers, of the Admiraltie for the time being, of such ship or shippes as they shall set foorth in the same voyage, and of the number of Mariners appointed to goe in the same ship or shippes, by the space, of fifteene dayes before the setting or going foorth of the same ship or shippes. And also the said Edward Osborne, Thomas Smith, Richard Staper and William Garret, and such other as shall be by them the saide Edward and Richard, nominated to be of the said trade, shall and will at the setting foorth of their ship, or shippes, for the same voyage, permit and suffer the Master of the Ordinance of us, our heires and successors, or some others, our or their principall officers of the Ordinance, to take a view of the number and quantitie of such Ordinance, powder, and munition as shall be caried in the said ship, or shippes, and shall also at the returne of the same ship, or shippes, suffer a view to be taken, and upon request made, make an accompt to the saide officers of our Ordinance, of the expenses, and wastes of the said Ordinance, powder, and munition, so to bee caried in the same ship or shippes.

Provided alwayes, that if any of the said trade or Company, or their servants, factors, or sailers, in any ship by them laden, shall commit any piracie or outrage upon the seas, and that, if the said Company or societie shall not, or do not, within reasonable time, after complaint made, or notice given to the said Company, or to any of them, either satisfie or recompense the parties that so shall fortune to be robbed, or spoiled by any of the said Company, or sailers, in the said ships, or els shall not do their endevour to the uttermost of their reasonable power, to have the parties so offending punished for the same their offences, that then, and from thencefoorth, these present letters patents shall be utterly voyd, cease, and determine.

Provided likewise, that if it shall hereafter appeare unto us, our heires, or successors, that this grant, or the continuance thereof in the whole, or in any part thereof, shall not be profitable to us, our heires, our successors, or to this our Realme, that then, and from thencefoorth, upon, and after one full yeeres warning, to be given unto the said Company, or to the Governour thereof, by us, our heires, or successors, this present grant shall cease, be voyd, and determine [sic], to all intents, constructions, and purposes.

Provided also, that we, our heires and successors, from time to time, during the said 7. yeeres, may lawfully nominate, appoint, and authorise two persons, being fit men, to be of the saide company, and for want or lacke of them, two others to be adventurers in the said trade, for such stocke and summe of money, as they shall put in, so that the said persons to bee nominated, or authorised, shall be contributorie to all charges of the said trade & adventure indifferently, according to their stockes: and as other adventurers of the said trade shall doe for their stockes, and so that likewise they doe observe the orders of the said Company, allowable by this our graunt, and that such persons so to be appointed by us, our heires or successors, shall, and may, with the saide Company, and fellowship, use the trade and feate of marchandise aforesaide, and all the liberties and privileges herein before granted, according to the meaning of these our letters patents, any thing in these our letters patents contained to the contrary notwithstanding.

And further of our speciall grace, certaine knowledge, and meere motion, we have condescended and granted, and by these presents for us, our heires and successors, doe condescend, and grant to the said Edward Osborne, Thomas Smith, Richard Staper, and William Garret, their executors, and administrators, that if at the ende of the said terme of seven yeeres, it shall seeme meete, and convenient unto the said Edward Osborne, Thomas Smith, Richard Staper, and William Garret, or the surviver of them, that this present grant shall be continued: and if that also it shall appeare unto us, our heires, or successors, that the continuance thereof shall not be prejudiciall, or hurtfull to this our Realme, that then we, our heires, or successors, at the instance and petition of the said Edward Osborne, Thomas Smith, Richard Staper, and William Garret, or the surviver of them, to be made to us, our heires, or successors, wil grant and make to the said Edward, Thomas, Richard and William, or the surviver of them, and to such other persons, as so shall be by the said Edward and Richard nominated and appointed, new letters patents, under the great seale of England, in due forme of lawe, with like covenants, grants, clauses, and articles, as in these presents, are contained, or with addition of other necessary articles, or change of these, in some part, for and during the full terme of seven yeeres then next following. Willing, and straightly commanding, and charging all and singuler our Admirals, Viceadmirals, Justices, Maiors, Sheriffes, Escheaters, Constables, Bailiffes, and all and singuler our other officers, ministers, liege men, and subjects whatsoever, to be aiding, favouring, helping, and assisting unto the said Governour, and company, and their successors, and to their Deputies, officers, servants, assignes, and ministers, and every of them, in executing and enjoying the premises, as well on land as on sea, from time to time, and at all times when you, or any of you, shall be thereunto required, any statute, act, ordinance, proviso, proclamation, or restraint heretofore had, made, set forth, ordained, or provided, or any other matter, cause or thing to the contrary, in any wise notwithstanding.

6. PROMISE BY SHAH 'ABBAS OF EXTRATERRITORIAL PRIVILEGES TO EUROPEANS
1600

[Malcolm, *History of Persia*, 1: 352–53]

In 1598 an English soldier of fortune, Sir Anthony Sherley, with a group of twenty-seven Englishmen, among them his brother Robert, reached the court of Shah 'Abbas

(1587–1629) at Qazvin. Ostensibly delegated by the earl of Essex, then the lord-lieutenant of Ireland, Sherley in reality sought to promote his personal affairs by presenting his services to the Persian monarch. The self-appointed Sherley mission was an early instance of European technical assistance, for its staff helped the shah effectively to reorganize the Persian army. So wholly had Sir Anthony ingratiated himself that in 1600 Shah 'Abbas dispatched the Englishman to Europe as special ambassador in search of European allies against the hostile Sunni Ottomans. 'Abbas permitted the envoy to publicize, as inducement, the following *farman* (royal decree), assuring all Europeans capitulatory privileges in perpetuity in Persia. Sir Anthony's roving assignment proved as total a failure as did the shah's promissory decree. Yet the abortive instrument is of interest, since it represented the unusual phenomenon of a strong Middle East monarch freely offering capitulations to European states as bait for a military alliance. Sykes, *History of Persia*, vol. 2, chap. 63; Foster, *England's Quest of Eastern Trade*, chap. 30; A. Wilson, *Persian Gulf*, chap. 9.; Chew, *The Crescent and the Rose*, chaps. 6, 7; Shirley, *Sherley Brothers*; Asian Circle, "Note on the Abolition of Extraterritoriality in Persia."

Our absolute commaundement, will, and pleasure, is, that our cuntries and dominions shall be, from this day, open to all Christian people, and to their religion: and in such sort, that none of ours, of any condition, shall presume to giue them any euil word. And, because of the amitie now ioyned with the princes that professe Christ, I do giue this pattent for all Christian marchants, to repaire and trafique, in and through our dominions, without disturbances or molestations of any duke, prince, gouernour, or captaine, or any, of whatsoeuer office or qualitie, of ours; but that all merchandize that they shall bringe, shall be so priuileged, that none, of any dignitie or authoritie, shall haue power to looke unto it: neyther to make inquisition after, or stay, for any use or person, the ualue of one asper. Neyther shall our religious men, of whatsoeuer sort they be, dare disturbe them, or speake in matters of their faith. Neyther shall any of our justices haue power ouer their persons or goodes, for any cause or act whatsoeuer.

If by chaunce a marchant shall die, none shall touch any thing that belongeth unto him; but if the marchante haue a companion, he shall haue power to take possession of those goodes. But if (by any occasion) he be alone, onely with his seruants, the gouernor, or whomsoeuer shall be required by him in his sickness, shall be answearable for all such goodes unto any of his nation, which shall come to require them. But if he die suddainly, and haue neyther companion nor seruant, nor time to recomende to any what he woulde haue done, then the gouernor of that place shall sende the goodes to the next marchant of his nation, which shall be abiding in any parts of our dominions.

And those within our kingdomes and prouinces hauing power ouer our tolles and customes, shall receiue nothing, or dare to speake for any receipt from any Christian marchant.

And if any such Christian shall giue credite to any of our subjectes, (of any condition whatsouer,) he shall, by this pattent of ours, haue authoritie to require any caddie, or gouernor, to do him justice, and thereupon, at the instant of his demaunde, shall cause him to be satisfied.

Neyther shall any gouernor, or justice, of what quality so euer he be, dare take any rewarde of him, which shall be to his expense: for our will and pleasure is, that they shall be used, in all our dominions, to their owne full content, and that our kingdomes and cuntries shall be free unto them.

That none shall presume to aske them for what occasion they are heere.

And although it hath bin a continuall and unchaungeable use in our dominions euery yeere to renue all pattentes, this pattent, notwithstanding, shall be of full effect and force for euer, without renuing, for me and my successors, not to be chaunged.

7. GRANT OF CAPITULATIONS TO THE NETHERLANDS
BY SHAH 'ABBAS
17 November 1623

(Registered with the States-General, 24 December 1624)
[Translated from the Dutch text in Valentijn, *Oud en nieuw Oost Indiën*, vol. 5, bk. 5, pp. 293–95]

With the expulsion of the Portuguese from Hurmuz in 1622 by the joint action of Persia and the English East India Company, the Dutch moved promptly into a position of supremacy in European commerce with Persia, which centered in the Persian Gulf, and retained the lead for well over a half-century. Shah 'Abbas was the first of the Safavi dynasty to negotiate with European merchants in explicit detail the conditions under which they might trade in his realm. Although promulgated as a *farman* (royal decree), the instrument framed with, and on behalf of the Dutch East India Company in 1623 more closely resembled in content and structure the capitulatory treaties of that period between the Ottoman Empire and the maritime states of Western Europe. The Dutch swiftly came into conflict with the English by refusing, on the strength of article 3 of the 1623 instrument, to pay duties at Bandar 'Abbas, where the English East India Company was supposed to have shared the customs revenue with the Persian government. The farman remained valid only for the reign of Shah 'Abbas; comparable decrees were granted by later shahs in 1642 and 1694. Dunlop, *Bronnen tot de Geschiedenis der Oostindische Compaagnie in Perzië*, vol. 1 (documents, with introductory essay by the editor); A Wilson, *Persian Gulf*, chap. 11; Bayani, *Les relations de l'Iran avec l'Europe occidentale*, pt. 2, chap. 3; Bonnassieux, *Les grandes compagnies de commerce*, bk. 1, chap. 2; Chardin, *Travels in Persia*, pp. 59–62, 277–87.

1. His Majesty grants freedom to the Netherlands Nation, allowing them to come and go through all the places under His Majesty's rule, to pursue their commerce [and] to buy and sell all sorts of merchandise, none being excepted, insofar as that Nation may deem it advantageous to their commerce.

2. The Netherlands Nation shall not be bound by anyone, whosoever it may be, to accept any kind of merchandise against their will, but may without compulsion deal in, buy and sell all manner of merchandise without the interference of any person of whatever quality.

3. The Netherlands Nation shall not have to pay any duty or toll on their imports or exports or specie, but all specie and merchandise which they import or export shall be free of all duties and charges, with the sole exception of the small duty of the Nazir [overseer or inspector] in accordance with ancient usage.

4. No minister shall have the power to impound and much less to consign to custom-houses the merchandise or the specie, whether import or export, of the Netherlanders; but the Netherlanders will be permitted to travel with their goods through all the cities, roads and fortified places without being molested or hindered by any governor or ruler, whosoever he may be; nor shall the latter be allowed to inspect [the Netherlanders'] goods.

5. The Netherlands Nation will be permitted to use in the purchase and sale of merchandise in their houses all such weights, ells and measures as may be in their possession for the purpose in the localities where they conduct their business; and the official weighers of the district shall not prevent this, much less shall they claim

any duty or weighing fee [that] His Majesty's subjects [must pay], apart from the [duty] on the receiving and weighing of silk or of large and substantial shipments.

6. If any Netherlander having no companion or compatriot with him should happen to pass away anywhere under the rule of His Majesty, the justice of the locality shall take into custody the goods found with the deceased, until a successor has filled the deceased's post or until a request comes from the deceased's chief, to whom the justice shall deliver everything intact. But if there should be others of the same Nation in the locality where the Netherlander happened to die, the justice will not be permitted to touch any of the goods.

7. His Majesty undertakes and promises to pay, make up and compensate for all that may be taken from the Netherlands Nation within his jurisdiction.

8. The Netherlanders also shall not be burdened in the loading of camels, mules or work-horses, but all muleteers and caravan chiefs are required to serve the [Netherlands] Nation at the rates prevailing among the natives of Persia.

9. All officials in Persia are obliged to provide the Netherlands Nation with a fortified house, food, horses and anything that may be requested, as well as with troops to accompany them from one locality to another for the greater safety of their persons and goods.

10. The house of the Netherlands Nation in Persia shall enjoy full freedom without exception; and no justice may enter [the premises] without the permission of the principal representative of the said Nation; and if anyone should seek forcibly to enter [the premises], the Netherlanders will be allowed to resist him with force.

11. The Netherlanders may acquire a place for the exercise of their religion and may perform their rites publicly without let or hindrance.

12. They will be allowed without hindrance to purchase and take out of the country and Christian slaves, especially natives and subjects of the sovereign Estates General of the United Netherlands Provinces.

13. If any Netherlander should become a Muslim, the chief or president will be al-

lowed, as he may deem proper, to take that person and his goods into custody and to send him away at the first opportunity.

14. If a member of the Netherlands Nation should (God forbid) strike dead another person, from whatever nation, or should commit any crime or infraction of the law, that person shall not be tried by any justice of the [Persian] Empire but shall be punished by his president or chief, according to the circumstances of the case and in the manner deemed appropriate.

15. If any Netherlander should be found in the company of a woman, [Persian] officers shall not be empowered to apprehend that person but he shall be punished by his own chiefs after having been found guilty.

16. The Netherlands Nation may acquire a place for the convenient and unhindered burial of their dead in their accustomed manner.

17. The interpreter or dragoman of the Netherlands house shall be privileged with no less freedom than a member of the Netherlands Nation; no one may ever accuse or displease him.

18. It is expressly forbidden to do harm or cause hindrance to any person in the service of the Netherlands Nation; but all persons, whether Persians, Armenians, Turks, Moors or Bengalis, shall be allowed freely to enter the service of the Netherlanders without molestation on this account.

19. Whenever a Netherlands ship should suffer an accident within the jurisdiction of His Majesty and the goods be fished out or salvaged by any imaginable method, the ministers who may receive such goods must return them without claim to the Netherlands Nation.

20. The Netherlanders shall be allowed to export from Persia horses or other kinds of beasts, as they see fit.

21. No custom toll under any pretext whatsoever shall be levied upon the present cargo of the Netherlanders in Shiraz and Hurmuz.

22. Rahdars [road guardians] shall not collect from the Netherlanders any tolls in any locality whatsoever.

23. His Majesty promises to grant privileges additional to those enumerated in the above articles as soon as His Princely Excellency is presented with reasoned and

proper request by the Netherlands Nation   Gentlemen the Estates General.
or by an ambassador of the Sovereign

8. TREATY OF PEACE AND COMMERCE, AND CORAL FISHERY CONCESSION: FRANCE AND THE GARRISON OF ALGIERS
19–29 December 1628

[Translated from the French texts in Rouard de Card, *Traités de la France*, pp. 15–22]

By the beginning of the seventeenth century the merchants of Marseilles had virtually cornered French trade with North Africa, as they had already done to French trade with the eastern Mediterranean. Marseilles's commercial relations with Algiers dated to the beginning of Algerine ties with the Ottoman Empire in the mid-sixteenth century. Coral fishing must have been a prosperous enterprise, for the Marseilles merchants had built in the Bône harbor area an impressive compound, known as the Bastion of France. The earliest surviving recorded recognition of French coral fishing rights off the Algiers-Tunis coast dates from the reign of the sultan Ahmed I (1603–17). "We also permit Frenchmen, named and avowed by their princes, to fish without let or hindrance for fish and coral in the Gulf of Stora-Courcouri, situated in our dependent Kingdom of Algiers and in all other places of our Barbary coasts, in particular in those places within the jurisdiction of our Kingdoms of Algiers and Tunis," runs article 21 of the third renewal by the Imperial Ottoman Government of the French capitulations, approved by Sultan Ahmed on 20 May 1604 (French text in Noradounghian, *Recueil d'actes internationaux de l'empire ottoman*, 1: 93–102). "We confirm all the permissions given by our forebears, and especially by our late father, relating to this fishing, without need for further confirmation than has already been made," the document continues. When the French "concessionaires" in the following month notified the authorities of Algiers of the sultan's decision, the Algerine Divan, or executive legislature, responded by ordering the immediate destruction of the Bastion of France. The interested Marseilles merchants had to cool their heels for nearly a quarter-century longer before they finally procured from the government of Algiers a formal concessionary contract, and, when they did, it was issued and approved by the government of Algiers without reference to the Ottoman padişah, or emperor. Explanation for the long delay and the independent behavior of the Algiers government is to be found in the loosening ties between the center and the periphery of the sprawling Ottoman Empire. The three Barbary provinces—Algiers, Tunis, and Tripoli—which from the start enjoyed a large degree of autonomy, became quasi-sovereign by the opening of the seventeenth century because of the degeneration of the Ottoman system after the death of Sultan Süleyman I (1520–66). Since the waning Ottoman power coincided with the distraction of Europe by the wars of the Reformation, culminating in the Thirty Years War (1618–48), the quasi-sovereign states could prosper. Their brilliant prosperity, however, did not long survive the Peace of Westphalia (1648). Still, in the first half of the seventeenth century, Algiers became a showplace on the Mediterranean. With an estimated population of 100,000 in 1650, the city, by contemporary European standards, boasted an orderly society and a respected government with a highly developed sense of public responsibility and an enviable opulence evidenced by gracious private homes, public baths with running hot and cold water, a sewage disposal system, imposing mosques, and even schools of quality. Few, if any, cities on the Continent could compete with Algiers in per capita wealth, general comfort, and the amenities of "modernization." Algiers set the standards to which Tunis and Tripoli, in that order, aspired. The three states were known as "regencies" in Europe but as "garrisons" (*ocaklar*) in North Africa itself. There, garrison had a dual meaning. One was moral, defense of the Islamic frontier against infidel Europe; and the other political, relating to polities run by military oligarchies. The oligarchs were always responsive to and sometimes captive to the wishes of the top commanders of the local armies, who chose the oligarchs, kept the peace, and collected the taxes. The following treaty of peace and commerce between France and Algiers reflected the condition of equality between the parties. Also reproduced below is the first concessionary contract the Garrison of Algiers issued to French nationals; it later served as a model for French-Algerine concessionary instruments. Masson, *Histoire des établissements et du commerce français dans l'Afrique barbaresque*, chaps. 1–2; G. Fisher, *Barbary Legend*, chaps. 1–5, 8–11; Abun-Nasr, *History of the Maghrib*, chap. 7; Julien, *Histoire de l'Afrique du Nord*, vol. 1, chap. 6.

1. Treaty of Peace and Commerce, 19 September 1628

1. All Musulman slaves, refugees from enemy countries, who may reach France, shall be free to return to Algiers, and all other persons living elsewhere in the Kingdom of France shall be prohibited from selling or returning Musulmans to their enemies.

2. On meeting, Algerine and French ships, having recognized each other, shall exchange news like true and good friends; Algerines shall not be permitted to board French ships or barks to take anything, or to change the sails, cables, cannons, munitions of war, or any other thing. They may neither threaten nor beat the owners, scriveners, men, or others on the ship or bark, so to compel them to say anything contrary to the truth.

3. French ships or barks laden with merchandise belonging to enemies of the Grand Seigneur [Ottoman Padişah], on discovery either by a manifest of the owners or scriveners or by sailors, shall to taken to Algiers, where they shall be paid the freight charge and then allowed to go wherever they may wish. They shall be warned never again to carry goods belonging to enemies, at the risk of losing the credit for their freight.

4. On warships belonging to enemies of Algiers, all Frenchmen who are married and living in the enemy countries, on being captured in such ships, shall be enslaved as enemies.

5. If French ships, after recognizing and parleying with Algerine ships and after clearing themselves, should seek to engage in combat and should be the ones to begin it, [their crews] shall be enslaved on capture, as is laid down in the orders of the Grand Seigneur.

6. No Algerine may force a Frenchman to recant, or may threaten him in any way. Any Frenchman wishing to recant voluntarily shall be taken before the Divan [Governing Council], where he may declare frankly and without constraint the law by which he wishes to be bound.

7. If occasionally Algerine ships or barks, on meeting French ships or barks, should not believe the testimony of the French captain and scrivener that the goods on board belong to Frenchmen, and should wish to take the vessels to Algiers, immediately on arrival there the captains and

scriveners shall be questioned in the Divan with words of friendship and without threats. If they persist [in stating] that the goods belong to Frenchmen, they shall be released at once and the corsair chief shall be punished severely.

8. No natives of states that are Algerine enemies, married and living in France, shall be enslaved. Similarly, as subjects of the Emperor of France, French passengers on enemy ships shall not be enslaved.

9. Members of the Algerine Militia who are corsair chiefs and captains of galleys and men-of-war shall never violate this Peace Treaty. But if evil people such as armed Moors or Togarins [Moorish refugees from Spain] should take French ships or barks to Salé or to any place belonging to enemies of the French, the integrity of the peace would be prejudiced, and blame might be laid upon the Algerines. Consequently, in order to forestall such inconveniences, a strict system shall be instituted requiring all [vessels] that leave Algiers to return there, and forbidding any stranger from serving as corsair chief of the galleys and ships.

10. Likewise, on both sides, we pledge by the present Treaty to observe and maintain point for point every article of the capitulations between our two monarchies—whose glory and virtue may God increase—in consequence of which no one, whether officer of the Divan or member of the Militia, may for any reason or object enter the house of the French Consul. If anyone should have a request to make of the Consul, the latter shall be taken with all honor in a carriage of the Divan before the Ağa, chief of the Divan, where justice shall be observed, so that the French Consul may live in peace and tranquillity, with all due honor and respect.

11. If an evil person, Algerine or French, should commit an act that violates the articles of the present Treaty, with prejudice to the imperial commands and capitulations, and should seek to break the peace, there being no grounds for so doing, he shall be punished by death, and all those who violate any of the present articles shall be beheaded.

12. For the observance of everything in the present articles, in the presence of the very illustrious Hüseyin Paşa, the Ağa of the Militia, the Müftü and the Kadi as defenders of the law, all the ulema and elders, all those who continually pray to the Very High God, and all members, great and small, of the Divan and Council of the invincible Militia of Algiers, with common accord and consent, to the glory and honor of the Emperors and in accordance with the imperial commands and capitulations, we have made and promised this peace, and given our solemn word, and [we] promise to maintain and keep it point for point. We have made several copies of the present Act, similarly sealed and signed by all three above mentioned. One copy shall be kept in the office of the sacred treasury of the Divan, another is for the Emperor of France, and the others are for those places where they must be made known. . . .

2. Concessionary Contract, 29 September 1628

. . . .Since the French formerly commanded the place called the Bastion [French fortress] along with the port of Bône, these are granted to them [again] for the consideration of 26,000 doubloons [Spanish], of which 16,000 doubloons are for the salary of the Janissaries and 10,000 doubloons for the glorious treasury of the Qasbah [citadel], as was promised by Captain Samson Napollon.

In consideration of this sum we have promised to give the King of France, with fishing rights, the Bastion and port of Bône, of which, as repayment for services, Captain Samson shall be chief. He shall be lifetime commander of these. After his death the King may appoint successors.

The vessels of Captain Samson may come and go at these places to sell, trade, buy, and carry off leathers, wax, wool, and all other such things, as formerly. Nor may any other vessel, of whatever ownership, be permitted to go there to sell, trade for, or buy wax, wool, and other merchandise without a written order from Captain Samson.

We understand that the vessels of Captain Samson may rightfully leave France, and on their return to the port [of Bône] we permit them to come and go freely.

If the vessels should encounter a corsair,

they shall not be subjected to annoyance or reproach, since they have the right to come and go.

The vessels will be permitted to visit any part of our coast, without interference, coming and going.

Since the Bastion Square and its associated buildings have been demolished, we permit them to be rebuilt and made as they were for protection against Moors and vessels and brigands of Majorca and Minorca. The [concessionnaires] shall also enjoy access to the leather warehouses of which the port of Bône is full.

They may rebuild as before the other positions and places that were customarily held for defense.

Coral-fishing boats being obliged by contrary winds to tie up at various places on the coast, such as Jijelli, Collo, and Bône, shall suffer no harm; nor shall slaves be taken for sale to Moors.

Any kind of ship, galley or frigate passing along this coast, either in trade or otherwise, going to or coming from the Kingdom of Tunis, may not harm or annoy the coral-fishing boats and shall in no way cause them injury. . . .

9. GRANT OF CAPITULATIONS TO ENGLAND BY SHAH SAFI
July-August 1629

[Foster, *Letters received by the East India Company*, 6: 293–97]

The English East India Company procured its first *farman* (royal decree) authorizing trade in Persia from Shah 'Abbas in October 1615, with the reluctant intervention of Sir Robert Sherley, who continued in Persian service as military adviser and "ambassador at large." The farman consisted of little more than a vague directive to Persian officials and subjects "to kindly receive and entertaine the English Frankes or Nation" (text in Purchas, *His Pilgrimes,* vol. 1, bk. iv, p. 524). Yet, on the strength of it, company factories were set up in 1617 at Shiraz and at Isfahan, then the capital of Persia. In the same year, Edward Connock, manager of the company's Persian operations, negotiated with the shah in the name of King James I, but without express authorization, an elaborate treaty of commerce, promulgated, as were all such documents, in the form of a royal decree. The original text appears to have been lost. In 1629, however, Shah Safi (1629–42) granted a farman that purported to confirm, unaltered, the provisions Shah 'Abbas had sanctioned a dozen years earlier. The two instruments, which probably differed in detail only, established the legal framework for English-Persian commercial relations for a full century, the terms having been confirmed by Shah Sultan Husayn (1694–1722), the last of the Safavi monarchs. Herbert, *Some Years Travels*; A. Wilson, *Persian Gulf*, chaps. 9–11; Foster, *England's Quest of Eastern Trade*, chaps. 30–31.

1. That in the behalf of the supreme Majesty of King James there might continually reside at the court of Shah Abas an ambassador; and at what time soever as the Majesty of the King of England shall, for the better establishing of amity, benevolence and correspondency, desire an ambassador from hence, we shall gladly send one, who being arrived in his country shall conserve and keep those amorous links and bands of friendship, live, unity and benevolence.

2. At that time soever as the said English nation shall arrive with their ships

to any of the ports belonging to the King of Persia, or shall travel by land with their merchandises, the Governors of the said ports or places wheresoever they come shall not exact from them one farthing more than the accustomed duties which my own subjects pay.

3. Whatsoever is necessary, as victuals, munition, etc., shall be sold unto the said nation for the furnishing [of] their shipping at the same rates and prices my own subjects pay.

4. If by chance there happen any torment or tempestuous storm where the English ships shall ride, and that any of the said ships suffer shipwreck (which God forbid), no man whatsoever shall pretend anything thereof, but shall suffer the said nation in the best manner they can to save their goods and make the most of all things thereof. If any person take anything thereof, they shall restore it again.

5. Whatsoever goods the said nation shall import [into?] our dominions, they may carry it to whatsoever place in my country they please, buying and selling freely, nobody molesting them, or offer-[ing?] them any force or violence.

6. They shall buy whatsoever sort of merchandise they list, nobody hindering them.

7. They shall live in their own laws and religion, and no man compel them by violence to turn Mussellmen: for as religion is a work which proceeds from the conscience and mind, which pleads between the creature and the Creator, so nobody but the high Majesty of God hath power to penetrate the said conscience; and God it is above unto whom all men are to render an account of their salvation. But if any of the said nation shall voluntarily turn Mussellman, he shall live an any part of my dominions he lists, possessing quietly what belongs unto him.

8. They shall keep whatsoever sort of arms or weapons in their houses; and if in their travels any person shall steal anything from them, and they in defence thereof kill him, the governors of that jurisdiction shall not molest them for it; but if they apprehend the thief and carry him before the magistrate, he shall in their presence give him punishment.

9. At what time soever any ambassador shall come from the high Majesty of the King of England, he hath power to constitute in any part of my dominions agents and factors for the negotiating their business; and our governors and supreme ministers of such places shall respect them and assist them in all occasions.

10. If any of their people shall commit any disorders, they shall be carried before the said Ambassador to have chastisement.

11. In whatsoever part any of the said nation shall reside, and anybody offer them force or violence, they shall acquaint the governor of those parts thereof. If he deny them justice, they shall appeal unto the Ambassador which is in my Court, and he informing our Royal Person thereof, We shall severely chastise such abuses.

12. If in any part whatsoever there shall be any servant or interpreter of the said nation in whom they themselves put trust and confidence, they [shall?] give credence unto him, and respect him in the like manner as if he were one of the said nation.

13. If from any parts of Turkie, or other places whatsoever, any man shall bring any slaves of the English nation, if he be not turned Mussellman, he shall be delivered unto the said nation, they paying only the price he cost.

14. If any of the said nation die in any part of my dominions, that no man offer to take one farthing of his goods, but that the said Ambassador dispose thereof as he see good, and that the corpse of the said deceased be interred in places where other Christians bury.

15. If the said English shall not find vent for such commodities as they bring, according to their content, they may transport it through my country into any other parts whatsoever, paying only the accustomed duties my own subjects pay, and as they do in Constantinople and Alepo and other parts of Turkie.

If anything be stolen from them on the way the governors of those parts shall make search for the thief; and, finding him, shall restore the said goods; if not, the said governors shall make good what was stolen.

16. If between the said nation and our subjects happen any difference or discord in buying or selling, they shall repair unto the Justice, who shall do them right according to the ancient laws of this land.

But if the said difference pass or exceed twenty tomands, the Justice shall send them to the Ambassador to be decided, that he in presence our Justices might do whatsoever shall be conformable to honourable and noble laws.

17. If any of the said nation shall marry a wife of any of those Christians in our country, if he have any issue, and should die, leaving the said children destitute of friends to protect them, they shall in such cases be delivered to the disposure of the Ambassador.

18. That no solider, merchant, rustic or whatsoever person in my dominions, nay, the said English themselves, shall not break these conditions, for that the high Majesty of Shah Abas, the conqueror of the world, hath accepted and allowed thereof.

10. GRANT OF EXTRATERRITORIAL PRIVILEGES TO PERSIAN MERCHANTS IN THE NETHERLANDS
7 February 1631

[Translated from the Dutch text in Valentijn, *Oud en nieuw Oost Indiën*, vol. 5, bk. 5, pp. 296–97]

A Dutch agent of Shah Safi, Johan van Hasselt, obtained—from "the Sovereign Gentlemen the Estates General of the United Netherlands," in 1631—a grant of extraterritorial privileges for Persian merchants in the Netherlands. These were patterned on the interstate arrangements in Europe at the time. However, the promise of the exchange of capitulatory rights on a reciprocal basis never materialized, because Persian merchants rarely established branches in Europe. Still, the following instrument is significant for evaluating the development of the capitulatory regimes in the Middle East and in demonstrating differences between the experience of Persia and that of the Ottoman Empire. For references, see Doc .7.

The Sovereign Gentlemen the Estates General of the United Netherlands, having granted permission to the Persian Nation to land here in the name of the Much-Revered King, now also allow that Nation to do so in private capacity and to have free access and passage to all places and cities located in the United Provinces or under their jurisdiction, and to move about freely, unhampered and unmolested, to come and go, and also to negotiate, to buy and sell all sorts of goods and merchandise, none excepted, insofar as that Nation may deem fit and may find such dealings profitable.

The same Persian Nation, whenever they may desire to engage in business, shall enjoy in these lands all the same freedoms and rights as those of the inhabitants of these lands, even as those of persons of quality who are invested in these lands with important functions and offices.

If the Persian Nation should buy or sell small quantities of goods or merchandise in their houses, they will be allowed to use their own ells and also their own weights and measures; but in transactions in which they may buy or sell a large quantity of goods or merchandise which must be weighed or measured, the weighing or measuring shall be regulated according to the wise and circumspect customs of the land, so that the buyer or seller may be neither cheated nor defrauded.

If any member of the Persian Nation should happen to pass away in these lands, leaving no one to assume responsibility for the goods of the King or those of the deceased himself, the Gentlemen Regents of the deceased's place of residence shall become responsible for taking proper inventory and placing in custody all the goods of the Persian King or of the deceased himself until the Much-Revered King may make alternative arrangements for His Majesty's goods or the friends of the deceased for the latter's private goods. In the meantime the consumable or perishable goods shall be redeemed by opportune transactions for the benefit of the Much-Revered King or especially of the private heirs of the deceased; proper accounts, proofs and records of the redeemed goods and merchandise shall be kept.

Whenever Persian merchants may arrive in these lands in suitable numbers and with sufficient capital for engaging in business, they will be provided jointly with comfortable dwelling and they will enjoy in their place of residence freedom from all imposts on consumable goods which may be consumed in their households; similarly, comfortable housing will be furnished, and the same exemption [from imposts] granted, to those who may be commissioned by the Much-Revered Persian King to represent that Nation [in the Netherlands] and to serve as chiefs of such merchant [communities].

The house of the Agent of His Royal Persian Majesty shall be and shall remain privileged, as are the houses of other Agents of Kings and Princes in Europe who reside at the court of the above-mentioned Estates General. And if the Persian Nation should establish in these lands a factory, properly staffed and provided with capital,

they will enjoy the same rights, advantages and equities in commercial and judicial matters as those enjoyed respectively by the English Court residing in the city of Delft and by the Scottish Nation residing in the city of Camperveen with whose King the above-mentioned Estates General have maintained commercial accords and intercourse from ancient times.

The Persian Nation will be granted in their houses full liberty in the exercise of relgion without hindrance, molestation or disturbance by anyone.

If a member of the Persian Nation should wish to change his religion, the Sovereign Gentlemen of the Estates shall not interfere; but in any event the King or anyone else who might have entrusted goods with such a person shall not thereby be deprived of their property and that person, as theretofore, shall [continue to] administer matters under his charge and judiciously settle them.

The Persian Nation shall be granted a place for the burial of their dead in accordance with their customs and usages.

If the Agent of the Much-Revered King should find that a member of the Persian Nation has committed a misdeed, a misdemeanor or an act of opposition against him and should request the judicial authorities of the locality in which the transgression occurred to support him so that he might effect justice with respect to such person or persons, the [requested] assistance shall be given to the agent in opportune time.

11. TREATY OF PEACE AND FRONTIERS: THE OTTOMAN EMPIRE AND PERSIA
17 May 1639

(Reaffirmed, 4 September 1746, 28 July 1823, 31 May 1847)
[*British and Foreign State Papers*, 105: 763–66]

With the rise of the Safavi dynasty in Persia at the opening of the sixteenth century, recurrent wars between the Sunni Ottomans and the Shi'i Persians produced frequent shifts in the boundaries between the two Muslim states. Sultan Murad IV (1623–40) finally recaptured Baghdad in 1638. In dictating the following conditions of peace which Shah Safi's representative accepted at Zuhab (in northern Persia), the sultan reincorporated Baghdad and the surrounding districts into the Ottoman Empire. These frontiers, although only roughly drawn, endured virtually unchanged (with brief exceptions) for more than two hundred years. In the mid-nineteenth century, when mixed commissions endeavored to demarcate the boundary with precision, the 1639 arrangement provided the point of departure. Sykes, *History of Persia*, vol. 2, chap. 66; Hekmat, *Essai sur l'histoire des relations politiques irano-ottomanes*, pp. 17–39; Achoube-Amini, *Le conflit de frontière irako-iranien*, chap. 3; Hammer, *Geschichte des osmanischen Reiches*, 5: 193–294.

Praise to God, the Holy, the Gracious, the bestower of Victory; who has opened the door of peace and concord with the key of the words: "Verily I wish nothing so much as reconciliation," and dispelled the darkness of war and fighting with the light of quiet and happiness. Blessings and benedictions, so long as flowers spread their perfume and daylight shines, upon his Prophet who has fully and clearly manifested the faith, and with whose auspicious advant Islamism was greatly rejoiced; and upon his family, children and companions who have been active in propagating that faith.

Now, whereas, by the will and good pleasure of Him who raised the skies without pillars, and by an effect of the wisdom and omnipotency of Him who composed all things from various elements, and who has no equal, good order in society, and the conservation of the world depend upon the justice and equity of the Sovereigns, and upon their good understanding and union, no less than upon their submission to the positive and to the negative divine Commands, the August Sultans have, in conformity to this sacred precept: "Fear God and reconcile yourselves," resorted to reconciliation, which is a source of happiness, and renounced to hostilities and war, the sword of mutual contrariety was put into the scabbard; and nations which were making war with each other, cordially reconciled themselves. "That is a favour of God. He grants it to whom He pleases: and God is most gracious."

I, therefore, the most humble of all the servants of God, being charged and authorized to do or undo whatever concerns the Empire and the nation, and to make, just as I choose, war or peace, an authority which I hold from the most glorious Padi-

shah who is the Defender of the faith, whose Majesty is as great as that of Solomon, who is the substitute of God in the world, and who has justified the maxim that "An equitable Sultan is the shadow of God on earth"; the asylum of the greatest Musulman Princes, the shelter of the most illustrious Turkish Sovereigns, the supporter of Islamism and of Musulmans, the exterminator of heresies and of the polytheists, the Soverign of the two lands and of the two seas, the Sovereign of the two Orients and of the two Occidents, the servant of the two Holy Cities, the treasure of Mankind and the apple of the age, who is protected by the Supreme Being whose divine assistance men implore, and favoured by the most High and propitious God; May His Imperial Majesty's Dynasty last till the end of the world, and their reign be prolonged till the consummation of ages! have, in virtue of my full powers and my real character of the Sultan's substitute, ordered the Turkish victorious troops to march from beneath Bagdad, and began [sic] to go forward with an intention of entering the Persian territory. On our arrival at a station called Haronia, the most distinguished among the Grandees Chems Uddin Mehmed Culy Bey, Great Equerry, arrived there in the capacity of Ambassador with a Letter from Him who is the ornament of the Persian Throne, the splendor of the Kingdom of Djem, and whose magnificence is equal to that of Darius, the great Prince and illustrious Lord, the Precious Pearl of the Sea of Royalty, the sun of the sky of Sovereignty, the noble Eagle of the high region of the Dignity of Shah, the most Illustrious and Majestic Prince whose troops are as numerous as the stars; may the most High God raise the banners of his strength from earth to Heaven, and exalt the edifice of his glory to the height of the vaulted sky! to our great and august Padishah, and also a flattering Letter to me. The Ambassador having asked that the fire of war should be extinguished and the dust of fighting dispersed, stating that His Majesty the Shah's will is that reconciliation and peace between the two Parties should take place, I, on my part too, wishing to act in conformity to the sacred text, to wit: "If they incline to peace, do ye also incline to it," have readily consented, for the sake of the safety and tranquillity of mankind to make Peace; and a letter was sent to the Shah to the end that His Majesty might send a Person of confidence with power to settle the conditions of the Peace, in a manner suitable to the honour and dignity of the two Governments. Consequently the Shah has appointed according to the established laws and rules, to negotiate and conclude this treaty of Peace, and establish and fix the state of the frontiers, the most excellent and faithful Saroukhan, may he always be fortunate in transacting affairs on which quiet and security depend! Saroukhan, on his arrival in the Imperial Camp at Zahab, was received with marks of hospitality; and on the 14th day of Muharem, in the year 1049 of the Hegira of the Prophet, upon whom be the best benedictions, a Divan was held in the Imperial Camp, in which were present the illustrious Vizirs, the Miri Miran, the Commanders and Agas, the Aga of the Janissaries, six Agas of six Companies, and other officers of the army. Saroukhan, the Plenipotentiary who was duly accredited, and the Ambassador Mehmed Culy Bey, were introduced in the Divan, and the preliminaries were discussed with them so as to put on a good footing the position of the Rayas and of the poor who are a trust imposed by the Author of all beings, and the result of the discussions on both Parties has been written down and is as follows: Tzanan, Bedrie, Mendelgeen, Derteuk and Dernai, in the Pashalik of Bagdad, will remain under the authority of our august Padishah, who will also take possession of the Plains between Mendelgeen and Derteuk, and the Mountain will remain under the authority of the Shah. Serminil is fixed as frontier between Derteuk and Dernai. That part of the country of Haronia, occu-

pied by the Tribes of Djaf and Zilja Uddin, will belong to the Sultan. Pezai and Zerdony remain to the Shah. The fortress of Zindjir, which lies on the top of the Mountain, shall be demolished; the Sultan will take possession of the Villages lying westward of it, and the Shah will take possession of those lying eastward. The Villages on the Mountain above Sailm Calè, near Chehrezor, will be in the possession of the Sultan, and the Villages lying on the East, will be in the possession of the Shah, who will also keep the Castle of Orman with the Villages which are dependent on it. The defile leading to Chehrezor has been established as a frontier. The fortress of Kizilidji with its dependencies shall remain in the possession of the Sultan; and Mihreban with the dependencies thereof, in that of the Shah. The fortresses of Cotour (Kotur) and Makoo on the frontier of Van, and the fortress of Magazberd towards Kars and Van, will be demolished by the two Parties, and so long as the Shah will not have molested the fortresses of Akiskha, Kars, Van, Chehrezor, Bagdad, Bassora and other Places within the limits, such as fortresses, forts, Districts, lands, hills and mountains, and to no such horrible act as provoking to rebellion shall have been committed by Him, on their part also His Majesty our Great Padishah will respect this Peace, and no molestation shall, contrary to Treaty, be done to the places which remain within the limits of the other side.

In order, therefore, that Merchants and travellers belonging to either Party may come and go and meet with a friendly reception, I have, in virtue of my full power and positive authority written down this egregious Treaty, the contents of which are true, and sent it to His Majesty the Shah, and to our most August Padishah. So long as the Shah shall, according to the Sacred text: "Do not violate an agreement after ye have done it" observe this treaty as it ought to be observed, His Imperial Majesty, our most Magnificent Padishah also, will act in obedience to the Holy Command: "Fulfil your agreement, for an agreement is obligatory."

This Happy Peace will last and be maintained, with the permission of God, till the day of resurrection: "And he who shall alter it after having heard it, verily this sin shall be upon those who shall have altered it."

Praise to God; He is the sole God, and

blessings upon him after whom there will be no Prophet. In the beginning; and in the end; and externally; and internally....

12. PROCLAMATION OF FRENCH PROTECTION OF THE MARONITE COMMUNITY IN LEBANON BY LOUIS XIV
28 April 1649

[Translated from the French text in Testa, *Recueil des traités de la Porte Ottomane*, 3: 140–41]

The preferential position of France, in its role as protector of European commerce in the Ottoman Empire, was progressively whittled away after 1580, when England, Holland, and other European states successively received their own capitulatory privileges from the Ottoman crown. At about this time, France came to be recognized as the guardian of European Catholicism in the sultan's realm, and after 1639 France claimed also the right to protect Ottoman Christian subjects—especially Catholics—throughout the Asian provinces. One of the earliest formal acts of this class was the "adoption," by Louis XIV in 1649, of the Maronite Community in Lebanon, thus establishing the precedent of close relations between the Maronites and France which has persisted into the twentieth century. Jouplain, *La question du Liban*, bk. 1, chap. 3; Hourani, *Syria and Lebanon*, chap. 8.

Louis, by the grace of God King of France and Navarre, to all to whom these presents come, greeting: Let it be known: that we, by the advice of the Queen Regent, our very honored Lady and Mother, having taken and placed, as by these signs of our hand we do take and place in our protection and special safeguard the Most Reverend Patriarch and all the prelates, ecclesiastics, and Maronite Christian laics, who dwell particularly in Mount Lebanon: we desire that they should be aware of this at all times and, to this end, we command our beloved and trusty Sieur la Haye de Pentetet, Councilor in our Councils and our Ambassador in the Levant, and all those who succeed him in this post, to show favor to these former, together or separately, by their care, good offices, entreaty and protection, either before the Porte of our very dear and perfect friend the Grand Seigneur, or elsewhere as needs be, so that there will not be accorded to them any ill treatment, but, on the contrary, that they

may continue freely their spiritual exercises and functions. We enjoin the Consuls and Vice-Consuls of the French Nation in the seaports of the Levant, or others flying the flag of France, now and in the future, to show all favor in their power to the said Lord Patriarch and to the said Maronite Christians of the said Mount Lebanon, and to assist to embark on French or other vessels the young men and all other Christian Maronites who might wish to go over into Christian lands, either to study or for any other business, without taking or requiring of them any fee other than that which they may be able to give, treating them with all possible gentleness and charity.

We request and require the illustrious and magnificent Lords the Pashas and officers of His Highness to show favor to and assist the Lord Archbishop of Tripoli and all prelates and Maronite Christians, offering on our part to do likewise for all those recommended by them.

13. TREATY OF PEACE AND COMMERCE, AND COMMERCIAL CONCESSION: FRANCE AND THE GARRISON OF TUNIS
25 November 1665–2 August 1666

[Translated from the French texts in Rouard de Card, *Traités de la France*, pp. 116–23, 126–29]

Beginning with the formation in 1585 of the Ligue des ports de la Provence contre les Barbaresques, French privateers and Tunisian corsairs engaged in a continuing "war" that lasted well over a century, interrupted from time to time by "peace treaties" and the exchange of slaves. In the circumstances, it was hardly astonishing that French relations with the Garrison of Tunis in the seventeenth century represented an exercise in unrelieved frustration. The first treaty, concluded as early as 1605 and designed to place French subjects under the Ottoman capitulatory umbrella, became a dead letter before it could even go into effect. The mutual piracy grew worse until it was briefly suspended by the signature in 1616 of yet another peace treaty, with the customary arrangement for the exchange of slaves and the solemn pledges for durable friendship. The French concessionaires in Bône (Doc. 8) tried in 1633 to capture Tabarca as a permanent base in the Garrison of Tunis, but the venture was abandoned when Samson Napollon, its leader, was killed in action. In 1639 Cardinal Richelieu sent an envoy to Tunis to negotiate the terms of a concession at Cap Nègre. This effort too was given up two years later, after the French failed to live up to their side of the preliminary bargain for full reciprocity in the exchange of slaves. Meanwhile, French subjects, without treaty protection, were establishing themselves in Cap Nègre and Tabarca to engage in fishing and commerce. In the quarter-century that followed the abortive Richelieu initiative, France and the Garrison fought an almost uninterrupted, if also still undeclared, war, and the buildings erected by the French factors on the Tunisian coast were destroyed. Starting in 1663 the French government mounted a major naval campaign, eventually placed under the command of the duc de Beaufort, who in the fall of 1665 compelled the Garrison to sue for peace. The terms of the treaty reflected Beaufort's views, and after its ratification by King Louis XIV a convention granted French merchants the long-sought concession in the Cap Nègre-Tabarca area. The two instruments, reproduced below, were hardly put into effect before the war of the pirates erupted once again, punctuated as always by short-lived treaties of peace (1672, 1685, and 1691) and by yet another concessionary instrument (1685). By then the Garrison had become involved in a prolonged civil war, which was not resolved until the rise of the Husayni dynasty in 1705. The following instruments are more valuable for their reflection of French aspirations than for their immediate practical effects. Masson, *Histoire des établissements et du commerce français dans l'Afrique Barbaresque*, chap. 4–5; Cambon, *Histoire de la régence de Tunis*, chap. 6; Abun-Nasr, *History of the Maghrib*, chap. 7; Julien, *Histoire de l'Afrique du Nord*, vol. 1, chap. 6; G. Fisher, *Barbary Legend*.

1. Treaty of Peace and Commerce, 25 November 1665

1. Henceforth, counting from the day of the signature of the present articles, there shall be a cessation of arms and of all hostility on both sides, and as soon as this Treaty is ratified by His Very Christian

Majesty, there shall be good understanding, friendship, and firm and stable peace between the subjects of His Very Christian Majesty, and the very illustrious and magnificent Paşa, Divan, and Dey, and the peoples of the Kimgdom [of Tunis]. In anticipation of the desired peace, their vessels, galleys, barks, and other ships shall sail in complete freedom. On land and sea, the subjects of both sides shall commit no act of hostility against one another. On the contrary, they shall assist and serve one another without injury, giving only help and comfort. Similarly, all merchants of both nations may trade in complete freedom in the Kingdom of France and Navarre and in that of Tunis, where they shall be treated with every expression of true and sincere friendship.

2. All French slaves in the town of Tunis and in the jurisdiction of that Kingdom, without exception, whatever their quality and condition, and all Janissary slaves of the Kingdom of Tunis shall be set free by both sides and returned in good faith.

3. All vessels of both sides on the high seas or in the roads, the harbors, or the ports, having unfurled their flags and been recognized, shall continue on their way without committing any hostile act. Since the vessels of Algiers, Tripoli, Salé and other places in Barbary carry the same flag as that of Tunis, to prevent any inconveniences that might occur, it is decreed that the vessels of Tunis (after those on board both ships have shown themselves on deck) may send a boat alongside the vessels of His Very Christian Majesty, with no more than one or two men over and above those necessary for its navigation, to assure themselves that [those on board] are truly Frenchmen. They may also board the ships, if they wish, after showing a certificate from the French Consul resident at Tunis. The Commanders of the ships of His Very Christian Majesty shall then be allowed to continue on their way in complete freedom, without damage to their persons, clothing, and merchandise, whether they be merchants, sailors, soldiers, or passengers of whatever nationality. All other visits and searches on both sides are forbidden. The same procedure shall be followed by the vessels of Tunis with regard to those of His Very Christian Majesty,

which must show a passport from the Admiral of France.

4. If any vessel, bark, or other merchantship of Tunis should be met at sea by warships or others of His Very Christian Majesty, and if, after lowering its flags, it should nevertheless be forced to defend itself by firing its cannons or *pierriers* [stone-firing guns], and then, having been pursued and captured, is afterward recognized as being from the Kingdom of Tunis, it shall not be considered a fair prize. On the contrary, it and its people, with all their property, merchandise, clothing, and effects, shall be returned. The same procedure shall be followed by Tunisian vessels toward merchantships of His Very Christian Majesty.

5. When His Very Christian Majesty's warships and others enter the ports or roads of the Kingdom of Tunis, they may sell prizes, except for those taken from the Turks, at their pleasure and without hindrance by natives of the country, and without having to pay and other duty than that paid by friends. If the vessels require live or dead victuals or other necessities, they may buy them freely in the local markets wherever they happen to be, at the regular prices paid by the inhabitants of the Kingdom, without payment of taxes to any officer. The same procedure shall be followed in France toward Tunisian vessels.

6. Any subject of His Very Christian Majesty, whether merchant or passenger, of whatever quality and condition, who happens to be in one of the ports or harbors in the jurisdiction of the Kingdom of Tunis, may remain on his vessel or leave it, and may come and go anywhere he wishes on land without hindrance. This shall also be permitted to vessels belonging to the Kingdom of Tunis when they are in the ports of His Very Christian Majesty.

7. If, by some ill fortune, vessels, galleys, barks, or other ships belonging to subjects of His Very Christian Majesty should be attacked by those of Algiers, Tripoli, Salé, or other enemies, in the ports or on the roads of the Kingdom of Tunis, the Commanders of these places shall be obliged to give them refuge in their ports and shall be required to send their men as reinforcements in one or more boats so to defend the French ships so far as possible.

8. All merchantmen and other ships belonging to subjects of His Very Christian Majesty going to Tunis, Sousse, Porto Farina, and other places of the Kingdom to sell their goods may do so in all liberty and surety, paying only ordinary duties. They may take on board again their unsold goods without payment of duty.

9. Vessels of war or commerce, even galleys and other ships, belonging to the Very Christian King or to his subjects may enter as they wish such ports, roads, or harbors in the jurisdiction of the Kingdom of Tunis for repairing, tarring, careening, greasing, or taking on water or refreshment without being refused or asked to pay duty. Nevertheless, as a precaution, galleys shall be obliged, before entering the port, to send a caïque ashore to explain their intentions to the Commanders of the fortresses. The caïque shall remain on land as a surety, while the boat belonging to the fortresses shall go to the galleys to learn their wishes.

10. Any vessel, galley, or other ship of His Very Christian Majesty or his subjects which by ill chance should be wrecked in the ports, roads, or coasts of the Kingdom of Tunis shall not be considered a fair prize. Nor shall its property be pillaged or its men, whether merchants or passengers, of whatever quality and condition, be considered slaves. On the contrary, the Governors of the fortresses and the peoples of the Kingdom of Tunis shall do their best to give it aid and comfort, to save its persons, its vessels, its goods and its merchandise, without the Paşa, the Divan, or the Dey making claims or transgressing in any way. The same procedure shall be followed in France toward the vessels of Tunis, should similar misfortunes befall them.

11. If any slave belonging to the Kingdom of Tunis or any nation whatsoever should escape by swimming to a French vessel, the Consul of France resident in Tunis may not be obliged to pay the buying-price of the slave, unless he had been warned in time of the flight of the slave, and unless he had time to make reparation [i.e., to return the slave]. If the Consul should neglect this warning, he shall be obliged to pay for the slave at the price that his owner paid in the market, but no more than 300 piasters for everything.

12. If any vessel from Tripoli, Algiers, Salé, or elsewhere should take to Tunis, Porto Farina, or any other road in the jurisdiction of the Kingdom vessels, barks, or other ships, sailors, passengers, or goods belonging to subjects of His Very Christian Majesty, they may not be sold. The same procedure shall be followed in France with regard to Tunisian vessels.

13. Henceforth no warships, galleys, or other ships of Tunis or the Kingdom of France may enslave any Frenchman or [individual of] other [nationality], not even the Knights of the Cross, nor similarly the subjects of the Kingdom of Tunis, under one or the other flag. But under other flags or foreign banners, the passengers, whatever their condition, and the merchants shall be free. However, French gunners, soldiers and sailors may be made slaves and, with the exception of the Knights of Malta, may be redeemed for 150 piasters per head. In return, Tunisians shall receive the same treatment.

14. Henceforth, subjects of the Kingdom of Tunis shall be free in France, no matter where they came from, and shall not be received as slaves, either for purchase or for sale. If by chance such a slave should be discovered, he shall be set free on the first demand, and all his clothing and property returned. The same shall be done for Frenchmen throughout the Kingdom of Tunis.

15. The French Consul resident in the town of Tunis shall be honored and respected and shall have precedence over all other Consuls. He shall continue to have a place in his house where he and the subjects of His Very Christian Majesty may practice their religion freely without hindrance, harm, or injury, by word or deed. The Consul may have and maintain a priest in his home, if he wishes, to serve his chapel, without the Dey and the Divan's preventing him from doing so.

16. On the change of French Consuls by His Very Christian Majesty, the Paşa, the Divan, and the Dey may not impede or hinder the process in any manner whatsoever, and the departing Consul may leave freely, on paying his debts. Henceforth, French Consuls with the cooperation of the Dey may change the *saccagi*, or

interpreter, every three months, according to the custom of the Divan. This will be granted him without difficulty.

17. Every nation trading in the town of Tunis and in the jurisdiction of the Kingdom, except the English and the Flemish, each of whom presently has a Consul in Tunis, shall recognize the French Consul and shall pay him the accustomed dues of the Consulate without difficulty.

18. There shall be no duties or taxes on the materials and victuals that the French Consul may import for his own use and as presents, nor on those that he may buy locally for the provision of his house.

19. Henceforth, all goods of the subjects of His Very Christian Majesty living in Tunis and within the boundaries of the Kingdom, in case of debt, absence, or misdeed, may not be seized or kept illegally by anyone of Tunis. On the contrary, the goods shall remain in the hands of the French Consul. The subjects of His Very Christian Majesty shall even be free to go to France, or wherever else they see fit, with their wives, children, servants, goods, and effects, without any hindrance whatsoever.

20. Neither the French Consul nor any subject of His Very Christian Majesty shall be responsible for the debts of any other Frenchman or of anyone of another nation, whoever he may be. Neither may they be imprisoned for this reason nor may the Consul's house be sealed. Neither may testimony be accepted against any of them, nor action taken, unless they have previously made an undertaking by an act signed by their own hands.

21. If any subject of His Very Christian Majesty should strike or ill-treat a Turk or a Moor, he may be punished if captured; but if he flees, no revenge may be taken on the French Consul or on any [other] subjects of His Very Christian Majesty.

22. No subjects of His Very Christian Majesty may be subjected, in case of disagreements that occur unexpectedly, to any other judgment than that of the Dey, not even that of the Divan or the Kadi.

23. In particular, subjects of His Very Christian Majesty or those of any other nation trading under the protection of the French Consul shall not be obliged to settle disagreements among themselves before anyone except the Consul, who alone shall receive the testimony.

24. If any French or other merchant under the protection of the French Consul should die in the Kingdom of Tunis, and if he has made a will, his property shall be assigned to the named testamentary executor to hold for the heirs or others in whose favor the goods have been disposed. But if he should die intestate, the French Consul shall seize his goods and property so to hold them in the same way for his heirs, without anyone of the Kingdom of Tunis being informed.

25. Henceforth, no subject of His Very Christian Majesty who is considered a slave, whether from the Levant or from the West, shall be sold in the bazaar or market.

26. If any warship, galley, merchantman, or other ship belonging to His Very Christian Majesty or his subjects should happen to run aground or be wrecked on some island or uninhabited place, and if by chance a vessel, galley, or other ship of Tunis should pass, it must go to the former's aid, even take its people, clothing, and merchandise, which it will put into the hands of the French Consul at Tunis, without being permitted to carry or sell them elsewhere. The same procedure shall be followed by the ships of France toward those of Tunis, should they suffer a similar misfortune.

27. When the present articles are signed and confirmed, all damage and deprivations suffered on both sides before the present peace was known shall be repaired forthwith, and full and entire satisfaction shall be given reciprocally. Everything found in its original state shall be given back. That is why, to prevent any inconvenience, the Commanders of the two parties shall be diligently warned of this.

28. If an injury should occur on either side, neither party may break the peace until fair justice had been refused.

29. If a difference of any sort should arise that might break the peace between the two parties, the Consul of the French nation resident in Tunis shall have complete freedom to leave and retire to his country, or elsewhere, when he thinks fit. When he leaves, he shall be allowed without hindrance to take with him his family and servants, even two slaves of his choice, and

his goods. In order to do this, he may come and go freely on the vessels in the ports, and may even remove his property in the country. . . .

2. Commercial Concession at Cap Nègre, 2 August 1666

1. The French merchants coming to reside at Cap Nègre will be there under the protection of the Divan, which will not permit them to be molested in their persons, in their effects, or in the commerce that they may carry on privately, without restriction, with all other Frenchmen.

2. They may repair the houses, shops, and other buildings which their predecessors enjoyed, without enlarging them or making them smaller, but leaving them as they were before. They may surround them with a wall eight Arab feet high and three palms thick. If the buildings shall not suffice for commerce, they will be allowed to build three other stores near the old ones, of the same shape and size, to restore the place destined for the chapel which was there before, and to practice their religion there. But in these places and walls, and on the houses, they may not erect battlements, embrasures, or anything else having the appearance of a fortress, except loopholes in the enclosure and four lookouts at the corners, each to accommodate two men who may keep watch for defense against thieves. It is also agreed that the tower at the head of the cape, where a guard is kept, will be repaired at Company expense, so that in case of need [the company] may take refuge there with its effects, without being stopped by the resident guard, who will have orders to protect their persons and effects.

3. Le sieur Emanuel Payen of Marseilles will be appointed to manage the above-mentioned places. Knowing the Arabic language very well, he will take care to give satisfaction to the people of the region who bring foodstuffs and to whom the Company shall give 1,000 piasters per year for its upkeep.

4. All trade which hitherto has taken place with the Frankish merchants residing at Tabarca will be transferred wholly to the Compagnie des Français. To prevent continued dealing, direct or indirect, with the merchants, the Beys shall order as many horsemen and foot-soldiers as is necessary to interdict it absolutely. If, in spite of precautions, such commerce should be carried on clandestinely, the French will be permitted to subtract 6,000 piasters from the 35,000 piasters mentioned below. If they should not find profit in the trade and should wish to abandon it and withdraw, they may do so by paying, over and above the 35,000 piasters, the 6,000 paid by the Genoese residing at Tabarca. It has also been agreed that the French may buy leather and wax only from the usual dealers at Tabarca. If by chance they should buy these [products] from the farmers of Béja, Testour, le Kef, and Bizerte, they shall have to return them, or to come to an understanding with [the farmers].

5. It has been agreed that the Company shall pay to Murad Bey and Ahmed Bey 35,000 piasters per year, which will be shared as follows: 12,000 to the Paşa for the pay of the Janissaries; 2,000 to the Dey; 13,000 for the pay and upkeep of the militia appointed for the security of the places of commerce; and 3,000 for the nobles and chiefs of the Arabs, the last sum being payable in two months in two equal installments. The 2,000 for the Dey shall be paid in advance, at the beginning of the year. The remaining 5,000 piasters for Murad Bey and Ahmed Bey will be explained in Article 14.

6. The period of payment, as explained in the preceding article, shall run from the day the Company is established at Cap Nègre and vicinity, after the ratification of the present agreement by the Duc de Beaufort, the Paşa, the Dey, and the Divan of Tunis.

7. The present Treaty shall remain valid for twenty consecutive years; after that, it will be renewed and ratified by both parties.

8. All the Arab principals or chiefs who are accustomed to selling wheat, barley, chick-peas, beans, and other vegetables to the Genoese of Tabarca shall sell these and other items to the French of Cap Nègre at current prices, without demanding more, although they may receive whatever may be given voluntarily as a gratuity. Whenever the people of the region do not carry out the terms of the Treaty, Murad Bey and Ahmed Bey shall send soldiers there to oblige them to do so.

9. Frenchmen residing at Cap Nègre and other places in its jurisdiction may go into the countryside to hunt and gather wood without hindrance. They may even take two or three soldiers along to prevent their being insulted. When the French wish to whiten their houses and repair their grounds and their stores, they shall be permitted to make as many lime ovens as necessary, and [they may] erect a windmill and a shed for two ovens, to bake bread for themselves and biscuits for the soldiers of the guard.

10. The Company may maintain as many boats, launches, or coral-fishing boats as it deems necessary for the fishing of coral.

11. If French vessels should be wrecked in the places mentioned in the present Treaty and their vicinities, the men and goods shall be returned to the Company, and the Divan or others may not lay claim to them for any reason.

12. The Company shall be allowed to build a windmill and two ovens on the lands specified in the present Treaty.

13. A customs duty of 10 percent shall be paid on all goods that the Company may import to Cap Nègre for sale in Tunis. On goods that it exports from Tunis and its dependencies, the Company shall pay the ordinary duty of Tunis according to ancient custom. On all goods bought at Tabarca, at Cap Nègre, and at other places mentioned in the present Treaty, no duty or tax shall be paid.

14. The remaining 5,000 piasters of the 35,000 mentioned in Article 5, which should be paid to Murad Bey and Ahmed[1] Bey, will not be paid in the first year, because they are refunding the sum, pure and simple, to the Company. The payment of the 5,000 piasters shall be due in the second year and thereafter, to the end of the twentieth year.

---

1. The French text reads "Mehemed."

14. FINAL TREATY OF CAPITULATIONS: THE OTTOMAN EMPIRE AND ENGLAND
September 1675

(Reaffirmed, 5 January 1809; terminated, 6 August 1924)
[Hertslet, *Treaties, etc., between Turkey and Foreign Powers*, pp. 247–66]

The Ottoman government progressively broadened English exterritorial rights by successive renewals of, and additions to, the earlier treaties in 1603, 1606, 1624, 1641, 1662, and 1675. The capitulations of 1675, which thus included all previous instruments, continued in force until the end of the Ottoman Empire. The first twenty articles, which correspond to the twenty-two articles[1] of the 1580 treaty (Doc. 4), have been omitted below, as have the several preambles. Sousa, *Capitulatory Regime of Turkey*, chap. 3; Wood, *History of the Levant Company*, and "English Embassy at Constantinople"; for negotiations of 1675, see Abbott, *Under the Turk in Constantinople*, chaps. 2, 9–11.

XXI. That duties shall not be demanded or taken of the English or the merchants sailing under the flag of that nation, on any piastres and sequins they may import into our sacred Dominions, or on those they may transport to any other place.

XXII. That our Beglerbegs, Judges, Def-terdars, and Masters of the mint, shall not interpose any hindrance or obstacle thereto by demanding either dollars or sequins from them, under the pretence of having

---

1. Articles 9 and 16 of the 1580 treaty do not appear in the 1675 version.

them recoined and exchanged into other money, nor shall give them any molestation or trouble whatever with regard thereto.

XXIII. That the English nation, and all ships belonging to places subject thereto, shall and may buy, sell, and trade in our sacred Dominions, and (except arms, gunpowder, and other prohibited commodities) load and transport in their ships every kind of merchandise, at their own pleasure, without experiencing any the least obstacle or hindrance from any one; and their ships and vessels shall and may at all times safely and securely come, abide, and trade in the ports and harbours of our sacred Dominions, and, with their own money, buy provisions and take in water, without any hindrance or molestation from any one.

XXIV. That if an Englishman, or other subject of that nation, shall be involved in any lawsuit, or other affair connected with law, the judge shall not hear nor decide thereon until the Ambassador, Consul, or Interpreter, shall be present; and all suits exceeding the value of four thousand Aspers shall be heard at the Sublime Porte, and nowhere else.

XXV. That the Consuls appointed by the English Ambassador in our sacred Dominions, for the protection of their merchants, shall never, under any pretence, be imprisoned, nor their houses sealed up, nor themselves sent away; but all suits or differences in which they may be involved shall be represented to our Sublime Porte, where their Ambassadors will answer for them.

XXVI. That in case any Englishman, or other person subject to that nation, or navigating under its flag, should happen to die in our sacred Dominions, our fiscal and other officers shall not, upon pretence of its not being known to whom the property belongs, interpose any opposition or violence, by taking or seizing the effects that may be found at his death, but they shall be delivered up to such Englishman, whoever he may be, to whom the deceased may have left them by his will; and should he have died intestate, then the property shall be delivered up to the English Consul, or his representative, who may be there present: and in case there be no Consul, or Consular Representative, they shall be sequestered by the judge, in order to his

delivering up the whole thereof, whenever any ship shall be sent by the Ambassador to receive the same.

XXVII. That all the privileges and other liberties already conceded, or hereafter to be conceded to the English, and other subjects of that nation sailing under their flag, by divers Imperial Commands, shall be always obeyed and observed, and interpreted in their favour, according to the tenor and true intent and meaning thereof; neither shall any fees be demanded by the fiscal officers and judges in the distribution of their property and effects.

XXVIII. That the Ambassadors and Consuls shall and may take into their service any janizary or interpreter they please, without any other janizary or other of our slaves intruding themselves into their service against their will and consent.

XXIX. That no obstruction or hindrance shall be given to the Ambassadors, Consuls, and other Englishmen, who may be desirous of making wine in their own houses, for the consumption of themselves and families; neither shall the janizaries our slaves, or others, presume to demand or exact any thing from them, or do them any injustice or injury.

XXX. That the English merchants having once paid the customs at Constantinople, Aleppo, Alexandria, Scio [Chios], Smyrna, and other ports of our sacred Dominions, not an Asper more shall be taken or demanded from them at any other place, nor shall any obstacle be interposed to the exit of their merchandise.

XXXI. That having landed their merchandise imported by their ships into our sacred Dominions, and paid in any port the customs thereon, and being obliged, from the impossibility of selling the same there, to transport them to another port, the Commandants or Governors shall not, on the landing of such merchandise, exact from them any new custom or duty thereon, but shall suffer them, freely and unrestrictedly, to trade, without any molestation or obstruction whatsoever.

XXXII. That no excise or duty on animal food shall be demanded of the English, or any subjects of that nation.

XXXIII. That differences and disputes having heretofore arisen between the Ambassadors of the Queen of England and the

King of France, touching the affair of the Flemish merchants, and both of them having presented memorials at our Imperial Stirrup, praying that such of the said merchants as should come into our sacred Dominions might navigate under their flag, *Hatti-sheriffs* were granted to both parties, but the Captain Pasha, Sinan, the son of Cigala, now deceased, who was formerly Vizir, and well versed in maritime affairs, having represented that it was expedient that such privilege should be granted to the Queen of England, and that the Flemish merchants should place themselves under her flag, as also the merchants of the four Provinces of Holland, Zealand, Friesland, and Guelderland, and all the other Vizirs being likewise of opinion that they should all navigate under the Queen's flag, and, like all the other English, pay the consulage and other duties, as well on their own merchandise as on those of others loaded by them, in their ships, to the Queen's Ambassadors or Consuls, it was by express order and Imperial authority accordingly commanded, that the French Ambassador or Consul should never hereafter oppose or intermeddle herein, but in future act conformably to the tenor of the present Capitulation. . . .

XXXIV. That the English merchants, and other subjects of that Nation, shall and may, according to their condition, trade at Aleppo, Egypt, and other ports of our sacred Dominions, on paying (according to ancient custom) a duty of three per cent. on all their merchandize, without being bound to the disbursement of an Asper more.

XXXV. That, in addition to the duty hitherto uniformly exacted on all merchandise, laden, imported, and transported in English ships, they shall also pay the whole of the consulage to the English Ambassadors and Consuls.

XXXVI. That the English merchants, and all others sailing under their flag, shall and may, freely and unrestrictedly, trade and purchase all sorts of merchandise (prohibited commodities alone excepted), and convey them, either by land or sea, or by way of the River Tanaïs, to the countries of Muscovy or Russia, and bring back from thence other merchandise into our sacred Dominions, for the purposes of traffic, and also transport others to Persia and other conquered countries.

XXXVII. That such customs only shall be demanded on the said goods in the conquered countries as have always been received there, without any thing more being exacted.

XXXVIII. That should the ships bound for Constantinople be forced by contrary winds to put into Caffa, or any other place of those parts, and not be disposed to buy or sell any thing, no one shall presume forcibly to take out or seize any part of their merchandise, or give to the ships or crews any molestation, or obstruct the vessels that are bound to those ports; but our Governors shall always protect and defend them, and all their crews, goods, and effects, and not permit any damage or injury to be done to them: and should they be desirous of purchasing, with their own money, and provisions in the places where they may happen to be, or of hiring any carts or vessels (not before hired by others), for the transportation of their goods, no one shall hinder or obstruct them therein.

XXXIX. That custom shall not be demanded or taken on the merchandise brought by them in their ships to Constantinople, or any other port of our sacred Dominions, which they shall not, of their own free will, land with a view to sale.

XL. That on their ships arriving at any port, and landing their goods and merchandises, they shall and may, after having paid their duties, safely and securely depart, without experiencing any molestation or obstruction from any one.

XLI. The English ships coming into our sacred Dominions, and touching at the ports of Barbary and of the Western Coast, used oftentimes to take on board pilgrims and other Turkish passengers, with the intention of landing them at Alexandria, and other ports of our sacred Dominions; on their arrival at which ports the Commandants and Governors demanded customs of them on the whole of their goods before they were landed, by reason of which outrage they have forborne receiving any more pilgrims; the more so as they were forced to take out of the ships that were bound to Constantinople the merchandise destined for other places, besides exacting the duties on those that were not landed: all English ships, therefore, bound to Constantinople, Alexandria, Tripoli of Syria, Scanderoon, or other ports of our sacred Dominions, shall in future be bound to pay duties, according to custom, on such goods only as they shall, of their own free will, land with a view to sale; and for such merchandise as they shall not discharge, no custom or duty shall be demanded of them, neither shall the least molestation or hindrance be given to them, but they shall and may freely transport them wherever they please.

XLII. That in case any Englishman, or other person navigating under their flag, should happen to commit manslaughter, or any other crime, or be thereby involved in a lawsuit, the Governors in our sacred Dominions shall not proceed to the cause until the Ambassador or Consul shall be present, but they shall hear and decide it together, without their presuming to give them any the least molestation, by hearing it alone, contrary to the Holy Law and these Capitulations.

XLIII. That notwithstanding it is stipulated by the Imperial Capitulations that the merchandise laden on board all English ships proceeding to our sacred Dominions shall moreover pay over consulage to the Ambassador or Consul for those goods on which customs are payable, certain Mahometan merchants, Sciots, Franks, and ill-disposed persons, object to the payment thereof; wherefore it is hereby commanded, that all the merchandise, unto whomsoever belonging, which shall be laden on board their ships, and have been used to pay custom, shall in future pay the consulage, without any resistance or opposition.

XLIV. That the English and other merchants navigating under their flag, who trade to Aleppo, shall pay such customs and other duties on the silks brought and laden by them on board their ships, as are paid by the French and Venetians, and not one Asper more.

XLV. That the Ambassadors of the King of England, residing at the Sublime Porte, being the representatives of His Majesty, and the interpreters, the representatives of the Ambassadors for such matters, therefore, as the latter shall translate or speak, or for whatever sealed

letter or memorial they may convey to any place in the name of their Ambassador, it being found that that which they have interpreted or translated is a true interpretation of the words and answers of the Ambassadors or Consul, they shall be always free from all imputation or fault of punishment; and in case they shall commit any offence, our Judges and Governors shall not reprove, beat, or put any of the said interpreters in prison, without the knowledge of the Ambassador or Consul.

XLVI. That in case any of the interpreters shall happen to die, if he be an Englishman proceeding from England, all his effects shall be taken possession of by the Ambassador or Consul; but should he be a subject of our Dominions, they shall be delivered up to his next heir; and having no heir, they shall be confiscated by our fiscal officers. . . .

XLVII. That whereas the Corsairs of Tunis and Barbary having, contrary to the tenor of the Capitulations and our Imperial Licence, molested the merchants and other subjects of the King of England, as also those of other Kings in amity with the Sublime Porte, and plundered and pillaged their goods and property, it was expressly ordained and commanded, that the goods so plundered should be restored, and the captives released: and that if after such commands, the Tunisians and Algerians should, contrary to the tenor of our Capitulations, again molest the said merchants, and pillage their goods and property, and not restore the same, but convey them to the countries and ports of our sacred Dominions, and especially to Tunis, Barbary, Modon, or Coron, the Beglerbegs, Governors, and Commandants of such places should, in future, banish and punish them, and not permit them to sell the same.

XLVIII. That it is written and registered in the Capitulations, that the Governors and officers of Aleppo and other ports of our sacred Dominions, should not, contrary to the tenor of the said Capitulations, forcibly take from the English merchants any money for their silk, under the pretence of custom or other duty, but that the said merchants should pay for the silk by them purchased at Aleppo, the same as the French and Venetians do, and no more. Notwithstanding which, the Commandants of Aleppo have, under colour of custom and duty, demanded *two and a half per cent.* for their silk, and thereby taken their money: wherefore we command that this matter be investigated and inquired into, in order that such money may be refunded to them by those who have taken the same; and for the future, the duty exacted from them shall be according to ancient custom, and as the Venetians and French were accustomed to pay, so that not a single asper more be taken by any new imposition.

XLIX. That the merchants of the aforesaid nation, resident at Galata, buy and receive divers goods, wares and merchandises, and after having paid to our customer the duties thereon, and received a *Teskéré*, ascertaining their having paid the same, preparatory to loading such goods in due time on board their ships, it sometimes happens that in the interim the customer either dies, or is removed from his station, and his successor will not accept the said *Teskéré*, but demands a fresh duty from the said merchants, thereby molesting them in various ways; wherefore we do command, that on its really and truly appearing that they have once paid the duties on the goods purchased, the customer shall receive the said *Teskéré* without demanding any fresh duty.

L. That the merchants of the aforesaid nation, after having once paid the duties, and received the *Teskéré*, for the camlets, mohair, silk, and other merchandise purchased by them at Angora, and transported to Constantinople and other ports of our sacred Dominions, and having deposited such goods in their own warehouses, have been again applied to for duties thereon; we do therefore hereby command that they shall no longer be molested or vexed on that head, but that when the said merchants shall be desirous of loading such goods on board their ships, and on its appearing by the *Teskéré* that they have already paid the duties thereon, no fresh custom or duty shall be demanded for the said goods, provided that the said merchants do not blend or intermix the goods which have not paid custom with those which have.

LI. That the merchants of the aforesaid nation, having once paid the customs on the merchandise imported into Constantinople and other ports of our sacred Dominions,

and on those exported therefrom, as silks, camlets, and other goods, and being unable to sell the said goods, are under the necessity of transporting them to Smyrna, Scio, and other ports; on their arrival there the Governors and Custom-house Officers of such ports shall always accept their *Teskérés*, and forbear exacting any further duty on the said merchandise.

LII. That for the goods which the merchants of the nation aforesaid shall bring to Constantinople, and other ports of our sacred Dominions, and for those they shall export from the said places, the *Mastarriagi* of Galata and Constantinople shall take their *Mastarria*, according to the old canon and ancient usage; that is to say, for those merchandises only whereon it was usually paid; but for such merchandises as have not been accustomed to pay the same, nothing shall be taken contrary to the said canon, neither shall any innovations be made in future with regard to English merchandise, nor shall one asper more be taken than is warranted by custom.

LIII. That the merchants of the aforesaid nation shall and may always come and go into the ports and harbours of our sacred Dominions, and trade, without experiencing any obstacle from any one, with the cloths, kerseys, spice, tin, lead, and other merchandise they may bring, and, with the exception of prohibited goods, shall and may, in like manner, buy and export all sorts of merchandise, without any one presuming to prohibit or molest them: and our customers and other officers, after having received the duties thereon, according to ancient custom and the tenor of these sacred Capitulations, shall not demand of them any thing more, touching which point certain clear and distinct Capitulations were granted, to the end that the Beglerbegs and other Commandants, our subjects, as also the Commandants and Lieutenants of our harbours might always act in conformity to these our Imperial Commands, and let nothing be done contrary thereto.
. . .

LIV. That the English merchants having once paid the duties on their merchandise, at the rate of *three per cent.* aud [sic] taken them out of their ship, no one shall demand or exact from them anything more without their consent: and it was moreover expressly commanded, that the English merchants should not be molested or vexed in manner aforesaid, contrary to the Articles of the Capitulations. . . .

LV. That the imperial fleet, galleys, and other vessels, departing from our sacred Dominions, and falling in with English ships at sea, shall in no wise molest or detain them, nor take from them any thing whatsoever, but always show to one another good friendship, without occasioning them the least damage or injury; and notwithstanding it is thus declared in the Imperial Capitulations, the said English ships are still molested by the ships of the Imperial fleet, and by the beys and captains who navigate the seas, as also by those of Algiers, Tunis, and Barbary, who, falling in with them whilst sailing from one port to another, detain them for the mere purpose of plunder, under colour of searching for enemy's property, and under that pretence prevent them from prosecuting their voyage; now We do hereby expressly command, that the provisions of the old canon be executed at the Castles and in the ports only, and nowhere else, and that they shall no longer be liable to any further search or exaction at sea, under colour of search or examination.

LVI. That the said Ambassador having represented that our customers, after having been fully paid the proper duties by the English merchants on their goods, delayed, contrary to the Articles and stipulations of the Capitulations, to give them the *Teskérés* of the goods for which they had already received the duty, with the sole view of oppressing and doing them injustice; We do hereby strictly command that the said customers do never more delay granting them the *Teskérés*, and the goods whereon they have once paid the duty being transported to another port, in consequence of no opportunity of sale having occurred in the former port, entire credit shall be given to the *Teskérés* ascertaining the payment already made, agreeably to the Capitulations granted to them, and no molestation shall be given to them, nor any new duty demanded.

LVII. That notwithstanding it is stipulated by the Capitulations that the English merchants, and other subjects of that nation, shall and may, according to their rank and condition, trade to Aleppo, Egypt, and other parts of our Imperial Dominions, and for all their goods, wares, and merchandise, pay a duty of *three per cent.* only, and nothing more, according to ancient custom, the customers having molested the English merchants, with a view to oppress them and the subjects of that nation, on their arrival with their goods laden on board their ships, whether conveyed by sea or land, at our ports and harbours, under pretence of the goods so brought by them not belonging to the English; and that for goods brought from England they demanded *three per cent.* only; but for those brought by them from Venice and other ports, they exacted more; wherefore, on this point, let the Imperial Capitulations granted in former times be observed, and our Governors and officers in no wise permit or consent to the same being infringed.

LVIII. That whereas it is specified in the Capitulations, that in case an Englishman should become a debtor or surety, and run away or fail, the debt shall be demanded of the debtor: and if the creditor be not in the possession of some legal document given by the surety, he shall not be arrested, nor such debt be demanded of him; should an English merchant, resident in another country, with the sole view of freeing himself of the payment of a debt, draw a bill of exchange upon another merchant, living in Turkey, and the person to whom the same is payable, being a man of power and authority, should molest such merchant who had contracted no debt to the drawer, and oppress him, contrary to law and the sacred Capitulations, by contending that the bill was drawn upon him, and that he was bound to pay the debt of the other merchant: now, We do hereby expressly command, that no such molestation be given in future; but if such merchant shall accept the bill, they shall proceed in manner and form therein pointed out; but should he refuse to accept it, he shall be liable to no further trouble.

LIX. That the interpreters of the English Ambassadors, having always been free and exempt from all contributions and impositions whatever, respect shall in future be paid to the Articles of the Capitulations stipulated in ancient times, without the fiscal officers intermeddling with the effects of any of the interpreters who may happen to die, which effects shall be distributed amongst his heirs.

LX. That the aforesaid King, having been a true friend of our Sublime Porte, his Ambassador, who resides here, shall be allowed ten servants, of any nation whatsoever, who shall be exempt from impositions, and in no manner molested.

LXI. That if any Englishman should turn Turk, and it should be represented and proved, that besides his own goods, he has in his hands any property belonging to another person in England, such property shall be taken from him and delivered up to the Ambassador or Consul, that they may convey the same to the owner thereof. . . .

LXII. That for every piece of cloth, called *Londra*, which, from ancient times, was always brought by the English ships to Alexandria, there should be taken in that place a duty of forty paras; for every piece of kersey six paras; for every bale of hareskins six paras; and for every quintal of tin and lead, Damascus weight, fifty-seven paras and a half.

LXIII. That on afterwards transporting the said goods from Alexandria to Aleppo, there should be demanded, by the customhouse officers of Aleppo, for every piece of *Londra* eighty paras; for a piece of kersey eight paras and two aspers; for every bundle of hare-skins eight paras and two aspers; and for every Aleppo weight of tin and lead one para.

LXIV. That on the goods purchased by the aforesaid nation at Aleppo, there should be paid for transport duty, on every bale of unbleached linen, cordovans, and *Chorasani-hindi*, two dollars and a half; for every bale of cotton yarn one dollar and a quarter; for every bale of galls one quarter; for every bale of silk ten osmans; and for rhubarb and other trifles, and various sorts of drugs, according to a valuation to be made by the appraiser, there should be taken a duty of *three per cent.*

LXV. That on carrying the said goods to Alexandria, and there loading them on board their ships, there should be taken for transport duty, on every bale of unbleached linen and cordovans one dollar and a half; for every bale of *Chorasani-hindi* and cotton-yarn, three quarters; for every bale of

galls one quarter; and for rhubarb and other trifles, and various sorts of drugs, after a valuation made thereof, there should be taken three quarters of a piastre: and that for the future no demand whatever to the contrary should be submitted to.

LXVI. That all commands issued by the Chamber contrary to the above-mentioned Articles should not be obeyed: but for the future, every thing be observed conformably to the tenour of the Capitulations and the Imperial Signet.

LXVII. It being stipulated by the Capitulations that the English merchants shall pay a duty of *three per cent.* on all goods by them imported and exported, without being bound to pay an asper more; and disputes having arisen with the customers on this head, they shall continue to pay duty as heretofore paid by them at the rate of *three per cent.* only, neither more nor less.

LXVIII. That for the *Londra* and other cloths manufactured in England, whether fine or coarse, and of whatsoever price, imported by them into the ports of Constantinople, and Galata, there shall be taken, according to the ancient canons, and as they have always hitherto paid, one hundred and forty-four aspers, computing the dollar at eighty aspers, and the leone at seventy, and nothing more shall be exacted from them; but the cloths of Holland and other countries, viz. serges, *Londrina* scarlets, and other cloths, shall pay, for the future, that which hitherto has been the accustomed duty; and at Smyrna likewise shall be paid, according to ancient custom, calculated in dollars and leones, for every piece of *Londra* or other cloth of English fabric, whether fine or coarse, one hundred and twenty aspers, without an asper more being demanded, or any innovation being made therein.

LXIX. It being registered in the Imperial Capitulations, that all suits wherein the English are parties, and exceeding the sum of four thousand aspers, shall be heard in our Sublime Porte, and no where else:

That if at any time the Commanders and Governors should arrest any English merchant, or other Englishman, on the point of departure by any ship, by reason of any debt or demand upon him, if the Consul of the place will give bail for him, by offering himself as surety until such suit shall be decided in our Imperial Divan, such person so arrested shall be released, and not imprisoned or prevented from prosecuting his voyage, and they who claim any thing from him shall present themselves in our Imperial Divan, and there submit their claims, in order that the Ambassador may furnish an answer thereto. With regard to those for whom the Consul shall not have given bail, the Commandant may act as he shall think proper.

LXX. That all English ships coming from the ports of Constantinople, Alexandria, Smyrna, Cyprus, and other ports of our sacred Dominions, shall pay three hundred aspers for anchorage duty, without an asper more being demanded from them.

LXXI. That should any Englishman coming with merchandise, turn Turk, and the goods so imported by him be proved to belong to merchants of his own country, from whom he had taken them; the whole shall be detained, with the ready money, and delivered up to the Ambassador, in order to his transmitting the same to the right owners, without any of our judges or officers interposing any obstacle or hindrance thereto.

LXXII. That no molestation shall be given to any of the aforesaid nation buying camlets, mohairs, or grogram yarn, at Angora and Beghbazar, and desirous of exporting the same from thence, after having paid the duty of *three per cent.*, by any demand of customs for the exportation thereof, neither shall one asper more be demanded of them.

LXXIII. That should any suit be instituted by an English merchant for the amount of a debt, and the same be recovered by means of the assistance of a *Chiaux*, he shall pay him, out of the money recovered, *two per cent.* and what is usually paid for fees in the *Mehkemé*, or court of justice, and not an asper more.

LXXIV. That the King, having always been a friend to the Sublime Porte, out of regard to such good friendship, His Majesty shall and may, with his own money, purchase for his own kitchen, at Smyrna, Salonica, or any other port of our sacred Dominions, in fertile and abundant years, and not in times of dearth or scarcity, two cargoes of figs and raisins, and after having paid a duty of *three per cent.* thereon, no obstacle or hindrance shall be given thereto.

LXXV. That it being represented to Us that the English merchants have been accustomed hitherto to pay no custom or scale duty, either on the silks bought by them at Brussa and Constantinople, or on those which come from Persia and Georgia, and are purchased by them at Smyrna from the Armenians; if such usage or custom really exists, and the same be not prejudicial to the Empire, such duty shall not be paid in future: and the said Ambassador having requested that the aforegoing Articles might be duly respected and added to the Imperial Capitulations, his request was acceded to; therefore in the same manner as the Capitulations were heretofore conceded by our Imperial *Hatti-sheriff*, so are they now in the like manner renewed by our Imperial Command; wherefore, in conformity to the Imperial Signet, We have again granted these sacred Capitulations, which We command to be observed, so long as the said King shall continue to maintain that good friendship and understanding with our Sublime Porte, which was maintained in the happy time of our glorious Ancestors, which friendship We, on our part, accept; and adhering to these Articles and Stipulations, We do hereby promise and swear, by the one Omnipotent God, the Creator of Heaven and Earth, and of all creatures, that We will permit nothing to be done or transacted contrary to the tenour of the Articles and Stipulations heretofore made, and these Imperial Capitulations; and accordingly every one is to yield implicit faith and obedience to this our Imperial Signet.

15. TREATY OF PEACE AND COMMERCE: FRANCE AND MOROCCO
29 January 1682

(Confirmed, 13 December 1682)
[Translated from the French text in Rouard de Card, *Traités de la France*, pp. 315–20]

France concluded its first treaties with Morocco in 1631 and 1635, but neither one produced lasting results, as attested by the total absence before 1683 of correspondence with Morocco in the archieves of the Foreign Ministry in Paris and of the Chamber of Commerce in Marseilles, the center of French trade with Morocco as with the rest of North Africa. This could be attributed in part to the disintegration of the twin kingdoms of Fez and Marrakesh under rival Sa'di dynasties, finally replaced in the 1660s by the 'Alawi dynasty, which was destined to keep Moroccan sovereignty alive until the eve of World War I and itself survived nearly half a century of French protectorate status. The combative Mawlay Isma'il (1672–1727), the second ruler of the 'Alawi line, became the real unifier of modern Morocco. Isma'il shoved the Portuguese and the English out of the fortified ports on the Atlantic coast and reduced to two—Ceuta and Melilla—the number of presidios that the Spaniards still clutched in his kingdom. In the sixteenth century, Morocco had provided safe ports for European privateers, particularly at al-Arish (Larash). As in the Barbary garrisons, in defense of Moroccan shipping, corsair guilds were formed to seize European vessels and enslave the crews and passengers. The Moroccan corsairs operated out of Salé and Tetuan, preying primarily on navigation in the Atlantic and at the entrance to the Mediterranean. After 1678 such slaves became the property of the mawlay. Meanwhile, French privateers turned over their Muslim slaves, including Moroccans, to the French government for impressment into the expanding French navy as galley slaves. This practice continued beyond the reign of Louis XIV (1643–1715), for only then did the French navy finally adopt the sailing vessel. Even without treaty protection, French merchants in the seventeenth century resided in Moroccan ports, particularly Salé, where they were assisted by self-styled French consuls. The provisions of the following treaty of peace and commerce were strung together in 1681–82 in Tetuan and Paris by Captain Lefèvre de la Barre and al-Hajj Muhammad Tammim. Article 20 limited the treaty to a period of six years. Morocco rejected a French proposal, made on delivery of the ratification, that the treaty be validated in perpetuity. The sticking point was the adamant refusal of Jean Baptiste Colbert and his successors to carry out the terms of slave exchange, manifestly because the French navy wished to hold on to its galley slave power. The treaty itself, well structured for its time, specified the extraterritorial privileges of French residents. The almost ceaseless piratical war, however, prevented its effective execution. Dealings between the two countries went from bad to worse in the opening years of the eighteenth century, and the French merchants and consuls had withdrawn from Salé and Tetouan by 1712. Formal relations were broken altogether in 1718 and were not resumed for nearly a half-century. Masson, *Histoire des établissements et du commerce français dans l'Afrique Barbaresque*, chaps. 7–8; Brignon et al., *Histoire du Maroc*, chap. 17; Abun-Nasr, *History of the Maghrib*, chap. 7; Julien, *Histoire de l'Afrique du Nord*, vol. 1, chap. 6; G. Fisher, *Barbary Legend*.

1. All acts of hostility shall cease in the future between the land and naval forces, the vessels, and the subjects of the Emperor of France and those of the Emperor of Morocco, King of Fez and of Sousse.

2. In the future there shall be peace between the Emperor of France and his subjects and the Emperor of Morocco, King of Fez and of Sus, and his subjects; and these subjects may reciprocally carry on commerce in the [two] Empires, Kingdoms and Countries and may navigate in full liberty, without hindrance for any reason and any pretext whatsoever.

3. Vessels armed for war in the ports of the Emperor of Morocco, meeting vessels and warships at sea under the French flag and carrying passports from the Admiral of France, conforming to the copy appended to the present treaty,[1] shall let them continue their voyage freely without hindering them in any way, and shall give them all the assistance they may need. French vessels shall treat in the same way vessels of the subjects of the Emperor of Morocco in possession of certificates from the French Consul who shall reside in Salé. A copy of this certificate is also appended to the present treaty.[1]

4. Vessels of war and commerce belonging to the two nations shall be reciprocally received in the ports and on the roads governed by the Emperor of France and the Emperor of Morocco. If necessary, they shall receive every kind of help for crew and passengers. Similarly, they shall be supplied with victuals, fruit, and in general all other necessities, at the customary prices in ports of call.

5. If any French merchantship in one of the ports or roads governed by the Emperor of Morocco is attacked by enemy warships, even by those of Algiers and Tunis and of other ports of the African coast, it shall be defended by the cannon of the citadels and fortresses. It shall be given sufficient time to move away from the ports and roads, and during that interval the enemy vessels shall be prevented from following. The Emperor of France shall do the same, on condition nevertheless that vessels armed for war by the Emperor of Morocco or his subjects may not take prizes within six leagues of the coasts of France.

6. All Frenchmen captured by enemies of the French Emperor and taken to any port or territory governed by the Emperor of Morocco shall be set free at once and shall not be kept as slaves. Even when the vessels of Algiers, Tunis, Tripoli, and others that are or may be at war with the Emperor of France put French slaves ashore, the Emperor of Morocco shall command all his Governors henceforth to retain the slaves and try to have them ransomed by the French Consul at the best possible price. The subjects of the Emperor of Morocco shall receive the same treatment in France.

7. All French slaves at present in the dominions of the Emperor of Morocco may be ransomed for three hundred pounds apiece, and their actual owners shall not be permitted to demand a higher price. The same rule shall apply to those slaves, subjects of the Emperor of Morocco who may be in France. In the draft truce made between le sieur de la Barre and al-Qaid 'Umar, the latter agreed in a note which he signed and gave to le sieur de la Barre to exchange the same number of French slaves for Moors on the vessel named *Aly Baudy*. The ambassadors have pledged that the Emperor of Morocco, as soon as he is informed of the note given by al-Qaid, will release sixty-five Frenchmen, so as, along with the twenty that al-Qaid has already released, to make up the number of eighty-five, the equivalent of the number of Moors released by le sieur de la Barre.

8. Neither foreign passengers on French vessels nor Frenchmen on foreign vessels may be enslaved under any pretext whatsoever, even when the captured vessel has defended itself. This will also apply to foreigners on Moroccan vessels, and subjects of the Emperor of Morocco on foreign vessels.

9. If any French vessel should lose its way off the coasts governed by the Emperor of Morocco, being either pursued there by enemies or driven there by bad weather, it will be given all necessary help to put back to sea, or to recover the goods of its cargo, paying by the day for the labor of those employed, without need to pay tax or tribute for goods put ashore unless these goods are sold in the ports of the dominions of the Emperor.

---

1. Not reproduced here.

10. All French merchants in the ports of Morocco or Fez may put their goods ashore to sell and buy freely at the market price of the subjects of the Emperor of Morocco. The same rule will apply in the ports of the dominions of the Emperor of France. When the merchants put their goods ashore for storage only, they may reload the goods without customs duties.

11. No help or protection against the French will be given to vessels belonging to Tripoli, Algiers, Tunis, or those armed under their commission. The Emperor of Morocco expressly forbids all his subjects from taking arms under the commission of any Prince or state that is an enemy of the French Crown. He will also prevent those with whom the Emperor of France is at war from arming in Moroccan ports to pursue French subjects.

12. The Emperor of France may appoint a Consul at Salé, Tetouan, or anywhere else that he deems fit, to assist French merchants in all their needs. The Consul shall be free to practice the Christian religion in his home, as much for himself as for all Christians who may wish to attend. Similarly, the subjects of the Emperor of Morocco who come to France may practice their religion at home. The Consul shall enjoy complete jurisdiction in differences which may arise among Frenchmen, without having to summon judges of the Emperor of Morocco.

13. If a difference should arise between a Frenchman and a Moor, they may not be tried by ordinary judges, but by a council of the Emperor of Morocco or his commander in the ports where the differences occur.

14. The Consul shall not be responsible for paying any debt for French merchants, unless obliged to do so in writing. The property of Frenchmen who may die in Morocco shall be given to the Consul for transfer to Frenchmen or others to whom it belongs. The same practice shall apply for the subjects of the Emperor of Morocco who settle in France.

15. The Consul shall be exempt from all duties for the provisions, victuals, and goods that he needs in his home.

16. No Frenchman who strikes a Moor may be punished until the Consul has been called to defend his cause. If such a Frenchman should flee, the Consul may not be held responsible.

17. If the present treaty should be violated, no act of hostility shall be made until after a formal denial of justice.

18. If any corsair of France or the Kingdom of Morocco should harm any French or Moroccan vessels at sea, he and the responsible shipowners shall be punished.

19. If the present treaty between the Emperors of France and Morocco should be broken—may it not please God—all French merchants in the dominions of the Emperor of Morocco may have three months to withdraw to wherever they please, without suffering arrest.

20. The above articles shall be confirmed and ratified by the Emperors of France and Morocco and shall be observed by their subjects for a period of six years. In order that no one may plead ignorance, the articles shall be read, published, and posted wherever necessary. . . .

16. TREATY OF PEACE AND COMMERCE: GREAT BRITAIN AND THE GARRISON OF ALGIERS
10 April 1682

[*British and Foreign State Papers*, 1:354–60]

Like France, Britain at first viewed its relations with the Barbary Garrisons as an extension of its relations with the Ottoman Empire. As monopolist of English trade with the Ottoman Empire, the Levant Company on its own tried to develop trade with the Garrisons, signing a treaty with Algiers in 1623 and appointing consuls there and at Tunis. But the effort to encompass the Barbary Coast in its commercial operations never took hold, and before 1640 the company abandoned it as useless. During the Civil War and under the Commonwealth, the British government directly promoted the establishment of formal relations with the Barbary states. But nothing came of the Barbary treaties of 1646 and 1658, because the rulers of the Garrisons, then at the zenith of their power, refused to be browbeaten by British privateers, who found the Mediterranean at the time a profitable hunting ground and did not consider themselves reciprocally bound by agreed terms, particularly as they applied to the exchange of slaves kidnapped by both sides. According to conventional maritime wisdom in Europe in the sixteenth and seventeenth centuries, handed down to historians of the subject, the difficulties of trading with the Barbary states could be attributed, not to the interaction of European privateers and Muslim corsairs, but wholly to the latter, who, it was held, by their disregard for innocent passage, had crowded out normal commerce between North Africa and Europe. To take one example from the most authoritative, and otherwise sound, historian of the Levant Company, power in the Barbary Garrisons "had passed into the hands of an undisciplined and turbulent body of soldiery who elected—and repeatedly removed by violence—their agas (commanders); and these agas presided, subject to the humour of their troops, over what was perhaps the richest collection of rascality ever assembled in so small a compass. For the native population of Moors, Turks, and Jews was continuously being recruited from the sweepings of all of Europe: renegades, outlaws, rebels, and pirates flocked to those military republics where the rest of human society was treated as fair prey, and most of the ordinary sanctions of morality were stayed; and the plunder of Christendom formed the main occupation of this community of outcasts" (Wood, *History of the Levant Company*, p. 59). Piracy there was, but the Barbary variety originated in response to and as a defense against the piracy of the European privateers—chiefly from England, France, and Holland—who infested the Mediterranean in the sixteenth and seventeenth centuries. Since in Islamic societies guilds managed specific economic activities, guilds of corsair captains (*taife reisleri*) were founded in each of the three capitals to establish rules of piratical conduct. Whereas in Europe piracy, as confirmed by its very name, was a form of private enterprise, in North Africa it was a form of collective enterprise in which the state was often a partner. Besides, the corsair guilds became powerful interest groups, and from time to time they even gained control of governments by participation in recurrent coups d'états, particularly in the period of precipitate decline after the middle decades of the seventeenth century. Through the sale of prize goods, the corsairs provided large public revenues, as taxes and profit sharing. The captured passengers, too, were sold as slaves or retained by the state in enforced government service. At the time, this was the practice on the Continent as well, for the privateers kidnapped Muslim passengers for enslavement in Europe. In France, for example, they often became galley slaves, and the French navy continued using the galley well into the eighteenth century, long after the galley had given way in the Barbary states to the sailing vessel. Galley slavery was a singularly unimaginative, uneconomical, and barbarous use of forced labor. By contrast, in the mid-seventeenth century the captured Europeans were constructively assimilated into the thriving economies of the Barbary Garrisons, where the slaves used their proved

skills or developed new ones in the service of private or public owners. The state benefited from the prosperous economy, and occasionally from the ransom which incidentally reduced the investment risk of the private slaveowner, who as a rule could be
assured a return of at least the purchase price, giving him yet another reason for doing
everything he could to keep his temporary slaves alive and healthy. Slavery was thus
good business, but it was not the only business of the Garrison economies. The Barbary markets imported cloth, metals, arms and gunpowder, spices, and luxury items,
for which they exchanged agricultural produce, livestock, wool hides, and leather.
This is a subject that remains to be investigated in depth, but even preliminary findings
indicate that Algiers and Tunis and probably also Tripoli were generally more opulent
and more advanced than most cities in Europe in the middle decades of the seventeenth century. The following treaty, which was renewed, confirmed, and from time
to time enlarged (in 1686, 1700, 1703, 1716, 1729, 1762, and 1800), fixed the pattern
of British relations with Algiers until after the Napoleonic wars. G. Fisher, *Barbary
Legend*; Wood, op. cit., chap. 4; Abun-Nasr, *History of the Maghrib*, chap. 7; Julien,
Histoire de l'Afrique du Nord, vol. 1, chap. 6.

Articles of Peace and Commerce between the Most Serene and Mighty Prince Charles the Second, by the grace of God King of Great Britain, France, and Ireland, Defender of the Christian Faith, &c., and the Most Illustrious Lords, the Bashaw, Dey, Aga, and Governors of the famous City and Kingdom of Algiers, in Barbary: concluded by Arthur Herbert, Esquire, Admiral of His Majesty's Fleet in the Mediterranean Seas, on the 10th day of April, old style, 1682.

ART. I. In the first place it is agreed and concluded, that from this day, and for ever forwards, there be a true, firm, and inviolable Peace between the Most Serene King of Great Britain, France, and Ireland, Defender of the Christian Faith, &c., and the Most Illustrious Lords, the Bashaw, Dey, Aga, and Governors of the City and Kingdom of Algiers, and between all the Dominions and Subjects of either side, and that the Ships or other Vessels, and the Subjects and People of both sides shall not henceforth do to each other any harm, offence, or injury, either in word or deed, but shall treat one another with all possible respect and friendship.

II. That any of the Ships, or other Vessels belonging to the said King of Great Britain, or to any of His Majesty's Subjects, may safely come to the Port of Algiers, or to any other Port or place of that Kingdom, there freely to buy and sell, paying the usual Customs of 10 per cent., as in former times,

for such goods as they sell; and the goods they sell not, they shall freely carry on board without paying any Duties for the same; and that they shall freely depart from thence whensoever they please, without any stop or hindrance whatsoever. As to contraband merchandises, as powder, brimstone, iron, planks, and all sorts of timber fit for building of Ships, ropes, pitch, tar, fusils, and other habiliments of War, His said Majesty's Subjects shall pay no Duty for the same to those of Algiers.

III. That all Ships, and other Vessels, as well those belonging to the said King of Great Britain, or to any of His Majesty's Subjects, as those belonging to the Kingdom or People of Algiers, shall freely pass the Seas, and traffic without any search, hindrance, or molestation from each other; and that all Persons or Passengers, of what Country soever, and all monies, goods, merchandises, and moveables, to whatsoever People or Nation belonging, being on board of any of the said Ships or Vessels, shall be wholly free, and shall not be stopped, taken, or plundered, nor receive any harm or damage whatsoever from either Party.

IV. That the Algier Ships of War, or other Vessels, meeting with any Merchants' Ships, or other Vessels, of His said Majesty's Subjects, not being in any of the Seas appertaining to His Majesty's Dominions, may send on board 1 single Boat, with 2 Sitters only, besides the ordinary Crew of

Rowers, and that no more shall enter any such Merchant Ship or Vessel, without express leave from the Commander thereof, but the 2 Sitters alone; and that upon producing a Pass under the Hand and Seal of the Lord High Admiral of England and Ireland, or of the Lord High Admiral of Scotland, for the said Kingdoms respectively, or under the Hands and Seals of the Commissioners for executing the office of Lord High Admiral of any of the said Kingdoms, that the said Boat shall presently depart, and the Merchant Ship or Vessel shall proceed freely on her voyage, and that although, for the space of 15 months next ensuing after the conclusion of this Peace, the said Commander of the Merchant Ship or Vessel produce no such Pass, yet if the major part of the Seamen of the said Ship or Vessel be Subjects of the said King of Great Britain, the said Boat shall immediately depart, and the said Merchant Ship or Vessel shall freely proceed on her voyage; but that, after the said 15 months, all Merchants' Ships or Vessels of His said Majesty's Subjects shall be obliged to produce such a Pass as aforesaid. And any of the Ships of War or other Vessels of His said Majesty, meeting with any Ships or other Vessels of Algiers, if the Commander of any such Algier Ship or Vessel shall produce a Pass firmed by the Chief Governors of Algiers, and a Certificate from the English Consul living there, or if they have no such Pass or Certificate, yet if for the space of 15 months next ensuing the conclusion of this Peace, the major part of the Ship's Company be Turks, Moors, or Slaves belonging to Algiers, then the said Algier Ship or Vessel shall proceed freely; but that, after the said 15 months, all Algier Ships or Vessels shall be obliged to produce such a Pass and Certificate as aforesaid.

V. That no Commander or other Person of any Ship or Vessel of Algiers shall take out of any Ship or Vessel of His said Majesty's Subjects, any Person or Persons whatsoever, to carry them anywhere to be examined, or upon any other pretence; nor shall they use any torture or violence to any Person, of what Nation or quality soever, being on board any Ship or Vessel of His Majesty's Subjects, upon any pretence whatsoever.

VI. That no Shipwreck belonging to the said King of Great Britain, or to any of His Majesty's Subjects, upon any part of the Coast belonging to Algiers, shall be made or become Prize, and that neither the goods thereof shall be seized nor the Men made Slaves; but that all the Subjects of Algiers shall do their best endeavours to save the said Men and their goods.

VII. That no Ship, nor any other Vessel of Algiers, shall have permission to be delivered up, or go to Sally, or any place in enmity with the said King of Great Britain, to be made use of as Corsairs or Sea Rovers against His said Majesty's Subjects.

VIII. That none of the Ships or other smaller Vessels of Algiers shall remain cruizing near or in sight of His Majesty's City and Garrison of Tangier, or of any other of His Majesty's Roads, Havens, or Ports, Towns and places, nor any ways disturb the peace and commerce of the same.

IX. That if any Ship or Vessel of Tunis, Tripoli, or Sally, or of any other place, bring any Ships, Vessels, Men, or Goods belonging to any of His said Majesty's Subjects, to Algiers, or to any Port or place in that Kingdom, the Governors there shall not permit them to be sold within the Territories of Algiers.

X. That if any of the Ships of War of the said King of Great Britain do come to Algiers, or to any other Port or place of that Kingdom, with any Prize, they may freely sell it, or otherwise to dispose of it at their own pleasure, without being molested by any; and that His Majesty's said Ships of War shall not be obliged to pay Customs in any sort; and that if they shall want provisions, victuals, or any other things, they may freely buy them at the rates in the market.

XI. That when any of His said Majesty's Ships of War shall appear before Algiers, upon notice thereof given by the English Consul, or by the Commander of the said Ships, to the Chief Governors of Algiers, Public Proclamation shall be immediately made to secure the Christian Captives; and if after that any Christians whatsoever make their escape on board any of the said Ships of War, they shall not be required back again, nor shall the said Consul or Commander, or any other His Majesty's Subjects, be obliged to pay anything for the said Christians.

XII. That from and after the time that the Ratification of this Treaty by the King of Great Britain shall be delivered to the Chief Governors of Algiers, no Subjects of His said Majesty shall be bought or sold, or made Slaves in any part of the Kingdom of Algiers, upon any pretence whatsoever. And the said King of Great Britain shall not be obliged, by virtue of this Treaty of Peace, to redeem any of his Subjects now in Slavery, or who may be made Slaves before the said Ratification; but it shall depend absolutely upon His Majesty, or the Friends and Relations of the said Persons in Slavery, without any limitation or restriction of time, to redeem such and so many of them, from time to time, as shall be thought fit, agreeing of as reasonable a price as may be with their Patrons or Masters for their redemption, without obliging the said Patrons or Masters, against their wills, to set any at liberty, whether they be Slaves belonging to the Beylicque or Gally, or such as belong to the Bashaw, Dey, Governor, Aga, or any other Persons whatsover [sic]. And all Slaves, being His Majesty's Subjects, shall, when they are redeemed, enjoy the advantage and benefit of abatements of the Duty due to the Royal House, and of the other charges, by paying such reasonable sums as any Slaves of other Nations usually pay when they are redeemed.

XIII. That if any Subject of the said King of Great Britain happen to die in Algiers, or in any part of its Territories, his goods or monies shall not be seized by the Governors, Judges, or other Officers of Algiers (who shall likewise make no inquiry after the same), but the said goods or monies shall be possessed or received by such Person or Persons whom the Deceased shall, by his last Will, have made his Heir or Heirs, in case they be upon the place where the Testator deceased. But if the Heirs be not there, then the Executors of the said Will, lawfully constituted by the Deceased, shall, after having made an inventory of all the goods and monies left, take them into their custody without any hindrance, and shall take care the same be remitted, by some safe way, to the true and lawful Heirs; and in case any of His said Majesty's Subjects happen to die, not having made any Will, the English Consul shall possess himself of his goods and monies upon inventory for the use of the Kindred and Heirs of the Deceased.

XIV. That no Merchants, being His Majesty's Subjects, and residing in or trading to the City and Kingdom of Algiers, shall be obliged to buy any merchandises against their wills, but it shall be free for them to buy such commodities as they shall think fit, and no Captain or Commander of any Ship or Vessel belonging to His said Majesty's Subjects shall be obliged, against his will, to lade any goods to carry them, or make a voyage to any place he shall not have a mind to go to; and neither the English Consul, nor any other Subject of the said King, shall be bound to pay the Debts of any other of His Majesty's Subjects, except that he or they become Sureties for the same by a public act.

XV. That the Subjects of His said Majesty in Algiers, or its Territories, in matter of controversy, shall be liable to no other jurisdiction but that of the Dey, or Duan, except they happen to be at difference between themselves, in which case they shall be liable to no other determination but that of the Consul only.

XVI. That in case any Subject of His said Majesty being in any part of the Kingdom of Algiers, happen to strike, wound, or kill a Turk or a Moor, if he be taken, he is to be punished in the same manner, and with no greater severity than a Turk ought to be, being guilty of the same offence; but if he escape, neither the said English Consul, nor any other of His said Majesty's Subjects, shall be in any sort questioned and troubled therefore.

XVII. That the English Consul now, or at any time hereafter living in Algiers, shall be there at all times with entire freedom and safety of his Person and estate, and shall be permitted to choose his own Druggerman and Broker, and freely to go on board any Ships in the Road, as often and when he pleases, and to have the liberty of the Country; and that he shall be allowed a place to pray in, and that no man shall do him any injury in word or deed.

XVIII. That not only during the continuance of this Peace and Friendship, but likewise if any breach of War happen to be hereafter between the said King of Great Britain and the Kingdom of Algiers, the said English Consul, and all other His said Majesty's Subjects inhabiting in the Kingdom of Algiers, shall always, and at all times, both of Peace and War, have full and absolute liberty to depart and go to their own, or any other Country, upon any Ship or Vessel, of what Nation soever, they shall think fit; and to carry with them all their estates, goods, families and servants, without any interruption or hindrance.

XIX. That no Subject of His said Majesty, being a Passenger, and coming or going with his baggage, from or to any Port, shall be any way molested or meddled with, although he be on board any Ship or Vessel in enmity with Algiers; and in like manner no Algerine Passenger being on board any Ship or Vessel in enmity with the said King of Great Britain, shall be any way molested, whether in his Person, or in his goods, which he may have laden on board the said Ship or Vessel.

XX. That at all times when any Ship of War of the King of Great Britain's, carrying His said Majesty's Flag at the main topmast head, shall appear before Algiers, and come to an anchor in the Roads; that immediately after notice thereof given by His said Majesty's Consul, or Officer, from the Ship unto the Dey and Government of Algiers, they shall in honour to His Majesty cause a Salute of 21 cannon to be shot off from the Castles and Forts of the City, and

that the said Ship shall return an answer by shooting off the same number of cannon.

XXI. That presently after the signing and sealing of these Articles, by the Bashaw, Dey, Aga, and Governors of Algiers, all injuries and damages sustained on either part, shall be quite taken away and forgotten, and this Peace shall be in full force and virtue, and continue for ever. And for all depredatious and damages that shall be afterwards committed or done by either side, before notice can be given of this Peace, full satisfaction shall immediately be made, and whatsoever remains in kind shall be instantly restored.

XXII. That in case it shall happen, hereafter, that anything is done or committed contrary to this Treaty, whether by the Subjects of the one or the other Party; the Treaty, notwithstanding, shall subsist in full force, and such Contraventions shall not occasion the breach of this Peace, friendship, and good correspondence; but the Party injured shall amicably demand immediate satisfaction for the said Contraventions, before it be lawful to break the Peace, and if the fault was committed by any private Subjects of either Party, they alone shall be punished as breakers of the Peace, and disturbers of the public quiet. And our faith shall be our faith, and our word our word. . . .

17. GRANT OF CAPITULATIONS BY SHAH SULTAN HUSAYN
TO FRANCE
7 September 1708

[Translated from the French text in Hauterive and Cussy, *Recueil des traités*, pt. 1, 2: 376–94]

The commercial relations of Persia with France began considerably later than those with England and the Netherlands (Docs. 3, 7, 9, 10), largely owing to the failures of successive French East India Companies in the first half of the seventeenth century. Instead, French religious orders—first the Capuchins, quickly followed by Jesuits, Carmelites, and Dominicans—established missions in Persia after 1628 with initial encouragement from Cardinal Richelieu. Throughout the remainder of that century, the religious interests of France bulked larger in Persia than the commercial. Thus, even after the successful French East India Company (1664–1769) obtained *farmans* (royal decrees) in February 1665 and December 1671 investing French merchants with trading privileges comparable to those of the English and the Dutch, no advantage was taken of the opportunity to open up a Persian market. The conclusion of the 1708 treaty, on the invitation of Shah Sultan Husayn (1694–1722), represented a belated effort by King Louis XIV to make up for lost time. Le sieur Michel, the French diplomat who negotiated the terms, returned to France in October 1709, but a French consulate was opened at Isfahan and another at Shiraz to handle French affairs. The treaty itself proved disappointing to its authors, for despite the promise of preferential treatment French trade with Persia did not flourish. Du Mans, *Estat de la Perse en 1660*, pp. i-cxv (introductory essay by C. Schefer); Bayani, *Les relations de l'Iran avec l'Europe occidentale*, pt. 2, chap. 4; Thieury, *Documents pour servir à l'histoire des relations entre la France et la Perse*, chap. 2; Herbette, *Une ambassade persane sous Louis XIV*, chap. 9; Sadre, *Relations de l'Iran avec l'Europe de l'antiquité, du moyen-age et la France*, pt. 2, chap. 3.

1. Merchants and others of the French nation who may come either by sea or by land to the ports and frontiers of the vast Persian Empire shall be pleasantly received and honestly treated by the Beglarbegis (Governors-General), Vazirs (Ministers), Governors, officers, and commissioners of the Divan (Treasury). This we herewith enjoin upon them as one of their principal duties, forbidding them to do anything that might be contrary to conditions of friendship, to tyrannize [or] to commit any excess against [French subjects], to covet their goods, or to exact anything belonging to them, whether merchandise or animals and carriages or anything else. Quite to the contrary, we order [Persian officials] to aid and help [French subjects] whenever they might require it, so that without fear or anxiety they will be free at all times to travel to every locality they choose without forcible exaction or insult. They may sojourn and remain as long as they desire in the ports and other places of our realm. Whenever they wish to leave, no one may hinder them. If something should happen to be taken from them by force or violence, after verification and conviction of the guilty, [the stolen property] shall be returned and the perpetrators fittingly punished.

2. The said Envoy, having demonstrated that the merchants would have to spend considerable sums in launching their enterprises and establishing commercial relations [between the two Empires], has requested that for several years they should be exempt from paying duty to the Divan

(Treasury) for goods that they might import into Persia under the [present] Convention. But [the Envoy promised] that [the French merchants], in gratitude for the exemption, would remit to the Royal Treasury an honest and agreeable present. In order to favor even more the said Lord Emperor [of France] of High Dignity, we have promised that for a period of five years [the French merchants] should be exempt from the duties specified below. But after the said five years they will execute the conditions that are hereafter laid down and agreed upon for the import into the lands of our realm of merchandise, and for its export to other Kingdoms.

3. It has been ordered and agreed that, upon the ratification of the articles of this treaty of friendship and the arrival of the factory chiefs of the said Lord Emperor of High Dignity, if [the French merchants] should want to stay at Isfahan, the Vazir and all the officers will assign to them from the Royal domain a suitable house in which they might reside and which, if they should desire, they might enlarge and repair as often as they please.

4. Whenever, following the arrival of the said factory chiefs and the ratification of the treaty, [the French merchants] should wish to erect hostels for their lodging in the ports of Bandar 'Abbas, Kung, and Bandar Rig, they may purchase a house with the consent of its owner and they may construct, with the knowledge of the Governor and the commander of the said ports, a suitable hostel which can accommodate them com-

fortably and in which they will reside. They may not, however, erect it larger than ordinary houses and buildings. No one may compel [the French merchants] to sell any hostel constructed for their own lodging, when they might desire to leave; instead, it shall remain in such condition as will enable them to use it again upon their return.

5. The Envoy has requested that the merchants should be permitted to fly the flag of France from the roofs of such hostels as they might acquire in each of the ports, following the example of other Europeans. Although the English for some time have rendered important services and so-to-say have sacrificed themselves, and although the Dutch have procured great advantages from which the Divan profits, and have placed great sums as gifts before this Throne, which is the support of the world, so that they have raised themselves above their equals by this honesty and this mark of distinction, nevertheless, in order to favor the said Lord Emperor, who has laid the foundations of our friendship, we have permitted and do now permit by these presents [French merchants] to fly their flag from each of the houses which they might acquire in the ports, in the manner of the other Europeans.

6. Since we and the officers of our August Throne recognize that the power, superiority, harmony, friendship, and grandeur of the said Emperor of High Dignity exceed [the comparable qualities] of the other Kings in Christendom, we agree and permit the Ambassadors and Envoys of that Lord Emperor to receive the honors and ceremonies suitable to each, whenever they might come to our Paradisiacal Audience Chamber.

7. It has been agreed that French merchants may import into and export from Persia wares of gold and silver in the amount of 300,000 Sevillian piasters, each piaster worth 100 *dinars* and the total 2,100 *tomans*. The present article [confers upon French merchants the right] to deal in wares of gold and silver. Concerning other kinds of merchandise, it has been agreed that:

8. Merchandise, from the Indies and other countries, which they might import into Persia will be valued at 100,000 piasters, which make 7,000 tomans.

Merchandise from Turkey and Europe, such as cotton and woolen cloth and other varieties [of goods] which have nothing in common with imports into Persia from the Indies, will be valued at 200,000 piasters, which make 14,000 tomans.

French merchants may bring each year, from their country to Persia, either by sea or by land, the sum of 100,000 Sevillian piasters and the value by weight of 50,000 piasters in silver ingots and additionally 60,000 gold sequins or the equivalent by weight of unminted gold ingots, on condition that both the piasters and the gold will be taken to our Royal Mint and will be sold to the Royal Treasury without delay at the prevailing price for the equivalent value in Persian currency. In the same manner the sequins will be sold for their [equivalent] value [in Persian currency]. If during the year [French merchants] should want to take sequins to the Indies, they must count the sequins in the presence of the Governor and of the mint-farmer. [The merchants] will be allowed to export no more than 30,000 sequins to such country as they wish; for these 30,000 no conditions will be stipulated. After the officers of the pertinent commissioner will have affixed their seals at the opening of the sacks, [the merchants] will be allowed to carry the sacks wherever they desire but will not be permitted to take out of the [Persian] Kingdom an amount greater [than 30,000 sequins]. The surplus must be sold in Persia, for if they wish to take it elsewhere, they shall pay to the Divan a duty of three percent. Nor will they be permitted to take out of the Persian Kingdom silver or gold in unminted ingots, unless they pay to the Divan the same duty of three percent and a supplementary duty of one percent as well as several other duties. However, since the [French] Envoy has requested a remission of some part of the duties, it has been agreed, as a token of favor to the Lord Emperor, with the approval of his Envoy, that the merchants shall pay a duty of three percent for the import and three percent for the export of piasters. sequins, gold, silver, cloth, aromatic drugs, cottons, woolens, and other items whose value and quantity have been specified above, and all kinds of goods that they may bring to Persia. In making this payment to the Divan, they shall obtain a receipt stamped with the commissioners' seal, on condition that the varieties of merchandise, if transported by sea, will be inspected in the presence of the customs officials in the port and, if transported by land, in the presence of the Beglarbegis, Governors, commanders and persons responsible for [conducting] the affairs of the Kingdom. After the opened parcels of merchandise and specie of gold and silver have been inspected, a clear, detailed, and specific statement of all items must be stamped with the seal of the Divan's commissioners. Without the seal, the items may neither enter nor leave [the country]. Those items brought to Isfahan will be inspected by the Divan's officers and commissioners in that city. The merchants will present a statement of their wares to the said officers and will receive from the latter another stamped statement, listing the quantity of effects, gold and silver as well as merchandise and textiles. If the merchants should bring to Persia goods and provisions in greater quantity than agreed upon, they will pay to the Divan the duty of each, whether import or export, at the rate of one-tenth, in accordance with the usage of the land.

9. Of all the goods that the merchants may import into or export from Persia every year, by whatever route, half when going and half when coming, the quantity equal to 500 loads shall be exempt from the duty of the *rahdars* [road guardians]. The latter will not be allowed to charge anything for this quantity, on condition that the merchants have in hand a statement signed by the officers and commissioners of the Divan in each place and bearing the number of parcels. If more should be found, the surplus will be subject to the ordinary duty of the said rahdars.

10. As much food as [the merchants] require for their sojourn in the cities and for their travels will be furnished against payment. Animals for haulage [will be provided] also at the same rate of hire and will be sold at the same price that they are ordinarily furnished to Muslims. [The merchants] may not be abused with requests for greater payment.

11. No tribute or *kharaj* (military-exemption tax) will be imposed on French subjects or French merchants, or on any Europeans who may be with them, or on their interpreters or household servants, or on Armenians or Indians, up to twenty persons, who may be in their retinue.

12. All the various goods that may be imported into Persia and exported from Persia to other Kingdoms shall be appraised and estimated at the prevailing rate. The [merchants] will pay duties in proportion to the destination. If they should want to pay the duties in merchandise instead of in ringing specie, they shall not be compelled to pay in minted silver.

13. After [the merchants] have paid the duties required in a port or other locality for the goods that they may import into Persia or export from Persia to such place as they please, and after they have obtained the receipts from the Divan's commissioners, nothing additional will be requested in any place for these goods.

14. Since the Emperor of High Dignity has promised, in the letter that he wrote to our Sacred Majesty, to carry out our requests, a memorandum sealed by the Ministers of this Magnificent Crown has been handed to the Envoy, so that His Majesty, following [the ratification of] this Convention, may cause to be executed that which is contained in the said memorandum.

15. The diverse goods, piasters, gold, silver, and materials which Frenchmen may bring will be sold with their consent at current prices. They will not be compelled to have the piasters or the gold minted.

16. If some difficulty should arise between two Frenchmen, the Consul shall see to it that their differences are settled according to the maxims of their law. If a difference should arise between Frenchmen and other nations, the Governors and officers of the land will establish the truth of the matter in the presence of the Consul and will settle it in conformity with Muslim justice and universal truth.

17. If a difference should arise between the Consul, who is the chief of the French merchants, and a person of some other nation, the Muslim judges will not be empowered to summon [the litigants] before them or before their Divan (Tribunal), without a prior request to the Sublime Throne. The said judges also will not place the seal of their authority upon the houses of Frenchmen. But after having submitted their request [to the Persian King], they will do as they have been commanded.

18. If an act of murder should occur among Frenchmen, the Consul will judge according to his maxims. If one should occur between Frenchmen and Muslims or other Europeans, the officers of Muslim justice will draw up the information according to Muslim maxims in the presence of the Consul. Frenchmen will not be imprisoned or fined without proof and conviction.

19. If a French vessel, having suffered in a storm, should encounter danger, the commanders and subordinates of Persian and European ships will give all manner of aid and help. The captains and chiefs of French factories, when in need, will also receive aid and help, paying the expenses incurred on their behalf. The effects and goods salvaged from the sea shall be returned without special payment.

20. If a French merchant, in the course of commercial transactions, should contract a debt and become insolvent, with no [other] Frenchman as guarantor of the debt, repayment may not be demanded from other Frenchmen, for this is contrary to justice and to the religion of the Twelve Imams (Shi'ah Islam), which it is forbidden to violate. It is thus prohibited to exact from the [French] nation [the sum of] the loan contracted by the individual, under the pretext that he is a Frenchman. The judges of civil justice may not press [the French] nation] in this matter. If an individual of the said nation should happen to die in Persia, the stipulations of his testament will be executed without modification. If he should die intestate, his effects and clothing will be placed in the custody of the Consul. Persian officers will not be allowed to take [formal] cognizance thereof, unless it is conclusively proved by legal means that [the deceased] is in debt. In such a case the debts will be paid with the movable [property] that [the deceased] may have left behind. The remainder will be given to the Consul, and no one will be allowed to interfere or to dispose of the goods or to seize the effects, without conclusive proof.

21. The Consul and the interpreter of the French nation will inform the *shahbandar* (mayor or warden of a port town) or the judges or the Vazirs or the *darugahs* (police officials) of [all instances] of purchase, sale, interest, trade, and endorsements [for debts among French merchants] and apprise [the Persian officials] of the manner in which each transaction was concluded. [The Consul and the interpreter] will obtain an authentic receipt, of which [the Persian officials] will retain a copy for registration purposes and for reference, when the need may arise. If someone should cause the French merchants anxiety on this account, he may not sue them upon simple allegation. If a Muslim should assert that a Frenchman has caused him injury, or has said unreasonable things to him, no anxiety will be caused to the Frenchman on this account, without conclusive judicial proof, since the complaint might have resulted from hatred and enmity.

22. If an enslaved Frenchman who had not become a Muslim should be found in the possession of a non-Muslim nation, he will so inform the Consul or factory chief, who will notify the Beglarbegi or the judge of the province where he may happen to be. [The Persian official], after establishing the truth, will deal justly with the slave as required by right and equity. If Frenchmen should be taken as slaves on the coast of Turkey or elsewhere for sale in Persia, and if these slaves should be recognized by Frenchmen as members of their nation, the masters will be obliged to surrender the said slaves—provided they have not embraced the Muslim religion—to the Frenchmen and will receive as reimbursement the price of purchase.

23. A factory chief, captain or Consul may reside in any port of Persia. When the Lord Emperor of France should [decide] to transfer them and appoint others to the posts, the [Persian] Governors will be obliged to render the same honors to the new incumbents as were accorded to the old, and to behave toward them in all matters with honesty and civility, in conformity with this treaty.

24. If a suit should be brought against a Frenchman, the plaintiff will refer his complaint to the judge of the locality. The judge will summon the Consul's interpreter and will send him to the Consul to settle the differences. If the Consul should be preoccupied with some other problem or if his interpreter should be absent and unable at the time to attend to the matter, [the Consul] will be given as much time as possible

to complete his [other] business. But he will submit a written statement, so that, if the suit is not settled by the time of the expiration of the deferment, the [Persian] judge may deal reasonably with it.

25. Whenever French merchants may travel in Persia, they will be assisted by [Persian] commanders and by rahdars [guardians of the roads]. If thieves should steal anything from them in transit, the said officers will be obliged to find and arrest the thieves and to return to the Frenchmen the stolen objects. If the thieves cannot be apprehended, the said officers, after conclusive proof, will be bound to make full restitution from their own resources.

26. Since under the reigns of our illustrious ancestors—may God illumine their graves!—several European ecclesiastics were received in Persia and edicts issued that they should be well treated, the Lord Emperor of France has requested, through the mouth of his Envoy, [comparable arrangements for the future]. We therefore promise that European bishops and ecclesiastics residing anywhere in our Empire will be free to devote themselves to their prayers and to exercise their religion in the places and houses where they may be lodged, without let or hindrance, on condition that outside their houses they shall do nothing which may be contrary to the religion of the Twelve Imams. No one may violate the edicts that have been issued on behalf of the Europeans living in Nakhichevan and other localities of our Empire, or cause them anxiety. Furthermore, we promise to confirm and ratify the edicts that have been issued on their behalf by our predecessors. If ecclesiastics of the Armenian nation or those of the other European nations should unjustly and unreasonably attack or mistreat [French clerics] in their district, they will be required, after conclusive proof, to pay to the Royal Divan a fine of fifty Tabrizi tomans. Carmelite, Dominican, Capuchin, Augustin, Jesuit, and other ecclesiastics established in the regions of Shirvan, Khalkhal, Ala Shur, Karabagh, Azarbayjan or Media, Isfahan, Tabriz, Tiflis, Ganja, Erivan, Nakhichevan, Shiraz, Bandar 'Abbas and in other regions and towns of our realm will be free to live in these localities and wherever else they may deem fit. No one may oppose or hinder the

Armenians and Christians and their children, if they should want to go and study with [the ecclesiastics] and listen to their lessons. Members of the [French] nation will be free to bury their dead in cemeteries set aside for them in accordance with their own religious customs. They will be free to present their complaints and to receive merited justice. If contrary to right and reason someone should deal with them unjustly, he shall be fined, chastised, corrected, and reprimanded, as he deserves.

27. We permit the Consul of France and the ecclesiastics in the houses designated as their lodging to make as much wine as they require for their own use, provided that they alone drink it and that they refrain from selling it to any Muslim. Apart from the two hundred fifty loads of merchandise and effects which we have exempted from the duties of the rahdars, we now add to the list wine, rose water, and *turshi* [pickles] (the last produced in Shiraz), which they may take to their vessels in the same tax-exempt quantity. No one may cause them anxiety, provided they refrain from taking to their vessels other foods not stipulated above. When the said foods are transported within Persia from town to town for the use of [French] officers and servants, no duty will be exacted from them.

28. Frenchmen will be permitted to buy eight stallions and four mares each year, with the consent of those to whom the animals belong, after inspection by His Excellency the *Mir Akhur Bashi* (Grand Equerry) at Isfahan, and by the judge or Governor elsewhere, provided that the horses are not from the King's stables or stud-farms. Frenchmen will be free to transport the animals to France without interference.

29. If a Frenchman should want to marry in our Kingdom, and should ask in marriage a Christian or an Armenian girl or another of the religion of Jesus, he will encounter no difficulty. If one of the two should die without having designated a guardian for the children of this marriage, they will be placed in the custody of the Consul, who may send them to France, if he should judge it proper.

30. The Envoy has promised that Frenchmen will receive on their vessels, at the ordinary passenger fare, Persian mer-

chants and traders who may be in Hindustan or in other lands under the hegemony of other Kings and who do not dare to cross the seas for fear of enemies of pirates. The merchants and their goods will be protected and brought [safely] to Persia.

31. All this has been written down and prescribed, so that the provisions will be executed in perpetuity from reign to reign between the two Emperors and no one, whether soldiers or civilians, merchants or other subjects of the said Empires, may violate [the undertakings].

A memorandum has been drawn up and given to the Ministers of this Heaven-like Throne for registration in the permanent archives and preservation among the royal protocols, so that the Lord Envoy's consent to the execution of certain articles of the agreement might become a matter of public knowledge. Our August Majesty, also in conformity with the said Lord Envoy's consent, have promised and do now promise that the magnificent Beglarbegis, Amirs (chief military officers) and illustrious judges, the Vazirs and all our venerable commanders and officers as well as the Darugahs, Shahbandars, caravan leaders, and all the officers of Divan (Treasury) affairs in the provinces of the Kingdom will

faithfully observe the Treaty that has just been concluded between Our August Imperial Majesty and the Very High and Excellent Emperor of the elevated throne, crowned by the Sun, the Emperor of France. We thus command, order and enjoin them to take care not to violate the provisions of the said treaty and that, guided by all the points and articles in conformity with the exact observation of friendship and union, they do nothing against the good and sincere understanding but that they observe this treaty which is the foundation thereof. Those who transgress the articles specified above shall know that they incur the anger and indignation of Our Redoubtable Majesty. Let them consider these articles indispensable orders that are to be executed in general and in particular, so that it may not become necessary to renew them each year by an edict to that effect. Therefore, as soon as the necessary command of obedience, august in this sovereign and happy order, will be adorned, garnished, adjusted, embellished and demonstrated by the authentic, sublime, formidable and most holy, most elevated, most redoubtable, most superior seal, let faith be added thereto.

18. OTTOMAN TERMS OF PEACE ACCEPTED BY RUSSIA AT PRUTH
10/21 July 1711

[Translated from the French text in Hertslet, *Treaties, etc., between Turkey and Foreign Powers*, pp. 434–35]

After wresting Azov from the Ottomans in 1696, Tsar Peter I, in renewed fighting a decade and a half later, faced ignorminious defeat at the hand of his southern neighbor and sued for peace. The terms, dictated by the Ottoman plenipotentiary at the Pruth River, although severe, proved far less exacting than the Russians had anticipated. The stipulations at Pruth provided the basis for the definitive peace, signed at Adrianople on 22 June/3 July 1713 (French text in Hertslet, op. cit., pp. 440–45), which delayed for more than sixty years the acquisition by Russia of the outlet it sought on the Black Sea and for seven years the restoration of a permanent diplomatic mission at the Sublime Porte (Ottoman Imperial Government), originally procured in 1701. Sumner, *Peter the Great and the Ottoman Empire*, chaps. 1–2, 5, 7–9; Florinsky, *Russia*, 1: 335–45; Übersberger, *Russlands Orientpolitik*, pp. 49–118.

Since it has pleased God, Sovereign Master of the Universe, to allow by His wise providence and His infinite mercy the victorious armies of the believers to encircle the Tsar of Russia and all his troops on the banks of the Pruth [River], where they have been so defeated that his Tsarist Majesty has been forced to seek peace and to sue for it publicly, this is the real reason which caused us to write these presents, the conditions of which are expressed as follows:

ART. 1. The fortress of Azov shall be returned to the Ottoman Empire in the state in which it was when captured, with all its dependent lands and jurisdictions.

ART. 2. The three fortresses of Tychan [Tsaritsyn?], Kamenny Zaton, and the new one [Taganrog] built near the Samara [River] shall be demolished. The cannon of the last-mentioned fort, with all its ammunition, shall be surrendered to the Empire. The rebuilding of forts in the three places mentioned shall never be allowed.

ART. 3. The Tsar shall refrain from molesting in any manner in the future the Barrabas and Potkali Cossacks, subjects of Poland, and those dependent on the very powerful Han Devlet Girey, Prince of the Crimea. The said Tsar shall let them enjoy their places of habitation, as always defined in the past.

ART. 4. In the future, with the exception of merchants who travel, the Tsar shall have no one in residence at Constantinople on his behalf with the rank of Ambassador or Minister.

ART. 5. All Turks who have been taken prisoner or enslaved, whatever their number, shall be freed, and returned to the Sublime Porte.

ART. 6. Since the King of Sweden has placed himself under the favorable protection of the Sublime Porte, no hindrance shall henceforth be caused him. When he should want to return to his states, he shall not be caused anxiety en route. Similarly, if he cannot [return], peace shall be concluded between the parties, once agreement can be reached on the conditions.

ART. 7. The Sublime Porte for its part and the Russians for theirs shall promise that the inhabitants, subjects, or other persons who may be under their protection shall nowhere be molested or caused anxiety. It is stipulated, however, that the Most Serene, Very High, and Very Clement Emperor, our Very Clement Lord and Master, will be supplicated to forget the irregular behavior of the Tsar and, at God's good pleasure, to ratify at Constantinople the treaty of alliance, a copy of which will be delivered to the Tsar, since he undertook on this basis to accept the obligation, approved in accordance with our full powers. The above articles will be executed after [the Sublime Porte] has received the hostages and four written engagements from the said Tsar, who will be permitted to withdraw to his states, without fear of trouble from the Tatars or other troops. As soon as the above conditions are implemented and the capitulation made and accepted, the Sublime Porte will allow Baron Peter Shafirov, Chancellor and secret Counselor of the Tsar, and Major-General Michel Borisovich Shermetev to return to their country without delay, after they have fulfilled the obligations for which they remained with our victorious army as hostages of the Tsar. To this end the present article has been inserted.

19. TREATY OF FRIENDSHIP AND COMMERCE: FRANCE AND PERSIA
13–15 August 1715

(Confirmed by Shah Sultan Husayn, 20 June 1722)
[Translated from the French text in Hauterive and Cussy, *Recueil des traités*, pt. 1, 2: 402–10]

"In 1708, M. Michel, sent out by Louis XIV, concluded a treaty with Shah Sultan Husein; and in 1715 Le Grand Monarque," observed the Honorable George N.

Curzon (*Persia and the Persian Question,* 2: 549), "was humbugged into signing another at Versailles by a Persian adventurer, named Mohammed Reza Bey." There is, indeed, basis for questioning the authenticity of Muhammad Riza's credentials. But the fact remains that the shah ratified the terms of the treaty in 1722. The French negotiators agreed to limited, but nonetheless reciprocal, exterritorial privileges for Persian merchants in France. Shah Sultan Husayn's surrender to the Afghan invaders in the fall of 1722 terminated the Safavi dynasty's rule over a united Persia, so that the terms of the 1708 and 1715 agreements were not binding on later Persian monarchs. For references, see Doc. 17, particularly Herbette, *Une ambassade persane sous Louis XIV.*

1. Treaty of Friendship and Commerce, 13 August 1715

ART. 1. The 1708 Treaty shall remain in force and shall be executed in all matters that are not contrary to the new articles below. With respect to those of its provisions that may be found contrary to the aforesaid articles, it shall be null and without effect.

2. Frenchmen and others engaging in commerce in Persia and bearing a French passport may import into or export from all the states under the hegemony of the King of Persia all sorts of merchandise in whatever quantity they deem desirable, either by sea or by land, from the Indies or from Europe, paying neither entry nor exit duties to the King of Persia or to the Governors of provinces and localities [or to] Persian Lords and communities possessing the right to exact duties from other nations.

3. If they should not find in Persia wares suitable for their commerce, they may exchange their gold and silver materials for sequins or other money which they may take away with them wherever they judge appropriate, without paying any duties and without being compelled to take the said materials to the mint.

4. The King of Persia will have the French merchants in his capital, in the ports of the Persian Gulf and on the boundaries of Turkey and Georgia, provided with buildings suitable for accommodating them and the Consul of the French nation and their factories and storehouses, without requirement of paying anything or offering any presents, and they will be allowed to fly therefrom the flag of France.

5. The Ambassador of His Very Chris-tian Majesty will enjoy first honors and precedence over all the other Ambassadors at the Court of the Kings of Persia. The Consuls, agents directors, and factors of the said merchants will in like manner enjoy precedence over all those of other nations.

6. The exemption from the capitation tax, from the *kharaj,* and from all other tributes and duties granted to Frenchmen by Article 11 of the Treaty of 1708, shall have effect for all Frenchmen generally, and for all their servants and slaves without limit.

7. Materials and goods which they may import or export will not be subject to inspection. The drivers thereof, provided with receipts certified by the Consul of the French nation, will be free to bring [the wares] in or take them out of the states under the domination of the King of Persia and to transport them from one place to another, without trouble or hindrance from the road guards [*rahdars*], who may not exact any duty or presents therefor, under penalty of their life.

8. If any gifts, for whatever cause or under whatever pretext, should be exacted from French merchants or from others provided with French passports, the King of Persia will have [the gifts] returned. If antthing should be taken from them in their houses or while they travel, the officers of the locality in charge of public safety will be held responsible for returning to the Frenchmen the stolen objects. Otherwise the value will be paid to [the Frenchmen] out of the funds of the domain of the King of Persia.

9. Frenchmen will be allowed to buy stallions and mares in the States of the King of Persia in such number as they may

find convenient. They will be permitted to export [the animals] to their own country or to the Indies; however, not before they have passed inspection by the Grand Equerry (if it is at Isfahan) or by the Governor of the city or of the district (if it is in another locality). The horses, moreover, may not come from the stables of the King of Persia or from his stud-farms. [Frenchmen] will not be compelled, in return, to hand out gifts.

10. Civil or criminal difference that may arise between Frenchmen and members of another nation will be investigated and decided by the officers of Muslim justice. However, the case will be neither investigated without [the participation of] the Consul of the French nation nor decided except in his presence or in the presence of such other person as he may commission, if he himself should be unable to assist in the matter. Differences that may similarly arise between the Consul or the interpreter of the French nation and persons of another nation will be decided by the King of Persia himself. The judges of the locality may not take formal congizance of such cases, nor may they, in any case, affix their seal upon the houses where the Frenchmen live.

11. Besides the immunities, franchises and privileges accorded to Frenchmen by the Treaty of 1708 and by the above articles, it has been agreed that they will enjoy all the other privileges, immunities, franchises, and exemptions that may hereafter be granted to other nations for whatever reason. . . .

2. Separate Articles of the Preceding Treaty, 15 August 1715

In addition, the said Ministers and Commissioners of His Imperial and Very Christian Majesty, in virtue of their full powers, have agreed on the following articles in favor of the Persian merchants.

ART. 1. Persian merchants, verily coming from the States of the King of Persia to the port of Marseilles, will enjoy the same privileges and exemptions as the other merchant subjects of His Very Christian Majesty, on condition, however, that they may not bring to France any goods whose entry is forbidden; that they will use French ships to transport the permissible goods; and that all the goods will be products of the States of the King of Persia, proved by a certificate that they will arrange to obtain from the Consul of the French nation.

2. [The Persian merchants] may have in Marseilles a Consul of their nation to whom the King will have a house given for [the Consul's] residence. The said Consul will enjoy exemption from the capitation tax.

3. The Consul will have sole right to decide any differences that may arise among Persian merchants. Investigation and decision of differences that may arise between Persians and subjects of His Very Christian Majesty or members of another nation, will belong to the judges of the locality established by His Very Christian Majesty. If a French merchant, debtor of a Persian, should happen to become bankrupt, the rights of the Persian will be guaranteed, and he will be permitted to exercise them against the person and the goods of the debtor in the same manner as the subjects of His Majesty and in conformity with the rules established in the Kingdom for such cases.

4. If a Persian merchant should happen to die in France, where he was engaged in commerce, his goods and effects will be placed in the custody of the Consul of [the Persian] nation for the heirs of the deceased. However, if it should be proved that the deceased was indebted to a Frenchman or to someone of another nation, the creditor will receive payent of his debt before the Persian consul may dispose of the goods and effects.

20. TREATY OF PEACE AND CAPITULATIONS: GREAT BRITAIN AND THE GARRISON OF TRIPOLI
19 July 1716

[*British and Foreign State Papers*, vol. 1, pt. 1, pp. 720–25]

Between 1620 and 1660, "war" was the common condition in British-Barbary relations. This was piratical war. British privateers such as Sir Robert Mansel and Robert Blake, with the blessing of the king and, during the Civil War and under the Commonwealth, of Parliament, were arrayed against Muslim corsairs going about their business with the sanction of the beys, deys, paşas, ağas, and divans, who in varying combinations managed the public affairs of the quasi-sovereign states. In the mid-seventeenth century, who started these wars no longer counted. European-Barbary piratical warfare had become institutionalized. Largely because of that, the warfare could not be brought under control. Basically, neither side tried to modify the rules, while commerce, religion, and strategy yielded pretexts enough for continuing to seize cargoes and kidnap crews and passengers. The European treaties with the Barbary states accordingly reflected the concerns of the maritime powers with arranging orderly sale of prize cargoes and agreed terms for the exchange, ransom, and release of enslaved subjects. Interspersed but concealed from ready view were clauses stipulating extraterritorial privileges for resident European consuls and merchants. While the consulship in the Barbary states, as everywhere in the Middle East, was unilateral, concern and provisions for managing the sale of prizes and the release of slaves were reciprocal. No sooner was peace achieved than both sides violated its conditions, because each had a vested interest in preserving the piratical institutions. Piracy thus dominated the formal relations, but trade and politics went on, often ignored by contemporary and later observers. Remarkable, then, was not the piracy but the continuing conduct of "normal" commercial and political relations. In these respects, while the styles differed among the European maritime powers as among the North African quasi-sovereignties, the underlying patterns were similar. When finally the British privateer disappeared after the restoration of the Stuarts in 1660, British trade with the Barbary states was not limited to members of a chartered company but was opened to individual merchants. In the absence of a chartered company, the government commissioned and paid—miserably—the "salaries" and expenses of the consuls. As early as 1658 Britain accredited a resident consul at Tripoli, becoming the first European power to do so. With the powerful support of the commanders of British naval squadrons on patrol in the Mediterranean, the consuls conducted the diplomacy, or rather consulship, of piratical war and peace. Between 1658 and 1694 Britain signed five treaties with Tripoli. The following, which was the first with the dynastic regime established in 1711 by Ahmed Karamanli, the commander of the cavalry, who was a *kuloğlu*, or son of a janissary through Ottoman-Arab intermarriage, remained the basic treaty in Britain's dealings with Tripoli until the end of the dynasty and the reintegration of the garrison into the Ottoman Empire after 1835. Abun-Nasr, *History of the Maghrib*, chap. 7; Masson, *Histoire des établissements et du commerce français dans l'Afrique Barbaresque*, chaps. 6, 11; G. Fisher, *Barbary Legend*.

ARTICLES of Peace between His Most Sacred Majesty, George, by the grace of God, King of Great Britain, France and Ireland, Defender of the Faith, &c., and the Most Excellent Lords, Mamet Bey, Isouf Dey, Siaban Rei, the Divan, and the rest of the Officers and People of the City and Kingdom of Tripoli; renewed, concluded and ratified this 19th of July, 1716, by John Baker, Esq. Vice-Admiral of the Blue Squadron of His Britannic Majesty's Fleet, and Admiral and Commander-in-Chief of His Majesty's Ships employed, and to be employed in the Mediterranean, being properly empowered for that purpose.

ART. I. In the first place it is agreed and concluded, that from this time forward for ever, there shall be a true and inviolable Peace between the Most Serene King of Great Britain, and the Most Illustrious Lords and Governors of the City and Kingdom of Tripoli, in Barbary, and between all the Dominious and Subjects of either side; and if the Ships and Subjects of either Party shall happen to meet upon the Seas, or elsewhere, they shall not molest each other, but shall show all possible respect and friendship.

II. That all Merchant Ships belonging to the Dominions of Great Britain, and trading to the City, or any other part of the Kingdom of Tripoli, shall pay no more than 3 per cent Custom for all kinds of goods they shall sell; and for such as they shall not sell, they shall be permitted freely to embark it again on board their Ships, without paying any sort of Duty whatsoever, and shall depart without any hindrance or molestation.

III. That all Ships and other Vessels, as well those belonging to the said King of Great Britain, or to any of His Majesty's Subjects, as also those belonging to the Kingdom or People of Tripoli, shall freely pass the Seas, and traffic where they please, without any search, hindrance, or molestation, from each other; and that all Persons or Passengers, of what Country soever, and all monies, goods, merchandises and moveables, to whatsoever People or Nation belonging, being on board of any the said Ships of Vessels, shall be wholly free, and shall not be stopped, taken, or plundered, nor receive any harm or damage whatso-

ever from either Party.

IV. That the Tripoli Ships of War, or any other Vessels there-unto belonging, meeting with any Merchant Ships, or other Vessels of the King of Great Britain's Subjects, (not being in any of the Seas appertaining to His Majesty's Dominions,) may send on board one single Boat, with 2 Sitters, besides the ordinary Crew of Rowers; and no more but the 2 Sitters to enter any of the said Merchant Ships, or any other Vessels, without the express leave of the Commander of every such Ship or Vessel; and then, upon producing to them a Pass under the Hand and Seal of the Lord High-Admiral of England, the said Boat shall presently depart, and the Merchant Ship or Ships, Vessel or Vessels, shall proceed freely on her or their voyage. And although the Commander or Commanders of the said Merchant Ship or Ships, Vessel or Vessels, produce no Pass from the Lord High Admiral of England, yet if the major part of the said Ship's or Vessel's Company be Subjects to the said King of Great Britain, the said Boat shall presently depart, and the Merchant Ship or Ships, Vessel or Vessels, shall proceed freely on her or their voyage; and if any of the said Ships of War, or other Vessels of His said Majesty, meeting with any Ship or Ships, Vessel or Vessels, belonging to Tripoli, if the Commander or Commanders of any such Ship or Ships, Vessel or Vessels, shall produce a Pass firmed by the Chief Governors of Tripoli and a Certificate from the English Consul living there; or if they have no such Pass or Certificate, yet if the major part of their Ship's Company or Companies be Turks, Moors, or Slaves belonging to Tripoli, then the said Tripoli Ship or Ships, Vessel or Vessels, shall proceed freely.

V. That no Commander, or other Person, of any Ship or Vessel of Tripoli, shall take out of any Ship or Vessel of His said Majesty's Subjects any Person or Persons whatsoever, to carry them anywhere to be examined, or upon any other pretence, nor shall use any torture or violence unto any Person of what Nation or quality soever, being on board any Ship or Vessel of His Majesty's Subjects, upon any pretence whatsoever.

VI. That no Shipwreck belonging to the

said King of Great Britain, or to any of His Majesty's Subjects, upon any part of the Coast belonging to Tripoli, shall be made or become Prize, and that neither the goods thereof shall be seized, nor the Men made Slaves; but that all the Subjects of Tripoli shall do their best endeavours to save the said Men and their goods.

VII. That no Ship, or any other Vessel of Tripoli, shall have permission to be delivered up, or to go to any other place in enmity with the said King of Great Britain, to be made use of as Corsairs at sea against His said Majesty's Subjects.

VIII. That if any Ship or Vessel of Tunis, Algier, Tetuan or Sally [Salé], or any other place being in War with the said King of Great Britain, bring any Ships, Vessels, Men or goods, belonging to His said Majesty's Subjects, to Tripoli, or to any Port or place in that Kingdom, the Governors there shall not permit them to be sold within the Territories of Tripoli.

IX. That if any Subject of the said King of Great Britain happens to die in Tripoli, or its Territories, his goods or money shall not be seized by the Governors, of any Ministers of Tripoli, but shall all remain with English Consul.

X. That neither the English Consul, nor any other Subject of the said King of Great Britain, shall be bound to pay the Debts of any other of His Majesty's Subjects, except that they become Surety for the same by a public act.

XI. That the Subjects of His said Majesty in Tripoli, or its Territories, in matter of Controversy, shall be liable to no other jurisdiction but that of the Dey, or Divan, except they happen to be at difference between themselves, in which case they shall be liable to no other determination but that of the Consul only.

XII. That in case any subject of His Majesty, being in any part of the Kingdom of Tripoli, happen to strike, kill, or wound a Turk or Moor; if he be taken, he is to be punished in the same manner, and with no greater severity than a Turk ought to be, being guilty of the same offence,; but if he escape, neither the said English Consul, nor any other of His said Majesty's Subjects, shall be in any sort questioned or troubled therefore.

XIII. That the English Consul now, or at any time hereafter, living in Tripoli, shall be there at all times with entire freedom and safety of his person and estate, and shall be permitted to choose his own Druggerman and Broker, and freely to go on board any Ship in the Road, as often and when he pleases, and to have the liberty of the Country; and that he shall be allowed a place to pray in, and that no Man shall do him any injury in word or deed.

XIV. That not only during the continuance of this Peace and friendship, but likewise if any breach or War happen to be hereafter between the said King of Great Britain and the City and Kingdom of Tripoli, the said Consul, and all other His Majesty's Subjects inhabiting in the Kingdom of Tripoli, shall always, and at all times, both of Peace and War, have full and absolute liberty to depart and go to their own Country, or any other, upon any Ship or Vessel of what Nation soever they shall think fit, and to carry with them all their estates, goods, Families and Servants, although born in the Country, without any interruption or hindrance.

XV. That no Subject of His said Majesty, being a Passenger from or to any Port, shall be any way molested or meddled with, although he be on board any Ship or Vessel in enmity with Tripoli.

XVI. That if any of the Ships of War of the said King of Great Britain do come to Tripoli, or to any other Port or place of that Kingdom, with any Prize, they may freely sell it, or otherwise dispose of it at their own pleasure, without being molested by any; and that His Majesty's said Ships of War shall not be obliged to pay Customs in any sort; and that if they shall want provisions, victuals, or any other things, they may freely buy them at the rates in the market.

XVII. That when any of His Majesty's Ships of War shall appear before Tripoli; upon notice thereof given to the English Consul, or by the Commander of the said Ships, to the Chief Governors of Tripoli, public proclamation shall be immediately made to secure the Christian Captives; and if after that any Christians whatsoever make their escape on board any of the said Ships of War, they shall not be required back again, nor shall the said Consul, or

Commander, or any other His Majesty's Subjects, be obliged to pay anything for the said Christians.

XVIII. That all Merchant Ships coming to the City and Kingdom of Tripoli, (though not belonging to Great Britain,) shall have free liberty to put themselves under the protection of the British Consul in selling and disposing of their goods and merchandise, if they shall think proper, without any hindrance or molestation.

XIX. That at all times, when any Ship of War of the King of Great Britain, &c., carrying His said Majesty's Flag, appears before the said City of Tripoli, and comes to anchor in the Road, immediately after notice thereof given by His said Majesty's Consul, or Officer from the Ship, unto the Dey and Government of Tripoli, they shall, in honour of His Majesty, cause a salute of 27 cannon to be shot off from the Castle and Forts of the City; and that the said Ship shall return an answer by shooting off the same number of cannon.

XX. That no Merchant Ship belonging to Great Britain, or any other Nation, under the protection of the British Consul, being in the Port of Tripoli, shall be detained from proceeding to sea on her voyage longer than 3 days, under the pretence of arming out the Ships of War of this Government, or any other whatsoever.

XXI. That no Subject of the King of Great Britain, &c., shall be permitted to turn Turk or Moor in the City and Kingdom of Tripoli, (being induced thereunto by any surprisal whatsoever,) unless he voluntarily appear before the Dey or Governor, with the English Consul's Druggerman, 3 times in 24 hours' space, and every time declare his resolution to turn Turk or Moor.

XXII. That the Most Serene King of Great Britain's Consul, residing in Tripoli aforesaid, shall have liberty at all times, when he pleaseth, to put up His said Serene Majesty's Flag on the flag-staff on the top of his house, and there to continue it spread as long time as he pleaseth; likewise the said Consul to have the same liberty of putting up and spreading the said Flag in his Boat when he passeth on the water, and no Man whatsoever to oppose, molest,

disturb, or injure him therein, either by word or deed.

XXIII. That whereas the Island of Minorca in the Mediterranean Sea, and the City of Gibraltar in Spain, have been yielded up and annexed to the Crown of Great Britain, as well by the King of Spain, as by all the several Powers of Europe engaged in the late War: now it is hereby agreed and fully concluded, that from this time forward, for ever, the said Island of Minorca and City of Gibraltar shall be esteemed in every respect by the Government of Tripoli to be part of His Britannic Majesty's own Dominions, and the Inhabitants thereof to be looked upon as His Majesty's natural Subjects, in the same manner as if they had been born in any other part of Great Britain; and they with their Ships and Vessels wearing British Colours, shall be permitted freely to trade and traffic in any part of the Kingdom of Tripoli, and shall pass without any molestation whatsoever, either on the Seas or elsewhere, in the same manner, and with the same freedom and privileges as have been stipulated in this and all former Treaties in behalf of the British Nation and Subjects.

XXIV. And whereas in the Treaty of Peace concluded in the Reign of King Charles II, in the year 1676, by Sir John Narbrough, Knight, an Article was inserted, by which the Ships and Vessels of Tripoli were not permitted to cruize before, or in sight of the Port of Tangier, then belonging to Great Britain; now it is hereby concluded and ratified, that in the same manner none of the Ships or Vessels belonging to Tripoli, shall cruize or look for Prizes, before or in sight of the Ports of the Island of Minorca, and the City of Gibraltar, to disturb or molest the trade thereof in any manner whatsoever.

XXV. That all and every the Articles in this Treaty shall be inviolably kept and observed between His Most Sacred Majesty of Great Britain, and the Most Illustrious Lords and Governors of this City and Kingdom of Tripoli, and all other matters not particularly expressed in this Treaty, and provided for in any former, shall still remain in full force, and shall be esteemed the same as if inserted here. . . .

21. TREATY OF PEACE AND COMMERCE: GREAT
BRITAIN AND MOROCCO
23 January 1721

[*British and Foreign State Papers*, vol. 1, pt. 1, pp. 428–31]

In almost all European treaties with the Garrisons, clauses on the sale of prize cargoes and captured Europeans as slaves automatically lumped Salé with Algiers, Tripoli, and Tunis as the primary centers of Muslim piracy. Salé was home base for most Moroccan corsairs, known in England as the Salé Rovers. The prevalence of piracy in Morocco added to the confusion among Europeans, who included it among the Barbary states. But Morocco, the only state of North Africa to escape Ottoman conquest, clung to its independence until the eve of World War I. Still, official Moroccan relations with Europe were conducted at the consular level as they were with the Garrisons. Official relations were unilateral. Among the states of the Maghrib, as the Barbary Coast is known to its Arab inhabitants, Britain's dealings with Morocco were the oldest. A Barbary Company received the monopoly of British trade with Morocco in 1585, but no attempt was made to renew the charter on its expiry a dozen years later. In the first half of the seventeenth century Moroccan ports, especially al-Arish (Larash), havened English and other European privateers. In 1662 Britain inherited from Portugal the port of Tangier. From there the British could protect their Mediterranean shipping at the straits. But Mawlay Isma'il (1672–1727), the Moroccan unifier, drove the Spaniards out of three presidios and made life so difficult for the British that they too withdrew from Tangier in 1684. The real basis for sustained dealings with Morocco came early in the eighteenth century. The conquest of Gibraltar in 1704 and the recurrent possession of Minorca (in the Balearic Archipelago) gave Britain and Morocco a common purpose. Hemmed in by Spain, which refused to traffic with the British military posts on former Spanish territory, the British had to seek food and other provisions elsewhere. Morocco thus became a primary source for the replenishment of the British fixed posts and patrolling naval vessels in the Mediterranean. Nor was this a one-way exercise, since Gibraltar became a lucrative market for the sale of English goods which found their way on small coastal vessels to Morocco's northern ports, particularly Tangier and Tetouan. The British also sold arms and ammunition to the Moroccan government—and to the governors of the ports in the thirty-year war of dynastic succession (1727–57) beginning immediately after the death of Isma'il, when rival military juntas attached themselves to rival claimants who seized the throne (a pair of them more than once) for brief and bloody reigns, reducing the kingdom to political anarchy. The treaty of 1721 became the enabling instrument for later British treaties with Morocco until the mid-nineteenth century. G. Fisher, *Barbary Legend*, pp. 324–25; Masson. *Histoire des établissements et du commerce français dans l'Afrique Barbaresque*, chap. 12; Abun-Nasr, *History of the Maghrib*, chap. 8; Julien, *Histoire de l'Afrique du Nord*, vol. 2, chap. 6; Coindreau, *Les corsaires de Salé*.

. . . ART. I. In order to establish Peace between the Powers, both by land and sea, and all their respective Dominions, it is agreed on, that the English may now, and always hereafter, be well used and respected by our Subjects, agreeable to the orders and commands of the Emperor.

II. That all English Men-of-War and Merchant Ships, that shall come to any part of the Emperor's Dominions, to trade or otherwise, and shall have on board a cargo not proper for vending in the place where they shall come, may depart with the same to any other part of the Emperor's Dominions, and shall pay Duty but once for the same; and that no Duty at all shall be paid for any War implements, such as fire arms, swords, and anything belonging to the Army, as also for materials of all kinds for Ship-building; and if any English Ship shall arrive at any of the Emperor's Ports, with any merchandise destined for any other part of the World, that no Duty shall be paid for such merchandise, but shall depart with the same without any manner of molestation. If any English Ship shall be thrown upon the Emperor's coasts, by stress of weather, or otherwise, the same shall be protected, and may safely depart without any ill usage or interruption: in like manner shall be treated the Emperor's Ships, happening to be thus thrown on the coast of Great Britain, or the Dominions thereto belonging.

III. That all the English Ships and Emperor's Ships may pass and repass the Seas without hindrance, interruption, or molestation, from each other; nor shall any money, merchandise, or any demand be made or taken by the Ships of either Power from each other; and if any Subjects of any other Nation shall be on board either the English or the Emperor's Ships, they shall be safely protected by both Sides.

IV. If the Emperor's Men-of-War meet with any English Ships, and shall want to see their Passports, they are to send a Boat, with 2 Men of fidelity to peruse the said Passports, who are to return without any further trouble, and then both Sides to proceed quietly on their respective voyages; the same usage to be received by the Emperor's Merchant Ships from the English Men-of-War, who shall allow the Passport made out by the English Consul; and if the Consul shall not be present to make them, then the Passports made out by the English Merchants to be good and valid.

V. If the English Men-of-War, Privateers, or Letter-of-Marque Ship, shall take Prizes from any Nation with whom they shall be at War, they shall have liberty to bring and dispose of the same in any of the Emperor's Dominions, without any Duty or charge whatsoever.

VI. If any English Ship shall, by storm, or in flying from her Enemy, come upon the Emperor's coasts, the same shall be safely protected, and nothing touched or taken away, but shall be under the direction of the English Consul, who shall send the goods and People where he shall think fit.

VII. It is the mutual agreement of the King of Great Britain and the Emperor, that the Emperor do issue out orders to all parts of his Dominions, for the well-using of all the English Subjects, and that particular places be appointed for the burial of their dead; that the Consul's Brokers shall freely go on board any Ship without interruption; that the English Consuls, Merchants, and other Subjects of Great Britain, may safely travel by land with effects, without any hindrance whatever; and if any English, settled in the Emperor's Dominions, shall be desirous to return home, that they may so do with their Families, goods, and effects, without interruption: if any English die, the effects of such to be taken under the care of the Consul, to be disposed of as directed by the Will of such Person, and if no Will, for the benefit of such Person's next Heir; and if any debts shall be owing to such deceased Person, the same to be paid by order of the Governor or other Person in power, where such Person shall die; and that a Subject of the Emperor's be appointed to demand and receive the same, and deposit the same in the hands of the English Consul for the aforesaid uses. If any English shall contract debts in the Emperor's Country, and remove from thence without satisfying the same, no other Person shall be liable to pay such debts. The like usage and treatment the Subjects of the Emperor are to receive in the King of Great Britain's Dominions;

and that the King may send as many Consuls to the Emperor's Dominions as he shall think necessary.

VIII. That no English Merchant, Captains of Ships, or other Person or Persons whatsoever, that are English Subjects, shall be forced to sell any of their goods for less then the real value; and that no Captain, Master, or Commander of any English Ship shall be compelled, without their own will and consent, to carry any goods or merchandises for any Person or Persons whatsoever; nor shall any Sailor be forced away from any English Ship.

IX. If any quarrel or dispute shall happen between any Englishman and a Musselman, by which hurt to either may ensue, the same to be heard before and determined by the Emperor only; and if an Englishman who may be the Aggressor shall make his escape, no other Englishman shall suffer upon his account; and if 2 Englishmen shall quarrel, to be determined by the English Consul, who shall do with them as he pleases; and if any quarrel or dispute shall happen between Musselmen in England, or in any of the English Dominions, by which hurt may ensure, the same to be heard before 1 Christian and 1 Musselman, and to be determined according to the Laws of Great Britain.

X. If it shall happen that this Peace by any means shall be broke, the Consul, and all other English, shall have 6 months' time to remove themselves with their Families and effects, to any place they please, without interruption; and that all debts owing to them shall be justly paid to them.

XI. If any English in the Emperor's Dominions, or the Emperor's Subjects in the English Dominions, shall maliciously endeavour to break the Peace, such of them who shall be proved so to intend, shall be each Power be punished for such offence; each Power to take cognizance of their own Subjects.

XII. If any of the Emperor's Subjects shall purchase any commodity in the English Dominions, they shall not be imposed upon in price, but pay the same as is sold to the English.

XIII. That not any of the Spanish, whether Captains, Sailors, or other Persons under the English Government in Gibraltar, or Port Mahon, shall be taken or molested, sailing under English Colours with Passports.

XIV. That no excuse be made, or ignorance pretended, of this Peace, the same shall be published and declared to all the Subjects of each Power, which Declaration shall be signed by each Power, and kept by them to prevent disputes.

XV. If any Men-of-War shall be on the Emperor's coasts, that are Enemies to the English, and any English Men-of-War, or other English Ships, shall happen to be or arrive there also, that they shall not in any manner be hurt or engaged by their Enemy; and when such English Ships shall sail, their Enemies' Ships shall not set sail under 40 hourse afterwards. And if after the conclusion of this Peace, any Ships shall happen to be taken by either Power within 6 months after the proclamation of the Peace, that the same, with the People and effects, shall be restored. . . .

22. RUSSIAN-OTTOMAN TREATY FOR THE PARTITION OF PERSIA'S NORTHWEST PROVINCES
13/24 June 1724

[Translated from the French text in Noradounghian, *Recueil d'actes internationaux de l'empire ottoman*, 1: 233–38]

The abdication of Shah Sultan Husayn on 22 October 1722 at Isfahan brought the Safavi dynasty to a humiliating end. The capital had suffered some seven months of

siege by Afghan troops under the command of the rebel Ghalzay chieftain of Qandahar, Mir Mahmud, who proved incapable of uniting the country. The sharpened
competition for the spoils between the Ottoman Empire and Russia contributed
substantially to the resulting chaos. Russian-Ottoman rivalry focused on the Transcaucasian districts. Tsar Peter I (1689–1725) seemed determined to transform the
Caspian Sea into a Russian lake. But the Ottomans had already taken under their
protection the Sunnis of Shirvan, recognizing as their khan, or tribal leader, Hajji
Daud, with Shamakhi as his headquarters. Russia signified its claims in an agreement
—never ratified—of 23 September 1723 with Tahmasp, son of the former shah.
Russia agreed to assist Tahmasp in crushing the Afghan rebellion in return for Darband, Baku, and their surrounding areas, together with the provinces of Gilan,
Mazandaran, and Astarabad along the southern Caspian shores. To prevent a head-
on clash between Russia and the Ottoman Empire, the French ambassador at the
Sublime Porte, the marquis de Bonnac, mediated the dispute, inducing the two powers
to divide between them the Transcaucasian and western provinces of Persia, and to
recognize Tahmasp as shah if be endorsed the treaty terms. A Russian-Ottoman war
was thereby averted, but the dismemberment of Persia proved short-lived. Of longer-
range significance, the following treaty represents one of the earliest examples of the
application of European practices to boundary demarcation in the Middle East.
Lockhart, *Nadir Shah*, chap. 1; Schefer, *L'ambassade de France à Constantinople par le
Marquis de Bonnac*, pp. 1-lxxviii, 155–284, esp. pp. 275–80; Shay, *Ottoman Empire
from 1720 to 1734*, chap. 4; Hekmat, *Essai sur l'histoire des relations politiques irano-
ottomanes*, pp. 83–169; Hanway, *British Trade over the Caspian Sea*, vol. 3, an abridg-
ment, with inadequate acknowledgement, of La Mamye-Clairac, *Histoire de Perse*;
Malleson, *History of Afghanistan*, chap. 7 (drawn from Hanway).

ART. 1. The Lazgis of the province of
Shirvan having as Muslims asked for the
protection of the Sublime Porte, the latter
has granted them protection and suggested
as Khan one Daud, giving him credentials
and assigning him Shamakhi as residence.
In order that this town, the Khan, and the
peoples under him may have their frontiers
known, the following is agreed upon: riders provided and furnished with good and
accurate timepieces will proceed on horseback, at a trot, along the quickest route
from Shamakhi to the border of the Caspian Sea; upon [their] arrival at that sea,
the number of hours taken from Shamakhi
will be calculated. That number will be divided by three; the riders will return by
the same route and, upon completing two
thirds of it, will post a marker at that point.
One-third—from that post to Shamakhi—
shall belong to the Sublime Porte under the
government of the said Khan; the other
two-thirds located between the post and
the sea shall belong to His Tsarist Majesty.

Similarly, riders, will proceed from the
town of Darband beginning at the seacoast
and moving toward the interior of the country, on horseback, at a trot, for a period
of twenty-two hours, at the end of which
a marker will be posted. From the marker
placed between Shamakhi and the sea, a
straight line will be drawn, with a sufficient
number of small markers, to the marker
placed at 22 hours' distance from Darband.
Another marker will be placed at the point
where the frontier of Shirvan ends and at
the point reached in trotting for twenty-
two hours in a straight line from the sea-
coast to the interior. Similarly, riders will
proceed at a trot from the marker placed
in leaving from Darband to the marker
placed at the frontier of Shirvan, this line
being thereby indicated with several small
markers. From the marker placed near
Shamakhi, in following the line up to the
frontiers of Shirvan, all areas toward
the interior from Shirvan shall belong to
the Sublime Porte; the rest from the line to

the Caspian Sea shall remain to the Tsar. A straight line will be drawn from the marker placed between Shamakhi and the Caspian Sea to the point where the Aras River flows into the Kura River; this line will serve as a boundary, so that all areas between the line and the interior shall belong to the Sublime Porte and all that are located from the line up to the Caspian Sea shall belong to the Tsar. But since at the point where the Aras flows into the Kura the territory belongs in part to the Sublime Porte, in part to the Tsar and in part to Persia, thereby constituting a point where three frontiers join, the Sublime Porte is free to build a fortress there and to furnish it with a garrison. The said Tsar is also at liberty to build a fortress on his territory. These fortresses shall, nevertheless, be established with the reciprocal knowledge of the two parties and shall be erected at three leagues from the frontier. In order that the boundaries may be determined in equity and good faith, and in order that the necessary markers may be placed, the parties shall appoint mutually acceptable Commissioners [who are] honest and peace loving and [who have had] prior experience in similar occupations. And since this treaty has been concluded through the mediation of the King of France, the two parties request that a third person be added for [assisting in the proposed] partition and [in the] establishment of the boundaries between the two Empires through his mediation. When, with the help of God, the boundaries will have been fixed by the two parties and their Commissioners will have framed an instrument to this end, its contents shall be explicitly observed in good faith and without difficulty. And since there are few strong points on these new frontiers, the two parties are permitted to construct fortresses in their respective territories for the safety of their subjects, and to maintain garrisons, on condition that they are located three leagues from the frontiers.

ART. 2. Since the Sublime Porte considers the areas belonging to it in the province of Shirvan as a special government having its special Khan, as stated above, Shamakhi shall be the residence of the Khan, who will govern the areas in the province of Shirvan belonging to the Sublime Porte.

Shamakhi will remain in its former state, without the erection of new fortifications, and the Sublime Porte will not furnish it with a garrison or send troops or a military command there, unless the Khan appointed by the Sublime Porte should renounce his loyalty and plot rebellion. If, without the knowledge of the Sublime Porte, difficulties, disorder, and confusion should arise; if, for example, its subjects should wish to lay siege to or disturb the countries and regions belonging to the Tsar, the Sublime Porte shall be responsible for taking remedial action to reestablish order and to punish the authors as disturbers of the public peace. In consequence, [the Sublime Porte], after notifying the Russian commanders, will be allowed to send troops beyond the Kura to suppress any confusion, revolt, and disorder; thereafter it will immediately evacuate its troops, without excepting a single military or civilian officer. And since the Sublime Porte controls the entire province of Georgia, where many garrisons with commanders named by the Sublime Porte are located, if it should become necessary to send a large number of troops to maintain order there, provisional notice will be given to the commanders appointed by the Tsar on the Caspian Sea, in order to avoid any suspicion. These troops may cross the Kura River at any point of their own choice. If the troops should be obliged to move close to the Russian frontiers, the [Ottoman] commanders shall receive the strictest orders to supervise their subordinates so that the frontiers of the Tsar will suffer no damage.

ART. 3. Concerning the frontiers of the provinces conquered by the Sublime Porte in the Persian Empire, the following is agreed upon: Starting at the town of Ardabil, which remains to Persia, riders will proceed at a trot for one hour toward Tabriz, where a marker will be placed From there a line will be drawn to the point where the three frontiers meet. All the points on the side of the line where Urdubad and Tabriz are located, such as Urdubad, Tabriz, Lake Tabriz [Urumiyah, now Rizaiyah], Marand, Maraghah, Urumiyah, Khuy, Churas, Salmas and other areas in the province of Azarbayjan, with their dependencies as well as points located on this direct line, Ganja, Barda'a, Karabagh,

Nakhichevan, the towns of Erivan and Uchkelis, and all the towns and inhabited places situated in the province of Erivan, shall belong to the Sublime Porte. Similarly, a line will be drawn from the marker placed at one hour's distance from Ardabil in a straight line to Hamadan; all the inhabited places and villages indicated by that line, with all their dependencies, as well as Harmandan itself with its dependencies, shall belong to the Sublime Porte; from Hamadan, the line goes to Kirmanshah, which the Sublime Porte already possesses. Such shall be the frontier. And since the territories of Ardalan and Kurdistan are located on this line, as well as all the other provinces and towns which the Sublime Porte already possesses, with their dependencies and districts, all these territories shall remain in the possession of the Sublime Porte; and this, as in the manner stated above, starting at the point where the two rivers meet and proceeding to Kirmanshah; all the provinces located beyond the two lines drawn from the marker placed one league from Ardabil, and from the point where the three frontiers meet, shall remain in the possession of the Sublime Porte; but the provinces situated on the Caspian Sea shall belong to the Tsar. Those located on that sea from the point where the two rivers meet to Kirmanshah, beyond the line drawn, shall remain to Persia as a buffer between the Sublime Ports and His Tsarist Majesty.

ART. 4. The Sublime Porte has sent a large army comprising three corps for the purpose of conquering the Persian provinces and by this means has already brought under its control many areas. Since the Tsar is the eternal friend of the Sublime Porte, he promises through mediation (in virtue of the treaties concluded with Tahmasp [the son of former Shah Sultan Husayn] to liberate him from the hegemony of the Sublime Porte) to see that Tahmasp gives up, either voluntarily or under compulsion, all the provinces named in Article 3. But if Tahmasp should oppose stubbornly the implementation of this treaty and refuse to surrender the provinces already conquered by the Sublime Porte from the Persian Empire, as well as those on the Caspian Sea which he has granted to the Tsar under the

treaties concluded between His Tsarist Majesty and Tahmasp, the Tsar and the Sublime Porte will take common action to place the Persian Empire, apart from the provinces already partitioned between themselves, under one ruler, who shall possess it in perpetuity with full and complete sovereignty, without dependence in any manner on another power and without and part thereof ever being detached by the Osmanlis or the Russians. But if Persia should undertake hostile action against any of the above-named provinces which the two Empires have conquered, the two Empires will unite to obtain redress with their combined forces.

ART. 5. If the provinces named above in Article 3 as belonging to the Sublime Porte are handed over to the latter without difficulty by Tahmasp through the mediation of the Tsar, the Sublime Porte will recognize Tahmasp as the Shah of Persia, render him all assistance, in fact come to his aid and address in imperial letter to him at the conclusion of peace. In conformity with the treaty concluded between His Tsarist Majesty and Tahmasp, His Tsarist Majesty will send the latter effective help and will fulfill his obligations, so that the Empire of Persia and the residence of Isfahan might be returned to him as a legitimate inheritance and taken away from the usurper Mir Mahmud. If, in that event, Mir Mahmud, son of Mir Ways, should oppose the Sublime Porte in any way or resort to fighting, and if it should consequently become necessary because of the duties of religion to send troops, the Sublime Porte will also act against him in accordance with the rules of the faith, will help in his expulsion from Persia, and will participate insofar as it lies within its power in crushing the rebellion and the hostilities to the last spark. In consequence, it will join the Tsar and will act in concert with him. When Isfahan has been liberated, the Sublime Porte, being at peace with Tahmasp, will act in concert with the Tsar and in conformity with this treaty to place the said Tahmasp on the throne of Persia.

ART. 6. If Tahmasp should refuse to furrender the provinces which, through the mediation of the Tsar, are to fall to the Sublime Porte or which have been forever surrendered to the Tsar, the two Powers will each first take the share belonging to it and, after pacifying Persia, will transfer the absolute and independent government of Persia to a Persian-born individual whom they may consider worthy of the position, and they will strengthen him on his throne; no one shall interfere in his affairs, major or minor, and he shall be honored, recognized, and treated as ultimate sovereign; and in order that he might be able to reign in peace and without fear, the two powers undertake to reject any representation from Mir Mahmud and to make

no arrangement whatsoever with him.

Conclusion

Since this treaty has for its purpose that all provinces of Persia that may fall to the Sublime Porte and to the Tsar shall remain forever under the hegemony of the two Empires and that the Empire of Persia shall be reestablished, strengthened, and stablized, the present treaty shall be accepted without reservation and irrevocably observed, so that perpetual peace might be more assuredly secured.

23. TREATY OF PEACE, AMITY, AND COMMERCE: PERSIA AND RUSSIA
21 January/1 February 1732

(Ratifications exchanged, Saint Petersburg, June 1732)
[Translated from the French text in Rousset de Missy, *Recueil historique d'actes, négotiations, mémoires et traités*, 7: 457–62]

After the death of Tsar Peter I in 1725, Russia's forward policy in the Transcaucasian districts of its southern neighbor was abandoned for three-quarters of a century, although a full decade passed before the occupied territory was returned to Persia. Within Persia itself, Nadir Quli Khan, who joined the service of Tahmasp, had destroyed the Ghalzay regime by 1730, dispersing the Afghan troops beyond the possibility of effective reorganization. Perturbed over the decimation by disease of Russian forces in Gilan, Empress Anne (1730–40) in the fall of 1730 informed Tahmasp of her readiness to negotiate the terms of a Russian withdrawal from the area. The consequent Russian-Persian parleys, begun in April 1731 and embracing commercial matters and the permanent exchange of diplomatic relations as well as the problems of evacuating Russian garrisons, were consummated at Rasht. A second agreement, signed at Ganja on 10/21 March 1735, was required before the Transcaucasian provinces were wholly restored to Persia. See references to Doc. 22 esp. Lockhart, *Nadir Shah*, chaps. 2–8; also Reading, *Anglo-Russian Commercial Treaty of 1734*, chap. 10.

1. All misunderstandings which occurred at the time of the unrest in Persia and the hostilities in which the two sides engaged will be forgotten forever. The ancient good and inviolable friendship that obtained between the two Empires will be reestablished in such a manner that each side will seek the good of the other inso-

far as it can and will carefully avoid all harm and damage.

2. Her Imperial Majesty of Russia, [desiring] to give His Majesty the Shah persuasive proof of her friendship, renounces of her own generous volition the rights acquired by treaty and conquest over the provinces of Persia, by her ancestors of

glorious memory, because of the great expenditures and preparations of war. She promises the Minister Plenipotentiary of His Majesty the Shah that, one month after the signature of the present treaty, she will evacuate and return to the Shah the province of Lagetshank [Lahijan or Daghistan?] with its dependencies, all of Ranakut [?], and [the area] that lies beyond the River called Safid Rud; and five months after the conclusion of the present treaty and the exchange of ratifications, the provinces of Gilan, Astarinsk [Astara?], and other lands between Astarabad and the Kura River, in the same good state on which they are under the guard of the troops of Her Imperial Majesty. The other provinces and places located on this side of the Kura will remain under the domination of Her Imperial Majesty, as they are at present, for the sole purpose of preventing the restless nations along the frontiers from joining the evil-intentioned subjects of the Shah and causing new troubles, if Her Imperial Majesty should withdraw her troops, by seizing forcibly the places now under Russian occupation. As for the remainder, His Majesty the Shah recognizes in the return of his provinces the generosity of Her Imperial Majesty and promises to demonstrate his gratitude by all sorts of expressions of amity.

3. In consequence, His Majesty the Shah undertakes on his own behalf and that of his successors to live in perpetual and inviolable amity and good neighborliness with Her Majesty and her Empire. He will regard as his own enemies those who may be enemies of Her Imperial Majesty. He will allow the subjects of Her Imperial Majesty to trade freely in all the lands and places under his domination without payment of duty on merchandise brought from Russia to Peria for sale or barter. To this end, the Shah will order all his officers in the cities and provinces not to exact either duty or gifts from Russian merchants but, upon seeing a declaration by Russian officers at the frontier that [the merchants] are truly Russian subjects, to allow them to trade in all localities of Persia, without payment of duty, and, if they should wish to cross over to the Indies or to another country in pursuit of trade, to permit them free passage by sea or by land, without

payment of duty or tax or [grant of] gift or present to the profit of His Majesty the Shah. [The Persian officials] are required to see that [the Russian merchants] obtain good justice and suffer not the least harm. Similarly, the said merchants are permitted to build in suitable places houses and stores to hold their merchandise. The Persian officers will designate the said places for this purpose and will give them all assistance. If a ship or vessel, loaded with Russian merchandise, should happen to meet with accident within the domain of His Majesty the Shah, those in danger will be given every assistance to save their goods. Pillage or theft in such circumstances is forbidden, under severest penalty. If a Russian subject should happen to die in Persia, his effects, against receipt, will be placed in the custody of his companions or relatives, without anything being mislaid or withheld.

4. Her Imperial Majesty promises that the subjects of the Shah coming to trade in her states or passing through her states for other lands will enjoy all freedoms and advantages that may be granted according to the customs and charters of her Empire. Upon application [the Persian merchants] will be given exact justice. To this purpose orders will be issued to all the officers of Her Imperial Majesty in the cities to grant [the merchants] every kind of liberty and to protect them and their trade. Her Imperial Majesty also promises that, when merchants of the Court of the Shah may come to Russia with good certification that they are sent to buy goods for His Majesty, they will pay no duty for goods belonging to the Shah. In conformity with ancient usage, the said merchants will be received with every kind of consideration, and in the same manner will be sent off, provided indeed that they are Persian and that they buy not for others but solely for the Shah.

5. Since in the recent troubles in Persia several Russian merchants were massacred by the rebel subjects of the Shah, who seized several thousand rubles, an act that plunged several persons into deepest misery, His Majesty the Shah promises to have these losses investigated for the benefit of the Russian subjects and to render them justice, when the culprits can be identified, by having the loss repaid from the

movable or immovable property of the guilty or of their heirs.

6. It has also been decided and enacted that the two signatories will be permitted to have, at the Court of Her Imperial Majesty and at the Court of His Majesty the Shah, Ministers of such character as the importance of the negotiations may dictate. Each of the parties will give the said Ministers such lodging and daily appointment as is suitable to their character. Similarly, the signatories will be allowed to have agents or Consuls in other cities where they may deem fit, and every respect commensurate with their duties will be shown them. The officers of these cities will be ordered to respect them as is proper and to protect them against every damage and insult. Also, upon their complaints, good justice will be administered, whenever any harm may have been done to the subjects of the two Sovereigns. The lawsuits will be settled without delay, and those who may have suffered damage will receive satisfaction.

7. It has also been agreed that His Majesty the Shah will not adjudge as unfaithful subjects those Persians who, during the invasion by Russian troops and their stay in the Persian provinces and cities, may have entered the service of or may otherwise have been employed by Her Imperial Majesty. After the withdrawal of the Russians, [the Persian subjects concerned] will not receive either corporal punishement of fine [for their earlier action]. They will not be troubled but will remain in peaceful possession of their goods. Her Imperial Majesty similarly promises that after the exchange of ratification no subject of the Shah will be taken away against his will, [and] all those who entered Russian service voluntarily will be allowed to resign and return home.

24. TREATY OF PEACE (BELGRADE): THE OTTOMAN EMPIRE AND RUSSIA
7/18 September 1739

(Ratifications exchanged, Istanbul, 17/28 December 1739)
[Translated from the French text in Noradounghian, *Recueil d'actes internationaux de l'empire ottoman*, 1: 258–65]

Disputes arising from ill-defined frontiers between the Ukraine and the Ottoman-dominated Tatar khanates furnished the pretext in 1735 for a renewed Russian endeavor to establish itself on the northern shore of the Black Sea and to assert control over the mouths of the Dniester, Bug, Dnieper, Don, and Kuban rivers. The consequent Russian-Ottoman war dragged on inconclusively for four years, largely the result of poor military planning and organization at Saint Petersburg and of Austria's half-hearted fulfillment of its 1726 alliance with Russia. The peace signed at Belgrade was chiefly the handiwork of the marquis de Villeneuve, French Ambassador at the Sublime Porte, who served as mediator. Russia retained Azov and the surrounding area on the express condition of the demilitarization of the district. Moreover, Russia was forbidden to engage in commerce on the Black Sea except on Ottoman vessels. The treaty of Belgrade, guaranteed by France, provided the basis for relatively stable relations between the signatories for more than a quarter of a century. Laugier, *Histoire des négociations pour la paix*; (analytical narrative and texts of principal supporting documents); Vandal, *Une ambassade française en orient*, chap. 7; Mischef, *La Mer Noire et les détroits de Constantinople*, chap. 1; Florinsky, *Russia*, 1: 462–65; Übersberger, *Russlands Orientpolitik*, pp. 157–240; G. Fisher, *Barbary legend*.

Art. 1. As of today all hostility and enmity between the two Parties shall remain suspended and annulled forever. All hostilities and acts of provocation committed by either Party, overtly or otherwise, shall be everlastingly forgotten, and [neither side] shall seek revenge. On the contrary, perpetual, constant, and inviolate peace shall be maintained on land and sea. Sincere harmony shall be preserved. Friendship shall remain unchangeable by the very precise fulfillment of the articles and conditions stipulated by the two High Contracting Parties, Her Imperial Majesty and His Sultanic Majesty, [binding] their heirs and successors and the empires, domains, lands, subjects, and inhabitants of the two nations, so that in the future the two Parties will avoid the commission of any hostility or act of provocation, public or secret. They shall also preserve between themselves faithful amity and sincere peace, wishing and providing for each other every kind of prosperity and happiness, so that peace and tranquility may remain inviolably safeguarded for the well-being and growth of the two Empires and of their subjects.

Art. 2. The two Parties sincerely intend to establish durable and constant peace, so that the subjects of the respective Empires may profit therefrom and live in blissful tranquillity. To extirpate every cause of dissension and dispute, it has been mutually agreed that the boundaries of the two Empires shall be the same as those established by preceding treaties and shall be precisely and clearly defined in a convention that will be concluded in consequence of the present treaty.

Art. 3. The fortress of Azov shall be entirely demolished. To insure peace in a most solid and durable manner, the territory of the said fortress shall remain deserted within the limits fixed by the treaty of 1700 and shall serve as a barrier between the two Empires. In compensation Russia will be permitted to erect a new fortress in the vicinity of the Circassian island situated in the Tanaïs (Don) River near Azov, an island that is the former frontier of Russia; and similarly the construction of an Ottoman fortress will be permitted on the Kuban frontier near Azov, after the establishment of the location of the two above fortresses by the Commissioners of the two

Parties, to whose equity and discretion the decision will be entrusted. It is further stipulated that the former fortress of Taganrog, already demolished, will not be rebuilt and that Russia will not be allowed to construct or maintain fleets or other ships on the Sivash Sea or on the Black Sea.

Art. 4. In order that the subjects of the two Empires may be more positively knowledgeable of the borders that will be determined, the two Empires will name, as soon as possible after the confirmation of the present treaty of peace, Commissioners having the required capacity and provided with full powers and sufficient instructions, so that their commissions will not be subjected to vain difficulties. [The Commissioners], coming together in virtue of the present treaty, will demarcate without delay the borders between the two Empires. After placing in the proper locations the markers and signals which will be used henceforth and forever, [the Commissioners] will confirm the said borders with the customary written instruments, specifying all the particulars. The Commissioners must fulfill and complete their commission in the space of six months from the day of the exchange of ratifications of the present treaty.

Art. 5. The Cossacks and the Kalmucks, subjects of Her Imperial Majesty and of the Empire of the Russias, as well as all other nations subject to the said Empire, shall not attempt any invasion of and shall commit no act of hostility against the Tatars of Crimea, subjects of the Ottoman Empire, or against the other nations and Tatar subjects of the same Empire, and shall do them no harm or damage. [Russian] subjects shall refrain from all such enterprise and from everything that would be contrary to this holy peace. If indeed they should commit any act of rashness, they shall be rigorously punished. Similarly, the subjects of the Ottoman Empire, the Tatars of Crimea and all other subjects of the Ottoman Porte in general, of whatever name and quality, shall not attempt any invasion of and shall commit no act of hostility against the cities, villages, and localities of the domain of Her Imperial Majesty of All the Russias, against her subjects of Great and of Little Russia, against the cities of the Cossacks subject to Her Imperial Majesty and their dwelling-places located on the Borysthenes (Dnieper), the Tanaïs (Don) and elsewhere, or against the small fortresses, villages, and their inhabitants within the borders of the Empire of All the Russias, as they may be agreed upon and fixed. [Ottoman subjects] shall commit no act of hostility and shall avoid causing any damage secretly or openly by making slaves, stealing animals, or causing [Russian subjects] anxiety in any manner. If they dare in any manner whatsoever to cause injury or damage to or act with hostility toward the subjects or vassals of Her Imperial Majesty, they shall not be protected but shall be rigorously punished according to Divine Law, the right of justice and the enormity of the crime. Everything that might have been taken forcibly by either side shall be sought and returned to its proprietors.

ART. 6. The two Parties agree that the two Kabardas, the greater and the lesser, and the nations that inhabit them shall remain free and shall not be subjected to either of the two Empires but shall serve as a barrier between them. The Sublime Porte for its part undertakes that neither Turks nor Tatars will interfere with these districts and cause them anxiety; and similarly the Russian Empire for its part undertakes not to molest the districts. Following the former custom, however, every time that the Empire of the Russias should take hostages from the two Kabardas for the sole purpose of maintaining tranquillity, the Ottoman Porte will be free to do the same for the same end. If the peoples of the Kabardas should give cause for complaint to either of the two Powers, each will be allowed to chastise and punish them.

ART. 7. All prisoners and slaves of a military or any other nature taken before or after the war in whatever circumstances and for whatever motive [and] hitherto detained in the two Empires shall be delivered and sent back immediately following the ratification of the present treaty of peace without exchange or ransom, without any exception whatsoever, as many as may be found at present or in the future in the two Empires—apart from those in the Empire of the Russias who may have embraced the Christian religion and those in the Ottoman Empire who may have em-

braced Islam. The most express orders shall be published in all the cities and provinces of the two Empires regarding the liberty of the said prisoners, so that their manumission and freedom may be effectively granted without difficulty or procrastination. All slaves who may have been taken furtively and led into captivity since the conclusion of this treaty or during this peace and who may be in Crimea, the Bujiak and the Kuban [districts], or elsewhere among the Turks, Tatars, and other subjects of the Sublime Porte shall be liberated and returned without ransom. No violence shall be done any persons with passports of Her Imperial Majesty who may go into these countries to deliver Russian slaves, provided that they limit themselves to the orderly execution of their commission. All those who contrary to Divine Law may do violence to them or cause them damage shall be punished.

ART. 8. If, after the conclusion and ratification of the present treaty of peace, subjects of either [Signatory] Power should commit crimes or acts of insubordination or treason and flee to [the territory] of the other Empire, they shall in no way be received or protected but—excepting only those who may have become Christians in the Empire of the Russias and those who may have become Muslims in the Ottoman Empire—shall at once be returned or at least expelled from the lands where they may happen to be, so that such infamous men may produce neither coolness nor dispute between the two Empires. Henceforth, if a subject of Russia should flee to the states of the Ottoman Porte, or if a subject of the Porte should flee to Russia, [the fugitive] shall be returned whenever his government requests [the extradition].

ART. 9. Merchants, subjects of the Sublime Porte, will be allowed to engage freely in commerce—the fruit of peace that provides states and peoples with every sort of abundance—in all the Russias in the same manner as merchants of other powers and with payment of the same duties. Reciprocally, merchants, subjects of the Empire of the Russias, will be allowed as freely to engage in commerce in the states of the Ottoman Porte. But the commerce of the Russians on the Black Sea shall be pursued on ships belonging to Turks.

ART. 10. If differences and dissensions should occur during this peace among subjects of the two Empires, the Governors and commanders of the frontiers shall conduct the necessary investigations as equitably as possible. Cases of litigation arising betweem [subjects] of the two Empires shall be settled by all suitable means, in order better to insure the preservation of peace and friendship. When these disputes [take place] among limitrophe subjects, neither side shall undertake acts of hostility. But the inalterable maintenance of tranquillity shall be realized by both sides with every sort of consideration and in an amicable manner.

ART. 11. Russian laymen and ecclesiastics will be allowed freely to visit the Holy City of Jerusalem and other places that deserve to be visited. No tributes or payment whatsoever may be levied on these passengers or pilgrims at Jerusalem or elsewhere by subjects of the Ottoman Empire. [Russian subjects] will be given the requisite passports, since the Sublime Porte customarily issues them to nations friendly to the Ottoman Empire. Moreover, in accorance with Divine Law, no injury or violence will be done to Russian ecclesiastics while they are in territories under Ottoman domination.

ART. 12. Friendly negotiations will be conducted regarding the imperial title that has been mentioned on behalf of Her Imperial Majesty of All the Russias, and agreement will be reached to the satisfaction of the two Parties, as the propriety and the supreme dignity and power of Her Imperial Majesty require.

ART. 13. In order further to strengthen the peace between the two Empires and the surety of the articles of the present treaty, and [more effectively to accomplish] everything that the affairs of the respective subjects may demand, the Ministers of Her Imperial Majesty are allowed to reside at the Porte with such rank as Her Imperial Majesty may deem suitable. The said Ministers and their households will enjoy the same privileges, franchises, and all the rest

as those of the Ministers of the other most distinguished powers.

ART. 14. In order that the present peace and good friendship between the two Empires may be even more firmly established by the two Parties, Ambassadors Extraordinary will be exchanged at a time to be determined later and fixed by agreement of the two Courts. The Ambassadors shall be exchanged on the frontier with equality. They shall be received, honored, and treated with the same ceremonies and formality and in the same manner as are observed in the exchange of Ambassadors between the most distinguished powers and the Ottoman Porte. As a friendly gesture, the Ambassadors will bear mutual presents, suitable to the dignity of Their Imperial Majesties.

ART. 15. Furthermore it has been agreed that in three months from the day of the signature of the present treaty the instruments of ratification will be exchanged through the medium of the most illustrious and most excellent Lord, the Ambassador of His Very Christian Majesty [the King of France], mediator of the present peace. Finally, for the greater clarification of the above articles, declaration is made that, since it was agreed in Article 4 that Commissioners will be named for the regulation of the borders and the execution of the convention that will be framed concerning the said borders, the Commissioners appointed by the Sublime Porte will be subordinated to the Khan of Crimea. If, on the part of either Empire, incidents capable of altering the peace should occur for which no provision has been made in the articles of the present treaty of peace, the two sides will seek remedy with justice and equity. In order that the conditions of this peace, stipulated in the preceding fifteen articles, may be implemented in the future by the two sides and maintained inviolable as they should be, it is declared that in virtue of the present treaty all previous treaties shall forever remain without force or validity, with the reservation of the borders that are to be determined.

25. TREATY OF PEACE AND CAPITULATIONS: FRANCE AND THE GARRISON OF TUNIS
9 November 1742

[Translated from the French text in Rouard de Card, *Traités de la France*, pp. 173–80]

The first half of the eighteenth century was not a placid period for the successive French Compagnies d'Afrique which acquired coral and commercial concessions in the Cap Nègre-Tabarca-La Calle coastal stretch of the Tunis Garrison. Years of high profits were interspersed with recurrent wars, even after the establishment by Husayn bin 'Ali (1705–35), an Islamized Greek, of a beylical dynasty that lasted into the twentieth century. France concluded its first treaty of peace and capitulations with the new dynasty on 16 December 1710 (French text in Rouard de Card, op. cit., pp. 161–63). The records show that in 1730, one of its best years, the Compagnie d'Afrique earned profits of more than 750,000 pounds from the coral fisheries and the purchase and resale chiefly of grains, hides, wax, and wool in its operations in the adjacent concessionary areas of Tunis and Algiers. Husayn Bey, meanwhile, was overthrown in 1735 by his nephew, 'Ali Paşa, with the help of Algiers. Husayn took refuge in al-Kayrawan in the center of the Tunis Garrison, where he tried with loyal troops to retake the beylical throne. Husayn was defeated and executed by his nephew in 1740. By then a new French-Tunisian "war" had broken out over inconsequentia. The French tempest in the Tunisian teapot reached its climax in July 1742, when a young French lieutenant commanding a bark attached to a squadron that was endeavoring to blockade the Tunisian coast "made a romantic but unsuccessful effort to obtain possession of Tabarca by stratagem" (Broadley, *Last Punic War*, 1: 70). The French vessel was overwhelmed by superior Tunisian forces, who then strung the severed heads of twenty-seven French sailors in front of the building that housed the resident French factors. The Tunisians also destroyed the French concessionary buildings in the three coastal towns and seized the stores. Distracted by the War of the Austrian Succession, France could not pay as close attention to the affairs of its subjects in the Tunis Garrison as it might otherwise have done. Although peace was restored on terms set forth in the following treaty, which with only minor modifications was a facsimile of the treaty of 1710, the Compagnie Royale d'Afrique (Royal Company of Africa)—as it was then known—found Marseilles merchants unenthusiastic about risking their capital in the Tunisian enterprise. Nevertheless, a convention renewing the concession was signed on 24 February 1743 (French text, Rouard de Card, op. cit., pp. 181–82). In the later decades of the eighteenth century, French trade with the Garrison progressively declined. Masson, *Histoire des établissements et du commerce français dans l'Afrique Barbaresque*, chaps. 11, 13; Cambon, *Histoire de la régence de Tunis*, chap. 7; Fitoussi and Benazet, *L'état tunisien et le protectorat français*, pp. 3–41; Julien, *Histoire de l'Afrique du Nord*, vol. 1, chap. 6; Abun-Nasr, *History of the Maghrib*, chap. 7; Lord, *England and France in the Mediterranean*, pp. 1–38; Broadley, *Last Punic War*, vol. 1, chap. 8; G. Fisher, *Barbary Legend*.

1. The present treaty shall be made known to all the subjects of the two Kingdoms, so that it may be carried out according to its form and its terms.

2. Vessels armed for war in Tunis and in the other ports of the Kingdom, meeting at sea vessels and warships sailing under the French flag and with passports of the Admiral of France, conforming to the copy which will be transcribed at the end of this instrument,[1] shall give them all the help and assistance they may need, being careful to send only two unarmed persons in the launches, over and above the sailors necessary to navigate them, and to give the order that no one other than these two persons may board the vessels without the express permission of the commander. Reciprocally, French vessels will act in the same way toward vessels belonging to private shipowners in the town and Kingdom of Tunis, carrying certificates of the French Consul established in that town. A copy of this certificate will also be attached to the end of the present instrument.[1]

3. Vessels of war and commerce of France and Tunis shall be reciprocally received in the ports and roads of the two Kingdoms, and in case of need the ships and crews will be given all kinds of aid. Similarly, they will be supplied with victuals, fresh fruit, and in general all other necessities, paying for them at the normal and customary prices of the places of call, without having to pay either duty or anchorage fees.

4. If a French merchantship, on the roads of Tunis or in any of the other ports of the Kingdom, is attacked by enemy warships from Algiers, Tripoli, and Salé or others, within range of the cannon of the fortresses, it shall be defended and protected by the citadels, and the commander must compel the enemy vessels to give the French ship sufficient time—at least two days—to get away from these ports and roads. In that period the enemy vessels or other warships shall be detained and shall not be permitted to pursue. The same thing will be done by the Emperor of France.

5. All Frenchmen captured by enemies of the Emperor of France and taken to Tunis and to other ports of the Kingdom shall be set free at once, and they may not be kept as slaves. Should the vessels of

Tripoli, Algiers, and others, which may similarly be at war with the Emperor of France, put French slaves ashore, they may not be sold within the confines of this Kingdom, unless the Consul of France wishes to buy them. In this case, the powers of Tunis will be obliged to help him obtain them at the best possible market price. The same practice will be followed in France toward the inhabitants of the Kingdom of Tunis.

6. Neither the foreign passengers on French vessels nor Frenchmen seized on foreign vessels may be made slaves, under any pretext whatsoever, even though the vessel on which they are captured should defend itself. Nor may their property and goods be retained, as soon as it is clear that they belong to Frenchmen and that the passengers are armed with a passport and their loading certificate. The same thing will be done to Tunisian passengers. It has been further agreed that French vessels and boats must have two-thirds of their French crew above deck.

7. If any vessel or other French ship should lose its way on the coasts of the Kingdom of Tunis, whether chased by enemy vessels or forced there by bad weather, it will be given all the help it needs to put back to sea and to recover the goods of its cargo, paying by the day for the work of those who were thereby employed, without demanding any duty or tribute for the merchandise put ashore, unless it is sold in the ports of the Kingdom. The same thing will be done in France for the subjects of that Republic [sic].

8. French merchant vessels, launches, barks, and tartans carrying the flag of France and arriving in the roads of Tunis and other places of the Kingdom, to load and unload their goods, shall pay at the most 25 piasters per ship as arrival duty for entry and exit, and 5 piasters for the çavuş [captain of the port] and the janissaries, providing that they actually serve, and in general for everything else, no matter what its nature.

9. Officers of the ports and citadels in the Kingdom of Tunis shall be forbidden to demand anything of the officers of the French merchantships. Even when the ships

---

1. Not reproduced here.

touch La Goulette or other ports of the Kingdom to replenish, they shall pay no arrival duty. Tunisians will enjoy the same favor in France.

10. All French merchantships which arrive at the coasts or ports of the Kingdom of Tunis may put their goods ashore to buy and sell everything freely, without paying more than 3.0 percent for entry into the Kingdom and for exit, even for wine and spirits, which will be on the same footing as the other goods, this being the same duty as the French nation pays at Constantinople, Smyrna, Candia, and other places in the dominions of the Grand Seigneur. Should the French merchants, captains, and owners carrying the flag of France not be able to sell their goods in the Kingdom of Tunis, they may load the goods on whatever ship they judge appropriate to transport them out of the Kingdom without payment of duty. The same will be done in the ports of the dominions of the Emperor of France. If the merchants should put their goods ashore only for storage, they may reload the goods without payment of duty, and they shall not be required to put their sails or their rudder ashore. The captains or owners may not load or unload contraband goods prohibited by both parties, unless the captains or owners should have express permission. Ships which have loaded goods in countries that are enemies of the Kingdom of Tunis, and which unload them in the ports of the Kingdom of Tunis, shall pay [a duty] of 10 percent, as has always been the practice.

11. No help or protection against the French will be given to the vessels of Barbary which are at war with them, nor to those who have armed under their commission, and the Pasa, the Bey, the Dey and the Divan shall forbid all their subjects to arm themselves under the commission of any prince or state enemy of the Crown of France. They shall also prevent those with whom the Emperor of France is or will be at war from arming themselves in their ports, in order to hunt his subjects. The same practice will prevail in France toward Tunisians. If the powers of Tunis should be at war with any nation, and if some of their subjects should be captured on French ships, the Emperor of France shall reclaim them with their property. The powers of

Tunis shall do the same thing with regard to Frenchmen and their property.

12. The French may not be constrained, for any reason or upon any pretext whatsoever, to load anything on their vessels against their will, nor to make any voyage to places where they do not intend to go.

13. The Emperor of France may continue the establishment of a Consul in Tunis to help French merchants with all their needs. The Consul may practice the Christian religion in his home freely, for himself and for all Christians who may wish to attend. Similarly, the Turks of the Town and Kingdom of Tunis who come to France may practice their religion in their homes. The [French] Consul will have precedence over the other Consuls, and complete power and jurisdiction over the differences which may arise among the French, without having to inform the judges of the Town of Tunis.

14. The Capuchin fathers and other religious missionaries in Tunis, whatever their nationality, shall henceforth be treated and regarded as subjects of the Emperor of France, who places them under his protection. In this capacity, they may not be harassed either in their persons, in their property, or in their chapel, but they shall be upheld by the French Consul as proper and true subjects of the Emperor of France.

15. The Consul will be permitted to choose his dragoman and his agent, and to change them as many times as he wishes, without being obliged in the future to accept one from the Bey, the Dey, and the Divan of the Town and Kingdom. He may also fly the white flag over his home, and carry it on his launch at sea, [and] when on the roads, where he may go as often as he pleases, en route to vessels.

16. If differences should arise between a Frenchman and a Turk or a Moor, they may be judged not by ordinary judges but by the Council of the Bey, the Dey, and the Divan, and in the presence of the Consul.

17. The Consul shall not be responsible for paying any debt for French merchants, unless he is obliged to do so in his name and writing. The effects of any Frenchman dying in the country shall be put in the hands of the Consul to dispose of for the profit of the Frenchmen or others to whom they belong. The same rule will apply for

Turks of the Kingdom of Tunis who settle in France.

18. The Consul shall be exempt from all duties on the provisions, victuals, and goods required for his home. However, he and all his nation shall be permitted to import only enough wine and spirits for their own consumption. Neither they nor the other Consuls and their nationals may sell any without express permission, under pain of confiscation.

19. Every Frenchman who strikes a Turk or a Moor may be punished only after the Consul has been called to defend the cause of the Frenchman. If the Frenchman should flee, the Consul may not be held responsible. Nor [shall he be held responsible] for slaves who escape to French warships. But if they escape to marchant-ships, the commander of Tunis may have them sought there, and the Consul will be obliged to help him.

20. If the present treaty should be violated, no act of hostility will be made until after a formal denial of justice.

21. If any corsair of France or of the Kingdom of Tunis should harm French vessels or corsairs of that Town encountered at sea, he and the responsible ship-owners will be punished very severely.

22. If the present treaty, concluded by le sieur Fort for the Emperor of France, and by the Paşa, the Bey, the Dey, the Divan, and the other powers and the militia of the Town and Kingdom of Tunis, should be broken—may it not please God—the Consul and all the French merchants within the confines of the Kingdom may withdraw to wherever they please without arrest for a period of three months.

23. Whenever a warship belonging to the Emperor of France anchors before the roads of Tunis, as soon as the Consul has advised the Governor, the said warship shall be saluted by the citadels and the forts of the Town, in proportion to the rank of its command, and by a greater number of cannon shots than those for all other nations. The salute shall be returned shot for shot. Naturally, the same practice will apply for warships meeting at sea.

24. In order that no surprise may occur in the explanation of the present treaty, a French copy certified by the Consul and the powers of the Kingdom shall be posted in the harbor of Tunis.

25. This article and the above comprise the conclusion of the peace made by le sieur Fort between the Emperor and the Paşa, the Bey, the Dey, the Divan, and the other powers and the Militia of the Town and Kingdom of Tunis, for observance by their subjects. To give sincere proof of the good union that they have just made for posterity with the Emperor of France, the powers of Tunis shall restore all Frenchmen, and passengers with passports, that they have captured on sea or on land during the war. They shall also return in their present condition all ships which have been held in the ports, as well as those captured at sea. In the name of the Emperor of France, le sieur Fort promises that all the slaves of the Kingdom of Tunis in his galleys, no matter when captured, until this day, shall similarly be given back. In addition, the powers of Tunis promise their protection to the French Consul, to all Frenchmen trading in their Kingdom, and even to those of Cap Nègre, who shall also be regarded as natives of the country. Wholly to define and maintain the good union promised by both parties, le sieur Fort, in the name of the Emperor of France, has abandoned all other claims against the Tunisians that His Majesty may have had in the past until this day.

The above articles shall be ratified and confirmed by the Emperor of France and the Paşa, the Bey, the Dey, the Divan, and the other powers and the Militia of the Town and Kingdom of Tunis, to be observed by their subjects for the period of one hundred years. In order that no one may claim ignorance, it will be published and posted wherever necessary. . . .

26. TREATY OF PEACE (KURDAN): THE OTTOMAN EMPIRE AND PERSIA
4 September 1746

(Confirmed by the treaty of Erzurum, 28 July 1823)
[Translated from the French text in Noradounghian, *Recueil d'actes internationaux de l'empire ottoman*, 1: 306–08]

Following the attempted Ottoman annexation of Persia's northwest provinces in the early 1720s, the two Muslim states remained technically at war for more than two decades. Actual campaigns, however, never endured beyond a few months. Sustained periods of military inactivity on the Ottoman-Persian front attested to the distraction of both powers by other problems. Efforts at adjustment in October 1727 and January 1732 failed because the principals—Ashraf and Tahmasp—in whose names the negotiations were successively conducted on the Persian side, did not long remain in positions of authority. Once Nadir Quli Khan came to power, as regent after September 1732 and as shah after March 1736, the shepherd-boy-turned-king laid down the Persian terms for coexistence. The parties indeed initiated several instruments—in December 1733, September 1736, and December 1743—but ratified none. The chief stumbling block was Nadir's insistence on Ottoman recognition of his artificially created fifth sect of Sunni Islam, which he labeled the Ja'fari, and on the installation by the Sublime Porte of a fifth column in the Ka'bah at Mecca for the Imam Ja'far after whom the sect was named. When a mutually acceptable peace was finally arranged in September 1746, it proved too late, for Nadir Shah was assassinated on 19 June 1747, before ratification of the treaty. Nevertheless, the terms were confirmed three-quarters of a century later in the treaty of Erzurum (Doc. 61). Lockhart, *Nadir Shah*, esp. chaps. 5–7, 10, 22, 24, 25; Hekmat, *Essai sur l'histoire des relations politiques irano-ottomanes*, pp. 201–55 (incorrectly dates the treaty January 1747); Hanway, *British Trade over the Caspian Sea*.

Basis of the Treaty

The treaty of peace concluded in the reign of Sultan Murad IV [at Zuhab on 17 May 1639], of glorious memory, shall be maintained as valid by the two Governments, and the frontiers and limits fixed by that treaty shall be preserved on the same footing, and there shall occur neither change nor alteration of the principles enunciated therein.

Condition

Henceforth all hostility must cease, and everything that is compatible with the dignity and honor of the two contracting parties shall be observed, and everything that may cause estrangement or may be contrary to peace and good understanding shall be avoided.

ART. 1. Persian pilgrims may go to the Holy Cities by way of Baghdad and Damascus. The Governors-General, the Judges and the Amirs al-Hajj [Commanders of the Pilgrimage] on this route shall conduct [the pilgrims] from place to place in full security and tranquility, and in entrusting them from one to the other, [the Ottoman functionaries] shall take every precaution for [the pilgrims'] comfort and protection.

ART. 2. In order to confirm the amit between the two Governments and to demonstrate their good harmony, every three years the Ottoman Imperial Government and the Persian Government shall accredit Ambassadors to each other's court. The attendant expenses shall be borne by the host Government.

ART. 3. Prisoners of war of the two contracting parties shall be liberated and may not by bought or sold [as slaves]. Those prisoners desiring to return to their homes shall not be impeded by either side.

Appendix

The limits and frontiers, established under Sultan Murad IV, shall be verified, and the frontier commanders shall abstain from measures detrimental to friendship. Moreover, the Persian people, having totally abandoned the unseemly innovations introduced in the time of the Safavis and having embraced the religion of the Sunnis, shall mention the Orthodox Caliphs, of blessed memory, with respect and veneration.

Henceforth Persians who may go in pilgrimage to Mecca, to Medina, and to other cities of the Ottoman Empire shall be received with the same friendliness as that [accorded] to Muslim pilgrims, travelers and inhabitants of the Empire. No tribute or tax, repugnant to the laws and regulations, may be levied on [the Persian pilgrims]. Similarly the authorities at Baghdad shall not levy any customs duty on Persian pilgrims who are not transporting merchandise. From those who are transporting merchandise, a customs duty no higher than that estimated according to ancient usage will be collected. Merchants and inhabitants of the Ottoman Empire shall be treated in the same manner in Persia.

If after the date of the conclusion of this treaty there should be those who wish to flee from Persia to Turkey or vice versa, they shall not receive asylum, and upon the demand for extradition, they shall be surrendered to the authorities of the pertiment signatory.

As long as the conditions stated above are mutually respected, the amity and good understanding between the two High Powers and their Illustrious Sovereigns shall be maintained and observed by them and their descendants.

27. TREATY OF PEACE AND COMMERCE: GREAT BRITAIN AND THE GARRISON OF TUNIS
19 October 1751

[*British and Foreign State Papers*, vol. 1, p. 1, pp. 739–44]

British trade with Tunis in the seventeenth and eighteenth centuries remained spasmodic. Britain's relations with Tunis on a sustained basis began in 1638 with the appointment of a consul by royal commission. After 1660, Britain's primary interest in Tunis, as in the neighboring Garrisons, became the regulation of piracy, particularly as it affected British subjects. Treaties with the Garrison in 1623 and 1658 had proved abortive. The first durable treaty, concluded in 1662, was later reaffirmed and enlarged in 1716 and 1751. The latest instrument, reproduced below, laid down in immense detail provisions for the avoidance of piracy and the management of its effects whenever, despite elaborate precautions, Tunisian corsairs nevertheless seized English subjects and properties. The right of search and the issuance of passes, formalized by treaty in the seventeenth century by Britain and the other maritime powers, still represented the procedure for inhibiting Barbary piracy. The 1751 treaty, negotiated by "the Honorable Augustus Keppel, Commander-in-Chief of His Britannic Majesty's

Ships and Vessels in and about the Mediterranean Seas and Charles Gordon, Esq. His said Serene Majesty's agent and Consul-General to the State of Tunis," routinized British relations with Tunis until the suppression of piracy in the nineteenth century. Abun-Nasr, *History of the Maghrib*, chap. 7; Broadley, *Last Punic War*, vol. 1, chap. 8; Cambon, *Histoire de la régence de Tunis*, chap. 7; G. Fisher, *Barbary Legend*, pp. 326–27.

Treaty of Peace and Commerce between the Most Serene and Mighty Prince George the Second, by the grace of God, of Great Britain, France, and Ireland, King, Defender of the Christian Faith, Duke of Brunswick and Lunenberg, Arch-Treasurer and Elector of the Holy Roman Empire, &c., &c., &c., and the Most Excellent and Illustrious Lord Ali Pasha, Begler Bey, and Supreme Commander of the State of Tunis, renewed, agreed on, and confirmed, by the Honourable Augustus Keppel, Commander-in-Chief of His Britannic Majesty's Ships and Vessels in and about the Mediterranean Seas, and Charles Gordon, Esq., His said Serene Majesty's Agent and Consul-General to the State of Tunis, furnished with His Majesty's Full Powers for that purpose.

ART. 1. That all former grievances and losses, and other pretences between both Parties, shall be void and of no effect; and from henceforward there shall be a firm Peace for ever, and free trade and commerce, between His Britannic Majesty's Subjects and the People of the Kingdom of Tunis, and Dominions thereunto belonging; but this Article shall not cancel or make void any just debt, either in commerce or otherwise, between the Subjects on both sides, but the same may be demanded and recovered as before.

II. That the Ships of either Party shall have free liberty to enter into any Port or River belonging to the Dominions of the other, where they shall pay Duties only for what they sell, and, for the rest, may freely export it again without molestation, and shall enjoy all other accustomed privileges; and the late exaction that hath been at Goletta and the Marine shall be reduced to the ancient Customs in those cases.

III. That there shall not be any seizure made of any of the Ships of either Party, either at Sea or in Port, but they shall pass without any interruption, they displaying their Colours; and to prevent any misunderstandings, the Ships of Tunis shall be furnished with Certificates, under the Hand and Seal of the British Consul, of their belonging to Tunis, which they are to produce on meeting with any English Ship, on board of whom they shall have liberty of sending 2 Men only, peaceably to satisfy themselves of their being English, who, as well as any Passengers of other Nations they may have on board, shall go free, both them and their goods.

IV. That if an English Ship receive on board any goods or Passengers belonging to the Kingdom of Tunis, they shall be bound to defend them and their goods, so far as lieth in their power, and not deliver them unto their Enemies; and the better to prevent any unjust demands being made upon the Crown of Great Britain, and to avoid disputes and differences that might arise, all goods and merchandise that shall from henceforward be shipped by the Subjects of Tunis, either in this Port or in any other whatsoever, on board the Ships or Vessels belonging to Great Britain, shall be first entered in the Office of Cancellaria, before the British Consul residing at the respective Port, expressing the quantity, quality, and value of the goods so shipped, which the said Consul is to manifest in the Clearance given to the said Ship or Vessel before she departs: to the end that if any cause of complaint should happen hereafter, there may be no greater claim made on the British Nation, than by this method shall be proved to be just and equitable.

V. That if any of the Ships of either Party shall, by accident of foul weather, or otherwise, be cast away upon any of the Coasts belonging to the other, the Persons shall be free, and the goods saved and delivered to the Proprietors thereof.

VI. That the English which do at present, or shall at any time hereafter, inhabit in the City or Kingdom of Tunis, shall have free liberty, when they please, to transport themselves, with their Families and Children, although born in the Country.

VII. That the People belonging to the Dominions of either Party shall not be abused with ill-language, or otherwise ill-treated, but the Parties so offending shall be punished severely according to their deserts.

VIII. That the Consul or any other of the English Nation residing in Tunis shall not be obliged to make their addresses, in any difference, unto any Court of Justice, but to the Bashaw himself, from whom only they shall receive judgment, in case the difference should happen between a Subject of Great Britain and another of this Government, or any other Foreign Nation; but if it should be between 2 of His Britannic Majesty's Subjects, then it is to be decided by the British Consul only.

IX. That neither the English Consul, nor any other of His Majesty's Subjects, shall be liable to pay the Debts of any other of the Nation, unless particularly bound thereto under his own hand.

X. That whereas the Island of Minorca in the Mediterranean Sea, and the City of Gibraltar in Spain, do now belong to His Majesty the King of Great Britain; it is hereby agreed and fully concluded, that from this time forward, for ever, the said Island of Minorca shall be esteemed (as likewise Gibraltar) by the Government of Tunis, to be, in every respect, part of His Britannic Majesty's Dominions, and the Inhabitants thereof shall be looked upon as His Majesty's natural-born Subjects, in the same manner as if they had been born in any other part of Great Britain; and they, with their Ships and Vessels wearing British Colours, shall be permitted freely to trade and traffic in any part of the Kingdom of Tunis, and shall pass, without any molestation whatsoever, either on the Seas or elsewhere, in the same manner, and with the same freedom and privileges that have been stipulated in this and all former Treaties in behalf of the British Nation and Subjects.

XI. That the better and more firmly to maintain the good correspondence and friendship that have been so long and happily established between the Crown of Great Britain, and the Government of Tunis, it is hereby agreed and concluded by the Parties before-mentioned, that none of the Ships and Vessels belonging to Tunis, or the Dominions thereof, shall be permitted to cruize or look for Prizes, of any nature whatsoever, before, or in sight of the aforesaid City of Gibraltar, or any of the Ports in the Island of Minorca, to hinder or molest any Vessels bringing provisions and refreshments for His Britannic Majesty's Troops and Garrisons in those places, or to give any disturbance to the trade and commerce thereof: and if any Prize shall be taken by the Ships or Vessels of Tunis, within the space of 10 miles of the aforesaid places, she shall be restored without any contradiction.

XII. That all Ships of War belonging to the Dominions of either Party, shall have free liberty to use each other's Ports, for washing, cleaning, and repairing any their defects, and to buy and ship off any sort of victuals, alive or dead, or any other necessaries, at the price the Natives buy at in the market, without paying Custom to any Officer. And whereas His Britannic Majesty's Ships of War do frequently assemble and harbour in the Port of Mahon, in the Island of Minorca; if, at any time, they, or His Majesty's Troops in Garrison there, should be in want of provisions, and should send from thence to purchase supplies in any part of the Dominions belonging to Tunis, they shall be permitted to buy cattle, alive or dead, and all other kinds of provision, at the prices they are sold in the market, and shall be suffered to carry it off without paying Duty to any Officer, in the same manner as if His Majesty's Ships were themselves in the Port.

XIII. That in case any Ships of War belonging to the Dominions of Tunis, shall take, in any of their Enemy's Ships, any Englishmen serving for wages, they are to be made Slaves; but if Merchants or Passengers, they are to enjoy their liberty and goods free.

XIV. That if any Slave of Tunis should make his escape from thence, and get on board an English Man-of-War, the said Slave shall be free, and neither the English Consul, nor any of his Nation, shall in any manner be questioned about the same.

XV. That the better to prevent any disputes that may hereafter arise between the

2 Parties about salutes and public ceremonies, it is hereby agreed and concluded, that whenever any Flag-Officer of Great Britain shall arrive in the Bay of Tunis, in any of His Majesty's Ships of War, there shall be shot off from the Castles of the Goletta, or other the nearest Fortifications belonging to Tunis, a number of guns according to custom, as a Royal salute to His British Majesty's Colours, and the same number shall be returned in answer thereto by His Majesty's Ships; and it is hereby stipulated and agreed, that all ceremonies of honour shall be allowed to the British Consul who resides here, to represent equal in every respect His Majesty's person, to any other Nation whatsoever, and no other Consul in the Kingdom to be admitted before him in precedency.

XVI. That the Subjects of His Most Sacred Majesty of Great Britain, &c., either residing in, or trading to the Dominions of Tunis, shall not, for the time to come, pay any more than 3 per cent Custom, on the value of the goods or merchandise which they shall either bring into or carry out of the Kingdom of Tunis.

XVII. It is moreover agreed, concluded, and established, that at whatsoever time it shall please the Government of Tunis to reduce the Customs of the French Nation to less than they pay at present, it shall always be observed, that the British Customs shall be 2 per cent less than any agreement that shall for the future be made with the said French, or that shall be paid by the Subjects of France.

XVIII. It is moreover agreed, concluded, and established, that in case any British Ship or Ships, or any of the Subjects of His Majesty of Great Britain, shall import at the Port of Tunis, or any Port of this Kingdom, any warlike stores, as cannons, muskets, pistols, cannon powder, or fine powder, bullets, masts, anchors, cables, pitch, tar, or the like; as also provisions, viz., wheat, barley, beans, oats, oil, or the like, for the said kinds of merchandise they shall not pay any sort of Duty or Custom whatever.

XIX. That in case a War should happen between His Britannic Majesty and any other State or Nation whatever, the Ships of Tunis shall not in any sort afford assistance to the Enemies of His Majesty or his Subjects.

XX. That if an Englishman kills a Turk, he shall be judged before the Caddi of the place, according to justice: if he is found guilty of the crime, he shall be punished with death; but if he escape, the Consul shall not be molested or called upon for that account; and the Consul shall always have timely notice, that he may have an opportunity of being present at the trial.

XXI. That if at any time a War or rupture happen between the 2 Contracting Powers, the English Consul and his Nation may freely depart with all their goods and effects; and this Article is to be reciprocal for the Subjects of Tunis.

XXII. That whereas Gibraltar and the Island of Minorca do belong to His Britannic Majesty, if at any time any of the Cruizers of Tunis should meet with any Vessels of the said places, under English Colours, furnished with proper Passports, they shall be treated in all respects like other English Ships, provided that there be no more than 1-third part of the Ship's Company who are not Subjects of His said Majesty; for, in such case, they (the said Strangers) shall be deemed as Prisoners: but it is allowed to embark as many Merchants or Passengers as they see good, be they of what Nation soever: and if at any time a Tunis Man-of-War shall take a Ship from their Enemies, on board of which may happen to be any English Subjects, they shall be immediately released, with all their goods and merchandise, provided always that they be provided with proper Passports; and this Article is to be observed reciprocally on the part of the English.

XXIII. That if any British Ships or Vessels meet with any of the Ships or Vessels belonging to the State of Tunis, and there should be any injury or offence given by either side, justice being properly demanded, shall be immediately done, and the Aggressor shall be severely punished, without it occasioning any breach or War.

XXIV. That His Britannic Majesty's Subjects shall be always treated, by the State of Tunis, with the highest degree of respect, love and honour, because the English, of all other Powers, are their first and best Friends.

XXV. That new Mediterranean Passes shall be issued out and given to His said

Majesty's trading Subjects, with all convenient speed; and that the time for the continuance of the old Passes, for the Ships in the Indies and remote parts, shall be 3 years; and for all other Ships and Vessels, 1 year; to commence from the delivery of the counter-tops of the new Passes at Algiers, of which His Majesty's Consul here shall give the earliest notice to this State; and it is hereby expressly agreed and declared, that the said new Passes shall, during the abovementioned spaces of time of 3 years and 1 year, be of full and sufficient force and effect to protect all Ships and Vessels of His said Majesty's Subjects, who shall be provided with the same.

XXVI. That all Packets bearing His Britannic Majesty's Commission, which shall be met by any of the Cruizers of Tunis, shall be treated with the same respect as His Majesty's Ships of War; and all due respect shall be paid to His Majesty's Commission, and both at meeting and parting they shall be treated as Friends; and if any of the Cruizers of Tunis commit the least fault or violence against them, the Captains or Raizes so offending shall, on their arrival at Tunis, and proper complaint being made of them, be most severely punished, without admitting of their excuses. . . .

28. GRANT OF SPECIAL PRIVILEGES AT BUSHIRE TO THE (BRITISH) EAST INDIA COMPANY
2 July 1763

[Aitchison, *Collection of Treaties . . . relating to India* (5th ed.), 13: 42–44]

The passing of the Safavi dynasty in 1722 brought to a close the capitulatory arrangements of the seventeenth century in Persia. Dutch, English, and French merchants alike failed to procure from Nadir Shah (1736–47) full renewals of their earlier privileges, and European trade with Persia languished. Indeed, Russia alone among the European powers attempted to maintain formal diplomatic relations with the self-made monarch. After Nadir's murder Persia literally fell apart. The Afghans finally broke away. Nadir's blind son, Shah Rukh, ruled in Khurasan, the northeast province, until 1796. Karim Khan (1750–79) of the Zand tribe, styling himself *vakil* (regent), reigned over most of southern Persia, selecting Shiraz as his capital. The Qajar tribesmen, establishing supremacy in Mazandaran, gradually extended their influence through the northwest provinces, which, however, for the greater part of the period remained essentially without government. During the Seven Years' War, in 1759, the French destroyed the British factory at Bandar 'Abbas, which for more than a century and a third had been the center of the East India Company's Gulf commerce. A company agent on 12 April 1763 concluded an agreement (text in Aitchison, op. cit., pp. 41–42) with Shaykh Sa'dun of Bushire, the port of Shiraz, for the erection of a factory. Less than three months later Karim Khan confirmed by *farman* (royal decree) Sa'dun's arrangements and amplified the special rights accorded the company. Bushire was destined to become the headquarters in the nineteenth and twentieth centries of British political as well as commercial activity in the Persian Gulf area. Lockhart, *Nadir Shah*, pp. 282–90; Sykes, *History of Persia*, vol. 2, chap. 73; A. Wilson, *Persian Gulf*, chap. 12.

The Great God having, of his infinite mercy, given victory unto Karem Khan, and made him Chief Governor of all the kingdoms of Persia, and established under him the peace and tranquillity of the said kingdoms, by means of his victorious sword, he is desirous that the said kingdoms should flourish and re-obtain their ancient grandeur by the increase of trade and commerce, as well as by a due execution of justice.

Having been informed that the Right Worshipful William Andrew Price, Esq., Governor-General for the English nation in the Gulf of Persia, is arrived with power to settle a factory at Bushire, and has left Mr. Benjamin Jervis, Resident, who, by directions from the said Governor-General, has sent unto me Mr. Thomas Durnford and Stephen Hermit, linguist, to obtain a grant of their ancient privileges in these kingdoms, I do, of my free will and great friendship for the English nation, grant unto the said Governor-General, in behalf of his king and Company, the following privileges, which shall be inviolably observed and held sacred in good faith:—

That the English Company may have as much ground, and in any part of Bushire, they choose to build a factory on, or at any other port in the Gulf, They may have as many cannon mounted on it as they choose, but not to be larger than six pounds bore; and they may build factory houses in any part of the kingdom they choose.

No customs shall be charged the English on any goods imported or exported by them at Bushire, or any other port in the Gulf of Persia, on condition that at no time they import or export other persons' goods in their names. They may also send their goods customs free all over the kingdom of Persia; and on what goods they sell at Bushire, or elsewhere, the Shaik, or Governor, shall only charge the merchants an export duty of three per cent.

No other European nation, or other persons, shall import any woolen goods to any port on the Persian shore in the Gulf, but the English Company only; and should any one attempt to do it clandestinely, their goods shall be seized and confiscated.

Should any of the Persian merchants, or others, become truly indebted to the English, the Shaik, or Governor of the place,

shall oblige them to pay it; but should he fail in his duty herein the English Chief may do his own justice and act as he pleases with the debtors to recover what owed him or them.

In all the kingdom of Persia the English may sell their goods to and buy from whomever they judge proper; nor shall the Governor, or Shaik, of any ports or places, prevent their importing or exporting any goods whatever.

When any English ship or ships arrive at any ports in the Gulf of Persia, no merchants shall purchase from them clandestinely, but with the consent and knowledge of the English Chief there resident.

Should any English ship or vessel be drove on shore, unfortunately wrecked, or otherwise lost in any part of the Gulf of Persia, the Shaiks, or Governors of the adjacent places, shall not claim any share of the said wrecks, but shall assist the English, all in their power, in saving the whole or any part of the vessel or cargo.

The English, and all those under their protection, in any part of the kingdom of Persia, shall have the free exercise of their religion, without molestation from any one.

Should soldiers, sailors, or slaves desert from the English in any part of Persia, they shall not be protected or encouraged, but, *bonâ fide,* delivered up, but not be punished for the first or second offence.

Wherever the English may have a factory in Persia their linguist, brokers, and all their other servants, shall be exempt from all taxes and impositions whatever, and under their own command and justice, without any one interfering therein.

Wherever the English are they shall have a spot of ground allotted them for a burying ground; and if they want a spot for a garden, if the king's property, it shall be given them *gratis*; if belonging to any private person, they must pay a reasonable price for it.

The house that formerly belonged to the English Company at Schyrash [Shiraz], I now redeliver to them, with the garden and water thereto belonging.

That the English, according to what was formerly customary, shall purchase from the Persian merchants such goods as will answer for sending to England or India, provided they and the Persians shall agree on reasonable prices for the same, and not export from Persia the whole amount of their sales in ready money, as this will impoverish the kingdom and in the end prejudice trade in general.

That the English, wherever they are settled, shall not maltreat the Mussulmen.

What goods are imported by the English into Persia they shall give the preference in sale of them to the principal merchants and men of credit.

The English shall not give protection to any of the king's rebellious subjects, nor carry them out of the kingdom, but deliver any up that may desert to them, who shall not be punished for the first or second offence.

The English shall at no time, either directly or indirectly, assist the king's enemies.

All our Governors of provinces, seaports, and other towns are ordered to pay strict obedience to these our orders, on pain of incurring our displeasure, and of being punished for their disobedience or neglect.

29. TREATY OF PEACE AND COMMERCE: GREAT BRITAIN AND THE GARRISON OF ALGIERS
3 August 1765

[*British and Foreign State Papers*, vol. 1, pt. 1, pp. 372–73]

That Britain in the late eighteenth century was not interested in the general suppression of piracy and of the practice of enslaving kidnapped Europeans but only in the insulation of British ships, goods, and subjects from the effects of piracy is amply confirmed in the following treaty. As Britain went, so went the other major maritime powers of Europe. Also revealing was the proposed procedure for discouraging adventurous British subjects from converting to Islam. For references, see Doc. 16.

ARTICLES of Peace and Commerce between the Most Serene and Mighty Prince, George the Third, by the grace of God, King of Great Britain, France and Ireland, Defender of the Christian Faith, Duke of Brunswick and Lunenburg, Arch Treasurer and Prince Elector of the Holy Roman Empire, &c., &c., and the Most Illustrious Lord Ally, Bashaw, Dey and Governor of the warlike City and Kingdom of Algier, in Barbary: concluded, ratified, confirmed and renewed by His Excellency Archibald Clevland, Esq., His Britannic Majesty's Ambassador to the Kingdom of Algier.

In the first place, it was expressly agreed upon and concluded, after a mature and regular deliberation with the Divan, that from henceforward, no Englishman taken by sea or by land, shall, upon any pretext whatsoever, be either bought, sold, or made Slave of, within the Dominions of this Kingdom, but [he shall] be immediately delivered up to His Britannic Majesty's Consul residing here; to which purpose orders were forthwith issued out to all the Governors of the several Provinces, that all Englishmen that hereafter may chance to be taken or found within the limits of their several Dependencies, be immediately forwarded to this Capital. To the more punctual compliance with this Treaty, and to the avoiding [of] the difficulties that may arise from Particulars buying English Subjects, and thereby believing themselves entitled to a ransom, notice has been given by the Common Crier in all the public places of this City, that from henceforward no Subject of His Britannic Majesty be either bought or sold by any body whatsoever.

Secondly, it is further concluded and agreed upon, that in case any of His Britannic Majesty's Subjects should, from liquor, or from any other motive, declare an intention of embracing the Mahometan religion, they shall forthwith be secured, sent to the Consul's house, and there 3 days allowed them for reflection, after which 3 days they shall be at liberty to put their design in execution, and no further constraint be put upon them;—this only case excepted: when they shall take refuge in the Casherias, or Soldiers' barracks, which being looked upon as sacred, any one taking refuge there cannot be meddled with. . . .

30. TREATY OF PEACE, AMITY, AND COMMERCE: FRANCE AND MOROCCO
28 May 1767

[Translated from the French text in Clercq, *Recueil des traités*, 1: 90–94]

France and Morocco resumed formal relations in 1767, after a lapse of nearly a half-century, during much of which Morocco was torn by a prolonged civil war over the 'Alawi succession (1727–57). Mawlay Muhammad bin 'Abdallah (1757–90), who finally restored order, deliberately but cautiously cultivated the friendship of the maritime powers of Europe by concluding treaties of peace and commerce and accrediting resident consular missions. As early as 1757, he conceded to Denmark a (short-lived) monopoly of trade at Safi, followed by commercial agreements with England (1760) and Sweden (1763). Not until 1767 did he finally negotiate a treaty of peace, amity, and commerce with France, which appears below; he concluded another in the same year with Spain. To stress the antiquity of the signatories' relations, article 1 of the French-Moroccan treaty stated that it was based on the one that Louis XIV had concluded with Mawlay Isma'il in 1682 (Doc. 15), and articles 2, 11, and 12 were modeled on its clauses. The inclusion of a most-favored-nation provision (art. 5) assured France of widening privileges as the capitulatory system in Morocco unfolded. France also won the right (art. 11) to name consuls anywhere in Morocco, not merely at Mogador, as Mawlay Muhammad had initially insisted (only two years before he had founded that port on the Atlantic, with the help of European architects, in the apparent hope of gathering all European resident consuls and merchants there and developing it into a center for the conduct of all external affairs). French merchants were allowed (art. 2) to travel at will throughout the country. Piracy also did not escape notice (arts. 3. 6, 9). The 1767 treaty became the enabling instrument for later French-Moroccan treaties and the basis for France's capitulatory privileges in the country. Still, by contrast with the detailed privileges in Morocco's treaty with Britain of 1760 (text in *British and Foreign State Papers,* vol. 1, pt. 1, pp. 436–45), the 1767 treaty was rudimentary. Chénier (French consul at Mogador under the 1767 treaty), *Present State of the Empire of Morocco,* 2: 294 ff; Penz, *Journal du consulat-général de France à Maroc*; Masson, *Histoire des établissements et du commerce français dans l'Afrique Barbaresque*, chaps. 22–23; Meakin, *Moorish Empire*, chap. 16; Terrasse, *Histoire du Maroc*, 2: 253–312; Abun-Nasr, *History of the Maghrib*, chap. 8; G. Fisher, *Barbary Legend.*

. . . ART 1. The present treaty has at its basis and foundation the one which was made and concluded [on 29 January 1682] between Louis XIV, Emperor of France of glorious memory, and the most elevated and the most powerful Emperor Sidi Isma'il, whom God has blessed.

ART. 2. The respective subjects of the two Empires may travel, trade, and navigate in full confidence and wherever they may wish, by land and by sea, within the dominions of the two Empires, without fear of being molested or hindered under any pretext whatsoever.

ART. 3. Whenever the naval forces of the Emperor of Morocco meet at sea merchant-ships carrying the flag of the Emperor of France and carrying passports from the Admiral in the form written below in the present treaty, they may not stop, visit, or require [these merchantships] to present anything but their passports, and having need of each other, they shall reciprocally render each other good services. Whenever the vessels of the Emperor of France meet those of the Emperor of Morocco, they shall give [the Moroccan ships] like treatment, and they shall not require anything but the certificate of the French Consul established in the state of the said Emperor in the form prescribed below in the present treaty. French war vessels, big or small, shall not require passports, since they do not as a rule carry them. Measures will be taken within six months to give the small ships in the royal service signs of recognition, of which the Consul shall give copies to the corsairs of the Emperor of Morocco. It has been further agreed that the launch which seamen are accustomed to send to acknowledge one another shall conform to the practice of the corsairs of the Regency of Algiers.

ART. 4. If the vessels of the Emperor of Morocco enter any port in the dominion of the Emperor of France, or if French vessels enter one of the ports of the Emperor of Morocco, the vessels of neither shall be prevented from taking on board all the edible provisions that they may need, and also all the rigging and other things necessary for the stores of their vessels. They shall pay for [these wares] at local prices, without further charge; they shall receive, moreover, the good treatment which amity and good relations require.

ART. 5. Subjects of the two nations may freely enter and leave, at their pleasure at all times, the ports in the dominions of the two Empires and may trade there with full confidence. If by chance the merchants should sell only part of their merchandise and should wish to take away the rest, they shall not be subjected to any duty for the export of the unsold products. French merchants, like [the merchants] of other nations, may buy and sell throughout the Moroccan Empire without paying any further duty. If it should ever happen that the Emperor of Morocco comes to favor other nations in rights of entry and departure, the French thereafter shall enjoy the same privilege.

ART. 6. If the peace existing between the Emperor of France and the Regencies of Algiers, Tunis, Tripoli, and others should be interrupted, and if a French ship pursued by its enemy should seek refuge in the ports of the Emperor of Morocco, the Governors of the said ports are under obligation to guarantee [the refuge] and to drive the enemy away or detain him in the port for a sufficient period, so as to allow the pursued vessel to withdraw in the customary way. Furthermore, the vessels of the Emperor of Morocco may not cruise along the coasts of France except at a distance of thirty thousand [meters].

ART. 7. If the vessel of an enemy of France should enter a port under the rule of the King of Morocco, and if French prisoners should go ashore, they shall be set free immediately and shall be rescued from the enemy. The same practice shall apply if vessels of an enemy of the Emperor of Morocco should enter a port of France and subjects of the said Emperor should go ashore. If the enemies of France, whosoever they might be, should enter the ports of the Emperor of Morocco with French prizes, or if, alternatively, the enemies of the Empire of Morocco should enter a port of France with [Moroccan] prizes, neither one may sell the prizes in the two Empires. Even if the passengers aboard the ships of the two Empires should be enemies, they shall be respected by both sides. Their persons and their goods may not be touched on any pretext. If by chance there should be French passengers among the prizes taken by the vessels of the Emperor of Morocco, the Frenchmen and their goods should be set free immediately. The same shall apply to the subjects of the Emperor of Morocco, whenever they find themselves as passengers on vessels taken by the French. But if either [group of passengers] should be sailors, they shall not enjoy this privilege.

ART. 8. French merchant vessels shall not be constrained to load what they do not wish, nor forcibly to undertake any voyage

ART. 9. In case of a rupture between the Emperor of France and the Regencies of Algiers, Tunis, and Tripoli, the Emperor of Morocco shall neither aid nor abet in any fashion the said Regencies, nor shall he permit any of his subjects to leave or to arm, under the flag of any of the said Regencies, so as to pursue the French. If one of the said subjects should happen to be disloyal, he shall be punished and [held] responsible for any damage. The Emperor of France, on his side, shall take similar action regarding the enemies of the Emperor of Morocco. He shall not help them, nor shall he permit any of his subjects to help them.

ART. 10. The French shall not be obliged to furnish any munitions of war, powder, cannons, or any other equipment that might be useful in the conduct of war.

ART. 11. The Emperor of France may establish in the Empire of Morocco as many Consuls as he wishes, to represent him in the ports of the said Empire, to assist the merchants, the captains, and the sailors in whatever they may need, to hear their differences, and to settle disputes which might arise between them, without the interference of any governor of the regions, wherever they may be. The said Consuls may have churches in their homes so as to perform Divine Service, and if a member of another Christian nation should wish to take part, he shall not be hindered in any way. The same shall apply to the subjects of the Emperor of Morocco, whenever they may be in France: they may freely pray in their homes. Those who may be in the service of the Consuls and of the merchants as secretaries and interpreters, as agents or otherwise, shall not be hindered in their functions. Those [who may be subjects] of the country shall be exempt from all imposts and personal obligations. No

duty shall be levied on the provisions which the Consuls buy for their own use, and they shall pay no duty on the provisions or other goods of whatever kind which they receive from Europe for their use. Furthermore, the French Consuls shall have precedence over the Consuls of other nations. Their houses shall be respected, and they shall enjoy the same immunities which may be accorded to others.

ART. 12. If a difference should arise between a Moor and a Frenchman, the Emperor, or his representative in the city where the incident occurs, shall settle the dispute, and the Qadi or the regular judge may not take cognizance of [the case]. The same shall apply in France, if a difference should occur between a Frenchman and a Moor.

ART. 13. If a Frenchman should strike a Moor, he shall not be judged except in the presence of a Consul who may defend his case, and it shall be decided with justice and impartiality. If the Frenchman should escape, the Consul may not be held responsible. If, on the contrary, a Moor should strike a Frenchman, he shall be punished in conformity with justice and the needs of the case.

ART. 14. If a Frenchman should be indebted to a subject of the Emperor of Morocco, the Consul shall not be responsible for the payment, unless he has given a guarantee in writing. For the same reason, if a Moor should be indebted to a Frenchman, he may not seek repayment from another Moor, unless the latter was the guarantor of the debtor.

If a Frenchman should die in some region of the Emperor of Morocco, his goods and effects shall be disposed of by the Consul, who may proceed at his pleasure to make the inventory and have [the goods and effects] sealed, without the least interference of the law or the government of the country.

ART. 15. If bad weather or the pursuit of enemy forces should cause a French vessel to run aground on the coast of the Emperor of Morocco, all the inhabitants of that coast must help the ship back to sea, if possible. If that cannot be done, they shall assist in removing the cargo which the Consul of the closest district (or his agent) shall arrange, according to local practice. The only payment that may be demanded is the salary of the day laborers employed in the salvage. Furthermore, no customs or any other fees shall be levied on merchandise which may be put ashore, except on that merchandise which may be sold.

ART. 16. French war vessels entering the ports and roadsteads of the Emperor of Morocco shall be received with the honors due their flag, in view of the peace between the two Empires. No duties shall be levied on the provisions and other things which the commanders and the officers might buy for their use, or for the service of the vessel. The same practice shall apply to the vessels of the Emperor of Morocco whenever they enter the ports of France.

ART. 17. On the arrival of a vessel of the Emperor of France in a port or a roadstead of the Empire of Morocco, the Consul shall inform the Governor of the district, so that he may take precautions against the escape of slaves in the said vessel. If a slave should take asylum [on the vessel], no search may be made, because of the immunity of the French flag. Furthermore, neither the Consul nor anyone else may be searched for this purpose. The same practice shall apply

in the ports of France, if a slave should escape to a war vessel of the Emperor of Morocco.

ART. 18. All articles which may have been omitted shall be understood and explained in the most favorable manner for the good and reciprocal advantage of the subjects of the two Empires, and for the maintenance of the best understanding and of peace.

ART. 19. If the articles and the conditions upon which peace has been made should be infringed, the peace shall not be altered in any way. But the dispute shall be thoroughly examined and justice shall be administered on both sides. The subjects of the two Empires unconnected [with the infringement] shall not become involved, and no act of hostility shall be committed, except in the case of a formal denial of justice.

ART. 20. If the present treaty of peace should be broken, all Frenchmen who may find themselves in the territory of the Emperor of Morocco shall be permitted to return to their country along with their goods and their families, and they may take up to six months to do this. . . .

31. TERMS OF PEACE: FRANCE AND THE GARRISON OF TUNIS
25 August–13 September 1770

[Translated from the French texts in Clerq and Clerq, *Recueil des traités*, vol. 15, supplement, pp. 93–96.]

When France annexed Corsica in 1768, it demanded that 'Ali Bey of Tunis (1759–82) release the Corsican ships, crews, and passengers seized by his corsairs. On the bey's refusal, France declared war, and its ships bombarded the ports of La Goulette, Bizerte, and Sousse. This punitive action had the desired effect. Following are the preliminary convention, which laid down the terms of peace, and the definitive peace treaty, which renewed and confirmed earlier treaties of 1720 and 1742 (Doc. 25). The convention of 13 September 1770, restoring to the (French) Royal Company of Africa coral fishery rights of 1768 off the Tunisian coast, is not reproduced; the French texts of 1768 and 1770 fishery conventions may be found in Rouard de Card, *Traités de la France*, pp. 184–87 and 192–93. From 1770 on, the official French resident in Tunis held the rank of consul-general. Broadley, *Last Punic War*, vol. 1, chap. 9, and, for a Tunisian description of the war, vol. 2, pp. 346–51; Fitoussi and Benazet, *L'état tunisien et le protectorat français*, pp. 3–41; Masson, *Histoire des établissements et du commerce français dans l'Afrique Barbaresque*, chaps. 17–19, 21; Ganiage, *Les origines du protectorat français en Tunisie*, chap. 1; Cambon, *Histoire de la régence de Tunis*, chap. 7; Julien, *Histoire de l'Afrique du Nord*, vol. 1, chap. 6; Abun-Nasr, *History of the Maghrib*, chap. 7; Lord, *England and France in the Mediterranean*, pp. 1–38; Debbasch, *La nation française en Tunisie*, pp. 13–34.

1. Preliminary Convention, 25 August 1770

ART. 1. The Tunisians shall suspend from this day the hostilities already started between our two nations. The French general shall [also] stop [hostilities] on ratifying the armistice which is being agreed.

ART. 2. The Bey recognizes in full and forever the reunion of the Island of Corsica to the states of the Empire of France. He undertakes to return, before the signature of peace, all the slaves of that nation who have been seized and brought into his Kingdom with the commission and flag of France, and to restore their ships and effects or equivalent damages.

ART. 3. This prince shall renew the fishing privileges which he granted to the Compagnie Royale d'Afrique. He submits and undertakes to pay at the same above-mentioned time all the damages caused to this company by the interruption of its treaty and the expulsion of its ships.

ART. 4. He undertakes [to pay] the reparations that the Emperor of France demands from the privateers and the chief of the corsairs of Tunis, about which [the French] officers have complained, and [the Bey] shall become solely responsible for the damages for which [the corsairs] shall be held accountable because of the harm caused to the French, whether in Corsica or at sea.

ART. 5. Confident of justifying his conduct to His Very Christian Majesty [Sa Majesté Très Chrétienne, or S.M.T.C.] the Bey begs him by letter to revoke for the present the order [that the French Emperor] gave to the General of his squadron and to his Consul to demand from [the Bey] all the expenses incurred for armaments for this war; and he is required on receipt of this order to send an Ambassador to S.M.T.C. to beg him to grant his august goodwill and to forget the past. This Ambassador shall at the same time be directed to frame with the Minister the article of his instructions on the cost of the armament.

ART. 6. On the cessation of hostilities, the High Contracting Parties shall restore to the commercial and peace treaties, interrupted between them, the rights and the force which they had before the declaration of war, and shall promise to confirm them with the changes and additions of the present preliminaries, or of any other article on which they may later agree. But, wishing to avoid delays or new obstacles to the conclusion of peace, they consent to fix to this single act their respective demands and to renounce and discharge each other of all claims, disputed between them or not, on objects cut out or omitted from the present preliminary articles. They also renounce and annul, on both sides, the affairs which preceded [this convention], as well as the right to return to them in the future and to reclaim, under any pretext whatsoever, the titles which they have reciprocally abandoned.

ART. 7. Prizes taken during the war and those which might still be taken in ignorance of the peace, shall be restored without delay and not kept because of the expense that might have been incurred. Confidence and order shall be reestablished between the subjects of the two nations, who may after this day resume their relations and their commerce.

ART. 8. On his return to the roadstead of Tunis, the French General shall lift the blockade [there] and in the other ports of the Kingdom. Similarly, the Bey shall fulfill his undertakings, either for himself or for those of his subjects obliged and interested in this act, of which the execution can be neither suspended nor limited by the addition to the treaty of peace, which with the aid of God shall be confirmed and assimilated, the present preliminary articles, drafted at the palace of Bardo by the Seigneur Bey and the Consul of France. . . .

2. Definitive Peace Treaty, 13 September 1770

Supplement to the treaties of France with the Regency of Tunis, agreed and granted in the name of the very powerful and invincible Emperor of France, Louis XV, the first and the greatest of Christian Emperors, by Count of Broves, Chief of the Squadron of his Naval Armies, and Barthélemy de Saizieu, his Consul at Tunis, both armed with the full powers of His Imperial Majesty to regulate and conclude with the very illustrious Pasha Bey of Tunis the present additions to the treaties of 1720 and 1742 which they renew and confirm in all their terms, neither party being permitted to claim that it was impaired because of differences and hostilities which suspended the execution and gave rise to the following articles, to wit:

ART. 1. The very illustrious 'Ali Pasha, in his quality of Bey, Possessor of the Kingdom of Tunis, guardian and representative of the Regency in whose name he acts and undertakes, as much for himself as for his heirs and successor Beys, to recognize the full and entire reunion of the two nations determined by the treaties, [herewith] gives up and renounces forever, insofar as is necessary, claims which he may have

formed on the navigation and commerce of the peoples of the said island, at the time when it passed under the domination of His Very Christian Majesty.

ART. 2. The Compagnie Royale d'Afrique is reestablished and will maintain all the rights of privilege of fishing which the Bey of Tunis had granted to it, and which this Prince guarantees to His Imperial Majesty with the changes and additions united and concluded by the express and separate convention which determines them and which shall have the same force as if it were inserted word for word in the present articles or in the treaties of peace which they recall and confirm.

ART. 3. Under the only reservation of rights recognized and acquired by France by the preliminary articles signed on twenty-fifth of the month of August last we depart mutually and expressly from those which might relate to matters which are neither recalled nor included there, and which we understand will be abandoned and relinquished without exception or return, as well as the titles which authorize them, which are annulled. This relinquishment, having for its object the reunion and the advantages of the subjects of the two nations in reestablishing between them the rights and the confidence of a solid and lasting peace, comprises and determines not only the disputes which preceded the rupture but also those to which the events of war might have given rise by reason of damages suffered until this day and abandoned by both parties. . . .

32. TREATY OF PEACE (KÜÇÜK KAYNARCA): RUSSIA AND THE OTTOMAN EMPIRE
10/21 July 1774

(Ratifications exchanged, Istanbul, 13/24 January 1775)
[Text of the public treaty from Great Britain, *Parliamentary Papers, 1854*, pp. 39–47; Separate Articles translated from the French text in Noradounghian, *Recueil d'actes internationaux de l'empire ottoman*, 1: 333–34.]

The instrument signed at Küçük Kaynarca (a village on the right bank of the Danube near Silistre), which ended a six-year war between tsarist Russia and the Ottoman

Empire, surpassed in significance all other treaties between the two states, fixing the pattern of their relations until the outbreak of World War I. Kükçük Kaynarca established Russia as a Black Sea power and assured Russian commercial vessels unrestricted navigation on the sea and free passage through the straits (art. 11). With the exclusive Ottoman ownership of the inland sea terminated, tsarist appetite for possession of the straits developed, creating a problem in Russian-Turkish relations that has outlasted World War II. Russia's claim to the protection of all Greek Orthodox subjects of the sultan, one of the immediate causes of the Crimean War, rested on a generous (and questionable) interpretation of articles 7 and 14 of the 1774 instrument. Küçük Kaynarca also promised Russian nationals most-favored-nation treatment in trade with the Ottoman Empire. Russia's capitulatory privileges, however were laid down in detail in a special commercial treaty concluded on 10/21 June 1783 (French text in Noradounghian, op. cit., 1: 351–73). The 1774 treaty, meanwhile, had been modified by a *convention explicative* of 10/21 March 1779 (French text, ibid., pp. 338–44). Included below are the public and secret clauses, with the exception of article 16 and the first paragraph of article 24 of the public treaty, which relate to the Balkans. Hurewitz, "Russia and the Turkish Straits"; A. Fisher, *Russian Annexation of the Crimea*; Holland, *Treaty Relations of Russia and Turkey*; Baddeley, *Russian Conquest of the Caucasus*, chaps. 2–3; Übersberger, *Russlands Orientpolitik*, chap. 3; Sorel, *La question d'Orient au dix-huitieme siecle*; Laloy, *Les plans de Cathérine II pour la conquéte de Constantinople*; M. Anderson, "Great Britain and the Russo-Turkish War"; Nolde, *La formation de l'empire russe*, chap. 9; Mischef, *La Mar Noire et les détroits de Constantinople*, chap. 2; Phillipson and Buxton, *Question of the Bosphorus and Dardanelles*, pt. 2, chap. 1; Shotwell and Deák, *Turkey at the Straits*, chap. 3; Arnold, *Caliphate*, pp. 165–66.

1. Public Treaty

ART. I. From the present time all the hostilities and enmities which have hitherto prevailed shall cease for ever, and all hostile acts and enterprises committed on either side, whether by force of arms or in any other manner, shall be buried in an eternal oblivion, without vengeance being taken for them in any way whatever; but, on the contrary, there shall always be a perpetual, constant, and inviolable peace, as well by sea as by land. In like manner there shall be cultivated between the two High Contracting Parties, Her Majesty the Empress of all the Russias and His Highness, their successors and heirs, as well as between the two Empires, their states, territories, subjects, and inhabitants, a sincere union and a perpetual and inviolable friendship, with a careful accomplishment and maintenance of these Articles; so that neither of the two Parties shall, in future, undertake with respect to the other any hostile act or design whatsoever, either secretly or openly. And in consequence of the renewal of so sincere a friendship, the two Contracting Parties grant respectively an amnesty and general pardon to all such of their subjects, without distinction, who may have been guilty of any crime against one or other of the two Parties; delivering and setting at liberty those who are in the gallies or in prison; permitting all banished persons or exiles to return home, and promising to restore to them, after the peace, all the honours and property which they before enjoyed, and not to subject them, nor allow others to subject them, with impunity, to any insult, loss, or injury under any pretext whatsoever; but that each and every of them may live under the safeguard and protection of the laws and customs of his native country in the same manner as his native fellow-countrymen.

II. If, after the conclusion of the Treaty and the exchange of the ratifications, any subjects of the two Empires, having committed any capital offence, or having been guilty of disobedience or of treason, should endeavour to conceal themselves, or seek an asylum in the territories of one of the two Powers, they must not be received or sheltered there under any pretext, but must be immediately delivered up, or at least expelled, from the States of the Power whither they had escaped, in order that, on account of such criminals, there should not arise any coolness or useless dispute between the two Empires, with the exception, however, of those who, in the Empire of Russia, shall have embraced the Christian religion, and, in the Ottoman Empire, the Mahometan religion. In like manner, should any subjects of the two Empires, whether Christians or Mahometans, having committed any crime or offence, or for any reason whatsoever, pass from one Empire into the other, they shall be immediately delivered up, so soon as a requisition to that effect is made.

III. All the Tartar peoples—those of the Crimea, of the Budjiac, of the Kuban, the Edissans, Geambouiluks and Editschkuls—shall, without any exception, be acknowledged by the two Empires as free nations, and entirely independent of every foreign Power, governed by their own Sovereign, of the race of Ghengis Khan, elected and raised to the throne by all the Tartar peoples; which Sovereign shall govern them according to their ancient laws and usages, being responsible to no foreign Power whatsoever; for which reason, neither the Court of Russia nor the Ottoman Porte shall interfere, under any pretext whatever, with the election of the said Khan, or in the domestic, political, civil and internal affairs of the same; but, on the contrary, they shall acknowledge and consider the said Tartar nation, in its political and civil state, upon the same footing as the other Powers who are governed by themselves, and are dependent upon God alone. As to the ceremonies of religion, as the Tartars profess the same faith as the Mahometans, they shall regulate themselves, with respect to His Highness, in his capacity of Grand Caliph of Mahometanism, according to the precepts prescribed to them by their law, without compromising, nevertheless, the stability of their political and civil liberty. Russia leaves to this Tartar nation, with

the exception of the fortresses of Kertsch and Jenicale (with their districts and ports, which Russia retains for herself), all the towns, fortresses, dwellings, territories, and ports which it has conquered in Crimea and in Kuban; the country situated between the rivers Berda, Konskie, Vodi, and the Dnieper, as well as all that situated as far as the frontier of Poland between the Boug and the Dniester, excepting the fortress of Oczakow, with its ancient territory, which shall belong, as heretofore, to the Sublime Porte, and it promises to withdraw its troops from their possessions immediately after the conclusion and exchange of the Treaty of Peace. The Sublime Ottoman Porte engages, in like manner, on its part, to abandon all right whatsoever which it might have over the fortresses, towns, habitations, &c., in Crimea, in Kuban, and in the island [sic] of Taman; to maintain in those places no garrison nor other armed forces, ceding these States to the Tartars in the same manner as the Court of Russia has done, that is to say, in full power and in absolute and independent sovereignty. In like manner the Sublime Porte engages, in the most solemn manner, and promises neither to introduce nor maintain, in future, any garrison or armed forces whatsoever in the above-mentioned towns, fortresses, lands, and habitations, nor, in the interior of those States, any intendant or military agent, of whatsoever denomination, but to leave all the Tartars in the same perfect liberty and independence in which the Empire of Russia leaves them.

IV. It is conformable to the natural right of every Power to make, in its own country, such dispositions as it may consider to be expedient: in consequence whereof, there is respectively reserved to the two Empires a perfect and unrestricted liberty of constructing anew in their respective States, and within their frontiers, in such localities as shall be deemed advisable, every kind of fortresses, towns, habitations, edifices, and dwellings, as well as of repairing and rebuilding the old fortresses, towns, habitations, &c.

V. After the conclusion of this happy peace, and the renewal of a sincere and neighbourly friendship, the Imperial Court of Russia shall always have, henceforth, at the Sublime Porte, a Minister of the second rank, that is to say, an Envoy or Minister Plenipotentiary; the Sublime Porte shall show to him, in his official character, all the attentions and respect which are observed towards the Ministers of the most distinguished Powers; and upon all public occasions the said Minister shall immediately follow the Emperor's Minister, if he be of the same rank as the latter; but if he be of a different rank, that is to say, either superior or inferior, then the Russian Minister shall immediately follow the Ambassador of Holland, and, in his absence, that of Venice.

VI. If any individual in the actual service of the Russian Minister during his stay at the Sublime Porte, having been guilty of theft or having committed any crime or act liable to punishment, should, for the purpose of escaping the penalty of the law, become Turk; although he cannot be prevented from so doing, yet after he has undergone the punishment be deserves, all the articles stolen shall be restored *in toto,* according to the specification of the Minister But those who, being intoxicated, might be desirous of adopting the turban, must not be allowed so to do until after their fit of drunkenness is over, and they have come to their right senses; and even then, their final declaration shall not be taken, unless in the presence of an interpreter sent by the Minister, and of some Musslman free from the suspicion of partiality.

VII. The Sublime Porte promises to protect constantly the Christian religion and its churches, and it also allows the Ministers of the Imperial Court of Russia to make, upon all occasions, representations, as well in favour of the new church at Constantinople, of which mention will be made in Article XIV, as on behalf of its officiating ministers, promising to take such representations into due consideration, as being made by a confidential functionary of a neighbouring and sincerely friendly Power.

VIII. The subjects of the Russian Empire, as well laymen as ecclesiastics, shall have full liberty and permission to visit the holy city of Jerusalem, and other places deserving of attention. No charatsch [ie., *haraç* or military-exemption tax], contribution, duty, or other tax, shall be exacted from those pilgrims and travellers by any one whomsoever, either at Jerusalem or elsewhere, or on the road; but they shall be provided with such passports and firmans as are given to the subjects of the other friendly Powers. During their sojourn in the Ottoman Empire, they shall not suffer the least wrong or injury; but, on the contrary, shall be under the strictest protection of the laws.

IX. The interpreters attached to the Russian Ministers resident at Constantinople, of whatever nation they may be, being employed upon State affairs, and consequently in the service of both Empires, must be regarded and treated with every degree of kindness; and they shall be subjected to no ill-treatment on account of the business with which they may be entrusted by their principals.

X. If between the signing of these Articles of Peace and the orders which shall thereupon be dispatched by the Commanders of the two respective armies, an engagement should anywhere take place, neither party shall be offended thereat, nor shall it be productive of any consequences, every acquisition made thereby being restored, and no advantage shall accrue therefrom to one party or the other.

XI. For the convenience and advantage of the two Empires, there shall be a free and unimpeded navigation for the merchantships belonging to the two Contracting Powers, in all the seas which wash their shores; the Sublime Porte grants to Russian merchant-vessels, namely, such as are universally employed by the other Powers for commerce and in the ports, a free passage from the Black Sea into the White Sea, and reciprocally from the White Sea into the Black Sea, as also the power of entering all the ports and harbours situated either on the sea-coasts, or in the passages and channels which join those seas. In like manner, the Sublime Porte allows Russian subjects to trade in its States by land as well as by water and upon the Danube in their ships, in conformity with what has been specified above in this Article, with all the same privileges and advantages as are enjoyed in its States by the most friendly nations, whom the Sublime Porte favours most in trade, such as the French and the English; and the capitulations of those two nations and others shall, just as if they were here inserted word for word, serve as a rule, under all circumstances and in every place, for whatever concerns commerce as well as Russian merchants, who upon paying the same duties may import and export all kinds of goods, and disembark their merchandize at every port and harbour as well upon the Black as upon the other Seas, Constantinople being expressly included in the number.

While granting in the above manner to the respective subjects the freedom of commerce and navigation upon all waters without exception, the two Empires, at the same time, allow merchants to stop within their territories for as long a time as their affairs require, and promise them the same security and liberty as are enjoyed by the subjects of other friendly Courts. And in order to be consistent throughout, the Sublime Porte also allows the residence of Consuls and Vice-Consuls in every place where the Court of Russia may consider it expedient to establish them, and they shall be treated upon a perfect footing of equality with the Consuls of the other friendly Powers. It permits them to have interpreters called Baratli, that is, those who have patents, providing them with Imperial patents, and causing them to enjoy the same prerogatives as those in the service of the said French, English, and other nations.

Similarly, Russia permits the subjects of the Sublime Porte to trade in its dominions, by sea and by land, with the same prerogatives and advantages as are enjoyed by the most friendly nations, and upon paying the accustomed duties. In case of accident happening to the vessels, the two Empires are bound respectively to render them the same assistance as is given in similar cases to other friendly nations; and all necessary things shall be furnished to them at the ordinary prices.

XII. When the Imperial Court of Russia shall have the intention of making any Commercial Treaty with the regencies of Africa, as Tripoli, Tunis, and Algiers, the Sublime Porte engages to employ its power and influence in order to accomplish the views of the above-named Court in this respect, and to guarantee, as regards those regencies, all the conditions which shall have been stipulated in those Treaties.

XIII. The Sublime [Porte] promises to employ the sacred title of the Empress of all the Russias in all public acts and letters, as well as in all other cases, in the Turkish language, that is to say, "Temamen Roussielerin Padischag."

XIV. After the manner of the other Powers, permission is given to the High Court of Russia, in addition to the chapel built in the Minister's residence, to erect in one of the quarters of Galata, in the street called Bey Oglu, a public church of the Greek ritual, which shall always be under the protection of the Ministers of that Empire, and secure from all coercion and outrage.

XV. Although, according to the manner in which the boundaries of the two Contracting Powers are arranged, there is every reason to hope that the respective subjects shall no longer find any occasion for serious differences and disputes amongst themselves, nevertheless, at all events to guard against whatever might occasion a coolness or cause a misunderstanding, the two Empires mutually agree that all such cases of disagreement shall be investigated by the Governors and Commanders of the frontiers, or by Commissioners appointed for that purpose, who shall be bound, after making the necessary inquiries, to render justice where it is due, without the least loss of time: with the express condition that events of this nature shall never serve as a pretext for the slightest alteration in the friendship and good feeling re-established by this Treaty.

XVI. The Empire of Russia restores to the Sublime Porte the whole of Bessarabia, with the cities of Ackermann, Kilija, Ismail, together with the towns and villages, and all contained in that Province; in like manner it restores to it the fortress of Bender. Similarly the Empire of Russia restores to the Sublime Porte the two Principalities of Wallachia and Moldavia, together with all the fortresses, cities, towns, villages, and all which they contain, and the Sublime Porte receives them upon the following conditions, solemnly promising to keep them religiously:

1. To observe, with respect to all the inhabitants of these Principalities, of whatever rank, dignity, state, calling, and extraction they may be, without the least exception, the absolute amnesty and eternal oblivion stipulated in Article I of the

Treaty, in favour of all those who shall have actually committed any crime, or who shall have been suspected of having had the intention of doing injury to the interests of the Sublime Porte, re-establishing them in their former dignities, ranks, and possessions, and restoring to them the property which they were in the enjoyment of previously to the present war.

2. To obstruct in no manner whatsoever the free exercise of the Christian religion, and to interpose no obstacle to the erection of new churches and to the repairing of the old ones, as has been done heretofore.

3. To restore to the convents and to other individuals the lands and possessions formerly belonging to them, which have been taken from them contrary to all justice, and which are situated in the environs of Brahilow, Choczim, Bender, &c., now called Rai.

4. To entertain for ecclesiastics the particular respect due to their calling.

5. To grant to families who shall be desirous to quit their country in order to establish themselves elsewhere, a free egress with all their property; and in order that such families may duly arrange their affairs, to allow them the term of one year for this free emigration from their country, reckoning from the day on which the present Treaty shall be exchanged.

6. Not to demand or exact any payment for old accounts, of whatever nature they may be.

7. Not to require from these people any contribution or payment for all the time of the duration of the war; and even, on account of the devastations to which they have been exposed, to relieve them from all taxes for the space of two years, reckoning from the day on which the present Treaty shall be exchanged.

8. At the expiration of the above-mentioned term, the Porte promises to treat them with all possible humanity and generosity in the monetary taxes which it shall impose upon them, and to receive them by means of deputies, who shall be sent to it every two years; and after the payment of these taxes, no Bacha, Governor, nor any other person whatsoever shall molest them, or exact from them any other payments or taxes of what description soever, but they shall possess all the advantages which they enjoyed during the reign of the late Sultan.

9. The Porte allows each of the Princes of these two States to have accredited to it a Chargé d'Affaires, selected from among the Christians of the Greek communion, who shall watch over the affairs of the said Principalities, be treated with kindness by the Porte, and who, notwithstanding their comparative want of importance, shall be considered as persons who enjoy the rights of nations, that is to say, who are protected from every kind of violence.

10. The Porte likewise permits that, according as the circumstances of these two Principalities may require, the Ministers of the Imperial Court of Russia resident at Constantinople may remonstrate in their favour; and promises to listen to them with all the attention which is due to friendly and respected Powers.

XVII. The Empire of Russia restores to the Sublime Porte all the islands of the Archipelago which are under its dependence; and the Sublime Porte, on its part, promises:

1. To observe religiously, with respect to the inhabitants of these islands, the conditions stipulated in Article I concerning the general amnesty and the eternal oblivion of all crimes whatsoever, committed or suspected to have been committed to the prejudice of the interests of the Sublime Porte.

2. That the Christian religion shall not be exposed to the least oppression any more than its churches, and that no obstacle shall be opposed to the erection or repair of them; and also that the officiating ministers shall neither be oppressed nor insulted.

3. That there shall not be exacted from these islands any payment of the annual taxes to which they were subjected, namely, since the time that they have been under the dependence of the Empire of Russia; and that, moreover, in consideration of the great losses which they have suffered during the war, they shall be exempt from any taxes for two years more, reckoning from the time of their restoration to the Sublime Porte.

4. To permit the families who might wish to quit their country, and establish themselves elsewhere, free egress with their property; and in order that such families may arrange their affairs with all due convenience, the term of one year is allowed

them for this free emigration, reckoning from the day of the exchange of the present Treaty.

5. In case the Russian fleet, at the time of its departure, which must take place within three months, reckoning from the day on which the present Treaty is exchanged, should be in need of anything, the Sublime Porte promises to provide it, as far as possible with all that may be necessary.

XVIII. The Castle of Kinburn, situated at the mouth of the Dnieper, with a proportionate district along the left bank of the Dnieper, and the corner which forms the desert between the Bug and the Dnieper, remains under the full, perpetual, and incontestable dominion of the Empire of Russia.

XIX. The fortresses of Jenicale and Kertsch, situated in the peninsula of Crimea, with their ports and all therein contained, and moreover with their districts, commencing from the Black Sea, and following the ancient frontier of Kertsch as far as the place called Bugak, and from Bugak ascending in a direct line as far as the Sea of Azow, shall remain under the full, perpetual, and incontestable dominion of the Empire of Russia.

XX. The city of Azow, with its district, and the boundaries laid down in the Conventions made in 1700, that is to say in 1113, between the Governor Tolstoi and Hassan Bacha, Governor of Atschug, shall belong in perpetuity to the Empire of Russia.

XXI. The two Cabardes, namely, the Great and Little, on account of their proximity to the Tartars, are more nearly connected with the Khans of Crimea; for which reason it must remain with the Khan of Crimea to consent, in concert with his Council and the ancients of the Tartar nation, to these countries becoming subject to the Imperial Court of Russia.

XXII. The two Empires have agreed to annihilate and leave in an eternal oblivion all the Treaties and Conventions heretofore made between the Two States, including therein the Convention of Belgrade, with all those subsequent to it; and never to put forth any claim grounded upon the said Conventions, excepting, however, the one made in 1700 between Governor Tolstoi and Hassan Bacha, Governor of Atschug,

on the subject of the boundaries of the district of Azow and of the line of demarcation of the frontier of Kuban, which shall remain invariably such as it has heretofore been.

XXIII. The fortresses which are standing in a part of Georgia and of Mingrelia, as Bagdadgick, Kutatis, and Scheherban, conquered by the Russian armies, shall be considered by Russia as belonging to those on whom they were formerly dependent; so that if, in ancient times, or for a very long period, they have actually been under the dominion of the Sublime Porte, they shall be considered as belonging to it; and after the exchange of the present Treaty the Russian troops shall, at the time agreed upon, quit the said Provinces of Georgia and Mingrelia. On its part, the Sublime Porte engages, conformably to the contents of the present Article, to grant a general amnesty to all those in the said countries who, in the course of the present war, shall have offended it in any manner whatsoever. It renounces solemnly and for ever to exact tributes of children, male and female, and every other kind of tax. It engages to consider such of these people only as its subjects as shall have belonged to it from all antiquity; to leave and restore all the castles and fortified places which have been under the dominion of the Georgians and Mingrelians, to their own exclusive custody and government; as also not to molest in any manner the religion, monasteries, and churches; not to hinder the repairing of dilapidated ones, nor the building of new ones; and it promises that these people shall not be oppressed on the part of the Governor of Tschildirsk, and other chiefs and officers, by exactions which despoil them of their property. But as the said people are subjects of the Sublime Porte, Russia must not, in future, intermeddle in any manner in their affairs, nor molest them in any way.

XXIV. Immediately upon the signing and confirmation of these Articles, all the Russian troops which are in Bulgaria on the right bank of the Danube shall withdraw, and within one month, reckoning from the day of the signature, they shall cross to the other side of the river. When all the troops shall have passed the Danube, the castle of Hirsow shall be delivered up to the Turks, the said castle being evacuated to them when all the Russian troops shall have completely passed over to the left bank of that river. After which, the evacuation of Wallachia and Bessarabia shall be effected simultaneously, the term of two months being allowed for that operation. After all the Russian troops shall have quitted these two Provinces, the fortresses of Giurgewo and afterwards Brahilow on the one side (of the river), and on the other, the town of Ismail and the fortresses of Kilia and Akkerman, shall be delivered up to the Turkish troops, from all which places the Russian garrisons shall withdraw for the purpose of following the other troops, so that for the complete evacuation of the said Provinces the term of three months shall be assigned. Lastly, the Imperial troops of Russia shall, two months afterwards, withdraw from Moldavia, and shall pass over to the left bank of the Dniester; thus, the evacuation of all the aforesaid countries shall be effected within five months, reckoning from the abovementioned signing of the Treaty of Perpetual Peace between the two contracting Empires. When all the Russian troops shall have passed to the left bank of the Dniester, the fortresses of Chotzum and of Bender shall be given up to the Turkish troops; upon this condition, however, that the castle of Kinburn with the district belonging to it, and the desert situated between the Dnieper and the Boug, shall have been already restored in full, perpetual and incontestable sovereignty to the Empire of Russia, conformably to Article XVIII of the Treaty of Perpetual Peace between the two Empires.

As to the islands of the Archipelago, they shall be left, as heretofore, under the legitimate dominion of the Ottoman Porte, by the fleet and the Imperial troops of Russia, as soon as the arrangements and peculiar necessities of the fleet shall permit, with regard to which it is not possible to assign here the precise time. And the Sublime Porte, in order to accelerate as much as possible the departure of the said fleet, already engages, as a friendly Power, to furnish it, as far as it can, with every necessary of which it may be in need.

During the stay of the Imperial troops of Russia in the Provinces to be restored to the Sublime Porte, the government and police shall remain there in the same vigour as at present and since the conquest, and the Porte must take no part whatever therein, during the whole of this time, nor until the entire withdrawal of all the troops. Up to the last day of their quitting these countries, the Russian troops shall be provided with all necessaries, as well provisions as other articles, in the same manner as they have hitherto been furnished with them.

The troops of the Sublime Porte must not enter the fortresses which shall be restored to it, nor shall that Power commence to exercise its authority in the countries which shall be given up to it, until at each place or country which shall have been evacuated by the Russian troops, the Commander of those troops shall have given notice thereof to the officer appointed for that purpose on the part of the Ottoman Porte.

The Russian troops may, at their pleasure, empty their magazines of ammunition and provisions which are in the fortresses, towns and wherever else they may be, and they shall leave nothing in the fortresses restored to the Sublime Porte but such Turkish artillery as is actually found there. The inhabitants in all the countries restored to the Sublime Porte, of whatever state and condition they may be, and who are in the Imperial service of Russia, have the liberty, besides the term allowed of one year, as assigned in the Articles XVI and XVII of the Treaty of Peace, of quitting the country and withdrawing with their families and property in the rear of the Russian troops; and conformably to the above-mentioned Articles, the Sublime Porte engages not to oppose their departure, neither then nor during the entire term of one year.

XXV. All the prisoners of war and slaves in the two Empires, men and women, of whatever rank and dignity they may be, with the exception of those who, in the Empire of Russia shall have voluntarily quitted Mahometanism in order to embrace the Christian religion, or in the Ottoman Empire shall have voluntarily abandoned Christianity in order to embrace the Mahometan faith, shall be, immediately after the exchange of the ratifications of this Treaty, and without any excuse whatever, be [sic] set at liberty on either side, and restored and delivered up without ransom or redemption money; in like manner, all the

Christians fallen into slavery, such as Poles, Moldavians, Wallachians, Peloponnesians, inhabitants of the islands, and Georgians, all, without the least exception, must be set at liberty without ransom or redemption money. Similarly all Russian subjects who, since the conclusion of this happy peace, shall by any accident have fallen into slavery, and who shall be found in the Ottoman Empire, must be set at liberty and restored in like manner; all which the Empire of Russia promises also to observe, on its part, towards the Ottoman Porte and its subjects.

XXVI. After having received in Crimea and in Oczakow intelligence of the signature of these Articles, the Commander of the Russian army in Crimea, and the Governor of Oczakow must immediately communicate with each on the subject, and within two months after the signing of the Treaty send, respectively, persons duly accredited for effecting, on the one hand, the cession, and on the other the taking possession, of the Castle of Kinburn, with the desert, as stipulated in Article XVIII above; and this the said Commissioners must absolutely effect within two months from the day of their meeting, in order that within four months, or even sooner, reckoning from the signing of the Treaty, the whole of this business be accomplished, and immediately after the said execution thereof, notice of the same shall be given to their Excellencies the Field-Marshal and the Grand Vizier.

XXVII. But in order that the present peace and sincere friendship between the two Empires be so much the more strongly and authentically sealed and confirmed, there shall be sent on both sides solemn and extraordinary Embassies with the Imperial ratifications signed, confirmatory of the Treaty of Peace, at such time as shall be agreed upon by both the High Contracting Parties. The Ambassadors shall be met on the frontiers in the same manner, and they shall be received and treated with the same honours and ceremonies as are observed in the respective Embassies between the Ottoman Porte and the most respectable Powers. And as a testimonial of friendship, there shall be mutually sent through the medium of the said Ambassadors presents which shall be proportionate to the dignity of their Imperial Majesties.

XXVIII. After these Articles of the perpetual peace shall have been signed by the said Plenipotentiaries, the Lieutenant General Prince Repnin, and on the part of the Sublime Porte the Nischandgi Resmi Achmet Effendi and Ibrahim Munib Effendi, all hostilities are to cease between the principal as well as between the separate corps, both by land and by sea, so soon as orders to that effect shall have been received from the Commanders of the two armies. For this purpose, couriers must first of all be dispatched on the part of the Field-Marshal and the Grand Vizier into the Archipelago, to the fleet which is in the Black Sea, opposite to the Crimea, and to all the places where hostilities are being mutually carried on, in order that by virtue of the concluded peace all warfare and hostile operations may cease and determine [sic]; and these couriers shall be provided with orders on the part of the Field-Marshal, and of the Grand Vizier, in such wise, that should the Russian courier arrive first at the quarters of the Commander to whom he is sent, he may, through his means, transmit to the Turkish Commander the orders of the Grand Vizier; and in like manner, if the courier of the latter should be the first to arrive, then the Turkish Commander may transmit to the Russian Commander the orders of the Field-Marshal.

And as the negotiation and accomplishment of this peace have been confided by the Sovereigns of the respective Empires to the care of the Commanders-in-chief of their armies, namely, the Field-Marshal Count Pierre de Roumanzow, and the Grand Vizier of the Sublime Porte, Mousson Zade Mechmet Bacha, the said Field-Marshal and Grand Vizier must, by virtue of the full power given to each of them by their Sovereigns, confirm all the said Articles of the perpetual peace as they are herein expressed, and with the same force as if they had been drawn up in their presence, sign them with the seal of their coat-of-arms, observe and faithfully and inviolably accomplish all that has been there stipulated and promised, do nothing, nor suffer anything whatsoever to be done in contravention of the said Treaty, and the copies, in every respect similar to the present one, signed by them, and having their seals attached, on the part of the Grand Vizier in the Turkish and Italian language, and on the part of the Field-Marshal in Russian and Italian, as well as the full-powers to them given by their Sovereigns, shall be respectively exchanged by the same persons above-mentioned, who have been sent, on the part of the Sublime Porte, to the Field-Marshal, within five days without fail, reckoning from the day of the signing of the present Treaty, and sooner if it be possible; it being, from this present time, determined that they shall receive the said copies from the Field-Marshal as soon as they shall have notified that those of the Grand Vizier have reached them. . . .

2. Separate Articles

ART. I. Although it is indicated in Article XVII of the Treaty of Peace signed today, that in three months the Imperial Russian fleet will evacuate the islands of the archipelago, in Article XXIV of the same Treaty it is explained that, taking such a distance into consideration, it is not possible to specify how much time may be necessary; we have agreed to hold ourselves to the latter Article. Accordingly, we repeat that the said Imperial Russian fleet will evacuate the archipelago as soon as possible, without setting a time limit; and to facilitate the evacuation, the Sublime Porte will provide [the Imperial Russian fleet] with all that it needs for its voyage, insofar as that depends upon [the Sublime Porte].

This separate Article will receive the same confirmation as the entire Treaty, and we shall give it the same force and validity as if it had been inscribed word for word in the Treaty executed today, in the faith of which we have signed it in our own hand and sealed it with our seals. . . .

ART. II. It is regulated and established by this separate Article that the Sublime Porte will pay the sum of 15,000 purses or 7.5 million piasters, which in Russian money equals 4.5 million rubles, to the Russian Empire in three periods, for the expenses of the war. The first payment will fall due on 1/12 January 1775; the second payment, on 1/12 January 1776; the third payment, on 1/12 January 1777. Each payment of 5,000 purses will be made by the Sublime Porte to the Russian Minister accredited to the said Sublime Porte; and if the Court of Russia should wish some other assurance beyond that, the Ottoman Porte solemnly obligates itself to satisfy [Russia] on that score. This separate Article will be confirmed, together with the entire Treaty signed today and we shall give it the same force and validity as if it had been inscribed word for word in the Treaty concluded today between the two respective Empires; in the faith of which we have signed it with our hand and sealed it with our seals. . . .

33. TREATY OF PEACE, FRIENDSHIP, AND SHIP-SIGNALS:
THE UNITED STATES AND MOROCCO
28 June and 15 July 1786

(Ratified by the United States, 18 July 1787; confirmed by Sidi Muhammad bin 'Abdallah, August 1788 [in the middle of the month of Dhu al-Qa'dah 1202]; reconfirmed by Mawlay Sulayman, 19 August 1795)
[The English translation of the original Arabic in Miller, *Treaties and Other International Acts*, 2: 212–19]

The 1786 treaty of peace and friendship with Morocco was the fourteenth treaty the United States concluded with a foreign power, and from the testimony it is clear that Sidi Muhammad bin 'Abdallah, the ruler of Morocco, made the first overtures to the

United States, probably for more than one reason. From the moment that Sidi Muhammad came to the throne in 1757, he cultivated friendly relations with maritime powers, as a stimulus to commerce and state revenue. Because of the tradition established by his grandfather, Mawlay Isma'il (1672–1727), Sidi Muhammad could also expect a handsome down payment for the treaty. When the United States government failed to respond to the overtures, the Moroccan ruler detained an American vessel at Tangier early in 1784. On 12 May of that year the Congress gave to John Adams, Benjamin Franklin, and Thomas Jefferson or to "a Majority of them full Powers to confer, treat and negotiate with the Ambassador, Minister or Commissioner of His Majesty The Emperor of Morocco concerning a Treaty of Amity and Commerce, to make and receive propositions for such Treaty and to conclude and sign the same, transmitting it to the United States in congress assembled for their final Ratification. . . ." A more specific Congressional authorization followed on 11 March 1785, empowering the American negotiators to spend up to $80,000 in concluding treaties with Morocco and other Barbary states. American merchants engaged in the Mediterranean trade enthusiastically endorsed the congressional action, for with the Declaration of Independence they had lost the immunity from corsair attack afforded them by British treaties, and the relatively brisk American trade with the Mediterranean later suffered a severe decline. Neither France nor the Netherlands, to say nothing of Britain itself, would place American vessels under its umbrella. The reluctance of the maritime states was largely commercial, since all found additional competition in the Mediterranean market unwelcome. Thomas Barclay, who negotiated the treaty, reached Morocco in June 1786, and by mid-July the draft proposals that he had brought with him (together with a present of $20,000), were approved by Sidi Muhammad with only minor exceptions. Conforming to the prevailing arrangements with the maritime states of Europe, the American treaty provided for: unilateral diplomatic relations at the consular level, permitting the consuls to take up residence at any seaport of their choice (art. 23), commerce on a most-favored-nation basis (art. 14), capitulatory privileges (arts. 20–22), and assurances against piracy (arts. 4, 6). The treaty liberated American shippers from anxiety about Moroccan piracy in the Atlantic, but could not possibly offer protection against the corsairs of the Barbary Garrisons, over which Morocco had little or no influence. On the death of Sidi Muhammad in April 1790, the treaty had to be reconfirmed, since the only unilateral advantage enjoyed by Morocco was the issuance of the treaty in the form of a royal edict binding on the ruler of the day but not on his successors. The Congress in March 1791 appropriated an additional $20,000, which was handed over to Mawlay Sulayman (1792–1822), who had risen to power in a civil war, a common phenomenon in Islamic dynasties of the day, in the absence of firm rules of succession. The treaty, with only minor textual changes, was renewed on 18 September 1836 for an additional period of fifty years. It was convented, in effect, into a perpetual treaty by article 25, which laid down that "the Treaty shall continue to be binding on both parties, until the one shall give twelve months notice to the other of an intention to abandon it; in which case, its operations shall cease at the end of the twelve months" (see full text with commentary in Miller, op. cit., vol. 4, doc. 81, pp. 60–69). International Court of Justice, *Case concerning Rights of Nationals of the United States of America in Morocco*, pp. 257–408; Irwin, *Diplomatic Relations of the United States with the*

Barbary Powers, chaps. 1–2; Field, America and the Mediterranean World, chap. 2; G. Allen, Our Navy and the Barbary Corsairs, chaps. 1–3; Terrasse, Histoire du Maroc, pp. 253–312: Abun-Nasr, History of the Maghrib, chap. 8; Julien, Histoire de l'Afrique du Nord, 2d ed., vol. 2, chap. 5.

1. Treaty of Peace and Friendship, 28 June 1786

1. We declare that both Parties have agreed that this Treaty consisting of twenty five Articles shall be inserted in this Book and delivered to the Honorable Thomas Barclay, the Agent of the United States now at our Court, with whose Approbation it has been made and who is duly authorized on their Part, to treat with us concerning all the Matters contained therein.

2. If either of the Parties shall be at War with any Nation whatever, the other Party shall not take a Commission from the Enemy nor fight under their Colors.

3. If either of the Parties shall be at War with any Nation whatever and take a Prize belonging to that Nation, and there shall be found on board Subjects or Effects belonging to either of the Parties, the Subjects shall be set at Liberty and the Effects returned to the Owners. And if any Goods belonging to any Nation, with whom either of the Parties shall be at War, shall be loaded on Vessels belonging to the other Party, they shall pass free and unmolested without any attempt being made to take or detain them.

4. A Signal or Pass shall be given to all Vessels belonging to both Parties, by which they are to be known when they meet at Sea, and if the Commander of a Ship of War of either Party shall have other Ships under his Convoy, the Declaration of the Commander shall alone be sufficient to exempt any of them from examination.

5. If either of the Parties shall be at War, and shall meet a Vessel at Sea, belonging to the other, it is agreed that if an examination is to be made, it shall be done by sending a Boat with two or three Men only, and if any Gun shall be fired and injury done without Reason, the offending Party shall make good all damages.

6. If any Moor shall bring Citizens of the United States or their Effects to His Majesty, the Citizens shall immediately be set at Liberty and the Effects restored, and in like Manner, if any Moor not a Subject of these Dominions shall make Prize of any of the Citizens of America or their Effects and bring them into any of the Ports of His Majesty, they shall be immediately released, as they will then be considered as under His Majesty's Protection.

7. If any Vessel of either Party shall put into a Port of the other and have occasion for Provisions or other Supplies, they shall be furnished without any interruption or molestation.

8. If any Vessel of the United States shall meet with a Disaster at Sea and put into one of our Ports to repair, she shall be at Liberty to land and reload her cargo, without paying any Duty whatever.

9. If any Vessel of the United States shall be cast on Shore on any Part of our Coasts, she shall remain at the disposition of the Owners and no one shall attempt going near her without their Approbation, as she is then considered particularly under our Protection; and if any Vessel of the United States shall be forced to put into our Ports, by Stress of weather or otherwise, she shall not be compelled to land her Cargo, but shall remain in tranquillity untill the Commander shall think proper to proceed on his Voyage.

10. If any Vessel of either of the Parties shall have an engagement with a Vessel belonging to any of the Christian Powers within gunshot of the Forts of the other, the Vessel so engaged shall be defended and protected as much as possible untill she is in safety; And if any American Vessel shall be cast on shore on the Coast of Wadnoon: or any Coast thereabout, the People belonging to her shall be protected, and assisted until by the help of God, they shall be sent to their Country.

11. If we shall be at War with any Christian Power and any of our Vessels sail from the Ports of the United States, no Vessel belonging to the enemy shall follow untill twenty four hours after the Depature of our Vessels; and the same

Regulation shall be observed towards the American Vessels sailing from our Ports—be their enemies Moors or Christians.

12. If any Ship of War belonging to the United States shall put into any of our Ports, she shall not be examined on any Pretence whatever, even though she should have fugitive Slaves on Board, nor shall the Governor or Commander of the Place compel them to be brought on Shore on any pretext, nor require any payment for them.

13. If a Ship of War of either Party shall put into a Port of the other and salute, it shall be returned from the Fort, with an equal Number of Guns, not with more or less.

14. The Commerce with the United States shall be on the same footing as is the Commerce with Spain or as that with the most favored Nation for the time being and their Citzens shall be respected and esteemed and have full Liberty to pass and repass our Country and Sea Ports whenever they please without interruption.

15. Merchants of both Countries shall employ only such interpreters, & such other Persons to assist them in their Business, as they shall think proper. No Commander of a Vessel shall transport his Cargo on board another Vessel, he shall not be detained in Port, longer than he may think proper, and all persons employed in loading or unloading Goods or in any other Labor whatever, shall be paid at the Customary rates, not more and not less.

16. In case of a War between the Parties, the Prisoners are not to be made Slaves, but to be exchanged one for another, Captain for Captain, Officer for Officer and one private Man for another; and if there shall prove a defficiency on either side, it shall be made up by the payment of one hundred Mexican Dollars for each Person wanting; And it is agreed that all Prisoners shall be exchanged in twelve Months from the Time of their being taken, and that this exchange may be effected by a Merchant or any other Person authorized by either of the Parties.

17. Merchants shall not be compelled to buy or Sell any kind of Goods but such as they think proper; and may buy and sell all sorts of Merchandise but such as are prohibeted to the other Christian Nations.

18. All goods shall be weighed and examined before they are sent on board, and to avoid all detention of Vessels, no examination shall afterwards be made, unless it shall first be proved, that contraband Goods have been sent on board, in which Case the Persons who took the contraband Goods on board shall be punished according to the Usage and Custom of the Country and no other Person whatever shall be injured, nor shall the Ship or Cargo incur any Penalty or damage whatever.

19. No vessel shall be detained in Port on any pretence whatever, nor be obliged to take on board any Article without the consent of the Commander, who shall be at full Liberty to agree for the Freight of any Goods he takes on board.

20. If any of the Citizens of the United States, or any Persons under their Protection, shall have any disputes with each other, the Consul shall decide between the Parties and whenever the Consul shall require any Aid or Assistance from our Government to enforce his decisions it shall be immediately granted to him.

21. If a Citizen of the United States should kill or wound a Moor, or on the contrary if a Moor shall kill or wound a Citizen of the United States, the Law of the Country shall take place and equal Justice shall be rendered, the Consul assisting at the Tryal, and if any Delinquent shall make his escape, the Consul shall not be answerable for him in any manner whatever.

22. If an American Citizen shall die in our Country and no Will shall appear, the Consul shall take possession of his Effects, and if there shall be no Consul, the Effects shall be deposited in the hands of some Person worthy of Trust, untill the Party shall appear who has a Right to demand them, but if the Heir to the Person deceased be present, the Property shall be delivered to him without interruption; and if a Will shall appear, the Property shall descend agreeable to that Will, as soon as the Consul shall declare the Validity thereof.

23. The Consuls of the United States of America shall reside in any Sea Port of our Dominions that they shall think proper; And they shall be respected and enjoy all the Privileges which the Consuls of any

other Nation enjoy, and if any of the Citizens of the United States shall contract any Debts or engagements, the Consul shall not be in any Manner accountable for them, unless he shall have given a Promise in writing for the payment or fulfilling thereof, without which promise in Writing no Application to him for any redress shall be made.

24. If any differences shall arise by either Party infringing on any of the Articles of this Treaty, Peace and Harmony shall remain notwithstanding in the fullest force, until a friendly Application shall be made for an Arrangement, and untill that Application shall be rejected, no appeal shall be made to Arms. And if a War shall break out between the Parties, Nine Months shall be granted to all the Subjects of both Parties, to dispose of their Effects and retire with their Property. And it is further declared that whatever indulgences in Trade or otherwise shall be granted to any of the Christian Powers, the Citizens of the United States shall be equally entitled to them.

25. This Treaty shall continue in full Force, with the help of God for Fifty Years. . . .

2. Additional Article, 15 July 1786

Grace to the only God
I the underwritten the Servant of God, Taher Ben Abdelhack Fennish do certify that His Imperial Majesty my Master /

whom God preserve/ having concluded a Treaty of Peace and Commerce with the United States of America has ordered me the better to compleat it and in addition of the tenth Article of the Treaty to declare "That, if any Vessel belonging to the United States shall be in any of the Ports of His Majesty's Dominions, or within Gunshot of his Forts, she shall be protected as much as possible and no Vessel whatever belonging either to Moorish or Christian Powers with whom the United States may be at War, shall be permitted to follow or engage her, as we now deem the Citizens of America our good Friends. . . .

3. Ship-Signals Agreement, 6 July 1786

The following Signals are agreed upon between Commodore Rais Farache, on the Part of His Majesty the Emperor of Morocco, and the Honorable Thomas Barclay Esquire Agent for the United States of America on their Part, to the End that the Vessels of both Parties may be known to each other at Sea.

For Vessels of two or of three Masts,
In the Day, a blue Pendant is to be hoisted on the End of the Main Yard, and in the Night a Lantern is to be hoisted on the same Place.

For Vessels of one Mast only,
In the Day, a blue Pendant is to be hoisted at the Mast-Head, and in the Night a Lantern is to be hoisted on the Ensign Staff. . . .

34. TREATY OF PEACE (JASSY): THE OTTOMAN EMPIRE AND RUSSIA
29 December 1791/9 January 1792

(Ratifications exchanged, 14/25 January 1792)
[Translated from the French text in Noradounghian, *Recueil d'actes internationaux de l'empire ottoman*, 2: 16–21]

After earlier failures Russia finally established itself as a Black Sea power under the treaty of Küçük Kaynarca of 1774 (Doc. 32), which ended a six-year war with the Ottoman Empire. But the legal basis for the Russian presence on that inland sea remained imperfect, for the Tartar khanates in and around the Crimea, which up to then had been Ottoman protectorates, did not pass at once into Russia's possession.

Instead only their ties to the Sublime Porte were broken, for they were declared "independent." The khanates, however, became de facto Russian protectorates, and in less than a decade, under the prodding of Field Marshal Grigori Alexandrovich Potemkin, Tsarina Catherine II (1762–96) unilaterally assimilated the principalities into her empire by decree on 28 December 1783/8 January 1784 and named Potemkin governor of the territory. This act, which the Sublime Porte refused to acknowledge as binding, together with Catherine's ostentatious visit to the Crimea early in 1787 contributed to the Ottoman declaration of war against Russia on 14 August of that year. By then, Russia had entered into a secret agreement with Austria providing for the division between them of the Ottoman provinces in the Balkans, and one with France providing for its acquisition of Syria and Egypt. In the event, Austria entered the war, while France did not, and even its political support vanished in 1789 after the start of the revolution. Meanwhile, once Selim III (1789–1807) acceded to the Ottoman throne that year, he won Sweden and Prussia as allies and enjoyed the political support of Britain. The war itself dragged on inconclusively for four years with substandard military performances on both sides, although on balance Russia gained the edge by occupying Bessarabia and Moldavia. Austria was the first to negotiate peace, signing the terms of 4 August 1791 at Sistova (French text in Noradounghian, op. cit., 2: 13–16), settling their dispute without territorial change in the Balkans. Four days before the signature of the Austrian treaty, the Ottoman and Russian governments agreed to a truce, confirming their mutual sincerity by an immediate exchange of prominent prisoners. The Russian-Ottoman peace negotiations took place at Jassy (Yaşi), Potemkin's headquarters and the capital of the Ottoman province of Moldavia (in present-day Rumania). Interrupted by Potemkin's death (5 October 1791), the negotiations were not resumed until 1 December. Under the treaty the Sublime Porte formally recognized Russia's annexation of the Tatar khanates (art. 2) and accepted the Kuban River in the north Caucasus as the "fixed" boundary between the two empires. Russia, on its side, returned all other territory occupied by its troops in the war, including Bessarabia and Moldavia. Russia had already acquired the right of free passage through the straits for its commercial vessels, a right still denied its naval vessels. The creeping territorial expansion along the coast of the Black Sea was manifestly designed to enable Russia to take possession of the straits, for only then would the tsarist empire finally break out of its landlocked condition in the southwest and be able to project its naval power into the Mediterranean. The aspiration for the seizure of the straits became a dominating theme of later Russian-Ottoman relations in the nineteenth century, and since the aspiration was never fulfilled, it came to bedevil Soviet-Turkish relations in the twentieth century. Shaw, *Between Old and New*, chaps. 3–7; Florinsky, *Russia*, vol. 1, chap. 20; Nolde, *La formation de l'empire russe*, chaps. 10–11; Hurewitz, "Russia and the Turkish Straits"; Soloveytchik, *Potemkin*, chaps. 15–18.

. . . ART. 1. All hostilities and enmity between His Highness the Grand Signor and Her Majesty the Empress of All the Russias, their heirs and successors, as well as between their empires and respective subjects, shall cease from today and for always. They shall be buried in eternal oblivion and in the future a solid and durable peace on land and on sea shall exist between them. A constant friendship and durable harmony shall be established and maintained, in as much as the Articles of the Treaty of Peace currently agreed upon shall be observed with frankness and sincerity, śo that neither of the two Parties may attempt, secretly or overtly, any scheme or expedition against the other. As a result of the renewal of such a sincere friendship, the two High Contracting Parties respectively grant an amnesty and general pardon, without exception, to all their subjects who may have offended either of them; [they] shall liberate those subjects who are in galleys or in prison, permitting, moreover, all those who have emigrated or been banished to return to their homes, and promising after the peace to restore to them the goods and honors which they had previously enjoyed, without making them suffer the least insult, prejudice, or offense, but on the contrary receiving them, as all their compatriots, under the protection of the laws and customs of the country.

ART. 2. The present Treaty of Peace confirms and ratifies the Treaty concluded and signed 10/21 July 1774, the Explanatory Convention of 10/21 March 1779 (3 Rebiyulevvel 1193),[1] the Treaty of Commerce of 10/21 June 1783 (21[2] Recep 1197) and the Act concluded 28 December 1783/8 January 1784 concerning incorporation into Russia of the Crimea and the Peninsula of Taman, establishing the Kuban River as a boundary; and the two High Contracting Powers undertake to observe solemnly and to execute exactly and faithfully all the Articles of these Treaties, that have in no way been changed by the present or by earlier Treaties.

ART. 3. In virtue of Article 2 of the preliminaries, which establishes that the Dnestr shall serve forever as the boundary separating their two Empires, the territory situated on the right bank of the river shall be returned to the Sublime Porte and shall remain forever incontestably under its domination, as, on the contrary, all the territory situated on the left bank of the same river shall remain forever incontestably under Russian domination.

ART. 4. In view of the said clause on the boundaries of the two Empires and of Article 4 of the Preliminaries, which establishes that all the other frontiers of the two Empires shall remain as they were at the beginning of the present war and that all the lands which during the hostilities were taken by Russian troops shall be returned to the Sublime Porte with all the fortifications in their present state, Her Majesty the Empress restores Bessarabia to [the Sublime Porte] as well as the localities of Bender, Akkerman, Kilya, and Ismail, and all the cities and villages that comprise this Province.

Moreover, Her Majesty the Empress returns to the Sublime Porte the Province of Moldavia with its cities and villages and all that it comprises, on the following conditions, which the Sublime Porte promises faithfully to fulfill:

1. To observe and execute solemnly all that has been stipulated in favor of the two Provinces of Wallachia and Moldavia in the Treaty of Peace concluded 10/21 July 1774, in the Explanatory Convention concluded 10/21 March 1779 (3 Rebiyulevvel 1193),[3] as well as in the Act of 28 December 1783/8 January 1784, which the Grand Vezir signed in the name of the Porte.

2. Not to demand from these Provinces any reimbursement of debts in arrears, of whatever nature.

3. Not to demand any taxes or payments from these districts for the duration of the war but, on the contrary, in consideration of the damages and devastation that they have suffered in the said war, to free them from all charges and taxation whatsoever for two years from the time of the ratification of the present Treaty.

4. To permit families that wish to establish themselves elsewhere freely to leave their districts and to take their goods with them; [to give] them time to inform their relatives, subjects of the Ottoman Empire, to sell their movable or immovable [goods] to other subjects of the Ottoman Empire according to the laws of the land; and, finally, to put their affairs in order, a reprieve of fourteen months shall be granted them, from the day of the exchange of the ratifications of the present Treaty.

ART. 5. As a proof of the sincerity with which the two High Contracting Parties

---

1. The Noradounghian text reads 20 Cemaziyelahir 1193, which was the date on which ratifications were exchanged.

2. The Noradounghian text reads "20."

3. See fn. 1 above.

desire to restore peace and good harmony betweeen them for the present and to consolidate [it] for the future and to banish everything that might furnish a pretext for dispute, the Sublime Porte promises, by renewing the *ferman* that it has already issued, severely to prohibit the commanders of the frontiers, [and] the Paşa of Akhaltsikhe [Georgia], from disturbing secretly or publicly from this day, under any pretext whatsoever, the country and the population under the domination of the Khan of Tiflis, and expressly to direct him not to interrupt in any way the friendly and neighborly relations.

ART. 6. The second Article of the present Treaty having confirmed, among other preceding Treaties, the Act of 28 December 1783/8 January 1784 on the incorporation of the Crimea and the peninsula of Taman into the Russian Empire, establishing the Kuban River as a boundary between the two Empires, the Sublime Porte solemnly promises and undertakes to employ all its authority and means to maintain order among the peoples inhabiting the right bank of the Kuban and to prevent them from crossing into the Russian Empire or from secretly or overtly carrying out prejudicial [acts], under any pretext whatsoever, against the Russian inhabitants of the right bank. For this purpose the Sublime Porte shall send to whoever is responsible the most express orders prohibiting, under the most severe penalty, the capture and enslavement of Russian subjects, and after the exchange of the ratifications of the present Treaty, it shall make these prohibitions public in the same localities. If after the arrangements a member of one of the tribes should cross into Russian territory, rob Russian subjects of cattle or any other property, or kidnap them, on the complaint brought against this subject prompt justice shall be done and the pillaged or stolen objects restored. No difficulty shall be made [in conducting] the investigation necessary to discover those who have captured Russian subjects and [to effect] their release. Moreover, the expenses incurred shall be charged to the Porte, and the acknowledged offenders shall be severely punished in the presence of the Russian Commis-

sioner to be named for this purpose by the frontier commander. If, despite all efforts, reparation shall not have been made six months after the date of the complaint, the Sublime Porte undertakes, one month after the demand of the Russian Minister, to pay all the expenses that shall have resulted from these raids. Compensation apart, it is understood that the penalties mentioned above against the disturbers of the peace and good understanding that must prevail between neighbors shall be applied in the field.

ART. 7. As proof of a sincere desire that commerce, the truest and most constant bond of mutual harmony, should flourish with security and profit for the subjects of the two Empires, the Sublime Porte herewith renews Article 6 of the Treaty of Commerce [of 1783] relating to the corsairs of Algiers, Tunis, and Tripoli and stipulates in particular that, if a Russian subject should be captured by an Algerian, Tunisian, or Tripolitan corsair, or if the corsairs should seize his ship or any goods belonging to Russian merchants, [the Sublime Porte] shall use its influence with the Regents to liberate the kidnapped Russian subjects, to restore their ship or goods, and fully to indemnify them. If it should be ascertained by confirmed reports that the fermans were not executed by the said Regencies, the Sublime Porte undertakes, on the demand of the Russian Minister of charge d'affaires, within two months from the date of his demand, or sooner if possible, to pay from its Imperial Treasury the amount of the indemnity.

ART. 8. All prisoners of war and those of both sexes kidnapped in the two Empires, with the exception of Christians in Turkey who have embraced Islam or Muslims in the Russian Empire who have embraced Christianity, shall be freed immediately after the ratification of the present Treaty and without ransom. So, too, shall all kidnapped Christians, without exception and without ransom, namely, ploes, Moldavians, Wallachians, inhabitants of the Peloponnesus and the islands, Georgians, and others. These arrangements shall apply equally, after the conclusion of the present Treaty, to all Russian subjects who may be kidnapped in the Ottoman Empire in any circumstance whatsoever, and Russia promises to act toward subjects of the Porte with the most perfect reciprocity.

ART. 9. To avoid any kind of misunderstanding or error after the armistice in which the present negotiations have been so happily consummated, the Grand Vezir of the Ottoman Porte and the Minister Plenipotentiary of Her Majesty the Empress shall, immediately after the signature of the present Treaty, make known to all commanders of the armies and of the fleets of both Empires that peace and friendship have been reestablished between the two Powers.

ART. 10. Better to cement the peace and friendship that shall unite the two Empires from now on, the High Contracting Parties shall at an agreed time exchange Ambassadors Extraordinary. They shall be received at the frontiers with all honor and ceremony granted by the two Courts to Ambassadors of the most favored Powers. Through the respective Ambassadors the two Sovereigns shall exchange presents in conformity with their dignity.

ART. 11. After the conclusion of this Treaty and the exchange of ratifications by the two Sovereigns, the Russian troops and galley fleet shall evacuate Ottoman territory. However, the obstacles of the advanced season obligating the deferment of this evacuation, the two High Contracting Parties have agreed to fix 15/26 May of the coming year 1792[4] as the final

date when all the troops of Her Majesty the Empress shall retire to the right bank of the Dnestr and the entire galley fleet shall leave the mouth of the Danube. So long as Russian troops shall occupy the districts and the fortresses which in virtue of the present Treaty shall be restored to the Ottoman Porte, the presently established administrative regime shall continue, and the Porte shall not interfere in any way until the moment of complete evacuation. The Russian troops shall continue to receive until then all the provisions, supplies, and necessary objects that have been furnished them up to now.

ART. 12. Fifteen days after the respective Plenipotentiaries gathered at Jassy shall have signed the present Treaty, or sooner if possible, they shall make the exchange that shall give full validity to this salutary work.

ART. 13. The present Treaty happily concluded, assuring perpetual peace to the two Empires, shall be confirmed by ratifications solemnly signed with the hand of their Majesties the Grand Sultan and the Empress of Russia, and the ratifications shall be exchanged in five weeks, or sooner if possible, by the Plenipotentiaries who have signed the Treaty. All the respective Plenipotentiaries have signed the present Treaty and, after having affixed their seals, have reciprocally exchanged [the instruments]. . . .

---

4. The Noradounghian text reads "1795."

35. TREATY OF PEACE AND AMITY: THE UNITED STATES AND THE GARRISON OF ALGIERS
5 September 1795

(Ratified by the United States, Philadelphia, 7 March 1796; Algerine entry into effect, 8 July 1796) [J. H. Kramers's 1930 English translation of the original Turkish text, in Miller, *Treaties and Other International Acts*, 1: 304–12]

The origins of the United States navy go back to a resolution of the House of Representatives on 2 January 1794 for the construction of "a naval force, adequate to the protection of the commerce of the United States against the Algerine corsairs" (as cited by G. Allen, *Our Navy and the Barbary Corsairs*, 1905 p. 48). Before the end of March, the Congress passed an enabling act. Public interest in the creation of a navy was aroused by the sudden recrudescence of piracy against American shipping, and its scale. In October and November 1793 the corsairs had seized eleven American ships; its 109 officers and men were imprisoned or assigned to slave labor in Algiers, pending the payment of ransom by the United States government. (The captives of the only prior incident, the seizure of two ships, which had occurred more than nine years earlier, were still held in Algiers, their number in the interval reduced by death from 21 to 10.) Meanwhile, the Congress also decided to play the Barbary game according to the rules accepted, or laid down, by the maritime states of Western Europe. The American negotiators agreed to pay to the Garrison of Algiers $585,000 for the ransom of the enslaved Americans and for the treaty, and an annual tribute of $21,600 in naval stores or gold, or both. Because the money did not arrive on schedule, the Dey and his Divan, or oligarchic council, raised the fees to $992,463.25. Comparable treaties were concluded with Tripoli on 4 November 1796 and 3 January 1797 (text, with explanatory notes, in Miller, op. cit., 2: 363–85) and with Tunis on 28 August 1797 and 26 March 1799 (text, ibid., pp. 402–26). Although all the Barbary Garrisons sought costly presents, the Algerine treaty was the only one in which the United states undertook to pay an annual tribute. Such treaties did not buy immunity for American—or European—nationals but merely increased the margin of safety for the commerce of the contracting maritime state. Pending the conclusion of the treaties with Tripoli and Tunis, *Claypoole's American Daily Advertiser* (Philadelphia) carried in its issue of 10 June 1796 a warning by the Secretary of State to "merchants and other citizens of the United States" to "see the hazard to which they will expose their property and the liberty of their fellow citizens by engaging, in the present state of things, in commerce within the straights of Gibraltar" [as cited by Miller, op. cit., p. 316]. Cathcart, *Captives*, chaps. 10–12; Miller, op. cit., pp. 312–17; Barnby, *Prisoners of Algiers*; F. Ross, "Mission of Joseph Donaldson, Jr., to Algiers,"; G. Allen, op. cit., chaps. 1–5; Irwin, *Diplomatic Relations of the United States with the Barbary Powers*, chaps. 3–7; Field, *America and the Mediterranean World*, chap. 2; Todd, *Life and Letters of Joel Barlow*; H. and M. Sprout, *Rise of American Naval Power*, chaps. 3–4; Smelser, *Congress Founds the Navy;* Macleod, "Jefferson and the Navy."

. . . The reason for the drawing up of this treaty and the motive for the writing of this convention of good omen, is that on Saturday, the twenty-first day of the month of Safar of this year 1210, there have been negotiations for a treaty of peace between the ruler and commander of the American people, living in the island called America among the isles of the ocean, and the frontier post of the holy war, the garrison of Algiers. To this purpose has been appointed as his Ambassador, Joseph Donaldson, who has, in confirmation of the articles and paragraphs of the present treaty, strengthened the mutual friendship and good understanding in the exalted presence of His Excellency the noble Vizier and powerful Marshal who sits on the throne of lordship, the destructor of tyranny and injustice and the protector of the country, Hassan Pasha—may God grant to him what he wishes; and in the presence of all the members of the Divan, of the chiefs of the victorious garrison, and of the victorious soldiers. This peace treaty has been concluded, together with the contractual promise to give annually to the garrison of Algiers 12,000 Algerian gold pieces, provided that, in equivalence of these 12,000 gold pieces, being the price of the peace, there may be ordered and imported for our garrison and our arsenal, powder, lead, iron, bullets, bombshells, bomb stones, gun stones, masts, poles, yards, anchor chains, cables, sailcloth, tar, pitch, boards, beams, laths, and other necessaries, provided that the price of all the ordered articles shall be accounted for, so that, if this is equal to 12,000 gold pieces, it shall be all right, but if the price of the articles is higher, it shall be paid to them, and if there remains something to our credit, they promise to complete it. If, before the conclusion of our peace, our vessels of war have captured vessels of the said nation, these shall not be restored and shall remain our prizes, but if our war vessels capture one of their ships after the date of the conclusion of the peace treaty, it is promised that this ship shall be given back.

All this have been put down in the present document, which shall be consulted whenever needed and according to which both parties shall act.

ART. 1. The statements of the first article are that in this year 1210 an agreement has been reached between the ruler of America, George Washington, President, our friend and actually the Governor of the States of the island of America, and the lord of our well-preserved garrison of Algiers, His Highness Hassan Pasha—may God grant to him what he wishes—the Dey, together with the Agha of his victorious army, his minister, all the members of the Divan, and all his victorious soldiers, and equally between the subjects of both parties. According to this agreement our peace and friendship shall be steady and has been confirmed. After this date nothing has been left that is contrary to our peace or that may disturb it.[1]

ART. 2. The statements of the second article are that when large or small ships belonging to our friend the ruler of America, and equally ships belonging to his subjects, arrive in the port of Algiers or in other ports dependent on Algiers, and they sell from their goods according to the ancient usage, there shall be taken a duty of 5 piasters from every 100 piasters, in the same way as this is paid, according to the treaties, by the English, the Dutch, and the Swedes, and that no more shall be taken. Also that if they wish to take back their unsold goods and reembark them, nobody shall require

anything from them, and equally that nobody in the said ports shall do them harm or lay hand upon them.

ART. 3. The statements of the third article are that if war vessels or merchant vessels belonging to our friend the American ruler meet on the open sea with war vessels or merchant vessels belonging to Algiers, and they become known to each other, they shall not be allowed to search or to molest each other, and that none shall hinder the other from wending its own way with honor and respect. Also, that whatever kind of travelers there are on board, and wherever they go with their goods, their valuables, and other properties, they shall not molest each other or take anything from each other, nor take them to a certain place and hold them up, nor injure each other in any way.

ART. 4. The statements of the fourth article are that if war vessels of Algiers meet with American merchant vessels, large or small, and this happens out of the places under the rule of America, there shall be sent only a shallop, in which, besides the rowers, two persons shall take place; on their arrival no more than two persons shall go on board the ship, the commander of the said ship having to give permission, and after the showing of the Government passport, these persons shall perform quickly the formalities with regard to the ship, and return, after which the merchant vessel shall wend its own way.

Further, that if war vessels of the American ruler meet with war vessels or merchant vessels of Algiers, and these vessels are in possession of a passport delivered by the ruler of Algiers or the American Consul residing in Algiers, nobody may touch anything belonging to the said vessel, but it shall wend its way in peace.

Further, that the war vessels of Algiers, large or small, shall not touch Americans not possessed of American passports within a period of eighteen months after the date of the passports given by reason of the peace treaty and after the date of the peace treaty, and they shall not hinder them

---

1. Each article concludes with the word "salaam," salutation or peace, which was left untranslated, and with the date "21 Safar 1210," which has been omitted.

from going their way. Equally, if the war vessels of the American ruler meet with Algerian ships, they shall not prevent them from continuing their journey in the same way, within a period of eighteen months, but they shall wend peacefully their way.

Further that our friend the American ruler shall not give a passport to any crew not being under his rule and not belonging to his own people; if an American passport is found in the hands of a crew not belonging to his own people, we shall take them as prize, for this is not covered by the stipulations of this peace treaty. This has been expressly stated in this article in order to prevent a rupture of peace; so it should not be neglected.

ART. 5. The statements of the fifth article are that none of the captains of Algerian ships or of their officers or commanders shall take anybody by force from American ships into their own ships or bring such a person to other places, that they shall not interrogate them on account of anything or do them harm, whatever kind of people they may be; as long as these are on American ships, they shall not molest them.

ART. 6. The statements of the sixth article are that if a ship of the American ruler or belonging to his subjects shall be stranded on one of the coasts of the territory under Algerian rule and is wrecked, nobody shall take anything from their properties or goods or plunder them.

Also, that if such a thing should happen, their goods shall not be taken to the customhouse, nor shall there be done any damage to their people, and if a similar thing should happen in the places that are under the rule of Algiers, the inhabitants shall do anything in their power to give every possible aid and assistance and help them to bring their goods on dry places.

ART. 7. The statements of the seventh article are that no Algerian ship, small or large, shall, with the permission and the authority of the ruler of Algiers, be equipped from countries at war with the ruler of America and commit acts of war against the Americans.

ART. 8. The statements of the eighth article are that if an American merchant buys a prize in Algiers, or if an Algerian cruiser captain who has taken a prize on the open sea sells his prize to an American merchant, either in Algiers or on the sea, so that it is bought immediately from the captain, and there is drawn up a document concerning this sale, and if he meets afterwards another war vessel from Algiers, nobody shall molest the merchant who has bought this prize, nor shall he prevent him from wending peacefully his way.

ART. 9. The statements of the ninth article are that the inhabitants of Tunis, Tripoli, Sale, or others shall in no wise bring the people or the goods of American ships, large or small, to the territory under the rule of Algiers, nor shall there be given permission to sell them nor shall they be allowed to be sold.

ART. 10. The statements of the tenth article are that if the warships of the American ruler bring to Algiers, or to ports under Algerian rule, prizes or goods captured by them, nobody shall hinder them from doing with their booty as they wish, namely, selling it or taking it with them.

Also, that American war vessels shall not pay any tithes or duties whatever.

Further, that if they wish to buy anything for provisions, the inhabitants shall give it to them at the same price as they sell it to others and ask no more.

Likewise, if those people want to charter ships for the transport of goods to whatever region, province, or port, be it to Smyrna or from Constantinople to this region, or for the transport of travelers from Smyrna or other provinces, or in order to convey pilgrims to Egypt, they may charter those ships at reasonable prices, in the same way as other peoples, and from our side they shall not be opposed by pretexts such as that it is contraband or that it is not allowed among us, so that we do not allow those ships to leave.

ART. 11. The statements of the eleventh article are that if war vessels belonging to our friend the American ruler come to anchor in front of Algiers, and a slave, being an American or of another nationality, takes refuge on board the said war vessel, the ruler of Algiers may claim this slave, at which request the commander of the war vessel shall make this fugitive slave leave his ship and deliver him into the presence of the ruler of Algiers. If the slave is not to be found and reaches a country of unbelievers, the commander of the ship shall pledge his word that he shall return and bring him to Algiers.

Art. 12. The statements of the twelfth article are that from this time onward the subjects of the American ruler shall not be bought, nor sold, nor taken as slaves, in the places under the rule of Algiers.

Also, that since there is friendship with the American ruler, he shall not be obliged to redeem against his will slaves belonging to him, but that this shall be done at the time he likes and that it shall depend on the generosity and the solicitude of the friends and relations of the slaves.

Further, that there shall be put no term or time for the redeeming of prisoners, that the amount which shall be found convenient shall be paid in due order, and that there shall be negotiations about the price with the masters of the slaves; nobody shall oblige the masters to sell their slaves at an arbitrary price, whether they be slaves of the State, of others, or of the Pasha; but if the redeemed persons are American subjects, there shall not be asked of them more than of other nations in similar circumstances.

Also, that if the Algerian vessels of war capture a ship belonging to a nation with which they are at war, and there are found Americans among the crew of this ship, these shall not be made slaves if they are in possession of a pass, nor shall there be done harm to their persons and goods; but if they are not in possession of a pass they shall be slaves and their goods and properties shall be taken.

Art. 13. The statements of the thirteenth article are that if one of the merchants of the American ruler or one of his subjects shall die in Algiers or in one of the dependencies of Algiers, the ruler of Algiers or other persons shall not touch in any way the deceased's money, property, or goods; if he has designated before his death an executor, nobody else shall touch any part of his property or goods, either if the executor mentioned is present in Algiers or if he is not there. Accordingly, the person designated as executor by the deceased shall take the properties and the goods, and nobody else shall touch the slightest part of it; so shall it be. The executor or the person delegated by him as his representative shall make an inventory of his money and property, take possession of it, and forward it in due time to the heir.

Further, that if no subject of the American ruler is present, the American Consul shall made an inventory of the said deceased's money and goods and take possession of them and keep them in charge until the arrival of his relations living in their own country.

Art. 14. The statements of the fourteenth article are that neither in Algiers itself nor in its dependencies shall the American merchants be obliged to purchase goods which they do not desire, but they shall be free to purchase the goods they desire.

Also, that the ships visiting the ports of Algiers shall not be molested in this way— that goods which they do not wish be put into the ships.

Further, that neither the American Consul nor anyone else, in case an American subject is unable to pay his debts, shall be held responsible for those debts and be obliged to pay, unless some persons, according to their free will, are bound for the debtor.

Art. 15. The statements of the fifteenth article are that if one of the subjects of the American ruler has a suit at law with a Mohammedan or with some one subjected to the rule of Algiers, the said suit at law shall be settled in the presence of His Excellency the Dey and the honored Divan, without intervention of anybody else. If there occurs a suit at law among those people themselves, the American Consul shall decide their disputes.

Art. 16. The statements of the sixteenth article are that should one of the subjects of the American ruler have a fight with a Mohammedan, so that one wounds the other or kills him, each one shall be punished according to the prescriptions of the law of his own country, that is, according to the custom in all other places. If, however, an American kills a Mohammedan and flies and escapes after the murder, neither the American Consul in Algiers nor other Americans shall be compelled to answer for him.

Art. 17. The statements of the seventeenth article are that the American Consul now and in future, without regard to who he is, shall be free to circulate without fear, while nobody shall molest his person or his goods.

Also, that he may appoint anyone whom he desires as dragoman or as broker.

Also, that whenever he wishes to go no board a ship or to take a walk outside, nobody shall hinder him.

Further, that a place shall be designated for the practice of their void religious ceremonies, that a priest whom they need for their religious instruction may dwell there, and that the American slaves present in Algiers, either belonging to the Government or to other peoples, may go to the house of the Consul and practice their vain religious ceremonies without hindrance from the chief slave guard or from their masters.

ART. 18. The statements of the eighteenth article are that now there reigns between us peace and friendship, but that if in future there should occur a rupture of our present state of peace and friendship, and there should be caused trouble on both sides, the American Consul, and besides him the subjects of the American ruler either in Algiers or in its dependencies, may not be hindered either in peace or in trouble, and that whenever they wish to leave, nobody shall prevent them from leaving with their goods, properties, belongings, and servants, even if such a person be born in the country of Algiers.

ART. 19. The statements of the nineteenth article are that a subject of the American ruler, to whatever country he goes or from whatever country he comes, and to whatever kind of people he belongs, shall not be molested in his person, goods, property, belongings, or servants, in case he meets with Algerian vessels, large or small.[2] Equally, if an Algerian is found on board a ship belonging to enemies of the American ruler, they shall not be molested in any way in their person, their property, their

goods, their money, or their servants, but the properties of these people shall not be regarded with disdain, and they shall always be treated in a friendly manner.

ART. 20. The statements of the twentieth article are that every time that a naval commander of the American King, our friend, arrives off Algiers, the American Consul shall inform the commander as soon as the vessel is seen; after the said captain has anchored before the port, the commander of Algiers shall, in honor of the American ruler, order a salute of twenty-one guns from the citadel, after which the captain of the American ruler shall answer gun for gun, and, as the said vessel is a vessel of the King, there shall be given provisions according to the custom, in honor of the King.

ART. 21. The statements of the twenty-first article are that there shall not be asked dity and taxes for goods that are destined for the house of the American Consul, consisting of eatables, drinkables, other necessaries, and presents.

ART. 22. The statements of the twenty-second article are that if there occurs from this time onward a disturbance of our peaceful relations, from whatever side this happens, this shall not rupture our peace, but the peace shall be maintained and our friendship shall not be disturbed. The person injured, to whatever party he belongs, shall claim justice. If, however, the fault and the guilt are on both sides, or on the side of a subject, and the matter is kept secret, our belief in our friendship shall remain and our word shall remain as good as ever.

---

2. The Turkish text does not mention the condition that these Americans and their goods are on ships belonging to enemies of Algiers, but this, of course, is the meaning.

36. DECREE OF THE FRENCH DIRECTORY INSTRUCTING NAPOLEON TO LAUNCH THE EGYPTIAN CAMPAIGN
12 April 1798

[Translated from the French text in Napoleon I, *Correspondance*, 4: 52–53]

"Napoleon's policies for the Near East," we are told by one Western authority, "account in great part for the ultimate collapse of his imposing empire." This assertion, accurate as far as it goes, relates the Western side of the story. Examining the same events from Istanbul, Tehran, and Cairo, we must conclude that Napoleon's schemes in the decade after 1798 for defeating England by occupation of, or alliance with and transit through, Middle East states produced basic changes in the internal politics of those states and in European diplomacy toward them. The French occupation (1798–1801) brought Mehmed 'Ali to Egypt and led to his personal transformation from an obscure Macedonian tobacco vendor into the founder of modern Egypt. This, in turn, helped hasten the modernization effort within the Imperial Ottoman Government. It also inaugurated the nineteenth-century phase of the Eastern Question among the European powers and, as regards their relations with the Muslim East, marked the transition in primary emphasis from commercial to political diplomacy. Napoleon himself drafted the following decree for the French Directory. But the Directory was pleased to have the popular general become enmeshed in an overseas venture. The literature on the French occupation of Egypt is enormous. Only a sample is mentioned here. Herold, *Bonaparte in Egypt*; Napoleon I, op. cit., vols. 4–6 (original documentation) and vols. 29–30 (Bonaparte's retrospective account of his Egyptian campaign); Jonquière, *L'expédition d'Egypte*, 5 vols. (documentation); Berthier, *Relation des campagnes du général Bonaparte*; Bertrand, *Napoléon Ier guerre d' orient*; Boulay de la Meurthe, *Le directoire et l'expédition d'Egypte*; Charles-Roux, *Les origines de l'expédition d'Egypte*, and *l'Angleterre et l'expédition française*, 2 vols. (the four preceding sources give French interpretative accounts); Ghorbal, *Beginnings of the Egyptian Question*, chaps. 1, 2, 6 (an Egyptian view); R. Wilson, *History of the British Expedition to Egypt*; Walsh, *Journal of the Late Campaign in Egypt*; Baldwin, *Political Recollections* (British attitudes); see also references to Doc. 37.

The Executive Directory,

Considering that the Beys who have sized the Government of Egypt have established intimate ties with the English and have placed themselves under [the English's] absolute dependence; that in consequence they have engaged in open hostilities and most horrible cruelties against the French, whom they vex, pillage, and assassinate daily;

Considering that it is the duty of the Republic to pursue its enemies wherever they may be and in any place where they engage in hostile activities;

Considering, in addition, that the infamous treason which enabled Britain to become mistress of the Cape of Good Hope has rendered access to India by the customary route very difficult to the vessels of the Republic, it is important to open to the Republican forces another route, to combat the satellites of the English Government, and to dry up the source of its corruptive riches;

Decrees as follows:

ART. 1. The General-in-Chief of the Army of the Orient shall direct the land and sea forces under his command to Egypt and shall take over that country.

ART. 2. He shall expel the English from all their possessions in the Orient which he can reach and shall in particular destroy all their factories [trading posts] on the Red Sea.

ART. 3. He shall have the Isthmus of Suez cut and shall take all necessary measures to insure to the French Republic the free and exclusive possession of the Red Sea.

ART. 4. He shall improve by all means at his disposal the conditions of the natives of Egypt.

ART. 5. He shall maintain, as much as this depends on him, good understanding with the Grand Seigneur [the Ottoman Sultan] and his immediate subjects.

ART. 6. The present decree shall not be printed.

37. NAPOLEON'S PROCLAMATION TO THE EGYPTIANS
2 July 1798

[Translated from the French text in Napoleon I, *Correspondance*, 4: 191–92]

Napoleon issued the following statement immediately upon his triumphant entry into Alexandria, proclaiming himself the protector of Islam and savior of the Egyptian people. The identical theme, it will be readily recognized, was employed by Kaiser Wilhelm II in 1898 in his visit to Damascus and by Mussolini and Hitler four decades later in their respective efforts to win friends and destroy the influence of Britain and France in the Middle East. Ghorbal, *Beginnings of the Egyptian Question*, chap. 2; Charles-Roux, *Bonaparte* (also, the English translation by E. W. Dickes); Lacroix, *Bonaparte en Egypte*; Dennis, *Eastern Problems*, chap. 3; Ingram, "Preview of the Great Game in Asia"; Turki, *Chronique d'Egypte*; see also references to Doc. 36.

Bonaparte, member of the National Institute, General-in-Chief:

For a long time, the Beys governing Egypt have insulted the French nation and its traders. The hour of their punishment has come.

For too long, this assortment of slaves bought in Georgia and the Caucasus has tyrannized the most beautiful part of the world; but God, on Whom all depends, has ordained that their empire is finished.

Peoples of Egypt, you will be told that I have come to destroy your religion; do not believe it! Reply that I have come to restore your rights, to punish the usurpers, and that more than the Mamluks I respect God, his Prophet, and the Quran.

Tell them that all men are equal before God; that wisdom, talents, and virtues alone make them different from one another.

But, what wisdom, what talents, what virtues distinguish the Mamluks, that they should possess exclusively that which makes life pleasant and sweet?

Is there a good piece of land? It belongs to the Mamluks. Is there a pretty slave, a fine horse, a beautiful house? They belong to the Mamluks.

If Egypt is their farm, let them show the lease which God has granted them. But God is just and merciful to the people.

All Egyptians will be called to administer all places; the wisest, the best educated, and the most virtuous will govern, and the people will be happy.

Of old, there used to exist here, in your midst, big cities, big canals, a thriving commerce. What has destroyed all this, but Mamluk avarice, in justice and tyranny?

Qadis, Shaykhs, Imams, Çorbacıs [commanders of Janissary regiments], tell the people that we are the friends of the true Mussulmans.

Did we not destroy the Pope, who said that war should be waged against the Mussulmans? Did we not destroy the Knights of Malta, because those insane people thought that God wanted them to wage war against the Mussulmans? Have we not been for centuries the friends of the Grand Seigneur (may God fulfill his wishes!) and the enemies of his enemies? Have not the Mamluks; on the contrary, always revolted against the authority of the Grand Seigneur, whom they still ignore? They do nothing but satisfy their own whims.

Thrice happy are those who join us! They shall prosper in wealth and rank. Happy are those who remain neutral! They will have time to know us and they will take our side.

But unhappiness, threefold unhappiness, to those who arm themselves for the Mamluks and fight against us! There shall be no hope for them; they shall perish.

ART. 1. All villages within a radius of three leagues from the locations through which the Army will pass will send a deputation to inform the Commanding General that they are obedient, and to notify him that they have hoisted the Army flag: blue, white, and red.

ART. 2. All villages taking up arms against the Army shall be burnt down.

ART. 3. All villages submitting to the Army will hoist, together with the flag of the Grand Seigneur, our friend, that of the Army.

ART. 4. The Shaykhs shall have seals placed on the possessions, houses, [and] properties belonging to the Mamluks, and will see that nothing is looted.

ART. 5. The Shaykhs, the Qadis, and the Imams shall continue to perform their functions. Each inhabitant shall remain at home, and prayers shall continue as usual. Each man shall thank God for the destruction of the Mamluks and shall shout Glory to the Sultan! Glory to the French Army, friend! May the Mamluks be cursed, and the peoples of Egypt blessed!

38. TREATIES OF ALLIANCE AND COMMERCE: BRITISH INDIA AND PERSIA
10 October 1799–28 January 1801

(Ratified by the acting governor general of India, 10 January 1807)
[Instructions to Malcolm from M. Martin, *Despatches, Minutes, and Correspondence of the Marquess of Wellesley*, 5: 82–90; treaty texts from Aitchison, *Collection of Treaties . . . relating to India* (5th ed.), 13: 45–53]

The Qajar dynasty (1796–1925) reunited Persia under a central government after a half-century of political anarchy. With the appearance of a new dynasty, the old commercial privileges lapsed, and the East India Company had to negotiate fresh ones. To the commercial interests were added political, after Napoleon's appearance in Egypt in the summer of 1798 and the company's fear of an attempted French invasion of India with possible Persian collaboration. The anxiety was compounded by the designs on northern India of Zaman Shah, the Afghan ruler at Kabul. The governor general of India on 10 October 1799 instructed a young Scottish captain named John Malcolm, whom he had appointed special ambassador to Tehran, the Qajar capital, to negotiate treaties that would serve the political interests of British India and the United Kingdom and the commercial interests of the company. Some thirteen months

passed before Malcolm reached his destination and was formally presented to Fath
'Ali Shah (1797–1834). The envoy's lavish gifts and the promise of arms hastened the
drafting of the desired agreements. Although the captain bargained better than
instructed, since the political as well as the commercial arrangements were designed
as permanent, the governor general nevertheless praised—but did not ratify—
Malcolm's treaties. Indeed, the company withheld formal ratification, sought by the
shah in 1802 and 1804. By the time the acting governor general finally ratified the
treaties early in 1807, the shah had lost interest and he repudiated them (see Kelly,
Britain and the Persian Gulf, p. 80). The dating of the treaties is based on that in
Malcolm's private diary, as reported by his official biographer, who was apparently
more precise on this point than was Aitchison. The preambular flourishes and commands of the shah enjoining his officials and subjects "cheerfully [to] comply and
execute the clear sense and meaning" of the two instruments have been omitted.
Kelly, ibid., chap. 2; Kaye, *Major-General Sir John Malcolm*, vol. 1, chap. 7; Sykes,
History of Persia, vol. 2, chap. 75; Rawlinson, *England and Russia in the East*, chap.
1; Ramazani, *Foreign Policy of Iran*, chap. 2.

1. Instructions to Captain John Malcolm, Fort William, 10 October 1799

1. The right honourable the Governor-
General having appointed you . . . [in]
August to be envoy from the Government-
General in India to the court of Baba
Khan, the present King of Persia, his
Lordship now directs me to furnish you
with the following instructions for the
regulation of your conduct in that mission.

2. You are to proceed with all convenient
expedition to Bombay, the government of
which will be directed to furnish you with
one of the honourable Company's cruizers
for the purpose of conveying yourself and
suite to Bussorah.

3. At Bombay you will also be furnished
by the Governor-in-Council with copies of
all the correspondence which has passed
between him and Mehdi Alli Khan, a native
agent employed for some time past by Mr.
Duncan, under the instructions of the
Governor-General, in opening and conducting a negotiation at the court of Persia,
with a view to preventing Zemaun Shah
from executing his frequently renewed
projects against Hindostan.

4. No accounts have yet been received of
the arrival of Mehdi Alli Khan at Tahiran,
where Baba Khan holds his court. It may
be expected, however, that before you can
leave Bombay such advices will be received
from Mehdi Alli Khan, as may be of considerable use in regulating the measures

proper to be pursued by you either before
or after you shall have reached your destination.

5. Mehdi Alli Khan is the Company's
Agent at Bushire, and may possibly have
returned thither from his temporary mission to the court of Persia by the time of
your arrival at Bushire, where it will be
proper you should touch on your way to
Bussorah. But however this may be, Mehdi
Alli will be directed by the Governor of
Bombay to place himself under your orders,
and you will accordingly either take him
with you from Bushire, should you find
him there, or retain him with you should
you find him at the court of Persia, or suffer
him to resume the duties of his station at
Bushire, as you may judge best for the
public service.

6. You must exercise your discretion
with regard to the degree of confidence to
be reposed in Mehdi Alli and to the manner in which he shall be employed. Some
circumstances make his circumspection
doubtful; but as there appears no ground
for questioning his integrity, or zeal for the
public service, his Lordship thinks it may
be in his power to afford you some useful
assistance in the progress of your mission.

7. If the season should admit of it, his
Lordship wishes you to touch at Muscat on
your way up the Gulph. You will be furnished with letters from his Lordship to be
eventually delivered to the Imaum of
Muscat and to his Minister. You will

receive from the government of Bombay copies of such parts of the correspondence of Mehdi Alli Khan as relates to his negotiation at Muscat in 1798. The Governor-General has but too much reason to believe, that, notwithstanding the engagements entered into on that occasion by the Imaum, that Prince has continued as favourably disposed as ever towards the French. During your stay therefore at Muscat, you must omit no endeavours to prevail on the government of that place to execute faithfully the condition of the treaty of 1798, and effectually renounce all sort of connection with the French. His Lordship deems it unnecessary to suggest to you the topics proper to be employed for this purpose. The government of Bombay will on your application communicate to you all the information in their possession relative to the grounds on which the fidelity of the Imaum to his engagements has been suspected.

8. The Persian Translator has been directed to furnish you with copies and extracts of all the correspondence of the Governor-Gerneral with the late Tippoo Sultaun, and of such of the papers found at Seringapatam as are calculated to prove the inimical designs entertained by that Prince against the English and their allies. You will make such use of these documents both at Muscat and every where else in the course of your mission as may appear to you to be necessary. You will particularly advert to the gross calumny which Tippoo Sultaun is now known to have industriously circulated in every Mahommedan state about the beginning of the present year; and which imputed to the British Government in India an avowed design of destroying every Mussulman Power in Asia. Mr. Edmonstone will point out to you the particular passage in his Lordship's letter of the 8th of November 1798 to Tippoo Sultaun, on which the latter affected to build this extraordinary accusation; and it will be easy for you to demonstrate its utter falsehood and absurdity even to the most bigoted Mahommedans.

9. You will endeavour to adjust while at Muscat any points relating to our interests at that place, which the government of Bombay may recommend particularly to your attention; but you are not to permit any object of this nature to delay your voyage to Persia.

10. From Bussorah you will proceed to the court of Persia either by the route of Bagdad, or by such other route as you may find to be most eligible. In case you should visit Bagdad, you will deliver to the Bashaw of that place the letter from the right honourable the Governor-General which you will receive with these instructions.

11. You will communicate fully and unreservedly both with Mr. Manesty the Company's Resident at Bussorah, and with Mr. Jones at Bagdad on the object of your mission, and you will arrange with those gentlemen the steps to be taken with a view to establishing as quick and secure a communication by letter between yourself and them as may be practicable.

12. You will apprize the court of Persia of your deputation as soon as possible after your arrival, either at Bussorah or at Bagdad, intimating in general terms, that the object of it is to revive the good understanding and friendship which antiently subsisted between the Persian and British Governments. It is not desirable that you should be more particular with any person who may be sent to meet you, or to ascertain the design of your mission; but if much pressed on the subject you may signify, that, among other things, you have been instructed to endeavour to extend and improve the commercial intercourse between Persia and the British possessions in India.

13. The primary purpose of your mission is to prevent Zemaun Shah from invading Hindostan; or should he actually invade it, to oblige him, by alarming him for the safety of his own dominions, to relinquish the expedition. The next object of his Lordship is to engage the court of Persia to act vigorously and heartily against the French in the event of their attempting at any time to penetrate to India by any route in which it may be practicable for the King of Persia to oppose their progress.

14. With respect to the first of these objects, your manner of negotiating it will necessarily turn, in a great measure, upon the progress which Mehdi Alli Khan shall have made previously to your arrival at the court of Persia in pursuit of the same end. Should he have succeeded in disposing that

court favourably towards his Lordship's views, you will confirm and improve this advantage by every means in your power. You will begin by expatiating on the mutual benefits which cannot fail to accrue to both nations from the establishment of a solid friendship between them, and of a commercial intercourse regulated on liberal and enlightened principles between the Persian dominions and the British possessions in India. The information necessary to enable you to state the advantages of a commercial connection in the most forcible manner cannot be any where better obtained than at Bombay; and accordingly that government will be directed to furnish you with such instructions and materials for this purpose as they may judge proper.

15. The period for agitating the question respecting Zemaun Shah must be regulated in some degree by the information which you may be in possession of relative to the motions of that Prince; and on this account it will be necessary that you should omit no means of obtaining the speediest and most authentic intelligence from his country. The government of Bombay will be instructed to transmit to you, by every opportunity, whatever information of this nature they may receive either from the Governor-General, or from the Residents at Poonah and with Dowlut Rao Scindiah, both of whom will be particularly directed to correspond punctually with Mr. Duncan on this subject.

16. If you should learn from authority to be depended on, that there is no probability of Zemaun Shah suddenly disturbing the tranquillity of Hindostan, there will be the less necessity for your immediately entering upon this point of your negotiation; but if you should be well assured of the contrary, no time must be lost in opening the business.

17. It is proper you should know, that the solicitude of the Governor-General with regard to Zemaun Shah arises at present almost solely from considerations which have reference to the actual circumstances of Oude: last year it was necessarily excited in a great degree by the nature of our situation with respect to Tippoo Sultaun. But now, if the civil and military branches of the Vizier's administration were upon that footing on which his Lordship is desirous (and not without hopes of being able) to place them, he would cease to feel any further degree of anxiety relative to the projects of Zemaun Shah, than what must always be raised by a prospect of any interruption to the tranquillity of our possessions in India.

18. It is this peculiar state of affairs with regard to Oude which renders it of the greatest importance, that Zemaun Shah should be prevented from making any attempt upon Hindostan for three years longer; by which time his Lordship expects that the Vizier's frontier will be put in such a respectable posture of permanent defence as, if it should not effectually discourage any invasion of his Excellency's territories, will at least render it difficult for a foreign enemy to make any serious impression upon them.

19. Upon this principle, his Lordship authorizes you, whenever circumstances shall appear to you to require the measure, to conclude a treaty with the court of Persia on the following basis;

First. The King of Persia to engage to prevent Zemaun Shah, by such means as shall be concerted between his Majesty and you, from invading any part of Hindostan, and in the event of his crossing the Attock, or of the actual invasion of Hindostan by that Prince, the King of Persia to pledge himself to the adoption of such measures as shall be necessary for the purpose of compelling Zemaun Shah to return immediately to the defence of his own dominions.

Second. The Company to engage to pay to the King of Persia for this service, either an annual fixed subsidy of three lacs of rupees during the period that this treaty shall continue in force; or a proportion, not exceeding one-third, of such extraordinary expense as his Majesty shall at any time actually and bonâ fide incur for the specific purposes stated in the foregoing article. His Lordship leaves it to your discretion to adjust the amount of subsidy on either of these principles, according as may appear to you to be most favourable to the interests of the Company. But he is of opinion, that by absolutely fixing the amount of subsidy in the first instance many grounds of dispute and dissatisfaction would be precluded, which would otherwise be liable to arise; while being fixed at the standard which has been mentioned, the total charge to the Company for the term of the treaty would probably fall very short of what might be justly claimed under the other arrangement in the course of a single year.

Third. The Company not to be entitled to a participation in any conquests or spoils which may be acquired from Zemaun Shah in the event of hostilities between him and the King of Persia.

Fourth. The subsidy to be discharged by the Company in money and merchandize in such proportions, and by such instalments, as you shall settle with the court of Persia.

Fifth. The duration of this treaty to be limited to three years, and to be afterwards renewable at the option of the contracting parties.

20. His Lordship in fixing the subsidy at three lacs of rupees per annum, has been governed by a general consideration of the high comparative value of money in Persia. But if the principle of a fixed subsidy should be adopted, and if you should find an augmentation of the sum absolutely necessary, his Lordship empowers you to increase it to three and an half, or even to four lacs of rupees.

21. It has occurred to the Governor-General, that you may possibly find it practicable, by the judicious distribution of presents, and offers of military and other supplies to accomplish his Lordship's objects with respect to Zemaun Shah without being obliged to bind the Company to the payment of any immediate or eventual subsidy; his Lordship recommends this point to your deliberate consideration, not doubting that you will exert yourself to the utmost to obtain the objects of your mission at as light a charge as possible to the Company.

22. With respect to the commercial points to be negotiated, his Lordship directs me to observe, that, when finally adjusted, they may either be included in a general treaty comprehending all the proposed objects of your mission, or be thrown into the form of a distinct convention, as you may find most convenient. The commercial arrangements, however, should be of a permanent and perpetual nature,

and should not be made to expire with the subsidiary treaty. You have already been referred generally to the government of Bombay for the information necessary on this head; and that government will be directed to form an outline of such commercial arrangements as may appear to them to be desirable, and to submit the same to the Governor-General in Council for the consideration and approbation of his Lordship previously to your finally concluding upon them.

23. In considering the different means by which Zemaun Shah may be kept in check during the period required, you will naturally pay due attention to those which may be derived from the exiled brothers of that Prince, now resident in Persia under the protection of Baba Khan. If occasion should offer, you will cultivate a good understanding with those Princes, but you are not to contract any positive engagements with them without the specific authority of the Governor-General.

24. With respect to the second object of your mission, or the engaging the court of Persia to act eventually against the French, his Lordship deems it unnecessary to furnish you with any detailed instructions. The papers with which you will be furnished, and your own knowledge and reflection will suggest to you all the arguments proper to be used for the purpose of convincing the court of Persia of the deep interest it has in opposing the projects of that nation, and of inducing it to take an active and decisive part against them. If in this event the co-operation of a British naval armament in the Gulph of Persia with the land forces of Baba Khan should be judged expedient, his Lordship directs me to say, that you may confidently promise it, as well as an ample supply of whatever arms or military stores may be required by his Majesty. His Lordship empowers you also, in the case here supposed, and on the condition of the most vigorous and decisive operations being undertaken against the enemy by Baba Khan, to engage to pay to that Prince, during the period of such operations, either a monthly subsidy to be previously fixed, or such a proportion of the expenses actually incurred by him on the occasion, as may be mutually agreed on between you and the court of Persia.

25. The subsidy which it may be stipulated to pay to Baba Khan, in either of the cases stated, must be discharged by funds which you will endeavour to raise by means of bills to be drawn by you either on the Supreme Government, or on the government of Bombay. In case of your being unable to raise the requisite funds by such means, the Governor-General will take the proper measures for making you the remittance from hence either in bills or specie.

26. You will be careful to regulate the conduct of the persons belonging to your mission, during your residence in Persia, in such manner as may most effectually conduce to the honour of the national character, and to the prevention of jealousy or misunderstandings.

27. His Lordship thinks it unnecessary to caution you against submitting to any ceremonies at the court of Persia which can have any tendency to degrade your representative character. He considers it sufficient to observe, that conformity to such usages as you shall find established in th cease of ambassadors from other independent powers can never have such a tendency.

28. With respect to the nature and amount of the presents which it will be proper you should make to the King of Persia and the principal persons of his court, his Lordship confides in your discretion for observing such a degree of economy on this head as may be practicable consistently with a due regard to the honour of the British Government and to the usages of the country.

29. His Lordship authorizes you to purchase on your arrival at Bussorah, or as soon after as you may judge expedient, a sufficient number of horses for the use of the party of dismounted native cavalry ordered to be furnished you from the Presidency of Fort St. George, and to provide them with saddles and the other necessary articles of equipment. His Lordship relies on your mounting, equipping, and maintaining this part of your escort at as moderate a charge as may be practicable.

30. You will endeavour during your residence at the court of Baba Khan to obtain an accurate account of the strength and resources of Zemaun Shah, and of his political relations with his different neighbours, and to establish some means of obtaining hereafter the most correct and speedy information on the subject of his future intentions and movements.

31. His Lordship desires you will keep a regular journal of your public transactions, and that you advise him by every opportunity of the progress of your negotiations and of all important occurrences. It is also his Lordship's direction that you correspond occasionally with the right honourable Henry Dundas and with the Secret Committee of the Court of Directors, on the affairs of your mission. A copy of the cypher No. 11 will be furnished you on application, by the government of Bombay.

32. In the event of the death of Baba Khan, or of any revolution in the government of Persia before you shall have entered into any engagements, you will either suspend or prosecute your negotiations with the new government according to the judgment which you may form of its character, its probable stability, and its means of fulfilling the ends of the proposed alliance.

2. The Political Treaty, 28 January 1801

ART. 1. As long as the sun, illuminating the circle of the two great contracting powers, shines on their sovereign dominions and bestows light on the whole world, the beautiful image of excellent union shall remain fixed on the mirror of duration and perpetuity, the thread of shameful enmity and distance shall be cut, conditions of mutual aid and assistance between the two States shall be instituted, and all causes of hatred and hostility shall be banished.

ART. 2. If the king of the Afghans should ever show a resolution to invade India, which is subject to the government of the monarch (above mentioned) the prince of high rank, the king of England, an army overthrowing mountains, furnished with all warlike stores, shall be appointed from the State of the conspicuous and exalted, high and fixed in power (the king of Persia), to lay waste and desolate the Afghan dominions, and every exertion shall be employed to ruin and humble the above mentioned nation.

ART. 3. Should it happen that the king of the Afghans ever becomes desirous of opening the gates of peace and friendship with the government of the king (of Persia), who is in rank like Solomon, in dignity like Jumsheed, the shade of God! who has bestowed his mercy and kindness on the earth; when negotiations are opened for an amicable adjustment, it shall be stipulated in the peace concluded that the king of the Afghans, or his armies, shall abandon all design of attack on the territories subject to the government of the king above mentioned, who is worthy of royalty, the king of England.

ART. 4. Should ever any king of the Afghans or any person of the French nation commence war and hostilities with the powerful of the ever enduring State (of the king of Persia), the rulers of the government of the king (of England), whose Court is like heaven, and who has been before mentioned, shall (on such event) send as many cannon and warlike stores as possible, with necessary apparatus, attendants, and inspectors, and such supply shall be delivered over at one of the ports of Persia, whose boundaries are conspicuous, to the officers of the high in dignity, the king of Persia.

ART. 5. Should it ever occur that an army of the French nation, actuated by design and deceit, attempts to settle with a view of establishing themselves on any of the islands or shores of Persia, a conjunct force shall be appointed by the two high contracting States to act in co-operation for their expulsion and extirpation, and to destroy and put an end to the foundation of their treason. It is a condition, if such event happens, and the conquering troops (of Persia) march, that the officers of the government of the king (of England), who is powerful as the heavens and as before mentioned, shall load, transport, and deliver (for their service) as great a quantity of necessaries, stores, and provisions as they possibly can. And if ever any of the great men of the French nation express a wish or desire to obtain a place of residence or dwelling on any of the islands or shores of the kingdom of Persia that they may there raise the standard of abode or settlement, such request or representation shall not be consented unto by the high in rank of the State encompassed with justice (the government of Persia), and leave for their residing in such a place shall not be granted.

While time endures, and while the world exists, the contents of this exalted Treaty shall remain an admired picture in the mirror of duration and perpetuity, and submission to the fair image on this conspicuous page shall be everlasting.

3. The Commercial Treaty, 28 January 1801

ART. 1. The merchants of the high contracting States are to travel and carry on their affairs in the territories of both nations in full security and confidence, and the rulers and governors of all cities are to consider it their duty to protect from injury their cattle and goods.

ART. 2. The traders and merchants of the kingdom of England or Hindoostan that are in the service of the English Government shall be permitted to settle in any of the seaports or cities of the boundless empire of Persia (which may God preserve from calamity) that they prefer; and no government duties, taxes, or requisitions shall ever be collected on any goods that are the actual property of either of the governments; the usual duties on such to be taken from purchasers.

ART. 3. Should it happen that either the persons or property (of merchants) are injured or lost by thieves or robbers, the utmost exertions shall be made to punish the delinquents and recover the property. And if any merchant or trader of Persia evades or delays the payment of a debt to the English Government, the latter are authorized to use every possible mode for the recovery of their demands, taking care to do so in communication and with the knowledge of the ruler or governor of the place, who is to consider it as his duty to grant, on such occasion, every aid in his power. And should any merchants of Persia be in India, attending to their mercantile concerns, the officers of the English Government are not to prevent them carrying on their affairs, but to aid and favour them, and the above-mentioned merchants are to recover their debts and demands in the mode prescribed by the customs and laws of the English Government.

ART. 4. If any person in the empire of Persia die indebted to the English Government, the ruler of the place must exert his power to have such demand satisfied before those of any other creditor whatever. The servants of the English Government, resident in Persia, are permitted to hire as many domestic natives of that country as are necessary for the transaction of their affairs; and they are authorised to punish such, in cases of misconduct, in the manner they judge most expedient, provided such punishment does not extend to life or limb; in such cases the punishment to be inflicted by the ruler or governor of the place.

ART. 5. The English are at liberty to build houses and mansions in any of the ports or cities of Persia that they choose, and they may sell or rent all such houses or mansions at pleasure. And should ever a ship belonging to the English Government be in a damaged state in any of the ports of Persia, or one of Persia be in that condition in an English harbour, the Chiefs and rulers of the ports and harbours of the respective nations are to consider it as their duty to give every aid to refit and repair vessels so situated. And if it happens that any of the vessels of either nation are sunk or shipwrecked in or near the ports or shores of either country, on such occasions whatever part of the property is recovered shall be restored to their owners or their heirs, and a just hire is to be allowed by the owners to those who recover it.

FINAL ARTICLE. Whenever any native of England or India, in the service of the English Government, resident in Persia, wishes to leave that country, he is to suffer obstruction from no person, but to be at full liberty to do so, and to carry with him his property.

The Articles of the Treaty between the two States are fixed and determined. That person who turns from God turns from his own soul.

ADDITIONAL ARTICLE. It is further written in sincerity that on iron, lead, steel, broadcloth, and purpetts that are exclusively the property of the English Government, no duties whatever shall be taken from the sellers; a duty not exceeding one per cent. to be levied upon the purchasers. And the duties, imports, and customs which are at this period established in Persia and India (on other goods) are to remain fixed and not to be increased.

Tlhe high in rank Hajee Kulleel Khan Mullick-oo-Tijjar is charged and entrusted with the arrangement and settlement of the remaining points relative to commerce.

39. EAST INDIA COMPANY'S AGREEMENT WITH THE IMAM OF MASQAT EXCLUDING THE FRENCH FROM HIS TERRITORIES
12 October 1798

(Approved by the governor-general of India in Council, 26 April 1800)
[Aitchison, *Collection of Treaties . . . relating to India* (5th ed.), 11: 287–88]

Agents of the East India Company first began to trade in the Persian Gulf area as early as the start of the seventeenth century. But the agreement with the imam of Masqat, concluded in October 1798 as a defensive measure against Napoleon's Egyptian campaign, was the first of a series of acts that gradually placed most of the principalities along the eastern and southern coasts of the Arabian Peninsula in varying degrees of dependence on Great Britain. An agreement of 18 January 1800 (text in Aitchison op. cit., p. 288) stipulated that "an English gentleman of respectability, on the part of the Honourable Company, shall always reside at the port of Muscat, and be an Agent through whom all intercourse between the States shall be conducted." Aitchison, op. cit. (basic documents); Kelly, *Britain and the Persian Gulf*, chap. 2; Rose, "Political Reactions of Bonaparte's Eastern Expedition"; Auzou,

"La France et Muscate"; Salil ibn Raziq, *History of the Imâms and Seyyids of 'Omân;* Maurizi, *History of Seyd Said;* Coupland, *East Africa and Its Invaders,* chap. 4; Curzon, *Persia and the Persian Question,* vol. 2, chap. 27; A. Wilson, *Persian Gulf,* chap. 15; Liebesny, "International Relations of Arabia, the Dependent Areas"; Brinton, "Arabian Peninsula"; Kaye, *Major General Sir John Malcolm,* vol. 1, chap. 7; Ingram, "Preview of the Great Game in Asia."

ART. 1. From the intervention of the Nawab Etmandi Edowla Mirza Mehedy Ally Khan Bahadoor Hurhmut Jung never shall there be any deviation from this Cowl-namah.

ART. 2. From the recital of the said Nawab my heart has become disposed to an increase of the friendship with that State, and from this day forth the friend of that Sircar is the friend of this, and the friend of the Sircar is to be the friend of that; and, in like manner, the enemy of that Sircar is the enemy of this, and the enemy of this is to be the enemy of that.

ART. 3. Whereas frequent applications have been made, and are still [being made] by the French and Dutch people for a Factory, *i.e.,* to seat themselves in either at Maskat or Goombroom [Bandar 'Abbas], or at the other ports of this Sircar, it is therefore written that, whilst warfare shall continue between the English Company and them, never shall, from respect to the Company's friendship, be given to them throughout all my territories a place to fix or seat themselves in, nor shall they get even ground to stand upon within this State.

ART. 4. As there is a person of the French nation, who has been for these several years in my service, and who hath now gone in command of one of my vessels to the Mauritius, I shall, immediately on his return, dismiss him from my service and expel him.

ART. 5. In the event of any French vessel coming to water at Muscat, she shall not be allowed to enter the cove into which the English vessels are admitted, but remain without; and in case of hostilities ensuing here between the French and English ships, the force of this State by land and by sea, and my people, shall take part in hostility with the English, but on the high seas I am not to interfere.

ART. 6. On the occurrence of any shipwreck of a vessel or vessels appertaining to the English, there shall certainly be aid and comfort afforded on the part of this Government, nor shall the property be seized on.

ART. 7. In the port of Abassy (Goombroom) whenever the English shall be disposed to establish a Factory, I have no objection to their fortifying the same and mounting guns thereon, as many as they list, and to forty or fifty English gentlemen residing there, with seven or eight hundred English Sepoys, and for the rest, the rate of duties on goods on buying and selling will be on the same footing as at Bussora [Basrah] and Abushehr [Bushire].

40. TRIPLE ALLIANCE: RUSSIA, GREAT BRITAIN,
AND THE OTTOMAN EMPIRE
23 December 1798/3 January 1799, and 5 January 1799

(Ratifications of the Russian-Ottoman treaty exchanged, Istanbul, 27 December 1798/7 January 1799; superseded, 11/23 September 1805; ratifications of the British-Ottoman treaty exchanged, Istanbul, 23 November 1799; expired, 2 January 1807)
[Russian-Ottoman instrument, translated from the agreed French text in the Turkish State Archives, Muahedeler Tasnifi, nos, 418/1–3; text of the British-Ottoman instrument from *Journals of the House of Commons*, vol. 57 (1801–02), app. (no. 11), p. 702]

Napoleon's invasion of Egypt temporarily dissolved Russian-Ottoman hostility, nurtured over the preceding 120 years by six major wars, and aroused in the British government for the first time genuine concern for preserving the territorial integrity of the sultan's realm. Russia contracted at Istanbul the first defensive alliance with its southern neighbor on 23 December 1798/3 January 1799. The old style date of the agreement commonly occurs in works on the subject, as if it were the new style. The texts of the public and secret treaties that follow appear for the first time in English translation. These instruments, discovered in the State Archives in Istanbul, were the ratified texts that the Tsarist government deposited at the Sublime Porte. The Ottoman government consented for the first time (arts. 1 and 2) to the passage of Russian war vessels through the straits for the prosecution of the war against France, but nevertheless insisted (art. 3 of the secret treaty) that this movement of ships "may not establish the right or serve as a pretext for claiming future free passage of war vessels through the Canal." Secret article 4 went on to stipulate the closure of the straits "to any flag of war or armed vessel of any Power whatsoever." To the Sublime Porte, this included Russia (except under the agreed conditions) and simply reaffirmed the prevailing regime, for no power, not even Russia, was challenging the Ottoman government's right of absolute discretion in locking or unlocking the straits. To the Russian-Ottoman alliance the United Kingdom adhered on the terms specified in the instrument reproduced below, which, as one British historian observed, represented "the most extensive pledge" Britain was ever to give the Ottoman Empire, for, unlike Russia, Britain at that time had no clearly defined strategic interests in the eastern Mediterranean. The significance for Britain's position in India of the continued survival of the Ottoman Empire was articulated only intermittently. Once the British-Ottoman treaty expired in January 1807, British policy toward the Ottoman Empire lapsed into its earlier state of ambiguity until resuscitated by Lord Palmerston in the 1830s. For the common war effort Britain welcomed the movement of Russian ships from the Black Sea into the Mediterranean, the only time it did so in the nineteenth century. Hurewitz, "Russia and the Turkish Straits"; Temperley, *England and the Near East*, pp. 43–46, 409–10; Goriainow, *Le Bosphore et les Dardanelles*, chaps. 1–2; Phillipson and Buxton, *Question of the Bosphorus and Dardanelles*, chap. 2; Headlam-Morley, *Studies in Diplomatic History*, chap. 8; Mischef, *La Mer Noire et les détroits de Constantinople*, chap. 3.

1. Russian-Ottoman Public Treaty, 23 December 1798/3 January 1799

. . . ART. 1. There shall always be peace, friendship, and good understanding between their Majesties the Emperor of All the Russias and the Ottoman Emperor, their Empires and their subjects on land and on sea, in such a way that they establish between them, in consideration of this Defensive Alliance, such a perfect intimacy that in the future they shall have only the same friends and the same enemies. For this reason their said Majesties promise to come to a frank understanding in all matters bearing upon their reciprocal peace and security, and to take by common consent the necessary measures to oppose every project hostile and prejudicial to themselves, and to bring about general tranquillity.

ART. 2. The Peace Treaty concluded at Jassy on 29 December 1791/9 January 1792, [corresponding to] 15 Cemaziyelevvel 1206, together with the other Treaties that are there [endorsed], is confirmed hereby in all [that] it embodies, as if it were inserted word for word in the present Treaty of Defensive Alliance.

ART. 3. In order to give this Alliance full and complete effect, the two High Contracting Parties mutually guarantee each other's possessions. His Majesty the Emperor of All the Russias guarantees all the possessions of the Sublime Porte, without exception, such as they were before the aggression against Egypt,[1] and His Majesty the Ottoman Emperor guarantees all the possessions of the Court of Russia, without exception, such as they are at present.

ART. 4. Although the two Contracting Parties reserve to themselves the full right to enter into negotiations with other Powers and to conclude with them all such Treaties as their interests may demand, they nevertheless pledge themselves in the most formal manner, each to the other, that such Treaties shall not contain anything that may ever, in any way, cause the least detriment, injury, or prejudice to either of the two, or impair the integrity of either's Dominions. They promise, on the contrary, to treat with care and to preserve to the best of their abilities each other's honor, security, and advantage.

ART. 5. If any harmful intention or act against the two Parties or against one of them should manifest itself, and the efforts employed to avert the aggression should prove insufficient, one Party shall be obliged to assist the other with land or naval forces, so as to act in concert or to divert [the enemy], or indeed to furnish financial help insofar as the common interest of the Allies and their security may require. Moreover, in such an event, after preliminary and frank discussions, the necessary arrangements shall be made promptly and this obligation shall immediately thereafter be carried out in good faith.

ART. 6. The attacked Party shall determine the [form] of assistance, either material or financial, and, if it should demand the first, the troops or squadron shall be sent no later than three months after the request; but if financial aid should be preferred it shall be computed on a yearly basis and the terms fixed from the day of the declaration of war by the attacked Power, or from the start of hostilities to the conclusion of peace.

ART. 7. Whenever the two High Contracting Parties shall take action in concert, either with all their forces or with the stipulated aid, neither Party shall conclude a peace or truce without including the other and without providing for [the other's] security; and in case of an attempt or an attack against the [aiding] Party in hostility toward the concluded Alliance and the aid furnished, the [petitioning] Party shall be obliged to fulfill in good faith and exactitude the same pledges for [the aiding Party's] defense.

ART. 8. In the circumstances of general cooperation, either with all the forces or with the stipulated aid, the two High Allies promise reciprocally to communicate with the most perfect sincerity the plans for their military operations, to facilitate their execution to the fullest extent possible, to share with each other their intentions on the duration of the war and the conditions of peace, and to reach agreement in this respect, conducting themselves in conform-

---

1. The French text reads "avant l'aggression de l'Egypte"; the Russian, "prezhde napadeniia na Egipet." The French text is manifestly erroneous.

ity with the principles of peace and moderation.

ART. 9. The auxiliary troops shall be equipped in proportion to their number with artillery and munitions and all that they require by their Sovereign, from whom they shall also receive their pay. As for subsistence, the petitioning Party must furnish provisions and provender in kind or in money according to the price jointly determined in advance from the day of their moving beyond their frontiers. The petitioning Party shall also procure for them quarters and all other commodities which its own troops enjoy, as well as those to which the requisitioned troops are accustomed in time of war.

ART. 10. According to agreement, the requesting Party must furnish the necessary provisions to the auxiliary squadron, from the day of its arrival in the Canal [and throughout] the period of its employment against the common enemy. The requesting Party shall also furnish without delay or difficulty, from its arsenals or its depots, at the ordinary price, all that [the auxiliary squadron] may require for repairs. For the duration of the common war, the warships and transports of the two Allied Courts shall have free entry to [each other's] ports for winter quarters or repairs.

ART. 11. The trophies and all the booty that may be taken from the enemy shall belong to the troops that have taken them.

ART. 12. Their Majesties the Emperor of all the Russias and the Emperor of the Ottomans, in concluding the present Treaty of Defensive Alliance, not with a view to conquest but solely to defend the integrity of their respective possessions and the security of their subjects, and to maintain the other Powers in the respectable state that has prevailed to the present and in the condition of political balance so essential for general peace, shall not fail to invite to adhere [to the present instrument] Their Majesties the Emperor of the Romans, King of Hungary and of Bohemia; the Kings of Great Britain and of Prussia; and other Sovereigns who may wish to take part in such innocent and salutary pledges.

ART. 13. Although the two High Contracting Parties are sincerely disposed to honor these pledges as long as possible,

circumstances may nevertheless dictate modification of the stipulations. It is [therefore] agreed to fix the period of the present Treaty of Defensive Alliance to the term of eight years from the day of the exchange of imperial ratifications. The two Parties shall hold themselves amicably disposed, at the approach of the expiry of this period, to the renewal of the Treaty in accordance with the state of affairs at that time.

ART. 14. The present Treaty of Defensive Alliance shall be ratified by His Majesty the Emperor of all the Russias and His Majesty the Emperor of the Ottomans, and the ratifications shall be exchanged at Constantinople in two months, or sooner, if possible. . . .

2. Russian-Ottoman Secret Treaty, 23 December 1798/3 January 1799

ART. 1. The Treaty of Defensive Alliance between their Majesties the Emperor of All the Russias and the Ottoman Emperor, now concluded, for the purpose of preserving the integrity of their possessions, maintaining the tranquillity of their respective subjects, and keeping the other Powers in the respectable state that has prevailed until the present, forming a political balance so necessary for the maintenance of general peace; their Imperial Majesties, taking into mature deliberation the present circumstances and considering that the present Government of France persists overtly in the pernicious design of destroying religion, toppling thrones, and upsetting all order until now viewed as the best, and that, after having subjugated different countries by its conquests and by the propagation of its destructive principles, it has turned its arms against the possessions of the Ottoman Porte to have them experience the same end, have believed it their duty to enter into negotiations and to establish between them frank communications such as those usually existing between two Sovereigns linked by the most sincere friendship and by the best understanding.

His Imperial Majesty of All the Russias, having consequently recognized that the present war is a legitimate reason for alliance and an object worthy of his solicitude for the restoration of tranquillity and the repression of the pernicious schemes of the

French, has resolved to come to the aid of his Ally, His Majesty the Emperor of the Ottomans. He has ordered to this effect, even before the execution of the Treaty of Alliance and at the first request of His said Majesty, that his naval forces of the Black Sea should pass into the Canal of Constantinople, after prior agreement with the Ottoman Porte, and that they should go in search of the common enemy in the Mediterranean in order to act against him. The aid which His Imperial Majesty of All the Russias reserves for the present situation, and that which in virtue of this Treaty of Alliance it will furnish for future situations, shall comprise the following number of warships: to wit, one vessel of 84 guns, two of 74 guns, three of 70 guns, and six of 50 guns, that is, twelve ships of the line, not including the light and smaller ships reserved for the service of the fleet. The said vessels and their crews must always be complete throughout the war. The Ottoman Porte shall permit these forces to pass through the Canal of Constantinople into the White [Marmara] Sea,[2] and as soon as the Russian and Ottoman fleets will have been conveyed there, their crossing and their operations against the common enemy shall be regulated in the manner found most convenient by the respective commanders for the purpose of defeating all the French projects and destroying their military and merchant navigation in the Mediterranean. The commanders of the [Allied] naval forces must maintain relations with the commander of the English fleet or detached squadrons in the Mediterranean and give them every assistance wherever the common utility may demand reinforcement or cooperation, since His Majesty the King of Great Britain, because of his war with the French, is making common cause with the two Allies.

ART. 2. His Majesty the Emperor of All the Russias promises to permit the sailing of his fleet from the Black Sea, for employment against the common enemy, so long as the war may last and the territories and possessions of His Majesty the Ottoman Emperor may be endangered. This fleet shall return after the conclusion of peace to the Russian ports of the Black Sea, and at the time of its return the Ottoman Porte shall lend it every assistance that it may require and that may be expected from a friendly and allied Power; but so long as the war may last and the Russian fleet of the Black Sea may be stationed in the Mediterranean, the warships and other armed Russian vessels, in view of the need for procuring munitions or reinforcements, shall have free entry and exit through the Canal of Constantinople. The same liberty shall exist for navigation in the White Sea and beyond, as well as for the return to the Black Sea. The warships and other vessels shall be subjected only to the single formality, at the entrance of the Canal either on the Mediterranean side or on that of the Black Sea, of identifying themselves as Russian, following the particular procedure that shall be agreed upon with the Russian Minister at the Ottoman Porte. Similarly, for the duration of the present war against the French, the ships of the line and other Russian vessels shall be [permitted] to enter into the ports and roadsteads of the Sublime Porte, for winter quarters or for shelter in bad weather or for repairs or for any other need whatsoever, by amicably giving notice of their entrance to the commander of the port.

ART. 3. In testimony of the sincerity with which His Majesty the Emperor of All the Russias has agreed to assist the Ottoman Porte to repel the unjust aggression of the enemy, His Imperial Majesty promises that the passage of his fleet and the free communication of the warships from the Black Sea into the White Sea via the Canal of Constantinople, as well as the return of the said fleet to the Russian ports of the Black Sea, stipulated in the second separate article, may not establish the right or serve as a pretext for claiming future free passage of war vessels through the Canal; this passage is solely reserved for the situation of a common war or the despatch of such aid as the Ottoman Porte might demand in virtue of the Treaty of Alliance and subject to prior agreement. Russian navigation in Ottoman waters, moreover, shall be bound by the same principles and stipulations proclaimed in the previous Treaties of the Russian Empire with the Ottoman Porte.

---

2. The White Sea (*bahr-i sefid*) in Turkish referred to either the Marmara or the Mediterranean.

ART. 4. The two Contracting Parties have agreed to consider the Black Sea closed and not to permit the appearance therein of any flag of war or armed vessel of any Power whatsoever, and if [any] should attempt to appear there in arms, the two High Contracting Parties undertake to view such an attempt as a *casus foederis* and to resist it with all their naval forces, as the only means of assuring their mutual tranquillity.

ART. 5. To complete and fix more positively the meaning of Article 10 of the Treaty of Defensive Alliance on the furnishing of provisions by the petitioning Party to the auxiliary squadron, the following arrangement has been agreed upon:

The Ottoman Porte shall furnish the Russian squadron, in kind, the victuals and provisions specified in the statement signed and returned to the Ottoman Porte and calculated [on the basis of] the number and strength of the vessels that presently comprise the squadron, as it has been laid down in the first separate article. This victualing shall take place on the arrival of the said squadron at Constantinople; it shall be done at first for four months and shall continue in such a manner that the squadron shall always have at least two months' provisions; and [the arrangement] shall terminate only after [the squadron's] departure from the Canal to return to the Russian ports of the Black Sea, following the restoration of peace. The victuals and provisions shall be delivered to the commander of the squadron or to the officer designated by him to receive them; they shall be choice and of good quality.

As for goods not included in the above statement, the Ottoman Porte shall make an equivalent monetary payment. This supplement has been evaluated at the sum of 1,200 purses, or 600,000 piasters; it shall be paid quarterly in advance to and receipted by the Minister of the Imperial Court of Russia at the Ottoman Porte; the payment shall begin on the first of September and shall continue for the same period as the furnishing of the provisions specified above. Vessels requiring repairs shall receive them in accordance with Article 10 of the Treaty of Alliance.

ART. 6. His Majesty the Emperor of All the Russias, unwilling to let any oppor-

tunity pass to demonstrate his sincere friendship and benevolent attitude toward His Majesty the Ottoman Emperor and toward the defense of his Empire against every attack, has made known in advance that, if the French Government should persist in its aggression against the Ottoman Porte to the point of causing it serious alarm, whether by an invasion of its territories or by incitement of its subjects with the support of French troops, His Majesty is prepared to send to the aid of His Highness, on his prior request, a corps of Russian troops of 75,000 to 80,000 men, with the necessary artillery, which, in case of need and in accordance with the Sublime Porte's [prior] agreement, shall enter into his realm and, by common agreement, shall move toward the points that may be assigned to it for subsequent operations. The provisions and provender for this corps, which must be delivered from the day of its crossing to the right bank of the Dnestr until it shall recross to the left bank of this river, shall be stipulated by agreement in a Special Act.

ART. 7. Since the present war has as its principal object the security and safeguarding of the territories of the Ottoman Porte, and [since] desertion weakens its armies and the auxiliary forces which it has requested, such a state of affairs would be harmful and should not be tolerated. The two High Contracting Parties [therefore] promise neither to receive nor to retain under any motive or pretext whatsoever deserters from their respective land and sea troops, religion being the only case excepted. Thus, if Russian subjects originally Muslims should desert, they shall be returned, and Russian Christian subjects who might embrace Islam shall continue to serve in the Russian fleet or armies until the conclusion of peace. At that time, action shall be undertaken in their behalf according to Article 8 of the Treaty of Jassy.

ART. 8. It has been stipulated by Article 7 of the Treaty of Defensive Alliance that the two High Contracting Parties, making common cause against the enemy, may not individually make either peace or truce without the participation of the other. This pledge as well as the rest of the said Article

7 must be upheld faithfully and without modification during the war.

ART. 9. In order to give His Majesty the Ottoman Emperor the most convincing proof of friendship and sincere affection for his Person and for his Empire, His Majesty the Emperor of All the Russias promises herewith, in the most formal manner, to act with all frankness and sincerity in negotiations which might take place to end the war and to restore peace, and not to countenance any indemnity or other compensation whatsoever, whether in his favor or that of his Allies, which might be detrimental to the possessions of the Porte. His Majesty the Ottoman Emperor reciprocally makes the same formal and friendly pledge and makes the same promise to his Ally, the Emperor of all the Russias, with reference to his Empire.

ART. 10. The two High Contracting Parties have agreed and resolved that when their fleets, squadrons, ships, and other vessels of war meet they shall salute each other, attention being paid on both sides, in [beginning] the salute, to superiority of rank, indicated by the flag of command hoisted; and that in case of an equality in rank the commanders shall not make any salute. The salute shall always be answered by the same number of guns as were fired by the first to salute. Consequently, in case of meeting, boats shall be sent reciprocally to reach agreement and avoid all dispute or misunderstanding.

ART. 11. The two High Contracting Parties have stipulated that if, in the period of their Defensive Alliance, a war should occur unexpectedly between one of them and some Power so far removed that assistance in land troops and maritime forces is absolutely not feasible, an equivalent monetary stipend shall be paid on an annual basis of 100 piasters for each infantryman and 150 piasters for each cavalryman. Thus, 2,000 infantrymen and 2,000 cavalrymen should yield aid at an annual rate of 3,000 purses, or 1,500,000 piasters. This sum, at the request of the Party attacked or requiring the assistance, shall be paid regularly by the assisting Party, quarterly, in advance, from the first month of the declaration of war until the conclusion of peace.

ART. 12. These Separate Articles shall be communicated, upon the agreement of the two High Allies, to those Courts only that, in taking part in the present war against the French, wish to accede to these stipulations.

ART. 13. The two High Contracting Parties are equally agreed that the above stipulations shall serve as a basis if, as a result of similar contingencies, the Emperor of the Russias and the Ottoman Porte should find it necessary [in the future again] to concert their action, whether for their own defense or for the preservation of the general peace, such additions being made as circumstances may require.

These Separate and Secret Articles shall have the same force and validity as if they had been inserted word for word in the Treaty of Defensive Alliance signed today, and the respective ratifications shall be exchanged at Constantinople in two months, or sooner if possible. . . .

3. Special Act on Maintaining Land Troops

In conformity with the stipulations of the Treaty of [Defensive] Alliance and of the Separate Articles of the said Treaty concluded on the same day, His Majesty the Ottoman Emperor promises and undertakes by this Special Act that the land troops of His Majesty the Emperor of All the Russias, designated to assist the Sublime Porte, the case mentioned in Separate Article 6 having occurred, shall be maintained at the expense and outlay [of the Ottoman Emperor] with provisions and forage in kind. This maintenance shall begin on the day of their crossing to the right bank of the Dnestr and shall end on their return to the left bank of this river; it shall be carried out according to the custom of the said troops in time of war, and the Russian Imperial Minister shall agree in advance with the Ottoman Ministry to the necessary arrangements, in conformity with Separate Article 5.

As for the provisions of maintenance which it might appear inconvenient to furnish in kind, the Imperial Russian and the Ottoman Ministers shall agree on [an equivalent] monetary payment at the prevailing price, being guided in this respect by all the considerations which would be promoted by the mutual friendship of the two Sovereigns and by the good will which His Majesty the Emperor of All the Russias has manifested in assisting the Ottoman Porte.

This Separate Act, [which shall be] known only to the two High Contracting Parties and which shall not be communicated to other Powers, shall have the same force and validity as if it had been inserted word for word in the Separate Articles signed today, and the respective ratifications shall be exchanged at the same time as those of the Treaty of [Defensive] Alliance. . . .

4. British-Ottoman Treaty, 5 January 1799

ART. I. His Britannic Majesty, connected already with his Majesty the Emperor of Russia by the Ties of the strictest Alliance, accedes, by the present Treaty, to the Defensive Alliance which has just been concluded between his Majesty the Ottoman Emperor and the Emperor of Russia, as far as the Stipulations thereof are applicable to the local Circumstances of his Empire, and of that of the Sublime Porte: And his Majesty the Ottoman Emperor enters reciprocally by this Treaty into the fame Engagements towards His Britannic Majesty, so that there shall exist for ever between the Three Empires, by virtue of the present Defensive Treaty, and of the Alliances and Treaties which already subsist, Peace, good Understanding, and perfect Friendship, as well by Sea as land, so that for the future the Friends of One of the Parties shall be the Friends of the Two others; and the Enemies of One shall, in like Manner, be considered as such by the others. On this Account the Two High Contracting Parties promise and engage to come to a frank and mutual Understanding in all Affairs in which their reciprocal safety and Tranquillity may be interested, and to adopt, by common Consent, the necessary Measures to oppose every Project hostile towards themselves, and to effectuate general Tranquillity.

II. In order to give to this Alliance a full and entire Effect, the Two High Contracting Parties mutually guarantee to each other their Possessions; His Britannic Majesty guarantees all the Possessions of the Ottoman Empire, without Exception, such

as they stood immediately before the Invasion of the French in Egypt: And his Majesty the Ottoman Emperor guarantees all the Possessions of Great Britain, without any Exception whatever.

III. Notwithstanding the Two Contracting Parties reserve to themselves the full Right of entering into Negociation with other Powers, and to conclude with them whatever Treaties their Interests may require, yet they mutually bind themselves in the strongest Manner, that such Treaties shall not contain any Condition which can ever produce the least Detriment, Injury, or Prejudice, to either of them, or affect the Integrity of their Dominions; on the contrary, they promise to regard and preserve, to their utmost, their reciprocal Honour, Safety, and Advantage.

IV. In every Case of an hostile Attack upon the Dominions of One of the Contracting Parties, the Succours which the other is to furnish shall be regulated by the Principles of good Faith, and in conformity with the close Friendship subsisting between the Two Empires, according to the Nature of the Case.

V. Whenever the Two Contracting Parties make common Cause either with all their Forces, or with the Succours furnished by virtue of this Alliance, neither Party shall make either Peace, or a durable Truce, without comprising the other in it, and without stipulating for its Safety; and in Case of an Attack against One of the Two Parties in hatred of the Stipulations of this Treaty, or of their faithful Execution, the other Party shall come to its Assistance in the Manner the most useful and the most conformable to the common Interest, according to the Exigency of the Case.

VI. The Two High Contracting Parties have agreed and resolved, that when their Fleets, Squadrons, Ships, and other Vessels of War, shall meet, they shall salute each other, Attention being paid on both Sides, in order to begin the Salute, to the Superiority of Rank of the Commanders, manifested by the Flag of Command; and in case of an Equality of Rank, no Salute shall be made. The Salute shall be answered by the same Number of Guns as were fired by the Party first saluting. Boats shall be reciprocally sent upon these Occasions for the Purpose of concerting the Mode of

Salute, in order to avoid all Misunderstanding.

VII. The Trophies, and all the Plunder taken from the Enemy, shall be the Property of the Troops making such Capture.

VIII. The Two High Contracting Parties being actually engaged in War with the common Enemy, have agreed to make common Cause, and not to conclude any Peace or Truce but by common Consent, as it has been stipulated in the Fifth Article; so that on the one Side the Sublime Porte, notwithstanding the Cessation of the Actual Attack directed against her Dominions, shall be bound to continue the War, and to remain attached to the Cause of her August Allies, until the Conclusion of a Peace just and honourable, as well for them as for herself; and, on the other Side, His Britannic Majesty shall be equally bound not to make Peace with the common Enemy without providing for the Interests, the Honour, and the Safety of the Ottoman Empire.

IX. The Two Allies, making thus common Cause, promise to communicate to each other their Intentions relative to the Duration of the War, and to the Conditions of Peace, governing themselves by just and equitable Principles, and having an Understanding with each other in this respect.

X. In order to render more efficacious the Succour to be furnished on both Sides during the War, according to the Spirit of the present Treaty of Alliance, the Two High Contracting Parties will concert together upon the Operations most suitable to be made in order to render abortive the pernicious Designs of the Enemy in general and especially in Egypt, and to destroy their Commerce in the Seas of the Levant, and in the Mediterranean; and for this Purpose his Majesty the Ottoman Emperor engages not only to shut all his Ports, without Exception, against the Commerce of the Enemy, but likewise to employ against them

in his Dominions (and in order to prevent the Execution of their ambitious Projects) an Army, consisting at least of 100,000 Men, and even to augment it, in case of Need, to the Extent of his whole Forces: He shall also put his Naval Forces in a State of Preparation to act in concert with those of his Allies in the Seas above-mentioned:—And His Britannic Majesty, on His Part, reciprocally engages Himself to employ in the same Seas, a Naval Force always equal to that of the Enemy, to annoy them; and to act in concert with the Fleets of His Allies, in order to impede the Execution of their Plans, and especially to prevent any Attack upon the Dominions or Provinces of the Ottoman Empire.

XI. In as much as the presence of the British Forces in the Seas of the Levant has for its principal Object the Defence of the Ottoman Coasts, and that Desertion, by weakening the Means, must unavoidably hurt the Cause, the Two High Contracting Powers promise not to tolerate it under any Pretext or Motive.

XII. Notwithstanding the Two High Contracting Parties desire to maintain these Engagements in Force as long as possible, nevertheless, as Circumstances might in Time require some Change, it is agreed to fix the Term of Eight Years for this Definitive Treaty of Defensive Alliance, to be computed from the Day of the Ratifications being exchanged. At the Expiration of this Term, the Two Parties shall enter into amicable Explanations for the Renewal of it, conforming themselves to the then Situation of Affairs.

XIII. The present Treaty of Defensive Alliance shall be ratified by His Majesty the King of Great Britain, and his Majesty the Emperor of the Ottomans; and the Ratifications shall be exchanged at Constantinople in Three Months, or sooner, if possible.

41. TREATY OF PEACE, FRIENDSHIP, NAVIGATION, COMMERCE, AND FISHING: MOROCCO AND SPAIN
1 March 1799

(Ratified by the king of Spain, Aranjuez, 3 April 1799)
[Translated from the French text in Martens, *Recueil des principaux traités*, supp., 3: 133–63] vol. 3, pp. 133–63]

Spanish treaty relations with the ʿAlawi dynasty started late. The treaty of peace and commerce which was signed at Marrakesh in 1767 (text in Rouard de Card, *Les relations de l'Espagne et du Maroc*, pp. 171–74) became the basic instrument for later Spanish-Moroccan relations. Peace did not last long, for in the 1770s Sidi Muhammad tried to expel Spain from its presidios, or fortified ports, of Ceuta and Melilla. The six-year war ended in a fresh accord in 1780 (text in ibid., pp. 175–79), conferring larger rights on Spain, because the British government at the time of the Spanish attack on Gibraltar (1779–83) refused to provide Sidi Muhammad with the military stores he requested as a price for the privilege of collecting from the Moroccan shore naval intelligence on Spanish movements. The new friendship persisted for a full decade, until the brief reign of the Anglophile Mawlay al-Yazid (1790–92), who declared war on Spain. Under Mawlay Sulayman (1792–1822) amity was restored when Spain and Britain became allies against Napoleon. The following inclusive treaty conferred on Spain in 1799 rights more generous than any received by European powers before. Ad valorem duty on imports from Spain was fixed at 10 percent (art. 27), and Spanish consular officers were given exclusive jurisdiction even over criminal disputes between Spaniards and Moroccans in which a Spanish national was the defendant (art. 6). Meakin, *Moorish Empire*, chap. 16; Terrasse, *Histoire du Maroc*, 2: 253–312; International Court of Justice, *Case concerning Rights of Nationals of the United States of America in Morocco*, 1: 257 ff; Barbour, *North West Africa*, pp. 137–43, 181–88.

. . . ART. 1. The Treaty of the year 1767, the Convention of 1780, and the Settlement of 1785 are renewed and confirmed in everything that is not contrary to the present Treaty.

ART. 2. Neither of the two High Contracting Parties shall, under any pretext, furnish provisions except what humanity demands, military stores including food as well as weapons, or any kind of arms to present or future enemies of one of the two Powers; nor shall it grant them passage of their troops through its territory, furnish them its flag or its passports, or permit them to arm while in its ports.

ART. 3. That peace and good friendship, consolidated once again by the present Treaty, may endure with the most perfect harmony, and that there may not be introduced into the reciprocal states subjects who by their actions, conduct, or opinions may trouble it, no Spaniard shall be allowed to pass through the states of Morocco or to settle there unless he obtains permission, or a passport which indicates the object or objects of his journey, from the commander or governor of the port where he embarks. On his arrival these documents shall be examined by the Consul General, the vice-consuls, or the commissioners of Spain. The same procedure shall take place in Spain regarding Moroccan subjects, who must be furnished with passports from the said Consul General, vice-consuls, or commissioners. Those who do not present the said documents shall not be admitted under any pretext; but if these documents are in order they shall be granted every protection and surety. In consequence, the Government shall take care that they do not suffer any bad treatment, or any other annoyance, punishing severely those who would molest them; to this purpose, His Catholic Majesty shall send the strictest orders to the governors of his ports. The same procedure shall take place on behalf of the Moroccan Government, under the threat that any officer who does not give a good welcome to each subject of His Catholic Majesty who passes through or who sojourns in the states of Morocco shall incur the indignation of the Government.

ART. 4. The Consul General, the vice-consuls, or [the] commissioners of Spain shall regulate with absolute jurisdiction the affairs of Spain in the states of Morocco; the Government shall furnish them with troops, armed launches, or anything else they desire to arrest and protect themselves from evil-doers, by which means good order and public tranquillity shall be preserved.

ART. 5. In all demands for payment of debts and for execution of contracts, or in all other differences which Moroccan subjects may have with Spaniards, they shall address themselves to the Consul General, to the vice-consuls, or [to the] agents of Spain in their respective districts, so that the latter may attempt directly to terminate and adjust the differences, constraining [both parties], if necessary, to fulfill their obligations. In the opposite case, the said [consular] employees shall notify the Moroccan Government so that its subjects shall pay to Spaniards what they owe them, doing so without delay, for the administration of justice must be reciprocal and in good faith, if it is to be a solid foundation for friendship and good harmony between the two nations and for the existence and well-being of all.

ART. 6. Every Spaniard who commits in the provinces of Morocco some scandal, injury, or crime which merits correction or punishment shall be handed over to his Consul General or vice-consuls so that he might be punished according to the laws of Spain or be sent back to his country with

the necessary surety, whenever circumstances make it necessary. The same procedure shall be observed reciprocally with regard to Moroccan delinquents in Spain, so that they may be sent to the first port under the authority of His Moroccan Majesty without a preliminary judicial inquiry or other formality other than that of an officer whom the commander, governor, or judge of the district where the crime is committed shall send to the Consul General of Spain to inform him of the crime or misdemeanor in order that the [Moroccan] Government may punish them according to its laws and statutes.

ART. 7. The said Consul General, vice-consuls, or commissioners shall continue to enjoy immunity from all duties on foodstuffs and other things which they need and which they may have sent from Spain or other countries for their consumption. The said Consul General shall be allowed to unfurl the royal flag of Spain at his house in Tangier and to board ships of his nation without hindrance when he deems it necessary, unfurling the large flag at the stern of the vessel or launch which takes him there. The consular house shall enjoy the immunity, prerogatives, and distinctions which it has enjoyed until now and which were granted to it by the late great king, Sidi Muhammad bin 'Abdallah.

ART. 8. If a Spaniard or his servant should die in Morocco, and if the latter should be the subject of a Christian nation, the Consul General, the vice-consuls, or [the] commissioners shall arrange his burial in the form that seems most appropriate to them, taking care of his property in order to restore them to his heirs.

If a Moroccan should die in Spain, the commander, governor, or judge of the district in which it happened shall put under guard what [the deceased] has left and shall advise the said Consul General of it, sending him a list of the property, so that his heirs may be informed and may recover [the property] without loss.

ART. 9. If Spaniards should buy land in Morocco legally, with the permission of the Government, they may build houses there for residence, storage, etc., [and] may rent and sell them as they see fit. Whenever [Spaniards] rent houses and warehouses for a fixed time or price, the rental shall not be raised during that [period] and they shall not be evicted, provided they pay the agreed price and they behave as expected. The same [terms] shall be observed in Spain toward the Moroccans.

Art. 10. Spaniards may leave Morocco with entire freedom whenever they see fit, without requiring the permission of the Government. Nevertheless, they must have the permission of the Consul General, the vice-consuls, or the commissioners so that the latter may know if they are free of debt or other kinds of obligations which they must discharge before their departure. This not only conforms to justice but will also preserve the good and due reputation of the Spanish name. In no way shall the Consul General, the vice-consuls, or the commissioners be made to pay the debts contracted by the said Spaniards in Morocco, if they are not expressly committed by their endorsement to discharge them; and the same procedure shall take place in Spain with regard to the Government of Morocco.

Art. 11. Neither the subjects of His Catholic Majesty who reside in the states of Morocco, nor those of Morocco residing in Spain, may be obliged to lodge or keep anyone in their homes.

Art. 12. The free worship of the Catholic religion shall be granted to all subjects of the King of Spain in the states of His Moroccan Majesty, and its rites may be practiced in the hospices of the missionary fathers established in the said Kingdom and protected by the Monarchs of Morocco for a long time. These missionaries shall enjoy in their hospices the safety, the distinctions, and the privileges which were granted to them by previous Sovereigns of Morocco and by the present Monarch. Considering that their ministry and works, far from displeasing the Moroccans, have always been agreeable and useful for their practical knowledge of medicine and for the humanity with which they have contributed to easing [the Moroccans] lot, His Moroccan Majesty undertakes to permit [these missionaries] to remain in his states with their establishments, even if one day the good harmony between the two nations is interrupted (which one has no reason to expect), as they have subsisted in the preceding reigns, notwithstanding the wars waged between the two monarchies. Similar-

ly, the Moroccans living in Spain may privately practice acts serving the worship of their religion, as they have until now.

Art. 13. Since we should try as far as possible to prevent misfortune resulting from unforeseen events, if relations between the two Sovereigns is ruptured again, they promise to grant one another reciprocally a period of six months or moons, counting from the day of the declaration of war in their states, so that the respective subjects might withdraw freely to their fatherland with all their property and effects.

His Moroccan Majesty, moreover, wishing that the odious name of slavery be wiped from the memory of man, promises that in the unexpected case of a rupture he will treat as prisoners of war the Spanish officers, soldiers, and sailors taken during the war, exchanging them, without distinguishing between persons, class, or rank, as promptly as possible, [and] in any case in no longer than a year counting from the time when they were captured, giving them a receipt at the time of their delivery, to establish a standard in the arrangement of successive exchanges. Children under twelve years of age, women of any age, or men above the age of sixty shall not be considered as such prisoners of war; since one may not expect any offense from these three classes of persons, they must not suffer the least injury or harassment. Therefore, as soon as they have been seized, they shall be set free and by means of trucial or neutral vessels shall be transported to their country by means of neutral vessels or those bearing the flag of truce, and the expenses of the transport shall be charged to the nation to which the prisoners belong. This His Catholic Majesty also promises to observe, [and] the two High Contracting Powers reciprocally give their royal word to accomplish exactly what is contained in this article. At the end of the war remaining prisoners [shall be set free without regard for their number], and the receipts [thereof] shall be handed over in the name of their custodian.

Art. 14. On reaching Moroccan territory, subjects of His Catholic Majesty who desert from Ceuta, Melilla, and the Alhucemas Islands shall be brought before the Consul General; he shall do with them what the Spanish Government orders and shall pay the expenses of their transport and keep. However, if before the said Consul they declare and confirm a desire to embrace the Muslim religion, the Moroccan Government shall keep them. But if accidentally someone should appear before the Sovereign and freely declare in front of the latter that he wishes to become a Moor, he need not be brought before the Consul General.

ART. 15. The limits of the camp of Ceuta and the stretch of land for the pasturage of flocks of that fort shall remain the same as when fixed and designated in 1781.

While there existed the best harmony between the said fort and the Moorish frontiers, it is well known how turbulent are those of Melilla and the Alhucemas islands, and how closely they are watched, which in spite of the repeated orders of His Moroccan Majesty, given to preserve the same [harmonious] relations with the said forts, has not ceased to inconvenience them continually. Although this seems to be a contravention of the general peace concluded by sea and by land, nevertheless it must not be considered as contrary to the good and amiable intentions of the two High Contracting Parties, but only as the effect of the bad inclinations of the said inhabitants. However, His Moroccan Majesty promises to use all the means which his wisdom and authority suggest to force the said neighbors to improve relations and to avoid the disagreements that arise over the violence, as much with the garrisons of the said forts as with the Moorish camps. However, if they continue without respite, which one must hope will not happen, as that would be contrary to justice and would also weaken the respect due to the Sovereignty of His Catholic Majesty, who must neither disregard nor tolerate such insults while only his own forts might restore order, it is agreed by this new Treaty that the Spanish fortresses may use cannon and mortars, should they be attacked, as experience has shown that musket fire is not sufficient to bring reason to the people.

ART. 16. *Navigation.* Merchantmen of the two nations may approach the ports of each of them, if furnished with appropriate sea papers sent by the respective authorities. The passports with which they should be furnished for their navigation shall be arranged in such a way that to examine them it will not be necessary to be able to read. Those not furnished with [such passports] shall be conducted by the vessel meeting them to the nearest port of its country without molesting them, so as to transfer them intact to its governor. Small fishing boats of either nation shall not be required to present passports. These [passports] may change form, but mutual care shall be taken to warn those concerned of each change made.

ART. 17. Warships of the two Powers shall not force [each other's] merchantships which they meet on the open sea, and of which they wish to examine the passports, to lower their boat or launch on the water; instead, the warships shall do so and shall not use more than a single trustworthy person to go aboard and make the said examination. The latter may not on any pretext visit or examine these ships, but shall limit himself solely to examining in the simplest fashion the passports with which the Moroccans should be furnished by the Consul General of Spain and the Spaniards those issued by their Government. Consequently, if one or the other should involuntarily cause any damage or inconvenience to any ship or its crew, the aggressor shall be punished for his crime and made to repair the damage he has caused.

ART. 18. Vessels of the two nations which meet on the open sea and need provisions of water or any other necessity to continue the journey shall furnish each other with what in the circumstances they judge themselves able to give, and the value of what they give shall be paid at market prices.

ART. 19. As proof of the good harmony which must reign between the two nations, it is stipulated that, any time Moroccan pirates take an enemy ship and find on board Spanish sailors or passengers [and] goods or anything else that may belong to them, they shall set [these Spanish subjects] free to their Consul General with all their property and effects, if they should be returning to the ports of His Moroccan Majesty; but if [this occurs] when Spanish subjects are en route to one of the Spanish ports, they should be handed over on the same basis to the commander or governor of the place. If verification cannot be made in one or another of these ways, they will leave [the Spanish subjects] with full safety in the first friendly port they approach. The same practice shall be observed by Spanish vessels as regards Moroccan subjects and property which they meet on captured enemy vessels. The good harmony and respect due to the flag of the two Sovereigns extends to the point of granting liberty to persons and property of subjects of enemy Powers of one or the other nation which sail in Spanish or Moroccan vessels with legitimate passports in which are shown the retinue and equipment belonging to them, provided that they are not those that are forbidden by the right of war.

ART. 20. If the vessels of any Barbary Power at war against Spain should take a vessel belonging to [Spain], or to its subjects, and should bring [the vessel] to one of the Moroccan ports, they will not be allowed to sell any individual captives or the cargo, either in its entirety or in part. The same [procedure] shall be observed reciprocally in Spain, if a Moroccan vessel seized by another enemy power of Morocco should be taken there.

ART. 21. Vessels of the two nations, warships and merchantmen, which might be attacked in the ports or within range of the cannon of the fortresses by any Power at war with one of them, shall be defended by fire from the said ports or fortresses; the enemy ships [shall be] detained without being permitted to commit any aggression or to leave the ports until twenty four hours after the friendly vessels have set sail. The two High Contracting Powers also undertake to obtain reciprocally from the enemy Power of one of them the restitution of prizes taken at a distance of two leagues from their coasts, or within view of [their coasts] if the seized ship was not able to approach land and had dropped anchor there. Finally, [the High Contracting Powers] forbid the sale in their ports of vessels or ships seized on the open sea by any enemy Power of Spain or Morocco; and if [an enemy Power] should enter there with any captured vessel of the two nations seized within sight of the coasts in the manner expressed above, [the Contracting Powers] shall declare it free immediately, obliging the captor to abandon it with all that he has seized of its effects, crew, etc.

ART. 22. If any Spanish ship should be wrecked on the River Nun and its bank, of which His Moroccan Majesty does not possess the sovereignty, he nevertheless promises, as a mark of the value that he attaches to the friendship of His Catholic Majesty, to use the swiftest and most efficient means to save and deliver the crews and other persons who have the misfortune to fall into the hands of the inhabitants of this place.

ART. 23. Into all Spanish ports open to commerce are admitted Moroccan ships that have taken the precautions and [observed the] formalities that the office of health requires to ensure the public of well-being. In the case of shipwreck or approach on a seaway not generally free, help will be given, as much as possible being done to rescue the persons, ships, and effects. This service will be paid for at the current price, as also the value of provisions bought, without the levying of duties on any object nor even on the goods which may have been saved and which they may wish to take to another place. Only when they are sold in [Spain] shall the customary duties be levied. The same shall be observed reciprocally without any difference on the coasts, seaways, and ports of His Moroccan Majesty with respect to Spanish ships.

ART. 24. Warships of the two nations shall not pay in any of the respective ports a duty for anchorage or for provisions, water, wood, coal, and refreshments which they may need for their consumption.

ART. 25. His Moroccan Majesty shall not reclaim the Christian slaves of any European Power who may seek refuge in Ceuta, Melilla, and the Alhucemas Islands, or on board Spanish warships. In the same manner His Catholic Majesty shall not demand the restitution of Muslims of any country who in Spanish ports seek refuge in Moroccan ships.

ART. 26. *Commerce.* Moroccans shall pay in Spain, for objects belonging to them of which importing and exporting is allowed, the same import and export duties as they have been paying until the present.

ART. 27. Whenever Spaniards import goods into Moroccan ports they shall not pay more than the established duty of 10 percent in silver or in specie, conforming without modification to the practice in the different customs offices.

ART. 28. The Spanish shall be asked to

pay from the port of Mogodor to that of Tetuan, inclusively, for the goods, cattle, and fruit specified below, only the following duties:

		Peso Fuerte	Ounces[1]
For each	*fanega* of every kind of vegetable	—	4
//	// head of horned cattle	3	—
//	// head of horned cattle with wool	—	5
//	// male head of horned cattle	8	—
//	// dozen chickens and other kinds of fowl	—	3
//	// thousand eggs	—	5
//	// hundredweight of dates	—	5
//	// hundredweight of wax, which [duty] H.M. of Morocco's own subjects pay	—	5
//	// thousand oranges and lemons	1	—
//	// dozen skins (from Tafilelt)	1	—
//	// hundredweight of wool	2	—
//	// hundredweight of almonds	1	—
//	// hundred wooden planks	12	—
//	// hundredweight of rice	—	8
//	// hundredweight of cowhides or goatskin with hair or tanned	2	—
//	// hundredweight of oil	2	—
//	// hundredweight of ivory	according to the charge in the port of Mogodor	
//	// hundredweight of copper		
//	// hundredweight of rubber		
//	// pound of white and black ostrich feathers		

1. A Spanish *fanega* equals 1.58 bushels. Ten ounces equaled one *peso fuerte*. And each ounce was equivalent to a Spanish *reale*, which was worth 2.5 English pence.

ART. 29. Since today the port of Santa Cruz of Barbary remains closed, the offer of His Moroccan Majesty previously made to Spain, that his subjects there should enjoy a decrease of 30 percent of the duties which other nations pay, cannot have effect; nevertheless this favor shall take effect whenever the port opens.

ART. 30. The company of five great merchant bodies of Madrid shall enjoy, as they have until now, the exclusive privilege of exporting wheat from the port of Derbeyda, paying sixteen *vellon reales* for each fanega of wheat and eight for each of barley; the conventions on this subject concluded previously with His Moroccan Majesty are retained in full force. However, His Cath-

olic Majesty may extend this said privilege to the advantage of some or all of his subjects, if he should deem it convenient, in view of His Moroccan Majesty's declaration that he granted this exclusive port not [as a mark of] respect for the said company but in deference to the King of Spain.

The privilege that the commercial house of Don Benito, Patron of Cadiz, possesses in the port of Mazagan shall be governed after the same principle and in the same circumstances, without exacting more duties than sixteen reales per fanega of wheat and eight per fanega of barley.

ART. 31. Despite the fact that a just motive be presented to His Moroccan Majesty to forbid the export of grain or any other merchandise or object of commerce from his states, that shall not prevent Spaniards from exporting what they may already have in their warehouses or may have bought and paid for before the interdiction (even though this should be in the possession of subjects of His Moroccan Majesty), as they would if no interdiction had been issued, without causing the least annoyance to them or prejudice to their interests. The same practices shall prevail in like cases in Spain with regard to the Moors of Morocco.

ART. 32. The collection of anchorage duty for merchantmen in the ports of Morocco shall be twenty to eighty vellon reales for each ship according to its class, its tonnage, etc., except those which come in and out, such as fishing boats, which shall be entirely free.

ART. 33. Permission is renewed to export hemp and wood for the use of the royal arsenals of His Catholic Majesty on payment of the first fifteen ounces of the country or thirty vellon reales in duties per hundredweight, and [on payment] of the last two hundred forty reales for each hundred planks; it is agreed, however, that no Spanish subject may make private use of the said privileges without obtaining special permission from His Catholic Majesty.

ART. 34. Experience having shown how constant are the frauds which the Spanish vessels commit, particularly in the export of coins from ports of His Catholic Majesty to those of Morocco, the Consul General [or] his vice-consuls or commissioners shall have the freedom to supervise this, and the

Moroccan Government shall give all requested help when needed, so that they might arrest or send to Spain the captains or owners of ships on which this fraud may be found and every other subject of His Catholic Majesty who may be guilty of this kind of misdemeanor. The Moroccan Government shall take the same care to examine if there are goods clandestinely loaded by Spaniards, even in ships of another nation coming from the state of Spain. In that case it shall inform the Consul General or vice-consuls so that they may report this to their Government. Every Moroccan caught in the act of importing or exporting contraband goods into Spanish ports shall be sent as a prisoner, with his goods, to the Government of Morocco, and the Consul General shall be informed so that the punishment may fit the crime. However, if the merchandise belongs to Christians, it shall be kept and confiscated in Spain, only the perpetrator of the fraud being sent back. If a Moroccan subject arrives in the said ports with goods of the said type, or if he enters with the said merchandise without knowing that it is forbidden, he must immediately declare it; if [he does] not, the punishment outlined above shall be applied to him.

ART. 35. *Fishing*. His Moroccan Majesty grants to the inhabitants of the Canary Islands and to all Spaniards the right to fish from the port of Santa Cruz of Barbary to the north.

ART. 36. Spaniards shall present the authorization which they must carry to leave the Spanish ports or those of the Canaries at Alcade to the Moorish governor nearest to the district in which they intend to fish, and the latter shall assign to them without delay or difficulty the limits within which they may do so.

ART. 37. Any Spanish ship which is seized by Moroccans on their coast without permission to fish, or which may go there in ignorance or with evil intent, shall immediately be handed over to the nearest Spanish Consul or commissioner, so that, having examined its case, the captain or owner may be absolved or punished by his respective superiors, according to the laws and decrees of Spain.

ART. 38. Spaniards and Moroccans who trade between Morocco and Spain must also make a declaration in the customs office of His Catholic Majesty by means of a certificate from the Consul General, the vice-consuls, or the commissioners resident in the ports of Morocco, [listing] the goods and effects that they may transport from one to the other with the precise intent to import [the merchandise]. Without this, the lower duties stipulated by Article 27 shall not apply to them, and they shall pay the same as nations which do not enjoy the privilege.

The present Treaty shall be ratified as soon as possible: three originals shall be signed and sealed in the Spanish and Arabic languages, one for His Catholic Majesty, a second for His Moroccan Majesty, and the third should remain in the care of the Spanish Consul General in Morocco. . . .

42. OTTOMAN GRANT OF COMMERCIAL PRIVILEGES IN THE BLACK SEA TO BRITISH MERCHANT VESSELS
30 October 1799

[*British and Foreign State Papers*, vol. 1, pt. 1, pp. 766–68]

In 1774 Russia acquired for its merchant vessels "a free and unimpeded navigation" in the Black Sea and a "free passage" through the straits (art. 11, treaty of Küçük Kaynarca). Austria received for its mercantile shipping identical advantages in a *senet* (bond) from Grand Vezir Hamid on 24 February 1784 (French texts of the

senet and Austrian note of acceptance in Noradounghian, *Recueil d'actes internationaux de l'empire ottoman*, 1: 379–86). Sultan Selim III (1789–1807), in the following
takrir, or official note, conferred the same rights on a most-favored-nation basis upon
the commercial vessels of Great Britain, the first Western maritime power to procure
them. Others followed—France (1802), Prussia (1806), Norway, Sweden, and Spain
(1827), the United States (1830), Tuscany (1833), and Belgium (1838)—until 1856,
when free transit through the straits for commercial vessels of all nations was enunciated as a universal principle in the treaty of Paris (art. 11–12) and reaffirmed
fifteen years later in the treaty of London (art. 3). Hurewitz, "Rusia and the Turkish
Straits," pp. 607–08; Great Britain, *Parliamentary Papers*, 1878, C. 1953. Turkey
no. 16: Wood, *History of the Levant Company*, chap. 10; Shotwell and Deak, *Turkey
at the Straits*, chap. 3.; Rose, "Political Reactions of Bonaparte's Eastern Expedition."

The friendship and concord which, since time immemorial, have subsisted between the Sublime Porte of steadfast glory, and the Court of England, being now happily improved into an Alliance established upon the firmest basis of truth and sincerity; and it being beyond doubt, that, in addition to the numerous advantages reaped hitherto by both Countries from the new ties so strongly formed between the 2 Courts, many more salutary effects will, by the pleasure of God, be witnessed in future.

Mature attention has, therefore, been paid to the representations, relative to the permission being graciously granted for the navigation of English Merchant Vessels in the Black Sea, which have been of late made, both verbally and in writing, by the English Minister at this Court, Mr. Spencer Smith, our most esteemed Friend, in con-formity to his instructions, and consistently with the confidence he is ever ambitious to manifest, in the inviolable attachment, which the Sublime Porte, of everlasting duration, professes towards his Court.

In fact, this being a means whereby to evince, in a still further degree, the attach-ment, the regard, and fidelity which are professed towards the Court of Great Brit-ain by the Sublime Porte, of steadfast glory, whose adherence to the obligations of Treaties, as well as faithful attention to fulfil the duties of friendship, are unexcep-tionable; and it being sincerely hoped, that many more salutary effects will hencefor-ward accrue from the close connexion so firmly contracted between the 2 Courts.

A cordial grant of the above point is hereby made, as an act springing from the sovereign breast of His Imperial Majesty himself. This privilege shall take effect with respect to the Merchant Vessels of Great Britain, exactly on the same footing ob-served with those of the most favoured Powers; it being understood, that its exe-cution be proceeded upon, immediately after the burden of the said Vessels, the mode of their transit through the Straits of Constantinople, and such other arrange-ments as appertain to this matter, shall have been settled in proper detail by friend-ly communication with the Minister before-named: and that the same Minister our Friend may notify this valuable concession to his Court, the present Memorial is writ-ten, and delivered to him by express com-mand.

43. CONVENTION (AL-'ARISH) FOR THE EVACUATION OF FRENCH TROOPS FROM EGYPT: FRANCE AND THE OTTOMAN EMPIRE
24 January 1800

(Ratified by General Paul Baptiste Kléber, al-Saliyah, 28 January 1800; repudiated by Kléber, 28 March 1800)
[Translated from the French text in Testa, *Recueil des traités de la Porte Ottomane*, 2: 7–11]

In the early morning hours of 23 August 1799, Napoleon set sail for France, leaving Alexandria secretly and without even discussing future plans with General Jean Baptiste Kléber, whom he had named commander of the French forces in Egypt. Instead, Napoleon strung together, in the words of one of the most readable historians of the subject, an "egregious collection of platitudes and pipedreams" (Herold, *Bonaparte in Egypt*, p. 342) as instructions for Kléber, with a categorical injunction against making peace with the Sublime Porte or arranging for the evacuation of French troops before the following spring, and then only if he had "received neither help nor news from France" and if in the intervening period, "despite all precautions, the plague should [have killed] more than 1,500 men" (cited in ibid., p. 343). Left with a decimated, demoralized, debt-ridden, disease-stricken, and mutinous army to administer a country that had been only partly and superficially subjugated, Kléber decided, less than a month after Napoleon had stolen away, to open negotiations with the Grand Vezir Yusuf, the Ottoman commander, who was approaching Egypt with a steadily enlarging—and motley—"army" that he recruited along the way as he moved down the Syrian coast toward Sinai. Mustafa Paşa, an Ottoman officer captured at Abuqir the year before, served as mediator until the end of October, when that task was taken over by Commodore Sir Sidney Smith, the British naval commander in the eastern Mediterranean, and coordinator with the Grand Vezir in joint British-Ottoman plans for driving the French out of Egypt. Kléber designated two aides to open preliminary negotiations with Smith aboard his flagship, the H. M. S. *Tigre*, on 22 December 1799. Meanwhile, ignoring the appeals of the French negotiators, the Grand Vezir moved his army from Gaza to al-Arish, the northernmost French outpost, which he seized with the help of the mutinous French garrison. At al-'Arish, which became his headquarters, the Grand Vezir entered into direct talks with the Frenchmen on 13 January 1800 in the presence of Smith. Eleven days later, the convention reproduced below was signed by the French and Ottoman negotiators. On Kléber's insistence, the withdrawing French forces were to be allowed to take with them arms and other possessions, on ships provided and victualed by the Sublime Porte; and until their actual withdrawal, the Sublime Porte agreed to cover the cost of maintaining the French army in Egypt. The Grand Vezir won his point that Ottoman troops should be permitted a phased entry into Egypt to coincide with a scheduled French withdrawal; and even Smith, who did not sign the convention, persuaded Kléber to give up the demand that the Sublime Porte end its alliance with Britain and Russia. The convention, which represented a mutual accommodation of the French and Ottoman negotiators—and even of the British mediator—was promptly put into effect. There were, however, major difficulties. The Grand Vezir alone had received full powers to negotiate. The British government, basing its decision on faulty information, had at first repudiated Smith's action. And Kléber was in an even more parlous situation, for Napoleon had become First Consul in Paris in November 1799, a development Kléber had no way of knowing of at the time he sponsored the search for a settlement at al-'Arish. As might have been expected, Napoleon rejected Kléber's action. But what caused the French general to stop the scheduled evacuation on 20 March and thus to invalidate the convention was not the directive from Paris but an arrogant letter from Admiral George Keith, the British naval commander in the Mediterranean, reflecting the initial attitude of the British government and calling for unconditional French surrender. Ironically, by that time the British government had changed its mind and in effect endorsed Smith's position. But with the slow communications of the day, further complicated by failure to inform Keith, the damage could not be undone. Kléber was killed by an assassin on 14 June, and his successor, General Jacques Menou, held out until final defeat by Ottoman and British forces, followed on 31 August 1801 by the involuntary French evacuation of Egypt. Herold, op. cit., chap. 10; Charles-Roux, "Une négociation pour l'évacuation de l'Egypte"; Rousseau, *Kléber et Menou en Egypte*; Turki, *Chronique d'Egypte*; Barrow, *Admiral Sir William Sidney Smith*, vol. 1, chaps. 10–11, and vol. 2, chap. 1; Sauzet, *Desaix, le "Sultan juste"*; Shaw, *Between Old and New*, chap. 17;

The French Army, wishing to give evidence of its desire to stop the bloodshed and to see the unhappy quarrels arising between the French Republic and the Sublime Porte cease, consents to evacuate Egypt in accordance with the arrangements of the present Convention, hoping that this concession will advance the general pacification of Europe.

ART. 1. The French Army shall withdraw with arms, baggage, and effects from Alexandria, Rashid [Rosetta], and Abuqir for embarkation and transport to France on its own ships as well as on those that it may be necessary for the Sublime Porte to provide; and in order that the said ships may be promptly prepared, it is agreed that one month after the ratification of the present [instrument] the Sublime Porte shall send a Commissioner to the palace of Alexandria with thirty persons.

ART. 2. There shall be a three months' armistice in Egypt from the day of the signing of the present Convention; however, if the truce should expire before the said ships to be furnished by the Sublime Porte are ready, the said truce shall be extended until the embarkation can be completely effected; [it is] understood by both parties that all possible means shall be employed to prevent upsetting the tranquillity of the armies and the inhabitants, which is the purpose of the truce.

ART. 3. The transportation of the French Army shall take place in conformity with the regulation of the Commissioners named for this purpose by the Sublime Porte and by General in Chief [Jean Baptiste] Kléber, and if after the embarkation some discussion should arise between the said Commissioners on this subject, Commodore [Sir] Sidney Smith shall designate [a third Commissioner], who shall decide the dispute according to the maritime regulations of England.

ART. 4. The localities of Kathye [al-Qatta?] and al-Salihiyyah shall be evacuated by the French troops between the eighth and the tenth days after the ratification of the present Convention. The city of al-Mansurah shall be evacuated on the fifteenth day; Dimyat [Damietta] and Bilbays on the twentieth day; Suez shall be evacuated six days before Cairo; the other localities situated on the east bank of the Nile shall be evacuated on the tenth day; the Delta shall be evacuated fifteen days after the evacuation of Cairo. The west bank of the Nile and its dependencies shall remain in French hands until the evacuation of Cairo;

however, since they must be occupied by the French Army until all the troops have descended from Upper Egypt, the said west bank and its dependencies shall be evacuated only at the expiration of the truce, if it should be impossible to evacuate them sooner. The localities evacuated by the Army shall be returned to the Sublime Porte in their present state.

ART. 5. The city of Cairo shall be evacuated within forty days, if possible, but no later than forty-five days from the day of the ratification of the present [Convention].

ART. 6. It is expressly agreed that the Sublime Porte shall take every precaution [to see] that the French troops from diverse places on the west bank of the Nile who shall withdraw, with all their belongings, toward their headquarters shall not along the route be disturbed or molested in their persons, goods, and honor either by the inhabitants of Egypt or by the troops of the Imperial Ottoman Army.

ART. 7. In view of the above article and for the prevention of disputes and hostilities, steps shall be taken always to separate the Turkish forces from the French forces.

ART. 8. Soon after the ratification of the present Convention, all Turks and [members of] other nations subject to the Sublime Porte [who are] detained or held in France or [held] in French custody in Egypt shall be freed, without exception, and reciprocally all Frenchmen held in all the cities and Levant ports of the Ottoman Empire as well as all the persons of whatever nation who may be attached to the French legations [sic] and consulates, shall also be freed.

ART. 9. The restitution of the goods and properties of the inhabitants and subjects on both sides, or equivalent compensation to the owners, shall begin immediately following the evacuation from Egypt and shall be regulated at Constantinople by the respective Commissioners named for this purpose.

ART. 10. No inhabitant of Egypt of whatever religion shall be disturbed, either in his person or in his goods, by the associations that he might have had with the French during their occupation of Egypt.

ART. 11. The necessary passports, safe conducts, and convoys shall be given to the French Army by the Sublime Porte and by the Courts of its Allies, Russia and Great Britain, to assure its return to France.

ART. 12. The Sublime Porte, as well as its Allies, promise that the French Army of Egypt, once embarked [and] until its return to the French mainland, shall not be disturbed. General in Chief Kléber, for his part, [together with] the French Army in Egypt, promises not to commit, during the said time, any hostility either against the fleets or against the territories of the Sublime Porte and its Allies, and, barring absolute necessity, not to stop the ships transporting the said Army at any coast other than that of France.

ART. 13. In view of the three months' truce with the French Army for the evacuation of Egypt, stipulated above, the Contracting Parties agree that, if, in the interval of the said truce several ships of France, without the knowledge of the commanders of the Allied fleets, should enter the port of Alexandria, they shall leave it after watering and provisioning and shall return to France provided by the Allied Courts with passports; and should several of the said ships require repairs, those alone might remain until the completion of the said repairs and then depart for France as the former, with the first favorable wind.

ART. 14. General in Chief Kléber shall be enabled to send without delay, and with the necessary safe conducts, a despatch vessel to France, so that it might inform the French Government of the evacuation of Egypt.

ART. 15. Having recognized that the French Army needs daily rations during the three months in which it must evacuate Egypt and for three more months from the day of embarkation, it is agreed that the necessary quantities of wheat, meat, rice, barley, and straw, at present provided by the French plenipotentiaries, shall be furnished [by the Sublime Porte] for the sojourn [in Egypt] and for the voyage, as circumstances may require. Whatever quantities [of the above-mentioned items] the Army will have withdrawn from its stores after the ratification of the present [Convention] shall be deducted from those to be furnished by the Sublime porte.

ART. 16. From the day of the ratification of the present Convention, the French Army shall not levy any tax whatsoever in

Egypt but, on the contrary, shall surrender to the Sublime Porte the ordinary demandable taxes—[otherwise] leviable [by the French Army] until its departure—as well as the camels, dromedaries, munitions, guns, and other objects belonging to it and judged inappropriate to carry away, as well as grain stores provided by taxes already levied, and finally victual stores. These goods shall be examined and evaluated by the Commissioners sent to Egypt for [this] purpose by the Sublime Porte and by the commander of the British forces, jointly with the officers in charge designated by General in Chief Kléber, and shall be delivered by the [French officers] at the price of evaluation thus made, not exceeding an amount of 3,000 purses, which the French Army shall need to accelerate its movements and its embarkation; and if the above designated goods should not produce this sum, the Sublime Porte shall advance the deficit as a loan, which the French Government shall reimburse on the note of the Commissioners appointed by General in Chief Kléber to receive the said sum.

ART. 17. The French Army, incurring expenses in the evacuation of Egypt, shall receive after the ratification of the present Convention the above-mentioned sum as follows:

On the fifteenth day, 500 purses; on the thirtieth day, 500 purses; on the fortieth day, 300 purses; on the fiftieth day, 300 purses; on the seventieth day, 300 purses; on the eightieth day, 300 purses; and finally on the ninetieth day, 500 purses.

All the said purses of 500 Turkish piasters each shall be received in advance from the persons commissioned for this purpose by the Sublime Porte; and to facilitate the execution of the said arrangements, the Sublime Porte immediately after the exchange of ratifications shall send Commissioners to the city of Cairo and to the other cities occupied by the [French] Army.

ART. 18. The revenues that the French will have collected after the ratification date and before the announcement of the present Convention in all the diverse places of Egypt shall be deducted from the amount of 3,000 purses stipulated above.

ART. 19. To facilitate and accelerate the evacuation of the localities, the navigation of the French transports that may be found in Egyptian ports shall be free in the three months of truce, from Dimyat and Rashid to Alexandria and from Alexandria to Rosetta and Damietta.

ART. 20. The security of Europe demanding the greatest precautions to prevent the spread of the plague, no person sick or suspected of attack by this malady shall embark; but those stricken with the plague or some other disease that does not permit their transportation in the period agreed for the evacuation shall remain in the hospitals where they may be under the safeguard of His Highness the Grand Vezir and shall be attended by French health officers, who shall stay with them until their cure may permit their departure, which shall take place as soon as possible. Articles 11 and 12 of this Convention shall be applied to them as to the rest of the Army, and the General in Chief of the French Army promises to give the strictest orders to the different officers commanding the embarking troops not to permit the ships to debark in ports other than those that shall be indicated by the health officers as offering the best facilities for putting into operation effective, customary, and necessary quarantine [measures].

ART. 21. All difficulties that may arise and that are not foreseen by the present Convention shall be amiably resolved by the Commissioners delegated for this purpose by the Grand Vezir and by General in Chief Kléber in such a manner as to facilitate the evacuation.

ART. 22. The present [Convention] shall not be valid until after the respective ratifications, which must be exchanged in the period of eight days, after which the present Convention shall be strictly observed by both parties. . . .

44. CONVENTION ON THE IONIAN ISLANDS:
RUSSIA AND THE OTTOMAN EMPIRE
21 March/2 April 1800

(Ratifications exchanged, Istanbul, 10 October 1800)
[Translated from the French text in Noradounghian, *Recueil d'actes internationaux
de l'empire ottoman*, 2: 36–41]

After four centuries of rule, Venice ceded the Ionian Islands to the French Republic under the treaty of Campo Formio (17 October 1797). In a joint naval campaign in the fall and winter of 1798–99, Russia and the Ottoman Empire drove the French forces out of the islands. The combined action, launched on the eve of the alliance, was later formalized by articles 1–4 of the alliance treaty (Doc. 39). The following convention transformed the archipelago, designated the Septinsular Republic, into an Ottoman protectorate under Russian military and naval occupation, ostensibly for underpinning the new regime. This role, we can see in retrospect, was designed to enable Russia to build a permanent military and naval presence in the Mediterranean, so as to provide a pretext for moving its naval vessels up and down the straits for the replenishment and reinforcement of its troops in the Septinsular Republic. The dual hegemony ended on the outbreak of war between Russia and the Ottoman Empire late in 1806, and at Tilsit on 7 July 1807 Tsar Alexander I surrendered the islands to to Napoleon. They passed into British possession in 1809 and were governed as a British protectorate from 1815 to 1864, when they were handed over to Greece. Pisani, "L'expédition russo-turque aux iles ioniennes"; see also references to Doc. 39.

The country originally subject to the Republic of Venice, after having fallen under French domination, having been delivered from this odious yoke, with the aid of the Sovereign Arbiter of Victory, by the combined squadrons of Russia and the Sublime Porte, seconded by the unanimous wish and efforts of the islanders; His Majesty the Emperor of All the Russias and His Majesty the Emperor of the Ottomans having agreed to observe the principles of equity, moderation, and distinterest, principles whose execution has been most solemnly and explictly stipulated in the Treaty of Defensive Alliance; and the dignity of the two Courts requiring that they should fulfill a promise made publicly by both; it has been resolved to establish in these countries such a Government whose proximity would not adversely affect the tranquillity and security of the dominions of the Sublime Porte and which conforms to the ancient practices, customs,

and religion of the country, being at the same time agreeable to the inhabitants delivered from the yoke of a Power that never ceases to use public and secret maneuvers to carry out its perverse design of destroying and overthrowing the laws and principles of all religion and human society. . . .

ART. 1. His Majesty the Emperor of All the Russias, considering that the above formerly Venetian Islands, in view of their proximity to Morea [Peloponnesus] and Albania, particularly affect the security and tranquillity of the dominions of the Sublime Porte, has agreed that the said Islands, like the Republic of Ragusa [Dubrovnik], should form a subject Republic under the suzerainty of the Sublime Porte and governed by the principals and notables of the country. His Imperial Majesty of All the Russias undertakes, on his own behalf and that of his successors, to guarantee the integrity of the dominions of the said Republic, to maintain its constitution, which shall be accepted and ratified by the two High Contracting Parties after having been submitted for their approval, as well as the perpetuity of the privileges which shall be granted to [the said parties]; His Majesty the Ottoman Emperor and his successors being suzerains of the above Republic, that is, Lords, Princes, and Protectors, and the said Republic being the vassal of the Sublime Porte, that is, dependent, subject, and protected, the duties of this protection shall be strictly observed by the Sublime Porte in favor of the above Republic.

ART. 2. In consequence of Article 1 above, the islands of Corfu, Zante, Cephalonia, Leukas [Santa-Maura], Ithaca, Paxos, Cerigo [Kithira], and all the large and small islands, inhabited and uninhabited, situated opposite the Morean and Albanian coasts that have been detached from Venice and have just been conquered, being subject to the Sublime Porte under the name of the Republic of the Seven United Islands, the said Republic and its subjects shall enjoy in their political affairs, in their internal constitution, and in their commerce all the privileges that the Republic of Ragusa and its subjects enjoy; and the two High Contracting Courts, properly to exercise their right of conquest over the said Islands, shall accept and ratify the internal constitution of the above Republic by solemn acts, after having approved it by mutual consent.

ART. 3. The above Republic of the Seven United Islands, by fulfilling precisely the duties of fidelity and obedience toward the Sublime Porte to which it is held by reason of its vassalage, shall enjoy in all its internal and external arrangements absolutely the same rights and privileges that the Republic of Ragusa customarily enjoys. The subjects of the said Republic who engage in commerce in the territories of the Sublime Porte, or who reside there, shall be under the direct control of their Consul or Vice-Consul. The same practices that existed in regard to the goods and persons of the Ragusans shall be exactly observed in whatever concerns [the Ionians]. The Sublime Porte shall employ all its efforts to protect the vessels and merchants of the above Republic against the Barbary Regents, in the same manner as it does the Ragusan vessels and merchants.

ART. 4. The above Republic, as a token of its vassalage toward the Sublime Porte and in recognition of its suzerainty, promises to pay 75,000 piasters to the Imperial Treasury every three years. This tribute shall be presented to the Sublime Porte by a solemn embassy, as is the tribute from the Republic of Ragusa. The above sum shall never be augmented or diminished. The above Republic shall not pay any other sort of tribute beyond the said sum, and its subjects, like those of the Republic of Ragusa, shall be exempt from the head tax and all other taxes in the territories of the Sublime Porte; the necessary orders to this end shall be issued throughout the Empire.

ART. 5. The existing fortresses and other [military] works in the above Islands must be returned to the above Republic. It must provide for their defense by stationing troops there in the manner judged appropriate. But if [the Republic] should by itself have insufficient forces to defend these Islands against all eventualities for the duration of the present war, the Courts of Russia and of the Sublime Porte, or even the commanders of their respective squadrons, shall be permitted to garrison the fortresses with regular troops, on the advice always of the said Republic and after a reciprocal agreement between the two High Contracting Parties or between the commanders of their naval forces. These troops shall be stationed there as long as required by the prevailing circumstances, but after the cessation of hostilities the two above High Courts shall terminate their military presence in the said Islands and shall without fail withdraw their squadrons and their troops.

ART. 6. The merchants and captains of the above Islands [having been] long permitted to navigate in the Black Sea, the two High contracting Parties agree that this permission shall be confirmed for the future, only under [the islanders'] own flag. Thus the purpose shall be served in the manner explained.

ART. 7. Since the Sublime Porte has at heart the security and tranquillity of the above islands, the previous regulation relating to free commerce and navigation in the Islands' waters shall be maintained as before in such a way that no harm shall be done to the articles which deal with the commerce and security and which have been inserted *ab antiquo* in the treaties of the Sublime Porte with the adjacent Powers; and the Sublime Porte severely and rigorously enjoins the Barbary Regents not to cross the maritime limits that have been assigned and demarcated for a great many years.

The Sublime Porte promises, as a shining favor and a signal act of kindness toward the above Republic, that [Ottoman] warships shall not go beyond the above maritime limits so long as there shall be no urgent necessity; but in case of urgent necessity and after having forewarned the above Republic and its Consul residing at the Sublime Porte, they shall be permitted to go there, and the dispatched warships shall conform to the quarantine and other regulations of the country in whose territory they shall go.

Art. 8. The localities of Preveza, Parga, Vonitsa, Butrinto, and their dependencies, situated on the mainland and detached from Venice, being contiguous with Albania, shall be annexed to the dominions of the Sublime Porte and shall belong to it henceforth. But since all the inhabitants of these areas are, without exception, Christian, the religious privileges and the administration of justice that have existed in the principalities of Moldavia and Wallachia, all of whose inhabitants are similarly Christian, shall also be assured to the inhabitants of the above areas. The customs of the country regarding civil and criminal procedures, property rights and inheritance shall therefore not be altered. Muslims shall still be forbidden from acquiring properties and from living there, since that is the practice in the above principalities of Moldavia and Wallachia. But since these lands belong fully to the Ottoman Empire, it shall be permitted to assign to them a commanding officer, who must be Muslim; and, in expectation that a great number of subjects of the Republic of the Seven United Islands will have possessions in the said regions, the Sublime Porte promises to determine henceforth the rank of this officer, the nature and rights of his functions, as well as the place of his residence, everything conforming to the will of the above Republic.

Art. 9. The Sublime Porte promises that everything relating to the religion of the *raiyye* [non-Muslim Ottoman subjects], inhabitants of the above territory, shall henceforth be maintained and observed in the same way that it has been to the present. They shall therefore have complete permission to repair their churches, to construct new ones, and to ring bells without hindrance.

Art. 10. According to the generous and beneficent sentiments of His Majesty toward his subjects, and above all according to the care that be takes to indulge and satisfy the said raiyye, who will become subjects of the Sublime Porte for the first time, only a moderate tribute shall be levied upon the raiyye, inhabitants of Preveza, Parga, Vonitsa, Butrinto, and their dependencies; for that reason the Sublime Porte promises that it will not levy upon them anything above those that they customarily paid to the former Republic of Venice. The above raiyye, having suffered all sorts of vexations while they were formerly dominated by the French, and having suffered a great deal also since then because of the calamities of war, shall be exempt from all taxes for two years from the date of the signing of the present Convention.

Art. 11. His Majesty the Emperor of All the Russias, in manifestation of the sincere friendship that he feels toward His Majesty the Ottoman Emperor and of the degree of his interest in the well-being of the Sublime Porte, promises, as its faithful Ally, once general peace [has been restored], to employ his good offices for the acceptance and guarantee by the Allied Powers and by others that may be invited, of all the principles stipulated in Articles 2, 5, 7, and 8 above and relating to the mode of political existence as much for the above islands as for the said regions of the Continent, all detached from Venice.

Art. 12. This Convention shall be ratified by their Majesties the Emperor of All the Russias and the Emperor of the Ottomans, and the respective ratifications shall be exchanged at Constantinople in two and a half months, or sooner if possible. . . .

45. TREATY OF PEACE: GREAT BRITAIN AND MOROCCO
14 June 1801

(Issued as an edict by Mawlay Sulayman, 14 June 1801; confirmed after modification of articles
7 and 8 by Mawlay 'Abd al-Rahman bin Hisham, 19 January 1824)
[*British and Foreign State Papers*, vol. 1, pt. 1, pp. 455–62.]

The conquest of Gibraltar in 1704 and the recurrent possession of Minorca (in the Balearic Archipelago) created for Britain in the eighteenth century a special interest in Morocco as a primary source of food for British garrisons deployed on former Spanish territory. The resultant commerce turned into a form of barter from which both sides profited, since the 'Alawi rulers willingly exchanged food for arms. On this foundation, British-Moroccan trade prospered, and in the eighteenth century Britain developed with Morocco more comprehensive treaty relations than any other maritime power in Europe. Britain and Morocco concluded five treaties between 1721 and 1791, augmented on three occasions by additional articles. The treaty of 28 July 1760 (text in *British and Foreign State Papers*, vol. 1, pt. 1, pp. 436–45) spelled out Britain's capitulatory privileges in Morocco in almost as much detail as comparable European treaties of the day with the Ottoman Empire. To commercial freedom were added in the eighteenth century a progressive immunity from all taxes and a stable duty on imports, fixed at 10 percent; a progressive recognition of the full jurisdiction of British consuls over all civil and criminal cases in which British nationals were defendants; and assurances of most-favored-nation treatment. The last provision, appearing in all Moroccan commercial treaties with European powers, led to the standardization of the capitulatory regime in Morocco by the start of the nineteenth century. The 1801 Anglo-Moroccan treaty, which best exemplified this trend, was modified by explanatory articles in 1824 and replaced by the commercial convention of 1856 (Doc. 107). Meakin, *Moorish Empire*, chap. 16; Terrasse, *Histoire du Maroc*, 2: 253–312; Abun-Nasr, *History of the Maghrib*, chap. 8; International Court of Justice, *Case concerning Rights of Nationals of the United States of America in Morocco*, 1: 257 ff.

This is the Patent Letter, containing, by the grace and power of God, the Treaties of Peace, Friendship, and Security; explained to the utmost, between His Imperial Majesty, Emperor of the Faithful Religion, proclaimed by the Almighty God, King of Agarb, Morocco, and all the Moorish Territories, Muley Soliman, Ben Mahomed, Ben-Abdala, may the Lord continue his grace over him and extol his Reign, through his Agent and Subject, Hadgi Abderhaman Ash Ash, now Governor of Tetuan; and the Agent of the English King, George the Third, whose Ambassador is James Maria Matra, now Consul at Tangier. To each of these Articles both Parties shall agree. These Articles have been made at Fez. May the Lord preserve them from all evil. Dated in the latter days of the month Moharam, 1216.

Herein we shall explain each Article:

ART. I. The English King may appoint one or more Consuls in the Dominions of the Emperor of Morocco and Fez; he or they may reside in any of the Emperor of Morocco's Ports, or in any of his Towns, at the election of the Consul, where he may think it convenient for his King's Subjects, or for the benefit of his commerce.

II. The Consul who may reside in the Dominions of the Emperor of Morocco, shall be treated with the utmost respect, according to his employment, and his house and family shall be taken care of; they shall not be molested by any body, nor affronted in any way whatever, and they who may be guilty of so doing shall be severely punished, in order that they may serve as an example to others; the said Consul may choose for his service either Moors or others, and none of his Dependants shall pay any Tax (which is commonly paid by the Jews), nor anything of the kind; the said Consul may establish a place of worship, and hoist his national colours at all times, either upon his House, within or without the Town, or in his Boat if he goes out to Sea. The said Consul shall be free from the payment of any Duties on whatever he may bring for his use, or the use of his house, in the Dominions of the Emperor of Morocco. Should the said Consul be called home to his King's service or otherwise, he shall not be hindered from going, or be stopped, either he or his Dependants, or anything that belongs to him: he shall be at free liberty to go and come when he pleases; he shall be treated with the utmost respect, and if anything more should be granted to any Consul of another Nation, it shall also be granted to him and his Agents.

III. English Subjects shall be permitted to come, with their Vessels and property of whatever kind, to any of the Dominions of the Emperor of Morocco; they shall also be permitted to reside therein as long as they please, and to build warehouses for their merchandise; the good friendship shall continue between the Subjects of both Nations for ever, so that no harm be done on either side.

IV. English Subjects or Merchants residing in the Dominions of the Emperor of Morocco, shall, themselves and their property, be in perfect security: they may follow their religion without being molested; they may also choose a place proper for a burying-ground for their dead, and may go out with a corpse to bury it, and return in safety. They are also at liberty to send any of their Agents, either by land or sea, for the purpose of their service, without their being hindered or stopped; and if any English Merchant should happen to have a Vessel in or outside the Port, he may go on board himself, or any of his People, without being liable to pay anything whatever.

V. English Subjects shall not be compelled to sell their property, or to make purchases unless at their own option, and no Moor shall take any property belonging to an English Subject, unless it be given by the goodwill of the Proprietor, or by mutual agreement; the same shall be practised towards Moorish Merchants in the English Dominions.

VI. No English Subject shall be answerable for any debts, contracted by another Individual, unless under his own hand he be responsible for the same.

VII. Disputes between Moorish Subjects and English Subjects shall be decided in the presence of the English Consul, provided the decision be conformable to the Moorish Law, in which case the English Subject shall not go before the Cadi or Hacam, as the Consul's decision shall suffice.

VIII. Should any dispute occur between English Subjects and the Moors, and that dispute should occasion a complaint from either of the parties, the Emperor of Morocco alone shall decide the matter; if the English Subject be guilty, he shall not be punished with more severity than a Moor would be; should he escape, no other Subject of the English Nation shall be arrested in his stead; and if the escape be made after the decision, in order to avoid punishment, he shall be sentenced the same as a Moor would be who had committed the same crime. Should any dispute occur in the English Territories, between a Moor and an English Subject, it shall be decided by an equal number of the Moors residing there and of Christians, according to the custom of the place, if not contrary to the Moorish Law.

IX. Moorish Subjects who escape from the Emperor of Morocco's Dominions, and go on board of any English Ship of War, or to any of the English Ports, shall be restored to their Country, without being sent as Prisoners; and English Subjects who come to the Dominions of the Emperor of Morocco, whether from their own Country, or from any other place near the Barbary Coast, such as Ceuta, from whence they may have made their escape, shall be delivered up to the Consul or his Agent, in order that they may be embarked for Gibraltar.

X. Renegades from the English Nation, or Subjects who change their religion to embrace the Moorish, they being of unsound mind at the time of turning Moors, shall not be admitted as Moors, and may again return to their former religion, but if they afterwards resolve to be Moors, they must abide by their decision, and their excuses will not be accepted.

XI. If any English Subject turn Moor, and have in his possession effects or papers belonging to English Subiects, he school deliver them up to the English Consul or his Agent, in order to their being returned to the respective Owners.

XII. English Subjects, resident in the Emperor of Morocco's Dominions, either in Peace or War, are at liberty to go to their own Country, or elsewhere, either in their own or in any other Vessel; they may dispose of their effects or houses, &c., and take their value with them, as also their Families and Servants, even though they should have been born in Barbary, without impediment whatever; and the same shall be practised towards Moorish Subjects residing in the English Dominions.

XIII. When an English Subject dies in the Emperor of Morocco's Dominions, his effects shall not be searched or touched by any of the Governors, but shall be delivered into the hands of his Executors, or his Heirs, if present; but if no Heir or Executor appear, the Consul or his Agent shall be Executor for the same, he taking an inventory of all such effects found, to be delivered to the Deceased's Heirs or Executors. If the Deceased made no Will, the Consul or Agent shall take charge of the effects, in whose possession they shall remain until the Heir appears. If any debts were owing to the Deceased, the Governor of the Place shall assist and compel the Debtors to pay their debts to the Consul, or his Agent, to be kept for the Heir.

XIV. All the Treaties concluded between the English and the Moorish Agent, are to be considered as extending to any Territories the English may have in Germany, and to their Inhabitants, the same as if they were Natives of England, as also to Gibraltar and its Inhabitants, who shall be considered as Natives of London; they shall also extend to any other Town and its Inhabitants, which may hereafter be under the Dominion or Protection of England, as if they were included, from the beginning, in the Treaties.

XV. English Subjects, in addition to what is mentioned in those Treaties, shall enjoy any other privileges which other Powers enjoy at present, and if hereafter any further indulgences be granted to any other Power, the greatest share shall be extended to this friendly Nation [by] the Emperor of Morocco.

XVI. The navigation between the English Subjects and Vessels and those of the Emperor of Morocco, shall be free, and if an English Man-of-War or Privateer meet at sea, with a Moorish Man-of-War or Merchantman, the latter shall not be hindered of their navigation, provided they are furnished with their Passes given to them by their respective Governors, certified by the English Consul or his Agent; but if no Passport be found on board, certified as above, the Vessel being under Moorish colours, and the greater part of the Crew being Moors, it shall not be molested or hindered of its navigation.

XVII. If a Morocco Man-of-War meet with an English Vessel at sea, not being in the English Sea, the Moorish Man-of-War may send his Boat, with 2 Officers, on board of the English Vessel to examine her Pass; the 2 Officers only shall be permitted to go on board; and, after so doing, the Boat shall return, and the Vessel continue its voyage: if an English Vessel come out of a Port with which the Emperor of Morocco may be at War, or go into it, no Mariners, Pilot, or Strangers shall, in either case, be taken from it; nor shall any one be allowed to search the said Vessel for the purpose of taking any ammunition or goods from the English Vessel, under the pretence of receiving them from the Captain as a present, or otherwise; and all Prizes taken by the King of England's Ships, and met with at sea by the Emperor of Morocco's Cruizers, even without a Pass, shall not be molested or hindered from their navigation, a Letter or Affidavit, either of the Captain by whom the Capture was made, or of the Governor of the place from whence she sailed, being deemed sufficient.

XVIII. The Emperor of Morocco's Cruizers, and his Subjects, shall not cruize near the English Ports, so that the commerce of the said Ports be interrupted, nor shall English Vessels so cruize near the Emperor of Morocco's Ports.

XIX. If a Moor, of the Emperor of Morocco's Subjects, be on board a Vessel of a Nation with which the King of England is at War, and the Vessel happen to be taken a Prize, neither the Moor nor his effects shall be seized, but shall be liberated; the same shall be observed, if an English Subject be found on board a Vessel, with whose Nation the Emperor of Morocco may be at War, and which may be taken as Prize, the English Subject and his effects being liberated.

XX. If an English Vessel capture a Prize, and bring it into any of the Emperor of Morocco's Ports, the Vessel or cargo may be sold without being hindered by any body, or the Prize taken away wheresoever they please.

XXI. If an English Vessel run from a Vessel with which it may be at War, and come within gun-shot of the Emperor of Morocco's Ports, the latter shall be fired upon, and the utmost shall be done to protect the former: the same condition shall be observed in respect of the Emperor of Morocco's Cruizers, when near the English Ports.

XXII. If a Morocco Cruizer meet with a Vessel of any Nation, under convoy of an English Cruizer, such Vessel shall be considered as belonging to the King of England, she being under the protection of the English, and the Morocco Cruizer shall not detain her, or hinder her navigation, on any pretext whatever; the same shall be practised by the English, if they find a Vessel under convoy or protection of the Emperor of Morocco's Cruizers.

XXIII. Cruizers belonging neither to Morocco nor England, but having a Pass from a Nation with which the Emperor of Morocco or the King of England may be at War, shall not be allowed to enter any Port of either Party, not to sell a Prize therein, neither shall they be allowed to take any stores or provisions, excepting only such a quantity of provisions as may be sufficient for their voyage home.

XXIV. If Vessels of a Nation with which the King of England is at War, enter any of the Emperor of Morocco's Ports or Bays, wherein there should happen to be English Vessels, it shall not be permitted to the Enemy to do violence to the English, or to molest them in any way, nor shall the Enemy be permitted to follow an English Vessel from the Harbour till 24 hours after her departure; the same shall be practised towards Vessels of the Emperor of Morocco in English Ports.

XXV. If an English Fleet, Cruizer, or Merchant-ship, come into a Port of the Emperor of Morocco, or into any of his Bays or Rivers and want provisions, they shall be allowed to buy what is necessary, at the current price paid by other Nations that are at Peace.

XXVI. Packet-boats, furnished with the King of England's Pass, or with a Passport from the Person authorized to dispatch King's Packets, shall be considered as Ships of War.

XXVII. The Inhabitants of Gibraltar, which is under the English command, as also the Inhabitants of any other Town which may hereafter be in possession of the English, shall be considered as native Englishmen, and be permitted to travel, and navigate, and fish, under English colours, with the Governor's Pass, without being hindered or molested.

XXVIII. Vessels of either Party, or its Subjects, that enter into the Ports or Bays of either Party, and do not choose to come into harbour, or to anchor in the Port, being bound for another place, shall not be obliged to exhibit their cargoes, nor to sell any part of them, nor shall they in such case be searched.

XXIX. If an English Vessel land part of its cargo in any of the Emperor of Morocco's Ports, it shall only pay the Duties inward, on the quantity landed, but not for the remaining part of the cargo, which has not been landed, and it shall be at liberty to depart with the latter to any place whatsoever.

XXX. No English Captain shall be compelled to take on board of his Vessel, any Passenger or Person, or goods belonging to any Person whatever, against his will, nor shall the Captain be compelled to go to any Port without his consent, nor be prevented from going where he pleases.

XXXI. If a Subject of the Emperor of Morocco freight an English Vessel, for the purpose of loading or taking Passengers from one of the Emperor's Ports to another; and, on his voyage, be driven by the wind and weather into another of the Emperor of Morocco's Ports, he shall not pay any Anchorage or other Duty whatever in such Port.

XXXII. English Vessels meeting with distress at sea, and entering any of the Emperor of Morocco's Ports to repair their damages, shall be allowed to come in, and shall be assisted with all requisite stores, &c., to continue their voyage to their destination.

XXXIII. If an English Vessel strand, or be wrecked on the Emperor of Morocco's coast, it shall be protected and assisted in every respect as becoming friendship; the Vessel, and what may be saved from such wreck, shall be delivered to the Consul or his Agent, for the use of the Owners, and the Crew shall be at liberty to depart when they please; the same shall be observed, in a similar case, towards the Emperor of Morocco's Vessels on the English coast; and if any English Vessel be cast away at Wadnun, or the Sands near, the Emperor of Morocco shall do his utmost to ensure the safety of the Crew, and their being sent to their Country; the English Consul or his Agent may also use his endeavours in procuring their liberty, and shall be assisted in that object by the Governor residing near the place.

XXXIV. If an English Subject, or Person under the King of England's protection, come to the Dominions of the Emperor of Morocco to load provisions, he shall be allowed, on payment of the existing Duties, to export them to other Christian Nations, with which he may be at Peace, it being understood that their coming over for that purpose shall be at proper seasons of the year, or once or more, according as may be agreed upon, as he is not permitted so to come and export without stipulation, and out of season.

XXXV. If English Ships come to a Port where Ships of other Nations happen also to be, and want a supply of provisions, and the place do not afford sufficient to satisfy both, it shall be divided in proportion to the number of Vessels, and shall be paid for at the current market price, without its being permitted to the Ships of other Nations to take more than their portion; and if, henceforward, the Garrison of Gibraltar should be in want of provisions, provided they be abundant in Barbary, the Emperor of Morocco shall permit their exportation, for the use of the Troops and the Inhabitants, at the same Duties that are paid by other Nations at the same period.

XXXVI. If an English Subject come to the Emperor of Morocco's Ports with ammunition or naval stores, he shall not pay any Duty for the same.

XXXVII. If an English Subject have imported any merchandise into the Emperor of Morocco's Ports, and have paid Duty thereon, and choose afterwards to remove the said merchandise to another of the Emperor of Morocco's Ports, he shall not pay any further Duty; and if any goods be smuggled by Subjects of either Party, the goods which they have smuggled shall be seized, but no other punishment shall be inflicted, to serve as an example to others.

XXXVIII. All the Treaties concluded with Muly Ishmael, Muly Abdala, and Muly Mahomed Ben Abdala, shall be in force without alteration; excepting such Articles as may be contrary to this Treaty between both Parties.

XXXIX. If any of the Subjects or Cruizers of either Party break through these Treaties, either by mistake or purposely, the Peace shall not, therefore, be disturbed, but shall continue until after a complaint be made to the respective King; and if any Subject of either Party be guilty of an infraction of these Treaties, he shall be severely punished by his King.

XL. If a rupture of the Peace happen, and War ensue, (which God forbid,) all English Subjects, as also all Morocco Subjects, of whatever description, may proceed to any part of the World they please, with their Families, property, and Servants, whether born in Barbary or not, on board the Vessel of any Nation, and 6 months' notice shall be given to them, in order that they may have time to dispose of their effects, and settle their affairs; and, during the said 6 months, they and their property shall continue in safety, without being molested or injured in any way, on account of the Declaration of War, and they shall be assisted by the respective Governors in recovering their debts without delay; the same shall be practised with the Emperor of Morocco's Subjects in the Dominions of the King of England.

XLI. This Treaty of Peace, concluded between the Emperor of Morocco and the King of England, shall be published to the Subjects of both Parties, that the Conditions may not be concealed, and Copies shall be given to the Governors and Commissioners of Imports and Exports of the Emperor of Morocco, and to the Captains of his Cruizers, this being the end of the above-mentioned Articles, concluded on the foregoing date, which corresponds with the 14th June, 1801, of the birth of Jesus, the Messiah, Son of Mary. Peace to Him.

46. TREATY OF PEACE (AMIENS): FRANCE AND THE OTTOMAN EMPIRE
25 June 1802

(Ratifications exchanged, Paris, 8 September 1802)
[Translated from the French text in Noradounghian, *Recueil d'actes internationaux de l'empire ottoman*, 2: 51–54]

The British-French treaty of peace signed at Amiens on 27 March 1802, thus ending the first phase of the Napoleonic wars, stipulated in article 8 that "The territories, possessions and rights of the Sublime Porte are preserved in their integrity, just as they were before the war." Article 19 invited the Ottoman government to accede to the instrument. Sultan Selim III formally accepted the offer in an imperial *ferman* (decree) of 13 May, which led to the conclusion six weeks later of the following treaty. Former capitulatory privileges were restored to France, and, what was of greater significance, French merchant vessels were expressly granted for the first time the right already enjoyed by Russia, Austria, and the United Kingdom to trade freely in the Black Sea (Doc. 42). Napoleon insisted upon this right, which delayed the signing of the treaty, so as to open up trade with Russia, the Danubian and Transcaucasian territories, and Persia. Nor was he unmindful of the political benefits vis-à-vis England and Russia that might accrue from the development of new markets in southeastern Europe and southwestern Asia. As for the reciprocal guarantee of territorial integrity (art. 5), Napoleon instructed the French negotiator to keep the assurances to the Ottoman Empire "vague, indeterminate, and general"; and to allay Ottoman fears, the Sublime Porte was exempted by a secret article from automatic involvement in wars between France and other states. Puryear, *Napoleon and the Dardanelles*, chap. 1; de Saint-Joseph, *Essai historique sur le commerce et la navigation de la Mer Noire*; Déhérain, *La vie de Pierre Ruffin*, vol. 1, chaps. 8–10, and vol. 2, chaps, 1–2; Coquelle, "L'ambassade du maréchal Brune"; Julliany, *Le commerce de Marseille*, vol. 2, chap. 5.

ART. 1. There shall be peace and friendship in the future between the French Republic and the Ottoman Sublime Porte. Hostilities shall cease now and for ever between the two states.

ART. 2. The Treaties or Capitulations which, prior to the war, determined respectively the relations of every kind that existed between the two Powers are all renewed.

In consequence of this renewal and in execution of the articles of the old Capitulations, by virtue of which the French enjoyed in the states of the Sublime Porte all the benefits accorded to other Powers, the Sublime Porte agrees that French vessels of commerce bearing the French flag henceforth shall enjoy without hindrance the right to enter into and navigate freely in the Black Sea.

The Sublime Porte agrees, furthermore, that the said French vessels, in their entrance into and departure from that sea and in everything that can favor their free navigation, shall be treated precisely like the merchant vessels of nations which navigate in the Black Sea. The Sublime Porte and the Government of the Republic will take, in concert, effective measures to purge of every sort of freebooters the seas serving the merchant vessels of both states. The Sublime Porte promises to protect the navigation of French merchant vessels on the Black Sea against all kinds of piracy.

It is understood that the benefits assured by the present article to the French in the Ottoman Empire are equally assured to the subjects and flag of the Sublime Porte in the seas and on the territory of the French Republic.

ART. 3. The French Republic shall enjoy in the Ottoman districts adjacent to the Black Sea, as much for its commerce as for the agents and commissioners of commercial relations which might be established in those places where French trade would render such establishment necessary, the same rights, privileges, and prerogatives enjoyed by France before the war in other parts of the states of the Sublime Porte, by virtue of the old capitulations.

ART. 4. The Sublime Porte accepts, insofar as it is concerned, the Treaty concluded at Amiens between France and England on 4 Germinal X (27 March 1802). All articles of that Treaty relating to the Sublime Porte are formally renewed in the present Treaty.

ART. 5. The French Republic and the Sublime Porte mutually guarantee to each other the integrity of their possessions.

ART. 6. The restitutions and compensations due the agents of both Powers, as well as those due the citizens and subjects whose properties have been confiscated or sequestrated during the war, shall be arranged with equity by a special agreement that the two Governments will negotiate in Constantinople.

ART. 7. While awaiting the new decisions that will be taken in concert on the customs, the two countries shall for the time being act in conformity with the old capitulations.

ART. 8. If there should remain additional prisoners still under detention as a result of the war between the two states, they shall be liberated immediately without ransom.

ART. 9. The French Republic and the Sublime Porte, desirous in the present Treaty of establishing themselves in each other's territory on the basis of the most favored Power, it is understood that they shall accord to each other in their respective states all the benefits which have been or might be accorded to other Powers, as if these benefits were expressly stipulated in the present Treaty.

ART. 10. The ratifications of the present treaty shall be exchanged in Paris within eighty days, or earlier if possible. . . .

Additional and Secret Article of the Foregoing Treaty

It is agreed by the Government of the French Republic and the Ottoman Sublime Porte that Article 5 of the open Treaty concluded between the two Powers on this day, by the same undersigned Ministers Plenipotentiary and expressing the mutual guarantee of the integrity of their possessions, shall not be binding on the Sublime Porte against its will in wars that France might have to wage against other Powers.

47. "WAR" AND PEACE: THE UNITED STATES AND THE
GARRISON OF TRIPOLI
23 February–10 June 1805

(Receipted by Yusuf Paşa, 19 June 1805; ratified by the United States, 17 April 1806)
[Text of the Eaton-Hamet convention from Miller, *Treaties and Other International Acts*, 2: 552–54;
text of treaty of peace and amity, ibid., pp. 529–35; Lear secret declaration, ibid., pp. 555–56]

The first United States treaty with Tripoli, signed in 1796, did not provide for tribute,
and when in April 1799 James L. Cathcart arrived to take up his post as consul,
Yusuf Paşa Karamanalı (1796–1832) refused to receive him until Cathcart promised
the bey, or ruler, of the Garrison of Tripoli a total of $23,550 in cash and gift equi-
valents. Yusuf Paşa seemed determined to extract a larger sum from the United States,
and to clinch his argument he seized an American brig in September 1800, detaining
it for a month. In the following February the bey insisted on a new treaty, for which he
requested payment of $250,000, with a provision for an annual tribute of $20,000.
Then, on 14 May 1801, Yusuf Paşa "declared war" on the United States, or, more
precisely, set his corsairs loose to seize American merchantships. At about the same
time, even before word reached Washington of Tripoli's hostile move, President
Jefferson ordered a squadron of four ships to the Mediterranean to ascertain the facts
and to take, if need be, appropriate punitive action against those harassing American
navigation. The American naval strategy of attempting to blockade the port of Tripoli
required a larger naval force, which was gradually assembled under successive commanders. Indeed, one of the side effects of the slow-motion punitive action against
Tripoli was the steady growth of the American navy under a president who had cam-
paigned for office by promising, among other things, to do away with the navy altogether. Meanwhile, under the treaties of 1795–97 with the Barbary Garrisons, the
United States consuls at Tunis and Tripoli and the consul general at Algiers were
expected to coordinate policies in dealing with the corsairs. This gave the consul at
Tunis, William Eaton (an apparently frustrated former army officer with good political connections in Washington), an opportunity to persuade the Jefferson Administration to permit him to organize in 1804–05 a mercenary force for a land offensive to be
synchronized with American naval action against the Tripoli Garrison. With this in
mind, Eaton concluded a convention on 23 February 1805 (reproduced below) with
Hamet (Ahmet) Paşa, who had been forcibly displaced from the beylical seat by his
younger brother Yusuf in 1796, "to reestablish the said Hamet Bashaw in the possession of his sovereignty of Tripoli, against the pretensions of Joseph Bashaw, who
obtained said sovereignty by treason, and who now holds it by usurpation" (art. 2).
In April 1805 some four hundred irregulars, mostly Arabs and Greeks, raised by
Eaton in Egypt and under his command, with the aid of three American fighting
ships, captured Darna, the first sizable settlement in the beylical jurisdiction, as the
Garrison was approached from the east. Eaton and his mercenaries held on to Darna,
despite counterattacks in May by the Garrison's forces, but before he could attempt to
proceed to Tripoli Yusuf signed with Tobias Lear, the American consul general at

Algiers, a new treaty of peace. Under it, the United States agreed to pay the Garrison $60,000 ransom for some two hundred American captives, but Lear successfully resisted Yusuf's efforts to include a tributary clause. Internal evidence shows that the treaty had been initially drafted in English, and the English and Arabic texts were both regarded as authentic. It should also be noted that in articles 6, 17, and 20 of the Arabic text the Turkish word for garrison (*ocak*) is used to refer to the government of Tripoli, and only once (art. 20) does the Arabic *dawlah* appear as a synonym. Also reproduced below is Lear's secret declaration, signed on 5 June 1805, about which the Jefferson Administration did not learn until two years later. Wright and Macleod, *First Americans in North Africa*; Cathcart, *Tripoli: Its First War with the United States*; Miller, op. cit., pp. 546–56; H. and M. Sprout, *Rise of American Naval Power*, chap. 5; Dupuy, *Américains et Barbaresques*, pp. 231–72; Knox, *History of the United States Navy*, chaps. 6–7; R. Anderson, *Naval Wars in the Levant*, chap. 14; Irwin, *Diplomatic Relations of the United States with the Barbary Powers*, chaps. 6–10; Field, *America and the Mediterranean World*, pp. 49–67; G. Allen, *Our Navy and the Barbary Corsairs*, chaps. 6–15.

1. The Eaton-Hamet Convention, 23 February 1805

God Is Infinite.

ART. 1. There shall be a firm and perpetual peace and free intercourse between the Government of the United States of America and His Highness Hamet Caramanly Bashaw, the legitimate sovereign of the kingdom of Tripoli, and between the citizens of the one and the subjects the other.

ART. 2. The Government of the United States shall use their utmost exertions, so far as comports with their own honor and interest, their subsisting treaties, and the acknowledged laws of nations, to re-establish the said Hamet Bashaw in the possession of his sovereignty of Tripoli, against the pretensions of Joseph Bashaw, who obtained said sovereignty by treason, and who now holds it by usurpation, and who is engaged in actual war against the United States.

ART. 3. The United States shall, as circumstances may require, in addition to the operations they are carrying on by sea, furnish the said Hamet Bashaw, on loan, supplies of cash, ammunition, and provisions, and if necessity require, debarkations of troops; also to aid and give effect to the operations of the said Hamet Bashaw, by land, against the common enemy.

ART. 4. In consideration of which friendly offices, once rendered effectual, His Highness Hamet Caramanly Bashaw engages, on his part, to release to the commander-in-chief of the forces of the United States, in the Mediterranean, without ransom, all American prisoners who are, or may hereafter be, in the hands of the usurper, said Joseph Bashaw.

ART. 5. In order to indemnify the United States against all expense they have or shall incur, in carrying into execution their engagements, expressed in the second and third articles of this convention, the said Hamet Bashaw transfers and consigns to the United States the tribute stipulated by the last treaties of His Majesty the King of Denmark, His Majesty the King of Sweden, and the Batavian republic, as the condition of peace with the regency of Tripoli, until such time as said expense shall be reimbursed.

ART. 6. In order to carry into full effect the stipulation expressed in the preceding article, said Hamet Bashaw pledges his faith and honor faithfully to observe and fulfil the treaties now subsisting between the regency of Tripoli and their Majesties the Kings of Denmark and Sweden, and with the Batavian republic.

ART. 7. In consideration of the friendly disposition of His Majesty the King of the Two Sicilies towards the American squadron, His Highness Hamet Bashaw invites His said Sicilian Majesty to renew their ancient friendship, and proffers him a peace on the footing of that to be definitively concluded with the United States of America, in the fullest extent of its privileges, according to the tenor of this convention.

ART. 8. The better to give effect to the operations to be carried on by land in the prosecution of the plan, and the attainment of the object pointed out by this convention, William Eaton, a citizen of the United States, now in Egypt, shall be recognised as general and commander-in-chief of the land forces which are or may be called into service against the common enemy; and His said Highness Hamet Bashaw engages that his own subjects shall respect and obey him as such.

ART. 9. His Highness, said Hamet Bashaw, grants full amnesty and perpetual oblivion towards the conduct of all such of his subjects as may have been seduced by the usurper to abandon his cause, and who are disposed to return to their proper allegiance.

ART. 10. In case of future war between the contracting parties, captives on each side shall be treated as prisoners of war, and not as slaves, and shall be entitled to reciprocal and equal exchange, man for man, and grade for grade; and in no case shall a ransom be demanded for prisoners of war, nor a tribute required, as the condition of peace, neither on the one part nor on the other. All prisoners on both sides shall be given up at the conclusion of peace.

ART. 11. The American consular flag in Tripoli shall for ever be a sacred asylum to all persons who shall desire to take refuge under it, except for the crimes of treason and murder.

ART. 12. In case of the faithful observance and fulfilment on the part of His Highness, said Hamet Bashaw, of the agreements and obligations herein stipulated, the said commander-in-chief of the American forces in the Mediterranean engages to leave said Hamet Bashaw in the peaceable possession of the city and regency of Tripoli, without dismantling its batteries.

ART. 13. Any article suitable to be introduced in a definitive treaty of peace between the contracting parties, which may not be comprised in this convention, shall be reciprocally on the footing of the treaties subsisting with the most favored nations.

ART. 14. This convention shall be submitted to the President of the United States for his ratification. In the mean time there shall be no suspense in its operations.

Done at Alexandria, in Egypt, February 23, 1805, and signed by said Hamet Bashaw, for himself and successors, and by William Eaton, on the part of the United States.

ADDITIONAL ARTICLE, SECRET.

His Highness Hamet Bashaw will use his utmost exertions to cause to surrender to the commander-in-chief of the American forces in the Mediterranean the usurper Joseph Bashaw, together with his family, and chief admiral called Maurad Rais, alias Peter Lisle, to be held by the Government of the United States as hostages, and as a guaranty of the faithful observance of the stipulations entered into by convention of the 23rd February, 1805, with the United States, provided they do not escape by flight.

2. Treaty of Peace and Amity: The United States and Tripoli, 4 June 1805

ART. 1. There shall be, from the conclusion of this Treaty, a firm, inviolable and universal peace, and a sincere friendship between the President and Citizens of the United States of America, on the one part, and the Bashaw, Bey and Subjects of the Regency of Tripoli in Barbary on the other, made by the free consent of both Parties, and on the terms of the most favoured Nation. And if either party shall hereafter grant to any other Nation, any particular favour or priviledge in Navigation or Commerce, it shall immediately become common to the other party, freely, where it is freely granted, to such other Nation, but where the grant is conditional it shall be at the option of the contracting parties to accept, alter or reject, such conditions in such manner, as shall be most conducive to their respective Interests.

ART. 2. The Bashaw of Tripoli shall deliver up to the American Squadron now off Tripoli, all the Americans in his possession; and all the Subjects of the Bashaw of Tripoli now in the power of the United States of America shall be delivered up to him; and as the number of Americans in possession of the Bashaw of Tripoli amounts to Three Hundred Persons, more or less; and the number of Tripoline Subjects in the power of the Americans to about, One Hundred more or less; The Bashaw of Tripoli shall receive from the United States of America, the sum of Sixty Thousand Dollars, as a payment for the difference between the Prisoners herein mentioned.

ART. 3. All the forces of the United States which have been, or may be in hostility against the Bashaw of Tripoli, in the Province of Derne, or elsewhere within the Dominions of the said Bashaw shall be withdrawn therefrom, and no supplies shall be given by or in behalf of the said United States, during the continuance of this peace, to any of the Subjects of the said Bashaw, who may be in hostility against him in any part of his Dominions; And the Americans will use all means in their power to persuade the Brother of the said Bashaw, who has co-operated with them at Derne &c, to withdraw from the Territory of the said Bashaw of Tripoli; but they will not use any force or improper means to effect that object; and in case he should withdraw himself as aforesaid, the Bashaw engages to deliver up to him, his Wife and Children now in his power.

ART. 4. If any goods belonging to any Nation with which either of the parties are at war, should be loaded on board Vessels belonging to the other party they shall pass free and unmolested, and no attempt shall be made to take or detain them.

ART. 5. If any Citizens, or Subjects with or [sic] their effects belonging to either party shall be found on board a Prize Vessel taken from an Enemy by the other party, such Citizens or Subjects shall be liberated immediately and their effects so captured shall be restored to their lawful owners or their Agents.

ART. 6. Proper passports shall immediately be given to the vessels of both the contracting parties, on condition that the Vessels of War belonging to the Regency of Tripoli on meeting with merchant Vessels belonging to Citizens of the United States of America, shall not be permitted to visit them with more than two persons besides the rowers, these two only shall be permitted to go on board said Vessel without first obtaining leave from the Commander of said Vessel, who shall compare the passport, and immediately permit said Vessel to proceed on her voyage; and should any of the said Subjects of Tripoli insult or molest the Commander or any other person on board a Vessel so visited; or plunder any of the property contained in her; On complaint being made by the Consul of the United States of America resident at Tripoli and on his producing sufficient proof to substantiate the fact, The Commander or Rais of said Tripoline Ship or Vessel of War, as well as the Offenders shall be punished in the most exemplary manner.

All Vessels of War belonging to the United States of America on meeting with a Cruizer belonging to the Regency of Tripoli, and having seen her passport and Certificate from the Consul of the United States of America residing in the Regency, shall permit her to proceed on her Cruize unmolested, and without detention. No passport shall be granted by either party to any Vessels, but such as are absolutely the property of Citizens or Subjects of said contracting parties, on any pretence whatever.

ART. 7. A Citizen or Subject of either of the contracting parties having bought a Prize Vessel condemned by the other party, or by any other Nation, the Certificate of condemnation and Bill of Sale shall be a sufficient passport for such Vessel for two years, which, considering the distance between the two Countries, is no more than a reasonable time for her to procure proper passports.

ART. 8. Vessels of either party, putting into the ports of the other, and having need of provisions or other supplies, they shall be furnished at the Market price, and if any such Vessel should so put in from a disaster at Sea, and have occasion to repair; she shall be at liberty to land and reimbark her Cargo, without paying any duties; but in no case shall she be compelled to land her Cargo.

ART. 9. Should a Vessel of either party be cast on the shore of the other, all proper assistance shall be given to her and her Crew. No pillage shall be allowed, the property shall remain at the disposition of the owners, and the Crew protected and succoured till they can be sent to their Country.

ART. 10. If a Vessel of either party, shall be attacked by an Enemy within Gun shot of the Forts of the other, she shall be defended as much as possible; If she be in port, she shall not be seized or attacked when it is in the power of the other party to protect her; and when she proceeds to Sea, no Enemy shall be allowed to pursue her from the same port, within twenty four hours after her departure.

ART. 11. The Commerce between the United States of America and the Regency of Tripoli; The Protections to be given to Merchants, Masters of Vessels and Seamen; The reciprocal right of establishing Consuls in each Country; and the priviledges, immunities and jurisdictions to be enjoyed by such Consuls, are declared to be on the same footing, with those of the most favoured Nations respectively.

ART. 12. The Consul of the United States of America shall not be answerable for debts contracted by Citizens of his own Nation, unless, he previously gives a written obligation so to do.

ART. 13. On a Vessel of War, belonging to the United States of America, anchoring before the City of Tripoli, the Consul is to inform the Bashaw of her arrival, and she shall be saluted with twenty one Guns, which she is to return in the same quantity or number.

ART. 14. As the Government of the United States of America, has in itself no character of enmity against the Laws, Religion or Tranquility of Musselmen, and as the said States never have entered into any voluntary war or act of hostility against any Mahometan Nation, except in the defence of their just rights to freely navigate the High Seas: It is declared by the contracting parties that no pretext arising from Religious Opinions, shall ever produce an interruption of the Harmony existing between the two Nations; And the Consuls and Agents of both Nations respectively, shall have liberty to exercise his Religion in his own house; all slaves of the same Religion shall not be impeded in going to said Consuls house at hours of Prayer. The Consuls shall have liberty and personal security given them to travel within the Territories of each other, both by land and sea, and shall not be prevented from going on board any Vessel that they may think proper to visit; they shall have likewise the liberty to appoint their own Drogoman and Brokers.

ART. 15. In case of any dispute arising from the violation of any of the articles of this Treaty, no appeal shall be made to Arms, nor shall War be declared on any pretext whatever; but if the Consul residing at the place, where the dispute shall happen, shall not be able to settle the same; The Government of that Country shall state their grievances in writing, and transmit it to the Government of the other, and the period of twelve Callendar months shall be allowed for answers to be returned; during which time no act of hostility shall be permitted by either party, and in case the grievances are not redressed, and War should be the event, the Consuls and Citizens or Subjects of both parties reciprocally shall be permitted to embark with their effects unmolested, on board of what vessel or Vessels they shall think proper.

ART. 16. If in the fluctuation of Human Events, a War should break out between the two Nations; The Prisoners captured by either party shall not be made Slaves; but shall be exchanged Rank for Rank; and if there should be a deficiency on either side, it shall be made up by the payment of Five Hundred Spanish Dollars for each Captain, Three Hundred Dollars for each Mate and Supercargo and One hundred Spanish Dollars for each Seaman so wanting. And it is agreed that Prisoners shall be exchanged in twelve months from the time of their capture, and that this Exchange may be effected by any private Individual legally authorized by either of the parties.

ART. 17. If any of the Barbary States, or other powers at War with the United States of America, shall capture any American Vessel, and send her into any of the ports of the Regency of Tripoli, they shall not be permitted to sell her, but shall be obliged to depart the Port on procuring the requisite supplies of Provisions; and no duties shall be exacted on the sale of Prizes captured by Vessels sailing under the Flag of the United States of America when brought into any Port in the Regency of Tripoli.

ART. 18. If any of the Citizens of the United States, or any persons under their protection, shall have any dispute with each other, the Consul shall decide between the parties; and whenever the Consul shall require any aid or assistance from the Government of Tripoli, to enforce his decisions, it shall immediately be granted to him. And if any dispute shall arise between any Citizen of the United States and the Citizens or Subjects of any other Nation, having a Consul or Agent in Tripoli, such dispute shall be settled by the Consuls or Agents of the respective Nations.

Art. 19. If a Citizen of the United States should kill or wound a Tripoline, or, on the contrary, if a Tripoline shall kill or wound a Citizen of the United States, the law of the Country shall take place, and equal justice shall be rendered, the Consul assisting at the trial; and if any delinquent shall make his escape, the Consul shall not be answerable for him in any manner whatever.

Art. 20. Should any Citizen of the United States of America die within the limits of the Regency of Tripoli, the Bashaw and his Subjects shall not interfere with the property of the deceased; but it shall be under the immediate direction of the Consul, unless otherwise disposed of by will. Should there be no Consul, the effects shall be deposited in the hands of some person worthy of trust, until the party shall appear who has a right to demand them, when they shall render an account of the property. Neither shall the Bashaw or his Subjects give hindrance in the execution of any will that may appear.

Whereas, the undersigned, Tobias Lear, Consul General of the United States of America for the Regency of Algiers, being duly appointed Commissioner, by letters patent under the signature of the President, and Seal of the United States of America, bearing date at the City of Washington, the 18" day of November 1803 for negociating and concluding a Treaty of Peace, between the United States of America, and the Bashaw, Bey and Subjects of the Regency of Tripoli in Barbary—

Now Know Ye, That I, Tobias Lear, Commissioner as aforesaid, do conclude the foregoing Treaty, and every article and clause therein contained; reserving the same nevertheless for the final ratification of the President of the United States of America, by and with the advice and consent of the Senate of the said United States. . . .

Having appeared in our presence, Colonel Tobias Lear, Consul General of the United States of America, in the Regency of Algiers, and Commissioner for negociating and concluding a Treaty of Peace and Friendship between Us and the United States of America, bringing with him the present Treaty of Peace with the within Articles, they were by us minutely examined, and we do hereby accept, confirm and ratify them, Ordering all our Subjects to fulfill entirely their contents, without any violation and under no pretext.

In Witness whereof We, with the heads of our Regency, Subscribe it.

Given at Tripoli in Barbary the sixth day of the first month of Rabbia 1220, corresponding with the 4th. day of June 1805.

(L. S.) Jusuf Caramanly *Bashaw*
(L. S.) Mohamet Caramanly *Bey*
(L. S.) Mohamet *Kahia*
(L. S.) Hamet *Rais de Marino*
(L. S.) Mohamet Dghies *First Minister*
(L. S.) Salah *Aga of Divan*
(L. S.) Selim *Hasnadar*
(L. S.) Murat *Dulartile*
(L. S.) Murat Rais *Admiral*
(L. S.) Soliman *Kehia*
(L. S.) Abdalla *Basa Aga*
(L. S.) Mahomet *Scheig al Belad*
(L. S.) Alli Ben Diab *First Secretary*

48. RENEWED TREATY OF DEFENSIVE ALLIANCE:
THE OTTOMAN EMPIRE AND RUSSIA
11/23 September 1805

(Russian ratification, Breslau, 3/15 November 1805; ratifications exchanged, Istanbul, 17/29 December 1805; denounced by the Sublime Porte, 2/14 November 1806)
[Open treaty translated from the French text in Noradounghian, *Recueil d'actes internationaux de l'empire ottoman*, 2: 70–77; secret treaty translated from the agreed text, ratified and deposited by Russia at the Sublime Porte, Turkey, State Archives, Istanbul, Dosya 886]

The renewed Russian-Ottoman defensive alliance of 1805, which seemed doomed from the moment of signature and lasted little longer than a year, would probably have had no more than antiquarian interest had the Soviet government not used the instrument in 1943–47 as a legal basis for pressing the Soviet claim to joint responsibility with Turkey for the defense of the straits, and to closure of the Black Sea to the naval vessels of all but the riparian powers. This was not a new claim, the Soviet government insisted, but a reaffirmation of an old principle, first enunciated in the Russian-Ottoman defensive alliance of 1805. It was later discovered, however, that the Russian evidence rested on a diplomatic and literary fraud, first perpetrated on the international community early in the twentieth century by Sergei Goriainov, the then director of the Central Imperial Archives in Saint Petersburg. The deception was set forth in 1907 in *Bosfor i Dardanelly*, which appeared three years later in French translation under the title *Le Bosphore et les Dardanelles*. Goriainov based his study almost entirely on unpublished documents in the Russian Foreign Ministry in Saint Petersburg, failing even to mention by name available books on the straits question. Manifestly framed as an official statement, the book was used as such. A political tract disguised as scholarship, the Goriainov book also served Russian, Turkish, and Western scholars as an authentic Russian source, for lack of alternative evidence. The key to the puzzle is article 7 of the secret treaty, which, according to Goriainov, included the following clause (absent from the Turkish text): "It is understood that the free passage through the Canal of Constantinople will continue in effect for the vessels of war and military transports of His Imperial Majesty of All the Russias, to which in every instance the Sublime Porte will furnish every assistance and grant every facility that may be required" (*Le Bosphore et les Dardanelles*, p. 6). As is demonstrated beyond contention by the text of the secret treaty, reproduced below in English for the first time, no such clause appeared in the agreed French text ratified by the tsarist government in November 1805 and deposited at the Sublime Porte. Article 7 of the 1805 secret treaty was identical with article 4 of the 1799 treaty, (Doc. 39), and under neither instrument did Russia share with the Ottoman Empire the defense of the straits and the Black Sea, much less did Russian naval vessels enjoy free transit through the straits, even in common action against the supposed common enemy. Had it not been for British mediation, the 1805 instrument would never have been signed. At the moment of signature, in fact, the Russian Foreign Ministry was unsure which alternative plan for aggrandizement at Ottoman expense it would attempt to execute: the forcible occupation of the Ottoman provinces of Moldavia and

Wallachia (in present-day Rumania), where Russia had acquired limited rights of intervention under the treaty of Küçük Kaynarca (art. 16), or a renewal of the 1799 alliance, which the Sublime Porte was resisting. Russia clearly preferred the second plan, in the hope that it might, together with the Russian-Ottoman convention of 1800 on the Ionian Islands (Doc. 44), enable the Russian navy to establish the precedent of free use of the straits. Despite the renewal of the alliance, Russia proceeded to occupy Moldavia and Wallachia in less than a year, precipitating war with the Ottoman Empire, which denounced the treaty in November 1806. For the Russian navy, denial of free transit through the straits kept the Black Sea a sealed body of water. Hurewitz, "Russia and the Turkish Straits"; Goriainov, *Le Bosphore et les Dardanelles*, chaps. 2–4; Puryear, *Napoleon and the Dardanelles*, chaps. 3–4; Phillipson and Buxton, *Question of the Bosphorus and Dardanelles*, pt. 2, chap. 2; Headlam-Morley, *Studies in Diplomatic History*, chap. 8; Muravieff, *L'alliance russo-turque, pp.* 197–202, and annex 17, p. 405.

1. Public Treaty

ART. 1. As a result of the peace, amity, and good understanding very fortunately existing between the Sultan of the Ottomans and the Emperor of All the Russias as well as between their respective states and subjects, the bonds of good relations based on their mutual security and prosperity shall not only be maintained but shall also be drawn closer by the present Defensive Alliance, so that the friend of one of the two states will be considered a friend of the other and the enemy of the one an enemy of the other. In consequence. His Imperial Majesty the Sultan and His Majesty the Emperor of Russia undertake to act loyally in concert on all questions affecting the peace and security of the two Contracting Parties, and to ally themselves n taking necessary measures to repel every aggression against their respective countries and to reestablish the common peace.

ART. 2. Whenever any power may manifest enmity toward one of the two Allied Powers or toward both, the Allied Power shall do everything that it can to prevent acts of hostility, but if it fails in its efforts to settle the litigation peacefully, and if the menaced state is not in a position to repel with its own means the attack launched against it, its Ally shall come to its assistance with land and sea forces. In the event, however, that the required state cannot furnish an army of assistance because of its geographic position or remoteness, it shall then be obliged to help its Ally financially in proportion to the costs involved in sending an auxiliary army. As regards naval forces, the number of warships placed by one Ally at the service of the other shall not be fewer than six ships of the line and four frigates; and as regards land forces, the troops shall consist of at least ten thousand infantrymen and two thousand cavalrymen; but the land and sea forces shall not be furnished without a preliminary understanding to that effect.

ART. 3. The choice between armed assistance or a financial subsidy rests with the attacked state. If the latter requests assistance in the form of troops and war vessels, they will be furnished within a maximum of three months from the date of request. If financial assistance is requested, it will be furnished in installments effective the date of the declaration of war by the aggressor state or the date of commencement of hostilities.

ART. 4. Armament in artillery, war munitions, and all the equipment of the assisting forces shall be at the expense of the expeditionary state. As to the rations of wheat, barley, straw, and hay, they will be furnished in kind by the state requiring [the forces], in same proportion and quality as those adopted in its own army in time of war, and this from the day the troops leave the frontiers of their country. To avoid any error or delay in this connection, the routes to be followed by these troops will be indicated in advance by the state requiring assistance. The state that has required assistance, for its part, will provide the troops of its Ally with the same facilities and accommodations as those which they enjoy in their country and those which are assured to its own troops.

ART. 5. The state that may require from its Ally the assistance of a naval force will be responsible for furnishing, this force with necessary rations, effective on the date of arrival of the force in its territorial waters or in the waters where it may be called to maneuver, and for as long a time as it may serve against the common enemy, subject to conditions to be agreed upon by the two Parties. In the event that it proves impossible to furnish the rations in kind, a financial subsidy proportional to the value of the rations agreed upon shall be paid. Furthermore, when the vessels of the assisting fleet may need repairs, the state requesting assistance will provide same in its own arsenals and stores, at current prices, without the least delay and without raising any difficulty. In addition to the vessels of the said fleet, the same treatment will also be assured, for the duration of the alliance, to other vessels of war and transport of the two Powers destined for common service. These vessels shall, therefore, have the right to enter without impediment the ports of one and the other Party for winter haven or for repair.

ART. 6. If the attacked state is unable, with its own forces or with the assistance of the land and sea forces furnished by its Ally in conformity with Article 2 of this Treaty, to repel the aggression directed against it, its Ally shall participate openly in the war, using all available forces until the conclusion of peace, provided, however, that this participation by land and by sea is possible in terms of its geographic position; but if the great distance separating the two countries renders impossible for one of the Allies direct participation in the war with all its forces, and if the attacked state signifies its desire to see the assisting contingent of land and sea forces augmented, the two states shall reach a common agreement on the scope and conditions of the necessary supplementary help.

ART. 7. The two High Contracting Parties undertake to communicate loyally to each other information pertaining to military measures taken, and mutually to facilitate their execution on all occasions when their collective action is necessary, using all available forces or furnishing each other the assistance stipulated in the present Treaty. They also obligate themselves to consult together concerning the prolongation of hostilities or the eventual conditions of peace. Neither of the two Allied States may conclude an armistice or peace with the enemy without including its Ally and without assuring the security of the two countries.

ART. 8. The two Contracting States agree that, in commencing the salute when their fleets or large vessels or other ships of war meet, account will be taken of the rank of the commanders, as evidenced by the flag hoisted to that effect. If the commanders of the two parties have the same rank, they will not exchange salutes. [In the case of unequal rank] the one receiving the salute will answer by firing an equivalent number of guns. When meeting, the parties involved will therefore act in concert, through the dispatch of launches, in order to avoid errors or misunderstanding on the subject.

ART. 9. The arms and munitions of war and the various effects taken from the enemy during the war will belong to the troops which seized them.

ART. 10. While the two High Contracting Parties have the right to negotiate and conclude, as in the past treaties and conventions with other Powers, they nevertheless undertake in a clear and precise manner not to conclude agreements which might adversely affect the interests of the Allied State or its territorial integrity, or to grant commercial advantages which might be harmful to the interests of the populations and subjects of the other country. On the contrary, each of the two Contracting Powers undertakes to defend to the extent possible in such a case the interests, the glory, and the security of the other Party.

ART. 11. Since His Imperial Majesty the Sultan and His Majesty the Emperor of Russia, in concluding the present Treaty of Defensive Alliance, seek no territorial expansion but only the maintenance of the integrity of their states, the security of their respective subjects, and the balance essential to public tranquillity, and since they wish in this respect to safeguard from danger the positions of other states, they have decided to invite to participate in the Alliance the King of England and other Powers which, guided by laudable purposes, might be desirous of entering into such an Alliance.

ART. 12. The Treaty of Peace concluded at Jassy on 29 December 1791/9 January 1792 and other conventions and acts mentioned therein plus the Treaty of Peace [relating to the Ionian Islands] signed on 21 March/2 April 1800 are confirmed, with the exception of clauses that have been modified by subsequent acts and by the clauses of the present Treaty of Alliance.

ART. 13. In order to strengthen their alliance, the two Contracting States mutually guarantee the integrity of all territories presently in their possession.

ART. 14. The two Contracting States have the firm desire to respect, as far as possible, the substance of the present Treaty of Defensive Alliance. Since, however, changes in time and circumstances may require the alteration of some clauses, it has been decided that [this Treaty] shall remain in force for a period of nine years following the date of the exchange of ratifications. At the approach of the expiry of this period, renewal of the act will be the subject of friendly negotiations between the two states. . . .

2. Secret Articles Annexed to the Public Treaty

ART. 1. Their Majesties the Emperor and Padişah of All the Russias and the Emperor of the Ottomans, taking into mature consideration the present circumstances in Europe and the conduct of the French Government which, dictated by its ambition and its projects of aggrandizement which are contrary to the principles of justice and of equity, has upset the political equilibrium and has rendered precarious the situation of all the states exposed to its hostile aggressions, [and] considering above all the existence of its views and its schemes against the dominions of the Sublime Porte, as well as the demands of Their Majesties' most sincere friendship, the preservation and solidity of which are affirmed for the future by the renewed Treaty of Defensive Alliance, have recognized the necessity of frank and unreserved

discussion between them on all these important questions. Following these overtures it was reciprocally agreed that if, to frustrate the ulterior schemes of aggrandizement of the French Government, to restore the political equilibrium, and to procure the security and tranquillity of all the states that the said Government menaces, several of the Great Powers of Europe should decide to unite their efforts and form a coalition, and if in this event His Imperial Majesty of All the Russias should decide for the good of his Allies and that of Europe as a whole to take an active part in such a defensive coalition from its inception, the Sublime Porte, desiring to contribute to the felicitous results of such a defensive coalition, which, in promoting the general welfare of Europe, would serve in particular to protect the Ottoman Empire against the sinister schemes of France, should make common cause with its august Ally, the Emperor of All the Russias, or should at least furnish His Imperial Majesty with the aid mentioned in Article 2 of the present Treaty of Defensive Alliance and in a manner conforming to the stipulations of the same Treaty. At the same time the Sublime Porte shall, for the duration of such a war, facilitate the passage through the Canal of Constantinople of warships and military transports that His Majesty the Emperor may be obliged to send into the Mediterranean, and [the Sublime Porte] shall comply with the salutary views of its Ally, His [Russian] Majesty.

ART. 2. His Majesty the Emperor and Padişah of All the Russias, proposing to invite the Courts of Vienna, Berlin, Stockholm, Copenhagen, and others to accede to the coalition that might be formed by him with England and one of the above-named Powers for the purpose of together compelling France to support the organization of a system that would restore the political balance of Europe and guarantee the sacred rights of nations and the general transquillity, undertakes simultaneously to inform them that His Majesty the Ottoman Emperor, his august Ally, will make common cause with him in order to contribute to the happy results of this defensive coalition. His Majesty the Ottoman Emperor reposes confidence in the wisdom of His Majesty the Emperor of

Russia on the means he believes should be employed for [issuing] these invitations and [this] information.

ART. 3. The Sublime Porte, desiring and intending that the stipulations of the earlier convention on the formerly-Venetian cities and districts in Albania that have been reunited with [the Ottoman] realm should be observed in their entirety and that the proper means of procuring the well-being and tranquillity of the inhabitants of the said cities should be provided [in accordance with] the privileges and prerogatives granted to them under the said convention, promises and pledges not to allow anyone to scorn its stipulations. [Neither] the paşas and the chiefs of the neighboring provinces nor the commanders and officers of the navy shall introduce armed men into the said cities and districts and impose taxes upon the population. The governing *voivoda* and his aides, may not abridge in any manner either the privileges and immunities of the population or the stipulations made in its favor. Finally, [the Sublime Porte], in conformity with the said stipulations, shall enable the [local population] to enjoy all the advantages that they enjoyed under the domination of the former Republic of Venice.

In a word, the convention concluded on 8 Zilkade 1214 A.H., that is, 21 March/2 April 1800, is confirmed by the present Treaty of [Defensive] Alliance as if it had been inserted [herein] word for word, and if, in breach of the present secret article, the servants and other subjects of the Sublime [Porte][1] should harass or cause damage to the population of the said formerly [Venetian][1] littora[ls of the Subli][1] me Porte, those responsible shall be obliged, on the remonstrances of the Minister of the Court of Russia, to make suitable reparations.

ART. 4. His Imperial Majesty of All the Russias, in virtue of the first article of the convention concluded between him and His Majesty the Ottoman Emperor on 21 March/2 April 1800, that is, on 8 Zilkade 1214 A.H., guarantees that he and his successors shall assure the integrity of the territories of the united Septinsular [Ionian] Republic. In view of the present circumstances in Italy, foresight demanding the presence of Russian troops in these

islands, it is agreed that they shall not be recalled until the situation that motivates their presence has been brought under control.

In exchange for this proof of sincere friendship by the Court of Russia, the Ottoman Porte, for the duration of the presence of Russian troops in the territory of the Septinsular Republic, shall facilitate the passage through the Canal of Constantinople of Russian warships destined to replace the naval forces in the said islands or to supply and relieve the troops stationed there.

ART. 5. The united Septinsular Republic, vassal of the Sublime Porte, must be viewed as a barrier [in defense of Ottoman] districts near the Italian coast. His Majesty the Ottoman Emperor, recognizing the need for this Republic to acquire a degree of stability and strength that might suffice for its own defense, and also wishing to attach himself to its population and to prove that it is to his dignity and his [sense of] justice no less than to his interest that this Republic should maintain itself in the political state procured for it by the convention of 8 Zilkade 1214 [A.H.], that is, 21 March/2 April 1800, between the two High Contracting Parties, promises to revoke those articles of the Imperial Statute, previously granted to this Republic, that contravene the text of the said convention concluded by the two Powers so that this Statute might be modified in a manner conforming to the previously cited stipulations and so that nothing in general might be neglected to enable this Republic to become firmly established and to acquire esteem.

ART. 6. Since this Alliance between the two Empires and the aid for which it provides in favor of both have as an object the mutual security and advantage [of the Parties], and [since] the desertion of their ships' crews and auxiliary troops can only weaken such aid, the two High Contracting Parties promise neither to receive nor to retain under any motive or pretext what-

---

1. These words in the original are partly illegible, occurring, as they do, at the bottom of a page that has been damaged. There is nevertheless no doubt about the accuracy of the reconstructed text.

soever deserters from their respective land and sea troops, religion being the only case excepted. Thus, if Russian subjects originally Muslims should desert, they shall be returned, and Russian Christian subjects who might embrace Islam shall continue to serve in the Russian fleet or armies until the time when these auxiliary land or sea forces shall return to the realm of the Power that has furnished them. At that time action shall be taken in their behalf, according to Article 8 of the Treaty of Jassy.

ART. 7. The two Contracting Parties have agreed to consider the Black Sea closed and not to permit the appearance therein of any flag of war or armed vessel of any Power whatsoever, and if [any] should attempt to appear there in arms the two High Contracting Parties undertake to view such an attempt as *casus foederis* and to resist it with all their naval forces, as the only means of assuring their mutual tranquillity.

ART. 8. If in hostility to the present Alliance French troops that are presently [stationed] adjacent to Denmark should seize the Straits of Sund on the Baltic Sea, which serves as an outlet for the most lucrative commerce of North Russia and is the indispensable passage for the dispatch of its fleets to distant parts, giving rise to a state of war between this Court [Russia]

and France, the Sublime Porte, reciprocating the lively interest and the general anxiety that His Imperial [Russian] Majesty has manifested in [Ottoman] affairs, promises and pledges that, after prior consultation with the Court of Russia, it will either make common cause with it or furnish the stipulated assistance.

ART. 9. The quality of financial aid stipulated in Article 3 of the patent provisions [of the present Treaty] shall be fixed as follows: This aid shall be paid in cash at the rate of 100 piasters annually for each infantryman and 150 for each cavalryman, and this sum shall be paid precisely every three months, in advance, by the assisting Power, at the request of the attacked and petitioning Party, from the first month of the declaration of war until the conclusion of peace.

If it should become necessary to act in conformity with Articles 1 and 8 of the secret provisions, financial aid shall be furnished in the same way until the situation that prompted the assistance shall cease to exist.

ART. 10. The present secret articles shall be concealed from the other Powers, to which nothing shall be divulged. The articles shall be shown upon agreement between the two Parties only to those Powers that might accede to this Alliance. . . .

49. THE END OF THE BRITISH-OTTOMAN ALLIANCE AND THE SEVERANCE OF RELATIONS
25–27 January 1807

[Ottoman record of proceedings translated by Halil Inalcik from the Osmanlı text in Turkey, State Archives, Istanbul, Hatt-ı Hümayunlar no. 6971; British report from Great Britain, Public Record Office, F.O. 78/55, Ambassador Charles Arbuthnot at Istanbul to Foreign Minister Viscount Howick, 27 January 1807, no. 9 and enclosure]

Having framed with Russia in 1798–99 an alliance to which Britain became linked on terms of full equality for the three signatories, the Ottoman government behaved accordingly. It accepted Russian naval cooperation against France in the Adriatic but did not invite the aid of Russian land forces to which it was entitled under article 6 of the 1799 secret treaty. From Britain the sultan procured military and naval aid in expelling French forces from Egypt. He also procured unlimited territorial guarantees, which, through palpably shaped with France in mind, might also be invoked against Russia, whose thinly disguised imperial policies, even under the alliance, gave the padişah's vezirs pause. Russia in turn comported itself as if the alliance were unequal, and General Vasilii Tomara, the tsarist ambassador, patronized and bullied the Sublime Porte. Lord Elgin, the British ambassador, on the other hand, treated the Ottoman Empire as an equal partner and hardly concealed his disapproval of Russia's excesses toward its formal ally. After the peace with France at Amiens (Doc. 46), the triple alliance fell apart, and in the next two years each of the three partners in rotation, as the shifting circumstances seemed to dictate, urged its resuscitation, Andrei J. Italinskii, the tsar's envoy after Amiens, did not deviate from Tomara's style and pursued identical policies under close instructions from Saint Petersburg. However, Charles Arbuthnot, Elgin's successor, went uninstructed during his service at Istanbul until just before the rupture of British-Ottoman relations early in 1807. Arbuthnot had no choice but to make his own decisions, and throughout his tour of duty he remained faithful to his original mission, to which he was appointed in June 1804, of promoting a British-Russian alliance against an expansionist France, while trying to keep the Sublime Porte a friendly third partner. But the new British ambassador did not take up duties until thirteen months after his appointment, by which time the international situation had changed radically. No longer first consul but now emperor, Napoleon was on the rampage, moving from victory to victory, with the exception in October 1805 of Trafalgar, where Nelson in any case had given his life. Little wonder that the uninstructed Arbuthnot, tucked away in the forgotten extremity of southeastern Europe, slavishly upheld Italinskii's imperial policies toward the Ottoman Empire and copied his arrogant style. This eased the mission of General Horace Sébastiani, Napoleon's flamboyant ambassador, who appeared in Istanbul in August 1806 with instructions to smash the triple alliance. Ironically, the first word from the Foreign Office, dated November 1806, came to Arbuthnot at the end of January 1807, generally endorsing his proposals. This prompted Arbuthnot to take the action explained in the documents below, which led at once to the severance of relations, followed by the disastrous naval diplomacy of Vice-Admiral Sir John Duckworth off the Istanbul coast, and then war between Britain and the Ottoman Empire for the first time since England had accredited a permanent diplomatic mission to the padişah at the end of the sixteenth century. These documents illumine not only the events of the day but even more significantly the sophistication of Ottoman diplomacy under Sultan Selim III (1789–1807), who was the first Ottoman ruler to experiment with reciprocal continuous diplomacy. Selim's vezirs, to judge from their report of the conversations with Arbuthnot, were well versed in the diplomatic and international rules of the European state system, three decades before the Ottoman government finally and fully entered that system. Hurewitz, "Russia and the Turkish Straits," and "Ottoman Diplomacy and the European State System"; Rose, *Indecisiveness of Modern War*, chap. 10; Lewis, *Emergence of Modern Turkey*, chap. 3; Shupp, *European Powers and the Near Eastern Question*; Mackesy, *War in the Mediterranean*, chap. 6; R. Anderson, *Naval Wars in the Levant*, p. 437 ff; M. Anderson, *Eastern Question*, p. 34 ff; Puryear, *Napoleon and the Dardanelles*, chaps. 6–7; and Coquelle, "Sébastiani, ambassadeur à Constantinople."

1. Proceedings of a Conference with the British Ambassador, Sunday, 16 Zilkade 1221 [25 January 1807]

The Ambassador requested the conference. The honorable Ismet Bey Efendi and Ibrahim Nesim Efendi met at the office of the Reis Efendi [the official chiefly concerned with foreign affairs] at the Porte, where the Kethuda Bey [the Grand Vezir's deputy] and the Reis Efendi were also present. The Ambassador arrived before noon on that day. After the usual formalities, the Ambassador began to speak gently, stating:

> When the Reis Efendi and I discussed the subject of Russia in the past, my strong representation derived from a sentiment, not of hostility toward, but of affection for the Imperial [Ottoman] Government and particularly from a desire to bolster the friendship between the Imperial Government and England. I wish that my representation at that time had not been viewed as strong and that my advice had been followed. Now, I am honored that a new meeting with the ministers of the Imperial Government has been granted. If my explanation once again appears angry and severe, this may be attributed to my sympathy and to the urgent instructions given me by my government. And if the reis efendi is disappointed, I beg his pardon.

At this point the reis efendi said that the matter had already been explored with [Count F.] Pisani [the British dragoman]. Both agreed that "the past is past." "In time of friendship," [continued the reis efendi], "such utterances are not taken into account. We must now turn to the business at hand."

The Ambassador, speaking again, said:

> In view of my latest instructions and the expectation that this may be our last meeting, what I say vehemently may be attributed to the requirements of official duty, since I am basically friendly [to your government] and unselfish in my character. Thus, should our present conference become heated because of the dictates of the situation, no other meaning must be given to it. You must also pardon any short-comings that I may have.
>
> Previously, in the Russian campaign, I warned the Sublime Porte that, if the Russian Ambassador, [Andrei] Italinskii, departed, I too would leave. At that time I did not have instructions from my government, but it seems to me now that I acted just like a fortune-teller. Now, first of all, I propose to treat the events of the past year in detail: It is observed that the triple alliance [which united the Ottoman Empire with Russia and Britain] previously yielded many good results. A proposal for renewing the alliance with England was thus expected to come from the Imperial Government.
>
> An English Ambassador was awaited for some time, and on my arrival the office of Reis Efendi inquired about my written authorization to conclude the alliance. I, too, wrote to my government, which issued the requested authorization. Upon presentation of this written authorization, I was told that [the negotiation] had to be deferred because Ramazan intervened and that the matter would be settled after the *bayram*, and I believed what was told me. After the bayram, when I asked about this, I received the reply "We are busy now," and the matter was [again] postponed.
>
> In this period of procrastination the Russian-Austrian War against France broke out. Although these campaigns had nothing to do with the English alliance, all my efforts to renew that alliance were fruitless. However, I did my best to interpret the delay in the most positive manner possible, by writing to my government that the term of the alliance had not expired and that upon its expiry it would be renewed. But the Imperial Government did not pay any attention to this situation. What is more, at that time, a Frenchman named Roux [Talleyrand's secretary] arrived and, even though of common origin, he was received as an honored ambassador and met with the Grand Vezir and the Reis Efendi.
>
> Furthermore, the English Government respectfully requested the Imperial Government, through me, not to

recognize Bonaparte's empire. After many exchanges on this subject and my delivery of the note, the news of the recognition of the empire suddenly reached me, and, what is more, the English Government considered my note wholly fitting. Moreover, the English Government pursued lengthy bilateral talks on the subjects of *berat* holders and protection. While the English Government expected more special favors than the other governments, it suffered instead worse treatment than the others. In the matter of the regulation of customs, the English Government also sought an arrangement, but this inevitably produced disadvantages for English nationals. Although it was explicitly noted that the tariff would be enforced throughout Ottoman dominions, it was not generally observed, and, most significantly, never in Egypt. We refrained from insisting on our rights by resort to force.

After this, the French sent [General Horace] Sébastiani, who was received with such extraordinary honor and warmth that on the anniversary of Bonaparte's birthday he was given five horses. This honor was never before displayed by the Imperial Government toward the officials of any other government. This became unbearable to the English King, who said, "I sent to the Imperial Government a ranking ambassador in the expectation that he would be honored more than the others by the Imperial Government, but Sébastiani was preferred. In particular, [this is insulting because] Bonaparte is not of noble origin, as I am, but is nothing more than a juggler." My purpose in mentioning all this, emphasizing that the successive actions of the Imperial Government caused great concern to the English King, is as an introduction to the following matters:

Thus, on arrival, Sébastiani presented to the Sublime Porte a note, copies of which were given by the late Vasif Efendi to me and to the Russian Ambassador. Included in this note were words that might provide a pretext for damaging the friendship between [our] two states, among them two clauses [which] might furnish cause for complaint. The first one called upon the Imperial Government to give up the Russian and English alliances and to permit French soldiers now in Dalmatia to pass through Albania and cross the Danube against the Russians. This suggestion may not be overlooked. The other one proposed that any enemy of France should be viewed as the enemy of the Imperial Government. These are matters giving rise to suspicions that might destroy friendship.

Sébastiani should not have been received at that time but should have been expelled at once. Besides, the said note requested that Russian ships should not be allowed to pass through the straits. The Imperial Government, adopting this suggestion, proposed it to the Russian Ambassador. In the meantime the question of the Beyler (the hospodars, or Ottoman governors, of Moldavia and Wallachia) became critical, and Russia advocated their retention. While immediate compliance with this proposal was required by the terms of the agreement, the Imperial Government waited three weeks before settling the issue. If this is added to the other actions of the Imperial Government, [it becomes apparent that] an estrangement between the two states was unavoidable.

Furthermore, in my recently received instructions, my assignment is that which was expressly stipulated in the previous alliance, [to wit,] that "the friend of one of the two states is the friend of the other, and the enemy of the one is the enemy of the other." But in the war with France, England and Russia consented to the Imperial Government's choice of neutrality. Yet nothing resulted from this.

Because the Imperial Government has been leaning toward France, the English Government has proposed to the Imperial Government the renewal of the alliance as it was before and the expulsion of Sébastiani. If the Imperial Government should not accept this proposal, in view of the present war with Russia, it is manifest that its friendship with England will become subject to change. Since my expectation is that the Imperial Government will give a negative reply, and since this is my government's view as well, I have been instructed to issue a circular to the English merchants advising them to wind up their affairs and prepare [for departure]. I am also instructed to give the same notice to English subjects throughout Ottoman dominions. Therefore, after sending [all English subjects] away, I shall remain alone. If the Russian fleet together with the English fleet should enter the straits as far as the forts, and if England is given equal treatment with Russia, I shall join the fleet, remain there, and act according to the circumstances.

To prove his statement the Ambassador displayed a document in English from the Prime Minister and pointed to the latter's signature and revealed its contents. Thereupon the dragoman of the Divan (the Ottoman Imperial Court) requested the document for translation after this discussion. He sent a copy of the Turkish translation,[1] which follows:

As a condition for unselfish help and strong assistance, the French demanded that the Imperial Government terminate its agreements with its former tested allies. Otherwise the places that were allegedly occupied as a means of defense would be transformed into bases for attack. All this puzzled the Ottomans. If the Imperial Court should fall under the sway of the French, its security would be jeopardized. The [evil] results that would necessarily issue from such an act of the Imperial Court were made clear in the notes presented to the Sublime Porte previously by the English Ambassador. These notes were approved by the English Government.

The Ambassador presented and read the instructions from his government. In the orally translated summary it was stated that "as regards the discussions that had taken place between the Russian Government and the Imperial Government and the resulting disagreements, the Ambassador's actions and views were fully approved by the English Cabinet. Although there is little prospect of the Imperial Government's modifying its present attitude, nevertheless every argument and means should be employed openly and clearly to induce it to render its policy favorable."

There is no need to comment on and analyze the serious consequences that spring from the influence of the French in the administration of other countries. From the evidence of the condition of the various peoples who once enjoyed responsible government and external sovereignty and who now have become French dependencies we conclude that, whenever the French are in a position to threaten and harm these nations that they promise to defend, the peoples are deprived of security and peace. We should be pleased, if this were not clearly so. This is also manifest from Sébastiani's careless words and writing and from the terms that he experssly used against every state and nation that sought [French] protection. In the notes that Sébastiani presented allegedly to protect the Imperial Government, he stated that in his view the *eyâlets* (provinecs) of Dalmatia and Croatia might cause harm to the Imperial Court.

It is futile to expect the continuation of mutual trust and sincerity between our two countries so long as the Ambassador, whose intrigues and nefarious influence damage so seriously our former good relations, remains at the Porte. Indeed, it was deplorable to see that Sébastiani's dangerous proposals and treasonable words were not repudiated by the Imperial Government. In view of the kind of language that Sébastiani has been using, the demands of the two allied states for his expulsion are manifestly well grounded. The English Ambassador has been

---

1. This translation, apparently prepared by the British dragoman, was in defective Turkish.

authorized by his government to insist that the Imperial Government [act] in this matter. He also was instructed to make representations [to the effect] that the justifiable demands of the Russians Government should be fully satisfied by the Imperial Government.

At the time that these instructions were addressed to the Ambassador, special instructions were also sent to the English naval arsenals to support the Ambassador's statements with coercion against the Imperial Government. A second fleet was assigned under the command of Lord Collingwood, the commander of the British Mediterranean Fleet. In view of the conduct of the Imperial Government, the hope of preserving peace was thereafter so slight that the Ambassador was firmly warned to do his best to secure the safe return of English merchants and all their possessions from Ottoman dominions. The other [Ottoman] side learned the contents of the note from the Ambassador's oral paraphrase. "Now, we have a question to ask," [we continued]. "Can it be that the misunderstanding between the Imperial Government and England stemmed from the note that Sébastiani presented? Is it because of this note that Russia has broken the agreement?"

"In the behavior of the Imperial Government," the Ambassador replied, "the Russian and English Government have seen their security destroyed. In accordance with the continuing firm alliance between Russia and England, they exchanged views and decided that one would send an army by land and the other a navy by sea, for the purpose of deflecting the Imperial Government from its course of action. Therefore, if you have any other question about the Russians, you must ask me about it, as if I were the Russian Ambassador."

In response to an inquiry from the other, [Ottoman] party, the Ambassador replied that the instructions from his government were dated thirty-three days earlier. Then the other party observed that "in this event, there has not been sufficient time for the news of the Russian campaign to reach London and for the receipt of a reply. Did this correspondence take place before or after the news of the reappointment of the Beyler?" The Ambassador answered that the correspondence took place after the news of the reappointment of the Beyler had reached London.

Thereupon the other [Ottoman] side replied, "When we previously discussed the question of the Beyler with the Ambassador, at Bebek Castle, most of the matters which the Ambassador now touches on were mentioned and the answers given. Since that meeting took place before the date of the reappointment [of the Beyler], the Ambassador has already forwarded his report to his government, explaining the situation. Nevertheless, since he alludes to these questions again, let us once more state our reply summarily."

At that instant the Ambassador, as was his wont, tried to confuse the issue. We did not listen to him and did not allow him to interrupt, saying,

Since we listened to the explanations of the Ambassador one by one, it is now our turn to reply. There is first the problem of the renewal of the alliance: previously, at the time of the conclusion of the triple alliance, first an alliance was consummated with Russia, and later England adhered to it. Before the expiry of the Russian alliance, it was renewed by the Imperial Government. Soon thereafter, France defeated Russia at Austerlitz, and the alliance became detrimental to Ottoman interests. Nevertheless, even at that time the Imperial Government openly exchanged ratifications to prove its sincerity toward its allies. In this manner the English alliance was also automatically prolonged. As is generally known, because of later unexpected developments, overt drafting of the formal instrument of the English alliance had necessarily to be deferred. What is obvious and essential is that the Russian alliance has been renewed, and that the alliance with England was automatically included. Since the English Government was aware of these developments, and particularly of the fact that the alliance had not yet expired, there was no need for haste.

In fact, a few days ago, the Ambassador sent word stating, "Let my sincerity be known from the fact that, when previously a document promising to renew the alliance was being prepared, I saw that this would harm the Imperial Government in its relations with France, and, not wanting this, I did not insist but chose silence."

Now, let us come to the question of the recognition of Napoleon's empire: This matter was left in abeyance for four to five months because of the opposition of the British and Russian Ambassadors to the [Ottoman] recognition of the empire. The French Ambassador, Marshal [Guillaume] Brune, finally left Istanbul because of nonrecognition. The French almost declared war on the Imperial Government. Even in this situation, in accordance with the opposition of the allied Ambassadors, the Imperial Government refused recognition and risked war. Did not this attitude conform to [the wishes of] our allies? Later, France roundly defeated Austria and Russia and, through the [French] seizure of Dalmatia, became a neighbor of the Imperial Government. This occurred because of France's victory and not because of the Imperial Government's search for such a neighbor on its boundaries. Once again France demanded the recognition of its empire. If there were to have been hesitation again, it would definitely have entailed war with France and a French offensive from this direction. Thus, we recognized the empire, assuming that our allies and freinds would not find it fitting for the Imperial Government to enter into a war with France over a single word [i.e., recognition].

Moreover, all that was said about the enthusiastic reception of Roux and Sébastiani is unwarranted, since honoring the subjects of states at peace with the Imperial Government is one of our ancient customs. Besides, sometimes for political reasons people are treated graciously according to existing circumstances. Let us ignore all of this. In the past the Imperial Government honored English ambassadors and subjects more than those of other states. As for the Imperial Government's presentation on Napoleon's birthday of horses as a gift to the French Ambassador, it should be stated now, as it was stated in the Bebek meeting, that this was not planned at all.

At this point the Ambassador could not refrain from interrupting and declared, "The French Ambassador has also been given a seaside house."

The [Ottomans] responded, "This was merely to reciprocate the extraordinary honor shown and the house given to Muhip Efendi, [the Ottoman] Ambassador to France. It is known that the Imperial Government has not built palaces for ambassadors of other countries, but only for the English Ambassador."

After this, the Ambassador mentioned the aid by land and sea given by His English Majesty in the Egyptian campaign.

The other side responded, "We are only answering the point raised by the Ambassador," and thus the topic of discussion was resumed.

All that the French Ambassador, Sébastiani, wrote in the note that he submitted to the Imperial Government after his arrival at the Porte is not relevant. Since France is actually at war with England, the French may say anything they wish against their enemy. Attention should be turned to the following: Did the Imperial government act in accordance with [Sébastiani's] note and desert its allies in the period before the outbreak of the Russian war? Did the Imperial Government try to establish ties with France against them? Even when Sébastiani proposed the closing of the Black Sea Straits and adduced arguments to prove that failing to do so violated the rule of neutrality, did the Imperial Government close them at once? [No.] However, because of the necessity for mutual assistance between allies, the Imperial Government informed Russia in a friendly way not to send its ships [through the straits]. In fact, until the advent of war Russian ships were permitted to pass through the narrows in both directions. This fact does not require proof. Moreover, from time to time France asked the Imperial Government's permission to send [through Ottoman territory], against Russia, French troops located in Dalmatia and Croatia. Despite the request of the French Ambassador and the state of war between Russia and the Imperial Government, whereby the passage of troops would serve Ottoman interests, the Imperial Government withheld its permission.

Moreover, according to the terms of the alliance, the friend of one of the parties is also the friend of the other, and the enemy of the one is the enemy of the other. However, our alliance is defensive and is limited to the needs of the war in which it was consummated. Thus, noninvolvement in the wars of others at the end of the present campaign is an essential corollary of the rules of a defensive alliance. From this standpoint, by electing to remain neutral, the Imperial Government has done nothing to violate its pledges and the neutrality that it chose.

With so much concrete evidence that the Imperial Government did not change its principles, there is no room for English suspicion. Even if there were suspicion, the English Government has now made known to the Ambassador the points which it viewed as grounds for suspicion. If you argue that Russia with such suspicions might break its pledge, we wonder whether the Russians first enumerated to the Imperial Government their grievances in order to remove these suspicions, and whether they received our reply before denouncing the agreement and invading our empire? The Russian military build-up along the Dnestr began in Safer 1221 [April-May 1806], that is, ten months ago. We still possess reports about this matter which the

Imperial Government received at that time. The Frenchman Sébastiani had not yet arrived nor submitted his notes. In the circumstances, what was the reason for the build-up? Even after the later Russian violations of Ottoman borders, and the sudden invasion of the empire, the Imperial Government remained silent for a month; and when the Russian Ambassador was questioned, he merely replied until the day of his departure, "I do not have any information." Does the English Ambassador know all this? If Russia harbored suspicions, why did it not question the Imperial Government or inform it in advance?

The Beyler were reappointed by the Imperial Government solely to prevent war and to be separated from its allies. The Imperial Government preserved its confidence in the alliance with Russia even after the alliance was no longer beneficial, and it hoped that Russia would act in conformity with Ottoman policies. That the Imperial Government did not contemplate war is manifest from the fact that it did not take [defensive] measures on the borders. The Ottoman garrisons and fortresses, such as those of Hotin, Bender, and other places, had no instructions but to observe friendship with the Russians, and steps were not taken to shore up [the fortresses]. Because of the Ottoman failure to take such precautions, the Russians invaded the fortresses by trickery. If the Imperial Government had any ulterior motives, it would have though in advance about the security of the Imperial boundaries, and Russia would not have been able to undertake its invasion so swiftly. In fact, General Michelson deceived the residents on the frontier by initiating tricky rumors to the effect that the friendship between Russia and the Imperial Government is known to all. Since the Ottoman subjects received no fresh instructions from the Imperial Government, other than those of friendship toward Russia, the invasion could take place. Since this is the truth of the matter, there is no need for further discussion.

The Ambassador, unable to find an appropriate reply, said, "According to my instructions, my final statement is that the Imperial Government must renew its alliance with Russia. If not, it will lead to the cessation of friendship with England."

The other side replied, "The news of the sudden Russian denunciation of the pledge and of the seizure of Ottoman fortresses must not have reached England yet. The instructions of which the Ambassador speaks were actually dispatched from England before these events."

The Ambassador: "Whatever action Russia pursues, England knows about because of the mutual alliance. Russia did not declare war, and the mutual pact was denounced by the Imperial Government. Moreover, the contents of General Michelson's note are also friendly."

Saying this he presented a documents, to which the other side replied: "What does friendship mean? Is it friendly to attack, without warning, the territory of another state? Is not this contrary to the law of all states and peoples? Is it not as clear as daylight that the denunciation of the pact and the declaration of war are Russia's? The Imperial Government waited for an answer and did not attack until a month after [the start of] the invasion. But when Russia intensified its attack the Imperial Government for its part was compelled to resist and expel the attacker."

The Ambassador: "Will the same be said if the English also come to Ottoman territory in the same friendly way? Let me state in advance that the English fleet will also come to Sarayburnu (the promontory on which the Imperial Palace and grounds were located)."

The other side: "If what you stated is a *fait accompli*, and if the English Government has come to an agreement with Russia [which will be upheld] regardless of what happens, the present discussion is unnecessary. If the purpose of the present discussion is to give and take in conformity with the rules of negotiation, let us talk accordingly."

The Ambassador: "I said what I did because I know about the present mission

of the English fleet, and [I also know] that British-Russian cooperation was agreed upon through correspondence. To prove my good intentions toward the Imperial Government, I am presenting to you a letter in which it is written that the Russian fleet will meet the English fleet at Bozcaada (Tenedos) and that the Russian Ambassador in London has ordered the Russian admiral at Corfu to attach half of the fleet under his command to the English Navy." After stating this, he presented the letter and repeated that the declaration of war was solely the responsibility of the Imperial Government.

The other side: "In the first place, we must know what is meant by denunciation of the pact and declaration of war."

The Ambassador: "Denunciation of the pact means violation of the terms of the treaty. While I was trying to stop the advance of the Russian soldiers and advising [the Imperial Government] not to expel the Russian Ambassador, I saw with my own eyes the Ottoman seizure of the Russian Government's ship and the raising of the Ottoman flag. The denunciation of the pact and the declaration of war resulted from such actions."

The other side: "These words may not be regarded as part of our negotiations, since the seizure of the Russian ship occurred after and not before the Russian aggression and invasion across the Imperial frontiers. Only after the outbreak of war may a ship be seized. Anything might be acceptable but the fallacy that the declaration of war was the responsibility of the Imperial Government. The facts are self-evident."

After this reply was given, the Ambassador stated: "When Michelson reached the Ottoman borders, I sent him a dispatch. While promising to wait for the answer, the Imperial Government declared war, thus breaking its word. Besides, my courier, who had previously been given permission to travel, is still being held up at Ruşçuk (on the Danube, in Bulgaria)."

The other side. "We made no such pledge. To be sure, the Ambassador did state that he was going to write to the Russian general. But we exerted no pressure on him one way or the other, and the matter was left entirely to his own discretion. In fact, we remember what the Ambassador once said during these talks: 'I am not the Russian Emperor. The Russian general follows his orders. But I think that the Russians might take my notes into consideration.' Russia invaded Bogdan (in Moldavia) and seized the fort of Hotin, causing bloodshed. Following the conquest of Bender and other places by trickery, the Russians reached Ismail (on the Danube, in Bulgaria). The Muslim soldiers did not resist until the Russians attacked with artillery and guns. Moreover, in a manner unprecedented in history, Russia published declarations to incite a revolt in Rumelia. If these actions do not mean denunciation of the pact and declaration of war, we do not know what they mean. Therefore, let us put these subjects to one side."

At this point the Ambassador confessed that the present Russian aggression was a logical outcome of the Russian alliance with England.

The other side: "If this is the situation, then all your talk of the evacuation of Russian soldiers as a result of your letter is manifestly absurd."

Unable to frame a pertinent reply, the Ambassador said, "Because of my great affection for the Imperial Government, I tried at that time to assume responsibility on my own initiative. If I were able to find a way, I should do my best to normalize the relations between Russia and the Imperial Government."

The other side: "The very structure of the Imperial Government rests on the Muslim Seriat. According to the dictates of our faith, if a state chooses to make peace and if it remains firm in its pledges, peace will not be withheld. The reverse is also true. In the face of Russia's tricks, the Imperial Government was forced by Muslim law to resist. The terms of alliance and peace are now useless. However, because England did not attack the Ottoman Empire as Russia aid, the Imperial Government recognizes [England] as an agreeable friend. Since no reply was received to the special letter sent to England about the reappointment of the Beyler, two Imperial letters were also addressed [to England] announcing the advent of war. The Imperial Government is now awaiting replies. In short, today the Imperial Gov-

ernment regards England as a friend and Russia as an enemy. This much is beyond contention."

The Ambassador: "The English Government also does not seek hostility with the Imperial Government. I read the instructions of my government as they are, and now it is known that it is not I but my government that does not want Sébastiani. Consequently, the English Government proposes to the Imperial Government that the alliance with Russia be renewed and that Sébastiani be sent away. I have been instructed, for the realization of these proposals, to submit a special memorandum."

The other side: "Do you want the Imperial Government to go to war with France?"

The Ambassador: "I cannot state anything beyond my written instructions, which call for the expulsion of Sébastiani."

The other side: "Basically, this means war with France. France will send part of its army in Poland to the Turla [Dnestr]. Moreover, it is known that [France] has an army in Dalmatia. If the French were to begin moving on these two fronts, how could the English come to the aid of the Imperial Government?" This questions was asked in an ironical and derogatory way.

Unable to answer the question, the Ambassador nevertheless declared: "The capacity of judgment of the ministers of the Ottoman state is well known to everybody. If France's potential harm [to the Ottoman state] is a weighed against English benefit, everything will become clear. The overriding purpose of England is the removal of the French Ambassador from Istanbul."

The other side: "Let us suppose that the Imperial Government will go to war with France, while already at war with Russia. It would then have to withdraw soldiers fighting against Russia. In the interval, the Russian Michelson will advance further, and, if he can, he will cross the Danube. If we ask the Ambassador about this, he will respond: Sufficient time has not yet elapsed for the message to come from England. The Russian general is acting according to his old instructions. A message is expected momentarily, and as soon as it arrives he will withdraw. In the meantime, the Russians will come as far as Edirne (Adrianople), if the opportunity presents itself. On the other front the French, too, will attack. What kind of a bargain is this? I do not see where there is friendship here."

The Ambassador: "The Imperial Government knows the best solution to this problem. The conclusion of the Russian campaign and the satisfaction of English wishes are dependent on the expulsion of Sébastiani and the acceptance of Russian demands. When these ends are accomplished, everything will be resolved and the troubles will be overcome."

The other side: "What are the Russian demands?"

The Ambassador: "Firstly, the restoration of the former Russian alliance in all its vigor. Secondly, the enjoyment of protection by Russian subjects in Ottoman dominions. Thirdly, those Russian subjects who hold berats should be free from all interference and should continue to be protected as in the past. Fourthly, the Seven [Ionian] Islands should be liberated from the oppression and tyranny of Ali Paşa, who must not interfere in the district of Butrinto (in Albania). Finally, there is the matter of the expulsion of Sébastiani. In fact, whatever Michelson has written conforms to these demands."

In the belief that a new dispatch from Michelson had arrived, the other side asked. "What has Michelson written? There is no harm in its disclosure. Let us hear it."

Thereupon, the Ambassador took out a paper, saying that this was the translation of a note that Michelson sent to Ruşçuk.

When he started to read the paper, the other side interrupted: "We know the contents; it is thus not necessary to read [the paper]." And we did not listen to it at all.

But the Ambassador continued without stopping: "In our previous talk it was believed that Russia might abandon England to join France. I act according to instructions, and my latest directives confirm that this belief was mistaken."

The other side: "That will be revealed by later events. The Imperial Government is firm is its conviction. But it is not necessary to discuss these things at present. The gist of the [present] discussion is that the Ambassador has explained the assignment given him by his government. In accordance with the instructions from our Master, the Ruler of the country, we state that today the Imperial Government is an enemy of Russia, and that, since we observe that there is no action by England showing a violation of the alliance, the Imperial Government is its friend. Whatever the Ambassador says, this is our answer. Since the three Imperial letters sent to the English Government have not yet been answered, replies to these are being awaited."

The Ambassador: "I cannot wait for the replies to the Imperial letters. I have to implement my instructions."

The other side: "If so, let the Ambassador present the note, and we shall submit it to the Padişah. Whatever the Majestic Master of our land commands, we will act accordingly."

The Ambassador: "I also am familiar with subtle matters. The ministers of the Sultanate cannot themselves take the responsibility for decisions in such important matters. However, considering that I presented the note in written form, I also request a written reply, because there is the probability of war. I wish to say at this very moment that England's first duty is to protect its commerce. I must therefore address a letter to the Minister of Commerce, so that he will be prepared for war. I hope that the Imperial Government will not regard me as inferior to the Russian Ambassador but will grant the permission of passage that I shall request for a few ships. These words should be taken seriously. Will the return of English merchants be facilitated by the Imperial Government? Will permission be granted for the safe and secure passage of English ships through the straits?"

The other side: "Until now English ships and subjects have been protected. The probabilities that you have imagined may be answered only after there is a real threat of war. We do not have an answer to your question because we did not consider this probability before."

In order to reinforce his position, the Ambassador said: "After the departure of the Russian Ambassador, I looked after Russian subjects. Since no one will be here as custodian [of English affairs] after my departure, the English merchants should be notified in advance."

The other side: "What strange words are these. The Imperial Government has not decided to go to war with England. Such thoughts ought not to be voiced. Let the essential problem be resolved first. Secondary problems will have their turn later."

Thereupon the Ambassador again pressed his views: "I previously wrote to the English admiral to leave the straits and proceed to Bozcaada (Tenedos). Now that affairs have reached their present state, another English fleet is about to arrive. The two fleets are to merge, proceed to the forts, and continue through the straits. If the Hadimzades (commanders of the straits) accord them friendly passage, they will proceed. If the Ottoman commanders refuse passage and attack, then it will become necessary for the English to force their way. How will your government act in this matter?"

The other side: "The Imperial Government's instructions to the straits officials are these: 'If a Russian ship arrives, it will be repelled. If an English warship tries to pass, it will be told that the straits are closed because of the Russian war. The ship will be held in friendly detention, and the government will be informed and asked for instructions.' "

The Ambassador: "It should be understood from my words that, if [at] this time England is rejected, the arriving fleet will be used against the Imperial Government. After that, the problems that divide us will be resolved not by negotiation but by war. The purpose of the present negotiations is simply to find an immediate solution to avoid the [above-mentioned] evil consequences. If the English fleet that is coming is sunk in the straits, so much the better. If it is not sunk and it arrives, it will do what it must do because it was attacked by artillery to prevent it from passing through the straits."

The other side: "If the straits are closed and the fleet of a friendly nation arrives, according to the rule it will be detained and investigated. This is what we are trying to tell the Ambassador."

The Ambassador: "My question stems from this fact: we are already semibelligerent today. Since the arriving admiral has been authorized by his government, if he has to fight his way through the straits when he comes here, I shall automatically be removed from my office, and the prospect of negotiation will vanish. But, if the fleet is not repelled at the straits and arrives in a friendly way, the prospect of negotiations, will remain. If new instructions have not been sent recently to the straits' commander, I shall write to the English admiral saying that 'the orders are as before.' Attention must be paid to this statement, because however strong the straits may be they present no difficulty to the English warships, which will pass through [the straits to their intended destination]."

After stating that "this subject is known only to Allah and, being dependent on predestination, it is not for humans to know," the other side remained silent.

The Ambassador: "All that I have said must be reported to His Imperial Majesty. The ministers of the Imperial government well know the dangers involved in the attempted repulsion of the English fleet. If the Advisory Council [Meclis-i Mesveret] meets, this matter must be explained to them. I plead that the demands of England be accepted in a friendly way, without a naval conflict."

The Ottoman representatives did not think an answer was necessary. They remained silent, and the meeting was ended. As [the facts of the case] become become to you, the command belongs to His Majesty who possesses the right to command.

2. Ambassador Charles Arbuthnot to Foreign Secretary Viscount Howick, 27 January 1807.

Late at night on the 23rd Instant, my Servant arrived with your Lordship's Dispatch of the 14th of last November.

It has been the highest gratification to me to learn from your Lordship that my Conduct has met with his Majesty's approbation. Your Lordship will have the goodness, I hope, to take an Opportunity of expressing to his Majesty my deep Sense of this distinguished favour, and you will allow me at the same time to offer my sincere thanks to yourself for the obliging manner in which you made to me so flattering a communication.

After the receipt of your Lordship's dispatch I lost no time in asking for a Conference. It was fixed for the 25th Instant; and on my arrival at the Porte I found Ismet Bey, the Reis Efendi, the Chiaya [Kethüda] Bey, and the Ex-Chiaya Bey all assembled.

As the Conference lasted more than four hours, it would require a length of time to set down on Paper all that was said on that Occasion. Being anxious to inform your Lordship without delay of my having received your Instructions, and having also to forward my eight preceding dispatches which have been detained till now by a contrary wind; I shall for the present do little more than refer to the Contents of the letter herewith inclosed, which was sent by me yesterday to the Reis Efendi. Indeed that letter may give a tolerable idea of what passed at the Conference; for the Ottoman ministers, who of late had been displeased at what they called my personal partiality to Russia, and who all along have expressed their Conviction that His Majesty was not acting in Concert with Russia, were now so amazed and dejected that they did not utter a single word which is worth repeating to your Lordship. They confined themselves entirely to their usual Professions of friendship for His Majesty; to the Complaints, which I had often heard before, of the treatment they had received from Russia; and to excuses for their own Conduct, grounded on the changes which have taken place in Europe. They declared however that they can give no official answer until the Sultan's pleasure had been known.

I have only to observe in addition to what your Lordship will find in my letter to the Reis Efendi, that as it was left to my discretion either to announce or to conceal the approaching arrival of a second Squadron, I determind on the former after some deliberation.

I was convinced that the only chance of opening the eyes of the Porte would arise from its being proved that His Majesty's final Resolution had been taken; and for this reason I made to the Ottoman Min-

isters the Communication in question, and read to them such parts of Your Lordship's Dispatch as would be right for them to know.

Your Lordship left it also to my discretion how to act with respect to the eventual departure of the merchants. I knew that many of them had outstanding debts to a considerable amount, and here in particular it would be impossible to settle their accounts at a short warning. I therefore informed the Porte that I should immediately prepare our Factories for their departure, which had likewise the effect of showing that His Majesty's Government was really serious; and I obtained a solemn Promise that, should it be necessary, the British Merchants, as had been the Case with the Russians, should have Firmans to pass the Dardanelles.

I have since made known to the Factory here the present state of things; and should His Majesty's Subjects be ultimately obliged to leave the Country, I will take every possible care to procure for them the means of departing in safety. I am no less attentive to the Factory at Smyrna, and to the British Commerical Establishments at other Scales of this Empire.

I shall not trouble your Lordship with any Conjectures as to the result of this negotiation. I might perhaps augur ill from the savage barbarity with which the Father of Prince Ipsilanty has been treated. After subjecting him to the most excruciating tortures successively inflicted for a long series of days, they at last beheaded him, and they chose the very hour which had been fixed for my Conference. They imagined I understand that I had demanded a Conference for the purpose of making an application in his favour; but I know the Turks too well not to be aware that no good could arise from such an interference.

This unfortunate Prince was above 80 years of Age, and was guilty of no other Crime than that of being Father to the Hospodar who is now with the Russians. His death was owing to the fury and indignation which prevail at the Porte against the Son. His tortures were inflicted with a view to discover what Property he possessed, and I am told that Sums of a great amount have been obtained.

I shall write to your Lordship again the very instant that I get a final answer from the Porte.

3. The British Ambassador to the Reis Efendi [Mehmed Galib], 26 January 1807

Your Excellency expressed a desire of receiving in writing the Substance of what I had the honour to state to you in our Conference of Yesterday. In compliance with this desire I shall recal[1] to your recollection the several topics which by my Sovereign's orders I had to lay before you; and in again pointing out the line of Conduct which His Majesty expects from the Porte. I shall in their very words repeat the orders I have now received; and which as they admit of but one construction, it will be my duty most literally and most faithfully to obey.

That your Excellency and the other Ministers who assisted at the Conference might understand more clearly the motives which had induced His Majesty, after a long enduring patience, to change His Conduct towards the Porte; it was necessary for me to allude to the first Conference I had after my arrival in this Country. I told you that Mahmood, who was then Reis Efendi, had scarcely given me time to leave the Frigate before he invited me to a Conference; that his first question was whether I was authorised to renew the Treaty; and that to give me a convincing proof of the Sultan's desire to continue that connexion with His Majesty which had already been productive of such inestimable benefits to this Empire, he read to me a Note from His Highness to the Vizer, which had been written as I was coming round the point of the Seraglio, and which, as I remember well, contained these words: "I see that the Ambassador of my Friend the King of England is arrived; let my Reis Efendi see him immediately; and let me know whether he has brought Powers to renew the Treaty." I should not presume to quote the words of the Sultan's Note, if even one of them had escaped my memory; but His Highness I am sure will own the accuracy of my statement, and in revolving in His mind the feelings by which he was then influenced, He will regret perhaps that new Counsellors soon inspired other sentiments.

I then informed you of the answer which I had given to Mahmood; and which, notwithstanding it contained the most satisfactory reasons for my not having been able to be myself the bearer of Full Powers, and was expressive of my conviction that they would soon arrive, was received however by that Minister with marks of mortification which could not but prove that he, no less than his Master, was aware that an alliance with England was the only means of insuring prosperity to this Empire.

To save your Excellency the trouble of reading the long details into which I was obliged to enter yesterday, I shall pass rapidly over all that intervened between that Conference with Mahmood and the arrival at Constantinople of the present French Ambassador. Not that I consider the events which happened during that period as of inferior importance, and [am] therefore inclined to notice them but slightly; I feel on the contrary that the Conduct of the Ottoman Government in regard to these events has been the cause of all the evil which we are now witnessing; and as that conduct has been no less lamented by Your Excellency than by me, it would be with yourself that I ought chiefly to discuss it: To you indeed I might with peculiar propriety express my feelings of sorrow that the wise principles which I heard from you on your first entrance into office have either been forgotten, or, what I think is more probable, have unfortunately been opposed by superior Influence.

But to save time and to save you trouble, I shall briefly observe that consistently with what I had declared to Mahmood, Full Powers for negotiating the Treaty did almost immediately arrive. Tho' Your Excellency was not then in office, you are not ignorant of the Joy which was expressed when it was known that my Sovereign was willing to renew his connexions with the Sultan. You remember well that the approach of the Ramazan [23 November–22 December 1805]—alone prevented the immediate commencement of the negotiation; and you are equally aware that when that time of Religious Retirement was expired, the sentiments of the Ottoman Ministers had entirely changed; and that without frankly confessing the real truth, there was an attempt to justify delay by the most absurd pretences. You know that the misfortunes which happened to Austria, instead of being considered as they ought to have been as additional reasons for consolidating that System which in times of danger had proved the surest bulwark of this Empire, were the signal on the contrary for abandoning the friendship which till then had influenced the Ottoman Councils, and as if total blindness had been produced by a sudden panic, this Government lost the security which had been derived from acting in conjunction with Its Allies; and imaginary perils gave place to real ones when a connexion with that Power was sought whose professions of friendship have uniformly been more baneful than Its open Enmity.

By referring to the minutes of the Conferences which I had at the time with your immediate Predecessor, Your Excellency will find that when I discovered the intention to deceive me, far from insisting upon a renewal of the Treaty, I expressed no more than the sense I justly entertained of the indignity which had been offered to my Sovereign; and only demanded an explicit avowal of the real determination of this Government.

Such an avowal the Ministers of that day were not inclined to make to me; nor even did they think it necessary to advise the Sultan to open His mind confidentially to my Sovereign; tho' some valid reasons were undoubtedly wanting as an explanation for declining to renew the Treaty which here and not in England had been so earnestly desired; tho' I as a friend had pointed out that a letter to that effect ought in prudence to be written; and tho', as recent facts have proved, there is not the same unwillingness to address His Majesty when His powerful Interference is wanted as was evinced when an offence against Him was to be accounted for and explained.

But the advisers of His Highness were then otherwise engaged. They were wholly occupied in receiving with signal marks of distinction the person who had come to demand the acknowledgment of Bonaparte's new Imperial Title; and in preparing the answer which was to announce to that chief of the French nation that his demand had without hesitation been agreed to.

It is true that Notes were presented to M. d'Italinsky and to me, in which we were informed of Bonaparte's overture; and as it came from the Head of a Government with which the Porte ought at least not to have considered Herself as on terms of Friendship, for Treaties with Great Britain and Russia were then existing by which She had expressly stipulated that their Enemies should be Hers, it was not unreasonable to suppose that in the Communication made to us there was a design to consult our opinions.

Our answers were not delayed, for the danger of becoming thus connected with the French Government was sufficiently evident without deliberation. With a warning, and as it now appears with a prophetic voice, we cautioned the Ottoman Government against the admission of a Minister whose unceasing efforts would be to sow dissension between the Porte and Her Allies; but tho' twenty four hours had not elapsed between the delivery of the Notes from the Porte and of our answers, the deed had been already done, and in an evil hour a last and fatal blow had been given to the system which the Sultan's Embassy as well as Ours had so long and so unceasingly been endeavouring [not?] to undermine.

It was then that the Triple Alliance was virtually dissolved; and there was prepared that new State of things which we are now witnessing, and which from the effects it has already produced does not argue great wisdom in its contrivers.

Tired out with such constant failure in our endeavours to save the Porte from the false measures She was pursuing the Russian Minister and I would both of us have gladly been relieved from long and unsuccessful labour. But still it was our duty to have constant discussion with the Porte; and still we had to lament that all our efforts to obtain justice for our Governments and to inspire Counsels wiser for Herself, were equally without avail.

Our commercial subjects; —on that of Protections, in regard to which my Sovereign in particular was treated with disrespect, for to gratify the Porte he had voluntarily abandoned long enjoyed privileges; —on the Right to carry the Russian Flag, which my colleague had to assert; —on the passage of Russian Ships of War thru' the Bosphorus, tho' it formed an article of a Treaty but just renewed; —on the conduct of Ali Pasha of Yannina towards the Septinsular Republic; —on all these subjects, and on various others which could be enumerated, I and the Russian Minister had daily to remonstrate with the Porte, and as your Excellency well knows, it was scarcely ever that we remonstrated with effect. Indeed so notorious was the disinclination of the late Ministers to give us satisfaction with respect to our just demands, that your Excellency at our first meeting assured me, in expressions which did you honour, that the time of evil conduct was gone by, and that the commencement of your Ministry should mark an epoch more worthy of the Sultan and more satisfactory to His Allies. Your Excellency I am confident, was sincere in these Professions. To give them effect you wanted only that influence which I wished you to obtain, but which was still possessed by persons who had had their share in separating the Sultan from His Allies; and who having now to work in secret unchecked by the responsibility attached to public situations, had thereby the means of baffling more effectually your Efforts as well as ours.

I come now to the event which was naturally to be the consequence to the acknowledgment of Bonaparte's title. I allude to General Sebastiani's arrival. He found the Ministers of the Allies offensively treated by the Porte; and it was not to be expected that, after he was present, the conduct towards their Governments would be improved. And in effect his arrival was the Signal for those more overt acts of aggression which have so justly excited the displeasure of our Sovereigns.

I shall pass by unnoticed the attentions shown to the new Ambassador. They were irregular and unprecedented; —but I feel that they were more disgraceful to those to whose instigation they were owing, than it has been disreputable to us not to share them. But I shall confine myself to those two acts by which the Embassy of M.

Sebastiani has been principally marked: To the Note he presented on the 16th of last September; and to the deposition of the Hospodars, which was so equally his deed that he did not scruple to take the glory of it.

Respecting the Note I need say the less as the Ottoman Ministers had at the time my written Sentiments on the Subject; —as your Excellency and your colleagues saw yesterday in the Instructions sent to me from England that those Sentiments had met with the most decided approbation of His Majesty's Government; and as, what is far more deserving your attention, you have from the very words of His Majesty's Cabinet Minister known the effect which the conduct of the Porte with regard to that Note had produced in England. You have seen that the insulting and faithless propositions made by M. Sebastiani ought, in the opinion of my Government, to have been immediately rejected with indignation; and you have perceived that little hope was entertained of preserving the relations of amity between the two Powers, whilst a Minister whose influence had already been so prejudicial to the friendship subsisting between them was suffered to remain at Constantinople.

On the other subject, that of the Hospodars, I mean, it will be necessary to restate to you as accurately as I am able what I mentioned yesterday. It is true that you did restore them; but may I not ask, as I have done before, whether the unwillingness manifested to repair the injury you had committed; and whether the time which was allowed to elapse before you could be persuaded to give new effect to violated Engagements were not sufficient grounds for suspicion; and sufficiently strong motives for demanding some more solid security? May I not ask whether this suspicion had not since been fully justified; and whether in your Notes and Manifestoes you have not avowed the reluctancy you felt in fulfilling your most solemn Treaties?

Our Governments were not to be deceived. The confidence I had placed in the assurances of Your Excellency, and your unqualified disapprobation of that conduct towards Russia which is now represented as perfectly justifiable, had led me to give the praise of sincerity to this Government which I find to have been ill deserved. But our Sovereigns did not partake of the delusion which, I must fairly own, had blinded their Ministers. They had not heard the strong and repeated professions of Your Excellency: They had only to calculate the time which had passed in negotiation, and to observe the difficulties which we had every instant to encounter, and they had already obtained two convincing proofs that the influence inimical to the friendship between the Sultan and His Allies still prevailed. They resolved therefore on such measures as would remove all doubt as to the real designs of the Porte; and these measures were to be accompanied with such declarations as cannot but prove that notwithstanding all that has happened, friendship and not enmity is their real object.

General Michelson marched into Moldavia, and in the Proclamation which he then issued you will have found the terms on which the Emperor has offered the renewal of His Friendship. You would have heard the same from his late Minister at this Court if you had not hurried him from Your Country; and, if in Contradiction to the solemn assurances given to me, You had not rashly committed an act of hostility by the seizure of the Russian Brig which had been bearer of dispatches.

Of what is expected from you by my Sovereign, I had the honour of informing you yesterday. You know the reasons why His Majesty feels Himself justified in requiring the removal of M. Sebastiani. He is convinced, as I have already told you that the presence of that Minister is incompatible with the existence of friendship between the Porte and the allies; and He thinks with the Emperor that a false and hollow Peace would be worse than open War.

It is therefore for the Porte to make Her choice between France and the Allies.

Should the boastings of France continue to be credited, should faith be placed in Her Professions of Friendship, and should her Menaces excite no alarm; then most probably His Majesty's offers will be rejected and General Sebastiani will remain.

Should there however be some recollection of what Russian armies have achieved and of what British Fleets have been seen to execute; it may occur to the Porte that Her late conduct has not been wise. She may, as I said yesterday, then wish to place Herself in that Situation, in which I found Her when I first arrived.

She has still the means of doing it. She has only to comply with the just demands of His Majesty and the Emperor; and both these Sovereigns will with greater joy concert Measures for Her defence, than they have now concerted those which they found essential for their interests.

I might now conclude for I have retraced to your Excellency nearly the whole of what I stated in my Conference, and I feel that I have fully executed all my Instructions. But I cannot close the last letter which perhaps I may ever write to Your Excellency, without exhorting you to exert that Influence which belongs to Your high and distinguished Situation. Make those feel, whose Errors have caused the Evil which is now impending, that whatever changes may have taken place in Europe, there are none which ought to affect the ancient System of this Empire. Make them understand that the armies of Russia from being concentrated are become more powerful, and that Great Britain has not lost the means of protecting Her Allies and of injuring Her Enemies. Your Excellency by enforcing these truths may be the Saviour of Your Country. You may renew the friendship which had existed between the Sultan and the Allies; and you may thus render even to my Sovereign a most grateful Service. His Majesty's regard for the Sultan remained unaltered. It has been with grief that He has been forced to measures so little consonant to His personal feelings; but he was aware that it was the duty of a Sovereign to make every Sacrifice to the Honour of His Crown, and the Interests of His People. He would rejoice if His private wishes could be made to accord with His public Sentiments; and it may I trust be Your Excellency's work to destroy the effects of evil Counsels, and to renew those happy days when Great Britain and Russia were united in successfully endeavouring to promote the Interests of this Empire.

50. TREATY OF ALLIANCE (FINKENSTEIN): FRANCE AND PERSIA
4 May 1807

(Ratifications exchanged, Tehran, 20 December 1807)
[Translated from the French text in Clerq, *Recueil des traités*, 2: 201–03]

Following the renewal of war with Russia in 1804, Fath 'Ali Shah (1797–1834) sent a mission to India to seek British aid under the British-Persian alliance (Doc. 41) in the hope of reconquering Georgia, which had been annexed by Russia in 1801. Discouraged by the failure of the mission, Fath 'Ali sent Mirza Muhammad Riza early in 1807 to treat with Napoleon at his temporary headquarters in Poland. Napoleon, for his part, had been trying to detach Persia from the British orbit since 1802. Once the alliance of the Sublime Porte with England and Russia had been destroyed, owing in part to the successful diplomacy of General Horace Sébastiani, the French ambassador at Istanbul, Napoleon's negotiations with the Persian envoy assumed added significance, especially since the outcome of the French-Russian fighting in eastern Europe still remained uncertain in the spring of 1807. The instrument signed at Finkenstein on 4 May was intended to form part of a projected tripartite alliance of France, Persia, and the Ottoman Empire against Russia and England. The French negotiations with the Ottoman envoy, however, dragged on inconclusively. Under the Safavi dynasty (ca. 1500–1722) Persia had been drawn into European politics only marginally by those powers most often at war with the Ottoman Empire (Venice, Austria, Poland). The maritime states of Western Eruope (Portugal, the Netherlands, France, and Britain) attempted to promote trade with Persia and received extraterritorial privileges for their nationals from successive shahs. But in these earlier centuries there were no European powers whose interest in Persia was both political and economic; and for the protection of limited interests ad hoc diplomacy, almost wholly of the one-sided European variety, seemed to suffice until the start of the nineteenth century. Technically, under article 5 of the Finkenstein treaty, France became the first European power to accredit a permanent diplomatic mission to Persia, but Napoleon's minister, Brigadier General Antoine Gardane, left Persia early in 1809, and France did not again appoint a resident minister to Tehran until nearly a half-century later. Kelly, *Britain and the Persian Gulf*, pp. 78–83; Hurewitz, "Ottoman Diplomacy and the European State, System"; Puryear, *Napoleon and the Dardanelles*, chap. 8 (based on the French archives); Déhérain, *La vie de Pierre Ruffin*, vol. 2, chaps. 3–4; Driault, *La politique orientale de Napoélon*; Hoskins, *British Routes to India*, chap. 3; Bertrand, *Lettres inédites de Tallyrand à Napoléon*, pp. 315–454; Jaubert, *Voyage en Arménie et en Perse*; Ramazani, *Foreign Policy of Iran*, chap. 2.

ART. 1. Peace, friendship, and alliance shall be constantly maintained between H.M. the Emperor of the French, King of Italy, and H.M. the Emperor of Persia.

ART. 2. H.M. the Emperor of the French, King of Italy, guarantees to H.M. the Emperor of Persia the integrity of his present territory.

ART. 3. H.M. the Emperor of the French, King of Italy, recognizes Georgia as belonging legitimately to H.M. the Emperor of Persia.

ART. 4. [H.M. the Emperor of the French, King of Italy] undertakes to direct every effort toward compelling Russia to withdraw from Georgia and Persian territory. This withdrawal will be the constant goal of his policies.

ART. 5. H.M. the Emperor of the French, King of Italy, will maintain at the Persian Court a Minister Plenipotentiary and Legation Secretaries.

ART. 6. H.M. the Emperor of Persia, desirous of organizing his infantry, his artillery and fortifications, according to the principles of the European system, H.M. the Emperor of the French, King of Italy, undertakes to supply as many field guns and rifles with bayonets as may be requested by H.M. the Emperor of Persia. Payment for these arms will be made in conformity with their value in Europe.

ART. 7. H.M. the Emperor of the French, King of Italy, undertakes to provide for H.M. the Emperor of Persia artillery, engineer, and infantry officers in such numbers as may be considered necessary by H.M. the Emperor of Persia to strengthen his fortresses and to organize Persian artillery and infantry in accordance with principles of European military art.

ART. 8. H.M. the Emperor of Persia for his part undertakes to sever all diplomatic and commercial relations with England, to declare war at once on the latter power, and to commence hostilities without delay. Accordingly, he will recall the Persian Minister accredited to Bombay. The consuls, factors, or other agents of the English Company residing in Persia and in the ports of the Persian Gulf will have to leave their places of residence immediately. H.M. the Emperor of Persia will seize all English merchandise and will forbid England communications in his territories, either by sea or by land. No minister, ambassador, or agent who might present himself on behalf of this power during the war will be recognized.

ART. 9. In any other war in which Britain and Russia may ally themselves against Persia and France, France and Persia will ally themselves equally against Britain and Russia. They shall act against the common enemy as soon as official notification is given by the Contracting Party menaced or attacked that a state of war exists. All diplomatic and commercial relations will be conducted in accordance with the preceding article.

ART. 10. H.M. the Emperor of Persia will use all his influence to persuade the Afghans and other peoples of Qandahar to add their armies to his in fighting England and, after obtaining passage on their territory, he will send an army against the English possessions in India.

ART. 11. If a French fleet should be dispatched to the Persian Gulf and to the ports of H.M. the Emperor of Persia, it will be granted all the facilities and help which it might need.

ART. 12. If it were the intention of H.M. the Emperor of the French to send an army by land to attack English possessions in India, H.M. the Emperor of Persia, as a good and faithful ally, would grant this army passage on his territories. In such event, a special convention will be concluded in advance by the two governments stipulating the route that must be taken by the troops, the food and transportation that will be provided, and the number of auxiliary troops that H.M. the Emperor of Persia will be prepared to attach to this expedition.

ART. 13. Everything furnished to either the fleets or the troops in accordance with the preceding two articles shall be offered at prices and under conditions prevailing among the [Persian] nationals themselves and shall be paid for by the said fleets and troops.

ART. 14. The stipulations enumerated in article 12 above shall be applicable only to France. They shall, accordingly, not be extended by future treaties to either England or Russia.

ART. 15. For the reciprocal advantage of both Powers, a treaty of commerce, to be negotiated in Tehran, will be concluded.

51. NAPOLEON'S INSTRUCTIONS TO THE CHIEF OF THE
FRENCH MISSION TO PERSIA
10 May 1807

[Translated from the French text in Napoleon I, *Correspondance*, 15: 210–14]

The instructions to Brigadier General Antoine Gardane, head of the French mission to Persia, amply attest to the seriousness with which Napoleon viewed the Persian alliance—at the time of its signature. They also shed light on Napoleon's grand design for the conquest of India via the Ottoman Empire and Persia; and Napoleon's comments on technical assistance have a marked contemporary quality. Once France had unexpectedly entered into a competing alliance with Russia at Tilsit on 7 July 1807, Napoleon abandoned his plans for invading India with Ottoman and Persian collaboration. But Gardane, already en route to his post by then, was not recalled. He arrived in Tehran on 4 December 1807 with a diplomatic and military deputation of approximately a dozen and a half and managed to score a series of initial successes. The French general persuaded Fath 'Ali Shah to repudiate the 1801 treaties (Doc. 41) and sever relations with Britain; and he negotiated by January 1808 a commercial treaty (text in Thieury, *Documents pour servir à l'histoire des relations entre la France et la Perse*, pp. 69–76) which more than reaffirmed the capitulatory arrangement of a century earlier [Docs. 17, 19]. With little guidance and no tangible support from his government, and with no prospect of fulfilling the shah's demands, Gardane nevertheless managed for well over a year to carry out Napoleon's original instructions by persuasion alone. By mid-February 1809, when Gardane withdrew to Tabriz on the arrival of British diplomats in Tehran, it was merely a matter of weeks before Napoleon's mission entirely retired, rendering the alliance meaningless. Gardane, *Mission du général Gardane en Perse* (documents); Puryear, *Napoléon and the Dardanelles*, chaps. 8, 11, 16; Driault, *La politique orientale de Napoléon*, chap. 8; Vandal, *Napoléon et Alexandre Ier*, vol. 1, chap. 6.

General Gardane will arrive as promptly as possible in Persia. Fifteen days after his arrival he will dispatch a courier, and a month later he will send one of the officers who accompanied him.

During his sojourn at Constantinople he shall take all measures to arrange that his correspondence with the Minister of Foreign Affairs and that of the Minister with him is expedited. If it is possible to have this service performed by agents of the Porte itself, he might write once a week. All dispatches of any importance, whether for the Minister of Foreign Affairs or for General Sébastiani, shall be written in code.

His initial dispatches should above all be those that are essential for making known a land about which no precise information exists. The geography and topography of the country, its coasts, population, finances, the military situation in its various details —these should constitute the primary objectives of General Gardane's inquiries. They should fill his dispatches and take volumes.

Persia must regard the Russians as her natural enemies: they have taken Georgia from her; they menace her finest provinces; they have not yet recognized the present dynasty, and since its accession they have constantly been at war with her. General Gardane will dwell upon all these grievances; he will support the enmity of the Persians for the Russians; he will stimulate.

them to renewed efforts, to more numerous levies. He shall give them, for purposes of their military operations, all the guidance that his experience might suggest, and to that end he will seek to align himself with Prince 'Abbas Mirza, who commands the army and who appears to enjoy its complete confidence. Persia must create a powerful diversion on the Russian frontier and, taking advantage of the fact that the Russians have weakened their army of the Caucasus by sending a part of it to Europe, reenter the provinces that have been captured by [Russian] armed forces or by intrigue. Georgia, whose last prince was compelled to cede the territory [to Russia], is in a poor state of defense; its inhabitants appear to feel nostalgic for their erstwhile rulers. The chain of mountains that guards the entrance into Persia and the Ottoman provinces is, moreover, situated to the north of Georgia. It is important that Russia should not remain in control of all its passes.

General Gardane shall employ every effort to ensure that Persia and the Ottoman Porte act in concert, insofar as it may prove possible, in their operations between the Black Sea and the Caspian Sea. The interests of the two empires are the same: all countries south of Russia are equally menaced, because she prefers a more fertile land and a better climate to her deserts and icy terrain. But Persia has yet another interest which is her very own: to halt the progress of England in India.

Persia is now crushed between Russia and English possessions. The further these possessions are extended toward the Persian frontiers, the more she has to fear eventual aggrandizement [of these powers]. She runs the risk of becoming an English province, like the north of India, if she does not seek immediately to prevent that danger, to stand in the way of England, and to facilitate all French operations against her.

France regards Persia from two points of view: as the natural enemy of Russia and as a means of transit for an expedition into India.

Because of this dual aim a large number of engineer and artillery officers have been attached to General Gardane's Mission. They should be employed to render Persian military forces more formidable to Russia and to institute inquiries, reconnaissance operations, and reports which might conduce to discerning the obstacles that an expedition would encounter in passing through Persia, a route that ought to be followed into India, whether the point of departure is Aleppo or one of the ports of the Persian Gulf. It is presumed that in the first case the French expedition would debark at Iskenderun with the Porte's consent; that in the second case it would round the Cape of Good Hope and proceed to debark at the entrance to the Persian Gulf. It is necessary to know in either case what the route to India might be from the point of debarkation; what its difficulties might be; whether the expedition might find sufficient means of transport and of what kind; whether artillery might train on the roads; and what means there might be for avoiding or overcoming obstacles; whether [the expedition] might find abundant provisions and, above all, water; and, in the second case, which might serve as appropriate ports of debarkation, that is, those which triple-decked vessels, ships of 80 guns, and ships of 74 guns could enter; those in which shore batteries could be established to protect the vessels from attack by an enemy squadron; lastly, those in which the squadron might find water and provisions for remuneration.

Finally, it will be equally necessary to know whether a sufficient number of horses might be found for remounts for the cavalry and artillery.

If General Gardane were alone, he could not answer any of these questions, since we find even in Europe, in the heart of Germany itself, that information given by the indigenous population is always imprecise and incomprehensible. But General Gardane will have at his command army and navy engineers and artillery officers, who will go over the routes, examine sites, visit the ports of the Persian Empire not only on the Persian Gulf but also on the Caspian Sea, prepare maps, and furnish him after a four-month stay with the material for detailed and trustworthy reports on the various purposes of these surveys.

Care must always be taken to send messages in duplicate, so that such valuable information should not be lost in the event of some mishap to a courier.

These officers should render themselves equally useful in instructing the Persians in European military science and in aiding them to construct new works for the defense of their positions.

The two principal objectives which we propose thus will be fulfilled, since the Persians will be rendered more formidable to the Russians, and the means of transit and all other information about the country will be well known to us. So much for the military sector.

As for the diplomatic sector, General Gardane is authorized to conclude agreements for the future dispatch by France of rifles with bayonets, cannons, and a number of officers and noncommissioned officers, sufficient to form the cadre for a corps of 12,000 men to be raised by Persia. The price of the arms shall be fixed by the artillery officers, according to the value in Europe. Payment for them will be stipulated. The intention of His Majesty in requesting payment for these arms is not to avoid the expenditure of 500,000 to 600,000 francs but to assure himself that the Persian Government will make more use of them if it pays than it would had they been donated. Moreover, if [the arms] are purchased, it will be certain that [the Persian Government] has the will to make use of them. These arms, the officers, and the noncommissioned officers will be transported by one of His Majesty's squadrons.

There shall be stipulated in the agreement the place of debarkation and means of payment, which might be made for the most part by provisions such as biscuits, rice, cattle, etc., for the arms for the squadron which, after having debarked the men and material it has brought, shall cruise these waters. The quantity of arms which [General Gardane] may undertake to furnish may run as high as 10,000 rifles and some 30 field pieces. The remuneration of officers and noncommissioned officers, those who accompany General Gardane as well as those who will be sent, should also be fixed by these agreements. His Majesty will accord them the payment they enjoy in France; but it is desirable that they receive in Persia extraordinary sums which are always necessary for Europeans who go abroad.

If the war in Russia continues, if Persia desires it and if General Gardane—once he knows the country well—thinks it useful, the dispatch of four or five battalions and two or three artillery companies to form a reserve for the Persian army may be requested by General Gardane, and the Emperor will give his approval.

The Minister understands the state of affairs well enough to know that it is only by means of great secrecy and an exact notion of the ports of debarkation that a squadron can be sent to provide help for Persia.

If an expedition of 20,000 French soldiers [should be sent] to India, it would be convenient to know the number of auxiliaries that Persia could add to that army, and above all, as has been said above, everything relating to the ports of debarkation, the routes to take, the provisions and water necessary for the expedition. It is also necessary to know which would be the favorable season for transit by land.

General Gardane's mission does not end there; he is to communicate with the Mahrattas [Marathas] and learn, as positively as possible, what support the expedition might find in India. This peninsula has so changed in the last ten years that matters concerning it are hardly known at all in Europe. Nothing will be more useful than all the information that can be gathered, all the contacts that can be made.

Finally, General Gardane should not lose sight of the fact that our important object is to establish a triple alliance between France, the Porte, and Persia, to open up a road to India, and to secure allies for ourselves against Russia. If the execution of the last aim could be taken as far as the borders of Tatary, it would be a matter worthy of attention; since Russia meddles in matters which concern our frontiers, we shall sooner or later derive the benefit of what we are prepared to do to stir dissension on her frontiers.

General Gardane shall examine the opportunities that Persia can offer to our commerce, which products of our manufacture will have success there, and what we might import in exchange. He is therefore authorized to negotiate a commercial treaty on the basis of those of 1708 and 1715. He shall correspond with Mauritius and shall encourage its trade with such care that Mauritius will become the principal waystation in the commerce of Metropolitan France with the Persian Gulf.

52. TREATY OF PEACE, COMMERCE, AND SECRET ALLIANCE (DARDANELLES): GREAT BRITAIN AND THE OTTOMAN EMPIRE
5 January 1809

(Ratifications exchanged, Istanbul, 27 July 1809)
[Great Britain, Public Record Office, F.O. 93/110/1B and 93/110/2; the translation of the secret articles from the French text was prepared by the Foreign Office in September 1833]

French intrigue at Istanbul drew the Ottoman Empire into war against Russia (1806–12) and England (1807–09). Napoleon's alliance with Tsar Alexander I at Tilsit upset the British-Russian entente and paved the way for a British-Ottoman rapprochement. The following treaty reaffirmed in full Britain's capitulatory rights and granted limited reciprocal privileges (art. 8) to the Sublime Porte. The United Kingdom became the first European power to acknowledge the right of the Sublime Porte to close the straits to foreign warships, on condition that "this ancient regulation of the Ottoman Empire is in future to be observed towards every Power in time of peace (art. 11)." General European recognition of the principle had to await the conclusion of the treaty of London of 13 July 1841 (Doc. 87). The renewed British-Ottoman defensive alliance against France was far more restricted in scope than that of a decade earlier (Doc. 39) and was essentially unilateral, since the Sublime Porte did not accept any obligations comparable to those binding the United Kingdom. The 1809 treaty was framed in French and Turkish. In forwarding the British ratification, Foreign Minister George Canning called the attention of Robert Adair, the British negotiator, to the fact that "a Treaty is usually drawn up either in a language which is not that of either Contracting Party, but which is adopted by mutual consent, or it is drawn up at the same time in the languages of both Powers" (25 April 1809, F.O. 78/63). Adair explained in self-defense that the Ottoman dragoman was "absolutely ignorant of English" and knew so little French that, "between his ignorance, his fears, and his suspicions, I could not obtain the alteration of a word, sometimes not even the transposition of a word, after the Article itself, to the substance of which I was obliged chiefly to attend, during discussions not always the most temperate, had once been admitted" (Adair, *Negotiations for the Peace of the Dardanelles*, 1: 229–30). The United Kingdom ratified the additional and secret article concerning the £300,000 grant-in-aid, but the ratification was not to be presented for exchange except "in the event of a War commenced against the Porte by France, and in that event alone" (Canning to Adair, 25 April 1809, F.O. 78/63). The exchange of ratifications of this article, in fact, never did take place. Adair, op. cit., 2 vols. (official and private letters, 1808–11); Puryear, *Napoleon and the Dardanelles*, chap. 16; Temperley, *England and the Near East*, pp. 46–49, 410; Mischef, *La Mer Noire*, chap. 3; Headlam-Morley, *Studies in Diplomatic History*, chap. 8; Wood, *History of the Levant Company*, chap. 10; Khadduri and Liebesny, *Law in the Middle East*, vol. 1, chap. 13 (by Liebesny).

I. From the moment of signing the present Treaty, every act of hostility between England and Turkey shall cease; and in furtherance of this happy peace, the prisoners on both sides shall be exchanged without distinction, in thirty-one days from the signature of this Treaty, or sooner, if possible.

II. Should any fortresses belonging to the Sublime Porte be in the possession of Great Britain, they shall be restored to the Sublime Porte, and given up, with all the cannons, warlike stores, and other effects, in the condition in which they were found at the time of their being occupied by England, and this restitution shall be made in the space of thirty-one days from the signature of the present Treaty.

III. Should there be any effects and property belonging to English merchants under sequestration, within the jurisdiction of the Sublime Porte, the same shall be entirely given up, and restored to the proprietors; and in like manner, should there be any effects, property, and vessels, belonging to merchants, subjects of the Sublime Porte, under sequestration at Malta, or in any other islands and possessions of His Britannic Majesty, they also shall be entirely given up and restored to their proprietors.

IV. The Treaty of Capitulations agreed upon in the Turkish year 1086, (A.D. 1675) in the middle of the month Gemmaziel Akir, as also the Act relating to the Commerce of the Black Sea, and the other privileges (*Imtiazat*) equally established by Acts at subsequent periods, shall continue to be observed and maintained as if they had suffered no interruption.

V. In return for the indulgence and good treatment afforded by the Sublime Porte to English merchants, with respect to their goods and property, as well as in all matters tending to facilitate their commerce, England shall reciprocally extend every indulgence and friendly treatment to the flag, subjects, and merchants of the Sublime Porte, which may hereafter frequent the Dominions of His Britannic Majesty for the purposes of commerce.

VI. The last custom-house tarif established at Constantinople, at the ancient rate of 3 per cent. and particularly the Article relating to the interior commerce, shall continue to be observed, as they are at present regulated, and to which England promises to conform.

VII. Ambassadors from His Majesty the King of Great Britain shall enjoy all the honours enjoyed by Ambassadors to the Sublime Porte from other nations; and Ambassadors from the Sublime Porte at the Court of London shall reciprocally enjoy all the honours granted to the Ambassadors from Great Britain.

VIII. Consuls (*Shahbenders*) may be appointed at Malta, and in the Dominions of His Britannic Majesty where it shall be necessary, to manage and superintend the affairs and interests of merchants of the Sublime Porte, and similar privileges and immunities to those granted to English Consuls resident in the Ottoman Dominions, shall be duly afforded to the "*Shahbenders*" of the Sublime Porte.

IX. English Ambassadors and Consuls may supply themselves, according to custom, with such Dragomen as they shall stand in need of: but as it has already been mutually agreed upon, that the Sublime Porte shall not grant the "*Barat*" of Dragoman in favour of individuals who do not execute that duty in the place of their destination, it is settled, in conformity with this principle, that in future, the "*Barat*" shall not be granted to any person of the class of tradesmen or bankers, nor to any shopkeeper or manufacturer in the public markets, or to one who is engaged in any matters of this description; nor shall English Consuls be named from among the subjects of the Sublime Porte.

X. English patents of protection shall not be granted to dependants, or merchants who are subjects of the Sublime Porte, nor shall any passport be delivered to such persons, on the part of Ambassadors or Consuls, without permission previously obtained from the Sublime Porte.

XI. As ships of war have at all times been prohibited from entering the canal of Constantinople, viz. in the straits of the Dardanelles and of the Black Sea, and as this ancient regulation of the Ottoman Empire is in future to be observed by every Power in time of peace, the Court of Great Britain promises on its part to conform to this principle. . . .

Separate and Secret Articles

The Secret Articles which the Court of England engaged to perform on her part in proof and fulfilment of her friendship and sincerity towards the Sublime Porte, and which were included in the conference that took place on the day of the signing of the Treaty of Peace [just] concluded between the Exalted Ottoman Court and the Court of England, are as follows—

ART. 1. Should France, unjustly, declare war against the Sublime Porte, or should he manifest any threats towards her, in consequence of the Peace that has been now so happily concluded between the Exalted Ottoman Court and the Court of Great Britain, His Majesty, the Honored King of England, engages to exert all his attention and inclination in affording the Sublime Porte assistance, and securing [protecting] the islands and harbours belonging to her in the White [Mediterranean] Sea, against the assaults of enemy, by sending into the [said] Sea a sufficient fleet for that purpose, the details and arrangements of which assistance shall be discussed at the High Court [of Constantinople].

ART. 2. Likewise, should France manifest any hostilities, or spread out menaces, against the Sublime Porte, His Majesty, the aforesaid King of England, engages to assist the Exalted Ottoman Court by supplying her, at the sea ports which she may point out, with guns, powder, and all necessary warlike stores, for the fortification or defence of the boundries of her Possessions in Bosnia and Dalmatzia.

ART. 3. The discussion of the agreements or covenants that took place between the Commanders of England and the authorized persons of the Sublime Porte, relative to the late entrance into, and evacuation of, Alexandria of Egypt, by Great Britain,

shall be brought into the Happy Court [of Constantinople], and the claims of both parties looked into and arranged, according to justice and equity, and shall be finally settled.

ART. 4. Should the Court of England conclude peace with Russia before the Ottoman Porte, His Majesty, the aforesaid King of England, engages to exert and use his good efforts to obtain, as far as circumstances may permit, an advantageous and honorable peace between the Exalted Court and the Court of Russia; honorable and beneficial to the Sublime Porte, and with independence to, and complete integrity of the Ottoman Dominions.

Conclusion—These Secret Articles shall be kept concealed from all the Courts, nor their secrecy shall ever be divulged. . . .

ADDITIONAL AND SECRET ARTICLE. The cause of writing these lines is as follows—

The ancient friendship and sincerity [that existed] between the Sublime Ottoman Porte and the Court of England, having been happily restored, His Majesty the Honored King of England, in confirmation of his friendship, will readily undertake to give the Exalted Ottoman Court, by way of assistance, Three Hundred Thousand Pounds Sterling, or Ten Thousand Two Hundred Purses of Turkish Money, in two instalments, in the course of about six months from the day of the exchange of the ratifications of the treaties of peace.

53. TREATY OF ALLIANCE AND MUTUAL DEFENSE: BRITISH INDIA AND AFGHANISTAN
17 June 1809

(Ratified by the governor general, Calcutta, 17 June 1809)
[India Office Library, Government of India, Political and Secret Department, Memoranda, vol. 2 (1898–1923), A 155, doc. no. 155, pp. 345–46]

Late in 1808 Lord Minto, the governor general of India, sent Mountstuart Elphinstone to conclude an alliance with Shah Shuja' al-Mulk (1803–09) for common defense against the French-Persian alliance that Napoleon had framed at Finkenstein in 1807 (Doc. 50). Elphinstone, bearing lavish gifts, reached Shah Shuja' at his winter capital in Peshawar at the end of February 1809. By the time the following instrument —the first formal British-Afghan agreement and the first Afghan agreement with a European power—was signed by Lord Minto, Persia had in effect already denounced its alliance with France. Moreover, soon after signing the treaty, Shah Shuja' was overthrown, making the pact with British India worthless and further weakening the Sadozay dynasty. This was the first dynasty of sovereign Afghanistan, which had arisen from the ruins of Nadir Shah's short-lived Persian Empire (1736–47). Before then Afghanistan had never constituted an independent political entity, and in modern times it passed back and forth in full or in part between the Safavi Empire in Persia and the Mughal Empire in India. Ahmad Shah (1747–73) established the Sadozay dynasty by uniting in his realm the Afghan and Indian provinces of Nadir Shah, and these remained nominally intact on the accession in 1793 of Zaman Shah, the grandson of the dynasty's founder. But the dethronement and blinding of Zaman by a half-brother in 1800 ushered in more than four decades of civil war, first among the surviving Sadozay princes and then between them and the related Barakzay clan. Shah Shuja' himself, after losing his throne, took refuge in British India, and in 1816 he became a pensioner of the East India Company. Elphinstone, *Account of the Kingdom of Caubul*; Kaye, *History of the War in Afghanistan*, bk.1, chap. 5; Archbold, "Afghanistan, Russia, and Persia"; Fraser-Tytler, *Afghanistan*, pt. 2, chap. 2; Norris, *First Afghan War*, chap. 1; Sykes, *History of Afghanistan*, vol. 1, chap. 26; entries for "Afghanistan," "Ahmad Shah Durrani," and "Dust Muhammad" in EI[2].

Whereas in consequence of the confederacy with the State of Persia, projected by the French for the purpose of invading the dominions of His Majesty the King of the Dooranees, and ultimately those of the British Government in India, the Hon'ble Mountstuart Elphinstone was despatched to the Court of His Majesty in quality of Envoy Plenipotentiary on the part of the Right Hon'ble Lord Minto, Governor-General, exercising the supreme authority over all affairs, civil, political, and military in the British possessions in the East Indies, for the purpose of concerting with His Majesty's Ministers the means of mutual defence against the expected invasion of the French and Persians, and whereas the said Ambassador having had the honor of being presented to His Majesty and of explaining the friendly and beneficial object of his mission, His Majesty, sensible of the advantages of alliance and co-operation between the two States, for the purpose above described, directed his Ministers to confer with the Hon'ble Mountstuart Elphinstone, and consulting the welfare of both States to conclude a friendly alliance, and certain articles of Treaty having accordingly been agreed to between His Majesty's Ministers

and the British Ambassador, and confirmed by the Royal Signet, a copy of the Treaty so framed has been transmitted by the Ambassador for the ratification of the Governor-General, who consenting to the stipulations therein contained without variation, a copy of those Articles as hereunder written is now returned, duly ratified by the seal and signature of the Governor-General and the signatures of the Members of the British Government in India, and the obligations upon both Governments both now and for ever shall be exclusively regulated and determined by the tenor of those Articles, which are as follows:—

ART. 1. As the French and Persians have entered into a confederacy against the State of Cabool, if they should wish to pass through the King's dominions, the servants of the Heavenly Throne shall prevent their passage, and exerting themselves to the extent of their power in making war on them and repelling them, shall not permit them to cross into British India.

ART. 2. If the French and Persians in pursuance of their confederacy should advance towards the King of Cabool's country in a hostile manner, the British State, endeavouring heartily to repel them, shall hold themselves liable to afford the expenses necessary for the above-mentioned service to the extent of their ability. While the confederacy between the French and Persians continues in force, these Articles shall be in force and [shall] be acted on by both parties.

ART. 3. Friendship and union shall continue for ever between these two States, the veil of separation shall be lifted up from between them, and they shall in no manner interfere in each other's countries, and the King of Cabool shall permit no individual of the French to enter his territories. . . .

54. TREATY OF PEACE (BUCHAREST): THE OTTOMAN EMPIRE AND RUSSIA
16/28 May 1812

[Translated from the French text in Noradounghian, *Recueil d'actes internationaux de l'empire ottoman*, 2: 86–92]

The Treaty of Bucharest ended a six-year war between Russia and the Ottoman Empire. The imminence of Napoleon's invasion of Russia, for which the elaborate military and diplomatic preparations could not be hidden from either belligerent in the eastern war, made Tsar Alexander I and his advisers increasingly anxious for a settlement with the Sublime Porte after the summer of 1811. But Sultan Mahmud II (1808–39) and his advisers were especially obdurate in insisting on the withdrawal of Russian forces from all Ottoman provinces in the Balkans and the Caucasus. In the end, Russia clung to Bessarabia as its only territorial gain in the Balkans, returning to the Ottoman Empire Moldavia and Wallachia (present-day Rumania) and stretches of Bulgaria across the Danube which tsarist forces had begun to penetrate before Saint Petersburg was overtaken by anxiety about Napoleon. In the Caucasus, the Russians had tried to fill the northern gap between the Kuban River, which had been fixed at Jassy in 1792 (Doc. 34) as the Ottoman-Russian boundary, and Eastern Georgia, which had been annexed in 1801. Here the Russian position was more precarious, for while the Sublime Porte surrendered its claims to the Rion basin the Russians had to relinquish a good part of the Black Sea coast, including the powerful fortress of Anapa. Russia requested, and received (art. 13), Ottoman assurances of good offices in seeking peace with Persia. However, that settlement (Doc. 55) was not consummated until long after Napoleon's disastrous retreat from Russia, so that the Qajars wrested far less favorable terms from their northern neighbor than had the Ottomans. Stratford Canning, who was to return to Istanbul thirty years later for an illustrious sixteen-year tour of duty (1842–58) as British ambassador, underwent in 1810–12 his baptism of diplomatic fire as chargé d'affaires with the rank of minister plenipotentiary, though still under twenty-five years of age. The Foreign Office, under the marquis Wellesley, completely ignored the young diplomat. Although Lane-Poole's account overstates the case, Canning nevertheless did display unusual skill in uninstructed mediation between the Ottoman and Russian governments in the peace negotiations that dragged on for about eight months, establishing his reputation as a talented diplomat. Lane-Poole, *Life of the Right Honourable Stratford Canning*, vol. 1, chap. 3; Temperley, *England and the Near East*, pp. 49–51; Allen and Muratoff, *Caucasian Battlefields*, chap. 1; M. Anderson, *Eastern Question*, chap. 2.

ART. 1. All hostilities and disputes that have until now occurred between the two Empires on land and on sea shall cease from today and for always in virtue of the present Treaty. Peace, friendship, and good understanding shall reign in perpetuity from now on between His Majesty the Emperor of All the Russias and His Highness the Ottoman Emperor, their successors, and the subjects of the two Empires. The two High Contracting Parties, equally animated by a sincere desire to avoid anything that might cause disagreement between their respective subjects, shall with the most scrupulous exactitude fulfill all the provisions of the present Treaty and shall apply themselves zealously in the future to prevent anything from happening, [perpetrated] by one party or the other, secretly or publicly, contrary to the said Treaty.

ART. 2. Thus reconciled, the High Contracting Parties grant an amnesty and general pardon to all their subjects who, in the course of the war, took part in military operations or who, in whatever manner, acted against the interests of their sovereign and country. Accordingly, they are freed from all responsibility; and all those who may return to their homes shall enjoy all the rights that they had previously acquired under the protection of the law, in the same manner as their compatriots.

ART. 3. All the treaties and conventions that have been concluded in several prior negotiations of peace and that have been recognized by the two [said] sovereigns are confirmed and shall remain in force, with the exception of those articles which, as a result of the passage of time, have suffered some change. Accordingly, the two High Contracting Parties promise faithfully and solemnly to observe not only the present Treaty but all prior treaties.

ART. 4. In Article 1 of the preliminaries it is stipulated that the Pruth, from the point where it enters Moldavia to its mouth at the Danube, and from the left bank of the Danube to Kilya and to its mouth at the Black Sea, shall form the frontier of the two Empires. However, the two peoples shall continue to share navigation rights. The small islands of the Danube, inhabited until the beginning of this war and located between Ismail and Kilya, must, being closer to the left bank, fall under Russian rule; but the High Contracting Parties are agreed that they shall remain deserted and that from now on no fortification whatsoever shall be constructed there; the subjects of the two Powers shall be free to fish and cut wood there. The large islands situated opposite Ismail and Kilya shall also remain deserted but only at one league's distance from the left bank of the Danube. This distance shall subsequently be fixed. The establishments that existed before the war, such as Old Kilya, shall not be included in this line of demarcation. In virtue of the other arrangements of this same article, the Sublime Ottoman Porte renounces in favor of Russia [all rights] to the lands situated on the left bank of the Pruth, all the fortresses, cities, and dwellings that are found there, as well as half the river Pruth, which forms the boundary of the two Empires. The merchantships of the two Powers shall be allowed to enter and leave by the mouth of and navigate the entire length of the Danube, but Russian warships shall never be allowed to ascend the Danube beyond the point of its confluence with the Pruth.

ART. 5. His Majesty the Emperor of All the Russias abandons and returns to the Sublime Porte the part of Moldavia situated on the right bank of the Pruth; the Great and the Small Wallachia, with its fortresses in their present condition and all the cities, boroughs, villages, and other establishments and all that this province may comprise; and the islands of the Danube, with the exception of those that are mentioned in the preceding article.

The treaties and conventions concerning the privileges of Moldavia and Wallachia are confirmed according to the principles of Article 5 of the preliminaries. The particular conventions and provisions of Article 4 of the Treaty of Jassy shall also remain in force, to wit: that the Porte shall not demand indemnities for the revenues that it has lost; that it shall not levy any tax for the entire duration of the war; that the inhabitants of these two provinces shall be exempt from all taxation for two years dating from the exchange of the ratifications of the present Treaty; and, finally, that those who may desire to emigrate shall obtain a reprieve of four months and that the Sublime Porte shall act in such a way that the future taxes of Moldavia shall be proportionate to the actual extent of its territory.

ART. 6. With the exception of the new boundaries formed by the Pruth, all the other frontiers of the two Empires in Asia and elsewhere shall remain as they were before the start of hostilities, and the Court of Russia, in virtue of Article 3 of the preliminaries, returns to the Sublime Ottoman Porte in their present condition all the conquered fortresses and forts included in these limits, with all the cities, boroughs, villages, and dwellings, and all that these districts comprise.

ART. 7. Ottoman subjects who, as a result of the war, have either come to or remained in the districts now ceded to Russia shall be allowed freely to pass into establish themselves there with their families and all their property without anyone preventing them from so doing. They shall be free to sell their goods to whomever they deem worthy and to take with them all that they may desire. This permission shall extend also to the inhabitants of the ceded districts who possess goods there and who are at present in the Ottoman provinces: and a reprieve of eighteen months, dating from the exchange of the ratifications of the present Treaty, shall be granted to all so they might put their affairs in order.

Also, the Tatars of the tribe of Kavusan who in this war crossed from Bessarabia into Russia shall, if they so desire, be permitted to return to the Ottoman provinces, always on condition that the Sublime Porte shall be obligated to indemnify Russia for the expenses that the emigration and establishment of these Tatars have entailed. Similarly, Christians who have possessions in the districts ceded to Russia or who were born there but who are at present in other parts of the Ottoman Empire may, if they so wish, return to the said ceded districts and establish themselves there with their families and goods, without anyone being permitted to oppose it. They shall also be permitted to sell whatever goods they possess in the Ottoman Empire and to transfer the product [of the sale] to the Russian provinces, and for this they shall enjoy the same reprieve of eighteen months from the date of the exchange of ratifications of the present Treaty.

ART. 8. Although it is not permissible to doubt that the Sublime Porte, faithful to its principles, treats the Serbians (people who have long been subservient and tributary) with clemency and generosity, it has been thought just, considering the part they have taken in this war, solemnly to agree to a clause concerning their security. Consequently, and in accordance with Article 4 of the preliminaries, the Sublime Porte grants a complete amnesty to the Serbians and promises that their tranquillity shall not be disturbed because of past events. The fortresses which did not previously exist but which were constructed in their district in this war shall be razed, since in the future they shall be useless, and the Sublime Porte shall as above, take possession of the other strongholds and shall place there the artillery, munitions, and garrisons it judges necessary. But, that these garrisons may not unjustly oppress the Serbians, the Sublime Porte shall treat this people with all due moderation, being guided solely by sentiments of mercy. In addition, the Sublime Porte shall, at the request of the Serbians, grant them the same advantages as those enjoyed by the subjects of the islands of the Archipelago and other parts of their provinces and shall also give them a proof of its magnanimity in leaving to them the care of their country's internal administration, in accepting from them immediately the amount of moderate taxes that it may levy upon them, and in acting in this regard in concert with this people.

ART. 9. All the prisoners found in the two Empires of every sex, nation, and rank shall be exchanged immediately after the ratification of the present Treaty and without the least ransom, always excepting Christians who, in the provinces of the Sublime Porte, shall have embraced Islam in good faith and Muslims who, in Russia, shall have also voluntarily embraced Chris-

tianity. These measures shall extend to all
Russian subjects who after the signature of
the present Treaty may be enslaved by any
event whatsoever and who may be found in
the Ottoman Empire. The Court of Russia
undertakes in this respect to treat subjects
of the Sublime Porte reciprocally. The two
High Contracting Parties may not issue
claims relating to the sums employed for
the maintenance of prisoners, who shall be
provided with all that is vitally necessary
until their arrival at the frontiers, where the
resepctive commissioners shall exchange
them.

ART. 10. All the affairs and [legal] proceedings of the respective subjects of the
two Empires which at the end of the war
may not be terminated shall not be abandoned but, on the contrary, shall be dealt
with and adjudicated after the peace. All
debts contracted by subjects of the two
Powers as well as revenue claims shall be
paid promptly.

ART. 11. As a result of the present Treaty
of Peace concluded between the two High
Parties and after the exchange of ratifications, the ground troops and fleets of His
Majesty the Emperor of Russia shall evacuate the provinces and waters of the Ottoman Emperor. But this evacuation not
being easily effected, owing to great distance and other obstacles, the two High
Contracting Parties agree to fix at three
months dating from the exchange of ratifications the period of the complete evacuation of Moldavia and Wallachia and of the
other [Ottoman] provinces in Europe and
Asia. When the Russian troops will have
left all those provinces restored by this
Treaty to the Sublime Porte, the Russian
fleets and warships shall retire from the
waters of the Ottoman Empire. The places
and strongholds occupied by the Russians
shall, until the moment of evacuation, continue to be administered by the Court of
Russia, as they are now. The Sublime Porte
shall not interfere until the expiration of the
agreed date and the entire evacuation of all
the troops, who shall be maintained and
provided with all their needs until the day
of their departure, just as they have been
to the present.

ART. 12. If the Minister or Plenipotentiary of the Court of Russia at Constantinople should demand in writing, and, in

virtue of Article 7 of the Treaty of Jassy,
damages for seizures from Russian subjects and merchants by the corsairs of the
Regencies of Algiers, Tunis, or Tripoli,
claims concerning the interest guaranteed
by the existing treaties of commerce shall be
made. The Sublime Porte shall see to it
that all the provisions of the said treaties
shall be observed and fulfilled and thus
avoid all cause for litigation and complaint,
without at any time damaging the established regulations and ordinances.

As for the commercial laws, the Court of
Russia shall observe the same conduct with
regard to the Sublime Porte.

ART. 13. After the conclusion of the
present Treaty the Court of Russia consents
to the Sublime Porte's offering its good
offices to its coreligionists, so that the war
between Russia and Persia may be terminated and a reciprocal accord may assure
peace to these two Powers.

ART. 14. As soon as possible after the
exchange of the ratifications of the present
Treaty, the generals commanding the respective armies of the two Empires shall
issue to all commanders of particular
corps the order to cease all hostilities on
land and sea; and if nevertheless [hostile
acts] should be committed after the signing
of the present Treaty, they shall be viewed
as not having occurred[1] and shall not yield
any change in this Treaty. Moreover, all
conquests that the troops of the two High
Contracting Parties may make in this interval shall be restored in the field.

ART. 15. After the plenipotentiaries of
the two sovereigns will have signed the
Treaty, the first plenipotentiary of His
Majesty the Emperor of All the Russias and
the Grand Vezir of the Sublime Ottoman
Porte shall confirm it, and ten days after
their signature, or sooner if possible, its
instruments shall be exchanged by these
plenipotentiaries.

ART. 16. The present Treaty of Perpetual
Peace shall be confirmed and ratified by His
Majesty the Emperor of All the Russias
and His Highness the Ottoman Emperor,
who shall sign it solemnly with their own

---

1. Noradounghian text reads, "elles seront
regardées comme non avenues," but clearly
"ont lieu" would be more accurate than
"avenues."

hand, and it shall be exchanged by their respective plenipotentiaries in the city where the Treaty was concluded within four weeks, or sooner if possible.

55. TREATY OF PEACE (GULISTAN): RUSSIA AND PERSIA
30 September/12 October 1813

(Ratifications exchanged, Tiflis, 3/15 September 1814)
[Aitchison, *Collection of Treaties . . . relating to India* (5th ed.), vol. 13, app. no. 5, pp. xv-xviii]

The treaty of Gulistan, negotiated through the good offices of the United Kingdom, ended a nine-year war with Persia and assured Russian possession of Georgia—the original cause of the war—and other districts then owing suzerainty to the shah. But the ambiguous terms of the territorial settlement kept alive the tensions between Persia and its northern neighbor for more than a dozen years, culminating in 1826 in renewed hostilities. The 1813 instrument, in article 5, also gave Russian war vessels the exclusive right to navigate in the Caspian Sea. Although artice 7 provided for the exchange of permanent diplomatic missions, this provision was not put into effect until after its reaffirmation by article 9 of the treaty of Turkmanchay (1828). Schlechta-Wssehrd, "Die Kämpfe zwischen Persien und Russland in Transkaukasien"; Krausse, *Russia in Asia*, chap. 5; Baddeley, *Russian Conquest of the Caucasus*, chaps. 4–5; W. Allen, *History of the Georgian People*, chap. 18; Sykes, *History of Persia*, vol. 2, chap. 76; Rawlinson, *England and Russia in the East*, chap. 1; Watons, *History of Persia*, chaps. 6–8.

ART. 1. After the conclusion of this Treaty the hostilities which have hitherto existed between the States of Russia and Persia shall cease, and peace shall be established between the respective sovereigns and their allies for ever.

ART. 2. The *status quo ad presentem* having been agreed on as the basis of treating in virtue of this arrangement, the several districts hitherto possessed by the respective States shall remain under their subjection, and the frontier is determined in the manner under written.

The line of demarcation is to commence from the plain of Aduna Bazar, running direct towards the plain of Moghan to the ford of the Anas at Yuln Bulook, up the Anas to the Junction of the Capennuk Chace at the back of the hill of Mekri; from thence the boundary of Karabagh and Nukshivan is from above the mountains of Alighuz to Dualighuz, and thence the boundary of Karabagh, Nukshivan, Erivand, and also part of Georgia, and of Kuzah and Shums-ud-deen Loo is separated by Eishuk Meidaun; from Eishuk Meidaun the line is the chain of mountains on the right and the river of Humya Chummun, and from the tops of the mountains of Alighuz it runs along the village of Shoorgil and between those of the village of Mystery until it reaches the river of Arpachahi; and as the district of Talish during the hostilities has been partially subjected by the contending parties, for the purpose of strengthening mutual confidence after the conclusion of the Treaty, Commissioners shall be appointed respectively, who, in concurrence with each other and with the cognizance of the Governors concerned, shall determine what mountains, rivers, lakes, villages, and fields shall mark the line of frontier, having first ascertained the respective possessions at the time of making the Treaty, and holding in view the *status quo ad presentem* as the basis on which the boundaries are to be determined.

If the possessions of either of the High Contracting Parties shall have been infringed on by the above-mentioned boundaries, the Commissioners shall rectify it on the basis of the *status quo ad presentem*.

ART. 3. His Majesty the King of Persia, in demonstration of his amicable sentiments towards the Emperor of Russia, acknowledges in his own name and that of his heirs the sovereignty of the Emperor of Russia over the provinces of Karabagh and Georgia, now called Elizabeth Paul, the districts of Shekie, Shiriwan, Kobek, Derbend, Bakoobeh, and such part of Talish as is now possessed by Russia, the whole of Degesten, Georgia, the tract of Shoorgil, Achook, Bash, Gooreea, Mingrelia, Abtichar, the whole country between the boundary at present established and the line of Caucasus, and all the territory between the Caucasus and the Caspian Sea.

ART. 4. His Majesty the Emperor of Russia, actuated by similar feelings towards His Majesty of Persia, and in the spirit of good neighbourhood wishing the Sovereign of Persia always to be firmly established on the throne, engages for himself and [his] heirs to recognise the Prince who shall be nominated heir-apparent, and to afford him assistance in case he should require it to suppress any opposing party. The power of Persia will thus be increased by the aid of Russia. The Emperor engages for himself and [his] heirs not to interfere in the dissensions of the Prince, unless the aid of the Russian arms is required by the King of the time.

ART. 5. The Russian merchantmen on the Caspian Sea shall, according to their former practice, have permission to enter the Persian harbours, and the Persians shall render to the Russian Marine all friendly aid in case of casualties by storm or shipwreck.

Persian merchantmen shall enjoy the same privilege of entering Russian harbours, and the like aid shall be afforded to the Persian Marine by the Russians in case of casualties by storm or shipwreck.

The Russian flag shall fly in the Russian ships-of-war which are permitted to sail in the Caspian as formerly; no other nation whatever shall be allowed ships-of-war on the Caspian.

ART. 6. The whole of the prisoners taken either in battle or otherwise, whether Christians or of any other religion, shall be mutually exchanged at the expiration of three months after the date of the signature of the Treaty. The High Contracting Parties shall give a sum to each of the prisoners for his expenses, and send them to Kara Ecclesia; those charged with the superintendence of the exchange on the frontiers shall give notice to each other of the prisoners being sent to the appointed place, when they shall be exchanged; and any person who either voluntarily deserted or fled after the commission of a crime shall have permission to return to his country, [or] shall remain without molestation. All deserters who return to their country shall be forgiven by both contracting parties.

ART. 7. In addition to the above articles, the two contracting sovereigns have been pleased to resolve to exchange Ambassadors, who at a proper period will be sent to their respective capitals, where they will meet with that honour due to their rank, and due attention shall be paid to the requests they may be charged to make. Mercantile agents shall be appointed to reside in the different cities for the purpose of assisting the merchants in carrying on their trade; they shall only retain ten followers; they shall be in no ways molested; they shall be treated with respect and attention, and parties of either nation injured in the way of trade may by their interference have their grievances redressed.

ART. 8. With regard to the intercourse of caravans, the merchants of either country must be provided with a passport that they may travel either by sea or land without fear, and individuals may reside in either country for the purpose of trade so long as it suits their convenience, and they shall meet with no opposition when they wish to return home. In regard to merchandise and goods, brought from Russia to Persia, or sent from Persia to Russia, the proprietors may at their own discretion either sell or exchange them for other property. Merchants having occasion to complain of failure of payment or other grievances will state the nature of their cases to the mercantile agents; or, if there are none resident in the place, they will apply to the Governor, who will examine into the merits of their representations, and will be careful that no injustice be offered this class of men. Russian merchants having entered Persia with merchandise will have permission to convey it to any country in alliance with that State, and the Persian Government will readily furnish them a passport to enable them to do so. In like manner, Persian merchants who visit Russia will have permission to proceed to any country in alliance with Russia. In case of a Russian merchant dying in Persia, and his goods remaining in Persia, as they are the property of a subject of a friendly State, they shall be taken charge of by the proper constituted authorities, and shall be delivered over, on demand, to the lawful heirs of the deceased, who shall have permission to dispose of them. As this is the custom among all civilised nations, there can be no objection to this arrangement.

ART. 9. The duties on Russian merchandise brought to Persian ports shall be in the proportion of five hundred dinars (or 5 per cent.) on property of the value of one toman, which having been paid at one city the goods may be conveyed to any part of Persia without any further demand of duty being made on any pretence whatever. The like percentage, and nothing more, will be paid on exports. The import and export duties from Persian merchants in Russia will be levied at the same rate.

ART. 10. On the arrival of goods at the seaport towns, or such as come by land-carriage to the frontier towns of the two States, merchants shall be allowed to sell or exchange their goods without the further permission of the Custom House Officers because it is the duty of Custom House Officers to prevent all sorts of delay, in the prosecution of trade, and to receive the King's customs from the buyer or seller as may be agreed between them.

ART. 11. After the signature of this Treaty the respective plenipotentiaries shall immediately announce the peace to the different frontier posts and order the suspension of all further hostilities; and two copies of this Treaty being taken with Persian translations, they shall be signed and sealed by the respective plenipotentiaries, and be exchanged.

56. (DEFINITIVE) TREATY OF DEFENSIVE ALLIANCE (TEHRAN): GREAT BRITAIN AND PERSIA
25 November 1814

(Ratifications exchanged, Tehran, September 1815)
[Aitchison, *Collection of Treaties . . . relating to India* (5th ed.), 13: 60–63]

The treaty of 1814, which established the pattern of British-Persian relations under the Qajar dynasty (1796–1925), consumed more than five years in its formulation. The East India Company and the British government in London independently matured plans for the arrangement, the first primarily concerned with defense against Russia and the second with defense against France. Indeed, each sent a separate delegation to Tehran in 1808. But the Foreign Office insisted on assuming charge of English affairs in Persia at the time, and the London representative signed in March 1809 a preliminary agreement (text in Aitchison, op. cit., pp. 53–55), which was superseded three years later by a second (ibid., pp. 56–59) and finally in 1814 by the following instrument. Under the alliance the United Kingdom, through the government of British India, furnished Persia between 1810 and 1815 with military training missions. In exchange for a British grant of 200,000 *tomans* (about £150,000) Fath 'Ali Shah in 1828 annulled by decree (ibid., p. 64) articles 3 and 4 of the 1814 agreement, providing for financial subsidies to Persia. Although none of the three treaties expressly provided for continuous diplomacy, Britain became in 1809 the first European power to accredit a permanent diplomatic mission to Persia; it remained responsible to the Foreign Office in London except for two interruptions—1823-35 and 1858-59—when the government of India managed British affairs in the shahdom. Kaye, *Major-General Sir John Malcolm*, vol. 1, chap. 15, and vol. 2, chap. 1; Brydges, *Transactions of His Majesty's Mission to the Court of Persia*; Lorimer, *Gazetteer of the Persian Gulf*, vol. 1, pt. 2, pp. 1894-1909; Kelly, *Britain and the Persian Gulf*, chap. 2; Hoskins, *British Routes to India*, chap. 3; Sykes, *History of Persia*, vol. 2, chap. 75; Rawlinson, *England and Russia in the East*, chap. 1.

ART. 1. The Persian Government judge it incumbent on them, after the conclusion of the definitive Treaty, to declare all alliances contracted with European nations in a state of hostility with Great Britain null and void, and hold themselves bound not to allow any European army to enter the Persian territory, not to proceed towards India, nor to any of the ports of that country, and also engage not to allow any individuals of such European nations entertaining a design of invading India, or being at enmity with Great Britain whatever, to enter Persia. Should any of the European powers wish to invade India by the road of Kharizen, Taturistan, Bokhara, Samarkand, or other routes, His Persian Majesty engages to induce the kings and governors of those countries to oppose such invasion, as much as is in his power, either by the fear of his arms or by conciliatory measures.

ART. 2. It is agreed that these Articles formed with the hand of truth and sincerity shall not be changed or altered, but there shall arise from them a daily increase of friendship which shall last for ever between the two most serene kings, their heirs, successors, their subjects, and their respective kingdoms, dominions, provinces, and countries; and His Britannic Majesty further engages not to interfere in any dispute which may hereafter arise between the Princes, Noblemen, and great Chiefs of Persia, and if one of the contending parties should even offer a province of Persia with a view of obtaining assistance, the English Government shall not agree to such a proposal, nor by adopting it possess

themselves of such part of Persia.

ART. 3. The purpose of this Treaty is strictly defensive, and the object is that from their mutual assistance both States should derive stability and strength, and this Treaty has only been concluded for the purpose of repelling the aggression of enemies; and the purport of the word aggression in this Treaty is an attack upon the teritorries of another State. The limits of the territories of the two States of Russia and Persia shall be determined according to the admission of Great Britain, Persia, and Russia.

ART. 4. It having been agreed by an Article in the preliminary Treaty concluded between the high contracting parties that in case of any European nation invading Persia, should the Persian Government require the assistance of the English, the Governor General of India, on the part of Great Britain, shall comply with the wish of the Persian Government by sending from India the force required, with officers, ammunition, and warlike stores, or, in lieu thereof, the English Government shall pay an annual subsidy, the amount of which shall be regulated in a definitive Treaty to be concluded between the high contracting parties; it is hereby provided that the amoung of the said subsidy shall be two hundred thousand (200,000) tomans annually. It is further agreed that the said subsidy shall not be paid in case the war with such European nation shall have been produced by an aggression on the part of Persia; and since the payment of the subsidy will be made solely for the purpose of raising and disciplining an army, it is agreed that the English minister shall be satisfied of its being duly applied to the purpose for which it is assigned.

ART. 5. Should the Persian Government wish to introduce European discipline among their troops, they are at liberty to employ European officers for that purpose, provided the said officers do not belong to nations in a state of war or enmity with Great Britain.

ART. 6. Should any European power be engaged in war with Persia when at peace with England, His Britannic Majesty engages to use his best endeavours to bring Persia and such European power to a friendly understanding. If, however, His Majesty's cordial interference should fail of success, England shall still, if required, in conformity with the stipulations in the preceding Articles, send a force from India, or in lieu thereof, pay an annual subsidy of two hundred thousand tomans for the support of a Persian army so long as a war in the supposed case shall continue, and until Persia shall make peace with such nation.

ART. 7. Since it is the custom of Persia to pay the troops six mosths in advance, the English minister at that Court shall do all in his power to pay the subsidy in as early instalments as may be convenient.

ART. 8. Should the Afghans be at war with the British nation, His Persian Majesty engages to send an army against them in such force and in such manner as may be concerted with the English Government. The expense of such an army shall be defrayed by the British Government in such manner as may be agreed upon at the pe-

riod of its being required.

ART. 9. If war should be declared between the Afghans and Persians, the English Government shall not interfere with either party unless their mediation to effect a peace shall be solicited by both parties.

ART. 10. Should any Persian subject of distinction showing signs of hostility and rebellion take refuge in the British dominions, the English Government shall, on intimation from the Persian Government, turn him out of their country, or, if he refuse to leave it, shall seize and send him to Persia.

Previously to the arrival of such fugitive in the English territory, should the Governor of the district to which he may direct his flight receive intelligence of the wishes of the Persian Government respecting him, he shall refuse him admission. After such prohibition, should such person persist in his resolution, the said Governor shall cause him to be seized and sent to Persia, it being understood that the aforesaid obligations are reciprocal between the contracting parties.

ART. 11. Should His Persian Majesty require assistance from the English Government in the Persian Gulf, they shall, if convenient and practicable, assist him with ships of war and troops. The expenses of such expedition shall be accounted for and defrayed by the Persian Government, and the above ships shall anchor in such ports as shall be pointed out by the Persian Government, and not at other harbours without permission, except from absolute necessity.

57. TREATY OF PEACE: THE UNITED STATES AND THE GARRISON OF ALGIERS
30 June 1815–22 December 1816

(Treaty of 1815 ratified by the United States, 26 December 1815; ratification rejected by the dey on 6 April 1816, but treaty allowed to enter into provisional effect; treaty renewed by fresh agreement, 22–23 December 1816; entered into effect, 23 December 1816; ratified by the United States, 11 February 1822)

[Text of 1815 treaty from Miller, *Treaties and Other International Acts*, 1: 585–91; texts of the dey's exchange of letters with the president, and the American commissioner's aide-mémoire to the dey, from Shaler, *Sketches of Algiers*, pp. 276–78, 295–97; text of additional and explanatory article of 1816 from Miller, op. cit., p. 623]

Caught between Napoleon's Continental System and Britain's Orders in Council, American commerce in the Mediterranean measurably declined after 1807 and then almost vanished after the outbreak of war with Britain in 1812, principally over the issue of the British navy's impressment of American seamen into British naval service. In 1810 the United States could not even deliver its annual tribute to the Garrison of Algiers. The dey, Haci 'Ali Paşa (1809–15), "declared war" on the United States in July 1812. Given the virtual disappearance of American shipping from the Mediterranean and its Atlantic approach, the dey's signal that American ships were liable to seizure netted the Algerine corsairs only token gain; their unique exploit was the capture in September 1812 of a small brig with a crew of eleven. The United States delayed taking punitive action until after the Congress approved the treaty of peace with Britain. Then, on 3 March 1815, Congress authorized naval operations against Algiers; two squadrons were deployed, one assembled in New York under the command of Commodore Stephen Decatur and the other in Boston under the command of Commodore William Bainbridge. Decatur's squadron left for the Mediterranean on 20 May, carrying aboard William Shaler, the consul general–designate for the Barbary Garrisons with residence at Algiers and joint commissioner with the commodores for negotiating the peace. In less than a month, Decatur captured the flagship of the Algerine squadron off the coast of Spain, killing the admiral and some thirty of his men, and taking more than four hundred prisoners. Two days later, Decatur seized an Algerine brig, bringing the total number of prisoners to nearly five hundred. Still worse for the Garrison, when the American squadron reached Algiers, the dey's major fighting ships were at sea. The American commissioners were thus able to dictate the terms of peace, including the abolition of the annual tribute, the unconditional release of American captives, and the payment of damages by Algiers. The treaty was signed by the dey, Ömer Paşa (1815–17), on 30 June, and by Shaler and Decatur on 3 July. The original signed treaty was lost at sea while en route to the United States for ratification; the ratified instrument for delivery to the dey therefore bore only the American president's signature. Using this as a pretext, the dey—with British encouragement, Shaler suspected—withheld endorsement, in the obvious expectation of getting better terms. In a letter of 24 April 1816 to President Madison, Ömer Paşa requested the renewal of the 1795 treaty, which had stipulated the annual payment of tribute by the United States. "It is a principle incorporated into the settled policy of America," replied President Madison four months later, "that as peace is better than war, war is better than tribute." By the time the new terms were negotiated in December 1816, the dey's position was even weaker than it had been a year and a half earlier, since the remnant of the Algerine naval force had been virtually wiped out by the British (Doc. 58). Included below are the treaty of peace of 1815 (which incorporated verbatim many of the clauses of the 1805 treaty with Tripoli [Doc. 47]), the exchange between the dey and the president, and the American commissioner's aide-mémoire. The treaty of 1816 (text in Miller, op. cit., pp. 617–23) simply repeated word for word the treaty of the preceding year, except for articles 2 and 3, the execution of which was acknowledged, and the transposition of articles 13 and 14. Therefore only the additional and explanatory article of 1816 appears below. Shaler, op. cit., chap. 5; Miller, op. cit., 2: 585–94, 617–42; G. Allen, *Our Navy and the Barbary Corsairs*, chaps. 16–17; Irwin, *Diplomatic Relations of the United States with the Barbary Powers*, chaps. 11–13; Abun-Nasr, *History of the Maghrib*, pp. 166–77; Grammont, *Histoire d'Alger sous la domination turque*, chaps. 24–25.

1. Treaty of Peace, 30 June and 3 July 1815

ART. 1. There shall be from the Conclusion of this treaty, a firm inviolable and universal peace and friendship between the President and Citizens of the United States of America on the one part, and the Dey and Subjects of the Regency of Algiers in Barbary, on the other, made by the free consent of both parties and upon the terms of the most favored nations; and if either party shall hereafter grant to any other nation, any particular favor or privilege in navigation or Commerce it shall immediately become common to the other party, freely when freely it is granted to such other nation; but when the grant is conditional, it shall be at the option of the contracting parties to accept, alter, or reject such conditions, in such manner as shall be most conducive to their respective interests.

ART. 2. It is distinctly understood between the Contracting parties, that no tribute either as biennial presents, or under any other form or name whatever, shall ever be required by the Dey and Regency of Algiers from the United States of America on any pretext whatever.

ART. 3. The Dey of Algiers shall cause to be immediately delivered up to the American Squadron now of Algiers all the American Citizens now in his possession, amounting to ten more or less, and all the

Subjects of the Dey of Algiers now in the power of the United States amounting to five hundred more or less, shall be delivered up to him, the United States according to the usages of civilized nations requiring no ransom for the excess of prisoners in their favor.

ART. 4. A just and full compensation shall be made by the Dey of Algiers to such citizens of the United States, as have been Captured, and detained by Algerine Cruizers, or who have been forced to abandon their property in Algiers in violation of the 22d article of the treaty of peace and amity concluded between the United States and the Dey of Algiers on the 5 September 1795.

And it is agreed between the contracting parties, that in lieu of the above, the Dey of Algiers shall cause to be delivered forthwith into the hands of the American Consul residing in Algiers the whole of a quantity of Bales of Cotton left by the late Consul General of the United States in the public magazines in Algiers; and that he shall pay into the hands of the said Consul the sum of ten thousand Spanish dollers.

ART. 5. If any goods belonging to any nation with which either of the parties are at war should be loaded on board of vessels belonging to the other party, they shall pass free and unmolested, and no attempt shall be made to take or detain them.

ART. 6. If any Citizens or subjects belonging to either party shall be found on board a prize vessel taken from an Ennemy by the other party, such Citizens or subjects shall be liberated immediately, and in no case or on any pretence whatever whatever shall any American Citizen be kept in Captivity or Confinement, or the property of any American Citizen found on board of any vessel belonging to any nation with which Algiers may be at War, be detained from its lawful owners after the exhibition of sufficient proofs of american Citizenship, and American property, by the Consul of the United States residing at Algiers.

ART. 7. Proper passports shall immediately be given to the vessels of both the Contracting parties, on condition that the vessels of war belonging to the Regency of Algiers on meeting with Merchant Vessels belonging to Citizens of the United States of America, shall not be permitted to visit them with more than two persons besides the rowers; these only shall be permitted to go on board without first obtaining leave from the Commander of said vessel, who shall compare the passports and immediately permit said vessel to proceed on her voyage; and should any of the subjects of Algiers insult or molest the Commander or any other person on board a vessel so visited, or plunder any of the property contained in her, on complaint being made to the Consul of the United States residing in Algiers, and on his producing sufficient proofs to substantiate the fact, the Commander or Rais of said Algerine ship or vessel of war, as well as the offenders shall be punished in the most exemplary manner.

All vessels of war belonging to the United States of America, on meeting with a Cruizer belonging to the Regency of Algiers, on having seen her passports, and Certificates from the Consul of the United States residing in Algiers shall permit her to proceed on her Cruize unmolested, and without detention. No passport shall be granted by either party to any vessels but such as are absolutely the property of Citizens or subjects of the said contracting parties, on any pretence whatever.

ART. 8. A Citizen or subject of either of the contracting parties having bought a prize Vessel condemned by the other party, or by any other nation, the Certificates of Condemnation and bill of sale shall be a sufficient passport for such vessel for six months, which, considering the distance between the two countries is no more than a reasonable time for her to procure passports.

ART. 9. Vessels of either of the contracting parties putting into the ports of the other and having need of provisions, or other supplies shall be furnished at the market price, and if any such Vessel should so put in from a disaster at sea and have occasion to repair, she shall be at liberty to land, and reembark her Cargo, without paying any customs, or duties whatever; but in no case shall she be compelled to land her Cargo.

ART. 10. Should a vessel of either of the contracting parties be cast on shore within the Territories of the other all proper assistance shall be given to her, and to her crew; no pillage shall be allowed. The property shall remain at the disposal of the owners, and if reshipped on board of any vessel for exportation, no customs or duties whatever shall be required to be paid thereon, and the crew shall be protected and succoured until they can be sent to their own Country.

ART. 11. If a vessel of either of the contracting parties shall be attacked by an enemy within Cannon shot of the forts of the other, she shall be protected as much as is possible. If she be in port she shall not be seized, or attacked when it is in the power of the other party protect her; and when she proceeds to sea, no Ennemy shall be permitted to pursue her from the same port within twenty four hours after her departure.

ART. 12. The Commerce between the United States of America and the Regency of Algiers, the protections to be given to Merchants, masters of vessels, and seamen, the reciprocal right of establishing Consuls in each country, the privileges, immunities and jurisdictions to be enjoyed by such Consuls, are declared to be upon the same footing in every respect with the most favored nations respectively.

ART. 13. On a vessel or vessels of war belonging to the United States of America anchoring before the City of Algiers, the Consul is to inform the Dey of her arrival when she shall receive the Salutes, which are by treaty or Custom given to the ships of war of the most favored nations on similar occasions, and which shall be returned gun for gun: and if after such arrival so announced, any christians whatever, Captives in Algiers make their escape and take refuge on board of the said ships of war, they shall not be required back again, nor shall the Consul of the United States, or commander of the said Ship be required to pay anything for the said Christians.

ART. 14. The Consul of the United States of America shall not be responsable for the debts Contracted by the Citizens of his own Country unless he gives previously written obligations so to do.

ART. 15. As the Government of the United States of America has in itself no character of enmity against the laws, religion, or tranquility of any nation, and as the said States have never entered into any voluntary war, or act of hostility, except in defence of their just rights on the high seas, it is declared by the Contracting parties that no pretext arising from religious opinions shall ever produce an interruption of Harmony between the two nations; and the Consuls and agents of both nations, shall have liberty to Celebrate the rights of their respective religions in their own houses.

The Consuls respectively shall have liberty and personal security given them to travel within the territories of each other, both by land, and by sea, and shall not be prevented from going on board of any vessel they may think proper to visit; they shall likewise have the liberty of apointing their own Dragoman, and Broker.

ART. 16. In Case of any dispute arrising from the violation of any of the articles of this Treaty no appeal shall be made to arms, nor shall war be declared, on any pretext whatever; but if the Consul residing at the place where the dispute shall happen, shall not be able to settle the same, the Government of that country shall state their grievance in writing, and transmit the same to the government of the other, and the period of three months shall be allowed for answers to be returned, during which time no act of hostility shall be permitted by either party; and in case the grievances are not redressed, and war should be the event, the Consuls, and Citizens, and subjects of both parties respectively shall be permitted to embark with their families and effects unmolested, on board of what vessel or vessels they shall think proper. Reasonable time being allowed for that purpose.

ART. 17. If in the Course of events a war should break out between the two nations, the prisoners Captured by either party shall not be made slaves, they shall not be forced to hard labor, or other confinement than such as may be necessary to secure their safe keeping, and they shall be exchanged rank for rank; and it is agreed that prisoners shall be exchanged in twelve months after their Capture, and the exchange may be effected by any private individual, legally authorized by either of the parties.

ART. 18. If any of the Barbary powers, or other states at war with the United States shall Capture any american Vessel, and send her into any port of the Regency of Algiers, they shall not be permitted to sell her, but shall be forced to depart the port on procuring the requisite supplies of provisions; but the vessels of war of the United States with any prizes they may capture from their Ennemies shall have liberty to frequent the ports of Algiers for refreshment of any kinds, and to sell such prizes in the said ports, without paying any other customs or duties than such as are customary on ordinary Commercial importations.

ART. 19. If any Citizens of the United States, or any persons under their protection, shall have any disputes with each other, the Consul shall decide between the parties, and whenever the Consul shall require any aid or assistance from the Government of Algiers to enforce his decisions it shall be immediately granted to him. And if any dispute shall arise between any citizens of the United States, and the citizens or subjects of any other nation having a Consul or agent in Algiers, such disputes shall be settled by the Consuls or agents of the respective nations; and any dispute or suits at law that may take place between any citizens of the United States, and the subjects of the Regency of Algiers shall be decided by the Dey in person and no other.

ART. 20. If a Citizen of the United States should kill wound or strike a subject of Algiers, or on the Contrary, a subject of Algiers should kill wound or strike a Citizen of the United States, the law of the country shall take place, and equal justice shall be rendered, the consul assisting at the tryal; but the sentence of punishment against an american Citizen, shall not be greater or more severe, than it would be against a Turk in the same predicament, and if any delinquent should make his escape, the Consul shall not be responsable for him in any manner whatever.

ART. 21. The Consul of the United States of America shall not be required to pay any customs or duties whatever on any thing he imports from a foreign Country for the use of his house & family.

ART. 22. Should any of the citizens of the United States die within the Regency of Algiers, the Dey and his subjects shall not interfere with the property of the deceased, but it shall be under the immediate direction of the Consul, unless otherwise disposed of by will; should there be no Consul the effects shall be deposited in the hands of some person worthy of trust until the party shall appear who has a right to account of the property; neither shall the Dey or his subjects give hindrance in the execution of any will that may appear. . . .

2. Ömer Paşa to President James Madison, 24 April 1816

With the aid and assistance of Divinity, and in the reign of our sovereign, the asylum of the world, powerful and great monarch, transactor of all good actions, the best of men, the shadow of God, director of the good order, king of kings, supreme ruler of the world, emperor of the earth, emulator of Alexander the Great, possessor of great forces, sovereign of the two worlds, and of the seas, king of Arabia and Persia, emperor, son of an emperor and conqueror, Mahmoud Khan, (may God end his life with prosperity, and his reign be everlasting and glorious,) his humble and obedient servant, actual sovereign Governor and Chief of Algiers, submitted forever to the orders of his Imperial Majesty's noble throne, Omar Pachaw, (may his government be happy and prosperous,)

To his Majesty, the Emperor of America, its adjacent and dependent provinces and coasts, and wherever his government may extend, our noble friend, the support of the kings of the nation of Jesus, the pillar of all Christian sovereigns, the most glorious amongst the princes, elected amongst many lords and nobles, the happy, the great, the amiable James Madison, Emperor of America, (may his reign be happy and glorious, and his life long and prosperous,) wishing him long possession of the seal of his blessed throne, and long life and health, Amen. Hoping that your health is in good state, I inform you that mine is excellent, thanks to the Supreme Being, constantly addressing my humble prayers to the Almighty for your felicity.

After many years have elapsed, you have at last sent a squadron, commanded by Admiral Decatur, your most humble servant, for the purpose of treating of peace with us. I received the letter of which he was the bearer, and understood its contents; the enmity which was between us having been extinguished, you desired to make peace as France and England have done. Immediately after the arrival of your squadron in our harbour, I sent my answer to your servant the Admiral, through the medium of the Swedish Consul, whose proposals I was disposed to agree to, on condition that our frigate and sloop of war, taken by you, should be returned to us, and brought back to Algiers; on these conditions we would sign peace according to your wishes and request. Our answer having thus been explained to your servant the Admiral by the Swedish Consul, he agreed to treat with us on the above mentioned conditions; but having afterwards insisted upon the liberation of all American citizens, as well as upon a certain sum of money, for several merchant vessels made prizes of by us, and of other objects belonging to the Americans, we did not hesitate a moment to comply with his wishes, and in consequence of which we have restored to the said Admiral, your servant, all that he demanded from us. In the mean time, the said Admiral having given his word to send back our two ships of war, and not having performed his promise, he has thus violated the faithful articles of peace which were signed between us, and by so doing a new treaty must be made.

I inform you, therefore, that a treaty of peace having been signed between America and us, during the reign of Hassan Pashaw, twenty years past, I propose to renew the said treaty on the same basis stipulated in it, and if you agree to it, our friendship will be solid and lasting.

I intended to be on higher terms of amity with our friends the Americans than ever before, [America] being the first nation with whom I made peace; but as they have not been able to put into execution our present treaty, it appears necessary for us to treat on the above mentioned conditions. We hope that with the assistance of God you will answer this our letter, immediately after you shall have a perfect knowledge of its contents. If you agree, according to our request, to the conditions specified in the said treaty, please to send us an early answer. If on the contrary, you are not satisfied with my propositions, you will act against the sacred duty of man, and against the laws of nations.

Requesting only that you will have the goodness to remove your Consul as soon as possible, assuring you that it will be very agreeable to us, these are our last words to you, and we pray God to keep you in his holy guard. . . .

3. President Madison to Ömer Paşa, 21 August 1816

I have received your letter, bearing date the twenty-fourth of April last. You represent that the two vessels of war captured by the American squadron were not restored, according to the promise of its Commodore, Decatur, and inferring that his failure violated the treaty of peace, you propose as an alternative, a renewal of the former treaty made many years ago, or a withdrawal of our Consul from Algiers. The United States being desirous of living in peace and amity with all nations, I regret, that an erroneous view of what has passed, should have suggested the contents of your letter.

Your predecessor made war without cause on the United States, driving away [the American] Consul, and putting into slavery the captain and crew of one of [the American] vessels, sailing under the faith of an existing treaty. The moment we had brought to an honourable conclusion our war with a nation the most powerful in Europe on the sea, we detached a squadron from our naval force into the Mediter-

ranean, to take satisfaction for the wrongs which Algiers had done to us. Our squadron met yours, defeated it, and made prize of your largest ship, and of a small one. Our commander proceeded immediately to Algiers, offered you peace, which you accepted, and thereby saved the rest of your ships, which it was known had not returned into port, and would otherwise have fallen into his hands. Our commander, generous as [he is] brave, although he would not make the promise a part of the treaty, informed you that he would restore the two captured ships to your officer. They were accordingly so restored. The frigate, at an early day, arrived at Algiers. But the Spanish government, alleging that the capture of the brig was so near the Spanish shore as to be unlawful, detained it at Carthagena, after your officer had received it into his possession. Notwithstanding this fulfilment of all that could be required from the United States, no time was lost in urging upon that government a release of the brig, to which Spain could have no right, whether the capture were or were not agreeable to the law of nations. The Spanish government promised that the brig should be given up, and although the delay was greater than was expected, it appears that the brig, as well as the frigate, has actually been placed in your possession.

It is not without great surprise, therefore, that we find you, under such circumstances, magnifying an incident so little important as it affects the interests of Algiers, and so blameless on the part of the United States, into an occasion for the proposition and threat contained in your letter. I cannot but persuade myself, that a reconsideration of the subject will restore you to the amicable sentiments towards the United States which succeeded the war so unjustly commenced by the Dey who reigned before you. I hope the more that this may be the case, because the United States, whilst they wish for war with no nation, will buy peace with none. It is a principle incorporated into the settled policy of America, that as peace is better than war, war is better than tribute.

Our Consul, and our naval Commander, Chauncey, are authorized to communicate with you, for the purpose of terminating the subsisting differences by a mutual recognition and execution of the treaty lately concluded. And I pray God that he will inspire you with the same love of peace and justice which we feel, and that he will take you into his holy keeping. . . .

4. American Commissioners William Shaler and Isaac Chauncey, to Ömer Paşa, 9 December 1816

The undersigned have the honour to transmit herewith to his Highness the Dey of Algiers, a letter addressed to him from the President of the United States, and to inform him that they have been appointed by the President Commissioners to treat of the renewal of the relations of peace and amity between the United States and Algiers.

Pursuant to these instructions, they have lost no time in proceeding to this bay, in the hope of adjusting the differences subsisting between the two countries by a treaty of peace, subject to the ratification of the President, by and with the advice and consent of the Senate.

As the promise of Commodore Decatur, to restore the ships captured from the Regency by the squadron under his command, previous to the negotiations for peace in June, 1815, has been fulfilled by the delivery of the vessels in question into the possession of officers of the Regency sent to Carthagena for that purpose, and by the actual return of those vessels to Algiers, the undersigned are instructed not to admit the unfounded claim, which has been brought forward by the Regency of Algiers upon that question, to a discussion. But, in order to demonstrate to his Highness that the American government has not been remiss in effecting the fulfilment of that promise of their naval commander in a manner the most scrupulously punctual, they here with transmit copies of a correspondence between the [American] Secretary of State, and the Minister of his Majesty the King of Spain, in America, upon that subject. This preliminary being agreed to, they are instructed to propose to his Highness the renewal of the relations of peace and amity between the two States, upon the following conditions, viz.

1st. The renewal of the treaty of peace of June, 1815, in the exact form and terms in which the same was concluded with the Regency by the Consul General, and Commodore Decatur; but as a proof of the conciliatory policy of the President, they are instructed to propose gratuitously to his Highness a modification of the eighteenth article of that treaty, by adding the following, explanatory of it;—viz. "The United States of America, in order to give the Dey of Algiers a proof of their desire to maintain the relations of peace and amity between the two powers, upon a footing the most liberal, and in order to withdraw any obstacle which might embarrass him in his relations with other States, agree to annul so much of the eighteenth article of the foregoing treaty, as gives to the United States any advantage, in the ports of Algiers, over the most favoured nations having treaties with the Regency."

2d. The Regency of Algiers having misunderstood the liberal principles upon which the treaty of June, 1815, was concluded, and, contrary to a distinct understanding between them and the American Commissioners, having introduced into the translation of that treaty an obligation on the part of the United States, to pay to the Regency a present on the presentation of their Consuls, the same is formally denied; and the undersigned declare in the most distinct and formal manner, that no obligation binding the United States to pay any thing to the Regency or to its officers, on any occasion whatsoever, will be agreed to.

The undersigned believe it to be their duty to assure his Highness that the above conditions will not be departed from; thus leaving to the Regency of Algiers the choice between peace and war. The United States, while anxious to maintain the former, are prepared to meet the latter.

In order to facilitate to the government of Algiers the understanding of this note, the undersigned herewith transmit to his Highness an informal translation of it into the Arabic language, and they expect that his Highness will cause a reply to be made to this communication in writing, in either the English, French, Spanish, or Italian language; or by a foreign Consul, authorized by him to vouch for the same. And they avail themselves of this occasion to offer to his Highness the homage of their high consideration and profound respect.

5. Additional and Explanatory Article, 22 December 1816

The United States of America in order to give to the Dey of Algiers a proof of their desire to maintain the relations of peace and amity between the two powers upon a footing the most liberal; and in order to withdraw any obstacle which might embarrass him in his relations with other States, agree to annul so much of the Eighteenth Article of the foregoing Treaty, as gives to the United States any advantage in the ports of Algiers over the most favoured Nations having Treaties with the Regency. . . .

58. TREATIES OF PEACE: THE GARRISON OF ALGIERS WITH GREAT BRITAIN AND THE NETHERLANDS
28 August–24 September 1816

[Text of the British treaty and accompanying documents from *British and Foreign State Papers*, 3: 516–21; text of the Dutch treaty translated from the French given in ibid., p. 549]

By the end of the Napoleonic wars, Britain's naval position in the Mediterranean had become preeminent. With the sharp reduction of French naval power and the total elimination of the Russian naval presence before it could anchor itself, in the Mediterranean, no possible combination of interested adversaries could for the time being challenge Britain's supremacy there. Yet Decatur's dictated treaty of 1815 (Doc. 57) had suddenly given the United States—a small and (as of only recently) enemy maritime power—a preferential position in the Algerine Garrison. That spurred Britain to seek to erase the American advantage either (as some American officials believed) by encouraging the dey to renege on his treaty pledge or by itself demanding most-favored-nation treatment. Given the uncontested prestige of the British navy, when Admiral Lord Exmouth, the British commander in chief in the Mediterranean, showed the flag along the Barbary coast in the spring of 1816 at the head of a massive fleet, he could hardly have failed to persuade (1) each of the corsair Garrisons to sign a treaty recognizing as British subjects the people of the Ionian islands; (2) the dey of Algiers to enter into a comparable arrangement on Hanover; and (3) the beys of Tunis and Tripoli to issue declarations on the abolition of Christian slavery (the texts of these instruments may be found in *British and Foreign State Papers*, 3: 509–16). Yet, significantly, Exmouth could not extract from Ömer Paşa a comparable declaration. Instead, the dey bought time by convincing the admiral to let him send a special emissary to the padişah at Istanbul for guidance in the matter. Meanwhile, on returning to England in June, Exmouth found Parliament agitated over reports on the massacre a few weeks earlier of Italians and Corsicans engaged in coral fishing under British license at Bône, a port under Algerine jurisdiction. This, in turn, gave added emphasis to the antislavery movement that had been gathering popular support in England, and in the public mind the movement to abolish slavery was aimed not only at the sub-Saharan traffic in blacks but also at the corsair enslavement of Christians for ransom. The Admiralty thereupon ordered Exmouth back to Algiers to extract from the Garrison, forcibly if necessary, a declaration abolishing slavery. At Gibraltar on 9 August Exmouth was joined by a small Dutch squadron under the command of Vice-Admiral Baron Theodore Frederic van der Capellen. Tension was heightened at Algiers by the dey's refusal to allow a British sloop, which had preceded the fleet, to take on board the British consul and his family. Instead, the consul, two naval officers, and some of the ship's crew were imprisoned after the consul's family had managed to escape to the sloop. Ömer Paşa rejected Exmouth's ultimatum on 27 August, and in a nine-hour battle later that day the British and Dutch fleets destroyed 33 of the 37 corsair ships in Algiers harbor and silenced about half of the shore batteries. On the morning of the twenty-eighth, the dey capitulated. Reproduced below are the second ultimatum to the dey, the British and Dutch treaties of peace, the dey's declaration on the abolition of Christian slavery, and Lord Exmouth's final report to the Admiralty. Lord, *England and France in the Mediterranean*, pp. 60–82; Shaler, *Sketches of Algiers*, chap. 5; Grammont, *Histoire d'Alger sous la domination turque*, chap. 25.

1. Admiral Lord Exmouth's Second Ultimatum to the Dey of Algiers, 28 August 1816

FOR your atrocities at Bona, on defenceless Christians, and your unbecoming disregard to the demands I made yesterday, in the name of the Prince Regent of England, the Fleet under my orders has given you a signal chastisement, by the total destruction or your Navy, Storehouses, and Arsenal, with half your Batteries.

As England does not war for the destruction of Cities, I am unwilling to visit your personal cruelties upon the inoffensive Inhabitants of the Country, and I therefore offer you the same terms of Peace, which I conveyed to you yesterday, in my Sovereign's name. Without the acceptance of these terms, you can have no Peace with England:

If you receive this offer as you ought, you will fire 3 guns; and I shall consider your not making this signal as a refusal, and shall renew my operations at my own convenience.

I offer you the above terms, provided neither the British Consul, nor the Officers and Men so wickedly seized by you from the Boats of a British Ship of War, have met with any cruel treatment, or any of the Christian Slaves in your power; and I repeat my demand, that the Consul, and Officers and Men, may be sent off to me, conformable to ancient Treaties.

2. Treaty of Peace: Great Britain and Algiers, 28 August 1816

Treaty of Peace between His Majesty the King of the United Kingdom of Great Britain and Ireland, and His Most Serene Highness Omar Bashaw, Dey and Governor of the warlike City and Kingdom of Algiers, made and concluded by the Right Honourable Edward Baron Exmouth, Knight Grand Cross of the Most Honourable Military Order of the Bath, Admiral of the Blue Squadron of His Britannic Majesty's Fleet, and Commander-in-Chief of a Squadron of His said Majesty's Ships and Vessels employed on a particular Service, being duly authorized by His Royal Highness The Prince Regent, acting in the name and on the behalf of His Britannic Majesty.

It is hereby agreed and concluded, that from this day and for ever there shall be a strict and inviolable Peace and Friendship between His Britannic Majesty and the Kingdom of Algiers, and that all the Articles and Treaties of Peace and Commerce subsisting between the Kingdom of Great Britain and its Dependencies, and the Kingdom of Algiers, previous to the 27th of August, 1816, are here by renewed, ratified, and confirmed; that the Ships and other Vessels, and the Subjects and People of both sides, shall not, from henceforward, do to each other any harm, offence, or injury, either in word or deed, but shall treat each other with all possible respect and friendship; and that all the transactions which took place on the 27th shall, from henceforward, be buried in oblivion, and the ancient friendship between the 2 Kingdoms restored.

Done in Duplicate, in the warlike City of Algiers, in the presence of Almighty God, the 28th day of August, is the year of Jesus Christ, 1816, and in the year of the Hegira, 1231, and the 6th day of the Moon Shawal.

3. Treaty of Peace: Algiers and the Netherlands, 28 August 1816

. . . ART. 1. It is agreed and concluded between Baron van der Capellen and His Highness the Dey of Algiers that from this day there shall be durable Peace and Amity between His Majesty the King of the Netherlands, his estates and his subjects, and that all the Articles of Peace and Amity formerly agreed since the year 1757 between Their High Powers the Estates General of the United Provinces and the Government and the Kingdom of Algiers are hereby renewed, ratified, and confirmed as if they were inserted word for word in the present Treaty; and that the war vessels and other ships as well as the subjects of the two Kingdoms shall not do to each other any harm or injury but shall treat each other from this day and forever with respect and friendship.

ART. 2. To regulate commercial affairs, a Consul of His Majesty the King of the Netherlands will be admitted to Algiers on the same footing as, and will be treated with the same respect as, the Consul of His Britannic Majesty; he will also be accorded the free exercise of his religion within his residence, as will also his servants and all other persons who may wish to enjoy this benefit.

4. Declaration by the Dey of Algiers on the Abolition of Christian Slavery, 28 August 1816

Declaration of His Most Serene Highness Omar Bashaw, Dey and Governor of the warlike City and Kingdom of Algiers, made and concluded with the Right Honourable Edward Baron Exmouth, Knight Grand Cross of the Most Honourable

Military Order of the Bath, Admiral of the Blue Squadron of His Britannic Majesty's Fleet, and Commander-in-Chief of His said Majesty's Ships and Vessels in the Mediterranean.

In consideration of the deep interest manifested by His Royal Highness the Prince Regent of England, for the termination of Christian Slavery, His Highness the Dey of Algiers, in token of his sincere desire to maintain inviolable his friendly relations with Great Britain, and to manifest his amicable disposition and high respect towards the Powers of Europe, declares, that in the event of future Wars with any European Power, not any of the Prisoners shall be consigned to Slavery, but treated with all humanity as Prisoners of War, until regularly exchanged according to European practice in like cases, and that, at the termination of hostilities, they shall be restored to their respective Countries without ransom; and the practice of condemning Christian Prisoners of War to Slavery is hereby formally and for ever renounced.

Done in Duplicate, in the warlike City of Algiers, in the presence of Almighty God, the 28th day of August, in the year of Jesus Christ, 1816, and in the year of the Hegira, 1231, and the 6th day of the Moon Shawal.

5. Admiral Lord Exmouth's Final Report to the Admiralty, 24 September 1816

On the 28th of August, Treaties of Peace were signed by the Dey of Algiers with His Majesty, and with His Majesty the King of The Netherlands.

On the same day also was signed, an Additional Article or Declaration, for the Abolition of Christian Slavery, to the following effect [see above].

The Dey also, in presence of his Divan, apologized to the British Consul for the personal restraint which had been imposed upon him during the late transactions; and he also paid to the Consul, a sum of 3,000 dollars, as a remuneration for depredations committed on his residence after his imprisonment.

After the Treaties and Article beforementioned had been negociated, and that the Dey had refunded 382,500 dollars, which he had lately received from the Governments of Naples and Sardinia, and had released 1,083 Christian Slaves who were at Algiers, it came to the knowledge of Lord Exmouth, that 2 Spaniards, the one a Merchant and the other the Vice-Consul of that Nation, had not been released, but were still held by the Dey in very severe custody, on pretence that they were Prisoners for debt.

The inquiries which his Lordship felt himself called upon to make into these cases, satisfied him that the confinement of the Vice-Consul was groundless and unjustifiable, and he therefore thought himself authorized to demand [the Vice-Consul's] release under the Articles of the Agreement for the deliverance of all Christian Prisoners.

It appeared that the Merchant was confined for an alleged debt, on the score of a contract with the Algerine Government; but the circumstances under which the contract was stated to have been forced on the Individual, and the great severity of the confinement which he suffered, determined his Lordship to make an effort in his favour also.

This his Lordship did, by requesting his release from the Dey, offering himself to guarantee to the Dey the payment of any sum of money which the Merchant should be found to owe to His Highness.

The Dey having rejected this demand and offer, his Lordship, still unwilling to have recourse to extremities, and the renewal of hostilities, proposed that the Spaniards should be released from irons, and the miserable dungeons in which they were confined; and that they should be placed in the custody of the Spanish Consul, or, at least, that the Consul should be permitted to afford them such assistance and accommodation as was suitable to their rank in life.

These propositions the Dey also positively refused; and Lord Exmouth then felt, that the private and pecuniary nature of the transactions for which these Persons were confined, must be considered as a pretence for the continuance of a cruel and oppressive system of Slavery, the total and bonâ fide abolition of which his instructions directed him to insist upon.

He, therefore, acquainted the Dey, that His Highness having rejected all the fair and equitable conditions proposed to him on this point, his Lordship had determined to insist on the unconditional release of the 2 Spaniards. He therefore desired an answer, yes or no; and in the event of the latter, stated, that he would immediately recommence hostilities; and his Lordship made preparations for that purpose.

These measures had the desired effect, and the 2 Persons were released from a long and severe captivity; so that no Christian Prisoner remained at Algiers at his Lordship's departure, which took place on the evening of the 3d instant, with all the Ships under his orders. . . .

59. IMPLEMENTATION OF THE AIX-LA-CHAPELLE DECISION ON THE SUPPRESSION OF BARBARY PIRACY
20 November 1818–9 September 1819

[Translation of the French text of protocol no. 30 of the Congress of Aix-la-Chapelle from Shaler, *Sketches of Algiers*, pp. 302–03; note by Freemantle and Jurien to the dey of Algiers and summary minutes of audiences with the dey from Great Britain, Public Record Office, London, F.O. 8/3]

The crushing defeat by British and Dutch naval forces on 27 August 1816 temporarily chastened the Algerine Garrison, brought about the release of all kidnapped Christians, and procured renewals of past treaties and assurances that in the future Christian captives would be treated as prisoners of war. Ömer Paşa (1815–17), the dey, with great energy and perseverance commandeered artillery pieces and technicians throughout the Garrison and personally supervised before the end of 1816 the repair of the stone wall and the restoration of the three tiers of artillery batteries that constituted the shore defense of the city of Algiers. He even hired Neapolitan divers to remove sunken ships from the harbor. By then too he had procured four new cruisers and had commissioned the building of other naval vessels. These emergency expenditures undoubtedly cut into the Garrison's reserves, but the resident European consular and merchant community was persuaded that the Deylical treasury was far from exhausted. Algiers remained the most powerful of the Barbary states, and even though Tunis and Tripoli had escaped physical destruction by the British-Dutch action, they nevertheless learned the lesson that, if determined, the European powers could impose their will. In brief, the Barbary Garrisons had been chastened in 1816 but not put out of business. It is therefore understandable that the issue appeared on the agenda of the Congress of Aix-la-Chapelle in 1818. For the first time all the major powers of Europe agreed, on paper, to take concerted action to put an end to Barbary piracy and instructed Britain and France to communicate this decision to the Garrisons. In September-October 1819 a combined British-French squadron under the joint command of Vice-Admiral Sir Thomas Freemantle and Rear-Admiral Jurien de la Gravière, the British and French naval commanders in the Mediterranean, issued a severe warning to each Garrison against continuing "a system so inimical to the peaceful Commerce." It palpably required more than a verbal warning to put an end to a system that the major maritime powers of Europe had tolerated, and occasionally nurtured, for so long. The conventional textbook wisdom that at Aix-la-Chapelle in 1818 the powers, by acting in concert, had at long last struck the deathknell of the garrisons and their piratical institutions is of course erroneous. The Garrisons continued operating for more than a decade longer. The steadily declining scale of piracy was due less to the policies of the maritime powers than to the Industrial Revolution. Following are the protocol of the Congress of Aix-la-Chapelle, the identic note presented to the dey of Algiers and the beys of Tunis and Tunisia, and the summary minutes of the British and French admirals' audiences with Hüseyin Paşa (1818–30), the last dey of Algiers. Shaler, op. cit., chap. 5; Julien, *Histoire de l'Afrique du Nord*, chap. 6.

1. Congress of Aix-la-Chapelle, Protocol No. 30

The Plenipotentiaries agreed, according to the Protocol of [20 November 1818], to continue, in the ministerial conferences of London, the examination of different plans proposed for effectually suppressing the piracies committed by the Barbary States. The Count of Capo d'Istria once more called the attention of the conference to this question; and it being acknowledged how important it was to oppose, as soon as possible, some barrier to the evils which these piracies bring on the commerce of Europe, and to lay before the Regencies on the coast of Africa, in some direct and imposing manner, the resolutions to be taken on this subject, the Plenipotentiaries of France and Great Britain, as the representatives of the two courts whose authority would naturally have most weight with those Regencies, were requested to cause them to be addressed in serious terms, and to be warned, that the unavoidable consequence of their perseverance in a system hostile to peaceful commerce, would be a general league among the powers of

Europe; on the results of which the Barbary States would do well to reflect in season, and which might eventually affect their very existence.

The Duke of Richelieu and Lord Castlereagh pledged themselves to give the instructions necessary to carry into execution such a measure; and to give notice to the other powers of the effect it should produce; and the five courts, as they may hereafter see fit, are to cause also the Ottoman Porte to be apprized, in a friendly way, of the danger to which the Barbary Regencies would expose themselves by persisting in their present system, and by provoking decisive measures on the part of the European powers.

2. Identic Note to the Dey of Algiers and the Beys of Tunis and Tunisia, 5 September 1819

The Sovereigns of the Powers of Europe who met last year at Aix la Chapelle, have entrusted to Great Britain and France on behalf of the whole, to make the most earnest representations to the States of Barbary, on the necessity of terminating the depredations and outrages committed by the armed Vessels of those Regencies.

We therefore come in the name of the King of the United Kingdom of Great Britain and Ireland, and the King of France and Navarre, to notify to your Serene Highness, the decision of all the Powers of Europe.

These powers have irrevocably determined to suppress a system of Piracy which is not only detrimental to the general Interests of their respective States, but even destructive to those who practise it.

Should the Regencies persist in a system so inimical to the peaceful Commerce, they will inevitably draw upon themselves a General league of all the European Powers, and it behooves them well to consider before it is too late, that such a combination may endanger their very existence.

But whilst we point out the dreadful effects that may arise from the continuance of those outrages which excite the complaints of all Europe, we wish to impress and assure Your Highness, that if the Regencies renounce this system, the Allied Powers are not only disposed to maintain good intelligence and friendship with them, but to encourage such Commercial intercourse, as may be equally advantageous to their respective subjects.

The Allied Powers in whose name we have the honour to address you are thoroughly united on the important object of this mission with which we are accredited to Your Highness, and we are the faithful interpreters of their intentions. We have to hope that your Highness, alive to your true interests, will not hesitate in giving a satisfactory answer.

The Allied powers insist that the States of Barbary will respect the Rights and usages considered as sacred by all civilized Nations. If the Regencies at their Caprice attempt to molest the Commerce of other States, they will most certainly draw upon themselves the Arms of all Europe.

We trust your Highness will give us such an assurance, as their Majesties the Kings of Great Britain and France expect and which they are so impatient to transmit to their Allies.

In an affairs of such importance and which they have so much at heart, verbal promises are not sufficient. It should be a sacred Deed for the security of the Navigation and Commerce of their respective States, and as we make this representation in writing, we look for a reply confirmed with your Seal.

We are most anxious to report to our Government your decision, and we repeat to Your Highness that we cannot bring ourselves to imagine, that you can reject propositions which are calculated to secure you the benefits resulting from Commerce guaranteed by a respect for the Rights of Nations.

3. Summary Minutes of the British and French Admirals' First Audience with Hüseyin Paşa, the Dey of Algiers, 5 September 1819

The Commissioners of Their Majesties the Kings of Great Britain and France met at eleven oclock in the forenoon at an audience of His Highness the Bey of Algiers accompanied by the Consuls General of their respective Nations, and two Staff Officers, His Highness having prescribed that there should be only three persons of each nation admitted to this audience.

Having arrived at the Palace, the Commissioners appeared before his Highness, who was sitting in a large arm chair placed in an alcove. They then informed His Highness they had the honor of presenting in the name of their Majesties, the Kings of Great Britain and France, the Copy of the protocol containing a decision taken by all the Powers of Europe, at the Congress of Aix la Chapelle, with a written explanatory note, praying His Highness to take them into consideration, and give them an answer in writing, that their Governments might transmit to their Allies.

His Highness received graciously the two notes from the Hands of the Commissioners, to which was joined a correct translation in the Turkish and Arabic languages equally signed by them both. His Highness in receiving them said very obligingly that the Commissioners were welcome and enquired particularly after their health: he ordered some Coffee to be brought to them, and took some himself; His Higness then read the translation of Commissioners' notes, as well as the Copy of the Protocol containing a decision of the Congress at Aix la Chapelle: after having read them very attentively, His Highness said, that he was surprized that such a representation had been made him, since the Regency of Algiers was in peace with all the Powers of Europe, and that since his accession to the Supreme Government of the Regency, no affair of the nature therein mentioned had occurred at Algiers, and that for this reason the representation appeared to him unnecessary.

The Commissioners replied that assuredly His Highness had been since his accession to the Regency in peace with all Europe, but that the decision of the Congress was founded upon the Complaints that had been made to them for acts of his Predecessors who had disturbed the tranquillity of Europe; that in the situation in which he was placed, he was consequently responsible for all deeds of his Predecessors which might some time or other be renewed, and that on this account the Powers of Europe desired to know his fixed and precise determination as a guarantee for the future.

His Highness assured them, he would never detain any Vessel or property of those European Powers whose Consuls were residing at Algiers; that he would certainly endeavour to continue the peace which happily subsisted between the Regency of Algiers and the Powers of Europe; but should any injustice or insult whatsoever be offered him from any other power, or from any of their Subjects, was he not at liberty to declare war and demand redress for the wrongs that should be offered to him?

The Commissioners observed that without doubt in such a case His Highness was to judge of the expediency of declaring War, and to obtain reparation for wrongs done him by any foreign power, but [they feared that], under pretext of War and to make reparation the Neutral States would be molested, and be searched by the Vessels of the Regency: that the purport of the Allied Powers of Europe was to secure for ever the entire and perfect tranquillity of European commerce as well as to protect those who navigate and trade under the faith of the law of Nations.

His Highness assured the Commissioners that neutral Vessels should never be molested in a War in which they had no concern, and that he perfectly agreed in opinion with the intentions of the High Powers of Europe to whom the Commissioners might transmit these assurances from him.

The Commissioners then asked His Highness to give them a written answer explaining his intentions.

His Highness answered that it was not necessary and that the Commissioners ought to be contented with the verbal assurances he gave them.

The Commissioners acquainted His Highness, that the instruction of their Courts prescribed to them a written document in answer: His Highness answered that he would think of it, and in a few days communicate to the Commissioners the result.

His Highness then expressed his doubts as to the powers granted to the Commissioners by their Courts and asked them, if these representations had not been combined by them, and it appeared this doubt was more particularly directed to the Commissioner from Great Britain since [it seemed that] (as His Highness affirmed) His Envoy who had just arrived from London had no communication on the subject, or any knowledge of such instructions being given by the British Cabinet which appeared to him singular.

The Commissioners assured His Highness that they had been sent expressly on this mission, by their respective Governments, and the English Commissioner added that it appeared to him that it would have been informal for the British Cabinet to have given information to the Algerine Envoy on the subject, as he was neither authorized, nor capable of giving any explanation or assurance that could be satisfactory. After this the Commissioners retired to wait the result.

4. Summary Minutes of British and French Admirals' Second Audience with Hüseyin Paşa, the Dey of Algiers, 9 September 1819

The Commissioners of their Majesties the King of Great Britain and France having yesterday the 8th of this Month through the medium of their respective Dragomen, demanded of His Highness the Dey, if he was disposed to give a categorical answer in writing, of his determination in answer to the demands of the High Powers, as inserted in the Protocol of Aix la Chapelle in their declaration.

His Highness desired the Dragoman to inform the Commissioner that he never had injured any European Nation, and from principle, it was his intention always to continue the same line of conduct with Foreign Powers, but that it did not appear necessary to give any answer in writing.

In consequence the Commissioner judged it proper to demand of His Highness another audience, in order to obtain a positive explanation on the subject of their demands. This second audience was fixed for today the 9th September at one o'clock in the afternoon, whither they proceeded on Horseback, and in the same manner as they did in their first audience.

When they appeared before His Highness the Commissioners presented him with a Copy of their declaration translated into Arabic, similar to that which had been transmitted through their Deagomen, requesting that he would read it with attention, and to approve of it, by annexing his Seal. The declaration was as follows:

The Commissioners of their Majesties The Kings of Great Britain and France request of His Highness the Dey of Algiers to certify by the placing of his Seal that since his accession to the Supreme Government of Algiers, he has never injured any European Nation, and that from principle it is his intention so to act towards Foreign Powers.

His Highness after having read with attention our communication, answered that the intentions contained in the aforesaid Note were precisely his own, that he confirmed them, and requested that the Commissioners would make such assurances to their respective Sovereigns, but he refused to sign any Document, giving as a reason, that he had received no notification from either the Kings of Great Britain or France and therefore he would not give any Document in writing.

The Commissioners observed to His Highness, that it was not customary for Sovereigns to write, when they sent Persons duly accredited and that these were authorized to give their demands in writing, and in like manner to have answers.

His Highness then replied, that such was his determination, and repeated that not having received any official documents, under the signature of their Sovereigns, he would not give any under his own.

The Commissioners requested to know if His Highness had read with attention the Protocol of the Congress of Aix La Chapelle, as well as the Note delivered in the name of their respective Courts: His Highness after answering in the affirmative, demanded if he had not the right to make war on his Enemies? To which the Commissioners replied that this Question was foreign to their Mission, but at the same time they observed that a War declared unjustly would draw upon him the Forces of the High Powers of Europe.

His Highness then demanded of the Commissioners to tell him honestly, if he should burn all his Vessels, as from the nature of their representations they would become entirely useless.

The Commissioners observed that His Highness might preserve his Vessels in the same manner as other Powers did, without molesting the peaceful Commerce of the European Nations.

His Highness declared that he certainly would maintain the treaties which he now had, with the Nations of Europe which were at peace with him, and had accredited Agents, and that he would positively forbid his Cruizers to molest them, but that he would not give up the right of examining the Vessels of all Nations without distinction, in order that he might know this friends from his Enemies, and to detain and confiscate all those found without having their papers regular.

The Commissioners represented that this was precisely the point on which the High Powers founded their demands, insomuch as the Owner of Vessels whose decuments may be found correct, suffer severely in their property, both by loss of time, as well as by an expensive and burthensome quarantine.

His Highness observed that if tomorrow he were to declare war with Tunis, then it was material to know his Enemies did not endeavour to evade by hoisting the flag of his Friends, and further that he would

acknowledge as such only those Nations who had Agents resident with him, and other states he would consider as Enemies, and treat them as such, until such time as they sent persons to negotiate for Peace with the Regency.

The Commissioners felt it their duty to speak freely on this subject to His Highness declaring in the names of their Governments that such conduct would endanger his very existence.

This conversation now appearing at an end, the Commissioners were about to retire when they judged it necessary to recall His Highness's attention to an object so important, by declaring that if it was really his intention to continue his System of Piracy against the Commerce of Europe he must expect the Arms of all the Allied Powers to fall on him.

To this declaration His Highness made no reply on which the Commissioners took their leave, His Highness wishing them with much politeness a good Voyage.

60. GENERAL TREATY SUPPRESSING PIRACY AND SLAVE TRAFFIC: GREAT BRITAIN AND THE ARAB TRIBES IN THE PERSIAN GULF
8 January–15 March 1820

[Aitchison, *Collection of Treaties . . . relating to India* (5th ed.), 11 : 245–49]

Piracy flourished in the Persian Gulf after the destruction of Portugese primacy in 1622 and the failure of Persia to establish enduring control over the inland sea. This had contributed to the downfall of the Safavi dynasty in 1722, and the disciplinary effects of Nadir Shah's reign (1736–47) did not long outlast his life. The consolidation of British supremacy in India toward the end of the eighteenth century roughly coincided with the appearance of the short-lived Wahhabi "empire" in the Arabian Peninsula. The Wahhabis brought under their sway the Qawasim (pronounced "Jawasim") tribesmen along the southeastern coast of the gulf, the organizing center for the piracy, which gave the locality the name of "pirate coast" in British-Indian annals. At first the Qawasim preyed only on local ships, but during the Napoleonic wars the pirates, emboldened by their Wahhabi associations, began to attack British ships. The East India Company accordingly ordered the Bombay Marine in 1806, 1809, and 1819 to take punitive action. After the last expedition, conducted in cooperation with the *imam* of Masqat, each of the tribal shaykhs of the pirate coast and the shaykh of Bahrayn undertook between 8 January and 15 March 1820 to abide by the conditions laid down in the present instrument. The 1820 agreement marked the formal beginning of British-Indian responsibility for policing the Persian Gulf. Lorimer, *Gazetteer of the Persian Gulf*, vol. 1, pt. 1, pp. 636–74; Kelly, *Britain and the Persian Gulf*, chaps. 3–4; Moyse-Bartlett, *Pirates of Trucial Oman*; Belgrave, *Pirate Coast*; A. Wilson, *Persian Gulf*, chap. 13; Adamiyat, *Bahrein Islands*, chap. 2; Low, *Indian Navy*, vol. 1, chap. 10; Liebesny, "International Relations of Arabia, the Dependent Areas"; Curzon, *Persia and the Persian Question*, 2: 446–52; Buckingham, *Travels in Assyria, Media, and Persia*, (1829 ed.), chaps. 23–25; Mignan, *A Winter Journey through Russia*, vol. 2, chaps. 8–10; Standish, "British Maritime Policy."

ART. 1. There shall be a cessation of plunder and piracy by land and sea on the part of the Arabs, who are parties to this contract, for ever.

ART. 2. If any individual of the people of the Arabs contracting shall attack any that pass by land or sea of any nation whatsoever, in the way of plunder and piracy and not of acknowledged war, he shall be accounted an enemy of all mankind and shall be held to have forfeited both life and goods. An acknowledged war is that which is proclaimed, avowed, and ordered by government against government; and the killing of men and taking of goods without proclamation, avowal, and the order of a government, is plunder and piracy.

ART. 3. The friendly (literally the pacificated) Arabs shall carry by land and sea a red flag, with or without letters in it, at their option, and this shall be in a border of white, the breadth of the white in the border being equal to the breadth of the red, as represented in the margin (the whole forming the flag known in the British Navy by the title of white pierced red), this shall be the flag of the friendly Arabs, and they shall use it and no other.

ART. 4. The pacificated tribes shall all of them continue in their former relations, with the exception that they shall be at peace with the British Government, and shall not fight with each other, and the flag shall be a symbol of this only and of nothing further.

ART. 5. The vessels of the friendly Arabs shall all of them have in their possession a paper (Register) signed with the signature of their Chief, in which shall be the name of the vessel, its length, its breadth, and how many Karahs it holds. And they shall also have in their possession another writing (Port Clearance) signed with the signature of their Chief, in which shall be the name of the owner, the name of the Nacodah, the number of men, the number of arms, from whence sailed, at what time, and to what port bound. And if a British or other vessel meet them, they shall produce the Register and the clearance.

ART. 6. The friendly Arabs, if they choose, shall send an envoy to the British Residency in the Persian Gulf with the necessary accompaniments, and he shall remain there for the transaction of their business with the Residency; and the British Government, if it chooses, shall send an envoy also to them in like manner; and the envoy shall add his signature to the signature of the Chief in the paper (Register) of their vessels, which contains the length of the vessel, its breadth, and tonnage; the signature of the envoy to be renewed every year. Also all such envoy shall be at the expense of their own party.

ART. 7. If any tribe, or others, shall not desist from plunder and piracy, the friendly Arabs shall act against them according to their ability and circumstances and an arrangement for this purpose shall take place between the friendly Arabs and the British at the time when such plunder and piracy shall occur.

ART. 8. The putting men to death after they have given up their arms is an act of piracy and not of acknowledged war; and if any tribe shall put to death any persons, either Muhammadans or others, after they have given up their arms, such tribe shall be held to have broken the peace; and the friendly Arabs shall act against them in

conjunction with the British, and God willing, the war against them shall not cease
until the surrender of those who performed
the act and of those who ordered it.

ART. 9. The carrying off of slaves, men,
women, or children from the coasts of Africa or elsewhere, and the transporting
them in vessels, is plunder and piracy, and
the friendly Arabs shall do nothing of this
nature.

ART. 10. The vessels of the friendly
Arabs, bearing their flag above described,

shall enter into all the British ports and
into the ports of the allies of the British
so far as they shall be able to effect it; and
they shall buy and sell therein, and if any
shall attack them the British Government
shall take notice of it.

ART. 11. These conditions aforesaid shall
be common to all tribes and persons, who
shall hereafter adhere thereto in the same
manner as to [sic] those who adhere to them
at the time present.

61. TREATY OF PEACE (ERZURUM): THE OTTOMAN EMPIRE AND PERSIA
28 July 1823

(Confirmed, Erzurum, 31 May 1847, in article 9 of the Persian-Ottoman boundary agreement)
[Hertslet, *Treaties . . . between Great Britain and Persia*, pp. 163–68]

Shi'i Persia and the Sunni Ottoman Empire engaged in intermittent wars from the
early sixteenth to the early nineteenth centuries. The latest conflict, in 1821–23,
resulted from Russian intrigue at Tehran. The treaty of peace at Erzurum reaffirmed
the treaty of Kurdan of 4 September 1746 (Doc. 26) and involved no change in boundaries, which however remained obscure and gave rise to recurrent disputes. A
Persian-Ottoman mixed boundary commission (1843–47), which for the first time
included British and Russian members, produced a boundary agreement (French
text in Hertslet, *Treaties . . . between Great Britain and Persia*, pp. 169–72), also
signed at Erzurum on 31 May 1847. Since precision was still lacking, adjustment of the
conflicting claims was assigned to yet another commission on which sat British and
Russian mediators. On the basis of the new body's detailed survey (1857–65) the two
Muslim states concluded a temporary boundary agreement (French and English texts,
ibid., pp. 176–78), but they did not formally accept the demarcation until the end of
October 1914. Sykes, *History of Persia*, vol. 2, chap. 79; Curzon, *Persia and the Persian
Question*, 1: 568–70; 2: 335–36, 339–40, 587; Achoube-Amini, *Le conflit de frontière
irako-iranien*, chap. 3.

Basis.—The Stipulations of the Treaty
concluded in the year of the Hegira 1159
[4 September 1746] respecting the ancient
Boundaries of the Two Empires, and the
former Agreements relating to Pilgrims,
Merchants, the delivery of Refugees, the
free egress of all Prisoners, and the residence of a Minister at the respective
Courts, are considered valid, and are to be

strictly observed. The slightest deviation
from the engagements therein detailed shall
not be permitted, and the amity between
the Two powerful States shall be for ever
preserved.

Stipulations.—Henceforward the Sword
of Enmity shall be sheathed, and every
circumstance shall be avoided, which may
produce coldness or disgust, and may be

contrary to friendship and perfect union. The Countries within the boundaries of the Ottoman Empire, which, during the war, or previously to the commencement of hostilities, have been taken possession of by Persia, including Fortresses, Districts, Lands, Towns, and Villages, to be restored in their present state, and, at the expiration of sixty days from the signature of this Treaty, to be delivered over to the Ottoman Government.

And in token of respect for this happy peace, the prisoners captured on both sides, without concealment or prevention, shall have free permission to depart. Provisions and other necessaries requisite for the journey shall be afforded them, and they shall be sent to the Frontiers of the two Countries.

ART. I. The Two High Powers do not admit each other's interference in the internal affairs of their respective States. From this period, on the side of Bagdad and Koordistan no interference is to take place, nor with any Districts of the Divisions of Koordistan within the Boundaries, is the Persian Government to intermeddle, or authorise any acts of molestation, or to assume any authority over the present or former Possessors of those Countries.

And on that frontier, should the Tribes of either side pass the boundaries for a summer or winter residence, the Agents of His Royal Highness the Heir Apparent, with the Pasha of Bagdad, shall arrange the tribute customary to be paid, the rent of the pasture lands, and other claims, in order that they may not cause any misunderstanding between the two Governments.

ART. II. Persian subjects proceeding to the Holy Cities of Mecca and Medina, as to other Mahomedan towns, such as Pilgrims, and persons travelling through the Ottoman Territories, are to be entirely exempted from all contributions; and other impositions at variance with lawful usage are not to be demanded from them.

In like manner the Pilgrims to Kerbelah and Nujuff, as long as they have no merchandize, neither tribute nor tax of any kind is to be extracted from them; but in case they have in their possession articles of commerce, the just rate of Customs is to be levied on such goods, and nothing extra is to be demanded.

The Persian Government is likewise bound to pursue the same line of conduct towards the Merchants and Subjects of the Ottoman Empire. In conformity with former Engagements, from this period, on the part of the Vizirs, the Emir-Elhadj, and other Commanders and Governors, the ancient Stipulations respecting the Persian Pilgrims and Merchants shall be considered as in full force and acted upon.

The Pilgrims shall be conducted from Damascus to the Holy Cities, and back to Damascus, and on the part of the Emir-Elhadj every attention shall be shown towards them; whilst no treatment at variance with the existing engagements shall be permitted; on the contrary, every exertion shall be made to afford them aid and protection. In case any disputes should arise amongst the Persian Pilgrims, the Emir-Elhadj, in conjunction with the chief persons among them, is to settle their differences. To the female attendants of His Persian Majesty, the wives of the Royal Princes, or of the Grandees of the Empire, who may be on pilgrimage to Mecca, or to Kerbelah and Nujuff, every respect and honour shall be paid according to their respective ranks. Persian Merchants and Subjects shall pay the same rate of Customs as those of the Ottoman Government. The duties are only to be exacted once, and they shall be at a computation of four piastres to a hundred on the value of the merchandize; *Teskérés* shall be given; and whilst the goods remain in the possession of the first proprietors, and are not disposed of to other Persons, no further duties are to be demanded.

The Persian Merchants, who carry the *Choobooks*, or Pipesticks of Sheeraz to Constantinople, shall be allowed to traffick them without any restrictions, and to sell them to whomsoever they may think proper. To the Merchants, Subjects, and Dependants of the Two High Powers, visiting the two Countries, in consideration of the Mahomedan religion, every friendly treatment shall be extended, and they shall be preserved from all molestation and injury.

ART. III. The Tribes of Hyderanloo and Sibbikee, which have been the cause of contention between the Two High Powers, and are now dwelling in the Territory of the Ottoman Empire, should they from thence transgress the boundary of Persia, and commit any ravages, the Turkish Frontier Authorities will endeavour to prevent such proceedings, and [will] punish the offenders. In case that these tribes continue to invade and molest the Persian Territory, and the Frontier Authorities do not put a stop to these aggressions, the Ottoman Government shall cease to protect them, and should these Tribes of their own will and choice return to Persia, their departure shall not be prohibited nor opposed. But after their arrival in Persia, should they again desert to Turkey, the Ottoman Government shall afford them no further protection, nor shall they be received. In the event of their return to Persia, should these tribes disturb the tranquillity of the Ottoman Territory, the Persian Frontier Authorities agree to use every effort to prevent these irregularities.

ART. IV. In conformity with ancient engagements, the deserters from either Country shall not be received; and in like manner, from this period, the wandering Tribes and others quitting Persia for Turkey, or Turkey for Persia, shall not received protection from either party.

ART. V. The property of the Persian Merchants sequestrated at Constantinople, with the cognizance of the Law and according to the public registers, from the date of this Treaty to the period of sixty days, wherever the sequestration may have taken place, shall be restored to the Proprietors. Besides the goods under sequestration, whatever effects during the way may have been taken by force from the Persian Pilgrims and Subjects throughout the Ottoman Dominions, by the different Vizirs and Governors, on the representations of the Persian Government, Firmans shall be delivered up to the Agents of such persons, who, on giving lawful proofs of the authenticity of their claims, shall receive the required restitutions.

ART. VI. On the demise of any Persian Subjects in the Ottoman Dominions, should the deceased have no lawful heir and executor present, the Officers of the Treasury (*Beit ul Mal*) shall, with the cognizance of the Law, register the property, and shall enter it upon the Records of the Court of Judicature. For the period of one year the effects shall be lodged in a secure place, until the lawful heir or administrator of the estate may arrive, when, according to the Register of the Courts of Judicature, the property shall be delivered up. The customary fees and the hire of the place for depositing the effects are to be paid, and should they be burnt or destroyed within the above stated period, no claims are to be advanced for the recovery of the property. If during the said period the heir of the executor of the deceased does not arrive, the Officers of the Treasury, with the knowledge of the Agent of the Persian Government, shall sell the property and keep the amount in deposit.

ART. VII. Agreeably to former Engagements, and for the purpose of adding fresh ties to the Alliance, a Minister shall be sent every three years to reside for that period at the respective Courts.

The subjects of the Two High Powers, who, during the War, may have deserted from either country, in consideration of this happy Peace, shall suffer no punishment for the offence committed.

Final Article.—The Capitulations detailed in the Basis of the Treaty, and the Stipulations and different Articles which have been the result of the Conferences, shall be approved of by both Parties. No claims shall be advanced on account of plunder and losses, or any indemnification required for the expenses of the War, and the principle adhered to by both Governments shall be to overlook all past occurrences.

62. TREATY OF PEACE AND RENEWAL OF CAPITULATIONS: FRANCE AND THE GARRISON OF TUNIS
21 May and 15 November 1824

(Ratified by the king of France, 31 July 1825)
[Translated from the French text in Clercq, *Recueil des traités*, 3 : 345–47]

The suppression of priacy in the Garrison of Tunis by the mid-1820s drew this North African principality into the politics of European expansion. With a major source of revenue gone, the principality swiftly adapted to the modes of external commerce, and later finance, imposed by the major maritime powers of Western Europe. For the first time the capitulatory system, as practiced in the Ottoman Empire, could be stablilized and made uniform for the treaty powers in what might henceforth be aptly labeled the Regency of Tunis, for with the pulling of the fangs of piracy, the rationale for a frontier garrison of Islam disappeared. The following instrument reflected the turn of events. From this time on, with capitulatory privileges assured, Europeans came to settle in Tunis. But Tunis was not destined to become a major object of commerce for concession hunters. This was window dressing for the strategic rivalry between Britain and France, complicated after 1860 by the conflicting territorial ambitions of France and a united Italy. Cambon, *Histoire de la régence de Tunis*, chap. 8; Julien, *Histoire de l'Afrique du Nord*, vol. 2, chap. 6; Fitoussi and Benazet, *L'état tunisien et le protectorat français*, pt. 1; Ganiage, *Les origines du protectorat français en Tunisie*, chap. 1; Abun-Nasr, *History of the Maghrib*, pp. 177–89.

ART. 1. The capitulations made and agreed upon between the Emperor of France and the Grand Seigneur or their predecessors, or those which may once more be agreed upon by the Ambassador of France at the Sublime Porte for the peace and union of the said states, shall be kept and observed exactly, without in any way being transgressed directly or indirectly.

ART. 2. All previous treaties and supplements are renewed and confirmed by the present [treaty] except for the changes and additions mentioned in the attached articles.

ART. 3. The French established in the Kingdom of Tunis shall continue to enjoy the same privileges and exemptions which had been accorded to them, and to be treated as belonging to the most favored nation, and, following the same capitulations and treaties, neither privilege nor advantage will be given to other nations which may not be equally shared by the French nation, even though they have not been specified in the said capitulations or treaties.

ART. 4. Goods coming from France or other countries under any flag whatsoever, even though the country may be an enemy of the Regency, so long as they are sent by a merchant or any other French national, shall pay only 3.0 percent customs duty, without any other contribution whatsoever. These customs duties shall be paid according to normal usage, until the establishment of a new tariff. And if goods belonging to [the subject] of another nation should be sent to a French national, the customs duty shall be paid according to the usage of the nation to which that individual belongs.

ART. 5. There will be imposed on the import by the French of rice, any kind of grain, and dried vegetables a fee of only one and a quarter piasters per Caffis, payable to the chief of the *rahbah* [market], without any customs duty.

ART. 6. In the preliminary articles, the request of the Chargé d'Affaires of H.M. the Emperor of France that a tariff of evaluation of goods be framed for the payment of customs duties has been granted.

As soon as this tariff has been definitively enacted and reciprocally adopted by the interested parties, it shall be attached to the present treaty.

ART. 7. According to the former treaties all goods which French merchants bring in and are unable to sell shall not [require] payment of either fees or customs duties if [the goods] are reshipped.

ART. 8. The French may transfer goods from one ship to another without setting them on the ground and may carry them from one place to another without liability for paying any fee.

ART. 9. Goods for which customs have been paid may be sent to another port of the states of the Regency without the imposition of [further] entry or exit fee wherever they may be unloaded.

ART. 10. The French bakery established in al-Funduq [al-Jadid] shall have the option, as of old, to supply *galettes*, or biscuits, to French ships and not to others; and, to enjoy this right, [they] shall pay two piasters per hundredweight to the biscuit farmer, without any other imposts.

ART. 11. The supposed Jews or others of the country in the service of the French either at Tunis or in the ports of the Regency shall continue to enjoy the same protection and the same advantages for commercial business that were granted to them by earlier treaties.

ART. 12. The Consul General, [i.e.,] the Chargé d'Affaires of France, may choose and change at his will the dragomans, janissaries, auditors, or scriveners in his service, without any opposition or restriction whatsoever.

ART. 13. In case of war between France and another power, the French merchants who send or receive goods under foreign and simulated names shall nevertheless enjoy the same favors and privileges that were granted to them; but they must make a sworn declaration before the Consul General of France and append to it their pledge.

ART. 14. In case of a dispute between a French national and a Tunisian subject over a commercial matter, the Consul General shall name French merchants, and an equal number of merchants of the country shall be chosen by the *amin* [chief of the corporation of merchants] or any other authority designated by His Excellency the Bey. If the plaintiff is a Tunisian subject, he shall have the right to ask the Consul General to be judged in this way, and if the commission cannot settle the dispute, by reason of disagreement or equal division of opinion, the matter shall be referred to His Excellency the Bey for his decision in agreement with the Consul General, in accordance with justice.

ART. 15. French ships shall in the future receive most-favored-nation treatment in anchorage and port dues.

ART. 16. In case of disagreement between the two governments, the two Powers expressly renounce reprisals against private individuals, who in no case shall be held responsible for the deeds of their governments.

ART. 17. All French nationals residing in the Kingdom of Tunis without exception shall be under the jurisdiction of the Consul General of France.

The present treaty shall be ratified and confirmed by His Majesty the Emperor of France.

63. ACT OF THE BRITISH PARLIAMENT DISSOLVING THE LEVANT COMPANY
10 June 1825

[*British and Foreign State Papers*, 12: 531–35]

The commencement of the Industrial Revolution in England a half-century ahead of its closest competitors, the dislocating effects on the Continent of the Napoleonic wars, and the unchallenged supremacy of the British fleet inaugurated after 1815 the most prosperous decade in the long history of the (English) Levant Company, which had received its first royal charter in 1581 (Doc. 5). By 1815, however, overseas commerce by monopoly had outlived its usefulness. Under the stress of the Napoleonic wars, the United Kingdom's political and military interests in the Ottoman Empire had assumed for the first time greater significance than the commercial. The government in 1804 relieved the company of its residual responsibilities for managing the British Embassy at Istanbul. But the British consular service in the Ottoman Empire remained under the company's direct control for two decades longer, when it was finally taken over by the Foreign Office in response to public demands for free trade and the growing complexity of British-Ottoman relations. Early in 1825 the company agreed in the public interest to surrender its remaining restrictive privileges. Wood, *History of the Levant Company*, chap. 10; Puryear, *France and the Levant*, chap. 2; Bailey, *British Policy and the Turkish Reform Movement*, chap. 3.

Whereas His late Majesty King *James* the First, by His Letters Patent bearing Date the 14th Day of *December*, in the 3rd Year of His Reign, did grant to several Persons therein named, and to their Sons, and such Others as should thereafter be admitted and made free, that they should be One Fellowship, and One Body Corporate and Politic, by the Name of "The Governor and Company of Merchants of *England* trading to the *Levant* Seas," and by the same Name should have perpetual Succession, with certain Rights and Privileges in the said Letters Patent specified: And whereas His late Majesty King *Charles* the Second, by His Letters Patent bearing Date the 2nd Day of *April*, in the 13th Year of His Reign, did ratify and confirm the said Letters Patent of King *James* the First, and did grant further Authorities and Privileges to the said Governor and Company: And where as by divers Acts certain Regulations have been made respecting the said Company, and the Dues and Duties payable to the said Company, that is to say, an Act made in the 26th Year of the Reign of His late Majesty King *George* the Second, [cap. 18], intituled *An Act for enlarging and regulating the Trade into the* Levant *Seas*; an Act made in the 20th Year of the Reign of His late Majesty King *George* the Third, [cap. 18,] among other things, for the allowing the Importation into and Exportation from *Ireland*, of such Goods as may be Imported into or Exported from *Great Britain* by the Merchants of *England* trading to the *Levant*

Seas; an Act made in the 43rd Year of the Reign of His said late Majesty King *George* the Third, [cap. 153], to permit the Importation into *Great Britain* and *Ireland*, of certain Goods, Wares, and Merchandize in Neutral Vessels; an Act made in the 55th Year of the Reign of His late Majesty King *George* the Third, [cap. 29,] intituled *An Act to regulate the Trade between* Malta *and its Dependencies and His Majesty's Colonies and Plantations in* America, *and also between Malta and the United Kingdom*; an Act made in the 57th Year of the Reign of His said late Majesty King *George* the Third, [cap. 4,] intituled *An Act to extend the Privileges of the Trade of Malta to the Port of* Gibraltar; and an Act made in the 59th Year of the Reign of His said late Majesty King *George* the Third, [cap. 110,] intituled *An Act to remove Doubts respecting the Dues payable to the* Levant *Company*: And whereas it would be beneficial to the Trade of the United Kingdom, and especially to the Trade carried on in the *Levant* Seas, that the exclusive Rights and Privileges of the said Governor and Company under the said Letters Patent and Acts of Parliament should cease and determine: And whereas the said Governor and Company are willing and desirous to surrender up the said Letters Patent into His Majesty's Hands: May it therefore please Your Majesty that it may be enacted, and be it enacted by the King's most Excellent Majesty, by and with the Advice and Consent to the Lords Spiritual and Temporal, and Commons, in this present

Parliament assembled, and by the authority of the same, That whenever and so soon as any Deed or Instrument by which the said Governor and Company shall so surrender up to His Majesty the said Letters Patent, and all Rights, Powers, and Privileges thereby granted or confirmed to the said Governor and Company, shall be made and executed under the Common Seal of the said Governor and Company, and shall be enrolled in His Majesty's High Court of Chancery, the said several Letters Patent and Grants hereinbefore recited, and every Matter, Clause, and Thing therein contained, shall be and become, and the same are hereby declared to be and become null and void; and that from and immediately after the Enrolment of such Deed or Instrument, the said Governor and Company shall cease to be a body Politic and Corporate, and the said Corporation shall be dissolved to all Intents, Contructions, and Purposes, whatsoever; and all Rights, Powers, and Privileges by the said Letters Patent, or by the said several hereinbefore recited Acts, or by any other Authority or Means granted to or possessed by the said Governor and Company, shall from henceforth cease and determine; anything in the said several Letters Patent and Acts, or any of them, to the contrary in anywise notwithstanding; and the said Governor and Company shall be and they are hereby divested of and from all Land, Houses, and Buildings, by whatever Tenure holden, at any Time heretofore purchased, acquired, or holden by the said Governor and Company, and which are holden, possessed, or claimed by the said Governor and Company, within the United Kingdom, or at *Smyrna* or elsewhere, and all such Land, Houses, Buildings, and all Right, Title, Estate, or Interest therein or thereto, holden, purchased, acquired, possessed, enjoyed, or claimed by the said Governor and Company, shall thenceforth be and the same and every of them are and is hereby declared and enacted to be fully and absolutely vested in His Majesty, His Heirs and Successors, for ever.

II. And whereas certain grants of money have been from time to time made to the said Governor and Company of Merchants of *England* trading to the *Levant* Seas, by sundry Acts, for the purpose of better enabling them to carry into effect the objects for which they were incorporated: And whereas it is just and expedient that all such property as shall belong to or be at the disposal of the said Governor and Company under or by virtue of the said Letters Patent and Acts, or any of them respectively, at the time of such their dissolution, should, after the payment of all debts and demands to which the said Governor and Company may be liable as such Corporation, be applied to the public Service, in the manner hereinafter directed; Be it therefore enacted, That from and immediately after the enrolment of any such Deed or Instrument as aforesaid, whereby the said Corporation shall be dissolved in manner directed by this Act, all monies in the Public Funds, and all other monies, goods, chattels, property, and other personal estate and effects whatsoever, in the possession or at the disposal of the said Governor and Company as such Corporation as aforesaid, or to which the said Governor and Company as such Corporation are or shall be entitled, or which shall or may be due to the said Governor and Company as such Corporation, shall be and become vested, and are hereby vested in the Commissioners of His Majesty's Treasury of The United Kingdom of *Great Britain* and *Ireland* for the time being; and that it shall and may be lawful for the said Commissioners of the Treasury now and for the time being, or any Three of the said Commissioners, to accept, receive, and recover, and to sell, transfer, and dispose of all such funds, monies, goods, chattels, property, and other personal estate and effects whatsoever, and to apply the produce thereof in the first place in and for the payment of all just debts and demands to which the said Governor and Company are or shall be liable at the dissolution of such Corporation, on account of any matter or thing relating to such Corporation; and from and after payment of all such debts and demands, it shall be lawful for the said Commissioners of the Treasury for the time being, or any Three or more of them, and they are hereby authorized and required to direct, that all the remainder and surplus of the produce of such public funds, monies, goods, chattels, property, and other personal Estate as aforesaid, shall be paid into the Receipt of His Majesty's Exchequer at *Westminster*, and shall be placed to the Account of and made part of the Consolidated Fund of the United Kingdom of *Great Britain* and *Ireland*.

III. And be it further enacted, That from and immediately after the enrolment in His Majesty's High Court of Chancery of Such Deed or Instrument as aforesaid. the said recited Act of the 26th Year of the Reign of His said late Majesty King *George* the Second, and also the said recited Act of the 59th Year of the Reign of His late Majesty King *George* the Third, and all Powers for the levying of any Duties or Dues heretofore payable to the said Governor and Company, shall be and the same are hereby repealed; and all such Duties and Dues, and all Powers for levying the same, shall cease and determine, except only so far as relates to the payment and recovery of any arrears of Duties and Dues which shall be payable to the said Company at the time of the enrolment of such Deed or Instrument; and also that from and after such enrolment of such Deed or Instrument, all and every clause, matter, and thing contained in the said several hereinbefore recited Acts made in the 20th, 43rd, 55th, and 57th Years of the Reign of His said late Majesty King *George* the Third, in any way extending or relating to the said Governor and Company, shall be and the same are from thenceforth hereby repealed; anything in the said recited Acts or any of them, or any other law, usage, or custom to the contrary in anywise notwithstanding.

IV. And be it further enacted, That from and immediately after the enrolment of any such Deed or Instrument as aforesaid, all such Rights and Duties of Jurisdiction and Authority over His Majesty's Subjects resorting to the Ports of the *Levant* for the purposes of Trade or otherwise, as were lawfully exercised and performed, or which the said recited Letters Patent or Acts, or any of them, authorized to be exercised and performed by any Consuls or other Officers appointed by the said Company, or which such Consuls or other Officers lawfully exercised and performed under and by virtue of any Power or Authority whatever, shall, from and after the enrolment of such Deed or Investment as aforesaid, be and become invested in, and shall be exercised and performed by such Consuls and other Officers respectively as His Majesty may be pleased to appoint, for the protection of the Trade of His Majesty's Subjects in the Ports and Places respectively mentioned in the said Letters Patent and Acts, or any or either of them.

V. And be it further enacted, That it shall and may be lawful for the Commissioners of His Majesty's Treasury, or any Three or more of them, and they are hereby empowered and authorized to grant reasonable allowances and Pensions to such of the Officers and Servants in *England* of the said Company, and to such other Person or Persons as, by reason of the dissolution of the said Company, may lose and be deprived of their Offices, Employments, and Pensions, and to charge the same upon the Consolidated Fund of the United Kingdom; and all such Allowances and Pensions to be so granted, shall be payable and paid Quarterly at the receipt of the Exchequer at *Westminster*, out of the said Consolidated Fund, free and clear of and from all taxes, charges, and deductions whatsoever; and the said Commissioners of His Majesty's Treasury shall yearly and every Year before the 25th Day of *March* in each Year, if Parliament be sitting, and in case Parliament shall not be sitting, then within 20 Days after the Meeting of Parliament then next following such 25th Day of *March*, cause an Account and Estimate to be laid before Parliament, of the total Amount of such Allowances and Pensions payable to such Officers and Servants in *England* of the said Company, and to such other Persons as are hereinbefore mentioned, for One Year ending on the 5th Day of *January* preceding every such 25th Day of *March* respectively.

64. REPORTS ON THE FLY-WHISK INCIDENT: THE GARRISON OF ALGIERS, FRANCE, AND THE OTTOMAN EMPIRE
30 April–19 December 1827

[Report of Pierre Deval, the French consul general in Algiers, to the baron de Damas, the minister of foreign affairs in Paris, translated from the French text in Bernard, *Les colonies françaises*, pp. 174–76; the report of the dey, Hüseyin Paşa translated from Ercümend Kuran's French translation of the original Turkish text, *Revue africaine*, 96 (1st and 2nd trimesters 1952): 189–95]

One major difference between the Maghrib and the Mashriq—between the Arab West and the Arab East—was demographic. From Libya to Morocco, the only native non-Muslims were Jews, as also in Yemen, but not elsewhere in the Arabian Peninsula. But, in Egypt and the Ottoman Arab provinces in Asia north of the peninsula, there were also Christians, who in fact outnumbered the Jews. Because of their commercial, financial, and cultural ties to Europe, native non-Mulsims until early in the nineteenth century were useful to the rulers in Morocco and to the quasi-sovereign Garrisons and paşaliks, as they were at the time to the Sublime Porte, for the conduct of external commerce and finance and occasional diplomacy with the maritime states of Europe. The prevailing literature on the Garrisons after the start of their decline late in the seventeenth century, when piracy became their main business and source of government revenue, commonly leads the reader to assume that the only diplomacy of the European powers toward the Barbary states related to tribute and ransom. But every now and then we get a glimpse of more "normal" activities. To supplement the food supplies of the Mediterranean districts of France, for example, and later to help meet the needs of the French armies for the Italian and Egyptian campaigns, the Republican government in 1793–98 bought grain on credit in the Algerien Garrison with the financial assistance of the dey's Jewish bankers, the Bakri and Bushnaq families. In a decade and a half of rule, Napoleon did not pay these Algerine debts, and the failure of the restored Bourbon monarchy after 1815 to settle the accounts permanently beclouded French-Algerine relations. Nor were matters improved by the choice of consul general at Algiers, since Pierre Deval, who remained at the post from 1815 to 1827, qualified primarily because of his familiarity with Turkish and Arabic, which he learned in his native Istanbul, where his father had been a dragoman, or interpreter, in the diplomatic service. Deval lived up to a shady reputation in his dealings with Hüseyin Paşa (1818–30), who as it turned out was the last dey of that quasi-sovereign Garrison. Instead of trying to reach an equitable settlement of the debts, which were compounded over the years by accrued interest, Deval allowed the quarrel to fester. The Barbary Garrisons, of course, continued their piratical raids, even after the Exmouth-Capellen punitive expedition of 1816 and the warning of the Congress of Aix-la-Chapelle presented in 1819 (Docs. 58, 59), but on a steadily diminishing scale. One of these piratical ventures, involving French ships, became entangled with the issue of unsettled debts. The claims and counterclaims could easily have been settled with a modicum of goodwill. But Deval's machinations gradually began to give those French policymakers who were manifestly seeking territorial expansion their excuse. Meanwhile, as the Garrison's fortunes declined, Hüseyin Paşa and his *divan*, or council, grew more and more sensitive to European slights to their quasi-sovereign status. When Deval appeared at a deylical audience on 29 April 1827, Hüseyin Paşa inquired why he had not received answers to the last three letters that he had addressed to the French government. The rest of the story, as far as the deylical audience went, is best told by the actors themselves. To say, however, as an English author did (Usborne, *Conquest of Morocco*, p. 17), that "the interview . . . had far-reaching consequences, for the stroke of the fly-whisk was destined to change profoundly the fate of all North Africa," was to employ literary license. Abun-Nasr, *History of the Maghrib*, chap. 9; Julien, *Histoire de l'Algérie contemporaine*, chap. 1; Lacoste, Nouschi, and Prenant, *L'Algérie passé et présent*, pp. 234–46; Piquet, *La colonisation française dans l'Afrique du Nord*, chap. 2; Lord, *England and France in the Mediterranean*, pt. 1; Grammont, *Histoire d'Alger sous la domination turque*, chap. 25; Usborne, op. cit., introd. chap.

1. The Deval Report, 30 April 1827

The privilege granted to Consuls of France in this town, of complimenting the Dey in private audience on the eve of the feats of *bayram*, led me to ask at what hour His Highness wished to receive me. The Dey sent word that he would receive me one hour after noon but that he wished to see Your Excellency's latest dispatch which the King's schooner, destined for the coral-fishing station, had brought to me. I sent an immediate reply with the Turkish dragoman of the Consulate that I had received no letter from Your Excellency on that occasion, and that I had received no other than that from His Excellency the Minister of the Navy relating to fishing. I was, however, not a little surprised at the Dey's pretension of personal knowledge about dispatches that Your cellency has done the honor of addressing to me, and I could not imagine what end he had in mind. Nevertheless, I went to the palace at the appointed hour. The Dey asked me, as soon as I was introduced into his audience, if it were true that England had declared war on France. I told him that this was only a false rumor, arising from troubles stirred up in Portugal, in which the Government of the King in its dignity and loyalty had not wished to meddle. "Thus," said the Dey, "France grants England whatever it wishes, and nothing at all to me!" "It seems to me, Lord, that the King's Government has

always granted you what it could." "Why has your Minister not replied to the letter I wrote him?" "I had the honor to bring you the reply as soon as I received it." "Why did he not reply directly? Am I a clodhopper, a man of mud, a barefoot tramp? You are a wicked man, an infidel, an idolater!" Then, rising from his seat, with the handle of his fly-whisk, he gave me three violent blows about the body and told me to retire.

If Your Excellency does not wish to give this affair the severe and well-publicized attention that it merits, he should at least be willing to grant me permission to retire with leave.

2. Report of the Dey Hüseyin Paşa, to the Ottoman Grand Vezir, 19 December 1827

His Lordship, my master, my very powerful Sultan, benefactor, merciful and magnificant disperser of favors, and master of the graces,

My very humble letter is the following:

Although on my humble behalf three friendly letters were written to the King of France requesting that the sums which the French owe the victorious Ocak [Garrison] be sent to the Muslim public treasury, these letters were ignored and I have received no reply. I therefore raised the matter with the French Consul who resides in our country, in courteous terms and with a deliberately friendly attitude, stating that, if the long friendship between the government of his country and the imperial

Ocak is to continue in accordance with the terms of the letters addressed to the paşas, my predecessors, and preserved in my archives, I am no less obliged by my office as delegated vezir to uphold the interests of the victorious Ocak of our master, the Padişah, fortunate, generous, [and] powerful asylum of the world, of whom I am the servant. "Why did no reply come to my letters written and sent to your [i. e., the French] Government?" The Consul, in stubbornness and arrogance, replied in offensive terms that "the King and state of France may not send replies to letters which you have addressed to them." He dared to blaspheme the Muslim religion and showed contempt for the honor of His Majesty, protector of the world. Unable to endure this insult, which exceeded all bearable limits, and having recourse to the courage natural only to Muslims, I hit him two or three times with light blows of the fly-whisk which I held in my humble hand. Impelled by intrigue and depravity [with] the vapors of the African coast mounting to [his] vicious brain (from which may God protect us), the Consul lit the fires of sedition day and night. A month later a schooner entered the port of Algiers and dropped anchor inside the bay. According to the regulation of the imperial Ocak, on the arrival of ships of foreign states in the bay, the coming and going to Consuls to their ships with the launch of our port commander is a current practice. After going to his schooner, the Consul unhappily declared that he would not leave it and sent our launch away. Early the next morning, their ships of evil omen—a ship with two bridges [besides] two frigates and a corvette—appeared on the surface of the sea, and their schooner which was in the bay raised anchor and joined them. This day passed, and on the next day their Admiral sent a letter, demanding a reply within twenty-four hours. After translation, it was learned that this letter demanded that the French flag be flown at the Qasbah [Citadel], which is my humble residence, and that the standard of Islam be raised beneath it; and the same was also to be done at the principal tower [Bure Mawlay Hasan] in the square of the Sultan's Castle, whose fame is universal. We were ordered, moreover, to fire a hundred cannon shots to announce to everyone from our towers that the chiefs of the imperial Ocak and the keepers of the arsenal, home of fighters for the faith, must go to the accursed [French] ships to offer apologies. [The ultimatum] laid down other unacceptable conditions, which would have prejudiced the honor of Islam. In conclusion, we were warned that "if these conditions are not accepted within twenty-four hours, hostilities will be declared." Your servant replied to this message with courage and firmness, [saying] that "intelligent statesmen do not lay down conditions of this kind which resemble the proposals of madmen committed to asylums. If [you seek an accurate account] of the incident, [send a man of good sense] to investigate it. Such an inquiry should convince him that the plotting Consul is suitable neither to you nor to us. Until the nomination of an experienced Consul, no consideration will be given to such insulting proposals, issued without prior request for an explanation. If you send a man within twenty-four hours, as suggested above, the dispute may be settled; if not, we shall enter into a state of hostility."

In the region of Bône, to the east of the victorious province, at the place called the Bastion of France, trade and coral fishing have been conceded to France for many years. A small building was erected there, large enough for three to five persons. During the rebellion of the late Bonaparte, this building was demolished. Despite a pledge never again to undertake such construction, the French applied themselves day and night for several years, putting to good use the time and the circumstances to build a solid fort, and within it they installed fourteen iron cannons, two brass cannons, and two mortars, manned by more than a hundred soliders and an officer. In their perversity, they manifestly nourished hostile designs. The disobedience of our Kabyles in the high mountain permitted the smuggling of powder, guns, and other arms of war, despite the prohibitions in our agreements. Informed of their conduct, I sent men who found in the above-mentioned post a large quantity of powder and guns. As [we did] a year ago, we [again] equipped and prepared our vessels to sail in the spring of good omen under the order of the imperial fleet in the service of His Majesty, our Padişah, our benefactor, our very fortunate, very generous, [and] magnificent master, benefactor of the world and all peoples. This obliged us to close our eyes to the activities of the cunning infidels. But when we declared war, they sent two of their ships of ill fortune to the Bastion, and, thanks to favorable weather, they were able to take away the infidels and the arms that were discovered there. Your servant had the fortress razed to the ground, and this was a great delight. [Then,] the enemy of the Islamic religion, with the illusion of stretching a hostile hand to our coasts in alliance with the Greek rebels, opened without valid reason hostilities against the victorious Ocak, and with his ships of ill fortune [the enemy] blockaded Algiers by sea. Because of the impossibility of bringing out our warships, the ships of the Greek brigands, more than fifteen in number, clearly could not be stopped from crossing from Tripoli to the Strait of Gibraltar, attacking Muslims and putting them to flight. Although until the present the worthless French infidels have blockaded the victorious Ocak by sea with six or seven powerful ships, thank God we luckily needed absolutely nothing, and, with the assistance and the grace of God and by the good will of His Imperial Majesty, we had the capacity, thanks to His Majesty the Padişah, to repel the attacks not only of the French but of the other nations, if they had laid seige to us together. May God defeat and wipe out the enemies of His Majesty, our Padişah, our very fortunate, generous, and powerful master, and may he assure victory to the armies of Islam. Amen!

For several years, the victorious Ocak has not received reinforcements from Anatolia. Since the Ocak, in any case, must have Turkish troops, and since its fame and glory depend on their abundance, we report their insufficiency to our benefactor adorned with science, and we solicit his consent to grant his high sovereign favors authorizing the dispatch at this time of additional troops from the town of Smyrna and other coastal regions. The French vessels, mirrors of contemptibility, a large frigate with two batteries equivalent to a two-bridge vessel, one other frigate, two brigs and one schooner, thus a total of five

powerful warships, which crossed day and night in front of Algiers with the illusion of laying seige by sea to the victorious Ocak, increased the ardor and the desire of your slave and of your slaves, the fighters of the faith, distinguished by their victories, to engage in combat.

We therefore equipped for action our eleven small warships which lay inside our port, comprising a little old frigate and a small corvette, with brigs making up the rest. The interior of these ships was crammed with Muslim warriors after sunset, on the eve of the twelfth day of Rebiyülevvel of the present year of victory [3 October 1827]. Putting their faith in God and asking for the intercession of the prophet of God, they took to sea, and the next day, holy day of the birth of the Prophet, the ships of the evil-doing infidels came into sight. Although our warships, resembling a seven-headed dragon, attacked them, the will of the Very High God opposing a favorable wind, our vessels had to hug the shore and reached only with great efforts the waters of the enemy, with whom they finally crossed swords. Immediately, they lit the fire of war, and by artillery duel of more than three hours they transformed the surface of the sea into a furnace. After exhausting its means of struggle and fearing to see its vessels become the prey of Muslims in whose favor the wind of victory was blowing, the enemy fled filled with sadness, as birds flee before the hunter, seeing in this day a day of bad luck. They fired three blank shots and took advantage of the favorable wind to end the fighting. Because of unfavorable winds, three of our vessels remained immobile and could not participate in the combat. With the assistance and the grace of God, the help and the spirituality of the Prophet, and the sacred favor of the caliph, a battle of this violence caused our vessels no damage; only one man of Arab nationality drank the cup of the martyr. We have, besides, six wounded. One month later, letters from the well-guarded town of Tunis and some Christian countries informed us that over and above the wounding of one of the great captains of the flagship, whose hand a bullet removed in a scathing fire, and besides the perverse infidels thrown into infernal fire, the wounded, transported to their hospital in Toulon, were fifty-six in number, even more, according to other versions. May God continue to assure victory to the Muslim armies and to plunge the enemy of the religion into misfortune. Amen, in honor of the Prophet! The events have been accurately written and presented to Your Excellency the Serasker. [Commander in Chief]. In this matter as always, the order and favor belong to His Lordship, my master, my Sultan, the benefactor, the very fortunate, gracious, clement, and magnificent dispenser of favors.

3. The Grand Vezir's Notation

This is the letter from your slave, the Beylerbeyi [governor general] of Algiers, Hüseyin Paşa. The opening of his communication exposes the facts of the war and the hositlities with the French. Because of the small number of Turkish troops, imperial permission is solicited to raise troops in sufficient number in Smyrna and other coastal regions. Although the Ocaks of the West have solicited similar concessions of imperial permission, the aforementioned letter was sent to your slave, the Serasker [Hüseyin] Paşa, because of his competence, to ask for his advice. While declaring that the citadel of Algiers is a very victorious fortress on the frontier which has nothing to fear from such hostilities with France and other nations, thanks to the assistance of God and the benediction of imperial goodwill, he has made it known that, if troops of which the enlistment is presently solicited should be sent to Algiers, the concession and permission to enlist these

troops by the deys charged with these functions of the said Ocak requires an imperial order. The letter from your slave, the said Hüseyin Paşa, is presented with two others sent to your servants the Kaptan Paşa [Ottoman naval commander] and the Kapi Kethudasi [the Dey's representative at the Sublime Porte] to be examined by His Imperial Majesty. When they have been seen by His Imperial Majesty, if it is judged to conform to the imperial order of His Majesty, a letter of permission will be written in the recommended manner by your slave, the Serasker Paşa, on behalf of your servant [i.e., Hüseyin Paşa] to your slave, the Governor of Smyrna, according to what may be judged necessary, and a similar reply will be made to the above-mentioned Paşa, your slave. The order and command belong to him who has the prerogative.

4. The Imperial Rescript of the Sultan

This letter and the others of the Beylerbeyi of Algiers, Hüseyin Paşa, and the note of the Serasker Paşa have been seen by my royal person. According to the contents they have been, thank God, victorious in the war with the French! In this way the happy outcome of an affair pursued with a sincere alliance is observed. May God grant this ardor and perseverance to all Muslims. Amen! Let there be written on your behalf according to need in the sense indicated, in the annotation in red ink and recommended by the Serasker Paşa, a letter to the Governor of Smyrna in reply to the said Paşa.

65. TREATIES OF PEACE AND COMMERCE (TURKMANCHAY): PERSIA AND RUSSIA
10/22 February 1828

[Childs, *Perso-Russian Treaties and Notes*, pp. 1–18]

The treaty of Gulistan in 1813 (Doc. 55) left neither side entirely happy. The Irredentist spirit in Persia did not fade away in the dozen years that followed. Despite large gains in Transcaucasia at Persian expense, Russia still sought the shah's districts north of the Aras River, which the tsarist government regarded as a more defensible frontier. Victory in the renewed war of 1826–28 enabled the Russians, under the treaty of peace concluded in the Persian village of Turkmanchay in Azarbayjan, to annex the coveted provinces of Erivan and Nakhichevan (art. 3), thus achieving a stable boundary with Persia west of the Caspian. In the same treaty the exclusive right of Russian naval vessels to sail on the Caspian Sea, first granted in Gulistan, was re-affirmed (art. 8), and under article 9 Russia became the second European power (after Britain) to establish a permanent diplomatic mission in Tehran. No less significant was the commercial treaty signed the same day, assuring Russian subjects extrater-ritorial privileges and establishing the pattern of the capitulatory regime for Euro-peans in Persia under the Qajar dynasty. Article 14 of the peace treaty was modified in 1844 (French text of the convention appears in *British and Foreign State Papers*, 33: 884), and the unpaid Persian indemnity (art. 6) was waived in 1853. Baddeley, *Russian Conquest of the Caucasus*, chaps. 6–11; Sykes, *History of Persia*, chap. 76; Rawlinson, *England and Russia in the East*, chap. 1; Allen and Muratoff, *Caucasian Battlefields*, pp. 20–21; Florinsky, *Russia,* 2: 830–31; Matine-Daftary, *La suppression des capitulations en Perse*, chaps. 2–3; Krausse, *Russia in Asia*, chap. 5; Watson, *History of Persia*, chaps. 8–9.

1. The Treaty of Peace

ART. I. There will be, dating from this day, peace, friendship and perfect under-standing between His Majesty the Emperor of all the Russias on one hand, and His Majesty the Shah of Persia on the other, their Heirs and Successors, their States and their respective Subjects, in perpetuity.

ART. II. Considering that the hostilities taken place between the High Contracting Parties, and happily terminated today, have brought to an end the obligations which the Treaty of Gulistan imposed upon them, His Majesty the Emperor of all the Russias and His Majesty the Shah in Shan [King of Kings] of Persia have judged it appro-priate to replace the said Treaty of Gulistan by the present Clauses and Stipulations, which are designed to regulate and to consolidate more and more the future relations of peace and friendship between Russia and Persia.

ART. III. His Majesty the Shah of Persia, both in his name as in that of his Heirs and Successors, cedes in entire ownership to the Russian Empire the Khanate of Erivan on both sides of the Araxe, and the Khanate of Nakhitchevan. In consequence of this cession, His Majesty the Shah under-takes to turn over to the Russian Authori-ties, within six months at the latest, from the date of signature of the present Treaty, all the archives and all public documents concerning the administration of the two Khanates above-mentioned.

ART. IV. The two High Contracting Parties agree to establish, as the frontier between the two States, the following line of demarcation: In parting from the point of the frontier of the Ottoman States, the nearest in a straight line from the summit of the little Ararat, this line will continue to the summit of this mountain from whence it will descend to the source of the river known as the Lower Karassou which flows from the southern side of the Little Ararat and it will follow its course until its discharge in the Araxe, opposite Cherour, Arrived at this point, this line will follow the bed of the Araxe to the Fortress of Abbas-Abad; around the exterior works of this place which are situated on the right bank of the Araxe, there will be traced a radius of a half agatch, or three versts and a half from Russia, which will extend in all directions; all the land which will be en-closed in this radius will belong exclusively to Russia and will be demarked with the greatest exactitude in the space of two months, dating from this day, From the locality where the eastern extremity of this radius will have rejoined the Araxe, the frontier line will continue to follow the bed of this river to the ford of Jediboulouk, from whence the Persian Territory will ex-tend the length of the bed of the Araxe for a distince of three agatch or twenty-one versts from Russia; arrived at this point, the frontier line will traverse in a direct manner the plain of Moughan to the bed of the river known as Bolgarou, to the place situated at three agatch or twenty-one versts below the conjunction of the two small rivers known as Odinabazar and Sarakamyche. From there, this line will reascend from the left bank of the Bolgarou to the junction of the said rivers Odinabazar and Sarakamyche and will extend the length of the right bank of the river of Odinabazar to its source and from there to the summit of the heights of Djikoir so that all the waters which flow towards the Caspian Sea will belong to Russia, and all those [whose] watershed is of the Persian side will belong to Persia. The limit of the two States being marked here by the crest of the mountains, it is agreed that the declination from the side of the Caspian Sea will belong to Russia and that their opposite slope will belong to Persia. From the crest of the heights of Djikoir, the frontier will follow the summit of Kamarkouia, the mountains which separate the Talyche from the district of Archa. The crests of the mountains, separating on all sides the watershed, will determine here the frontier line in the same manner as stated above concerning the distance included between the source of the Odinabazar and the summits of Djikoir. The frontier line will follow thereafter, from the summit of Kamarkouia, the crests of the mountains which separate the district of Zouvante from that of Archa to the limit of that of Welkidji, always conforming to the principle enunciated in connection with the watershed. The district of Zouvante, with the exception of the part situated on the opposite side of the summit of the said mountains, will fall in this way in division to Russia. Beginning with the limit of the district of Welkidji, the frontier line between the two States will follow the summits of Klopouty and of the principal chain of mountains which traverse the district of Welkidji to the northern source of the river called Astara, always observing the principle relative to the watershed. From there the frontier will follow the bed of this river to its discharge in the Caspian Sea, and will complete the line of demarcation which will separate in future the respective possessions of Russia and Persia.

ART. V. His Majesty the Shah of Persia in testimony of his sincere friendship for His Majesty the Emperor of all the Russias, solemnly recognizes by the present Article, both in his name as in that of his Heirs and Successors to the throne of Persia, as belonging forever to the Russian Empire, all the countries and all the islands situated between the line of demarcation designated by the preceding Article on the one side, and the crest of the mountains of the Caucasus, and the Caspian Sea on the other, as well as the peoples, nomads and others who inhabit these countries.

ART. VI. With a view to recompensing the considerable sacrifices that the war, which occurred between the two States, has occasioned to the Russian Empire, as well as the losses and damages which have resulted therefrom for Russian subjects, His Majesty the Shah of Persia undertakes to make them good by means of a pecuniary indemnity. It is agreed between the two High Contracting Parties that the total of this indemnity is fixed at ten kupours of silver tomans or 20,000,000 silver roubles and that the method, the terms and the guarantees of payment of this sum will be regulated by a special arrangement which shall have the same force and value as if it were inserted word for word in the present Treaty.

ART. VII. His Majesty the Shah of Persia having judged it fitting to appoint as his Successor and Heir Presumptive his August Son Prince Abbas Mirza, His Majesty the Emperor of all the Russias, with a view to giving to His Majesty the Shah public evidence of his friendly dispositions and of his desire to contribute to the consolidation of this order of succession, undertakes to recognize as from today, in the August Person of His Royal Highness Prince Abbas Mirza, the Successor and Heir Presumptive of the Crown of Persia and to consider Him as the Legitimate Sovereign of this Kingdom from his ascension to the throne.

ART. VIII. Russian merchant vessels will enjoy, as in the past, the right to navigate freely on the Caspian Sea and along its coasts and to land there. They will find in Persia aid and assistance in case of shipwreck. The same right is accorded to Persian merchant vessels to navigate on the old footing in the Caspian Sea and to enter Russian Rivers where, in case of shipwreck, the Persians will receive reciprocally aid and assistance.[1]

As for war vessels, those which bear the Russian military flag being *ab antiquo* the only ones which have had the right to navigate on the Caspian Sea, this same exclusive privilege is, for this reason, equally reserved and assured today, so that, with the exception of Russia, no other Power shall be able to have war vessels on the Caspian Sea.

ART. IX. His Majesty the Emperor of all the Russias and His Majesty the Shah of Persia, having at heart to strengthen by all means the ties so happily reestablished between them, are agreed that the Ambassadors, Ministers, and Chargés d'Affaires, who may be reciprocally delegated near the respective High Courts, whether to discharge a temporary Mission or to reside there permanently, will be received with the honors and distinction befitting their rank and conformable with the dignity of the High Contracting Parties, as with the sincere friendship which unites them and conformable with the customs of the country. An understanding to this effect will be reached by means of a special Protocol regarding the ceremonial to be observed by both sides.

ART. X. His Majesty the Emperor of all the Russias and His Majesty the Shah of Persia, considering the reestablishment and the extension of commercial relations between the two States as one of the first benefactions which the return of peace should produce, have agreed to regulate in a perfect accord all provisions relative to the protection of commerce, and to the safety of the respective subjects, and to embody them in a separate Act annexed hereto, drawn up between the respective Plenipotentiaries and which is and will be considered as forming an integral part of the present Treaty of Peace.

His Majesty the Shah of Persia reserves to Russia, as in the past, the right of appointing consuls or commercial agents wherever the good of commerce will demand it, and he undertakes to endow these consuls and agents, none of which shall have a suite of more than ten persons, with the protection, the honors and the privileges belonging to their public character. His Majesty the Emperor of all the Russias promises on His side to observe a perfect reciprocity in respect of the consuls and commercial agents of His Majesty the Shah of Persia. In case of well-founded complaint on the part of the Persian Government against one of the Russian consuls or agents, the Minister or Chargé d'Affaires of Russia, residing at the Court of His Majesty the Shah, and under the immediate orders of whom they will be placed, will suspend him from his functions and will confer provisionally the office upon whom he will deem fitting.

ART. XI. All the affairs and suits of the respective subjects, suspended by the intervention of the War, will be resumed and terminated in accordance with justice after the exclusion of Peace. The debts that the respective subjects may have the one in favor of the other, as well as to the treasury, will be promptly and entirely liquidated.

ART. XII. The High Contracting Parties agree by common accord in the interest of their respective subjects to fix a term of three years in order that those among them who (own) immobile property on both sides of the Araxe may have the right to sell or exchange it freely. His Imperial Majesty of all the Russias excepts, however, from the benefit of this provision, so far as it concerns Him, the former Sardar of Erivan, Houssein Khan, his brother Hassen Khan and Kerim Khan, the former Governor of Nakhitchevan.

ART. XIII. All prisoners of war made in one way or another, whether in the course of the last War, or before, as well as the subjects of the two Governments reciprocally fallen into captivity, at no matter what time, will be freed within a period of four months and, after having been provided with food and other necessary objects, they will be directed to Abbas Abad in order to be turned over there into the hands of Commissioners, respectively

---

1. On 24 November 1869, a decision of the Council of the Empire of Russia was published, prohibiting the establishment of companies for the navigation of the Caspian Sea, except by Russian subjects, and the purchase by foreigners of shares in such companies (Hertslet, *Treaties . . . between Great Britain and Persia*).

charged with receiving them and to decide upon their eventual return to their homes The High Contracting Parties will undertake the same in respect of all prisoners of War and all Russian and Persian subjects reciprocally fallen into captivity, who may not have been freed within the period above-mentioned, whether by reason of the isolated distance where they are to be found, or for any other cause or circumstance. The two Governments reserve expressly the unlimited right to reclaim them at no matter what time, and they obligate themselves to restore them mutually in the measure that they may present themselves for that purpose, or in the measure that they may reclaim them.

ART. XIV. The High Contracting Parties will not demand the extradition of fugitives and deserters who shall have passed under their respective jurisdiction before or during the war. At the same time, in order to prevent the mutually prejudicial consequences which might be able to result from the correspondence which some of these deserters may seek to hold with their former compatriots, or vassals, the Persian Government undertakes not to tolerate in its Possessions, situated between the Araxe and the line formed by the River known as Tohara, by Lake Urumiah, by the River called Djakatou and by the River known as Kizil-Ozane, to its descent into the Caspian Sea, the presence of individuals who will be designated now by name or who may be nominated to it in the future. His Majesty the Emperor of All the Russias promises equally on His side not to permit Persian deserters to establish themselves or to remain fixed in the Khanats of Karbag or of Nakhitchevan or in the part of the Khanat of Erivan situated on the right bank of the Araxe. It is, however, understood, that this clause is and will only be obligatory in respect of individuals possessing a public character of a certain dignity, such as the Khans, the Begs and the spiritual leaders or mullahs, whose personal example, intrigues and clandestine correspondence may be able to exercise a pernicious influence on their former compatriots, those formerly under their administration or their vassals. In so far as concerns the mass of the population in the two countries, it is agreed between the High Contracting Parties that the respective subjects who shall have passed or who may pass in the future from one State into the other, will be free to establish themselves or to sojourn wherever the Government under whose domination they will be placed will find it proper.

ART. XV. With the beneficent and salutary aim of restoring tranquility in his States and of removing from his subjects all that may aggravate the evils which have brought on them the war to which the present Treaty has put an end so happily, His Majesty the Shah accords a full and complete amnesty to all the inhabitants and functionaries of the province known as Azerbaijhan. No one of them, without exception of category, may be either pursued, nor molested for his opinions, for his acts or for the conduct which he may have pursued, either during the war or during the temporary occupation of the said province by Russian troops. There will be, moreover, accorded them a period of one year dating from this day in order to transport themselves freely with their families from Persian States into Russian States, to export and to sell their movable property, without the Governments or the local authorities being able to place the least obstacle in the way thereof, nor to deduct previously any tax or any recompense on the goods and objects sold or exported by them. As for their immovable property there will be accorded a term of five years to sell or to dispose thereof as may be desired. There are excepted from this amnesty those who may have rendered themselves culpable within the period of time above-mentioned of one year of some crime, or misdemeanor liable to penalties punished by the Courts.

ART. XVI. Immediately after the signature of the present Treaty of Peace, the respective plenipotentiaries will hasten to send the necessary notices and injunctions in all localities for the immediate cessation of hostilities.

2. The Commercial Treaty

ART. I. The two High Contracting Parties desiring to make their respective subjects enjoy all the advantages which result from a reciprocal liberty of commerce, have agreed upon the following:

Russian subjects provided with passports in proper order shall be able to engage in commerce throughout the whole extent of the Persian Kingdom, and to proceed equally in the neighboring States of the said Kingdom.

In reciprocity thereof Persian subjects shall be able to import their merchandise into Russia, either by the Caspian Sea or by the land frontier which separates Russia from Persia, to exchange it or to make purchases for exportation, and they will enjoy all the rights and prerogatives accorded in the States of His Imperial Majesty to the subjects of the most favored friendly Powers.

In case of the decease of a Russian subject in Persia, his movable and immovable property, as belonging to the subject of a friendly Power, will be turned over intact to his relatives or associates, who will have the right to dispose of the said property as they may judge fitting. In the absence of relatives or associates the disposition of the said property will be confided to the Mission or to the Consuls of Russia without any difficulty on the part of the Russian authorities.

ART. II. Contracts, bills of exchange, bonds and other written instruments between the respective subjects for their commercial affairs will be registered with the Russian Consul and with the Hakim (Civil Magistrate) and there, where there is no Consul, with the Hakim alone, so that in case of dispute between the two parties one can make the researches necessary in order to decide the difference in conformity with justice.

If one of the two parties without being provided with the documents drawn up and legalized as stated above, which will be valid before every court of justice, should desire to institute a suit against the other in producing only proofs of testimonials, such pretensions will not be admitted at all unless the defendant himself may recognize the legality thereof.

Every undertaking entered into between the respective subjects in the forms above prescribed will be religiously observed and the refusal to give satisfaction therein which may occasion losses to one of the parties will give place to a proportional indemnity of the part of the other. In case of bankruptcy of a Russian merchant in Persia, his creditors will be recompensed with the goods and effects of the bankrupt, but the Russian Minister, the Chargé

d'Affaires or the Consul shall not refuse if demanded their good offices to assure themselves whether the bankrupt has not left in Russia available properties which may serve to satisfy the same creditors.

The provisions drawn up in the present Article will be reciprocally observed in respect of Persian subjects who engage in commerce in Russia under the protection of its laws.

ART. III. With a view to assuring to the trade of the respective subjects the advantages which are the object of the previous stipulations, it is agreed that merchandise imported into Persia or exported from that Kingdom by Russian subjects and equally the products of Persia imported into Russia by Persian subjects, whether by the Caspian Sea or by the land frontier between the two States, as well as Russian merchandise which Persian subjects may export from the Empire by the same means, will be subject, as in the past, to a duty of five per cent, collected one time for all at entry or departure, and will not be subject thereafter to any other customs dues. If Russia may judge it necessary to draw up new customs regulations or new tariffs, it undertakes however not to increase even in this case the rate above-mentioned of five per cent.

ART. IV. If Russia or Persia find themselves at war with another Power it will not be forbidden to the respective subjects to cross with their merchandise the territory of the High Contracting Parties to proceed into the confines of the said Power.

ART. V. Seeing that after existing usages in Persia it is difficult for foreign subjects to find for rent houses, warehouses or premises suitable as deports for their merchandise, it is permitted to Russian subjects in Persia not only to rent but also to acquire in full ownership houses for habitation and shops as well as premises to store therein their merchandise.

The employees of the Persian Government shall not be able to enter by force in the said houses, shops or premises, at least without having recourse in case of necessity to the authorization of the Russian Minister, Chargé d'Affaires or Consul who will delegate an employee or dragoman to assist in the visit to the house or the merchandise.

ART. VI. At the same time the Minister

or the Chargé d'Affaires of His Imperial Majesty, the employees of the Russian Mission, Consuls and Dragomans, finding for sale in Persia neither the effects to serve for their clothing nor many objects of food which are necessary to them, shall be able to introduce free of tax and of dues, for their own account, all objects and effects which may be destined solely to their use.

The public servants of His Majesty the Shah residing in the States of the Russian Empire will enjoy perfect reciprocity in this regard.

Persian subjects forming part of the suite of the Minister or Chargé d'Affaires or Consuls, and necessary for their service, will enjoy, so long as they shall be attached to them, their protection on an equality with Russian subjects, but if it may happen that one amongst them renders himself culpable of some misdemeanor and that he makes himself liable thereby to punishment by the existing laws, in this case the Persian Minister or Hakim and, in his absence, the competent local authority, shall address himself immediately to the Russian Minister, Chargé d'Affaires or Consul, in the service of which the accused is to be found in order that he may be delivered to justice; and if this request is founded on proofs establishing the culpability of the accused, the Minister, Chargé d'Affaires or Consul will interpose no difficulty for the satisfaction thereof.

ART. VII. All suits and litigations between Russian subjects will be subject exclusively to the examination and decision of the Russian Mission or Consuls in conformity with the laws and customs of the Russian Empire; as well as the differences and suits occurring between Russian subjects and those of another Power where the parties shall consent thereto.

When differences or suits shall arise between Russian subjects and Persian subjects, the said suits or differences will be brought before the Hakim or Governor and will be examined and judged only in the presence of the Dragoman of the Mission or the Consulate.

Once juridically terminated, such suits may not be instituted a second time. If, however, the circumstances were of a nature to demand a second examination, it may not take place without notification to the Russian Minister, Chargé d'Affaires or Consul and in this case the affair will only be considered and judged at the Defter, that is to say, in the Supreme Chancellery of the Shah at Tabriz or at Teheran, likewise in the presence of a Dragoman of the Russian Mission or Consulate.

ART. VIII. In case of murder or other crime committed between Russian subjects the examination and the decision of the case will be the exclusive concern of the Russian Minister, Chargé d'Affaires or Consul by virtue of the jurisdiction over their nationals conferred upon them.

If a Russian subject is found implicated with individuals of another nation in a criminal suit be cannot be pursued nor harried in any manner without proofs of his participation in the crime, and in this case even as in that where a Russian subject may be accused of direct culpability, the courts of the country may only proceed to take cognizance and give judgment concerning the crime in the presence of a delegate of the Russian Mission or Consulate, and if they are not to be found at the place where the crime has been committed, the local authorities will transport the delinquent there where there is a constituted Russian Consul or Agent.

Testimonies for the prosecution and for the defense of the accused will be faithfully collected by the Hakim and by the Judge of the locality, and invested with their signature; transmitted in this form there where the crime has to be judged, these testimonies will become authentic documents or parts of the suit unless the accused proves clearly their falsity.

When the accused shall have been duly convicted and sentence shall have been pronounced, the delinquent will be turned over to the Minister, Chargé d'Affaires or Consul of His Imperial Majesty who will return him to Russia to receive there the punishment prescribed by the laws.

ART. IX. The High Contracting Parties will take care that the stipulations of the present Act may be strictly observed and fulfilled, and the Governors of their Provinces, Commandants and other respective authorities will not permit themselves in any case to violate them, under penalty of a grave responsibility and even of dismissal in case of complaint duly proven.

66. POLICY GUIDELINES ON CENTRAL ASIA: THE EAST INDIA COMPANY BOARD OF CONTROL TO GOVERNOR GENERAL IN COUNCIL
12 January 1830

[India Office Library, Board's Drafts of Secret Letters and Dispatches, 1st ser., vol. 7, no. 208]

British India pushed its northwest frontier from the Sutlej to the Indus in the second quarter of the nineteenth century, completing the last major conquest in the subcontinent. The Russian advance into Central Asia took place for the most part in the 1860s and 1870s. But British-Indian anxiety over Russian territorial ambitions in Central Asia developed early. "The Chairs [i.e., the East India Court of Directors] lend themselves most willingly," Lord Ellenborough, the president of the East India Company Board of Control and chairman of its Court of Directors, informed the duke of Wellington, then prime minister, "to the project of repelling the Russian commerce from Cabul and Bokhara, by carrying our goods directly up the Indus. . . . The Chairs enter thoroughly into your view of the nature of the danger to be apprehended from the advance of the Russians towards the frontier of India" (cited by Norris, *First Afghan War*, p. 37). Briefly, in the British Indian perspective, Afghanistan formed part of Central Asia, and, since policy on Afghanistan from the start of the nineteenth century through the end of World War I was framed for the most part either in the subcontinent or by its spokesman in Whitehall, it is essential to bear this perspective in mind in analyzing the unfolding British policies on Afghanistan. Although the following statement, which has been characterized as "the master plan," ties the fate of Afghanistan to Central Asia, the Russian pressures in the next three decades, as we shall see, came less from the north than from the west. Norris, op. cit., chap. 3; Yapp, *British Policy in Central Asia*; Fraser-Tytler, *Afghanistan*, pt. 2, chap. 4; Kaye, *History of the War in Afghanistan*, bk. 1, chaps. 7–8, and bk. 2, chaps. 1–3.

1. We refer you to our letter dated the 19th December 1829 in which we directed you to instruct your Envoy in Persia to obtain information for you on the several Points upon which H.M.'s Ambassador at St. Petersburgh had been instructed to obtain it for H.M.'s Government.

2. We now direct you to adopt measures for obtaining information upon the several points therein specified through such other Channels as may seem to you best calculated to afford it.

3. In our opinion such information will be best obtained through native merchants trading between India and the several Countries beyond the Indus and the Hindoo-Coosh; but if on deliberate reflection, you should think that it would be adviseable for the purpose of obtaining the information we require, or for the other purposes to which we shall presently advert, to send a Diplomatick Mission to Bochara, or to send any European in the character of a merchant to that Country, you will do so.

4. We wish you however before you adopt either of these measures to consider well whether the first may not be misinterpreted as the mark of ambitious designs, or injuriously represented as proceeding from unjustified & excessive apprehension of the designs of other Powers.

5. In adopting the second measure every precaution must be taken to protect the Person of the European you may send, without giving reason for suspicion that he bears any character but that of a Private Merchant.

6. When we advert to the Policy which

has for many years marked the Counsels of Russia, and to the open indication of her views in the Missions to Chiva and Bochara —when we further consider the actual condition of those States, and the nature of the Country between the last Russian Post on the side of the Sir Deria and the mountains which separate Cabul from Central Asia— we can neither feel justified in reposing upon the good faith and moderation of Russia, nor in permitting the apprehensions her Policy and her Power are calculated to excite to be altogether done away by reflection upon the difficulties she would have to encounter in the attempt to approach the Indus.

7. We know that these difficulties would be great—we believe that a Russian army, recruited as it might be in the Countries through which it passed, would yet arrive in Cabul diminished in real force, and in a very defective state of equipment—We trust that the Military means at our disposal would enable us to destroy any such army before it could reach our own Provinces.

8. We dread therefore not so much actual Invasion by Russia, as the moral effect which would be produced amongst our own Subjects in India and amongst the Princes with whom we are allied by the continued apprehension of that event—We look with dismay on the financial embarrassments in which we should be involved by the necessity of constant military preparation, not only to meet an European Army in the field but to preserve tranquillity in our own Provinces and in our Tributary Stales.

9. If such would be the consequences of any approximation of the Russians to the North of India, it is our interest to take measures for the prevention of any movement on their part beyond their present limits—But the efficacy of such measures must depend upon their being taken promptly, and you cannot take them promptly unless you are kept constantly informed of every thing which passes on the Russian frontier in Asia, in Chiva and in Bochara.

10. It must be borne in mind that Russia, even without any intention of engaging in an expensive and hopeless invasion of India, may yet be desirous of taking up such a position in Central Asia, by reducing either Chiva or Bochara under her rule, as would place her Army within a single campaign of Cabul, and thus not only occasion so large an Expenditure on our part as would be ruinous to our Finances in India, but operate in a material degree as a Check upon the free course of our Policy in Europe.

11. It is therefore not only as an Asiatick but as an European Power that England is interested in preventing the further extension of the Russian Empire in Asia. Russia may desire the possession of Chiva or of Bochara for purposes purely Commercial; but no Commercial benefits which would result to her from their occupation would be sufficient to cover the expense their conquest and occupation would cause.

12. Be her object however what it may, we must look only to the effect her advance would produce upon our interests—We must consider that advance to indicate the hostile designs which it would afford the means of conducting, and against that advance we must adopt the measures of counteraction dictated to us by a view of our own interests, and by a regard for our own safety as an Asiatick Power.

13. In the adoption however of such measures of counteraction you will confine yourselves to the employment of your Pecuniary means in such manner as may seem best calculated to raise up obstacles to the views of Russia and to impede her advance; you will employ those means with caution but without parsimony when their employment shall become necessary.

14. You will not undertake any military movement, or enter into any Treaty by which you would be bound to afford military aid without previous authority from us—and while you take such measures for your own future safety as a commanding necessity may require, you will be careful not to adopt a line of conduct which might needlessly lead to collision in Europe.

15. It cannot however be doubted that H.M.'s Government will watch over the interests of British India, and make any movement of the Russians in Asia, which could originate only in hostile intentions against our Asiatick dominions the subject of their serious and effective intervention.

16. In considering the means which Russia has at her disposal for the establishment

of a preponderating influence in Central Asia we cannot be insensible to the advantage she derives from her commercial intercourse with Bochara; nor can we on considering our own position despair of being able to substitute our own influence for hers in as far as that influence may be connected with Commerce.

17. As long as our manufactures are conveyed to the North Western Provinces of India by the long and tedious navigation of the Ganges and then through the Punjab and Cabul to Bochara, we may doubt whether manufactures of a similar description, and even our own, may not be conveyed at a less cost by the Caravans which pass from Orenberg to Bochara; but if the produce of England and of India could be sent at once up the Indus to such points as might be most convenient for their transport to Cabul we cannot but entertain the hope that we might succeed in underselling the Russians and in obtaining for ourselves a large portion at least of the internal Trade of Central Asia.

18. This is a subject to which we wish you to direct your attention with a view to the Political effects which would be the result of success.

19. If you should upon consideration determine upon the experiment, we desire that you will take care to give it a purely Commercial character, and avoid doing anything which can excite the apprehensions of the Ameers of Sinde or of Runjeet Singh, and induce them to believe that Commerce is intended to be the precursor of Conquest.

20. Our first object being to introduce English goods and not Englishmen into Cabul and Central Asia, and our desire being to effect this object silently, you will consider whether, with a view to the effect of the enterprize upon your Political relations it may not be advisable that it should in the first instance at least be conducted in the name and apparently on the account of some native Mercantile House connected with such Trade as is now carried on with the Countries on the right bank of the Indus.

21. With a view to your information upon the Trade of Bochara we send you the work of the Baron de Meyendorf who accompanied the Russian Mission to that Country in 1820.

22. You have other and later information with respect to that State in your own Records.

23. We are informed that it is the intention of H.M.'s Government to send very shortly a Present to Runjeet Singh in H.M.'s name in return for Presents transmitted by him to His Majesty.

24. At the suggestion of Lord Amherst the present to Runjeet Sing[h] will consist of Dray horses, which will be sent to Bombay.

25. We are desirous that this opportunity should be taken of navigating the Indus as far as Lahore.

26. The Horses will thus be sent to Runjeet Singh in the only manner by which they can reach the Punjab in safety; and you will assign this reason for the adoption of that mode and line of conveyance.

27. You will send an Envoy to Runjeet Singh to apprize him of the intended measure, and to make previous arrangements with him for the secure passage of the vessel through his Dominions.

28. You will select for this purpose an able and discreet officer who may take advantage of his visit to Lahore to acquire a knowledge of the present state of the Sikh dominions and Army, and to obtain all such information as may enable you to form a Judgement of the probable consequences of Runjeet Singh's decease.

29. Your Envoy will represent the British Government as more than satisfied with the extent of Dominion they possess, as secure in the confidence of their own invincible strength, and as having now no object but that of improving their own Territories and of preserving peace with and amongst all their neighbours.

30. He will express the satisfaction with which they regard the friendship which has for so many years subsisted between them and Runjeet Singh, and his own confidence that relations so manifestly in accordance with the mutual interests of both Powers will ever continue.

31. He will put forth these sentiments and opinions as his own—he will say that he knows they are yours—but he will not give it to be understood that he states them as yours by your direction.

32. He will assume no ostensible character but that of an Agent deputed solely for the purpose of arranging the safe passage of the Horses and of presenting them to Runjeet Singh.

33. He will take occasion from the circumstance of their transmission from England by water to Lahore, to observe as if from himself, upon the great advantage of the position of the Punjab, traversed by so many fine rivers all terminating in the Indus and giving an easy communication with the Sea to every part of the Country.

34. He will not at one formal interview but as opportunities may offer in the more familiar intercourse he will endeavour to establish try to lead the mind of Runjeet Singh to consider how much wealth would flow into his Country if the Commerce were established which once existed on the Indus and its tributary streams, and if by the renovation of the Canals which in distant times joined the Sutledge to the Jumna, the Gulf of Persia were united by internal navigation with the Bay of Bengal, and both Seas made accessible to the Sikhs. We cannot but think that Runjeet Singh is too enlightened not to see the benefits which would result to him from the realization of such Projects and not to assist in their accomplishment.

35. The Report of your Envoy will enable you to judge how far it may be expedient at the present moment to give him authority to enter into a negociation with Runjeet Singh for securing to us the free navigation of the Rivers which traverse or bound his dominions, and at the same time to propose to him stipulations of mutual Support in the event of any obstacle being raised by the Ameers of Sinde to the free navigation of the Indus where it passes through their Territory.

36. It will be necessary to make some notification to the Ameers of Sinde of your intention to send Presents to Runjeet Singh by the Indus, and to take some steps for the Security of the vessel in traversing their Territory.

37. Whether any Envoy should be sent to Hyderabad for this purpose, or your intention communicated in some less formal manner we must leave to your discretion.

38. We are far from desirous of having any collision with the people of Sinde, but we cannot permit any jealous feeling on their parts to close the navigation of the Indus, should it appear to offer results not only Commercially but Politically important which but for them would be attained.

39. It will be for your consideration whether it may not be expedient to send the Horses up the Indus in a Steam vessel.

40. Whatever vessel or vessels may be employed you should take measures for their entire security. They should be so well armed and manned as not to invite and to be able to resist attack.

41. Should any Commercial experiment be made at the same time, you may be able, without giving the appearance of any connection between that Experiment and the transmission of the Presents, to afford the protection of Convoy to a considerable distance.

42. You will feel that we desire ultimate Success, not to make a hurried and premature venture.

43. You will therefore carefully advert to every circumstance which may affect the final Success of the measures we have indicated, and while you do nothing rashly, still wish something for the attainment of a great object.

44. We shall transmit a Copy of this Dispatch to the Governor in Council at Bombay for his information.

67. THE FRENCH CONQUEST OF ALGIERS
12 March–5 July 1830

[Instructions from the French premier and foreign minister to the French ambassador in London, in English translation, from Lord, *England and France in the Mediterranean*, pp. 108–12; convention for the delivery of the cities and the forts, translated from the French text in Clercq, *Recueil des traités*, 3: 577–78]

The efforts of Charles X (1824–30) to restore government on the model of the *ancien régime* created a domestic crisis in France from which the king's principal advisers, notably his premier and foreign minister starting in August 1829, Prince Jules Armand de Polignac, sought to distract the opposition by a foreign adventure. In opting for the conquest of the Algerine Garrison, de Polignac won the support of those politicians and military officers who saw a strategic advantage for France in a North African possession and of those merchants—primarily in Marseilles, the traditional center of French commerce in the Mediterranean—who saw an opportunity for procuring a new protected market. This explained the studied overreaction of the French government, beginning with the Fly-Whisk Incident of April 1827 (Doc. 64). Hüseyin Paşa, the dey of Algiers, encouraged by the British consul, reacted with characteristic obstinacy. The three-year French blockade affected life in Algiers only marginally. Hüseyin Paşa rejected out of hand French tactics aimed at extracting a public apology or compelling him to settle the differences with France under duress. The latter effort, made on 2 August 1829 by the commander of the blockading fleet on instructions from Paris, gave rise to a fresh incident, when Algerine batteries fired on the French flagship on orders from the *wakil al-kharj*, or naval chief. In this instance, Hüseyin Paşa did apologize for an act that was not of his making. It was at that juncture that de Polignac was recalled from London, where he had been ambassador for six years, to organize a new government. With the full support of Russia and Prussia and the neutrality of Austria, de Polignac took up with vigor the plans for the conquest of the Algerine garrison. To escape the wrathful opposition of Britain, which was alert to the adverse changes in the Mediterranean military balance that would clearly occur if a European power should anchor itself on the North African coast, de Polignac at first supported a scheme that called for the annexation of the three Barbary Garrisons by Mehmed 'Ali, the paşa of Egypt, with French economic and military grants-in-aid, on the assumption that a grateful paşa would then ally himself with France. But the haggling over the price of the venture discouraged the de Polignac government, which finally decided to do the annexing itself. On 7 February 1830, Charles X ordered the mobilization of the armed forces and the creation of an expeditionary force at Toulon. By 25 May the 37,000 officers and men with supplies and munitions were loaded on some 572 vessels plus a convoying fleet of 96 sail- and 7 steamboats to cross the Mediterranean. The troops landed at Cape Sidi Ferruch (twelve miles west of Algiers) on 14 June and, after overcoming the resistance of the dey's forces by the end of June, reached the outskirts of Algiers. It was the assault on the Sultan's Castle, which the French later called the Emperor's Fort, on 4 July that forced Hüseyin's capitulation. The original French texts of de Polignac's letters of 12 March and 12 May, which appear below, may be found in *British and Foreign State Papers* (19: 943–44, 957–58). The terms of the convention of 5 July were dictated by the triumphant commander, Lieutenant-General Count Louis de Bourmont. For references see Doc. 64; also Esquer, *Les commencements d'un empire*; d'Ault-Dumesnil, *Relation de l'expédition d'Afrique*; Berthezène, *Dix-huit mois à Alger*; Swain, "Occupation of Algiers in 1830," and *Struggle for the Control of the Mediterranean*, chap. 5.

1. Prince de Polignac, Premier and Foreign Minister, to the Duc de Laval, French Ambassador (London), 12 March 1830

When we communicated to our allies the destination of the armaments now preparing in the forts of France, we spoke of the results to which they might lead, with a reserve which appeared to us to be called for by the uncertainty of the chances of war. Many Cabinets having since invited us to declare to them, in a more precise manner, the object which we propose to attain by our expedition against the Regency of Algiers, His Majesty is pleased to comply with this desire, so far as depends upon him; and he authorizes me to give to the several Cabinets the following explanations; you may address them, M. le Duc, to the Government of His Britannic Majesty.

The public insult offered by the Dey to our Consul was the immediate cause of a rupture, which was moreover but too well justified by numerous infractions of treaties, by the violation of rights which a possession of many ages' duration had consecrated, and by the injury done to interests of very high value and importance.

To obtain satisfaction for the insults offered to one of his agents, suitable reparation for the injuries experienced by France, and the performance of the engagements which the Dey refused to fulfil—such was at first the object which the king proposed to attain.

Events have subsequently given a more extended development to the projects of His Majesty.

The Dey has ruined and utterly destroyed all our establishments on the coast of Africa; a three years' blockade has only increased his insolence, and instead of the reparation due to us, he has spoken only of claims and pretensions which he himself reckoned upon making good against France. In short, he has replied to the pacific propositions, which one of the commanders of our navy was sent to convey to him, even in his own palace, by an absolute refusal; and at the moment when the vessel employed for the negotiation, and carrying a flag of truce, was preparing to leave the port, it was suddenly attacked by the fire of all the nearest batteries, upon a signal given from the very castle which was occupied by the Chief of the Regency.

The king, M. le Duc, has therefore been compelled to acknowledge that no arrangement could be practicable with the Dey, and that even if it should be possible to induce him to conclude any treaty whatsoever, the previous conduct of the Regency, compared with more recent events, left no security that such an arrangement would be better observed than our conventions, so often renewed and so often violated by the Algerine Government.

These considerations have convinced us of the necessity of giving a more extended development to the war. From that period also it became incumbent upon us to consider how to give to this war an object, the importance of which would correspond with the extent of the sacrifice which it would impose upon us; and the king, no longer confining his projects to obtaining reparation for the particular wrongs of France, determined to turn to the advantage of all Christendom the expedition for which he was ordering the preparations to be made, and His Majesty adopted as the object and recompense of his efforts—

The complete destruction of piracy.

The total abolition of Christian slavery.

The suppression of the tribute which Christian Powers pay to the Regency.

Such, if Providence assist the arms of the king, will be the result of the enterprise for which preparations are now making in the ports of France. His Majesty is determined to prosecute it by the employment of all the means which may be necessary to secure its success; and if, in the struggle which is about to take place, it should happen that the existing Government at Algiers should ever be dissolved, in that case, Monsieur le Duc, the king, whose views upon this important question are perfectly disinterested, will concert with his allies for the purpose of deciding what shall be the new order of things which may be substituted, with the greatest benefit to Christendom, for the system which has been destroyed, and which may be best calculated to secure the triple object which His Majesty proposes to attain.

You may convey these communications, M. le Duc, to the knowledge of the Government of His Britannic Majesty; and if Lord Aberdeen wishes to have a copy of the present despatch, the king authorizes you to give it to him.

2. Prince de Polignac to the Duc de Laval, 12 May 1830

At the moment when the fleet which conveys our army to Africa is leaving France, the king feels the necessity of making known to his allies how sensible he has been of the marks of interest and friendship which he has received from them during the important conjuncture of circumstances which preceded the departure of the expedition against Algiers. His Majesty has applied for their concurrence with perfect confidence; he has treated, it may be said, publicly a question which he has thought fit to make common to all Europe; his allies have responded to his confidence, and they have afforded him sanction and encouragement, the remembrance of which will never be effaced from his mind.

To make a return for conduct so loyal and friendly, His Majesty is now desirous of laying before them again, at the moment of the departure of the French fleet, the object and aim of the expedition which he is sending against the Regency of Algiers.

Two interests, which by their nature are distinct, but which are closely connected in the mind of the king, have led to the armaments which have been prepared in our ports. The one more especially concerns France; it is to vindicate the honour of our flag, to obtain redress of the wrongs which have been the immediate cause of our hostilities, to preserve our possessions from the aggressions and acts of violence to which they have been so often subjected, and to obtain for us a pecuniary indemnity which may relieve us, so far as the State of Algiers will allow, from the expense of a war which we have not provoked; the other, which regards Christendom in general, embraces the abolition of slavery, of piracy, and of the tribute which Europe still pays to the Regency of Algiers.

The king is finally resolved not to lay down his arms, or to recall his troops from Algiers, until this double object shall have been obtained and sufficiently secured; and it is with the view of coming to an understanding as to the means of arriving at this end, so far as regards the general interests of Europe, that His Majesty on the 12th of March last announced to his allies his desire to take measures in concert with them, in the event of the dissolution of the Government actually existing at Algiers, in the struggle which is about to take place. It would be the object of this concert to discuss the new order of things which it might be expedient to establish in that country for the greater benefit of Christendom. His Majesty thinks it right at once to assure his allies that he would enter into those deliberations prepared to afford all the explanations which they might still desire— disposed to take into consideration the rights and interests of all parties, himself unfettered by any previous engagements— at liberty to accept any proposition which might be considered proper for the attainment of the object in question, and free from any feeling of personal interest; and as the state of things foreseen by His Majesty may very shortly be realized, if Providence deigns to protect our arms, the king now invites his allies to furnish their Ambassadors at Paris with contingent instructions on this subject.

You will have the goodness, M. le Duc, to make this proposition to Lord Aberdeen; and if that Minister wishes it, you will give him a copy of this despatch.

3. Convention for the Delivery of the Cities and the Forts: France and the Dey of Algiers, 5 July 1830

The fort of the Qasbah [Citadel], all the other forts that depend on Algiers, and the port of that city will be delivered to the French troops this morning at 10 o'clock (French time).

The General in Chief of the French Army undertakes to grant His Highness the Dey of Algiers the freedom and possession of that which belongs to him personally.

The Dey will be free to retire with his family and with whatever belongs to him to the place that he may fix; and, as long as he remains in Algiers, he and his entire family will enjoy the protection of the General in Chief of the French Army. A guard will guarantee the security of his person and that of his family.

The General in Chief assures all [the Dey's] militia the same advantages and the same protection.

The practice of the Muhammadan religion will remain free. The freedom of the inhabitants of every class, their religion, their properties, their commerce, and their industry, will suffer no damage; the General in Chief pledges on his honor that their women will be respected.

The exchange of this Convention will take place before 10 o'clock this morning, and the French troops will enter, as soon as possible thereafter, the Qasbah and successively all the other wharves of the city and of the naval administration.

68. TREATY OF COMMERCE AND NAVIGATION: THE UNITED STATES AND THE OTTOMAN EMPIRE
7 May 1830

(Ratifications exchanged, Istanbul, 5 October 1831)

[United States, *Treaty Series*, no. 267; the unratified separate and secret article was translated from the Turkish original in 1931 by J. H. Kramers and printed in Miller, *Treaties and Other International Acts*, 3: 580–81]

Capitulatory rights of American nationals in the Ottoman Empire derived from the treaty of 1830, which was framed in the Turkish language with an official and agreed French version. The United States later abandoned the French text and relied wholly upon the Turkish. Differences over the meaning of article 4, arising from English translations persisted until 1917 and strained American-Ottoman relations, particularly after the 1880's. The two governments concluded a commercial convention on 25 February 1862 (United States, *Treaty Series*, no. 268), modeled on the British-Ottoman agreement of 1861. But the Sublime Porte in 1884 repudiated the convention with the United States, which thereafter based its claims to most-favored-nation treatment on the 1830 instrument. The separate article, the first proposed secret arrangement presented by an American president to the Senate, attested to the anxiety of the Ottoman government over its naval losses in the war for Greek independence (1821–30). As one of the American negotiators commented when the treaty was sent to Washington, "It was necessary to shew The Sultan that *something* had been granted for the concessions he had made." The secret article, he went on, "is a *perfect nullity*, giving only the privilege of *consulting* with our Minister about the best mode of making a Contract to procure Ships or Ship Timber and moreover The Reis Effendi [Foreign Minister] said that if The President was not disposed to sign the article, it would be of no consequence, and the Treaty would be ratified without it," (as cited in Miller, *Treaties and Other International Acts*, 3: 575). Ibid., pp. 541–98 (which contains on pp. 551–57 Kramers's 1931 translation of the full text of the treaty); Paullin, *Diplomatic Negotiations of American Naval Officers*, chap. 5; Gordon, *American Relations with Turkey*, chaps. 2, 12; P. Brown, *Foreigners in Turkey*; Hurewitz, *Middle East Dilemmas*, chap. 5; Van Dyck, *Report on the Capitulations*; Ravndal, *Origin of the Capitulations*.

ART. I. Merchants of the Sublime Porte, whether Mussulmans or Rayahs' going and coming, in the countries, provinces, and ports, of the United States of America, or proceeding from one port to another, or from the ports of the United States to those of other countries, shall pay the same duties and other imposts that are paid by the most favored nations; and they shall not be vexed by the exaction of higher duties; and in travelling by sea and by land, all the privileges and distinctions observed towards the subjects of other Powers, shall serve as a rule, and shall be observed towards the merchants and subjects of the Sublime Porte. In like manner, American merchants who shall come to the well defended countries and ports of the Sublime Porte, shall pay the same duties and other imposts, that are paid by merchants of the most favored friendly Powers, and they shall not, in any way, be vexed or molested. On both sides, travelling passports shall be granted.

ART. II. The Sublime Porte may establish *Shahbenders* (Consuls) in the United States of America; and the United States may appoint their citizens to be Consuls or Vice Consuls, at the commercial places in the dominions of the Sublime Porte, where it shall be found needful to superintend the affairs of commerce. These Consuls or Vice Consuls shall be furnished with *Berats* or *Firmans*; they shall enjoy suitable distinction, and shall have necessary aid and protection.

ART. III. American merchants established in the well defended States of the Sublime Porte, for purposes of commerce, shall have liberty to employ *Semsars*, (brokers) of any nation or religion, in like manner as merchants of other friendly Powers; and they shall not be disturbed in their affairs, nor shall they be treated, in any way, contrary to established usages. American vessels arriving at, or departing from, the ports of the Ottoman Empire, shall not be subjected to greater visit, by the officers of the Customhouse and the Chancery of the Port, than vessels of the most favored nations.

ART. IV. If litigations and disputes should arise between subjects of the Sublime Porte and citizens of the United States, the parties shall not be heard, nor shall judgment be pronounced unless the American Dragoman be present. Causes in which the sum may exceed five hundred piastres, shall be submitted to the Sublime Porte, to be decided according to the laws of equity and justice. Citizens of the United States of America, quietly purusing their commerce, and not being charged or convicted of any crime or offense, shall not be molested; and even when they may have committed some offence they shall not be arrested and put in prison, by the local authorities, but they shall be tried by their Minister of Consul, and punished according to their offence, following, in this respect, the usage observed towards other Franks.

ART. V. American merchant vessels that trade to the dominions of the Sublime Porte, may go and come in perfect safety with their own flag; but they shall not take the flag of any other Power, nor shall they grant their flag to the vessels of other Nations and Powers, nor to the vessels of rayahs. The Minister, Consuls, and Vice Consuls of the United States, shall not protect, secretly or publicly, the rayahs of the Sublime Porte, and they shall never suffer a departure from the principles here laid down and agreed to by mutual consent.

ART. VI. Vessels of war of the two Contracting Parties, shall observe towards each other, demonstrations of friendship and good intelligence, according to naval usage; and towards merchant vessels they shall exhibit the same kind and courteous manner.

ART. VII. Merchant vessels of the United States, in like manner as vessels of the most favored nations, shall have liberty to pass the Canal of the Imperial Residence, and go and come in the Black Sea, either laden or in ballast; and they may be laden with the produce, manufactures and effects of the Ottoman Empire, excepting such as are prohibited, as well as of their own country.

ART. VIII. Merchant vessels of the two Contracting Parties shall not be forcibly taken, for the shipment of troops, munitions and other objects of war, if the captains or proprietors of the vessels, shall be unwilling to freight them.

ART. IX. If any merchant vessel of either of the Contracting Parties, should be wrecked, assistance and protection shall be afforded to those of the crew that may be saved; and the merchandise and effects, which it may be possible to save and recover, shall be conveyed to the Consul, nearest to the place of the wreck, to be, by him, delivered to the proprietors.

Separate and Secret Article

The reason of the writing of this document and the motive of the drawing up of this writ are as follows:

As there has not been concluded heretofore any kind of official treaty between the everlasting Sublime Government and the Government of the United States of America, now, as we, the undersigned functionary occupying the elevated degree of Chief of the Secretaries of the ever-stable Sublime Government and of the exalted Sultanate, eternally enduring, have been authorized by the Most Noble Imperial Excellency, there have been negotiations between us and our friend Charles Rhind, who has been charged and commissioned with complete authority by the aforesaid Government, separately by coming to the Gate of Felicity and jointly with the functionaries named Commodore Biddle and David Offley, now being in the town of Smyrna.

The documents containing the treaty articles that have been drawn up and established as a result of these negotiations, have been exchanged and will be under signed hereafter by the two aforesaid functionaries.

Now that in this way a new treaty and an increased friendship and amity have been established between the two Governments, in observance of the principles of mutual profit and common interest and with regard to the fact that in the state of America timber is abundant and strong and that the building expense are there light and small, the aforesaid functionary, our friend, in confirmation of the sincere feelings of the said Government towards the glorious Imperial Sultanate, has contracted the obligation that, whenever the Sublime Government shall order the building and construction in the dominion of America of whatever quantity of war vessels, such as two-deckers, frigates, corvettes, and brigs, this shall be communicated and notified by the office of the Chief (of the Secretaries) to the functionary of the said Government who will be at that time at the Gate of Felicity; that there shall be drawn up a contractual document stating in which way it has been negotiated and agreed upon with regard to the building expenses, the time of construction, and also to the mode of sending and conveying to the Gate of Felicity, according to which contract the required ships shall be built and constructed after the design and model to be fixed and explained by the Imperial Arsenal, so as to be as strong and tight as the Government ships of the said Government, and provided that the building expenses be not higher than the expenses of the war ships of the said Government; and that, in case of an order being given, and so as to prevent the required ships from arriving empty at the Imperial Arsenal, there shall be negotiations between the functionaries of both parties, according to which there shall be laden and sent in each ship the timber necessary for the construction of another ship like that ship itself, provided that the price be in accordance with the official price of the said Government and that the material be calculated carefully and prepared in its place, after having been cut and well executed according to the measure.

This separate article, after having been signed by the two aforesaid functionaries, is destined to be a secret article and to be counted as a part of the mentioned treaty. By the exchange of the ratifications within ten months after the day of this document, it shall be observed in every way.

69. TREATY OF NAVIGATION AND COMMERCE:
FRANCE AND THE REGENCY OF TUNIS
8 August 1830

[Translated from the French text in Clercq, *Recueil des traités*, 3: 578–80]

In less than a half-dozen years, the Regency of Tunis had lost its quality as a Barbary Garrison, as becomes clear from a comparison of the 1824 French treaty renewing capitulations (Doc. 62) with the 1830 instrument, reproduced below. In the two treaties France invoked its capitulations in the Ottoman Empire as binding on Tunis, a practice soon abandoned as French expansionists looked covetously eastward over their Algerian shoulder. For references, see Doc. 62.

. . . ART. 1. The Bey of Tunis renounces entirely and forever, for himself and his successors, the right to conduct or authorize privateering, in time of war, against the vessels of powers which may deem it appropriate to renounce the same right toward Tunisian commercial vessels.

When the Regency is at war with a power which has communicated that such is its intention, the merchantmen of the two nations may sail freely without being harassed by enemy warships, so long as they do not wish to penetrate a blockaded port or do not carry soldiers or contraband war goods; in these two cases, they may be seized, but their confiscation may be decided only by a legal judgment. With these exceptional cases, any Tunisian warship which should stop a merchantship, being considered by this deed alone to have placed itself beyond the orders and authority of the Bey, should be treated as a pirate by any other power and by the Regency of Tunis.

ART. 2. The Bey abolishes forever in his states the enslavement of Christians. All existing Christian slaves shall be freed, and the Bey undertakes to reimburse the owners. If, in the future, the Bey should be at war with another state, the soldiers, merchants, transients, or any other subjects whatever of this state who may fall under his power shall be treated as prisoners of war, after the manner of European nations.

ART. 3. Any foreign ship which might be stranded on the coasts of the Regency shall receive, as far as possible, the assistance, help, and provisions which it may need.

The Bey shall take the most prompt and severe measures to assure the safety of the passengers and crew of this ship and respect for the property it carries. If any proved murders of passengers or crew were committed, the guilty should be pursued and punished as murderers, according to the justice of the land. Moreover, the Bey should pay to the Consul of the nation to which the victim belonged a sum equal to the value of the ship's cargo. If several proved murders were committed, the Bey should pay a sum equal to twice the value of the cargo, and in the case of the murder of individuals of different nations, the Bey shall divide between the Consuls of these nations, and in proportion to the persons assassinated, the sum which he would have paid, in such a way that this sum might be transmitted directly to the families of those who perished. If the property and the merchandise carried by the wrecked vessels should be looted, the deed having been ascertained, the Bey shall repay the price to the Consul of the nation to which the ship belongs, independently of what he must pay for the murders of crew or passengers of the said ship.

ART. 4. Henceforth, foreign powers may establish Consuls and commercial agents wherever they may wish in the Regency, without having to give any present to local authorities. In general, all tribute, presents, donations, and other rents which the governments or their agents paid in the Regency of Tunis under whatever title, circumstance, or name, especially at the conclusion of a treaty, or at the installation of a consular agent, are considered abolished and may neither be demanded nor reestablished in the future.

ART. 5. The Bey of Tunis returns to France the exclusive right to coral fishing, from the boundary of French possessions to the Nègre Promontory, such as it possessed before the war of 1796. France shall pay no rent for the enjoyment of this right. The ancient properties, edifices, buildings, and different constructions of the Island of Tabarca, shall also be returned [to France].

ART. 6. Foreign subjects may freely traffic with Tunisian subjects, making use of the established rights. They may buy and sell, without hindrance, goods coming from their respective countries, and the Tunisian Government may not claim [such goods] for its own account, or make a monopoly of them. France does not claim for itself any new commercial advantage. However, the Bey undertakes, for the present and the future, to see that [France] shares all the advantages, favors, facilities, and privileges which have been or may be granted, no matter in what title, to a foreign nation. France shall acquire these advantages by the simple claim of its Consul.

ART. 7. The capitulations concluded between France and the [Sublime] Porte, as well as ancient treaties and conventions between France and the Regency of Tunis, and especially the treaty of 15 November 1824, shall be confirmed and shall continue to be observed with all their provisions from which the present act should not depart.

ART. 8. The present treaty will be published immediately in the town of Tunis and, within one month, in all the provinces and towns of the Regency, according to the formula and usages adopted in the country. . . .

70. CONVENTION PLACING THE BEYLIK OF CONSTANTINE UNDER TUNISIAN RULE AND FRENCH SOVEREIGNTY
18 December 1830

[Translated from the French text in Rouard de Card, *Traités de la France*, pp. 217–18]

France mounted the Algerine campaign, as one French authority on North Africa put it, "without idea of conquest, without plan of organization in case of victory, without knowledge, except superficial, of the country" (Le Tourneau, *L'évolution politique de l'Afrique du Nord musulmane*, p. 302). To make matters worse, less than a month after Hüseyin Paşa, the Algerine dey, capitulated, the conservative Charles X was forced to abdicate, and the liberal upper bourgeoisie and journalists who staged the July revolution placed the duc of Orleans on the throne, as King Louis Philippe (1830–48). Understandably, the July Monarchy was preoccupied in the initial months with establishing its authority at home, paying no more than incidental attention to cross-Mediterranean developments. Without firm political guidance from Paris, the commanders in the field simply improvised. Possession of the town of Algiers and its immediate coastal neighborhood, which was all that France acquired on 5 July 1830 (see Doc. 67), freed the beys of Oran, Constantine, and Titteri to govern their provinces autonomously. Lieutenant-General Count Bernard Clauzel, Bourmont's successor as of 2 September 1830, widened the French coastal position by capturing Oran in the west and Bône in the east and by making unsuccessful probes into the interior. In doing so, he virtually destroyed the provincial administration, thereby creating a political vacuum, which without carefully executed plans the French could not themselves fill. In consultation with the French consul in Tunis, Mathieu de Lesseps, Clauzel framed a scheme for indirect French rule by inviting Husayn bin Mahmud, the bey of Tunis (1824–35) to nominate relatives as Algerine beys to govern the provinces as French vassals. With this in mind, Clauzel concluded on 18 December 1830 the following convention with Sidi Mustafa, the brother of the Tunisian ruler, and on 6 February 1831 he negotiated a similar instrument with Sidi Ahmad, Mustafa's son, recognizing him as the bey of Oran. The French commander in Algiers had failed to notify the metropole in advance on the ground, as he later explained, that such conventions were simply internal administrative arrangements. The foreign minister, General Horace Sébastiani, persuaded the king not to ratify either convention. Even if ratified, the arrangements could not have been put into operation, since the Tunisians proved incapable of establishing their authority in the two Algerine beyliks. Julien, *Histoire de l'Algérie contemporaine*, chap. 2; Clauzel, *Observations du général Clauzel*, and *Rapport du maréchal Clazuel*; Azan, *L'expédition d'Alger*.

. . . ART. 1. The General in Chief, in virtue of his stated powers, having named as Bey of Constantine Sidi Mustafa, designated by His Highness the Bey of Tunis, his brother; and His said Highness Sidi Mustafa, the Bey-designate, Guard of the Seals and Minister, having been authorized by the full powers already cited to guarantee in the name of His Highness [the Bey of Tunis] and of the Bey-designate the conditions already agreed between the Contracting Parties and in the same way their execution, it has been agreed to draft these conditions by means of the present act; which, written in the two languages, [French and Arabic], will be signed by the two Parties in their respective qualities indicated in the preamble.

These conditions are the following:

1. His Highness the Bey of Tunis guarantees and personally obligates the payment at Tunis of the tax of 800,000 francs for the province of Constantine for the year 1831. The first payment, consisting of one-fourth of the tax, will be made next July and the others at successive times in such a way that the entire sum will be paid before the end of December 1831; and for the regularity of the accounts, Sidi Mustafa, Guard of the Seals, one of the Contracting Parties, agrees in the name of the Bey of Tunis to make four payments of 200,000 francs each for the benefit of the French treasury at Algiers.

2. The payments of the following years, also quarterly, will amount to 1,000,000 francs, divided into quarter payments, without prejudice to later arrangements that might be made after the province of Constantine has been pacified.

3. Asylum will be given, without cost, by the Government of Tunis, in the island of Tabarka, to French coral and other fishing boats.

4. In the ports of Bône, Stora, Bougie, and others in the province of Constantine, the French will pay only half the customs duties imposed on other nations.

5. All revenues of the province of Constantine, of whatever nature, will be collected by the Bey.

6. Every protection will be given to Frenchmen and other Europeans who may become domiciled in the province of Constantine as merchants or farmers.

7. No French garrison will be deployed in the ports or towns of the Beylik until the province has been entirely subjugated; and, in any case, measures for [the establishment of] order in the reciprocal interest will be taken only by common accord.

8. If His Highness the Bey of Tunis should recall the Bey of Constantine, his brother, he will designate another prince possessing the necessary qualities, who will receive the commission as the Bey of Constantine with the prior approval of the General in Chief.

ART. II. The present act, drafted in two languages, has been signed in duplicate by the General in Chief and Sidi Mustafa, each according to the qualities set forth above, one copy remaining with the Gen- eral in Chief and the other with Sidi Mustafa. . . .

71. RESTORATION OF EXCLUSIVE PRIVILEGES FOR CORAL FISHING: FRANCE AND TUNIS
24 October 1832

[Translated from the French text in Clercq, *Recueil des traités*, 4: 202–04]

Article 5 of the 1830 treaty of navigation and commerce (Doc. 68) stipulated the return to France of the exclusive right to coral fishing off Cape Nègre. The conditions for the renewed concession were set forth in the following instrument. For references see Doc. 62.

. . . ART. 1. The French will pay for the farming of the coral 13,500 Tunisian piasters, according to usage and in conformity with the former treaties, and they shall not be subject to any fees and imposts whatsoever.

ART. 2. The French may fish the coral in all the coastal waters of our kingdom.

ART. 3. The coral-fishing boats shall be given French licenses, of which the number will not be limited, and they shall be admitted into all the ports of our kingdom without harassment by anyone. We will give the most formal orders that [the French boats] should be respected and protected. The French shall ensure that no one fishes without a license.

ART. 4. The French shall assign agents in the coral-fishing ports, and if they need warehouses in which to keep the equipment of the coral-fishing boats and the necessary provisions, they may rent warehouses in the fishing area and shall pay rentals for them to their owners. They shall not be liable to any customs duty on provisions bought for the coral-fishing boats, or for fishing equipment, or for the coral which they gather, unless they wish to import the said coral for sale in our kingdom, in which event they shall pay customs duty on the [same] basis [as] other goods. Each boat shall carry only the amount of provisions that it may need, and this through the medium of our agent in the said places.

ART. 5. We shall give the French agent at Tabarka the place which normally serves as lodging, so that he may live there according to custom.

ART. 6. Sardinia shall pay to the French fishermen license fees, at the same rate that they formerly paid them to our court, because that was our agreement with that at the conclusion of the treaty between us through the mediation of England.

ART. 7. The present treaty as stipulated above will enter into effect only when it receives the approval of the French Government. . . .

72. TREATY OF DEFENSIVE ALLIANCE (HÜNKÂR İSKELESİ): THE OTTOMAN EMPIRE AND RUSSIA
26 June/8 July 1833

(Ratifications exchanged, Istanbul, 20 August 1833; superseded, 15 July 1840)
[Great Britain, *Parliamentary Papers, 1836*, vol. 50, no. 85]

Facing almost certain defeat by the insurgent Mehmed 'Ali Paşa of Egypt and the probable end of the Ottoman dynasty, Sultan Mahmud II (1808–39), after requests for assistance had been turned down by Austria, Britain, and France, accepted Russian military aid early in 1833. For this he paid with a defensive alliance. The British Embassy procured a copy of the secret article almost before the drafter's ink had dried, and when the text reached London Foreign Secretary Lord Palmerston took a dim view of the provision, fearing that its literal execution would convert the Ottoman Empire into an appendage of Russia. The arrangement explicitly stipulated that, on activation of the alliance, the Sublime Porte would be spared "the expense and inconvenience . . . [of] affording substantial aid," being required instead only to shut the Dardanelles to all foreign naval vessels. However, England—and France—suspected that Russian naval vessels, excepted from this prohibition, would enjoy free transit in both directions through the entire length of the straits. Although the treaty did not give Russia such exclusive rights, the instincts of the maritime powers were nevertheless sound, since there is no doubt that the tsar and his advisers were trying to extract from a beleaguered sultan a privileged position at the straits. Webster, *Foreign Policy of Palmerston*, 1: 301–19; Mosely, *Russian Diplomacy and the Opening of the Eastern Question*, chap. 2; Temperley, *England and the Near East*, pp. 69–74, 412–14; Florinsky, *Russia*, 2: 834–41; Hurewitz, "Russia and the Turkish Straits"; Goriainow, *Le Bosphore et les Dardanelles,* chap. 8; Phillipson and Buxton, *Question of the Bosphorus and Dardanelles*, pt. 2, chap. 3; Mischef, *La Mer Noire et les détroits de Constantinople*, chap. 4; Cattaui, *Histoire des rapports de l'Egypte avec la Sublime Porte*, pt. 2, chaps. 1–2.

ART. 1. There shall be for ever peace, amity and alliance between His Majesty the Emperor of all the Russias and His Majesty the Emperor of the Ottomans, their empires and their subjects, as well by land as by sea. This alliance having solely for its object the common defence of their dominions against all attack, their Majesties engage to come to an unreserved understanding with each other upon all the matters which concern their respective tranquillity and safety, and to afford to each other mutually for this purpose substantial aid, and the most efficacious assistance.

ART. 2. The Treaty of Peace concluded at Adrianople, on the 2d of September 1829, as well as all the other Treaties comprised therein, as also the Convention signed at St. Petersburg, on the 14th of April 1830, and the arrangement relating to Greece concluded at Constantinople, on the 9 & 21 July 1832, are fully confirmed by the present Treaty of Defensive Alliance, in the same manner as if the said transactions had been inserted in it word for word.

ART. 3. In consequence of the principle of conservation and mutual defence, which is the basis of the present Treaty of Alliance, and by reason of a most sincere desire of securing the permanence, maintenance and entire independence of the Sublime Porte, his Majesty the Emperor of all the Russias, in the event of circumstances occurring which should again determine the Sublime Porte to call for the naval and military assistance of Russia, although, if it please God, that case is by no means likely to happen, engages to furnish, by land and by sea, as many troops and forces as the two high contracting parties may deem necessary. It is accordingly agreed, that in this case the land and sea forces, whose aid the Sublime Porte may call for, shall be held at its disposal.

ART. 4. In conformity with what is above stated, in the event of one of the two powers requesting the assistance of the other, the expense only of provisioning the land and the sea forces which may be furnished, shall fall to the charge of the power who shall have applied for the aid.

ART. 5. Although the two high contracting parties sincerely intend to maintain this engagement to the most distant period of time, yet, as it is possible that in process of time circumstances may require that some changes should be made in this Treaty, it has been agreed to fix its duration at eight years from the day of the exchange of the Imperial Ratifications. The two parties, previously to the expiration of that term, will concert together, according to the state of affairs at that time, as to the renewal of the said Treaty. . . .

Separate and Secret Article

In virtue of one of the clauses of the first Article of the Patent Treaty of Defesive Alliance concluded between the Imperial Court of Russia and the Sublime Porte, the two high contracting parties are bound to afford to each other mutually substantial aid, and the most efficacious assistance for the safety of their respective dominions. Nevertheless, as his Majesty the Emperor of all the Russias, wishing to spare the Sublime Ottoman Porte the expense and inconvenience which might be occasioned to it, by affording substantial aid, will not ask for that aid if circumstances should place the Sublime Porte under the obligation of furnishing it, the Sublime Ottoman Porte, in the place of the aid which it is bound to furnish in case of need, according to the principle of reciprocity of the Patent Treaty, shall confine its action in favour of the Imperial Court of Russia to closing the strait of the Dardanelles, that is to say, to not allowing any foreign vessels of war to enter therein under any pretext whatsoever.

The present Separate and Secret Article shall have the same force and value as if it was inserted word for word in the Treaty of Alliance of this day.

73. PROTEST AGAINST THE TREATY OF HÜNKÂR İSKELESI PRESENTED TO THE SUBLIME PORTE BY THE BRITISH AMBASSADOR
26 August 1833

[Great Britain, Public Record Office, F.O. 28/220]

On 7 August 1833 Foreign Minister Lord Palmerston sent to Istanbul a note of protest against the Russian-Ottoman secret alliance, directing the British ambassador to present the note to the Sublime Porte if the ratifications of the treaty had already been exchanged or if his representations against ratification were to prove ineffectual. This note, and a comparable one from the French ambassador, were transmitted to the Ottoman government on 26 August. For references, see Doc. 72.

The Undersigned has been instructed to express to the Sublime Porte the deep concern with which the British Government has learnt the conclusion of the Treaty of the 8th of July between the Emperor of Russia and the Sultan. That Treaty appears to His Majesty's Government to produce a change in the relations between Turkey and Russia, to which other European States are entitled to object; and the undersigned is

instructed to declare that if the stipulations of that Treaty should hereafter lead to the armed interference of Russia in the internal affairs of Turkey, the British Government will hold itself at liberty to act upon such an occasion, in any manner which the circumstances of the moment may appear to require, equally as if the Treaty above-mentioned were not in existence.

74. CONVENTION (MÜNCHENGRÄTZ) ON COMMON ACTION ON THE EASTERN QUESTION: AUSTRIA AND RUSSIA
6/18 September 1833

[Translated from the French text in Martens, *Recueil des traités et conventions*, 4: 445–49]

Tsar Nicholas I feared that Mehmed 'Ali's revolt (1831–33) was encouraging republicanism in Europe. Russian aid to Sultan Mahmud II early in 1833 could be viewed partly in this light. To win European allies animated by the same spirit of conservatism and to induce them to forge a common policy on the Eastern Question, either by keeping the Ottoman Empire alive under the existing dynasty or by agreeing in advance on who was to get what, should the empire collapse, constituted the principal motivation of the secret Russian-Austrian entente arranged at Münchengrätz. Although Austria's Metternich did not regard the convention with the same reverence as Nicholas I and favored making it public, the terms of the private accord proved to be a better kept secret than those adopted at Hünkâr İskelesi. Webster, *Foreign Policy of Palmerston*, 1: 301–19; Temperley, *England and the Near East*, pp. 78–82, 414; Florinsky, *Russia*, 2: 840–41; Molden, *Die Orientpolitik des Fürsten Metternich*, pp. 92–118; Beer, *Die orientalische Politik Österreichs*, chap. 6; Schiemann, *Geschichte Russlands unter Kaiser Nikolaus I*, vol. 3, chap. 7.

ART. 1. The Courts of Austria and Russia undertake mutually to implement their resolution to maintain the existence of the Ottoman Empire under the present dynasty, and to devote to this end, in perfect accord, all the means of influence and action in their power.

ART. 2. In consequence, the two Imperial Courts undertake to oppose in common any combination affecting the independence of sovereign authority in Turkey, whether by the establishment of a provisional regency, or by a complete change of dynasty. If either of these situations

should occur, the two High Contracting Parties will not only refuse to recognize such an order of things but will also consult immediately on the most effective measures to adopt in common, so as to prevent the dangers which a change in the existing Ottoman Empire might entail for the safety and interests of their own states adjacent to Turkey. . . .

Separate and Secret Articles

ART. 1. The High Contracting Parties intend to apply specifically to the Pasha of Egypt the stipulations of Article 2 of today's Convention, and they undertake in common expressly to prevent the authority of the Pasha of Egypt from extending, directly or indirectly, to the European provinces of the Ottoman Empire.

ART. 2. In signing today's Convention, the two Imperial Courts do not overlook the possibility that, despite their wishes and joint efforts, the present order of things in Turkey may be upset; and it is their intention, in such a case, not to alter the principle of unity in Eastern affairs which forms the basis of today's Convention. It is understood therefore that, in such an eventuality, the two Imperial Courts will act only in concert and in a perfect spirit of solidarity

in all matters pertaining to the establishment of a new order of things, destined to replace that which now exists, and that they will assume point responsibility in making certain that the change occurring in the internal situation of this Empire does not endanger either the safety of their own states and the rights assured them respectively by treaties or the preservation of the European balance.

These separate and secret articles, having the same force and validity as that of today's Convention, will be exchanged at Vienna at the same time as those of the aforementioned Convention.

75. TREATY OF AMITY AND COMMERCE: THE UNITED STATES AND MASQAT
21 September 1833

(Ratifications exchanged, Masqat, 30 September 1835; superseded, 20 December 1958)
[United States, *Treaty Series*, no. 247]

The ruler of Masqat, who at that time was styled in Arabic the Hami, or Protector, of Masqat and its Dependencies, but is labeled "Sultan" in the present instrument, invited the United States in 1832 to conclude a commercial treaty in a letter "directed to the [American] president, and forwarded by one of . . . [the American] vessels lately trading in these seas." The following instrument was the shaykhdom's first capitulatory treaty with a Western power; later France (1844) and the Netherlands (1877) also acquired extraterritorial privileges for their nationals. The existence of the capitulatory treaties prevented the full assimilation of Masqat into the British system of quasi protectorates in the Persian Gulf. E. Roberts, *Embassy to the Eastern Courts*, chap. 23; Miller, *Treaties and Other International Acts*, 3: 789–810 (see pp. 799–801 for a fresh translation of the Arabic text by C. Snouck Hurgronje, with comments on differences between the Arabic and English official texts); Kelly, *Britain and the Persian Gulf*, pp. 235–37; Ruete, *Said bin Sultan*, pp. 122–29; Ruschenberger, *Narrative of a Voyage Round the World*, vol. 1, chap. 9; Sanger, *Arabian Peninsula*, chap. 14.

ART. 1. There shall be a perpetual Peace between the United States of America and Seyed Syeed bin Sultan and his dependencies.

2. The Citizens of the United States shall have free liberty to enter all the Ports of His Majesty Seyed Syeed bin Sultan, with their

Cargoes of whatever kind the said cargoes may consist, & they shall have the liberty to sell the same, to any of the subjects of the Sultan, or others who may wish to buy the same, or to barter the same for any produce or manufactures of the Kingdom, or other articles that may be found there—no price shall be fixed by the Sultan or his Officers on the articles to be sold by the Merchants of the United States, or the merchandize they may wish to purchase—but the trade shall be free on both sides, to sell, or buy, or exchange on the terms, & for the prices the owners may think fit—and whenever the said Citizens of the United States may think fit to depart they shall be at liberty so to do—and if any Officer of the Sultan shall contravene this Article, he shall be severely punished. It is understood & agreed however, that the articles of Muskets, Powder and Ball can only be sold to the Government in the Island of Zanzibar—but in all the other ports of the Sultan, the said munitions of war may be freely sold, without any restrictions whatever to the highest bidder.

3. Vessels of the United States entering any port within the Sultan's dominions, shall pay no more than Five per centum Duties on the Cargo landed; and this shall be in full consideration of all import & export duties, tonnage, license to trade, pilotage, anchorage, or any other charge whatever. Nor shall any charge be paid on that part of the cargo which may remain on board unsold, & re-exported—nor shall any charge whatever be paid on any vessel of the United States which may enter any of the Ports of His Majesty for the purpose of re-fitting, or for refreshments, or to enquire the state of the market.

4. The American Citizen shall pay no other duties on export or import, tonnage, license to trade, or other charge whatsoever, than the nation the most favored shall pay.

5. If any vessel of the United States shall suffer Shipwreck on any part of the Sultan's Dominions, the persons escaping from the wreck shall be taken care of and hospitably entertain'd at the expense of the Sultan, until they shall find an opportunity to be return'd to their country—for the Sultan can never receive any remuneration what-

ever for rendering succour to the distress'd—and the property saved from such wreck, shall be carefully preserv'd and delivered to the owner, or the Consul of the United States, or to any authorized Agent.

6. The Citizens of the United States resorting to the Ports of the Sultan for the purpose of trade, shall have leave to land, & reside in the said Ports, without paying any tax or imposition whatever for such liberty, other than the General Duties on Imports which the most favored nation shall pay.

7. If any citizens of the United States, or their vessels, or other property shall be taken by Pirates, and brought within the Dominions of the Sultan, the persons shall be set at liberty, and the property restored to the owner if he is present, or to the American Consul, or to any authorized agent.

8. Vessels belonging to the subjects of the Sultan which may resort to any port in the United States, shall pay no other or higher rate of Duties, or other charges, than the nation the most favored shall pay.

9. The President of the United States may appoint Consuls to reside in the Ports of the Sultan where the principal commerce shall be carried on; which Consuls shall be the exclusive judges of all disputes or suits wherein American Citizens shall be engaged with each other. They shall have power to receive the property of any American Citizen dying within the Kingdom, and to send the same to his heirs, first paying all his debts due to the subjects of the Sultan. The said Consuls shall not be arrested, nor shall their property be seized.

Nor shall any of their household be arrested, but their persons, and property, & their houses, shall be inviolate—Should any Consul however, commit any offence against the laws of the Kingdom, complaint shall be made to the President who will immediately displace him.

76. TREATY OF PEACE AND FRIENDSHIP: THE
FRENCH MILITARY GOVERNOR OF ORAN AND ʿABD AL-QADIR
26 February 1834

(Formal ratifications not exchanged; the French government authorized General
Desmichels to inform Amir ʿAbd al-Qadir that the king approved the treaty.)
[Translated from the French text in Clercq, *Recueil des traités*, 4: 262]

The lingering French ambivalence over Algerine policy under the July Monarchy
deprived the military commanders in the field of essential political guidance. Without
firm instructions, the commanders persisted in political and military improvisation.
Still, the French military strategy was clear enough. Until the metropole made up its
mind, the generals tried by every means to tighten the French grip on the territory of
the former Garrison. Since movement into the interior was impeded by mountainous
terrain, even more by stiffening Muslim opposition, and most of all by unfamiliarity
with the country, the French officers took the line of least resistance. They hugged the
coast, moving east and west out of Algiers. By June 1831 they had subjugated Oran
and Bône, and two months later the Tunisians in both towns returned home, winding
up the short-lived experiment in managing the former Algerine beyliks through Tunisian vassals. The most stubborn opposition in the early years of the French presence
in Algeria—indeed the first seventeen of them—came from the former beylik of Oran.
There, many tribes, closely tied by membership in Sufi orders with tribes owing allegiance to the ʿAlawi regime in Morocco, sought that monarchy's support in attempting to organize a jihad against the invading Christians to defend the *dar al-Islam*
against the infidel. The Moroccans at first sent armed tribesmen to assist the Algerians,
only to recall the troops on the receipt of a French ultimatum. As a result, the Algerian
tribesmen organized their own government of Oran. In November 1832, al-Hajj
ʿAbd al-Qadir bin Muhyi al-Din al-Hasani, the twenty-four-year-old son of one of the
leaders of the Hashim tribal federation, together with two allied federations (the
Banu ʿAmir and the Gharaba)—all members of the Qadiriyyah, a popular Sufi order
in the western Maghrib—was proclaimed amir, or head, of the new Arab state.
ʿAbd al-Qadir exhibited military and political talents of high quality. With personal
courage, he led the tribesmen in attacking French outposts and ambushing French
columns. His victories rallied more and more tribesmen, thus frustrating every French
effort in 1833 to penetrate the interior of the former beylik of Oran. Over this territory
ʿAbd al-Qadir created his own government, organized into provinces and military
subdistricts, and through it he enforced an economic blockade of the French coastal
positions, compelling the invaders to import their provisions from the metropole.
The French military governor, Brigadier General Baron Louis Alexis Desmichels,
who had taken up his post on 23 April 1833, decided to break the blockade by recognizing ʿAbd al-Qadir. The following treaty, under which Desmichels acknowledged
the existence of the Arab government, was negotiated without advance notice to his
military, to say nothing of his political, superiors. The French and Arabic versions of
the treaty were given equal validity, producing an early misunderstanding. In the

Arabic version, the only one that 'Abd al-Qadir accepted as valid, article 1 entitled the amir to send consuls to Oran, Mostaganem, and Arzew, the coastal towns in French possession; and this the amir used to support his claim to sovereignty. The French version, translated below, simply speaks of "representatives." Julien, *Histoire de l'Algérie contemporaine*, chap. 2; Azan, *L'emir Abd el-Kader*; C. Churchill, *Life of Abdel Kader*; Blunt, *Desert Hawk*; Emerit, *L'Algérie à l'époque d'Abd el-Kader*.

The commanding general of the French troops in the city of Oran and the Prince of the Faithful, Sidi al-Hajj 'Abd al-Qadir bin Muhyi al-Din, have reached agreement on the following terms:

ART.1. From today's date, the hostilities between the French and the Arabs shall cease. The general commanding the French troops and the Amir 'Abd al-Qadir shall do everything possible to promote the union and friendship which must exist between the two peoples that God has destined to live under the same sovereignty. For this purpose and for the prevention of any conflicts between the French and the Arabs, representatives of the Amir shall reside at Oran, Mostaganem, and Arzew [while] French officers shall reside at Mascara.

ART. 2. The religion and customs of the Arabs shall be respected and protected.

ART. 3. Prisoners shall immediately be exchanged between the two sides.

ART. 4. Freedom of commerce shall be full and complete.

ART. 5. Soldiers of the French army who may desert their units shall be returned by the Arabs. Similarly, Arab malefactors who, to avoid just punishment, may run away from their tribes and seek refuge with the French shall be returned immediately to the representatives of the Amir in the three maritime cities occupied by the French.

ART. 6. For aid and protection throughout the province, every European who may happen to be traveling in the interior shall be furnished with a passport visaed by the representatives of the Amir and approved by the commanding general.

77. OTTOMAN *FERMAN* PERMITTING NAVIGATION OF THE EUPHRATES RIVER BY BRITISH STEAM VESSELS
29 December 1834

[Aitchison, *Collection of Treaties . . . relating to India* (4th ed.), 13: 16–17]

British interest in establishing shorter routes to India, aroused by the Napoleonic wars, was further stimulated after 1825 by the development of the steam vessel. Parliament authorized in August 1834 the expenditure of £20,000 to finance an exploratory expedition to the Euphrates River and named Colonel (later General) Francis Rawdon Chesney, who had conducted a preliminary survey in 1830–31, as head of the mission, for which the following *ferman* (decree)was procured. The ferman later served as the enabling act of a British firm—known after 1860 as the Euphrates and Tigris Steam Navigation Company—which enjoyed a virtual monopoly of steam navigation on the twin rivers. The company, which in 1863 began receiving an annual mail subsidy of £2,400 from the government of Bombay, continued in operation until 1949. Kelly, *Britain and the Persian Gulf*, chap. 12; Hoskins, *British Routes to India*, chaps. 6–7, 17; Longrigg, *Four Centuries of Modern Iraq*, chaps. 10–11; A. Wilson, *Persian Gulf*, chap. 16; Chesney, *Narrative of the Euphrates Expedition*.

To their Excellencies the Viziers, Pashas of three tails, to the illustrious Miri Mirans, Pashas of two tails, to the learned Judges, to the Wainadas, Captains of Ports, and other Magistrates of places situated on both banks of the Euphrates, health.

On receiving the imperial command, you will know as follows:—The Ambassador Extraordinary and Plenipotentiary of Great Britain at Constantinople, Lord Ponsonby, one of the most illustrious personages among the Christian nations, has presented at our Sublime Porte an official note, by which he intimates that the British Government requires permission to cause to navigate by turns two steam boats on the river Euphrates which flows at a small distance from the city of Bagdad, for the purpose of facilitating commerce.

We in consequence issued to our very illustrious governor of Bagdad and Bus-sora, Ali Reza Pasha, an order to furnish our Sublime Porte with information of the proposed navigation.

Although the answer of the Pasha had not arrived, the Ambassador made representations on this point, informing our Sublime Porte [that] the British Government awaited our reply.

For this reason we have and do permit two steam boats to navigate the Euphrates by turns, and this navigation is to continue as long as, conformably to what has been represented to us, it may prove useful to the two powers, and no inconvenience result therefrom, and it is to this purpose that an official rule has been transmitted to the British Ambassador.

A firman couched in the same terms has been addressed to the Pasha of Bagdad and Bussora.

78. TREATY OF MUTUAL RECOGNITION (TAFNA): FRANCE AND THE ARAB AMIRATE IN ALGERIA
30 May 1837

(Authentic texts in Arabic and French; ratified by King Louis Philippe, 15 June 1837)
[Translated from the French text in Clercq, *Recueil des traités de la France*, 4: 375–77]

The peace and friendship for which the Desmichels treaty with 'Abd al-Qadir (Doc. 76) ostensibly provided did not long endure. The amir continued enlarging his principality by winning the allegiance of more and more tribes, including some uncomfortably close to Algiers, as the French generals viewed it. In the serious fighting that broke out in the summer of 1835 between the French forces and 'Abd al-Qadir's tribesmen, each side could claim victories. But it proved much easier for the amir to regroup tribal troops after defeat than for the French, for whom reinforcement of men and supplies from the metropole posed major logistical problems. Moreover, the French were spreading their forces thin, since in the east Ahmet Bey still clung stubbornly at Constantine to the beylik, shorn of its coastal towns, as the last major remnant of the Algerine Garrison. The decision to amass French forces in Algeria for the conquest of Constantine induced the metropole to find a basis for ending the war with 'Abd al-Qadir, and for this purpose the French government sent to Oran Lieutenant-General (later marshal) Robert Bugeaud (later Duc d'Isly) as commander of the troops in the west. Bugeaud came to terms with 'Abd al-Qadir in May 1837 by recognizing the enlargement of the amirate to include the beylik of Titteri in the south and even some inland districts of the beylik of Algiers. This time peace lasted for nearly two and a half years before it broke down over conflicting interpretations of the boundary between French-held districts in the beylik of Algiers and those claimed by the amir, who refused to accept the French governor general's proposal for a precise definition of the boundary. It was 'Abd al-Qadir's tribesmen who fired the first shots in November 1839 in a war that seesawed for more than a year before Bugeaud became governor general in December 1840. During his governorship (1840–47), Bugeaud inaugurated a plan for pacification by military colonization. His program called for the erection of a chain of strategic villages on land granted only provisionally to colons on condition that they or their designees work and reside on the land. Bugeaud's soldiers furnished the hard core of settler recruits for the avowed goal of populating the country "with colons who might reproduce the image of the metropole" (Emile Labiche, "Rapport sur la colonisation de l'Algérie," p. 41). Holding the previous policy of *refoulement* (i.e., the "forcing back" of natives to make room for colons) to be unjust, Bugeaud insisted that his practice of *resserrement* (i.e., contraction, or the obligatory surrender by Muslims of part of their landholdings) was more equitable because it was compensated and because it offered the natives the benefits of irrigation and other services furnished the Europeans. In establishing the military villages at strategic points, Bugeaud progressively destroyed the amirate by capturing its major towns one after another and twice forcing the amir to cross into Morocco. Even then the French had to suffer seven years of hard fighting before 'Abd al-Qadir finally surrendered on 23 December 1847. After five years of internment in France, 'Abd al-Qadir was released with a pension from the French government. He settled first in Brusa and then in 1855 in Damascus, where he lived until his death in 1883. Julien, *Histoire de l'Algérie contemporaine*, chaps. 3–5; Agéron, "Administration directe ou protectorate"; see also references to Doc. 76.

. . . ART. 1. Amir 'Abd al-Qadir recognizes the sovereignty of France in Algeria.

ART. 2. France reserves for itself:
—In the province of Oran, Mostaganem, Mazagram, and their territories: Oran, Arzew, plus a territory bounded as follows: on the east by the river al-Makta and the marsh from which it rises; on the south by a line proceeding from the above-mentioned marsh, passing along the southern shore of the lake and continuing to al-Wadi [Oued] Maleh in the direction of Sidi Sa'id and from this river to the sea, in such a manner that all of the territory enclosed within this perimeter shall be French territory;
—In the Province of Algiers: Algiers, al-Sahil, the Plain of al-Matija, bounded on the east as far as al-Wadi [Oued] Kaddara, and beyond; on the south by the crest of the first chain of the Small Atlas, as far as al-Chiffa, encompassing Blidah and its territory; on the west by al-chiffa, as far as the bend of Mazafran, and from there by a straight line, as far as the sea, comprehending Koleah and its territory, in such a manner that all of the territory enclosed within this perimeter shall be French territory.

ART. 3. The Amir will administer the province of Oran, that of Titteri, and the part of [the province] of Algiers that is not included on the east within the boundaries indicated by Article 2. He may not enter into any other part of the regency.

ART. 4. The Amir will have no authority over Muslims who might wish to live in the territory reserved for France; but these [Muslims] shall remain free to go to live within the territory which the Amir will administer, just as the inhabitants of the Amir's territory may take up residence in French territory.

ART. 5. Arabs living in French territory may practice their religion freely. They may build mosques there and follow in every respect their religious discipline, under the authority of their spiritual chiefs.

ART. 6. The Amir will give to the French

army: 30,000 Oran *fanegas* of wheat; and
30,000 Oran fanegas of barley; [and]
5,000 oxen. The delivery of these commodities will be made in Oran in three
[stages]: the first will take place between 1
and 15 September 1837, and the two others
at [later] two-month intervals.

ART. 7. The Amir will purchase in France
the powder, the sulphur, and the arms that
he might need.

ART. 8. The *kuluglis*[1] who may wish to
remain in Tlemsen or elsewhere may own
their properties freely and shall be treated
like the *hadar*s [townsmen]. Those who
wish to withdraw to French territory may
sell and rent their properties freely.

ART. 9. France cedes to the Amir:
Rachgoun, and Tlemsen, the Citadel and
the cannons that were formerly in it; the
Amir undertakes to transport from the
garrison of Tlemsen to Oran all effects,
together with the munitions of war and the
provisions.

ART. 10. Commerce will be free between
the Arabs and the French who may wish to
take up residence on one territory or the
other.

ART. 11. The French will be respected by
the Arabs just as the Arabs will be by the

French. The farms and the properties which
the French have acquired or may acquire
on Arab territory will be guaranteed to
them; they will be in free possession of
[these properties], and the Amir undertakes to reimburse [the French] for any
damages which the Arabs may inflict upon
them.

ART. 12. Criminals of the two territories
will be reciprocally surrendered.

ART. 13. The Amir undertakes not to
cede any point of the coast to any power
whatsoever without the authorization of
France.

ART. 14. The commerce of the regency
will not be conducted except through the
ports occupied by France.

ART. 15. France may accredit agents to
the Amir and in the towns under his
administration to serve as intermediaries
between him and French subjects in case of
commercial and other disputes which they
may have with the Arabs. The Amir shall
enjoy the same privilege in the French
towns and seaports.

---

1. In Algeria, Muslims born of Turkish
fathers and Arab mothers.

79. INTERPRETATION OF HÜNKÂR İSKELESI BY COUNT NESSELRODE, THE RUSSIAN MINISTER OF FOREIGN AFFAIRS
4/16–18/30 January 1838

[Translated from the French text in Mosely, *Russian Diplomacy and the Opening of the Eastern Question*, pp. 141–47; original text from *Reports to the Emperor*, fol. 66, pp. 2–16, in the Russian Diplomatic Archives]

The maritime powers, particularly Britain, continued to suspect that Russia had extracted a privileged position at the straits from the beleaguered Sultan Mahmud II (1808–39) in the secret and separate article of the Russian-Ottoman treaty of defensive alliance concluded at Hünkâr İskelesi in 1833 (Doc. 72). The advisers of Tsar Nicholas I (1825–55) were clearly divided on how to expedite a Russian solution of the straits question. The naval advisers seemed prone to force the issue, resorting to the practice used at the start of the century under the Russian-Ottoman treaty of alliance of 1798–99 of inuring the Sublime Porte and the maritime powers to the movement of Russian war vessels through the straits in both directions in the hope that eventually the

Russian navy might establish an acceptable precedent for such an exclusive privilege (Doc. 39). The Sublime Porte, on its side, was determined to keep the straits closed to the war vessels of all states, including Russia, a position that Britain categorically endorsed after Hünkâr İskelesi, having already accepted it in principle in 1809 in article 11 of the treaty of the Dardanelles (Doc. 52). In the following report to Tsar Nicholas I, Foreign Minister Count Nesselrode leaves no doubt that in his view the significance of Hünkâr İskelesi lay in the fact, not that the Sublime Porte opened the straits to Russian naval vessels while closing it to those of all other states, but that for the first time it accepted as a *"direct engagement to us . . .* to maintain the closure of the Dardanelles *in case of war* between Russia and other powers" (italics in original). This assurance, received from Saint Petersburg more than once, carried little conviction in London to Foreign Minister Lord Palmerston. Still, in the Nesselrode position lay the basis for an agreement between Russia and Britain which was finally reached at the end of 1839, as the prelude to the general guarantee by the European Concert of the Ottoman closure of the straits to the war vessels of all states. Hurewitz, "Russia and the Turkish Straits"; Mosely, *Russian Diplomacy and the Opening of the Eastern Question*,; see also references to Doc. 40.

1. Prince Menshikov to Count Nesselrode, 4/16 January 1838

The Emperor has instructed me to inform you, my dear Count, that in the coming spring His Majesty intends to dispatch two ships of the line, with one or two sloops, which will leave the Baltic under the pretext of conducting maneuvers and will then proceed to the Dardanelles in order to pass into the Black Sea.

The length of this voyage requires calling at a port to refresh the crews and to take on provisions and water. In the present circumstances, the ports of the Sardinian Islands seem to me the only ones [among which] to designate this port of call. I shall await your communications on the Emperor's subsequent decisions before drafting the instructions to the commanding officer of this squadron.

2. Nesselrode's report to Tsar Nicholas I, 16/28 January 1838

Prince Menshikov has informed me that it is Your Majesty's intention to dispatch in the coming spring two ships of the line, with one or two sloops, which will leave the Baltic, call at one of the Sardinian ports, and proceed from there to the Dardanelles in order to pass into the Black Sea.

In acquainting me eventually with these provisions by the attached note, the honorable Minister of the Navy has kindly informed me that he awaits my communication on Your Majesty's subsequent decisions, so that his instructions to the commander of the squadron might comply with them.

I feel it my duty, Sire, consequently to solicit your orders on this subject, insofar as the concurrence of the Minister of Foreign Affairs is demanded.

I dare, on this occasion, to observe above all that the amicable relations happily established between the Imperial Cabinet and that of Turin authorize us to count on the speed with which the King of Sardinia will greet the steps that our Minister might be instructed to take in announcing the arrival of our squadron and in obtaining, during its call at the Sardinian ports, all desirable facilities. With this expectation in mind, I have no doubt of a completely satisfactory result from the overtures that Mr. d'Obrescov may make as soon as Your Majesty deigns to instruct me to transmit the order to him.

As for the passage of our squadron through the Bosphorus, the sentiments of duty and profound devotion that guide me in your service, Sire, command me to elaborate upon several considerations that are connected with the general system of your politics; very grave considerations that my own responsibility as Your Majesty's faithful servant obliges me to submit in advance of your decisions, with respectful and complete frankness.

In the difficult and often dangerous state of Oriental affairs, Your Majesty has invariably adopted the principle of safeguarding the security of Russia's southern provinces by rigorously ensuring that the entrance to the Dardanelles remain closed to foreign flags of war.

This principle, in agreement with the well-understood interests and ancient political traditions of the Porte, has been consecrated formally by the treaty concluded between Turkey and England in 1809.

By this transaction, the principle of the closure of the Dardanelles is clearly recognized as "an ancient rule of the Ottoman Empire which must be observed in time of peace by every Power whatsoever, a principle to which the British Court also promises to conform."

However, until then no *direct engagement to us* existed by which the Porte was bound also to maintain the closure of the Dardanelles *in case of war* between Russia and other Powers.[1]

It is this gap that our Treaty of Alliance of 26 June/8 July 1833 served to fill.

The secret article of this treaty stipulates that Turkey, "instead of the assistance that it must lend to Russia in virtue of the Public Treaty, shall limit its action in favor of the Imperial Court [and Russia] to closing the strait of the Dardanelles, that is to say, to not permitting any foreign vessel of war to enter there under any pretext whatsoever."

The maritime Powers have sought in vain to invalidate our Treaty of Alliance. Our efforts have succeeded in inspiring the Sultan with the firmness and courage to maintain his engagements to us in all their integrity.

But, in order to encourage the Porte to persist in this attitude, Your Majesty has always adhered loyally to the axiom[2] neither to stipulate nor to demand for us this same right of passage through the Dardanelles that it is in our great interest to see denied to all other Powers.

The treaties oblige Turkey, as a result of the actual state of our relations, *to close* the entrance of the Dardanelles to foreign flag[s] of war, but these instruments do not oblige it in any way *to open* [that entrance] to us.

The Treaty of Adrianople, confirmed by that of Constantinople [Hünkâr İskelesi], stipulates explicitly in our favor the free passage of *merchantships* only; but no stipulation authorizes us to demand the admission of our vessels of war into the Bosphorus.

Such is the general principle that serves as the basis for our instruments on this important matter.

It is only as a special exception and in pure deference that the Ottoman Government accords us, from time to time, the right to relieve our station in Greece and issues to us *fermans* of passage for the light ships returning from the Archipelago as well as for those coming from the Black Sea to replace them.

Thus far, the Porte has never refused this privilege, although it definitely has that right, according to the strict letter of our treaties.

On our side, we have used this right only with caution, at long intervals, without public announcement. In this way, the transit of our ships coming from the Archipelago to return to the Black Sea has passed, until now, and continues to pass unnoticed, as an exceptional measure, justified by the need periodically to reinforce the station of light ships that are destined to maintain the service of our regular communication with Greece.

But it would be an entirely different matter with a Baltic squadron that, after having made the tour of Europe and attracted the attention of all the maritime Powers, might appear before the Dardanelles and demand [the right] to pass through the Canal of Constantinople.

One of two things would then necessarily occur: either the Porte would refuse us passage; or it would decide to grant it to us.

In the first instance, we should not, as I have already observed, have any positive right to *insist on* this passage. In refusing our demand the Porte would base its action

---

1. Italics throughout appear in original.
2. The French reads, "a toujours eu loyalement en vue."

on the [principle of] strict execution of the treaties. It would be legally within its rights. We would have no basis for objecting to its refusal. But, however circumspectly [the Porte's refusal] might be phrased, it is not less true that in the eyes of Europe such a refusal would injure Russia's dignity. We should suffer a double disadvantage: on the one hand, perceptible injury would have been done to our influence; on the other hand, a grievance would have been created and a motive provoked for a misunderstanding that could not fail to react in a trying manner on our direct relations with Turkey.

In the second case, admitting that the Sultan grants us passage, England and France in their turn would rapidly seize this pretext to demand the Porte's permission to send several warships into the Black Sea. England would profit more from this circumstance, as it would pretend to have need of granting the protection of a naval station to its commerce in these parts, a scheme that has been bruited already in Parliament and that the Minister, supported by public opinion, would doubtless be happy to realize the moment we might furnish him with the reason. The Ottoman Government, we must understand, would not then have either the force or the courage to resist this demand of the maritime Powers. Our mission would be forced in vain to object that the Black Sea is surrounded everywhere by provinces subject to the rule of only two Powers, Russia and the Porte; that our warships return to *our* ports without their presence menacing any third Power, whereas the appearance of a French or English warship in these same parts could manifestly be directed only against us. All these arguments which our mission would certainly not fail to put forward with the language of truth and reason would nevertheless fall before an invincible objection: that the Porte does not have the power to refuse to England and France a concession that we ourselves have demanded outside the letter of the treaties. Thus, in order to justify its weakness, to excuse its pusillanimity, the Porte would tell us that our Cabinet cannot blame [the Porte] if, in opening the entrance of the Dardanelles to England and France, it is resigned to deviate, de-

spite itself, from a principle whose observance we had been the first to transgress.

In the two suppositions which I have just analyzed, we should not be able to conceal the fact that the result would be equally unfavorable for us; for, in short, we should have to expect from the Porte either a *refusal*, compromising our dignity, or a *concession* whose immediate consequence would be the entrance of a British and French squadron into the Black Sea.

Both of these results are so grave that, before deciding to run the risk, the interests of Your Majesty's service demand serious examination of the consequences for which we must be prepared; the sacrifices that Russia must make [and] the precautionary mecsures which would enable us to come, whatever the event, to the support of Russia's dignity if it is compromised, to the defense of its security if it is exposed to menace!

In submitting these reflections to Your Majesty there is one more [point] that I dare finally to set forth here, in the hope that, in elaborating upon it, I shall not fail, Sire, to meet with your approval. I think that the system of loyal and generous politics that Your Majesty has adopted toward the Sultan suggests that the Imperial Cabinet should not face this sovereign, our Ally, with the painful necessity of making a concession to us which would inevitably invlove [the Sublime Porte] in a dangerous complication. In its present state of weakness and decadence, Turkey has in effect an equal need to rely on the protection of Russia and at the same time to treat with caution the susceptibility of the maritime Powers. To force the Porte from this position is to cause its ruin. Assuming that the Sultan, in opening the Dardanelles to us, might wish to close them to the English and the French, we should be placing Turkey in danger and imposing on ourselves the absolute obligation to come to its aid; we should consequently be accepting the risks of a most unfavorable war, a war in which we should have nothing to win and great commercial interests to lose. Assuming, on the other hand, that the Sultan, ceding to the maritime Powers, might grant them passage, we should be destroying with our own hands the barrier that constitutes our security;

we should be losing an ally faithful until now and we should hand Turkey over to the influence of England and France; in a word, we are in danger of compromising in a single day the results that the persevering politics and generosity of Your Majesty have obtained in the seven [sic] years from the Peace of Adrianople to the signature, despite England and France, of the memorable arrangement concluded by Count Orlov for the glory of Russia.

To consolidate the work of preservation and peace that we owe to the moderation of Your Majesty; to assure the tranquillity of Russia in removing all that may trouble Turkey in its present state; finally, to maintain instead of destroying this political and moral barrier that the Dardanelles establishes between us and the maritime Powers in the Orient seems to me to be a faithful expression of the thought and wishes of Your Majesty. It also seems to me [to meet] the true needs and real interests of Russia.

3. Menshikov to Nesselrode, 18/30 January 1838.

I am very grateful to you for the communication of this model piece of logic and great truth.

80. COMMERCIAL CONVENTION (BALTA LIMAN): BRITAIN AND THE OTTOMAN EMPIRE
16 August 1838

[Great Britain, *Parliamentary Papers, 1839*, 50: 291–95]

During the Napoleonic wars, the United Kingdom moved into first place in the external trade of the Ottoman Empire; it remained there for a full century. In approving the liberal terms of the 1838 commercial convention, Sultan Mahmud II was motivated by the desire to subdue with British support his rebellious vassal, Mehmed 'Ali Paşa of Egypt. The convention provided the pattern for similar agreements later concluded with the Sublime Porte by France (25 November 1838) and the Netherlands (31 March 1840) and led to the destruction of Mehmed 'Ali's commercial monopolies immediately after the Egyptian settlement of 1841. Platt, *Finance, Trade, and Politics in British Foreign Policy*, pp. 181–218; Issawi, *Economic History of the Middle East*, pt. 2, chap. 3; Hurewitz, *Middle East Politics*, chap. 3; Temperley, *England and the Near East*, pp. 31–39, 406–08; Webster, *Foreign Policy of Palmerston*, 2: 548–57; Bailey, *British Policy and the Turkish Reform Movement*, chap. 3, esp. p. 120 ff.; Puryear, *International Economics and Diplomacy in the Near East*, chaps. 3–4; Robinson, *David Urquhart*, chap. 2; *British and Foreign State Papers*, 34: 280–415 (correspondence).

ART. I. All rights, privileges, and immunities which have been conferred on the subjects or ships of Great Britain by the existing Capitulations and Treaties, are confirmed now and for ever, except in as far as they may be specifically altered by the present Convention: and it is moreover expressly stipulated, that all rights, privileges, or immunities which the Sublime Porte now grants, or may hereafter grant, to the ships and subjects of any other foreign Power, or which may suffer the ships and subjects of any other foreign Power to enjoy, shall be equally granted to, and exercised and enjoyed by, the subjects and ships of Great Britain.

ART. II. The subjects of Her Britannic Majesty, or their agents, shall be permitted to purchase at all places in the Ottoman Dominions (whether for the purposes of internal trade or exportation) all articles, without any exception whatsoever, the produce, growth, or manufacture of the said Dominions; and the Sublime Porte formally engages to abolish all monopolies of agricultural produce, or of any other articles whatsoever, as well as all *Permits* from the local Governors, either for the purchase of any article, or for its removal from one place to another when purchased; and any attempt to compel the subjects of Her Britannic Majesty to recieve such *Permits* from the local Governors, shall be considered as an infraction of Treaties, and the Sublime Porte shall immediately punish with severity any Vizirs and other officers who shall have been guilty of such misconduct, and render full justice to British subjects for all injuries or losses which they may duly prove themselves to have suffered.

ART. III. If any article of Turkish produce, growth, or manufacture, be purchased by the British merchant or his agent, for they purpose of selling the same for internal consumption in Turkey, the British merchant or his agent shall pay, at the purchase and sale of such articles, and in any manner of trade therein, the same duties that are paid, in similar circumstances, by the most favoured class of Turkish subjects engaged in the internal trade of Turkey, whether Mussulmans or Rayahs.

ART. IV. If any article of Turkish produce, growth, or manufacture, be purchased for exportation, the same shall be conveyed by the British merchant or his agent, free of any kind of charge or duty whatsoever, to a convenient place of shipment, on its entry into which it shall be liable to one fixed duty of nine per cent. *ad valorem*, in lieu of all other interior duties.

Subsequently, on exportation, the duty of three per cent., as established and existing at present, shall be paid. But all articles bought in the shipping ports for exportation, and which have already paid the interior duty at entering into the same, will only pay the three per cent. export duty.

ART. V. The regulations under which Firmans are issued to British merchant vessels for passing the Dardanelles and the Bosphorus, shall be so framed as to occasion to such vessels the least possible delay.

ART. VI. It is agreed by the Turkish Government, that the regulations established in the present Convention, shall be general throughout the Turkish Empire, whether in Turkey in Europe or Turkey in Asia, in Egypt, or other African possessions belonging to the Sublime Porte, and shall be applicable to all the subjects, whatever their description, of the Ottoman Dominions: and the Turkish Government also agrees not to object to other foreign Powers settling their trade upon the basis of this present Convention.

ART. VII. It having been the custom of Great Britain and the Sublime Porte, with a view to prevent all difficulties and delay in estimating the value of articles imported into the Turkish Dominions, or exported therefrom, by British subjects, to appoint, at intervals of fourteen years, a Commission of men well acquainted with the traffic of both countries, who have fixed by a tariff the sum of money in the coin of the Grand Signior, which should be paid as duty on each article; and the term of fourteen years, during which the last adjustment of the said tariff was to remain in force, having expired, the High Contracting Parties have agreed to name conjointly fresh Commissioners to fix and determine the amount in money which is to be paid by British subjects, as the duty of three per cent upon the value of all commodities imported and exported by them; and the said Commissioners shall establish an equitable arrangement for estimating the interior duties which, by the present Treaty, are established on Turkish goods to be exported, and shall also determine on the places of shipment where it may be most convenient that such duties should be levied.

The new tariff thus established, to be in force for seven years after it has been fixed, at the end of which time it shall be in the power of either of the parties to demand a revision of that tariff; but if no such demand be made on either side, within the six months after the end of the first seven years, then the tariff shall remain in force for seven years more, reckoned from the end of the preceding seven years; and so it shall be at the end of each successive period of seven years.

81. BRITISH POLICY TOWARD THE OTTOMAN EMPIRE: FOREIGN MINISTER PALMERSTON TO HER MAJESTY'S AMBASSADOR AT VIENNA
28 June 1839

[Great Britain, *Parliamentary Papers*, 1841, 29: 117–19]

Profound fear of Russian designs on the straits and of French support of Mehmed 'Ali in Egypt initiated Palmerston in Eastern affairs in the years immediately after Hünkâr İskelesi (Doc. 72). In response to the dual challenge to British imperial communications, the foreign minister pursued a policy of internationalizing the Eastern Question by making the European powers responsible for preserving the territorial integrity and political independence of the Ottoman Empire. This policy lasted for forty years. Palmerston's instruction to Viscount Beauvale, shortly after the outbreak of the second Syrian war between the sultan and his recalcitrant paşa in Egypt, defined concisely the British position at the time and foreshadowed the terms of the final settlement of the Egyptian question two years later. Temperley, *England and the Near East*, chaps. 3–5; Webster, *Foreign Policy of Palmerston*, vol. 2, chaps. 7–8; Driault, *L'Egypte et l'Europe*; Mosely, *Russian Diplomacy and the Opening of the Eastern Question*; Rodkey, *Turco-Egyptian Question in the Relations of England, France, and Russia*, chaps. 3–6; Sabry, *L'empire égyptien sous Mohamed-Ali*, chaps. 10–12; Hasenclever, *Die orientalische Frage*; Dodwell, *Founder of Modern Egypt*, chaps. 6–7; Hoskins, *British Routes to India*, chap. 11.

The general view which Her Majesty's Government, as at present informed, entertain of the affair in question, may be stated as follows:

The Great Powers are justified in interfering in these matters, which are, in fact, a contest between a sovereign and his subject, because this contest threatens to produce great and imminent danger to the deepest interests of other Powers, and to the general peace of Europe. Those interests and that peace require the maintenance of the Turkish Empire; and the maintenance of the Turkish Empire is, therefore, the primary object to be aimed at. This object cannot be secured without putting an end to future chances of collision between the Sultan and Mehemet Ali. But as long as Mehemet Ali continues to occupy Syria, there will be danger of such collision. Mehemet Ali cannot hold Syria without a large military force constantly stationed there. As long as there is an Egyptian force in Syria, there must necessarily be a Turkish army in that part of Asia Minor which borders on Syria. Each party might agree at present to reduce those forces to a given amount, but neither could be sure that the other was not, after a time, secretly increasing his amount of force; and each party would, beyond a doubt, gradually augment his own force; and thus, at no distant period, the same state of things which has existed of late, would again recur: for the motives and passions which have led to it would still be in action. Mehemet Ali, or Ibrahim, would still desire to add more territory to their Pashalics; the Sultan would still burn to drive them back into Egypt.

It appears then to Her Majesty's Government, that there can be no end to the danger with which these affairs menace the peace of Europe, until Mehemet Ali shall have restored Syria to the direct authority of the Sultan; shall have retired into Egypt; and shall have interposed the Desert between his troops and authorities and the troops and authorities of the Sultan. But Mehemet Ali could not be expected to consent to this, unless some equivalent advantage were granted to him; and this equivalent advantage might be hereditary succession in his family to the Pashalic of Egypt: Mehemet Ali and his descendants being secured in the Government of that Province in the same way that a former Pasha of Scutari and his family were so secured; the Pasha continuing to be the vassal of the Porte, paying a reasonable tribute, furnishing a contingent of men, and being bound like any other Pasha by the treaties which his sovereign might make. Such an arrangement would appear to be equitable between the parties, because, on the one hand, it would secure the Sultan against many dangers and inconveniences which arise from the present occupation of Syria by the Pasha; while, on the other hand, it would afford to the Pasha that security as to the future fate of his family, his anxiety about which, he has often declared to be the main cause of his desire to obtain some final and permanent arrangement.

It appears to Her Majesty's Government that if the Five Powers were to agree upon such a plan, and were to propose it to the two parties, with all the authority which belongs to the Great Powers of Europe, such an arrangement would be carried into effect, and through its means, Europe would be delivered from a great and imminent danger.

82. COLLECTIVE NOTE TO THE SUBLIME PORTE FROM THE GREAT POWERS' DIPLOMATIC REPRESENTATIVES
27 July 1839

[Great Britain, *Parliamentary Papers*, 1841, 29: 297]

The Ottoman Empire appeared in July 1839 to be moving swiftly toward disaster. Mahmud II died on 1 July without hearing the full details of the defeat his forces had sustained in their battle against the Egyptian troops. On 7 July the Ottoman admiral handed over to Mehmed 'Ali the sultan's entire fleet. By the month's end fear had spread in Europe, particularly England, that the new sultan, sixteen-year-old 'Abdülmecid, might grant the Egyptian paşa almost all his demands. To forestall such a move, the ambassadors at Istanbul of the five major European powers presented to the Sublime Porte the following collective note. But the harmony was destined to be short-lived, for France was then backing the position of Egypt and not that of the Ottoman government. For references, see Doc. 84.

The undersigned have this morning received instructions from their respective Governments, in virtue of which they have the honour to inform the Sublime Porte, that agreement between the Five Powers upon the Eastern question is ensured, and to invite the Porte to suspend any final determination without their concurrence, awaiting the result of the interest which those Powers feel for the Porte.

83. THE HATT-I ŞERIF OF GÜLHANE
3 November 1839

[Translated, by Halil Inalcik, from the Osmanlı text in *Takvim-i Vekayi* as reproduced in *Tanzimat* (Istanbul, 1940) after p. 48; checked, against the text in Latin Turkish characters in A. Şerif Gözübüyük and Suna Kili, eds., *Türk Analyasa Metirleri*(Ankara, 1957), pp. 3–5, a text that appeared in *Düstür*, 1st ser. 1: 4–7.]

The Ottoman Westernization movement, to which Sultan Selim III (1789–1807) had given fillip by employing French and British technicians in the reorganization of his army and navy, quickened under Mahmud II (1808–39), particularly after the suppression in 1826 of the Janissary Corps. Nevertheless, Mahmud II's consuming but abortive efforts after 1834 to restrain Mehmed 'Ali distracted the sultan from his program of innovation, except as it affected the army. The *hatt-ı şerif* (noble rescript)— or *hatt-ı hümayun* (imperial rescript), as Turkish historians call it—proclaimed in Gülhane square of Istanbul in the presence of the European diplomatic community, who were "for the first time associated with Turks in a public ceremony"(Temperley, *England and the Near East*, p. 161), was essentially the handiwork of Foreign Minister Reşid Paşa, who sought by this means to wheedle material assistance out of Britain. The explicit promises of 1839—fundamental changes in the conduct of the courts, the assessment and collection of taxes, and the terms of military service for Ottoman subjects—were never wholly executed. Yet the hatt-ı şerif of Gülhane set in motion a series of administrative innovations and, in thus inaugurating the period of the Tanzimat, or reforms, that culminated in the promulgation of a constitution in 1876, represented a landmark in the Ottoman Westernization movement of the nineteenth century. Lewis, *Emergence of Modern Turkey*, chap. 4; Berkes, *Development of Secularism in Turkey*, chap. 5; Hurewitz, *Middle East Politics*, chap. 5; Temperley, op. cit., chaps. 6, 9; Engelhardt, *La Turquie et le Tanzimat*, 2 vols. (summary of legislative acts); Bailey, *British Policy and the Turkish Reform Movement*, chaps. 4–5; Assad Efendi, *La destruction du corps des janissaires*; Ubicini, *Letters on Turkey*, 1: 27–50.

All the world knows that since the first days of the Ottoman State, the lofty principles of the Kuran and the rules of the Şeriat were always perfectly observed. Our mighty Sultanate reached the highest degree of strength and power, and all its subjects [the highest degree] of ease and prosperity. But in the last one hundred and fifty years, because of a succession of difficulties and diverse causes, the sacred Şeriat was not obeyed nor were the beneficent regulations followed; consequently, the former strength and prosperity have changed into weakness and poverty. It is evident that countries not governed by the laws of the Şeriat cannot survive.

From the very first day of our accession to the throne, our thoughts have been devoted exclusively to the development of the empire and the promotion of the prosperity of the people. Therefore, if the geographical position of the Ottoman provinces, the fertility of the soil, and the aptitude and intelligence of the inhabitants are considered, it is manifest that, by striving to find appropriate means, the desired results will, with the aid of God, be realized within five or ten years. Thus, full of confidence in the help of the Most High and certain of the support of our

Prophet, we deem it necessary and important from now on to introduce new legislation to achieve effective administration of the Ottoman Government and Provinces. Thus the principles of the requisite legislation are three:

1. The guarantees promising to our subjects perfect security for life, honor, and property.
2. A regular system of assessing taxes.
3. An equally regular system for the conscription of requisite troops and the duration of their service.

Indeed there is nothing more precious in this world than life and honor. What man, however much his character may be against violence, can prevent himself from having recourse to it, and thereby injure the government and the country, if his life and honor are endangered? If, on the contrary, he enjoys perfect security, it is clear that he will not depart from the ways of loyalty and all his actions will contribute to the welfare of the government and of the people.

If there is an absence of security for property, everyone remains indifferent to his state and his community; no one interests himself in the prosperity of the country, absorbed as he is in his own troubles and worries. If, on the contrary, the individual feels complete security about his possessions, then he will become preoccupied with his own affairs, which he will seek to expand, and his devotion and love for his state and his community will steadily grow and will undoubtedly spur him into becoming a useful member of society.

Tax assessment is also one of the most important matters to regulate. A state, for the defense of its territory, manifestly needs to maintain an army and provide other services, the costs of which can be defrayed only by taxes levied on its subjects. Although, thank God, our Empire has already been relieved of the affliction of monopolies, the harmful practice of tax-farming [iltizam], which never yielded any fruitful results, still prevails. This amounts to handing over the financial and political affairs of a country to the whims of an ordinary man and perhaps to the grasp of force and oppression, for if the tax-farmer is not of good character he will be interested only in his own profit and will behave oppressively. It is therefore necessary that from now on every subject of the Empire should be taxed according to his fortune and his means, and that he should be saved from and further exaction. It is also necessary that special laws should fix and limit the expenses of our land and sea forces.

Military matters, as already pointed out, are among the most important affairs of state, and it is the inescapable duty of all the people to provide soldiers for the defense of the fatherland [vatan]. It is therefore necessary to frame regulations on the contingents that each locality should furnish according to the requirements of the time, and to reduce the term of military service to four or five years. Such legislation will put an end to the old practice, still in force, of recruiting soldiers without consideration of the size of the population in any locality, more conscripts being taken from some places and fewer from others. This practice has been throwing agriculture and trade into harmful disarray. Moreover, those who are recruited to lifetime military service suffer despair and contribute to the depopulation of the country.

In brief, unless such regulations are promulgated, power, prosperity, security, and peace may not be expected, and the basic principles [of the projected reforms] must be those enumerated above.

Thus, from now on, every defendant shall be entitled to a public hearing, according to the rules of the Şeriat, after inquiry and examination; and without the pronouncement of a regular sentence no one may secretly or publicly put another to death by poison or by any other means. No one shall be allowed to attack the honor of any other person whatsoever. Every one shall possess his property of every kind and may dispose of it freely, without let or hindrance from any person whatsoever; and the innocent heirs of a criminal shall not be deprived of their hereditary rights as a result of the confiscation of the property of such a criminal. The Muslim and non-Muslim subjects of our lofty Sultanate shall, without exception, enjoy our imperial concessions. Therefore we grant perfect security to all the populations of our Empire in their lives, their honor, and their properties, according to the sacred law.

As for the other points, decisions must be taken by majority vote. To this end, the members of the Council of Judicial Ordinances [Meclis-i Ahkam-ı Adliyye], enlarged by new members as may be found necessary, to whom will be joined on certain days that we shall determine our Ministers and the high officials of the Empire, will assemble for the purpose of framing laws to regulate the secruity of life and property and the assessment of taxes. Every one participating in the Council will express his ideas and give his advice freely.

84. CONVENTION (LONDON) FOR THE PACIFICATION OF THE LEVANT: AUSTRIA, GREAT BRITAIN, PRUSSIA, AND RUSSIA WITH THE OTTOMAN EMPIRE
15 July-17 September 1840

(Ratifications exchanged, London, 17 September 1840)
[Convention and attached instruments signed on 15 July 1840, from Great Britain, *Parliamentary Papers, 1841*, 29: 691–93, 696–98, 700; self-denying protocol signed in London on 17 September 1840, from Holland, *European Concert in the Eastern Question*, p. 97]

European intervention into internal Ottoman affairs in the summer of 1840 inaugurated nearly four decades of successful conference diplomacy by the European Concert of major powers in dealing with the Eastern Question, as the European repercussions of the progressive disintegration of the Ottoman Empire became known on the Continent. Lord Palmerston, the British foreign secretary during the two Egyptian-Ottoman crises (1832–33 and 1839–41), saw in the threat to the Ottoman dynasty a threat also to British interests. With the appearance of the steam vessel, the British government belatedly discovered what the East India Company had begun learning more than a half-century earlier—that through the Ottoman Empire coursed developing primary routes of communication and transportation between the metropole and the empire in India. In the regional quarrel of the 1830s, Russia backed the sultan, and France the viceroy. The main problem, as Palmerston diagnosed it, was to keep Russia and France apart, for if they joined hands Britain would suffer along with the Ottoman dynasty. Since Palmerston preferred a weak Ottoman Empire to a powerful Egypt astride the developing imperial arteries, he responded favorably to tsarist initiatives for a British-Russian rapprochement over the Eastern Question, which was reached in the last week of December 1839. Tsar Nicholas I agreed to give up the treaty of Hünkâr İskelesi (Doc. 72) and assented to Palmerston's condition that the fleets of Russia and the maritime powers should be allowed simultaneous entry into the Sea of Marmara, as an exceptional measure in case of need to defend the integrity of the Ottoman Empire. In return, Palmerston accepted the Russian condition that the powers should act in concert in the Ottoman-Egyptian dispute. The British government did not endorse these arrangements for more than six months, and then only after Palmerston had threatened to resign, for with France still giving its blessing to

Mehmed 'Ali the action implied the dissolution of the existing British-French alliance. At the meeting of 8 July 1840 when the British Cabinet took the decision in support of Palmerston, Lords Clarendon and Holland formally appended their dissent to the minute communicated to Queen Victoria (text in Maxwell, *Life and Letters of George William Frederick*, 1: 196–97; and Temperley, *England and the Near East*, pp. 86–88). The principal instruments were signed a week later; to these were added on 17 September 1840 a self-denying protocol. The Ottoman Empire, along with Austria and Prussia, joined Britain and Russia in signing the following instruments, which explained the purposes and laid down the rules of the collective European intervention into internal Ottoman affairs. Although it was not recognized by statesmen at the time or by scholars later on, the convention of 1840 signaled the start of the Ottoman Empire's unqualified participation in the European state system. Hurewitz, "Ottoman Diplomacy and the European State System"; Webster, *Foreign Policy of Palmerston*, 2: 644–94; Temperley, op. cit., pp. 111–16; Charles-Roux, *Thiers et Méhémet-Ali*, chaps. 1–3; Maxwell, op. cit., vol. 1, chaps. 7–8; see also references to Doc. 86.

1. Convention

ART. 1. His Highness the Sultan having come to an agreement with their Majesties the Queen of the United Kingdom of Great Britain and Ireland, the Emperor of Austria, King of Hungary and Bohemia, the King of Prussia, and the Emperor of all the Russias, as to the conditions of the arrangement which it is the intention of His Highness to grant to Mehemet Ali, conditions which are specified in the Separate Act hereunto annexed; Their Majesties engage to act in perfect accord, and to unite their efforts in order to determine Mehemet Ali to conform to that arrangement; each of the High Contracting Parties reserving to itself to co-operate for that purpose, according to the means of action which each may have at its disposal.

ART. 2. If the Pasha of Egypt should refuse to accept the above-mentioned arrangement, which will be communicated to him by the Sultan, with the concurrence of Their aforesaid Majesties; Their Majesties engage to take, at the request of the Sultan, measures concerted and settled between Them, in order to carry that arrangement into effect. In the meanwhile, the Sultan having requested his said Allies to unite with him in order to assist him to cut off the communication by sea between Egypt and Syria, and to prevent the transport of troops, horses, arms, and warlike stores of all kinds, from the one province to the other; Their Majesties the Queen of

the United Kingdom of Great Britain and Ireland, and the Emperor of Austria, King of Hungary and Bohemia, engage to give immediately to that effect, the necessary orders to their naval Commanders in the Mediterranean. Their said Majesties further engage, that the naval Commanders of their squadrons shall, according to the means at their command, afford, in the name of the Alliance, all the support and assistance in their power to those subjects of the Sultan who may manifest their fidelity and allegiance to their Sovereign.

ART. 3. If Mehemet Ali, after having refused to submit to the conditions of the arrangement above-mentioned, should direct his land or sea forces against Constantinople, the High Contracting Parties, upon the express demand of the Sultan, addressed to their Representatives at Constantinople, agree, in such case, to comply with the request of that Sovereign, and to provide for the defence of his throne by means of a co-operation agreed upon by mutual consent, for the purpose of placing the two Straits of the Bosphorus and Dardanelles, as well as the Capital of the Ottoman Empire, in security against all aggression.

It is further agreed, that the forces which, in virtue of such concert, may be sent as aforesaid, shall there remain so employed as long as their presence shall be required by the Sultan; and when His Highness shall deem their presence no longer necessary, the said forces shall simultaneously withdraw, and shall return to the

Black Sea and to the Mediterranean, re-specitively.

ART. 4. It is, however, expressly under-stood, that the co-operation mentioned in the preceding Article, and destined to place the Straits of the Dardanelles and of the Bosphorus, and the Ottoman Capital, un-der the temporary safeguard of the High Contracting Parties against all aggression of Mehemet Ali, shall be considered only as a measure of exception adopted at the express demand of the Sultan, and solely for his defence in the single case above-mentioned; but it is agreed, that such mea-sure shall not derogate in any degree from the ancient rule of the Ottoman Empire, in virtue of which it has at all times been pro-hibited for ships of war of Foreign Powers to enter the Straits of the Dardanelles and of the Bosphorus. And the Sultan, on the one hand, hereby declares that, excepting the contingency above-mentioned, it is his firm resolution to maintain in future this principle invariably established as the ancient rule of his empire; and as long as the Porte is at peace, to admit no foreign ship of war into the Straits of the Bosphorus and of the Dardanelles; on the other hand, their Majesties the Queen of the United Kingdom of Great Britain and Ireland, the Emperor of Austria, King of Hungary and Bohemia, the King of Prussia, and the Em-peror of all the Russias, engage to respect this determination of the Sultan, and to conform to the above-mentioned prin-ciple. . . .

2. Separate Act

§ 1. His Highness promises to grant to Mehemet Ali, for himself and for his de-scendants in the direct line, the administra-tion of the Pashalic of Egypt; and His Highness promises, moreover, to grant to Mehemet Ali, for his life, with the title of Pasha of Acre, and with the command of the fortress of St. John of Acre, the admin-istration of the southern part of Syria, the limits of which shall be determined by the following line of demarcation:—

This line, beginning at Cape Ras-el-Nakhora, on the coast of the Mediterran-ean, shall extend direct from thence as far as the mouth of the river Seisaban, at the northern extremity of the Lake of Tiberias; it shall pass along the Western shore of

that Lake, it shall follow the right bank of the river Jordan, and the western shore of the Dead Sea; from thence it shall extend straight to the Red Sea, which it shall strike at the northern point of the Gulf of Akaba, and from thence it shall follow the western shore of the Gulf of Akaba, and the east-ern shore of the Gulf of Suez, as far as Suez.

The Sultan, however, in making these offers, attaches thereto the condition, that Mehemet Ali shall accept them within the space of ten days after communication thereof shall have been made to him at Alexandria, by an agent of His Highness; and that Mehemet Ali shall, at the same time, place in the hands of that agent the necessary instructions of the Commanders of his sea and land forces, to withdraw im-mediately from Arabia, and from all the Holy Cities which are therein situated; from the Island of Candia; from the dis-trict of Adana; and from all other parts of the Ottoman Empire which are not com-prised within the limits of Egypt, and within those of the Pashalic of Acre, as above defined.

§ 2. If within the space of ten days, fixed as above, Mehemet Ali should not accept the above-mentioned arrangement, the Sul-tan will then withdraw the offer of the life administration of the Pashalic of Acre; but His Highness will still consent to grant to Mehemet Ali, for himself and for his de-scendants in the direct line, the administra-tion of the Pashalic of Egypt, provided such offer be accepted within the space of the ten days next following; that is to say, within a period of twenty days, to be reck-oned from the day on which the communi-cation shall have been made to him; and provided that in this case also, he places in the hands of the agent of the Sultan, the necessary instruction to his military and naval Commanders, to withdraw immedi-ately within the limits, and into the ports of the Pashalic of Egypt.

§ 3. The annual tribute to be paid to the Sultan by Mehemet Ali, shall be propor-tioned to the grater or less amount of ter-ritory of which the latter may obtain the administration, according as he accepts the first or the second alternative.

§ 4. It is, moreover, expressly under-stood, that, in the first as in the second alternative, Mehemet Ali (before the expiration of the specified period of ten or of twenty days), shall be bound to deliver up the Turkish Fleet, with the whole of its crews and equipments, into the hands of the Turkish Agent who shall be charged to receive the same. The Commanders of the Allied Squadrons shall be present at such delivery.

It is understood, that in no case can Mehemet Ali carry to account, or deduct from the tribute to be paid to the Sultan, the expences which he has incurried in the maintenance of the Ottoman Fleet, during any part of the time it shall have remained in the ports of Egypt.

§ 5. All the Treaties, and all the laws of the Ottoman Empire, shall be applicable to Egypt, and to the Pashalic of Acre, such as it has been above defined, in the same manner as to every other part of the Ottoman Empire. But the Sultan consents, that on condition of the regular payment of the tribute above-mentioned, Mehemet Ali and his descendants shall collect, in the name of the Sultan, and as the delegate of His Highness, within the provinces the administration of which shall be confided to them, the taxes and imposts legally established. It is moreover understood, that in consideration of the receipt of the aforesaid taxes and imposts, Mehemet Ali and his descendants shall defray all the expences of the civil and military administration of the said provinces.

§ 6. The military and naval forces which may be maintained by the Pasha of Egypt and Acre, forming part of the forces of the Ottoman Empire, shall always be considered as maintained for the service of the State.

§ 7. If, at the expiration of the period of twenty days after the communication shall have been made to him (according to the stipulation of § 2), Mehemet Ali shall not accede to the proposed arrangements; and shall not accept the hereditary Pashalic of Egypt, the Sultan will consider himself at liberty to withdraw that offer, and to follow, in consequence, such ulterior course as his own interests, and the counsels of his Allies may suggest to him.

§ 8. The present Separate Act shall have the same force and validity, as if it were inserted, word for word, in the Convention of this date. It shall be ratified, and the ratifications thereof shall be exchanged at London at the same time as those of the said Convention. . . .

3. Protocol

In affixing his signature to the Convention of this date, the Plenipotentiary of the Sublime Ottoman Porte declared:

That in recording by Article IV. of the said Convention the ancient rule of the Ottoman Empire, by virtue of which, it has been at all times forbidden to Foreign Vessels of War to enter within the Straits of the Dardanelles and of the Bosphorus, the Sublime Porte reserves to itself, as heretofore, to deliver passes to light vessels under Flag of War, which may be employed according to custom, for the service of the correspondence of the Legations of Friendly Powers.

The Plenipotentiaries of the Courts of Great Britain, Austria, Prussia, and Russia, took note of the above Declaration, for the purpose of communicating it to their respective Courts.

4. Reserved Protocol

The Plenipotentiaries of the Courts of Great Britain, Austria, Prussia, Russia, and Turkey, having, in virtue, of their full powers, concluded and signed this day a Convention between their respective Sovereigns, for the pacification of the Levant;

Considering that, in consequence of the distances which separate the Capitals of their respective Courts, a certain space of time must necessarily elapse before the ratifications of the said Convention can be exchanged, and before orders founded thereupon can be carried into execution;

And the said Plenipotentiaries being deeply impressed with the conviction, that by reason of the present state of things in Syria, the interests of humanity, as well as the grave considerations of European policy which constitute the object of the common solicitude of the Contracting Parties to the Convention of this day, imperiously require that, as far as possible, all delay should be avoided in the accomplishment of the pacification which the said Convention is intended to effect;

The said Plenipotentiaries, in virtue of their full powers, have agreed, that the preliminary measures mentioned in Article II. of the said Convention, shall be carried into execution at once, without waiting for the exchange of the ratifications; the respective Plenipotentiaries recording formally, by the present Instrument, the consent of their Courts to the immediate execution of these measures.

It is moreover agreed between the said Plenipotentiaries, that His Highness the Sultan will proceed immediately to adress to Mehemet Ali, the communication and offers specified in the Separate Act annexed to the Convention of this day.

It is further agreed, that the Consular Agents of Great Britain, Austria, Prussia, and Russia, at Alexandria, shall place themselves in communication with the Agent whom His Highness may send thither to communicate to Mehemet Ali the above-memtioned offers; that the said Consuls shall afford to that Agent all the assistance and support in their power; and shall use all their means of influence with Mehemet Ali, in order to persuade him to accept the arrangement which will be proposed to him by order of His Highness the Sultan.

The Admirals of the respective squadrons in the Mediterranean shall be instructed to place themselves in communication with the said Consuls on this subject.

5. Self-denying Protocol

The Plenipotentiaries of the Courts of Great Britain, Austria, Prussia, and Russia, after having exchanged the ratifications of the Convention concluded on the 15th of July last, have resolved, in order to place in its true light the disinterestedness which has guided their Courts in the conclusion of that Act, to declare formally:

That in the execution of the engagements resulting to the Contracting Powers from the above-mentioned Convention, those Powers will seek no, augmentation of territory, no exclusive influence, no commercial advantage for their subjects, which those of every other nation may not equally obtain.

The Plenipotentiaries of the Courts above-mentioned have resolved to record this Declaration in the present Protocol.

The Plenipotentiary of the Ottoman Porte, in paying a just tribute to the good faith and disinterested policy of the allied Courts, has taken cognizance of the Declaration contained in the present Protocol, and has undertaken to transmit it to his Court.

85. SULTAN'S *FERMAN* NAMING MEHMED 'ALI GOVERNOR FOR LIFE OF THE SUDANESE PROVINCES
13 February 1841

[*Foreign Relations of the United States*, 1899, p. 1027]

At the time of the negotiation of the London convention of 15 July 1840, Palmerston insisted on the inclusion of the reserved protocol authorizing the immediate application of the instruments even before the exchange of ratifications. Since Mehmed 'Ali did not accept the proffered arrangements, Austrian and British forces intervened early in September and defeated the Egyptian troops by the year's end, although hostilities continued until 17 January 1841. The Egyptian paşa finally agreed to evacuate his soldiers from the Ottoman Asian provinces and from Crete and to surrender the Ottoman fleet. In the flush of victory Sultan 'Abdülmecid issued on 13 February 1841 two *fermans* (decrees), one on Egypt and the other on the Sudan. Mehmed 'Ali objected to the provisions of the initial ferman on Egypt, especially to the sultan's retention of the right on each vacancy to select the successor. This decree was replaced on 1 June 1841 by another (see Doc. 86). While the ferman on the Sudan was neither withdrawn nor modified, Mehmed 'Ali's successors were confirmed as governors of these provinces as well. Cocheris, *Situation internationale de l'Egypte et du Soudan*, chap. 2. See also references to Doc. 86.

As is contained in another imperial firman, I have confirmed you in the government of Egypt, with a hereditary tenure thereof, under some conditions and certain limitations. More than that, I have granted to you, without hereditary tenure, the government of the provinces of Nubia, Darfour, Kordofan, and Sennaar, with all their dependencies—that is to say, with all their adjoining regions outside of the limits of Egypt. Guided by the experience and wisdom that distinguish you, you will apply yourself to administer and organize these provinces according to my equitable views, and to provide for the welfare of the inhabitants.

Each year you will transmit to my Sublime Porte the exact list of all the yearly revenues.

From time to time the troops attack the villages of the aforenamed provinces, and the young of both sexes that are taken remain in the hands of the soldiers in payment of their wages.

Not only does the ruin and depopulation of the country result therefrom, but moreover such a state of things is contrary to the holy law of right. This abuse, and that other no less baneful abuse of mutilating men for the guarding of concubine houses, being wholly reprobated by my equitable will, and in complete opposition to the principles of justice and humanity proclaimed since my coming to the throne, you will carefully deliberate as to the means for hindering and repressing in the future acts so culpable.

You will not forget that, with the exception of a few known individuals who went to Egypt with my imperial fleet, I have pardoned without distinction all the officers, soldiers, and other employés that are to be found there.

Although according to my other firman the appointment of your officers above the rank of adjustant must be submitted to my decision, you will send to my Sublime Porte a list of such officers in order that their firmans of confirmation be sent to them. Such is my sovereign will, with which you will hasten to comply.

86. SULTAN'S *FERMAN* TO MEHMED 'ALI STIPULATING CONDITIONS OF HEREDITARY GOVERNORSHIP OF EGYPT
1 June 1841

[Great Britain, *Parliamentary Papers, 1879,* 78; 36–39]

In the intervention of 1840 France refused to join the European Concert and continued instead to uphold the viceroy, Mehmed 'Ali. Once the Egyptian troops were pushed out of the Asian Arab provinces of the Ottoman Empire and Mehmed 'Ali sued for peace, the problem became one of finding a durable settlement that would sustain the Ottoman dynasty and protect its future, while enabling France and its protégé to save face. In three months of negotiations, the European powers, now joined by France, mediated between the sultan and the viceroy, generally inducing the sultan to modify in Mehmed 'Ali's favor the terms under which he and his heirs were to govern Egypt.

The sultan gave up the right to select the successors; nor was the governor-elect required to "proceed in person to Constantinople, there to receive investiture of his office." The Sublime Porte was relieved of responsibility for domestic legislation in the province, and the annual tribute was fixed by a separate *ferman* in May at 80,000 purses, or the equivalent of $1,775,600, instead of one-fourth the total revenue of the Egyptian government. But Mehmed 'Ali was forced to accept the stipulation that "all the Treaties concluded and to be concluded between my Sublime Porte and the friendly Powers, shall be completely executed in the Province of Egypt likewise." This clause brought into effect the British-Ottoman convention of Balta Liman (Doc. 80) and the others modeled on it, which, by destroying Mehmed 'Ali's commercial and industrial monopolies and thus depriving him of essential revenues, ended his integrated program of modernization. Although altered in detail by subsequent edicts (see Doc. 127), the ferman of 1 June 1841 established the basic pattern of the formal Ottoman-Egyptian relationship that existed until 1914. Webster, *Foreign Policy of Palmerston*, 2: 753–58; Temperley, *England and the Near East*, pp. 137–43; Bréhier, *L'Egypte*, chap. 4; Hasenclever, *Geschichte Ägyptens*, pp. 116–39; Cattaui, *Histoire des rapports de l'Egypte avec la Sublime Porte*, 2. chaps. 10–11; Owen, *Cotton and the Egyptian Economy*, chap. 3; Mustafa, "Breakdown of the Monopoly System in Egypt."

The act of submission which thou hast just made, the assurances of fidelity and devotion which thou hast given, and the upright and sincere intentions which thou hast manifested, as well with regard to myself as in the interests of my Sublime Porte, have come to my sovereign knowledge, and have been very agreeable to me.

In consequence, and as the zeal and sagacity by which thou art characterized as likewise the experience and knowledge which thou hast acquired in the affairs of Egypt during the long space of time that thou hast held the post of Governor of Egypt, give reason to believe that thou hast acquired a title to the favour and to the confidence which I may grant to thee, that is to say, that thou wilt be sensible of their full extent, and all the gratitude which thou shouldst have for them, that thou wilt apply thyself to cause these feelings to descend to thy sons and thy nephews, I grant unto thee the Government of Egypt within its ancient boundaries, such as they are to be found in the map which is sent unto thee by my Grand Vizier now in office, with a seal affixed to it, together with the additional privilege of hereditary succession, and with the following conditions:—

Henceforth, when the post shall be va-cant, the Government of Egypt shall descend in a direct line, from the elder to the elder, in the male race among the sons and grandsons. As regards their nomination, that shall be made by my Sublime Porte.

If at any time fate should decide that the male line should become extinct, as in that case it will devolve upon my Sublime Porte to confer the Government of Egypt on another person, the male children, issue of the daughters of the Governors of Egypt, shall possess no right to, no legal capacity for, the succession of the Government.

Although the Pashas of Egypt have obtained the privilege of hereditary succession, they still must be considered, as far as precedency is concerned, to be on a footing of equality with the other Viziers, they shall be treated like the other Viziers of my Sublime Porte, and they shall receive the same titles as are given to the other Viziers when they are written to.

The principles founded on the laws of security of life, of the security of property, and the preservation of honour, principles recorded in the salutary ordinances of my Hatti Sheriff of Gulhané; all the Treaties concluded and to be concluded between my Sublime Porte and the friendly Powers, shall be completely executed in the Province of Egypt likewise.

In Egypt, all the taxes, all the revenues, shall be levied and collected in my sovereign name; and all the regulations made and to be made by my Sublime Porte shall also be put in practice in Egypt, reconciling them in the best way possible with the local circumstances and with the principles of justice and of equity. Nevertheless, as the Egyptians are likewise the subjects of my Sublime Porte, and in order that they may not one day be oppressed, the tithe, the duties, and the other taxes which are levied there, shall be so, in conformity with the equitable system adopted by my Sublime Porte; and care shall be taken to pay, when the period for payment shall arrive, out of the customs duties, the capitation tax, the tithe, the revenues, and other produce of the Province of Egypt, the annual tribute of which the amount is inserted and defined in another Imperial Firman.

It being customary to send every year from Egypt provisions in kind to the two Holy Cities, the provisions and other articles, whatever they may be, which have up to this time been sent thither, shall continue to be sent to each place separately.

As my Sublime Porte has taken the resolution of improving the coin, which is the soul of the operations of society, and of effecting this in such manner that henceforth there can be no variation either in the alloy, or in the value, I grant permission for money to be coined in Egypt; but the gold and silver monies which I permit thee to coin shall bear my name, and shall resemble in all respects, as regards their determination, value, and form, the monies which are coined here.

In time of peace, 18,000 men will suffice for the internal service of the province of Egypt; it shall not be allowed to increase their numbers. But as the land and sea forces of Egypt are raised for the service of my Sublime Porte, it shall be allowable, in time of war, to increase them to the number which shall be deemed suitable by my Sublime Porte.

The principle has been adopted that the soldiers employed in the other parts of my dominions shall serve for five years, at the end of which term they shall be exchanged for recruits.

That being the case, it would be requisite that the same system should also be observed in Egypt in that respect. But with regard to the duration of the service, the dispositions of the people shall be attended, to, observing what is required by equity with regard to them.

Four hundred men shall be sent every year to Constantinople to replace others.

There shall be no difference between the distinguishing marks and the flags of the other troops which shall be employed there, and the distinguishing marks and the flags of the other troops of my Sublime Porte. The officers of the Egyptian navy shall have the same distinguishing marks of ranks, and the Egyptian vessels shall have the same flags as the officers and vessels of this place.

The Governor of Egypt shall appoint the officers of the land and sea forces up to the rank of Colonel. With regard to the appointments to ranks higher than that of Colonel, that is to say, of Pashas *Mirliva* (Brigadier-Generals), and of Pashas Ferik (Generals of Division), it will be absolutely necessary to apply for permission for them, and to take my orders thereupon.

Henceforth the Pashas of Egypt shall not be at liberty to build vessels of war without having first applied for the permission of my Sublime Porte, and having obtained from it a clear and positive authority.

As each of the conditions settled as above is annexed to the privilege of hereditary succession, if a single one of them is not executed, that privilege of hereditary succession shall forthwith be abolished and annulled.

Such being my supreme pleasure on all the points above specified, thou, thy children, and thy descendants, grateful for this exalted sovereign favour, ye shall always be diligent in scrupulously executing the conditions laid down, ye shall take heed not to infringe them, ye shall be careful to ensure the repose and the tranquillity of the Egyptians by protecting them from all injury and from all oppressions, ye shall report to this place, and ye shall apply for orders on all matters of importance which concern those countries, it being for these purposes that the present Imperial Firman, which is decorated with my sovereign signature, has been written, and is sent to you.

87. CONVENTION (LONDON) REGARDING THE STRAITS:
AUSTRIA, FRANCE, GREAT BRITAIN, PRUSSIA, RUSSIA,
AND THE OTTOMAN EMPIRE
13 July 1841

[Great Britain, *Parliamentary Papers, 1942*, 45: 350–56]

The end of the Egyptian crisis restored unity among the Big Five in Europe, for France initialed on 15 March 1841 the London Convention of 15 July 1840 (Doc. 84). The new unity found expression in the following convention, establishing a regime for the straits that survived without major change until the outbreak of World War I. The new arrangement disposed at last of the treaty of Hünkâr İskelesi (Doc. 72) and thus pleased England. Russia was equally satisfied, for the convention laid down that the straits were to be closed to all foreign war vessels. Hurewitz, "Russia and the Turkish Straits"; Temperley, *England and the Near East*, 144–50; Webster, *Foreign Policy of Palmerston*, 2: 758–76; on the straits regime, Mischef, *La Mer Noire et les détroits de Constantinople*, chap. 5; Phillipson and Buxton, *Question of the Bosphorus and Dardanelles*, pt. 2, chap. 4; Goriainow, *Le Bosphore et les Dardanelles*, chap. 10; Shotwell and Deák, *Turkey at the Straits*, chap. 4.

ART. I. His Highness the Sultan, on the one part, declares that he is firmly resolved to maintain for the future the principle invariably established as the ancient rule of his Empire, and in virtue of which it has at all times been prohibited for the Ships of War of Foreign Powers to enter the Straits of the Dardanelles and of the Bosphorus; and that, so long as the Porte is at peace, His Highness will admit no foreign Ship of War into the said Straits.

And their Majesties the Queen of the United Kingdom of Great Britain and Ireland, the Emperor of Austria, King of Hungary and Bohemia, the King of the French, the King of Prussia, and the Emperor of all the Russias, on the other part, engage to respect this determination of the Sultan, and to conform themselves to the principle above declared.

ART. II. It is understood that in recording the inviolability of the ancient rule of the Ottoman Empire mentioned in the preceding Article, the Sultan reserves to himself, as in past times, to deliver firmans of passage for light vessels under flag of war, which shall be employed as is usual in the service of the Missions of foreign Powers.

ART. III. His Highness the Sultan reserves to himself to communicate the present Convention to all the Powers with whom the Sublime Porte is in relations of friendship, inviting them to accede thereto.

88. TREATY OF COMMERCE: THE UNITED KINGDOM AND PERSIA
28 October 1841

(Ratified by the shah on signature; unilaterally abrogated by Persia, 10 May 1928)
[Great Britain, *Parliamentary Papers, 1842*, 45: 357–58]

"What relates to commerce, trade, and other affairs will be drawn up and concluded in a separate commercial Treaty," the negotiators hopefully inserted into the preamble of the 1814 British-Persian alliance (Doc. 56), after the Persians had turned down a British proposal that trade between the two countries should be regulated by the commercial treaty of 1801 (Doc. 41). Twenty-seven years elapsed before the fresh instrument—"annexed and united . . . to the original Treaty [of 1814]"—was framed, placing British merchants in Persia on the same footing as Russian merchants under the commercial treaty of Turkmanchay (Doc. 65). Curzon, *Persia and the Persian Question*, vol. 2, chap. 29, pt. 2; Kelly, *Britain and the Persian Gulf*, pp. 347–38; also Miller, *Treaties and Other International Acts*, 7: 453–82.

ART. 1. The merchants of the two mighty States are reciprocally permitted and allowed to carry into each other's territories their goods and manufactures of every description, and to sell or exchange them in any part of their respective countries; and on the goods which they import or export, custom duties shall be levied, that is to say, on entering the country the same amount of custom duties shall be levied, once for all, that is levied on merchandise imported by the merchants of the most favoured European nations; and at the time of going out of the country, the same amount of custom duties which is levied on the merchandise of merchants of the most favoured European nations shall be levied from the merchants, subjects of the High Contracting Parties; and except this, no claim shall be made upon the merchants of the two States in each other's dominions on any pretext or under any denomination; and the merchants or persons connected with or dependent upon the High Contracting Parties in each other's dominions, mutually, shall receive the same aid and support, and the same respect, which are received by the subjects of the most favoured nations.

ART. II. As it is necessary, for the purpose of attending to the affairs of the merchants of the two Parties respectively, that from both Governments Commercial Agents should be appointed to reside in stated places; it is therefore arranged that two Commercial Agents on the part of the British Government shall reside, one in the Capital, and one in Tabreez, and in those places only, and on this condition, that he who shall reside at Tabreez, and he alone, shall be honoured with the privileges of Consul-General; and as for a series of years a Resident of the British Government has resided at Bushire, the Persian Government grants permission that the said Resident shall reside there as heretofore. And, in like manner, two Commercial Agents shall reside on the part of the Persian Government, one in the Capital London, and one in the port of Bombay, and shall enjoy the same rank and privileges which the Commercial Agents of the British Government shall enjoy in Persia.

89. REPUDIATION OF THE BRITISH-INDIAN INTERVENTION IN AFGHANISTAN: PROCLAMATION AT SIMLA BY GOVERNOR GENERAL LORD ELLENBOROUGH
1 October 1842

[India Office Library, L/P & S/5, Secret Letters from Bengal and India, vol. 27, 1842]

The British-Indian attempt in 1839–42 forcibly to install as a puppet on the Afghan throne Shah Shuja' al-Mulk, ended after a preliminary success, in an unmitigated disaster. Shah Shuja' and the British principals, Lieutenant-General Sir Alexander Burnes and Sir William Hay Macnaghten, were murdered, and the British-Indian troops and their families were virtually wiped out. Meanwhile, hardly less conclusive were the failure of a Russian-advised Persian campaign in 1838 to capture the Afghan khanate of Herat, defended with British advice, and a Russian attempt to seize the khanate of Khiva in 1839–40. "All we want of Khiva is that it should be a non-conducting body between Russia and British India, and separated from both by a considerable interval of space," observed Foreign Minister Lord Palmerston in January 1840, at the time of the brief initial Russian thrust into the principality (cited by Webster, *Foreign Policy of Palmerston*, 2: 749). In contemplating Central Asia from the vantage point of Saint Petersburg, Nesselrode might well have nourished a similar thought, simply substituting Afghanistan for Khiva. In any case, the ruckus over Afghanistan, Persia, and Central Asia was essentially an extension of the diplomatic dispute precipitated in the Ottoman Empire by the treaty of Hünkâr İskelesi in 1833 (Doc. 72), for British-Russian rivalry cut across the Asian Middle East in the 1830s. Once the two powers reached a détente on Egypt and the Turkish straits in 1840–41 (Docs. 84, 87), British-Russian relations in Persia and over Afghanistan and Central Asia calmed down for about a dozen years. Lord Ellenborough's repudiation in the proclamation reproduced below did not erase the memory either in Afghanistan and British-India or in Britain of the ill-fated policy of his predecessor, Lord Auckland. But it did destroy once and for all the Sadozay dynasty and make possible the slow rebuilding of a fresh relationship with the new Barakzay rulers of Afghanistan under the leadership of Dust Muhammad Khan, who regained control of Kabul, and his half-brother Kohandil Khan, who resumed rule over Qandahar. Norris, *First Afghan War*; Webster, op. cit., 2: pp. 738–52; Singhal, *India and Afghanistan*, chap. 1; Kaye, *History of the War in Afghanistan*; Fraser-Tytler, *Afghanistan*, pt. 2, chaps. 4–6; Archbold, "Afghanistan, Russia and Persia," in *Cambridge History of the British Empire*, vol. 4, chap. 28; Burnes, *Cabool*; Lal, *Life of Amir Dost Mohammed Khan*; Durand, *First Afghan War and Its Causes*.

The Government of India directed its army to pass the Indus in order to expel from Afghanistan a Chief believed to be hostile to British interests, and to replace upon his throne a Sovereign represented to be friendly to those interests, and popular with his former subjects.

The Chief believed to be hostile became a prisoner, and the Sovereign represented to be popular was replaced upon his throne; but, after events which brought into question his fidelity to the Government by which he was restored, he lost by the hands of an assassin the throne he had only held amidst insurrections, and his death was preceded and followed by still existing anarchy.

Disasters unparalleled in their extent, unless by the errors in which they originated, and by the treachery by which they were completed, have in one short campaign been avenged upon every scene of past misfortune; and repeated victories in the field, and the capture of the cities and citadels of Ghuznee and Cabool, have again attached the opinion of invincibility to the British arms.

The British army in possession of Afghanistan will now be withdrawn to the Sutlej.

The Governor General will leave it to the Afghans themselves to create a Government amidst the anarchy which is the consequence of their crimes.

To force a Sovereign upon a reluctant people would be as inconsistent with the policy as it is with the principles of the British Government, tending to place the arms and resources of that people at the disposal of the first invader, and to impose the burthen of supporting a Sovereign without the prospect of benefit from his alliance.

The Governor Gereral will willingly recognize any Government approved by the Afghans themselves, which shall appear desirous and capable of maintaining friendly relations with neighbouring States.

Content with the limits nature appears to have assigned to its empire, the Government of India will devote all its efforts to the establishment and maintenance of general peace, to the protection of the Sovereigns and Chiefs its allies, and to the prosperity and happiness of its own faithful subjects.

The rivers of the Punjab and the Indus, and the mountainous passes and the barbarous tribes of Afghanistan, will be placed between the British army and an enemy approaching from the West, if indeed such enemy there can be, and no longer between the army and its supplies.

The enormous expenditure required for the support of a large force, in a false military position, at a distance from its own frontier and its resources, will no longer arrest every measure for the improvement of the country and of the people.

The combined army of England and of India, superior in equipment, in discipline, in valour, and in the Officers by whom it is commanded, to any force which can be opposed to it in Asia, will stand in unassailable strength upon its own soil, and for ever, under the blessing of Providence, preserve the glorious empire it has won, in security and in honor.

The Governor General cannot fear the misconstruction of his motives in thus frankly announcing to surrounding States the pacific and conservative policy of his Government.

Afghanistan and China have seen at once the forces at his disposal, and the effect with which they can be applied.

Sincerely attached to peace for the sake of the benefits it confers upon the people, the Governor General is resolved that peace shall be observed, and will put forth the whole power of the British Government to coerce the State by which it shall be infringed.

90. OTTOMAN ACCEPTANCE OF THE GREAT POWERS' PROPOSAL
FOR THE ADMINISTRATION OF LEBANON
7 December 1842

[Translated from the French text in Testa, *Recueil des traités de la Porte Ottomane*, 3: 66–68. Serim Efendi, the Ottoman foreign minister, addressed identical notes to the chiefs of the diplomatic missions of Austria, France, Great Britain, Prussia, and Russia at Istanbul. The note to the British ambassador is reproduced here.]

The population of Lebanon became progressively more restive in the last year of Egyptian rule, partly because of the efforts by Ibrahim Paşa, Mehmed 'Ali's son and governor general of Syria, to disarm the district and augment the tax revenue, and partly because of the courtship of the Maronites by France and the Druzes by Britain. Following the defeat and departure of the Egyptians, the European powers also brought to a close the long and harsh rule over Lebanon by Amir Bashir II al-Shihabi (1788–1840). It also ended the Shihabi provincial dynasty, which had governed Lebanon since the close of the seventeenth century, for the Sublime Porte deposed the incompetent Amir Bashir III in January 1842. Having asserted its political supremacy in Lebanon, the Sublime Porte tried to manage affairs there by playing the Maronites off against the Druzes. The plan for communal autonomy for the Maronites and the Druzes under a dual kaymakamate represented a compromise between the French and the Ottoman proposals which was advocated by Prince Metternich, the chancellor of Austria, and was accepted by the Concert. Salibi, *Modern History of Lebanon*, chaps. 3–4; Hurewitz, "Lebanese Democracy in Its International Setting"; Harik, *Politics and Change*, chap. 9; Kerr, *Lebanon in the Last Years of Feudalism;* Polk, *Opening of South Lebanon*; Ferah, "Lebanese Insurgence of 1840"; Temperley, *England and the Near East*, chap. 7; Jouplain, *La question du Liban*, 247–353; for a contemporary account, see C. Churchill, *The Druzes and the Meronites*, chaps. 1–3.

I read with care the translation of the instruction of 23 November [1842] to Mr. Pisani, the first interpreter of the British Embassy, a copy of which was given me by him.

Your Excellency expresses in the instruction the desire to confer with me, jointly with your colleagues, to inform me in full of the inclinations of the Great Powers on the question of Lebanon.

I myself wish to have a meeting with you to let you know as promptly as possible my intentions on the subject. I therefore hastened to apprise the Ministry of His Highness [the Sultan] of the views expressed by the Great Powers on the said question, of which I was informed by the explanations and observations given me in the conferences that I have previously had the honor

to hold with Your Excellency and the Barons de Bourqueney [of France] and von Klezl [of Austria] and by the tenor of the notes that I have received on the subject from Their Excellencies Mr. Butenev [of Russia] and Mr. Wagner [of Prussia].

At a ministerial meeting on the question, attended by the Serasker Paşa [Ottoman supreme commander in Syria], the latter persistently limited himself to the communications and observations that he has incessantly presented to the Sublime Porte. Mustafa Paşa [Serasker of Syria until October 1842] declared that he was wholly convinced that the measure adopted, providing for the appointment by the *müşür* [commander; in this case, governor] of Sidon of two *kaymakams* [deputy governors], one for the Druzes and one for the

Maronites, previously enacted to ensure the unanimously desired tranquillity of the Mountain, would not fulfill the purpose unless the kaymakams were chosen from among foreigners. But at the same time he stressed that this tranquillity would not be achieved, if the kaymakams were chosen from among the Druzes and the Maronites themselves.

The Ottoman Minister most strongly regrets to observe that this aspect of the question has given rise to so much discussion and negotiation in the past year and that his friends and allies the Great Powers have never changed their views on the subject, despite the sound administration that he has succeeded in reestablishing in the Mountain, a claim for which he can produce convincing proof.

Nevertheless, prompted by the sentiments of respect toward its dearest friends and allies, the five Great Powers, by which it has constantly been animated, the Sublime Porte, in the search for a solution of so delicate a question, which is simultaneously a matter of domestic jurisdiction, prefers to conform itself to their wishes rather than oppose them.

It is clear, however, that since the object of the Sublime Porte and that of the Great Powers are identical—the reestablishment of law and order in the Mountain—the system proposed for adoption by the two parties ought to have been considered in the first place as an experiment.

If [the desired] result could be obtained by means of the [proposed] system, the Sublime Porte would accomplish its wish and could hardly fail to be grateful. But if it should not be possible to reestablish tranquillity in Syria, as [the Ottoman Government] has reason to fear on the basis of information that has accumulated, the objections previously raised by the Sublime Porte would clearly have been justified and the government of His Highness [the Sultan] would be acknowledged by everyone to have been right.

Therefore, the Sublime Porte, desirous of conforming to the friendly advice proffered by its friends, has decided to issue to Es'ad Paşa [the new Serasker of Syria] an order to select and appoint two kaymakams, one for the Druzes and the other for the Maronites, from among the natives other than those belonging to the Shihabi family, in conformity with the measure already approved by the Great Powers, for the administration of the different classes of subjects who inhabit Mount Lebanon, placed under his jurisdiction. Simultaneously [the Sublime Porte] has urged [Es'ad Paşa] to devote his full efforts to the maintenance of tranquillity in Syria.

This decision of the Ottoman Ministry has also received the imperial sanction of His Highness, and I believe it is my duty to inform Your Excellency that this question has been resolved without [need for] further negotiations.

91. TREATY OF FRIENDSHIP: GREAT BRITAIN AND THE SULTAN OF LAHIJ
11 February 1843

[Aitchison, *Collection of Treaties* . . . *relating to India* (5th ed.), 11 : 58–60]

The British first entered into political relations with the shaykhs of the Aden area in 1799, as a defensive measure against possible French attempts to reach the Indian Ocean via the Red Sea. On 6 September 1802 the East India Company concluded a commercial treaty (text in Aitchison, op. cit., pp. 53–56) with the Sultan of Lahij, who owned the port of Aden. When the company was preparing to start a monthly steam service to Egypt in 1837, the British for the first time sought permanent possession of the site as a coaling station. Its value to the United Kingdom was enhanced by strategic considerations, for Foreign Minister Palmerston seemed somewhat disturbed by the presence of Egyptian troops in the immediate hinterland. Efforts to purchase the port from Sultan Muhsin proved fruitless, so that ultimately on 19 January 1839 two British armed vessels forcibly occupied the small peninsula. Despite the two treaties of 2 and 4 February and a bond of 18 June 1839, signed by the sultan or his agent and acknowledging British possession of Aden in return for an annual subsidy of $6,500 (ibid., pp. 56–58), the Arab chieftain tried several times to recapture the port. Not until 11 February 1843 did Sultan Muhsin finally acquiesce in British contorl of Aden. The adjacent territory of Shaykh 'Uthman, which later formed part of the Crown Colony of Aden, was purchased from the Sultan of Lahij by India in the name of the British government on 7 February 1882 (text of agreement, ibid., pp. 70–72). Hoskins, *British Routes to India*, chap. 8, and "British Position in Arabia"; Hunter, *British Settlement of Aden*, pt. 5; Dodwell, *Founder of Modern Egypt*, pp. 145–51; Reilly, "Aden and Its Links with India"; Laws, "Capture of Aden"; Robbins, "Legal Status of Aden"; Jacob, *Kings of Arabia*, chaps. 2–3; Low, *Indian Navy*, vol. 2, chap. 3; Apelt, *Aden*, chap. 8.

ART 1. In consideration of the respect due to the British Government, Sultan Muhsin Fadhl agrees to restore the lands and property of all kinds belonging to the late Hassan Abdoolah Khateeb, Agent to the British at Lahej, after such property shall be proven. But the Sultan Muhsin expects in return that certain revenue and territorial books styled Deiras, said to be in the possession of the Khateeb family, should be restored to the government of Lahej, and then their persons shall be safe should they wish to go inland.

ART. 2. The Sultan will, on the same consideration, and has, in the presence of witnesses, settled all claims made by Shumaiel, the Jew, and he will also attend to all claims that may be brought against him during his fifteen days' residence in Aden.

ART. 3. Such transit duties as shall be hereafter specified shall be exacted by the Sultan, who binds himself not to exceed them. The Sultan will also, by every means in his power, facilitate the intercourse of merchants, and he shall in return be empowered to levy a moderate export duty.

ART. 4. The Sultan engages to permit British subjects to visit Lahej for commercial purposes and to protect them, allowing toleration of religion with the exception of burning the dead.

ART. 5. Should any British subject become amenable to the law, he is to be made over to the authorities at Aden; and in like manner are the subjects of the Sultan to be made over to his jurisdiction.

ART. 6. The bridge at Khor Maksar is English property, and as such shall be kept in order by them; but should it be proved that it is destroyed by the followers of the Sultan, he shall repair it.

ART. 7. The Sultan binds himself, as far as he can, to keep the roads clear of plundering parties and to protect all merchandize passing through his territories.

ART. 8. British subjects may, with the permission of the Sultan, hold in tenure land at Lahej, subject to the laws of the country; and in like manner may the ryots of the Sultan hold property in Aden subject to the British laws.

ART. 9. Such articles as the Sultan may require for his own family shall pass Aden free of duty; and in like manner all presents and all government property shall pass the territories of the Sultan free from transit duty.

ART. 10. With regard to the stipend of the Sultan, it entirely rests with Captain Haines and the British Government. The Sultan considers the British his true friends; and likewise the British look upon the Sultan of Lahej as their friend.

92. CONVENTION (TANGIER) FOR THE RESTORATION OF FRIENDLY RELATIONS: FRANCE AND MOROCCO
10 September 1844

(Ratifications exchanged, 26 October 1844)
[Translated from the French text in Clercq, *Recueil des traités*, 5: 200–03]

Bugeaud's strategy of pacification by military colonization (Doc. 78) virtually destroyed the Arab amirate by mid-1843, and before the end of the year 'Abd al-Qadir was forced to cross the Moroccan border. There the *mujahid*, or religious warrior, received asylum, while he recruited fresh tribesmen for the struggle against the infidel French and the restoration of the territorial integrity of the amirate. He also succeeded in widening the jihad by drawing Morocco into the war. Mawlay 'Abd al-Rahman (1822–59), in fact, attacked the French at Lalla Maghnia (present-day Marnia) in Algeria late in the spring of 1844 but was repulsed. The extension of the war into Morocco aroused the anxiety of Britain, which had not yet acquiesced in the French conquest of Algeria. For Britain, the French presence there was bad enough, since it had already modified the military balance in the Mediterranean. But the possible French subjugation of Morocco appeared even more ominous, since if successful it would install a major maritime power on the African shore of the straits and deprive Britain of its predominant position at the chokepoint of a major international sealane, so important for the defense of British imperial interests in peace and in war. Alive to British sensitivities, King Louis Philippe and his government had little stomach for testing British resolve, particularly at a time when the pacification of Algeria was inching inland in the face of determined Muslim resistance. Bugeaud, however, and the French naval commander, the prince de Joinville, Louis Philippe's son, ignored instructions from Paris not to use force in persuading Mawlay 'Abd al-Rahman to stop at once all aid to 'Abd al-Qadir. Despite the presence off Tangier of a British naval squadron equal in size and power to that of France, de Joinville issued an ultimatum to the mawlay, which was ignored. The French squadron thereupon bombarded Tangier (6 August 1844) and Mogador (15 August). Meanwhile Bugeaud ordered his troops into Morocco, routing the mawlay's regular and tribal forces at Isly (14 August). Unable to prevent the brief war, Britain nevertheless, with the bribe of recognition of the French presence in Algeria, inhibited France from dictating the terms of peace. Still, Bugeaud realized his major objective of procuring the mawlay's pledge to outlaw the elusive 'Abd al-Qadir. Flournoy, *British Policy towards Morocco*, chaps. 3–4; Usborne, *Conquest of Morocco*, chap. 2; Julien, *Histoire de l'Algérie contemporaine*, chap. 4; Cossé-Brissac, *Les rapports de la France et du Maroc*; Latreille, *La campagne de 1844 au Maroc*.

. . . ART. 1. The extraordinary concentration of Moroccan troops at the frontier of the two Empires or in the vicinity of the said frontier shall be disbanded. His Majesty the King of Morocco undertakes to avoid any such [military] buildup in the future. There shall remain only one military unit, with a customary strength not exceeding two thousand men, under the command of the *qaid* [chief] of Oueschda [Oudjda]. This number may nevertheless be increased if, in the view of the two governments, extraordinary circumstances render it necessary in the common interest.

ART. 2. An exemplary punishment shall be imposed on those Moroccan chiefs who led or tolerated aggressive acts in time of peace on the territory of Algeria against the troops of His Majesty the Emperor of the French.

The Moroccan Government shall inform the French Government of the measures taken to implement the present clause.

ART. 3. His Majesty the Emperor of Morocco undertakes once again, in the most formal and most absolute manner, neither to give nor to permit others in his realm to give assistance, financial aid, munitions, or any kind of war materials to any refractory subject or enemy of France.

ART. 4. Al-Hajj 'Abd al-Qadir is outlawed throughout the empire of Morocco as well as Algeria. He shall therefore be pursued at gun-point by the French on Algerian territory and by the Moroccans on their territory, until he shall be expelled or captured by either country. If French troops should capture 'Abd al-Qadir, the government of His Majesty the Emperor of the French Pledges to treat him with respect and magnanimity. Should 'Abd al-Qadir fall into the custody of Moroccan troops, His Majesty the King of Morocco promises to place him under arrest in a village on the western seacoast of the Empire until the two governments have adopted in concert the necessary measures for preventing 'Abd al-Qadir from taking up arms again and disturbing once again the tranquillity of Algeria and Morocco.

ART. 5. The boundaries between the possessions of His Majesty the Emperor of the French and those of His Majesty the King of Morocco remain fixed and agreed in conformity with the state of things recognized by the Moroccan Government at the time of Turkish rule in Algeria. The full and precise execution of the present clause shall be the object of a special agreement negotiated and concluded on the spot by the plenipotentiaries designated for this purpose by His Majesty the Emperor of the French and a representative of the Moroccan Government. His Majesty the King of Morocco pledges to take without delay suitable measures with this end in view, and to keep the French Government informed.

ART. 6. Immediately after the signing of the present convention, the two parties shall cease hostilities. As soon as the stipulations in Articles 1, 2, 4, and 5 are executed to the satisfaction of the French Government, the French troops shall evacuate the island of Mogador as well as the city of Oueschda [Ujdah], and all prisoners taken by the two Parties shall be returned to their respective countries.

ART. 7. The two High Contracting Parties undertake in good faith and as promptly as possible to conclude a new treaty which, based on agreements presently in force, shall be designed to strengthen and fulfill them in the interest of the political and commercial relations of the two Empires. In the meantime, all provisions of past treaties shall be scrupulously respected and observed, and France shall enjoy most-favored-nation treatment in every matter and on every occasion.[1]

ART. 8. The present Convention shall be ratified and the ratifications shall be exchanged within two months, or sooner if possible. . . .

1. France enjoyed these privileges under art. 5 of the treaty of 28 May 1767 and the additional article of 28 May 1825.

93. TREATY OF COMMERCE: FRANCE AND MASQAT
17 November 1844

(Ratifications exchanged 4 February 1846)
[Aitchison, *Collection of Treaties . . . relating to India* (5th. ed.), 11: app. 2, pp. xxix-xxxiv]

Britain concluded on 31 May 1839 its capitulation with Masqat (text in Aitchison, op. cit., pp. 292–99), whose shaykh—variously styled Hami (Protector), Imam, and

Sultan—also ruled over the island of Zanzibar. But Masqat never became as dependent on Britain as did the neighboring principalities. This was confirmed by the 1833 Masqati treaty with the United States (Doc. 75) and the following capitulation with France. The commercial agreement of 1844, of which the Arabic text was regarded as binding, accorded France inclusive extraterritorial rights and most-favored-nation treatment. A comparable treaty was concluded with the Netherlands on 7 April/27 August 1877 (ibid., app. 4, pp. xxxix-xl). Liebesny, "International Relations of Arabia, the Dependent Areas"; Auzoux, "La France et Muscate"; for British views, see A. Wilson, *Persian Gulf*, chap. 15; Curzon, *Persia and the Persian Question*, 2: 433–46; Ruete, *Said bin Sultan*, pp. 93–111.

ART. 1. There shall always be good understanding and friendship between the King of the French, his heirs and successors, and His Highness Syud Sueed bin Sultan, the Sultan of Maskat, his heirs and successors, as also between their respective subjects.

ART. 2. The subjects of Syud Sueed bin Sultan, the Sultan of Maskat, shall be at liberty to enter, reside in, trade with, and pass with their merchandize through France; and the French shall, in like manner, have similar liberty with regard to the territories of Syud Sueed bin Sultan, the Sultan of Maskat. The subjects of both the Governments shall have all the privileges which are or may be conceded by the respective Governments to the subjects of the most favoured nations.

ART. 3. The French shall be at liberty to purchase, sell or rent land, houses or warehouses, in the dominions of Syud Sueed bin Sultan, the Sultan of Maskat. The houses, warehouses, or other premises occupied by the French, or by persons in their service, shall not be forcibly entered without the permission of the French Consul. [Frenchmen] shall not be prevented from leaving the dominions of Syud Sueed bin Sultan whenever they wish to do so.

ART. 4. The subjects of Syud Sueed bin Sultan, the Sultan of Maskat, actually in the service of the French, shall enjoy the same privileges which are granted to the French themselves; but if such subjects of His Highness shall be convicted of any crime or infraction of the law, they shall be discharged by the French, and delivered over to the authorities of the place.

ART. 5. The two high contracting parties acknowledge reciprocally the right of ap-

pointing Consuls to reside in each other's dominions, wherever the interests of commerce may require the presence of such officers; and such Consuls shall at all times be placed in the country in which they reside on the footing of the Consuls of the most favoured nations. Each of the high contracting parties further agrees to permit his own subjects to be appointed to Consular offices by the other contracting party, provided always that the persons so appointed shall not begin to act without the previous approbation of the sovereign whose subjects they may be. The public functionaries of either Government, residing in the dominions of the other, shall enjoy the same privileges, immunities, and exemptions which are enjoyed within the same dominions by similar public functionaries of other countries. The French Consul shall be at liberty to hoist the French flag over his house.

ART. 6. The authorities of the Sultan of Maskat shall not interfere in disputes between the French, or between the French and the subjects of other Christian nations. When differences arise between a subject of the Sultan of Maskat and a Frenchman, if the former be the complainant, the cause shall be heard by the French Consul; but if a Frenchman be the complainant against any of the subjects of the Sultan at Maskat, or against any Mahomedans, then the cause shall be decided by the authorities of the Sultan of Maskat, or by his deputy: but in such case the cause shall not be decided, except in the presence of the French Consul, or his deputy, who shall attend at the Court. In causes between a Frenchman and a subject of the Sultan of Maskat the evidence of a man proved to have given false testimony on a former occasion shall not be received. A cause to be decided by the French Consul shall be tried in the presence of the Sultan of Maskat, or a person acting for him.

ART. 7. The property of a French subject who may die in any part of the dominions of the Sultan of Maskat, or of a subject of the Sultan of Maskat who may die in any part of the French dominions, shall be delivered over to the executor or administrator of the deceased, or, in default of such executor or administrator, to the respective Consuls of the contracting parties.

ART. 8. If a Frenchman shall become bankrupt in the dominions of the Sultan of Maskat, the French Consul shall take possession of all the property of such bankrupt, and shall give it up to the creditors of the bankrupt to be divided among them. This having been done, the bankrupt shall be entitled to a full discharge from his creditors, and he shall not at any time afterwards be required to make up the deficiency, nor shall any property he may afterwards acquire be considered liable for that purpose. But the French Consul shall use his endeavours to obtain for the benefit of the creditors all the property of the bankrupt. It shall also be incumbent upon the Consul to ascertain that everything possessed by the bankrupt at the time when he became insolvent has been given up.

ART. 9. If a subject of the Sultan of Maskat owes a debt to a Frenchman, the Sultan or his deputies shall urge the former to pay the claim of the latter. In like manner, the French Consul shall enjoin a Frenchman to pay a debt due by him to a subject of the Sultan of Maskat.

ART. 10. No duty exceeding five per cent. shall be levied on goods imported by French vessels into the dominions of Syud Sueed bin Sultan, the Sultan of Maskat. If a vessel of other nations imports any goods into the territories of the Sultan of Maskat, and pays less duty than five per cent., the same duty only shall be levied on similar goods imported by a French vessel into the said territories. A French vessel after she has paid the duty of five per cent., shall not be subject to any other charges, such as anchorage, pilotages, etc., nor shall any charge be made on that part of the cargo

which may remain on board a French vessel; but if the vessel shall go to another part of the dominions of the Sultan of Maskat, duty shall be levied at five per cent. The above-mentioned duty having once been paid, the goods may be sold, by wholesale or retail, without paying any further duty. No charge whatever shall be made on French vessels which may enter any of the ports of the Sultan of Maskat for the purpose of refitting, or for refreshments, or to inquire about the state of the market; and they shall enjoy the same privileges which are enjoyed (by the vessels) of the most favoured nations.

ART. 11. No vessel shall be prohibited from importing into, or exporting from, the territories of the Sultan of Maskat any kind of merchandise. The trade shall be perfectly free in the said territories, subject to the above-mentioned duty and to no other. The French shall be at liberty to buy and sell from whomsoever and to whomsoever they choose; but they shall not trade in the articles of ivory and gum copal on that part of the East Coast of Africa from the port of Tongate, situated in 5½ degrees of south latitude, to the port of Culva, lying in 9 degrees south of the equator, both ports inclusive. But if the English or Americans, or any other Christian nation, should carry on this trade, the French shall, in like manner, be at liberty to do so.

ART. 12. If any disputes should arise in the dominions of the Sultan of Maskat as to the value of goods which shall be imported by French merchants, and on which the duty of five per cent. is to be levied, the Custom Master, or other person acting on the part of the Sultan of Maskat, shall, when practicable, receive one-twentieth part of the goods, and the merchant shall then be subject to no further demand on account of customs on the remaining goods in any part of the dominions of the Sultan of Maskat to which he may transport them. But if the Custom Master should object to levy the duty in the manner aforesaid, [i.e.,] by taking one-twentieth part of the goods, or if the goods should not admit of being so divided, then the point in dispute shall be referred to two competent persons, one chosen by the Custom Master, and the other by the merchant, who shall make a valuation of the goods; and if they shall differ in opinion, they shall appoint an arbitrator, whose decision shall be final, and the duty shall be levied according to the value thus established.

ART. 13. It shall not be lawful for any French merchant to expose his goods for sale for the space of three days after the arrival of such goods, unless the Custom Master and the merchant shall have agreed as to the value of such goods. If the Custom Master shall not within three days have accepted one of the two modes proposed for ascertaining the value of the goods, the authorities on the part of the Sultan of Maskat, on an intimation being made to them on the subject, shall compel the Custom Master to choose one of the two modes for the levy of the duty.

ART. 14. If it shall happen that either the King of the French or the Sultan of Maskat should be at war with another country, the subjects of the King of the French and the subjects of the Sultan of Maskat shall nevertheless be allowed to trade with, and to take to, such country, merchandise of every description, except war-like stores, but they shall not be allowed to enter any port or place actually blockaded or besieged.

ART. 15. Should a vessel under the French flag enter a port in the dominions of the Sultan of Maskat in distress, the local authorities at such port shall afford all necessary aid to enable the vessel to refit and to prosecute her voyage; and if any such vessel should be wrecked on the coasts of the dominions of the Sultan of Maskat, the authorities on the part of the Sultan of Maskat shall render all the assistance in their power to recover and deliver over to the owner, or the Consul, the property that may be saved from such wreck. The same assistance and protection shall be afforded to vessels of the dominions of the Sultan of Maskat, and property saved therefrom under similar circumstances, in the ports and on the coasts of the French dominions.

ART. 16. If any person not belonging to the Christian nations shall steal any article from a French vessel, and take it to the dominions of the Sultan of Maskat, it shall be recovered from the robber and delivered over to the Consul.

ART. 17. The French shall be at liberty to hire or erect houses and warehouses at Zanzibar or anywhere else.

ART. 18. Any engagements which may have been entered into previously to this are null and void, and are not to be acted upon or attended to.

94. RUSSIAN (NESSELRODE) MEMORANDUM TO THE BRITISH GOVERNMENT RECOMMENDING JOINT POLICY TOWARD THE OTTOMAN EMPIRE
3 December 1844

[Great Britain, *Parliamentary Papers, 1854*, vol. 71, pt. 6]

During a state visit to England in June 1844 Tsar Nicholas I sought to broaden the Austrian-Russian alliance of September 1833 (Doc. 74) to include Great Britain as the third partner. The tsar was convinced that France was the source of the revolutionary spirit which he felt threatened the established order in Europe. The proposed alliance, based on a common policy toward the Ottoman Empire, was transparently aimed at holding France in check. The Nesselrode memorandum, submitted to the British government on 3 December 1844 by Baron Ernest Philip Brunnow, the Russian ambassador in London, elaborated upon the Russian version of the projected accord on the Ottoman Empire, as clarified in the discussions between the tsar and members of the British Cabinet the preceding June. While avoiding any British pledges, the foreign minister, Lord Aberdeen, agreed that the memorandum was an essentially accurate summary of the British-Russian conversations. Tsar Nicholas and his advisers, however, believed that Aberdeen's assent implied "something more binding." The misunderstanding was later to contribute to the outbreak of the Crimean War. Temperley, *England and the Near East*, chap. 10; Florinsky, *Russia*, 2: 844–50; Goryainov, "Secret Agreement of 1844"; Puryear, *England, Russia, and the Straits Question*, chaps. 1–4; Rodkey, "Anglo-Russian Negotiations about a 'Permanent' Quadruple Alliance."

Russia and England are mutually penetrated with the conviction that it is for their common interest that the Ottoman Porte should maintain itself in the state of independence and of territorial possession which at present constitutes that Empire, as that political combination is the one which is most compatible with the general interest of the maintenance of peace.

Being agreed on this principle, Russia and England have an equal interest in uniting their efforts in order to keep up the existence of the Ottoman Empire, and to avert all the dangers which can place in jeopardy its safety.

With this object the essential point is to suffer the Porte to live in repose, without needlessly disturbing it by diplomatic bickerings, and without interfering without absolute necessity in its internal affairs.

In order to carry out skilfully this system of forbearance, with a view to the well-understood interest of the Porte, two things must not be lost sight of. They are these:

In the first place, the Porte has a constant tendency to extricate itself from the engagements imposed upon it by the Treaties which it has concluded with other Powers. It hopes to do so with impunity, because it reckons on the mutual jealousy of the Cabinets. It thinks that if it fails in its engagements towards one of them, the rest will espouse its quarrel, and will screen it from all responsibility.

It is essential not to confirm the Porte in this delusion. Every time that it fails in its obligations towards one of the Great Powers, it is the interest of all the rest to make it sensible of its error, and seriously to exhort it to act rightly towards the Cabinet which demands just reparation.

As soon as the Porte shall perceive that it is not supported by the other Cabinets, it will give way, and the differences which have arisen will be arranged in a conciliatory manner, without any conflict resulting from them.

There is a second cause of complication which is inherent in the situation of the Porte; it is the difficulty which exists in reconciling the respect due to the sovereign authority of the Sultan, founded on the Mussulman law, with the forbearance required by the interests of the Christian population of that Empire.

This difficulty is real. In the present state of feeling in Europe the Cabinets cannot see with indifference the Christian populations in Turkey exposed to flagrant acts of oppression and religious intolerance.

It is necessary constantly to make the Ottoman Ministers sensible of this truth, and to persuade them that they can only reckon on the friendship and on the support of the Great Powers on the condition that they treat the Christian subjects of the Porte with toleration and with mildness.

While insisting on this truth it will be the duty of the foreign Representatives, on the other hand, to exert all their influence to maintain the Christian subjects of the Porte in submission to the sovereign authority.

It will be the duty of the foreign Representatives, guided by these principles, to act among themselves in a perfect spirit of agreement. If they address remonstrances to the Porte, those remonstrances must bear a real character of unanimity, though divested of one of exclusive dictation.

By persevering in this system with calmness and moderation, the Representatives of the great Cabinets of Europe will have the best chance of succeeding in the steps which they may take, without giving occasion for complications which might affect the tranquillity of the Ottoman Empire. If all the Great Powers frankly adopt this line of conduct, they will have a well-founded expectation of preserving the existence of Turkey.

However, they must not conceal from themselves how many elements of dissolution that Empire contains within itself. Unforeseen circumstances may hasten its fall, without its being in the power of the friendly Cabinets to prevent it.

As it is not given to human foresight to settle beforehand a plan of action for such or such unlooked-for case, it would be premature to discuss eventualities which may never be realized.

In the uncertainty which hovers over the future, a single fundamental idea seems to admit of a really practical application; it is that the danger which may result from a catastrophe in Turkey will be much diminished, if, in the event of its occurring, Russia and England have come to an understanding as to the course to be taken by them in common.

That understanding will be the more beneficial, inasmuch as it will have the full assent of Austria. Between her and Russia there exists already an entire conformity of principles in regard to the affairs of Turkey, in a common interest of conservatism and of peace.

In order to render their union more efficacious, there would remain nothing to be desired but that England should be seen to associate herself thereto with the same view.

The reason which recommends the establishment of this agreement is very simple.

On land Russia exercises in regard to Turkey a preponderant action.

On sea England occupies the same position.

Isolated, the action of these two Powers might do much mischief. United, it can produce a real benefit: thence, the advantage of coming to a previous understanding before having recourse to action.

This notion was in principle agreed upon during the Emperor's last residence in London. The result was the eventual engagement, that if anything unforeseen occurred in Turkey, Russia and England should previously concert together as to the course which they should pursue in common.

The object for which Russia and England will have to come to an understanding may be expressed in the following manner:

1. To seek to maintain the existence of the Ottoman Empire in its present state, so long as that political combination shall be possible.

2. If we foresee that it must crumble to pieces, to enter into previous concert as to everything relating to the establishment of a new order of things, intended to replace that which now exists, and in conjunction with each other to see that the change which may have occurred in the internal situation of that Empire shall not injuriously affect either the security of their own States and the rights which the Treaties assure to them respectively, or the maintenance of the balance of power in Europe.

For the purpose thus stated, the policy of Russia and of Austria, as we have already said, is closely united by the principle of perfect identity. If England, as the principal Maritime Power, acts in concert with them, it is to be supposed that France will find herself obliged to act in conformity with the course agreed upon between St. Petersburgh, London, and Vienna.

Conflict between the Great Powers being thus obviated, it is to be hoped that the peace of Europe will be maintained even in the midst of such serious circumstances. It is to secure this object of common interest, if the case occurs, that, as the Emperor agreed with Her Britannic Majesty's Ministers during his residence in England, the previous understanding which Russia and England shall establish between themselves must be directed.

95. BOUNDARY TREATY: FRANCE AND MOROCCO
18 March 1845

(Ratifications exchanged, 6 August 1845)
[Translated from the French text in Clercq, *Recueil des traités*, 5: 271–75]

Article 5 of the convention of Tangier (Doc. 92) stipulated that a mixed French-Moroccan boundary commission should delimit the frontier between the two countries "in conformity with the state of things recognized by the Moroccan Government at the time of Turkish rule in Algeria." The commission completed its task swiftly by producing the following boundary treaty. The condition on the frontier was left vague. Article 1 stipulated that the boundary "shall not be marked by stones. In brief, it shall remain just as it always was before the conquest of the Algerian Empire by France." Since there never had been fixed boundaries in the earlier period, none manifestly became fixed in 1845. This opened the door to later trouble, since the treaty permitted the armed forces of either side to enter the other's territory in hot pursuit, enabling France to build up over time a case for the eventual annexation of Morocco. The ambiguities of 1845 plagued the relations of Algeria and Morocco after each won its independence, as the lightning war between the two in October 1963 amply demonstrated. Trout, *Morocco's Saharan Frontiers*, chap. 1; see also references to Doc. 92.

. . . ART. 1. The two Plenipotentiaries have agreed that the boundaries that existed formerly between Morocco and Turkey shall remain the same between Algeria and Morocco. Neither of the two Emperors shall cross the boundary of the other; neither of them shall build new structures on the boundary line in the future; it shall not be marked by stones. In brief, it shall remain just as it alway was before the conquest of the Algerian Empire by the French.

ART. 2. The plenipotentiaries have traced the boundary by means of the places through which it passes, and concerning which they have reached an agreement, so that this boundary has become as clear and manifest as a traced line would be. What lies to the east of this frontier line belongs to the Empire of Algeria. Everything that lies to the west belongs to the Empire of Morocco.

ART. 3. The description of the beginning of the boundary and the places through which it passes is as follows: This line starts at the mouth of the *oued* [*wadi*] (that is, the watercourse) Adjeroud on the sea, and follows this watercourse as far as the ford where it is known as the Kis; then it follows again the same watercourse as far as the source that is called Ras-el-Aioun, which is located at the foot of three hills called Menasseb-Kis, which, because of their situation to the east of the wadi, belong to Algeria. From Ras-el-Aioun, this same line follows on the crest to the neighboring mountains as far as Drâ-el-Doum; it then descends to the plain called el-Aoudj. From there, it goes almost in a straight line toward Haouch-Sidi-Aiêd. Haouch itself, however, remains approximately 500 cubits [250 meters], on the east side, within the Algerian limits. From Haouch-Sidi-Aied, it continues to Djerf-el-Baroud, situated on the wadi Bou-Nâim; from there it reaches Kerkour-Sidi-Hamza; from Kerkour-Sidi-Hamza to Zoudj-el-Beghal; then running along on the left the country of the Ouled-Ali-ben-Talha as far as Sidi-Zahir, which is in Algerian territory, where it follows the highway as far as Ain-Takbalet, which is located between the wadi Bou-Erda and the two olive trees called el-Toumiet that lie in Moroccan territory. From Ain-Takbalet, it follows the wadi Roubban until Ras-Asfour; it continues beyond Kef, passing on the east the *marabout* [*murabit*] Sidi-Abd-Allah-ben-Mehammed-el-Hamlili [Sayyid 'Abdallah bin Muhammad al-Hamlili]; then, turning toward the west, following the defile of el-Mechêmiche, it goes in a straight line to the marabout Sidi-Aissa, which forms the end of the plain of Missiouin. This marabout and its appendages lie on Algerian territory. From there, it runs toward the south as far as Koudiet-el-Debbagh, a hill situated on the far side of the Tell (i.e., the cultivated land). From there, the boundary takes a southerly direction as far as Kheneg-el-Hada to Teniet-el-Sassi, a defile the enjoyment of which belongs to the two Empires.

In order to establish more clearly the boundary from the sea to the start of the desert, mention must be made of the land to the east of the line denoted above and the name of the tribes established there.

The first lands and tribes nearest the sea are those of Beni-Mengouche-Tahta and Aâttia. These two tribes are composed of Moroccan subjects who have come to live on Algerian territory following serious disputes between them and their brothers of Morocco. Because of these arguments, they withdrew to seek refuge on the land that they occupy today with the permission of the sovereign of Algeria, in return for a yearly rental.

But the Plenipotentiary Commissioner of the Emperor of the French, desiring to give to the representative of the Emperor of Morocco a proof of French generosity and of his willingness to draw closer the bonds of friendship and to maintain good relations between the two states, consented to the remittance of this annual rental (500 francs for each of the two tribes) as a gift of hospitality, so that these two tribes will not have to pay anything for any reason whatsoever to the Government of Algiers, so long as peace and good understanding persist between the two Emperors of the French and of Morocco.

After the territory of the Aâttia is that of the Messirda, the Achâche, the Ouled-Mellouk, the Beni-Bou-Sâid, the Beni-Senous, and the Ouled-el-Nahr. The last six tribes form part of those under the rule of the Empire of Algiers.

It is also necessary to mention the territory immediately adjoining on the west the boundary designated above and to mention the tribes that live in this district. Nearest the sea the first territory and the first tribes are the Ouled-Mansour-Rel-Trifa, the Beni-Iznêssen, the Mezaouir, the Ouled-Ahmed-ben-Brahim, the Ouled-el-Abbês, the Ouled-Ali-ben-Talha, the Ouled-Azouz, the Beni-Bou-Hamdoun, the Beni-Hamlil, and the Beni-Mathar-Rel-Ras-el-Ain. All these tribes belong to the Empire of Morocco.

Art. 4. In the Sahara (desert) there is no territorial boundary to establish between the two countries, since the land is not arable and serves only as pasture for the Arabs of the two Empires who came there to find the pasturage and water that they need. The two sovereigns shall exercise in the manner they please the plenitude of their rights over their respective subjects in the Sahara. Nevertheless, if one of the two sovereigns has to pursue his subjects at a time when they are mingled with those of the other state, he shall pursue as he wishes his own [subjects], but shall forbear pursuing the subjects of the other government.

The Arabs of the Empire of Morocco are: the M'bèia, the Beni-Guil, the Hamian-Djenba, the Eûmour-Sahara, and the Ouled-Sidi-Cheikh-el-Gharaba.

The Arabs of Algeria are: the Ouled-Sidi-Cheikh-el-Cheraga, and all the Hamian, except the Hamian-Djenba named above.

Art. 5. This article pertains to the designation of the *qusurs* [desert villages] of the two Empires. In this regard, the two sovereigns shall follow the ancient time-hallowed custom of according, in consideration of each other, deference and goodwill to the inhabitants of these qusurs.

The qusurs that belong to Morocco are Yiche and Figuigue.

The qusurs that belong to Algeria are: Ain-Safra, S'fissifa, Assla, Tiout, Chellala, el-Abiad, and Bou-Semghoune.

Art. 6. With regard to the district that is south of the qusurs of the two governments, since there is no water there, it is unhabitable and it is strictly speaking desert [and therefore] the delimitation of the boundary would be superfluous.

ART. 7. Any individual who may take refuge from one state in another shall not be returned to the government that he has left, for as long as he wishes to remain there.

But if on the contrary he should desire to return to his state, the authorities of the place of refuge may not interfere with his departure. If he wishes to remain, he shall obey the laws of the land and shall find protection and security for his person and his property. By this provision, the two sovereigns wish to express their mutual respect.

It is understood that this article does not pertain to the tribes, the Empire to which they belong having been sufficiently defined in the preceding articles.

It should also be noted that al-Hajj 'Abd al-Qadir and his supporters shall not enjoy the benefits of this convention, since that would prejudice Article 4 of the agreement of 10 September 1844, while the express intention of the High Contracting Parties is to continue to give force and vigor to this stipulation desired by the two sovereigns, and its fulfillment will affirm the friendship and ensure forever peace and good relations between the two states. . . .

96. OTTOMAN CIRCULAR INFORMING THE GREAT POWERS OF CHANGES IN THE ADMINISTRATION OF LEBANON
28 July 1845

[Translated from the French text in Testa, *Recueil des traités de la Porte Ottomane*, 3: 68–73]

Despite the institution of autonomy for Maronites and Druzes in Lebanon at the end of 1842 (Doc. 90), relations between the communities continued to be tense. To this situation the Ottoman officials contributed by their favoritism toward the Druzes, as did the agents of the European powers, who by 1844 lost all semblance of harmony and once more intrigued against one another among the local population. In the circumstances, civil strife between the communities became ominous in the spring and summer of 1845, thus giving the Sublime Porte an opportunity for forcible intervention. Şekip Paşa's circular of 28 July was issued six weeks before his actual arrival in Lebanon accompanied by eighteen Ottoman battalions with which he quickly restored order and inaugurated a program of disarming the populace, particularly the Maronites. Autonomy was preserved in form, but, in the decade and a half that followed, the powers of the two communities were considerably reduced while those of the Sublime Porte were correspondingly enlarged. See references to Doc. 111.

As is universally known. His Highness the Sultan, in paternal solicitude for his peoples, seeks to find and perfect the means that will ensure the well-being, tranquillity, and security of all classes of subjects placed under his equitable authority. He wishes that the inhabitants of Mount Lebanon should also share in these bounties. Tokens of goodwill and favor of every kind have

been bestowed upon them, their ancient privileges have been maintained, and the administration of the Mountain has been endowed with its own particular structure. In order that no further cause for disaffection should remain, each village whose population consists of Druzes and Maronites has recently been allowed to have a *vekil* [agent] as well as a *mukata'aci* [lease-

holder or landlord who frequently also
served as tax-farmer]. The decree has been
issued to all [villages concerned] to put the
measure promptly into effect.

It would seem that the inhabitants of the
Mountain, in appreciation for the favors
that His Highness unremittingly bestows
upon them, should have shown themselves
grateful and, in their quality as subjects,
should have hastened to submit to the
edicts of the Sublime Porte. But, yielding
to the rudeness of their character, they
hesitated to accept [the edicts] and have
made difficulties: some found the favors
beneath their expectations and others believed themselves betrayed. Moreover, seizing the enactment of a decision taken to
ensure the peace and security of the country as an occasion in which to give vent to
their mutual hatred and to carry out their
evil designs, they have dared to attack one
another and to shed one another's blood.
The government of His Highness has not
only been shocked to hear of it but has also
been surprised by the claim that their deeds
were authorized by the Sublime Porte.

However, it is the definite will of the
Sublime Porte to establish completely and
without delay the administrative structure
for mixed villages which is the result and
the complement of the previous imperial
decisions on the local administration of the
Mountain. That is why it has become necessary to take immediate and efficacious steps
that will demonstrate to the inhabitants of
the Mountain [the Porte's] high solicitude,
authority, and power, make its goodwill
and good spirit manifest to the high courts
of its allies, and terminate this question of
Lebanon once for all. In view of the past
behavior of the inhabitants of the Mountain, it is clear that they will hesitate to
accept the bounties and favors bestowed
upon them as long as the possibility of
using force has not been demonstrated to
them. Besides, their hesitation is certain to
last until they realize that the decision is
immutable and until they are given to
understand that whatever further wishes
they may still nurture have no chance of
realization. The government of His Highness thus believes that the circumstances
demand that a man having full understanding of the true significance of the matter
and of the pure intentions of the Sublime

Porte should be dispatched to Lebanon, the
seat of the problem, on a special and
absolute mission and accompanied by adequate forces to settle and terminate the
matter without leaving any cause for further difficulties or complaints. Since the
[Ottoman] Ministry of Foreign Affairs has
for some time been the center of the deliberations and the actions required in this
matter, it naturally favors the decision
taken here. Accordingly, I have the honor
to inform Your Excellency that I [Şekip
Paşa, Minister of Foreign Affairs] have
been charged by His Highness personally
to proceed to Syria on a special and absolute mission for the purpose of regulating
the matter promptly and completely and
demonstrating that no cause for hesitation
or friction remains.

The crux of the problem and the goal of
my mission are to apply fully and completely the arrangements and the more recent
enactments on local administration while
preserving the particular privileges granted
by His Majesty the Sultan and to succeed in
ensuring the peace of the district and the
tranquillity of the subjects of the government in all matters. To facilitate its execution, one needs, as I have said above, a
demonstrable force which can intimidate
and which can be used effectively against
those who will have brought this action
upon themselves by refusing to accept the
above decision. The government hopes that
this situation will not arise. But it is essential to increase the effectiveness of the
coercive forces stationed in the Mountain,
so that the projected goal can be attained.
Therefore, Namık Paşa, müşür [command-
er] of the imperial camp in Arabia, has been
ordered to augment the regular army under
his command by the requisite number of
troops, move with them to Lebanon, take
up suitable military positions, and make the
necessary movements dictated by circumstances and by the instructions that I shall
give him. If the forceful and efficacious
steps which the government proposes to
undertake are considered with fairness, it
will be seen that the mission which I have
received as a member of the ministry of
His Highness—to settle this question completely and without hesitation according to
the pure intentions of the government of
His Highness—will hasten the moment of

solution. It will also be seen that the inclusion of Namık Paşa and the deployment of the intimidating force will persuade the inhabitants of the Mountain of the necessity of returning within the bounds of obedience. As for the indemnities, they have been accorded previously to show that His Highness can employ force as benefaction and to prove that the aim of the measures taken by his government has been solely to grant a favor and a token of generosity and simultaneously to display his power to those unwise inhabitants who were ignorant of their true interest. The decision taken today to distribute a portion of these indemnities and at the same time to begin tackling the question itself and to apportion the balance after the matter has been settled provides renewed proof of the equitable intentions of the government of His Highness. The inhabitants of Lebanon will come to understand that the more they conform to the duties of obedience and of their status as subjects, the more they will obtain tokens of goodwill and of graciousness from His Highness. This consideration, together with the steps previously taken, must lead to a prompt and final solution of the question. Since the various groups of inhabitants of the Mountain, whenever they are reluctant to accept the orders of the Sublime Porte, find moral support of various forms for their resistance and commit acts that disturb the tranquillity of the district; since, whenever decisions taken here are implemented in Syria, the Consuls under pretext of renewed negotiations express doubts and thus give rise to difficulties; and since, as is witnessed by the mission that I am personally to fulfill, the present decision shall not be modified in any manner, it is important that the Consuls refrain from meddling in any fashion in what I may say say and abstain from injecting themselves into the matter, whether in spirit or in form. Convinced as I am that the moral support of Your Excellency in this matter will be forthcoming in conformity with the request of the Sublime Porte, I have the honor to appeal to your solicitude for the execution of all that is necessary.

The hesitation and the delays in effecting the last decision taken on mixed villages were, it may be presumed, caused by inadequate local appreciation of the degree of competence of the mukata'acis and of the Maronite vekils. In order to avoid all further reason for discussion of this subject in Lebanon, it is necessary to dissipate uncertainties. Accordingly, I shall now explain and clarify what the intention of the Sublime Porte, is in this matter.

In the administration of mixed villages, matters fall into three classes:

1. Questions of law (*hukukiye*)
2. Administrative affairs (*siyasiye*)
3. Executive or police power (*zaptiye*)

As for the first category, every suit or difference between individuals of the same nation shall be judged solely by its vekil. If the litigants belong to different nations, the vekil of the one and the mukata'aci of the other shall jointly judge the case. Recourse will be had to the *kaymakam* [deputy governor], if they cannot agree. Regarding administrative matters, that is, general affairs such as the execution of orders sent by the government or emanating from the provincial governor and the collection of the taxes of the district, the vekils shall serve as intermediaries between their nations and the mukata'acis for the execution of orders and the maintenance of defense. As for the executive or police power, the division of which would hinder its exercise, the vekil shall not be associated therewith, and the task of the maintenance [of law and order] and of reprimand shall be entrusted solely to the mukata'aci, as is the practice elsewhere. But if the mukata'aci should arrest and imprison a person of another nation in punishment, the deserved penalty shall be endorsed by and executed jointly with the vekil. In case of disagreement recourse will be had to the kaymakam. The vekils shall have the right to see that the imprisoned man suffers no ill treatment until the execution of his punishment has been decreed.

These provisions conform to the principles of justice and equity and to the body of administrative regulation in the district. To supervise their full and entire execution and to investigate individual crimes, such as cases of murder which occurred from time to time in the Mountain before the latest troubles and the perpetrators of which have escaped punishment because of regrettable events—these are the goals that the government of His Highness wishes to reach and that are included in the mission entrusted to me. I have the honor to inform Your Excellency that I shall leave in a few days to fulfill my mission. I shall do my utmost to implement the beneficent wishes of His Highness the Sultan, my sovereign. Since the [Great] Powers, sincere friends of and moved by well-known sentiments of goodwill toward the Sublime Porte, are equally anxious to see the organization of tranquillity in the Mountain, and since the present decision of the government of His Highness is manifestly an efficacious means for attaining this goal, I have the honor to request Your Excellency to entrust to me unsealed formal instructions, in harmony with the above-mentioned resolutions, that I may forward to your Consul in Bayrut.

97. CONVERSATIONS BETWEEN TSAR NICHOLAS I AND SIR GEORGE HAMILTON SEYMOUR, THE BRITISH MINISTER TO RUSSIA
22 January–21 February 1853

[Letters of 22 January and 9 February 1853 from Great Britain, *Parliamentary Papers, 1854*, vol. 71, pt. 5; letter of 21 February 1853, Public Record Office., F.O. 65/424, no. 87]

By the time Tsar Nicholas I renewed his overtures to England (see Doc. 94) in January–April 1853, relations between Russia and France were rapidly deteriorating. The repercussions of the contest in the Ottoman Empire centered in the dispute, which grew increasingly serious after February 1852, between the Greek Orthodox Christians (with the support of Russia) and the Roman Catholics (with the support of France) over special privileges in the Church of the Holy Sepulcher at Jerusalem and the Church of the Nativity at Bethlehem. Encouraged by the fact that Lord Aberdeen —with whom the tsar had negotiated in 1844—had just become prime minister, Nicholas began his personal diplomatic approaches to England through the British minister to Saint Petersburg on 9 January 1853. The Seymour correspondence informs the policies of Britain as well as Russia toward the Ottoman Empire in the mid-nineteenth century. To this correspondence the sobriquet "sick man of Europe," which thereafter became a cliché in the West for the Ottoman Empire, owes, if not its origin, at least its popularity. Yet it should be noted that the tsar used as his metaphor "the bear is dying, you may give him musk, but even musk will not long keep him alive," and that apparently Seymour in his letter of 11 January and the Foreign Office in publishing the minister's letter of 21 February substitued "man" for "bear," as Harold Temperley has pointed out, "from a mistaken sense of decorum" (*England and the Near East*, p. 272). Only two of Seymour's letters and the first reply of Foreign Minister Lord Russell are reproduced here. The remaining published correspondence may be found in *Parliamentary Papers, 1854*, vol. 71, pt. 5. Temperley, op. cit., pp. 270–279, and "Stratford de Redcliffe and the Origins of the Crimean War"; Conacher, *Aberdeen Coalition*, chaps. 7–8; Henderson, *Crimean War Diplomacy*, pp. 1–14; Florinsky, *Russia*, 2: 858–69; Puryear, *England, Russia and the Straits Question*, chaps. 4–5; Schmitt, "Diplomatic Preliminaries of the Crimean War."

1. Seymour to Lord Russell, 22 January 1853[1]

On the 14th instant, in consequence of a summons which I received from the Chancellor, I waited upon the Emperor, and had the honour of holding with His Imperial Majesty the very interesting conversation of which it will be my duty to offer your Lordship an account, which, if imperfect, will, at all events, not be incorrect.

I found His Majesty alone; he received me with great kindness, saying, that I had appeared desirous to speak to him upon Eastern affairs; that, on his side, there was no indisposition to do so, but that he must begin at a remote period.

You know, His Majesty said, the dreams and plans in which the Empress Catherine was in the habit of indulging; these were handed down to our time; but while I inherited immense territorial possessions, I did not inherit those visions, those intentions if you like to call them so. On the contrary, my country is so vast, so happily circumstanced in every way, that it would be unreasonable in me to desire more territory or more power than I possess; on the contrary, I am the first to tell you that our great, perhaps our only danger, is that which would arise from an extension given to an Empire already too large.

Close to us lies Turkey, and in our present condition, nothing better for our interests can be desired; the times have gone by when we had anything to fear from the fanatical spirit or the military enterprise of the Turks, and yet the country is strong enough, or has hitherto been strong enough to preserve its independence, and to insure respectful treatment from other countries.

Well, in that Empire there are several millions of Christians whose interests I am called upon to watch over (surveiller), while the right of doing so is secured to me by Treaty. I may truly say that I make a moderate and sparing use of my right, and I will freely confess that it is one which is attended with obligations occasionally very inconvenient; but I cannot recede from the discharge of a distinct duty. Our religion, as established in this country, came to us from the East, and there are feelings, as well as obligations, which never must be lost sight of.

Now Turkey, in the condition which I have described, has by degrees fallen into such a state of decrepitude that, as I told you the other night, eager as we all are for the prolonged existence of the man (and that I am as desirous as you can be for the continuance of his life, I beg you to believe), he may suddenly die upon our hands (nous rester sur les bras); we cannot resuscitate what is dead; if the Turkish Empire falls, it falls to rise no more; and I put it to you, therefore, whether it is not better to be provided beforehand for a contingency, than to incur the chaos, confusion, and the certainty of an European war, all of which must attend the catastrophe if it should occur unexpectedly, and before some ulterior system has been sketched; this is the point to which I am desirous that you should call the attention of your Government.

Sir, I replied, your Majesty is so frank with me, that I am sure you will have the goodness to permit me to speak with the same openness. I would then observe, that deplorable as is the condition of Turkey, it is a country which has long been plunged in difficulties supposed by many to be insurmountable.

With regard to contingent arrangements, Her Majesty's Government, as your Majesty is well aware, objects, as a general rule, to taking engagements upon possible eventualities, and would, perhaps, be particularly disinclined to doing so in this instance. If I may be allowed to say so, a great disinclination (répugnance) might be expected in England, to disposing by anticipation (d'escompter) of the succession of an old friend and ally.

The rule is a good one, the Emperor replied, good at all times, especially in times of uncertainty and change, like the present; still it is of the greatest importance that we should understand one another, and not allow events to take us by surprise; "Now I desire to speak to you as a friend and as a *gentleman*; if England and I arrive at an

---

1. A postscript of no pertinence to this collection was omitted from the Blue Book and is not reproduced here; otherwise the published letter conforms to F.O. 65/424, no. 24.

understanding of this matter, as regards the rest, it matters little to me; it is indifferent to me what others do or think. Frankly then, I tell you plainly, that if England thinks of establishing herself one of these days at Constantinople, I will not allow it. I do not attribute this intention to you, but it is better on these occasions to speak plainly; for my part, I am equally disposed to take the engagement not to establish myself there, as proprietor that is to say, for as occupier I do not say: it might happen that circumstances, if no previous provision were made, if everything should be left to chance, might place me in the position of occupying Constantinople."

I thanked His Majesty for the frankness of his declarations, and for the desire which he had expressed of acting cordially and openly with Her Majesty's Government, observing at the same time, that such an understanding appeared the best security against the sudden danger to which His Majesty had alluded. I added that, although unprepared to give a decided opinion upon questions of such magnitude and delicacy, it appeared to me possible that some such arrangement might be made between Her Majesty's Government and His Majesty, as might guard, if not for, at least against, certain contingencies.

To render my meaning more clear I said further: I can only repeat, Sir, that in my opinion, Her Majesty's Government will be indisposed to make certain arrangements connected with the downfall of Turkey, but it is possible that they may be ready to peldge themselves against certain arrangements which might, in that event, be attempted.

His Imperial Majesty then alluded to a conversation which he had held, the last time he was in England, with the Duke of Wellington, and to the motives which had compelled him to open himself to his Grace; then, as now, His Majesty was, he said, eager to provide against events which, in the absence of any concert, might compel him to act in a manner opposed to the views of Her Majesty's Government.

The conversation passed to the events of the day, when the Emperor briefly recapitulated his claims upon the Holy Places, claims recognised by the Firman of last February, and confirmed by a sanction to which His Majesty said he attached much more importance—the word of a Sovereign.

The execution of promises so made, and so ratified, the Emperor said he must insist upon, but was willing to believe that his object would be attained by negotiation, the last advices from Constantinople being rather more satisfactory.

I expressed my belief that negotiation, followed, as I supposed it had been, by the threats of military measures, would be found sufficient to secure a compliance with the just demands of Russia. I added, that I desired to state to His Majesty what I had previously read from a written paper to his Minister, viz., that what I feared for Turkey were not the intentions of His Majesty, but the actual result of the measures which appeared to be in contemplation. That I would repeat, that two consequences might be anticipated from the appearance of an Imperial army on the frontiers of Turkey,—the one the counter-demonstration which might be provoked on the part of France; the other, and the more serious, the rising, on the part of the Christian population, against the Sultan's authority, already so much weakened by revolts, and by a severe financial crisis.

The Emperor assured me that no movement of his forces had yet taken place (n'ont pas bougé), and expressed his hope that no advance would be required.

With regard to a French expedition to the Sultan's dominions, His Majesty intimated that such a step would bring affairs to an immediate crisis; that a sense of honour would compel him to send his forces into Turkey without delay or hesitation; that if the result of such an advance should prove to be the overthrow of the Great Turk (le Grand Turc), he should regret the event, but should feel that he had acted as he was compelled to do.

To the above report I have only, I think, to add, that the Emperor desired to leave it to my discretion to communicate or not to his Minister the particulars of our conversation; and that before I left the room, His Imperial Majesty said, You will report what has passed between us to the Queen's Government, and you will say that I shall be ready to receive any communication which it may be their wish to make to me upon the subject.

The other topics touched upon by the Emperor are mentioned in another despatch. With regard to the extremely important overture to which this report relates, I will only observe, that as it is my duty to record impressions, as well as facts and statements, I am bound to say, that if words, tone, and manner offer any criterion by which intentions are to be judged, the Emperor is prepared to act with perfect fairness and openness towards Her Majesty's Government. His Majesty has, no doubt, his own objects in view; and he is, in my opinion, too strong a believer in the imminence of dangers in Turkey. I am, however, impressed with the belief, that in carrying out those objects, as in guarding against those dangers, His Majesty is sincerely desirous of acting in harmony with Her Majesty's Government.

I would now submit to your Lordship that this overture cannot with propriety pass unnoticed by Her Majesty's Government.

It has been on a first occasion glanced at, and on a second distinctly made by the Emperor himself to the Queen's Minister at his Court, whilst the conversation held some years ago with the Duke of Wellington proves that the object in view is one which has long occupied the thoughts of His Imperial Majesty.

If, then, the proposal were to remain unanswered, a decided advantage would be secured to the Imperial Cabinet, which, in the event of some great catastrophe taking place in Turkey, would be able to point to proposals made to England, and which, not having been responded to, left the Emperor at liberty, or placed him under the necessity, of following has own line of policy in the East.

Again, I would remark that the anxiety expressed by the Emperor, even looking to his own interests, for an extension of the days "of the dying man," appears to me to justify Her Majesty's Government in proposing to His Imperial Majesty to unite with England in the adoption of such measures as may lead to prop up the falling authority of the Sultan.

Lastly, I would observe that even if the Emperor should be found disinclined to lend himself to such a course of policy as might arrest the downfall of Turkey, his declarations to me pledge him to be ready to take beforehand, in concert with Her Majesty's Government, such precautions as may possibly prevent the fatal crisis being followed by a scramble for the rich inheritance which would remain to be disposed of.

A noble triumph would be obtained by the civilization of the nineteenth century, if the void left by the extinction of Mahommedan rule in Europe could be filled up without an interruption of the general peace, in consequence of the precautions adopted by the two principal Governments the most interested in the destinies of Turkey.

2. Lord Russell to Seymour, 9 February 1853

I have received, and laid before the Queen, your secret and confidential despatch of the 22nd of January.

Her Majesty, upon this as upon former occasions, is happy to acknowledge the moderation, the frankness, and the friendly disposition of His Imperial Majesty.

Her Majesty has directed me to reply in the same spirit of temperate, candid, and amicable discussion.

The question raised by His Imperial Majesty is a very serious one. It is, supposing the contingency of the dissolution of the Turkish Empire to be probable, or even imminent, whether it is not better to be provided beforehand for a contingency, than to incur the chaos, confusion, and the certainty of an European war, all of which must attend the catastrophe if it should occur unexpectedly, and before some ulterior system has been sketched; this is the point, said His Imperial Majesty, to which I am desirous that you should call the attention of your Government.

In considering this grave question, the first reflection which occurs to Her Majesty's Government is that no actual crisis has occurred which renders necessary a solution of this vast European problem. Disputes have arisen respecting the Holy Places, but these are without the sphere of the internal government of Turkey, and concern Russia and France rather than the Sublime Porte. Some disturbance of the relations between Austria and the Porte has been caused by the Turkish attack on Montenegro; but this, again, relates rather to dangers affecting the frontier of Austria than the authority and safety of the Sultan; so that there is no sufficient cause for intimating to the Sultan that he cannot keep peace at home, or preserve friendly relations with his neighbours.

It occurs further to Her Majesty's Government to remark, that the event which is contemplated is not definitely fixed in point of time. When William the Third and Louis the Fourteenth disposed, by treaty, of the succession of Charles the Second of Spain, they were providing for an event which could not be far off. The infirmities of the Sovereign of Spain, and the certain end of any human life, made the contingency in prospect both sure and near. The death of the Spanish King was in no way hastened by the Treaty of Partition. The same thing may be said of the provision, made in the last century, for the disposal of Tuscany upon the decease of the last prince of the house of Medici. But the contingency of the dissolution of the Ottoman Empire is of another kind. It may happen twenty, fifty, or a hundred years hence.

In these circumstances it would hardly be consistent with the friendly feelings towards the Sultan which animate the Emperor of Russia, no less than the Queen of Great Britain, to dispose beforehand of the provinces under his dominion. Besides this consideration, however, it must be observed, that an agreement made in such a case tends very surely to hasten the contingency for which it is intended to provide. Austria and France could not, in fairness, be kept in ignorance of the transaction, nor would such concealment be consistent with the end of preventing an European war. Indeed, such concealment cannot be intended by His Imperial Majesty. It is to be inferred that, as soon as Great Britain and Russia should have agreed on the course to be pursued, and have determined to enforce it, they should communicate their intentions to the Great Powers of Europe. An agreement thus made, and thus communicate, would not be very long a secret; and while it would alarm and alienate the Sultan, the knowledge of its existence would stimulate all his enemies to increased violence and more obsti-

nate conflict. They would fight with the conviction that they must ultimately triumph; while the Sultan's generals and troops would feel that no immediate success could save their cause from final overthrow. Thus would be produced and strengthened that very anarchy which is now feared, and the foresight of the friends of the patient would prove the cause of his death.

Her Majesty's Government need scarcely enlarge on the dangers attendant on the execution of any similar Convention. The example of the Succession War is enough to show how little such agreements are respected when a pressing temptation urges their violation. The position of the Emperor of Russia as depositary, but not proprietor, of Constantinople, would be exposed to numberless hazards, both from the long-cherished ambition of his own nation, and the jealousies of Europe. The ultimate proprietor, whoever he might be, would hardly be satisfied with the inert, supine attitude of the heirs of Mahomet the Second. A great influence on the affairs of Europe seems naturally to belong to the Sovereign of Constantinople, holding the gates of the Mediterranean and the Black Sea.

That influence might be used in favour of Russia; it might be used to control and curb her power.

His Imperial Majesty has justly and wisely said: My country is so vast, so happily circumstanced in every way, that it would be unreasonable in me to desire more territory or more power than I possess. On the contrary, he observed, our great, perhaps our only danger, is that which would arise from an extension given to an Empire already too large. A vigorous and ambitious State, replacing the Sublime Porte, might, however, render war on the part of Russia a necessity for the Emperor or his successors.

Thus European conflict would arise from the very means taken to prevent it; for neither England nor France, nor probably Austria, would be content to see Constantinople permanently in the hands of Russia.

On the part of Great Britain, Her Majesty's Government at once declare that they renounce all intention or wish to hold Constantinople. His Imperial Majesty may be quite secure upon this head. They are likewise ready to give an assurance that they will enter into no agreement to provide for the contingency of the fall of Turkey without previous communication with the Emperor of Russia.

Upon the whole, then, Her Majesty's Government are persuaded that no course of policy can be adopted more wise, more disinterested, more beneficial to Europe than that which His Imperial Majesty has so long followed, and which will render his name more illustrious than that of the most famous Sovereigns who have sought immortality by unprovoked conquest and ephemeral glory.

With a view to the success of this ploicy it is desirable that the utmost forbearance should be manifested towards Turkey; that any demands which the Great Powers of Europe may have to make, should be made matter of friendly negotiation rather than of peremptory demand; that military and naval demonstrations to coerce the Sultan should as much as possible be avoided; that differences with respect to matters affecting Turkey, within the competence of the Sublime Porte, should be decided after mutual concert between the Great Powers, and not be forced upon the weakness of the Turkish Government.

To these cautions Her Majesty's Government wish to add, that in their view it is essential that the Sultan should be advised to treat his Christian subjects in conformity with the principles of equity and religious freedom which prevail generally among the enlightened nations of Europe. The more the Turkish Government adopts the rules of impartial law and equal administration, the less will the Emperor of Russia find it necessary to apply that exceptional protection which His Imperial Majesty has found so burthensome and inconvenient, though no doubt prescribed by duty and sanctioned by Treaty.

You may read this despatch to Count Nesselrode, and, if it is desired, you may yourself place a copy of it in the hands of the Emperor. In that case you will accompany its presentation with those assurances of friendship and confidence on the part of Her Majesty the Queen, which the conduct of His Imperial Majesty was so sure to inspire.

3. Seymour to Lord Russell, 21 February 1853

The Emperor came up to me last night, at a party of the Grand Duchess Hereditary's, and in the most gracious manner took me apart, saying that he desired to speak to me. After expressing, in flattering terms, the confidence which he has in me, and his readiness to speak to me without reserve upon matters of the greatest moment, as, His Majesty observed, he had proved in a late conversation, he said: And it is well it is so; for what I most desire is, that there should be the greatest intimacy between the two Governments: it never was so necessary as at present. Well, the Emperor continued, so you have got your answer, and you are to bring it to me to-morrow?

I am to have that honour, Sir, I answered; but your Majesty is aware that the nature of the reply is very exactly what I had led you to expect.

So I was sorry to hear; but I think your Government does not well understand my object. I am not so eager about what shall be done when the bear dies, as I am to determine with England what shall not be done upon that event taking place.

But, Sir, I replied, allow me to observe, that we have no reason to think that the Bear (to use your Majesty's expression) is dying. We are as much interested as we believe your Majesty to be in his continuing to live; while for myself, I will venture to remark that experience shows me that countries do not die in such a hurry:— I have seen by our Archives both in Turkey and Portugal that these two countries have for years past been considered in a perishing state, and yet there they remain, and there Turkey will remain for many a year, unless some unforeseen crisis should occur. It is precisely, Sir, for the avoidance of all circumstances likely to produce such a crisis, that Her Majesty's Government reckons upon your generous assistance.

Then, rejoined the Emperor, I will tell you, that if your Government has been led to believe that Turkey retains any elements of existence, your Government must have received incorrect information. I repeat to you that the Bear is dying, you may give him musk, but even musk will not long keep him alive, and we can never allow such an event to take us by surprise. We must come to some understanding; and this we should do, I am convinced, if I could hold but ten minutes' conversation with your Ministers—with Lord Aberdeen, for instance, who knows me so well, who has full confidence in me, as I have in him. And remember, I do not ask for a Treaty or a Protocol; a general understanding is all I require—that between gentlemen is sufficient; and in this case I am certain that the confidence would be as great on the side of the Queen's Ministers as on mine. So no more for the present; you will come to me to-morrow, and you will remember that as often as you think your conversing with me will promote a good understanding upon any point, you will send word that you wish to see me.

I thanked His Majesty very cordially, adding that I could assure him that Her Majesty's Government, I was convinced, considered his word, once given, as good as a bond.

It is hardly necessary that I should ob-serve to your Lordship, that this short conversation, briefly but correctly reported, offers matter for most anxious reflection.

It can hardly be otherwise but that the Sovereign who insists with such pertinacity upon the impending fall of a neighbouring State, must have settled in his own mind that the hour, if not of its dissolution, at all events for its dissloution, must be at hand.

I will only remark to your Lordship, as a point of evidence which goes far towards establishing a settled purpose, that the expression of Musk being insufficient to keep alive the sinking Turk was used to me ten days ago by one of the Emperor's most confidential Servants.

Then, as now, I reflected that this assumption would hardly be ventured upon unless some, perhaps general, but at all events intimate, understanding, existed between Russia and Austria.

Supposing my suspicion to be well founded, the Emperor's object is to engage Her Majesty's Government, in conjunction with his own Cabinet and that of Vienna, in some scheme for the ultimate partition of Turkey, and for the exclusion of France from the arrangement.

98. UNDERTAKING BY PERSIA NOT TO ATTACK HERAT
25 January 1853

[Aitchison, *Collection of Treaties . . . relating to India* (5th ed.), 13: 77–78]

Persian-Afghan relations were unaffected by European politics until the nineteenth century. Lying in the path of Russian expansion to the south and British-Indian expansion to the north, Persia and the three khanates or principalities of Afghanistan became objects of British-Russian rivalry, which first became critical in the 1830s. The Qajar dynasty did not abandon hope of reasserting Persian sovereignty over Afghanistan, briefly exercised in the reign of Nadir Shah (1736–47). Russia encouraged Persian interest in Herat after 1828 to distract the Qajars from their unhappiness over the loss of the northwest provinces to the tsar. During the British-Russian rapprochement the contest died down for more than a decade (1840–52), only to start up again as a result of the interplay of regional and international politics. It began in 1851 when Sayyid Muhammad Khan, the new ruler of Herat, sought Persian protection against the khans of Kabul and Qandahar. Ever mindful of the defense of India, the British resisted Persia's eastward expansion. A major reason for British anxiety at the time lay in the Russian right, established in the treaty of Gulistan (1813), to appoint consuls throughout the shahdom, a right repeatedly denied to Britain, even in the commercial convention of 1841, which authorized British consulates in Tehran and Tabriz only (art. 2). British-Indian officials had visions of the establishment of a tsarist consulate in a Persian-ruled Herat to foment hostility toward Britain among the Afghan tribesmen. The following pledge, which the British minister at Tehran wrung from a reluctant Nasir al-Din Shah (1848–96) on Palmerston's instructions, was designed to calm British-Indian anxiety. But the pledge not to send forces to Herat unless it was beseiged by foreign troops and not to interfere in the internal affairs of the khanate opened the door to Russian intrigue in Tehran, as British-Russian rivalry in the Persian-Afghan area was rekindled before and during the Crimean war. Kelly, *Britain and the Persian Gulf*, pp. 452–54; *British and Foreign State Papers*, 45: 642–71 (correspondence); Rawlinson, *England and Russia in the East*, pp. 44–89; Kaye, *History of the War in Afghanistan* (for background through 1842); Sykes, *History of Persia*, vol. 2, chaps. 77–78, and *History of Afghanistan*, vol. 1, chap. 27, vol. 2, chaps. 28–33; Popowski, *Rival Powers in Central Asia*; Curzon, *Russia in Central Asia*, chap. 9, and *Persia and the Persian Question*, vol. 2, chap. 30; Krausse, *Russia in Asia*, chap. 10; Ferrier. *Voyages en Perse*.

The Persian Government engages not to send troops on any account to the territory of Herat, excepting when troops from without attack that place, that is to say, troops from the direction of Cabool, or from Candahar, or from other foreign territory; and in case of troops being despatched under such circumstances, the Persian Government binds itself that they shall not enter the city of Herat, and that immediately on the retreat of the foreign troops to their own country, the Persian force shall forthwith return to the Persian soil without delay.

The Persian Government also engages to abstain from all interference whatsoever in the internal affairs of Herat, likewise in (regard to) occupation or taking possession, or assuming the sovereignty or government, except that the same amount of interference which took place between the two in the time of the late Zuheer-ood-Dowlah, Yar Mahomed Khan, is to exist as formerly. The Persian Government, therefore, engages to address a letter to Syed Mahomed Khan, acquainting him with these conditions, and to forward it to him (by a person) accompanied by some one belonging to the English mission, who may be in Meshed.

The Persian Government also engages to relinquish all claim or pretension to the coinage of money and to the "Khootbeth", or to any other mark whatever of subjection or of allegiance on the part of the people of Herat to Persia. But if, as in the time of the late Kamran and in that of the late Yar Mahomed Khan, they should, of their own accord, send an offering in money and strike it in the Shah's name, Persia will receive it without making any objection. This condition will also be immediately communicated to Syed Mahomed Khan. They also engage to recall Abbas Koolee Khan, Peeseean, after four months from the date of his arrival, so that he may not reside there permanently; and hereafter no permanent agent will be placed in Herat, but intercourse will be maintained as in the time of Yar Mahomed Khan. Neither will they maintain a permanent agent on the part of Herat in Teheran. There will be the same relations and privileges which existed in Kamran's time, and in that of the late Yar Mahomed Khan. For instance, if at any time it should be necessary for the punishment of the Toorkomans, or in case of disturbance or rebellion in the Shah's dominions, that the Persian Government should receive assistance from the Heratees, similar to that afforded by the late Yar Mahomed Khan, they may, as formerly, render assistance of their own accord and free-will, but not of a permanent nature.

The Persian Government further engages, unconditionally and without exception, to release and set free all the Chiefs of Herat who are in Meshed or in Teheran or in any other part of Persia, and not to receive any offenders, prisoners, or suspected persons whatsoever from Syed Mahomed Khan, with the exception of such persons as having been banished by Syed Mahomed Khan from Herat may come here and themselves desire to remain, or to enter the service. These will be treated with kindness and favour as formerly. Distinct orders will be issued immediately to the Prince Governor of Khorassan to carry out these engagements.

The above six engagements on the part of the Persian Government are to be observed and to have effect; and the Persian ministers, notwithstanding the rights which they possess in Herat, solely out of friendship, and to satisfy the English Government, have entered into these engagements with the English Government so long as there is no interference whatsoever on its part in the internal affairs of Herat and its dependencies; otherwise these engagements will be null and void, and as if they never had existed or been written. And if any foreign (State), either Afghan or other, should desire to interfere with or encroach upon the territory of Herat or its dependencies and the Persian ministers should make the request, the British Government are not to be remiss in restraining them and in giving their friendly advice, so that Herat may remain in its own state of independence.

99. PERPETUAL MARITIME TRUCE CONCLUDED BY THE SHAYKHS OF THE PIRATE COAST
4 May 1853

(Approved by the governor general of India in Council, 24 August 1853)
[Aitchison, *Collection of Treaties . . . relating to India* (5th ed.), 11: 252–53]

The general treaty of 1820 for the suppression of piracy and slave traffic (Doc. 60) did not proscribe war among the signatories, and "under the name of acknowledged war many acts of piracy were committed, especially during the pearl-fishing season." The British therefore persuaded the shaykhs (excluding the shaykh of Bahrayn, who had signed the 1820 instrument) in 1835 to accept a six-month maritime truce on the understanding that Her Majesty's government would not interfere with their wars on land. The truce was renewed annually (for twelve-month periods starting in 1838) until 1843, when the shaykhs agreed to a ten-year extension (text, Aitchison, op. cit., pp. 250–51), at the expiration of which it was decided to prolong the agreement in perpetuity. Kelly, *Britain and the Persian Gulf*, chaps. 6 and 9; Lorimer, *Gazetteer of the Persian Gulf*, vol. 1, pt. 1, 694–719; A. Wilson, *Persian Gulf*, chap. 13; Curzon, *Persia and the Persian Question*, 2: 446–52; Low, *Indian Navy*, vol. 2, chap. 6; Liebesny, "International Relations of Arabia, the Dependent Areas"; Brinton, "Arabian Peninsula"; Hawley, *Trucial States*, chap. 6; Standish, "British Maritime Policy."

We, whose seals are hereunto affixed, Sheikh Sultan bin Suggur, Chief of Rassool-Kheimah, Sheikh Saeed bin Tahnoon, Chief of Aboo Dhebbee, Sheikh Saeed bin Butye, Chief of Debay, Sheikh Hamid bin Rashed, Chief of Ejman, Sheikh Abdoola bin Rashed, Chief of Umm-ool-Keiweyn, having experienced for a series of years the benefits and advantages resulting from a maritime truce contracted amongst ourselves under the mediation of the Resident in the Persian Gulf and renewed frm time to time up to the present period, and being fully impressed, therefore, with a sense of the evil consequence formerly arising, from the prosecution of our feuds at sea, whereby our subjects and dependants were prevented from carrying on the pearl fishery in security, and were exposed to interruption and molestation when passing on their lawful occasions, accordingly, we, as aforesaid have determined, for ourselves, our heirs and successors, to conclude together a lasting and inviolable peace from this time forth in perpetuity and do hereby agree to bind ourselves down to observe the following conditions:—

ART. 1. That from this date, *viz.*, 25th Rujjub 1269, 4th May 1853, and hereafter, there shall be a complete cessation of hostilities at sea between our respective subjects and dependants, and a perfect maritime truce shall endure between ourselves and between our successors, respectively, for evermore.

ART. 2. That in the event (which God forbid) of any of our subjects or dependants committing an act of aggression at sea upon the lives or property of those of any of the parties to this agreement, we will immediately punish the assailants and proceed to afford full redress upon the same being brought to our notice.

ART. 3. That in the event of an act of aggression being committed at sea by any of those who are subscribers with us to this engagement upon any of our subjects or dependants, we will not proceed immediately to retaliate, but will inform the British Resident or the Commodore at Bassidore, who will forthwith take the necessary steps for obtaining reparation for the injury inflicted, provided that its occurrence can be satisfactory proved.

We further agree that the maintenance of the peace now concluded amongst us shall be watched over by the British Government, who will take steps to ensure at all times the due observance of the above Articles, and God of this is the best witness and guarantee.

100. TREATY FOR MILITARY AID TO THE SUBLIME PORTE: FRANCE, GREAT BRITAIN, AND THE OTTOMAN EMPIRE
12 March 1854

(Ratifications exchanged, Istanbul, 8 May 1854)
[Great Britain, *Parliamentary Papers, 1854*, 72: 105–07]

If any uncertainty remained by the mid-nineteenth century that Ottoman affairs had become inseparable from those of Europe, these doubts should have been dissipated by the Crimean War. The Sublime Porte, with the backing of the British ambassador at Istanbul, refused in March 1853 to accede to Russian demands for the right to protect all Greek Orthodox subjects of the sultan. This led to the Russian occupation in July of Moldavia and Walachia, Ottoman Danubian provinces (forming part of present-day Rumania). The Porte's declaration of war on 4 October was followed by that of the tsarist regime precisely four weeks later. The Russians destroyed the Ottoman fleet at Sinop on 30 November. British and French warships, which had already passed the Dardanelles to give moral support to the sultan, entered the Black Sea in January 1854, In justifying the tripartite treaty, which preceded by fifteen days their formal declaration of war, England and France stated in the preamble that they had consented to the sultan's request for assistance "in repelling . . . [Russian] aggression by which the integrity of the Ottoman Empire and the independence of the [sultan's] throne . . . are menaced," for the Western signatories were "fully persuaded that the existence of the Ottoman Empire in its present limits is essential to the maintenance of the balance of power among the States of Europe." Temperley, *England and the Near East*, chaps. 12–14; Anderson, *Eastern Question*, chap. 5; Conacher, *Aberdeen Coalition*, chap. 10, and "New Light on the Origins of the Crimean War"; Holland, *Treaty Relations of Russia and Turkey*; Florinsky, *Russia*, 2: 869–78; Puryear, *England, Russia and the Straits Question*, chap. 5; Bapst, *Les origines de la guerre de Crimée*; Jomini, *La guerre de Crimée*; B. Martin, *Triumph of Lord Palmerston*, chaps. 7–8; Lane-Poole, *Life of the Right Honourable Stratford Canning*, vol. 2, chaps. 25–28; Gooch, "Century of Historiography on the Origins of the Crimean War," and "Crimean War"; Hösch, "Neuere Literatur über den Krimkrieg"; for questions relating to the straits, see references to Doc. 105.

ART. I. Her Majesty the Queen of the United Kingdom of Great Britain and Ireland, and His Majesty the Emperor of the French, having already, at the request of His Imperial Majesty the Sultan, ordered powerful divisions of their naval forces to proceed to Constantinople, and to afford to the Ottoman territory and flag such protection as the circumstances might admit of, their said Majesties undertake by the present Treaty still further to cooperate with His Imperial Majesty the Sultan for the defence of the Ottoman territory in Europe and in Asia against Russian aggression, by employing for that purpose such an amount of their land forces as may appear necessary to attain the said object; which land forces their said Majesties will immediately dispatch to such point or points of the Ottoman territory as shall be deemed expedient: and His Imperial Majesty the Sultan agrees, that the British and French land forces thus sent for the defence of the Ottoman territory, shall meet with the same friendly reception, and shall be treated with the same consideration, as the British and French naval forces, which have for some time past been employed in the waters of Turkey.

ART. II. The High Contracting Parties severally engage to communicate to each other, without loss of time, any proposition which any one of them may receive on the part of the Emperor of Russia, either directly or indirectly, with a view to the cessation of hostilities, to an armistice, or to peace;

and His Imperial Majesty the Sultan engages, moreover, not to conclude any armistice, nor to enter on any negotiation for peace, and not to conclude any preliminary of peace, nor any Treaty of Peace, with the Emperor of Russia, without the knowledge and consent of the High Contracting Parties.

ART. III. As soon as the object of the present Treaty shall have been attained by the conclusion of a Treaty of Peace, Her Majesty the Queen of the United Kingdom of Great Britain and Ireland, and His Majesty the Emperor of the French, will forthwith make arrangements for the immediate withdrawal of all their military and naval forces which shall have been employed to accomplish the object of the present Treaty; and all the fortresses or positions in the Ottoman territory which shall have been temporarily occupied by the military forces of England and France, shall be delivered up to the authorities of the Sublime Ottoman Porte in the space of forty days, or sooner if possible, after the exchange of the ratifications of the Treaty by which the present war shall be terminated.

ART. IV. It is understood that the auxiliary armies shall retain the power of taking such part as they may deem expedient in the operations directed against the common enemy, without the Ottoman authorities, civil or military, having any pretension to exercise the slightest control over their movements: on the contrary, every aid and facility shall be afforded to them by those authorities, especially for their landing, their march, their quarters or encampment, their subsistence and that of their horses, and their communications, whether they act together or whether they act separately.

It is understood, on the other hand, that the commanders of the said armies undertake to maintain the strictest discipline in their respective troops, and shall cause them to respect the laws and usages of the country.

As a matter of course property shall be everywhere respected.

It is moreover understood, on either side, that the general plan of campaign shall be discussed and settled between the Com-manders-in-chief of the three armies, and that if any considerable portion of the allied troops should be acting in conjunction with the Ottoman troops, no operation shall be undertaken against the enemy without its having been previously concerted with the commanders of the allied forces.

Finally, attention shall be paid to any demand relative to the wants of the service which may be addressed by the Commanders-in-chief of the auxiliary troops, either to the Ottoman Government through their respective Embassies, or, in case of urgency, to the local authorities, unless insuperable objections, to be clearly explained, should prevent compliance with such demands...

101. DEED OF THE MASQATI SULTAN CEDING THE KURIA MURIA ISLANDS TO THE BRITISH CROWN
14 July 1854

[Aitchison, *Collection of Treaties . . . relating to India* (5th ed.), 11: 302]

The British appear to have sought possession of the Kuria Muria Islands, which the French had also tried to acquire, for their guano deposits and for use as a cable station in a projected telegraph line to India. Coupland, *East Africa and Its Invaders*, chap. 17; also references to Doc. 93.

From the humble Saeed bin Sultan, to all and every one who may see this paper, whether Mahomedans or others—

There has arrived to me from the powerful nation (England) Captain Fremantle, belonging to the Royal Navy of the Great Queen, requesting from me the (Jesairi bin Colfaim) Koria Moria Islands, *viz.*, Helaneea, Jibleea, Soda, Haski and Gurzond; and I hereby cede to the Queen Victoria the above-mentioned Islands, to be her possessions, or her heirs and successors after her. In proof whereof I have hereunto affixed my signature and seal, on behalf of myself and my son after me, of my own free will and pleasure, without force, intimidation, or pecuniary interest whatsoever.

102. TREATY OF PERPETUAL PEACE AND FRIENDSHIP:
BRITISH INDIA AND THE AMIR OF KABUL
30 March 1855

(Ratified by the governor general of India, Octakamund, 1 May 1855)
[India Office Library, Political and Secret Department, Memoranda, vol. 2 (1898–1923), A 155, doc. no. 158, pp. 349–50]

After the disastrous First Afghan War (1838–42), British India kept its hands off the three khanates of Kabul, Qandahar, and Herat into which Afghanistan disintegrated. However, in 1848–49 when Dust Muhammad Khan (1826–38, 1842–63), the amir of Kabul, joined the Sikhs in their war with British India, hoping to acquire the district of Peshawar as a reward in the event of victory, the Afghan tribesmen, along with the Sikhs, were crushed in the battle of Gujrat on 21 February 1849. It was then that British India finally annexed the Punjab and Peshawar, establishing a de facto boundary with Afghanistan that was not formalized for more than forty years. During the Crimean War British India approached Dust Muhammad as a precautionary measure "to make Afghanistan an effectual barrier against Russian aggression," by inducing "the Afghan tribes to make a common cause . . . against an enemy whose success would be fatal to the common interests of both Afghan and British power" (as cited in India Office Library, Political and Secret Department, Memoranda, vol. 1, no. A 21, "Afghanistan: Historical Sketch," by A. W. Moore, 30 November 1878, p. 3). The British-Indian initiative Dust Muhammad welcomed, for he was becoming anxious over Persian meddling—with Russian encouragement, it was suspected—in the khanates of Herat and Qandahar. The outcome of the exchanges was the following instrument, which signaled the start of sustained diplomatic relations between British India and Afghanistan. The treaty was signed by John Lawrence, the chief commissioner of the Punjab, and the Sardar Ghulam Haydar Khan, the heir apparent of Amir Dust Muhammad Khan of Kabul. Fraser-Tytler, *Afghanistan*, pt. 2, chap. 7; Singhal, *India and Afghanistan*, chap. 1; Sykes, *History of Afghanistan*, vol. 2, chap. 23; Rawlinson, *England and Russia in the East*, chap. 2.

. . . ART. 1. Between the Honorable East India Company and His Highness Ameer Dost Mohummud Khan, Walee of Cabool and of those countries of Affghanistan now in his possession, and the heirs of the said Ameer, there shall be perpetual peace and friendship.

ART. 2. The Honorable East India Company engages to respect those territories of Affghanistan now in His Highness's possession, and never to interfere therein.

ART. 3. His Highness Ameer Dost Mohummud Khan, Walee of Cabool and of those countries of Affghanistan now in his possession, engages on his own part, and on the part of his heirs, to respect the territories of the Honorable East India Company, and never to interfere therein; and to be the friend of the friends and enemy of the enemies of the Honorable East India Company. . . .

103. DEFINITIVE CONCESSION FOR THE CONSTRUCTION OF THE SUEZ CANAL
5 January 1856

[United States, *Suez Canal Problem*, pp. 4–9, translated by the Department of State from the French text in *British and Foreign State Papers*, 55: 976–81]

From the time of Napoleon I, French interest in piercing the Isthmus of Suez for sea-borne traffic grew progressively more articulate. The British government resisted French efforts at every turn, fearing that a canal linking the Mediterranean and Red seas and severing the Asian and African continents could hardly fail to become a second Ottoman Straits in European politics. The British line was defined by Palmerston, who held office as foreign or prime minister throughout most of the period in which the canal scheme became a practical possibility. He promoted, as an alternative to the canal, the erection of a railroad from Alexandria to Cairo and Suez. Despite British opposition, Ferdinand de Lesseps, a former French consul with a long record of service in Egypt, obtained on 30 November 1854 from Sa'id Paşa (1854–63), Mehmed 'Ali's youngest son, who had just succeeded to the governorship, an act of concession for building the canal (English translation in Fitzgerald, *Great Canal at Suez*, pp. 293–97). De Lesseps's triumph derived as much from persistence as from personal friendship with Sa'id. The original act of concession was replaced by a definitive and more detailed one on 5 January 1856, when the statutes of the Compagnie Universelle du Canal Maritime de Suez were adopted (French text of statutes in *British and Foreign State Papers*, 55: 981–95; English abstract in Fitzgerald, op. cit., pp. 310–23). British diplomatic opposition stiffened after work on the canal commenced in 1859, and it was not finally overcome until nearly seven years later. Hallberg, *Suez Canal*, chaps. 1–12; A. Wilson, *Suez Canal*, chaps. 1–2; Fitzgerald, op. cit., Schonfield, *Suez Canal*, chaps. 1–5; Hoskins, *British Routes to India*, chaps. 12–14; Kinross, *Between Two Seas*; De Lesseps, *Lettres, journal et documents pour servir à l'histoire du canal de Suez*; Beatty, *Charles De Lesseps*; Compagnie Universelle du Canal Maritime de Suez, *Des actes constitutifs de la Compagnie Universelle du Canal Maritime de Suez*; Sammarco, *Précis de l'histoire d'Egypte*, vol. 4, chaps. 3–6, 9; Farnie, *East and West of Suez*, chaps. 1–5; Rivlin, "Railway Question."

We, Mohammed Said Pasha, Viceroy of Egypt.

In view of our Act of Concession dated November 30, 1854, by which we gave to our friend, Mr. Ferdinand de Lesseps, exclusive power for the purpose of establishing and directing a universal company to cut through the Isthmus of Suez, to operate a passage suitable for large vessels, to establish or adapt two adequate entrances, one on the Mediterranean, the other on the Red Sea, and to establish one or two ports:

Mr. Ferdinand de Lesseps having represented to us that, in order to establish the aforementioned company in the form and under the conditions generally adopted for companies of this nature, it is desirable to stipulate in advance, in a more detailed and more complete act, on the one hand, the responsibilities, obligations, and charges to which such company will be subject and, on the other hand, the concessions, immunities, and advantages to which it shall be entitled, as well as the faciliies that will be granted to it for its administration.

We have laid down as follows the conditions for the concession which forms the subject of these presents.

Obligations

ART. I. The company founded by our friend, Mr. Ferdinand de Lesseps, by virtue of our grant of November 30, 1854, must execute at its own expense, risk, and peril, all work, including construction, necessary for the establishment of:

(1) A canal for large seagoing vessels, between Suez on the Red Sea and the Bay of Pelusium in the Mediterranean Sea;

(2) An irrigation canal also suitable for use by Nile shpping, connecting the river with the maritime canal above-mentioned;

(3) Two irrigation and feeder branches leading off from the above-mentioned canal and flowing in the two directions of Suez and Pelusium.

The work will be carried out so as to be finished within a period of six years, except in the event of hindrances and delays resulting from *force majeure.*

II. The company shall be empowered to carry out the work with which it is charged by itself under State supervision or to cause it to be carried out by contractors through competitive bids or on an agreed-price basis. In all cases at least four-fifths of the workmen employed in this work are to be Egyptians.

III. The canal suitable for large seagoing vessels shall be dug to the depth and width fixed by the program of the International Scientific Commission.

In conformity with this program it shall start from the port of Suez itself; it shall use the basin known as the Bitter Lakes Basin and Lake Timsa; it shall have its outlet in the Mediterranean, at a point on the Bay of Pelusium to be determined in the final plans to be drawn up by the company's engineers.

IV. The irrigation canal suitable for river shipping under the conditions of the said program shall begin near the city of Cairo, follow the valley (wadi) of Tumilat (ancient land of Goshen) and meet the large maritime canal at Lake Timsa.

V. The branches of the said canal are to lead off from it above the outlet into Lake Timsa; from that point they will be made to flow in the one case toward Suez and in other case toward Pelusium, parallel to the large maritime canal.

VI. Lake Timsa will be converted into an inland port capable of receiving vessels of the largest tonnage.

The company will be bound, moreover, if necessary: (1) to construct a harbor at the point where the maritime canal enters the Bay of Pelusium; (2) to improve the port and roadstead of Suez, so as also to afford shelter to vessels there.

VII. The maritime canal and ports belonging to it, as well as the canal connecting with the Nile and the lead-off canal, shall at all times be kept in good condition by the company, at its expense.

VIII. Owners of riparian property wishing their land to be irrigated by water from the canals constructed by the company may obtain permission from it for this purpose through payment of compensation or a fee the amount of which shall be fixed by the conditions of Art. XVII hereinafter mentioned.

IX. We reserve the right to appoint at the administrative headquarters of the company a special commissioner, whose salary shall be paid by it, and who will represent with its administration the rights and interests of the Egyptian Government for the execution of the provisions of these presents.

If the company's administrative headquarters is established elsewhere than in Egypt, the company shall have itself represented at Alexandria by a superior agent vested with all powers necessary to see to the proper functioning of the service and the company's relations with our government.

Concessions

X. In return for the construction of the canals and appurtenances mentioned in the foregoing articles, the Egyptian Government allows the company, without tax or fee, to enjoy the use of all such land, not belonging to private parties, as may be necessary.

It also allows it to enjoy the use of all now uncultivated land not belonging to private parties, which will be irrigated and cultivated by its efforts and at its expense, with this difference: (1) That the portions of land included in this last category shall be exempt from all taxes for ten years only, dating from their connection with the undertaking; (2) That after that period, and until the expiration of the concession, they shall be subject to the obligations and taxes to which the land of the other Egyptian provinces is subject under the same circumstances; (3) That the company can, subsequently, acting itself or through its assigns, retain the right to enjoy possession of this land and of the water-supply facilities necessary for its fertilization, subject to payment to the Egyptian Government of the taxes levied upon land under the same conditions.

XI. To determine the extent and limits of the land granted to the company, under the conditions of (1) and (2) of Article X above, reference is made to the plans annexed hereto,[1] it being understood that on the said plans the lands granted for the construction of the canals and appurtenances free of tax or fee in conformity with (1) are shown in black, and the lands granted for cultivation through payment of certain fees in conformity with (2) are shown in blue.

All acts executed subsequent to our act of November 30, 1854 shall be considered null and void if they would result in creating for private parties as against the company either rights to compensation which did not exist at the time with respect to those lands, or rights to compensation that are more extensive than those which they were able to claim at that time.

XII. The Egyptian Government will make over to the company, if desirable, privately-owned land the possession of which may be necessary to the execution of the work and the exploitation of the concession, provided the company pay fair compensation to the owners.

Compensation for temporary occupation or for definitive expropriation shall be settled amicably in so far as possible; in case of disagreement, it shall be fixed by a court of arbitration acting in summary proceedings and composed of: (1) an arbitrator chosen by the company; (2) an arbitrator chosen by the interested parties, and (3) a third arbitrator appointed by us.

The decisions of the court of arbitration shall become executory immediately and shall not be subject to appeal.

XIII. The Egyptian Government grants the concessionary company, for the entire life of the concession, the right to extract from mines and quarries beloning to the public domain, without payment of any fee, tax, or compensation, all materials necessary for the work of constructing and maintaining the installations and establishments belonging to the company.

Furthermore, it exempts the company from all customs, entry, and other duties on the importation into Egypt of all machinery and material of any kind that it may bring in from abroad for the needs of its various services during construction or operation.

XIV. We solemnly declare, for ourselves and our successors, subject to ratification by His Imperial Majesty the Sultan, that the great maritime canal from Suez to Pelusium and the ports belonging to it shall be open forever, as neutral passages, to every merchant vessel crossing from one sea to the other, without any distinction, exclusion, or preference with respect to persons or nationalities, in consideration of the payment of the fees, and compliance with the regulations established by the universal company, the concession-holder, for the use of the said canal and its appurtenances.

XV. In consequence of the principle laid down in the foregoing article, the universal company holding the concession may not, in any case, give to any vessel, company, or private party any advantage or favor not given to all other vessels, companies, or private parties on the same terms.

XVI. The life of the company is fixed at 99 years, counting from the completion of the work and the opening of the maritime canal to large vessels.

At the expiration of that period, the Egyptian Government will resume possession of the maritime canal constructed by the company, and it shall be its responsibility, in this case, to take over all materials and supplies used in the company's maritime service and, in return, to pay the

---

1. Not reproduced here.

company the value to be fixed, either by amicable agreement or on the basis of an opinion of experts.

Nevertheless, should the company retain the concession for successive periods of 99 years, the levy for the benefit of the Egyptian Government stipulated in Article XVIII below shall be increased for the second period to 20 percent, for the third period to 25 percent, and so on, at the rate of 5 percent for each period; but such levy shall, however, never exceed 35 percent of the net profits of the company.

XVII. In order to compensate the company for the expenses of construction, maintenance, and operation for which it is made responsible by these presents, we authorize it, henceforth and for its entire term of possession, as specified in paragraphs 1 and 3 of the foregoing article, to establish and collect, for passage in the canals and the ports belonging thereto, navigation, pilotage, towage, and anchorage fees, according to rate-schedules which it may change at any time, subject to the express condition that it shall:

(1) Collect these fees without exception or favor from all vessels, under the same terms

(2) Publish the rate-schedules three months before they become effective, in the capitals and principal commercial ports of the countries concerned

(3) Not exceed for the special navigation fee the maximum figure of ten francs per ton of burden for vessels and ten francs a head for passengers.

The company may, also, for all water-supply facilities granted at the request of private parties, by virtue of Article VIII above, collect, according to rate-schedules which it will fix, a fee proportionate to the quantity of water used and the area of the land irrigated.

XVIII. At the same time, in view of the land grants and other advantages accorded the company in the foregoing articles, we shall make, for the benefit of the Egyptian Government, a levy of 15 percent of the net profits for each year as determined and apportioned at the general meeting of shareholders.

XIX. The list of charter members who contributed by their work, their studies, and their capital to the accomplishment of the undertaking, before the founding of the company, shall be prepared by us.

After deduction of the amount levied for the Egyptian Government stipulated in Article XVIII above, 10 percent of the annual net profits of the enterprise is to be alotted to the charter members or their heirs or assigns.

XX. Independently of the time necessary for the execution of the work, our friend and representative, Mr. Ferdinand de Lesseps, will preside over and direct the company as first founder for ten years from the time when the period of the enjoyment of the 99-year concession begins, under the terms of article XVI above.

XXI. The articles of incorporation of the company thus created under the name of Universal Company of the Maritime Canal of Suez are hereby approved; this approval constitutes authorization for establishment in the form of a corporation, effective on the date on which the capital of the company shall have been subscribed in full.

XXII. In token of the interest we attach to the success of the enterprise, we promise the company the loyal cooperation of the Egyptian Government and by these presents expressly request the officials and agents of all the departments of our Government to accord it assistance and protection under all circumstances.

Our engineers, Linant Bey and Mougel Bey, whom we place at the company's disposal for the direction and management of the work laid out by it, shall be in charge of the supervision of the workers and shall be responsible for enforcement of the regulations for putting the work programs into operation.

XXIII. All provisions of our *ordonnance* of November 30, 1854 are hereby revoked, together with any others which may be in conflict with the clauses and terms of the present articles and conditions, which alone shall govern the concession to which they apply.

104. SULTAN 'ABDÜLMECID'S *ISLAHAT FERMANI* REAFFIRMING
THE PRIVILEGES AND IMMUNITIES OF THE
NON-MUSLIM COMMUNITIES
18 February 1856

[United States, 46th Cong., spec. sess. (March 1881), Senate, Exec. Documents, vol. 3, no. 3, *The Capitulations*, by E. A. Van Dyck, pt. 1, pp. 108–11]

In a reform decree of 18 February 1856 Sultan 'Abdülmecid reaffirmed the traditional rights of his non-Muslim subjects and promised them complete religious liberty and equality. After prodding by the all-powerful British ambassador, Viscount de Redcliffe (formerly Stratford Canning), the sultan issued his latest decree on the eve of the peace conference at Paris. The decree was obviously designed to weaken Russian claims to the right of protecting all Greek Orthodox Christians in the Ottoman Empire, a claim that had been one of the principal immediate causes of the Crimean War. In article 9 of the treaty of Paris (see Doc 105). the European powers recognized "the high value of this communication. It is clearly understood that it cannot, in any case, give to the said Powers the right to interfere, either collectively or separately, in the relations of His Majesty the Sultan with his subjects, nor in the internal administration of his Empire." The islahat fermani of 1856, one observer noted, "left nothing to be desired but its execution." He might have made the same comment with equal validity on article 9 of the treaty of Paris. Davison, *Reform in the Ottoman Empire*, chap. 2, and "Turkish Attitudes concerning Christian-Muslim Equality in the Nineteenth Century"; Lewis, *Emergence of Modern Turkey*, chap. 4; Berkes, *Development of Secularism in Turkey*, chap. 5; Englehardt, *La Turquie et le Tanzimat*, 1: 115–51; Creasy, *History of the Ottoman Turks* (2d ed.), chap. 25; Lane-Poole, *Life of the Right Honourable Stratford Canning*, 2: 439–45.

Let it be done as herein set forth.

To you, my Grand Vizier Mehemed Emin Aali Pasha, decorated with my imperial order of the medjidiye of the first class, and with the order of personal merit; may God grant to you greatness and increase your power.

It has always been my most earnest desire to insure the happiness of all classes of the subjects whom Divine Providence has placed under my imperial sceptre, and since my accession to the throne I have not ceased to direct all my efforts to the attainment of that end.

Thanks to the Almighty, these unceasing efforts have already been productive of numerous useful results. From day to day the happiness of the nation and the wealth of my dominions go on augmenting.

It being now my desire to renew and enlarge still more the new institutions ordained with a view of establishing a state of things conformable with the dignity of my empire and the position which it occupies among civilized nations, and the rights of my empire having, by the fidelity and praiseworthy efforts of all my subjects, and by the kind and friendly assistance of the great powers, my noble allies, received from abroad a confirmation which will be the commencement of a new era, it is my desire to augment its well being and prosperity, to effect the happiness of all my subjects, who in my sight are all equal, and equally dear to me, and who are united to each other by the cordial ties of patriotism, and to insure the means of daily increasing the prosperity of my empire.

I have therefore resolved upon, and I order the execution of the following measures:

The guarantees promised on our part by the Hatti-Humayoun of Gulhané, and in conformity with the Tanzimat, to all the subjects of my empire, without distinction of classes or of religion, for the security of their persons and property, and the preservation of their honor, are to-day confirmed and consolidated, and efficacious measures shall be taken in order that they may have their full entire effect.

All the privileges and spiritual immunities granted by my ancestors *ab antiquo*, and at subsequent dates, to all Christian communities or other non-Mussulman persuasions established in my empire, under my protection, shall be confirmed and maintained.

Every Christian or other non-Mussulman community shall be bound within a fixed period, and with the concurrence of a commission composed *ad hoc* of members of its own body, to proceed, with my high approbation and under the inspection of my Sublime Porte, to examine into its actual immunities and privileges, and to discuss and submit to my Sublime Porte the reforms required by the progress of civilization and of the age. The powers conceded to the Christian patriarchs and bishops by the Sultan Mahomet II and to his successors shall be made to harmonize with the new position which my generous and beneficient intentions insure to these communities.

The principle of nominating the patriarchs for life, after the revision of the rule of election now in force, shall be exactly carried out, conformably to the tenor of their firmans of investiture.

The patriarchs, metropolitans, archbishops, bishops, and rabbins shall take an oath, on their entrance into office, according to a form agreed upon in common by my Sublime Porte and the spiritual heads of the different religious communities. The ecclesiastical dues, of whatever sort or nature they be, shall be abolished and replaced by fixed revenues of the patriarchs and heads of communities, and by the allocations of allowances and salaries equitably proportioned to the importance, the rank, and the dignity of the different members of the clergy.

The property, real or personal, of the different Christian ecclesiastics shall remain intact; the temporal administration of the Christian or other non-Mussulman communities shall, however, be placed under the safeguard of an assembly to be chosen from among the members, both ecclesiastics and laymen, of the said communities

In the towns, small boroughs, and villages where the whole population is of the same religion, no obstacle shall be offered to the repair, according to their original plan, of buildings set apart for religious worship, for schools, for hospitals, and for cemeteries.

The plans of these different buildings, in case of their new erection, must, after having been approved by the patriarchs or heads of communities, be submitted to my Sublime Porte, which will approve of them by my imperial order, or make known its observations upon them within a certain time. Each sect, in localities where there are no other religious denominations, shall be free from every species of restraint as regards the public exercise of its religion.

In the towns, small boroughs, and villages where different sects are mingled together each community inhabiting a distinct quarter shall, by conforming to the above-mentioned ordinances, have equal power to repair and improve its churches, its hospitals, its schools, and its cemeteries. When there is question of their erection of new buildings, the necessary authority must be asked for, through the medium of the patriarchs and heads of communities, from my Sublime Porte, which will pronounce a sovereign decision according that authority, except in the case of administrative obstacles.

The intervention of the administrative authority in all measures of this nature will be entirely gratuitous. My Sublime Porte will take energetic measures to insure to each sect, whatever be the number of its adherents, entire freedom in the exercise of its religion. Every distinction or designation pending to make any class whatever of the subjects of my empire inferior to another class, on account of their religion, language, or race, shall be forever effaced from administrative protocol. The laws shall be put in force against the use of any injurious or offensive term, either among private individuals or on the part of the authorities.

As all forms of religion are and shall be freely professed in my dominions, no subject of my empire shall be hindered in the exercise of the religion that he professes, nor shall he be in any way annoyed on this account. No one shall be compelled to change their religion.

The nomination and choice of all functionaries and other employes of my empire being wholly dependent upon my sovereign will, all the subjects of my empire, without distinction of nationality, shall be admissible to public employments, and qualified to fill them according to their capacity and merit, and conformably with rules to be generally applied.

All the subjects of my empire, without distinction, shall be received into the civil and military schools of the government, if they otherwise satisfy the conditions as to age and examination which are specified in the organic regulations of the said schools. Moreover, every community is authorized to establish public schools of science, art, and industry. Only the method of instructions and the choice of professors in schools of this class shall be under the control of a mixed council of public instruction, the members of which shall be named by my sovereign command.

All commercial, correctional, and criminal suits between Mussulmans and Christians, or other non-Mussulman subjects, or between Christian or other non-Mussulmans of different sects, shall be referred to mixed tribunals.

The proceedings of these tribunals shall be public; the parties shall be confronted and shall produce their witnesses, whose testimony shall be received without distinction, upon an oath taken according to the religious law of each sect.

Suits relating to civil affairs shall continue to be publicly tried, according to the laws and regulations, before the mized provincial councils, in the presence of the governor and judge of the place.

Special civil proceedings, such as those relating to successions or others of that kind, between subjects of the same Christian or other non-Mussulman faith, may, at the request of the parties, be sent before the councils of the patriarchs or of the communities.

Penal, correctional, and commercial laws, and rules of procedure for the mized tribunals, shall be drawn up as soon as possible and formed into a code. Translations of them shall be published in all the languages current in the empire.

Proceedings shall be taken, with as little delay as possible, for the reform of the penitentiary system as applied to houses of detention, punishment, or corrrection, and other establishments of like nature, so as to reconcile the rights of humanity with those of justice. Corporal punishment shall not be administered, even in the prisons, except in conformity with the disciplinary regulations established by my Sublime Porte, and everything that resembles torture shall be entirely abolished.

Infractions of the law in this particular shall be severly repressed, and shall besides entail, as of right, the punishment, in conformity with the civil code, of the authorities who may order and of the agents who may commit them.

The organization of the police in the capital, in the provincial towns and in the rural districts, shall be revised in such a manner as to give to all the peaceable subjects of my empire the strongest guarantees for the safety both of their persons and property.

The equality of taxes entailing equality of burdens, as equality of duties entails that of rights, Christian subjects, and those of other non-Mussulman sects, as it has been already decided, shall, as well as Mussulmans, be subject to the obligations of the law of recruitment.

The principle of obtaining substitutes, or of purchasing exemption, shall be admitted. A complete law shall be published, with as little delay as possible, respecting the admission into and service in the army of Christian and other non-Mussulman subjects.

Proceedings shall be taken for a reform in the constitution of the provincial and communal councils in order to insure fairness in the choice of the deputies of the Mussulman, Christian, and other communities and freedom of voting in the councils. My Sublime Porte will take into consideration the adoption of the most effectual means for ascertaining exactly and for controlling the result of the deliberations and of the decisions arrived at.

As the laws regulating the purchase, sale, and disposal of real property are common to all the subjects of my empire, it shall be lawful for foreigners to possess landed property in my dominions, conforming themselves to the laws and police regulations, and bearing the same charges as the native inhabitants, and after arrangements have been come to with foreign powers.

The taxes are to be levied under the same denomination from all the subjects of my empire, without distinction of class or of religion. The most prompt and energetic means for remedying the abuses in collecting the taxes, and especially the tithes, shall be considered.

The system of direct collections shall gradually, and as soon as possible, be substituted for the plan of farming, in all the branches of the revenues of the state. As long as the present system remains in force all agents of the government and all members of the medjlis shall be forbidden under the severest penalties, to become lessees of any farming contracts which are announced for public competition, or to have any beneficial interest in carrying them out. The local taxes shall, as far as possible, be so imposed as not to affect the sources of production or to hinder the progress of internal commerce.

Works of public utility shall receive a suitable endowment, part of which shall be raised from private and special taxes levied in the provinces, which shall have the benefit of the advantages arising from the establishment of ways of communication by land and sea.

A special law having been already passed, which declares that the budget of the revenue and the expenditure of the state shall be drawn up and made known every year,

the said law shall be most scrupulously observed. Proceedings shall be taken for revising the emoluments attached to each office.

The heads of each community and a delegate, designated by my Sublime Porte, shall be summoned to take part in the deliberations of the supreme council of justice on all occasions which might interest the generality of the subjects of my empire. They shall be summoned specially for this purpose by my grand vizier. The delegates shall hold office for one year; they shall be sworn on entering upon their duties. All the members of the council, at the ordinary and extraordinary meetings, shall freely give their opinions and their votes, and no one shall ever annoy them on this account.

The laws against corruption, extortion, or malversation shall apply, according to the legal forms, to all the subjects of my empire, whatever may be their class and the nature of their duties.

Steps shall be taken for the formation of banks and other similar institutions, so as to effect a reform in the monetary and financial system, as well as to create funds to be employed in augmenting the sources of the material wealth of my empire. Steps shall also be taken for the formation of roads and canals to increase the facilities of communication and increase the sources of the wealth of the country.

Everything that can impede commerce or agriculture shall be abolished. To accomplish these objects means shall be sought to profit by the science, the art, and the funds of Europe, and thus gradually to execute them.

Such being my wishes and my commands, you, who are my grand vizier, will, according to custom, cause this imperial firman to be published in my capital and in all parts of my empire; and you will watch attentively and take all the necessary measures that all the orders which it contains be henceforth carried out with the most rigorous punctuality.

105. THE TREATY OF PEACE (PARIS) TERMINATING THE CRIMEAN WAR, WITH PERTINENT ANNEXED CONVENTIONS AND A TREATY OF GUARANTEE
30 March–15 April 1856

(Ratifications exchanged, Paris: treaty of peace, 27 April 1856; treaty of guarantee, 29 April 1856; treaty of peace unilaterally abrogated by the Sublime Porte, 13 November 1916)
[Great Britain, *Parliamentary Papers, 1856*, 61: 19–34, 444–45]

The treaty of Paris took formal note of what had already become fact a decade and a half earlier (see Doc. 84): the unqualified admission of the Ottoman Empire into the European state system. The European signatories—Austria, France, Great Britian, Prussia, Russia, and Sardinia—engaged jointly to respect and guarantee the integrity and independence of the Ottoman Empire. The Black Sea was neutralized. Sardinia participated in the negotiations because it had entered the war in January 1855; Austria because beginning in June 1854 the Sublime Porte had permitted Austrian troops to occupy Moldavia and Walachia (forming part of present-day Rumania) for the war's duration; and Prussia because it had been a party to the straits convention of 13 July 1841 (see Doc. 87). Omitted from the main treaty below are articles 15–29 (relating to the Balkans) and 33–34 (relating to the Aland Islands). Annexed to the treaty were three separate conventions: the first signed by all the parties, reaffirming the 1841 straits convention; the second by Russia and Turkey, stipulating the kinds and number of war vessels which the two powers were authorized to maintain in the Black Sea; and the third (not reproduced here) by Britain, France, and Russia, concerning the demilitarization of the Aland Islands. Moreover, a fortnight later Britain, France, and Austria reinforced the Crimean system with a separate treaty explicitly guaranteeing the sovereignty and integrity of the Ottoman Empire. Marriott, *Eastern Question*, pp. 249–84; Driault, *La question d'orient*, pp. 166–84; Eversley and Chirol, *Turkish Empire*, chap. 20; on the straits question, see Mischef, *La Mer Noire et les détroits de Constantinople*, chap. 6; Goriainow, *Le Bosphore et les Dardanelles*, chap. 11; Phillipson and Buxton, *Question of the Bosphorus and Dardanelles*, pt. 2, chap. 5; Shotwell and Deák, *Turkey at the Straits*, chap. 5; Anchieri, *Constantinopoli e gli stretti*, pp. 39–46; Puryear, *England, Russia and the Straits Question*, chaps. 6–7; Temperley, "Treaty of Paris of 1856 and Its Execution"; Mosse, *Rise and Fall of the Crimean System*.

1. General Treaty

ART. 1. From the day of the exchange of the ratifications of the present Treaty, there shall be Peace and Friendship between Her Majesty the Queen of the United Kingdom of Great Britain and Ireland, His Majesty the Emperor of the French, His Majesty the King of Sardinia, His Imperial Majesty the Sultan, on the one part, and His Maj-

esty the Emperor of all the Russias, on the other part; as well as between their heirs and successors, their respective dominions and subjects, in perpetuity.

ART. II. Peace being happily reestablished between their said Majesties, the territories conquered or occupied by their armies during the war shall be reciprocally evacuated.

Special arrangements shall regulate the

mode of the evacuation, which shall be as prompt as possible.

ART. III. His Majesty the Emperor of all the Russias engages to restore to His Majesty the Sultan the town and citadel of Kars, as well as the other parts of the Ottoman territory of which the Russian troops are in possession.

ART. IV. Their Majesties the Queen of the United Kingdom of Great Britain and Ireland, the Emperor of the French, the King of Sardinia, and the Sultan, engage to restore to His Majesty the Emperor of all the Russias, the towns and ports of Sebastopol, Balaklava, Kamiesch, Eupatoria, Kertch, Jenikale, Kinburn, as well as all other territories occupied by the allied troops.

ART. V. Their Majesties the Queen of the United Kingdom of Great Britain and Ireland, the Emperor of the French, the Emperor of all the Russias, the King of Sardinia, and the Sultan, grant a full and entire amnesty to those of their subjects who may have been compromised by any participation whatsoever in the events of the war in favour of the cause of the enemy.

It is expressly understood that such amnesty shall extend to the subjects of each of the belligerent parties who may have continued, during the war, to be employed in the service of one of the other belligerents.

ART. VI. Prisoners of war shall be immediately given up on either side.

ART. VII. Her Majesty the Queen of the United Kingdom of Great Britain and Ireland, His Majesty the Emperor of Austria, His Majesty the Emperor of the French, His Majesty the King of Prussia. His Majesty the Emperor of all the Russias, and His Majesty the King of Sardinia, declare the Sublime Porte admitted to participate in the advantages of the public law and system (concert) of Europe. Their Majesties engage, each on his part, to respect the independence and the territorial integrity of the Ottoman Empire; guarantee in common the strict observance of that engagement; and will, in consequence, consider any act tending to its violation as a question of general interest.

ART. VIII. If there should arise between the Sublime Porte and one or more of the other signing Powers, any misunderstanding which might endanger the maintenance of their relations, the Sublime Porte, and each of such Powers, before having recourse to the use of force, shall afford the other Contracting Parties the opportunity of preventing such an extremity by means of their mediation.

ART. IX. His Imperial Majesty the Sultan, having, in his constant solicitude for the welfare of his subjects, issued a firman [decree] which, while ameliorating their condition without distinction of religion or of race, records his generous intentions towards the Christian population of his Empire, and wishing to give a further proof of his sentiments in that respect, has resolved to communicate to the Contracting Parties the said firman, emanating spontaneously from his sovereign will.

The Contracting Parties recognize the high value of this communication. It is clearly understood that it cannot, in any case, give to the said Powers the right to interfere, either collectively or separately, in the relations of His Majesty the Sultan with his subjects, nor in the internal administration of his Empire.

ART. X. The Convention of the 13th of July, 1841, which maintains the ancient rule of the Ottoman Empire relative to the closing of the Straits of the Bosphorus and of the Dardanelles, has been revised by common consent.

The Act concluded for that purpose, and in conformity with that principle, between the High Contracting Parties, is and remains annexed to the present Treaty, and shall have the same force and validity as if it formed an integral part thereof.

ART. XI. The Black Sea is neutralized: its waters and its ports, thrown open to the mercantile marine of every nation, are formally and in perpetuity interdicted to the flag of war, either of the Powers possessing its coasts, or of any other Power, with the exceptions mentioned in Articles XIV and XIX of the present Treaty.

ART. XII. Free from any impediment, the commerce in the ports and waters of the Black Sea shall be subject only to regulations of health, customs, and police, framed in a spirit favourable to the development of commercial transactions.

In order to afford to the commercial and maritime interests of every nation the security which is desired, Russia and the Sublime Porte will admit Consuls into their ports situated upon the coast of the Black Sea, in conformity with the principles of international law.

ART. XIII. The Black Sea being neutralized according to the terms of Article XI, the maintenance or establishment upon its coast of military-maritime arsenals becomes alike unnecessary and purposeless: in consequence, His Majesty the Emperor of all the Russias, and His Imperial Majesty the Sultan engage not to establish or to maintain upon that coast any military-maritime arsenal.

ART. XIV. Their Majesties the Emperor of all the Russias and the Sultan having concluded a Convention for the purpose of settling the force and the number of light vessels, necessary for the service of their coasts, which they reserve to themselves to maintain in the Black Sea, that Convention is annexed to the present Treaty, and shall have the same force and validity as if it formed an integral part thereof. It cannot be either annulled or modified without the assent of the Powers signing the present Treaty. . . .

ART. XXX. His Majesty the Emperor of all the Russias and His Majesty the Sultan maintain, in its integrity, the state of their possessions in Asia, such as it legally existed before the rupture.

In order to prevent all local dispute the line of frontier shall be verified, and, if necessary, rectified, without any prejudice as regards territory being sustained by either Party.

For this purpose a Mixed Commission, composed of two Russian Commissioners, two Ottoman Commissioners, one English Commissioner, and one French Commissioner, shall be sent to the spot immediately after the reestablishment of diplomatic relations between the Court of Russia and the Sublime Porte. Its labours shall be completed within the period of eight months after the exchange of the ratifications of the present Treaty.

ART. XXXI. The territories occupied during the war by the troops of Their Majesties the Queen of the United Kingdom of Great Britain and Ireland, the Emperor of Austria, the Emperor of the French, and the King of Sardinia, according to the terms of the Conventions signed at Constantinople on the twelfth of March, one thousand eight hundred and fifty-four, between Great Britain, France, and the Sublime Porte; on the fourteenth of June of the same year between Austria and the Sublime Porte; and on the fifteenth of March, one thousand eight hundred and fifty-five, between Sardinia and the Sublime Porte; shall be evacuated as soon as possible after the exchange of the ratifications of the present Treaty. The periods and the means of execution shall form the object of an arrangement between the Sublime Porte and the Powers whose troops have occupied its territory.

ART. XXXII. Until the Treaties or Conventions which existed before the war between the belligerent Powers have been either renewed or replaced by new Acts, commerce of importation, or of exportation shall take place reciprocally on the footing of the regulations in force before the war; and in all other matters their subjects shall be respectively treated upon the footing of the most favoured nation. . . .

ADDITIONAL AND TRANSITORY ARTICLE. The stipulations of the Convention respecting the Straits, signed this day, shall not be applicable to the vessels of war employed by the belligerent Powers for the evacuation, by sea, of the territories occupied by their armies; but the said stipulations shall resume their entire effect as soon as the evacuation shall be terminated. . . .

2. Convention on the Straits, Signed by All Parties to the General Treaty

ART. I. His Majesty the Sultan, on the one part, declares that he is firmly resolved to maintain for the future the principle invariably established as the ancient rule of his Empire, and in virtue of which it has, at all times, been prohibited for the ships of war of foreign Powers to enter the Straits of the Dardanelles and of the Bosphorus; and that, so long as the Porte is at peace, His Majesty will admit no foreign ship of war into the said Straits.

And Their Majesties the Queen of the United Kingdom of Great Britain and Ireland, the Emperor of Austria, the Emperor of the French, the King of Prussia, the Emperor of all the Russias, and the King of Sardinia, on the other part, engate to respect this determination of the Sultan, and to conform themselves to the principle above declared.

ART. II. The Sultan reserves to himself, as in past times, to deliver firmans of passage for light vessels under flag of war, which shall be employed, as is usual, in the service of the Missions of Foreign Powers.

ART. III. The same exception applies to the light vessels under flag of war, which each of the Contracting Powers is authorised to station at the mouths of the Danube in order to secure the execution of the regulations relative to the liberty of that river, and the number of which is not to exceed two for each Power.

3. Convention Limiting Naval Force in the Black Sea, Signed by Russia and the Ottoman Empire

ART. I. The High Contracting Parties mutually engage not to have in the Black Sea any other vessels of war than those of which the number, the force, and the dimensions are hereinafter stipulated.

ART. II. The High Contracting Parties reserve to themselves each to maintain in that sea six steam-vessels of fifty metres in length at the line of floatation, of a tonnage of eight hundred tons at the maximum, and four light steam or sailing vessels of a tonnage which shall not exceed two hundred tons each.

4. Treaty of Guarantee: Britain, France, and Austria, 15 April 1856

ART. I. The High Contracting Parties guarantee, jointly and severally, the independence and the integrity of the Ottoman Empire, recorded in the Treaty concluded at Paris on the thirtieth of March, one thousand eight hundred and fifty-six.

ART. II. Any infraction of the stipulations of the said Treaty will be considered by the Powers signing the present Treaty as *casus belli*. They will come to an understanding with the Sublime Porte as to the measures which have become necessary, and will without delay determine among themselves as to the employment of their military and naval forces.

106. LEASE BY PERSIA TO MASQAT OF BANDAR 'ABBAS, QISHM AND HURMUZ
17 November 1856

[Hertslet, *Treaties . . . between Great Britain and Persia*, pp. 112–15]

Persia in 1798 leased to the ruler of Masqat for an annual payment of 6,000 *tomans* (approximately $15,000) Bandar 'Abbas and the islands of Qishm and Hurmuz, which had figured prominently in European trade with the Persian Gulf from the sixteenth to the eighteenth century. The Masqati shaykh in 1822 permitted the British to establish a naval base at Basidu, at the northwest end of Qishm, which served until 1879 as the headquarters of the Indian naval squadron maintained in the Persian Gulf to suppress piracy and the slave traffic and, after 1835, to supervise the maritime truce. The Persians expelled the Masqati governor from Bandar 'Abbas in 1853 and did not renew the arrangement until 17 November 1856, when the annual payment was increased to 14,000 tomans (about $35,000). This agreements was superseded on 4 August 1868 by yet another (text in Aitchison, *Collection of Treaties . . . relating to India* [4th ed.], 12: cxlii-iv), which again more than doubled the yearly tribute, bringing it to 30,000 tomans (about $75,000). "In the same year [October 1868], however, the Sultan was expelled from Muscat by a successful revolt," reports G. N. Curzon

(*Persia and the Persian Question*, 2: 424), "and the Persian Government, taking advantage of a clause in the lease [art. 12], allowing them to cancel the contract if a conqueror obtained possession of Muscat, installed their own governor at Bunder Abbas, and have retained possession of the place ever since" (ibid., pp. 410–27). Kelly, *Britain and the Persian Gulf*, chaps. 12 and 14; see also references to Doc. 114.

I. The Ruler of 'Bender-Abbas, who is on the part of the 'Imam, possessed of magnificence, the Seyyid Sa'id, over [in] Bender-'Abbas, and Shemil and Mina, and the two islands El-Qishm ("Kishm") and Hurmuz ("Ormuz"), together with the appended territories, is appointed and commissioned, and shall deliver to the Agents of the Exalted Government [of Persia] a document to the following effect, namely:—

Bender-'Abbas, with all its Dependencies, as well as the appendages of that frontier, is [shall be] placed [accounted] as a portion of the territories of Persia (or, "Fars"), and the Ruler of the whole of that frontier is subject to the exalted Government of Iran (Persia).

II. The said Ruler, when there shall proceed from him a derogatory act in the affair of the frontiers, when upon investigation, a derogatory act shall have proceeded from him, [then], by the mere notification from His Highness the Governor-General (Ferman-ferma, Command-issuer) of Fars to His Highness the Imam, the said Ruler shall be deposed and another appointed speedily.

III. In the said sea-port town ("bender") there shall be no new building erected, such as castles or towers; but, if repair be needed, it shall be repaired, and any repeated digging of the moat shall not be, the former castles with the towers being sufficient without erection of new castles or digging of a moat.

IV. If at any time His Highness the Governor-General of Fars shall move towards the Territories of Bender-'Abbas in view of relaxation, the Ruler of Bender-'Abbas shall arise and continue at his service like other Rulers of towns [or countries] in the parts requiring services, meeting him with ceremonial honours and respect, and receiving him with the most sacred, most holy attentions and marks of favour.

V. On the days of the Festivals, on Fridays, and on the birthday of the centre of the aspect of the Universe, the very great Shah, on which the flag of the Badshah shall be hoisted in Bender-'Abbas for the sake of a blessing and of joy, there shall also be appointed a sufficient number of workmen to execute this service, so that there be no negligence in this respect.

VI. [In] the villages and parishes which may be in the jurisdiction of the Ruler of Bender-'Abbas, in a more general sense, of the territory of Fars or Kirman, the Ruler of Bender-'Abbas shall not exercise any control or interference therein.

And if it be that troops, on the part of the exalted Government [of Persia], be on their way to the countries of the Bulush (Belooches), or any other parts, passing the frontiers of Bender-'Abbas, then the Rulers who may be [acting] on your part shall give them provisions and a guide for the heaven-assisted [Persian] forces, taking from them a receipt. They shall render them requisite services, as also the subjects (Riaya) of Mina and Shemil, and of those parts which, in the space of the last two years, have served the exalted Government in fidelity, and are known to His Highness the most sacred and holy.

From this day forward, the Ruler of Bender-'Abbas shall not turn against them any evidence, or seek to cavil against them on the subject of damage or the like.

VII. If any one of the subjects of Fars should run away and flee to the said frontiers, and join you, [then], on the mere indication of his most sacred Highness the Governor-General, the fugitives shall be delivered over to him.

VIII. The regular revenue and the *honorarium* are 14,000 tomans; in this wise: the revenue is 12,000 tomans, and the *honorarium* 2,000 tomans, in every year; this being paid in four instalments, delivered, and receipts shall be given to all the Rulers.

IX. The properties of Persian merchants impounded in Kishm shall be entirely and totally released and delivered to their representatives, who shall give receipts on delivery of their goods.

X. From the tenour of what the merchants, subjects of the exalted Government of Persia, have represented, that formerly one of the Baniyans (Banians), who farmed the dues of the Bay of Masgat (Muscat), had some one on his part, who resided in Bender-'Abbas, over the commercial effects belonging to the subjects of the exalted Government of Iran, which were carried from Bender-'Abbas to India and other parts, and who used to collect from them the Muscat duties, &c., at Bender-'Abbas. And that, in all countries [towns], and with all Governments, this custom [due] does not exist [that], a thing which does not enter the country [town], they [should nevertheless] take tithes therefrom. And this is contrary to the rule and the law; indeed, it is an evident innovation [that] property which does not enter the country [town] should be made liable to tithes. It is necessary that His Highness the Imam should do away with this innovation altogether. And whosoever introduces commercial effects into Bender-'Abbas from any places henceforward, let them deliver up the tithes [thereof] in like manner as took place in the time of Seyf, son of Mihnan, not more.

107. GENERAL TREATY AND COMMERCIAL CONVENTION: GREAT BRITAIN AND MOROCCO
9 December 1856

[*British and Foreign State Papers*, 46: 176–95.]

European commerce with Morocco never reached the scale of European commerce with the Ottoman Empire, even relatively, but in the limited Moroccan market Britain remained in first place through the mid-nineteenth century. Gibraltar continued as a center of commercial exchange and its garrison still found Morocco the most convenient source of food. So, too, did the British navy, for Britain deployed in the Mediterranean on a regular basis naval forces which expanded and contracted as international crises came and went but always on a rising curve, especially after the mid-1830s, when France once again was becoming a rival. To uphold its commercial and strategic interests, Britain was not prepared to try to annex Morocco; it simply insisted on preventing other major maritime powers from doing so. Commerce and strategy thus became the twin elements of concern in Britain's French North African policy as laid down by Lord Palmerston, the dominant articulator of the British position on international issues in the middle decades of the nineteenth century. In his view, Britain had to keep France out of Morocco and, while reluctantly recognizing the French presence in Algeria, confine it there by keeping it out of Tunis and Tripoli as well. French expansionists seemed prepared to move in both directions, even before the French position had been consolidated in Algeria. But on each occasion, whether the action was disguised (as in Tunis) or open (as in Morocco), London let Paris know that it would not abide French expansion beyond Algeria. Bugeaud tried to ignore the vigor of Britain's reaction to the hot pursuit of 'Abd al-Qadir into Morocco in the early 1840s, but King Louis Philippe and his foreign minister, François Guizot, got the message. Again and again in these years, Britain extracted assurances from France that it had no intention of taking over Tripoli, Tunis, or Morocco. In the words of Guizot in 1845, France recognized that Morocco "had for a long time been under the especial protection of Great Britain" (as cited by Flournoy, *British Policy towards Morocco*, p. 60). Meanwhile, in the mid-1840s a new factor intruded to impede British commerce with Morocco, this time within Morocco itself. Mawlay ʿAbd al-Rahman (1822–59) permitted his friends to create monopolies in the sale of cattle, wax, and other commodities, imposed restrictions on the export of hides, bark, and olive oil, and prohibited altogether the sale of wool to foreigners. British traffic in these goods was handled by importers in Gibraltar, who complained to the Foreign Office in 1852. Soon thereafter the foreign minister instructed the British chargé d'affaires—a permanent title created in 1846 to replace "diplomatic agent"—and consul general at Tangier, John Drummond Hay, to negotiate fresh agreements with Morocco, so as to modernize the British relationship with that country, since the last comprehensive arrangement, dating from more than a half century earlier, rested on the relics of mercantilism and piracy. It took nearly four years for Hay, using alternate bribes and threats, to persuade Mawlay ʿAbd al-Rahman and his divan to accept the details of a general treaty and a commercial convention. Hay, who had served his diplomatic apprenticeship in Istanbul, recalled to good effect how commercial monopolies and other restrictions on Ottoman trade with Britain were eliminated at Balta Liman in 1838 (Doc. 80). The British-Moroccan instruments of 1856 regulated later commercial and capitulatory relations between the two countries, and from its explicit privileges all other maritime states benefited on the basis of most-favored-nation treatment. Flournoy, op. cit., chaps. 3–6; Hay and Brooks, *Memoir of Sir John Drummond Hay*; Piquet, *La colonisation française dans l'Afrique du Nord*, chap. 14; International Court of Justice, *Case concerning Rights of Nationals of the United States of America in Morocco*, pp. 263–77.

1. The General Treaty

. . . ART. I. There shall be perpetual peace and friendship between Her Majesty the Queen of the United Kingdom of Great Britain and Ireland, her heirs and successors, and His Sherifian Majesty the Sultan of Morocco and Fez, and between their respective dominions and subjects.

II. Her Majesty the Queen of Great Britain may appoint one or more Consuls in the dominions of the Sultan of Morocco and Fez; and such Consul or Consuls shall be at liberty to reside in any of the sea-ports or cities of the Sultan of Morocco which they or the British Government may choose, and find most convenient for the affairs and service of Her Britannic Majesty, and for the assistance of British merchants.

III. The British Chargé d'Affaires, or other political agent accredited by the Queen of Great Britain to the Sultan of Morocco, as also the British Consuls who shall reside in the dominions of the Sultan of Morocco, shall always have respect and

honour paid to them, suitable to their rank. Their houses and families shall be safe and protected. No one shall interfere with them, or commit any act of oppression or disrespect towards them, either by words or by deeds; and if any one should do so, he shall receive a severe punishment, as a correction to himself and a check to others.

The said Chargé d'Affaires shall be at liberty to choose his own interpreters and servants, either from the Mussulmans or others, and neither his interpreters nor servants shall be compelled to pay any capitation tax, forced contribution, or other similar or corresponding charge. With respect to the Consuls or Vice-Consuls who shall reside at the ports under the orders of the said Chargé d'Affaires, they shall be at liberty to choose 1 interpreter, 1 guard, and 2 servants, either from the Mussulmans or others; and neither the interpreter, nor the guard, nor their servants, shall be compelled to pay any capitation tax, forced contribution, or other similar or corresponding charge. If the said Chargé d'Affairs should appoint a subject of the Sultan of Morocco as Vice-Consul at a Moorish port, the said Vice-Consul, and those members of his family who may dwell within his house, shall be respected, and exempted from the payment of any capitation tax, or other similar or corresponding charge; but the said Vice-Consul shall not take under his protection any subject of the Sultan of Morocco except the members of his family dwelling under his roof. The said Chargé d'Affaires, and the said Consuls, shall be permitted to have a place of worship, and to hoist their national flag at all times on the top of the houses which they may occupy, either in the city or out of it, and also in their boats whenever they go to sea. No prohibition nor tax shall be put upon their goods, furniture, or any other articles which may come to them for their own use and for the use of their families, in the dominions of the Sultan of Morocco; but the said Chargé d'Affaires, Consuls, or Vice-Consuls, shall be required to deliver to the officers of the Customs a note of hand, specifying the number of articles which they shall require to be passed. This privilege shall only be accorded to those Consular Officers who are not engaged in trade. If the service of their sovereign should require their attendance in their own country, or if they should depute another person to act for them in their absence, they shall not be prevented in any way from so doing; and no impediment shall be offered either to themselves, their servants, or their property, but they shall be at liberty to go and come, respected and honoured; and both they themselves and their deputies or Vice-Consuls shall be entitled, in the most ample sense, to every privilege which is now enjoyed, or may in future be granted, to the Consul of any other nation.

IV. With respect to the personal privileges to be enjoyed by the subjects of Her Britannic Majesty in the dominions of the Sultan of Morocco, His Sherifian Majesty engages that they shall have a free and undoubted right to travel and to reside in the territories and dominions of his said Majesty, subject to the same precautions of police which are practised towards the subjects or citizens of the most favoured nations.

They shall be entitled to hire, on lease or otherwise, dwellings and warehouses; and if a British subject shall not find a house or warehouse suitable for his dwelling or for his stores, the Moorish authorities shall assist him in finding a site, within the localities generally selected for the habitations of Europeans, if there be a suitable site within the town, for building a dwelling or stores, and an agreement shall be entered upon, in writing, with the authorities of the town, regarding the number of years that the British subject shall retain possession of the land and buildings, in order that he shall thus be repaid the expenses of the outlay he shall have made; and no person shall compel the British subject to give up the dwelling or warehouses until the time mentioned in the said document shall have expired. They shall not be obliged to pay, under any pretence whatever, any taxes or impositions. They shall be exempt from all military service, whether by land or sea; from forced loans, and from every extraordinary contribution. Their dwellings, warehouses, and all premises appertaining thereto, destined for purposes of residence or commerce, shall be respected. No arbitrary search of or visit to the houses of British subjects, and no arbitrary examination or inspection whatever of their books, papers, or accounts, shall be made; but such measures shall be executed only in conformity with the orders and consent of the Consul-General or Consul. And, generally, His Majesty the Sultan engages that the subjects of Her Britannic Majesty residing in his states or dominions shall enjoy their property and personal security in as full and ample manner as subjects of the Emperor of Morocco are entitled to do within the territories of Her Britannic Majesty.

Her Britannic Majesty, on her part, engages to ensure the enjoyment of the same protection and privileges to the subjects of His Majesty the Sultan of Morocco within her dominions, which are or may be enjoyed by the subjects of the most favoured nations.

V. All British subjects and merchants who may wish to reside in any part of the dominions of the Sultan of Morocco shall have perfect security for their own persons and property; and they shall be free to exercise the rites of their own religion, without any interference or hindrance, and to have a burial-place for their dead; and they shall be allowed to go out to bury them with safety and protection in going and in returning. They shall be free to appoint any one whom they may choose of their own friends or servants for the transaction of their affairs, either on land or at sea, without any prohibition or interruption; and if a British merchant shall have a ship in or outside of one of the harbours of the Sultan of Morocco, he shall be permitted to go on board of her, either by himself or with any whom he likes of his own friends or servants, without either himself or his friends or servants being subjected to any forced contribution for so doing.

VI. Any person subject to the Queen of Great Britain, or under her protection, shall not be compelled to sell or to buy anything without his own free will; nor shall any of the Sultan of Morocco's subjects have a claim or right upon any goods of a British merchant, but what such merchant may give them voluntarily; and nothing shall be taken away from any British merchant but what shall be agreed upon between the respective parties.

The same rule shall be observed with regard to Moorish subjects in the dominions of the Queen of Great Britain.

VII. No subject of the Queen of Great Britain, nor any person under her protection, shall, in the dominions of the Sultan of Morocco, be made liable to pay a debt due from another person of his nation, unless he shall have made himself responsible or [provided a] guarantee for the debtor, by a document under his own handwriting; and, in like manner, the subjects of the Sultan of Morocco shall not be made liable to pay a debt due from another person of his nation to a subject of Great Britain, unless he shall have made himself responsible or [provided a] guarantee for the debtor by a document under his own handwriting.

VIII. In all criminal cases and complaints, and in all civil differences, disputes, or causes of litigation which may occur between British subjects, the British Consul-General, Consul, Vice-Consul, or Consular Agent, shall be sole judge and arbiter. No Governor, Kadi, or other Moorish authority, shall intermeddle therein; but the subjects of Her Britannic Majesty shall, in all matters of criminal or civil cognizance arising or existing between British subjects exclusively, be amenable to the tribunal of the Consul-General, Consul, or other British authority only.

IX. All criminal cases and complaints, and all civil differences, disputes, or causes of litigation arising between British subjects and subjects of the Moorish Government, shall be adjusted in the following manner.

If the plaintiff be a British subject and the defendant a Moorish subject, the Governor of the town or district, or the Kadi, according as the case may appertain to their respective Courts, shall alone judge the case; the British subject making his appeal to the Governor or Kadi, through the British Consul-General, Consul, or his deputy, who will have a right to be present in the Court during the whole trial of the case.

In like manner, if the plaintiff be a Moorish subject, and the defendant a British subject, the case shall be referred to the sole judgment and decision of the British Consul-General, Consul, Vice-Consul, or Consular Agent; the plaintiff shall make his appeal through the Moorish authorities; and the Moorish Governor, Kadi, or other officer who may be appointed by them shall be present, if he or they so desire, during the trial and judgment of the case. Should the British or Moorish litigant be dissatisfied with the decision of the Consul-General, Consul, Vice-Consul, Governor, or Kadi (according as the case may appertain to their respective Courts), he shall have a right of appeal to Her Britannic Majesty's Chargé d'Affaires and Consul-General, or to the Moorish Commissioner for Foreign Affairs, as the case may be.

X. A British subject suing, in a Moorish court of law, a subject of the Sultan of Morocco, for a debt contracted within the dominions of the Queen of Great Britain, shall be required to produce an acknowledgment of the claim written either in the European or Arabic characters, and signed by the Moorish debtor in the presence of, and testified by the Moorish Consul, Vice-Consul, or Consular Agent, or before 2 witnesses whose signatures shall have been at the time, or subsequently, certified by the Moorish Consul, Vice-Consul, or Consular Agent, or by a British Notary in a place where no Moorish Consul, Vice-Consul, or Consular Agent resides. Each document so witnessed or certified by the Moorish Consul, Consular Agent, or British Notary, shall have full force and value in a Moorish tribunal. Should at any time a Moorish debtor escape to any town or place in Morocco where the authority of the Sultan may be established, and where no British Consul or Consular Agent may reside, the Moorish Government shall compel the Moorish debtor to come to Tangier, or other port or town in Morocco where the British creditor may desire to prosecute his claim before a Moorish court of law.

XI. Should the British Consul-General, or any of the British Consuls, Vice-Consuls, or Consular Agents, have at any time occasion to request from the Moorish Government the assistance of soldiers, guards, armed boats, or other aid for the purpose of arresting or transporting any British subject, the demand shall immediately be complied with, on payment of the usual fees given on such occasions by Moorish subjects.

XII. If any subject of the Sultan be found guilty before the Kadi of producing false British subject, he shall be severely punished by the Moorish Government according to the Mahometan law. In like manner, the British Consul-General, Consul, Vice-Consul, or Consular Agent, shall take care that any British subject who may be convicted of the same offence against a Moorish subject, shall be severely punished according to the law of Great Britain.

XIII. All British subjects, whether Mahometans, Jews, or Christians, shall alike enjoy all the rights and privileges granted by the present Treaty and the Convention of Commerce and Navigation which has also been concluded this day, or which shall at any time be granted to the most favoured nation.

XIV. In all criminal cases, differences, disputes or other causes of litigation arising between British subjects and the subjects or citizens of other foreign nations, no Governor, Kadi, or other Moorish authority shall have a right to interfere, unless a Moorish subject may have received thereby any injury to his person or property, in which case the Moorish authority, or one of his officers, shall have a right to be present at the tribunal of the Consul.

Such cases shall be decided solely in the tribunals of the foreign Consuls, without the interference of the Moorish Government, according to the established usages which have hitherto been acted upon, or may hereafter be arranged between such Consuls.

XV. It is agreed and covenanted that neither of the High Contracting Parties shall knowingly receive into or retain in its service any subjects of the other party who have deserted from the naval or military service of that other party; but that, on the contrary, each of the Contracting Parties shall respectively discharge from its service any such deserters, upon being required by the other party so to do.

And it is further agreed, that if any of the crew of any merchant-vessel of either Contracting party, not being slaves, nor being subjects of the party upon whom the demand is made, shall desert from such vessel within any port in the territory of the other party, the authorities of such port and territory shall be bound to give every assistance in their power for the apprehension of such deserters, on application being made by the Consul-General or Consul of the party concerned, or by the deputy or representative of the Consul-General or Consul; and no person whatever shall protect or harbour such deserters.

XVI. No British subject professing the Mahometan faith, or who may have professed the Mahometan religion, shall be considered as having in any manner lost, or as being by reason thereof in any degree less entitled to, the rights and privileges, or the full protection, enjoyed by British subjects who are Christians; but all British subjects, whatever their religion may be, shall enjoy all the rights and privileges secured by the present Treaty to British subjects, without any distinction or difference.

XVII. Any subjects of the Queen of Great Britain who may be found in the dominions of the Sultan of Morocco, either in time of peace or in time of war, shall have perfect liberty to depart to their own country, or to any other country, in their own ships or in the ships of any other nation; and they shall also be free to dispose as they please of their goods and property of every kind, and to carry away with them the value of all such goods and property, as well as to take their families and domestics even though born and brought up in Africa or elsewhere out of the British dominions, without any one interfering with or preventing them under any pretence. All these rights shall be likewise granted to the subjects of the Sultan of Morocco who may be in the dominions of the Queen of Great Britain.

XVIII. If any subject of Her Britannic Majesty, or any native of a State or place under British protection, should die in the dominions of the Sultan of Morocco, no Governor or officer of the Sultan shall, under any pretence, dispose of the goods or property of the deceased, nor shall any one interfere therewith; but all the property and goods belonging to the deceased, and all that was under his hands and in his possession, shall be taken possession of by the persons chosen by him for that purpose, and named in his will as his heirs, if they should be present; but in case such heir or heirs should be absent, then the Consul-General, Consul, or his deputy, shall take possession of all the property and effects, after making a list or inventory thereof, specifying every article correctly, until he delivers the same to the heir of the deceased. But should the deceased die without making any will, the Consul-General, Consul, or his deputy, shall have the right to take possession of all the property left by him, and to preserve it for the persons entitled by law to the property of the deceased; and if the deceased should leave behind him debts due to him from individuals, then the Governor of the town, or those who have such a power, shall compel the debtors to pay what is due from them either to the Consul-General, Consul, or his deputy, for the benefit of the estate of the deceased; and likewise, if the deceased should leave behind him debts due from him to a subject of the Sultan of Morocco, the Consul-General, Consul, or his deputy shall assist the creditor in the recovery of his claim upon the estate of the deceased.

XIX. The present Treaty shall apply generally to all the dominions of Her Britannic Majesty, and to all subjects who are under her obedience, and all those who inhabit any town or place which is considered part of her kingdom, as also to all her subjects in Gibraltar and its inhabitants, and likewise to the inhabitants of the United States of the Ionian Islands which are under her protection; and all those who are called or described as English shall be considered as British subjects, without any distinction between those born in and those born out of Great Britain; and if the Queen of Great Britain should hereafter possess a town or a country which, either by conquest or by Treaty, shall enter under her authority, all its people and inhabitants shall be considered as British subjects, even if only for the first time subjected to Great Britain.

XX. The subjects of the Queen of Great Britain, and those who are under her government or protection, shall have the full benefit of the privileges and of the particular favours granted by this Treaty and which may be allowed to the subjects of other nations that are at war with Great Britain; and if after this date any other privileges sall be granted to any other Power, the same shall be extended and apply to and in favour of all British subjects in every respect, as to the subjects of such other Power.

XXI. If a subject of the Sultan of Morocco should ship himself and his goods on board of a vessel belonging to a nation at war with the Queen of Great Britain, and that ship should be taken by a British man-of-war, the said Moroquine subject, and also his goods, provided they be not contraband of war, shall not be molested or interfered with, but both he and the goods which he has on board the vessel thus taken, shall be let free, and he shall be set at liberty to go where he pleases. In like manner, if a British subject should take his passage on board of a vessel belonging to a nation at war with the Sultan of Morocco, and that vessel be taken by a Moroquine cruizer, such British subject shall not be molested, nor shall his goods, if not contraband of war, which he may have with him on board of the vessel thus taken, be interfered with, but he shall have his liberty, and be left free to go where he pleases, with his goods without impediment or delay.

XXII. If any duly commissioned British vessel should capture a ship, and take her to a harbour in the dominions of the Sultan of Morocco, the captors shall be allowed to sell such prize or the goods taken in her, without impediment from any one; or they shall be at liberty to depart with their prize and take her to any other place they please.

XXIII. If a British vessel should be chased by an enemy to within gun-shot from the seaports or shores of the dominions of the Sultan of Morocco, the local authorities shall respect and defend her as much as they can; and, in like manner, the ships of Morocco shall be protected in all the seaports or coasts of the dominions of the Queen of Great Britain.

XXIV. If a cruizer not belonging either to the Queen of Great Britain or to the Sultan of Morocco should possess letters of marque from a nation at war with Great Britain or with Morocco, that cruizer shall not be permitted to remain in any of the harbours or seaports of either of the 2 parties, nor to sell its prizes therein, nor to exchange such prizes or their cargo for other merchandize; nor shall any such cruizer be allowed to purchase stores or provisions, except as much as may be absolutely necessary for the voyage to the nearest port of its own country.

XXV. If an armed ship of a nation at war with Great Britain should be found in any of the harbours or seaports of the Sultan of Morocco, and at the same time a British ship should happen to be also there, such ship of the enemy of Great Britain shall not be allowed to seize upon the British vessel, nor to cause it any injury; and the enemy's ship shall not be allowed to sail in the track of the British vessel till 24 hours shall have elapsed after the departure of the said vessel, if the authorities of the port or harbour have the power of detaining the vessel of the enemy. The same rule shall be observed towards the ships of the Sultan of Morocco or his subjects, in all the harbours and seaports of the Queen of Great Britain.

XXVI. If any British vessels of war or merchant-vessels should enter one of the harbours or seaports of the Sultan of Morocco, and be in want of provisions or refreshments, such vessels shall be at liberty to buy what they require at the current prices of the time, free of duty; but the quantity shall not exceed that which may be sufficient for the sustenance of the master and crew during the voyage to the port

whither the vessel may be bound, and also the necessary provisions required for the daily maintenance of the crew during the time the vessel remains at anchorage in the Moorish port.

XXVII. Vessels or boats freighted by order of the British Government for the conveyance of mails, or employed by the British Government under contract for the same service, shall be respected, and shall have the same privileges as ships of war, if they do not bring or take articles of merchandize to or from a port of the Sultan of Morocco; but if they carry any merchandize from a port of these dominions, they shall pay the same charges as any other merchant-vessel.

XXVIII. If any vessel belonging to the subjects or to the inhabitants of the dominions of either Contracting Party should enter one of the seaports of the other, and should not wish to go into harbour nor to declare nor sell her cargo there, she shall not be compelled to do so, nor shall any one inquire or search in any way to know what she contains; but a guard may be placed on board by the Custom-House officers, as long as the vessel remains at anchor, to prevent any illegal traffic.

XXIX. If a British vessel with a cargo should enter one of the harbours of the Sultan of Morocco, and should wish to land a part of her cargo which may be destined for that place, she shall not be compelled to pay duties upon more than the landed part of her cargo, and shall not be required to pay any duty upon the rest of the cargo which is left on board, but she shall be at liberty to depart with the remainder of her cargo to any place she pleases. The manifest [i.e., invoice] of the cargo of each vessel shall, on her arrival, be delivered up to the Moorish Custom-House officers, who will be permitted to search the vessel on her arrival and departure, or to place a guard on board the vessel to prevent any illegal traffic.

The same rule shall be observed in British ports with regard to Moorish vessels.

The master of each vessel, on departure from a Moorish port, shall be required to present a manifest of the cargo of articles exported, certified by the Consul or the Vice-Consul, and shall exhibit the manifest to the administrators of Customs when required to do so, in order that they may verify that no goods have been embarked in contraband.

XXX. No captain of a British vessel in a Moorish port, and no captain of a Moorish vessel in a British port, shall be in any way compelled to carry any passengers or any kind of goods against his own will, nor shall he be forced to sail for any place which he does not wish to go to; and his ship shall not be molested in any way whatever.

XXXI. If any of the subjects of the Sultan of Morocco should hire a British vessel to carry goods or passengers from one place to another within the dominions of Morocco, and if in the course of her voyage such British vessel should be forced by stress of weather or accident of the sea to enter a different port in the same dominions, the captain shall not be obliged to pay anchorage or any other duty on account of his entering such port; but if such vessel should discharge or take on board at such port any cargo, the said vessel shall be treated like any other.

XXXII. Any British ships or vessels which may be damaged at sea, and may enter one of the harbours of the Sultan of Morocco for repairs, shall be received and assisted in all their wants during their stay in such harbour, during their refit, or at their departure for the place of their destination, if the articles required for the repairs of the vessel shall be found for sale in such harbour, and in such case they shall be bought and paid for at the same prices as are usually paid by others; and the British ships or vessels shall not be in any way whatever molested or prevented from proceeding on their voyage.

XXXIII. If a ship belonging to the Queen of Great Britain, or to any of her subjects, should get on shore, or be wrecked on any part of the dominions of the Sultan of Morocco, she shall be respected and assisted in all her wants, in accordance with the rules of friendship; and such ship, and all her contents, cargo, or any goods which may be saved from her at the time or after the wreck, shall be preserved and given up to the owners, or to the British Consul-General, Consul, or his deputy, without the loss or concealment of anything whatever. Should the wrecked vessel have on board any goods which the proprietors desire to sell within the dominions of Morocco, the proprietors shall pay upon these goods the requisite duties; but if the goods on board the vessel had been embarked from any port of the dominions of Morocco, no other duties in addition to those which may already have been paid, shall be demanded, either on importation or on exportation, and the proprietors shall have the right either of selling the goods in Morocco, or of embarking them, as they please. The captain and crew shall be at liberty to proceed to any place they please, and at any time they may think proper, without any hindrance. In like manner, the ships of the Sultan of Morocco, or of his subjects, shall be treated in the dominions of the Queen of Great Britain; it being understood that such ships are to be subject to the same lawful charges for salvage to which British ships are subject. If a British vessel should be wrecked at Wadnoon, or on any part of its coast, the Sultan of Morocco shall exert his power to save and protect the captain and crew, till they return to their own country; and the British Consul-General, Consul, or his deputy, shall be allowed to inquire and ascertain, as much as they can, about the captain and crew of any such ship, in order that they may obtain and save them from those parts of the country; and the Governors appointed in those places by the Sultan of Morocco shall also assist the Consul-General, Consul, or deputy, in his researches, agreeably to the rules of friendship.

XXXIV. Her Majesty the Queen of Great Britain and His Majesty the Sultan of Morocco engage to do all in their power for the suppression of piracy; and the Sultan especially engages to use his utmost efforts to discover and punish all persons on his coasts or within his dominions who may be guilty of that crime, and to aid Her Britannic Majesty in so doing.

XXXV. If any of the subjects or of the ships of either of the 2 Parties should do anything contrary to any of the conditions of this Treaty, whether intentionally or unintentionally, the peace and friendship thereby stipulated for shall not be disturbed but shall remain preserved, fixed, and always durable upon the basis of sincerity, till communication shall be forwarded to the Sovereign of the aggressor, without his being in the mean time molested; and if any of the subjects of either party should wish or attempt to violate this Treaty, or any of its conditions his Sovereign shall be bound to chastise and punish him severely for his conduct.

XXXVI. If this Treaty of Peace and Friendship between the 2 Cotracting Parties should be infringed, and if, in consequence of such infringement (which God forbid!), war should be declared, all the country and subjects of the Queen of Great Britain, and those under her protection, of whatever degree or class, who may happen to be found in the dominions of the Sultan of Morocco, shall be permitted to depart to any part of the world they choose, and to carry with them their goods and property, their families and their servants or establishments, whether they be British born or not; and they shall be allowed to embark on board of any ship of another nation which they may select. Moreover, a period of 6 months shall be granted them, if they ask for it, for the arrangement of their affairs, the sale of their goods, or for doing what they please with their property; and during such period of 6 months they shall have full liberty and perfect security for their persons and property, without any interference, injury, or hindrance in any way, by reason of such war; and the Governors or authorities shall assist and help them in the arrangemet of their affairs, and attend them in the recovery of the debts due to them, without delay, dispute, or postponement. In like manner, all this shall be granted to the subjects of the Sultan of Morocco in all the dominions of the Queen of Great Britain.

XXXVII. This Treaty shall be declared and made public to the subjects of both parties, lest any one of them should remain ignorant of its conditions, and copies shall be prepared and sent to the Governors and men of authority who are entrusted with the revenue and the expenditure; and also to all the seaports and the captains of cruizers belonging to the Sultan of Morocco. . . .

2. The Commercial Convention

. . . ART. I. There shall be reciprocal freedom of commerce between the British dominions and the dominions of the Sultan of Morocco. The subjects of Her Britannic Majesty may reside in and trade to any port of the territories of the Sultan of Morocco to which any other foreigners are or shall be admitted.

They shall be permitted to hire houses, and to build houses, stores, or warehouses, as stipulated in Article IV of the general Treaty of this date.

They shall enjoy full protection for their persons and properties, as specified in Article IV of the General Treaty: they shall be allowed to buy from, and to sell to, whom they like, all articles not prohibited in Article II of this Convention, either by wholesale or retail, at all places in the Moorish dominions, without being strained or prejudiced by any monopoly, contract, or exclusive privilege of purchase or sale whatever, except the articles of export and those of import enumerated in Article II; and they shall, moreover, enjoy all other rights and privileges which hereafter may be granted to any other foreigners, subjects, or citizens of the most favoured nation.

The subjects of the Sultan of Morocco shall, in return, enjoy in the dominions of Her Britannic Majesty the same protection and privileges which are or may be enjoyed by the subjects or citizens of the most favoured nation.

II. The Sultan of Morocco engages to abolish all monopolies or prohibitions on imported goods, except tobacco, pipes of all kinds used for smoking, opium, sulpur, powder, saltpetre, lead, arms of all kinds, and ammunition of war; and further to abolish all monopolies of agricultural produce, or of any other article whatsoever in the dominions of the Sultan, except leeches, bark, tobacco, and other herbs used for smoking in pipes.

III. No tax, toll, duty, or charge whatsoever, beside the export duty hereinafter mentioned shall, under any pretext or on any account, be imposed by any person whatsoever, in any part of the dominions of Morocco, upon or in respect of any goods or produce whatsoever which may have been purchased for exportation by or on behalf of any British subject; but the said goods or produce, when so purchased, shall be conveyed from any place in Morocco to, and embarked from, any port therein, absolutely free and exempt from all other taxes, tolls, duties, or charges whatsoever. No permit, or any similar document, shall be requisite to enable them to be so conveyed or embarked, nor shall any officer or subject of the Sultan offer any impediment to, or lay any restriction on, the conveyance or embarkation of such goods (except those goods or produce which the Sultan of Morocco shall prohibit from being exported, as arranged in Article V), or, on any pretext, demand or receive any money in respect or on account of such goods; and should any such officer or subject act contrary to this stipulation, the Sultan shall immediately punish with severity the Governor, officer, or other subject who shall have been guilty of such misconduct, and render full justice to British subjects for all injuries or losses which they may duly prove themselves to have suffered thereby.

IV. The subjects of Her Britannic Majesty within the dominions of His Majesty the Sultan shall be free to manage their own affiairs themselves, or to commit those affairs to the management of any persons whom they may appoint as their broker, factor, or agent, nor shall such British subjects be restrained in their choice of persons to act in such capacities; nor shall they be called upon to pay any salary or remuneration to any person whom they shall not choose to employ; but those persons who shall be thus employed, and who are subjects of the Sultan of Morocco, shall be treated and regarded as other subjects of the Moorish dominions. Absolute freedom shall be given in all cases to the buyer and seller to bargain together, and no interference on the part of the Sultan's officers shall be permitted. Should any Governor or other officer interfere in the bargains between British and Moorish subjects, or place any impediments in the lawful purchase or sale of goods or merchandize imported into, or to be exported from, the Sultan's dominions, His Sherifian Majesty shall severely punish the said officer for such misconduct.

V. Should the Sultan of Morocco at any time think proper to prohibit the exportation of any kind of grain or other article of commerce from his dominions, British subjects shall in no manner be prevented from embarking all the grain or other articles which they may have in their magazines, or which may have been bought previously to the said prohibition; but they shall be allowed to continue to export all they may have in their possession, during the term of 6 months from the time the prohibition was publicly made known; but on the day when the order of the Sultan of Morocco regarding the prohibition shall arrive, and shall be published to the merchants, British subjects shall, within the term of 2 days, declare and give proofs of the amount of produce they shall possess in their stores, on which the prohibition is imposed, and they shall also present legal certificates regarding the amount of the said produce which they shall have bought in the interior, or elsewhere, previously to the promulgation of the order for the prohibition. No prohibition, either as to the exportation or importation of any article, shall apply to British subjects, unless such prohibition shall apply to subjects of every other nation.

VI. Merchandize or goods, except the articles enumerated in Article II, imported by British subjects in any vessel, or from any country, shall not be prohibited in the territories of the Sultan of Morocco, nor be subject to higher duties than are levied on the same kind of merchandize or goods imported by the subjects of any other foreign Power, or by native subjects, after the date of this Convention.

All articles, except those enumerated in Article II, the produce of Morocco, may be exported therefrom by British subjects in any vessels, on as favourable terms as by the subjects of any other foreign country, or by native subjects.

VII. In consideration of the favourable terms upon which the produce of Morocco is admitted into the territories of Her Britannic Majesty, and with a view to the extension of commercial intercourse between Great Britain and Morocco, for their mutual advantage, His Majesty the Sultan of Morocco hereby agrees that the duties to be levied on all articles imported into the territories of His Majesty by British subjects, shall not exceed 10 per cent. in cash on their value, at the port of their disembarkation; and that the duties to be levied on all articles exported from the territories of His Majesty by British subjects, shall not exceed in amount the duties marked in the following tariff:

TARIFF OF EXPORTS

Articles of Exportation.	Quantity.		Dollars.	Ounces.
Wheat	Per	strike fanega	1	
Maize and Durra	„	full fanega	½	
Barley	„	strike fanega	½	
All other grain	„	cantar	½	
Flour	„	„	..	30
Birdseed	„	„	..	12
Dates	„	„	..	40
Almonds	„	„	..	35
Oranges, lemons, and limes	„	1,000	..	12
Wild Marjoram	„	cantar	..	10
Cummin seed	„	„	..	20
Oil	„	„	..	50
Gums	„	„	..	20
Henna	„	„	..	15
Wax	„	„	..	120
Rice	„	„	..	16
Wool (washed)	„	„	..	80
Wool (in grease)	„	„	..	55
Hides, sheep, and goat skins	„	„	..	36
Tanned skins called Felaly, Zawany, and Cochinea	„		..	100
Horns	„	1,000	..	20
Tallow	„	cantar	..	50
Mules	„	head	25	
Donkeys	„	„	5	
Sheep	„	„	1	
Goats	„	„	..	15
Fowls	„	dozen	..	22
Eggs	„	1,000	..	51
Slippers	„	100	..	70
Porcupine quills	„	1,000	..	5
Grasool	„	cantar	..	15
Ostrich feathers	„	1b.	..	36
Baskets	„	100	..	30
Carraway seed	„	cantar	..	20
Combs of wood	„	100	..	5
Hair	„	cantar	..	30
Raisins	„	„	..	20
Woolen sashes, called Karazy	„	100	..	100
Taekawt (a dye)	„	cantar	..	20
Tanned fleeces	„	„	..	36
Hemp and flax	„	„	..	40

The Sultan of Morocco has the right of prohibiting any article of exportation; but when a prohibition on any article shall be imposed, it shall be in conformity with what is arranged in Article V; but upon the exportation of articles the prohibition of which shall be taken off, the duties noted in the tariff shall alone be paid. With regard to wheat and barley, should the Sultan think proper to prohibit the exporation of these articles, but should desire to sell to merchants the grain which belongs to Government, it shall be sold at the price the Sultan thinks proper to impose. Should the Sultan augment or diminish the price of the grain, there shall be granted to the purchaser for exporting that which he shall have bought, the term stated in Article V; but should the grain be free for exportation, the duties imposed thereon shall be in conformity with what is stated in the tariff.

Should the Sultan of Morocco think proper to reduce the duties on articles of exportation, His Majesty shall have the right of doing so, on condition that British subjects shall pay the lowest duty that shall be paid by any other foreign or native subjects.

VIII. Should a British subject, or his agent, desire to convey by sea, from one port to another in the dominions of the Sultan of Morocco, goods upon which the 10 per cent duty has been paid, such goods shall be subject to no further duty, either on their embarkation or disembarkation, provided they be accompanied by a certificate from a Moorish Administrator of Customs.

IX. If any article of Moroquine produce, growth, or manufacture, except the articles enumerated in Article II, be purchased for exportation, the same shall be conveyed by the British merchant, or by his agent, free of any kind of charge or duty whatsoever, to a convenient place of shipment. Subsequently, on exportation, the export duty according to the tariff in Article VII shall alone be paid on it.

X. No anchorage, tonnage, import, or other duty or charge, shall be levied in the dominions of the Sultan of Morocco on British vessels, or on goods imported or exported in British vessels, beyond what is, or may be, levied on national vessels, or on the like goods imported or exported in national vessels; they shall not, however, exceed in amount the rates of the following scale, viz.:

Six moozoonats per ton shall be levied upon every British vessel (except steam-vessels) that does not exceed 200 tons in measurement. Upon every vessel (not a steam-vessel) measuring more than 200 tons, the following charge shall be made, viz., 6 moozoonats per ton shall be paid for 200 of her tons, and 2 moozoonats per ton for the remainder. Should the Administrator of Customs have any doubt regarding the tonnage of a British vessel, as declared by the master, the British Consul or Vice-Consul shall, on appeal being made to him, cause the ship's papers, whereon the tonnage is formally stated, to be exhibited. The same charges shall be made in all the ports of Morocco except Rabat and Laraiche, at which ports 4 moozoonats per ton shall be paid for pilotage into the river, should the vessel enter the river, and 4 moozoonats per ton for pilotage out of the river; 3 moozoonats per ton shall also be levied

upon each vessel entering the river, on account of anchorage. Should a vessel, however, not enter the river, the same charges shall be levied upon her as those which are paid at the other ports. At Mogadore, 4 moozoonats per ton shall be paid on British vessels for pilotage on their entering the port only, and 6 moozoonats per ton for anchorage.

Should the master of a British vessel require, at any other port, a pilot, he shall pay for him at the rate of 2 moozoonats per ton; but this charge shall not be exacted except when the master of a vessel requires a pilot.

The sum of 16 dollars shall be levied, on account of anchorage, on a steam-vessel entering a port in the Moorish dominions for the purpose of discharging or embarking cargo. If, afterwards, the said steam-vessel proceed from that port to any other port or ports in the Moorish dominions, and on her arrival at the latter embark or discharge cargo, the aforesaid charge of 16 dollars for anchorage shall again be levied; but if the said steam-vessel, on her return voyage, should enter a Moorish port at which the said anchorage dues shall have already been paid, no further charge on account of anchorage shall be levied upon her unless the said steam-vessel depart on a second voyage to a Moorish port, or unless during her return voyage she shall have touched at any port other than a port of the Moorish dominions, in which case the aforesaid charge of 16 dollars shall again be levied. The charge, however, for anchorage on a steamer of 150 tons burthen, or less, shall not exceed what is due from a sailing-vessel of the same size.

The masters of all vessels shall pay, in addition to the aforesaid charges, the following sums to officers of the ports, but no other payments shall be demanded of them; viz.:

A vessel measuring 25 tons or less, 20 ounces; a vessel exceeding 25 and not over 50 tons, 40 ounces; a vessel exceeding 50 and not over 100 tons, 60 ounces; a vessel exceeding 100 and not over 200 tons, 80 ounces; a vessel exceeding 200 tons, 100 ounces.

In addition to these charges, the master of every British vessel visiting the port of

Tetuan shall pay 10 ounces for the messenger who shall convey the ship's papers from the port of Marteen to Tetuan; 5 ounces to the trumpeter who shall announce the arrival of the vessel; and 3 ounces to the public crier; but no other payments shall be demanded at the port of Tetuan. No charge for anchorage shall be levied on account of British vessels which may enter the ports of Morocco for the purpose of seeking shelter from the weather, and which do not embark or discharge cargo, nor shall any charge for anchorage be levied upon fishing vessels.

And, in like manner, no anchorage, tonnage, import, or other duty or charge, shall be levied in the British dominions on Moorish vessels, or on goods imported or exported in Moorish vessels, beyond what is or may be levied on national vessels, or on the like goods imported or exported in national vessels.

XI. Should British subjects desire to embark in or discharge goods from vessels arriving in the ports of Morocco, they shall employ the Moorish Government boats for that purpose; but if within 2 days after the arrival of a vessel the Moorish Government boats are not placed at their disposal for the aforesaid purpose, the British subjects shall have the right of employing private boats, and shall not pay, in such case, to the port authorities more than one-half of what would have been paid, had they employed the Government boats. This regulation shall not be applicable to the ports of Tangier and Tetuan, inasmuch as there is a sufficient number of Government lighters at those 2 ports.

The charges now paid for lighterage at the different ports of Moroceo shall not be augmented, and the Administrator of Customs at each port of Morocco shall deliver to the British Vice-Consul a tariff of the charges now demanded for lighterage.

XII. The Articles of this Convention shall be applicable to all the ports in the Empire of Morocco; and should His Majesty the Sultan of Morocco open the ports of Mehedea, Agadeer, or Wadnoon, or any other ports within the limits of His Majesty's dominions, no difference shall be made in the levying of duties, or anchorage, between the said ports and other ports in the Sultan's dominions.

XIII. If a British subject be detected in smuggling into the Moroquine territories goods of any description, the goods shall be confiscated to the Sultan; and such British subject shall, on conviction before the British Consul-General, Consul, Vice-Consul, or Consural Agent, be liable to be fined in an amount not exceeding treble the amount of duties leviable on such goods, or in case of goods not admitted to importation, treble the value of the goods at the current price of the day; and failing payment of such fines, such British subject shall, on conviction before the British Consul-General, Consul, Vice-Consul, or Consular Agent, be liable to be imprisoned; or, without being fined, any British subject on conviction as aforesaid may be imprisoned, but in either case for a time not exceeding one year, in such place as the Consul-General, Consul, Vice-Consul, or Consular Agent may determine.

XIV. In order that the 2 High Contracting Parties may have the opportunity of hereafter treating and agreeing upon such other arrangements as may tend still further to the improvement of their mutual intercourse, and to the advancement of the interests of their respective subjects, it is agreed that at any time after the expiration of 5 years from the date of the exchange of the ratifications of the present Convention of Commerce and Navigation either of the High Contracting Parties shall have the right to call upon the other to enter upon a revision of the same; but until such revision shall have been accomplished by common consent, and a new Convention shall have been concluded and ratified, the present Convention shall continue and remain in full force and effect.

XV. The present Convention shall be ratified by Her Majesty the Queen of Great Britain and by His Majesty the Sultan of Morocco, and the ratifications shall be exchanged at Tangier, at the same time as the ratifications of the General Treaty signed this day between the High Contracting Parties.

When the ratifications of the present Convention and of the said General Treaty shall have been exchanged, the stipulations of the said Convention and Treaty shall come into operation within 4 months, and shall be substituted for the stipulations of all preceding Treaties between Great Britain and Morocco. . . .

108. TREATY OF FRIENDSHIP AND COMMERCE:
THE UNITED STATES AND PERSIA
13 December 1856

(Ratifications exchanged, Istanbul, 13 June 1857; unilaterally terminated by Persia, 10 May 1928)
[United States, *Treaty Series*, no. 273]

The American minister at Istanbul on 9 October 1851 signed with the chargé d'affaires of the Persian legation a treaty of amity commerce and navigation (text in Miller, *Treaties and other International Acts*, 7: 453–57), patterned after that of 1842 between Persia and Spain (text in Hertslet, *Treaties . . . between Great Britain and Persia*, pp. 140–43). The treaty with the United States, framed on Persian initiative, never entered into force because of the shah's failure in the spring of 1852 even to respond to the Senate's recommended inclusion of an additional article that would assure American and Persian subjects most-favored-nation treatment on a reciprocal basis. American officials at the time attributed to British intrigue the shah's unexplained silence. Late in 1854 the Persian chargé d'affaires at Istanbul again approached the American minister, this time proposing the negotiation of a fresh commercial agreement and suggesting that the shah also desired "to buy or have constructed in the United States several vessels of war and to procure the services of American officers and seamen to navigate them." The Persian government simultaneously attempted to open conversations for the same end with the American minister at Vienna. The secretary of state in mid-May 1855 instructed the American minister at Saint Petersburg to seek the friendly intervention of Russia's Count Nesselrode, who was probably one of the principal instigators of the Persian overtures of 1854–55. In two years of interrupted parleys, which finally centered in Istanbul, the United States appeared overly suspicious of the United Kingdom, from which it tried, unsuccessfully, to keep all intelligence of the negotiations. Thus, almost without realizing it, the United States was drawn into European politics over the Eastern Question during the Crimean War. In the end the United States managed to obtain a treaty of friendship and commerce, unencumbered by the naval aid agreement that Nasir al-Din Shah and his councillors so ardently desired. The commercial instrument with the United States virtually replicated the one that Persia concluded with France on 12 July 1855 (French text in *British and Foreign State Papers*, 45: 869–71), which had set a record in Persia for the exchange of ratifications: only forty-eight hours after signature. The haste could be explained, in part, by France's frustrations with earlier Persian commercial treaties in 1708 and 1715 (Docs. 17, 19), which never went into practical effect because of the fall of the Safavi dynasty, and in 1808 (Doc. 51) and 1847, for which the ratifications were never exchanged. On Persian-American negotiations, see Miller, op. cit., pp. 429–89; Adamiyat, *Bahrein Islands*, pp. 144–54; Kelly, *Britain and the Persian Gulf*, pp. 455–58; on French negotiations, see Siassi, *La Perse au contact de l'Occident*, chap. 13; Vadala, *Le Golfe Persique*.

ART. I. There shall be hereafter a sincere and constant good understanding between the Government and citizens of the United States of North America and the Persian Empre and all Persian subjects.

ART. II. The Ambassadors or Diplomatic

agents, whom it may please either of the two high contracting parties to send and maintain near the other, shall be received and treated, they and all those composing their Missions, as the Ambassadors and Diplomatic agents of the most favored nations are received and treated in the two respective countries: and they shall enjoy there, in all respects, the same prerogatives and immunities.

ART. III. The citizens and subjects of the two high contracting parties, travellers, merchants, manufacturers and others, who may reside in the Territory of either Country, shall be respected and efficiently protected by the authorities of the Country and their agents, and treated in all respects as the subjects and citizens of the most favored Nation are treated.

They may reciprocally bring by land or by sea into either Country, and export from it all kinds of merchandise and products, and sell, exchange or buy, and transport them to all places in the Territories of either of the high contracting parties. It being however understood that the merchants of either nation, who shall engage in the internal commerce of either country, shall be governed, in respect to such commerce by the laws of the country in which such commerce is carried on; and in case either of the High contracting powers shall hereafter grant other privileges concerning such internal commerce to the citizens or subjects of other Governments the same shall be equally granted to the merchants of either nation engaged in such internal commerce within the territories of the other.

ART. IV. The merchandise imported or exported by the respective citizens or subjects of the two high contracting parties shall not pay in either country on their arrival or departure, other duties than those which are charged in either of the countries on the merchandise or products imported or exported by the merchants and subjects of the most favored Nation, and no exceptional tax under any name or pretext whatever shall be collected on them in either of the two Countries.

ART. V. All suits and disputes arising in Persia between Persian subjects and citizens of the United States shall be carried before the Persian tribunal to which such matters are usually referred at the place where a Consul or agent of the United States may reside, and shall be discussed and decided according to Equity, in the presence of an employé of the Consul or agent of the United States.

All suits and disputes which may arise in the Empire of Persia between citizens of the United States, shall be referred entirely for trial and for adjudication to the Consul or agent of the United States residing in the Province wherein such suits and disputes may have arisen, or in the Province nearest to it, who shall decide them according to the laws of the United States.

All suits and disputes occurring in Persia between the citizens of the United States and the subjects of other foreign Powers shall be tried and adjudicated by the intermediation of their respective Consuls or agents.

In the United States Persian subjects in all disputes arising between themselves, or between them and citizens of the United States or Foreigners shall be judged according to the rules adopted in the United States respecting the subjects of the most favored nation.

Persian subjects residing in the United States, and citizens of the United States residing in Persia shall when charged with criminal offences be tried and judged in Persia and the United States in the same manner as are the subjects and citizens of the most favored nation residing in either of the above-mentioned countries.

ART. VI. In case of a citizen or subject of either of the contracting parties dying within the Territories of the other, his effects shall be delivered up integrally to the family or partners in business of the Deceased, and in case he has no relations or partners, his effects in either Country shall be delivered up to the Consul or agent of the Nation of which the Deceased was a subject or citizen, so that he may dispose of them in accordance with the laws of his country.

ART. VII. For the protection of their citizens or subjects and their commerce respectively, and in order to facilitate good and equitable relations between the citizens and subjects of the two countries, the two high contracting parties reserve the right to maintain a Diplomatic Agent at either seat of Government, and to name each three Consuls in either Country, those of the United States shall reside at Teheran, Bender Bushir, and Tauris; those of Persia at Washington, New York and New Orleans.

The Consuls of the high contracting parties shall reciprocally enjoy in the territories of the other, where their residences shall be established, the respect, privileges and immunities granted in either country to the Consuls of the most favored Nation.

The Diplomatic Agent or Consuls of the United States shall not protect secretly or publicly the subjects of the Persian Government, and they shall never suffer a departure from the principles here laid down and agreed to by mutual consent.

And it is further understood, that if any of those Consuls shall engage in trade, they shall be subjected to the same laws and usages to which private individuals of their Nation engaged in commercial pursuits in the same place are subjected.

And it is also understood by the High contracting parties, that the Diplomatic and Consular Agents of the United States shall not employ a greater number of domestics than is allowed by Treaty to those of Russia residing in Persia.

ART. VIII. And the high contracting parties agree that the present Treaty of Friendship and Commerce cemented by the sincere good feeling, and confidence which exists between the Governments of the United States and Persia, shall be in force for the term of ten years from the exchange of its ratification, and if before the expiration of the first ten years neither of the high contracting parties shall have announced, by official notification to the other, its intention to arrest the operation of said Treaty, it shall remain binding for one year beyond that time, and so on until the expiration of twelve months, which will follow a similar notification, whatever the time may be at which it may take place; and the Plenipotentiaries of the two high contracting parties further agree to exchange the ratifications of their respective Governments at Constantinople in the space of six months or earlier if practicable.

109. DEFENSIVE ALLIANCE AGREEMENT: THE EAST INDIA COMPANY AND THE AMIR OF BALKH, KABUL, AND QANDAHAR
26 January 1857

[India Office Library, Government of India, Political and Secret Department, Memoranda, vol. 2 (1898–1923), no. A 155, doc. no. 159, pp. 350–52]

In March 1856 the government of India decided that the independence of the khanate of Herat was "an important element in the defense of British India against the possible machinations of Russia" (as cited by Fraser-Tytler, *Afghanistan*, p. 123). The policy was tested the following October, when Persia seized the principality. In December British India attacked Persia, and in January 1857 the East India Company concluded a defensive alliance with Dust Muhammad Khan, by the amir of Qandahar as well as Kabul, undertaking to pay him a monthly stipend of one lakh (100,000) of rupees for the duration of the war with Persia in return for the amir's active participation in the fighting. The agreement also provided for the continuous exchange of quasi-diplomatic agents, with the Indian government consenting to the condition that its agent would not be a European. The arrangement lasted a half-dozen years, until Dust Muhammad's conquest of Herat on 27 May 1863, after a ten-month siege of the town.

Dust Muhammad did not enjoy the fruits of a reunited Afghanistan, because he died only a fortnight after the fall of Herat, leaving the amirate to one of his younger sons, Shir 'Ali Khan. For references, see Doc. 102.

1. Whereas the Shah of Persia contrary to his engagement with the British Government, has taken possession of Herat, and has manifested an intention to interfere in the present possessions of Ameer Dost Mohommud Khan, and there is now war between the British and Persian Governments, therefore the Honorable East India Company, to aid Ameer Dost Mohommud Khan, to defend and maintain his present possessions in Balkh, Cabool, and Candahar against Persia, hereby agrees out of friendship to give the said Ameer one lakh of Company's Rupees monthly during the war with Persia, on the following conditions:—

2. The Ameer shall keep his present number of Cavalry and Artillery, and shall maintain not less than 18,000 Infantry, of which 13,000 shall be Regulars divided into 13 Regiments.

3. The Ameer is to make his own arrangements for receiving the money at the British treasuries and conveying it through his own country.

4. British Officers, with suitable native establishments and orderlies, shall be deputed, at the pleasure of the British Government, to Cabool, or Candahar, or Balkh, or all three places, or wherever an Afghan army be assembled to act against the Persians. It will be their duty to see generally that the subsidy granted to the Ameer be devoted to the military purposes for which it is given, and to keep their own Government informed of all affairs. They will have nothing to do with the payment of the troops, or advising the Cabool Government; and they will not interfere in any way in the internal administration of the country. The Ameer will be responsible for ther safety and honorable treatment, while in his country, and for keeping them acquainted with all military and political matters connected with the war.

5. The Ameer of Cabool shall appoint and maintain a Vakeel at Peshawur.

6. The subsidy of one lakh per mensem [i.e., month] shall cease from the date on which peace is made between the British and Persian Governments, or at any previous time at the will and pleasure of the Governor-General of India.

7. Whenever the subsidy shall cease the British Officers shall be withdrawn from the Ameer's country; but at the pleasure of the British Government, a Vakeel, not a European Officer, shall remain at Cabool on the part of the British Government, and one at Peshawur on the part of the Government of Cabool.

8. The Ameer shall furnish a sufficient escort for the British Officers from the British border when going to the Ameer's country, and to the British border when returning.

9. The subsidy shall commence from 1st January 1857, and be payable at the British treasury one month in arrears.

10. The five lakhs of Rupees which have been already sent to the Ameer (three to Candahar and two to Cabool), will not be counted in this Agreement. They are a free and separate gift from the Honorable East India Company. But the sixth lakh now in the hands of the mahajuns of Cabool, which was sent for another purpose, will be one of the instalments under this Agreement.

11. This Agreement in no way supersedes the Treaty made at Peshawur on 30th March 1855 (corresponding with the 11th of Rujjub 1271), by which the Ameer of Cabool engaged to be the friend of the friends and enemy of the enemies of the Honorable East India Company; and the Ameer of Cabool, in the spirit of that Treaty, agrees to communicate to the British Government any overtures he may receive from Persia or the allies of Persian during the war, or while there is friendship between the Cabool and British Governments.

12. In consideration of the friendship existing between the British Government and Ameer Dost Mohommud Khan, the British Government engages to overlook the past hostilities of all the tribes of Afghanistan, and on no account to visit them with punishment.

13. Whereas the Ameer has expressed a wish to have 4,000 muskets given him in addition to the 4,000 already given, it is agreed that 4,000 muskets shall be sent by the British Government to Tull, whence the Ameer's people will convey them with their own carriage.

110. TREATY OF PEACE (PARIS): GREAT BRITAIN AND PERSIA
4 March 1857

(Ratifications exchanged, Baghdad, 2 May 1857)
[Aitchison, *Collection of Treaties . . . relating to India* (5th ed.), 13: 81–86]

Although Persia remained neutral throughout the Crimean War, the enforced engagement of 1853 not to annex Herat (Doc. 98) continued to irk Nasir al-Din Shah. Growing tension between Britain and Persia, fanned by Russia, produced a rupture of British-Persian relations later in 1855. The shah then felt free to attack Herat, which his troops invested and eventually entered on 26 October 1856. British military units from India retaliated by occupying on 4 December the island of Kharak at the head of the Persian Gulf and landing three days later on the Persian mainland. The shah, meanwhile, had appointed Farrukh Khan Amin-al-Mulk as plenipotentiary to Paris to negotiate, through the good offices of France, a settlement of British-Persian differences. Reaching Istanbul on 16 October 1856, Farrukh Khan opened conversations with Viscount Stratford de Redcliffe. The Istanbul negotiations, however, led nowhere, despite the Persian envoy's assent to de Redcliffe's stiff conditions—the abandonment of Herat and of Persian claims to Afghanistan, the dismissal of the *sadri a'azam* (the shah's chief councillor), the appointment of British consuls in places additional to those listed in the 1841 treaty (Doc. 88), and "the acknowledgement of the Sovereign rights of the Imam of Muscat over certain towns hitherto held by him under the Shah." Farrukh Khan finally proceeded on 22 December 1856 to Paris, where less than two and one-half months later he and Lord Cowley, the British ambassador, agreed upon the terms of the treaty below. Because of inadequate communications, British-Persian fighting continued for several weeks after the signature of the treaty. British extraterritorial and consular privileges in Persia rested thereafter on the most-favored-nation principle, unconditionally reaffirmed in article 9. A Persian account of Farrukh Khan's mission, written by Mirza Husayn ibn 'Abdallah, a member of the delegation, still remains in manuscript. Kelly, *Britain and the Persian Gulf*, chap. 11; English, *John Company's Last War*; Standish, "Persian War of 1856–1857"; Miller, *Treaties and Other International Acts*, 7: 47–82; Watson, *History of Persia*, chaps. 14–15; Outram, *Outram's Persian Campaign*; Trotter, *Bayard of India*, chap. 15; Low, *Indian Navy*, vol. 2, chap. 7; Hunt, *Outram and Havelock's Persian Campaign*.

ART. 1. From the day of the exchange of the ratifications of the present Treaty there shall be perpetual peace and friendship between Her Majesty the Queen of the United Kingdom of Great Britain and Ireland on the one part and His Majesty the Shah of Persia on the other, as likewise between their respective successors, dominions and subjects.

ART. 2. Peace being happily concluded between their said Majesties, it is hereby agreed that the forces of Her Majesty the Queen shall evacuate the Persian territory, subject to conditions and stipulations hereafter specified.

ART. 3. The high contracting parties stipulate that all prisoners taken during the war by either belligerent shall be immediately liberated.

ART. 4. His Majesty the Shah of Persia engages, immediately on the exchange of the ratifications of this Treaty, to publish a full and complete amnesty, absolving all Persian subjects who may have in any way been compromised by their intercourse with the British forces during the war from any responsibility for their conduct in that respect, so that no persons, of whatever degree, shall be exposed to vexation, persecution, or punishment on that account.

ART. 5. His Majesty the Shah of Persia engages further to take immediate measures for withdrawing from the territory and city of Herat, and from every other part of Afghanistan, the Persian troops and authorities now stationed therein; such withdrawal to be effected within three months from the date of the exchange of the ratifications of this Treaty.

ART. 6. His Majesty the Shah of Persia agrees to relinquish all claims to sovereignty over the territory and city of Herat and the countries of Afghanistan, and never to demand from the Chiefs of Herat, or of the countries of Afghanistan, any marks of obedience, such as the coinage, or "Khootbeh", or tribute.

His Majesty further engages to abstain hereafter from all interference with the internal affairs of Afghanistan. His Majesty promises to recognise the independence of Herat and of the whole of Afghanistan, and never to attempt to interfere with the independence of those States.

In case of differences arising between the government of Persia and the countries of Herat and Afghanistan, the Persian Government engages to refer them for adjustment to the friendly offices of the British Government, and not to take up arms unless those friendly offices fail of effect.

The British Government, on their part, engage at all times to exert their influence with the States of Afghanistan, to prevent any cause of umbrage being given by them, or by any of them, to the Persian Government; and the British Government, when appealed to by the Persian Government, in the event of difficulties arising, will use their best endeavours to compose such differences in a manner just and honourable to Persia.

ART. 7. In case of any violation of the Persian frontier by any of the States referred to above, the Persian Government shall have the right, if due satisfaction is not given, to undertake military operations for the repression and punishment of the aggressors; but it is distinctly understood and agreed to that any military force of the Shah which may cross the frontier for the above-mentioned purpose shall retire within its own territory as soon as its object is accomplished, and that the exercise of the above-mentioned right is not to be made a pretext for the permanent occupation by Persia, or for the annexation to the Persian dominions, of any town or portion of the said States.

ART. 8. The Persian Government engages to set at liberty without ransom, immediately after the exchange of the ratifications of this Treaty, all prisoners taken during the operations of the Persian troops in Afghanistan, and all Afghans who may be detained either as hostages or as captives on political grounds in any part of the Persian dominions shall, in like manner, be set free; provided that the Afghans, on their part, set at liberty, without ransom, the Persian prisoners and captives who are in the power of the Afghans.

Commissioners on the part of the two contracting powers shall, if necessary, be named to carry out the provisions of this Article.

ART. 9. The high contracting parties engage that, in the establishment and recognition of Consuls-General, Consuls, Vice-Consuls and Consular Agents, each shall be placed in the dominions of the other on the footing of the most favoured nation; and that the treatment of their respective subjects and their trade shall also, in every respect, be placed on the footing of the treatment of the subjects and commerce of the most favored nation.

ART. 10. Immediately after the ratifications of this Treaty have been exchanged the British mission shall return to Tehran when the Persian Government agrees to receive it with the apologies and ceremonies specified in the separate note signed this day by the plenipotentiaries of the high contracting parties.

ART. 11. The Persian Government engages, within three months after the return of the British mission to Tehran, to appoint a Commissioner, who, in conjunction with a Commissioner to be appointed by the British Government, shall examine into and decide upon the pecuniary claims of all British subjects upon the government of Persia, and shall pay such of those claims as may be pronounced just, either in one sum or by instalments, within a period not exceeding one year from the date of the award of the Commissioners, and the same Commissioners shall examine into and decide upon the claims on the Persian Government of all Persian subjects, or the subjects of other powers, who, up to the period of the departure of the British mission from Tehran, were under British protection, which they have not since renounced.

ART. 12. Saving the provisions in the latter part of the preceding Article, the British Government will renounce the right of protecting hereafter any Persian subject not actually in the employment of the British mission, or of British Consuls-General, Consuls, Vice-Consuls, or Consular Agents, provided that no such right is accorded to or exercised by any other foreign powers; but in this, as in all other respects, the British Government requires, and the Persian Government engages, that the same privileges and immunities shall in Persia be conferred upon and shall be enjoyed by the British Government, its servants and its subjects, and that the same respect and consideration shall be shown for them, and shall be enjoyed by them, as are conferred

upon and enjoyed by and shown to the most favoured foreign government, its servants and its subjects.

ART. 13. The high contracting parties hereby renew the agreement entered into by them in the month of August 1851 (Shawal 1267) for the suppression of the slave trade in Persian Gulf, and engage further that the said agreement shall continue in force after the date at which it expires, that is, after the month of August 1862, for the further space of ten years and for so long afterwards as neither of the high contracting parties shall, by a formal declaration, annul it; such declaration not to take effect until one year after it is made.

ART. 14. Immediately on the exchange of the ratifications of this Treaty, the British troops will desist from all acts of hostility against Persia, and the British Government engages further that as soon as the stipulations in regard to the evacuation by the Persian troops of Herat and the Afghan territories, as well as in regard to the reception of the British mission at Tehran, shall have been carried into full effect, the British troops shall, without delay, be withdrawn from all ports, places, and islands belonging to Persia; but the British Government engages that, during this interval, nothing shall be designedly done by the Commander of the British troops to weaken the allegiance of the Persian subjects towards the Shah, which allegiance it is, on the contrary, their earnest desire to confirm; and further the British Government engages that, as far as possible, the subjects of Persia shall be secured against inconvenience from the presence of the British troops, and that all supplies which may be required for the use of those troops, and which the Persian Government engages to direct its authorities to assist them in procuring, shall be paid for, at the fair market price, by the British Commissariat immediately on delivery.

111. CONVENTION ON MEASURES FOR PACIFYING SYRIA (AND LEBANON): AUSTRIA, FRANCE, GREAT BRITAIN, PRUSSIA, RUSSIA, AND THE OTTOMAN EMPIRE
3 August–5 September 1860

(Ratifications exchanged, Paris, 18 October 1860)
[Great Britain, *Parliamentary Papers, 1861*, 68: 5–8]

The preamble of the 1860 convention declared that "His Imperial Majesty the Sultan" wished "to stop, by prompt and efficacious measures, the effusion of blood in Syria, and to show his firm resolution to establish order and peace amongst the populations placed under his sovereignty," and to this end "accepted" the "active co-operation" of the European signatories. The massacre by Druzes of thousands of Christians in Lebanon (27 May–10 July 1860) and by Muslims of thousands more in Damascus (9–11 July 1860) could be traced in part to the complicity of Ottoman officials and in part to internal social ferment. Once the crisis broke, European rivalry sharpened, as France rallied behind the Maronites and Britain behind the Druzes (Docs. 90, 96). European intervention, however, stemmed largely from the initiative of France, which the other powers suspected of seeking to annex the territory. For this reason Britain, in particular, insisted upon the issuance by the European signatories of a self-denying protocol, when the terms of the convention were framed in Paris on 3 August 1860. Salibi, *Modern History of Lebanon*, chap. 5; Kerr, *Lebanon in the Last Years of Feudalism*; Holt, *Egypt and the Fertile Crescent*; Hourani, *Syria and Lebanon*, pp. 27–33; Jouplain, *La question du Liban*, pp. 386–451; C. Churchill, *Druzes and the Maronites*, chaps. 4–9; Reid, "Syrian Troubles and Mission"; Abkarius, *Lebanon in Turmoil* (contemporary); Mange, *Near Eastern Policy of the Emperor Napoleon III*, chap. 4.

1. Self-denying Protocol, 3 August 1860

The Plenipotentiaries of Great Britain, Austria, France, Prussia, Russia, and Turkey, desirous of establishing, in conformity with the intentions of their respective Courts, the true character of the assistance afforded to the Sublime Porte by the provisions of the Protocol signed this day, the feelings which have dictated the clauses of this Act, and their perfect disinterestedness; declare in the most formal manner, that the Contracting Powers do not intend to seek for, and will not seek for, in the execution of their engagements, any territorial advantages, any exclusive influence, or any concession with regard to the commerce of their subjects, such as could not be granted to the subjects of all other nations.

Nevertheless, in recalling here the Acts issued by His Majesty the Sultan, the great importance of which was established by Article IX of the Treaty of the 30th of March, 1856, they cannot refrain from expressing the value which their respective Courts attach to the fulfilment of the solemn promises of the Sublime Porte, that serious administrative measures should be taken to ameliorate the condition of the Christian population, of every creed, in the Ottoman Empire.

The Plenipotentiary of Turkey takes note of this declaration of the Representatives of the High Powers, and undertakes to transmit it to his Court; pointing out that the Sublime Porte has employed, and will continue to employ, her efforts in the sense of the wish expressed above.

2. Convention, 5 September 1860

ART. I. A body of European troops, which may be increased to twelve thousand men, shall be sent to Syria to contribute towards the re-establishment of tranquility.

ART. II. His Majesty the Emperor of the French agrees to furnish, immediately, the half of this body of troops. If it should become necessary to raise its effective force to the number stipulated in the preceding Article, the High Powers would come to an understanding with the Porte without delay, by the ordinary course of diplomacy, upon the designation of those among them who would have to provide it.

ART. III. The Commander-in-chief of the expedition will, on his arrival, enter into communication with the Commissioner Extraordinary of the Porte, in order to concert all the measures required by circumstances, and to take up the positions which there may be occasion to occupy in order to fulfil the object of the present Convention.

ART. IV. Their Majesties the Queen of the United Kingdom of Great Britain and Ireland, the Emperor of Austria, the Emperor of the French, His Royal Highness the Prince Regent of Prussia, and His Majesty the Emperor of all the Russias, promise to maintain sufficient naval forces to contribute towards the success of the common efforts by the re-establishment of tranquillity on the coast of Syria.

ART. V. The High Parties, convinced that such a period will be sufficient to attain the object of pacification which they have in view, fix at six months the duration of the occupation of the European troops in Syria.

ART. VI. The Sublime Porte undertakes to facilitate, as far as lies in her power, the furnishing supplies and provisions for the expeditionary corps.

112. CONVENTION PROLONGING THE FRENCH OCCUPATION OF LEBANON: THE EUROPEAN POWERS AND THE OTTOMAN EMPIRE
19 March 1861

(Ratifications exchanged, Paris, 18 May 1861)
[Great Britain, *Parliamentary Papers, 1861*, 68: 14–15]

A French military force landed in Lebanon on 16 August 1860 on the strength of the preliminary instruments signed at Paris a fortnight earlier. These were the only European troops actually deployed, for the Sublime Porte had already taken energetic—and effective—measures to pacify the provinces. By January 1861 the British government showed signs of restiveness and began to press for the evacuation of French units from Bayrut. Overruled by the other powers, Britain reluctantly agreed in the following convention to prolong the French occupation until 5 June 1861. For references, see Doc. 111.

ART. I. The duration of the European occupation in Syria shall be prolonged until the 5th of June of the present year, at which date it is understood between the High Contracting Parties that it shall have reached its term, and that the evacuation shall have been effected.

ART. II. The stipulations contained in the second Article of the Convention of the 5th of Setember, 1860, in so far as they have not yet been executed, or as they are not modified by the present Convention, shall continue in force during the period which will elapse between the date of the signature of the present Act and the 5th of June of the present year.

113. REGULATION FOR THE ADMINISTRATION OF LEBANON
9 June 1861

[Translated from the French text in Great Britain, *Parliamentary Papers, 1861*, 68: 683–86]

A commission of the Big Five created to investigate the causes of the massacres of 1860 and to recommend changes in the administration of Lebanon arrived in Bayrut on 26 September and completed its report on 4 May 1861. On the basis of the commission's recommendations, the diplomatic representatives of the powers at Istanbul and of the Sublime Porte drew up the regulation that is reproduced below, providing for a non-Lebanese, Ottoman Christian governor nominated by the Porte after consultation with the European governments. The regulation was modified on 6 September 1864 (French text in Holland, *European Concert in the Eastern Question*, pp. 212–18). The special regime transformed Lebanon into the best administered Ottoman province and endured until October 1914, when it was unilaterally terminated by the Sublime Porte. The governor's tenure, at first limited to three years, was extended in 1864 to five and in 1868 to ten. The confessional basis of mid-twentieth-century politics in Lebanon may be found in precedents established in the period of the special Ottoman regime. Spagnolo, "Constitutional Change in Mount Lebanon," and "Mount Lebanon, France and Daud Pasha"; Salibi, *Modern History of Lebanon*, chap. 6; Hurewitz, "Lebanese Democracy in Its International Setting"; Hourani, *Syria and Lebanon*, pp. 33–40; Jouplain, *La question du Liban*, bk. 3; Mange, *Near Eastern Policy of the Emperor Napoleon III*, chap. 4; Young, *Corps de droit ottoman*, 1: 139–59 (regulations).

1. Protocol Adopted by the Sublime Porte and the European Powers

Article 1 gave rise to the following declaration, issued by His Highness 'Ali Paşa and accepted by the five Representatives:

"The Christian Governor entrusted with the administration of Lebanon shall be chosen by the Porte, to which he shall be directly responsible. He shall have the title of Müşür [commander], and he shall reside normally at Dayr al-Qamar, which will again fall under his direct authority. Invested for a three-year term, he will nevertheless be removable at pleasure, but his dismissal shall not take place without a trial. Three months prior to the expiration of his term, the Porte, before taking action, shall seek a new agreement with the Representatives of the Great Powers."

It has also been understood that the power granted by the Porte to this official to appoint on his own responsibility Administrative Agents shall be conferred upon him but once, at the time that he himself shall be invested with authority, and not in connection with each appointment.

Regarding Article 10, which deals with suits between the subjects or protégés of a foreign power, on the one hand, and the inhabitants of the Mountain, on the other, it has been agreed that a Mixed Commission sitting at Bayrut will be charged with verifying and reviewing titles of protection.

In order to maintain the security and freedom of the highway from Bayrut to Damascus at all times, the Sublime Porte will establish a blockhouse at the point of the said highway which may be deemed most suitable.

The Governor of Lebanon may proceed with the disarmament of the Mountain at such time as he shall consider the circumstances favorable.

2. Regulation for the Administration of Lebanon

ART. 1. Lebanon shall be administered

by a Christian Governor appointed by and directly responsible to the Sublime Porte.

This official, holding office at pleasure, shall be invested with all the attributes of executive power, shall maintain order and public security throughout the Mountain, shall collect taxes, and shall appoint on his own responsibility Administrative Agents with authority that he shall receive from His Imperial Majesty the Sultan; he shall appoint judges, shall summon and preside over the Central Administrative Council (Meclis), and shall assure the execution of all sentences legally rendered by the courts, except as limited by the provisions of Article 9.

Each of the constituent elements of the population of the Mountain shall be represented before the Governor by an Agent (Vekil) appointed by the chiefs and notables of each community.

ART. 2. There shall be for the entire Mountain one Central Administrative Council comprision twelve members: two Maronites, two Druzes, two Greek Orthodox, two Greek Catholics, two Matawilah, and two Muslims; it shall be charged with assessing taxes, adminstering revenues and expenditures, and rendering its advisory opinion on all questions submitted to it by the Governor.

ART. 3. The Mountain shall be divided into six Administrative Districts:

(1) Al-Kura, including the lower sections, as well as other such sections of territory in which the population adheres to the Greek Orthodox sect, but ecxluding the city of al-Qalamun, situated on the coast and inhabited almost exclusively by Muslims.

(2) The northern part of Lebanon, except for al-Kura, to the Nahr al-Kalb.

(3) Zahlah and its territory.

(4) Al-Matn, including Christian Sahal and the territories of Kata and Salima.

(5) The territory to the south of the Damascus-Bayrut road to Jazzin.

(6) Jazzin and Taffah.

The Governor shall appoint to each of these Districts an Administrative Agent, selected from that religious group which predominates either in size or in the importance of its properties.

ART. 4. There shall be in each District a Local Administrative Council comprising from three to six members [and] representing the various elements of the population and landed interests in the District.

The local Council, presided over and convoked annually by the chief of the District, shall in the first instance resolve all matters of administrative litigation, shall hear the claims of the inhabitants, shall provide the necessary statistical information for tax assessment in the District, and shall give its advisory opinion on all questions of local interest.

ART. 5. The Administrative Districts shall be divided into Subdistricts, the territory of which shall be based roughly on that of the former *iklims* (zones), and shall be insofar as possible of homogeneous population; the Subdistricts shall be divided into communities, each with at least five hundred inhabitants. At the head of each Subdistrict there shall be an Agent appointed by the Governor upon the recommendation of the Chief of the District; and at the head of each community there shall be a shaykh selected by the inhabitants and appointed by the Governor.

In mixed communities, each constituent element of the population shall have its own shaykh, who will exercise authority over only his correligionists.

ART. 6. [There shall be] equality of all before the law; all feudal privileges, especially those appertaining to the Mukata'aci (leaseholder or landowner, who was also frequently the local tax farmer), are abolished.

ART. 7. There shall be in each Subdistrict one justice of the peace for each religious group; there shall be in each District a Lower Judicial Council (Meclis), comprising from three to six members [and] representing the diverse elements of the population; and at the seat of the government a Higher Judicial Council, comprising twelve members, two from each of the six communities enumerated in Article 2, to which will be added a representative of the Protestant or the Jewish religion whenever the interests of a member of these communities may be involved in a lawsuit.

The presidency of the Judicial Council will rotate every three months among all of their members.

ART. 8. Justices of the peace shall pass judgment without appeal in cases involving no more than five hundred piasters. Cases involving more than five hundred piasters shall fall under the jurisdiction of the Lower Judicial Councils.

Mixed cases, that is, cases involving persons not of the same sect, whatever the value at stake in the suit, shall be brought directly before the Lower Judicial Council, unless the parties agree to recognize the competence of the defendant's justice of the peace.

In principle all cases shall be tried by the entier membership of the Council However, when all the parties of the particular suit shall belong to the same sect, they shall have the right to challenge a judge belonging to a different sect; but even in such a case the challenged judges shall participate in the trial.

ART. 9. In criminal matters, there shall be three degrees of jurisdiction. Contraventions shall be tried before justices of the peace; delicts before Lower Judicial Councils; and crimes before the Higher Judicial Council, whose sentences shall be executed only in conformity with formal usage in the rest of the Empire.

ART. 10. All suits of a commercial nature shall be brought before the commercial tribunal of Bayrut, and every suit, even in civil matters, between a subject of or person protected by a foreign power and an inhabitant of the Mountain shall be submitted to the jurisdiction of the same tribunal.

ART. 11. All the members of Judicial and Administrative Councils, without exception, and the justices of the peace will be chosen and designated by the heads of their respective communities after consultation with the notables and will be appointed by the Governor.

Half of the personnel of the Administrative Councils will be changed every year; outgoing members will be eligible for reappointment.

ART. 12. All judges shall be paid. If, after investigation, it is proved that one of them has been partial, or has committed any act of any nature unworthy of his office, he shall be dismissed and in addition shall be subject to a penalty proportionate to the misdeed committed by him.

ART. 13. The sessions of all Judicial Councils shall be public, and a verbatim report of their proceedings shall be kept by

a clerk appointed ad hoc. In addition, the clerk shall maintain a register of all contracts of sale of real estate; the contracts shall not become valid until they have been formally registered.

ART. 14. Inhabitants of Lebanon who have committed a crime or delict in another Sancak (provincial district) shall be tried by that Sancak, just as the inhabitants of other Districts who have committed a crime or delict within the limits of Lebanon shall be tried by the tribunals of the Mountain.

Accordingly, indigenous or nonindigenous individuals who have committed a crime or delict in Lebanon and who have escaped to another Sancak shall be arrested, upon the request of the authorities of the Mountain, by those of the Sancak where they may be found, and they shall be handed over to the administration of Lebanon.

Similarly, persons indigenous to the Mountain or inhabitants of other Districts who have committed a crime or delict in a Sancak other than Lebanon and who may have taken refuge there shall be arrested without delay by the authorities of the Mountain, upon the request of the interested Sancak, and shall be handed over to the authorities of the latter.

Agents of the authorities who are guilty of negligence or of nonjustifiable delays in the execution of orders relating to the return of guilty persons to the competent tribunals shall be punished according to the law, like those who would seek to shelter guilty persons from the police.

Finally, the relations of the Administration of Lebanon with the respective Administrations of the other Sancaks shall be precisely the same as the relations which exist and which shall be maintained among all the other Sancaks of the Empire.

ART. 15. In ordinary times the maintenance of order and the enforcement of law shall be the exclusive responsibility of the Governor, assisted by a mixed police force recruited on a voluntary basis and comprising about seven men for every thousand inhabitants.

[The practice of] arrest by troops shall be abolished and replaced by other methods of constraint, such as attachment and imprisonment; exaction by policemen of payments in money or in kind from the inhabitants shall be prohibited and most severely punished. Policemen shall wear a uniform or other external sign of their office, and in the execution of any order whatsoever the authorities shall use as far as possible agents belonging to the nation or the sect of the individual against whom the order is directed. United the time that the Governor may declare the local police force capable of fulfilling all the duties for which it is responsible in normal times, the roads from Bayrut to Damascus and from Sidon to Tripoli shall be occupied by imperial troops. The troops shall be subject to the command of the Governor of the Mountain.

Whenever the need may arise in extraordinary circumstances, the Governor, after consultation with the Central Administrative Council, may request from the military authorities of Syria the assistance of regular troops.

The officer commanding the troops shall reach agreement with the Governor of the Mountain on the measures to be taken, and for the duration of his stay in Lebanon he shall be subordinated to the Governor of the Mountain, acting under the latter's responsibility; he shall, however, retain his rights of initiative and evaluation in all purely military questions, such as strategy and discipline. The troops shall withdraw from the Mountain as soon as the Governor will have officially notified their commanding officer of the fulfillment of the mission for which they were called to the Mountain.

ART. 16. The Ottoman Porte reserves for itself the right to collect, through the medium of the Governor of Lebanon, the 3,500 purses (about $75,000) which constitute at present the tax burden of the Mountain and which may be augmented to 7,000 purses (about $150,000) when circumstances allow it; it is understood, however, that the proceeds of the tax will first be applied to the administrative expenses of the Mountain and to its outlays for public service, only the surplus, if there is any, becoming revenue of the state.

If the general expenses absolutely essential for the regular conduct of the administration should exceed the revenue from taxes, the Porte will provide the necessary balance.

However, it is understood that the Sublime Porte will be responsible for public works or other extraordinary expenditures only if approved in advance by the Porte.

ART. 17. As soon as possible a census of the population by communities and by sect shall be taken, and a land register drawn up for all cultivated lands.

114. DECLARATION BY GREAT BRITAIN AND FRANCE GUARANTEEING THE INDEPENDENCE OF MASQAT AND ZANZIBAR
10 March 1862

[Great Britain, *Parliamentary Papers, 1899*, 109: 124]

Sayyid Sa'id (1807–56), the *imam* of Masqat, established permanent residence in 1840 at Zanzibar, whose islands the Masqatis had conquered in the seventeenth century. On Sa'id's death, in accordance with his prior wishes, the succession was divided between two sons, Thuwayni becoming ruler of Masqat and Majid of Zanzibar. Thuwayni promptly tried to assert supremacy over his brother's patrimony. The dispute, arbitrated in 1861 by Lord Canning on behalf of the governor general of India, was resolved by the imposition upon Zanzibar of an annual tribute to Masqat.

The payment was "not to be understood as a recognition of the dependence of Zanzibar upon Muscat," but merely as compensation to "the ruler of Muscat for the abandonment of all claims upon Zanzibar" (text in Aitchion, *Collection of Treaties . . . relating to India* (5th ed.), 11: 303). The arrangement lasted until the death of Thuwayni in 1866, after which the United Kingdom continued the annual payments to Masqat. The 1862 declaration represented, implicitly, a recognition by France of the validity of the arbitral award and a joint assurance by the two powers not to infringe the sovereignty of the shaykhdoms. In 1890 Zanzibar was declared a British protectorate. Kelly, *Britain and the Persian Gulf,* chap. 12; Landen, *Oman since 1856,* chap. 5; Coupland, *East Africa and Its Invaders,* chaps. 5–16; Ingrams, *Zanzibar,* chaps. 13 and 14; Kajare, *Le sultanat d'Omân, pp.* 83–185; Aitchison, op. cit., pp. 269–86; see also references to Doc. 93.

Her Majesty the Queen of the United Kingdom of Great Britain and Ireland and His Majesty the Emperor of the French, taking into consideration the importance of maintaining the independence of His Highness the Sultan of Muscat and of His Highness the Sultan of Zanzibar, have thought it right to engage reciprocally to respect the independence of these Sovereigns.

The Undersigned, Her Britannic Majesty's Ambassador Extraordinary and Plenipotentiary [Lord Cowley] at the Court of France, and the Minister Secretary of State for Foreign Affairs [E. Thouvenel] of His Majesty the Emperor of the French, being furnished with the necessary powers, hereby declare, in consequence, that their said Majesties take reciprocally that engagement.

115. AGREED PROTÉGÉ REGULATIONS: FRANCE AND MOROCCO WITH THE ADHESION OF THE POWERS
19 August 1863

[English translation from Malloy, *International Acts, Protocols, and Agreements,* 1: 1226–27]

The unilateralism of the capitulations in Morocco, as in the Ottoman Empire and Persia, was not by itself a mark of weakness. In the early years, it made Moroccan diplomacy and commerce with Europe possible, by providing resident nationals (mostly merchants and—unlike the Ottoman Empire—only exceptionally missionaries and prelates) as well as diplomats with extraterritorial privileges that exempted them from local laws and taxes and permitted them to organize their own religious and cultural institutions. Almost from the outset, limited extraterritorial privileges were also conferred on Moroccan subjects in the employ of the European diplomatic and consular officers and even of merchants, who for reasons of personal safety tended to conduct their commerce in the interior of the country through native brokers, known as *samsars.* This practice went by the name of protection, and the privileged Moroccans, called protégés, to all intents and purposes became nominal citizens of the European protecting state. The theory of Moroccan governance at the time remained monarchical absolutism; the practice was often characterized by arbitrary decision making. In the circumstances, the protégé system was bound to be perverted, as wealthy Moroccans came to see in European protection a means of ensuring security of their persons and property against the increasingly arbitrary forms of taxation, justice, and military service of the *makhzan*, or governing establishment of Morocco, which essentially commanded the allegiance of the Arabized lowlands but neutralized the Berber highlands into reluctant subordination by manipulating tribal quarrels. Still, there was no denying that the protégé system also promoted corruption by depriving the makhzan of its fair share of revenue and its proper right to regulate justice, and by shielding criminals from Moroccan justice, thereby encouraging crime. More than that, it gave the European powers yet another means of penetrating the Moroccan society and economy to enlarge the political influence of the imperial rivals as they maneuvered to build claims to territory or to thwart the territorial claims of others. The three leading rivals were Britain, France, and Spain. As late as 1850, the rights of protection were based on custom, not on treaty, although some treaty clauses had implied the existence of such rights. In treaties concluded with Britain in 1856 (Doc. 107) and with Spain five years later (English translation in *British and Foreign State Papers*, 53: 1089–1108), the government of Morocco tried expressly to limit the number of protégés, and the types of employment that might warrant protection, to employees of diplomatic and consular officers. But existing lists of protégés in the employ of merchants—and in the case of Spain employed also by religious institutions—were not modified. Then, in 1863, France reached an agreement with the government of Morocco on the regulations reproduced below, which were designed to define the protégé system explicitly and give it formal status. To this arrangement the other interested powers—Belgium, Great Britain, Sardinia, Spain, Sweden and Norway, and the United States—later adhered. The regulations, however, instead of inhibiting the practice of protection, stimulated its further growth. Le Boeuf, *De la protection diplomatique et consulaire des indigènes au Maroc*; Wendel, "Protégé System in Morocco"; Stuart, *International City of Tangier*, chap. 2; Hall, *United States and Morocco*, chap. 5; Cruickshank, *Morocco*, chap. 1; International Court of Justice, *Case concerning Rights of Nationals of the United States of America in Morocco*, 1: 263–78; Miège, *Le Maroc et l'Europe*, 2: 261–410; Flournoy, *British Policy towards Morocco*, chap. 8.

Protection is individual and temporary.

It consequently does not in general apply to the relatives of the person protected.

It may apply to his family, that is to say, to his wife and children living under the same roof. It lasts at the longest for a person's lifetime and is never hereditary, with the single exception of the Benchimol family, which has furnished for several generations and still furnishes persons who act in the capacity of Brokers and interpreters for the post at Tangier.

Protected persons are divided into two classes.

The first class comprises natives employed by the Legation and by the various French consular officers.

The second class consists of native factors, brokers, or agents, employed by French merchants for their business affairs. It is proper here to refer to the fact that the term merchant is only applied to a person carrying on the import or export trade on a large scale, either in his own name or as the agent of others.

The number of native brokers enjoying French protection is limited to two for each commercial house.

By way of exception commercial firms having establishments in different ports may have two brokers attached to each of these establishments, who may as such enjoy French protection.

French protection is not extended to natives employed by French citizens in agricultural occupations.

Nevertheless, in consideration of the existing state of things, and by agreement with the authorities of Morocco, the benefit of the protection which has hitherto been granted to the persons referred to in the foregoing paragraph shall be extended to the said persons for two months from the first of September next.

It is, moreover, understood that agri-cultural laborers, herdsmen, or other native peasants, in the service of French citizens shall not be legally prosecuted without immediate information thereof being communicated to the competent consular officer, in order that the latter may protect the interests of his country-men.

The list of all protected persons shall be delivered by the proper consulate to the competent magistrate of the place, who shall likewise be informed of any changes that may subsequently be made in the said list.

Each protected person shall be furnished with a card in French and in Arabic, mentioning his name and stating the services which secure this privilege to him.

All these cards shall be issued by the Legation of France at Tangier.

116. CONVENTION AUTHORIZING BRITISH SUBJECTS TO HOLD REAL PROPERTY IN TUNIS: GREAT BRITAIN AND TUNIS
10 October 1863

[*British and Foreign State Papers*, 53: 46–50]

Competition with Britain in the Regency of Tunis intensified as France progressively "pacified" the inland districts of Algeria. The overriding anxiety of the maritime rivals, as noted elsewhere (Doc. 107), was strategic. Security planners in Paris saw a threat to French hegemony in Algeria and, to check that threat, tried building up a dominant position in the regency, thereby preventing Britain from doing so. Britain, on its side, feared that the conquest of the regency by France might make possible the transforma-tion of Bizerta into a North African Toulon, giving France command of the narrows between the western and eastern basins of the Mediterranean and neutralizing in the process the British base on Malta. Since Britain had no desire to annex Tunis, it dis-guised its hostility to French expansion by encouraging the Sublime Porte to press its claims to the regency and to institute direct rule, as it had in Tripoli in 1835, and then by upholding the territorial integrity of the Ottoman Empire. Responding in kind, France resisted the Porte's efforts to reimpose an Ottoman administration on the regency by defending the bey's title to quasi independence. Behind the contesting maneuvers, the two European powers nurtured all forms of interest which might bol-ster their respective demands for a voice in policy on Tunis. Meanwhile, once piracy had been suppressed in the 1820s, European immigration into the regency became feasible, and by 1856 the number of permanent settlers had grown to twleve thousand. The largest single group—close to 60 percent of the total—consisted of Maltese, and as such British subjects; the second largest—more than 30 percent—were Italians; far behind both trailed the French resident community of fewer than sixty families. On the basis of article 11 of the constitution promulgated by Muhammad al-Sadiq Bey (1859–82) on 26 April 1861, Britain concluded the following convention, establishing the conditions for land ownership by British subjects permanently residing in the regency. France never entered into a comparable agreement and, as it turned out, did not have to, since after the creation of the protectorate it was able to rewrite the land ownership laws in favor of French settlers and to subsidize French immigration. Ganiage, *Les origines du protectorat français en Tunisie*, chap. 1; Langer, "European Powers and the French Occupation of Tunis"; Estournelles de Constant, *La politique française en Tunisie*; Hofstetter, *Die Vorgeschichte des französischen Protektorats in Tunis bis zum Bardovertrag*; Broadley, *Last Punic War*, vol. 1, chap. 12.

. . . Whereas, by Article XI of the Organic Laws of the Regency of Tunis, foreigners have acquired the right to possess immovable property so soon as their respective Governments shall enter into an arrangement with the Government of Tunis, establishing the conditions which shall entitle them to exercise the right conceded to them; and whereas it is expedient to prevent in future the abuses, contentions, and confusion that have arisen in consequence of the means to which foreigners have had recourse, in order to evade the regulations and customs which prohibited them from holding immovable property in their own names, the following stipulations have been entered into and concluded. . . .

ART. I. It being henceforward lawful for British subjects to purchase and possess immovable property of every description in the Regency of Tunis, the Ecclesiastical and other legal Courts and authorities shall be empowered, upon the application of the purchaser, to proceed to the verification of the title-deeds, and to transfer the same in his name, according to the usages of the country, in order to give them the validity required by law.

II. British subjects possessing immovable property shall pay the same municipal and fiscal taxes which are paid by natives, and shall discharge in general the obligations which are by law attached to, and are discharged by, the like property held by natives.

III. Every proprietor of houses, magazines, or other tenements, shall conform to the municipal regulations now existing, or which shall hereafter exist.

IV. All cases of litigation respecting immovable property, and relating to the ownership or occupation of houses or lands, between a British and a Tunisian subject, shall be referred for adjudication to the competent legal tribunals, whose summons for the appearance of the British subject shall be transmitted through the British Consul-General, or, in his absence, through his deputy, in order that he or his deputy may be present at the trial. And the condemned party shall have the right to appeal to the courts constituted for that purpose, until the appeal shall have reached the Meglis Elakbar (Legislative Assembly); and whatever decision might be given by the last tribunal, the authority of the condemned party shall carry it out. But in cases where the dispute is between British subjects, it shall be optional for them, or either of them, to have their difference heard and determined by their Consul-General, or his deputy, whose decision, however, shall be governed by the laws and usages of the country, so far as they can be ascertained, and so far as the conditions expressed in the contract will permit,.

V. British subjects holding immovable property shall be free to sell, dispose of, and convey their property to natives; but they shall not sell, transfer, or convey their property to foreigners, except to subjects of such friendly Governments as have, by Convention or other agreement with His Highness the Bey, acquired for their subjects the right to purchase and hold immovable property in the Regency of Tunis; and, in order to guard against any infraction of the present Article, as well as to avoid any dispute or litigation that may arise therefrom, it is agreed that in all cases of a sale or conveyance of immovable property from a British to a foreign subject, the instrument of transfer shall have affixed to it the seals of the Ecclesiastical Court, or those of the competent native authorities, to render the sale valid and lawful.

VI. If a British proprietor die, either wholly intestate or intestate as to his immovable property, the succession to his immovable property shall be governed by the same law as the succession, *ab intestato*, to his movable property, without any let or hindrance on the part of the Tunisian authorities.

VII. It being established at all times that the Consul-General, or, in his absence, his deputy, do administer the estate of a British subject dying intestate in the Regency of Tunis, it is further established and agreed that the same right of administration shall extend to the lands, houses, and tenements of a British subject so dying. And it is moreover established, that upon the written declaration of Her Majesty's Agent and Consul-General, or, in his absence, [upon that] of his deputy, given under the seal of his office, that he has sold, disposed of, or conveyed the immovable property belonging to the deceased, the courts and legal authorities shall recognize such sale; and shall, upon the testimony of two notaries that the sale was made in due and legal form, furnish the purchaser, being a native or a foreigner coming within the provision of Article V of the present Convention, with such legal instruments or deeds as will enable the said purchaser, in case of contention, sale, conveyance, or mortgage, to prove his right over the said property.

VIII. The stipulations of the foregoing Article, and the rights therein reserved, shall also apply to, and shall be exercised by, the Consul-General, or his deputy in his absence, with regard to the immovable property of a British subject who has become involved in pecuniary difficulties, or who has declared himself insolvent in order to the payment of his debts and liabilities.

IX. The written declaration of Her Majesty's Agent and Consul-General, or, in his absence, of his deputy, that he has disposed of the immovable property of a British subject, for the reasons and for the purposes specified in Articles VII and VIII, shall be held to free from responsibility, the legal authorities and courts recognizing and confirming the transfer of such property; and for the satisfaction of the courts that the transaction has been made in due form, it shall be optional for them to depute their own notaries to assist at such sales and conveyances.

X. In all transactions relating to immovable property, British subjects shall pay the notarial and other fees which are fixed by law and are paid by natives.

XI. No British subject shall be forced to dispose of his immovable property, except for objects of public utility. But in all cases of expropriation, Article XI and XII of the Municipal Law of Tunis shall be the rule for effecting the compulsory expropriation for any public purpose in a lawful manner, and for fixing the amount of the indemnity to be paid; and such indemnity shall be paid in full, and to the satisfaction of the proprietor, before the act of expropriation can be carried out.

XII. As a further protection, however, to proprietors, the Decree declaring the public object for which the expropriation has been rendered necessary shall emanate from His Highness the Bey. The Consul-General, or in his absence, his Deputy, shall have due information thereof, so that he may have it in his power to watch over the execution of the provisions of Article XI of the Municipal Law heretofore established and agreed upon with reference to the mode of ascertaining and fixing the amount of the indemnity.

XIII. With a view to prevent complaints, abuses, or a misconstruction being put upon an act of expropriation, it is agreed that should the Bey's Decree, specifying the object of public utility for which the expropriation has been made, be not executed at the expiration of one year after its date, the owner of the immovable property shall have the right to recover the same by reimbursing in full the amount of the indemnity.

XIV. Whenever a British subject shall desire to introduce machinery, or establish a manufactory in the Regency of Tunis, he shall be bound to apply for and obtain the permission of the Bey for that purpose, and His Highness, in according such permission, shall specify in the body of the Decree or Concession the conditions upon which it has been granted, in order that the Decree shall serve, in case of litigation or of an infraction of any of the conditions, as a rule and a guidance for the equitable adjustment of the point of points at issue.

XV. The building and appurtenances of manufactories being immovable property, are subject to the conditions and stipulations relating to such property in general. But as a further security to the local Government and to the public revenue, it is moreover established and agreed that, upon the written requisition of the Minister for Foreign Affairs, or of the President of the Municipal Council, to the Consul-General, or, in his absence, to his deputy, the fiscal officers shall have the right to ascertain, by personal inspection, that the manufactory has not been diverted from the purpose for which permission was given, and that the internal taxes and imposts levied upon raw materials, either previously to or after their being manufactured, are duly paid.

XVI. British subjects holding, or here-after becoming possessed of property called *anzal* (leasehold), shall continue to enjoy the conditions which constitute and are attached to that description of property, and which conditions are hereby established and confirmed.

XVII. British subjects holding immovable property in the Regency of Tunis shall, in conforming to the local laws and regulations, exercise and enjoy the same immunities, privileges, and rights that are accorded to Tunisian proprietors; and for that purpose the right of British subjects to hold immovable property being derived from the enactments founded upon the organic laws (*Aad-el-Aman*) the said enactments are hereby confirmed; and their observance being considered necessary for the more efficient protection of the immovable property held as aforestated, it has been further agreed that they shall be maintained, as a greater security for the due performance of the conditions of the present Convention. And they shall be furthermore entitled to all the immunities, privileges, and exemptions accorded, or to be hereafter accorded, to the subjects or citizens of the most favoured nation. . . .

117. *SENATUS-CONSULTE* ON THE NATURALIZATION OF MUSLIMS AND JEWS IN ALGERIA AND THE PUBLIC ADMINISTRATIVE REGULATION FOR ITS EXECUTION
14 July 1865–21 April 1866

[Translated from the French texts in France, *Le Moniteur Universel*, 24 July 1865 and 26 April 1866]

Despite the lack of clear purpose in initiating the conquest of Algeria in 1830 (Docs. 68, 70) and the continuing ambiguity of successive French regimes and governments over how best to rule the territory (Docs. 76, 78), Algeria was transformed, in effect, into a settlement dependency. In such dependencies, the interests of the immigrants invariably transcend those of the indigenous population. This was reflected primarily in the laws and practices relating to land procurement in Algeria, for without the inducement of cheap land, especially in rural areas, Europeans would hardly have been drawn to a territory where many of the natives were forcibly resisting the expropriation of their properties by alien settlers. In the metropole, coping with such militant resistance went under the label of "pacification," a euphemism for secondary conquest, that is, the piecemeal annexation of the country. In Algeria, this process lasted until about 1890. Before the appearance of the French, landed property in Algeria fell into four classes: beylical, or that belonging to the dey and his provincial governors; *habous* (from the Arabic *hubus*), or land in mortmain; large estates collectively owned by settled or migrant tribes; and individually owned plots. The conversion of beylical land into state domain as a preliminary step in its distribution to European immigrants or colons created no special difficulty, since this was an accepted consequence of conquest. Similarly, the individually owned lands, once the right of possession had been confirmed, need not have created much trouble, because their sale to Europeans could be regulated under French law without violence to local traditions. But the holdings in these two categories were smaller and less desirable thean the habous and tribal properties. Successive French administrations improvised modes of transferring land titles for the latter from Muslims to Europeans. The game was essentially the same—driving Muslim tribesmen off their lands—but the name changed from *refoulement* (forcing back) in the 1830s, to *resserrement* (contraction or compression) in the 1840s (see Doc. 78), and then to *cantonnement* in the 1850s and early 1860s. Under cantonnement, which differed little from the American practice of creating reservations for Indians, the tribes were compelled to surrender part— usually the choicest—of their collectivized lands to the state for their "more efficient" use by Europeans. European colonization by confiscation and ejection intensified the Muslim resistance, so that the metropole had commonly to impose their settlement policies on an aroused population. No less an improvisor than his predecessors, Napoleon III (1852–70) nevertheless shifted to a more compassionate program in the second half of his reign. A *sénatus-consulte* (senate decree) of 22 April 1863 (for the French text, see *Le Moniteur Universel*, 25 April 1863) put an end to the practice of cantonnement and pledged that the existing Muslim landed property would remain in Muslim possession. Indeed, in the remaining years of the Second Empire no new colon villages were established. Meanwhile, by 1863, Napoleon III had begun to refer to Algeria as his "Arab Kingdom," and he came to endorse the doctrine of the political assimilation of the native population, Jewish as well as Muslim. With this in mind, the following sénatus-consulte was issued, declaring as French subjects all native Algerians and opening up the possibility of the voluntary adoption of French citizenship by individuals. The complicated conditions and procedures for enfranchisement, set forth in the administrative regulation below, hardly encouraged the process. An even greater impediment was the requirement that Muslim applicants for citizenship accept French civil law, which implied an abandonment of Islam, since the shari'ah, or Islamic canon law, closely regulates all matters of personal status such as marriage, divorce, and inheritance. Consequently very few Muslims became French citizens—only 194 by 1870, 736 by 1890, and 1,362 by 1906. On the status of Jews in Algeria, see Doc. 123. Roberts, *History of French Colonial Policy*, chap. 26; Julien, *Histoire de l'Algérie contemporaine*, pp. 424–34; Martin, *L' histoire de l'Algérie française*, pt. 2, chaps. 9–10; Confer, *France and Algeria*, chaps. 1–3; Gooch, *Reign of Napoleon III*, chap. 3; Bury, *Napoleon III and the Second Empire*, chap. 8; Priestley, *France Overseas*, chaps. 6, 9; Cordier, *Napoléon III et l'Algérie*.

1. The Sénatus-Consulte, 14 July 1865

ART. 1. The Muslim native is French; nevertheless he shall continue to be governed under Muslim law.

He shall be allowed to serve in the army and navy. He may hold civil service positions in Algeria.

He may, on application, be granted the rights of French citizenship; in this case, he shall be governed under the civil and political laws of France.

ART. 2. The Israelite native is French; nevertheless, he shall continue to be governed under his [religious laws of] personal status.

He shall be allowed to serve in the army and the navy. He may hold civil service positions in Algeria.

He may, on application, be granted the rights of French citizenship; in this case, he shall be governed by French law.

ART. 3. The foreignor who gives proof of three years' residence in Algeria may be admitted to all the rights of French citizenship.

ART. 4. In conformity with Articles 1, 2, and 3 of the present Senate decree, French citizenship may be obtained only after the age of twenty-one. It is conferred by imperial decree given in the Council of State.

ART. 5. A public administrative regulation shall determine: (1) the conditions of admission into service and of promotion of Muslim and Israelite natives in the army and the navy; (2) the civil service positions to which the Muslim natives and the Israelite natives may be nominated in Algeria; [and] (3) the forms in which the applications provided for in Articles 1, 2, and 3 of the present Senate decree shall be made.

2. The Regulation, 21 April 1866

Chap. I. *Admission to and Service and Promotion of Algerian Natives in the Army*

ART. 1. Native troops of Algeria form part of the French Army.

They are to be considered as combatant troops.

ART. 2. They are subject only to voluntary recruitment.

ART. 3. Any native may enlist in a native corps, if he satisfies the following conditions.

He must: (1) be between seventeen and thirty-five years of age, and not less than one meter fifty-six centimeters tall; (2) be physically fit for military service; [and] (3) be judged worthy in conduct and morality to serve in the French Army.

ART. 4. Age is to be determined by usage in Algeria.

Physical fitness will be established by a military doctor of the corps.

Conduct and morality will be assessed, on the basis of the report of the chief of the Arab Bureau of the district, by the commander of corps, who will give his opinion and send the application and the supporting papers to the commander of the subdivision, who will take the decision.

ART. 5. Enlistment will be for four years.

It will be received by the deputy military officer of the district in the presence of an interpreter and two witnesses chosen from among the native officers, NCOs, corporals, or sergeants.

It carries the right to a bonus, the amount of which is fixed each year by an order of the Minister of War, issued on the proposal of the Governor General of Algeria, one-half payable on the day of enlistment and the other half two years later.

The interpreter is to explain the conditions of service to the enlistee, who is to declare that he will comply with them, and take the oath on the Quran.

ART. 6. In the last quarter of the fourth year of service, the native may be allowed by the administrative council of the corps to reenlist either in the native corps or in the French corps.

This reenlistment will be completed under the conditions stipulated in Articles 11, 12, 13, 14, 16, 17, and 18 of the law of 26 April 1855 on the endowment of the army.

However, a special bonus will be given for this reenlisment; it is fixed annually by an order of the Minister of War issued on the proposal of the higher commission of the endowment.

ART. 7. Promotion of natives in the army will take place exclusively by choice, in conformity with the provisions of the law of 14 April 1832 on the length of service required in each grade for promotion to the next higher grade.

ART. 8. Applicable to native soldiers are: the military judicial code of the army, and in general all regulations on military service and discipline; the law of 19 May 1834 on the status of officers; [and] the law of army pensions, on condition, however, that, insofar as it concerns widows and orphans, the marriage was contracted under French civil law.

Chap. II. *Admission to and Service and Promotion in the Navy*

ART. 9. The conditions of admission to and of service and promotion in the native marine and naval units are the same as those framed in Chapter I above for the army.

The imperial decision of 25 June 1864 which dispenses with forced recruitment and considers as being on active service the native fishermen or sailors off the Algerian coast remains in force.

Those native sailors wishing to serve in the naval reserves must register at the port or Toulon.

Chap. III. *Admission to Civil Service Positions*

ART. 10. If the Muslim or Israelite native fulfills the conditions of age and aptitude fixed by the French regulations especially for each service, he may apply in Algeria for civil service positions designated in the list annexed to the present decree.

He does not qualify for civil service positions other than those provided for in this table merely on the condition of having obtained the rights of French citizenship.

Native civil servants have a right to retirement pension under the conditions, in the forms, and according to the rates that regulate civil servants in France.

Their widows, however, are not entitled to pensions unless the marriage was performed under French civil law.

Chap. IV. *Provisions for the Naturalization of Natives*

ART. 11. The Muslim or Israelite native who wishes to enjoy the rights of French citizenship in conformity with paragraph 3 of Articles 1 and 2 of the Senate decree of 14 July 1865 must present himself in person either before the mayor of the commune of his domicile or before the chief of the Arab Bureau of the district in which he resides, to present his application and to declare that he agrees to be governed by the civil and political laws of France.

A record of the application and the declaration will be drawn up.

ART. 12. The mayor or the chief of the Arab Bureau, by virtue of his office, will proceed to inquire into the past morality of the applicant. The result of this inquiry will be transmitted with the report containing the application to the military commander of the province, who will send all paper with his opinion to the Governor General of Algeria.

ART. 13. The Governor General will transmit the application to our Keeper of the Seals, Minister of Justice and of Religions, on whose report we shall enact the law, the Council of State agreeing.

ART. 14. If the applicant is already in military service, the report provided for in Article 11 will be drawn up by the commander of the corps or by the ranking officer of the detachment to which he belongs and will be transmitted to the commander of the province with (1) a report on the applicant's service: (2) a certificate on his morality and conduct.

The paper will be forwarded by the commander of the province with his opinion to the Governor General of Algeria, to be followed up in conformity with Article 13 of the present decree.

Chap. V. *Provisions on the Naturalization of Foreigners Residing in Algeria*

ART. 15. The foreigner residing in Algeria who wishes to obtain French citizenship must file his application before the mayor of the commune of his domicile or before the person who fulfills the functions of the mayor in his place of residence. A report of of the application will be drawn up.

ART. 16. For attachment to the application, the foreigner will deposit such documents as will establish the fact of his residence in Algeria at the time and for at least three years previous.

This proof will be made by official and public documents or those bearing a specific date and, in lieu of these, by an affidavit drawn up by the local justice of the peace on the affirmation of four witnesses.

ART. 17. Time spent by the foreigner in Algeria in the [military] service will be counted in the legal length of residence laid down in the preceding article.

ART. 18. The application will then be handled in conformity with the provisions of Articles 11, 12, 13, and 14 of the present decree.

ART. 19. Only those Muslim and Israelite natives and foreigners residing in Algeria above the age of twenty-one may file the applications specified in Articles 11 and 15 of the present decree.

They must prove their age by a birth certificate or in lieu of that by an affidavit made by four witnesses before a justice of the peace, or by the Qadi of the place of residence if the applicant is a native, or before the justice of the peace, if the applicant is a foreigner.

ART. 20. The charge for the seal and for registration is fixed at one franc for natives and for foreigners who are granted the rights of French citizenship under the Senate of 14 July 1865.

ART. 21. Our Ministers, State Secretaries for War, Navy, and Colonies, Finance, Justice, and Religions and for Public Instruction, and our Governor General of Algeria are charged, each as pertains to his functions, with the execution of the present decree, which will appear in the Law Bulletin and Official Bulletin of the Governor General of Algeria.

3. List of Civil Positions in Algeria Open to Muslim and Israelite Native Who Are Not French Citizens

Department of Justice
Copy clerk or clerk of the court and tribunals
Judicial interpreter and translator
Notary
Counsel
Bailiff
Appraiser
General and Municipal Administration
Member of the General Council
Clerk, assistant chief clerk, and chief clerk of any class in prefectures and sub-prefectures, and civil commissioners
Employee of any grade among the administrative personnel of jails, departmental prisons, and penitentiaries
Member of the inspecting commission of prisons
Employee of any grade among the administrative personnel of hospitals, asylums, or orphanages, employment agencies, and other welfare institutions
Member of the administrative commission of hospitals
Municipal councillor
Municipal collector
Inspector, secretary, or police commissioner
Administrator of savings bank
Administrator of (municipal) pawnshop
Administrator of the bureau of welfare
Militiaman, NCO, or officer of the militia up to but not including the grade of captain
Collector of local duties (*octrois*)
Constable
Guard of waterworks
And generally all positions in the general and communal administration over which prefects and mayors have the direct nominative power
Telegraph Service
Inspector and office worker
Office director
Public Instruction
Member of academic council
Master, director, and inspector of Arab-French schools
Holder of a publicly endowed chair in Arabic
Schoolmaster, assistant master, and teacher in a lycée
Public Works Service
Clerk of any class, draftsman, and storekeeper in the Service of Bridges and Roads, of Mines, and of Civil Buildings
Foreman and driver in the Service of Bridges and Roads
Mine guard
Ordinary inspector of public buildings
Service of Finance
Clerk of any class in the offices of:
Registration and property
Taxes
Customs
Postal Service
Forests
Tobacco Administration
In the Postal Service:
Letter carrier
Distributing Clerk
Foreman, customs inspector, collector, and officer up to but not including the grade of captain

Forestry guard and sergeant
Surveyor of any class in the Topographical
  Field Service
Service of Ports and Sanitation
Fishery guard

Pilot
Wharf inspector
Guard and secretary of the sanitation
  department

118. CONVENTION ON TELEGRAPHIC COMMUNICATION BETWEEN EUROPE AND INDIA: GREAT BRITAIN AND PERSIA
23 November 1865

(Ratifications exchanged, Tehran, 1 May 1866)
[Aitchison, *Collection of Treaties . . . relating to India* (5th ed.), 13: 179–83]

The Indian mutiny of 1857–58 pressed the governments in Britain and India to promote the development of a comprehensive telegraphic system in the Asian subcontinent that would connect with the rapidly multiplying lines in Europe. The early submarine cables in the Red and Arabian seas failed altogether to function. It therefore
became necessary to fall back on overland routes. The requisite agreements, however,
were only slowly reached. A convention with the Sublime Porte for the construction
of a line connecting India with the Ottoman Empire was concluded on 3 September
1864 (text in *British and Foreign State Papers*, 54: 20–25). A comparable convention,
reproduced below, was negotiated with Persia. The Persian government undertook to
build at its own expense a cable system from Khanaqin, on the Ottoman border, to
Tehran, Isfahan, and Shiraz, joining the Bushire (Abu Shahr)-Khanaqin line which
had been erected by the British under an agreement of 17 December 1862 (text in
Hertslet, *Treaties . . . between Great Britain and Persia*, pp. 23–25; see also the
Persian-Ottoman agreement of 28 November 1863, ibid., pp. 173–75). Telegraphic
communications in Persia were later extended by German and Russian firms, so that
the British-Indian service embraced alternative routes to Baghdad (via lower Mesopotamia or Persia) and to Europe (via the Ottoman Empire or Persia and Russia).
The interest of the shah and the sultan in telegraphy was no less than that of the
European powers, for they equally realized its value as a means of exercising close
administrative supervision over provincial governors. Hoskins, *British Routes to
India*, chap. 15; Sykes, *History of Persia*, vol. 2, chap. 80; Bright, *Submarine Telegraphs*; E. and C. Bright, *Sir Charles Tilston Bright*, vol. 2, chap. 5; Goldsmid,
Telegraph and Travel; Kelly, *Britain and the Persian Gulf*, pp. 554–63; Litten, *Persien*,
chaps. 1 and 2.

ART. 1. In order to improve the telegraphic communication between Europe
and India, the Persian Government agrees
to attach another wire to the poles now
standing from Bushire to Khannikeen, and

to bring it into working order as soon as
possible. The wire [is] to be used solely for
international messages sent in European
languages.

ART. 2. In order that the second wire

may be attached in a complete and effective manner, the Persian Government also agrees that it shall be done under the direction and supervision of an English Engineer Officer and staff; and the Persian Government will use its best endeavours to collect the necessary materials and lay down the wire with all expedition.

ART. 3. The British Government agrees to procure for the Persian Government at a reasonable price, and with the cognizance of a Persian Commissioner, all the wire insulators, Morse instruments, etc., that may be requisite for this work inclusive of two hundred iron posts for the marshy tracts of Bushire, and to deliver them over to the Government Commissioners at any seaports or frontier towns of Persia that may be suitable, receiving payment in five years in five instalments.

ART. 4. The Persian Government, moreover, agrees that an English Telegraph Officer with the necessary staff not exceeding (50) fifty in number, exclusive of families, shall be engaged, from the opening of the telegraphic communication through the new wire, for (5) years in organizing the Persian line of telegraph and giving instructions in telegraphy. And the British Government agrees that the English Officer and his staff shall, at the expiration of the prescribed period, make over the said line to the Persian Government and cease connection with Persian Telegraph.

ART. 5. The conditions under which the English Officer shall exercise control over the second wire during the prescribed period are stated in the following rules:—

1.—His Royal Highness the Itizad-es-Sultaneh, Minister of Science, or any other person who, by the Shah's order, may be appointed in his place, is to be considered the head and absolute chief of all the Persian Government Telegraphs.

2.—Any order which His Royal Highness or such other person in his place may issue concerning the protection of the line, its working, and the Persians employed on it, shall be given through and with the approval of the English Telegraph Officer.

3.—For the protection of the line the whole distance from the Turkish frontier to Bushire shall be divided from station to station into six sections as follows:—

From the Turkish Frontier to Hamadan.

From Hamadan to Tehran.
" Tehran " Cashan.
" Cashan " Ispahan.
" Ispahan " Shiraz.
" Shiraz " Bushire.

To each of these divisions the Itizad-es-Sultaneh shall appoint a Persian Officer, who will be responsible to His Royal Highness for the protection of the line situated within his limits. To enable the said Persian Officer, or Yaver, of each division to carry out his duties efficiently, a certain number of horsemen shall be stationed under his orders along the line. The Yaver will, of course, accept any suggestions which the English Telegraph Officer may give with reference to his charge, due regard being had to the customs of Persia and her power of carrying out such suggestions.

4.—The organization of offices and instruction of employé's shall be exclusively in charge of the English Superintending Officers, who will be responsible for the working of the line in these respects; and the Persian signallers shall be ordered to obey implicitly the instructions which the English Officers may given in the performance of their duties.

5.—In case of insubordination or misconduct on the part of the Persian signallers, His Royal Highness the Itizad-es-Sultaneh engages to use his best endeavours in lawfully supporting the authority of the English Superintending Officer, exercised under the last rule. On the other hand, the English Officer engages that the bounds of that authority shall in no way be exceeded.

6.—The English Officer shall have nothing whatever to do with receipts of money. A Mirza will be appointed at each station, who will be directly responsible for the accounts to the Itizad-es-Sultaneh. But the English Superintending Officer shall render to His Royal Highness or any person who may be appointed by the Persian Government, such account of the telegrams despatched under his authority as may be sufficient for full information.

These rules, however general in some sense, are understood to have special application to the second wire.

ART. 6. In filling up vacancies which may occur among the signallers employed under Article 4 the English Telegraph Officer shall give the preference to natives of Persia, provided they be qualified, in his estimation, by knowledge of the English language and other attainments necessary for this service, to perform the duties required.

ART. 7. As the Telegraph Offices of these two wires ought to be distinct, the Persian Government shall build a new office adjoining the existing one wherever there are not separate rooms.

ART. 8. If any injury befall the second wire, or delay occur through press of traffic, the first wire, which, is specially used for internal communication in Persia, shall give assistance to the second wire, and *vice versa*.

ART. 9. For every message of twenty words or less from Khannikeen to Bushire, or *vice versa*, 1 toman, 5 kerans and 8 shahis in Persian money, or 14 shillings in English money, shall be charged, with proportionate rates for the intervening towns. The Persian Government accepts the tariff laid down in the last convention between Turkey and England so far as regards the rates of messages sent by the two governments from Bushire to India and from Khannikeen to Constantinople or Europe.

ART. 10. The yearly receipts will be credited to the Persian Treasury, but should they reach a higher sum than thirty thousand (30,000) tomans, the surplus will be made over to the Officers of the English Government for the cost of their establishment.

ART. 11. All Indian messages at whatever part of the line, or from whatever place received, shall be given over to the second wire, and the accounts regularly kept.

ART. 12. Should the traffic so continuously increase as to demand more than in one day the fair day's work on the second wire, the excess of telegrams shall be handed over for despatch to the first wire, the money received on them being separately credited to the Persian Government. The adjustment of this matter shall rest with the Itizad-es-Sultaneh and the English Superintending Officer. This Article is quite irrespective of the provision for mutual assistance in the event of a slight and temporary delary.

ART. 13. The cost of all other than In-dian or Submarine cable messages shall be separately credited to the Persian Treasury, although conveyed by the second wire.

ART. 14. The relative value of coin shall be calculated for purposes of account at the following rates:—

One pound sterling = 25 francs = 22 kerans.

One shilling = 1 franc − 25 centimes = 1 keran − 2 shahis.

One penny = 10 centimes = 2 shahis.

As a rule, accounts shall be kept in English and payments made in Tehran in Persian currency.

ART. 15. The telegraph accounts shall be made up by the English Superintending Officer monthly and sent to Constantinople, where, by comparison with the Cable and Turkish accounts, they will be checked by the British Commissioner appointed for that purpose. On the return to Tehran of the audited accounts from Constantinople, the amount due to the Persian Government will be certified by the English Officer and speedily paid every six months, as stated in the last Article. The above account shall always be open to the inspection of the Telegraph Agent of the Persian Government at Constantinople, or any person recognized by the Persian Minister at the Ottoman Court for the settlement of accounts of international traffic on the Persian Turkish Line.

ART. 16. The Telegraph Regulations drawn up at Paris on the thirteenth of April Anno Domini one thousand eight hundred and sixty-five shall be carried out under the superintendence of the Persian Government so far as not opposed to the terms of the present convention of the institutions of Persia.

ART. 17. Any disagreement arising between the telegraphic employes of the two governments shall be referred to their Excellencies the Persian Minister for Foreign Affairs and the British Minister at Tehran, in order that, after necessary investigation, a just decision may be pronounced.

ART. 18. This convention shall take effect from the opening of correspondence on the second wire, and remain in force for five years from the day that a telegram is first despatched hereby. At the expiration of the five years it shall be null and void. If at any time within the term appointed the capabilities of Persian telegraphers for their work shall be proved to the satisfaction of the Chief of the Persian Telegraphs and the English Telegraph Officer, the full period shall be curtailed, and the line made over altogether to the Persian Government.

119. FIRST SA'UDI ASSURANCES TO GREAT BRITAIN
21 April 1866

[Aitchison, *Collection of Treaties . . . relating to India* (5th ed.), 11 : 206]

Local tribes in league with a branch of the Wahhabis in 1865 plundered British property at the port of Sur, technically owing allegiance to Masqat. British protests, and naval action, finally elicited a promissory statement from 'Abdallah bin Faysal, who had just succeeded to the rulership of the Sa'udi amirate, that his subjects would refrain from interfering with British interests in the area. Aitchison, op. cit., pp. 182–90; Winder, *Saudi Arabia in the Nineteenth Century*, chap. 8; Lorimer, *Gazetteer of the Persian Gulf*, vol. 1, pt. 1, pp. 1051–1128; Philby, *Sa'udi Arabia*, chaps. 7–8.

I, Mahomed bin Abdullah bin Maneh, am certain on the following points:—

I am authorized by Imaum Abdullah bin Fysul to request the Sahib, the Resident in the Persian Gulf, to become the medium of friendship between Imaum Abdullah bin Fysul and the British Government;

Secondly.—I assure the Resident in the Persian Gulf on the part of Imaum Abdullah bin Fysul that he will not oppose or injure British subjects residing in territories under the authority of Abdullah bin Fysul; and

Thirdly.—I assure the Resident in the Persian Gulf on the part of Imaum Abdullah bin Fysul that he will not injure or attack the territories of the Arab tribes in alliance with the British Government, specially on the Kingdom of Muscat, further than in receiving the zukat that has been customary of old.

120. TREATY OF FRIENDSHIP, COMMERCE, AND NAVIGATION: ITALY AND TUNIS
8 September 1868

[*British and Foreign State Papers*, 59: 1280–90]

The Italian city-states were slow to merge, but once united in 1861 Italy made up for lost time in accumulating the status symbols of a major power. The search for an empire, the predominant symbol, evoked in some Italian leaders memories of ancient Rome, since within the narrowing range of conquerable territories were the former Barbary Garrisons of Tunis and Tripoli. Tunis in particular appealed to the Italian imperialists because of its proximity, its identity as the seat of ancient Carthage, and its attraction as a place of settlement for Italian farmers (chiefly from Sicily). By 1870, an estimated 15,000 Europeans—nearly half of them Italians—resided in the Regency of Tunis, where only a half-century earlier the most common form of European immigration had been involuntary. Indeed, at the time of the Exmouth-Capellen expedition in 1816 (Doc. 58), all 781 European "slaves" liberated in Tunis had come from Sicily, Naples, Sardinia, and Genoa. In the spring of 1864 Italy joined Britain and France in sending a naval squadron to Tunisian waters to protect the interests of its nationals in a domestic insurrection which spread through the towns and the tribal areas against the government's reforms, and the fiscal policies devised to pay for them. The rebellion was suppressed before any physical intervention took place, but it is a matter of record that the Italians in Turin (united Italy's capital until 1864) and in Tunis were carried away by high imperial expectations and were therefore far less cautious than either Britain or France about the actual use of the naval power they had deployed off the regency's coast. The Italian imperialists, even after the settlement of the domestic crisis and the prompt recall of the activist consul general, kept their eyes trained on the regency. Meanwhile, Italy as such had had no prior treaty relations with Tunis; therefore, to regulate these relations and to legalize the ownership of the land that Italian farmers cultivated, Italy negotiated the following instrument. Ganiage, *Les origines du protectorat français en Tunisie*, chaps. 1, 4, 5; Langer, "European Powers and the French Occupation of Tunis"; Julien, *La question italienne en Tunisie*; Toscano, "Tunis."

. . . ART. I. All the rights, privileges, and immunities which are conferred on the Italian representatives, citizens, and vessels, by the usages and by the Treaties previously existing between the Regency of Tunis and the States which now form the Kingdom of Italy, are confirmed and extended to the whole of Italy, with the exception of those clauses which would not agree with any of the Articles of the present Convention; and it is, moreover, expressly understood that all the rights, privileges, and immunities of which the Regency of Tunis grants at present, or may grant or allow in future, the enjoyment by whatever title, to the representatives, to the citizens, to the ships, and to the commerce of any other foreign Power, shall be understood as granted *ipso facto* to the representatives, to the citizens, to the ships, to the commerce, and to the navigation of the Kingdom of Italy.

In the same manner Tunisian subjects and vessels in Italy shall continue to enjoy the rights granted to them by the previous Treaties, and they shall be admitted to the enjoyment of the rights and favours which are or which shall be granted to any other foreign Power whatever.

II. There shall be, reciprocally, complete and perfect freedom of navigation and of commerce between all the territories belonging to His Majesty the King of Italy, and all the territories belonging to His Most Serene Highness the Bey of Tunis.

The subjects and citizens of the two Contracting Parties may, with all freedom and security, arrive with their vessels and cargoes at all those places, ports, and rivers of Italy and of Tunis, where the arrival of the vessels and cargoes of any foreign Power is now, or shall be in future, permitted.

Italians at Tunis, and Tunisians in Italy, shall enjoy in this respect the same freedom and security as the natives, and their vessels shall not be subjected to tonnage, lighthouse, port, pilotage, quarantine, and other dues higher than or different from those to which the national vessels are subject.

Italian ships of war shall be received treated, in the waters and the ports of the Regency of Tunis, in the same manner as the ships of war of the most respected and privileged Power.

The treatment of the most favoured

foreign nation is assured by way of reciprocity to Tunisian ships of war in the waters and the ports of Italy.

III. In carrying on the port to port and coasting trade the subjects or citizens of both the Contracting Parties shall be respectively treated as the natives.

That is, the vessels of each of the two Parties may take in or unload a portion of their cargo in a port or territory of the other, and complete in the first case their cargo for abroad, or unload, in the second case, the remainder of their cargo, coming from abroad, in one or more ports of the same territory, and they may, likewise, make up their cargo in one or more ports of the other State, and unload it in one or more ports of the same State, without having, in any case, to ask any permission of the local authorities, or to pay dues higher than or different from those to which the national vessels are subject.

IV. The following shall be entirely exempt from tonnage and clearance dues in the respective ports:

1. Ships which having entered in ballast also leave in ballast.

2. Ships which, on passing from a port of one of the two States, to one or more ports of the same State, whether to dispose there of the whole or part of their cargo, or to take in or complete their cargo, shall prove that they have already paid the above-mentioned dues.

3. Ships which, having entered a port with a cargo, whether voluntarily or under stress, shall leave it without engaging in commercial operations.

In the case of entry under stress, the loading and reloading of the goods for the repair of the ship, the transhipment to another vessel in case of the unseaworthiness of the first, the necessary expenses of provisions for the crew, and the sale of the damaged goods when the Custom-house authorities have given permission, and the said goods are not intended for home consumption, shall not be considered as commercial operations.

V. In all the territories and dominions of one of the two States, the vessels of the other shall be allowed to complete their crews to enable them to continue their voyage with sailors engaged in the country,

provided that the local regulations be observed and that the engagement be voluntary.

If a Tunisian vessel should wish to complete its crew in the ports of its own country, or in those of a third Power, with sailors who are Italian subjects, it can only do so after having obtained permission in writing from the Consular Agent of His Majesty the King of Italy.

VI. If a ship of one of the two Contracting Parties should be wrecked, run aground, or suffer damage on the coast or anywhere else within the jurisdiction of the other Party, the respective citizens shall receive for themselves and for their vessels, effects, and merchandise, the same assistance from the local authority as would be afforded to the inhabitants of the country where the accident occurs.

The operations relative to the salvage of Italian vessels shall, however, be directed by the Consular Agents of His Majesty the King of Italy, and for that purpose the authorities of the Regency of Tunis are to give notice of the accident as soon as possible to the said Agents, and to confine their intervention to the preservation of order and the protection of the interests of those engaged in the salvage, if they do not belong to the shipwrecked crews, and to secure the observation of the regulations concerning the entry and issue of the goods saved.

VII. Ships, merchandise, and effects belonging to the citizens of one of the Contracting Parties, which may be taken by pirates, whether within the limits of the respective jurisdiction, or in the territorial waters of the other State, or on the high seas, and be brought to or found in the ports, rivers, on the coasts, or in the dominions of the other Party, shall be given up to their owners on payment only of the expenses incurred in retaking them.

In these cases the action of recovery must be brought within the space of two years before the Courts by the interested parties, who may for that purpose be represented by special advocates, or by the Consuls of their nation.

VIII. The subjects and citizens of each of the Contracting Parties may reciprocally enter with full freedom any part of the respective territories, reside there, travel, sell, and buy, trade by wholesale and retail, hire and hold warehouses and shops, send away goods and money, receive consignments, both from inland and abroad, conduct their affairs themselves, and present their own declarations at the Custom-houses, or, in the course of their business, get the assistance of whomsoever they please under the name of commissioners, factors, agents, consignees, interpreters, or any other, as well for the acquisition and for the sale of their effects, property, and merchandise, as for the loading unloading, and clearance of their vessels; they shall also have to the right of exercising those functions on account of their countrymen, or of foreigners, or of natives of the country, and they shall enjoy, in fine, the fullest freedom in fixing the price of the goods which they may intend to sell or to buy. It is understood, however, that in all this they must conform to the laws and regulations of the country, in so far as they are not contrary to the freedom of commerce stipulated in this Article; and they must be subject to all the taxes which are paid by the natives or to those which the most privileged foreigners pay, in case the latter should be less onerous than those paid by the natives.

IX. The citizens of each of the two Contracting States may export from the territory of the other the articles, commodities, and merchandise produced by the soil and the industry of the country, without asking permission from any local authority, and without paying higher Customs or dues than those paid for the exportation of the same articles to the foreign country most favoured in this respect, and by vessels under the national flag.

In like manner they may import any article, commodity, or merchandise produced by the soil and the industry of the other State, without paying higher Customs or dues than those imposed on the similar goods coming from the most favoured State, and under the national flag.

The same freedom shall be granted for transit.

The payment of the Customs duties on importation at the frontier of the Regency of Tunis shall free the goods from any internal commercial tax. The same exemption shall be granted to goods intended for exportation. The Government of His Most Serene Highness the Bey undertakes not to increase, in regard to Italy, the present Customs duties on importation and the maritime dues, without having come to an understanding with the Italian Government on the subject; and it also promises not to subject the exportation, importation, and commerce of goods and articles of any kind to prohibitions or monopolies, excepting only arms and munitions of war, and reserving the monopolies of the mint, of salt, and of tobacco. The Italian Government, on its part, undertakes not to lay any prohibition on the importation into and the exportation from Italy of any goods, excepting such as are provided for by the existing laws and regulations.

His Most Serene Highness the Bey of Tunis reserves to himself, however, the right of forbidding, in case of necessity, and as a general measure of public service, the exportation of grain, barley, and other cereals from his States; but in this case, in so far as Italian commerce is concerned, His Majesty's Agent or Consul-General must have 3 months' notice before such a measure comes into operation.

X. Every right of deposit and any permission and drawback of duty which may be granted in the territory of one of the two Contracting Parties on the importation or exportation of any article, shall be likewise granted to the articles of the same nature produced by the soil or the industry of the other Contracting Party, and to the importation and exportation of the products themselves.

XI. The Contracting Parties agree to appoint Commissioners for the purpose of establishing by common agreement the average value of the goods of every kind produced by the soil and the industry of Italy and imported into the States of His Most Serene Highness the Bey of Tunis, as well as of articles of every kind produced by the soil and the industry of the Regency of Tunis, which Italian merchants obtain from the Tunisian territory for importation into Italy and other places.

The tariff of prices shall remain in force for 7 years, reckoned from the day of the promulgation thereof; but if, during the 7th year, neither of the Parties shall have demanded the revision of the tariff, it shall continue in force for 7 years longer, and so on for every successive period of 7 years.

In case of disagreement between the Custom-House and the merchant as to the price to be put upon goods which are to pass the frontier of the Regency of Tunis, the merchant may pay the duty thereon in the most equitable manner. If the merchant cannot or will not exercise this right, the Custom-House shall have power to take the goods for itself, paying for them the price put on them by the merchant, with an addition of 5 per cent.

In default of those two methods of settling the difficulty, a jury shall be formed, composed of two merchants, one chosen by His Most Serene Highness the Bey and the other by the Consul-General, who shall decide the question as arbitrators in the shortest possible time. If the votes of the two arbitrators be different, they shall nominate a third, also a merchant, whose judgment shall be decisive.

XII. The Government of Tunis is to consider as Italian vessels, and the Italian Government as Tunisian vessels, those which shall navigate under the respective flag, and shall be furnished with the ship letters and other documents required by the laws of the respective States for vouching the nationality of merchant vessels.

XIII. Those who shall have retained Italian or Tunisian nationality in accordance with the laws of their country, shall be considered as Italian citizens at Tunis, and as Tunisians in Italy.

Italian citizens who may enter the service of the Tunisian Government, with the permission of their own Government, shall not lose their original citizenship nor the protection of the Italian Government and Consulate.

XIV. The citizens of each of the Contracting States shall enjoy in the territory of the other the most constant protection and security, and they shall enjoy, in this respect, the same rights and privileges as are or shall be granted to the natives, being liable to the conditions, taxes, and other burdens imposed on the latter, saving the provision at the end of Article VIII.

Nevertheless they shall be exempt, in the States of the other Party, from obligatory military service, either in the army or navy, in the national guard or in the militia; they shall also be exempt from every judicial and municipal office, as well as from every contribution in money or in kind imposed as a charge instead of personal service.

No innovation is made in regard to the protection and guardianship exercised by the Italian Consul in Tunis over his own fellow-countrymen, nor in regard to the superior rights, immunities, or privileges, which the latter enjoy in virtue of the Treaties, laws and usages.

The most extended and complete protection shall be secured by the Tunisian Government to the exercise of any worship professed by the Italian citizens.

XV. The citizens of each of the two Contracting Parties may exercise in the States of the other any kind of art, profession, and industry, open workshops and manufactories, and introduce machines moved by steam or any other motive power, without being liable to other formalities, or to taxes different from or higher than those which the general laws and regulations require from the natives.

The buildings of the workshops and their appurtenances, being immovable property, shall be subject in the Regency of Tunis to the stipulations of the present Treaty relative to such property in general.

The officers of the Tunisian Government, on a previous written request from the Minister for Foreign Affairs of His Most Serene Highness the Bey, or from the President of the Municipal Council, to the Consul-General or, in his absence, to the person acting for him, may visit the manufactory and make all necessary investigations to ascertain any infractions of the general or municipal laws and regulations respecting salubrity, police, finance, or other matters, and report them to the Government of His Most Serene Highness the Bey, which may take the necessary measures to put an end to the irregularities complained of, and to inflict the penalties imposed by the laws in a legal manner and by competent judges; but in no case can the lawful exercise of the manufacturing industry, for which the building is intended, be hindered, curtailed, or suspended.

XVI. Each of the two Contracting Parties undertakes not to grant in its own State any monopoly, indemnity, or privilege, properly so called, to the injury of the industry, the commerce, and the flag of the citizens of the other.

The provisions of this Article do not extend to the privileges for the articles of which the trade belongs to the two respective Governments, nor to patents of invention.

XVII. With regard to the fishery trade, the Government of Tunis recognizes the right of the Italians to exercise it in the waters and ports, and on the coasts of the Regency, without the necessity of asking leave from the authorities of the country, and without being liable to other dues and taxes besides those paid by the native fishermen.

The Italian Government, on its part, undertakes to allow Tunisian vessels to fish in the waters and ports, and on the coasts of the Kingdom of Italy, to the same extent and on the same conditions as such a right shall hereafter be conceded to the most favoured nation.

XVIII. The citizens of each of the two Contracting Parties may freely establish, in the States of the other, commercial, industrial, and banking societies, mutual and participating associations, and any other kind of partnership, among themselves or with Tunisian subjects, or subjects of a third Power, provided that their aims be lawful, and that they be subject to the laws in force in the country where they are established.

Nevertheless, joint stock societies, whose capital is divided into nominal shares, or shares to bearer, and anonymous societies, cannot be established in the respective territories without the sanction of the local Government.

XIX. Tunisian subjects in Italy are admitted, without condition or restriction of any kind, and wherever they may reside, to the enjoyment of civil rights, in the same way as the Italians, according to the rules of the civil code, and the other laws in force in Italy. The same treatment shall be observed in the territory of the Regency of Tunis in regard to the Italians, whether they reside there or elsewhere, in consequence whereof they shall be admitted in the Regency of Tunis, to the enjoyment of the same civil rights as the Tunisians, in so far as this may be compatible with their personal condition, and with the prohibitive laws of their country; therefore they may acquire and possess, in the same manner as the natives, houses, lands, olive plantations, and any kind of immovable property, as well as movable, self-moving, and any other kind of property. The competent local authorities shall be authorised, on demand of the person acquiring the property, to verify the titles of acquisition, and to transfer the estates to the name of the new proprietor, according to the usages of the country, so as to give the contract the validity required by the law.

They may likewise cede the property, and let it on lease, and in general dispose of it by agreement between living persons, or by last will, and transmit it to their heirs, without other limitation than that arising from the prohibition to cede or to lease landed property to foreigners who have not, by diplomatic Convention, by law, or by custom, the right of acquiring real estates in the Regency of Tunis. And in order to prevent any infringement of that prohibition, as well as to avoid any dispute or litigation that might arise therefrom, it is agreed that, in every case of sale or transfer of landed property by an Italian subject to a foreign subject, the deed of transfer must be furnished with the seals of the competent local authorities.

With regard to immovable property situated in the Regency of Tunis, Italians must submit to the laws and imposts, and to the jurisdiction of the local magistrates, saving the declarations or exceptions contained in the following Articles:

XX. Immovable property possessed in the Regency of Tunis by Italian citizens is, like movable property, inviolable, saving only the right of expropriation for public utility.

The exercise of the right of expropriation shall be subject to the following conditions;

1. The Decree declaring the public utility for which the expropriation has become necessary, must emanate from His Most Serene Highness the Bey, and be communicated to the Italian Representative.

2. Articles XI and XII of the municipal law of Tunis are to serve as the rule for effecting the expropriation, and liquidating the indemnity.

3. The indemnity must be wholly paid to the proprietor before the act of expropriation can be carried into execution.

4. If the Decree of His Most Serene Highness the Bey, which sepecifies the object of public utility for which the expropriation has been made, should not be put in execution at the expiration of a year after its date, the proprietor of the immovable property shall have a right to recover it on reimbursing the whole amount of the indemnity received.

XXI. The assimilation with the natives in matter of land-taxes shall not exclude Italian owners, who may demand it, from the right of discharging the tax upon the lands by an annual payment in money, corresponding to 40 Tunisian piastres for every "mescia," cultivated or not, computed at 10 hectares.

The owners of olive plantations shall have the same right, with the difference only that the amount of the annual tax shall be fixed for them on an equality with that of the impost now laid upon olive plantations of the coast.

XXII. Every question relative to immovable property between an Italian and a Tunisian shall be brought before the local tribunals, in conformity with the usages and laws of the country; but the summons to court cannot be transmitted excepting through the medium and on the order of the Italian Consul, who must intervene personally, or by means of a delegate, in the proceedings in the case, on pain of nullity of the judgment.

The condemned party shall have a right to appeal to the competent magistrates, and finally to His Most Serene Highness the Bey.

The definitive decision shall be carried into execution by the Italian authority, if the defeated party is an Italian, and by the local authority, if the defeated party is a Tunisian.

But if the dispute should arise between two Italians, or between an Italian and a subject of a third Power, the party that is summoned before the local magistrate shall have the right to have the case taken before the respective Consular authority, to be tried there in the ordinary way.

The laws to be applied for the decision of the case, if the dispute is to be resolved by the local tribunals and authorities, shall be those of the country, unless the question be to establish the personal state and capacity of the Italian party, or other matters for which it may be necessary to have recourse to other laws, in accordance with the commonly accepted rules and distinctions of private international law.

Donations and successions, even though the object of them be immovable property, shall be regulated in conformity with the Italian or Tunisian laws, according as the donor or the deceased may belong to either nation, saving in every case the prohibition to transmit immovable property to foreigners who are incapable of possessing it in the Regency of Tunis.

XXIII. The right appertaining to the Italian Consul to interpose in the administration of the estate of his deceased countrymen, when the heir or his attorney is not present, or is incapacitated, or [when] there is no testamentary executor at hand, the right of taking cognisance in his countrymen's insolvencies, and all the rights of voluntary jurisdiction attributed by the Italian laws, by Conventions and by usages, to the Consul and the Consular Tribunal, are maintained to their full extent, and are to embrace every kind of property whatever, not excluding immovable property possessed in the Regency of Tunis.

XXIV. If any doubt should arise as to the interpretation, or as to the application of any of the Articles of this Treaty, or of the preceding Treaties mentioned in Article I, it is agreed that at Tunis the interpretation most favourable to Italian citizens is to be adopted, and in Italy that most favourable to the Tunisians.

XXV. The present Treaty shall remain in force for 28 years, to be reckoned from the day of the exchange of the ratifications; but if it should not be denounced by one of the two High Contracting Parties 12 months before that term, it shall be understood as renewed for an equal time. Nevertheless, His Majesty the King of Italy and His Most Serene Highness the Bey of Tunis reserve to themselves the right of proposing, at the end of every 7 years, the modifications suggested by experience.

XXVI. The present Treaty, composed of 26 Articles, shall be ratified by His Majesty the King of Italy and by His Most Serene

Highness the Bey, possessor of the Regency of Tunis, in the manner indicated by the laws and the usages of the two countries; and the ratifications shall be exchanged at the Goletta, or at the Bardo, in the term of 3 months from the day of the signature, or even sooner if possible. . . .

121. LORD CLARENDON'S FORMULA OF THE BRITISH POSITION ON THE BAHRAYN ISLANDS
29 April 1869

[Great Britain, Public Record Office, F.O. 248/251]

"This is another instance of the evils of divided authority in the Persia Gulf," observed Sir John W. Kaye, secretary of the Political and Secret Department in the India Office, in December 1868, "and I would most strenuously recommend that something should be done to put an end to the conflicts of authority which are so frequently embarrassing to Her Majesty's Government" (cited by Kelly, *Britain and the Persian Gulf*, p. 676). The instance was the latest quarrel between Persia and Britain over the Bahrayn Islands. As the islands fell increasingly under British influence in the nineteenth century, Persia protested to Britain against its engagements with the Arab shaykhs of the archipelago, to which the shahdom laid claim. The divided authority, over which Kaye mourned, arose from the fact that the Foreign Office in London had handled relations with Persia ever since 1809—except in 1823-35 and 1858-59, when the East India Company and later the India Office temporarily took over—while the India Office (and the government of India) framed policy on the Persian Gulf. The fact that Persia fell within the jurisdiction of the Foreign Office, we can see in retrospect, reduced the likelihood of an attempt by Britain to absorb the shahdom, for disputes arose within the British government whenever Persia opposed British-Indian expansionist policy on the gulf; the Foreign Office, with its international perspective, responded with greater sensitivity to the Persian position than did the India Office, with its regional perspective. The British-Indian replacement in September 1868 of the Bahrayni shaykh Muhammad Al Khalifah by his brother 'Ali precipitated the latest dispute within the British government and between Britain and Persia. The deposed shaykh had violated his convention with Britain of 31 May 1861 (text in Aitchison, *Collection of Treaties . . . relating to India* [5th ed.], 11: 234-36) under which he had pledged (art. 2) "to abstain from all maritime aggressions of every description, from the prosecution of war, piracy, and slavery by sea, so long as I receive the support of the British Government in the maintenance of the security of my own possessions against similar aggressions directed against them by the Chiefs and tribes of this Gulf." Trying to wheedle out of Whitehall an acknowledgment of Persian possession of Bahrayn, the Persian foreign minister protested against the forcible change of its rulers as an infringement of Persian sovereignty. In reply, Foreign Secretary Lord Clarendon articulated the position of the British government in a note addressed to General Hajji Muhsin Khan, the Persian chargé d'affaires in London.

Lord Clarendon's original draft contained a marginal note, presumably by one of his aides, which stated, "This draft seems to me to go beyond the views of the India Office as expressed in their letter, and also to invite the Shah to set on foot a Persian naval force in the Gulph which he wishes to do, but of which the India Council [?] and the Admiralty I believe both dislike the idea." In later protests to Britain, the Persian government continued to refer to the Clarendon note as constituting a statement of British recognition of Persian sovereignty over Bahrayn. Britain placed precisely the reverse construction on the Clarendon formula. Kelly, op. cit., pp. 672–85, and his "Persian Claim to Bahrayn"; Adamiyat, *Bahrein Islands*, chap. 5; Tadjbakhche, *La question des îles Bahrein*; Khadduri "Iran's Claims to . . . Bahrayn"; Faroughy, *Bahrein Islands*, pp. 73–93; Rawlinson, *England and Russia in the East*, pp. 108–10; Esmaili, *Le Golfe Persique*, chaps. 5–7.

With reference to my Note of the 16th instant in which I acknowledged the receipt of your Note of the 13th enclosing two Letters from the Sheikh of Bahrein, I have now the honour to state to you that I have considered in communication with Her Majesty's Secretary of State for India, the whole question of the position of the Shikh of Bahrein, and I avail myself of this opportunity to make known to you the views of Her Majesty's Government on the subject.

The British Government readily admit that the Government of the Shah has protested against the Persian right of sovereignty over Bahrein being ignored by the British Authorities; and they have given due consideration to that Protest. But it is the fact, as yourself and the Government of the Shah are undoubtedly aware, that the Sheikhs of Bahrein have at different periods entered directly into engagements with the British Government; and I beg to assure you that the British Government hold the Sheikhs to these engagements solely for the purposes of preventing piracy and Slave Trade, and of maintaining the police of the Gulf. If the Persian Government are prepared to keep a sufficient force in the Gulf for these purposes, this country would be relieved of a troublesome and costly duty, but if the Shah is not prepared to undertake these duties, Her Majesty's Government cannot suppose His Majesty would wish that in those waters disorder and crimes should be encouraged by impunity.

I need scarcely assure you of the friendly feelings entertained by Her Majesty's Government towards Persia, and their desire on all occasions to meet as far as possible the wishes of the Shah; and in regard to this question I have the honour to state to you that whenever it is practicable to do so, Her Majesty's Government will cause the Persian Government to be informed beforehand of any measures of coercion against himself which the conduct of the Sheikh of Bahrein may have rendered necessary. But the British Government cannot consent to debar its officers, to whom the superintendence of the Police of the Persian Gulf is entrusted, from the exercise of the right of punishing by prompt measures any violation of treaty engagements [with] the Sheikh of Bahrein, on occasions when a reference to the Court of Teheran would be attended with embarrassing delays which might endanger the present peace of the Gulf—but whenever such a necessity shall arise a full communication respecting it shall be made to the Persian Government.

122. BEYLICAL DECREE ESTABLISHING A FINANCIAL
COMMISSION IN TUNISIA
5 July 1869

[Translated from the French text in France, Ministère des Affaires Etrangères, *Documents diplomatiques*, no. 13, pp. 161–63]

Once the garrison had been transformed into a regency, Tunis experienced much of what Egypt and the Ottoman Empire had earlier gone through. Ahmad Bey (1837–55) fended off efforts by the Sublime Porte to reimpose direct rule on the regency by attempting to create a Europeanized army and a supporting Europeanized industry. However, with meager resources and limited opportunities, Ahmad Bey's accomplishments failed in comparison with those in Egypt of Mehmet 'Ali, who had inspired Tunisian modernization. For identical reasons in both cases, the modernizing Islamic quasi-sovereign rulers received technical aid from France, which lost no chance to enlarge its influence in North Africa, and political opposition from Britain, which aimed to enlarge its influence by upholding the claims of an allied Ottoman Empire. The pattern of European interests in Tunis became more complex after 1860 because of Italy's entry into the competition. In 1857 Muhammad Bey (1855–59), with British-French encouragement, enacted by decree a fundamental law along the lines of the Ottoman reform decree of the preceding year (Doc. 104), assuring all Tunisians, whether Muslims or Jews, equality, religious liberty, and commercial freedom and permitting foreigners to own land and to engage in all economic pursuits. To help finance governmental reorganization, the bey introduced an annual poll tax, or *majbah*, of thirty-six piasters for all adult males. The next bey, Muhammad al-Sadiq (1859–82), an even more zealous reformer, promulgated in April 1861 a Europeanized constitution, the first in any Islamic state, providing for a legislative council and regular law courts. He also sponsored public works such as the restoration of a Carthaginian aqueduct and the paving of the first road in the regency from Tunis to Bardo, a distance of four kilometers; he also built lavish premises at Tunisian expense for the French and British agents and consuls general. When profligate spending at state expense by many of the bey's relatives was added to these outlays at inflated prices, borrowing became the only way to balance the budget. By 1862 the Bey and his finance minister, or *khaznadar*, Mustafa, who lined his own pockets, had exhausted the possibilities of raising local loans. In the following year the bey fell into the hands of foreign money sharks, who with Mustafa Khaznadar's cooperation, floated a loan with the banking firm of Emile Erlanger in Paris on disastrous terms. For an effective loan of 37.8 million francs, Muhammad al-Sadiq Bey undertook to repay more than 65 million francs. As a stopgap to defray the costs of administration, Mustafa Khaznadar had already suspended payment of salaries to civil servants and army officers. Then, in September 1863, the rate of the poll tax, which had been pledged to redeem the loan, was doubled, and it was imposed on all subjects, including those previously exempt (civil servants, soldiers, students, 'ulama, and Jews as well as residents of the major towns). This was a proximate cause of the short-lived rebellion of 1864 (Doc. 120), which added to the financial crisis. Further loans from Erlanger were raised in 1865 and 1867, each succeeding loan used largely to meet payments on earlier ones. In 1867, French diplomats had begun to think of a French solution to the Tunisian problem, either annexing it to Algeria or creating a protectorate or, as the very least, compelling the bey through armed intervention to honor his financial commitments. In 1868 the French foreign minister, the marquis de Moustier, proposed a plan for a foreign debt commission, composed primarily of French bankers. However, on vigorous protest from Italy and Britian, it was agreed to internationalize the commission along the lines laid down in the bey's decree, reproduced below. Thus, Tunisia became the first of the Islamic states to surrender external fiscal sovereignty to an international commission; it was followed in 1876 by Egypt and five years later by the Ottoman Empire. Ganiage, *Les origines du protectorat français en Tunisie*, chaps. 1–7; Langer, "European Powers and the French Occupation of Tunis"; Woolf, *Empire and Commerce in Africa*, pt. 2, chap. 3; Estournelles de Constant, *La politique française en Tunisie*, pt. 1, chaps. 2–3; Staley, *War and the Private Investor*, chap. 12; Safwat, *Tunis and the Great Powers*, chap. 1.

Praise God. May God's prayer be [recited] for our Lord and Master Muhammad, for his family, for his companions, and greetings to him.

From the servant who entrusts himself and leaves the care of his destiny to God Glorified, al-Mushir Muhammad al-Sadiq, Pasha-Bey, possessor of the Kingdom of Tunis, may God protect him.

To all those who may see these presents, greetings!

It has seemed fitting to us in the interest of the finances of our Kingdom, in that of our subjects, and of commerce, to establish a Financial Commission, based on the plan of the decree of 4 April of last year, confirmed by another decree of ours, of the following 29 May, and we have settled on the following:

ART. 1. The Commission established by our decree of 4 April 1868 shall meet in our capital within one month of the date of the present decree.

ART. 2. The above-mentioned Commission is divided into two separate committees: an Executive Committee and a Control Committee.

ART. 3. The Executive Committee shall be composed in the following manner: two officials of our government named by ourself, and a French inspector of finances also named by ourself and previously nominated by the government of His Majesty the Emperor [of France].

ART. 4. The Executive Committee is instructed to ascertain the actual state of the several credits constituting the debt of the Kingdom and the resources with which our government should repay it.

ART. 5. The Executive Committee shall keep a register in which to enter all debts contracted outside the Kingdom and within it, consisting of treasury *tezkeres* [notes] and bonds of the loan of 1863 and that of 1865. As for the debts that are not controlled by contracts, the bearers of the claims must present themselves within two months, and the Executive Committee shall see that a notice to this effect is published in Tunisian and European newspapers.

ART. 6. The Minister of Finance shall facilitate the examination by the Executive Committee of all authenticated documents of receipts and expenditures.

ART. 7. After comparing the budget of receipts and the budget of expenditures, increased by the amounts of the debt, the Executive Committee shall seek ways of dividing the public revenues equitably, making allowance for a just share for all interests. It shall also draw up a list of revenues which might be added to the total of the guarantees already given to the creditors.

ART. 8. The Executive Committee shall make all arrangements regarding the general debt and shall give us all the necessary and most complete assistance to ensure that the measures are carried out.—

ART. 9. The Executive Committee shall

collect all the revenues of the Kingdom, without exception. Our government may not issue treasury tezkeres, under any form whatsoever, without the prior consent of the said Committee, duly authorized by the Control Committee. If the government must contract a [new] loan, it may not do so without the approval of the two committees. All tezkeres issued in the sum appropriated by the [Financial] Commission for the expenses of the government shall be written in the name of the Commission and shall bear the endorsement of the Executive Committee. These tezkeres must not exceed the amount fixed in the budget of expenditures.

ART. 10. The Control Committee is composed in the following manner: two French members, representing the bearers of the bonds of the year 1863 and the year 1865; two English members and two Italian members representing bearers of claims of the internal debt. Each of the delegates will receive his mandate from the bearers of the claims of the two loans and the bearers of the claims to the funding [of the debts] of our Kingdom. They shall receive notice from us through the Executive Committee.

ART. 11. The Control Committee must be informed of all transactions of the Executive Committee; it is instructed to verify and approve them, wherever necessary. This approval is required to execute measures of general interest decided by the Executive Committee.

ART. 12. We order our Prime Minister to execute the contents of the above eleven articles. We shall name the two officials, and we request [the appointment] as soon as possible [of] the French inspector of finances, in accordance with Article 3 of the present decree. . . .

123. THE CREMIEUX DECREE: CONFERRAL OF FRENCH CITIZENSHIP ON ALGERIAN JEWS
24 October 1870–7 October 1871

[Translated from the French texts in République Française, Gouvernement de la Défense Nationale, *Bulletin des Lois*, 12th ser., 1: 109 (Crémieux decree) and 3: 344–45 (provisional reinstatement); and Assemblée Nationale, *Annales*, 4 (12 July-18 August 1871), annex 412, pp. 90–91 (Lambrecht proposal)]

The *sénatus-consulte* of 14 July 1865 (Doc. 117) declared native Muslims and Jews in Algeria French subjects and invited them to become French citizens, provided they agreed to be bound by French civil law. This offer, however, was taken up by only a handful by 1870—fewer than two hundred Muslims and a little more than three hundred Jews. Of the latter, slightly more than half came from Tunisia and Morocco. The Algerian Jews, who constituted the only non-Muslim native community in Algeria found patrons in the Jewish Consistory of Paris and in the person of Adolphe Crémieux (1796–1880), a prominent lawyer, politician, deputy, and crusader in the movement for sponsoring the political emancipation of Jews wherever they suffered civil and political disabilities. Immediately after the downfall of the Second Empire early in September 1870, following the defeat of the French army at Sédan and the capitulation of Napoleon III, a provisional Government of National Defense was formed. When German armies invested Paris in mid-September, the government sent a delegation to Tours, headed by Crémieux, then, minister of justice, to organize resistance in the provinces. At Tours, Crémieux assumed responsibility for Algerian affairs and took steps to end military rule by transferring from the Ministry of War to the Ministry of the Interior in Paris responsibility for governing the dependency; to provide for full legal and political integration of Algeria into mainland France; to divide the dependency into three departments, each under a prefect and each represented in the Assembly in Paris by elected deputies; and to modify the judicial regime by the introduction of assize courts and the jury system. As a leader in Jewish communal affairs and a patron of the Jews of Algeria, Crémieux included a decree, reproduced below, for the obligatory mass enfranchisement of all members of the Jewish consistories of the departments of Algiers (11,000), Constantine (8,000), and Oran (14,000), in whose creation in the 1840s he had played a major role. That the Algerian Jews were not ready for instant enfranchisement had been confirmed in April 1869 at a countrywide conference called expressly to consider the subject. There the Oran consistory voted against the proposal; and even in the two others there was opposition to acceptance of French civil law for precisely the same reason given by the Muslims, since in orthodox Judaism matters of personal status are regulated by rabbinical law. The French settlers welcomed the civilianization of the governing system and the legal-political integration of Algeria into the metropole. The remaining Europeans (Spaniards, Italians, and Maltese, in order of size), almost as numerous as the French immigrants, may have had reservations about the administrative reorganization because it was introduced at the height of the French-Prussian War (19 July 1870-1 March 1871), when France's massive defeat was already recognized and the expectation that the transfer of Algeria's political ownership might be part of the price for peace was not wholly unreasonable. But none of the European immigrants, whether from France or elsewhere, paid immediate attention to the decree on the group naturalization of the Jews. Only later, in the 1880s and 1890s, did the act stir up controversy among them, as European radicals of the Right became devotees of a vigorous anti-Jewish movement in Algeria. For the Muslims, however, the group enfranchisement seemed from the outset discriminatory. Under Muslim rule, before the advent of the French, the native Jews had been a tolerated minority, with second-class social and political status. The resentment and anger of Muslims arose, not from the denial to them of the right of enfranchisement, since very few had sought that right under the 1865 decree, but from the fact that the group naturalization suddenly reversed the political status of Jews and Muslims. But to go on to claim, as some French historians and observers of Algeria have done, that the Crémieux decree was the primary cause of the massive insurrection (March 1871-January 1872) in the Kabylia, the predominantly Berber mountain interior of the Algiers Department, is to ignore the degree to which the mountain tribesmen had been stirred up long before October 1870 by the French confiscatory land policies. Nevertheless, the Crémieux decree did add another irritant, and in the midst of the rebellion, headed by the powerful Muqrani family, the provisional Government of National Defense in July 1871 approved the proposal of the minister of the interior to rescind the Crémieux decree, only to reverse itself in October, in response to the vigorous reaction of Crémieux and the other leaders of the Jewish Consistory in Paris. These two documents are reproduced below along with the Crémieux decree. Martin, *Les israélites algériens* and *L' histoire de l'Algérie fran-*

çaise, pp. 157–203, 225–43; Cohen, *Les israélites de l'Algérie et le décret Crémieux*; Posener, *Adolphe Crémieux*, vol. 2, chap. 9 (in the abridged English edition, see chap. 11); Forest, *La naturalisation des juifs algériens*; Ageron, *Les algériens musulmans et la France*, 1: 583–608.

1. The Crémieux Decree, 24 October 1870

Indigenous Israelites of the departments of Algeria are declared [to be] French citizens. Consequently, their actual status and their personal status shall, from the promulgation of the present decree, be regulated by French law. All rights acquired up the this day shall remain inviolate.

Every legislative provision, sénatus-consulte, decree, regulation, or ordinance to the contrary is abolished.

2. The Lambrecht Proposal for Abrogating the Crémieux Decree, 21 July 1871

EXPLANATION OF MOTIVES

The number of Jews in the Regency of Algiers has increased substantially since the conquest; many have come from neighboring countries to place their property and persons under the guarantee of a regular government.

Moreover, they have preserved the traditional customs and institutions which have allowed their race, with one single exception, to come down through the ages without mingling with the others, and in general they in no way view themselves as forming part of the political community. Their preoccupations permit them to remain somewhat as strangers to this community and do not attach them to the country in which they reside more or less permanently. This particular situation explains why the Algerian Jews, in spite of their number, have never claimed collective naturalization. The initiative for measure has come from the French themselves.

Early in 1870, M. Emile Ollivier, then Keeper of the Seal, without preliminary instruction presented to the Council of State a draft law proposing to bestow French nationality on native Algerian Jews. The Council instituted a local inquiry, sought the opinions of Governor General Marshal [Marie Edme Patrice] de Mac-Mahon, the chiefs of the court of Algiers, the prefects, and the generals commanding divisions, and, having verified the results,

shelved the proposal whcih in any case the consistories had received more than coldly.

However, some months later, the delegation of Tours, with views useless to specify, by a measure wholly foreign to the national defense decided that "indigenous Israelites of the departments of Algeria are declared French citizens. Consequently," added the decree, "their actual status and their personal status shall, from the time of the promulgation of the present decree, be regulated by French law. All rights acquired up to this day shall remain inviolate."

The administration of Algeria had not been consulted. The officials responsible for the application sought to limit and attenuate the consequences of an act of which they disapproved. But the Arab insurrection soon demonstrated the inadequacy of these palliatives and underlined everything dangerous and impolitic in the decree of 24 October. Its abrogation was energetically demanded, under their separate titles, by the general government and the Ministry of War.

Assimilation cannot be decreed. It is achieved over time, and even in quite a short time when it is desired in the interest of the peoples on whom it is conferred. But in the case in point it was not desired or even accepted with all its consequences.

At the time of the Arab insurrection, the Jews entered military service most reluctantly. Everyone knows that in Algeria by temperament and custom the Jews, with very few exceptions, absolutely refuse effective recruitment into the ranks of our army. The few who did join refused to accommodate themselves to the daily routine of the soldier on active duty, on grounds of the violation of religious law. They had to be released all the more promptly because Muslim riflemen and tribal units could not accept the idea of shooting their Arab coreligionists with Jews in our ranks. Thus for their own reasons or because of their relations with other races, the Jews are incapable of performing military service.

Their presence as jurors in the courts is similarly ruled out. Apart from the fact that the largest number understands or speaks French only most imperfectly, it must be taken into consideration that the Arabs would never patiently bear the sight of native Jews sitting among their judges. The insurrection broke out late in January 1870 at the very moment when the Muslim peoples saw Jews serving as jurors. Only then did these people, who had not understood the implications of the theoretical declaration of 24 October, understand that they might become defendants before native Jews. If this interpretation of the facts is contested, it will be recalled that the Kalifah of al-Medjana, Si Mokrani [Muqrani], returning his cross [designating him] an officer of the *Légion d'honneur*, made it known that he preferred to die weapon in hand rather than tolerate the insult to his race in having the Jews placed above it. The conferral on the latter of the right to sit among the jurors is therefore premature and dangerous, and it was at least one of the causes of the insurrection.

From the viewpoint of the electorate, the inconveniences are no less serious. They arise from causes analogous to those that have been recorded previously.

One would not expect from the Jews votes dictated by either political considerations or the appreciation of municipal interests, as seen from the perspective of the majority of the local residents. Thus, as has already been said, they form and will continue to form a body apart, considering themselves as having been gifted with a separate existence. Consequently, under their present religious leaders, they will always bring to bear as a united group all the influence at their disposal. This state of affairs can only be serious. For example:

At Oran the French population is	8,958 souls
The Jewish population is	5,653
At Constantine, the French population is	7,887
The Jewish population is	4,396
At Tlemcen, the French population is	3,264
The Jewish population is	3,185

It is easy to see that, the Jewish votes not being spread about like those of the French, the municipal councils will be made up wholly of native Jews in their quality as Frenchmen. Alongside them, it is true, there will be foreign and Muslim councillors, since the Arabs and foreigners will always keep the number of candidates allowed them. It would therefore not be impossible for native-born Frenchmen to see themselves wholly excluded from a French municipal council.

The same result might be foreseen in the general councils that have at their disposal half of the Arab taxes, the sole resource of the departmental budgets.

Seen from the French viewpoint, this situation is bad. It is even worse from the viewpoint of the traditions, customs, and antipathies of the Muslim populations, which will never understand the relegation of 2.5 million Muslims to the rank of simple subjects, while raising 35,000 Jews to the dignity of French citizens. This inequity is intolerable. It must disappear through the retraction of political rights so imprudently conferred.

Must one on the contrary preserve the decree of 24 October by virtue of which the real status and the personal status of native Jews shall henceforth be regulated no longer by rabbinical but by French law?

We believe that the decree of the delegation of Tours should be abrogated in its entirety.

The civil status of the Jews arises from the same source as their religious status and governs them with an almost equal authority. It follows that to take it from them by a general measure represents in part an attack on their freedom of conscience. With regard to civil rights, it can assuredly occur to no one to prefer rabbinical law to French law. But, in refusing the Jews citizenship rights, it is assuredly just to leave them what pleases them most in their present condition, to know they have the right to settle according to their own traditions all matters relating to marriage, divorce, and inheritance.

Besides, here again it may be said that assimilation cannot be decreed, and that in this regard, in imposing the laws of the metropole, one is liable to create the ever dangerous conflict between custom and institutions. To avoid this conflict, it is enough to know that time and education will make the Jews seek naturalization, which must be offered them individually as a favor.

It must not be forgotten: in Algeria, this favor is still easier to obtain than in France; admission to domicile is not obligatory; seal and registration duties are reduced to one franc, and anyone who has resided in the colony for three years enjoys the right of naturalization without difficulty and expense, on the sole condition of proving his morality. It is the continuous and rational application of this liberal legislation that will gradually break up the class of native Jews and assimilate its elements into the overall French unity, while mass naturalization tends only to perpetuate the original distinctions and seems to have had no other aim than to create an instrument in the service of passions and interests against which there can be no sufficient warning.

PROPOSED LAW

Sole Article: The decree issued on 24 October 1870 by the delegation of Tours declaring the native Jews of Algeria [to be] French citizens is abrogated.

3. Provisional Reinstatement of the Crémieux Decree, 7 October 1871

ART. 1. Provisionally, and until the National Assembly has legislated on the maintenance or abrogation of the decree of 24 October 1870, Jews born in Algeria before the French occupation or since that time of parents already established in Algeria shall be considered natives and, in this capacity, shall remain registered on the electoral rolls, if they also fulfill other civil conditions.

ART. 2. Consequently, any Jew wishing to register or remain on the electoral rolls must declare, within twenty days of the promulgation of the present decree, that he has satisfied one of the conditions defined in Article 1.

ART. 3. This declaration shall be made before a justice of the peace at the Jew's place of residence. It shall take the form of either the written declaration or the verbal testimony of seven persons who have been living in Algeria for at least ten years, or any other proof that the justice of the peace may accept as conclusive.

The decision of the justice of the peace shall serve as a certificate for the Jew; he shall immediately be given a copy free of charge. If the Jew has no fixed family and first names, he shall be obliged to adopt them and declare them before the justice of the peace as a preliminary condition for the transfer of this certificate.

For each decision thus taken, a file, which shall be deposited in the town hall of the native's domicile, shall be kept in the form of police records to serve either in the compilation of electoral rolls or as an attested affidavit.

ART. 4. The Jew whose claim is not accepted by the justice of the peace may appeal within three days of the pronouncement of the decision by means of a simple request addressed to the President of the tribunal in the *arrondissement*. The President shall grant a hearing within three days of that date. The tribunal, having heard the Jew or his defense, shall make a final decision. The lodging of an appeal shall not be a bar to later proceedings.

ART. 5. Any Jew presently registered on the electoral rolls who does not carry out the formalities and satisfy the conditions required by the preceding articles shall be struck from [these rolls] and may not be reinstated until the next revision.

ART. 6. All judicial acts entered into under the present decree and in its execution shall be exempt from stamp and registration duties.

ART. 7. The convocation of electoral colleges shall not take place less than a month following the promulgation of the present decree.

ART. 8. The Ministers of Justice and the Interior and the civil Governor General of Algeria are charged, each within his own sphere of responsibility, with the execution of the present decree.

124. TREATY (LONDON) REVISING THE BLACK SEA CLAUSES OF THE TREATY OF PARIS (1856): THE EUROPEAN POWERS AND THE OTTOMAN EMPIRE
1/13 March 1871

(Ratifications exchanged, London, 15 May 1871; formally superseded, 6 August 1924)
[Great Britain, *Parliamentary Papers, 1871*, 72: 169–71]

Tsar Alexander II (1855–81) viewed the clauses of the treaty of Paris (Doc. 105) calling for the neutralization of the Black Sea as "a blot on his reign." At the height of the French-Prussian War, when France was preoccupied and thus could not join England in opposition, the tsar, on 31 October and 1 November 1870, issued two notes (texts in Hertslet, *Map of Europe by Treaty*, 3: 1892–97), declaring that the arrangement placed Russia at a distinct disadvantage as against the other signatories. He therefore deemed "himself both entitled and obliged to denounce to His Majesty the Sultan the Special and Additional Covention appended to the said Treaty, which fixes the number and size of the Vessels of War which the two Powers bordering on the Black Sea shall keep in that Sea." The Russian notes disturbed the British, who, while deploring the unilateral action and upholding the principle of the sanctity of treaties, nevertheless accepted Bismarck's proposal that the original signatories confer for the purpose of revising the 1856 arrangement (British text, ibid., 1898–1900). The conference, held in London (17 January–13 March 1871), produced a treaty annulling the neuralization clauses adopted in Paris and enlarging the sultan's discretionary power to admit through the straits naval vessels of friendly governments. Appended to the treaty was a Russian-Ottoman convention expressly abrogating their earlier convention (1856) which had limited the number and force of Russian and Ottoman warships in the Black Sea (Doc. 105, Sec. 3). The 1871 convention and the articles in the principal treaty relating to the Danube are omitted below. Mosse, "End of the Crimean System"; Rheindorf, *Die Schwarze-Meer(Pontus)-Frage*; Mertz, *Die Schwarze Meer-Konferenz*; Shotwell and Deák, *Turkey at the Straits*, chap. 6; Mischef, *La Mer Noire*, chap. 7; Goriainow, *Le Bosphore et les Dardanelles*, chap. 12; Phillipson and Buxton, *Question of the Bosphorus and Dardanelles*, pt. 2, chap. 6.

ART. I. Articles XI, XIII, and XIV of the Treaty of Paris of March 30, 1856, as well as the special Convention concluded between Russia and the Sublime Porte, and annexed to the said Article XIV, are abrogated, and replaced by the following Article.

ART. II. The principle of the closing of the Straits of the Dardanelles and the Bosphorus, such as it has been established by the separate Convention of March 30, 1856, is maintained, with power to His Imperial Majesty the Sultan to open the said Straits in time of peace to the vessels of war of friendly and allied Powers, in case the Sublime Porte should judge it necessary in order to secure the execution of the stipulations of the Treaty of Paris of March 30, 1856.

ART. III. The Black Sea remains open, as heretofore, to the mercantile marine of all nations. . . .

ART. VIII. The High Contracting Parties renew and confirm all the stipulations of the Treaty of March 30, 1856, as well as of its annexes, which are not annulled or modified by the present Treaty.

125. OTTOMAN *FERMAN* ENLARGING THE POWERS OF THE
BEY OF TUNIS
23 October 1871

[Translated from the French text in *British and Foreign State Papers*, 61: 104–06]

The doctrine of upholding the territorial integrity and political sovereignty of the Ottoman Empire, which Palmerston resurrected late in the 1830s, remained consistent principle of Britain's Mediterranean policy for four decades. Although the doctrine informed Britain's policies toward Tunisia at the time, the Foreign Office was unable to win the European Concert's approval of its applicability to the regency. The position of each European power turned on its interpretation of the status of the regency in relation to the Ottoman Empire. Since France, and after 1860 Italy also, aspired to take possession of Tunisia, each insisted that Ottoman claims to sovereignty had become purely nominal. Britain, however, nurturing no territorial ambitions but seeking simply to keep France and Italy out, contended that Tunisia formed an integral part of the padişah's realm; and, from the time of the Ottoman termination of the Karamanli dynasty in Tripoli in 1835 and the resumption of direct rule there by the Sublime Porte, Britain supported Ottoman efforts to replicate that policy in Tunisia. In these efforts Whitehall had to face the resistance of the beys as well as the two European powers. Muhammad al-Sadiq (1859–82) became the first bey to respond to British and Ottoman initiatives when he and his advisers recognized in the Tunisian insurrection of 1864 how narrowly their regime had escaped from the dual threat of internal and external enemies. Khayr al-Din, a trusted beylical aide and later principal minister, reached an understanding with the Sublime Porte to tighten the political and legal ties of the regency with the Ottoman Empire, while clarifying the residual autonomous powers of the bey. France and Italy raised such a diplomatic fuss, however, that this mutually accepted instrument never went into effect. The issue then lay dormant until 1871, when Italy precipitated an artificial crisis: an Italian concessionaire who had leased an estate belonging to Mustafa Khaznadar, the bey's principal financial minister, for an elaborate development scheme—including an olive oil refinery, a distillery, and a credit bank for Tunisian peasants as well as a commercial agricultural project with tenant farmers—engaged in high-handed practices and quarreled with the Tunisian agents and functionaries. When, in January 1871, the bey refused to accede to impossible demands, the Italian consul general broke relations with Tunisia and the Italian government upheld the concessionaire, who sued the regency for a sum exceeding the capitalization of the development company. Italy's diplomatic behavior in Tunisia was more immature than usual because it had the field to itself, since France was still dazed over the massive defeat by Germany and the rebellion that it had sparked in Algeria. With these two European powers immobilized, Richard Wood, the British consul general, was able to presuade the Tunisian government to reopen negotiations with the Sublime Porte. In September 1871, Khayr al-Din once again went to Istanbul, where Sultan Abdülaziz, with Muhammad al-Sadiq's approval, issued the following ferman, virtually a carbon copy of the terms framed seven years earlier. France and Italy protested loudly and refused to recognize its validity. Less than seven years later (see Dec. 144), Britain itself repudiated the policy it had strived for so long to bring into effect. Ganiage, *Les origines du protectorat français en Tunisie*, chap. 8; Raymond, "Les tentatives anglaises de pénétration économique en Tunisie"; Julien, *La question italienne en Tunisie*; Estournelles de Constant, *La politique française en Tunisie*, pt. 1, chap. 3; Cambon, *Histoire de la régence de Tunis*, chap. 9.

To our Vezir Muhammad al-Sadiq Pasha, who presently governs in Tunis, decorated with the Order of Mecidiye First Class, and the Imperial Order of Osmaniye in diamonds.

You will learn on receiving our present high imperial writ that it has come to our notice that you have not ceased to show competence and to act in the most dignified manner ever since the management of the affairs of the Eyâlet [province] of Tunis, which forms part of the realm of our hereditary Empire, was committed to you by our Sublime Imperial Authority, as it had been committed in the past to your predecessors, and that you have given equal proofs of loyalty and faithfulness to our August Sovereign Person. We hope therefore that you will continue on this path which has been marked out for you by the praiseworthy qualities which distinguish you and which have earned our approval.

We desire that you use all your energy to help the growth of the prosperity of our said Kingdom and the well-being, the happiness, and the prosperity of its inhabitants, who are dependents of our sublime government, in order that by so doing you may continue to merit the imperial goodwill and confidence which we have always shown you, and that, realizing their importance, you will express your gratitude.

Our principal aim and our real desire incline constantly toward the development of the prosperity and the guarantee of the tranquillity of this important Eyâlet which forms part of our realm as well as to the progressive establishment of solid bases which ensure confidence and order to its inhabitants; to attain this end, the [Ottoman] Imperial Government manifestly does not interrupt, because of any difficulty, the pursuit of anything that affects [the Eyâlet's] fundamental rights.

Also, regarding the request that you recently presented to our sublime government, the Eyâlet of Tunis, having as boundaries its ancient frontiers, shall continue to be committed to you with the privileges of heredity in the succession of its government, which we confirm to you and maintain under the following conditions:

Our sovereign desire being, as decreed above, the growth of the prosperity of the said Kingdom and the well-being of its inhabitants, and having seen that this Kingdom is at present in a state of [financial] difficulty because of the lack of revenue for its government and for its inhabitants and consequently moved by a feeling of mercy toward the latter, we are postponing the tribute which, because of the recognized dependence of this Eyâlet, was paid in the past to our Imperial Government under a special designation.

The said Eyâlet being an integral part of our realm, it is our benevolent sovereign intention that its governor should have the right of nomination of worthy persons to religious, military, and administrative [civil and financial] employment and the right of dismissal in conformity with law and justice; that his relations should continue as in the past with foreign powers except in political matters, that is to say, the conclusion of political and military treaties, the modification of boundaries, or other similar acts which lie within our sovereign and sacred jurisdiction.

When the seat of government falls vacant and the oldest member of your family requests a ferman from our sublime Imperial Government, this ferman will be sent to him at the same time as his nomination to the dignity of Vezir and Müşür [field marshal], as has been the practice to this day, on condition, however, that the *hutbe* [sermon and public prayer] should continue to be made in our imperial name and that coins struck in Tunis should equally be in our name. As public witness of ancient legal ties which attach the Eyâlet of Tunis to the sublime *hilâfet* [caliphate], the flag shall preserve its colors and form.

In the event of war between our empire and a foreign country, the Eyâlet of Tunis shall send a military contingent in proportion to its means, as has been the practice in the past.

Under these arrangements, the government of Tunis shall belong exclusively by hereditary descent to your family, on condition that the relations which attach the country to the sublime government shall continue to be observed on the same basis as in the past, and that the domestic administration shall conform to the commands of the glorious Seriat and the laws of justice, the necessity of which circumstance and time will bring about and which would guarantee the security, fortune, and honor of the individual.

To make manifest that which precedes, this high ferman has been issued by our Sublime Porte and invested with our imperial signature. The aim of our imperial solicitude is to improve the state of this important Eyâlet and the condition of your family, to consolidate improvement now and in the future, and to assure the means

of well-being, prosperity, and security to the different classes of the population which are dependent on us and which live under the care and protection of our justice. Our greatest and sole desire is consequently that you should employ all your efforts to attain this end.

As the fundamental and recognized condition of hereditary privilege in the government of Tunis consists in safeguarding the rights of our empire established from time immemorial over the Eyâlet of Tunis, entrusted to your loyalty, and of the continuation of that which inspires the security of its population as regards their persons, their goods, and their honor and all other general rights, these same rights must be maintained intact forever, and every incident and act that might injure them must be avoided.

In imbuing you with this idea, [we direct] you and the members of your family who may follow you by right of succession to understand the importance of this high imperial favor and to welcome it with gratitude. You must in consequence exert yourself to merit our benevolent approval by the zeal and the great efforts that you employ to put into effect the arrangements and conditions established above.

126. REUTER AND FALKENHAGEN DRAFT RAILROAD CONCESSIONS IN PERSIA
25 July 1872–17/29 October 1874

(Reuter concession, annulled by Nasir al-Din Shah, Tehran, 5 November 1873; Falkenhagen concession, as modified by the Persian Government, rejected by the concessionaire on 5 May 1875)
[Reuter concession translated from the French text in Iran, Archives of the Ministry of Foreign Affairs, Tehran; translation of the Falkenhagen concession from Great Britain, Public Record Office, F.O. 539/10, "Persia: Correspondence respecting the Reuter and Falkenhagen Concessions, 1872–75," pp. 97–101]

Most of the population of Iran is clustered in the north, cut off by high mountains and wide deserts from easy access to the Persian Gulf and the open sea, and in the north itself even from access to the inland Caspian Sea. The economic and social development of the country was thus dependent on the prior creation of a modern internal transportation system. What was therefore astonishing was not the growth of an interest in railroad construction but the long delay in its realization, for the main north-south line was not completed until 1938. Actually, the first railroad schemes for Iran originated in British India, which explored the possibility of linking the subcontinent to the Mediterranean by a line that would cut through Persia and the Ottoman Arab provinces. But none of the proposals, which first received serious attention in the 1850s, was sufficiently realistic to attract the needed capital or governmental support. Since the major part of such a line along the shortest route would have to pass through desert, and since almost all the materials would have to be imported from Europe, the costs for amortization of the investment within a reasonable period were prohibitive and the strategic interest was inadequate for a governmental guarantee. The introduction and rapid development of telegraph lines by British-Indian and Russian companies in the 1860s focused the attention of Nasir al-Din Shah and a handful of his close advisers on their own promotion of railroad development. Starting in 1866, the shah's minister in London, Mushin Khan, tried to recruit private entrepreneurs. After several false starts with Prussian and British businessmen, Muhsin Khan finally persuaded Baron Julius de Reuter, the successful German-born entrepreneur of an international telegraphic news service, to seek a global and exclusive concession for building and operating railroads, tramways, and irrigation facilities, for developing mines, and for using state forests; he was also given a first option for creating a bank in Persia. No sooner was the concessionary instrument that provided for these multiple activities signed by the Persian prime minister and Reuter's agent, than the scheme became hopelessly tangled in the shahdom's domestic and external politics. Viewing the proposal as a promoter's deal and not as a sound business venture, the British government withheld its endorsement and in effect encouraged the shah in November 1873 to repudiate the concession on the technicality that the work was not started on schedule, the delays for which the Persian government itself was largely responsible. The Russian government, which had actively supported the shah in defaulting on the agreement, then vigorously backed a more modest scheme, ostensibly framed by a retired Russian general, Adolf von Falkenhagen, for building a railroad from Julfa, on the Russian-Persian border, to Tabriz, with coal-mining rights reserved in a fifty-mile zone on each side of the projected line. At this juncture, the British government took up Reuter's cause, not because of genuine interest but as a tactic for persuading the shah to cancel the Falkenhagen concession. This it achieved, for the Persian government laid down terms unacceptable to the Russians. What the Shah and his ministerial advisers clearly wanted was railroad construction sponsored by private enterprise with European political backing, not a European political maneuver disguised as private enterprise. Issawi, *Economic History of Iran*, chap. 4; Kazemzadeh, *Russia and Britain in Persia*, chap. 2; Frechtling, "Reuter Concession in Persia"; Farman Farmayan, "Forces of Modernization in Nineteenth Century Iran"; Curzon, *Persia and the Persian Question*, vol. 1, chap. 15; Ramazani, *Foreign Policy of Iran*, chap. 4.

1. Draft of the Reuter Concession

Between the Government of His Imperial Majesty the Shah of Persia, on the one hand, and Baron Julius de Reuter, residing in London, on the other hand, the following has been agreed and determined:

ART. 1. The Government of His Imperial

Majesty the Shah by these presents authorizes the said Baron de Reuter to establish in London, under such name and statutes as he may determine, one or more societies to bring into being and manage throughout the empire the public utilities that are the object of this concession.

ART. 2. The Persian Government grants to the said Baron de Reuter and to his associates or representatives for a period of seventy years the exclusive and definitive concession for a railroad line extending from the Caspian Sea to the Persian Gulf, with exclusive and definitive right to make any branches that he may judge suitable either to link the provinces and cities in the interior of the empire or to connect the Persian lines with foreign railroads at any point whatever along the frontiers facing Europe or India.

ART. 3. The exclusive privilege is also granted to the present concessionaires to build "tramways" at all points that they may judge suitable, either to connect different centers of population or to link them with the railroads or with different enterprises of the company. The company shall enjoy, for the establishment and exploitation of these tramways, the privileges granted to the railroads (in Art. 4, 5, and 6).

ART. 4. Within the state's domain, the government grants to the concessionaires gratis all the lands necessary for the construction and working of a double-track line, sidings, stations, workers' houses, factories, railroad yards, and offices. For lands belonging to individuals, the company must arrive at a mutual agreement with the owners; but the government shall employ all its means to enable [the company] to obtain [such lands] at the price prevailing in the country, using if necessary the right of expropriation by force. Aside from the normal size of the track, the government grants the company gratis, along the length and on each side of the line, thirty meters of land taken from undeveloped and uncultivated state lands. If, outside the most important cities and villages where it is in the interest of the company to build stations, the necessities of the line require the building of stations at several isolated and uncultivated points, the government shall grant to the company gratis

an area of four square kilometers at those places designated [by the company] for these stations, in order to ensure comfortable living conditions for the workers whom it may be obliged to assign there.

ART. 5. The company is authorized to take from the state's domains gratis the materials necessary for the erection and maintenance of the track, such as stones, sand, gravel, etc. As regards secondary materials, such as utensils, provisions, beasts of burden, etc., which the company may have to purchase on the spot at the different locations of its work, the government shall prevent its being harassed and charged prices exceeding those current in the country.

ART. 6. All the materials necessary for the construction or the operation of the line shall enter Persia free of fees, either customs duties, or landing or storage fees, or finally at the frontier or on the road any other particular duty whatsoever. The customs office, however, reserves the right of control, but in such a way that the prompt and rapid arrival of the materials at their destination shall in no way be hindered. The same privilege of exemption shall apply to the materials for all undertakings and activities of the company. Its employees shall be exempt from all taxes whatsoever in the interior, [and] all their lands shall be free of all imposts or taxes whatsoever; and the products of the company's activities of all kinds shall enjoy free circulation within the empire and free exports, exempt from all taxes and duties.

ART. 7. The mode of construction and operation of the line and the date at which each section must be opened to traffic shall be mutually determined by arrangement with the Persian Government in the schedule of expenses that will be annexed to the present concession.

ART. 8. Caution money in the amount of £ 40,000 sterling[1] shall be deposited in the Bank of England, in the name of the Persian Government and the concessionaires, on the day the contract is signed. It shall be confiscated should work not begin within fifteen months from the date of the present contract, except in case of a force majeure,

---

1. The Foreign Ministry text reads £40 sterling, but this is obviously an error.

or obstacles independent of the company's volition, such as war, shipwreck, or suspension of transportation in foreign countries. The caution money shall be returned to the company against a receipt of the Governor of Resht, attesting to the arrival at Enzeli of the quantity of rails necessary for the construction of the line from Resht to Tehran.

ART. 9. The company undertakes to pay the government for the entire duration of the concession an annual premium of 20 percent of the net profits from the line's operation.

ART. 10. At the expiration of the present concession's term (seventy years) the concessionaires shall come to an understanding with the government in advance on the continuation of their enjoyment of the line. If they should not reach an agreement on some new arrangement, all the lines constructed under the present concession, with their fixed and rolling stock, shall revert to the government. As for the buildings and sheds on the line, the general rules followed in concessions made by states with the most favorable conditions on these points shall be observed. The concessionaires shall not have the right to demand any reimbursement or indemnity whatsoever from the government for the reversion of the line.

ART. 11. The government by these presents grants to the said concessionaires for the duration of the concession the exclusive and definitive privilege of developing throughout the empire mines of coal, iron, copper, lead, petroleum, etc., and all other mines, at their pleasure, with the exception of those actually being developed by individuals [already, in which case] the company must, if it desires to buy them, come to a mutual agreement with the owners. It is firmly agreed that no civil or religious authority or individual may establish valid title to ownership of a mine unless its development had been undertaken previously on a regular basis and with public knowledge for a period of at least five years. Apart from these considerations, every mine discovered by the company shall be treated as common land and bought as such at the price prevailing in the province in which it is situated. The government reserves to itself mines of gold, silver, and previous stones, for the development of

which it may frame special arrangements with the company.

ART. 12. The government shall receive an annual fixed premium of 15 percent of the net profits of every mine developed by the company.

ART. 13. The land necessary for the working of these mines and for their connection with the railroad, highway, or tramway shall be given gratis to the company, on state lands. For the working of these mines the company shall enjoy the privilege mentioned in Article 6 and shall be subject to the engagement stipulated for the railroad in Article 10.

ART. 14. Under the present contract the government grants to the concessionaires for the duration of the concession the exclusive and definitive right to use state forests throughout the empire. This right of use may be exercised in general on all land not cultivated up to the date of the present contract. Wherever the company has cleared the forest, [the company] shall have the right of first purchase from the government of those lands that [the government] may consent to sell. The government shall annually collect the fixed sum of 15 percent of the net profits from the use of the forests.[2]

ART. 15. Finally, the government grants the concessionaires for the duration of this concession the exclusive right to bring into being throughout the empire works necessary to divert rivers or streams, construct dams, and erect reservoirs, artesian wells, and canals, in order to take and bring to different places where they may find advantageous those waters for which the government has not yet granted any rights. No property owner may prevent the passage of this water, and the government on its side exempts the company from the need to indemnify any property owner who may suffer from this passage. The government accords the company gratis the necessary land for all its hydraulic works and fixtures, and additionally twenty meters of land on

---

2. Articles 14 and 15 of the French text in Tehran were transposed in the French text sent to London; cf. "Persia: Correspondence Respecting the Reuter and Falkenhagen Concessions, 1872–27," Great Britain, Public Record Office, F.O. 539/10, p. 13.

each side of the current of water that it may establish. The company shall have the right to cultivate and freely dispose of all uncultivated lands developed by its conveyed waters. The company may fix, upon mutual agreement with the government, the price for the sale of water. The government shall receive an annual premium of 15 percent of the net profits.

ART. 16. For the construction of the railroad line granted by the present concession and the works required by the above-mentioned undertakings, Baron de Reuter and his associates or representatives are authorized by the Persian Government, in virtue of these presents, to raise an initial capital of 150 million francs (15 million *tomans* or £6 million sterling) in shares or bonds whose price, mode, and conditions of issue the concessionaires shall determine later.

ART. 17. The Persian Government guarantees to the company by these presents, for all the capital issued or to be issued, an annual interest of 5 percent plus an annual sum of 2 percent as a sinking fund.

ART. 18. The said guarantee of 7 percent shall be backed by the revenues from the mines, forests, waters, and customs of the empire. It shall become valid only after the completion of the line from Resht to Isfahan, according to the form determined in the schedule of expenses. Until that time, the company shall pay to its stockholders an annual interest on the initial capital issued or on any new capital that it may be authorized to issue at its convenience.

ART. 19. The government pledges by these presents to grant to the concessionaires the management of the customs regime from March 1874 for a period of twenty-five years. For this lease of the customs, the concessionaires shall pay to the government the sum presently paid for this lease plus an annual premium of 500,000 francs (50,000 tomans, or £20 thousand sterling). These conditions shall be fixed for the first five years. From the sixth year the premium of 500,000 francs shall be replaced by a premium of 60 percent of the net profits over and above the price of the lease.

ART. 20. If the Persian Government should decide in the future to grant the privilege for a bank or institution of credit, this privilege, from today, is reserved and assured by the present contract to the present company in preference to any other party.

ART. 21. The concessionaires shall have the right of preference over any other party, and may excerise this right at a later date, for enterprises such as gas, decorating and beautifying the capital, roads, highways, post offices, telegraphs, mills, factories, manufacturing plants, etc.

ART. 22. The concessionaires may, at any time, transfer to any other party the rights granted by the present concession, with the obligations that these rights entail.

ART. 23. The concessionaires undertake to begin the above-mentioned works (mines, waters, forests) at the same time as the railroad works and to bring them into being with all possible dispatch. Apart from foreign labor that the company may employ as it wishes, the government on its side shall procure for the company, at the price prevailing in the country, all labor that it may need for its different enterprises. It may promulgate all regulations and authorize all measures necessary for preserving the security of all the land or places granted to the company for each of its enterprises, as well as the perfect security of each of its representatives, agents, or employees.

ART. 24. The present concession shall be translated into the Persian language, but in case of disagreement between the two contracting parties the French text alone shall be authoritative. . . .

Explanatory appendix to Article 18 which must be inserted into the schedule of charges:

It is firmly understood and clearly stipulated that, even at the time of the completion of the [railroad] line from Resht to Isfahan, the Persian Government shall not be responsible for the payment of the 7 percent interest. The company, however, shall be obligated to place the mines, waters, forests, and customs, with the surplus from their revenue, in such a state as to produce a revenue equal to the guaranteed interest on the capital. If the concessionaires should not obtain such a result at the time fixed above, they shall have no claim against the government nor shall they make any modification or delay in the payment of the said interest on the initial capital issued or, if they should wish, issue new capital with guarantees similar to those stipulated in the present concession. . . .

2. Draft of Falkenhagen Concession

The following Articles respecting the construction of a railway from the Aras to the town of Tabreez have been agreed upon between his Excellency Hassan Ali Khan, Persian Minister of Public Works, and Mirza Yousuf Khan, Counsellor of the (Foreign) Office, being both furnished with full powers from their Government, on the one side, and his Excellency Major-General Falkenhagen of the Engineers, who has retired from the Imperial Russian service, on the other hand:—

ART. 1. Major-General Falkenhagen, of the Engineers, having retired from the service of the Russian Government, engages to construct and to work, at his own cost and risk, a railway between the River Aras, near the village of Julfa, and the town of Tabreez. It will be named the Tabreez line.

In order that he may connect this line with those of Europe, the Government of His Majesty the Shah promises to request the Government of His Majesty the Emperor of Russia to construct a railway from Tiflis to the Persian frontier at Julfa, or to some other point on the Aras near Julfa. In this case the aforesaid General engages to connect his own railway with that of the Russian Government, and to pay to its Directors half the cost of the bridge which will be constructed over the River Aras.

ART. 2. General Falkenhagen has no right to transfer this Concession, which the Government of His Majesty the Shah has granted to him for the construction and working of the railway, to any other party excepting to a Company, which the said General will himself form for this special purpose. He must himself be regarded as the Agent of that Company during the whole period (of the construction) of the railway. When this has been completed, the Company will be at liberty to confide [i.e., entrust] the administration with the working of the railway either to Falkenhagen or to another person. This Company must conform itself to the laws of Russia, which regulate the formation of railway companies.

ART. 3. Major-General Falkenhagen engages that the Company which he will form for this purpose will, eight months after the exchange of this Concession, commence the construction of the railway, the intention being that such commencement is not to represent work of a trifling nature, but to be effected in a serious and earnest manner, so that competent persons may admit that the work has been thoroughly undertaken.

If the Company should wish to commence the work sooner than eight months after the exchange of this Concession it will be at liberty to do so. The Company also engages entirely to complete and to work the railway within five years at the outside from the date of its commencement. It engages in the meantime that if the Government of His Majesty the Emperor should complete the railway from Tiflis to Julfa before the expiration of the aforesaid period, General Falkenhagen's Company will entirely complete its railway within six months after that from Tiflis to Julfa has commenced to work. The Government of His Majesty the Shah promises that, conformably to the statement contained in the 1st Article of this Concession, it will request the Government of His Majesty the Emperor of Russia to hasten to commence and bring to a completion the line from Tiflis to Julfa. As a security for the fulfilment of its engagements by the said Company, General Falkenhagen, the founder of this Company, four months after the ratification of the exchange of this Concession, will deposit at any one of the banks of Russia which the Persian Government may indicate, in accordance with the usages established in Russia, the sum of 100,000 ducats. This deposit will, in proportion to the work done, be returned to the Company in the following manner:—

	Ducats
After levelling the line	25,000
After laying the sleepers	25,000
After fixing the rails	25,000
After starting the engines	25,000

ART. 4. The constructions must be solid and in accordance with the present rules of architecture and engineering which are adopted for railways in Russia. The gradients and curves must be adapted to the

ground so that, in working the line, difficulties may not arise. The line is to be a
single one, and the width between the inner
sides of the rails must be five English feet.
The length of the sidings to be constructed
for the purpose of fixing wheels, placing
reserved waggons, and turning engines,
must be in accordance with the requirements of the stations for the working of the
line. Altogether, it must not be less than a
seventh of the whole length of the line. As
to the weight of the rails, if they are made of
iron it must not be less than 66 English
pounds for every English yard; and if they
are made of steel, each yard must not weigh
less than 54 English pounds. The bridges
and water pipes must be constructed either
of stone, of bricks, or of metal, or partly of
stone and partly of iron. The stations,
called in French "gares," the engine sheds,
and the workshops must be built either of
stone or of bricks. The other buildings,
whether at the stations or along the line,
may be constructed of the materials and in
the manner used in those places. The
stations must be properly supplied with
water and must not be less than nine in
number. There must be the requisite number of crossings and houses along the line.
The following rolling stock must be ready
on the line at the time that it is opened:—

Engines 27
Carriages of three classes............. 80
Trucks 400

The Company must increase the rolling
stock in proportion to the increase of
passengers and traffic so as fully to meet
all the requirements of the line.

ART. 5. The exact length of the railway
will be fixed after a survey of the line based
upon a detailed investigation.

ART. 6. The Company shall have the
right to maintain, at its own cost and risk,
possession of the Tabreez Railway, both
during the period specified in Article 3 and
for the space of seventy years, according to
the European calendar, dating from the
opening of the said line.

ART. 7. The nominal capital of the Company is fixed at 3,440,000 Russian ducats,
and is to be formed by the issue of "actions" (shares). The Company shall be at
liberty to exchange a portion of the shares
for "obligations" (bonds); and, as no

guarantee being given, the Persian Government will not in any way attend to this
matter, the responsibility of the expenditure
and of exchanging bonds, shares, &c., shall
rest entirely with the Company.

ART. 8. The Government of His Majesty
the Shah promises to request the Government of His Majesty the Emperor to support the Company in the sale in its dominions of the shares referred to in Article
7.

ART. 9. After the expiration of the term
during which, as specified in Article 6, the
Company is to hold the line, the Government of His Majesty the Shah shall take
possession of the same with all its plant.
But in that case, the price of the engines,
carriages, &c., which the Company shall
have added to those existing when the line
was first completed, as set forth in Article
4, shall, according to their value at the time,
be paid to the Company. The Persian Government shall restore to the Company the
real value of all the said additional rolling
stock, which will be settled upon the estimation of competent assessors, or by
mutual agreement. In like manner, the
Company shall make over all the fuel and
other materials to the Persian Government,
the price thereof being settled in either of
the ways above quoted.

ART. 10. The Company shall have the
right to fix the fares of passengers and the
rates of transport of merchandise on the
Tabreez line, according to the exigencies of
trade and to the amount of traffic. It is the
duty of the Company to conform its regulations for the acceptance and transport of
goods and passengers to those which are
established on the railways of Russia and
other European States.

ART. 11. The Company is bound to erect
alongside of the line of railway two telegraph wires, which are necessary for the
maintenance of order, and for the safety of
the trains.

ART. 12. The Company is at liberty to
engage, as it pleases, for every branch of its
service, the persons it may require, whether
they be Persian or foreign subjects, provided that such persons consent to serve the
Company.

ART. 13. The Persian Government engages to give, gratis, to the Company out of
the State lands, situated on the railway line

from Tabreez to the river Aras, the ground which may be required for the railway, with its stations, &c. The breadth of this ground from each side of the rails must be 20 French metres; but in the places where store-rooms and stations are to be built the ground will be 100 French metres in width, by 100 French metres in length. And if it should become necessary to extend small branches of railway from the main line, the above conditions are to be similarly observed. If any ground belonging to private individuals should anywhere be required for the railway or for its stations, &c., or should it become necessary that any building belonging to the State or to private individuals should be demolished, the Government will afford its support to the Company for the purchase of such private grounds, and for the destruction of buildings, provided that the Company shall pay their fair value.

Should any person not agree to the sale of his lands or to the destruction of his buildings upon payment of their usual price, the Government will induce him, in the manner it may deem fit, to consent to evacuate the grounds, to destroy the buildings in question, and to accept their fair price based upon a fair estimation. Mosques, burial-grounds, and holy places are exempted from destruction.

Art. 14. The Company will be at liberty to use gratis any materials found on the stipulated borders of the lands which may be evacuated for the railway and its buildings, which may be required for the construction of the same.

If on the borders of the lands evacuated for the Company or withn a distance not exceeding fifty English miles from the railway, or from the grounds acquired for it, a coal mine should be discovered, the Persian Government agrees to grant to the Company the right of working it. And the Company engages not to injure the rights of the proprietors of the surface of the ground. Should the said proprietors, however, oppose the working of such mine by the Company the Government of His Majesty the Shah will support the Company in the same manner as has been stipulated above with reference to the evacuation of lands required for the railway, and will induce the proprietors to give their consent.

Art. 15. The Persian Government agrees, should it possess it, to grant to the Company at the usual price the water which may be required at the time of constructing the line and while it is worked.

Should the Company find it expedient to acquire water from some quarter where it may be useless, or by digging an artesian well, or by clearing out old kanats (acqueducts) which have no owners, and which may not be likely to injure in any way other persons' kanats, in such case the water thus acquired shall become the property of the railway.

Art. 16. The implements and materials specially required for the railway, whether at the time of its construction or while it is worked, shall be exempted from Customs dues and other taxes.

Art. 17. The lands, money, and income of the Tabreez Railway are to be free from all taxation. The Company is also exempted from fees on transactions and documents connected with the construction and the working of the line. For the transport of passengers, merchandize, and other articles by the railway, beyond the fares and freight fixed by the Company, neither the Government nor its agents, nor any other party, are to claim or levy any kind of fee or tax excepting the established and customary Customs duty.

Art. 18. The Company makes over the administration of the affairs connected with the regulating and the working of the railway and its offices and accounts to a Board composed of three Directors, for whom a place will be selected on the line. This Board is to represent the Company both before the Persian Government, its officials, and other persons, who may have to deal with the Company. All matters, therefore, connected with the Company must be referred to this Board.

Art. 19. For the investigation and settlement of all discussions and complaints which may arise in the affairs of the Company in carrying out the Articles of the Concession, whether proceeding from the Governments of Persia and Russia, or from their subjects, or from the Company, a permanent Commission is to be formed, consisting of a President of rank, of two persons representing the Persian Government, of a Member of the Russian Consulate-General at Tabreez, and of two persons representing the Company, who are to settle such matters whenever their opinions coincide. Should there be a difference of opinion the majority of votes is to decide. Should they be equally divided the question is to be referred to the Deputy Governor of Azerbijan and to the Russian Consulate-General. If these two high functionaries can settle such matters between them, well and good; otherwise, the two parties are to make a reference to Tehran.

ART. 20. If the Persian Government should wish to construct a railway from some point of the Tabreez line to another point of the same, it must be done with the Company's permission. For the construction of railways which during the term of this Concession the Persian Government, or another company, may find it advisable to lay down within a distance of 100 English miles from any point of the Tabreez line, the Persian Government shall give the preference to the Tabreez Railway Company, should the conditions be equal.

ART. 21. If General Falkenhagen's Company should not complete the Tabreez Railway within the time specified in Article 3, and should be owing not to any fault of its own, but to circumstances beyond its control, such as the occurrence of war, the blockading of ports, rebellion, and contagious diseases, which may at the time prevent the prosecution of the work, or other calamities; the loss of ships conveying materials for the railway; or engineering difficulties, which may be admitted by the Commission; (in that case) the term for the opening of the line shall be extended in proportion to the nature of such impediments and difficulties. But should the Company, through its own fault or that of its agents, not complete the railway within the specified time, the Persian Government will, in the first instance, give it a warning, and three months after it will repeat that warning. Should the Company, six months after the issue of this second warning, fail to fulfil its engagements, it shall forfeit all the rights conceded to it in the Concession, and shall pay over to the Persian Government the deposited sum of 100,000 ducats, which is mentioned in Article 3; and it must, within the space of one year, liquidate its accounts. In this case the Company shall

have the right to sell all its property to whomsoever it pleases.

ART. 22. As, in accordance with the terms of this Concession, this Company must be formed in Russia, General Falkenhagen engages, within six months at the outside from the commencement of the construction of the railway, as set forth in Article 3 of this Concession, to present to the Persian Government a copy of the byelaws of the Company, called in French "statuts," drawn up and ratified in conformity with the usages in Russia.

The Persian Government, it order to facilitate the Company's operations, promises to make arrangements with the Government of Russia, that the Russian Government should anthorize that the Company's byelaws be drawn up in Russia, and that the Company's shares ("actions") and bonds ("obligations") be circulated in that country.

ART. 23. The Company itself is to prepare its paper, denominated "actions" and "obligations," which must be written either in one foreign language, opposite the Persian, or in several European languages in addition to the Persian, so that it may bear the registered seal of the Persian Government. But this condition is to be observed, that the Company is to insert in the writing of its paper that the Company is responsible for the payment of the same and of the interest thereon, and that the Persian Government is not concerned therein.

ART. 24. General Falkenhagen's Company engages that in the waggons separate compartments shall be assigned to women; that Mussulman cooks, coffee men, and sherbet-makers, shall be placed at the stations, and that places reserved for prayers shall also be built therein.

ART. 25. The Persian Government engages that after the exchange of this Concession, it shall forthwith issue the necessary orders to the Governors and Superintendents stationed on the road, to afford all necessary support to the engineers and agents who may be appointed by the Company for the purpose of examining, surveying, and laying down the railway line.

ART. 26. All the contents of this Concession having been submitted to His

Majesty the Shah, and confirmed by his Royal hand, Major-General Falkenhagen, of the Russian Engineers, is authorized to take all necessary steps for carrying the same into effect; and the Government of His Majesty the Shah agrees to afford to General Falkenhagen and to the Company which he will form, at all times and in every way, all the support in its power for the construction and the working of the Tabreez Railway. This Concession having received the auspicious seal and signature of His Majesty the Shah, has been delivered to Major-General Falkenhagen, so that by possessing this deed he may do what is necessary to give effect to its contents.

ART. 27. This Concession has been written in duplicate. One copy, bearing the auspicious signature and seal of His Majesty the Shah of all the Dominions of Persia, has been delivered to Major-General Falkenhagen, of the Russian Engineers; and the second copy, bearing the signature of the aforesaid General, is kept at Her Majesty's Foreign Office. And it is decided, if within four months from the date of the exchange of this Concession, Major-General Falkenhagen, having obtained the acceptance and signature of his partners thereto, shall notify the same to the (Persian) Foreign Office, either by telegraph, or by an official letter from the Russian Legation at Tehran, in that case the present Concession shall remain in force; and the date of the commencement (of the work), as specified in the first [part] of Article 3, shall count from the day the (aforesaid) announcement reaches the Persian Foreign Office from the (Russian) Mission. Otherwise this Concession, whatever it may be, shall be null and void, and shall cease to be of any value.

127. OTTOMAN *FERMAN* CONSOLIDATING THE SPECIAL PRIVILEGES CONFERRED ON THE KHEDIVE OF EGYPT
8 June 1873

[Great Britain, *Parliamentary Papers, 1879*, 78: 625–27]

Isma'il Paşa, who acceded to the governorship of Egypt in 1863, lived lavishly, but he also resumed the efforts of his grandfather, Mehmed 'Ali Paşa, to improve the condititons in his province through public works. He constructed irrigation canals, bridges, railroads, and lighthouses; modernized Alexandria harbor; and contributed to the cost of constructing the Suez Canal. He also extended the zone of Egyptian rule in the Sudan. To finance such an ambitious program Isma'il borrowed heavily, and unwisely, from European and Levantine bankers at exorbitant discount and interest rates. In consequence, the public debt of his semisovereign province grew from some £3 million to nearly £100 million in about a decade and a half, and Isma'il was compelled in 1876 to set up a Public Debt Commission under the dual control of Britain and France to supervise the finances of Egypt. He was finally deposed by Sultan 'Abdülhamid II (1876–1909) in 1879. Nevertheless Isma'il left his province considerably more independent of the Sublime Porte than he had found it. In return for raising his annual tribute in 1866 from 80,000 purses (about £1.7 million) to 150,000 purses (about £3.2 million), he was allowed to alter the principle of succession from seniority to primogeniture and to enlarge his army from 18,000 to 30,000 troops. In the following year he acquired for himself and his heirs the Persian title of *khedive*, thereby elevating his status from governor to viceroy, with almost unrestricted legislative autonomy and full control over nonpolitical external affairs. These and other special privileges granted in later decress were finally brought together in a single *ferman*, reproduced below. Vatikiotis, *Modern History of Egypt*, chap. 5; Holt, *Egypt and the Fertile Crescent*, chap. 14; Landes, *Bankers and Pashas*; Douin, *Histoire du règne du khédive Ismail*; Nahoum Efendi, *Recueil des firmans impériaux ottomans addressés aux valis et aux khédives d'Egypte, 1597–1904* (French translations of Turkish texts); Crabitès, *Ismail*; Sabry, *L'empire égyptien sous Ismail, et l'ingérénce anglo-française*; Sammarco, *Précis de l'histoire d'Egypte*, vol. 4, chap. 11; Hasenclever, *Geschichte Ägyptens*, chap. 4; Bréhier, *L'Egypte*, chaps. 6–7; Cocheris, *Situation internationale de l'Egypte et du Soudan*, chap. 3.

Be it known that we have taken thy request into consideration, and that we have decided to unite in one single Firman all the Firmans and Khats Houmayoun which, since the Firman which granted the Egyptian succession to thy grandfather, Mehemet Ali, have been granted to the Khedives of Egypt, either in order to modify the manner of succession, or to accord to Egypt fresh immunities and privileges in harmony with the customs of the inhabitants, and with the character and nature of the country. It is our will that the present Firman, with all the modifications and necessary explanations included in it, and with the principles and regulations which it establishes, shall henceforth be executed and respected, and shall also in future replace the other Imperial Firmans, and that in the following manner:—

The order of succession to the Government of Egypt granted by our Imperial Firman dated the 2nd Rehib-ul-ewel, 1257, has been so modified that the Khedivate of Egypt passes to thy eldest son, and after him to his eldest son, and in like manner as regards others, that is to say, that the succession is to proceed by primogeniture in the interests of the good administration of Egypt and of the welfare of its inhabitants. Again, as I have noted the care which thou bestowest on Egypt and the efforts thou art making for its prosperity, the greatness and importance of which are obvious to me, as well as the fidelity and devotion which thou hast always evinced to me, I have given thee my entire good grace and confidence, and, in order to give thee a striking proof of this, I have resolved to establish as law that the sucession to

the Khedivate of Egypt and its dependencies, with the Kaimakamats of Souakin and Massowa, and their dependencies, shall pass, as aforesaid, to thy son, and after him, in conformity with the law of primogeniture, to the eldest sons of future Khedives. In the event of a Khedive leaving no male children, the Khedivate shall pass to his younger brother, and, in case he should not be surviving, to the eldest son of such younger brother. This rule is established definitely, and does not apply to the male children of the female line.

In order completely to insure the security of this order of succession, the Regency which shall govern Egypt in the event of a minority is regulated as follows: If, at the death of the Khedive, his eldest son is a minor, that is to say, if he is under 18 years of age, as by right of succession he will be actually Khedive in spite of his minority, his Firman will be immediately sent to him. If the deceased Khedive has, in his lifetime, appointed a Regency in a document which must be countersigned by two high functionaries, whose names shall appear as witnesses in the document, the Regent and the members of the Regency who have been thus named shall immediately take in hand the administration of affairs, and shall inform my Sublime Porte thereof, and my Imperial Government will confirm the Regent and the members of the Regency in their office. If the Khedive has not provided for a Regency during his life, one will be formed of the persons who may at the time be at the head of the Departments of the Interior, of War, of Finance, of Foreign Affairs, of the Council of Justice, of the Army, and of the General Inspection. They shall proceed to the nomination of a Regent in the following manner. These different Chiefs of the Administration shall elect the Regent from among themselves; this election will be made either unanimously, or by the vote of the majority. In the case of two persons obtaining an equal number of votes, the one occupying the most important office, beginning with the Department of the Interior, shall be elected Regent, and the other members shall form the Council of Regency. They shall take in hand the administration of affairs, [and] inform my Sublime Porte, who will confirm them in their office. Whether the Regent and the Council of Regency have been instituted by the Khedive during his lifetime, or whether the Regency shall have been constituted by election, in neither case can any of the members be changed. If one of the members should happen to die, the surviving members shall choose and name another Egyptian functionary to replace him. If it is the Regent who happens to die, the Members of the Council shall choose his successor from among themselves, and shall appoint another Egyptian functionary to the place which the new Regent occupied in the Council. When the Khedive who is a minor has attained the age of 18, he shall be considered of age, and shall administer the affairs of the Government.

I attach the greatest importance to the prosperity of Egypt, to the well-being, tranquillity, and security of its population, and since these are matters which depend on the civil and financial administration of the country, as well as upon the development of the material and other interests of the country, which are under the control of the Egyptian Government, we mention as follows, with modifications and explanations, all the privileges which my Imperial Firman has accorded, whether formerly or for the first time, to the Egyptian Government, in order that they may be for ever possessed by succeeding Khedives:—

The civil and financial administration of the country, and all interests, material or otherwise, are in every respect under the control of the Egyptian Government, and are confided to it, and as the administration, the maintenance of order in any country, and the development of the riches and prosperity of the population spring from the harmony to be established between the facts, the general relations, the condition and the nature of the country, as well as the disposition and the customs of the inhabitants, the Khedive of Egypt is authorized to make internal regulations and laws as often as it may be necessary.

He is also authorized to renew and to contract (without interfering with the political Treaties of my Sublime Porte) Conventions with the Agents of foreign Powers for customs and trade, and for all relations which concern foreigners, and all the affairs of the country, internal or otherwise, with the object of developing commerce and industry, and to arrange the police for foreigners as well as their position, and all their relations with the Government and the population.

The Khedive has complete and entire control over the financial afiairs of the country. He has full power to contract, without leave, in the name of the Egyptian Government, any foreign loan, whenever he may think it necessary.

The first and most essential duty of the Khedive being to guard and defend the country, he has full and entire authority to provide for all the means and establishments for defence and protection according to the exigencies of time and place, and to increase or diminish the number of my Imperial Egyptain troops as may be required, without any restriction being imposed upon him.

The Khedive will retain, as before, the privilege of conferring ranks in the military Order up to the rank of Colonel, and in the civil Order up to the rank of Raubci Sanick. The money coined in Egypt should be struck in my Imperial name; the flags of the land and sea forces will be the same as the flags of my other troops; and, as regards ships of war, iron-clads alone shall not be constructed without my permission.

By my Imperial order reproducing the above provisions, I cause this illustrious Firman, headed by my Imperial signature, to be transmitted to thee by my Imperial Divan. This Firman comprises and completes (with explanations and modifications) all the Firmans and Imperial Khats which have hitherto been granted to the Egyptian Government, whether instituting the order of succession and the form of the Regency in case of necessity, or for the civil, military, and financial administration, as well as for the interests of the country, whether material or otherwise.

It is in accordance with my Imperial wish that the rules and principles contained in this Firman should be for ever observed and executed, instead of and in place of all others contained in my previous Firmans.

As for thyself, thous wilt faithfully execute the conditions stipulated in this Firman in accordance with thy character full

of uprightness and zeal, and with the knowledge which thou hast acquired of the condition of Egypt, and thou wilt endeavour to administer the country well, and to assure by all possible means the tranquillity of the inhabitants, and thereby show thy gratitude for my favours any my Imperial kindnesses towards thee.

Thou wilt also pay great attention to remitting to my Imperial Treasury, every year, without delay, and in its entirety, the fixed tribute of 150,000 purses.

128. BRITISH TREASURY MINUTE ON ARRANGEMENTS FOR A LOAN TO PURCHASE THE KHEDIVE'S INTEREST IN THE SUEZ CANAL COMPANY
25 November 1875

[Great Britain, *Parliamentary Papers, 1876*, 83: 139]

Britain's predominance in the trade with India and the Far East established its primacy in the Suez Canal traffic from the very outset, as attested by the fact that more than 70 percent of the ships using the waterway in its first few years flew the Union Jack. Owing to British failure to invest in the canal company, however, London could exercise no control over the company's policy, which, in the view of English shipping firms, often discriminated against their vessels. The desire for a voice in the company's management prevailed especially among the Conservatives. When Disraeli became prime minister in 1874 he immediately began to explore the prospects of acquiring at least part ownership. The opportunity came in the fall of 1875, when word reached London that French financial circles were negotiating for the shares owned by Khedive Isma'il, who was then in desperate need of funds to meet interest payments on his loans. Having ascertained that the khedive would part with his substantial holdings, the British government was in a quandary. Such a transaction required parliamentary authorization, but the legislature was then in recess. Disraeli succeeded in overcoming the opposition within his cabinet to obtaining a £4 million loan from the House of Rothschild, pending final parliamentary approval. The line of action taken by the Lords Commissioners of Her Majesty's Treasury is presented in the following minute. Hoskins, *British Routes to India*, chap. 18; Hallberg, *Suez Canal*, chap. 15; A. Wilson, *Suez Canal*, chap. 4; Fitzgerald, *Great Canal at Suez*, vol. 2, chap. 19; Lesage, *L'invasion anglaise en Egypte*; Monypenny and Buckle, *Life of Benjamin Disraeli*, vol. 5, chap. 12; Jenks, *Migration of British Capital*, pp. 320–25; Thompson, *Public Opinion and Lord Beaconsfield*, 1: 237–52; Blake, *Disraeli*; Farnie, *East and West of Suez*, chap. 14; see also references to Doc. 103.

The First Lord and the Chancellor of the Exchequer state to the Board, that Her Majesty's Government have received a telegram from Her Majesty's Consul-General in Egypt, to the effect that the Khedive has offered to sell his shares in the Suez Canal to Her Majesty for the sum of 100,000,000 fr., and that His Highness will pay interest at the rate of 5 per cent, upon the amount paid upon the shares until the coupons are free, His Highness having disposed of his interest in the coupons for some time to come.

The First Lord and the Chancellor further state that they have been in communication with Messrs. N. de Rothschild and Sons, who, in the event of the offer being accepted, are prepared to carry out the operation as the agents of Her Majesty's Government in London; with that object Messrs. Rothschild will undertake to hold 1,000,000l. sterling at the disposal of the Egyptian Government, on the 1st of December next, as soon as they receive an assurance from Her Majesty's Government that the shares in question have been handed over to Her Majesty's Consul-General in Egypt. They will provide the remaining 3,000,000l. sterling in the months of December and January, and hold them at the disposal of the Khedive in such manner as may be arranged between His Highness and themselves.

Meessrs. Rothschild will charge a commission of 2½ per cent. upon the 4,000,000l. sterling which they thus undertake to provide, and they will receive the 5 percent interest which the Khedive undertakes to pay upon the amounts advanced, from the date of the advance thereof, until the date of repayment by Her Majesty's Government.

The First Lord and the Chancellor inform the Board that these several proposals have been considered and accepted by Her Majesty's Advisers, and that they have telegraphed to Her Majesty's Consul-General in Egypt that they agree to purchase the shares, 177,642 in number, held by the Khedive, for the sum of 4,000,000l. sterling, and that the money will be provided in the manner proposed by Messrs Rothschild.

The First Lord and the Chancellor point out that Messrs. Rothschild undertake this heavy liability on the pledge of Her Majesty's Government that they will submit the engagement for the sanction of Parliament, and endeavour to obtain the necessary powers to enable them to repay the advance, and pay Messrs. Rothschild's commission as soon as may be practicable after the meeting of Parliament; and they recommend that a letter embodying that pledge in an official form should be written to Messrs. Rothschild without delay.

My Lords approve.
Write to Messrs. Rothschild.

129. ANGLO-EGYPTIAN AGREEMENT FOR THE PURCHASE OF THE KHEDIVE'S SUEZ CANAL COMPANY SHARES, WITH EXPLANATORY LETTER OF THE BRITISH AGENT AND CONSUL GENERAL
25 and 27 November 1875

[Great Britain, *Parliamentary Papers, 1876*, 83: 140–42]

At the time that Disraeli arranged for the Rothschild loan, the khedive was believed to possess 177,642 shares of the canal company. It was soon discovered, however, the Isma'il had disposed of 1,040 shares in Paris several years earlier. Account was taken of the discrepancy in the agreement for the sale of the khedive's interest to the British government, concluded by the British agent and consul general in Cairo, Major General Edward Stanton, and the Egyptian minister of finance, Isma'il Sadiq Pasha. For references, see Doc. 128.

1. General Stanton's Explanatory Letter

My telegram of yesterday aftermoon will have informed your Lordship of the conclusion of the negotiations which had been entrusted to me for the purchase of the Khedive's Suez Canal shares, by the deposit of these shares in Her Majesty's Consulate in this town, and I have little to add to the information already conveyed to your Lordship on this matter.

On the receipt of your Lorship's telegram of the 23rd, which reached me on the morning of the 24th instant, I lost no time in proceeding to the palace to inform his Highness of the acceptance of his offer to dispose of his Canal shares to Her Majesty's Government. I was unable at that hour to see the Khedive; but I informed the Minister of Finance, whom I saw in the presence of Nubar Pasha and of the Khedive's "Garde des Sceaux," of the nature of the communication I had to make, and shortly afterwards received the assurance that the terms were agreed to. Being, however, anxious to prevent any misunderstanding on the subject, and also to prevent the possibility of any successful intrigue interfering with the arrangement, I told the Minister I would draw up an agreement for signature, specifying the terms of the engagement entered into.

Before leaving the palace, however, Nubar Pasha had told me that he believed the number of shares in the Khedive's possession did not quite tally with the number specified by your Lordship, as a few of the shares had been disposed of in Paris some ten or twelve years since. I therefore left a blank in the agreement to be filled up when the actual number of shares in His Highness' possession should be ascertained; and when, shortly afterwards, the Minister of Finance informed me that the shares were 176,602 in number instead of 177,642, as specified by your Lordship. I provided that the value of the 1,040 shares short of the last-named number should be deducted from the amount agreed to be paid by Her Majesty's Government.

I also, as your Lordship will perceive, stipulated that the 5 per cent. interest to be paid by the Egyptian Government to Her Majesty's Government until the coupons were liberated from the existing engagement with the Canal Company, should be charged on the revenues of Egypt, and the amount paid in London by equal half-yearly payments of 100,000l. on the 1st of June and 1st of December of each year.

Yesterday morning the Egyptian Government sent me seven large cases containing the shares in question, which cases (having previously verified the fact that they contained Suez Canal shares) I caused to be fastened up and corded in my presence, and then sealed with the seals of the Egyptian Minister of Finance, Her Majesty's Agency and Consulate-General, and of the Consular Court for Cairo, leaving the verification of the numbers till I had received further instructions from your Lordship, and I gave the Egyptian Government a receipt for the seven cases, which are now deposited in Her Majesty's Consulate in this town, pending the receipt of instructions for their disposal.

2. Agreement Concluded by Stanton and Sadiq

Whereas, His Highness, the Khedive has proposed to sell to Her Britannic Majesty's Government the whole of his shares in the Suez Canal Company, and whereas Her Britannic Majesty's Government has proposed to purchase from His Highness the Khedive 177,642 shares in the said Suez Canal Company, for the sum of 4,000,000l. sterling.

Now it is hereby witnessed that His Highness the Khedive agrees to sell to Her Britannic Majesty's Government the whole of his shares in the Suez Canal Company, being to the number of 176,602 shares, not, as supposed by Her Britannic Majesty's Government, 177,642 shares; and Her Britannic Majesty's Government agrees to purchase the same for the sum of 4,000,000l. sterling, less the proportionate value of the 1,040 shares, the difference between 177,642, and 176,602, and Her Britannic Majesty's Government agrees to recommend to Parliament to sanction the contract.

Her Britannic Majesty's Government undertakes that on the 1st of December next, on the deposit of the shares in the hands of Her Majesty's Agent and Consul-General in Egypt, the sum of 1,000,000*l*. sterling shall be held at the disposal of the Egyptian Government, in the hands of Messrs. N. de Rothschild and Sons of London; and that the remaining 3,000,000*l*. sterling, less the amount to be deducted for the value of the 1,040 shares above mentioned, shall be provided in the months of December and January next, as may be arranged between the Egyptian Government and Messrs. Rothschild and Sons.

The Egyptian Government undertakes to pay to Her Britannic Majesty's Government interest at the rate of 5 per cent. per annum on the whole amount of the purchase money of the said 176,602 shares, in equal half-yearly payments,—the said payments to be made in London on the 1st of June and the 1st of December in each year, until such time as the coupons of the said shares shall be liberated from the engagement now existing with the Suez Canal Company; and the Egyptian Government further engages that the amount of the said interest shall be charged on the revenues of Egypt.

130. DISRAELI'S DEFENSE BEFORE THE HOUSE OF COMMONS OF HIS SUEZ ACTION
21 February 1876

[Great Britain, *Parliamentary Debates, Commons*, 3d ser., vol. 227, cols. 652–61]

Although Parliament passed a bill on 15 August 1876 approving the government's action on Suez (text in *British and Foreign State Papers*, 67: 541 ff.), the matter first came before the legislature the preceding February. The opposition, whose chief spokesman was Gladstone, focused on the manner of the purchase and the alleged lack of benefits to Britain from the transaction. In the statement reproduced below, Disraeli replied to both charges and left no doubt that his original motive was not commercial but political. For references, see Doc. 128.

Sir, although, according to the noble Lord, we are going to give a unanimous vote, it cannot be denied that the discussion of this evening at least has proved one result. It has shown, in a manner about which neither the House of Commons nor the country can make any mistake, that had the right hon. Gentleman the Member for Greenwich been the Prime Minister of this country, the shares in the Suez Canal would not have been purchased. The right hon. Gentleman, in his numerous observations upon the Vote before the House, has divided them under two heads—what he calls the operation and the policy. The right hon. Gentleman found great fault with the conduct of the operation; and though that is not the more important portion of the business, and though it is one which I could have wished to refrain from touching, from the personal details that must be involved necessarily in such a discussion, still as the question has been not only noticed by the two right hon. critics of the evening, but by some who followed them, I have no wish to avoid it, and I certainly shall encounter that question. The right hon. Gentleman defies me to produce an instance of a Ministry negotiating with a private firm. Well, I think the right hon. Gentleman must be in error. [MR. GLADSTONE: Those were not at all my words.] Unfortunately, we are all on this side under the impression that those were the words. I listened attentively to the right hon. Gentlemen, but it is unnecessary to dwell upon the topic. I was only going to say that I doubted the accuracy of the statement; but I conceive it has nothing to do with the matter before us, which is of an unprecedented character, as I was going to show. The right hon. Gentleman found great fault with the amount of the commission which has been charged by the Messrs. Rothschild and admitted by the Government; and, indeed, both the right hon. Gentlemen opposite took the pains to calculate what was the amount of interest which it was proposed the Messrs. Rothschild should receive on account of their advance. It is, according to both right hon. Gentlemen, 15 per cent; but I must express my surprise that two right hon. Gentlemen, both of whom have filled the office of Chancellor of the Exchequer, and one of whom has been at the head of the Treasury, should have shown by their observations such a lamentable want of acquaintance with the manner in which large amounts of capital are commanded when the Government of a country may desire to possess them under the circumstances under which we appealed to the House in question. I deny altogether that the commission charged by the Messrs. Rothschild has anything to do with the interest on the advance; nor can I suppose that two right hon. Gentlemen so well acquainted with finance as the Member for Greenwich and the Member for the University of London can really believe that there is in this country anyone who has £4,000,000 lying idle at his bankers. Yet one would suppose, from the argument of the right hon. Gentleman the Member for Greenwich, that such is the assumption on which he has formed his opinion in this matter. In the present instance, I may observe, not only the possibility, but the probability, of our having immediately to advance the whole £4,000,000 was anticipated. And how was this £4,000,000 to be obtained? Only by the rapid conversion of securities to the same amount. Well, I need not tell anyone who is at all acquainted with such affairs that the rapid conversion of securities to the amount of £4,000,000 can never be affected without loss, and sometimes considerable loss; and it is to guard against risk of that kind that a commission is asked for before

advances are made to a Government. In this case, too, it was more than probable that, after paying the first £1,000,000, following the signature of the contract, £2,000,000 further might be demanded in gold the next day. Fortunately for the Messrs. Rothschild they were not; but, if they had, there would in all likelihood have been a great disturbance in the Money Market, which must have occasioned a great sacrifice, perhaps the whole of the commission. The Committee, therefore, must not be led away by the observations of the two right hon. Gentlemen, who, of all men in the House, ought to be the last to make them. But the right hon. Gentleman the Member for Greenwich says we ought to have gone to our constitutional financiers and advisers, the Governor and Deputy Governor of the Bank of England, and, of course, the hon. Member for Galway (Mr. Mitchell Henry), who rose much later in the debate, and who spoke evidently under the influence of strong feeling, also says that we ought to have asked the Governor of the Bank of England to advance the £4,000,000, But they forget that it is against the law of this country for the Bank to advance a sum of money to the Ministry. But then it may be said—"Though the Bank could not have advanced the £4,000,000, you might have asked them to purchase the shares." But how could they have purchased the shares? They must have first consulted their legal adviser, who probably would have told them that they had not power to do it; but, even if that doubtful question had been decided in the affirmative, they must have then called a public Court in order to see whether they could be authorized to purchase those shares to assist the Government. Now, I ask the Committee to consider for a moment what chance would we have had of effecting the purchase which we made under the circumstances, and with the competitors we had to encounter, and the objects we had to attain, if we had pursued the course which the right hon. Gentleman opposite has suggested? "But," says the Member for the University of London—and this also has been echoed by his late right hon. Colleague—"you would have avoided all this, if you adopted the course which we indicate, and which I have just reminded the Committee is illegal, if you had only taken the illegal course we recommend, you would have got rid of this discreditable gambling, because although the Messrs. Rothschild, some of whom have been Members of this House, are men of honour, yet they have a great number of clerks who were all gambling on the Stock Exchange." Now, my belief is that the Messrs. Rothschild kept the secret as well as Her Majesty's Government, for I do not think a single human being connected with them knew anything about it. And, indeed, it was quite unnecessary for the Messrs. Rothschild to have violated the confidence which we reposed in them, and quite unnecessary even for the Members of Her Majesty's Government to hold their tongues, for no sooner was the proposal accepted than a telegram from Grand Cairo transmitted the news to the Stock Exchange, and it was that telegram which was the cause of all the speculation and gambling to which the right hon. Gentleman has referred. It is a fact that while the matter was a dead secret in England, the news was transmitted from Cairo. That was the intelligence on which the operations occurred. But I wish to say one word respecting the moral observations which have been made. As to gambling on the Stock Exchange, are we really to refrain from doing that which we think is proper and advantageous to the country because it may lead to speculation? Why, not a remark was made by the noble Lord, who has just addressed the House, the other night, or by me in reply, that would not affect the funds. On the one side people would say—"The Government are in great difficulty, and probably a Vote of Censure will arise out of this Suez Canal speculation," while other persons would observe—"There is evidently something coming about Egypt, and he is not going to let it all out." Ought we to refrain from doing what is necessary for the public welfare because it leads to stock-jobbing? Why, there is not an incident in the history of the world that led to so much stock-jobbing as the battle of Waterloo, and are we to regret that that glorious battle was fought and won because it led to stock-jobbing? So much for the operations on the Stock Exchange. I think we have been listening all night to remarks on this transaction that

have very little foundation. We have been admonished for conduct which has led to stock-jobbing and we have been admonished because we applied to a private firm when from the state of the law, I have shown that it was absolutely necessary from the character of the circumstances we had to deal with that a private firm should be appealed to. And now I come to the policy of the two right hon. Gentlemen, for on that portion of the subject they appear to agree very much. The right hon. Gentleman the Member for the University of London says—"You have your shares, but you have no dividends." And the right hon. Gentleman the Member for Greenwich says—"You have your shares, but you have no votes." That is the great lamentation of the two right hon. Gentlemen. Shrieking and screaming out—"You have no votes and no dividends, though you have the shares," they account for conduct on the part of the Government so totally devoid of sense and calculation as that the Government should become encumbered with all these shares, and yet possess neither the advantage of dividends nor of voting power. They say this is due to the simple circumstance that we acted in total ignorance, that we were innocent—nay, more than innocent—and that the most becoming thing for us to do would be to acknowledge and, at the same time, to regret our fault. Instead of that, they say we triumph in our ignorance, and they absolutely pretend that we were aware of the immense blunder we have committed. It is very remarkable that the two right hon. Gentlemen should have ventured to take up such a position in this case. What is this question of the Suez Canal? From the numerous Papers which have been placed before the House, the House must be tolerably aware that during the whole period of the existence of the present Parliament the question of the Suez Canal has more or less been before us. I am not sure that in the first Cabinet Council we held some decision was not come to on the subject. Then the International Commission at Constantinople had either just terminated, or was involving the Government in a painful and difficult Correspondence. We were represented at the International Commission by Colonel Stokes, who is completely master of the subject, an invaluable public servant, and a man of great intelligence, and who had completely mastered all the details of what was then a very complicated question. From that time until we made the purchase in October last Colonel Stokes has been in almost constant attendance at the Foreign Office. The question of the Suez Canal was constantly before us, and therefore I need not go further to show to the Committee that, although it happened to be a subject upon which we were called in the present instance to decide hastily, we had the advantage of much previous knowledge. Why, my right hon. Friend the Chancellor of the Exchequer was intimately acquainted with the subject, and was himself present at the opening of the Suez Canal. Nothing, in short, can be more unfounded than the assumption of the two right hon. Gentlemen, who wished to convey to the House that Her Majesty's Government had entered into their agreement in perfect ignorance of all the circumstances of the case. This, in fact, was the style of the whole speech of the right hon. Gentleman (Mr. Lowe). Take this away; convince the right hon. Gentleman—or convince, what is easier and more satisfactory, the Committee—that we were aware of these circumstances, and the right hon. Gentleman himself confesses that he might as well have made no speech at all. Then the right hon. Gentleman the Member for Greenwich (Mr. Gladstone) proceeds in his attack in his own way, and makes a great many objections, but takes up two great positions as grounds of condemnation. "First of all," he says, "I object to this purchase, because it will give you no influence." That is the assertion of the right hon. Gentleman. I might meet it with a counter assertion. I might offer many arguments to show that it will give us a great deal of influence. I might refer to that which has already occurred, and which, though not in its results very considerable, shows some advantage from what has been done, while before a year has elapsed it will possibly show much more. I might refer to the general conviction and the common sense of society that such an investment cannot be treated as absolutely idle and nugatory, as the right hon. Gentleman wishes to treat

it. The right hon. Gentleman takes a position from which it is certainly difficult to dislodge him, because it is perfectly arbitrary. He says—"You have no votes." He views the question abstractly. He says—"Here is a company, and you have a great many shares in it, but you are not allowed to vote, and therefore it follows you can have no influence." But everybody knows that in the world things are not managed in that way, and that if you have a large amount of capital in any concern, whatever may be restrictions under which it is invested, the capitalist does exercise influence. Then the right hon. Gentleman says—"You have no real control over the purchase you have made; and yet that purchase will lead to great complications." Sir, I have no doubt that complications will occur. They always have occurred, and I should like to know the state of affairs and of society in which complications do not and will not occur. We are here to guard the country against complications, and to guide it in the event of complications; and the argument that we are to do nothing—never dare to move, never try to increase our strength and improve our position, because we are afraid of complications is certainly a new view of English policy, and one which I believe the House of Commons will never sanction. I think under these two heads all the criticisms of the right hon. Gentleman are contained. But the noble Lord who has just addressed us says many points were made by the right hon. Gentleman which the Chancellor of the Exchequer did not answer. There is no precedent of a British Ministry treating with a private firm; my right hon. Friend did not answer that. [MR. GLADSTONE: I did not say so.] The right hon. Gentleman, however, says he made no observation of the kind. Then the noble Lord says my right hon. Friend never answered the charge about speculations in Egyptian Stock. Well, I have answered that charge. The noble Lord says my right hon. Friend never touched upon the amount of the commission. I have touched upon it. He says that we never thoroughly cleared ourselves from the charge of not buying the 15 per cent shares. I am here to vindicate our conduct on that point. In purchasing the shares we did, we purchased what we wanted, we gained the end we wished, and why we should involve the country in another purchase, when we should thereby only have repeated the result we had already achieved I cannot understand. The noble Lord says my right hon. Friend never expressed what expectations we had of receiving the £200,000 a-year from the Khedive. We certainly do expect to receive the £200,000 a-year from the Khedive, but we do not suppose that interest which is at the rate of 5 per cent is quite as secure as it would be if it were at the rate of $3\frac{1}{4}$ per cent. Then the noble Lord says that my right hon. Friend never met the charge of the right hon. Gentleman that our policy would lead to complications with other nations. We believe, on the contrary, that, instead of leading to complications with other nations, the step which we have taken is one which will avert complications. These are matters which to a great degree must be matters of opinion; but the most remarkable feature of the long harangue of the right hon. Gentleman the Member for Greenwich is that it was in a great degree a series of assumptions, abstract reasonings, and arbitrary conclusions, after which he sat down quite surprised that the Vote should be passed unanimously, and requesting his allies to attack us for not answering that which we have felt not to be substantial, but to consist of assumptions which we believe experience will prove to be entirely false. The right hon. Gentleman charged us, lastly, with not having answered a charge of having abandoned a strong position. The right hon. Gentleman pictured us as having been in a good position before this—a position which he charged us with having abandoned for one of a more doubtful character. Here again, what proof does he bring of the charge he makes? We found ourselves in a position which has been called a strong position, but we could not for a moment think that our position with regard to the Canal was satisfactory. The International Commission sat, as hon. Members know, before the Conservatives acceded to power, and the work it did was greatly assisted by our Predecessors, and by a number of other able and eminent men; but, as I have said, no one who remembers all the circumstances of the case and what has occurred

since, can for a moment pretend that our position with regard to the Canal was then satisfactory. At that moment Turkey was in a very different position from that which she occupies at present, as far as authority is concerned. The Khedive himself was in a very good position; and yet those who are familiar with what occurred at that time know the great difficulties which the Government experienced, and the very doubtful manner in which, for a considerable time, affairs looked with regard to the whole business. Therefore I do not agree with the right hon. Gentleman. I feel that at this moment our position is much stronger, and for the reason that we are possessors of a great portion of the capital invested in the Canal. The noble Lord himself has expressed great dissatisfaction, because I have not told him what the conduct of the Government would be with regard to the Canal in a time of war. I must say that on this subject I wish to retain my reserve. I cannot conceive anything more imprudent than a discussion in this House at the present time as to the conduct of England with regard to the Suez Canal in time of war, and I shall therefore decline to enter upon any discussion on the subject. Then the noble Lord passed to the mission of Mr. Cave, and says we have no good account to give of it. It is impossible to give a good account of a mission which is not yet finished. I believe the mission of Mr. Cave to be a wise and a beneficial one, and I look with confidence to satisfactory results flowing from it; but really that mission has nothing to do with the Vote of the evening, and it will be much better to defer any discussion concerning it until we have fuller information before us, and when the Envoy is himself—as I hope he soon will be—in his place in Parliament. What we have to do tonight is to agree to the Vote for the purchase of these shares. I have never recommended, and I do not now recommend this purchase as a financial investment. If it gave us 10 per cent of interest and a security as good as the Consols, I do not think an English Minister would be justified in making such an investment; still less if he is obliged to borrow the money for the occasion. I do not recommend it either as a commercial speculation, although I believe that many of those who have looked upon it with little favour will probably be surprised with the pecuniary results of the purchase. I have always, and do now recommend it to the country as a political transaction, and one which I believe is calculated to strengthen the Empire. That is the spirit in which it has been accepted by the country, which understands it though the two right hon. critics may not. They are really seasick of the "Silver Streak." They want the Empire to be maintained, to be strengthened; they will not be alarmed even it be increased. Because they think we are obtaining a great hold and interest in this important portion of Africa—because they believe that it secures to us a highway to our Indian Empire and our other dependencies, the people of England have from the first recognized the propriety and the wisdom of the step which we shall sanction tonight.

131. INSTRUCTIONS ON AFGHANISTAN: THE SECRETARY OF STATE FOR INDIA TO THE VICEROY DESIGNATE
28 February 1876

[India Office Library, Government of India, Political and Secret Department, MSS. Eur., E218/11]

Shir ʿAli, the amir of Afghanistan (1863–66, 1868–78), named heir apparent by Dust Muhammad, took five years to consolidate his rule. He was forcibly displaced from Kabul in May 1866 and later from Qandahar by his oldest brother, Muhammad Afdal. Only Herat remained to him, and even this district was governed not by Shir ʿAli but by his oldest son, Muhummad Yaʿqub. Then Muhammad Afdal died in October 1867 and was succeeded by the next oldest brother, Muhammad Aʿzam, who in turn was driven out of Qandahar by Yaʿqub Khan in May 1868 and out of Kabul by Amir Shir ʿAli in September. By then, the Russian conquest of Bukhara had brought the tsarist realm into direct contact with Afghanistan on the north, with no clear boundary separating the two. In the south, British India had already been pushing against Afghanistan for more than thirty years. Shir ʿAli's problem of political survival, after reuniting Afghanistan in 1868, was thus a massive one: how to keep the power that he had forcibly wrested from immediate kin, including his oldest son, and how to defend that domain against acquisitive foreign neighbors. Having won the throne the hard way, he was determined to establish a firm line of succession and promptly chose as heir his younger son, the *sardar*[1] ʿAbdallah Jan Khan. In a meeting at Ambala in the Punjab in March 1869, Shir ʿAli failed to persuade the British viceroy to conclude an alliance and failed even to budge Lord Mayo from the fixed British-Indian policy of strict neutrality among the domestic contenders in Afghanistan and the conduct of relations only with the actual rulers. However, the government of India did give to Shir ʿAli, then and later, occasional modest grants of money and arms. Even less successful were the negotiations launched in 1873 on the initiative of the next viceroy, Lord Northbrook. On that occasion Shir ʿAli simply refused to go to Simla, sending instead a trusted adviser, for the amir was still smarting from the decision made the previous year by the British arbitrator, who had ruled, on the Sistan border dispute,

---

1. Military-political chief, a title used by the amir's sons.

largely in favor of Persia. At the same time, Her Majesty's Government sought from Russia a clear understanding on its aspirations in Central Asia, letting Saint Petersburg know in forceful but correct diplomatic idiom that Russia would not be allowed to interfere in Afghanistan or in any other state contiguous with India. Indeed, assurances that Afghanistan lay outside the sphere of Russian action were repeatedly given to Britain in these years. Russia even agreed that it would refrain from appointing agents to Afghanistan and that it would not object to the presence there of British agents. The issue of representation became a central one almost from the moment that Lord Salisbury took over the management of the India Office in February 1874 in Disraeli's Conservative government, for Shir 'Ali refused even to consider the accreditation of a British instead of an Indian Muslim agent. In January 1875 Salisbury informed the prime minister that he was "getting uneasy about our lack of information from Afghanistan," and when Disraeli replied that he shared the apprehension the secretary of state for India told the viceroy, "Our position with respect to Afghanistan is so anomalous that some steps must soon be taken to set it right. It is the only Power on the face of the earth that, professing to be friendly, will not admit a representative in its territory from us" (as cited by Cecil, *Life of Robert, Marquis of Salisbury*, 2: 71–72). To Salisbury, representation looked like nothing more than providing a secure means of communication, but in Shir 'Ali, it evoked suspicions that the acceptance of a permanent British mission to Kabul would simply convert Afghanistan into another Indian princely state, with total loss of external, and substantial abridgement of internal, sovereignty. Reproduced below are Salisbury's instructions to Lytton, which marked the beginning of the end of the policy of "masterly inactivity." Fraser-Tytler, *Afghanistan*, p. 2, chaps. 7–8; Gregorian, *Emergence of Modern Afghanistan*, chap. 4; Sykes, *History of Afghanistan*, vol. 2, chaps. 34–37; Rawlinson, *England and Russia in the East*, chaps. 5–6; Balfour, *Lord Lytton's Indian Administration*, chap. 5; Singhal, *India and Afghanistan*, chaps. 1–2.

1. The tranquillity of the British power in India is so far dependent on its relations with the Trans-frontier States, that Her Majesty's Government cannot view without anxiety the present unsatisfactory condition of those relations. The increasing weakness and uncertainty of British influence in Afghanistan constitutes a prospective peril to British interests; the deplorable interruption of it in Khelat inflicts upon them an immediate inconvenience by involving the cessation of all effective control over the turbulent and predatory habits of the Trans-Indus tribes.

2. In view of these considerations, Her Majesty's Government have commended to the consideration of the Governor General of India in Council arrangements for promoting unity of purpose and consistency of conduct in the administration of the Sindh frontier. They have also instructed the Viceroy to find an early occasion for sending to Caubul a temporary mission, furnished with such instructions as may, perhaps, enable it to overcome the Amir's apparent reluctance to the establishment of permanent British Agencies in Afghanistan, by convincing His Highness that the Government of India is not coldly indifferent to the fears he has so frequently urged upon its attention; that it is willing to afford him material support in the defence of his territories from any actual and unprovoked external aggression, but that it cannot practically avert or provide for such a contingency without timely and unrestricted permission to place its own Agents in those parts of his dominions whence they may best watch the course of events.

3. It appears to Her Majesty's Government that the present moment it favourable for the execution of this last-mentioned instruction. The Queen's assumption of the

Imperial title in relation to Her Majesty's Indian subjects, feudatories, and allies will now for the first time conspicuously transfer to Her Indian dominion, in form as well as in fact, the supreme authority of the Indian Empire. It will, therefore, be one of your earliest duties to notify to the Amir of Afghanistan and the Khan of Khelat your assumption of the Viceregal office, under these new conditions.

4. A special mission, having for this purpose a twofold destination, might perhaps be advantageously despatched from Jacobabad, up the Bolan Pass, to Quetta, where the Khan could be invited to meet and receive it. After delivering your letter to the Khan, the mission might proceed to Kandahar, and thence, under an escort furnished by the Amir, continue its journey to Cabul. From Cabul it would return to India, either through the Koorum Valley or the Khyber Pass, according to circumstances.

5. Her Majesty's Government, however, only suggest this plan to your consideration, with due reference to the circumstances of the moment as they arise. You may possibly find it advisable, on your arrival at Calcutta, to communicate indirectly with the Amir through your Commissioner at Peshawur. This officer might privately inform Shere Ali of your intention to send a complimentary letter to him, as well as to the Khan of Khelat, and ascertain the route by which it would be most agreeable to His Highness that the mission charged with the delivery of that letter should approach his capital. If the Amir expresses any preference for the northern route, the mission could proceed directly to Cabul by the Khyber Pass, returning to India through Kandahar and Khelat.

6. To invite the confidence of the Amir will be the primary purpose of your Agent. To secure that confidence must be the ultimate object of your Government. But to invite confidence is to authorise the frank utterance of hopes which it may be impossible to satisfy, and fears which it may be dangerous to confirm. Whether these hopes and fears be reasonable or the reverse, their open avowal is, in the opinion of Her Majesty's Government, preferable to their concealment.

7. The maintenance in Afghanistan of a strong and friendly power has at all times been the object of British policy. The attainment of this object is now to be considered with due reference to the situation created by the recent and rapid advance of the Russian arms in Central Asia towards the northern frontiers of British India. Her Majesty's Government cannot view with complete indifference the probable influence of that situation upon the uncertain character of an Oriental Chief whose ill-defined dominions are thus brought, within a steadily narrowing circle, between the conflicting pressures of two great military empires, one of which expostulates and remains passive, whilst the other apologises and continues to move forward.

8. It is well known that not only the English newspapers, but also all works published in England upon Indian questions, are rapidly translated for the information of the Amir, and carefully studied by His Highness. Sentiments of irritation and alarm at the advancing power of Russia in Central Asia find frequent expression through the English press, in language which, if taken by Shere Ali for a revelation of the mind of the English Government, must have long been accumulating in his mind impressions unfavourable to its confidence in British power. Whether the passivity of that power, in presence of a situation thus unofficially discussed with disquietude, be attributed by the Amir to connivance with the political designs, or fear of the military force, of his Russian neighbours,—the inference, although erroneous, is in either case prejudicial to our influence in Afghanistan.

9. The Russian Ambassador at the Court of St. James has been officially informed by Her Majesty's Principal Secretary of State for Foreign Affairs that the objects of British policy as regards Afghanistan are—

1st. To secure that State against aggression.

2nd. To promote tranquillity on the borders of that country, by giving such moral and material support to the Amir, without interfering in the internal affairs of his country, as may enable Her Majesty's Government to prevent a recurrence of the disturbances and conflicts between rival candidates for power among his own family, or the Meers of the different Provinces.

10. Her Majesty's Government would not, therefore, view with indifference any attempt on the part of Russia to compete with British influence in Afghanistan; nor could the Amir's reception of a British Agent (whatever be the official rank of function of that Agent) in any part of the dominions belonging to His Highness afford for his subsequent reception of a Russian Agent similarly accredited any pretext to which the Government of Her Majesty would not be entitled to except as incompatible with the assurances spontaneously offered to it by the Cabinet of St. Petersburg. You will bear in mind these facts when framing instructions for your mission to Cabul. To demands which you have no intention of conceding your Agent will oppose a frank and firm refusal. You will instruct him to prevent such demands from becoming subjects of discussion. Others which, under certain conditions, you may be willing to entertain, he will undertake to refer to your Government, with such favourable assurances as may induce the Amir to recognize the advantage of facilitating, by compliance with your wishes, the fulfilment of his own.

11. If the language and demeanour of the Amir be such as to promise no satisfactory result of the negotiations thus opened, His Highness should be distinctly reminded that he is isolating himself, at his own peril, from the friendship and protection it is his interest to seek and deserve.

12. The requests which may be made by Shere Ali in connexion with his reception of permanent British Agents in Afghanistan will probably raise the question of granting to His Highness—

1st. A fixed and augmented subsidy.

2nd. A more decided recognition than has yet been accorded by the Government of India to the order of succession established by him in favour of his younger son, Abdullah Jan.

3rd. An explicit pledge, by Treaty or otherwise, of material support in case of foreign aggression.

13. The first of these questions is of secondary magnitude. You will probably deem it inexpedient to commit your Government to any permanent pecuniary obligation on behalf of a neighbour whose conduct and character have hitherto proved uncertain. On the other hand, you may possibly find it worth while to increase from time to time the amount of pecuniary assistance which up to the present moment the Amir has been receiving. But your decision on this point can only be determined by circumstances which have not arisen, and considerations which must be left to your appreciation of such circumstances.

14. With regard to the recognition of Abdulla Jan, whose selection as legitimate successor to the throne of his father has been made with much solemnity by Shere Ali, and ostensibly acquiesced in by the most influential of the Afghan Chiefs, Her Majesty's Government in considering this question have before them the solemn and deliberate declaration made in 1869 by Lord Northbrook's predecessor to the present Amir, viz., that "the British Government does not desire to interfere in the internal affairs of Afghanistan, yet considering that the bonds of friendship between that Government and your Highness have been lately more closely drawn than heretofore, it will view with severe displeasure any attempts on the part of your rivals to disturb your position as Ruler of Cabul, and rekindle civil war; and it will further endeavour from time to time, by such means as circumstances may require, to strengthen the Government of your Highness to enable you to exercise with equity and with justice your rightful rule, and to transmit to your descendants all the dignities and honours of which you are the lawful possessor."

15. The Government of India having in 1869 made that declaration, which was approved by Her Majesty's advisers, have not based upon it any positive measures; while to the Amir, who had received that declaration under circumstances of some solemnity and parade, it appears to have conveyed a pledge of definite action in his favour. It is not surprising that these conflicting interpretations of an ambiguous formula should have occasioned mutual disappointment to His Highness and the Government of India.

16. Her Majesty's Government do not desire to renounce their traditional policy of abstention from all unnecessary interference in the internal affairs of Afghanistan. But the frank recognition of a *de facto* order in the succession established by a *de facto* Government to the throne of a foreign State does not, in their opinion, imply or necessitate any intervention in the internal affairs of that State.

17. You may also find it in your power to bring about a reconciliation between the Amir and his nephew, Abdul Rahman Khan, who is now a refugee at Samarcand, under Russian protection. The order of succession established by Shere Ali would derive increased solidity from the support of this powerful malcontent, whose adhesion to it might, perhaps, be secured through the friendly assistance of your Government.

18. Any of these arrangements might strengthen the position of the Government of India in Afghanistan, by securing its influence over the present Ruler of that country, and exhausting some of the sources of the political and social confusion which his death is now likely to occasion. But you will fully understand that, in adverting to them, I am only suggesting points to which your consideration should be directed, and am in no way limiting your discretion with respect to them.

19. It remains to consider the question of giving to the Amir a definite assurance of material support in case of external aggression upon those territories over which Her Majesty's Government has publicly recognized and officially maintained his right of sovereignty.

20. With or without any such assurance, England would be impelled by her own interests to assist His Highness in repelling the invasion of his territory by a foreign power. It is, therefore, on all accounts desirable that the Government of India should have at its disposal adequate means for the prevention of a catastrophe which may yet be averted by prudence, and the fulfilment of an obligation which, should it ever arise, could not be evaded with honour. The want of such means constitutes the weakness of the present situation.

21. In the year 1873, Lord Northbrook gave to the Envoy of the Amir the personal assurance that, in the event of any aggression upon the territories of His Highness which the British Government had failed to avert by negotiation, that Government would be prepared "to assure the Amir that they will afford him assistance in the shape of arms and money, and will also, in case of necessity, assist him with troops."

22. The terms of this declaration, however, although sufficient to justify reproaches on the part of Shere Ali if, in the contingency to which it referred, he should be left unsupported by the British Government, were unfortunately too ambiguous to secure confidence or inspire gratitude on the part of His Highness. The Amir, in fact, appears to have remained under a resentful impression that his Envoy had been trifled with, and his attitude towards the Government of India has ever since been characterized by ambiguity and reserve.

23. If, therefore, Shere Ali be frank with your Envoy, he will probably renew to him the demand addressed in 1873, through his own Envoy, to Lord Northbrook, "that in the event of any aggression of the Amir's territories, the British Government should distinctly state that it regards the aggressor as its enemy; and, secondly, that the contingency of an aggression by Russia should be specifically mentioned in the written assurance to be given to the Amir."

To answer this renewed demand in terms identical with those of the answer formerly given to it would prejudice, instead of improve, your relations with the Amir, by the evasion of an invited confidence.

24. Her Majesty's Government are, therefore, prepared to sanction and support any more definite declaration which may, in your judgment, secure to their unaltered policy the advantages of which it has been hitherto deprived by an apparent doubt of its sincerity. But they must reserve to themselves entire freedom of judgment as to the character of circumstances involving the obligation of material support to the Amir, and it must be distinctly understood that only in some clear case of unprovoked aggression would such an obligation arise.

25. In the next place, they cannot secure the integrity of the Amir's dominions, unless His Highness be willing to afford them every reasonable facility for such precautionary measures as they may deem requisite. These precautionary measures by no means involve the establishment of British garrisons in any part of Afghanistan, nor do Her Majesty's Government entertain the slightest desire to quarter British soldiers upon Afghan soil; but they must have, for their own Agents, undisputed access to its frontier positions. They must also have adequate means of confidentially conferring with the Amir upon all matters as to which the proposed declaration would recognize a community of interests. They must be entitled to expect becoming attention to their friendly counsels; and the Amir must be made to understand that, subject to all fair allowance for the condition of the country, and the character of the population, territories ultimately dependent upon British power for their defence must not be closed to those of the Queen's officers or subjects who may be duly authorized to enter them.

26. Her Majesty's Government are also of opinion that the establishment, if possible, of a telegraph from some point on the Indian frontier to Cabul, *viâ* the Koorum Valley, is an object deserving of your consideration, and the permanent presence at the Viceregal Court of a properly accredited Afghan Envoy is much to be desired, as a guarantee for the due fulfilment of counter obligations on the part of the Amir, and the uninterrupted facility of your confidential relations with His

Highness. Subject to these general conditions, Her Majesty's Government can see no objection to your compliance with any reasonable demand on the part of Shere Ali for more assured support and protection, such as pecuniary assistance, the advice of British officers in the improvement of his military organization, or a promise, not vague, but strictly guarded and clearly circumscribed, of adequate aid against actual and unprovoked attack by any foreign power. Such a promise personally given to the Amir will probably satisfy His Highness, if the terms of it be unequivocal. But Her Majesty's Government do not wish to fetter your discretion in considering the advantages of a treaty on the basis above indicated.

27. The conduct of Shere Ali has more than once been characterised by so significant a disregard of the wishes and interests of the Government of India, that the irretrievable alienation of his confidence in the sincerity and power of that Government is a contingency which cannot be dismissed as impossible. Should such a fear be confirmed by the result of the proposed negotiation, no time must be lost in reconsidering, from a new point of view, the policy to be pursued in reference to Afghanistan.

28. On the other hand, the success of those efforts (which, if they be made at all, cannot be safely delayed) will be pregnant with results so advantageous to the British power in India that Her Majesty's Government willingly leave to the exercise of your judgment every reasonable freedom in carrying out the present instructions.

132. KHEDIVAL DECREE ESTABLISHING A PUBLIC DEBT COMMISSION IN EGYPT
2 May 1876

[Great Britain, *Parliamentary Papers, 1876*, 83: 71–72]

The purchase by the British government of the khedive's interest in the Suez Canal Company gave Isma'il only a few months' grace from his creditors. No longer able to contract new loans, Isma'il suspended payment of treasury bills in early April 1876.

In less than a month he issued, under the influence of French and Italian advisers, the following decree providing for a public debt commission. On 7 May the khedive promulgated a "unification decree" (text in *Parliamentary Papers, 1876*, 83; 69–71) calling for the consolidation of all Egyptian debts at 7 percent interest. To the specific arrangements laid down in the latter act, the British took exception, and their resistance ultimately led to the issuance of a fresh decree on 18 November 1876 (French text in *British and Foreign State Papers*, 67: 1024–32), in which Egyptian finances were placed under French and British controllers general, who supervised the revenue and expenditures of the Egyptian government. Landes, *Bankers and Pashas*; Haekal, *La dette publique égyptienne*; Elliot, *Life of George Joachim Goschen*, vol. 1, chap. 5; Langer, *European Alliances and Alignments*, chap. 8; C. Wilson, *Chapters from my Official Life*, chaps. 11–14; Cromer, *Modern Egypt*, vol. 1, chaps. 2–3; Duflot, *La caisse de la dette et les finances égyptiennes*; Sammarco, *Précis de l'histoire d'Egypte*, vol. 4, chaps. 16–18; Mulhall, "Egyptian Finance"; Jenks, *Migration of British Capital*, pp. 311–25; McCoan, *Egypt As It Is*, chaps. 6–7; Dicey, *Story of the Khedivate*, pp. 47–188.

We, the Khedive of Egypt, desiring to take definitive and opportune measures for obtaining the unification of the different debts of the State and those of the Daira Sanieh, and also desiring the reduction of the excessive charges resulting from these debts, and wishing to bear solemn testimony to our firm intention to secure every guarantee to all persons interested, have resolved to establish a special Treasury charged with the regular service of the public debt, and to appoint to its management foreign Commissioners, who at our request will be indicated by the respective Governments as fit officials to fill the post to which they will be appointed by us in the quality of Egyptian officials, and under the following conditions. Having consulted our Privy Council, we have decreed, and do hereby decree, as follows:—

ART. 1. A Treasury of the Public Debt is established, charged with receiving the funds necessary for the interest and the redemption of the debt, and with applying them to this object exclusively.

ART. 2. The officials, the local Treasuries, or the special Administrations, after collecting, receiving, or accumulating the revenues specially devoted to the payment of the debt, are or shall be in future charged to pay them into the Central Treasury or to keep them at the disposal of the Intendants of Public Expenditure ("Ordonnateurs des Dépenses de l'Etat"). The Intendants of Public Expenditure are,

by virtue of the present Decree, bound to pay these revenues on account of the State Treasury into the special Treasury of the Public Debt, which will be considered in this respect as a special Treasury. These officials, treasuries and administrations can only procure a valid discharge by means of the vouchers which will be delivered to them by the said Treasury of the Public Debt. Any other order or voucher will not be valid. These same officials, treasuries or administrations will every month send to the Minister of Finance a statement of the receipts or collections made by themselves directly or paid in by the receivers of the revenues specially devoted to the debt and the payments made into the special Treasury of the Public Debt. The Minister of Finance will communicate these statements to the Administration of the Treasury of the Public Debt.

The Treasury of the Public Debt shall receive from the Daira Sanieh the entire sum necessary for the interest and redemption of the amount of its unified debt, and it shall likewise receive the funds for the yearly payment due to the English Government, and representing the interest on the Suez Canal shares.

ART. 3. If the payments of the revenue devoted to the debt be insufficient to meet the half-yearly charges, the special Public Debt Department will demand from the Treasury, through the intermediary of the Minister of Finance, the sum required to complete the half-yearly payments; the Treasury will have to deliver this sum a fortnight before the payments are due. If the funds in hand constitute a surplus over the amount necessary for the payment of the interest and the sinking fund, the special Treasury of the Public Debt will pay this surplus at the end of each year to the general Treasury of the Exchequer. The Treasury of the Public Debt will submit its accounts, which will be examined and reported upon according to law.

ART. 4. The suits which the Treasury and its Directors, on its behalf, acting in the name and in the interests of the creditors, mostly of foreign nationality, may consider they have to bring against the financial administration represented by the Minister of Finance in so far as regards the guardianship of the guarantees of the debt which we have confided to the said Treasury, will be brought in the terms of their jurisdiction before the new tribunals which, in conformity with the agreement entered into with the Powers, have been instituted in Egypt.

ART. 5. The Commissioners selected as stated above will have the direction of the special Treasury of the Public Debt. They will be appointed by us for five years, and will sit in Cairo. Their functions may be continued after the five years have expired, and in case of the death or resignation of one of them the vacancy will be filled by us in the manner of the original appointment. They may intrust one of themselves with the functions of President, and the latter will notify his nomination to the Minister of Finance.

ART. 6. The cost of exchange, insurance, and conveyance of specie abroad, as well as the commission for the payment of the coupons, will be borne by the Government. The Directors of the Treasury will come to a previous arrangement with the Ministers of Finance with regard to all these operations, but the Minister will decide whether the despatch of these sums is to be effected in specie or by letters of exchange.

ART. 7. The Treasury will not be allowed to employ any funds, disposable or not, in operations of credit, commerce, industry, &c.

ART. 8. The Government will not be able, without an agreement with the majority of the Commissioners directing the Treasury of the Public Debt, to effect in any of the taxes specially devoted to the Debt any changes which might result in a diminution of the revenue from these taxes. At the same time, the Government may farm out one or several of these taxes, provided that the contract entered into insure a revenue at least equal to that already existing, and may also conclude Treaties of commerce introducing modifications in the Customs duties.

ART. 9. The Government undertakes not to issue any Treasury Bonds or any other new bonds, and not to contract any other loan of any nature whatsoever. This same engagement is entered into in the name of the Daira Sanieh. Nevertheless, in case the Government, from urgent national reasons, should find itself placed under the necessity of having recourse to credit, it may do so within the limits of strict necessity, and without doing anything to affect the employment of the revenues set apart for the Treasury of the Public Debt, or to cause their diversion from their destination. These totally exceptional loans can only be contracted after an agreement on the subject with the Commissioners directing the Treasury.

ART. 10. In order that the arrangements stated in the preceding article shall not place obstacles in the way of the Administration, the Government may open a running account with a bank to facilitate its payments by means of anticipations to be regulated in accordance with the year's receipts. The debit or credit balance will be settled at the end of each year. This current account must never be overdrawn during the year by more than 50,000,000 fr.

133. SUEZ CANAL COMPANY ASSEMBLY'S RESOLUTION ON BRITISH PARTICIPATION IN THE COMPANY'S COUNCIL
27 June 1876

[Great Britain, *Parliamentary Papers, 1876*, 83: 379]

Title to the khedive's shares gave the British government a 44 percent interest in the Suez Canal Company and made it the largest single stockholder. The United Kingdom, however, was not automatically vested with, and indeed never acquired, command of the company's management. Power to revise the statutes of the company rested in the general meeting or assembly of the stockholders. But article 51 of the statutes stipulated that each owner could cast one vote in the assembly for every twenty-five shares in his possession up to an absolute maximum of ten votes. England, it was clear, could not revise the statutes at will. Still, as soon as the khedive's shares were purchased, Britain began to press for participation in the company's council or board of directors, which was charged with formulating policy. Originally comprising 32 members, the council was reduced in 1871 to 21. When the assembly voted in 1876 to accept 3 directors chosen by the British government, the size of the policy-making body was augmented to 24. Not until 1884, when the council was restored to its initial size of 32 members, did England at last secure 7 additional seats, which it allocated to ship owners. For references, see Doc. 128.

The Assembly, taking into account the XXIVth Article of the Statutes, and considering that there is occasion to ensure the representation of English interests in the Council, on account of the important share in the capital of the Company acquired by Great Britain;

Considering that, with a view of securing this representation, an Agreement has been entered into between the Government of Her Britannic Majesty and the Council of Administration, proposing the creation of three new Administrators' places, and considering the engagement to reserve these places as long as Her Majesty's Government shall remain the possessor of the shares it has acquired, to candidates nominated by the aforesaid Government, presented by the Council, and appointed by the Assembly in accordance with the customary formalities;

Adopts the following Resolution:

The number of Administrators, fixed at twenty-one by the XXIVth Article of the Statutes; as modified by a resolution of the General Assembly of the 24th of August, 1871, is increased to twenty-four.

The three places thus created shall be, from henceforth, and according as vacancies, occur, filled up in accordance with the conditions above specified.

134. THE CYPRUS CONVENTION: GREAT BRITAIN AND THE OTTOMAN EMPIRE
4 June 1878–3 February 1879

[Great Britain, Public Record Office, F.O. 93/110/27B]

Cyprus was the first province that Britain detached—significantly, on a de facto and not a de jure basis—from the Ottoman Empire, thus bringing to an end four decades of intimate cooperation with the Sublime Porte in resisting encroachment on its territory by the major European powers. This British action was one of the side effects of the Russian-Ottoman war of 1877–78. The war, in which the sultan's forces suffered decisive defeat, concerned primarily issues in the Balkans. Still, Russian troops occupied the northeast corner of Anatolia; and, in the preliminary treaty of peace of 3 March 1878 (text of San Stefano in Hertslet, *Map of Europe by Treaty*, 4: 2672–94), the Sublime Porte ceded Batum, Ardahan, Kars, Bayezit, and their immediate environs (art. 29). This, Disraeli and most of his cabinet feared, merely presaged a Russian drive toward the Gulf of Alexandretta which, if consummated, would have threatened British imperial communications in the Middle East. Indeed, less than a fortnight after the Russian declaration of war on 24 April 1877, London had warned Saint Petersburg against attempting any blockade of the Suez Canal, temporary occupation of Egypt or alteration of the straits regime (text, ibid., pp. 2615–17). By November, Disraeli began examining the question of procuring from the Sublime Porte, by purchase or otherwise, a naval base in the eastern Mediterranean. The cabinet formally considered the matter late in February 1878, but three more months elapsed before Cyprus was selected. Cyprus, Foreign Minister Lord Salisbury informed Austen Henry Layard, the British ambassador at Istanbul, on 16 May, "has the double advantage of vicinity both to Asia Minor and Syria; it would enable us without any act of overt hostility and without disturbing the peace of Europe, to accumulate material of war and, if requisite, the troops necessary for operations in Asia Minor or Syria, while it would not excite the jealousy which other Powers would feel at any acquisitions on the mainland" (Cecil, *Life of Robert, Marquis of Salisbury*, 2: 269). A week later, on instructions from London, Layard handed Sultan ʿAbdülhamid II (1876–1909) a draft agreement in the form of a defensive alliance, which he was given two days to accept. Ratifications of the principal instrument were exchanged at Istanbul on 15 July 1878. But in the preamble the sultan phrased the conditions of the alliance so broadly that Britain might have been held liable to defend his provinces in Europe as well as in Asia. To this Salisbury objected. Nonetheless, after prolonged but fruitless efforts to have the phraseology altered, the Foreign Office apparently acquiesced by mid-May 1880 in the form of ratifications as originally signed by the sultan. Cecil, op. cit., pp. 263–71; Monypenny and Buckle, *Life of Benjamin Disraeli*, 6: 291–303; Lee, *Great Britain and the Cyprus Convention Policy of 1878*; Medlicott, *Congress of Berlin*, and "Gladstone Government and the Cyprus Convention"; Hill, *History of Cyprus*, vol. 4, chaps. 7, 9; Headlam-Morley, *Studies in Diplomatic History*, chap. 7; Langer, *European Alliances and Alignments*, chap. 5; Temperley "Disraeli and Cyprus"; Loomie, "Cyprus Convention of June 4, 1878."

1. Convention of Defensive Alliance, 4 June 1878

ART. I. If Batoum, Ardahan, Kars, or any of them shall be retained by Russia, and if any attempt shall be made at any future time by Russia to take possession of any further territories of His Imperial Majesty the Sultan in Asia, as fixed by the Definitive Treaty of Peace, England engages to join His Imperial Majesty the Sultan in defending them by force of arms.

In return, His Imperial Majesty the Sultan promises to England to introduce necessary reforms, to be agreed upon later between the two Powers, into the government, and for the protection, of the Christian and other subjects of the Porte in these territories; and in order to enable England to make necessary provision for executing her engagement, His Imperial Majesty the Sultan further consents to assign the Island of Cyprus to be occupied and administered by England.

2. Annex to the Convention, 1 July 1878

It is understood between the two High Contracting Parties that England agrees to the following conditions relating to her occupation and administration of the Island of Cyprus:—

I. That a Mussulman religious Tribunal (Mehkéméi Shéri) shall continue to exist in the island, which will take exclusive cognizance of religious matters, and of no others, concerning the Mussulman population of the island.

II. That a Mussulman resident in the Island shall be named by the Board of Pious Foundations in Turkey (Evkaf) to superintend, in conjunction with a Delegate to be appointed by the British Authorities, the administration of the property, funds, and lands belonging to mosques, cemeteries, Mussulman schools, and other religious establishments existing in Cyprus.

III. That England will pay to the Porte whatever is the present excess of revenue over expenditure in the island; this excess to be calculated upon and determined by the average of the last five years, stated to be 22,936 purses, to be duly verified hereafter, and to the exclusion of the produce of State and Crown lands let or sold during that period.

IV. That the Sublime Porte may freely sell and lease lands and other property in Cyprus belonging to the Ottoman Crown and State (Arazii Miriyé vé Emlaki Houmayoun) the produce of which does not form part of the revenue of the island referred to in Article III.

V. That the English Government, through their competent authorities, may purchase compulsorily, at a fair price, land required for public improvements, or for other public purposes, and land which is not cultivated.

VI. That if Russia restores to Turkey Kars and the other conquests made by her in Armenia during the last war, the Island of Cyprus will be evacuated by England, and the Convention of the 4th of June, 1878, will be at an end.

3. Additional Article of Legislation, 14 August 1878

It is understood between the High Contracting Parties, without prejudice to the express provisions of the Articles I, II, and IV of the Annex of the 1st July, 1878, that His Imperial Majesty the Sultan, in assigning the Island of Cyprus to be occupied and administered by England, has thereby transferred to and vested in Her Majesty the Queen, for the term of the occupation and no longer, full powers for making Laws and Conventions for the government of the Island in Her Majesty's name, and for the regulation of its commercial and Consular relations and affairs free from the Porte's control.

4. Declaration on Land, 3 February 1879

It having been agreed between Her Britannic Majesty's Government and that of His Imperial Majesty the Sultan that all the rights reserved to the Ottoman Crown and Government under Article IV of the Annex to the Convention signed at Constantinople on the 4th June, 1878, shall be commuted by a fixed annual money payment, the Undersigned, the Right Honourable Austen Henry Layard, Her Britannic Majesty's Ambassador Extraordinary and Minister Plenipotentiary to the Sublime Porte, and his Excellency Alexandre Carathéodory Pasha, His Imperial Majesty's Minister for Foreign Affairs, being duly authorized so to do, hereby declare that—

All property, revenues, and rights reserved to the Ottoman Crown and Government in the said Article IV of the Annex to the Convention of the 4th June, includ-ing all revenue derived from tapous, mahloul, and intikal are commuted hereby for a fixed annual payment of 5,000*l.* to be made by Her Britannic Majesty's Government to that of His Imperial Majesty the Sultan every year during the British occupation of Cyprus, to be calculated from the beginning of next financial year.

135. THE TREATY OF BERLIN
13 July 1878

(European ratifications exchanged, Berlin, 3 August 1878; Ottoman ratification, 28 August 1878; unilateral denunciation by the Sublime Porte, 13 November 1916)
[Great Britain, *Parliamentary Papers, 1878*, 83: 690–705]

The Congress of Berlin in 1878 was the European Concert's fifth and final major conference on Ottoman affairs, convened to mitigate the harsh terms that Russia had imposed on its adversary at San Stefano on 3 March 1878 (text in Hertslet, *Map of Europe by Treaty*, 4: 2672–94). The premiers and their foreign ministers represented the powers at Berlin, thus exemplifying diplomacy at the summit. The Congress of Berlin did not signal the end of conference diplomacy on Ottoman affairs, which had become institutionalized in Istanbul by the late 1870s in the "little concert," comprising the heads of the resident diplomatic missions of the great powers under the chairmanship of the Ottoman premier or foreign minister of the day. The "little concert," to which was entrusted the supervision of the cumulative arrangements made by the major powers in the middle decades of the nineteenth century, met almost continuously after the 1870s. The pertinent events leading to the Congress of Berlin were these: British-Russian relations had deteriorated markedly during the Russian-Ottoman War and its preliminary peace settlement at San Stefano. To restore European unity on the Ottoman Empire and bring Russia and England into line, Bismarck proposed that all the signatories of the treaty of Paris of 1856 (Doc. 105) assemble in Berlin to review the terms of the provisional peace Russia had imposed on the Sublime Porte. Once England had obtained the right to occupy Cyprus—an arrangement not immediately disclosed—in the event of Russia's retention of Ottoman territory in Asia, Disraeli consented to participate in the Congress of Berlin (13 June–13 July 1878). The resulting treaty laid down the definitive conditions of the Russian-Ottoman settlement, later formally endorsed by the two powers in a separate instrument of 27 January/8 February 1879 (text in ibid., pp. 2845–51). Apart from the articles appearing below, the treaty of Berlin related exclusively to the Balkans and Crete. Medlicott, *Congress of Berlin*; Langer, *European Alliances and Alignments*, chap. 5; Anderson, *Eastern Question*, chap. 7; Allen and Muratoff, *Caucasian Battlefields*, chaps. 7–15 (on the military campaigns in the Caucasus in 1877–78); Thompson, *Public Opinion and Lord Beaconsfield*, 2: 464–96; Holborn, *Deutschland und die Türkei*, chap. 1.

ART. LVIII. The Sublime Porte cedes to the Russian Empire in Asia the territories of Ardahan, Kars, and Batoum, together with the latter port, as well as all the territories comprised between the former Russo-Turkish frontier and the following line:—

The new frontier starting from the Black Sea, and coinciding with the line laid down by the Treaty of San Stefano as far as a point to the north-west of Khorda, and to the south of Artwin, continues in a straight line as far as the River Tchoroukh, crosses this river and passes to the east of Aschmichen, going in a straight line to the south so as to rejoin the Russian frontier indicated in the Treaty of San Stefano, at a point to the south of Nariman, leaving the town of Olti to Russia. From the point indicated near Nariman the frontier turns to tïe east, passes by Tebrenec, which remains to Russia, and continues as far as the Pennek Tschaï.

It follows this river as far as Bardouz, then turns towards the south, leaving Bardouz and Jönikioy to Russia. From a point to the west of the village of Karaougan, the frontier takes the direction of Medjingert, continues in a straight line towards the summit of the Mountain Kassadagh, and follows the line of the watershed between the affluents of the Araxes on the north and those of the Mourad Sou on the south, as far as the former frontier of Russia.

ART. LIX. His Majesty the Emperor of Russia declares that it is his intention to constitute Batoum a free port, essentially commercial.

ART. LX. The valley of Alaschkerd and the town of Bayazid, ceded to Russia by Article XIX of the Treaty of San Stefano, are restored to Turkey.

The Sublime Porte cedes to Persia the town and territory of Khotour, as fixed by the mixed Anglo-Russian Commission for the delimitation of the frontiers of Turkey and of Persia.

ART. LXI. The Sublime Porte undertakes to carry out, without further delay, the improvements and reforms demanded by local requirements in the provinces inhabited by the Armenians, and to guarantee their security against the Circassians and Kurds.

It will periodically make known the steps taken to this effect to the Powers, who will superintend their application.

ART. LXII. The Sublime Porte having expressed the intention to maintain the principle of religious liberty, and give it the widest scope, the Contracting Parties take note of this spontaneous declaration.

In no part of the Ottoman Empire shall difference of religion be alleged against any person as a ground for exclusion or incapacity as regards the discharge of civil and political rights, admission to the public employments, functions and honours, or the exercise of the various professions and industries.

All persons shall be admitted, without distinction of religion, to give evidence before the tribunals.

The freedom and outward exercise of all forms of worship are assured to all, and no hindrance shall be offered either to the hierarchical organization of the various communions or to their relations with their spiritual chiefs.

Ecclesiastics, pilgrims, and monks of all nationalities travelling in Turkey in Europe, or in Turkey in Asia, shall enjoy the same rights, advantages, and privileges.

The right of official protection by the Diplomatic and Consular Agents of the Powers in Turkey is recognized both as regards the above-mentioned persons and their religious, charitable, and other establishments in the Holy Places and elsewhere.

The rights possessed by France are expressly reserved, and it is well understood that no alterations can be made in the status quo in the Holy Places.

The monks of Mount Athos, of whatever country they may be natives, shall be maintained in their former possessions and advantages, and shall enjoy, without any exception, complete equality of rights and prerogatives.

ART. LXIII. The Treaty of Paris of March 30, 1856, as well as the Treaty of London of March 13, 1871, are maintained in all such of their provisions as are not abrogated or modified by the preceding stipulations.

136. DRAFT TREATY OF FRIENDSHIP AND ASSISTANCE:
RUSSIA AND AFGHANISTAN
9/21 August 1878

[Translated by Oles M. Smolansky from the Russian text in Terent'ev, *Istoriia zavoevaniia Srednei Azii*, 2: 451–54]

Russia became a next-door neighbor of Afghanistan in the late 1860s, when tsarist forces under the command of General Konstantin Petrovich von Kaufmann opened the final phase in their conquest of Central Asia. Von Kaufmann owed his appointment to General Dimitrii Alekseevich Miliutin, the minister for war at Saint Petersburg and the tsar's hawkish counselor on Central Asia. While prone to follow Miliutin's advice, Tsar Alexander II also occasionally listened to his dovish chancellor, Prince Alexandr Mikhailovich Gorchakov. Gorchakov well understood the source of British anxiety, because Afghanistan was the one "country" whose frontier the makers of Indian policy—whether in Britain or on the subcontinent, whether as advocates of the doctrine of "masterly inactivity" or as advocates of the forward policy—were persuaded was vulnerable. The chancellor sought recurrently to allay British fears by urging the tsar to slow the pace of Central Asian conquest and by assuring Britain that Afghanistan lay wholly outside the sphere in which the tsar aspired to exercise his influence. Between the outbreak of the Russian-Ottoman war in April 1877 and the signing of the treaty of Berlin (Doc. 135) fifteen months later, the tsar pursued a policy of threatening British India in Afghanistan in the hope of dissuading Britain from supporting the Sublime Porte. The climax came in the summer of 1878 when von Kaufmann named Major General Nikolai Grigor'evich Stoletov head of a mission to Kabul to keep alive Shir 'Ali's distrust of Britain's efforts to establish itself in Afghanistan. Shir 'Ali was no more desirous of entangling himself with Russia than with British India, but von Kaufmann simply ignored the amir's pleas to abandon the idea of a mission. Instead, the Russian governor general accepted Shir 'Ali's offer to send an ad hoc mission to Tashkent as a "decision" to accredit a permanent Afghan mission. As for Stoletov, von Kaufmann stated that the party was already on its way and that the amir would be held accountable for its safety and proper reception. In signing the following instrument with Shir 'Ali, Stoletov allegedly acted on his own authority. But the action came too late to enable the Russian hawks to derive any lasting benefit. Once a definitive Russian-Ottoman peace had been reached the preceding month at the Congress of Berlin, the tsar was no longer willing to provoke Britain in Afghanistan. Kazemzadeh, *Russia and Britain in Persia*, chap. 1; Fraser-Tytler, *Afghanistan*, chap. 8; Singhal, *India and Afghanistan*, chap. 3; Balfour, *Lord Lytton's Indian Administration*, chap. 7; Gregorian, *Emergence of Modern Afghanistan*, chap. 4; Alder, *British India's Northern Frontier*, chap. 4.

ART. 1. The Russian Imperial Government regards the state of Shir 'Ali Khan, the Amir of Afghanistan, as a sovereign state and, because of ancient friendship, wishes to maintain friendly relations with it, as with other independent states.

ART. 2. Viewing Afghanistan as a state in which order and authority have been established to such a degree that the ruler of the country has sufficient power to deal with internal enemies in case of need, the Russian Imperial Government will not interfere in the internal affairs of the country. Only if the state of the Amir or of his successor (when he becomes Amir) should be exposed to danger by an internal or external enemy might the Russian Imperial Government, at the request of the Amir or his successor (when he becomes Amir), intervene in the internal affairs [of Afghanistan, including] even the granting of proper aid.

ART. 3. The Russian Imperial Government, following the example prevailing in other countries, has readily recognized as the successor to the Afghan throne the *Sardar* 'Abdallah Khan, the son chosen by the Amir. The Amir solemnly communicated [his choice] to the Governor General of Turkistan, through whom the news has been joyfully received by the Russian Imperial Government.

Thus, in acknowledgment of the friendly relations between Afghanistan and Russia, the chosen successor, along with his successors, from generation to generation, has been recognized by the Imperial Government.

Since, however, the appointed successor has now, by the will of God, passed away, the Russian Imperial Government, following past practices and according to established custom, will recognize that successor whom the Amir finds worthy.

ART. 4. If any complications should arise between Afghanistan and another foreign state, the Russian Imperial Government, upon request by the Amir, will use those means and methods which, as a result of the Amir's request, it may deem necessary to eliminate [such] misunderstandings and collisions, either through direct influence on the foreign state which is threatening Afghanistan or through the mediation of other states.

ART. 5. Should—may God forbid it—some foreign state enter and occupy the territory of Afghanistan by military means, the Imperial Government will give [Afghanistan] military aid, in recognition of the friendship between Russia and Afghan-istan, if the Amir should request [such] military support and if [the Imperial Government] should find it impossible to prevent a military confrontation by means of peaceful advice and suggestion. Then, if a war should break out, reliance on the Almighty Creator of the universe, the friendship between Afghanistan and Russia and the military support of the Russian Imperial Government will enable the Afghan Amir to regain, by victories and the sword, his former territories which previously had passed by conquest under the control of another state.

ART. 6. If the events set forth in Article 5 should occur, the Amir of Afghanistan shall approach the Governor General of Turkistan, presenting him with a detailed description of the extent, means, and plans of the military aid requested of the Russian Imperial Government. The Governor General of Turkistan has been granted by the Russian Imperial Government appropriate powers to act in response to the above-mentioned requests by the Amir.

ART. 7. In view of the friendly relations between Afghanistan and the Russian Imperial Government, the ruler of Afghanistan may send to Russia persons of his own choice for [technical], including military, training. In sending such persons [to Russia], the Amir of Afghanistan shall in each instance inform the Governor General of Turkistan.

ART. 8. Persons who may, in accordance with Article 7, be sent from Afghanistan to Russia as a result of orders issued in each instance by the Russian Imperial Government, shall enjoy the cooperation of the responsible military and civilian authorities and shall be received and feasted everywhere as persons chosen by the ruler of a friendly state.

ART. 9. Should the ruler of Afghanistan require technicians of various types, including military, the Imperial Government shall give its full cooperation.

ART. 10. In view of the friendly relations between Russia and Afghanistan, the Russian Imperial Government, in the person of the Governor General of Turkistan, and the government of the Afghan state shall, by mutual consent, take the necessary steps to encourage, facilitate, and guarantee the safety of their mutual trade relations.

ART. 11. Since relations between the two states may increase as a result of their friendship, it is necessary to establish the frequent exchange of all information and news which might be of interest to both parties.

Any friend of Shir 'Ali Khan, Amir of Afghanistan, must be regarded as a friend of the Russian Imperial Government, and any enemy of the state of Shir 'Ali Khan, Amir of Afghanistan, must be regarded as an enemy of the Russian Imperial Government, and vice versa.

Therefore, on the basis of the terms above stated from this day and forever, the Russian Imperial Government deems it essential to extend to the Amir of the Afghan state such aid, assistance, and support as it may deem necessary bye very means, overt and covert, external and internal, and mutually useful and expedient. . . .

137. TREATY OF PEACE AND AMICABLE RELATIONS (GANDAMAK) BRITISH INDIA AND AFGHANISTAN
26 May 1879

(Ratified by the viceroy at Simla, 30 May 1879)
[From the text presented to Parliament, "Despatch from Government of India, no. 136 of 1879, forwarding Treaty of Peace," Afghanistan no. 6, C. 2362]

The Stoletov mission brought no advantages to Russia, and by pressing too hard on British India's sensitive nerve it helped precipitate the second British-Afghan war (21 November 1878–26 May 1879). More than six weeks before Stoletov and his retinue actually reached Kabul, the government of India learned about Shir 'Ali's acceptance of the Russian mission and began amassing troops along the Afghan border. Late in August the viceroy, the earl of Lytton, sent a former Indian Muslim agent in Kabul as special envoy to notify the amir that General Sir Neville Chamberlain would head a mission to the Afghan capital to resume negotiations, which had been suspended nearly a year and a half earlier, and that, as befit the dignity of a viceregal envoy, he would have an escort of about two hundred men. Shir 'Ali refused to receive Chamberlain, however, and even turned back an advance party on 21 September at the Khyber Pass, then part of Afghanistan. This the government of India viewed as a hostile act, coming as it did after the reception of the Russian envoy and after formal assurances that the Chamberlain mission was a friendly one. On 2 November Lytton issued an ultimatum to Shir 'Ali, advising him of "the assemblage of Her Majesty's forces on your frontier" and demanding "a full and suitable apology" and the acceptance of a permanent British diplomatic agency. The term of the ultimatum ran out on 20 November without word from Kabul, and on the following day British-Indian troops entered Afghanistan in force. Shir 'Ali, after naming his son Ya'qub regent, left Kabul on 22 December with the remaining members of the Russian mission and took refuge in Russian territory, where he received no material support; he later returned to northern Afghanistan and died in Mazar-i Sharif in February 1879. The following treaty imposed on Amir Ya'qub conditions that the earl of Lytton had earlier failed to achieve through negotiations: the surrender to

Britain of Afghanistan's external sovereignty and the accreditation of a permanent British mission at Kabul. Moreover, the amir was forced to cede to British India districts held important for its defense, including the Khyber Pass. Fraser-Tytler, *Afghanistan*, pt. 2, chap. 8; Singhal, *India and Afghanistan*, chaps. 2–3; Gregorian, *Emergence of Modern Afghanistan*, chap. 4; Balfour, *Lord Lytton's Indian Administration*, chaps. 7–8; Ghose, *England and Afghanistan*, chap. 2; Hanna, *Second Afghan War*; Argyll, *Afghan Question*; Bellew, *Afghanistan and the Afghans*.

The following Articles of a Treaty for the restoration of peace and amicable relations have been agreed upon between the British Government and His Highness Muhammad Yakub Khan, Amir of Afghanistan and its dependencies:—

ART. 1. From the day of the exchange of the ratifications of the present Treaty there shall be perpetual peace and friendship between the British Government on the one part and His Highness the Amir of Afghanistan and its dependencies, and his successors, on the other.

ART. 2. His Highness the Amir of Afghanistan and its dependencies engages, on the exchange of the ratifications of this Treaty, to publish a full and complete amnesty, absolving all his subjects from any responsibility for intercourse with the British Forces during the war, and to guarantee and protect all persons of whatever degree from any punishment or molestation on that account.

ART. 3. His Highness the Amir of Afghanistan and its dependencies agrees to conduct his relations with Foreign States, in accordance with the advice and wishes of the British Government. His Highness the Amir will enter into no engagements with Foreign States, and will not take up arms against any Foreign State, except with the concurrence of the British Government. On these conditions the British Government will support the Amir against any foreign aggression with money, arms, or troops, to be employed in whatsoever manner the British Government may judge best for this purpose. Should British troops at any time enter Afghanistan for the purpose of repelling foreign aggression, they will return to their stations in British territory as soon as the object for which they entered has been accomplished.

ART. 4. With a view to the maintenance of the direct and intimate relations now established between the British Government and His Highness the Amir of Afghanistan and for the better protection of the frontiers of His Highness' dominions, it is agreed that a British Representative shall reside at Kabul, with a suitable escort in a place of residence appropriate to his rank and dignity. It is also agreed that the British Government shall have the right to depute British Agents with suitable escorts to the Afghan frontiers, whensoever this may be considered necessary by the British Government in the interests of both States, on the occurrence of any important external fact. His Highness the Amir of Afghanistan may on his part depute an Agent to reside at the Court of His Excellency the Viceroy and Governor-General of India, and at such other places in British India as may be similarly agreed upon.

ART. 5. His Highness the Amir of Afghanistan and its dependencies guarantees the personal safety and honourable treatment of British Agents within his jurisdiction; and the British Government on its part undertakes that its Agents shall never in any way interfere with the internal administration of His Highness' dominions.

ART. 6. His Highness the Amir of Afghanistan and its dependencies undertakes, on behalf of himself and his successors, to offer no impediment to British subjects peacefully trading within his dominions so long as they do so with the permission of the British Government, and in accordance with such arrangements as may be mutually agreed upon from time to time between the two Governments.

ART. 7. In order that the passage of trade between the territories of the British Government and of His Highness the Amir of Afghanistan, may be open and uninterrupted, His Highness the Amir of Afghanistan agrees to use his best endeavours to ensure the protection of traders, and to facilitate the transit of goods along the well-known customary roads of Afghanistan. These roads shall be improved and maintained in such manner as the two Governments may decide to be most expeident for the general convenience of traffic, and under such financial arrangements as may be mutually determined upon between them. The arrangements made for the maintenance and security of the aforesaid roads, for the settlement of the duties to be levied upon merchandize carried over these roads, and for the general protection and development of trade with and through the dominions of His Highness, will be stated in a separate Commercial Treaty, to be concluded within one year, due regard being given to the state of the country.

ART. 8. With a view to facilitate communications between the allied Governments and to aid and develop intercourse and commercial relations between the two countries, it is hereby agreed that a line of telegraph from Kurram to Kabul shall be constructed by and at the cost of the British Government, and the Amir of Afghanistan hereby undertakes to provide for the protection of this telegraph line.

ART. 9. In consideration of the renewal of a friendly alliance between the two States which has been attested and secured by the foregoing Articles, the British Government restores to His Highness the Amir of Afghanistan and its dependencies the towns of Kandahar and Jellalabad, with all the territory now in possession of the British armies, excepting the districts of Kurram, Pishin, and Sibi. His Highness the Amir of Afghanistan and its dependencies agrees on his part that the districts of Kurram and Pishin and Sibi, according to the limits defined in the schedule annexed,[1] shall remain under the protection and administrative control of the British Government: that is to say, the aforesaid districts shall be treated as assigned districts, and shall not be considered as permanently severed from the limits of the Afghan kingdom. The revenues of these districts after deducting the charges of civil administration shall be paid to His Highness the Amir.

The British Government will retain in its own hands the control of the Khyber and Michni Passes, which lie between the Peshawur and Jellalabad Districts, and of all relations with the independent tribes of the territory directly connected with these Passes.

ART. 10. For the further support of His Highness the Amir in the recovery and maintenance of his legitimate authority, and in consideration of the efficient fulfilment in their entirety of the engagements stipulated by the foregoing Articles, the British Government agrees to pay to His Highness the Amir and to his successors an annual subsidy of six lakhs of Rupees.

---

1. Omitted here and in the text presented to Parliament.

138. BRITISH POLICY ON EGYPT
16 October 1879

[Great Britain, Public Record Office, F.O. 78/2997, no. 275]

Khedive Isma'il's attempt in April 1879 to terminate the British-French Dual Control (Doc. 132) cost him the viceroyship of Egypt. England and France, joined by the other European powers, brought pressure to bear on the sultan, who on 26 June deposed Isma'il and named as khedive his eldest son, Tawfiq. In September the British and French controllers general were reappointed on the express condition that they could not again be dismissed without the approval of the two Eruorpean governments. The following letter of instructions from Foreign Secretary Lord Salisbury to Edward Malet, Her Majesty's new agent and consul general in Cairo, illumines British policy toward Egypt in the twilight period between the purchase of the Suez shares in 1876 and the occupation of the country six years later. Langer, *European Alliances and Alignments*, chap. 8; Vatikiotis, *Modern History of Egypt*, chaps. 5–7; Holt, *Egypt and the Fertile Crescent*, chaps. 14–15; Haekal, *La dette publique égyptienne*, chap. 4; Sabry, *La génèse de l'esprit national égyptien*, chap. 4; Freycinet, *La question d'Egypte*, chap. 2; Kleine, *Deutschland und die ägyptische Frage*, pp. 17–32.

As you will shortly proceed to Egypt to take up the appointment of Her Majesty's Agent and Consul-General in that country, I think, it right to address to you some observations as to the principles by which your conduct should be guided.

The leading aim of our policy in Egypt is the maintenance of the neutrality of that country, that is to say, the maintenance of such a state of things that no great Power shall be more powerful there than England.

This purpose might, of course, be secured by the predominance of England itself, or even by the establishment of the Queen's authority in the country. Circumstances may be conceived in which this would be the only way of attaining the object; but it would not be the best method. It would not in the present state of affairs confer any other advantages than opportunities of employing English people and introducing English capital; and these would be outweighed by the responsibilities, military and financial, it would entail. The only justification of such a policy would consist in its being the only available mode of assuring the neutrality of Egypt towards us.

With this object in view it is obvious that we can have no jealousy of Native rule in itself. On the contrary, its continuance is, for us, the easiest solution of the problem. But it must not degenerate into anarchy, or perpetuate the oppression of recent years. Egypt is too much in view of the whole world, and there are too many interests attaching to it, to be suffered to relapse into the barbarous administration which in Persia and Burmah has resulted in misery so acute as to produce depopulation. An opinion would grow up in Europe in favour of intervention, which, in this case, would mean occupation; and if England could not satisfy it, she would not be able to prevent some other Power from doing so.

For this reason there is a value in the present relations between Egypt and the Porte, however anomalous they may appear to be. In case of extreme misgovernment, they furnish a machinery for changing the ruler, without any violation of Treaties or breach of diplomatic comity. They enable us to exercise a general control without taking over the government.

We have no present reason, therefore, for wishing any formal change in the position or institutions of Egypt; and the only change in the present, or rather the recent practice which we desire is, that these institutions shall be worked with tolerable honesty, and with economy and humanity. Thus worked, they furnish what we want— an Egyptian neutrality which has a fair chance of permanence. Our Representatives in Egypt should, therefore, do all in their power to sustain the Native Government in its efforts to govern the country well; and this, for the present, must be an object with which no other should be allowed to interfere. So long as the country is formally independent, the Natives only can govern it. If they cannot do it, no one else can do it—without military occupation, It has been sufficiently proved that the Mussulmans will not willingly obey a Government which is nominally European, or of which the prevailing and most conspicuous elements are European. Their reluctance can only be overcome by force; and force the Europeans do not possess without military occupation.

It becomes, therefore, matter of great moment to make the Native Government succeed. For this purpose it should, in its own interest, employ Europeans largely, and should be pressed to do so, if insensible to its own interest in that respect; but they must be kept as much in the background as possible. They should not be used in sufficient numbers to destroy the apparent authority of the Native Government; and the employments to which they are named should be selected rather with a view to the effective exercise of power, than to the possession of conspicuous official rank. The posts which confer the greatest influence, and excite the least jealousy, are the posts which should be sought for Europeans.

In the performance of their duty as counsellors of the Egyptian Government, the Representaives of Her Majesty will be distinguished by one peculiar mark from those of any other Power. The policy they counsel will not be shaped by the interests of any particular class of creditors. It is their duty to do what they properly can to secure any rights Englishmen may possess in the country; they will not exclude English creditors from the benefit of this rule; and, for the sake of Egypt herself, they will wish that she should pay her debts. If, therefore, it shall appear that any particular claim, or class of claims, in which Englishmen are largely interested, is being unfairly treated by reason of the diplomatic support given to competing creditors of other nationalities the English Agent cannot refuse to interfere. But the protection of the private interests of creditors or others will be an object of a merely secondary kind, and will not compete with the important political aims which it is their chief duty to secure.

This singularity of their attitude in regard to the Egyptian debts is likely to be brought speedily into view. One of the questions which will be the most hotly debated in the ensuing winter at Cairo will be the proportion in which the various classes of creditors are to be paid. Almost all must forego some portion of their claim, and the sacrifices demanded may be larger than any of them expect. It will of course be the duty of the English Agent to interpose if any English claimant should be subjected to manifest injustice. But, save in such a contingency, which is improbable, the controyversy will not affect English interests; and the English Agent will do wisely to be sparing of his advice in respect to it so long as it concerns the interests of the creditors alone.

It cannot, however, be long restircted within these limits. It must either at first, or in the end, take the form of an issue between the interests of the creditors and the interests of the Egyptian Administration. The amount of the assets which will remain for the creditors to divide will depend on the amount which is first taken out of the revenue to pay the costs of Government. It will be for the interest of the creditors to put this sum at as low a figure as they can, and their zeal to do so may possibly lead them to proposals incompatible with the efficiency of the Administration. The present attitude of the Governments of Austria, France, Germany, and Italy, favour [sic] the conjecture that in this dispute they will lean rather to the side of the creditors than to that of the Government.

In such a policy, if they pursue it, Her Majesty's Government cannot follow them. To England the efficiency of the Administration is of paramount importance; in comparison with it the interests of the creditors must take an inferior place. On this point Her Majesty's Representative will be forced to separate himself very decidedly from his colleagues, if they take the course I have anticipated. Without favouring extravagance, he must urge on the Khedive the reservation of a sufficient sum to ensure the preservation of order, the due administration of justice, and the efficient maintenance of the public works on which the prosperity of the country depends.

What I have said refers to the present order of things; it serves the interest of England better than any that apparently could be subsituted for it, and the efforts of Her Majesty's Agent must be chiefly directed to insure that it shall work efficiently, and thus continue to exist.

But the contigency of a failure in these efforts must be contemplated. The character of the present Khedive gives ground for hope; on the other hand, the character and capacity of the men by whom he is surrounded, and from whom his Ministers must be chosen, justify apprehension as to the future. It may be that the causes of decay which at present threaten all the Mahommedan countries of the world will prove incurable in Egypt also. Such an issue is, however, in any case, probably distant, and the conditions under which it may take place cannot be foreseen now. But the possibility of it must be borne in mind. When it comes, if it is to come, it must find England as strong as any other country in substantial influence.

If any tendency betrays itself so to arrange the European appointments that a preponderance either in importance or number is assigned to other European nations, a state of things is being created which in the case of a collapse of Egypt would be dangerous to English interests. Her Majesty's Agent should, therefore, watch these appointments with vigilance, and interpose on any symptom of a hostile inclination on the part of the Government in this respect. I should be disposed to attach less importance to the distribution of Native appointments. In all Oriental countries where Embassies are powerful, the Native competitors for place are very ready to enrol themselves as clients of one Power or the other. But their friendship is not trustworthy, and their success of little real value to the Power of whom they are nominally partisans. Foreign Representatives in supporting them are apt to allow their exertions to degenerate into a race for small diplomatic victories, and in the struggle the object of appointing the best man is entirely forgotten. To us, whose chief interest in Egypt is that the Government should last and work well, it is much more important that the best men should be employed than that the partisans of England should be promoted. This princi-

ple, however, must not be stretched so far as to sanction the abandonment of Native statesmen or officials who, by listening to the advice of England, had exposed themselves to the resentment either of some other Agency or of the Native authorities.

It should further be borne in mind that if the Ottoman Empire were to fall to pieces and Egypt become independent, the part of Egypt which interests England is the sea-coast, including the railway and other communications across the Isthmus. If it should happen that Egypt were divided, and the sea-coast and communications remained under the dominant influence of England, while the interior were to be otherwise disposed of—supposing the stability of such an arrangement could be guaranteed—England would have no reason to be dissatisfied with it.

In the disposal, therefore, of European appointments, it is of primary importance to keep in English hands, as far as may be possible, the harbours, customs, lighthouses, and the communications by land and water from sea to sea. It is only of course to a limited extent that this can be done; and the necessity is not sufficiently urgent at present to justify steps which would awaken the jealousy of other Powers. But the extension and consolidation of English influence upon these points is the object which, as regards the future, must be kept in view. Whether it shall be pursued slowly or energetically must depend upon the circumstances of the moment.

139. CONVENTION (MADRID) ON PROTECTION IN MOROCCO[1]
3 July 1880

(Entered into effect on signature; ratifications exchanged, Madrid, 1 May 1881; adherence of Russia, 4 May 1881; ratification by the president of the United States, 10 May 1881)
[Translated English text from *United States Statutes at Large*, 22 (Dec. 1881-March 1883), 817–25]

By legalizing the protection of Moroccan samsars, or brokers, in the employ of European commercial firms, the French-Moroccan agreement of 1863 on regulating the protégé system to which all interested powers adhered (Doc. 115) had the effect

---

1. Signed with Morocco by Austria-Hungary, Belgium, Denmark, France, Germany, Great Britain, Italy the Netherlands, Portugal, Spain, Sweden and Norway, and the United States.

of multiplying the number of protégés, for, in the decade and a half that followed, European commerce with Morocco expanded swiftly. Inescapably, the rapid growth of the protégé lists resulted also in the continuing widespread abuse of the system by the grant of protection to spurious samsars, who evaded Moroccan laws for their own private benefit. In 1876 Mawlay al-Hasan (1873–94) appealed to the European diplomats in Tangier to help put an end to the corrupt practices. As dean of the diplomatic corps, the British minister, Sir John Drummond Hay, presided over conferences of the resident European diplomats in the summer of 1877 and again in 1879 to consider the Moroccan government's twenty demands for modifying the system of native protection. After the failure of both conferences, Hay proposed to the Foreign Office that the issue be submitted to an international conference in Europe. Accordingly, on 7 October 1879, the Foreign Office sent a circular to its missions in all capitals maintaining diplomatic relations with Morocco and to Saint Petersburg (even though Russia had no mission in Tangier) inquiring about their willingness to review the problem. By March 1880 the Foreign Office had received favorable replies from all interested governments; Russia alone declined to take part. Spain consented to serve as host, and its Foreign Ministry issued the formal invitations. The conference, which met in Madrid from 19 May to 3 July 1880, framed the convention reproduced below. While ostensibly discussing native protection, the major European powers sparred for position. France insisted and in the end succeeded, with the active support of Germany, in receiving the formal confirmation of the 1863 instrument. But the adoption of the convention perhaps proved more useful to Britain—and in the end also to Germany—than to France. The internationalization of the "Moroccan question" complicated the later expansionist efforts of France and Spain, which coveted possession of Morocco, since all the major powers along with the other interested powers were assured a voice in any future steps to modify the existing system of Moroccan relations with Europe. Cruickshank, *Morocco*; Le Boeuf, *De la protection diplomatique et consulaire des indigènes au Maroc*, pp. 45–145; Wendel, "Protégé System in Morocco"; France, Ministère des Affaires Etrangères, *Documents diplomatiques: Question de la protection diplomatique et consulaire au Maroc*; Great Britain, *Parliamentary Papers, 1880,* Morocco no. 1, Cd. 2707; see also references to Doc 115.

ART. 1. The conditions under which protection may be conceded are those established in the British and Spanish treaties with the Government of Morocco, and in the convention made between that Government, France and other powers in 1863, with the modifications introduced by the present convention.

ART. 2. Foreign Representatives at the head of a Legation may select their interpreters and employees from among the subjects of Morocco or others.

These protected persons shall be subject to no duty, impost or tax whatever, other than those stipulated in articles 12 and 13.

ART. 3. Consuls, Vice consuls or Consular Agents having charge of a post, and residing within the territory of the Sultan of Morocco, shall be allowed to select but one interpreter, one soldier and two servants from among the subjects of the Sultan, unless they may require a native secretary.

These protected persons shall, in like manner, be subject to no duty, impost or tax whatever, other than those stipulated in articles 12 and 13.

ART. 4. If a Representative shall appoint. a subject of the Sultan to the office of Consular Agent in a town on the coast, such agent shall be respected and honored, as shall the members of his family occupying the same dwelling with him, and they, like him shall be subject to no duty, impost or tax whatever, other than those stipulated in articles 12 and 13; but he shall not have the right to protect any subjects of the Sultan other than the members of his own family.

He may, however, for the exercise of his functions, have a protected soldier.

Officers in acting charge of Vice Consulates being subjects of the Sultan, shall, during the exercise of their functions, enjoy the same rights as Consular Agents who are subjects of the Sultan.

ART. 5. The Government of Morocco recognizes the right of Ministers, Chargés d'Affaires and other Representatives, which is granted to them by treaties, to select the persons whom they employ, either in their own service or that of their governments, unless such persons shall be sheiks or other employees of the Government of Morocco, such as soldiers of the line or of the cavalry, in addition to the Maghaznias in command of their guard. In like manner they shall not be permitted to employ any subject of Morocco who is under prosecution.

It is understood that civil suits commenced before protection, shall be terminated before the courts which have instituted such proceedings. The execution of the sentence shall suffer no hindrance. Nevertheless, the local authorities of Morocco shall take care to communicate, without delay, the sentence pronounced, to the Legation, Consulate or Consular Agency upon which the protected person is dependent.

As to those persons formerly protected, who may have a suit which was commenced before protection was withdrawn from them, their case shall be tried by the court before which it was brought.

The right of protection shall not be exercised towards persons under prosecution for an offense or crime, before they have been tried by the authorities of the country, or before their sentence, if any has been pronounced, has been executed.

ART. 6. Protection shall extend to the family of the person protected. His dwelling shall be respected.

It is understood that the family is to consist only of the wife, the children, and the minor relatives dwelling under the same roof.

Protection shall not be hereditary. A single exception, which was established by the convention of 1863, but which is not to create a precedent, shall be maintained in favor of the Benchimol family.

Nevertheless, if the Sultan of Morocco shall grant another exception, each of the contracting powers shall be entitled to claim a similar concession.

ART. 7. Foreign representative shall inform the Sultan's Minister of Foreign Affairs, in writing, of any selections of an employee made by them.

They shall furnish annually to the said Minister a list of the names of the persons protected by them or by their Agents throughout the States of the Sultan of Morocco.

This list shall be transmitted to the local authorities, who shall consider as persons enjoying protection only those whose names are contained therein.

ART. 8. Consular officers shall transmit each year to the authorities of the district in which they reside a list, bearing their seal, of the persons protected by them. These authorities shall transmit it to the Minister of Foreign Affairs, to the end that, if it be not conformable to the regulations, the Representatives at Tangier may be informed of the fact.

A consular officer shall be required to give immediate information of any changes that may have taken place among the persons protected by his Consulate.

ART. 9. Servants, farmers and other native employees of native secretaries and interpreters shall not enjoy protection. The same shall be the case with Moorish employees or servants of foreign subjects.

Nevertheless, the local authorities shall not arrest an employee or servant of a native officer in the service of a Legation or Consulate, or of a foreign subject or protected person, without having notified the authority upon which he is dependent.

If a subject of Morocco in the service of a foreign subjects shall kill or wound any person, or violate his domicile, he shall be arrested immediately, but the diplomatic or consular authority under which he is shall be notified without delay.

ART. 10. Nothing is changed with regard to the situation of brokers, as established by the treaties and by the convention of 1863, except what is stipulated, relative to taxes, in the following articles.

Art. 11. The right to hold property is recognized in Morocco as belonging to all foreigners.

The purchase of property must take place with the previous consent of the Government, and the title of such property shall be subject to the forms prescribed by the laws of the country.

Any question that may arise concerning this right shall be decided according to the same laws, with the privilege of appeal to the Minister of Foreign Affairs stipulated in the treaties.

Art. 12. Foreigners and protected persons who are the owners or tenants of cultivated land, as well as brokers engaged in agriculture, shall pay the agricultural tax. They shall send to their Consul annually, an exact statement of what they possess delivering into his hands the amount of the tax.

He who shall make a false statement, shall be fined double the amount of the tax that he would regularly have been obliged to pay for the property not declared. In case of repeated offense this fine shall be doubled.

The nature, method, date and apportionment of this tax shall form the subject of a special regulation between the Representatives of the Powers and the Minister of Foreign Affairs of His Shereefian Majesty.

Art. 13. Foreigners, protected persons and brokers owning beasts of burden shall pay what is called the gate-tax. The apportionment and the manner of collecting this tax which is paid alike by foreigners and natives, shall likewise form the subject of a special regulation between the Representatives of the Powers and the Minister of Foreign Affairs of His Shereefian Majesty.

The said tax shall not be increased without a new agreement with the Representatives of the Powers.

Art. 14. The mediation of interpreters, native secretaries or soldiers of the different Legations or Consulates, when persons are concerned who are under the protection of the Legation or Consulate, shall be permitted only when they are the bearers of a document signed by the head of a mission or by the consular authority.

Art. 15. Any subject of Morocco who has been naturalized in a foreign country, and who shall return to Morocco, shall after having remained for a length of time equal to that which shall have been regularly necessary for him to obtain such naturalization, choose between entire submission to the laws of the Empire and the obligation to quit Morocco, unless it shall be proved that his naturalization in a foreign country was obtained with the consent of the Government of Morocco.

Foreign naturalization heretofore acquired by subjects of Morocco according to the rules established by the laws of each country, shall be continued to them as regards all its effects, without any restriction.

Art. 16. No irregular of unofficial protection shall be granted in future. The authorities of Morocco will recognize no protection, or any kind whatever, save such as is expressly provided for in this convention.

Nevertheless, the exercise of the customary right of protection shall be reserved for those cases only in which it may be desired to reward signal services rendered by a native of Morocco to a foreign power, or for other altogether exceptional reasons.

The Minister of Foreign Affairs at Tangier shall be previously informed of the nature of the services, and notified of the intention to reward them, in order that he may, if need be, present his observations thereon; yet the final decision shall be reserved for the Government to which the service shall have been rendered.

The number of persons thus protected shall not exceed twelve for each power, and this number is fixed as the maximum unless the consent of the Sultan shall be obtained.

The status of persons who have obtained protection in virtue of the custom which is henceforth to be regulated by this stipulation shall be without limitation of the number of persons belonging to this class and now so protected, the same for themselves and their families as that which is established for other protected persons.

Art. 17. The right to the treatment of the most favored nation is recognized by Morocco as belonging to all the powers represented at the Madrid conference.

Art. 18. This convention shall be ratified. The ratifications shall be exchanged at Tangier with as little delay as possible.

By exceptional consent of the high contracting parties the stipulations of this

convention shall take effect on the day on
which it is signed at Madrid. . . .

140. ESTABLISHMENT OF A PRECLUSIVE PROTECTORATE: BRITISH INDIA IN AFGHANISTAN
20 July 1880—16 June 1883

[Letter from the secretary of the government of India to the commander in northern and eastern
Afghanistan, 20 July 1880, India Office Library, Government of India, Foreign Department, L/P &
S/7/28; remaining instruments from Public Record Office, F.O. 93.3/1]

The peace at Gandamak (Doc. 137) proved fragile. On 3 September 1879 mutinous
Afghan soldiers murdered Major Sir Louis Cavagnari, head of the British mission
installed at Kabul under the treaty, along with most of his staff. In October Amir
Ya'qub abdicated, soon after British-Indian troops reoccupied the major towns.
The British government in December approved a proposal long favored by the earl
of Lytton and his principal viceregal advisers. Afghanistan was to be divided into at
least three parts: Qandahar going under British-Indian protection to a khan of the
Sadozay clan, which had ruled Afghanistan before the rise of the Barakzay clan
under Dust Muhammad in the second quarter of the nineteenth century; Herat (and
Sistan) to Persia, as soon as the Foreign Office negotiated the terms of transfer; and
Kabul to a suitable candidate, also chosen by the government of India and under its
protection. In April 1880 the government of India began exploring the possibility
of designating as amir of Kabul the sardar 'Abd al-Rahman Khan, a son of Shir
'Ali's elder half-brother who was then living in exile in Russian Turkistan. The
arrangements were concluded at Zimma (about sixteen miles north of Kabul) on 31
July/1 August; in return for recognition as amir of Kabul, 'Abd al-Rahman surrendered external sovereignty to British India, which on its part pledged that it would
satisfy its diplomatic needs in the amirate through a Muslim agent rather than an
English resident. To help him launch his regime 'Abd al-Rahman received a grant of
close to 20 lakhs of rupees (£200,000 sterling), nearly half of it from the captured
treasury of Amir Ya'qub. In the final exchanges with Lepel Griffin, the British-
Indian negotiator, 'Abd al-Rahman sought a formal treaty. Griffin, however, rejected the idea of a treaty, for the time being at least, on the ground that until 'Abd
al-Rahman could demonstrate staying powers it was premature. On the other hand,
he encouraged the amir to annex Herat (since negotiations with Persia had fallen
through and the district was ruled by Ayyub Khan, a son of Amir Shir 'Ali) but to
keep away from Qandahar. However, the British-Indian forces withdrew from
Qandahar in April 1881. 'Abd al-Rahman, who was allowed to take over, proved
incapable at first of holding Qandahar against attack by Ayyub, but he rallied and
defeated Ayyub decisively at Qandahar in September and at Herat in October. After
reuniting Afghanistan, 'Abd al-Rahman continued to govern the amirate under the
terms of the 1880 agreement until his death in 1901. Indeed, in 1883 the viceroy
reaffirmed the existing arrangements and pledged to the amir an annual subsidy of
12 lakhs of rupees (£120,000 sterling) for "the payment of your troops and . . .

other measures required for the defence of your north-western frontier" (see sec. 4, below). The preclusive protectorate admittedly did not give British India full control over the amir, but it kept other powers out and prevented the amir from establishing formal or even informal relations with them, while enabling the British to escape internal entanglements in Afghanistan. Reproduced below are the viceroy's instructions for a political settlement in Kabul, the actual terms of the settlement, and the 1883 confirmatory instruments. Singhal, *India and Afghanistan*, chaps. 4–6; Fraser-Tytler, *Afghanistan*, chap. 9; Gregorian, *Emergence of Modern Afghanistan*, chap. 5; Ghose, *England and Afghanistan*, chap. 4; Adamec, *Afghanistan*, chap. 1.

1. Instructions from A. C. Lyall, Foreign Secretary, Government of India to Lieutenant General D. M. Stewart, Commander, Northern and Eastern Afghanistan, 20 July 1880

The latest reports from Kabul of the movements of Sirdar Abdul Rahman Khan show that he has now arrived in Kohistan, and that he may be expected very shortly to proceed towards Kabul. So far as his wishes and intentions can be judged from his recent actions and letters, there is fair ground for supposing that he has fully apprehended the nature and objects of the invitation sent to him in April last, and that his inclinations, as well as his needs and interests, are bringing him toward an arrangement with the British Government. It has therefore become expedient that you and Mr. Griffin should be furnished with instructions empowering you to conclude the political arrangements which must precede your departure from Kabul, since the evacuation of the city by our troops cannot, in any event, be much longer delayed.

2. In their correspondence with Abdul Rahman, the Government of India have throughout held steadily to two cardinal points. In the first place, it has been declared from the beginning, and throughout maintained, that our measures for withdrawing our troops from Northern Afghanistan are in no essential degree dependent upon the result of our correspondence with the Sirdar. In the instructions transmitted by my letter of the 27th April, regarding the terms of our communications with Abdul Rahman, it was laid down that our evacuation of Kabul cannot constitute any subject for proposals in Mr. Griffin's correspondence with the

Sirdar. Nevertheless, since the Government were willing to carry out this evacuation in the manner most conducive to Abdul Rahman's interests, Mr. Griffin was directed to inform the Sirdar of our intention to quit the place, and of our desire, in the interests of order and the restoration of tranquillity to the country, to transfer the government to him. In my letter of the 8th May to Mr. Griffin the same line of policy was adhered to, and it was said that we could not materially alter our plans for evacuation upon considerations affecting a new Amir. On the 15th May, also, I telegraphed to Mr. Griffin that he should bear steadily in mind that our policy of withdrawal from Kabul is in no way dependent on establishing a friendly Amir, or on an adjustment of friendly relations, however desirable, with any Kabul ruler. The early retirement of our forces was held to be the main object of all political and military measures, an object to which the establishment of a settled government at Kabul must, in case of necessity, be subordinated.

3. In the second place, it was decided, in authorizing correspondence with Abdul Rahman, that this correspondence must not take the form of negociations, in the sense of proposing or entertaining conditions, or of discussing a bargain. The suggestion that conditions should be offered to the Sirdar was definitely negatived; and the scope of the instructions give regarding this correspondence was carefully limited to authorizing an unconditional invitation and offer. The Government informed the Sirdar that if he came to Kabul upon a friendly understanding he should be recognized as Amir and assisted to establish himself before the departure of our troops. Subsequently, upon your special recom-

mendation, the Sirdar received a distinct statement of the views and intentions of the British Government upon certain additional points. But this statement, although of high importance to the Sirdar, was given him unconditionally; and while it conveys a declaration of the policy and intentions of Government, the Sirdar's assent has been neither asked nor expected.

4. In regard, therefore, to the plan of early withdrawal of our troops from Kabul, and to the continuance of our correspondence with Abdul Rahman, the lines of instruction originally traced have been substantially adhered to. You are thus free, as matters now stand, to complete the arrangements, political and military, preliminary to the retirement of the British forces; while as Abdul Rahman has accepted your invitation to Kabul, the time may have arrived for the fulfilment of our offers to him of recognition and assistance. Upon these points I am now to convey to you instructions in continuation and expansion of the orders already telegraphed. The Government of India agree with the opinion of yourself and Mr. Griffin that it will probably be advisable that the Sirdar should not enter Kabul immediately; but that he should remain for the present within a distance convenient for intercourse and for personal conference, if necessary, upon the arrangements for his assumption of authority. First, then, in regard to the Sirdar's recognition as Amir, (which, as well as any subsequent arrangement with him, is of course dependent upon your being satisfied that he is dealing with us in good faith, and in a friendly spirit) he will be recognized under the title of Amir of Kabul; and whenever the announcement shall have been publicly made, it should be understood as entitling him, thereafter, to your full countenance and political support, but not to any co-operation by British troops in his measures for establishing his authrotity. It will consequently be your duty to discountenance and discourag eall claims of candidates and combinations of parties, adverse to, or inconsistent with, the recognition of Abdul Rahman's Amirship.

5. You have been already instructed that for the purpose of establishing the Sirdar at Kabul, he may be provided with some artillery, and with money sufficient to meet his immediate wants. The precise number of guns to be given, and their calibre, must be left to your judgment, upon consideration of the Amir's position at Kabul, and of his own resources; the general view of the Government being that the guns should be serviceable, and sufficient to strengthen effectively his occupation of the city. In regard to money, it is important to place the Amir beyond the necessity of levying exactions upon the country, in order to collect funds for the maintenance of the troops he may require, and for the payment of his officials; and your disbursements to him will be proportioned, within a maximum of ten lacs of Rupees, to your estimate of his actual wants at the time. But the Sirdar should understand that we can engage ourselves to no regular subsidy or continuous supply of either arms or money, and that after he has taken possession of his capital, he must rely, for holding it, upon his own resources.

6. It would be manifestly premature at present to discuss the question whether any formal engagement should hereafter be made with the Amir's Government before the Sirdar has established himself in Kabul, or has shown what disposition toward the British Government, or capacity for rule, he may possess. Nevertheless, since the point has been raised, and since it has been argued that the Amir may have some claim to be admitted into some such engagement, it may be well that you should receive explicit instructions on the matter. The Government of India, I am to say, see no reason for diverging from the line of policy which has, from the beginning of these transactions with the Sirdar, positively excluded any question of a Treaty with him. It is true that in transmitting to the Sirdar the replies of the Government to certain questions regarding his future position, Mr. Griffin added, under authority, that if the Sirdar desired these matters to be stated in formal writing, he should first accept or refuse our invitation to Kabul. This formal statement, if he asks for it (but not otherwise), can now be given to him; and I am accordingly to inclose a letter which may be delivered, after the Sirdar's recognition, to him as Amir. But it appears to His Excellency the Governor-General in Council that it would

be highly inadvisable to enter into any other engagement at the present time. The actual state of Afghanistan would render futile any attempt to introduce regular diplomatic relations with its ruler; and all questions of reciprocal engagements between the two Governments must necessarily be postponed until some settled and responsible administration shall have been consolidated in North Afghanistan. This is the explanation which, if any reference is made to the question of a Treaty, may be given to Sirdar Abdul Rahman Khan.

7. It will be necessary, before evacuating Kabul, to determine what measures are possible for the protection of the tribes and individuals, who have assisted us there, from injury in consequence of their friendly conduct. Upon the subject of individuals who may claim our protection, and may not desire to remain in Afghanistan, you will receive a separate letter. You will, however, probably see fit to address some admonition to Abdul Rahman, intimating that if he seeks to retain our good will, he can give not better proof of his friendly disposition than by his behaviour toward those in whom the British Government is interested. But experience has shown the inutility of making, in favor of individuals, precise stipulations which can easily be evaded, and can very rarely be enforced; while the case of tribes, who, like the Hazaras, may have compromised themselves by taking part against the Afghans in the recent disturbances, must be reserved for separate consideration.

8. The foregoing instructions will have conveyed to you the views of the Government of India on such questions as may be expected to arise in concluding the transfer of the Kabul Government to Sirdar Abdul Rahman. When in the opening of the present year, it was determined to withdraw the British troops from North Afghanistan in the autumn, the Government of India considered that an invitation to Sirdar Abdul Rahman Kahan to assume the Amirship afforded the best prospect of replacing the country under some settled and durable rule. As the Sirdar has accepted this invitation, the most desirable issue from the present situation at Kabul lies, beyond doubt, in the direction of concluding arrangements with him. Nevertheless, in the present unstable position of affairs in North Afghanistan, where the course of events is still liable to sudden changes, it is necessary to provide against the contingency of a failure to bring the correspondence with the Sirdar to a satisfactory termination. Your instructions, under my telegram of the 29th June, are that if a breach with Abdul Rahman occurs, you can assemble the leaders of the party which would restore Sher Ali's family to power, offer to recognize any *de fucto* government they may be able to establish, and transfer Kabul to that government. My telegram of the 15th July, moreover, has empowered you, in the case of rupture with the Sirdar, to use all practical means, in the interval before your complete evacuation of Kabul, to communicate with the leaders of any substantial party in the country, who may be able to organize some administration at Kabul capable of discharging the functions of a government. With this object, you would proceed to notify to the Sirdars and to other representatives of the wishes and feelings of the people round Kabul, with whom it may be possible for you to communicate, that your correspondence with Abdul Rahman is at an end, and that the British Government wishes them to undertake the organizations of some ruling authority. You would explain that, if no attempts are made on their part, or with their collusion, to embarrass the movement of your troops, their endeavours to restore order will be supported by your influence, so long as you remain at Kabul, and that if they succeed in setting up a government *de facto*, you will recognize it by transferring the capital to its charge. But you are not authorized to make any further offers of assistance or specific support; and the Government of India must reserve full discretion to act, upon all ulterior questions according to the future course of events in Afghanistan.

9. On the other hand, while the Government of India do not disguise their reluctance to leave Kabul unprotected and to relinquish as unsuccessful their endeavours to promote the restoration of order under some recognized ruler, it would be in the highest degree imprudent to allow your arrangements for the withdrawal of your

troops to be materially delayed or de-
ranged. In the eventuality contemplated it
is probably that considerable confusion will
prevail in the country, and it might take a
long time to bring together the leading men
of the alternative party. The prospect of
any stable government being formed within
the short period to which your stay can in
any case be limited, is uncertain; and in a
former letter I have pointed out the need
of great caution in taking steps which
might implicate us unprofitably, and,
possibly against the wishes of the country,
in struggles among equally matched fac-
tions. Subject, therefore, to the foregoing
general instructions and limitations, the
Government desire to leave you free to use
your own discretion as to the measures to
be adopted under the circumstances for
the establishment of a *de facto* government
in Kabul.

2. Arrangements for a Preclusive Protectorate, 31 July/1 August 1880

His Excellency the Viceroy and Governor
General in Council has learnt with pleasure
that Your Highness has proceeded toward
Kabul, in accordance with the invitation
of the British Government. Therefore, in
consideration of the friendly sentiments by
which your Highness is animated, and of
the advantage to be derived by the Sirdars
and people from the establishment of a
settled government under your Highness's
authority, the British Government recognizes your Highness as Amir of Kabul.

I am further empowered, on the part of
the Viceroy and Governor General of
India, to inform your Highness that the
British Government has no desire to interfere in the internal government of the
territories in the possession of your Highness, and has no wish that an English
Resident should be stationed anywhere
within those territories. For the convenience of ordinary friendly intercourse,
such as is maintained between two adjoining States, it may be advisable that a
Muhammedan Agent of the British Government should reside, by agreement, at
Kabul.

Your Highness has requested that the
views and intentions of the British Government with regard to the position of the
ruler at Kabul in relation to foreign powers,
should be placed on record for your Highness' information. The Viceroy and Governor General in Council authorizes me
to declare to you that since the British
Government admits no right of interference
by foreign powers within Afghanistan, and
since both Russia and Persia are pledged to
abstain from all interference with the affairs
of Afghanistan, it is plain that your Highness can have no political relations with
any foreign power except with the British
Government. If any foreign power should
attempt to interfere in Afghanistan, and
if such interference should lead to unprovoked aggression on the dominions of
your Highness, in that event the British
Government would be prepared to aid
you, to such extent and in such manner as
may appear to the British Government
necessary, in repelling it; provided that
your Highness follows unreservedly the
advice of the British Government in regard
to your external relations.

3. Reaffirmation of the 1880 Understanding, 22 February 1883

Many vague rumours are doubtless
afloat, but they are, for the most part,
without foundation, and need cause your
Highness no uneasiness, more expecially
as, under the engagements of 1880, which
are embodied in the Memorandum presented to your Highness by Sir Lepel
Griffin in that year, your Highness is in
possession of the assurance of the British
Government that, if any foreign Power
should attempt to interfere in Afghanistan,
and if such interference should lead to
unprovoked agression on the dominions of
your Highness, in that event the British
Government would be prepared to aid
you—to such extent and in such manner as
may appear to the British Government
necessary—in repelling it, provided that
your Highness follows unreservedly the
advice of the British Government in regard
to your external relations.

Under these circumstances your Highness need be under no apprehension, but
may rest in secure reliance that the British
Government has both the will and the
power to make good all its engagements
with your Highness.

I beg to express the high consideration
I entertain for your Highness, and to

subscribe myself your Highness' sincere friend.

4. Viceroy's Grant of an Annual Subsidy, 16 June 1883

Your Highness will remember that, at Sir Lepel Griffin's interview with you at Zimma on the 31st July, 1880, he said that the Government of India could only start your Administration by giving you a grant to pay your army and officials and your immediate expenses; and that, having recognized you as Ameer, it was anxious to see you strong; but after you had taken possession of Cabul, you must rely on your own resources.

I have always interested myself so much in your Highness' success, and have felt so great a desire for the establishment of a strong and friendly Power under your Highness' auspices in Afghanistan, that I have on various occasions gone beyond the determination then communicated to you, and have from time to time aided your Highness with sums of money and arms, besides devoting some lakhs a-year to the support of Afghan refugees and detenus, whose presence in Afghanistan is, I understand, regarded by your Highness as dangerous to your power. Still my view of the relations to each other of the two countries has throughout been that, in matters of internal policy and finance, India should not seek to interfere with Afghanistan, but should confine herself to the part of a friendly neighbour and ally. On these conditions, it would be in accordance with the practice of nations that Afghanistan should regulate her own finance and bear her own burdens, as she has always done heretofore.

As regards matters of external policy, your Highness was informed in the communication from the Foreign Secretary to the Government of India, dated the 20th July, 1880, and again in my letter of the 22nd February, 1883, that if any foreign Power should attempt to interfere in Afghanistan, and if such interference should lead to unprovoked aggression on the dominions of your Highness, in that event the British Government would be prepared to aid you to such extent and in such manner as might appear to the British Government necessary in repelling it; provided that your Highness follows unreservedly the advice of the British Government in regard to your external relations.

On consideration, however, of your accounts of the condition of your northwest frontier, I have been satisfied that your Highness has to contend with exceptional difficulties in that quarter. I have understood that, owing to various untoward circumstances, your Highness has not yet been able to reduce the important frontier province of Herat to the orderly and secure condition so essential for the protection of Afghanistan as a whole; and therefore that, for the settlement of the affairs of that frontier, some friendly assistance may be needful to you. I further observe, with satisfaction, your Highness' assurances of good faith and loyalty to the British Government; and your Highness' language convinces me that you realize how much it is to the interest of Afghanistan to maintain friendly relations with the Government of India.

Impressed by these considerations, I have determined to offer to your Highness personally, as an aid towards meeting the present difficulties in the management of your State, a subsidy of 12 lakhs of rupees a-year, payable monthly, to be devoted to the payment of your troops, and to the other measures required for the defence of your north-western frontier. I feel that I may safely trust to your Highness' good faith and practised skill to devote this addition to your resources to objects of such vital importance as those which I have above mentioned.

141. AGREEMENT BETWEEN GREAT BRITAIN AND THE SHAYKH
OF BAHRAYN
22 December 1880

(Ratified by the British government, 1881)
[Aitchison, *Collection of Treaties . . . relating to India* (5th ed.), 11: 237]

Following the occupation of Cyprus, British-Ottoman relations cooled everywhere, including the Persian Gulf, where the Sublime Porte had begun to reassert its authority along the Arabian coast with the reconquest of al-Hasa in 1871. In 1879–80 the Sublime Porte showed interest in setting up a coaling station on the Bahrayn archipelago. This, the British-Indian government suspected, was intended merely as the first step in claiming Ottoman sovereignty over the islands. The suspicion was not unfounded, for a discontented branch of the ruling shaykhly clan, resident in al-Hasa, was promising to accept Ottoman suzerainty if their clan was restored to power. However, the British political resident in the Persian Gulf, Lieutenant Colonel E. C. Ross, received pledges in June 1879 and March 1880 from al-Shaykh 'Isa bin 'Ali Al Khalifah that he would not permit the Sublime Porte to erect a coaling station without first consulting the British government. In December al-Shaykh 'Isa, on Ross's initiative, signed the following agreement, surrendering his external sovereignty to Britain. This was the first in a series of such instruments that over the next twenty-six years brought the shaykhdoms along the Arabian coast of the gulf into a British quasi-protectorate system. Kelly, *Britain and the Persian Gulf*, chap. 16; Lorimer, *Gazetteer of the Persian Gulf, 'Oman and Central Arabia*, vol. 1, pt. 1, pp. 902–26; Curzon, *Persia and the Persian Question*, 2: 454–58; Aitchison, op. cit., pp. 190–97; see also references to Doc. 121.

I, Isa bin Ali Al Khalifeh, Chief of Bahrein, hereby bind myself and successors in the Government of Bahrein to the British Government to abstain from entering into negotiations or making treaties of any sort with any State or Government other than the British without the consent of the said British Government, and to refuse permission to any other Government than the British to establish diplomatic or consular agencies or coaling depots in our territory, unless with the consent of the British Government.

This engagement does not apply to or affect the customary friendly correspondence with the local authorities of neighbouring States on business of minor importance.

142. THE FRENCH OCCUPATION OF TUNISIA (TREATY OF BARDO): FRENCH, BRITISH, AND OTTOMAN POLICIES
9 May–16 June 1881

(Treaty of Bardo signed by Muhammad al-Sadiq, the bey of Tunis; approved by special French law, 27 May 1881; formally ratified by France, 9 June 1881; amplified by the convention of Marsa, 8 June 1883)
[French circular, translated from the text in Clercq, *Recueil des traités*, 13: 19–25; Ottoman statement, translated from the French text in Fitoussi and Benazet, *L'état tunisien et le protectorat français*, app., doc. no. 4, pp. xxxvii-xl; treaty, translated from the French text in France, *Journal Officiel: Documents parlementaires, sénat* (May 1881), annex no. 268, 25 May 1881, pp. 375–76; translation of Ottoman protest against the French treaty, presented to the British government, 15–16 May 1881, and British views on Ottoman protest, 16 June 1881, from Hertslet, *Map of Africa by Treaty*, 3: 1187–90]

The political fate of Tunisia was decided at the Congress of Berlin in July 1878, when Lord Salisbury, the British foreign minister, privately informed William H. Waddington, the French foreign minister, that Britain had concluded a convention with the Sublime Porte for the occupation of Cyprus (Doc. 134) and that insofar as Her Majesty's government was concerned France was free to absorb Tunisia. Thus ended Britain's unwavering fidelity to Palmerston's doctrine of protecting the territorial integrity and political sovereignty of the Ottoman Empire, a doctrine which for four decades had served British interests well in the Middle East and which had been extended to Tunisia so recently and with such difficulty (Doc. 125). This was the price that London had to pay for the procurement of a base to preserve its naval superiority in the eastern Mediterranean, in the event of a Russian seizure of the Turkish straits or an eventual French possession of the Suez Canal or both. The British withdrawal from the Tunisian contest aimed at softening French hostility to the British occupation of Cyprus; and, of the two contenders for the Tunisian prize, France must have seemed the less threatening to Britain in the long run, since the alternative would have placed Italy on both sides of Malta and of the narrows joining the western basin of the Mediterranean to its eastern basin. The Salisbury-Waddington plan had received the prior blessings of the German chancellor, Otto von Bismarck, who saw in the Tunisian venture a means of distracting France from its preoccupation with Alsace-Lorraine and who supported France without wavering until the occupation of Tunis. Waddington would have liked to cash his Tunisian check promptly, but opinion in France split on the issue of the likely Italian reaction. Besides, according to Lord Lyons, the British ambassador in Paris, Waddington wanted to have the oral assurances of Salisbury "in a written, official and so to speak binding shape" (as cited by Raymond, "Salisbury and the Tunisian Question," p. 124). As for Salisbury, while willing, under pressure, to confirm his assurances in tautological language he firmly refused for domestic and international political reasons to issue a binding commitment for public announcement, which he found "a little difficult" since Britain could not give "other people's property away" (as cited idem). Salisbury's evasiveness and Italian anger gave Waddington and his immediate successors pause, but in the end it was fear of an Italian preemptive move that led France in the spring of 1881 to use as a pretext for the military occupation of the regency an incursion into Algeria by tribesmen from Tunisia—an almost daily occurrence in an area where nomadic and seminomadic beduin would hardly have been likely to observe international boundaries that cut through their grazing lands. On 4 April Premier Jules Ferry informed the Chambre that France would send an expeditionary force to Tunisia to prevent the recurrence of such incidents. Ferry had already received unequivocal support from Bismarck and the acquiescence of the Liberal Gladstone government which had replaced the Conservatives in 1880. France warned the Sublime Porte crisply that any naval squadron sent to rescue the bey would be shut out of Tunisian waters. In these circumstances, the Italian government, the most vehement European critic of the French action, was effectively isolated. French troops moved into Tunisia on 24 April, and by 12 May Muhammad al-Sadiq Bey had surrendered his external sovereignty to France. Reproduced below are the French foreign minister's circular to the heads of the French diplomatic missions explaining the government's rationalization for the annexation of Tunisia; the protest of the Sublime Porte presented to the Quai d'Orsay by the Ottoman ambassador in Paris; the treaty of Bardo, which the French dictated to the bey; the Ottoman protest as conveyed to the British government; and the British foreign minister's reply. Raymond, op. cit., pp. 101–38; Langer, "European Powers and the French Occupation of Tunis"; Estournelles de Constant, *La politique française en Tunisie*, pt. 2; Power, *Jules Ferry*, chap. 2; Ganiage, *Les origines du protectorat français en Tunisie*, chaps. 10–13; Abun-Nasr, *History of the Maghrib*, pp. 276–84; Safwat, *Tunis and the Great Powers*; Cambon, *Histoire de la régence de Tunis*, chap. 10; Waddington, "Le rôle de la diplomatie française dans la question tunisienne"; Woolf, *Empire and Commerce in Africa*, pt. 2, chaps. 3–4; Toscano, "Tunis"; Staley, *War and the Private Investor*, chap. 12; Schuman, *War and Diplomacy in the French Republic*, chap. 4.; Broadley, *Last Punic War*.

1. Circular from the French Foreign Minister (Barthélemy Saint-Hillaire) to the Heads of French Diplomatic Missions, 9 May 1881

I have the honor to send you a collection of documents on Tunis, and I wish to specify in a general way the causes of the present expedition and the results we expect from it. On several occasions the government of the Republic has already made known its motives and intentions. You will recall particularly the declaration which the President of the Council solemnly issued in the National Tribunal [Parliament]. They cannot leave the least doubt by their clarity and precision. Nevertheless, I wish to submit to you a few considerations, which you may find useful in your relations with the government to which you are accredited.

The policy of France on the Tunisian question has been inspired by only a single principle, and that principle, which is sufficient to explain our entire conduct toward the Regency for half a century, is the absolute obligation to ensure the security of our great Algerian colony. Since 1830, none of the successive governments in France has neglected this essential responsibility. The duty devolves on us with such irresistible evidence that nobody in Europe contests our right to take all measures that we deem necessary to safeguard our African possession against a turbulent and hostile neighbor. Since the battle of Isly in 1884 we have been peaceful on the western, or Moroccan, side, where our frontier is protected by the desert; we have had to repress only passing disorders there. But on the east, on the Tunisian side, the disorder is permanent, having persisted for ten years despite all our efforts. It has in fact grown each year, from the revolt in

1871 of the Sipahis of Soukarrhas, who, after having massacred their officers under the orders of Kablouti, sought refuge on Tunisian territory, to the plundering of the Auvergne in 1878 and the recent raid of the Khoumirs and yesterday's plundering of the Santoni. We have been patient to a point that has sometimes astonished the world. We do not regret it, but after suffering so many injuries and such patience we have been forced to decide to settle things by durably pacifying our frontier and by regulating things with the Bey of Tunis in such a way that the danger will not recur in any form.

On looking over the documents that I am sending you, one is surprised at the frequency of the incidents of which we have had to complain and of the hopeless impotence of the state on whose territory they occur and which is incapable of preventing them. On the borders of Tunisia and Algeria there is an entire zone of insubordinate and bellicose tribes which are perpetually at war, raiding one another, and creating in these naturally difficult districts a sanctuary for raids, brigandage, and murder. Most commonly it is the tribes under our rule that are the victims, because, owing to the gentler rule of which we have given them the benefit, they have become more sedentary and more peaceful as they grow progressively more civilized. But the Tunisian tribes are more barbarous and warlike; and among them the Ouchtétas, the Freichichs, and the Khoumirs are especially prominent. It is not known exactly how many fighting men—or, as they are called, rifles—they comprise. But our operations, requiring at this moment an army of twenty thousand men, give proof enough of the strength of the enemy, entrenched in an almost inaccessible district.

Since there are no natural frontiers between Tunisia and Algeria, the border has remained unclear and has never been regularized. [Regularization] was attempted in 1842, and the [settlement based on that] survey, which the presence of our troops facilitated, lasted not less than three years. The map made at that time was approved in 1847 even by the Bey of Tunis, Ahmad, on his journey to France. But no official agreement between the Regency and our-selves resulted from these preliminaries, and the frontier remains vague, as it was under the Beys of Constantine. This is a gap that must be filled as soon as possible. The Regency will find this as much to its advantage as to ours.

Thus, the first object of our expedition is the definitive pacification of our eastern frontier.

However, it would be to no avail to restore order and calm if the adjacent state remained hostile and menacing. We cannot fear a serious attack from the Bey of Tunis, so long as he is limited to his own army. But the simplest prudence instructs us to watch over the obsessions by which he may be surrounded and which, according to circumstances, might create a very serious embarrassment for us in Algeria, since their repercussions may reach France. We must therefore at any price have in the Bey of Tunis an ally with whom we can loyally come to an agreement. We must have a neighbor who reciprocates the sincere goodwill we show him and who does not acquiesce in foreign suggestions seeking to harm us and compromise our legitimate power. We have shown for more than forty years that, if we were obliged, for the security of Algerian France, to claim in the Regency a preponderant position, we knew how to respect scrupulously the interests of other nations, which may in all confidence live and develop alongside our people and under their protection. The Powers know well that our sentiments toward [the protected peoples] will not change.

Until recently, we were on excellent terms with the government of His Highness the Bey; and if sometimes our relations have been troubled by the settlement of indemnities due to our injured tribes, peace was promptly reestablished, and even consolidated, following slight disagreements. But lately, and for reasons which would be too delicate to enter into, the disposition of the Tunisian Government toward us has totally changed. A war, covert at first, then more and more manifest and audacious, has been waged against all French enterprises in Tunisia, with the perseverance of evil intent, which has brought the situation to its present point.

The *Livre jaune* which you receive with this letter will show you the various phases which this stubborn resistance has presented, sometimes simply troublesome and annoying, most often unjust and injurious. You will see by these authentic documents the questions: of the railroad from Goletta to Tunis; of the submarine cable, which they wished to make independent of all our telegraph lines, defying all our rights; of the Enfida estate, which they tried to seize by illegal means from an honest and energetic Marseilles company; of the Soussa road, whose construction they hinder as if it were a pleasure; and [of] so many other affairs in which justice with the spirit of conciliation and even of compliance has not ceased to exist on our side. Nothing has prevailed, and before a party so tenacious and so little justified, we have had to recognize to our great regret that an understanding is no longer possible and that to modify such unfavorable tendencies it is necessary to have recourse to means other than frank discussion and persuasion, which have become absolutely useless.

That is the second motive for the expedition, which we had hoped to be able to avoid but into which we have been forced by malpractices we have borne perhaps for too long.

If we hold the Bey of Tunis responsible for claims thus founded, it is that we have always considered Tunisia an independent kingdom, in spite of a few barely noticeable traces of an ancient vassalage, which the suzerains, almost purely nominal, had themselves neglected for centuries, which were revealed only at very rare intervals, and which in the intervening periods counted much fewer years of effective submission than of oblivion and absolute emancipation. Taken and retaken three or four times in the sixteenth century by the famous Khayr al-Din Barbarossa (conqueror of the Spaniards in 1534), by Charles V the following year and again in 1553, by the Dey of Algiers in 1570, by Don Juan of Austria in 1573, Tunisia suffered throughout the seventeenth century under the anarchic oppression of the Janissaries, of whom the chiefs, or Deys, numbering forty, divided the country among themselves, almost as the Mamluks divided Egypt. But in 1705 one of them, Husayn bin'Ali, a Greek or Corsican renegade cleverer than the rest, was able to procure unity of power by

destroying his rivals. Proclaimed Bey by his companions in arms, he founded the Husayni dynasty, which since then has not ceased to reign, in the form of a Muslim seniority [system]. Tunisia has had by now nearly two hundred years of independence, and the only real tie with the Ottoman Porte that it has preserved in this long interval is a religious one. It has recognized the Caliph, without being a subject of the Sultan and especially without paying any tribute, with the exception that, on the accession of each Bey, by respectful custom rich presents were sent to the chief of the religion residing in Constantinople; in the rest of the reign no political act except for this voluntary homage recalled that the Bey of Tunis still owed anything to the Commander of the Faithful. Also, the Regency negotiated along and in its own sovereign right with all foreign Powers; it concluded with them conventions which were given the force of the law by the sole agreement of the Bey. Such were notably the conventions concluded with France in 1742, in the year III, the year X, in 1824; such also was the famous treaty of 8 August 1830 [providing] for the abolition of privaterring and slavery, not to mention other less important acts, like that which concerned the coral fishery.

The Porte seemed to have participated so fully in the irrevocable emancipation of this province, of which its possession had always been so transitory, that throughout the eighteenth century it refused to receive the claims against the Barbary pirates that were always being addressed to it by Europe. It took no action against them and, as it was not their master, it did not agree to reply to their plundering, so formidable and so costly to all the navies of the Mediterranean.

The Powers of Europe made war twenty times against the Regency without being in the very least at war with the Ottoman Porte. In 1819, the Congress of Aix-la-Chapelle called on Tunis to cease piracy and did not insist that Turkey intervene as being responsible for its pretended vassal. In 1833, the Kingdoms of Sardinia and the Two Sicilies were at war with the Regency without being so with the Porte, because Tunisia was independent in their eyes as in ours. All relations of France with Tunis since the conquest of Algiers have taken place in the same way, directly, without the mediation of Turkey. When Ahmad Bey came here in 1847, he was received with all the honors due to a king. Was the Ottoman Porte shocked by any of the royal pomp with which he was surrounded? By no means, and Europe was no more shocked than it, because Europe held the same opinion as Lord Aberdeen, who in his famous protest [23 March 1831] against our conquest of Algiers nonetheless declared that "the European states had for a long time treated with the Barbary [regencies] as independent powers."

Moreover, Tunisia itself has never had any other idea about its relation to Turkey than that of complete freedom. An authentic document, which is of the highest importance and which cannot be challenged, proves this sufficiently: it is the Tunisian constitution [*buyrultu*], sworn to by the present Bey of Tunis, Muhammad al-Sadiq, when he ascended the throne (23 September 1859), just as his predecessors had sworn to it. In the 114 articles of the constitution, entitled the Organic Law of the Tunisian Kingdom, published in Arabic and French, at Tunis and Bône, there is not one word about the [Ottoman] Sultan; and, that no one may question the sovereignty of the Bey, it proclaims in the preamble (page 4) that "it is the high Tunisian officials who have chosen [the Bey] unanimously as chief of state, in accordance with the law of succession practiced in the Kingdom." Entire chapters are devoted to setting forth the rights and duties of the King, the position of the princes of the Husayni family, the rights and duties of the subjects, the functions of the Ministers, the organization of their services, the Supreme Council of the Regency, taxes, budgets, and so on. Without doubt, this singular document may be criticized, if one wishes to judge it only according to our European ideas; but it is no less decisive for showing in all unforeseen intent that the Kingdom of Tunisia rises only from within itself without owing anything to an external sovereignty. All the treaties concluded in the last three centuries by the European states with Tunisia spoke only of the Kingdom and the King of Tunis. Fifteen or twenty treaties of 1662[1] to 1863 and 1875 where this al-

legiant expression has been used carry the signature of England; thirty others of 1604 to 1832 bear the signature of France. In 1868, an Italian treaty was again concluded with the Kingdom of Tunis. Thus, Tunisia in its organic law has given it the name that the world gave it unanimously; and in calling itself Kingdom, it wanted to emphasize that it had all the prerogatives of independence and the power that this brilliant title implies.

In view of such numerous and decisive precedents, the Ottoman Porte must not be very astonished that France should refuse to recognize [the Porte's] sovereignty every time it has been invoked, as it is today. We have no difficulty in acknowledging that the Porte for half a century has been constant enough in its claims. In 1835, it reasserted sovereignty over Tripoli, after having repressed terrible disorders; this occasion appeared favorable to extend its sovereignty to Tunis. However, faced with the energetic opposition of France, it renounced the project. Ten years later, in 1845, a Chamberlain of the Sultan having come to bring to Tunis a *ferman* [decree] of investiture, the Bey refused to submit. Twenty years passed without a fresh attempt being made. But toward the end of 1864, the old designs were taken up again; and this time it was the Regency itself that requested the investiture. The move was, to say the least, strange on the part of a prince who until then had seemed to attach much importance to his independence. But powerful counsels had frightened the Bey about his situation relative to the Porte, and General Khayr al-Din was sent to Constantinople to propose and obtain the ferman. Once more France imposed its veto; and, instead of an act emanating from the Sultan, the Bey and his councillors had to be content with a simple vezirial letter which contained identical clauses. They took advantage of our disasters in 1871 to accomplish what they had not been able to do either under the reign of Louis Philippe, when the French fleet had several times forbidden the Turkish fleet passage in the direction of Tunis, or under the Empire, which did not show itself any less resolute.

---

1. The French text reads 1862, which is obviously a typographical error.

The ferman of 25 [sic] October 1871, obtained in the shadow of our misfortunes, was proclaimed at Bardo on 18 November by Khayr al-Din in the name of the Sultan and accepted by the Bey, who had solicited it more or less spontaneously. Be that as it may, France protested as before, declaring the ferman null and void; and for ten whole years it has not ceased to show its opposition every time circumstances demanded it. It was not certain that the Porte itself, despite its success, would assert its right; the ferman of 1871, which destroyed the securlar independence of the Tunisian Kingdom, though receiving some publicity, remained generally unknown except to a few powers directly interested.

In the system established by the ferman of 1871, whatever might have been its origin, Tunis was partly reinstated under the authority of the Porte. The power of the Bey of Tunis is still recognized as hereditary, as it has been for two centuries; but the Bey of Tunis becomes a simple *vali,* that is to say governor general, of the *eyâlet* of Tunis. As a necessary consequence of this profound modification, the power is no longer really hereditary in the Husayni family, whatever the literal text of the ferman may say. A governor general, a vali, can be dismissed at the will of his suzerain, and it is possible that the present Bey will learn at his expense, at the expense of his throne, of his liberty, perhaps of his life, what an enormous error he was made to commit by his ill-advised councillors. Muhammad al-Sadiq has nothing to fear from France which, despite serious grievances, holds no grudge against either his dynasty, his person, or his realm. With the Porte, on the contrary, he can fear anything and his fate is delivered to the hazard of circumstances.

In the present state of our relations with the Ottoman Porte, [i.e.,] relations of sincere friendship and sympathy, we had wished to be able to envisage the situation of Tunis in another light. But the truth is irrefutable for us, after the precedents we have cited. We can even ask the Porte why, if the Bey is its vali, it has not stopped him for two years from acting toward France as he has done, and why it has not sought to prevent a crisis, which for our part we have tried to avert.

This crisis, the effects of which we are trying to limit insofar as we can, must end in a treaty which will guarantee us at the same time against the attacks from which our frontiers suffer without cease and against the disloyal plots of which the Bardo is too often the instrument or the center. Therein lies the double goal of our expedition; and I am not afraid to say that we have in Europe general approval, wherever unfounded prejudices do not blind the spirits.

Such is our attitude toward the Porte and toward Tunisia. For the one and for the other, we are full of goodwill, and all that we ask of the Bey is not to be hostile to us. If the Regency well understands its interests, it might profit by our alliance infinitely more than we can by alliance with it. We can bring it all the benefits of the civilization which we enjoy. Since 1847 we have established there a telegraph service; in 1877 and 1878, a railroad fifty leagues in length from the Algerian frontier to Tunis. We are building for it now two new railroads: the one which will link Tunis with Bizerta in the north, twenty leagues in length; the other, which will link Tunis with Soussa in the south. Next we are going to begin the most difficult work of [constructing] a port in Tunis itself, which will enable ships to arrive from the roads and from Goletta to the capital. Of the Tunisian debt, French funds (apart from English and Italian funds) account for three-fifths. The magnificent aqueduct of Adrien, which brought excellent water to Tunis, has been restored by a French engineer.

We are ready, as soon as good relations are restored, to carry out a multitude of other enterprises no less generous: lighthouses on the coasts; interior roads to link well-populated and prosperous towns to one another properly; vast irrigation works in a country where rivers are not lacking, but where they are no better turned to account than the forests; the exploitation of abundant mines for all kinds of metals; an improved cultivation on the lands that Europeans may acquire in the Regency, or even on the lands of the natives; the and use of the hot springs that the Romans once discovered and worked. The Regency of Tunis is in general very fertile, as the prodigious richness of ancient Carthage

demonstrates. Under the protection of
France, all the natural gifts of the country
can be developed again with all the energy
and intensity of modern methods and
practices.

We may add that, if the Bey wishes to
entrust it to us, the internal administration
of the Regency may receive improvements
no less necessary and assured. It would be
an incontestable and relatively easy service
to him to introduce there, either for the
raising of taxes, the management of funds,
or the keeping of accounts, the regularity
that the administration of our finances has
attained. It would also be a no less valuable
service to improve the administration of
justice in accordance with principles that
the Powers adopted for judicial reform in
Egypt.

It is not France alone that would profit
from all the progress the Regency may
achieve if it wishes. All the [other] civilized
nations as well as we ourselves would
benefit by it; and nothing hinders us from
doing in Tunisia, without conquest and
fighting, what we are doing in Algeria and
what England is doing in India. It is a
sacred duty that a superior civilization contracts toward less advanced peoples.

Such are the considerations that I com-
mend to your attention. They will enable
you to enlighten the spirits of those
around you who are desirous of learning
impartially the designs of the French
Republic in Tunisia.

2. Ottoman Foreign Minister ('Asim Paşa) to the Ottoman Ambassador in Paris (Es'ad Paşa), 10 May 1881

My several communications have already
brought to your attention the phases
through which the Tunisian question has
just passed.

After the uprisings of the Berber tribes of
Algeria, uprisings which the Tunisian
authorities declared themselves ready to
crush without delay, the French Government deemed it necessary to send a considerable number of troops, which after
seizing the largest part of the province have
come to within only a few leagues from the
center.

Notwithstanding our assurances of the
effective repressive measures taken by His
Highness the Paşa and of the prompt re-

establishment of calm in the disturbed
part of the country, the Republican Government simply ignored [our pledges. Instead
it] characterized from a completely different
point of view the secular relations which
united Tunisia integrally with the Ottoman
Empire and appeared to reject our proposal for a friendly understanding with it
which would avert the emerging difficulties
and reconcile the rights of the Sublime
Porte with the interests of France in this
circumstance.

The order of things established ab antiquo in Tunisia, I cannot repeat enough,
is the undisputed sovereignty of the Sultan
over this province, a sovereignty equally
undisputed by the Powers in general.

This right has remained intact to the
present, without interruption, ever since
the conquest of the country in 1534 by
Hayreddin Paşa and in 1574 by Kilic 'Ali
and Sinan Paşa, whom the sovereign
[Ottoman] court had sent to those places
with imposing sea and land forces.

Since that time, in virtue of the principles
established by the Sublime Porte, all the
valis of Tunis have descended from the
first vali nominated by the Sultan and have
invariably received their investiture from
the sovereign. The fermans of nomination
are recorded at the chancellery of the
Divan, as is also the continuous correspondence which they have had with the
Sublime Porte on their political relations
with the European governments and on the
affairs of their internal administration.

Until recently, the Sublime Porte reserved for itself the right, together with
nominating the governor general, to send
directly from Constantinople to that place
the grand judge, or kadi and the secretary
general of the province; and it is only by an
act which the sovereign court has granted
spontaneously that the Paşa has been
authorized to nominate these two officials
himself. In the ceremonies following the
rite and as a tribute to the sovereignty of the
Sultan, the public prayer, or *hutbe*, is recited in the mosques in the name of His
Imperial Majesty; also [in his name] is the
money coined. In time of war, moreover,
Tunisia has always sent its contingent to
the metropolis, and according to custom
from time immemorial, official personages
were frequently sent to Constantinople to

repeat the acts of submission and devotion of the governors general at the foot of the throne of their sovereigns and to receive from the Sublime Porte the necessary authorizations and instructions on important affairs of the province. Thus, the present Paşa, with the Tunisian people, has solicited and obtained an increment of the privileges granted to His Highness by the ferman of 1871, recognized to the present by the Powers. Even now he makes pressing appeals to his legitimate sovereign to come to his aid in the critical situation in which Tunisia finds itself.

Such are the actual facts, which no one may dispute. Does one now wish to see their sanction by history and by authentic documents? I limit myself to citing only a few examples among so many, in view of the restricted limits of this dispatch.

The ancient treaties concluded between Turkey and France contain the entire enumeration of the titles of the Sultan, among which is that of Sovereign of Tunis (see for example the treaty of 10 Sefer 1084, [which corresponds to 27 May] 1673[2] in the Christian Era). In these same documents it was stipulated that all the treaties concluded between the two states must be equally executed in Tunisia.

Toward the middle of the seventeenth century, that is to say, on the date of 15 Sefer 1066, a ferman was addressed by the Sultan to the Beys and grand judges of the Regency concerning the exequatur that the Sublime Porte had issued to the French Consul in Tunis, authorizing the latter to exercise the functions of Consul of the Powers not represented at the time in Constantinople, such as Portugal, Catalonia, Spain, Venice, Florence, and so on. The Consul had the task of protecting under the French flag the commerce and navigation of the subjects of these governments in the principal ports of Tunisia, and the ferman forbade the interference of the English, the Dutch, and the other Consuls in the exercise of the functions of the French agent.

A *sened*, or convention, concluded between the Sublime Porte and Austria on 9 Ramadan 1197 of the Hicret, confirmed by the treaty of Sistu of 3 Rebiyülâhir 1265, charged the authorities [*ocaklar*, or Garrisons] of Algiers, Tunis, and Tripoli of the Barbary [Coast] with protecting in the name of the Sultan the merchantships of

the Holy Roman Empire. Similarly, in the act which preceded the sened and which was concluded on 15 Şevval 1161 of the Hicret by the order of the Sultan, between the said Ocaklar and the said Empire, the governor general of Tunis having the rank Beylerbeyi and carrying the name of 'Ali Paşa clearly mentioned in the preamble he signed the following words, "Our sovereign Sultan Mehmed the Conqueror." As for contemporary facts, I shall cite for example the order addressed by the Sublime Porte, on 15 Rebiyülevvel 1245 (the year 1829[3] in the Christian Era), to the authorities of Algiers, Tripoli of the Barbary [Coast], and Tunis not to interfere in the difference arising between the Empires of Austria and Morocco. An order was also sent from Constantinople to the vali of Tunis on 24 Sefer 1247 (1831[4] A.D.) for new organization of the regular militia of the province, conforming to the system adopted at that time for the regular Ottoman army. Lastly, [I will mention] the act of submission of the Paşa of Tunis, presented in 1860 to His Imperial Majesty the Sultan, who had named him governor general, an act published at the time in the European journals without raising any objections.

I shall also add that in 1863, when the Tunisian loan was contracted in Paris without the authorization of the Sublime Porte, [Edouard] Drouyn de Lhuys, Minister of Foreign Affairs of the Emperor Napoleon III, at the instance of the Ottoman Government, suggested the idea of having the Paşa of Tunis and the issuing banker elicit a request from the Sublime Porte, as he said, to legitimize the operation so as to safeguard the right claimed by the Ottoman Porte. The French Minister even made overtures in this vein to the banker in question.

With the utmost confidence we submit the preceding considerations to the justice and equity of the signatory Powers of the treaty of Berlin.

Anxious on more grounds than one about the international obligations regarding all these solemn acts, they would be willing, we are persuaded, to offer their

---

2. The French text reads 1668, which would have corresponded to 1079.

3. The French text reads 1825.

4. The French text reads 1830.

impartial mediation regarding the sense of the proposal that we have already submitted to them, with a view to safeguarding the other rights of the Sublime Porte, guaranteed by the same treaty, and to bringing about the conciliation of the reciprocal interests of the two great states in this unhappy Tunisian province, which is an integral part of the [Ottoman] Empire.

I request Your Excellency to explain to the [French] Minister of Foreign Affairs [the main thrust of] the present dispatch, sharing with him all the details that you judge useful. You are authorized even to present a copy to His Excellency, if he expresses the wish to have one.

3. Treaty of Guarantee (Bardo), 12 May 1881

The Government of the French Republic and that of His Highness the Bey of Tunis, wishing to prevent forever renewal of the disorders that have occurred recently on the frontiers of the two states and on the coast of Tunisia, and being desirous of strengthening their former relations of friendship and good-neighborhood, have resolved in the interest of the two High Contracting Parties to conclude a convention to this effect.

Accordingly, the President of the French Republic has named as his Plenipotentiary General [Jules-Aimé] Bréart, who has reached agreement with His Highness the Bey on the following clauses:

ART. 1. The treaties of peace, of friendship, and of commerce and all other conventions currently in force between the French Republic and His Highness the Bey of Tunis are expressly confirmed and renewed.

ART. 2. With a view to facilitating the realization of the measures which the Government of the French Republic will have to take to attain the goal that the High Contracting Parties propose, His Highness the Bey of Tunis consents to the occupation of those places that the French military authority may deem necessary to assure the restoration of order and security on the frontier and the coast.

This occupation shall cease when the French and Tunisian military authorities recognize, in common accord, that the local administration can guarantee the maintenance of order.

ART. 3. The Government of the French Republic undertakes to lend constant support to His Highness the Bey of Tunis against any danger which may threaten the person or the dynasty of His Highness or which may compromise the tranquillity of his realm.

ART. 4. The Government of the French Republic guarantees the execution of the treaties currently in force between the Government of the Regency and the several European Powers.

ART. 5. The Government of the French Republic shall be represented near His Highness the Bey of Tunis by a Minister Resident, who will oversee the execution of the present instrument and who will be the intermediary in the relations of the French Government with the Tunisian authorities in all matters common to the two countries.

ART. 6. The diplomatic and consular agents of France in foreign countries shall be responsible for protecting the interests of Tunisia and the nationals of the Regency.

In return, His Highness the Bey pledges to conclude no act of an international character without first informing the Government of the French Republic and without its prior agreement.

ART. 7. The Government of the French Republic and the Government of His Highness the Bey of Tunis reserve the right to fix, by common accord, the principles of a financial organization of the Regency, which shall be of such a nature as to assure the service of the public debt and to guarantee the rights of the creditors of Tunisia.

ART. 8. A war contribution shall be imposed upon the refractory tribes of the frontier and the coast. A later convention will determine the amount and the mode of collection, for which the Government of His Highness the Bey holds itself responsible.

ART. 9. In order to protect the Algerian possessions of the French Republic against smuggling of arms and munitions of war, the Government of His Highness the Bey of Tunis pledges to prohibit any introduction of arms or of munitions of war via the island of Djerba, the port of Gabès, or the other ports of southern Tunisia.

ART. 10. The present treaty shall be submitted to the Government of the French Republic for ratification, and the instrument of ratification will be returned as soon as possible to His Highness the Bey of Tunis.

4. Ottoman Foreign Minister to the Ottoman Ambassador in London (Müsürüs Paşa), Protesting against the Treaty of Bardo

A. TELEGRAM OF 15 MAY 1881

I hasten to transmit herewith to your Excellency the telegram which His Highness the Pasha of Tunis addressed to us under date of yesterday:—

"I informed your Highness that the General in command of the French column which was, as I announced to your Highness, at Gedeida, approached my residence on Thursday evening. He then came to my Palace accompanied by a force of cavalry, and submitted for my signature a Protectorate Treaty, while declaring that he would not leave the Palace without my answer, for which he only gave me four hours.

"Seeing myself under the pressure of force, owing to the presence of an army near my residence, I was bound, by my honour, and in order to avoid blooshed, to sign this Treaty, without examining or in any way discussing it, while I declared to him that I signed it under the pressure of force."

As you will observe, the Pasha declares categorically that he signed the document in question in spite of himself, and under the influence of the pressure which was being exercised upon his Highness.

Conformably to the tenour of your various telegrams, the Sublime Porte had warned Méhemmed Sadik Pasha not to accept or sign any Treaty without having previously referred it to the Sovereign Court, and had ordered him at the same time to acquaint the English Consul-General at Tunis with this fact, and, in case of need, to consult him.

To-day the Governor-General is forced by violent proceedings to append his signature to a Treaty which entirely reverses the order of things established in Tunis, thereby completely violating the *status quo* to a modification of which the English Cabinet declared its inability to consent.

In any case so grave and unexpected an occurrence could hardly, we should think, be passed over by Her Britannic Majesty.

Please, therefore, to call Lord Granville's most serious attention thereto, and tell him that we are convinced that his Lordship could not view with indifference a mode of procedure so contrary to the rights of nations, as well as to general interests, and that he will be so good as to intervene with a view to bring about the understanding which we have so often proposed. We are awaiting with the keenest impatience the measures which the British Government intend taking to bring about the modification of a Treaty which, as I have just said, not only ignores the principles of international law, but is further of a nature to create an unfortunate precedent.

B. TELEGRAM OF 16 MAY 1881

We did not fail, when the events which have just taken place at Tunis occurred, repeatedly to bring to the notice of the Signatories of the Berlin Treaty the full and entire sovereign rights of the Sublime Porte over that province, an integral portion of the Ottoman Empire. Those rights, established *ab antiquo,* have been exercised by the Turkish Government without interruption up to the present day, and have obtained recognition from the Powers in general.

Nor did we fail, both before and after the entry of French troops into Tunis, to propose that a friendly understanding should be come to between the Sublime Porte and the Government of the French Republic with the view of reconciling our rights with the interests of France, and of thus removing all grounds for the complaints made by the latter country of the raids of certain Berber tribes, which raids the authorities of Tunis had declared themselves ready to repress without delay from the first commencement of the quarrel.

The Pasha of Tunis and the people entrusted to his government by Imeprial Firman, on their side, appealed, as was their duty, to the Suzerain Court [of the Ottoman Empire] for the purpose of laying before it the critical situation in which they found themselves placed by the advance of French troops into their country, and of urgently requesting us, as their legitimate rulers, to come to their assistance.

No attention was paid to our markedly concilatory proposals, nor to the irrefutable proofs which we adduced in support of our rights; nay, more, the Government of the French Republic thought fit to deny the existence of the immemorial ties of vassalage which bind Tunis to the Ottoman Empire, by asserting the alleged independence of that country, and thus to run counter to all our remonstrances, and in spite of the protests of the Governor-General and people, by gradually occupying the greater part of the territory of Tunis, and, finally, by forbidding us, in a peremptory and threatening manner, to send a single ship to the spot.

By way of supplementing a line of action which, we regret to say, we cannot refrain from regarding as utterly contrary to all international obligations, the Government of the Republic has just presented to the French Chambers the Treaty concluded by it on the 12th instant with His Highness the Pasha of Tunis. This Treaty the Pasha was forcibly compelled to submit to in the face of the pressure which was being brought to bear upon the country and the imminent danger which threatened it.

It is a duty which we owe to ourselves and to the country to repudiate this document, all the clauses of which overthrow the legitimate order of things established in Tunis, and deal the most serious blow to the sovereign authority and integrity of the Empire, both of which are guaranteed by Treaties.

The Sublime Porte therefore regards it as a duty to protest in the most emphatic terms and in the most solemn manner against the validity of this Treaty, which it declares to have been concluded under circumstances abnormal in their character and in contravention of the rights of the Sultan, and to possess, in consequence, in his eyes, as well as in those of His Highness the Pasha, and of the people of Tunis, the subjects of His Imperial Majesty, no value or legal force, either in its whole, or in any of its parts.

I request you to communicate this protest, official and without the slightest delay, to His Excellency Her Britannic Majesty's Minister for Foreign Affairs.

5. British Views on the Ottoman Protest: The British Foreign Minister (Earl of Granville) to the Ottoman Ambassador, 16 June 1881

When your Excellency did me the honour of calling at the Foreign Office on the 14th instant you expressed a wish to be furnished with a written answer to the communications respecting Tunis which you were good enough to leave with me on the 18th ultimo.

The first of those communications seems to have been intended to be received in the nature of a protest, and has, I presume, been addressed to all the other Powers as well as Her Majesty's Government. It does not call for any expression of opinion on the part of Her Majesty's Government, and under the actual circumstances I abstain from offering any.

With regard to the second despatch, in which Assim Pasha states that Her Majesty's Government had declared that they would not consent to a modification of the *status quo* in Tunis, I have the honour to point out to your Excellency that Her Majesty's Government have only said that they were favorable to its maintenance, but they have never stated that they would not consent to any change in it.

I have to add that Her Majesty's Government would have been quite ready to offer their mediation, in common with the other Powers who signed the Treaty of Berlin had they had any reason to believe that those Powers would have agreed to join in such an offer, or that France would have accepted it had such an agreement been arrived at.

143. BRITISH-FRENCH (GAMBETTA) NOTE TO THE KHEDIVE AND ITS IMMEDIATE CONSEQUENCES
8 January–11 February 1882

[Great Britain, *Parliamentary Papers, 1882*, 82: 6–7, 148–49, 182]

The operations of the Dual Control placed a major financial burden on the Egyptians and gave rise to local restiveness. Egyptian civil servants and military officers particularly resented external interference in the domestic affairs of the country and preferential treatment of Europeans in government employ and Turkish Circassians in the army. On 9 September 1881, Egyptian army officers, led by Colonel Ahmad 'Urabi, staged a demonstration before the viceregal palace and, by forcing Khedive Tawfiq to accept their demands for representative government and a larger army, gained substantial mastery over the government. The British-French communication of 8 January 1882, commonly known as the Gambetta Note after its author, Léon Gambetta, the French foreign minister of the day, was intended to restore effective authority to the khedive. Instead, the move evoked protests from the Sublime Porte and the other European powers, so that in less than five weeks, on London's initiative, Britain and France repudiated the purposes of their earlier action. Thus, British-French indecisiveness further undermined the khedive's position. Langer, *European Alliance and Alignments*, chap. 8; Robinson, Gallagher, and Denny, *Africa and the Victorians*, chap. 4; Daniel, *Islam, Europe, and Empire*, chap. 14; Freycinet, *La question d'Egypte*, pp. 205–30; Bioves, *Français et anglais en E'gypte*; Deschanel, *Gambetta*, pp. 303–20; Sabry, *La génèse de l'esprit national égyptien*, chaps. 4–5; Blunt, *English Occupation of Egypt*, chap. 8; Kleine, *Deutschland und die ägyptische Frage*, pt. 2, chap. 1; Cocheris, *Situation internationale de l'Egypte et du Soudan*, chap. 4; L. Roberts, "Italy and the Egyptian Question"; Abu-Lughod, "Transformation of the Egyptian Elite"; Ahmed, *Intellectual Origins of Egyptian Nationalism*, chap 1, Farnie, *East and West of Suez*, chap. 16.

1. British-French Note, 8 January 1882

You have already been instructed on several occasions to inform the Khedive and his Government of the determination of England and France to afford them support against the difficulties of various kinds which might interfere with the course of public affairs in Egypt.

The two Powers are entirely agree on this subject, and recent circumstances, especially the meeting of the Chamber of Notables convoked by the Khedive, have given them the opportunity for a further exchange of views.

I have accordingly to instruct you to declare to the Khedive that the English and French Governments consider the maintenance of His Highness on the throne, on the terms laid down by the Sultan's Firmans, and officially recognized by the two Governments, as alone able to guarantee, for the present and future, the good order and the development of general prosperity in Egypt in which France and Great Britian are equally interested.

The two Governments being closely associated in the resolve to guard by their united efforts against all cause of complication, internal or external, which might meance the order of things established in Egypt, do not doubt that the assurance publicly given of their formal intentions in this respect will tend to avert the dangers to which the Government of the Khedive might be exposed, and which would certainly find England and France united to oppose them. They are convinced that His Highness will draw from this assurance the confidence and strength which he requires to direct the destinies of Egypt and its people.

2. Protest from the Sublime Porte to the British Foreign Secretary, 13 January 1882

Your Excellency is aware that the Consuls-General of France and England in Egypt have just made simultaneous and identic communications to His Highness the Khedive, in accordance with the instructions of their Governments.

In view of the Imperial Firman which the Sublime Porte has promulgated relative to this province, and the proceedings of the recent Turkish Special Mission, the step taken by the two Consulates-General shows that the reiterated assurance of the Imperial Government have not been appreciated. We cannot, therefore, disguise the painful impression which it has made upon us, and we find ourselves compelled to submit some observations upon it to the sentiments of justice and equity of the English Government.

Always to protect the immunities granted to Egypt, and thus to preserve the order and properity of this province, is the sincere wish and interest of the Imperial Government, whose efforts up till now have been directed towards this end. It would be impossible, we believe, to affirm that there exists the slightest indication, material or moral, of anything opposed to this end, nor are there any circumstances in Egypt which could serve as a motive for foreign assurances of this kind. Nothing, therefore, justifies the collective communication which has just been made to His Highness Tewfik Pasha, especially since Egypt forms an integral part of the possessions of His Imperial Majesty the Sultan, and since the power conferred upon the Khedive for the maintenance, if necessary, of order and public security, and for the proper administration of the country, as well as the strengthening of his authority for this purpose, comes essentially within the rights and prerogatives of the Sublime Porte.

From the moment that such a step was considered necessary it seems to us only natural that the opinion of the sovereign Power should be first obtained regarding it, and that this channel alone should have been employed to make the declaration, and give the desired assurances, Consequently, we think ourselves justified in considering the direct communication made to the Khedive improper, and the Sublime Porte finds itself obliged to inquire the reasons which induced the English Government to assoicate itself with the Government of the French Republic in a step which it considers as infringing upon its rights of sovereignty over Egypt.

The observations mentioned above have been transmitted also to the Imperial Embassy at Paris.

I have to request you to speak to the Minister for Foreign Affairs in the above sense, extending it, as you may think opportune, and to bring clearly before his Excellency the pressing necessity of our receiving explanations and assurances which may free the Imperial Government from the difficult position in which if finds itself in consequence of what has just taken place at Cairo.

3. The British Ambassador at Istanbul to Foreign Secretary Granville, 2 February 1882

The Representatives of Russia, Italy, Austria, and Germay made to-day at the Porte an identic communication in the form of a *pro-memoriâ* in reply to that in which the Porte conveyed to the Government in question its telegram to London and Paris concerning the identic note to the Khedive.

The communication of the four Powers states that the above Governments desire the preservation of the *status quo* in Egypt on the basis of the European arrangements and of the Firmans of the Sultan; and that they are of opinion that the *status quo* could not be modified except by an accord between the Great Powers and the Suzerain Power.

4. Foreign Office Circular Instructions to British Diplomatic Representatives in Berlin, Vienna, Rome, and Saint Petersburg, 11 February 1882

The reports at present received from

Egypt are not of a nature to excite apprehension of early disorder and anarchy. But
we are in presence of a crisis which may
give rise to an encroachment upon the order
of things establsihed by the Firmans of the
Sultan and by the international engagements of Egypt, whether with England and
France alone, or with all the other Powers.
Her Majesty's Government are informed
that the answer of the four Powers to the
recent protect of the Porte against the Declaration made to the Khedive by the English and French Government on the 8th
January is based on a recognition of existing arrangements in Egypt.

Her Majesty's Government are now
agreed with the Government of France that,
in view of events which might occur in
Egypt, it is desirable to ascertain whether
the other Powers would be willing to enter
upon an exchange of views as to the best
most of dealing with the question on the
basis of the maintenance of the rights of
the Sovereign and of the Khedive; of international engagements and the arrange-

ments existing under them, whether with
England and France alone or with those
two nations and the other Powers; the
preservation of the liberties secured by the
Firman of the Sultan; together with the
prudent development of Egyptian institutions.

The Governments of England and France
do not consider that a case for discussing
the expendiency of an intervention has at
present arisen, since on the part of the
Chamber of Notables and of the new Government the intention is avowed to maintain international engagements; but, should
the case arise, they would wish that any
such eventual intervention should represent
the united action and authority of Europe.

In that event it would also, in their opinion, be right that the Sultan should be a
party to any proceeding or discussion that
might ensue.

Your Excellency will read this despatch
to the Minister for Foreign Affairs, and
leave a copy with him should he desire it.

144. FOREIGN SECRETARY GRANVILLE'S CIRCULAR OUTLINING
BRITISH POLICY IN EGYPT
3 January 1883

[Great Britain, *Parliamentary Papers, 1883*, 83: 38–40]

The nationalists became more entrenched in Egypt in the first half of 1882. Fearing
that the army might be tempted to depose Tawfiq, Britain and France in May
strengthened their fleets off the Egyptian coast. This display of unusual naval force
merely intensified the resentment of the nationalists. Anti-European disorders spread
swiftly from Alexandria, where they first occurred on 11 June, through the larger
cities in the Delta. In England, the Liberal Gladstone government vacillated between
joint action with France and full internationalization of the Egyptian question. Indeed, early in the summer of 1882, when the British alone sent troops ashore, warships
of all the principal powers crowded Alexandria harbor, the European diplomats at
Istanbul were conferring formally on the issue, and the British were engaging in bilateral talks with the Sublime Porte on measures that that government might adopt.
In the end, France wavered and so did Italy, which the United Kingdom had also
invited to cooperate. The Istanbul conference failed to produce a formula, while the
Ottomans gave a consummate performance of their customary diplomacy by defer-

ment. England thus blundered into exclusive management of Egypt. But once the Foreign Office took the plunge, it left no doubt of its policy: British authority in the land would continue supreme for the duration of the occupation. This Lord Granville made clear in circular instructions, reproduced below, to the British diplomatic representatives in Paris, Berlin, Vienna, Rome, and Saint Petersburg. Langer, *European Alliances*, chaps. 8–9; Robinson, Gallagher, and Denny *Africa and the Victorians*, chaps. 4–5; Holt, *Egypt and the Fertile Crescent*, chap. 15; Vatikiotis, *Modern History of Egypt*, chaps. 8–10; Tignor, *Modernization and British Colonial Rule in Egypt*, chap. 3; Hallberg, *Suez Canal*, chaps. 16–17; Headlam-Morley, *Studies in Diplomatic History*, chap. 3; Freycinet, *La question d'Egypte*, pp. 230–353; Fitzmaurice, *Life of Granville*, vol. 2., chaps. 7, 9; Maurice and Arthur, *Life of Wolseley*, chap. 7; Kamel, *La conférence de Constantinople et la question égyptienne*; Kleine, *Deutschland und die ägyptische Frage*, p. 2, chap. 1; Cocheris, *Situation internationale de l'Egypte et du Soudan*, chaps. 5–6.

The course of events has thrown upon Her Majesty's Government the task, which they would willingly have shared with other Powers, of suppressing the military rebellion in Egypt, and restoring peace and order in that country. The object has happily been accomplished; and although for the present a British force remains in Egypt for the preservation of public tranquillity, Her Majesty's Government are desirous of withdrawing it as soon as the state of the country, and the organization of proper means for the maintenance of the Khedive's authority, will admit of it. In the meanwhile, the position in which Her Majesty's Government are placed towards His Highness imposes upon them the duty of giving advice with the object of securing that the order of things to be established shall be of a satisfactory character, and possess the elements of stability and progress.

The subjects to be treated may be divided into two categories: those which concern other countries, and are matters for the consent or concurrence of the European Powers; and those which are matters of internal administration.

To begin with the former class: one result of recent occurrences has been to call special attention to the Suez Canal, firstly, on account of the danger with which it was threatened during the first brief success of the insurrection, secondly, in consequence of its occupation by the British forces in the name of the Khedive, and their use of it as a base of the operations carried on in His Highness' behalf, and in support of his authority; and thirdly, because of the attitude assumed by the Direction and officers of the Canal Company at a critical period of the campaign.

As regards the first two of these points, Her Majesty's Government believe that the free and unimpeded navigation of the Canal at all times, and its freedom from obstruction or damage by acts of war, are matters of importance to all nations. It has been generally admitted that the measures taken by them for protecting the navigation, and the use of the Canal on behalf of the territorial Ruler for the purpose of restoring his authority, were in no way infringements of this general principle.

But to put upon a clearer footing the position of the Canal for the future, and to provide against possible dangers, they are of opinion that an agreement to the following effect might with advantage be come to between the Great Powers, to which other nations would subsequently be invited to accede:—

1. That the Canal should be free for the passage of all ships, in any circumstances.

2. That in time of war a limitation of time as to ships of war of a belligerent remaining in the Canal should be fixed, and no troops or munitions of war should be disembarked in the Canal.

3. That no hostilities should take place in the Canal or its approaches, or elsewhere in the territorial waters of Egypt, even in the event of Turkey being one of the bellige rents.

4. That neither of the two immediately

foregoing conditions shall apply to measures which may be necessary for the defence of Egypt.

5. That any Power whose vessels of war happen to do any damage of the Canal should be bound to bear the cost of its immediate repair.

6. That Egypt should take all measures within its power to enforce the conditions imposed on the transit of belligerent vessels through the Canal in time of war.

7. That no fortifications should be erected on the Canal or in its vicinity.

8. That nothing in the agreement shall be deemed to abridge or affect the territorial rights of the Government of Egypt further than is therein expressly provided.

Passing to the financial arrangements which have been the subject of agreement with all the Powers in connection with the Law of Liquidation, Her Majesty's Government are induced to believe that greater economy and simplicity may be attained in regard to the management of the Daïra Estates and some other Administrations by certain changes of detail which would not diminish the security of the creditors. They trust shortly to be a position to lay before the Powers definite proposals for this purpose.

A question in which all the Powers are interested, and which connects itself with the general subject finance, is that of the equal taxation of foreigners and natives. Her Majesty's Government feel convinced that the Powers will be prepared to join them in accepting any equitable proposals of the Egyptian Government for the purpose of placing foreigners on the same footing as natives in regard to taxes from which they are at present exempt.

As regards the Mixed Tribunals which have been established in Egypt by international agreement for the decision of civil suits between natives and foreigners, you are aware that the prolongation of the present system, which was agreed to in January last, would naturally expire on the 1st February next. Her Majesty's Government have advised the Egyptian Ministry to propose a further prolongation of a year, in order to give time for the discussion of amendments in the Codes and procedure which was interrupted by the events of the present year.

This concludes the list of questions which are matters of direct international arrangement with the Powers.

Her Majesty's Government communicate this outline of their views, as the initiative seems, after what has occurred, to fall on them, and submit it for the consideration of the Powers, in the hope that it will meet with their approval.

With reference to the second class of questions, the first and most pressing of the measures of internal administration is the organization of a force for the maintenance of public security against external or internal attack. Both on grounds of economy and of safety, Her Majesty's Government think it desirable that the Egyptian army should be a small one, and that the duty of maintaining order within the country should be discharged, as far as possible, by a separate force of gendarmerie and of police. The Khedive and his Ministers have expressed a strong wish that British officers should be lent, to fill certain posts in the army, under the Commander-in-chief of the Khedive, and to this Her Majesty's Government have expressed their willingness to agree for a time, and on a system which would give Egyptian officers access to some of the higher commands. The details of the scheme are still under consideration, but the general principles are sufficiently indicated in what I have stated.

Among the administrative arrangements of recent years, one of great importance was the institution of the English and French Controllers-General, with certain attributions in relation to the revenue and expenditure of the State, to which the French Government, and more recently that of England, became parties.

Upon this subject I inclose, for your information, and for communication to the Government to which you are accredited, a copy of a note officially delivered by the Egyptian Government to the British and French Agents in Egypt on the 7th November, containing a proposal for the abolition of the Control, and a statement of the grounds on which that course is advocated. I also inclose a copy of the instructions which Her Majesty's Government have addressed to the Earl of Dufferin in reply to this communication, from which it will be seen that, for the reasons therein stated, and subject to a reservation as to the appointment for the present of an European official as financial adviser to the Khedive, Her Majesty's Government are prepared to accede to the proposal of the Egyptian Government. In this measure they earnestly desire the concurrence of France.

Her Majesty's Government have urged strongly upon the Khedive the necessity of at once introducing an improved system for the administration of justice to natives throughout the ountry, and they trust that in a short time effective measures will be taken for this purpose.

The question of the suppression of the Slave Trade, and of the abolition, as far as possible, of slavery in Egypt, is one which Her Majesty's Government have much at heart. They will lose no favourable opportunity of advising the Khedive to take such steps as may be judicious for the attainment of these objects.

There remains the question of the development of political institutions in Egypt. It is one of great importance and complexity, and requires for its treatment careful study of the circumstances of the country

and people. Her Majesty's Government are of opinion that the prudent introduction of some form of representative institutions may contribute greatly to the good government of the country and to the safety and regularity of the Khedive's rule. But they await further Reports from their Representatives in Egypt before coming to a conclusion as to the shape which would be best suited to the present occasion, while affording opportunities for future growth.

Her Majesty's Government have wished to give full information to the Powers on all these matters, which are immediately connected with the peace, security, and social order of Egypt, and on which, accordingly, they have thought it their duty to adivise the Khedive as to the best mode of exercising his governing power. They trust that the spirit in which they have proceeded will be found to be in consonance with the views of the other Governments who take an interest in the welfare of that country.

You will communicate a copy of this despatch to the Government to which you are accredited.

145. PROTECTORATE CONVENTION (MARSA):
FRANCE AND TUNISIA
8 June 1883

(Approved by French law, 10 April 1884)
[Translated from the French text in France, *Journal Officiel: Documents parlementaires, sénat* (June 1884), annex no. 128, 4 April 1884, p. 125]

The Treaty of Bardo (Doc. 142), which authorized the French military occupation of Tunisia and provided for the surrender to France of Tunisia's external sovereignty, nevertheless did not formally designate the regency a French protectorate. The following convention made the protectorate status explicit. empowering France to reorganize the administration of the country. With the bey's pledge (art. 1) "to undertake such administrative, judicial, and financial reforms as the French Government may deem useful," France sought to contain and then to eliminate the influence of the other European powers, or, to put it differently, to win their formal recognition of the protectorate. This took more than a dozen years. The first and most obvious line of attack was against the capitulations, which gave each concerned European power judicial autonomy. Even before the signature of the protectorate convention, the bey had been induced to issue a decree on the creation of a court system along French lines to adjudicate disputes involving European nationals. The French government did not wait for parliamentary approval of the convention, which came in April 1884, but immediately proceeded to negotiate with each capitulatory power arrangements for suspending the consular courts in Tunisia, as a major step toward the abrogation of extraterritorial privileges in the protectorate. This initiative Italy resisted, for it was still smarting from the French seizure of the territory, where the Italian settlers far outnumbered the French (11,000 to 700 in 1881), giving rise in Italy at the time to the claim that Tunisia was "an Italian colony governed by the French." When Italy finally gave its consent in August 1884 (after ten other capitulatory powers, indeed all but the Netherlands, had done so), it expressly reaffirmed in the protocol (art. 2) the validity of "all the other immunities, advantages, and guarantees, assured by the capitulations, usages, and treaties" (from the French text in A. and J. de Clercq, *Recueil des traités,* vol. 15, supp., pp. 720–23). The later weakness of the Italian position lay not in the size of the Italian settler community in Tunisia under French rule, since by 1896 there were 55,000 Italian immigrants as against 16,000 French immigrants, but in the fact that the Italian capitulatory privileges rested on the treaty of 1868 (Doc. 120), which was a term rather than a perpetual treaty. As assimilator of the external sovereignty of Tunisia, France in August 1895 exercised its right under article 25 of giving one year's notice that it would denounce the treaty on its expiry at twenty-eight years. The third largest group of European-protected settlers in Tunisia comprised the 10,000 Maltese, who were British subjects. Italy could successfully resist French pressure to end the capitulations only by procuring the cooperation of Britain. Yet Britain, which had a perpetual treaty with Tunis, notified France in January 1896 that it was prepared to enter into a new arrangement. In August, Austria went even further by becoming the first major power to recognize the French protectorate over Tunisia. Italy finally gave way by concluding with France on the eve of the expiry of the 1868 treaty three conventions regarding Tunisia: commerce and navigation, rights and status of Italian nationals and consuls, and extradition (for texts see Basdevant, *Traités et conventions,* 2: 731–55). By these acts Italy formally acknowledged France as protecting power in Tunisia, and France formally acquiesced in the continuance of capitulatory privileges for Italian settlers. Eubank, *Paul Cambon,* chap. 2; Julien, *La question italienne en Tunisie;* Billot, *La France et l'Italie,* 2: 332–73; Cambon, *Histoire de la régence de Tunis,* chaps. 11–12; Estournelles de Constant, *La politique française en Tunisie,* pt. 3; Cataluccio, *Italia e Francia in Tunisia;* Toscano, "Tunis"; S. Roberts, *History of French Colonial Policy,* chap. 7.

His Highness to Bey of Tunis, considering the necessity of improving the internal situation of Tunisia in the circumstances foreseen by the treaty of 12 May 1881, and the Government of the [French] Republic, profoundly wishing to respond to this desire and thereby to consolidate the friendly relations happily existing between the two countries, have agreed to conclude a special convention to this effect: therefore, the President of the French Republic

has named as his Plenipotentiary M. Pierre Paul Cambon, his Resident Minister in Tunis, officer of the Legion of Honor, decorated with the Haïd and the Grand Cross of Nishan Iftiqar, etc., etc., who, after having presented his full powers, found in good and sufficient form, has worked out with His Highness the Bey of Tunis the following arrangements:

ART. 1. To facilitate fulfillment of the Protectorate by the French Government,

His Highness the Bey of Tunis pledges to undertake such administrative, judicial, and financial reforms as the French Government may deem useful.

ART. 2. The French Government guarantees, at the time and under the conditions that may appear best to it, to issue a loan to His Highness the Bey, for the conversion or the repayment of the funded debt up to the sum of 125 million francs and of the floating debt up to the maximum amount of 17.55 million [francs].

His Highness the Bey is forbidden in the future to contract any loan on behalf of the Regency without the authorization of the French Government.

ART. 3. From the revenues of the Regency, His Highness the Bey will set aside: (1) the sums necessary to assure the service of the loan guaranteed by France [and] (2) the sum of two million piasters (1.2 million francs), a total [drawn] from the civil list. The surplus of revenues must be applied to the expenses of administering the Regency and to the repayment of the cost of the protectorate.

ART. 4. The present arrangement confirms and completes, as needed, the treaty of 12 May 1881. It will not modify the arrangements previously instituted for regulating war taxes.

ART. 5. The present convention will be submitted to the Government of the French Republic for ratification and the instrument of ratification will be delivered as soon as possible to His Highness the Bey of Tunis. . . .

146. CONVENTION ON EGYPTIAN AFFAIRS: GREAT BRITAIN AND THE OTTOMAN EMPIRE
24 October 1885

(Ratifications exchanged, Istanbul, 24 November 1885)
[Great Britain, *Parliamentary Papers*, *1886*, 74: 41–43]

No sooner had England launched its occupation of Egypt than the Sublime Porte, aided and abetted by France and Russia, sought to have the occupation terminated. Despite the contrary views of Queen Victoria and of the imperialist faction of the Liberal Party, the Gladstone government nevertheless gave repeated assurances that the presence of British forces in Egypt was only a temporary measure. But the occupation itself had been motivated chiefly by anxiety over defense of the Suez Canal, so vital to British imperial communications. To this was added British apprehension over the Mahdi Muhammad Ahmad's revolt against khedival administration in the Sudan, which endangered the security of Egypt's southern frontier and multiplied the financial burdens of a government already heavily in debt. To allay Ottoman fears and European jealousies while safeguarding British interests, Sir Henry Drummond Wolff was sent to Istanbul in mid-August 1885 to negotiate a settlement with the Sublime Porte. Lord Salisbury, once again foreign minister, this time in a Conservative government that he headed, instructed Wolff to accept the principle of evacuation but without binding Britain "to a fixed date" or to "the formal consent of the Powers to anything we do" and to acquire "a treaty right to occupy Alexandria when we pleased." Salisbury was even prepared, he informed the British ambassador at Vienna, "to get Turkish soldiers—they need not be in any very great numbers—sent to Egypt,

452   THE MIDDLE EAST AND NORTH AFRICA IN WORLD POLITICS

both for the obvious convenience of using soldiers who will stand the heat better than ours, and who are of the same religion as the natives—but also and still more for a political reason. . . . It seems to us that small bodies of Turkish troops, sent there to stay as long as the English, and go when they go, will regularise our position" (Cecil, *Life of Robert, Marquis of Salisbury*, 2: 235–36). Robinson and Gallagher, *Africa and the Victorians*, chap. 8; Hornik, "Mission of Sir Henry Drummond-Wolff to Constantinople"; Wolff, *Rambling Recollections,* vol. 2, chaps. 59–62; Freycinet, *La question d'Egypte*, pp. 333–73; M. Anderson, *Eastern Question*, pp. 240–53; Kleine, *Deutschland und die ägyptische Frage*, pt. 2, chaps. 2–3; Hallberg, *Suez Canal*, chap. 17; Cocheris, *Situation internationale de l'Egypte et du Soudan*, chaps. 7–8; Marlowe, *Cromer in Egypt*, chap. 6.

ART. I. Her Britannic Majesty and His Imperial Majesty the Sultan will respectively send a High Commissioner to Egypt.

ART. II. The Ottoman High Commissioner will consult with His Highness the Khedive, or with the functionary who shall be designated for that purpose by His Highness, upon the best means for tranquillizing the Soudan by pacific measures.

The Ottoman High Commissioner and His Highness the Khedive will keep the English High Commissioner currently informed of the negotiations, and as the measures to be decided upon form part of the general settlement of Egyptian affairs, they shall be adopted and placed in execution in agreement with the English High Commissioner.

ART. III. The two High Commissioners will reorganize, in concert with His Highness the Khedive, the Egyptian army.

ART. IV. The two High Commissioners, in concert with His Highness the Khedive, will examine all the branches of the Egyptian Administration, and may introduce into them the modifications which they may consider necessary, within the limits of the Imperial Firmans.

ART. V. The international engagements contracted by His Highness the Khedive will be approved by the Ottoman Government in so far as they shall not be contrary to the privileges granted by the Imperial Firmans.

ART. VI. So soon as the two High Commissioners shall have established that the security of the frontiers and the good working and stability of the Egyptian Government are assured, they shall present a Report to their respective Governments, who will consult as to the conclusion of a Convention regulating the withdrawal of the British troops from Egypt in a convenient period.

147. CONVENTION ON EGYPT: GREAT BRITAIN AND THE OTTOMAN EMPIRE
22 May 1887

[Great Britain, *Parliamentary Papers, 1887*, 92: 538–45]

In accordance with the 1885 convention (Doc. 146), Wolff and Muhtar Paşa, its negotiators, were named high commissioners by Britain and the Sublime Porte, respectively to study the situation in Egypt. On the basis of their inquiry British-Ottoman negotiations were resumed in an attempt to frame a more explicit agreement that would, without compromising basic British interests, reaffirm Ottoman sovereignty and satisfy the demands of France and Russia for a full British withdrawal. The United Kingdom promptly ratified the latest convention. But the Sublime Porte did not follow suit, primarily because of the inflexible opposition of France and Russia which were annoyed by the ambiguity of article 5. The British, it is clear, were not displeased with the outcome, for they could point to their accommodating attitude. The annexes of the 1887 convention are not reproduced here. Cecil, *Life of Robert Marquis of Salisbury*, vol. 4, chap. 2; see also references to Doc. 146.

ART. I. The Imperial Firmans at present in force in Egypt are confirmed, except in so far as they may be modified by the present Convention.

ART. II. The Khediviate of Egypt comprises the territories set forth in the Imperial Firmans concerning Egypt.

ART. III. The Imperial Ottoman Government will invite the Powers parties to the Treaty of Berlin to approve a Convention for better securing the freedom of navigation through the Suez Canal.

By such Convention the Imperial Ottoman Government will declare that this maritime Canal shall be always free and open, whether in time of peace or of war, for ships of war and merchant-vessels passing from one sea to the other, without distinction of flag, on payment of the dues and in conformity with the regulations actually in force, or with those which may hereafter be promulgated by the competent administration.

The Convention shall provide that the Great Powers shall undertake on their side never to impede the free passage of the Canal in time of war, and to respect the property and establishments belonging to the Canal.

It shall also provide that the Canal shall never be subjected to blockade, and that no right of war or act of hostility shall be exercised either within the Canal, or within a radius of 3 marine miles from the ports of Suez and Port Saïd.

It shall also be laid down that the Diplomatic Agents of the Signatory Powers in Egypt shall watch over the execution of the Convention whenever circumstances may arise of a nature to threaten the safety or freedom of passage of the Canal; that these Agents shall assemble when convened by one of their body, under the presidency of the special Commissioner named for that purpose by the Sublime Porte, or by the Khedive, in order to verify and record the cases of danger, and they shall inform the Egyptian Government thereof, in order that it may adopt proper measures to insure the protection and free passage of the Canal; that in any case they shall assemble once a-year, in order to record that the Convention has been duly observed.

It shall moreover be provided that no obstacle can be placed in the way of any measures which may be necessary for the defence of Egypt and the security of the Canal, and, finally, that the two High Contracting Parties shall also invite the other Powers to adhere thereto in the same manner as the Powers parties to the above mentioned Convention.

ART. IV. Inasmuch as the abnormal state of the Soudan, and the troubles caused by political events in Egypt may for some time render necessary the adoption of ordinary precautions for the safety of the frontiers, and the internal security of Egypt, Her Britannic Majesty's Government will superintend the military defence and organization of the country.

For this purpose, it will maintain in Egypt the number of British troops it may consider necessary, and will continue to exercise a general inspection of the Egyptian army.

The conditions concerning the withdrawal of the British troops, and the cessation of all supervision exercised by the Government of Her Britannic Majesty over the Egyptian army, shall be fulfilled in conformity with the stipulations of Article V of the present Convention.

ART. V. At the expiration of three years from the date of the present Covnention, Her Britannic Majesty's Government will withdraw its troops from Egypt. If at that period the appearance of danger, in the interior or from without, should render necessary the adjournment of the evacuation, the

British troops will withdraw from Egypt immediately after the disappearance of this danger, and two years after the aforesaid evacuation the provisions of Article IV above shall completely cease to have effect.

On the withdrawal of the British troops, Egypt shall enjoy the advantages of the principle of territorial immunity ("sûreté territoriale"), and on the ratification of the present Convention the Great Powers shall be invited to sign and Act recognizing and guaranteeing the inviolability of Egyptian territory.

Under such Act no Power shall have the right, under any circumstance, to land troops on Egyptian territory except in the cases provided for in the Regulations annexed to the present Convention.

Nevertheless, the Imperial Ottoman Government will make use of its right of occupying Egypt militarily if there are reasons to fear an invasion from without, or if order and security in the interior were disturbed, or if the Khediviate of Egypt refused to execute its duties towards the Sovereign Court, or its international obligations.

On its side, the Government of Her Britannic Majesty is authorized by this Convention to send, in the above-mentioned cases, troops into Egypt, which will take the measures necessary to remove these dangers. In taking these measures, the Commanders of these troops will act with all the regard due to the rights of the Sovereign Powers.

The Ottoman troops as well as the British troops will be withdrawn from Egypt as soon as the causes requiring this intervention shall have ceased.

If, by reason of hindrances, the Ottoman Government should not send troops to Egypt, it will send a Commissioner to remain during the period of the sojourn of the British troops with their Commander.

Whenever the two States may consider it necessary to send troops into Egypt, they will notify the circumstance one to the other, and will act in conformity with the present Convention.

ART. VI. When the present Convention shall have been ratified, the two High Contracting Parties shall notify the fact in the first instance to the Powers parties to the Treaty of Berlin, and subsequently to the other Governments who have made or accepted arrangements with the Khediviate of Egypt, inviting them to give to it their adhesion.

148. CONVENTION ON FREE NAVIGATION OF THE SUEZ CANAL: THE EUROPEAN POWERS AND THE OTTOMAN EMPIRE
29 October 1888

(Became effective 1905; repudiated by Egypt, 1956)
[Great Britain, *Parliamentary Papers, 1889*, Commercial no. 2, C. 5623]

To the conditions for regulating the Suez Canal laid down in the Granville circular (Doc. 144) the French objected, proposing instead the creation of an international commission of the powers chiefly interested in the waterway. As early as June 1885, an instrument was drafted incorporating the proposals of Britain and France. But the representative of Britain appended a reservation which, in effect, suspended the application of the clauses on the international commission for the duration of the occupation of Egypt. Although the convention was finally signed in 1888 by Austria, Germany, Italy, the Netherlands, the Ottoman Empire, Russia, and Spain, as well as Britain and France, it did not become operative—because of Britain's insistence on its reservation of 1885 and France's opposition thereto—until after the conclusion of the British-French understanding of 1904 (Doc. 162). The 1888 convention continued in force until 1956. Hallberg, *Suez Canal,* chap. 17; Robinson and Gallagher, *Africa and the Victorians,* chap. 8; Huang, "Suez Canal Question"; Avram, *Evolution of the Suez Canal Status*; A. Wilson, *Suez Canal,* chap. 6; Schonfield, *Suez Canal,* chap. 6; Farnie, *East and West of Suez,* chap. 18.

ART. I. The Suez Maritime Canal shall always be free and open, in time of war as in time of peace, to every vessel of commerce or of war, without distinction of flag.

Consequently, the High Contracting Parties agree not in any way to interfere with the free use of the Canal, in time of war as in time of peace.

The Canal shall never be subjected to the exercise of the right of blockade.

ART. II. The High Contracting Parties, recognizing that the Fresh-Water Canal is indispensable to the Maritime Canal, take note of the engagements of His Highness the Khedive towards the Universal Suez Canal Company as regards the Fresh-Water Canal; which engagements are stipulated in a Convention bearing date the 18th March, 1863, containing an *exposé* and four Articles.

They undertake not to interfere in any way with the security of that Canal and its branches, the working of which shall not be exposed to any attempt at obstruction.

ART. III. The High Contracting Parties likewise undertake to respect the plant, establishments, buildings, and works of the Maritime Canal and of the Fresh-Water Canal.

ART. IV. The Maritime Canal remaining open in time of war as a free passage, even to the ships of war of belligerents, according to the terms of Article I of the present Treaty, the High Contracting Parties agree that no right of war, no act of hostility, nor any act having for its object to obstruct the free navigation of the Canal, shall be committed in the Canal and its ports of access, as well as within a radius of 3 marine miles from those ports, even though the Ottoman Empire should be one of the belligerent Powers.

Vessels of war of belligerents shall not revictual or take in stores in the Canal and its ports of access, except in so far as may be strictly necessary. The transit of the aforesaid vessels through the Canal shall be effected with the least possible delay, in accordance with the Regulations in force, and without any other intermission than that resulting from the necessities of the service.

Their stay at Port Saïd and in the roadstead of Suez shall not exceed twenty-four hours, except in case of distress. In such case they shall be bound to leave as soon as possible. An interval of twenty-four hours shall always elapse between the sailing of a belligerent ship from one of the ports of access and the departure of a ship belonging to the hostile Power.

ART. V. In time of war belligerent Powers shall not disembark nor embark within the Canal and its ports of access either troops, munitions, or materials of war. But in case of an accidental hindrance in the Canal, men may be embarked or disembarked at the ports of access by detachments not exceeding 1,000 men, with a corresponding amount of war material.

ART. VI. Prizes shall be subjected, in all respects, to the same rules as the vessels of war of belligerents.

ART. VII. The Powers shall not keep any vessel of war in the waters of the Canal (including Lake Timsah and the Bitter Lakes).

Nevertheless, they may station vessels of war in the ports of access of Port Saïd and Suez, the number of which shall not exceed two for each Power.

This right shall not be exercised by belligerents.

ART. VIII. The Agents in Egypt of the Signatory Powers of the present Treaty shall be charged to watch over its execution. In case of any event threatening the security or the free passage of the Canal, they shall meet on the summons of three of their number under the presidency of their Doyen, in order to proceed to the necessary verifications. They shall inform the Khedivial Government of the danger which they may have perceived, in order that that Government may take proper steps to insure the protection and the free use of the Canal. Under any circumstances, they shall meet once a year to take note of the due execution of the Treaty.

The last-mentioned meetings shall take place under the presidency of a Special Commissioner nominated for that purpose by the Imperial Ottoman Government. A Commissioner of the Khedive may also take part in the meeting, and may preside over it in case of the absence of the Ottoman Commissioner.

They shall especially demand the suppression of any work or the dispersion of any assemblage on either bank of the Canal, the object or effect of which might be to interfere with the liberty and the entire security of the navigation.

ART. IX. The Egyptian Government shall, within the limits of its powers resulting from the Firmans, and under the conditions provided for in the present Treaty, take the necessary measures for insuring the execution of the said Treaty.

In case the Egyptian Government should not have sufficient means at its disposal, it shall call upon the Imperial Ottoman Government, which shall take the necessary measures to respond to such appeal; shall give notice thereof to the Signatory Powers of the Declaration of London of the 17th March, 1885; and shall, if necessary, concert with them on the subject.

The provisions of Articles IV, V, VII, and VIII shall not interfere with the measures which shall be taken in virtue of the present Article.

ART. X. Similarly, the provisions of Articles IV, V, VII, and VIII shall not interfere with the measures which His Majesty the Sultan and His Highness the Khedive, in the name of His Imperial Majesty, and within the limits of the Firmans granted, might find it necessary to take for securing by their own forces the defence of Egypt and the maintenance of public order.

In case His Imperial Majesty the Sultan, or His Highness the Khedive, should find it necessary to avail themselves of the exceptions for which this Article provides, the Signatory Powers of the Declaration of London shall be notified thereof by the Imperial Ottoman Government.

It is likewise understood that the provisions of the four Articles aforesaid shall in no case occasion any obstacle to the measures which the Imperial Ottoman Government may think it necessary to take in order to insure by its own forces the defence of its other possessions situated on the eastern coast of the Red Sea.

ART. XI. The measures which shall be taken in the cases provided for by Articles IX and X of the present Treaty shall not interfere with the free use of the Canal. In the same cases, the erection of permanent fortifications contrary to the provisions of Article VIII is prohibited.

ART. XII. The High Contracting Parties, by application of the principle of equality as regards the free use of the Canal, a principle which forms one of the bases of the present Treaty, agree that none of them shall endeavour to obtain with respect to the Canal territorial or commercial advantages or privileges in any international arrangements which may be concluded. Moreover, the rights of Turkey as the territorial Power are reserved.

ART. XIII. With the exception of the obligations expressly provided by the clauses of the present Treaty, the sovereign rights of His Imperial Majesty the Sultan, and the rights and immunities of His Highness the Khedive, resulting from the Firmans, are in no way affected.

ART. XIV. The High Contracting. Parties agree that the engagements resulting from the present Treaty shall not be limited by the duration of the Acts of Concession of the Universal Suez Canal Company.

ART. XV. The stipulations of the present Treaty shall not interfere with the sanitary measures in force in Egypt.

ART. XVI. The High Contracting Parties undertake to bring the present Treaty to the knowledge of the States which have not signed it, inviting them to accede to it.

149. REUTER CONCESSION FOR THE IMPERIAL BANK OF PERSIA
30 January 1889

[Translated from the French text in Iran, Archives of the Ministry of Foreign Affairs, Tehran]

As early as 1866, the House of Erlanger in Paris turned down an offer of a concession that it had sought to extend its banking facilities to Persia, because Nasir al-Din Shah refused to guarantee deposits against arbitrary governmental seizure. So far as is known, that was the first effort to open a modern bank in the shahdom. The New Oriental Banking Corporation, a British-owned firm operating in the Middle East, opened branches in Tehran and a half-dozen other towns in Persia in 1888–89 without an explicit concession. In 1890 all these branches were purchased by the Imperial Bank of Persia, which had received its concession in January of the preceding year. The Imperial Bank of Persia was the brainchild of Baron Julius de Reuter, who had never surrendered his claim to rights given him in the stillborn omnibus concession of 1872 (Doc. 126), particularly since the shah had retained the performance bond of £40,000 sterling. The Foreign Office and the British Legation in Tehran, which had come to look upon Reuter's claim as a national interest, in view of the sharpening British-Russian rivalry in Persia and Central Asia, mediated the negotiations that led to the shah's award of a new sixty-year concession, reproduced below, authorizing Reuter to establish the Imperial Bank of Persia with the exclusive right to issue bank notes. What is more, the shah agreed (art. 8) to accept as a valid guarantee for the fulfillment of the new contract the sequestered £40,000 sterling performance bond of 1872, it being understood that the bond would be returned to the concessionaire, once the bank was established. In the 1889 concession, no mention was made of railroad construction, although the exclusive mining rights of the earlier instrument were renewed. Incorporated in London in September 1889 under a royal charter, and its issue in the following month oversubscribed, the Imperial Bank of Persia started its career with assurance of immediate success as fiscal agents of the Persian government. However, its mining rights, which were never effectively exercised, were abandoned at the end of a decade. Meanwhile, the launching of Reuter's banking enterprise touched off a lively competition with Russia, which actively supported the application for concessions made by the Poliakov brothers, Russian Jewish subjects active in trade with Persia. They procured in December 1890 an exclusive concession to own and operate an insurance and transportation company. The Comptoire d'Assurance et de Transport, as it was called, developed essentially into a contracting agent for the Russian Ministry of Finance for road construction in northern Persia. The Poliakovs obtained a further concession in 1891 to open a Banque de Prêts, which never fulfilled its original design of providing small-scale loans to Persians soon degenerating instead into little more than a chain of pawn shops, as historian Firuz Kazemzadeh has observed. The bank was sold in 1894 to the Russian Ministry of Finance, and under its new name, Banque d'Escompte de Perse, it pursued the deliberate policy of offering generous mortgages to wealthy landowners in the north as a means of enlarging Russian influence in what the tsarist regime was coming to consider its sphere of influence.

Ronall, "Beginnings of Modern Banking in Iran"; Issawi, *Economic History of Iran*, chap. 8; Kazemzadeh, *Russia and Britain in Persia*, chap. 4; Curzon, *Persia and the Persian Question*, vol. 1, chap. 15.

The difficulties pending for a long time between the Government of His Imperial Majesty the Shah of Persia and Baron Julius de Reuter having been definitely overcome and the concession granted to the said Baron Julius de Reuter on 25 July 1872 annulled, the following has been mutually agreed upon:

ART. 1. By the present concession the Government of His Imperial Majesty the Shah of Persia grants to Baron Julius de Reuter and his associates or representatives the right to found a state bank in the Persian Empire under the name of Imperial Bank of Persia. This right is granted for a period of sixty years from the date of signature of the present concession by His Imperial Majesty the Shah. The seat of the association and the residence of the Bank shall be established at Tehran, and the Bank may establish branches in other cities in Persia or abroad. In order to develop Persia's commerce and augment its wealth, the Imperial Bank, aside from the purposes that an institution of credit serves, may undertake on its own behalf or on behalf of a third [party], any kind of financial, industrial, or commercial endeavor it believes favorable to this end, on condition that none of these enterprises shall be contrary to the treaties, laws, customs, or religion of the country and that the Persian Government shall be informed in advance. The Imperial Bank shall not have the right to accept a mortgage, or to buy immovable [property such as] lands, villages, etc., in the territory of the Empire, with the exception of land needed for the construction of a suitable establishment in Tehran and branches in the provinces. It is equally forbidden for the Bank to discount or to make advances on Government drafts that shall not have been drawn on the Bank.

ART. 2. The capital of the Imperial Bank shall be 100 million francs, or £4 million sterling. Consequently, a certain number of securities may be created that the Bank shall issue in series. The Bank shall be considered established when the first series of 25 million francs, or £1 million sterling, has been subscribed. The subscription shall be opened in various capitals, such as Tehran, Berlin, London, Paris, Saint Petersburg, and Vienna, if the governments of the several Powers permit it. The securities shall be [payable] to the bearer and the Bank may also issue registered securities. The Bank, when it is judged advantageous, may augment its capital and the number of its securities on agreement with the Government.

ART. 3. The Imperial Bank shall have the exclusive right as State Bank to issue notes payable to the bearer on demand. It shall never issue notes amounting to more than 20 million francs, or £800 thousand sterling, without informing the Persian Government. In order to further the development of public credit and place a limit on the circulation of silver money, while augmenting that of gold, the Imperial Bank accepts in principle the establishment of a single standard based on the *toman*, but within ten years after the Bank's establishment the Government of His Imperial Majesty and the Directors of the Bank shall agree on the most proper ways and means to attain this end. However, taking into consideration the demands of the actual monetary situation, the issuance of Imperial Bank notes shall be based primarily on the silver *kran*.

These notes shall be accepted by all agents and employees of the Imperial Government and shall be [considered] legal tender in all transactions in Persia. However, should the Bank not be able to redeem one of these notes, the circulation of Bank notes shall be forbidden throughout the Empire and the Bank shall be forced to redeem all its notes. To guarantee this reimbursement, the Bank expressly promises to maintain for two years from the time it begins its operations a cash balance equal to half [the value] of its notes in circulation, and after this period of two years, equal to at least one-third. The difference between the cash balance in specie and the amount of the notes issued shall be guaranteed by the titles to movable and immovable valuables belonging to the bank and deposited in its coffers in Persia.

The Imperial Bank shall be obligated to pay its notes on sight at the place of their issuance. Nevertheless, its branches' notes may be reimbursed in Tehran. The bank notes shall be in the Persian language. Paper money [of denominations] less than two tomans may not be issued without the authorization of the Government. The bank notes shall carry a sign or stamp indicating their inspection by the Persian Government and shall be signed by a Director or Administrator and by the principal cashier of the establishment where they were issued.

The Government of His Imperial Majesty the Shah pledges not to issue any sort of paper money for the duration of this concession nor to authorize the creation of any other bank or establishment having similar privileges.

ART. 4. The Imperial Government does not guarantee the capital of the Bank. It may, if it wishes, subscribe to it or promote the subscription of Persian subjects to the amount of one-fifth of the capital called for, or [it may choose not to] participate in any way.

The division of the capital into securities, the number and value of bank notes conforming to the provisions of Article 3 of the present instrument, the organization and administration of the Bank, the nomination of managers and employees of the Bank in Persia or abroad, and the financial management of the Bank with the profits that it may make or the losses it may suffer shall be entirely in the hands of the concessionaire and his associates or representatives, at their risk and peril.

The Government of His Imperial Majesty the Shah shall exercise its high surveillance on the Bank by appointing an Imperial High Commissioner. This High Commissioner shall have the right to acquaint himself with the management of the Bank and to see that the affairs of the Bank are conducted in conformity with this instrument of concession. He shall officially attend General Meetings as well as gatherings of the Council of Administration at Tehran whenever invited. He shall control the issuance of bank notes with strict observance of the provisions of Article 3 of the present concession. He shall super-

vise relations between the Bank and the Imperial Treasury. He may not interfere with the administration and management of the Bank's affairs and his duties shall not impose any responsibility on the Imperial Government.

ART. 5. The purpose of [establishing] this Bank as a national institution being the public welfare and the welfare of the State, the Government of His Imperial Majesty grants it the military protection indispensable to the security of its principal seat and branches.

The Government as protector of the enterprise shall facilitate, wherever possible, the acquisition of necessary lands and sites upon which the Bank shall establish its principal seat and branches, intervening equitably between [the Bank] and the landowners. The Bank, its premises and branches, shall be entirely exempt from any kind of tax or duty. The same shall be true for its securities, notes, receipts, and checks and for all documents emanating from it on its affairs and transactions. But if the Imperial Government should introduce a stamp tax the Bank shall not accept any bill of exchange or other instrument circulating in Persia without a State stamp.

ART. 6. The Imperial Bank shall facilitate the payments of the Imperial Treasury in Persia or abroad. For each service the Government demands of [the Bank] the Government and the Bank's Directors shall mutually determine the commission to be paid to the Bank. After its establishment and the payment of its capital, the Imperial Bank undertakes to lend the Government of His Imperial Majesty the Shah for a period of ten years the sum of 1 million francs, or £40 thousand sterling, at an [interest] rate of 6 percent. The interest and amortization, shall, according to His Imperial Majesty's wishes, be deducted from the 6 percent of the Bank's net profits assured to the Government by Article 7 of the present instrument. Moreover, the Bank, after its establishment, shall also place itself at the disposal of the Imperial Government for all loans or advances that [the Imperial Government] may need, against such collatoral as may be agreed upon in each case by the Imperial Government and the Bank. Otherwise, these advances or loans shall be considered an equivalent guarantee for the sum of the notes issued. The Government shall repay these loans or advances within a period specified by the respective conventions. The total interest shall be discharged regularly at the end of each Persian fiscal year, to wit, on 20 March. The first of these advances above the aforementioned sum of 1 million francs shall be 5 million francs, or £200,000 sterling, at the current rate of exchange, i.e., at the rate of 8 percent.

ART. 7. At the end of each Persian fiscal year, on 20 March, the Imperial Bank must turn over to the Government of His Imperial Majesty the Shah, or transfer to his credit, 6 percent of the annual net profits. Should this share of the profits, fixed at 6 percent, not reach an annual sum of 100 thousand francs, or £4 thousand sterling, the Bank must furnish the balance, charging it [alone] or the total sum to its trade expenses without the right of any deduction whatsoever in the said share of profits resulting from the balance sheet of the following year.

ART. 8. The guarantee of £40 thousand sterling that was deposited in 1872 in the Bank of England by Baron Julius de Reuter shall serve the Persian Government as a guarantee for the establishment of the Imperial Bank. The day after its establishment, the Persian Government shall return to the said Baron the aforementioned sum of £40 thousand sterling. If the Imperial Bank is not founded within a period of nine months from His Imperial Majesty's signature of the present instrument, the said guarantee shall fall to the Persian Government, and the present concession shall be considered null and void [*non avenues*] unless a war erupts in Europe between the Great Powers or Persia finds itself engaged [in war] or in any other situation [caused by] an act of God.

ART. 9. At the moment of the establishment of the Imperial Bank, its principal Administrators shall publish the statutes by which the Bank is to be regulated. These statutes must conform strictly to the stipulations of the present concession. After the establishment of the Bank the said statutes may be modified only by the decision of a General Assembly of stockholders, who in any modifications must always respect the stipulations of the present instrument.

ART. 10. The Imperial Bank shall be under the high protection of His Imperial Majesty the Shah and of his Government for the exercise and maintenance of the rights granted to it by the present concession, and [the Bank] pledges to respect the general laws of the country in their entirety. Should a dispute arise between the Persian Government and the Bank or between the Bank and individuals, the two parties shall each choose one or two arbitrators and the decision of these arbitrators shall be final. Should the votes be split, the said arbitrators shall name a referee to judge in the last instance.

ART. 11. The Imperial Bank being ready immediately to undertake the sacrifices necessary to employ the resources of the country for the exploitation of its natural wealth, the Persian Government grants to the said Bank, for the entire duration of the present concession, the exclusive and definitive privilege to exploit throughout the Empire mines of iron, copper, lead, mercury, coal, petroleum, manganese, borax, [and] asbestos [that] belong to the State and [have] not previously [been] ceded to other [parties]. As an annex to the concession the Persian Government shall give Baron de Reuter an official list of the mines already granted, on the day the present [instrument] is signed. [Since] mines of gold, silver, and precious stones, etc., belong exclusively to the State, [any] Bank engineers who [should] discover them shall be obliged immediately to inform the Government of His Imperial Majesty the Shah. Except for indispensable engineers and foremen, all the minor laborers that the Bank may engage shall be chosen from among the subjects of His Imperial Majesty the Shah. The Persian Government shall, by all the means in its power, aid the Bank to procure labor at the price prevailing in the country. All mines that the Bank may not have begun to exploit ten years from its establishment shall be considered abandoned and the State may dispose of them without the concessionary Bank being able to [oppose its actions].

ART. 12. The land necessary for the exploitation of these mines and the establishment of a means of communication with the nearest and most rapid lines of transport shall be given to the Imperial

Bank from State lands. The Imperial Government shall aid the Bank by all the means in its power to deal with individual landowners in the most favorable conditions, should there be any along the said road of communications. The materials necessary for the exploitation shall enter Persia without any duty whatsoever. The lands and buildings of the said exploitations shall be free of all duties and taxes.

ART. 13. The Persian Government shall levy an annual premium of 16 percent on the net profits of all mines exploited by the Imperial Bank. At the expiration of the term of the present concession the lands exploited by the mines, with their buildings, offices, and material, shall be returned to the Persian Government according to the general rules followed by the Powers who have stipulated the most favorable conditions in this matter.

ART. 14. In return for the rights guaranteed to him by the present contract, Baron Julius de Reuter formally and completely renounces without reserve all other rights and privileges that had been granted him by the previous concession of 25 July 1872 [which is] annulled by the present [instrument]. . . .

150. CONCESSION OF THE TOBACCO *REGIE* IN PERSIA
8 March 1890

[Great Britain, *Parliamentary Papers, 1892*, 79: 211–13]

Ever since the early nineteenth century, Persia—later Afghanistan and Tibet as well—lay in the path of British and Russian expansion in Asia. Strategically, Russia aimed at consolidating its hold over the annexed territories contiguous with Persia, England at strengthening, in defense of India, the British grip over the northwest provinces of the subcontinent and the exclusive British position in the Persian Gulf area. In the last quarter of the century nationals of each of the two powers obtained a series of concessions that bid fair to subordinate the Persian economy to the concessionaires. The grant to a British subject, Major G. F. Talbot, of a monopoly on the production, domestic sale, and export of tobacco—including the *tunbaku* used in the *qalyan* or Persian water pipe—aroused throughout the realm such a storm of protest, organized by the *mujtahids* and *mullas* (members of the religious class) and encouraged by the Russians, that Nasir al-Din Shah (1848–96) annulled the contract on 5 January 1892. In April the shah borrowed the £500,000 damages that he had paid to Talbot at 6 percent interest from the (British-owned) Imperial Bank of Persia, "thus gratuitously imposing on the Persian people, who had been entirely ignored by both parties to the original agreement, an utterly unremunerative additional yearly expenditure of £30,000" (Browne, *Persian Revolution*, p. 57). To the fiasco of the Tobacco Régie (Administration), in Browne's view, may be traced the origin of the national awakening in Persia, which culminated a decade and a half later in the constitutional revolution. Browne, op. cit., chap. 2; Keddie, *Religion and Rebellion in Iran*; Kazemzadeh, *Russia and Britain in Persia,* chap. 4; Avery, *Modern Iran*, chap. 7; Feuvrier, *Trois ans à la cour de Perse*, chap. 5; Litten, *Persien*, pp. 195–97; Curzon, *Persia and the Persian Question*, vol. 2, chaps. 29 (ii), 30; Thornton, "British Policy in Persia," Brockway, "Britain and the Persian Bubble"; Lambton, "Tobacco Regie."

The monopoly of buying, selling, and manufacturing all the tootoon and tobacco in the interior or exterior of the Kingdom of Persia is granted to Major Talbot by us for fifty years from the date of the signing of this Concession, in accordance with the following stipulations:—

1. The concessionnaires will have to pay 15,000*l.* per annum to the exalted Imperial Treasury whether they benefit or lose by this business, and this money shall be paid every year, five months after the beginning of the year.

2. In order merely to ascertain the quantities of tootoon and tobacco produced in the protected provinces (of Persia) the concessionnaires will keep a register of the cultivators who wish to work under the conditions of this Concession, and the Persian Government will issue strict orders to the local Governors to compel the cultivators of tobacco and tootoon to furnish such a registration.

Permission for sale, &c., of tootoon, tobacco, cigars, cigarettes, snuff, &c., is the absolute right of the concessionnaires, and no one but the proprietors of this Concession shall have the right to issue the above-mentioned permits.

The Guilds of the sellers of tobacco and tootoon who are engaged in this trade will remain permanent in their local trade and transactions, on condition of possessing permits which will be given to them by the concessionnaires.

3. After deducting all the expenses appertaining to this business and paying a dividend of 5 percent. on their own capital to the proprietors of this Concession, one quarter of the remaining profit will yearly be paid to the exalted Imperial Treasury, and the Persian Government will have the right to inspect their (the concessionnaires') yearly books.

4. All the materials necessary for this work which the proprietors of this Concession import into the protected provinces (Persia) will be free of all customs duties, taxes, &c.

5. Removal and transfer of tootoon and tobacco in the protected provinces (of Persia) without the permission of the proprietors of this Concession is prohibited, except as such quantities at travellers may have with them for their own daily use.

6. The proprietors of this Concession must purchase all the tootoon and tobacco that are produced in the protected provinces and pay cash for it. They must purchase all the tobacco, &c., fit for use that is now in hand, and the price that is to be given to the owner or the producer will be settled in a friendly manner between the producer or the owner and the proprietors of this Concession, but in case of disagreement between the parties the case will be referred to an Arbitrator accepted by both sides, and the decision of the Arbitrator will be final and will be carried out.

7. The Persian Government engages not to increase the revenues, taxes, and customs that are now levied on tootoon, tobacco, cigars, cigarettes, and snuff for fifty years from the date of the signing of the Concession, and the proprietors also undertake that all the customs that the Persian Government now obtain from tobacco shall be continued as they are.

8. Any person or persons who shall attempt to evade (the rules) of these Articles will be severely punished by the Government, and any person or persons found to be secretly in possession of tobacco, tootoon, &c., for sale or trade, will also be fined the severely punished by the Government. The Government will give its utmost help and support in all the business of the proprietors of this Concession, and the proprietors of this Concession undertake in no way to go beyond their own rights consistent with these Articles.

9. The proprietors of this Concession are permitted, should they wish, to transfer all their rights, Concessions, undertakings, &c., to any person or persons, but, prior to this, they must inform the Persian Government.

10. The producer or owner of tootoon and tobacco, whenever his crop of tobacco and tootoon is gathered, shall at once inform the nearest agent of the proprietors of this Concession of the quantity, in order that the proprietors of this Concession may be able to carry out the engagement in above-mentioned Article 6, and to purchase it quickly.

11. The proprietors of this Concession have no right to purchase lands, except to the necessary extent, for store-houses and abodes, and what may be necessary to carry out this Concession.

12. The cultivators, in accordance with certain conditions which will be made in conjunction with the Government, are entitled to be given an advance to a limit for their crop.

13. If, from the date of the signing of this Concession until one year, a Company to carry it out is not formed, and the work does not begin, this Concession will be null and void, except that war or such like may prevent the formation of a Company.

14. In case of misunderstanding arising between the Persian Government and the proprietors of this Concession, that misunderstanding shall be referred to an Arbitra-tor accepted by both sides, and in case of the impossibility of consent to the appointment of an Arbitrator, the matter will be referred to the arbitration of one of the Representatives, resident at Tehran, of the Government of the United States, Germany, or Austria, to appoint an Arbitrator, whose decision shall be final.

15. This Concession is exchanged in duplicate with the signature of His Imperial Majesty, registered in the Foreign Ministry, between Major Talbot and the Persian Government, and the Persian text of it is to be recognized.

151. RUSSIAN-PERSIAN RAILROAD AGREEMENT
28 October/10 November 1890[1]

[Aitchison, *Collection of Treaties . . . relating to India* (5th ed.), 13: app. xxiii, p. lxxxi]

Russian influence in Persia in many respects topped that of England as the nineteenth century drew to a close. Persian cities, the capital included, were bunched in the northern provinces, where Russian mastery was generally acknowledged. Though still minuscule a dozen years after its formation in 1879, the Persian Cossack Brigade developed into the most effective military force in the shahdom by the eve of World War I; the brigade was trained and commanded by Russian officers, who received instructions from Saint Petersburg and salaries from Tehran. Furthermore, a Russian subject first procured the Caspian Sea fisheries concession—the source of Russia's best caviar—in 1876 and managed by frequent renewal to retain it through World War I. Therefore, when, in 1889, Nasir al-Din Shah awarded Baron Julius de Reuter, a British citizen, the concession for the Imperial Bank of Persia with the exclusive right to issue bank notes (see Doc. 149), Russia promptly demanded, and in 1891 obtained, a concession to open the Banque des Prêts, later called the Banque d'Escompte de Perse, an offshoot of the Russian Ministry of Finance. It is in this context of British-Russian rivalry that the restrictive railroad concession below must be viewed. The tsarist government was determined to prevent the construction of railroads in Persia by any but Russian nationals, for fear that one day the rails might convey British troops toward Asian Russia. All these activities were conducted with no concern whatsoever for the interests of Persia or the Persians. Browne, *Persian Revolution*; Kazemzadeh, *Russia and Britain in Persia*, chap. 3, and "Russian Imperialism and Persian Railways"; Sumner, "Tsardom and Imperialism in the Far East and the Middle East; Treue, "Russland und die persische Eisenbahnbauern"; Terenzio,

---

1. This document has been dated in accordance with the Persian date on the instrument.

La rivalité anglo-russe en Perse et en Afghanistan; Litten, *Persien,* chaps. 3–31; Lorini, *La Persia economica contemporanea e la sua questione monetaria*, chaps. 13–14; Curzon, *Persia and the Persian Question*, vol. 2, chaps. 29 (ii), 30.

As the Ministers of the Government of His Most Sacred Majesty the Shah have declared that there are difficulties in the way of their carrying out the engagements entered into in Rejeb 1306 (March 1888) regarding the construction of railways in Persia by Russian Companies, the Ministers of the Government of His Imperial Majesty the Czar of all the Provinces of Russia have agreed to alter the above-mentioned engagements as follows; and His Highness the Amin-es-Sultan, Grand Vizier of the Government of His Most Sacred, Sublime and Absolute Shah of all the Provinces of Persia, and His Excellency Monsieur de Butzow, Minister Plenipotentiary and Envoy Extraordinary of His Imperial Majesty the Most Mighty Emperor of all the Provinces of Russia, empowered by their respective Government have drawn up the following conditions:—

(1) The Persian Government engages, for the space of ten years, beginning from the date of the signature of this agreement, neither itself to construct a railway in Persian territory, nor to permit nor grant a concession for the construction of railways to a Company or other persons; and after the expiration of ten years the renewal of the prolongation shall be immediately discussed between the two parties.

(2) By railway lines is understood those upon which steam or any other power is used, of which all kinds are included in this agreement.

(3) Tramway lines worked by horses are excluded from this agreement, but only those in towns and on roads near towns.

(4) A railway line from Tehran to Shemran, where the summer residences of His Most Sacred Sublime Majesty are situated, the most distant of which is two farsakhs from Tehran, is excluded from this engagement and agreement.

(5) After the signature of this agreement that portion of the document, dated Rejeb 1306 (March 1888) relating to railways, becomes null and void.

152. MASQATI NONALIENATION BOND GIVEN TO GREAT BRITAIN
20 March 1891

(Ratified by Viceroy of India, Simla, 23 May 1891)
[Aitchison, *Collection of Treaties . . . relating to India* (5th ed.), 11: 317–18]

Masqat, alternatively called 'Uman or Masqat and 'Uman, "may, indeed, be justifiably regarded as a British dependency," observed G. N. Curzon in 1892 (*Persia and the Persian Question,* 2: 443). "We subsidize its ruler; we dictate its policy; we should tolerate no alien interference. I have little doubt myself that the time will some day come when, as these petty native states crumble before the advance of a friendly civilisation, a more definite possession will be required, and the Union Jack will be seen flying from the castles of Muscat." Lord Curzon's crystal ball was clouded. British influence in the sultanate, as the shaykhdom was then commonly designated by Europeans, became by the end of the nineteenth century paramount but not exclusive. The new commercial treaty concluded on 19 March 1891 (text in Aitchison, op cit., pp. 310–17) replaced the earlier instrument of 1839 and amplified the extraterritorial privileges of British and Indian nationals. Accompanying the latest agreement was the following secret nonalienation bond, which curtailed, but did not eliminate, the sultan's external sovereignty. The capitulatory treaties with the United States, France, and the Netherlands remained in force, and the British political agent was styled consul. In extracting the nonalienation bond from the Masqati *imam*, Britain violated the 1862 British-French declaration (Doc. 114), in which the two European powers undertook to respect the sovereignty of Masqat and Zanzibar. The United Kingdom and Masqat concluded fresh commercial agreements in 1939 (Great Britain, Treaty Series no. 29 (1939), Cmd. 6037) and in 1951 (Treaty Series no. 44 (1952), Cmd. 8633). Landen, *Oman since 1856,* chaps. 5–6; Kelly, "British Position in the Persian Gulf"; Lorimer, *Gazetteer of the Persian Gulf*, vol. 1, pt. 1, pp. 525–50; Liebesny, "International Relations of Arabia, the Dependent Areas"; A. Wilson, *Persian Gulf*, chap. 15; Curzon, op. cit., pp. 433–46; Aitchison, op. cit., pp. 269–86; Graves, *Life of Sir Percy Cox*, chaps. 5–8; Kajare, *Le sultanat d'Omân*, pp. 186–205; Busch, *Britain and the Persian Gulf*, chap. 2.

The object of writing this lawful and honourable Bond is that it is hereby covenanted and agreed between His Highness Seyyid Feysal bin Turki bin Seyyid, Sultan of Muscat and Oman, on the one part, and Colonel Edward Charles Ross, Companion of the Star of India, Her Britannic Majesty's Political Resident in the Persian Gulf, on behalf of the British Government, on the other part, that the said Seyyid Feysal bin Turki bin Saeed, Sultan of Muscat and Oman, does pledge and bind himself, his heirs and successors never to cede, to sell, to mortgage or otherwise give for occupation save to the British Government, the dominions of Muscat and Oman or any of their dependencies.

In token of the conclusion of this lawful and honourable Bond Seyyid Feysal bin Turki bin Saeed, Sultan of Muscat and Oman, and Colonel Edward Charles Ross, Companion of the Star of India, Her Britannic Majesty's Political Resident in the Persian Gulf, the former for himself, his heirs and successors, and the latter on behalf of the British Government, do each, in the presence of witnesses affix their signatures on this ninth day of Shaaban one thousand three hundred and eight (A.H.) corresponding to the twentieth day of March (A.D.) 1891.

153. EXCLUSIVE AGREEMENT: THE BAHRAYNI SHAYKH AND GREAT BRITAIN
13 March 1892

(Ratified by the viceroy of India, Simla, 12 May 1892; superseded, 14 August 1971)
[Aitchison, *Collection of Treaties . . . relating to India* (5th ed.), 11: 238]

In the undertaking reproduced below the Bahrayni shaykh reaffirmed in more explicit terms his original surrender of external sovereignty in 1880 (Doc. 141) and added thereto a general nonalienation clause. Liebesny, "International Relations of Arabia, the Dependent Areas"; Kelly, "British Position in the Persian Gulf"; Lorimer, *Gazetteer of the Persian Gulf*, vol. 1, pt. 1, pp. 902–46; see also references to Doc. 121.

I, Esau bin Ali, Chief of Bahrein, in the presence of Lieutenant-Colonel A. C. Talbot, C.I.E., Political Resident, Persian Gulf, do hereby solemnly bind myself and agree, on behalf of myself, my heirs and successors, to the following conditions, *viz.:*—

1st.—That I will on no account enter into any agreement or correspondence with any Power other than the British Government.

2nd.—That without the assent of the British Government, I will not consent to the residence within my territory of the agent of any other Government.

3rd.—That I will on no account cede, sell, mortgage or otherwise give for occupation any part of my territory save to the British Government.

154. PROGRAM OF THE WORLD ZIONIST ORGANIZATION (BASLE)
29 August 1897

[Sokolow, *History of Zionism*, 1: 268–69]

Jewish immigration into Palestine grew steadily in the second half of the nineteenth century and accounted, in the main, for the enlargement of the local Jewish community from about 10,000 in 1839 to some 24,000 in 1882. As a result of the persecution of Jews in Russia and the consequent formation of the Love of Zion (Hibbat Ziyyon) movement for promoting Jewish settlement in Palestine, the Jewish population again doubled by 1897. In that year the World Zionist Organization came into being, largely under the leadership of a Viennese Jewish journalist, Theodor Herzl, and transformed Zionism into a political movement. The constituent congress of the organization in Basle, Switzerland (27–29 August 1897), adopted as its basic aims the following platform. Böhm, *Die zionistische Bewegung*; Cohn, *Zionist Movement*; Sokolow, op. cit., and *Theodor Herzl*; Halpern, *Idea of a Jewish State*, chaps. 3–5; A. Taylor, *Prelude to Israel*; Parkes, *History of Palestine*; Esco Foundation, *Palestine*, vol. 1, chap. 1: Hurewitz, *Middle East Dilemmas*, chap. 4; Laqueur, *History of Zionism*, chap. 3.

The aim of Zionism is to create for the Jewish people a home in Palestine secured by public law. The Congress contemplates the following means to the attainment of this end:—

1. The promotion, on suitable lines, of the colonization of Palestine by Jewish agricultural and industrial workers.

2. The organization and binding together of the whole of Jewry by means of appropriate institutions, local and international, in accordance with the laws of each country.

3. The strengthening and fostering of Jewish national sentiment and consciousness.

4. Preparatory steps towards obtaining Government consent, where necessary, to the attainment of the aim of Zionism.

155. AGREEMENT ESTABLISHING A CONDOMINIUM IN SUDAN: GREAT BRITAIN AND EGYPT
10 November 1898–10 July 1899

[Cromer's memorandum of 10 November 1898 from Great Britain, Public Record Office, F.O. 78/4957; the two agreements of 19 January and 10 July 1899 from *British and Foreign State Papers*, 91: 19–22]

In 1820 Mehmed 'Ali Paşa, in the name of his suzerain, Sultan Mahmud II, embarked on the conquest of Sudan and forged the links between Egypt and Sudan in modern times. In the Egyptian settlement of 1841 the sultan nominally preserved a greater degree of control over Sudan than over Egypt (Docs. 85, 86). Sudan was evacuated by Egyptian and British troops in the early years of the British occupation at the time of the mahdi Muhammad Ahmad's insurrection (1881–85). Britian organized the reconquest of the territory in 1896–98 with Anglo-Egyptian forces primarily to forestall French designs. The United Kingdom rested its claim to take part in the administration of Sudan on its participation in the reconquest. But Baron (raised to earl, 1901) Cromer, Her Majesty's agent and consul general in Egypt (1883–1907), had to devise a formula for Sudan that would placate France, preclude Ottoman interference, exclude the European powers from the enjoyment of capitulatory privileges, admit Egypt to a role in the administration, and establish British paramountcy, "It was manifest," noted Lord Cromer (*Modern Egypt*, 2: 115), "that these conflicting requirements could not be satisfied without the creation of some hybrid form of government, hitherto unknown to international jurisprudence." (Cromer's final phrase was incorrect, because the tiny state of Andorra in the Pyrenees had been governed as a condominium since 1258, under the joint suzerainty of the head of the French state and the Spanish bishop of Urgel.) The condominium over Sudan became Anglo-Egyptian. On Cromer's recommendation, article 6 of the provisional draft, dealing with financial and security matters, was dropped. Perhaps the best statement of the meaning of the Anglo-Egyptian agreement on Sudan is Lord Cromer's explanatory memorandum sent with the draft instrument to Foreign Secretary Lord Salisbury on 10 November 1898. Together with this memorandum the two Anglo-Egyptian agreements on the Sudan of 19 January and 10 July 1899 are reproduced below. Abbas, *Sudan Question*; Shibeika, *British Policy in the Sudan*; Holt, *Mahdist State in the Sudan*; Theobald, *Mahdiya*; Sanderson, *England, Europe, and the Upper Nile*, chaps. 10–17; Giffen, *Fashoda*; Robinson and Gallagher, *Africa and the Victorians*, chap. 12; Kennedy, "Fashoda"; O'Rourke, *Juristic Status of Egypt and the Sudan*; Erian, *Condominium*; Cromer, op. cit., chap. 33 (for background, vol. 1, chaps. 19–27, and vol. 2, chaps. 28–32); W. Churchill, *River War*; MacMichael, *The Sudan*; Baratier, *A travers l'Afrique*; also his *Souvenirs de la mission Marchand*, vol. 3; Emily, *Mission Marchand*; Bobichon, *La mission Marchand*; R. Brown, *Fashoda Reconsidered*; Freycinet, *La question d'Egypt*, pp. 391–421; Cocheris, *Situation internationale de l'Egypt et du Soudan*, chaps. 11–14; Warburg, *Sudan under Wingate*, chap. 1; Marlowe, *Cromer in Egypt*, chap. 9;

1. Lord Cromer's Memorandum, 10 November 1898

It is becoming a matter of much importance to settle the future political status of the Soudan. I have carefully considered whether it would not be possible to allow matters to drift on, and to settle each point of difficulty on its own merits as it comes up for solution. If we only had to deal with the natives of the Soudan, much might be said in favour of the adoption of this course. The purely native requirements are, in fact, very simple.

A light system of taxation, some very simple forms for the administration of civil and criminal justice, and the appointment of a few carefully selected officials with a somewhat wide discretionary power to deal with local details, are all that for the time being is necessary. Gradually, as was done in what used to be called the "Non-regulation" provinces in India, a more regular and complex system could be substituted for the somewhat patriarchal forms of Government which, for the present, would suffice to meet the circumstances of the case.

We have, however, not merely to deal with the natives of the Soudan. Numerous demands have been received from Europeans who wish to reside, to invest capital, to trade with, and to acquire real property in the country. It is obviously both impossible to exclude them and undesirable to do so, for without European capital and assistance, no real progress can be made. One of the main difficulties of the situation, therefore, consists in the very marked contrast between the primitive institutions which, suitable to the native population, and the more complex administrative and judicial machinery which the presence of Europeans in the country will in some degree necessitate. Under these circumstances, we shall, I think, be obliged to some extent to fall back, for a while at all events, on the argument that if Europeans choose to trade with, or reside in a country only just emerging from barbarism, they must rest content with the best judicial and administrative institutions that the Government can give them—and the best will certainly be, for the time being, defective if judged, not merely by an European but by an Egyptian standard. It is possible that some special court will have to be eventually created for the trial of civil and criminal affairs in which Europeans are interested. I need not, however, dwell on this point now. It is one which will require very careful consideration before any action is taken. The question which demands more immediate treatment is somewhat different. It is how by timely action to prevent the acquisition of rights and the recognition of privileges to Europeans, similar to the rights and privileges which exist in Egypt. I cannot but think that, if we allow Europeans to trade with, and, still more, to reside and to hold real property in the Soudan, without some distinct declaration of the general political, administrative and judicial régime which is for the future to exist in that country, we shall be laying the seeds of much future trouble. It is only just and politic that Europeans should have some foreknowledge of what they have to expect. In default of any authoritative declaration, they may not unnaturally consider—and many of them will certainly consider—that the status of Europeans resident in the Soudan is similar to that which obtains in Egypt.

On these grounds, as well as for the reason that, from a political point of view, it would seem desirable from the outset to define the British position in the Soudan with as great precision as is possible, I venture to think that some public act laying down the political status of the Soudan is necessary.

What, therefore, is the political status of the country to be? Annexation by England would, of course, solve all the difficulties of which I am now treating. But I understand that, for many obvious political and financial reasons, we do not wish to annex. On the other hand, the recognition of the Soudan as a portion of the Ottoman Dominions in no way distinct from the rest of Egypt, would perpetuate all the international difficulties and obstruction of which, during the last 15 years, we have had such an unfortunate experience in dealing with Egyptian affairs. Under these circumstances, we have to find a compromise between the two extremes. Such a compromise may, I think, be found; but it is to be remembered that we shall be creating a status hitherto unknown to the law of Europe, and that, therefore—more especially in view of the extreme complication of some of the details—it is no easy matter to put down on paper any arrangement which may confidently be predicted to be workable in practice, and perfectly capable of defence in all its parts by valid and logical argument.

I think the arrangement had better take the form of a convention, or agreement, with the Egyptian Government.

The validity of any such convention may, and, without doubt, will be challenged.

In the first place, it may be argued that under the Imperial Firmans, the Khedive has no right to make any treaty with a Foreign Power, other than commercial and customs conventions, and those which concern the relations of foreigners with the internal administration of the country.

Moreover, it is laid down in the Firman to the present Khedive that he "shall not, on any pretext or motive, abandon to others, in whole or in part, the privileges accorded to Egypt, which are entrusted to him and which pertain to the inherent rights of the Sovereign Power, nor any portion of the territory".

To arguments based on these considerations a twofold answer may be given.

In the first place, it may be said that the convention is no treaty properly so-called; that in signing it the Khedive will not perform any act of external sovereignty; that he will merely be exercising his acknowledged right of making arrangements for the internal administration of the territory accorded to him by the Firmans; and that the fact of the Egyptian flag continuing, in concert with the British, to fly everywhere in the Soudan, shows that the suzerainty of the Sultan is, in part at all events, still recognised in that country.

This argument is, however, in my opinion, weak, for the more we dwell on whatever fragment of the Sultan's suzerainty which will remain, the more difficult will it be to differentiate the Soudan from the rest of the Ottoman Dominions in respect to the treatment of Europeans and other subjects.

I prefer, therefore, to take our stand boldly on the second argument, and that is that the Egyptian army, which forms part of the Ottoman army, was unable to maintain its position in the Soudan, and would unaided have been quite unable to reconquer that country; that the reconquest has been effected by English money, English troops, and Egyptian troops officered and trained by Englishmen; that this fact confers on Her Majesty's Government, on the recognised principles of international law, predominant rights in the determination of the future régime of the country; that the question of whether the Khedive is acting within his rights is therefore beside the mark, for that, rather than ceding anything to England, he is obtaining concessions from England.

I now procede to offer some explanatory remarks on the various articles of the draft convention annexed to this Memorandum.

PREAMBLE. In the preamble allusion is made incidentally and inferentially to the rights of the Khedive anterior to the Mahdist rebellion, but more prominence is given to the rights of the British Government accruing from the fact of the reconquest. It appears necessary to state these rights, as they alone constitute the real justification for the creation of a political and administrative status in the Soudan different to that which exists in Egypt.

ART. 1. This article gives a definition of the territories which, for the purposes of the present convention, will be comprised in the Soudan. I should mention, by way of explanation, that the 22nd parallel of latitude runs a few miles North of Wadi Halfa. Suakin is well South of this line.

If we wish to be perfectly consistent with the principles more or less explicitly set forth in the preamble, the term Soudan should be strictly limited to the territories which formerly belonged to Egypt, which were subsequently held by the Dervishes, and which, at one time or another, have been reconquered with British assistance. To do this, however, will create great administrative inconvenience, for we shall then have to exclude Suakin and Wadi Halfa from the Soudan. Neither of these towns has ever been occupied by the Dervishes, although it would be perfectly correct as a matter of fact to say that, but for the defensive action taken from time to time by British troops and under British auspices, they would certainly have been lost to Egypt during the rebellion.

It will be observed that in this article

the territories comprised in the Soudan are divided into three categories. These are:

(1) Those "which have never been evacuated by Egyptian troops since the year 1882". This formula has been adopted in order to include Wadi Halfa and Suakin.

(2) Those "which, having before the late rebellion in the Soudan been administered by the Government of His Highness the Khedive, were temporarily lost to Egypt and have been reconquered by Her Majesty's Government and the Egyptian Government acting in concert". Under this heading will be included all the territory recently reconquered. There is an objection to saying "all the territory which formerly belonged to Egypt" (or words to that effect) without any limitation as to reconquest by an Anglo-Egyptian force, as the use of these words might be held to include part of the Equatorial Province, and even possibly Zeyla and Berbera, which, of course, are not intended to be included in the present agreement.

(3) Those "which may hereafter be reconquered by the two Governments acting in concert". This provision has been so worded as to include extensions southwards or westwards, acquired by Anglo-Egyptian action, and at the same time to exclude extensions from Uganda northwards, made by the English Government acting alone.

ART. 2. At present the English and Egyptian flags are flying together at Khartoum. It is now proposed, in order to indicate that the political status of the whole of the Soudan is to be the same, to adopt a similar measure throughout the whole country, except at Suakin.

It would raise a great outcry to hoist the British flag at Suakin and it is really hardly necessary to do so. As I shall presently explain, it is proposed to make a difference between Suakin and the rest of the Soudan in respect to the jurisdiction of the Mixed Tribunals.

ARTS. 3 and 4 may conveniently be considered together. They are in some respects the most important portions of the proposed convention. They regulate the manner in which both the supreme legislative and executive authority in the Soudan shall be exercised.

1. It is proposed to vest the supreme military and civil command in the hands of one officer, who will be termed the "Governor-General of the Soudan". Of the desirability of this measure there can, I conceive, be little doubt. It is suggested that he should be appointed "by Khedivial decree on the recommendation of Her Majesty's Government". This is much the same formula as is adopted in the case of nominating the Commissioners of the Debt and some other officials. I should add that I should prefer that allusion should be specifically made in the preamble of the decree to the fact that English sanction has been obtained to the nomination, though the adoption of this course is not altogether necessary, for the Khedive is under an obligation to follow English advice in all important matters so long as the occupation lasts.

2. It is proposed that all proclamations issued by the Governor-General shall have the force of law, but that, in respect to all important matters, the previous consent of the Khedive "acting under the advice of his Council of Ministers",[1] and of the British Government, acting through their representative, should be obtained. It is obviously necessary that the Governor-General should be under some control, and the only really effective control will be that of the English Government acting through their Consul-General, but the Khedive must also be mentioned, both because, *ex-hypothesi*, the Soudan, though possessing a separate political status, is still to be Egyptian territory, and because the financial responsibilities assumed by Egypt render it both necessary and desirable that the voice of the Egyptian Government should be heard.

Whether, in the case of each proclamation, it should be stated that the British and Egyptian consent has been obtained, is an open question. I do not think the adoption of this procedure absolutely necessary, and perhaps it would be as well to do whatever is possible to make the

---

1. It is not absolutely necessary to introduce this phrase, as, under Ismail Pasha's Rescript of August 1878, the Khedive is always supposed to act under the advice of his Council of Ministers, but, inasmuch as the Khedive constantly endeavours to escape from this obligation, I think it would be advisable to allude to the point. [Note: This is Cromer's footnote.]

Governor-General absolutely supreme in the eyes of the population of the Soudan.

3. Although, as I have already said, it is necessary that some effective control should be exercised over the action of the Governor-General, it would be a great mistake to centralise the administration of the Soudan in the hands of any authority, British or Egyptian, at Cairo. It is proposed, therefore, to take power in the convention to dispense with the previous assent of the Khedive and of the English diplomatic Agent in certain matters. The detailed points in respect to which a free hand shall be left to the Governor-General, can form the subject of subsequent discussion.

ART. 5. This article deals with the body of laws which shall be applicable in the Soudan.

In the course of the discussions which have taken place here, it was at first proposed that no Egyptian law should be valid in the Soudan unless it had been specially applied to that country by proclamation of the Governor-General. The objection to this course is that, for the time being—that is to say, until a body of laws can be framed for the Soudan—there would be a condition of complete lawlessness. It has been thought better, therefore, to allow such Egyptian legislation as may, on legal principles, be held to be in force in the Soudan to hold good. I am advised that, on the legal principle applicable to the case, only Egyptian legislation previous to the year 1884—the first year in which the Soudan fell completely under Dervish control—is legally in force in the Soudan. This would include the Egyptian Codes as promulgated in June 1883. At the same time it is proposed to limit the application of all future Egyptian laws to Egypt proper, unless they are specially applied to the Soudan. It will be borne in mind that, under Article 4, all existing Egyptian laws may be altered or abrogated by proclamation of the Governor-General.

ART. 6. This Article deals with the important question of Finance.

It is obviously undesirable that the Caisse de la Dette should be allowed to interfere in Soudan affairs, but after fully discussing this matter with Mr. Gorst, I have come to the conclusion that it would be best to make no allusion to this subject in the convention. As matters at present stand, the net charge on account of the Soudan appears on the expenditure side of the Egyptian accounts. To this arrangement the Caisse has agreed. No question can, therefore, arise with the Caisse until the Soudan yields a surplus of revenue over expenditure, and if—as a mere matter of account—we charge as much as possible to the Soudan, as it will be our interest to do, a long time will elapse before any real surplus accrues. Moreover, should any difficulties arise with the Caisse, I doubt whether any provision made in this agreement will much help towards a settlement. On the whole, therefore, I think we had better leave this branch of the question alone for the present.

Turning to another point—it is proposed that the whole of the Soudan revenue shall be placed at the disposal of the Egyptian Government, and that, on the other hand, that Government shall be "solely responsible for the civil and ordinary military expenditure".

So far as I can yet see, the Soudan figures work out much more favourably than I anticipated. I have no doubt that the Egyptian treasury will be able to bear all the ordinary expenditure, civil and military, without making any call for British assistance.

On the other hand, it will be observed that the Article now under discussion contains the following provision: "Her Britannic Majesty's Government undertakes to bear the whole cost of any British troops who may be stationed in the Soudan, other than special expeditionary forces".

Both Sir Francis Grenfell and Lord Kitchener are strongly of opinion that a small British force of, say, two companies, or about 250 men, should be permanently stationed at Khartoum. I entirely agree with them. Their presence will give confidence to every one, and will be a very useful counterpoise in the event of any difficulties occuring with the native, notably the black, troops.

I cannot at present say what would be the extra expenditure involved, but it will certainly be a small sum, more especially as the two companies can be detached from Cairo, without increasing the total British force in Egypt.

I earnestly hope that Her Majesty's Government will consent to bear this small charge. It would produce a very bad effect were I to ask the Egyptian Government for the money. Moreover, under all the circumstances of the case, it would seem to me a fair charge on the English Treasury.

Lastly, I do not in any way anticipate that the necessity for sending any further expeditionary force to the Soudan will arise. Should, however, anything of the kind unfortunately occur, the division of cost between England and Egypt may, I think, best be settled at the time and according to the special circumstances of the case. Hence the last paragraph in Article 6.

ART. 7. In this Article the right to lay down the conditions under which Europeans shall trade with, reside in, or hold property in the Soudan is asserted. For the reasons which I have already stated, this right will almost certainly be contested. This is unfortunate, but it cannot be helped. We are in possession, and shall be able to assert our rights, even although we may not be able to convince others of the regularity of our position or the validity of our arguments. In the meanwhile, we may perhaps do something towards mitigating hostility if we proclaim the commercial policy now known as that of the "open door", and if we state that in all other respects Europeans, of whatsoever nationality, will be treated alike.

ART. 8. This Article deals with the question of Customs duties.

I should explain briefly what is the present Egyptian régime in these matters.

Under the Imperial Firmans, the Khedive has a right to make commercial conventions with other Powers. As a matter of fact, during the last few years such conventions have been concluded with England, Germany, Austria, Italy and some of the minor Powers, but inasmuch as a provision common to all these conventions is that they shall not come into force unless conventions have been signed with all the Powers, and inasmuch as France, Russia and some other Powers have concluded no conventions, the whole of the conventions signed by the Egyptian Government are at present inoperative. Customs duties in Egypt are, therefore, at present levied exclusively under the conventions existing between Turkey and the various European Powers. Under these circumstances, an *ad valorem* import duty of 8%, and an export duty of 1% are levied.

The proposed Article 8 is conceived in a sense from which the right to separate the commercial régime of the Soudan from that of Egypt may be inferred, even if it be not expressly stated. As in other similar cases, this right will, of course, be contested, and we must again fall back on the right of conquest argument.

As a matter of fact, however, I do not propose that any extra import duty should be levied on goods entering the Soudan from Egypt or from any of the ports of the Red Sea which will now be comprised in the term "Soudan". On the other hand, care has been taken to draft Article 8 in such a manner as to preserve complete liberty of action in respect to trade entering the Soudan, not from Egypt or the Red Sea, but from other directions.

The export duties stand on a somewhat different footing. It may become necessary and desirable to impose a higher duty than 1% on some articles such as gum and ostrich feathers. It is proposed, therefore, to maintain our liberty of action on that point.

ART. 9. This Article lays down that the jurisdiction of the Mixed Courts will not be recognised anywhere in the Soudan, except in the town of Suakin.

In connection with this subject I append to this Memorandum two documents prepared by Mr. McIlwraith, from which it appears that some doubt exists as to whether, even supposing no change to be made in the political status of the Soudan, the jurisdiction of the Mixed Courts extends to that country. The decisions of the Court of Appeal on this subject have been contradictory. For my own part, I may say that the balance of argument seems to me decidedly in favour of the view that the Mixed Courts have no jurisdiction. However this may be, it must be remembered that the tendency of the Courts is to extend their jurisdiction, that they practically are under no legislative control, and that, if they assume jurisdiction over the Soudan, the only means of resisting their encroachments is to refuse to serve their writs or execute their judgments. I think, therefore, it would be advisable not to rely on the arguments adduced by Mr. McIlwraith, which are based on the original Charter of Organization and cognate considerations, but to fall back again on the special political status of the Soudan as the main reason for refusing to admit the jurisdiction of the Courts.

It will be observed that it is proposed to exempt Suakin from the operation of this Article. Rightly or wrongly, the jurisdiction of the Mixed Courts at Suakin has for many years past been recognized. It would raise a great outcry to make any change, neither do I think that any change is much required. I am inclined, therefore, to leave matters alone in respect to this special point.

ART. 10. This Article provides that, for the time being, martial law shall prevail in the Soudan, except in the town of Suakin.

I am advised that, for reasons which are familiar to all who have studied this question, "martial", and not "military" law is the proper term to use in this connection.

I may remark incidentally that the proclamation of martial law will strengthen our case as regards declining to admit the jurisdiction of the Mixed Courts, for I conceive that many judges, who would refuse to admit the validity of our rights based on reconquest, would recognize that, so long as the ordinary civil law was in abeyance, the Courts could exercise no jurisdiction.

It is not, however, mainly on this account that I advocate the proclamation of martial law. I do so because, for the time being, I think that the adoption of this course is necessitated by the state of the country. It is still very disturbed. I hear of frequent cases of brigandage. Under the circumstances, I think that very ample powers for the maintenance of order must be vested in the hands of the Governor-General. Notably, he should have the right of expelling any individual, European or native, from the country.

I should add that the proclamation of martial law does not necessarily imply that all matters are to be settled by the simple order of the Governor-General, or of some military officer to whom he may have delegated his powers. Lawcourts, the nature of which I need not now describe in detail, have been already instituted in the Dongola province. They appear to be working fairly well. Provision has been made in the Soudan budget for an extension of these institutions. The spirit, therefore, in which I propose the proclamation of martial law is this—that the extreme powers which will thus be vested in the Governor-General shall only be used in exceptional cases, and further that, as time goes on, every endeavour shall be made to bring the administration of the law in the Soudan into harmony with the generally recognized principles of civil jurisprudence.

ART. 11. This Article provides that no Consular Authorities are to reside in the Soudan without the permission of Her Majesty's Government. This seems to me to be necessary, but our right to make this provision will, of course, be challenged by those who hold that the political status of the Soudan in no way differs from that of other parts of the Ottoman dominions.

ART. 12. I think we may at once go so far as to forbid the importation and exportation of slaves into and from the Soudan. The question of how to deal with domestic slavery in the Soudan is much more difficult. For the moment we had better leave it alone.

ART. 13. Although such a course is not absolutely necessary, it may perhaps be as well to draw special attention to the provisions of the Brussels Act as regards the sale and importation of arms and spirituous liquors.

2. Condominium Agreement, 19 January 1889

Whereas certain provinces in the Soudan which were in rebellion against the authority of His Highness the Khedive have now been reconquered by the joint military and financial efforts of Her Britannic Majesty's Government and the Government of His Highness the Khedive;

And whereas it has become necessary to decide upon a system for the administration of, and for the making of laws for, the said reconquered provinces, under which due allowance may be made for the backward and unsettled conditions of large portions thereof, and the varying requirements of different localities;

And whereas it is desired to give effect to the claims which have accured to Her

Britannic Majesty's Government, by right of conquest, to share in the present settlement and future working and development of the said system of administration and legislation;

And whereas it is conceived that for many purposes Wadi Halfa and Suakin may be most effectively administered in conjunction with the reconquered provinces to which they are respectively adjacent:

Now, it is hereby agreed and declared by and between the Undersigned, duly authorized for that purpose, as follows:—

ART. 1. The word "Soudan" in this Agreement means all the territories south of the 22nd parallel of latitude, which—

1. Have never been evacuated by Egyptian troops since the year 1882; or

2. Which, having before the late rebellion in the Soudan been administered by the Government of His Highness the Khedive were temporarily lost to Egypt, and have been reconquered by Her Britannic Majesty's Government and the Egyptian Government, acting in concert; or

3. Which may hereafter be reconquered by the two Governments acting in concert.

II. The British and Egyptian flags shall be used together, both on land and water, throughout the Soudan, except in the town of Suakin, in which locality the Egyptian flag alone shall be used.

III. The supreme military and civil command in the Soudan shall be vested in one officer, termed the "Governor-General of the Soudan." He shall be appointed by Khedivial Decree on the recommendation of Her Britannic Majesty's Government, and shall be removed only by Khedivial Decree, with the consent of Her Britannic Majesty's Government.

IV. Laws, as also orders and regulations with the full force of law, for the good government of the Soudan, and for regulating the holding, disposal, and devolution of property of every kind therein situate, may from time to time be made, altered, or abrogated by Proclamation of the Governor-General. Such laws, orders, and regulations may apply to the whole or any named part of the Soudan, and may, either explicitly or be necessary implication, alter or abrogate any existing law or regulation.

All such Proclamations shall be forthwith notified to Her Britannic Majesty's Agent and Consul-General in Cairo, and to the President of the Council of Ministers of His Highness the Khedive.

V. No Egyptian Law, Decree, Ministerial Arrêté, or other enactment hereafter to be made or promulgated shall apply to the Soudan or any part thereof, save in so far as the same shall be applied by Proclamation of the Governor-General in manner hereinbefore provided.

VI. In the definition by Proclamation of the conditions under which Europeans, of whatever nationality, shall be at liberty to trade with or reside in the Soudan, or to hold property within its limits, no special privileges shall be accorded to the subjects of any one or more Powers.

VII. Import duties on entering the Soudan shall not be payable on goods coming from Egyptian territory. Such duties may, however, be levied on goods coming from elsewhere than Egyptian territory; but in the case of goods entering the Soudan at Suakin, or any other port on the Red Sea littoral, they shall not exceed the corresponding duties for the time being leviable on goods entering Egypt from abroad. Duties may be levied on goods leaving the Soudan at such rates as may from time to time be prescribed by Proclamation.

VIII. The jurisdiction of the Mixed Tribunals shall not extend, nor be recognized for any purpose whatsoever, in any part of the Soudan, except in the town of Suakin.

IX. Until and save so far as it shall be otherwise determined by Proclamation, the Soudan, with the exception of the town of Suakin, shall be and remain under martial law.

X. No Consuls, Vice-Consuls, or Consular Agents shall be accredited in respect of nor allowed to reside in the Soudan, without the previous consent of Her Britannic Majesty's Government.

XI. The importation of slaves into the Soudan, as also their exportation, is absolutely prohibited. Provisions shall be made by Proclamation for the enforcement of this Regulation.

XII. It is agreed between the two Governments that special attention shall be paid to the enforcement of the Brussels Act of the 2nd July, 1890, in respect to the import, sale, and manufacture of fire-arms and their munitions, and distilled or spirituous liquors.

3. Agreement on Sawakin, 10 July 1899

Whereas under our Agreement made the 19th day of January, 1899, relative to the future administration of the Soudan, it is provided by Article VIII that the jurisdiction of the Mixed Tribunals shall not extend nor be recognized for any purpose whatsoever in any part of the Soudan except in the town of Suakin;

And whereas no Mixed Tribunal has ever been established at Suakin, and it has been found to be inexpedient to establish any such Tribunal in that locality, by reason notably of the expense which the adoption of this measures would occasion;

And whereas grievous injustice is caused to the inhabitants of Suakin by the absence of any local jurisdiction for the settlement of their disputes, and it is expedient that the town of Suakin should be placed upon the same footing as the rest of the Soudan;

And whereas we have decided to modify our said Agreement accordingly in manner hereinafter appearing:

Now, it is hereby agreed and declared by and between the Undersigned duly authorized for that purpose, as follows:—

ART. I. Those provisions of our Agreement of the 19th day of January, 1899, by which the town of Suakin was excepted from the general régime established by the said Agreement for the future administration of the Soudan, are hereby abrogated.

156. EXCLUSIVE AGREEMENT: THE KUWAYTI SHAYKH AND GREAT BRITAIN
23 January 1899

(Ratified by Britain, 16 February 1899; superseded, 19 June 1961)
[Text of agreement from Aitchison, *Collection of Treaties . . . relating to India* (5th ed.), 11: 262; text of accompanying letter from Lorimer, *Gazetteer of the Persian Gulf*, vol. 1, pt. 1, pp. 1049–50]

The town of Kuwayt was probably founded as a fortress, as its name suggests, by the Al Sabah clan of the 'Utub tribe early in the eighteenth century. Ottoman influence had almost vanished form the Persian Gulf, so that the question of sovereignty did not arise at that time. By the middle decades of the nineteenth century, as the interest of the Sublime Porte in the gulf reawakened, Kuwayt nominally acknowledged Ottoman suzerainty; to the Sublime Porte the shaykh "paid an annual tribute of 40 bags of rice and 400 Frasilahs of dates," and from his suzerain "he received every year a dress of honour" (Lorimer, op. cit., p. 1008). In 1871, Shaykh 'Abdallah al-Sabah Al Sabah (1866–92) participated in the Ottoman reconquest of al-Hasa, and Midhat Paşa, the *vali*, or governor, of Baghdad who had organized the campaign, later invested the shaykh "probably with the rank of Qaim-Maqam," or deputy governor (ibid., p. 1014). Relations with Britain, on the other hand, started in 1775, when the principality was used briefly as a station of a British overland mail service from India to the Mediterranean. In subsequent years, on the infrequent occasions when conditions in Basrah became inhospitable, the East India Company moved its factors to Kuwayt. From about the 1840s Britain implicitly acknowledged Ottoman sovereignty over the shaykhdom. It was not until the end of the century that Kuwayti and British interests began to converge. In May 1896, Mubarak (1896–1915) seized power in Kuwait by murdering his half-brother. The sons of the slain ruler and of another brother killed with him found asylum in the Ottoman *vilâyet* of Basrah and from there tried to organize the removal of the new shaykh. Although Mubarak's authority was formally confirmed by the Sublime Porte in December 1897, Mubarak himself felt insecure and sought British protection. The government of India, which had turned down Mubarak's initial overtures, reversed its position early in 1899. Disturbed by the scheme of Count Kapnist, a Russian subject, for a railroad from the Mediterranean coast of Syria to Kuwayt, the government of India procured from Mubarak the following secret bond, which included a nonalienation clause and the surrender of external sovereignty; in return the government of India pledged to protect Mubarak and his shaykhly dynasty. Britain preferred to avoid formal disclosure to the Sublime Porte that Kuwayt had been brought into the British quasi-protectorate system in the Persian Gulf, even after the appointment of a British political agent to the principality in 1904. By then, however, Britain had prevented Russia and Germany from establishing themselves in the shaykhdom. Lorimer, op. cit., vol. 1, pt. 1, pp. 1000–51; Kelly, "British Position in the Persian Gulf"; Busch, "Britain and the Status of Kuwayt," and *Britain and the Persian Gulf*, chap. 3; Liebesny, "International Relations of Arabia, the Dependent Areas"; Brinton, "Arabian Peninsula"; A. Wilson, *Persian Gulf*, chap. 15; Philby, *Sa'udi Arabia*; Fraser, *India under Lord Curzon and After* pp.78–115; Ronaldshay, *Life of Lord Curzon*, Vol. 2, chaps. 2, 23; Chirol, *Middle Eastern Question*, chap. 20; Kumar, *India and the Persian Gulf Region,* chap. 5.

1. The Exclusive Agreement

The object of writing this lawful and honourable bond is that it is hereby covenanted and agreed between Lieutenant-Colonel Malcolm John Meade, I.S.C., Her Britannic Majesty's Political Resident, on behalf of the British Government on the one part, and Sheikh Mubarak-bin-Sheikh Subah, Sheikh of Koweit, on the other part, that the said Sheikh Mubarak-bin-Sheikh Subah of his own free will and desire does hereby pledge and bind himself, his heirs and successors not to receive the Agent or Representative of any Power or Government at Koweit, or at any other place within the limits of his territory, without the previous sanction of the British Government; and he further binds himself, his heirs and successors not to cede, sell, lease, mortgage, or give for occupation or for any other purpose any portion of his territory to the Government or subjects of any other Power without the previous consent of Her Majesty's Government for these purposes. This engagement [is] also to extend to any portion of the territory of the said Sheikh

Mubarak, which may now be in the possession of the subjects of any other Government. . . .

2. Letter from Lieutenant Colonel M. J. Meade to Shaykh Mubarak

In view of the signing to-day of the agreement, so happily concluded between you, Sheikh Mubarak-bin-Subah, on behalf of yourself, your heirs and successors, on the one part, and myself, on behalf of Her Britannic Majesty's Government, I now assure you, as Sheikh of Koweit, of the good offices of the British Government towards you, your heirs and successors as long as you, your heirs and successors scrupulously and faithfully observe the conditions of the said bond.

The three copies of the bond will be sent to India to be ratified by His Excellency Lord Curzon of Kedleston, Her Imperial Majesty's Viceroy and Governor-General in Council, and, on their return, one copy, duly ratified, will be conveyed to you, when I will take measures to send you, as agreed, a sum of Rs. 15,000 from the Bushire Treasury. A most important condition of the execution of this agreement is that it is to be kept absolutely secret, and not divulged or made public in any way without the previous consent of the British Government.

157. ENTENTE ON MOROCCO AND TRIPOLI: FRANCE AND ITALY
14 December 1900–1 November 1902

[Translated from the French texts in France, Ministère des Affaires Etrangères, *Documents diplomatiques français, 1871–1914*. 2d ser., vol. 1, no. 17, pp. 20–23, and vol. 2, pp. 390–95]

"In Moroccan affairs," wrote French Foreign Minister Théophile Delcassé in August 1902 (op. cit., 2: 458–59), "I am interested . . . in distinguishing the international question from the French-Moroccan question, and to settle the former separately and successively with each power in order ultimately to enjoy full freedom to settle the latter directly [with Morocco]." The international question that Delcassé had in mind was the system erected by the convention of Madrid in 1880 (Doc. 139), which tried to regulate the European practice of protecting Moroccan subjects. To undo that system, which assured the major powers of Europe a voice in the Moroccan question, France had to offer Italy, Britain, Spain, and Germany compensation before each of its opponents in Morocco could be expected to acquiesce in the French forward policy. The process, initiated in 1900, took a dozen years to complete. Delcassé opened negotiations with Italy soon after he entered office in 1898, but the first phase of the talks broke down in April 1899, when the Italian foreign minister of the day, Admiral Felice Napoleone Canevaro, insisted on written assurances that France would be prepared to give Italy a free hand in Tripolitania and Cyrenaica (present-day Libya). In retrospect, it is clear that Delcassé was primarily concerned about British opposition to any French forward policy in Morocco. The first opportunity for the French arose in the fall of 1899, when Britain became distracted by the Boer War, which was to drag on for over two and one-half years. The talks, reopened with a new and friendly Italian foreign minister, Marquis Emilio Visconti-Venosta, moved slowly. As early as 23 October 1899 Delcassé was ready to give Italy written assurances on Tripoli, but for the first time he demanded a quid pro quo on Morocco. Reproduced below are the reports of the French ambassador at Rome, Camille Barrère, on the sets of negotiations and his exchange of letters with the Italian foreign minister of the day: (1) those signed on 4 January 1901 but predated 14 and 16 December 1900, and (2) those signed on 30 June 1902 but dated 10–11 July and intended to take effect on 1 November 1902. Under the first accord Barrère thought that Italy had given France full liberty in Morocco, without, however, acquiescing in the modification of the political and territorial integrity of the Islamic kingdom. But Visconti-Venosta believed that he was simply agreeing to full liberty of action for France in defense of Algeria. By June 1901 Barrère and Giulio Prinetti, the new Italian foreign minister, had reached an oral understanding that the freedom of Italy in

Tripoli would be equal to that of France in Morocco, each recognizing the other's right to establish a sphere of influence in the coveted territory. Nevertheless, a year passed before the oral agreement was converted into a written one. Andrew, *Théophile Delcassé*, chap. 7; E. Anderson, *First Moroccan Crisis*, chap. 2; Leaman, "Influence of Domestic Policy on Foreign Affairs in France"; Dethan, "Le rapprochement franco-italien"; Saint-Réné Taillandier, *Les origines du Maroc français*; Askew, *Europe and Italy's Acquisition of Libya*, chap. 1; Rouard de Card, *Accords secrets entre la France et l'Italie*.

1. Camille Barrère, French Ambassador in Rome, to Théophile Declassé, French Foreign Minister, 10 January 1901

With the resumption of normal relations between France and Italy after an interruption of ten years, and the appeasement of feelings that flowed from this reconciliation, Your Excellency has considered that French policy on the [Italian] Peninsula is locked in a vicious circle and that it would neither make sense nor have importance were it not applied to eliminating the causes of political dissent which have contributed to dividing the two nations. Outraged interest forms the essence of the peoples' feelings. You thought, with discerning wisdom, that such a proposition was all the more commendable because its execution entailed no sacrifice or renunciation of our legitimate ambitions. It is this fundamental idea that has inspired us to settle old disputes with Italy on the Red Sea coast; and since that time, no more has been heard in that country's press of rivalry of interest or of incidents, of which it was formerly full.

However, the most difficult point in French-Italian relations was less distant. The situation in the Mediterranean was the cornerstone of Italian action; in the past, that was what had contributed to the formation of alliances directed against us, and it was that too which had pushed Italy into concluding agreements with England. Since our establishment at Tunis, France has been constantly suspected here of wishing to extend its hegemony not only to Morocco but also to Tripolitania, an eventual object of the envious desires of the young kingdom. On this question, the most serious that might arise between the two countries, Your Excellency again deemed

it necessary to reassure the Government of Rome and to give guarantees against territorial expansion on the Tripoli side, which does not lie in our sphere of action and which French colonial policy excludes. But this friendly settling of accounts, in your judgment, would be incomplete if it did not include parallel recognition by Italy of our rights and action regarding the Moroccan Empire.

The signing of the African Convention of London of 20 March 1899 and the return of Marquis [Emilio] Visconti-Venosta have created an opportunity of opening this important negotiation, which I undertook confidentially on instructions that agreed completely with my own views. The discussion dragged on laboriously, lasting a year and a half; and this delay is fully explained by the extreme difficulty in finding terms that suited our mutual interest in defining dissimilar situations with measure and precision. This would not have been possible without Marquis Visconti-Venosta, I am pleased to concede, and I count it a duty to pay homage here to his friendly and benevolent disposition.

The discussions ended in the exchange of communications of which you will find the authentic text annexed to this dispatch (Marquis Visconti-Venosta wrote his own letter by hand). Under the terms of these written explanations, the Government of the Republic reiterates to the Italian Government its intention of not expanding its frontier or sphere of influence to the province of Tripoli. It expresses, moreover, the intention of respecting the caravan communications of Tripoli with French territory. Nevertheless, it does not recognize Italy's right to expand its influence into the province of Tripoli without [France's] consent. On the other hand, the Italian

Government, by the pen Marquis Visconti-Venosta and in terms that are worth noting, recognizes France's right to expand its influence in Morocco in whatever form may be convenient, with the reservation that, if its action should modify to its own advantage the political and territorial integrity of the Sharifi Empire, Italy will consider itself free to assert its influence in Tripoli. The result of this text is that Italy may not enjoy the stipulated advantage unless France should impose direct sovereignty or [French] protectorate [status] on Morocco.

Reading these two texts will help Your Excellency appreciate their intrinsic value to our European interests.

It is very unlikely that Italy will attempt to seize Tripoli, even if we should take possession of Morocco; to do so, soldiers, money, a solid interior situation, and the goodwill of the Powers, especially the Allies, would be necessary—all things which Italy lacks in such a large undertaking. But even should it undertake such an enterprise, the action would urgently require our consent and goodwill, any Mediterranean expansion necessarily placing Italy in a somewhat tributary position to us. The agreement of 16 and 18 December [predated 14 and 16 December 1900 but actually signed on 4 January 1901] has yet another remarkable advantage for us. It gets rid of a cause in the Peninsula of fear and jealousy, which, had it persisted, would have made impossible any sincere and serious reconciliation in the future. Moreover, it removes the purpose of Mediterranean coalitions between Italy and England, such as those of the not distant past which were directed against us. In a word, it profoundly modifies to our advantage the position of the active forces in the Mediterranean. I therefore communicate it to Your Excellency in the hope that you will approve of the efforts I have made to reply to your intentions and confidence.

2. Barrère to Marquis Visconti-Venosta, Italian Foreign Minister, 14 December 1900 [4 January 1901]

Following the conclusion of the Convention of 21 March 1899 between France and Great Britain, my Government, replying to your honorable predecessor, had occasion through me to give him explanations dispelling any ambiguity about the purpose of this instrument.

Since then Your Excellency has expressed the opinion that these assurances, [if] reiterated in a more explicit manner, would help affirm the good relations between our countries.

I was consequently authorized by the [French] Ministry of Foreign Affairs to inform Your Excellency that, by reason of the friendly relations that have been established between France and Italy, and with the thought that this explanation would help to improve them even more, the Convention of 21 March 1899, apart from the division of influence that it sanctions for the vilâyet of Tripoli, fixes for the sphere of French influence in Tripolitania-Cyrenaica a limit that the Government of the Republic has no intention of crossing; and that it is not a part of its plan to intercept caravan communication from Tripoli to the regions specifically mentioned in the aforesaid convention.

These explanations, which we have agreed to keep secret, will, I have no doubt, help to consolidate friendly relations between our two countries on this and other points.

3. Visconti-Venosta to Barrère, 16 December 1900 [4 January 1901]

The present situation in the Mediterranean and the possibilities that might emerge therefrom have formed the subject of an exchange between us of friendly ideas, our Governments being equally desirous in this matter to avoid anthing likely to compromise our mutual good understanding now and in the future.

In that which concerns Morocco in particular, it has become clear from our discussions that the action of France has the purpose of exercising and safeguarding the rights that arise from the proximity of its territory to [the sharifi] Empire.

I have recognized that in our eyes such an action, thus defined, is not of a kind to impair the interests of Italy as a Mediterranean Power.

It has also been agreed that, if there should result any modification of the political or territorial condition of Morocco, Italy would reserve the right, as a reciprocal measure, eventually to develop its influence in Tripolitania-Cyrenaica.

These explanations, which we have agreed to keep secret, will, I have no doubt, help to consolidate friendly relations between our two countries.

4. Barrère to Delcassé, 10 July 1902

I have the honor of transmitting to you, as annexes to this letter, the authentic texts of the declarations which I have exchanged with the King's Minister of Foreign Affairs and which define the general relations of the two countries on the continent and in the Mediterranean.

These documents present one particularity that requires an explanation. They comprise two copies of the same acts, each bearing different dates. I have already informed Your Excellency of the reluctance of M. [Giulio] Prinetti to sign simultaneously with the renewal of the Triple Alliance declarations which form the counterpart of that instrument and severely weaken its impact. This reluctance the King has shared. To persuade his Minister to sign, I made a proposal which he finally accepted, that the documents exchanged be postdated, and it was agreed that they would bear the date 1 November 1902. However, I did not hide the drawbacks of such an expedient. Besides the fact that the subscribed undertakings might be applied before I November, the retirement or death of one of the signatories before the agreed date inevitably entailed the annullment of the acts bearing their signatures. I therefore persuaded M. Prinetti to sign an identical instrument dated 10 July, in addition to the acts of 1 November. The same course was followed in the exchange of letters in which M. Prinetti defined, at my request, the exact meaning he attributed to the word "direct" in the clause relating to the case of provocation.

It was mutually agreed that on 1 November next we would return to each other and destroy the acts bearing the date of 10 July 1902, which would thereafter lose their validity; only those [instruments] dated 1 November would remain valid. I should therefore be obliged if Your Excellency would return to me in good time the documents dated 10 July 1902.

I propose, Mr. Minister, in a forth-coming communication to continue the long diplomatic campaign of which the attached declarations form the final act and sanction. . . .

5. Giulio Prinetti, Italian Foreign Minister, to Barrère, 10 July 1902 [1 November 1902]

Following the conversations we have had touching the reciprocal positions of Italy and France in the Mediterranean basin, and touching more especially the respective interests of the two nations in Tripolitania-Cyrenaica and Morocco, it has seemed appropriate to define the obligations resulting from the letters exchanged on this subject between Your Excellency and Marquis Visconti-Venosta on 14 and 16 December 1900, in the sense that each of the two Powers might freely develop its sphere of influence in the above-mentioned regions when it judges the time opportune, without either one's action being necessarily subordinate to that of the other. It had been explained on that occasion that the limit of French expansion in North Africa, set forth in Your Excellency's letter of 14 December 1900, cited above, is clearly understood [to mean] the Tripolitanian frontier indicated on the map annexed to the declaration of 21 March 1899 and the British-French Convention of 14 June 1898.

We have confirmed that this interpretation actually does not permit any disagreement between our two Governments on their respective interests in the Mediterranean.

At the time of these discussions, to eliminate conclusively any possible misunderstanding between our two countries over the definition of their general relarelations, I do not hesitate to make the following declarations spontaneously to Your Excellency in the name of the Government of His Majesty the King:

Should France be the object of direct or indirect aggression on the part of one or several Powers, Italy shall observe a strict neutrality.

The same will apply in the event that France, as a result of provocation, should be forced to take the initiative of a declaration of war in order to defend its honor or its security. In that eventuality the Government of the Republic must communicate its intention to the Royal Government in advance, so that the latter may verify that it is truly a case of direct provocation.

In fidelity to the spirit of friendship that has inspired the present declarations, I am also authorized to declare to you that Italy has not concluded nor will it conclude any protocol or military disposition of an international contractual nature that would be at variance with the present declarations.

I must add that, except for the interpretation of the Mediterranean interests of the two Powers which have a definite character conforming to the spirit of the correspondence exchanged on 14 and 16 December 1900 between Your Excellency and Marquis Visconti-Venosta, the preceding declarations being in harmony with Italy's actual international obligations, the Royal Government understands that they will remain fully valid for as long as it has not notified the Government of the Republic that these obligations have been modified.

I should be obliged if Your Excellency would acknowledge receipt of the present communication, which must remain secret, and give it effect in the name of the Government of the Republic.

6. Barrère to Prinetti, 10 July 1902 [1 November 1902]

By your letter of today, Your Excellency has been pleased to remind me that following our conversations on the reciprocal position of France and Italy in the Mediterranean basin, and more especially on the respective interests of the two countries in Tripolitania-Cyrenaica and Morocco, it has seemed appropriate to us to define the obligations resulting from the letters exchanged on this subject on 14 and 16 December 1900 between Marquis Visconti-Venosta and me, in the sense that each of the two Powers might freely develop its sphere of influence in the above-mentioned regions when it judges the time opportune, without either one's action being necessarily subordinate to that of the other.

It had been explained on that occasion that the limit of French expansion in North Africa, as set forth in my letter of 14 December 1900, cited above, is clearly understood [to mean] the Tripolitanian frontier indicated on the map annexed to the declaration of 21 March 1899 and to the British-French convention of 14 June 1898.

This interpretation, as we have con-firmed, does not permit any disagreement at the present time between our Governments on their respective interests in the Mediterranean, and, with the aim of eliminating conclusively any possible misunderstanding between our two countries, you have been authorized by the Government of His Majesty spontaneously to formulate certain declarations defining the general relations of Italy vis-à-vis France.

I have the honor to acknowledge receipt of Your Excellency's letter and to give its declarations effect in the name of my Government.

I am authorized, in return, to formulate in the following manner the conditions which France, on its side, understands in the same friendly spirit [as necessary] to regulate its general relations vis-à-vis Italy.

Should Italy be the object of direct or indirect aggression on the part of one or several Powers, France shall observe a strict neutrality.

The same will apply in the even that Italy, as a result of direct provocation, should be forced to take the initiative of a declaration of war in order to defend its honor or its security. In that eventuality, the Royal Government must communicate in advance its intention to the Government of the Republic, so that the latter may verify that it is truly a case of direct provocation.

I am also authorized to declare to you that France has not concluded nor will it conclude any military disposition of an international contractual nature at variance with the present declarations.

Finally, it is understood that, except for what concerns the interpretation of the Mediterranean interests of the two Powers, which have a definite character conforming to the spirit of the correspondence exchanged on 14 and 16 December 1900 between Marquis Visconti-Venosta and me, the preceding declarations, which must remain secret, being in harmony with Italy's actual international obligations, will remain fully valid for as long as the Royal Government has not informed the Government of the Republic that these obligations have been modified.

7. Barrère to Prinetti, 11 July 1902

On the subject of the declarations that we have exchanged by our letters of yesterday's date on the general relations between

France and Italy, it seems necessary to me, in order to avoid all possibility of misunderstanding, to define the meaning and scope that should be attributed to the word "direct" in the expression "direct provocation" employed in the said declarations.

I should be obliged if you would confirm your opinion of the interpretation contained in the term in question.

8. Prinetti to Barrère, 11 July 1902

By your letter of today, you have clearly expressed your desire, in order to avoid all possibility of misunderstanding, that I

should define the meaning and scope to be attributed to the word "direct" in the expression "direct provocation" used in the declarations which I made to you by my letter of yesterday's date.

I hasten to confirm to you on this subject what I have had occasion to say to you by word of mouth. The word "direct" has this meaning and scope, that the events which might eventually be invoked as constituting provocation must concern the direct relations between the Power provoking and the Power provoked.

158. THE WILLIAM KNOX D'ARCY OIL CONCESSION IN PERSIA
29 May 1901

[League of Nations, *Official Journal*, 13 (December 1932), 2305–08]

Oil has become synonymous with the Middle East (including North Africa) only since World War II. Between 1945 and 1972 the region's share of the world's "published proved" reserves had risen from 40 to 65 percent and its portion of the total production from 8.1 to more than 40 percent. But statistics alone do not begin to tell the story. The 1889 Reuter concession in Persia embraced, apart from the bank and note-issuing privileges, the exclusive right to exploit all minerals, among them oil (see Doc. 149). Reuter set up a Persian Bank Mining Rights Corporation, which proved unsuccessful in its search for oil, and in 1899 the Persian government withdrew his mineral development privileges. Two years later Muzaffar al-Din Shah (1896–1907) granted a sixty-year oil concession to William Knox D'Arcy, a wealthy British speculator with Australian gold-mining experience. The precise terms of the D'Arcy contract, given below, bear little relation to those currently operative in the Middle East oil-producing zone. Still, the 1901 model served as the prototype for later concessions in the region through World War II. The first commercial well in Persia was bored in 1908, and in the following year the Anglo-Persian Oil Company was formed in London to exploit the concession. Kazemzadeh, *Russia and Britain in Persia* chap. 5; Longrigg, *Oil in the Middle East*, chaps. 1–2; Shwadran, *Middle East, Oil and the Great Powers*, chap. 2; Mikesell and Chenery, *Arabian Oil*, chap. 4; Fanning, *Foreign Oil*, chap. 5; Staff Report to the Federal Trade Commission, *The International Petroleum Cartel* (U.S., 82d Cong., 2d sess., Senate, Select Committee on Small Business, Subcommittee on Monopoly, Committee Print no. 6; hereafter cited by title only), chap. 4; Litten, *Persien*, chap. 6; A. Zangueneh, *Le pétrole en Perse*, pp. 79–94.

Between the Government of His Imperial Majesty the Shah of Persia, of the one part, and William Knox d'Arcy, of independent means, residing in London at No. 42, Grosvenor Square (hereinafter called "the Concessionnaire"), of the other part;

The following has by these presents been agreed on and arranged—viz.:

ART. 1. The Government of His Imperial Majesty the Shah grants to the concessionnaire by these presents a special and exclusive privilege to search for, obtain, exploit, develop, render suitable for trade, carry away and sell natural gas petroleum, asphalt and ozokerite throughout the whole extent of the Persian Empire for a term of sixty years as from the date of these presents.

ART. 2. This privilege shall comprise the exclusive right of laying the pipe-lines necessary from the deposits where there may be found one or several of the said products up to the Persian Gulf, as also the necessary distributing branches. It shall also comprise the right of constructing and maintaining all and any wells, reservoirs, stations and pump services, accumulation services and distribution services, factories and other works and arrangements that may be deemed necessary.

ART. 3. The Imperial Persian Government grants gratuitously to the concessionnaire all uncultivated lands belonging to the State which the concessionnaire's engineers may deem necessary for the construction of the whole or any part of the above-mentioned works. As for cultivated lands belonging to the State, the concessionnaire must purchase them at the fair and current price of the province.

The Government also grants to the concessionnaire the right of acquiring all and any other lands or buildings necessary for the said purpose, with the consent of the proprietors, on such conditions as may be arranged between him and them without their being allowed to make demands of a nature to surcharge the prices ordinarily current for lands situate in their respective localities.

Holy places with all their dependencies within a radius of 200 Persian archines are formally excluded.

ART. 4. As three petroleum mines situate at Schouster, Kassre-Chirine, in the Province of Kermanschah, and Daleki, near Bouchir, are at present let to private persons and produce an annual revenue of two thousand tomans for the benefit of the Government, it has been agreed that the three aforesaid mines shall be comprised in the Deed of Concession in conformity with Article 1, on condition that, over and above the 16 per cent mentioned in Article 10, the concessionnaire shall pay every year the fixed sum of 2,000 (two thousand) tomans to the Imperial Government.

ART. 5. The course of the pipe-lines shall by fixed by the concessionnaire and his engineers.

ART. 6. Notwithstanding what is above set forth, the privilege granted by these presents shall not extend to the provinces of Azerbadjan, Ghilan, Mazendaran, Asdrabad and Khorassan, but on the express condition that the Persian Imperial Government shall not grant to any other person the right of constructing a pipe-line to the southern rivers or to the South Coast of Persia.

ART. 7. All lands granted by these presents to the concessionnaire or that may be acquired by him in the manner provided for in Articles 3 and 4 of these presents, as also all products exported, shall be free of all imposts and taxes during the term of the present concession. All material and apparatuses necessary for the exploration, working and development of the deposits, and for the construction and development of the pipe-lines, shall enter Persia free of all taxes and Custom-House duties.

ART. 8. The concessionnaire shall immediately send out to Persia and at his own cost one or several experts with a view to their exploring the region in which there exist, as he believes, the said products, and, in the event of the report of the expert being in the opinion of the concessionnaire of a satisfactory nature, the latter shall immediately send to Persia and at his own cost all the technical staff necessary, with the working plant and machinery required for boring and sinking wells and ascertaining the value of the property.

ART. 9. The Imperial Persian Government authorises the concessionnaire to found one or several companies for the working of the concession.

The names, "statutes" and capital of the

said companies shall be fixed by the concessionnaire, and the directors shall be chosen by him on the express condition that, on the formation of each company, the concessionnaire shall give official notice of such formation to the Imperial Government, through the medium of the Imperial Commissioner, and shall forward the "statutes", with information as to the places at which such company is to operate. Such company or companies shall enjoy all the rights and privileges granted to the concessionnaire, but they must assume all his engagements and responsibilities.

ART. 10. It shall be stipulated in the contract between the concessionnaire, of the one part, and the company, of the other part, that the latter is, within the term of one month as from the date of the formation of the first exploitation company, to pay the Imperial Persian Government the sum of £20,000 sterling in cash, and an additional sum of £20,000 sterling in paid-up shares of the first company founded by virtue of the foregoing article. It shall also pay the said Government annually a sum equal to 16 per cent of the annual net profits of any company or companies that may be formed in accordance with the said article.

ART. 11. The said Government shall be free to appoint an Imperial Commissioner, who shall be consulted by the concessionnaire and the directors of the companies to be formed. He shall supply all and any useful information at his disposal, and he shall inform them of the best course to be adopted in the interest of the undertaking. He shall establish, by agreement with the concessionnaire, such supervision as he may deem expedient to safeguard the interests of the Imperial Government.

The aforesaid powers of the Imperial Commissioner shall be set forth in the "statutes" of the companies to be created.

The concessionnaire shall pay the Commissioner thus appointed an annual sum of £1,000 sterling for his services as from the date of the formation of the first company.

ART. 12. The workmen employed in the service of the company shall be subject to His Imperial Majesty the Shah, except the technical staff, such as the managers, engineers, borers and foremen.

ART. 13. At any place in which it may be proved that the inhabitants of the country now obtain petroleum for their own use, the company must supply them gratuitously with the quantity of petroleum that they themselves got previously. Such quantity shall be fixed according to their own declarations, subject to the supervision of the local authority.

ART. 14. The Imperial Government binds itself to take all and any necessary measures to secure the safety and the carrying out of the object of this concession of the plant and of the apparatuses, of which mention is made, for the purposes of the undertaking of the company, and to protect the representatives, agents and servants of the company. The Imperial Government having thus fulfilled its engagements, the concessionnaire and the companies created by him shall not have power, under any pretext whatever, to claim damages from the Persian Government.

ART. 15. On the expiration of the term of the present concession, all materials, buildings and apparatuses then used by the company for the exploitation of its industry shall become the property of the said Government, and the company shall have no right to any indemnity in this connection.

ART. 16. If within the term of two years as from the present date the concessionnaire shall not have established the first of the said companies authorised by Article 9 of the present agreement, the present concession shall become null and void.

ART. 17. In the event of there arising between the parties to the present concession any dispute or difference in respect of its interpretation or the rights or responsibilities of one or the other of the parties therefrom resulting, such dispute or difference shall be submitted to two arbitrators at Teheran, one of whom shall be named by each of the parties, and to an umpire who shall be appointed by the arbitrators before they proceed to arbitrate. The decision of the arbitrators or, in the event of the latter disagreeing, that of the umpire shall be final.

ART. 18. This Act of Concession, made in duplicate, is written in the French language and translated into Persian with the same meaning.

But, in the event of there being any dispute in relation to such meaning, the French text shall alone prevail.

159. BOUNDARY PROTOCOL AND AGREEMENT: FRANCE AND MOROCCO
20 July 1901–20 April 1902

(Agreement ratified, 16 December 1902)
[Translated from the French texts in Clercq, *Recueil des traités*, 22: 32–34, 120–22]

The 1845 French-Moroccan treaty (Doc. 95) "demarcated" by a tribal and not a territorial "line" the sparsely inhabited nomadic Saharan zone which represented the major part of the Algerian frontier. Article 4 gave each signatory the right of hot pursuit of its own subjects fleeing from security forces. The near absence of serious friction between France and Morocco along the ill-defined frontier for more than a half-century could be ascribed less to the efficacy of the 1845 agreement than to France's preoccupation with the conquest of Algeria, which dragged on until about 1890. The later adoption by France of a program of peaceful penetration into Morocco required dismantling the international system erected at Madrid in 1880 (Doc. 139). Hardly accidental was the timing of the forward policy. Three oases (Touat, Gourara, and Tidikelt) unquestionably located in Morocco but coveted by France were seized early in 1900, ostensibly for a link in a projected trans-Saharan railroad. Distracted by the Boer War, Britain, as principal antagonist to the growth of French influence in Morocco, turned a deaf ear to appeals for help from the youthful but ineffective ruler, Mawlay 'Abd al-'Aziz (1894–1908). Moreover, Italy was neutralized by a secret deal with France on Morocco and Tripoli (Doc. 157), while Spain was negotiating a comparable understanding on the division of Morocco itself (Doc. 165). Meanwhile, early in 1901 tension mounted as a result of incidents along the Saharan segment of the frontier. In particular, raids into Algeria by Moroccan beduin brought sharp warnings from France to the mawlay, whose renewed appeals to Britain and Germany for aid proved unavailing. In the circumstances, the Moroccan ruler sent a mission to Paris to negotiate a fixed territorial boundary, but France insisted on leaving the frontier unmarked so as to establish the principle of joint French-Moroccan policing of the contested area and thereby to extend its influence. The latter principle was embodied in the protocol of July 1901 and the agreement of execution of April 1902, reproduced below; omitted is a second agreement of 7 May 1902 (French text in ibid., pp. 123–25). Andrew, *Théophile Delcassé*, chaps. 7, 13; E. Anderson, *First Moroccan Crisis*, chap. 1; Trout, *Morocco's Saharan Frontiers*, chap. 1; Rouard de Card, "La frontière franco-marocaine"; Saint-Réné Taillandier, *Les origines du Maroc français*; Abun-Nasr, *History of the Maghrib*, pp. 292–303; Rolo, *Entente Cordiale*, chap. 7; Gourdin, *La politique française au Maroc*, pp. 121–38.

1. Boundary Protocol, 20 July 1901

The French Government and the Sharifi Government have agreed on the following terms for the purpose of consolidating the bonds of amity existing between them and of developing good reciprocal relations, basing the effort on respect for the integrity of the Sharifi Empire and on the improvement of the immediate neighborhood existing between them, by all the special arrangements which such neighborhood may require.

ART. 1. The provisions of the treaty of peace, good friendship, and boundary concluded by the two Powers in 1845 continue in force with the exception of the points endorsed in the following articles.

ART. 2. The Makhzan [i.e., the Sharifi Government] may establish guard and customs stations made of stone or other material at the periphery of the tribal territories forming part of His [Sharifi Majesty's] Empire from the place known as Teniet-essassi to the *qsar* [fortified desert village] of Isch and the district of Figuig.

ART. 3. The people of the qusur [fortified desert villages] of Figuig and of the tribe of Amour-Sahra shall continue, as in the past, to use their irrigated lands, cultivated fields, pastures, etc., and if they possess them beyond the railroad on the eastern side, they may use them in their entirety as in the past, without let or hindrance.

ART. 4. The Moroccan Government may establish whatever guard and customs stations it wishes within the Moroccan Empire beyond the line that is considered, approximately, as the boundary of the grazing area of the Doui Menia and of the Ouled Djerir, running from the end of the district of Figuig to Sidi-Eddaher across the Oued Elkheroua and reaching, beyond the place known as Elmorra, the confluence of the Oued Telzaza and the Oued Guir. It may also establish guard and customs stations on the west bank of the Oued Guir, between the confluence of the two streams and fifteen kilometers above the qsar of Igli.

Similarly, the French Government may establish guard and customs stations on the line adjoining Djenan-Eddar, on the eastern slope of Djebel Bechar, and continuing in that direction as far as the Oued Guir.

ART. 5. The position of the inhabitants of the territory, situated between the lines of the stations of the two countries as indicated above, shall be regulated in the following manner:

As for the people of the tribes of the Doui Menia and the Ouled Djerir, the two governments shall name Commissioners to reside there and give [the tribes] the right to choose which of the two governments they will accept as their authority. Those who choose the French authority shall remain in their place of residence, and those who choose the Moroccan authority shall be moved from that territory to the locality which the Moroccan government may as-sign to them as a residence in its Empire. They shall have the option of keeping their properties and having them administered by agents or of selling them to whomever they wish.

The nomadic people other than the Doui Menia and the Ouled Djerir settled in the above-mentioned territory shall remain under the authority of the Moroccan Empire and shall be allowed to keep their residence there.

The peoples of the qusur of the above-mentioned territory shall choose the authority to administer them and may, in any case, continue to reside in their territory.

ART. 6. All the peoples dependent on the Algerian authority who possess properties, plantations, water, fields, etc., in the territory of the Moroccan Empire shall be permitted to administer them as they see fit. It shall be the same for those dependent on the Moroccan authority and possessing properties in Algerian territory.

ART. 7. For the purpose of maintaining good relations between neighboring tribes dependent on the two governments and of establishing peace and developing commerce between them, the two governments have stipulated that their respective subjects may proceed freely to the territory included between the stations of the two countries, as indicated in Articles 4 and 5, to conduct commerce there or for any other purpose, and without any denial of their rights.

ART. 8. The two governments have agreed that the Commissioners indicated in Article 5 shall determine in the field for the Moroccan Government all the points of guard and customs [stations] specified in Articles 2 and 4.

ART. 9. The two governments have agreed that henceforth they shall not accuse each other of responsibility for disputes which may occur in the future between the tribes of the two countries and shall not claim any monetary indemnity from each other for such occurrences, so as to avoid such difficulties, which have periodically beset the two governments.

Each of the two governments shall designate annually two Commissioners, one for the northern region and the other for the southern region, to discuss and settle tribal disputes in the best and most expeditious manner, and the respective local authorities shall lend the necessary support to render justice between the interested parties.

The Commissioner of the Makhzen in the north shall go to Marnia to examine and settle the claims of the Moroccan tribes with the Commissioner of the Algerian Government in accordance with the stipulated conditions. Similarly, the Commissioner of the Makhzan in the southern region shall go to the region of Djenan-Eddar to examine and settle the complaints of the Moroccan tribes with the French Commissioner in accordance with the stipulated conditions.

Similarly, the Commissioner of the Algerian government shall go to Oudjda [to hear] the complaints of the Algerian tribes in the northern region, while the Commissioner [hearing] the complaints of the southern region shall go to Figuig.

2. Agreement on the Execution of the Protocol, 20 April 1902

With a view to realizing the results of the protocol concluded in Paris between the Minister of Foreign Affairs of the Sharifi Government and the Minister of Foreign Affairs of the French Government in the month of July 1901, and in order to succeed in formally establishing peace, security, and commercial progress intended to enrich and populate the contiguous Moroccan and Algerian regions, General [Auguste-Constant] Cauchemez, chief of the French Mission, and the Féquih Si Mohammed el-Guebbas, First Secretary of the Moroccan Minister of War and chief of the Moroccan Mission, after having examined the situation on the spot, have agreed on the following arrangements:

These arrangements complete the treaties of friendship, good neighborhood, and reciprocal accord concluded in 1844 and 1845 between the two governments and are intended to affirm definitively their understanding of the double and mutual support that they give in the special circumstances which correspond to their respective situations, in order to assure the prosperity and development of the two countries.

ART. 1. The Sharifi Government will, by all possible means, consolidate throughout its territory, from the mouth of the Oued

Kiss and the Teniet-Sassi as far as Figuig, its Makhzani authority over the Moroccan tribes, as it has been established since the treaty of 1845. The French Government, because of its proximity, shall go to its aid in case of need.

The French Government shall establish its authority and peace in the Saharan regions, and the Moroccan Government, its neighbor, shall help it with all its power.

ART. 2. With a view to developing commercial transactions, each of the governments shall establish in the contiguous regions markets together with posts for the collection of fees, which shall be established to augment the resources and the means of action of the two countries.

The collection rights in the posts mentioned above and in the markets shall be the object of a commercial agreement annexed to the present provisions.

ART. 3. In the Tell, the points where the markets will be installed for the benefit of the two governments are fixed as follows:

The Sharifi Government will establish a market (suq) at Cherraa near the Oued Kiss in the district of Angad; a second at Oudjda; a third at the qasbah of Aioun Sidi Mellouk; and a fourth at Debdou.

A mixed market will be established at Ras el-Ain, a point known to belong to the Beni Mattar Ahel Ras el-Ain, of which mention is made in Article 3 of the treaty of 1845, as living to the west of the boundary line.

The French Government will establish markets at Adjeroud of Algeria, at Marnia, and at el-Aricha.

In the Sahara, the two governments will also establish markets. A French market will be established at Ain Sefra; a Moroccan market at Figuig; and mixed markets, with tax collection or marketing rights, along the railroad to Beni Ounif and to Kenadsa.

Furthermore, because of the commercial relations between Figuig and and Duveyrier, the French Government agrees to the installation of a mixed office of tax collection at the latter point.

Each government will name a Controller to represent it in each mixed market and in each collection office, and to collect taxes for the benefit of the two governments.

ART. 4. The following are the points between Adjeroud and Teniet-Sassi where tax collection offices will be set up:

For Morocco:

1. Saidia of Adjeroud or el-Heimer.
2. Oudjda
3. A point in the tribe of the Mehaia, opposite Magour

For France:

1. Adjeroud of Algeria
2. Marnia
3. El-Aricha

ART. 5. The chiefs of the two missions have examined with care the question of the customs regime to be established between Teniet-Sassi and Figuig and have endeavored to find a satisfactory solution.

It has appeared to them impossible to set up customs on the line indicated above. They have agreed to make an estimate of the quantity of merchandise which enters annually into Moroccan territory between these two points, and the sum on this head which accrues to the Sharifi Government. This sum will be paid, at the end of each year, to the agent designated by the Makhzan [the Moroccan Government] to receive it.

The French Government, on its side, undertakes to estimate the receipts which seem to it most proper to recover. By this clause of the present arrangement, [the French Government] intends to prove the pure and sincere friendship which exists between the two countries and their intention to make mutual use of their authority in these regions.

However, the representative of the Makhzan at Figuig should watch over the merchandise which enters Figuig from the regions referred to above. If customs fees have been paid for these goods and if the caravan drivers have a valid receipt, they will not be bothered. In the opposite case, they will be compelled to pay the fees to the Amin [Director] of the Makhzan at Figuig, who will immediately so inform the representative of the French Government. The latter will have the right to receive these fees annually, or to receive a proportionate share of them while giving a receipt, or relinquishing them to the Sharifi Government.

ART. 6. Similarly, since it has been recognized as impossible to set up customs and guard posts in the region between Teniet el-Sassi and Figuig, the two governments renounce the establishment of the guard posts and customs foreseen in Article 4 of the protocol of Paris referred to above.

The Makhzan will install at Figuig the guard post specified below in Article 8. It will also set up offices for the collection of fees, which will be indicated in the commercial agreement mentioned above.

ART. 7. The chiefs of the two missions agree to set up permanent guard posts between Saidia of Adjeroud and Teniet-Sassi in order to achieve peace and free movement between the two countries and to help the collection service.

The French Government will set up its [permanent guard posts] at the following points:

1. Adjeroud of Algeria
2. Marnia
3. El-Aricha

The Moroccan Government will set up its [permanent guard posts] at the following points:

1. Saidia of Adjeroud
2. Oudjda
3. A point on the Oued Za

ART. 8. The Moroccan guard posts at Figuig will be located between the qusur and the defiles in such a way as to assure security and help to agents entrusted with the collection of fees, which will be determined in the aforementioned commercial agreement.

The French Government shall assure the supervision of the railroad on both sides in the Sahara, but between the line and the qusur of Figuig it shall not carry out any military construction.

Crimes of every kind, particularly murders, take place frequently in the Djebel of the Beni Smir and in the neighboring region where the Oulad Abdallah, part of the Amour placed under Moroccan authority, camp; the chiefs of the two missions have zealously sought means to end this series of crimes, which deeply afflict the two friendly countries, and to restore tranquillity in this region.

The only method which to them has appeared effective for realizing this result consists of establishing in the Djebel of the Beni Smir two separate guards, one supplied by the French Government and the other by the Moroccan Government.

All offenders stopped in this region shall be judged according to the laws and justice of the legal authority under which the guard who carries out the arrest operates.

This will be the procedure for all the inhabitants of the mountain in question and for all those who normally take refuge there.

As for the others, they shall be judged according to the customs and treaties which exist between the two countries.

ART. 9. A Khalifah [Deputy] of the Amel [Governor] of Figuig shall be designated to represent the Moroccan Government in one of the three qusur: Kenadsa, Béchar, or Ouakda.

He shall be responsible for assisting the Algerian authorities against offending subjects who take shelter in the qusur.

ART. 10. The Commissioners of the two neighboring governments, foreseen in Article 9 of the protocol signed in Paris, shall endeavor by all possible means in their power to resolve as soon as possible all legal disputes which may arise between the inhabitants of the two countries.

The French Commissioners shall be: the commander of the Arab office at Marnia and the chief commander of native affairs at Djenan-eddar or at Beni Ounif, or any other agent named by the French Govern-

ment.

The Moroccan Commissioners shall be: the Khalifah of the Amel of Figuig; the Khalifah of the Amel of Oudjda, or any other agent named by the Makhzan.

The chiefs of the two missions shall affix their signatures to the present agreement, which will be arranged in two dispatches, each including the two texts, French and Arabic, placed side by side.

One of the dispatches shall be sent to the French Government and the other shall be addressed to the Sharifi Makhzan, so that they may be examined and approved by the Foreign Ministers of the two countries. . . .

To this document was added, by a later accord, the following note:

The Moroccan Government, after examining the present agreement, has found it conforming to the necessities of neighbors. Since the establishment of the customs for the collection of fees foreseen in the Paris protocol is impossible in the present circumstances, it has been decided to postpone it until such time as it may become possible, and to be limited in reality to collecting the market and transit fees in the posts for these purposes according to the articles of the present agreement. With this reservation, ratification is given on 16 December 1902.

160. BRITISH POLICY ON PERSIA
6 January 1902

[Gooch and Temperley, *British Documents on the Origins of the War*, 4: 369–70]

At the turn of the twentieth century, Britain and Russia appeared to be fumbling toward a reciprocal recognition of spheres of influence in Persia. Because of mutual fears, these policies were essentially reactive and defensive in relation to each other, although the rival policymakers often adopted offensive plans as preclusive actions, so as to shut the other side out. Whatever shape the British and Russian policies took, the effects invariably loomed as offensive and threatening to the emerging group of Persian nationalists. Actually, Whitehall would have preferred to establish Persia as a buffer between the British and Russian empires, much as Afghanistan had been, but the rival interests in Persia had already grown too large for that. The Foreign Office in

London therefore seemed to be willing to settle for second best. For the sake of keeping Russia out of Persia's southern provinces and the Persian Gulf, the British foreign secretary, as early as 1902, was prepared to acknowledge Russian supremacy in the northern provinces. Russia, however, continued to return confusing signals. The Russian government and Russian nationals, on the one hand, appeared to be seeking concessions and exclusive economic privileges that were geographically limited to northern Persia. The Caspian Sea fisheries franchise originally granted in 1876 to Russian nationals and later renewed at three-year intervals created no problem because of its fixed location. As for the preclusive railroad concessions, the road-building contracts, and even the mortgage banking operations, all were concentrated largely in Persian provinces adjacent to Russia. On the other hand, Russia was opening consulates for the first time in the gulf ports of Persia and even sought coaling stations there. Moreover, in the Russian loan agreement with Persia of 1901, the pledge of customs as surety did not expressly omit the gulf ports until after a strong British protest. No less serious in British eyes was the 1879 agreement which had provided for the formation of a Persian Cossack Brigade under the command of Russian officers, as an elite unit to protect the person of the shah and the royal family. Although after nearly a quarter-century the brigade remained well below its permissible and intended size, such a Europeanized force under European command looked menacing. But this was one of the realities to which Britain would have to accommodate itself in any spheric division of the shahdom. The population in Persia and therefore its major cities, including the capital, were bunched in those northern provinces in which Russia was building a preponderant position. The price of accommodation with Russia would inescapably have to include Britain's acceptance of this demographic reality together with the geographic reality of the long Russian-Persian border as tsarist strategic advantages. In preparation for the desired agreement, Britain seemed to be trying insofar as possible to limit to southern Persia its activities and claims to exclusive rights, particularly in view of the fiasco of the Tobacco Régie of the early 1890s (Doc. 150). It was thus not an accident that the D'Arcy oil concession of May 1901 (Doc. 158) expressly excluded the five northern provinces from the concessionary area. Above all, Britain had become sensitive to the importance of the Persian Gulf in the defense of India and seemed bent on securing international recognition of its exclusive position there. These points the marquess of Lansdowne developed with precision and clarity in the following memorandum, which he addressed to Sir Arthur H. Hardinge, the British minister in Tehran, for his guidance. Britain was clearly ready in 1902 to acknowledge a Russian sphere of influence in the Persian north; but it took five years longer before a formal understanding with Russia could be reached for reciprocal acknowledgment of a British sphere in the south (Doc. 170). Kazemazdeh, *Russia and Britain in Persia*, chaps. 5–6; Monger, *End of Isolation*, chaps. 3–4; Busch, *Britain and the Persian Gulf*, chap. 4; Greaves, "British Policy in Persia"; Hardinge, *Diplomatist in the East*, chap. 9; Kumar, *India and the Persian Gulf Region*, chap. 6.

The policy of His Majesty's Government in regard to the various Persian questions which most interest this country has from time to time been clearly indicated on the occasions when those questions have come under discussion. It may, however, be useful to recapitulate the salient features of that policy in a statement, which you may, at your discretion place before the Grand Vizier and other Ministers of the Shah, or even before His Majesty himself, if a suitable opportunity should present itself.

The Persian Government must be well aware, from the experience of 100 years, that Great Britain has no designs upon the sovereignty of the Shah or the independence of his State. It has, on the contrary, been one of our principal objects to encourage and strengthen the States lying outside the frontier of our Indian Empire, with the hope that we should find in them an intervening zone sufficient to prevent direct contact between the dominions of Great Britain and those of other great military Powers. We could not, however, maintain this policy if in any particular instance we should find that one of these intervening States was being crushed out of national existence, and falling practically under the complete domination of another Power. It would be necessary in that case, before the intervening State had virtually disappeared, to consider what alternative course our interests might demand now that the object to which our efforts had hitherto been directed was no longer attainable.

Applying these principles to Persia, we have long recognized the superior interest of Russia in the northern portion of the Shah's dominions, which must naturally result from the long extent of her conterminous frontier. Whatever steps we may have taken to maintain our position in Northern Persia have therefore been taken as much in the interests of Persia herself and of her national independence as in our own, which are not directly threatened by Russian superiority in those regions, except in so far as it might affect the Persian capital and seat of government.

In the south, on the other hand, for fully a century our efforts have been successfully devoted to building up a substantial and preëminent mercantile position, with the result that we have acquired an altogether exceptional interest in that part of Persia.

Persia herself has benefited immensely by these labours. We have cleared the waters adjoining her coasts of pirates, and have kept them constantly policed. It may be stated without exaggeration that the development of the whole southern trade of Persia is due to British enterprise, and that it is by this agency that Bushire and Bunder Abbas have been converted into flourishing ports.

The system of telegraphs which has been introduced by the British Indian Telegraph Administration, with the permission and assistance of the Persian Government, has tended not merely to industrial and commercial progress, but also in a remarkable degree to the consolidation of the Shah's authority over the centre and south of the country.

It cannot reasonably be supposed that Great Britain would abandon a position attained by so many years of constant effort, or would acquiesce in attempts on the part of other Powers to acquire political predominance in the south of Persia. Although, therefore, His Majesty's Government have no desire to obstruct in any way the efforts of Russia to find a commercial entrance for her trade in the Persian Gulf, or to oppose any obstacle to the passage of her commerce from the north for export from Persian ports, they could not admit that such commercial facilities should form the pretext for the occupation by Russia of points possessing strategical importance or for the establishment of such an ascendancy in the south as she already enjoys in the north.

The Persian Government should therefore distinctly understand and bear in mind that Great Britain could not consent to the acquisition by Russia of a military or naval station in the Persian Gulf, for the reason that such a station must be regarded as a challenge to Great Britain and a menace to her Indian Empire.

If the Persian Government were at any time to make such a concession to Russia, it would be necessary for His Majesty's Government to take in the Persian Gulf such measures as they might consider necessary for the protection of British interests: measures which, in view of their naval strength in those waters, would be attended with no serious difficulty.

Nor, again, could His Majesty's Government acquiesce in the concession to Russia of any preferential political rights or advantages, or any commercial monopoly or exclusive privilege in the southern or south-eastern districts of Persia, including Seistan. British interests must inevitably suffer by such concessions, and the Persian Government have themselves recognized and acquiesced in this view on more than one occasion. They gave in October 1897 a written promise to Her Majesty's Minister at Tehran that the customs of Southern Persia should never be placed under foreign control and supervision. When in 1900 the customs revenues were pledged as security for the loan obtained from the Russian Banque des Prêts, a special exception was made of the revenues and ports of Southern Persia, and when Her Majesty's Chargé d'Affaires in April 1900 called the attention of the Persian Minister for Foreign Affairs to the interest which the British Government had in the ports of Mohammerah, Bushire, Bunder Abbas, and other ports of the Persian Gulf, and insisted on the right of Her Majesty's Government to be consulted before any change was made in the administration of the Customs at Mohammerah or in the position of the Sheikh, his Excellency replied that not only in Mohammerah, but in every part of Persia where British interests were concerned, the Persian Government, before taking any steps of importance, would consult the British Government. His Majesty's Government have taken note of this assurance with satisfaction, and have only to add that a hypothecation of the internal revenues of any of the southern or south-eastern provinces of Persia as security for a foreign loan would be even more detrimental to Persian interests, and not less objectionable from a British point of view than that of the Customs of the southern ports.

As regards railways, I may remind you that in March 1889 the Shah of Persia gave a distinct promise in writing that Great Britain should have priority in the construction of a southern railway to Tehran; that if concessions for railways were given to others in the north a similar concession should be granted to an English Company in the south; and that no southern railway concession should be granted to any foreign Company without consultation with the British Government. This pledge was brought to the notice of the present Shah in April 1900, and was acknowledged by His Majesty to be of continued and binding validity.

As regards Seistan, I have quite recently, in my despatch of the 9th July, 1901, directed you to call the attention of the Persian Government to the interest which this district has for Great Britain on account of its proximity to India and its position on an important trade route between India and Persia, and to state that we regard it as of the utmost importance that it should remain free from the intrusion of foreign authority in any shape.

In all these matters His Majesty's Government have consistently sought to maintain the continued national existence and the territorial integrity of Persia, and to develop her resources. Their policy in this respect is in strict accordance with the understanding arrived at between Great Britain and Russia in 1834, which was reaffirmed by an exchange of assurances in 1888, pledging the two Governments to respect and promote the integrity and independence of Persia. So long as the Persian Government will work with us cordially upon the lines indicated in this despatch, they will find His Majesty's Government ready to support them in the promotion and protection of what are, in fact, common objects, to the advantage of both countries alike.

If, on the other hand, in the face of our warnings, the Persian Government should elect to encourage the advance of Russian political influence and intervention in these regions in any of the forms which I have indicated above, His Majesty's Government would necessarily have to reconsider their policy; and they would regard themselves as justified in taking such measures as might appear to them best calculated to protect the interests so endangered, even though in the adoption of such measures it might no longer be possible to make the integrity and independence of Persia their first object as hitherto.

161. RUSSIA, CONSTANTINOPLE, AND THE STRAITS: AN ASSESSMENT OF THE BRITISH INTEREST BY THE COMMITTEE OF IMPERIAL DEFENSE
14 February 1903

[Great Britain, Public Record Office, CAB 24/1, 11 March 1915, pp. 2–4]

With the exception of the brief period of the Triple Alliance which united Britain, Russia, and the Ottoman Empire against Napoleon at the turn of the nineteenth century (Doc. 39), Whitehall opposed repeated efforts by tsarist Russia to establish a naval presence in the Mediterranean, to say nothing of its persistent opposition to Russian plans for the seizure of Istanbul (Constantinople) and the straits. At the dawn of the nineteenth century, Britain had welcomed Russian naval cooperation in the war against Napoleon, although British diplomats at Istanbul looked askance at the subterfuge that Russia used at the time in trying to pry the straits open to its warships on a permanent basis. From the time of the treaty of Hünkâr İskelesi in 1833 (Doc. 73), the United Kingdom consistently favored the closure of the straits to all war vessels, and the British position was a major factor in the creation of an international regime for the straits, under which that principle was enforced. While Russia, under that system, did not enjoy free naval transit through the narrows, it at least had the negative satisfaction of shutting the naval vessels of the maritime powers out of the Black Sea in time of Ottoman peace. Despite recurrent frustration, Russia did not abandon its hopes for possession of the straits, and its latest attempt to seize the waterway had been made as recently as 1896. Thus, the conclusion of the newly formed Committee of Imperial Defense (CID) in 1903 represented a reversal of the British position that had remained fixed for nearly three-quarters of a century. The new policy, which was not publicly disclosed, gave Britain greater flexibility in later negotiations with Russia, especially in March-April 1915, when Britain, France, and Russia—on Russian initiative—negotiated the Constantinople agreement. Then, for the first time, Britain formally agreed to support tsarist claims to possession of Istanbul and the straits. Reproduced below is Prime Minister Arthur James Balfour's report on the CID assessment. Headlam-Morley, *Studies in Diplomatic History*, chap. 8; Shotwell and Deák, *Turkey at the Straits*, chaps. 8–9; Goriainow, *Le Bosphore et les Dardanelles*; Hurewitz, "Russia and the Turkish Straits"; Langer, "Russia, the Straits Question, and the European Powers."

The subject of the Dardanelles and Constantinople was discussed on the 11th February in connection with two different but closely allied problems.

The first of these may be stated as follows:—

What difference would it make to the balance of power in the Mediterranean if Russia were to obtain, through the possession of Constantinople, free egress from the Black Sea through the Dardanelles, these remaining closed, as at present, against other Powers?

The answer to this question, unanimously accepted by the Committee, was that while Russia would no doubt obtain certain naval advantages from the change, it would not fundamentally alter the present strategic position in the Mediterranean.

This view is based on the assumption

that Russia, with France as an ally, would, in the case of conflict with England, have no hesitation in forcing the Dardanelles, and would find no serious difficulty in carrying out such an operation, with, or without, the consent of the Turks. Whether she would obtain that consent would depend, of course, upon political and diplomatic considerations, which it is impossible to foresee. But, even were Turkey unwilling to consent to this violation of European Treaties, we must proceed on the assumption that Russia, in the stress of a great conflict, would not hesitate, did it seem otherwise expedient, to effect a junction between her Black Sea Squadron and the French Fleet in the Mediterranean. In the opinion of the Admiralty, the rapidity of the current flowing from the Sea of Marmora would render it a comparatively safe operation for them to force the Dardanelles and though the return journey could not be easy—and might even be impossible[1]— this would make comparatively little difference, as all the French ports in the Mediterranean would be available for their ships, either to coal or to refit.

No doubt, if Russia were established at Constantinople, co-operation with a foreign fleet would become somewhat easier. The 400 miles of protected waters between Sebastopol and the Sea of Marmora would be saved, and any risks and complications arising out of a forced passage of the Dardanelles would be avoided. But these advantages, though not to be ignored, do not constitute, so far as we are concerned, any fundamental or even very important, change in the naval problem, and would not require us to make any substantial alternation in the number and distribution of our Mediterranean Fleet.

Throughout the above argument, it has been assumed that Russia is acting as the ally of France. Were she fighting against us single-handed, it is certain that her fleet would not venture to leave the Black Sea so long as the relative sea power of Russia and Great Britain remained unchanged.

The most important corollary of the foregoing argument is, that the maintenance of the *status quo* as regards Constantinople is not one of the primary interests of this country. It would carry with it, as has been pointed out above, some naval advantages to Russia, and some naval disadvantages to ourselves; but these are not of the decisive character which has sometimes been supposed.

The second question discussed at the meeting was suggested in a private letter of January 1901 by Sir Nicholas O'Conor, His Majesty's Ambassador at Constantinople, who was present during this part of the discussions of the Defence Committee.

Sir Nicholas had asked what course this country was likely to pursue if, as might well happen, disorder and anarchy broke out at Constantinople, and if Russia, proclaiming herself to be acting in the interests of public order, were by a sudden *coup de main* to occupy the city. It is to be presumed that such an occupation would be (professedly at least) of a temporary character; but in Sir Nicholas's opinion, when the situation it produced came to be diplomatically dealt with by other Powers, it would be found that Russia had practically acquired a position from which diplomacy alone would be powerless to dislodge her. It is well known that the Russians are constantly practising in the Black Sea the rapid embarkation and disembarkation of troops, that they have a number of men-of-war and transport sufficient to make the maritime portion of the operation a very simple one, and that we could not count on more than a week at the outside, and more probably only on a few days, between our first notice that the attempt was to be made and its successful consummation.

Sir Nicholas O'Conor seemed to contemplate the possibility of meeting a sudden contingency of this kind by a British occupation of Gallipoli; and schemes have been from time to time suggested under which 5,000 British soldiers and marines, supported by the fleet, are to hold the peninsula, thus making an effective counter-stroke to the Russian occupation of Constantinople.

In the opinion, however, of the Defence Committee, this scheme is, in existing circumstances, impracticable. Even granting that 5.000 men would be sufficient for

---

1. The current flowing through the Dardanelles makes a difference of 7 knots between the speed of a ship going up and going down the Straits. [Footnote to the orginal.]

such an operation, which is probably not the case (see note at the end of the Paper), it seems more than doubtful whether they would be forthcoming. The fleet could supply no large number of marines, and it would be most unwise, at what would certainly be a crisis of European policy, to denude either the ships of the Mediterranean Fleet of an important portion of their complements, or Malta or Egypt of an equally important portion of their necessary garrison.

The occupation of Lemnos, near the mouth of the Dardanelles, would, on the other hand, be easy: but it could not, with advantage, be made permanent. The British naval position in the Mediterranean would be weakened, not strengthened, by the possession of another naval base, which could not be self-sufficing without costly fortifications and a large garrison, and which, if it were not self-sufficing, would merely be an additional anxiety to the Admiral Commanding-in-chief.

No doubt these disadvantages would not attach to a temporary occupation, but an occupation known to be temporary would be of very little use as a coercive threat to Russia, whose Government is presumably as well acquainted as we are both with the strength and with the weakness of our Mediterranean position.

Hence it appears that there is at the command of Great Britain no effective naval or military retort to a *coup de main* on Constantinople. Nor, if the arguments developed in the first part of this Paper are sound, is there any reason why Great Britain should take upon herself the burden of protecting by her solitary exertions what is first a Turkish and then a European interest. Our Ambassador at the Porte should be instructed, if the emergency arises to urge the Sultan, or whoever on the spot seems capable of taking a decision, to adopt active measures of resistance, either at Constantinople or Gallipoli; and in the meanwhile, if a fitting opportunity occurs, it would be desirable to consult with Austria, Italy, and possibly France, and other European Powers as to the part which each was to play in the case of any such eventuality as Sir N. O'Conor fears; it being intimated to them that Great Britain was prepared to take her share in any common action that might be agreed on, but was not prepared single-handed to do the work of Europe.

162. BAGHDAD RAILROAD CONVENTION
5 March 1903

[Great Britain, *Parliamentary Papers, 1911,* Baghdad Railway no. 1, Cd. 5635, pp. 37–48]

As late as the 1880s Bismarck was still discouraging official promotion of German interests in the Ottoman Empire. Thus, in 1881, when Germany sent its first military mission to Istanbul, on the Sublime Porte's invitation, he insisted on the severance of official ties with the German government. All this changed upon the accession of Kaiser Wilhelm II in 1888. The basis for the change was economic. German industry had made such rapid strides by the turn of the century that it began to seek new markets, and the Ottoman Empire offered a logical outlet. Betwen 1886 and 1910 Germany jumped from fifteenth to second place in Ottoman foreign trade, outstripped only by England. Sultan 'Abdülhamid II espoused as a favored cause the Baghdad railroad scheme. He felt that the line, once in operation, would contribute to the economic development, unification, and defense of his Asian domains. Following a second visit to the Ottoman Empire late in 1898, Wilhelm II persuaded the Deutsche

Bank to promote the project as a German national interest, and the sultan issued a preliminary concession in 1899. The Deutsche Bank, however, limited its interest chiefly to the commercial side of the venture and invited the participation of banks of other nationality, especially those in Britain. The definitive concession, granted in 1903 to the Ottoman Anatolian Railroad Company, which was owned for the most part by the Deutsche Bank and by French investors, was never wholly executed. The line itself, however, was finally completed during World War II under other auspices. The scheme has more than antiquarian interest. The award of the contract intensified European rivalries in the Middle East. The political importance of any undertaking as comprehensive as that of the projected Konya to Basrah railroad, sponsored and therefore ultimately dominated by Germany, could hardly fail to stir the suspicion and resentment of the entrenched powers. France sought to safeguard its status in Syria; Russia, its position along the Russian-Ottoman and Persian-Ottoman frontiers and at the straits—for the projected railroad would merely prolong one that was already linked with the German system; and Britain wanted to protect its commercial primacy in Ottoman Asia and its strategic primacy in the Persian Gulf. In the decade before World War I, European diplomacy, insofar as it encompassed the Middle East, strove to adjust these differences. Langer, *Diplomacy of Imperialism*, vol. 2 chap. 19; Chirol, *Middle Eastern Question*, chaps. 17–19; Earle, *Turkey, the Great Powers and the Bagdad Railway*; Wolf, *Diplomatic History of the Bagdad Railroad*; Chapman, *Great Britain and the Bagdad Railway*; Ragey, *La question du chemin de fer de Bagdad*; Helfferich, *Georg von Siemens*, vol. 3, chaps. 2–7; Sitki, *Das Bagdad-Bahn Problem*; Holborn, *Deutschland und die Türkei*, chap. 2 (German background); Trumpener, *Germany and the Ottoman Empire*, chap. 9; Mühlmann, "Die deutschen Bahnunternehmungen in der asiatischen Türkei"; Conker, *Les chemins de fer en Turquie*; Busch, *Britain and the Persian Gulf*, chap. 7; Pressel, *Les chemins de fer en Turquie*.

Between his Excellency Zihni Pasha, Minister of Commerce and Public Works, acting in the name of the Imperial Ottoman Government, of the first part; M. Arthur Gwinner, president of the board of directors, Dr. Kurt Zander, director-general, and M. Edouard Huguenin, assistant director-general of the Ottoman Anatolian Railway, acting in the name and on behalf of the Ottoman Anatolian Railway Company at Constantinople, of the second part. it has been decided as follows:—

ART. 1. The Imperial Ottoman Government grant the concession for the construction and working of an extension of the line from Konia to Bagdad and Busra, passing through, or as near as possible to, the towns of Karaman, Eregli, Kardash-Beli, Adana, Hamidieh, Osmanieh, Bagtcheb, Kazanali, Killis, Tel-Habesh, Harran Ras-ul-Ain, Nisibin, Avniat, Mosul, Tekrit, Sadidjeh, Bagdad, Kerbela, Nedjef, Zobeir, and Busra, as well as the following branches:—

1. From Tel-Habesh to Aleppo.
2. From a neighbouring point on the main line, to be agreed upon, to Urfa.

The Imperial Ottoman Government will not grant a guarantee, under any form, for the construction of this branch line, about 30 kilom. in length, nor any appropriation for working expenses, but the gross recepts of every description from the branch line shall belong exclusively to the concessionnaires.

3. From Sadidjeh to Khanikin.
4. From Zobeir to a point on the Persian Gulf to be agreed upon between the Imperial Ottoman Government and the concessionnaires, as well as everything appertaining to the said lines. The main line and its branches shall follow a route to be ap-

proved by the Imperial Ottoman Government—to the Ottoman Anatolian Railway Company on the following conditions:—

ART. 2. The duration of this concession shall be ninety-nine years. A similar period shall be adopted for the lines of Angora and Konia, and shall commence to run from the date of the issue of the firman and the exchange of the present convention.

As regards the new lines, this period of ninety-nine years shall commence to run separately for each section from the date on which the Imperial Government shall have issued the Government bonds to the concessionnaires in accordance with article 35 of the present convention.

ART. 3. These lines, taken collectively, are divided, as regards the submission of the final plans and designs, into sections of 200 kilom. in length. The concessionnaires shall, within three months from the date of the issue of the firman granting the concession and the exchange of the present convention and the specification (and after the conditions of article 35 have been fulfilled), submit to the Ministry of Public Works, after the survey has taken final shape, and in accordance with the terms of the specification full plans and designs of the first section of 200 kilom. in length, starting from Konia and passing through, or as near as possible to, Karaman and Eregli, i.e., along the contemplated route of the Bagdad line. As regards the other sections, the plans and designs relating thereto shall be submitted within eight months from the date on which the concession for each section commences in pursuance of the provisions of article 35 which relate to each section.

The plans and designs must be examined by the Ministry, and, according to circumstances, approved as they stand, or modified if necessary, within three months from the date of their submission. After that period, if the Imperial Government have not notified their decision to the concessionnaires, the latter may consider the designs which they have submitted as having been approved, and they shall proceed to put the work in hand. If the Imperial Government introduce such modifications into the designs as will involve a delay of more than one month in the approval of the plans, the period allowed for construction shall be extended by a period equal to the delay caused by the examination of those modifications and approval of the plans.

The special assignments intended for the first section of 200 kilom. starting from Konia and passing through or as near as possible to Karaman and Eregli, are set forth in Annex I (Financial Convention),[1] which forms an integral part of the present convention.

ART. 4. The concessionnaires undertake to commence work on the first section, at their own expense, risk, and peril, within three months from the date of approval of the plans and designs of those first 200 kilom., and likewise to complete it not later than two years from that same date.

The concessionnaires undertake to commence work within three months from the date of approval of the plans and designs of the other sections, and to complete the whole of the lines and branches within eight years from the date of the issue of the firman and the exchange of the present convention. Notwithstanding, any period of delay in carrying out the terms of article 35, for any section, that is to say any period of delay in the issue of the bonds by the Imperial Government to the concessionnaires, shall be added to the said period of eight years. The works must be carried out in accordance with standard practice and the terms of the annexed specifications, as well as with the approved plans and designs; notwithstanding, in case of *vis major*, the periods for completion shall be extended by a period equal to that of the interruption of the work, provided that the concessionnaires immediately notify the local authorities as well as the Ministry of Public Works.

The term *vis major* shall be understood to include the case of a war between European Powers, as also a radical change in the financial situation of Germany, England, or France.

ART. 5. The Ministry of Public Works shall control the works by one or more commissioners both during execution, on completion of the works, and before their reception. This control shall likewise apply

---

1. Not reproduced here.

to the working of the line and the maintenance of the works during the period of concession.

The concessionnaires shall deposit each year, to the order of the Ministry of Public Works, and in respect of expenses of control, a sum of 270 gold piastres per kilometre, payable monthly, from the date fixed for the commencement of the works until the termination of the concession.

ART. 6. The enterprise being of public utility, land necessary for the building of the railway and everything appertaining thereto, quarries, and gravel-pits for balast necessary for the railway and belonging to private persons shall be taken over in accordance with the law on expropriation, whenever it has not proved possible to come to an understanding between the concessionnaires and the owners for the purchase of such land.

The Government shall expropriate and hand over to the concessionnaires land necessary for the building of the line and everything appertaining thereto after the location of the railway has been approved and staked out. The land shall be handed over by the Government within two months

The land necessary for temporary occupation during the work shall be handed over to the concessionnaires by the local authorities on condition that the former shall indemnify the owners.

If in the said land necessary for the building of the railway and everything appertaining thereto there should be land called Arazii-Emirei-Halie, it shall be handed over free of charge to the concessionnaires.

If within a zone 15 kilom. each side of the railway there should be land called Arazii-Emirei-Halie which contains quarries and gravel-pits for ballast, the concessionnaires may work them free of charge, during the period of construction, provided that they close them down on the completion of the work; should the concessionnaires desire to make use of these quarries and gravel-pits during the period of working they shall conform to the regulations governing the matter and pay the specified royalty.

The temporary occupation of such land during the work of construction shall likewise be granted to them free of charge.

ART. 7. The railway shall be built for a single line; but land shall be acquired in view of the construction of a second line. As soons as the gross kilometric receipts shall have reached 30,000 fr. per annum, the Imperial Government shall have the right to demand the construction of the second line which the concessionnaires will be bound to build at their own expense.

ART. 8. Manufactured material for the permanent way and the materials, iron, wood, coal, engines, carriages and waggons and other stores necessary for the initial establishment as well as the general enlargement and development of the railway and everything appertaining thereto which the concessionnaires shall purchase in the Empire or import from abroad shall be exempt from all inland taxes and customs duties. The exemption from customs duties shall also be granted for the coal necessary for working the line which is imported from abroad by the concessionnaires until the gross receipts of the line and its branches reach 15,500 fr. per kilometre. Likewise, during the entire period of the concession the land, capital, and revenue of the railway and everything appertaining thereto shall not be taxed, neither shall any stamp duty be charged on the present convention or on the specification annexed thereto, the additional conventions, or on any subsequent instruments, or for the service of the Government bonds to be issued; nor on the amounts encashed by the concessionnaires on account of the guarantee for working expenses, nor shall any duty be levide on their shares, preference shares, and bonds, nor on the bonds which the Imperial Ottoman Government shall issue to the concessionnaires.

The concessionnaires shall be liable to stamp duty for all their transactions other than those for which exemption is granted to them in the present article.

The concessionnaires shall form an Ottoman joint-stock company, under the name of "Imperial Ottoman Bagdad Railway Company," which shall take the place of the Ottoman Anatolian Railway Company in all that concerns the new line from Konia to the Persian Gulf with its branches, and which shall be governed by the annexed statutes.

The Ottoman Anatolian Railway Company undertakes never to cede or transfer to any other company the existing lines from Haidar-Pasha to Angora and to Konia.

The Imperial Ottoman Bagdad Railway Company which will be formed undertakes likewise not to cede or transfer the lines to be constructed from Konia to Bagdad and to Busra and their branches.

ART. 9. The building and other materials necessary for the construction and working of this line and its branches, as also the officials and workmen, shall be conveyed, but only during the period of construction and under the supervision of the Ministry of Marine, on the Shatt-el-Arab, the Tigris, and Euphrates, in steam or sailing ships, or other craft which shall be acquired or hired by the company.

Material thus conveyed shall be exempt from customs duty, taxes, &c.

ART. 10. The wood and timber necessary for the construction and working of the railway may be cut in the forests of the neighbouring districts which belong to the State, in accordance with the regulations relating thereto.

ART. 11. As soon as the concessionnaires shall have notified to the Ministry of Public Works the completion of the work on one section the latter shall cause an inspection of the works already completed to be made by a technical commission appointed for that purpose, and shall accept them provisionally if approved; one year after they have been provisionally passed, a second inspection of the works shall be made by a technical commission, and, should it be reported that the works have been carried out in accordance with standard practice and the terms of the specification, the Ministry of Public Works shall pronounce their final acceptance as a result of the commission's report.

The concessionnaires shall have the right to open the lines to traffic in successive sections after they have been accepted provisionally. The length of the completed sections, from Konia, Adana, Bagdad, Busra, as also from the different intermediate points, shall be at least 40 kilom. and shall finish at a station.

ART. 12. Should the Imperial Government decide upon the construction of branches joining the railway which forms the subject of this convention with the sea at a point situated between Mersina and Tripoli in Syria, they shall grant the concession for the said branches exclusively to the concessionnaires, provided, however, that the rights already granted to the Damascus-Hamah Railway Company and extensions are safeguarded.

Notwithstanding, should the concessionnaires, within a maximum period of one year from the date of the notification made to them by the Imperial Government, not agree to construct the branch or branches in question in accordance with the clauses and terms of the present concession, or, having agreed to do so, fail to execute them within the time agreed on by the Imperial Government and the concessionnaires, the latter shall forfeit all rights to the said branches, and the Imperial Government may grant the concession for them to third parties.

The concessionnaires shall, further, have the preferential right on equal terms to construct the following branches:—

(*a*.) Towards Marash.
(*b*.) Towards Aintab.
(*c*.) Towards Birijik.
(*d*.) Towards Mardin.
(*e*.) Towards Erbil.
(*f*.) From the Diala towards Salakié and Tuz-kharmati.
(*g*.) From El-Badj to Hit.

This preferential right for the seven branches specified above is dependent for its validity on the following conditions:—

Should the Imperial Government decide definitely to grant the concession of one of these branches to third parties, the concessionnaires shall be obliged, within nine months from the date of the notification made to them by the Ministry of Commerce and Public Works, to inform the Imperial Ottoman Government whether they desire to take up that concession upon the conditions accepted by the third parties mentioned above.

ART. 13. The concessionnaires shall have the right to establish and work tile and brick works on the line with the permission of the local authorities. Machinery and tools for the use of the said works shall enjoy the same exemption as that granted to the material and tools for the railway. The coal consumed in those works shall be exempt from customs duty.

The works shall revert free of charge to the State on the expiration of the concession.

ART. 14. During the entire period of the concession, the concessionnaires shall be bound at their own expense to maintain in perfect condition the railway and everything appertaining thereto, as well as its fixtures and rolling stock, in default of which the procedure provided for by article 16 of the specifications shall be adopted.

ART. 15. The concessionnaires are bound to conform, as regards the policing and safety of the line, to the laws and regulations now in force, or to be enacted hereafter in the Ottoman Empire.

The Imperial Government shall take all necessary measures for the maintenance of order along the line and in the construction yards.

In the case of interruption of the traffic on part or whole of the line through the fault of the concessionnaires, the Imperial Government shall take, at the expense, risk, and peril of the concessionnaires, all necessary steps in accordance with article 16 of the specification with a view to ensuring the temporary working of the line.

ART. 16. The concessionnaires shall have the right to levy tolls in accordance with the tariff of the specification from the date on which each section of the railway is provisionally accepted until the expiration of the concession.

ART. 17. The transport of officers and men, both naval and military, travelling collectively or separately, whether in time of war or peace, as well as that of war material and stores, prisoners and convicts, State officials, and mails, shall be effected in accordance with the terms of Chapter V of the specification.

ART. 18. As guarantee for the fulfilment of the present engagements the concessionnaires shall, within three months from the day on which they receive official notice of the issue of the firman granting the concession, deposit as security in a bank at Constantinople, approved by the Government, a sum of £T. 30,000 either in cash or Government bonds, or the bonds of an Ottoman joint-stock company, or else guaranteed by the State at the current price.

If the deposit is made in bonds the bank shall obtain an undertaking that any deficiency caused by a fall in the price shall be made good. Immediately after the deposit of the security the firman granting the concession shall be issued to the concessionnaires.

The security shall be returned only when the works have been finally accepted and in proportion to the length of the sections opened to traffic; if within the three months above mentioned the concessionnaires do not make the said deposit, they shall, without any previous summons, forfeit all concession rights.

In the event of it proving impossible to carry out the terms of article 35, the concessionnaires shall have the right to recover their security without any formality or obligation to ask the previous consent of the Government.

ART. 19. The Imperial Ottoman Government reserve the right of withdrawing at any time the concession of the line from Konia to Busra and branches on payment to the concessionnaires, for the remaining period of the concession, of an annual sum equivalent to 50 per cent. of the average gross recepts for the five years preceding the year in which the concession is withdrawn, provided always that the said annual sum is not less than 12,000 fr. per kilometre. In this case the Imperial Ottoman Government shall repay in one payment the whole of the Government bonds issued to the concessionnaires which have not been previously redeemed, and from the annual sum to which, under the present article, the concessionnaires are entitled there shall be deducted the annuity of the said loans. viz., 11,000 fr. per kilometre. The Government shall guarantee to the concessionnaires the regular payment at the specified periods of the balance due to them on account of the withdrawal of the concession, which shall form the subject of a special convention.

The lines and everything appertaining thereto shall then be handed over to the Government, and the Government shall then proceed to purchase the existing rolling stock and fixtures, materials, and stores, in accordance with article 19 of the specification.

In the event of the concession for the

railway being withdrawn, and should the Imperial Government not deem it desirable to work it through their own officials, they shall not grant the right of working it to another company, but undertake to cause it to be worked on lease by the concessionnaires.

ART. 20. On the expiration of the concession for each section the Imperial Government shall acquire all rights of the concessionnaires over the railway and everything appertaining thereto, as well as in regard to plant and materials, and shall become entitled to all the proceeds derived therefrom.

The lines and everything appertaining thereto shall be handed over free of all debt and liability to the Imperial Government, and the latter shall effect the purchase of plant and stores in accordance with article 20 of the specification.

ART. 21. The railway employés and officials shall wear the uniform approved and adopted by the Imperial Government; they shall all wear the fez, and shall as far as possible be selected among Ottoman subjects.

Five years after the date of the opening of each section to traffic the whole of the executive working staff, except the higher officials, shall be exclusively composed of Ottoman subjects.

ART. 22. The concessionnaires may work any mines which they shall discover within a zone of 20 kilom. each side of the middle of the line, provided that they conform with the laws and regulations relating thereto, but this shall not give them a privilege or monopoly.

They may likewise cut wood in the forests adjoining the line, either for timber or for charcoal, on application to the competent authorities and if they conform to the regulations governing the matter.

ART. 23. The concessionnaires shall have the right to build at their own expense at Bagdad, Busra, and at the terminus of the branch from Zobeir, harbours with all necessary arrangements for bringing ships alongside the quay and for the loading, unloading, and warehousing of goods.

The plan of these harbours shall be submitted within eight years at the latest from the date of exchange of the present convention, and the works on each harbour shall be finished within twelve years at the latest from the date at which the work is begun on the section adjacent to each harbour respectively.

A scale of tariffs shall be annexed to the plans.

These three ports shall form an integral part of the railway, and the net receipts derived therefrom shall be carried to the account of the gross receipts of the railway.

On expiration of the concession these harbours and everything appertaining thereto shall revert free of charge to the State.

Should the concessionnaires fail to construct any one of these harbours within the above-mentioned period, the Imperial Government shall be entitled to grant the concession to third parties.

In any case the concessionnaires may during the period of construction of the railway establish at these three points, as well as at the port of Kostambul, temporary structures for the unloading of materials for the railway.

These structures shall, if the Imperial Government require it, be demolished on the completion of the works.

ART. 24. The concessionnaires shall be entitled to set up and open, wherever the need is felt, on the land belonging to the railway depôts and warehouses which shall be available for use by the public.

These depôts, warehouses, and other plant shall become the property of the Government on the expiration of the concession in accordance with article 20 of the specification.

The Government shall have a share of 25 per cent. in the net receipts of these depôts and warehouses.

ART. 25. The concessionnaires shall be entitled to use on the lines free of charge natural hydraulic power, the right of using which is not already appropriated, or which will be created, for the purpose of generating electricity for the driving of trains, for their lighting, or for other purposes in the working of the railway. The plans and designs of the works which are to be carried out for this purpose shall be submitted for the approval of the Ministry of Commerce and Public Works.

Should use be made of this electric power, 50 per cent. of the savings under this head in the working expenses shall be carried to the credit of the Imperial Ottoman Government.

All plant of this kind shall revert free of charge to the State on the expiration of the concession.

ART. 26. The Government shall be entitled to construct at their own expense entrenchments and works of defence on the points of the main line or its branches and wherever they shall deem it necessary.

ART. 27. Works of art and antiquities discovered during construction shall be subject to the regulations relating thereto.

Nevertheless the concessionnaires shall be exempt from the formality of presenting an application and obtaining permission for research.

ART. 28. The concessionnaires shall be bound to submit to the Ministry of Public Works a monthly statement of all receipts; these statements shall be drawn up in the manner prescribed by article 17 of the specification.

ART. 29. The railway being considered as divided into sections of 200 kilom. in length, should the concessionnaires, except in an established case of *vis major*, not have commenced the works within the appointed time or should they not complete the work on one section within the appointed time or should they interrupt the traffic, or should they not, on any one section, fulfil the other principal engagements under the present convention, the Imperial Government shall issue a summons to the concessionnaires stating the undertakings which remain to be fulfilled by them, and should they within a period of eighteen months from the date of the summons not have taken such steps as are necessary, they shall forfeit their concessionary rights for every section of the line in regard to which they shall have been found in default, and procedure provided for by article 18 of the specification shall be adopted.

It is agreed that, so long as the main line between Konia and Bagdad is not entirely completed, the concessionnaires may not open to traffic the parts of the line from Bagdad to Busra which they may have constructed.

During the period in which the sections between Bagdad and Busra are not open to traffic the concessionnaires shall refund to the Imperial Government, at the dates when the annual instalments fall due, the annuity of 11,000 fr. per kilometre for interest on and redemption of the bonds which the Imperial Government shall have issued to them for the said sections, and they shall not, of course, receive anything on account of working expenses; but these clauses do not in any way prejudice the other rights of the concessionnaires on the line from Bagdad to Busra.

The forfeiture of the concession for one or several sections of the railway shall not prejudice the rights of the concessionnaires as regards the remaining sections of the new lines, nor as regards the whole of the old lines.

ART. 30. The concessionnaires shall construct free of charge at the points selected by the Government the necessary premises for the offices of the Imperial Railway Commissioners and of the customs, postal, and police officials.

The concessionnaires shall construct at important stations, after arrangement with the Ministry of Commerce and Public Works, two rooms with water-closet for the postal service.

ART. 31. The concessionnaires may instal at their own expense on the whole extent of the line telegraph poles and wires; this line shall not be used for private correspondence which has no connection with the working of the railway.

The Imperial Government reserve to themselves the right of control at all times by inspectors appointed by the Ministry of Posts and Telegraphs of all telegraphic correspondence carried over the wires of the company.

The Government shall be entitled to make use of the poles belonging to the railway for the erection of one or, if necessary, two telegraphic wires, and the poles on the railway shall be erected so that they are capable of supporting these two additional wires, as well as those of the company. In case of need the Government shall have the right of erecting, at their own expense, other poles throughout the extent of the line or, in case of breakage or interruption of their lines, placing telegraphists in the stations for the transmission of important and urgent official telegrams on the telegraph lines of the railway, provided always that the railway service is not obstructed.

ART. 32. The concessionnaires shall be

entitled to convey by their own means of transport and without paying any tax to the postal administration of the Empire correspondence and bags concerning exclusively the railway service; but on condition that they shall submit them, according to rule, to the control of the officials of the postal administration. Private letters of the staff shall be subject to postage. The concessionnaires shall only carry letters of this nature on their lines on condition that they comply with the terms of the inland postal regulations in force within the Empire. They shall also be entitled to carry free of charge stores, such as coal, lubricants, and materials and plant required for the construction, maintenance, and working of the railway, both on the existing lines and on those lines which form the subject of the present convention.

ART. 33. The Imperial Government undertake that the service of the line connecting Haidar-Pasha with Sirkedji and the bridge of Karakeuï shall be carried on by the Mahsoussé Administration, by means of three new boats, of an average service speed of at least 14 miles (of 1,855 meters) per hour.

If within one year from the date of exchange of the present convention the Mahsoussé Administration should not organise the service under the above-mentioned conditions, the concessionnaires shall have the right to carry passengers and goods between the two points, provided that they select the crews of these boats from retired officers and men of the Imperial fleet, or from cadets of the Imperial Naval School who are eligible for commissions.

The boats of the concessionnaires shall carry on their service in the place and instead of those of the Mahsoussé Company while being exclusively appropriated to the said transport service, and the concessionnaires shall pay yearly to that administration a sum equal to 5 per cent. of the gross receipts derived from the transport of passengers and goods carried on by them between the above-mentioned points.

From the balance of the gross receipts there shall be deducted:—
1. Working expenses;
2. An annuity of 8.30 per cent. of the initial capital appropriated to the acquisition of boats; after deduction of the said sums, the remainder shall be carried to the account of the gross receipts of the new guaranteed lines.

The amount of initial capital shall be determined after the boats have been purchased.

It is understood that if the gross receipts of one year do not allow of the above-mentioned expenses being met the company shall have no claim upon the Imperial Government.

It may, however, make good the deficit from the receipts of the following years.

The boats of the concessionnaires, being considered as a section of the Mahsoussé, shall enjoy the same rights as the latter.

ART. 34. The concessionary company and the company about to be formed by it being Ottoman joint-stock companies, all disputes and differences which may arise, either between the Imperial Government and the concessionnaires or the company, or between the concessionnaires or the company and private persons, as a result of the execution or interpretation of the present convention and the specification attached thereto, shall be carried before the competent Ottoman courts.

The new company, being Ottoman, must correspond with the State departments in the Turkish language, which is the official language of the Imperial Ottoman Government.

ART. 35. The Imperial Government guarantee to the concessionnaires an annuity of 11,000 fr. per kilometre constructed and worked, and also a contract sum of 4,500 fr. per annum for working expenses in respect of each kilometre worked.

This annuity of 11,000 fr. shall be met by an Ottoman State loan bearing interest at 4 per cent., with a sinking fund of 0.087538 per cent., redeemable during the period of the concession. Consequently the concessionnaires will be entitled to a nominal sum of 269,110 fr. 65 c. of this State loan for each kilometre constructed and opened to traffic, and the concessionnaires shall be debarred from demanding other amounts on this head from the Imperial Ottoman Government.

The total nominal amount of Government bonds accruing to the concessionnaires by the terms of the foregoing arrangement shall be issued to them by the Imperial Ottoman Government on the signature of each special convention for each section; but the concessionnaires shall make good to the Imperial Ottoman Government the sums which the latter have paid during the period of construction for the service of the bonds issued to the concessionnaires, viz., till the date on which each section of the railway is provisionally accepted. These sums shall be placed by the concessionnaires in the hands of the Public Debt for the account of the Imperial Ottoman Government.

The Imperial Government reserve the right of modifying at any moment the system of payment of the kilometric annuity of 11,000 fr. fixed in the first paragraph of the present article, after redemption of the bonds issued in respect of the said annuity.

As soon as the growth of the traffic and receipts and the financial situation permit the issue by the concessionnaires themselves of bonds of their own to replace the Government bonds which have been issued to them by the Imperial Government, the concessionnaires shall come to an agreement with the Imperial Government for the purpose of carrying out this arrangement.

For the first section of 200 kilom. beyond Konia the face value of the bonds to be issued by the Imperial Ottoman Government to the concessionnaires is fixed at 54,000,000 fr. But as soon as this section is finally accepted and the length of the completed line is fixed, the exact nominal value of the bonds accruing to the concessionnaires for that section shall be calculated at the rate of 269,110 fr. 65 c. per kilometre. Any surplus over this nominal amount shall be calculated at the issue price, plus interest at 4 per cent. accrued up to the date of payment, and the sum thus ascertained shall be paid in cash by the concessionnaires into the Imperial Treasury. The calculation shall be made at a minimum of $81\frac{1}{2}$ per cent.

The Ottoman Anatolian Railway Company guarantees to the Imperial Ottoman Government the construction of the aforesaid first section of 200 kilom. until the work on this section is completed.

In the event of the Imperial Ottoman Government deeming it necessary, they may also require the Ottoman Anatolian Railway Company to guarantee other sections, and the Ottoman Anatolian Railway Company shall have the right so to do.

The contract sum of 4,500 fr. per annum for working expenses in respect of each kilometre opened to traffic will be guaranteed to the concessionnaires by a special convention for each section simultaneously with the convention regulating the annuity of 11,000 fr.

As regards the first section of 200 kilom. beyond Konia, the above-mentioned contract sum of 4,500 fr. per kilometre per annum is secured to the concessionnaires on the surplus of the guarantees already assigned to the lines of the Ottoman Anatolian Railway Company.

The service of the Government bonds which are to be issued for the aforesaid kilometric annuity of 11,000 fr. shall be secured on the special appropriations agreed on with the Imperial Government before work is begun on each section.

The Imperial Ottoman Bagdad Railway Company, on its part, further pledges, irrevocably and inalienably, to the holders of the said bonds the line from Konia to the Persian Gulf and its branches with their rolling stock. Similarly, and for the same purpose, it assigns its share in the receipts from this line after payment of the working expenses, but the bondholders shall not be entitled to intervene in the administration of the company.

The aforesaid share of the receipts, after deducting working expenses—both the said share and the amount of expenses to be determined by the company's books— shall be paid annually, if need be, by the company to the Administration of the Ottoman Public Debt for the service of the bonds. The Imperial Ottoman Government shall refund to the company any sums that the latter may have supplied under this head for the service of the bonds issued. The Imperial Ottoman Government further assign, irrevocably and inalienably, to the holders of the aforementioned Government bonds their share of the gross receipts of the said line.

If the gross kilometric receipts of the line exceed 4,500 fr. but do not exceed 10,000 fr., the surplus above 4,500 fr. shall belong entirely to the Government.

If the gross kilometric receipts exceed 10,000 fr., the portion up to 10,000 fr. being always divided as stated above, 60 per cent. of the surplus over and above the

10,000 fr. shall pass to the Imperial Government, and 40 per cent. to the Company.

It is agreed that if the gross kilometric receipts do not reach 4,500 fr. the sum required to make good the deficiency in this amount shall be paid to the concessionnaires by the Government at the same time as the annuity of 11,000 fr. from the special assignments to be agreed on between the Imperial Government and the concessionnaires before the fulfilment by the concessionnaires of the clauses of the present convention relative to each section.

The above assignments shall be collected and paid through the agency of the Administration of the Ottoman Public Debt.

As regards the Government bonds to be issued for the construction of the different sections of the railway, the receipts accruing to the Imperial Government shall be pooled in such a manner that the amount available shall be assigned to the whole of the said bonds in proportion to the original nominal value of each issue.

Immediately after the payment of the coupons and the sinking fund of the Government bonds issued, the surplus of the receipts accruing to the Imperial Ottoman Government shall be paid to the latter annually after the completion of the formalities provides for by article 40 of the present convention.

ART. 36. For the purpose of determining the average of the kilometric receipts of the new Bagdad lines, all the receipts from every portion of the new lines, together with the net receipts referred to in articles 23 and 33 of the present convention, shall be pooled as and when the new lines are opened to traffic.

The average of the gross kilometric receipts thus obtained shall serve as the basis for ascertaining the total of the sums to be paid in accordance with article 35.

ART. 37. The concessionnaires undertake to carry out at their own expense all the improvements on the old lines from Haidar-Pasha to Angora and Eskishehr to Konia required for the introduction of an express train service, but the expenditure involved shall not exceed a sum of 8,000,000 fr.

In return for this expenditure and for the new extraordinary charges for working expenses involved in the introduction of the express train service, the Imperial Government assign to the concessionnaires—

1. An annuity of 350,000 fr. for thirty years for interest and sinking fund in respect of the capital sum of 8,000,000 fr. mentioned above.

This annuity shall be paid from the commencement of the works of improvement.

2. An annuity of 350,000 fr. for the establishment of the express trains.

This latter annuity shall not become payably till the main line reaches Aleppo.

The annuities provided for in the persent article shall be paid to the Ottoman Anatolian Railway Company out of the existing assignments for the guarantees of the old railway system and in the same manner as the latter.

ART. 38. The concessionnaires undertake to construct and work, as soon as the Imperial Government shall require them to do so, on the conditions of the present convention, a branch line starting from the Konia-Busra line and ending at Diarbekr and Kharput.

ART. 39. The proposed junction of the Damascus-Hamah line and its extensions with the railway system forming the subject of the present convention shall take place at Aleppo.

ART. 40. The concessionnaires shall submit to the Ministry of Public Works, in the course of the month of January of each year, an account of the receipts, after it has been audited and approved by the Imperial Commission, and this shall be the basis on which the sums accruing to the Imperial Government and the company shall be determined in conformity with article 35 of the present convention.

As soon as the amount of the Government's share of these receipts is determined, the Imperial Ottoman Bagdad Railway Company shall remit it to the Administration of the Ottoman Public Debt for the account of the service of the Government bonds, and the latter shall deliver in cash to the Imperial Government any surplus which remains available over and above the sums required for the payment of the coupon which matures on the 1st July of the current financial year.

The Imperial Government, on their part, undertake to inform the Administration of the Public Debt within two months of the presentation of the account of receipts for a financial year of the amount of the sums acknowledged to be due to the company for immediate payment.

ART. 41. The concessionnaires shall have the right to establish between Hamidieh and the port of Kostambul a temporary branch line for the transport of the plant and materials required for the railway. It is nevertheless understood that after the completion of the works which form the subject of the present convention the concessionnaires shall, if the Imperial Government signify their demand for it, have to remove the rails from this temporary branch line.

It is understood that during this temporary working the Imperial Government will not pay either annuity or working expenses for the said branch line.

ART. 42. The land and the quarries which are expropriated in virtue of article 6 of the present convention shall be such area as is strictly necessary for the works of the railway and everything appertaining thereto, and may not be of greater extent. The expropriations shall be carried out under the supervision of the Ministry of Public Works.

ART. 43. All the plant and materials required for the construction of the new lines and everything appertaining thereto referred to in article 8 of the convention, being free of all taxes and customs duties, shall, on arrival, be inspected in the usual manner by the Customs officials.

ART. 44. The stores and warehouses to be constructed on the station premises in accordance with article 24 of the convention shall be used only for the storage of goods to be transported.

Such warehouses and stores shall be built in accordance with designs which will be submitted by the concessionnaires and approved by the Ministry of Public Works.

ART. 45. The concessionnaires must erect at their own expense and up to a total outlay of 4,000,000 fr., such military stations as may be deemed necessary by the Ministry of War. The number, the site, and the arrangements of these military stations and everything appertaining thereto shall be settled by agreement between the concessionnaires and the Ministry of War.

ART. 46. The concessionnaires undertake to pay annually a sum of £T. 500 to the Poorhouse as soon as the main line is opened to traffic.

163. BRITISH POSITION IN THE PERSIAN GULF: THE LANSDOWNE STATEMENT OF POLICY
5 May 1903

[Great Britain, *Parliamentary Debates, Lords*, 4th ser., vol. 121 (1903), col. 1348]

In winding up a debate in the House of Lords on the projected Baghdad Railroad, Foreign Secretary Lord Lansdowne took occasion to state explicitly the principles that guided British policy in the Persian Gulf. More than once in the preceding five years, Britain had had to threaten the use of naval force to discourage France and Russia from attempting to create coaling stations in or near the gulf. Now that the Sublime Porte had granted to a German-controlled firm a definitive concession for the construction of a railroad that would terminate in Kuwayt at the head of the gulf, the foreign secretary, with cabinet approval, notified all interested European powers, without mentioning any by name, that Britain would not abide in the gulf any rival political or military presence. Busch, *Britain and the Persian Gulf*, esp. chap. 8; Plass, *England zwischen Russland und Deutschland*; Kazemzadeh, *Russia and Britain in*

Persia, chap. 6; Staley, "Business and Politics in the Persian Gulf"; Mahan, "Persian Gulf and International Relations"; Martin, *German-Persian Diplomatic Relations*; Standish, "British Maritime Policy."

The noble Lord asked me for a statement of our policy with regard to the Persian Gulf. I think I can give him one in a few simple words. It seems to me that our policy should be directed in the first place to protect and promote British trade in those waters. In the next place I do not think that he suggests, or that we should suggest, that those efforts should be directed towards the exclusion of the legitimate trade of other Powers. In the third place—I say it without hesitation—we should regard the establishment of a naval base, or of a fortified port, in the Persian Gulf by any other Power as a very grave menace to British interests, and we should certainly resist it with all the means at our disposal. I say that in no minatory spirit, because, so far as I am aware, no proposals are on foot for the establishment of a foreign naval base in the Persian Gulf. I at least have heard of none; and I cannot help thinking that the noble Lord waxed almost unneccessarily warm at the idea of such a foreign intrusion, with which, so far as I am aware, we are not at present threatened. . . .

164. DECLARATION ON EGYPT AND MOROCCO: FRANCE AND GREAT BRITAIN
8 April 1904

[Great Britain, *Treaty Series, 1911*, no. 24, Cd. 5969]

After the British occupation of Egypt, English-French relations deteriorated. France kept needling Whitehall to set a definite date for the evacuation of its forces from the khedivate, while Britain no less adamantly refused to ratify the 1888 convention on the Suez Canal. Meanwhile, the French foreign minister, Théophile Delcassé, unfolding his diplomacy for the liquidation of Morocco, encountered the unbending resistance of London to any modification in the status quo. Manifestly, Britain had not lost interest in preserving its commercial primacy in Morocco and in keeping any other major maritime power from installing itself on Morocco's bank of the Strait of Gibraltar. The *parti colonial*, which became the most assertive pressure group in France advocating expansion into Morocco, suspected that Britain's obstinacy concealed an ambition to establish a protectorate over that territory, possibly by dividing it with Germany. The deadlock at both ends of North Africa created the opportunity for a deal through the barter of interests in Egypt and Morocco. France paid the higher price for the exchange. Britain, it is true, abandoned the diplomacy of upholding the status quo as a means of defending strategic and commercial interests in Morocco by acquiescing in the French demand for freedom to proceed with plans for sharing the Arab kingdom with Spain. One major consequence for Britain was loss of its traditional commercial primacy in Morocco. On the other hand, it was able to protect strategic interests by supporting the move for the transfer of the Mediterranean coast of Morocco to Spain, which did not represent a serious threat to Britain's command of the straits. Moreover, while Britain adhered (in art. 6 of the 1904 declaration) to the 1888 Suez Canal convention (Doc. 148), it did so only on condition that the international supervisory commission for the execution of the convention should not function for the duration of the British occupation of Egypt. Before the end of 1904, Germany, Russia, Italy, and Austria gave assurances not to press for British withdrawal from Egypt and accepted the British reservation on the 1888 convention. The public and secret articles of the British-French declaration of April 1904 made express provision for Spanish adherence, which was arranged by a French-Spanish convention signed in the following October (Doc. 165). The secret articles of the declaration were not released until after the Agadir crisis of 1911. Omitted below is a khedival decree, annexed to the 1904 agreement, on the administration and liquidation of the Egyptian debt, which finally assured Britain exclusive management of the finances of Egypt. Andrew, *Théophile Delcassé*, chaps. 9–10; Monger, *End of Isolation*, chap. 6; Rolo, *Entente Cordiale*; Mathews, *Egypt and . . . the Anglo-French Entente*; Hallberg, *Suez Canal*, chap. 17; Freycinet, *La question d'Egypte*, pp. 421–47; A. Taylor, "British Policy in Morocco"; Nicolson, *Portrait of a Diplomatist*, chap. 6; Newton, *Lord Lansdowne*, chap. 10; Tardieu, *France and the Alliances*, chap. 2; E. Anderson, *First Moroccan Crisis*, chap. 6; Abun-Nasr, *History of the Maghrib*, pp. 292–303; Farnie, *East and West of Suez*, chap. 26.

ART. 1. His Britannic Majesty's Government declare that they have no intention of altering the political status of Egypt.

The Government of the French Republic, for their part, declare that they will not obstruct the action of Great Britian in that country by asking that a limit of time be fixed for the British occupation or in any other manner, and that they give their assent to the draft Khedivial Decree annexed to the present arrangement,[1] containing the guarantees considered necessary for the protection of the interests of the Egyptian bondholders, on the condition that, after its promulgation, it cannot be modified in any way without the consent of the Powers signatory of the Convention of London of 1885.

It is agreed that the post of Director-Gerneral of Antiquities in Egypt shall continue, as in the past, to be entrusted to a French *savant*.

The French schools in Egypt shall continue to enjoy the same liberty as in the past.

ART. 2. The Government of the French Republic declare that they have no intention of altering the political status of Morocco.

His Britannic Majesty's Government, for their part, recognise that it appertains to France, more paticularly as a Power whose dominions are conterminous for a great distance with those of Morocco, to preserve order in that country, and to provide assistance for the purpose of all administrative, economic, financial, and military reforms which it may require.

They declare that they will not obstruct the action taken by France for this purpose, provided that such action shall leave intact the rights which Great Britian, in virtue of treaties, conventions, and usage, enjoys in Morocco, including the right of coasting trade between the ports of Morocco, enjoyed by British vessels since 1901.

ART. 3. His Britannic Majesty's Government, for their part, will respect the rights which France, in virtue of treaties, conventions, and usage, enjoys in Egypt, including the right of coasting trade between Egyptian ports accorded to French vessels.

ART. 4. The two Governments, being equally attached to the principle of commercial liberty both in Egypt and Morocco, declare that they will not, in those countries, countenance any inequality either in the imposition of customs duties or other taxes, or of railway transport charges.

The trade of both nations with Morocco

---

1. Not reproduced here. For text of this draft decree and related correspondence, see *Treaty Series, 1905*, no. 6, Cd. 2384.

and with Egypt shall enjoy the same treatment in transit through the French and British possessions in Africa. An agreement between the two Governments shall settle the conditions of such transit and shall determine the points of entry.

This mutual engagement shall be binding for a period of thirty years. Unless this stipulation is expressly denounced at least one year in advance, the period shall be extended for five years at a time.

Nevertheless, the Government of the French Republic reserve to themselves in Morocco, and His Britannic Majesty's Government reserve to themselves in Egypt, the right to see that the concessions for roads, railways, ports, &c., are only granted on such conditions as will maintain intact the authority of the State over these great undertakings of public interest.

ART. 5. His Britannic Majesty's Government declare that they will use their influence in order that the French officials now in the Egyptian service may not be placed under conditions less advantageous than those applying to the British officials in the same service.

The Government of the French Republic, for their part, would make no objection to the application of analogous conditions to British officials now in the Moorish service.

ART. 6. In order to ensure the free passage of the Suez Canal, His Britannic Majesty's Government declare that they adhere to the stipulations of the treaty of the 29th October, 1888, and that they agree to their being put in force. The free passage of the Canal being thus guaranteed, the execution of the last sentence of paragraph 1 as well as of paragraph 2 of article 8 of that treaty will remain in abeyance.

ART. 7. In order to secure the free passage of the Straits of Gibraltar, the two Governments agree not to permit the erection of any fortifications or strategic works on that portion of the coast of Morocco comprised between, but not including, Melilla and the heights which command the right bank of the River Sebou.

This condition does not, however, apply to the places at present in the occupation of Spain on the Moorish coast of the Mediterranean.

ART. 8. The two Governments, inspired by their feeling of sincere friendship for Spain, take into special consideration the interests which that country derives from her geographical position and from her territorial possessions on the Moorish coast of the Mediterranean. In regard to these interests the French Government will come to an understanding with the Spanish Government.

The agreement which may be come to on the subject between France and Spain shall be communicated to His Britannic Majesty's Government.

ART. 9. The two Governments agree to afford to one another their diplomatic support, in order to obtain the execution of the clauses of the present Declaration regarding Egypt and Morocco.

Secret Articles

ART. 1. In the event of either Government finding themselves constrained, by the force of circumstances, to modify their policy in respect to Egypt or Morocco, the engagements which they have undertaken towards each other by articles 4, 6, and 7 of the Declaration of to-day's date would remain intact.

ART. 2. His Britannic Majesty's Government have no present intention of proposing to the Powers any changes in the system of the Capitulations, or in the judicial organisation of Egypt.

In the event of their considering it desirable to introduce in Egypt reforms tending to assimilate the Egyptian legislative system to that in force in other civilised countries, the Government of the French Republic will not refuse to entertain any such proposals, on the understanding that His Britannic Majesty's Government will agree to entertain the suggestions that the Government of the French Republic may have to make to them with a view of introducing similar reforms in Morocco.

ART. 3. The two Governments agree that a certain extent of Moorish territory adjacent to Melilla, Ceuta, and other *présides* should, whenever the Sultan ceases to exercise authority over it, come within the sphere of influence of Spain, and that the administration of the coast from Melilla as far as, but not including, the heights on the right bank of the Sebou shall be entrusted to Spain.

Nevertheless, Spain would previously

have to give her formal assent to the provisions of articles 4 and 7 of the Declaration of to-day's date, and undertake to carry them out.

She would also have to undertake not to alienate the whole, or a part, of the territories placed under her authority or in her sphere of influence.

ART. 4. If Spain, when invited to assent to the provisions of the preceding article, should think proper to decline, the arrangement between France and Great Britain, as embodied in the Declaration of to-day's date, would be none the less at once applicable.

ART. 5. Should the consent of the other Powers to the draft Decree mentioned in article 1 of the Declaration of to-day's date not be obtained, the Government of the French Republic will not oppose the repayment at par of the Guaranteed, Privileged, and Unified Debts after the 15th July, 1910.

165. DECLARATION AND CONVENTION ON MOROCCO: FRANCE AND SPAIN
3 October 1904

[Translated from the French texts in Rivière, *Traités, codes, et lois du Maroc*, 1: 79–81]

When the French foreign minister, Theophile Delcassé, launched his slow-motion diplomacy for expansion into Morocco, he aimed at neutralizing the international system created in 1880 (Doc. 139) by winning over France's main contenders one by one through the offer of compensation. The French understanding with Italy, providing for mutual recognition of respective ambitions in Morocco and Tripoli, was reached in two stages in 1900 and 1902 (Doc. 157). The exchanges with Italy were still in an early phase when Delcassé started treating with Spain to spell out the details of their prospective accommodation. Spain was the only European power already physically present in Morocco. The presidios, or fortified ports, of Ceuta and Melilla and scattered islands along the North African coast formed, by the standards of European expansion at the time, an irrefutable basis for the claim to territory in Morocco if it should be put on the imperial auction block. In support of such claims, the Spanish imperialists insisted that it would halt their country's declining prestige and would shore up its strategic defense by keeping other European powers from establishing themselves on the other side of the narrows that join the Atlantic to the Mediterranean. A convention incorporating the promise of the division of Morocco between France and Spain had been initialed for signature by December 1902, only to be left dangling as an unsigned draft because an unexpected change of government at Madrid yielded an abrupt reversal of Spanish diplomacy. The new Conservative government under Francisco Silvela refused to sign the convention, seeking instead the guidance of Lord Lansdowne, the British foreign minister, who advised stalling for time and offered assurances of support from London. Soon thereafter France and Britain opened their own negotiations for the barter deal on Morocco and Egypt concluded in April 1904 (Doc. 164). Only then were the French talks with Spain resumed; they ended in the issuance of the following public declaration and secret convention. In the declaration the signatories announced their adherence to the British-French entente of the preceding April, confirmed by an exchange of letters between Paul Cambon, the French ambassador in London, and the marquess of Lansdowne, the British foreign minister (texts in Great Britain, *Parliamentary Papers, 1912,* Morocco no. 4 [1911], Cd. 6010, pp. 6–7) Andrew, *Théophile Delcassé,* chaps. 7, 9, 11; E. Anderson, *First Moroccan Crisis,* pp. 35–40, 118–25; Tardieu, "France et Espagne"; Rouard de Card, *Les relations de l'Espagne et du Maroc,* and *La question marocaine;* Maura y Gamazo, *La question du Maroc au point de vue espagnol;* Gourdin, *La politique française au Maroc,* pp. 169–82; Touron, *Notre protectorat marocain,* chap. 6; Donnadieu, *Les relations diplomatiques de l'Espagne et du Maroc,* pp. 103–18; Vidal, *La politique de l'Espagne au Maroc,* pp. 137–69.

1. The French-Spanish Declaration

The Government of the French Republic and the Government of His Majesty the King of Spain, having agreed to determine the scope of rights and the guarantee of interests which accrue to France from its Algerian possessions and to Spain from its possessions on the coast of Morocco, and the Government of His Majesty the King of Spain consequently having adhered to the French-English Declaration on Morocco and Egypt of 8 April 1904, which has been communicated to him by the Government of the French Republic, declare that they remain firmly attached to the integrity of the Moroccan Empire under the sovereignty of the Sultan.

In faith of which the undersigned, His Excellency the Minister of Foreign Affairs and His Excellency the Ambassador Extraordinary and Plenipotentiary of His Majesty the King of Spain accredited to the President of the French Republic, duly authorized to this effect, have prepared the present declaration to which they have affixed their seals. . . .

2. French-Spanish Convention on Morocco

The President of the French Republic and His Majesty the King of Spain, wishing to determine the scope of rights and the guarantee of interests which accrue to France from its Algerian possessions and to Spain from its possessions on the coast of Morocco, have decided to conclude a Convention and have appointed to that end as their Plenipotentiaries, that is to say:

The President of the French Republic:

His Excellency Théophile Declassé, Deputy, Minister of Foreign Affairs of the French Republic, etc. . . .

And His Majesty the King of Spain: His Excellency de Léon y Castillo, Marquis del Muni, His Ambassador Extraordinary and Plenipotentiary to the President of the French Republic, etc. . . .

Who, after having communicated to each other their full powers, found to be in good and due form, have agreed upon the following articles:

ART. 1. Spain adheres, in the terms of the present Convention, to the French-English Declaration of 8 April 1904 on Morocco and on Egypt.

ART. 2. The region situated to the west and to the north of the line designated below constitutes the sphere of influence which accrues to Spain from its possessions on the Moroccan coast of the Mediterranean.

In this zone the same [right of] action is reserved for Spain which is acknowledged for France by the second paragraph of Article 2 of the Declaration of 8 April 1904 on Morocco and on Egypt.

However, bearing in mind the present difficulties and the interest which the two parties have in overcoming them, Spain declares that it will not exercise this [right of] action except after agreement with France in the first period of the application of the present Convention, a period which shall not exceed fifteen years from [the date of] the signature of the Convention.

France, on its side, in the same period, wishing that the rights and interests acknowledged for Spain by the present Convention shall always be respected, will notify the Government of the King in advance of its action toward the Sultan of Morocco in whatever concerns the Spanish sphere of influence.

After the expiration of the first period and for the duration of the status quo, [any] action of France toward the Moroccan Government in whatever concerns the sphere of influence reserved to Spain shall be carried out only after agreement with the Spanish Government.

In the first period the Government of the French Republic shall do its utmost in order that, in two of the customs ports of the region designated below, the delegate of the bondholders of the Moroccan loan of 12 July 1904 shall be of Spanish nationality.

Starting from the mouth of the Muluya in the Mediterranean Sea, the line referred to above shall follow the thalweg of this river to the alignment of the crest of the heights closest to the left bank of the Wadi [River] Defla. From this point, and without in any case interrupting the course of the Muluya, the line of demarcation shall follow as directly as possible the actual line separating the basins of the Muluya and the Wadi Inawin from that of the Wadi Kirt; it shall then continue toward the west following the actual line that separates the basins of the Wadi Inawin and Wadi Sibu from those of the Wadi Kirt and the Wadi Wirgha, so as to reach Jabal Mawlay Bou-Chta through the northernmost crest. It shall then rise toward the north, keeping a distance of at least 25 kilometers east the road from Fez to Qsar al-Kabir [Alcazar] through Wazzan until it reaches the Wadi Lukkos or the Wadi al-Kus, whose thalweg it shall descend for a distance of 5 kilometers downstream from the intersection of that river with the aforementioned route from Qsar al-Kabir through Wazzan. From this point it shall reach as directly as possible the coast of the Atlantic Ocean above the lagoon of al-Zirga.

This delimitation conforms to the delimitation marked on the map annexed to the present Convention under no. 1.*

ART. 3. If the political state of Morocco and the Sharifi Government should deterio-

rate, or if, because of the weakness of the government and its persistent inability to assure security and public order, or for any other reason ascertained by common agreement, the maintenance of the status quo should become impossible, Spain may exercise freely its [right of] action in the region delimited in the preceding article, which from now on shall constitute its sphere of influence.

ART. 4. The Moroccan Government having, under Article 8 of the treaty of 26 April 1860, ceded to Spain an establishment in Santa Cruz de Mar Pequeña (Ifni), it is agreed that the territory of that establishment will not extend beyond the stream of the Wadi Tazerwalt, from its source to it confluence with the Wadi Mesa and following the stream of the Wadi Mesa from this confluence to the sea, in accordance with Map No. 2, annexed to the present Convention.*

ART. 5. In order to complete the delimitation indicated in the first Article of the convention of 27 June 1900, it is agreed that the demarcation between the French and Spanish spheres of influence shall start from the intersection of the meridian 14° 20′ west of Paris with the 26th degree of the north latitude, which it shall follow toward the east until its meeting with the 11th meridian west of Paris. It shall follow this meridian until its junction with the Wadi Draa, then the thalweg of the Wadi Draa until its junction with the 10th meridian west of Paris, finally the 10th meridian west of Paris, until the actual line between the basins of the Wadi Draa and of the Wadi Sus, and then between the coastal basins of the Wadi Mesa and of the Wadi Nun to the point closest to the source of the Wadi Tazerwalt. This delimitation conforms to the delimitation traced on Map No. 2 already cited and annexed to the present Convention.*

ART. 6. Articles 4 and 5 shall come into force at the same time as Article 2 of the present Convention.

However, the Government of the French Republic agrees that Spain may establish itself at any moment in the section defined by Article 4, on condition that it first

---

* Not reproduced here.

reaches an understanding with the [Ottoman] Sultan.

Similarly, the Government of the French Republic shall henceforth acknowledge that the Spanish Government [enjoys] full liberty of action in the region included between the 26° 40′ north latitude and the 11th meridian west of Paris, which lie outside Moroccan territory.

ART. 7. Spain pledges neither to alienate nor to cede in any form, even temporarily, the whole or part of the territories designated in Articles 2, 4, and 5 of the present Convention.

ART. 8. If in the application of Articles 2, 4, and 5 of the present Convention a military action should be forced on one of the two Contracting Parties, it shall immediately inform the other Party. In any case, it shall not seek the assistance of a foreign Powers.

ART. 9. The town of Tangier shall keep its special character, which the presence of the diplomatic corps and its municipal and sanitary institutions give it.

ART. 10. So long as the present political status lasts, schemes for public works, railroads, roads, [and] canals, starting at a point in Morocco and ending in a district envisaged in Article 2, and vice versa, shall be carried out by such companies as may be formed by Frenchmen and Spaniards.

Similarly, Frenchmen and Spaniards in Morocco may form partnerships for the working of mines, quarries, and economic enterprises in general.

ART. 11. Existing Spanish schools and establishments in Morocco shall be respected. The circulation of Spanish currency shall be neither stopped nor hindered.

Spaniards shall continue to enjoy in Morocco the rights which the treaties, conventions, and existing customs assure them, including the right of navigation and of fishing in the waters and ports of Morocco.

ART. 12. Frenchmen shall enjoy in the districts designated in Articles 2, 4, and 5 of the present Convention the same rights as are reserved in the preceding article for Spaniards in the rest of Morocco.

ART. 13. If the Moroccan Government should prohibit the sale [of arms and ammunition] within its territory, the two Contracting Powers engage to take the necessary measures in their African possessions to prevent the smuggling of arms and ammunition into Morocco.

ART. 14. It is understood that the zone envisaged in the first paragraph of Article 7 of the French-English Declaration of 8 April 1904 on Morocco and on Egypt begins on the coast 30 kilometers southeast of Melilla.

ART. 15. If the notice of termination foreseen in paragraph 3 of Article 4 of the French-English Declaration on Morocco and on Egypt takes place, the French and Spanish Governments shall work together for the establishment of an economic regime which particularly responds to their reciprocal interests.

ART. 16. The present Convention will be published when the two governments shall judge by common agreement that this may be accomplished without harm.

In any case, it might be published by one of the two governments at the expiration of the first period of its application, a period that is defined in paragraph 3 of Article 2. . . .

166. EXCHANGE OF NOTES AND DECLARATION ON A CONFERENCE ON MOROCCO: FRANCE AND GERMANY
8 July 1905

[Translated from the French text in Rivière, *Traités, codes, et lois du Maroc*, 1: 86–87]

From the time that French Foreign Minister Delcassé had framed the strategy of undoing the international system on Morocco, which had been fixed at Madrid in

1880 (Doc. 139), by buying off—or compensating, to use the terminology of political science in the analysis of the diplomacy of balanced power—the primary opponents of French aspirations in Morocco, they were being accommodated one by one. Thus Delcassé had agreed in 1902 that Italy might be paid off in Libya (Doc. 157); in 1904 Britain, in Egypt (Doc. 164); and later in the same year Spain, in part of Morocco itself (Doc. 165). Germany, the last of the major European adversaries of French annexation in Morocco, revealed Delcassé's blind spot. He at first rejected the pleas of his advisers and of the *parti colonial*, or pressure group for imperial expansion, to clear the plans with Germany too. The French foreign minister seemed unwilling to negotiate directly with Germany for fear that such exchanges might be interpreted by fellow Frenchmen as endorsement of the German annexation of Alsace-Lorraine and by Germany as a signal to expand its influence in the Mediterranean. Thus Delcassé gambled on a bypass. The German government, however, refused to play a passive role. Foreign Minister Prince Bernhard von Bülow accordingly resolved to turn the tables on Delcassé. On instructions from Berlin, the German chargé at Tangier encouraged Mawlay 'Abd al-'Aziz (1894–1908) to resist French plans for the military, economic, and fiscal reorganization of his realm. To emphasize German interest, Bülow staged with appropriate fanfare at the end of March 1905 a visit to Tangier by Kaiser Wilhelm II, who informed the French chargé that Germany would insist on viewing Morocco as a sovereign state and on upholding the principles of free trade and equal rights for all concerned outside powers. When Delcassé finally consented in mid-April 1905 to bilateral talks with Germany on Morocco, Bülow responded by demanding an international conference. Moreover, in response to German pressure, Delcassé was dismissed on 8 June as minister of foreign affairs, a post that he had filled for eight years. German obstinacy, which persisted even after Delcassé's dismissal, rallied Britain to France's support, forcing the German Foreign Ministry to reach an understanding with France; this was confirmed in an exchange of letters between Maurice Rouvier, the premier and foreign minister, and Prince Hugo von Radolin, the German ambassador at Paris, and in a joint declaration, both reproduced below. For references, see Doc. 168.

1. Rouvier to Radolin

The Government of the Republic is convinced, as a result of the conversations that have taken place in Paris and Berlin between the representatives of the two countries, that the [German] Imperial Government will not pursue at the conference proposed by the Sultan of Morocco any goal which might compromise the legitimate interests of France in that country or which might prejudice the rights of France resulting from its treaties or arrangements, and in harmony with the following principles:

[the] sovereignty and independence of the Sultan;

[the] integrity of his Empire;

economic freedom without inequality;

[the] usefulness of police reforms and of financial reforms, the introduction of which shall be regulated for a short period by international accord; [and]

recognition of the situation caused France in Morocco by the contiguity of Algeria and the Sharifi Empire over a long distance, by the particular relations between the two limitrophe countries resulting therefrom, and by the special interest of France in the stability of the Sharifi Empire.

Consequently the Government of the Republic [of France] drops its initial objections to the conference and agrees to attend it.

2. Radolin to Rouvier

The Government of the Republic, agreeing to attend the conference proposed by the Sultan of Morcco, the Imperial Government has instructed me to confirm to you its verbal declarations according to which it will not pursue at the conference any goal which might compromise the legitimate interests of France in Morocco or which might prejudice the rights of France resulting from its treaties or arrangements, and in harmony with the following principles:

[the] sovereignty and independence of the Sultan;

[the] integrity of his Empire;

economic liberty without inequality;

[the] usefulness of police reforms and financial reforms the introduction of which will be regulated for a short period by international accord; [and]

recognition of the situation caused France in Morocco by the contiguity of Algeria and the Sharifi Empire over a long distance, by the particular relations between the two limitrophe countries resulting therefrom, and by the special interest of France in the stability of the Sharifi Empire.

3. Joint Declaration

The Government of the Republic [of France] and the German Government agree:

1. to recall simultaneously to Tangier their missions now in Fez as soon as the conference is convened; [and]

2. to have their representatives by common accord advise the Sultan of Morocco, on fixing the agenda, that he should propose to the Conference the terms stipulated in the letters exchanged on 8 July between the [Franch] President of the Council [and] Minister of Foreign Affairs and the German Ambassador in Paris.

167. AGREEMENT TO REGULATE THE APPLICATION OF THE 1904 CONVENTION ON MOROCCO: FRANCE AND SPAIN
1 September 1905

[Translated from the French text in Rivière, *Traités, codes, et lois du Maroc*, 1: 82–3]

In preparation for the international conference on Morocco, which was scheduled to meet in Spain at an early date, France and Spain decided in the secret agreement reproduced below to concert plans for joint but exclusive technical aid to Morocco in the "reorganization" of its administration of police, finance, currency, customs, and economic and social policy. By this means, the two powers with articulated territorial designs on Morocco hoped to frustrate Germany's scheme for keeping the Moroccan question internationalized and to prevent Germany from taking part in the technical aid program. More than that, they hoped to prepare the ground for the seizure of power in Morocco and the division between them of its territory. For references, see Doc. 165.

ART. 1. *Police of Ports.* The corps of military police which must be organized as soon as possible in the ports of the Sharifi Empire shall be recuited among native troops. In accord with Spain, France agrees that all the chiefs, officers, and noncommissioned officers who may be charged with the instruction and command of the said troops in the ports of Tetouan and Larache must be of Spanish nationality. In accord with France, Spain on its side agrees that all the chiefs, officers, and noncommissioned officers who may be charged with the instruction and command of police troops in the ports of Rabat and Casablanca must be of French nationality. In accordance with the provisions of Article 9 of the treaty of 3 October 1904, it is agreed that the policing of the port of Tangiers shall be entrusted to a French-Spanish corps commanded by a Frenchman This regime shall be revised at the expiration of a period of fifteen years, as the convention of 3 October 1904 provides.

ART. 2. *Supervision and Repression of the Smuggling of Arms.* In conformity with the spirit of Article 13[1] of the said treaty, and with a view to ensuring its execution, it is agreed that the supervision and the repression of arms smuggling on land remains the responsibility of France in the sphere of its Algerian frontier, and the responsibility of Spain in the sphere of all its African localities and possessions.

The supervision and the repression of such smuggling at sea shall be assigned to a naval division of the two Powers which will determine the types [of vessels to use]. Naval officers of the two Powers shall alternately command that division. The command shall be exercised in the first year by an officer of the French navy.

The two government by common accord shall establish rules to be observed for the repression of this smuggling when the right of visitation is exercised, if the exercise of that right should become indispensable to the effectiveness of the repression.

ART. 3. *Economic and Financial Interests.* With a view to assuring on both sides, in the most amicable sense, the exact interpretation of Articles 10, 11, and 12 of the convention of 3 October 1904, it remains understood:

(1) That schemes for public works, railroads, roads and canals, exploitation of mines and quarries, and for all other [proejcts] that are commercial and industrial in nature in the territory of Morocco might be carried out by groups comprising Spaniards and Frenchmen. The two governments mutually undertake to favor by the means at their disposal the creation of these mixed enterprises on the basis of equal rights for the partners according to the proportion of committed capital.

At the expiration of the fifteen-year period for which the convention of 3 October 1904 provides, the two High Contracting Parties shall execute the works to which the preceding paragraph refers in conformity with the rules that they lay down in their respective zones of influence.

(2) Spaniards and Frenchmen, together with their existing establishments and schools in the Moroccan Empire, shall be respected. In any case, they shall always enjoy in Morocco, in the exercise of their professions and in the conduct of their commerical and industrial activities, existing or planned, the same rights and privileges, so that the juridical status of subjects under the jurisdiction of these two nations shall be consistently the same. The merchandise of the two countries shall enjoy identical treatment in its import, distribution, and sale within the Empire. The two High Contracting Parties shall employ all the peaceful means in their power and shall lend each other their mutual assistance with the Sultan and the Makhzan [Government of Morocco] with a view to avoiding now and in the future the modification of this clause by Moroccan authorities as a result of the framing of different rules for the juridical status of persons and the conditions to which the merchandise of the two nations may be subject.

(3) Spanish silver coinage shall continue as in the past to be imported into the Empire [with the assurance that no] measures, direct or indirect, already taken or to be taken in the future, may interfere with such freedom of import, circulation, and value of the said coinage.

The two governments pledge respectively not to allow the creation of direct or indirect obstacles to the provision in the preceding paragraph by commercial or industrial institutions organized in the Moroccan Empire by their respective subjects, and to employ all peaceful means at the disposal of each in order that a share in the capital and the public works of all public enterprises may be offered to the subjects of the two nations.

(4) The Spanish and French governments, agreeing on the necessity to create in Morocco an establishment of credit under the name of the State Bank or any establishment whose presidency shall be

---

1. Mistakenly called Article 18 in the French text.

reserved for France because of the greater number of shares subscribed by it, also agree on the following points:

(a) The ownership of stocks of all kinds and the share of profit reserved for Spain shall be greater than the share of the other Powers taken separately, France excepted.

(b) Spanish personnel in the administration of this establishment and its branches shall be proportionate to the share of capital subscribed by Spain.

(c) This establishment may undertake public works and services in the Moroccan Empire with the assent of or by agreement with the Sultan. It may either conduct them directly or transfer them to other groups and enterprises. However, for the conduct of all these public works and services, the stipulations of paragraphs (a) and (b) above must be observed.

(5) The two governments, Spanish and French, shall enlarge by common accord the present number of Spanish subjects delegated to the customs service of the Empire, reorganized to guarantee the loan recently contracted by the Sultan with French banks a loan which absorbs the loan previously contracted by His Sharifi Majesty with Spanish banks.

ART. 4. The Powers pledge to observe this accord, even if the provisions of Article 17 of the convention of Madrid of 1880 should be extended to all economic and financial matters. They shall endeavor, through their constant pacific actions toward the Sultan and the Makhzan, to ensure the faithful execution of all the stipulations of the present agreement.

Moreover, Spain having firmly decided to move in complete accord with France in the deliberations of the projected conference, and France resolving to act similarly toward Spain, the two governments agree that they will mutually assist each other and will proceed in common agreement in the said deliberations concerning the stipulations of the convention of 3 October 1904, in its most generous and most amicable interpretation, and concerning the different objectives of the present agreement.

They pledge finally to lend each other reciprocally the fullest peaceful assistance on all matters of a general nature concerning Morocco, as the cordial and amicable understanding that exists between them on the affairs of the Sharifi Empire requires.

168. GENERAL ACT AND ADDITIONAL PROTOCOL: INTERNATIONAL CONFERENCE ON MOROCCO AT ALGECIRAS
7 April 1906

(Ratifications deposited in Madrid, 31 December 1906)
[English translated text from Great Britain, *Treaty Series, 1907*, no. 4, Cd. 3302, pp. 37–78]

When France acquiesced in the German demand for an international conference on Morocco, and Germany reciprocated by acknowledging France's special interests there (Doc. 166), the two powers decided nothing except to conduct their sparring match before an international audience comprising Austria-Hungary, Belgium, Great Britain, Italy, Morocco, the Netherlands, Portugal, Russia, Spain, Sweden, and the United States. Germany's tactical aim at the conference was to win decisive reaffirmation of the international system in Morocco. But the undermining of that system had already gone too far, with four of the five contenders committed to European imperial annexation. Besides, given these conditions, Germany had nowhere to go within Morocco itself except by trying to frustrate French ambitions. Ostensibly, the thirteen powers attending the conference at Algeciras (Spain), which opened on 16 January 1906, had accepted Mawlay 'Abd al-'Aziz's invitation to help him frame a program for the repair of the machinery of his government. The Makhzan, as the 'Alawi dynastic establishment was known, had already slid far downhill, partly because of its own diminishing ability to cope with the administration of a truculent tribal society divided by language along lines roughly coinciding with the cleavage between mountain (Berber) and valley (Arab), and partly because of the growing European interference in internal Moroccan affairs, which precluded effective governmental reorganization. The European powers agreed that the Mawlay needed outside help. The questions at issue therefore were the sources of such aid. Would France and Spain procure the exclusive right to draft and execute the plans for governmental revitalization, or would the conferring states, through a third power, seek to exercise superivisory jurisdiction? Almost from the start of the conference, it became manifest that the contest would be decided, if at all, by the arrangements made for the reorganization of the police and for the creation of a state bank. If France (and Spain) alone received either the right to the first or the franchise to the second, it would simply be a matter of time before the aspiring partitioners could reach their goal. Discussion of the subsidiary issues—the introduction of arms transfer controls, tax and customs reforms, and regulations to rationalize public services and the award of concessions—aroused little controversy, and the decisions were swiftly reached. The conference then stalled over rival proposals for restructuring the police force. France advocated that it be assigned that responsibility together with Spain, if need be under the general supervision of Italy. Germany supported a variety of suggestions, all of which had the single object of excluding France from any predominant role. The deadlock was finally broken by a vote on 3 March, when all the conferees except Austria, Germany, and Morocco supported France. Thus isolated, Germany slowly gave way until in the end the management of the police was entrusted to France and Spain under the nominal supervision of a Swiss inspector. All Germany saved from the exercise was face, by mention in the preamble of the following general act of an explicit endorsement of "the triple principle of the sovereignty and independence of His Majesty the Sultan [of Morocco], the integrity of his domains, and economic liberty without any inequality." Having won the contest over the restructuring of the police, France consented to the plans for the management of the projected state bank by its stockholders under the general surveillance of four censors appointed by the national banks of Britain, France, Germany, and Spain. E. Anderson, *First Moroccan Crisis*, chaps. 16–18; Monger, *End of Isolation*, chaps. 8–10; Nicolson, *Sir Arthur Nicolson*, chap. 7; Tardieu, *La conférence d'Algéciras*; Rüdiger, *Die Bedeutung der Algeciras-Konferenz*; L. Maurice, *La politique marocaine de l'Allemagne*, chap. 2; Vidal, *La politique de l'Espagne au Maroc*, pp. 171–200; Hajoui, *Histoire diplomatique du Maroc*, chaps. 5–6; Diercks, *Die Marokkofrage;* Williamson, *Germany and Morocco before 1905*; Manger, "La crise marocaine de 1905"; Bérard, *L'affaire marocaine*, pp. 321–437; Morel, *Morocco in Diplomacy*, pp. 81–121.

. . . Inspired by the interest which attaches to the reign of order, peace, and prosperity in Morocco, and having recognized that this desirable end could only be attained by means of the introduction of reforms based upon the threefold principle of the sovereignty and independence of His Majesty the Sultan, the integrity of his dominions, and economic liberty without any inequality, [the contracting parties] have resolved, on the invitation which has been addressed to them by His Shereefian Majesty, to assemble a Conference at Algeciras, in order to arrive at an understanding respecting the said reforms, as well as to examine the means of providing the resources necessary for their application. . . .

Chapter I.—Declaration Relative to the Organization of the Police

ART. 1. The Conference, called by His Majesty the Sultan to pronounce on the measures necessary for the organization of the police, declares that the measures to be taken are as follows.

ART. 2. The police shall be under the sovereign authority of His Majesty the Sultan. It shall be recruited by the Makhzen from among Moorish Mussulmans, commanded by Moorish Kaïds, and distributed in the eight ports open to commerce.

ART. 3. In order to assist the Sultan in the organization of this police, Spanish officers and non-commissioned officers acting as instructors, and French officers and non-commissioned officers acting as instructors, shall be placed at his disposal by their respective Governments, which shall submit their nominations for the approval of His Shereefian Majesty. A contract drawn between the Makhzen and the instructors in accordance with the regulations contemplated by Article 4, shall determine the conditions of their engagement and fix their pay, which shall not be less than double the pay corresponding to the rank of each officer or non-commissioned officer. They shall be paid, in addition, house allowance, varying according to the locality. Suitable quarters shall be placed at their disposal by the Makhzen, who shall likewise provide the necessary mounts and forage.

The Governments of the countries to which the instructors respectively belong reserve the right to recall them, and to replace them by others approved of and engaged on the same conditions.

ART. 4. These officers and non-commissioned officers shall, for a period of five years from the date of the ratification of the Act of the Conference, give their services to the organization of the Shereefian police forces. They shall be responsible for the instruction and discipline of those forces in accordance with the regulations to be drawn up on the subject; they shall likewise see that the men enrolled are fit for military service. Generally, they shall superintend the administration of the force and the issue of pay, which shall be in the hands of the Amin, assisted by the instructor acting as accounting officer. They shall give technical assistance to the Moorish authorities invested with the command of these forces, in the exercise of that command.

Regulations for the proper working of the recruiting, discipline, instruction, and administration of the police force shall be drawn up by common agreement between the Shereefian Minister of War or his delegate, the Inspector referred to in Article 7, and the French and Spanish instructors of the highest rank.

The regulations shall be submitted to the Diplomatic Body at Tangier, which shall formulate its opinion within one month. On the expiration of such period the regulations shall come into force.

ART. 5. The total strength of the whole effective police force shall not exceed 2,500 men nor be less than 2,000. It shall be distributed according to the importance of the ports, in detachments varying from 150 to 600 men. The number of Spanish and French officers shall be from 16 to 20; that of the Spanish and French non-commissioned officers, from 30 to 40.

ART. 6. The funds necessary for the maintenance and payment of the men and of the officers and non-commissioned officers acting as instructors shall be advanced to the Shereefian Treasury by the State Bank, within the limits of the annual budget assigned to the police, which shall not exceed 2,500,000 pesetas for a strength of 2,500 men.

ART. 7. The working of the police shall, during the same period of five years, be subject to a general inspection, which shall be intrusted by His Shereefian Majesty to a superior officer of the Swiss army, the choice of whom shall be submitted for his approval by the Swiss Federal Government.

This officer shall be styled "Inspector-General," and shall have his residence at Tangier.

He shall inspect the several police detachments at least once a-year, and, as a result of such inspection, draw up a report addressed to the Makhzen.

Apart from the regular reports, he may, if he consider it necessary, draw up special reports on any question concerning the working of the police.

Without intervening directly in the command or the instruction of the force, the Inspector-General shall take note of the results achieved by the Shereefian police as regards the maintenance of order and security in the districts in which such police shall be installed.

ART. 8. A copy of the reports and communications addressed to the Markzen by the Inspector-General on the subject of his mission shall at the same time be handed to the dean of the Diplomatic Body at Tangier, in order that the Diplomatic Body may be in a position to satisfy itself that the Shereefian police are working in accordance with the decisions arrived at by the Conference, and to observe whether they afford, in a manner effective and conformable to the Treaties, security to the persons and property of foreigners as well as to commercial transactions.

ART. 9. In the case of complaints which may be brought before the Diplomatic Body by the Legation interested, the Diplomatic Body may, on advising the Sultan's Representative, request the Inspector-General to make an inquiry and to draw up a report on such complaints, available for any purposes.

ART. 10. The Inspector-General shall receive a yearly salary of 25,000 fr. He shall be granted in addition an allowance of 6,000 fr. for travelling expenses. The Makhzen shall place at his disposal a suitable residence, and provide for the upkeep of his horses.

ART. 11. The material conditions of his engagement and of his establishment, as laid down in Article 10, shall form the subject of a contract between him and the Makhzen. A copy of such contract shall be communicated to the Diplomatic Body.

ART. 12. The staff of instructors of the

Shereefian police (officers and non-commissioned officers) shall be Spanish at Tetuan, mixed at Tangier, Spanish at Laraiche, French at Rabat, mixed at Casablanca, and French at the three other ports.

Chapter II.—Regulations concerning the Detection and Suppression of the Illicit Traffic in Arms

ART. 13. Throughout the whole extent of the Shereefian Empire the importation of, and trade in, warlike arms, parts of arms, ammunition of all kinds, whether loaded or unloaded, powder, saltpetre, guncotton, nitro-glycerine, and all materials destined exclusively for the manufacture of ammunition are prohibited, except in the cases specified in Articles 14 and 15.

ART. 14. Explosives necessary for industrial purposes and for public works may, however, be imported. Regulations on the lines indicated in Article 18 shall determine the conditions on which such importation may take place.

ART. 15. Arms, parts of arms, and ammunition intended for the forces of His Shereefian Majesty shall be admitted on the following formalities being observed:—

A declaration, signed by the Moorish Minister for War, stating the number and kind of such supplies ordered from foreign industries, must be presented to the Legation of the country of origin, which shall affix its *visa*.

Cases and packages containing arms and ammunition, delivered to the order of the Moorish Government, shall be cleared through the Customs on the presentation of—

1. The declaration aforesaid;

2. The bill of lading, specifying the number and weight of the packages, and the number and kind of the arms and ammunition which they contain. This document must be certified by the Legation of the country of origin, which must indorse thereon the successive amounts previously cleared through the Customs. Such certification shall be refused so soon as delivery of the whole of the order has been completed.

ART. 16. The importation of sporting and high-priced arms, parts of arms, and cartridges, loaded or empty, is likewise prohibited. Provided, however, that such importation may be authorized—

1. For the strictly personal requirements of the importer;

2. For the supply of the arms-stores licensed in conformity with Article 18.

ART. 17. Sporting and high-priced arms and ammunition shall be admitted for the strictly personal requirements of the importer on presentation of a permit issued by the Representative of the Makhzen at Tangier. If the importer be a foreigner, the permit shall only be made out on the demand of his Legation.

As regards sporting ammunition, each permit shall be for not more than 1,000 cartridges, or the materials necessary for the manufacture of not more than 1,000 cartridges.

Such permit shall be given to such persons only as shall not have been convicted of an offence.

ART. 18. The trade in non-rifled sporting or high-priced arms of foreign make, and in ammunition for the same, shall be regulated, as soon as circumstances permit, by a Shereefian Order made in conformity with the advice of the Diplomatic Body at Tangier, whose decision shall be declared by a majority of votes. The same procedure shall be followed with regard to Orders made with the object of suspending or restricting this traffic.

Only persons who shall have obtained a special and temporary licence from the Moorish Government shall be permitted to open and carry on the businesses of retail stores for the sale of sporting arms and ammunition. Such licence shall only be granted on receipt of a written request from the applicant, supported by a recommendation from his Legation.

The number of retail stores which may be opened at Tangier, and eventually in such ports as may hereafter be specified, shall be determined by regulations drawn up in the manner provided in the first paragraph of this Article. Such regulations shall prescribe the formalities to be observed in connection with the importation of explosives intended for industrial purposes and for public works, and of arms and ammunition to be stocked in the retail

stores, and shall determine the maximum quantities that may be so stocked.

In cases of infraction of the regulations, the licence may be withdrawn, either temporarily or definitively, without prejudice to such further penalties as may be incurred by the offenders.

ART. 19. The penalty for importing, or attempting to import, prohibited goods shall be the confiscation of such goods, in addition to the penalties and fines specified below, which shall be inflicted by the competent courts.

ART. 20. The penalty for importing, or attempting to import, prohibited goods at a port open to commerce, or at a custom-house, shall be—

1. A fine of not less than 500 and not exceeding 2,000 pesetas, and a supplementary fine equal to three times the value of the imported goods;

2. Imprisonment for a period of not less than five days and not exceeding one year;

Or one of these two penalties only.

ART. 21. The penalty for importing, or attempting to import, prohibited goods at a place other than a port open to commerce or a custom-house shall be—

1. A fine of not less than 1,000 and not exceeding 5,000 pesetas, and a supplementary fine equal to three times the value of the imported goods;

2. Imprisonment for a period of not less than three months and not exceeding two years;

Or one of these two penalties only.

ART. 22. The penalties for fraudulently selling, receiving, or retailing goods prohibited by the present regulations shall be those laid down in Article 20.

ART. 23. Accessories to the offences specified in Articles 20, 21, and 22 shall be liable to the same penalties as the principal offenders. The question of what consitutes complicity shall be determined in accordance with the law administered by the court before which the particular case is heard.

ART. 24. Whenever there is good reason to suspect that a vessel anchored in a port open to commerce is carrying arms, ammunition, or other prohibited goods with a view to their importation into Morocco, the Shereefian Customs officers shall so inform the competent consular authority, in order that the latter may, with the assistance of an officer delegated by the Shereefian Customs, proceed to such inquiries, inspection, or search as many be deemed necessary.

ART. 25. In cases of the importation, or attempted importation, of prohibited goods by sea, at a place other than a port open to commerce, the Moorish Customs authorities may take the vessel to the nearest port, to be there handed over to the consular authority, who shall have the right to seize and retain it until payment of the prescribed fines. The vessel shall, however, be released at any stage of the proceedings on the deposit with the consular authority of the maximum amount of the fine, or on good security for the payment of the same being accepted by the Customs, provided such release do not impede the judicial investigation.

ART. 26. The Makhzen shall retain the confiscated goods for the purpose of sale in a foreign country or for its own use, if the goods are serviceable, provided always that the subjects of the Empire shall not obtain possession of them.

Boats used for illicitly landing goods may be confiscated, and shall, if so confiscated, be sold for the benefit of the Shereefian Treasury.

ART. 27. The sale of arms discarded by the Moorish Government shall be prohibited throughout the Shereefian Empire.

ART. 28. Rewards, payable out of the proceeds of the fines imposed, shall be granted to imformers who shall have been instrumental in discovering prohibited goods, as well as to the officials who shall have effected their seizure; such rewards shall be paid in the following manner, viz.: after deduction, if necessary, of the costs of the proceedings, one-third to be divided by the Customs authorities amongst the imformers, one-third amongst the officials who shall have seized the goods, and one-third to go to the Moorish Treasury.

If the seizure have been effected without the intervention of an informer, one-half of the amount of the fines shall be awarded to the officials who seized the vessel, and the remaining half to the Shereefian Treasury.

ART. 29. The Moorish Customs authorities shall notify direct to the foreign diplomatic or consular authorities any cases of infraction of the present regulations committed by persons under their jurisdiction, in order that such persons may be prosecuted before the competent court.

Cases of similar infractions committed by Moorish subjects shall be notified by the Customs Administration direct to the Shereefian authorities.

An officer delegated by the Customs shall be charged with the duty of watching the proceeding in cases pending before the different courts.

ART. 30. In the region adjoining the Algerian frontier the enforcement of the regulations respecting the illicit trade in arms shall be the exclusive concern of France and Morocco.

Similarly, in the Riff country, and in the regions adjoining the frontier of the Spanish possessions generally, the enforcement of the regulations respecting the illicit trade in arms shall be the exclusive concern of Spain and Morocco.

Chapter III.—Act of Concession for a State Bank

ART. 31. A bank shall be established in Morocco, under the name of "The Morocco State Bank," to exercise the rights hereinafter specified, which are granted to it by His Majesty the Sultan for a period of forty years from the date of the ratification of the present Act.

ART. 32. The Bank, which shall have power to carry on all business within the proper province of banking, shall have the exclusive privilege of issuing notes to bearer, payable on presentation, and receivable as legal tender at the public treasuries of the Moorish Empire.

The Bank shall, for a period of two years from the date of starting business, maintain a each reserve equal to not less than one-half the value of its notes in circulation, and, after the expiration of the said period of two years, equal to not less than one-third of such value. Not less than one-third of such each reserve shall be in gold bullion or gold coin.

ART. 33. The Bank shall, to the exclusion of any other bank or financial establishment, discharge the duties of disbursing Treasurer of the Empire. To this end the Moorish Government shall take the necessary measures to effect the payment into the Bank of the proceeds of the customs, except that portion thereof which is hypothecated for the service of the loan of 1904, as well as of such other revenues as the Government may indicate.

As regards the proceeds of the special tax established with a view to carry out certain public works, the Moorish Government shall cause them to be paid into the Bank, together with such revenues as it may eventually hypothecate as security for its loans, the Bank being specially charged with the service thereof, with the exception, however, of the loan of 1904, which is governed by a special contract.

ART. 34. The Bank shall be the financial agent of the Government both within and outside the Empire, without prejudice to the right of the Government to apply to other banking houses or financial establishments for its public loans. In respect of the said loans, however, the Bank shall enjoy a right of preference, other conditions being equal, over any other banking houses or financial establishments.

But, as regards Treasury bonds and other short term Treasury bills which the Moorish Government may desire to negotiate without having recourse to a public issue, the Bank shall, to the exclusion of any other establishment, be charged with their negotiation on behalf of the Moorish Government, whether in Morocco or abroad.

ART. 35. The Bank shall make advances to the Moorish Government on current account to an amount not exceeding 1,000000 fr., chargeable against Treasury receipts.

The Bank shall likewise, for a period of ten years from its constitution, open a credit account for the Government, which shall not exceed two-thirds of its initial capital. The amounts so credited shall be spread over several years, and employed primarily to meet the expenses of the establishment and upkeep of the police forces organized in accordance with the decisions arrived at by the Conference, and, secondarily, to meet the expenditure on such works of public interest as may not be charged to the special fund contemplated by the Article next following.

The rate of interest for these two advance shall be at most 7 per cent., including bankers' commission, and the Bank shall be at liberty to require the Government to place in its hands, as security for the amount, an equivalent sum in Treasury bonds.

If the Moorish Government contract a loan before the expiration of a period of ten years, the Bank shall be entitled to the immediate repayment of the advances made in accordance with the second paragraph of the present Article.

ART. 36. The proceeds of the special tax (Articles 33 and 66) shall form a special fund, for which the Bank shall keep a separate account. This fund shall be employed in accordance with the rules laid down by the Conference.

In case of an insufficiency of funds, and chargeable to subsequent receipts, the Bank may open a credit for such fund, of which the amount shall not exceed the total receipts for the preceding year.

The conditions respecting the rates of interest and commission shall be the same as those laid down in the preceding Article as regards the advance to the Treasury on current account.

ART. 37. The Bank shall adopt such measures as it may deem expedient for ameliorating the monetary situation in Morocco. Spainish money shall be permitted as heretofore to circulate as legal tender.

Consequently, the Bank shall exclusively be charged with the purchase of the precious metals, with the minting and melting-down of coins, as well as with all other monetary operations, which it shall carry out on account and for the profit of the Moorish Government.

ART. 38. The Bank, of which the head office shall be at Tangier, shall establish branches and agencies in the principal towns of Morocco, and in such other places as it may deem expedient.

ART. 39. The sites necessary for the premises of the Bank, and of its branches and agencies in Morocco, shall be placed at its disposal gratis by the Government, and, on the expiration of the Consession, the Government shall resume possession thereof, and shall repay to the Bank the cost of the erection of such premises. The Bank shall, morevoer, be entitled to acquire any building or site which it may need for the same purpose.

ART. 40. The Shereefian Government shall insure and be responsible for the security and protection of the Banks, its branches and agencies. With this view, it shall in each town place an adequate guard at the disposal of every such establishment.

ART. 41. The Bank, its branches and agencies shall be exempt from all taxes or dues, ordinary or extraordinary, whether now in force or to be hereafter imposed; this provision shall apply equally to the real property appropriated to its use as well as to the certificates and coupons of shares and to its notes. The importation and exportation of bullion and coin intended for the operations of the Bank shall be authorized, and shall be exempted from all duty.

ART. 42. The Shereefian Government shall exercise its high control over the Bank through a Moorish High Commissioner, whom it shall appoint after previous agreement with the board of directors of the Bank.

The High Commissioner shall have the right to examine into the management of the Bank; he shall control the issue of bank see that the provisions of the Concession are strictly observed.

The High Commissioner shall sign or affix his seal to every note; he shall be charged with the supervision of the relations between the Bank and the Imperial Treasury.

He shall not be at liberty to interfere in the administration or business of the Bank, but the shall always have the right to attend the meetings of the Censors.

The Shereefian Government shall appoint one or two Assistant Commissioners, who shall be specially charged with the control of the financial dealings of the Treasury with the Bank.

ART. 43. Regulations determining the relations between the Bank and the Moorish Government shall be drawn up by the Special Committee contemplated in Article 57, and shall be approved by the Censors.

ART. 44. The Bank, constituted, with the approval of His Shereefian Majesty, as a Limited Liability Company, shall be subject to the law of France governing the matter.

ART. 45. Actions instituted by the Bank in Morocco shall be tried before the Consular Court of the defendant, or before the Moorish courts, in accordance with the rules of competence laid down in the Treaties and Shereefian Firmans.

Actions brought against the Bank in Morocco shall be tried before a special court composed of three Consular magistrates and two assessors. The Diplomatic Body shall draw up annually the list of magistrates and assessors, and of their substitutes.

This court shall in such actions apply the rules of law, procedure, and competence laid down by French law in matters of commerce. Appeals from judgments pronounced by this court shall lie to the Federal Court at Lausanne, whose decision shall be final.

ART. 46. In case of dispute over the terms of the Concession, or of litigation between the Moorish Government and the Bank, the issue shall be referred to the Federal Court at Lausanne without appeal or recourse.

In like manner, all disputes which may arise between the shareholders and the Bank as to the observance of the statutes or the conduct of the Bank's business, shall be referred to the same court, without appeal or recourse.

ART. 47. The statutes of the Bank shall be drawn up, in accordance with the following bases, by a special committee, as provided for in Article 57. They shall be approved by the Censors and ratified by the general meeting of shareholders.

ART. 48. The general meeting at which the company is constituted shall decide upon the place at which the meetings of shareholders and those of the board of directors shall be held; the latter shall, however, be at liberty to meet in any other town if it sees fit to do so.

The head office of the Bank shall be at Tangier.

ART. 49. The Bank shall be administered by a board of directors consisting of as many members as there are allotted portions in the initial capital.

The directors shall have the most extensive powers for the administration and management of the company; in particular, they shall appoint the managers, sub managers, and members of the committee referred to in Article 54, as well as the managers of branches and agencies.

The staff of the company shall, as far as possible, be recruited from among the nationals of the several Powers which have participated in the subscription of the capital.

ART. 50. The directors, who shall be appointed by the general meeting of shareholders, shall, subject to the approval of such meeting, be nominated by the groups subscribing the capital.

The first board shall remain in office for five years. On the expiration of this period, it shall be renewed at the rate of three members annually. The order in which the directors retire shall be determined by lot; they shall be eligible for re-election.

On the constitution of the company, each of the subscribing groups shall have the right to nominate as many directors as it shall have subscribed allotted protions of the capital, provided such groups shall be under no obligation to choose candidates of their own nationality.

The subscribing groups shall only preserve their right of nominating directors, on the occasion of the latter being replaced or their mandate renewed, so long as they are able to give proof of still being in possession of at least one-half of each allotted portion in respect of which they exercise such right.

In the event of a subscribing group ceasing, in virtue of these provisions, to be in a position to nominate a director, the general meeting of shareholders shall itself make the nomination.

ART. 51. Each of the following institutions, viz., the German Imperial Bank, the Bank of England, the Bank of Spain, and the Bank of France, shall, with the approval of its Government, appoint a Censor to the State Bank of Morocco.

The Censors shall remain in office for four years. Retiring Censors may be reappointed.

In the event of death or resignation, the vacancy shall be filled by the bank which had appointed the previous holder, but only for the unexpired term of the vacated office.

ART. 52. The Censors, who shall exercise their functions in virtue of the present Act of the Signatory Powers, shall, in the interests of the latter, watch over the proper working of the Bank and insure the strict observance of the clauses of the Concession and the statutes. They shall see that the provisions respecting the issue of notes are strictly carried out, and shall superintend the operations tending to place the monetary situation on a sound basis; but they shall not at any time, or under any pretext whatsoever, be allowed to interfere in the conduct of the business or in the internal administration of the Bank.

Each of the Censors may at any time examine the accounts of the Bank, call upon either the board of directors or the manager's office for information respecting the conduct of the business of the Bank, and attend at the meetings of the board of directors, but only in an advisory capacity.

The four Censors shall meet at Tangier in the exercise of their functions at least once in every two years at a date to be fixed by common agreement. Other meetings at Tangier or elsewhere shall be held on the demand of three of the Censors.

The four Censors shall draw up, in common agreement, an annual report which shall be annexed to that of the board of directors. The board of directors shall, without delay, forward a copy of such report to each of the Governments signatories of the Act of the Conference.

ART. 53. The emoluments and travelling allowances to be assigned to the Censors shall be fixed by the committee charged with the task of preparing the statutes. They shall be paid directly to these officials by the banks who appoint the latter, and shall be reimbursed to those banks by the Morocco State Bank.

ART. 54. A committee shall be set up at Tangier and attached to the head office, the members of which shall be selected by the board of directors, without distinction of nationality, from amongst the persons of position residing at Tangier who hold shares in the Bank.

Such committee, which shall be presided over by one of the managers or submanagers, shall give advice in matters of discounts and the opening of credit accounts.

It shall submit to the board of directors

a monthly report on these different questions.

ART. 55. The capital, of which the amount shall be fixed by the special committee provided for in Article 57, but which shall not be less than 15,000,000 fr. nor more than 20,000,000 fr., shall be composed of gold coin, and the shares, the certificates of which shall represent a value equivalent to 500 fr., shall be expressed in the different gold currencies at a fixed rate of exchange, as determined by the statutes.

This capital may eventually be increased at one or more times by decision of the general meeting of shareholders.

The subscription of such increases of capital shall be reserved to all the shareholders, without distinction of groups, in proportion to the number of shares held by each of them.

ART. 56. The initial capital of the Bank shall be divided into as many equal portions as there are participants amongst the Powers represented at the Conference.

To this end each Power shall designate a bank which shall exercise, either on its own behalf or on behalf of a group of banks, the right of subscription above specified, as well as the right to nominate the directors under Article 50. Every bank selected as the head of a group may, with the authorization of its Government, be replaced by another bank belonging to the same country.

Those States which desire to avail themselves of their right of subscription shall notify their intention to do so to the Spanish Government within four weeks from the date of the signature of the present Act by the Representatives of the Powers.

Two portions, however, of the capital equal to those reserved to each of the subscribing groups shall be assigned to the syndicate of banks signatories of the contract of the 12th June, 1904, as compensation for the cession by the syndicate to the State Bank of Morocco—

1. Of the rights specified in Article 33 of the contract;

2. Of the right specified in Article 32 (§ 2) of the contract with regard to the available balance of the customs receipts, with the express reservation of the general preferential right to the total revenue from customs granted to the bondholders under Article 11 of the same contract.

ART. 57. Within three weeks from the date of the closing of the subscription, as notified by the Spanish Government to the Powers interested, a special committee composed of delegates appointed by the subscribing groups, under the conditions laid down in Article 50 for the appointment of directors, shall meet for the purpose of drawing up the statutes of the Bank.

The general meeting for constituting the company shall be held within two months from the date of the ratification of the present Act.

The functions of the special committee shall cease immediately after the formation of the company.

The special committee shall itself determine the place of its meetings.

ART. 58. No alteration shall be made in the statutes except on the proposal of the board of directors and with the previous approval of the Censors and of the Imperial High Commissioner.

Such alterations must be voted at a general meeting of shareholders by a majority of three-quarters of the members present or represented.

Chapter IV.—Declaration concerning an Improved Yield of the Taxes and the Creation of New Sources of Revenue

ART. 59. As soon as the *tertib* shall have been regularly enforced on Moorish subjects, the Representatives of the Powers at Tangier shall impose it upon their nationals within the Empire. It is, however, understood that the said tax shall not be imposed on foreigners, except—

(*a.*) Under the conditions prescribed by the regulations made by the Diplomatic Body at Tangier under date of the 23rd November, 1903;

(*b.*) In the localities where it shall be actually collected from Moorish subjects.

The Consular authorities shall retain a proportion of the amounts levied upon their nationals, in order to cover the expenses incurred in drawing up the lists and collecting the tax.

The rate of such deduction shall be fixed by agreement between the Makhzen and the Diplomatic Body at Tangier.

ART. 60. In accordance with the right

recognized as belonging to them by Article 11 of the Madrid Convention, foreigners shall be free to acquire real property throughout the whole extend of the Shereefian Empire, and His Majesty the Sultan shall give the necessary instructions to the administrative and judicial authorities to insure that authorization to execute the deeds shall not be refused without good cause. Subsequent transfers by deed between living persons or after decease shall continue to be effected without any impediment.

In the ports open to trade, and within a radius of 10 kilometres around such ports, the consent required by Article 11 of the Madrid Convention is granted by His Majesty the Sultan in a general manner, and without such consent having henceforth to be obtained specifically in respect of each purchase of real property by foreigners.

At Ksar-el-Kebir, Arzila, Azemur, and eventually in other localities on the coast or in the interior, the general authorization mentioned above is likewise granted to foreigners, but only for purchases within a radius of 2 kilometres around these towns.

Wherever foreigners have acquired real property, they shall be at liberty to erect buildings, provided they conform to the regulations and usages.

Before authorizing the execution of deeds of transfer of real property, the Cadi shall satisfy himself, in conformity with Mussulman law, that there is a good title.

The Makhzen shall designate, in each of the towns and districts specified in the present Article, the Cadi who shall be charged with the duty of effecting such verifications.

ART. 61. With the object of creating new sources of revenue for the Makhzen, the Conference recognizes, in principle, that a tax may be imposed on town buildings.

A portion of the revenue thus raised shall be set aside to meet the requirements of municipal roads and hygiene, and, in a general manner, to cover the cost of improvements and of conservancy in towns.

The tax shall be leviable on Moorish or foreign proprietors without any distinction; but the tenant or custodian of the key shall be responsible therefor to the Moorish Treasury.

Regulations made by common agreement between the Shereefian Government and the Diplomatic Body at Tangier shall fix the rate of the tax, lay down the manner of collecting and applying it, and determine what proportion of the resources thus created shall be devoted to meeting the cost of improvements and of conservancy in the towns.

At Tangier such proportion shall be paid to the International Sanitary Council, which shall determine the manner of its application until a municipal organization shall have been created.

ART. 62. His Shereefian Majesty having decided in 1901 that the Moorish officials charged with the collection of the agricultural taxes should no longer receive from the people either *sokhra* or *mouna,* the Conference is of opinion that this rule should be made general as far possible.

ART. 63. The Shereefian Delegates have drawn attention to the fact that certain *habou* property or Crown lands, notably estates belonging to the Makhzen, occupied at a rental of 6 per cent., are held by foreigners without regular title-deeds, or in virtue of contracts subject to revision. The Conference, desirous of remedying this state of affairs, charges the Diplomatic Body at Tangier to bring about an equitable settlement of these two questions in agreement with the Special Commissioner whom His Shereefian Majesty may be pleased to appoint for this purpose.

ART. 64. The Conference takes note of the proposals formulated by the Shereefian Delegates respecting the establishment of new taxes on certain trades, industries, and professions.

If, as the result of the collection of such taxes from Moorish subject, the Diplomatic Body at Tangier should consider that their levy should be extended to foreigners, it is hereby stipulated that the said taxes shall be exclusively municipal.

ART. 65. The Conference accepts the proposal made by the Moorish Delegation to introduce, with the co-operation of the Diplomatic Body—

(*a.*) A stamp duty on contracts and notarial acts signed before an *adul*;

(*b.*) A transfer tax, not exceeding 2 per cent., on sales of real estate;

(*c.*) A statistical and weighing due, not exceeding 1 per cent. *ad valorem,* on goods transported by coasting vessels;

(*d.*) A passport fee, to be levied from Moorish subjects;

(*e.*) Eventually, quay and lighthouse dues, of which the proceeds shall be devoted to the improvement of the harbours.

ART. 66. As a temporary measure, goods of foreign origin shall, on their entry into Morocco, pay a special tax of $2\frac{1}{2}$ per cent. *ad valorem.* The total revenue derived from this tax shall form a special fund, which shall be devoted to meeting the expenditure on, and execution of, public works undertaken for the development of navigation and trade generally in the Shereefian Empire.

The programme of the works and the order of their execution shall be settled by agreement between the Shereefian Government and the Diplomatic Body at Tangier.

All surveys, estimates, plans, and specifications relating thereto shall be prepared by a competent engineer appointed with the concurrence of the Diplomatic Body by the Shereefian Government. Such engineer may, if necessary, be assisted by one or more assistant engineers. Their salaries shall be charged to the special fund.

The moneys belonging to the special fund shall be deposited in the Morocco State Bank, which shall keep the accounts thereof.

Public contracts shall be awarded in the form and according to the conditions laid down in regulations which it shall be the duty of the Diplomatic Body at Tangier to draw up conjointly with the Representative of His Shereefian Majesty.

The board of awards shall consist of a Representative of the Shereefian Government, five delegates of the Diplomatic Body at Tangier, and the engineer.

The contract shall be awarded to the person or persons who, while complying with the terms of the specifications, shall have submitted the most generally advantageous offer.

As regards the sums yielded by the special tax which would be collected at the custom-houses established in the districts indicated in Article 103 of the Customs

Regulations, their employment shall, in agreement with the conterminous State, be determined by the Makhzen in accordance with the provisions of the present Article.

ART. 67. The Conference expresses the hope, subject to the observations submitted to it on this subject, that the export duties on the articles mentioned below may be reduced to the following extent:—

	Per cent.
Chick-peas	20
Maize	20
Barley	50
Wheat	34

ART. 68. His Shereefian Majesty agrees to increase from 6,000 to 10,000 the number of cattle which each Power has the right to export from Morocco. Such exportation may be effected through any custom-house. If, owing to unfortunate circumstances, a dearth of cattle should make itself felt in any particular district, His Shereefian Majesty may temporarily prohibit the export of cattle from the port or ports of such district. Such prohibition shall not exceed in duration a period of two years, nor shall it be enforced at all the ports of the Empire at one and the same time.

It is, moreover, understood that the preceding provisions do not modify the other conditions governing the export of cattle which are laid down in the Firmans of earlier date.

The Conference further expresses the hope that a system of veterinary inspection may be organized in the seaports as soon as possible.

ART. 69. In accordance with the former decisions of His Shereefian Majesty, and notably with that of the 28th September, 1901, the coasting trade in cereals, grains, vegetables, eggs, fruit, poultry, and generally in goods and animals of every kind, whether of Moorish origin or otherwise, with the exception of horses, mules, asses, and camels, for which a special permit from the Makhzen shall be required, is authorized between all the ports of the Empire. Such coasting trade may be carried on by vessels of any nationality, without the above-named articles being liable to pay export duty, but subject to the special duties and to the observance of the regulations governing this matter.

ART. 70. The scale of berthage or anchorage dues levied from vessels in Moorish harbours being fixed by treaties with certain Powers, these Powers are prepared to consent to a revision of the said dues. The Diplomatic Body at Tangier is charged with the duty of drawing up, in agreement with the Makhzen, the conditions of such revision, which shall not be effected until after the improvement of the harbours.

ART. 71. In all ports where sufficient warehouse accommodation exists, warehouse dues on articles in bond shall be levied in accordance with the regulations drawn up, or to be drawn up, on this subject by the Government of His Shereefian Majesty in agreement with the Diplomatic Body at Tangier.

ART. 72. Opium and kiff shall continue to be a monopoly of the Shereefian Government. Nevertheless, the importation of opium specially destined for medicinal purposes shall be authorized by a special permit, issued by the Makhzen at the request of the Legation of the country to which the importing chemist or doctor belongs. The Shereefian Government and the Diplomatic Body shall, by common agreement, determine the maximum quantity that may be imported.

ART. 73. The Representatives of the Powers take note of the intention of the Shereefian Government to extend to tobacco of all kinds the monopoly which at present exists in the case of snuff. They reserve the right of their nationals to due compensation for any losses which the said monopoly may inflict on such of them as carry on a tobacco business under the present system. Failing an amicable arrangement, the amount of such compensation shall be fixed by exports nominated jointly by the Makhzen and the Diplomatic Body, who shall be guided by the provisions agreed upon in the matter of expropriations in the public interest.

ART. 74. The principle of awarding contracts without regard to nationality shall be applied to the farming of the opium and kiff monopoly. The same course shall be adopted in respect to the tobacco monopoly if such be introduced.

ART. 75. Should occasion arise to modify any of the provisions of the present Declaration, an understanding on the subject must be arrived at between the Makhzen and the Diplomatic Body at Tangier.

ART. 76. In all the cases dealt with by the present Declaration in which the intervention of the Diplomatic Body is required, decisions shall be taken by a majority of votes, except in respect of Articles 64, 70, and 75.

Chapter V. —Regulations respecting the Customs of the Empire and the Suppression of Fraud and Smuggling

ART. 77. Every captain of a merchant-vessel coming from a foreign or a Moorish port shall, within twenty-four hours of his receiving pratique at any of the ports of the Empire, deposit at the customhouse an exact copy of his manifest signed by himself and certified to be correct by the consignee of the vessel. He shall, moreover, if required to do so, produce before the Customs officers the original of his manifest.

The Customs authorities shall have power to place one or more watchmen on board to prevent all illicit traffic.

ART. 78. The following are exempted from the obligation to deposit the manifest:—

1. Men-of-war or vessels chartered on behalf of a Power.

2. Boats belonging to private individuals kept by them for their personal use, and not employed in the carriage of merchandize.

3. Boats or vessels used for fishing within sight of the shore.

4. Yachts solely used for pleasure cruises and registered as such at their home ports.

5. Vessels specially fitted out for the laying and repair of telegraphic cables.

6. Boats exclusively employed in life-saving operations.

7. Hospital-ships.

8. Training-vessels of the mercantile marine which do not engage in commercial enterprise.

ART. 79. The manifest deposited at the custom-house shall state the nature and origin of the cargo, together with the marks and numbers of the cases, bales, packages, barrels, &c.

ART. 80. Should there be material grounds for mistrusting the correctness of the manifest, or should the captain of the vessel refuse to allow the visit and inspection of the Customs officers, the case shall be notified to the competent Consular authority, in order that the latter may proceed, with the assistance of a delegate of the Shereefian Customs, to such inquiries, search, and inspection as may be deemed necessary.

ART. 81. If, after the expiration of the period of twenty-four hours allowed under Article 77, the captain have not deposited his manifest, he shall, unless the delay be due to circumstances beyond control, be liable to a fine of 150 pesetas for each day's delay, provided that such fine shall not exceed 600 pesetas. If the captain fraudulently present an inaccurate or incomplete manifest, he shall be personally liable to pay a sum equal to the value of the goods for which he has failed to produce a manifest as well as a fine of not less than 500 and not exceeding 1,000 pesetas, and the vessel and its cargo shall, moreover, be liable to seizure by the competent Consular authority as security for such fine.

ART. 82. Every person shall, at the time of clearing goods through the Customs, whether for import or for export, file a detailed statement in the custom-house specifying the kind, quality, weight, number, size, and value of the goods, as well as the kind, marks, and numbers of the packages containing the same.

ART. 83. Should the Customs officers, on inspection, find that there are fewer packages or less merchandize than have been declared, the declarant, unless able to prove that he has acted in good faith, shall pay double the amount of the duty on the missing goods, and the goods declared shall be detained as security for this double duty; if, on the contrary, an excess be found at the time of the visit, either in the number of packages or in the quantity or weight of the goods, such excess shall be seized and confiscated for the benefit of the Makhzen, unless the declarant can prove his good faith.

ART. 84. If the declaration should be found to be incorrect as to either kind or quality, and if the declarant be unable to prove his good faith, the goods incorrectly declared shall be seized and confiscated by the competent authority for the benefit of the Makhzen.

ART. 85. Should the declaration be found to be incorrect as regards the value declared, and should the declarant be unable to prove his good faith, the Customs Administration may either levy the duty in kind there and then, or, in case the goods be indivisible, acquire the said goods on an immediate payment to the declarant of the declared value, plus 5 percent.

ART. 86. If the declaration be found to be false as regards the nature of the goods, the latter shall be considered as not having been declared, and the offence shall be dealt with as laid down in Articles 88 and 90 herein below, and the penalties shall be those provided in the said Articles.

ART. 87. The penalty for smuggling or attempting to smuggle dutiable goods into or out of the country, whether by sea or by land, shall be the confiscation of the goods, without prejudice to such penalties and fines hereinafter provided as may be inflicted by the competent courts.

In addition, vehicles or animals employed in transporting smuggled goods by land shall be seized and confiscated in all cases where such goods constitute the principal part of the load.

ART. 88. The penalty for illicitly importing, or attempting illicitly to import or export, at a port open to commerce, or through a custom-house, shall be a fine not exceeding three times the value of the goods so illicitly dealt with, and imprisonment for a period of not less than five days and not exceeding six months, or one only of these penalties.

ART. 89. The penalty for illicitly importing or exporting, or attempting illicitly to import or export, at places other than a port open to commerce, or a custom-house, shall be a fine of not less than 300 and not exceeding 500 pesetas, and a supplementary fine equal to three times the value of the goods, or imprisonment for a period of not less than one month and not exceeding one year.

ART. 90. Accessories to the offences specified in Articles 88 and 89 shall be liable to the same penalties as the principal offenders. The question of what constitutes complicity shall be determined in accordance with the law administered by the court before which the particular case is heard.

ART. 91. Any vessel importing or attempting to import, or exporting or attempting to export, merchandize illicitly at or from a place other than a port open to trade may be taken by the Moorish Customs authorities to the nearest port, to be handed over to the Consular authority, which may seize such vessel and detain it in custody until it shall have paid the amount of the fines imposed.

The vessel shall be released at any stage of the proceedings, on the deposit with the Consular authority of the maximum amount of the fine, or upon good security for payment being accepted by the Customs, provided such release do not impede the judicial investigation.

ART. 92. The provisions of the preceding Articles shall be applicable to vessels engaged in the coasting trade.

ART. 93. Goods not liable to export duty and embarked at a Moorish port for shipment by sea to another port in the Empire shall be accompanied by a certificate of export issued by the Customs, on pain of having to pay the import duty or even of being confiscated, if not entered in the manifest.

ART. 94. Shipment by coasting-vessels of goods liable to export duty shall not be effected except after deposit at the custom-house of the place of shipment, against receipt, of the amount of the export duties payable on such goods. Such deposit shall be repaid to the depositor by the custom-house into which it was paid, on production of a declaration on which the Customs authorities shall have indorsed the arrival of the goods, and the receipt for the amount of the duties deposited. The documents proving the arrival of the goods shall be produced within three months of their shipment. On the expiration of this term, the sum deposited shall be appropriated by the Makhzen unless the delay be due to circumstances beyond control.

ART. 95. Import and export duties shall be paid in ready money at the custom-house where the clearance has been effected.

The *ad valorem* duties shall be paid on the basis of the cash and wholesale value of the goods entered at the custom-house, free of customs and warehouse duties. In the case of damaged goods, the depreciation they have undergone shall be taken into account in their valuation. Goods shall not be removed except after payment of customs and warehouse duties.

A formal receipt, to be made out by the official charged with the business, shall be given for all goods and payments received.

ART. 96. The value of the principal goods taxed by the Moorish Customs Administration shall be fixed annually in accordance with the conditions laid down in the preceding Article, by a Customs Valuation Committee, sitting at Tangier, and consisting of—

1. Three members nominated by the Moorish Government.

2. Three members nominated by the Diplomatic Body at Tangier.

3. One delegate of the State Bank.

4. One agent of the Commission representing the Moorish 5 per Cent. Loan of 1904.

The committee shall nominate from twelve to twenty honorary members, resident in Morocco, whom it shall consult in connection with the valuation, and whenever it may see fit. Such honorary members shall be chosen from the lists of prominent residents, drawn up in the case of foreigners by the respective Legations, and, in the case of Moorish subjects, by the Representative of the Sultan.

They shall be nominated, as far as possible, in numbers proportionate to the importance of the trade of the respective nations.

The committee shall be appointed for three years.

The schedule of values fixed by the committee shall serve as a basis for the valuations which shall be made at every custom-house by the Moorish Customs Administration. It shall be posted up in the custom-houses and in the chanceries of the Legations or consulates at Tangier.

The schedule shall be subject to revision at the end of six months if any notable change shall have taken place in the value of certain goods.

ART. 97. A permanent committee, styled the "Customs Committee," shall be organized at Tangier, and appointed for a term of three years. It shall consist of a Special Commissioner of His Shereefian Majesty, of a member of the Diplomatic or Consular Body nominated by the Diplomatic Body at Tangier, and of a delegate of the State Bank. The committee may add to its number one or several representatives of the Customs Administration, with a consultative voice.

This Committee shall watch over the proper working of the Customs Administration, and shall have power to propose to His Shereefian Majesty such measures as would, in their opinion, tend to improve the service, and to assure the regularity and proper control of the transactions and charges (landing, loading, land transport, handing, import and export of goods, warehousing, valuation, payment and collection of duties). The rights stipulated for in favour of the bondholders by Articles 15 and 16 of the loan contract of the 12th June, 1904, shall be in no way impaired by the establishment of the "Customs Committee."

Detailed provision as to the application of Article 96 and of the present Article shall be made by means of instructions to be drawn up by the Customs Committee and the services interested; such instructions shall be submitted to the Diplomatic Body for their opinion.

ART. 98. At custom-houses having sufficient warehouse accommodation the Customs Administration shall take charge of the goods landed, from the time when they are handed over, against receipt, by the captain of the vessel to the officials in charge of the lighterage service, until the time when they are formally cleared.

The Customs Administration shall be responsible for any damage caused by loss of or injury to goods due to the fault or negligence of its officials. It shall not be responsible for damage due either to natural deterioration of the goods, or to their having been stored too long in the warehouse, or to circumstances beyond control.

At custom-houses not having sufficient warehouse accommodation, the officials of the Makhzen are only bound to employ such means of preservation as may be at the disposal of the custom-house.

The Warehousing Regulations at present in force shall be revised in agreement with the Shereefian Government, by the Diplomatic Body, whose decision shall be taken by a majority of votes.

ART. 99. Confiscated goods and boats or transport vehicles or animals shall be sold by the Customs within eight days from the pronouncement of the final judgment by the competent court.

ART. 100. The net proceeds of the sale of confiscated goods and articles definitely become the property of the State; those of the money fines, as well as any amounts paid by way of compounding, shall, after deduction of costs of every kind, be divided between the Shereefian Treasury and such persons as may have aided in the prevention of fraud or smuggling.

One-third to be divided by the Customs among the informers;

One-third to go to the officials who seized the goods; and

One-third to the Moorish Treasury.

If the seizure have been effected without the intervention of an informer, one-half of the amount of the fines shall be awarded to the officials who seized the goods, and the other half to the Moorish Treasury.

ART. 101. The Moorish Customs authorities shall notify direct to the Diplomatic or Consular officials any case of infringement of the present regulations by their respective nationals, with a view to the latter being proceeded against before the competent court.

Cases of similar infringements by Moorish subject shall be brought by the Customs before the Shereefian authorities direct.

A delegate of the Customs shall be charged with the duty of watching the proceding in cases pending before the different courts.

ART. 102. Every confiscation, fine or penalty shall be pronounced, in the case of foreigners, by the Consular courts, and in the case of Moorish subjects by the Shereefian courts.

ART. 103. In the region bordering on the Algerian frontier, the application of the present regulations shall remain the exclusive concern of France and Morocco; similarly in the Riff country and in the regions bordering on the Spanish possessions the application of the present regulations shall remain the exclusive concern of Spain and Morocco.

ART. 104. The provisions of the present regulations, other than those respecting penalties, shall, on the expiration of a period of two years from their coming into force, be open to revision by the Diplomatic Body at Tangier, whose decisions shall be unanimous, acting in agreement with the Makhzen.

Chapter VI.—Declaration relative to the Public Services and Public Works

ART. 105. With a view to insure the application of the principle of economic liberty without inequality, the Signatory Powers declare that in no case shall the rights of the State over the public services of the Shereefian Empire be alienated for the benefit of private interests.

ART. 106. Should the Shereefian Government consider it necessary to have recourse to foreign capital or to foreign industries for the working of public services or for the execution of public works. roads, railways, ports, telegraphs, or other, the Signatory Powers reserve to themselves the right to see that the control of the State over such large undertakings of public interest remain intact.

ART. 107. The validity of such concessions as may be granted for the purposes specified in Article 106, or for furnishing supplies to the State, shall, throughout the Shereefian Empire, be subject to the principle of public awards on tenders, without respect of nationality, as regards all matters which, by the rules observed under the laws of foreign countries, admit of the application of that principle.

ART. 108. So soon as it shall have been decided to proceed to the execution of particular public works by calling for tenders, the Shereefian Government shall notify such decision to the Diplomatic Body, to which it shall, in due course, communicate the plans, specifications, and all documents annexed to the call for tenders, so that the nationals of all the Signatory Powers may obtain information respecting the projected works, and be in a position to compete for them. A sufficient time limit shall be fixed for this purpose in the call for tenders.

ART. 109. The specifications shall not contain, either explicitly or implicitly, any condition or provision of a nature to violate the principle of free competition, or to place the competitors of one nationality at a disadvantage as against the competitors of another.

ART. 110. The contracts shall be made in the form and according to the general conditions prescribed by regulations to be drawn up by the Shereefian Government, with the assistance of the Diplomatic Body.

The contract shall be awarded by the Shereefian Government to the person or persons who, while complying with the terms of the specifications, shall have submitted the most generally advantageous offer.

ART. 111. The rules laid down in Articles 106 to 110 shall be applied to concessions for the working of cork-tree forests, in accordance with the laws governing this matter in the respective foreign countries.

ART. 112. A Shereefian Firman shall lay down the conditions of the concession and of the working of mines, ores, and quarries. In drawing up this Firman the Shereefian Government shall be guided by the laws governing this matter in foreign countries.

ART. 113. If, in the cases mentioned in Articles 106 to 112, it should be necessary to occupation of particular properties, it shall be lawful to proceed to expropriation, conditionally upon the previous payment of proper compensation and the observance of the following rules.

ART. 114. Expropriation shall not take place except on the ground of public interest, and provided the necessity for it shall have been established by an administrative inquiry, held in accordance with rules to be laid down in Shereefian regulations drawn up with the assistance of the Diplomatic Body.

ART. 115. Where the owners of property are Moorish subjects, His Shereefian Majesty shall take the necessary measures to insure that no obstacles are placed in the way of the execution of such works as he may have declared to be of public interest.

ART. 116. Where the owners are foreigners, expropriation shall be effected in the following manner:—

In case of disagreement between the competent Government Department and the owner of the property to be expropriated, the amount of compensation shall be determined by a special jury, or, if need be, by arbitration.

ART. 117. Such jury shall consist of six expert valuers, of whom three shall be chosen by the owner and three by the Government Department interested in the expropriation. The opinion of the absolute majority shall prevail.

If no majority can be formed, the owner and the Government Department shall each appoint an arbiter, and these two arbiters shall nominate a third arbiter.

Failing an agreement as to the nomination of the third arbiter, the latter shall be appointed by the Diplomatic Body at Tangier.

ART. 118. The arbiters shall be chosen from a list drawn up at the beginning of each year by the Diplomatic Body, and, as far as possible, from such experts as are not resident in the locality where the work is to be carried out.

ART. 119. The owner shall have the right to appeal to the competent court against the award pronounced by the arbiters. Such appeal shall be lodged in accordance with the rules laid down in the matter of arbitration by the laws of the country to which the owner belongs.

Chapter VII.—General

ART. 120. With a view to bring their respective legislations, if nceessary, into harmony with the engagements entered into by virtue of the present General Act, all the Signatory Powers undertake, so far as they are severally concerned, to promote such legislation as may be necessary.

ART. 121. The present General Act shall be ratified in accordance with the constitutional laws peculiar to each individual State; the ratification shall be deposited at Madrid as soon as may be, and at the latest on the 31st December, 1906.

Such deposit shall be recorded in a protocol, of which a copy, certified to be correct, shall be transmitted to the Signatory Powers through the diplomatic channel.

ART. 122. The present General Act shall come into force on the day on which all the ratifications shall have been deposited, and at the latest on the 31st December, 1906.

Should the special legislative measures which may be necessary in certain countries in order to insure the application of some of the provisions of the present General Act

to the nationals of such countries residing in Morocco not have been enacted before the date fixed for ratification, such provision shall not become applicable, so far as such nationals are concerned, until after the promulgation of such legislative measures.

ART. 123, AND LAST. All existing Treaties, Conventions, and Arrangements between the Signatory Powers and Morocco remain in force. It is, however, agreed that, in case their provisions be found to conflict with those of the present General Act, the stipulations of the latter shall prevail. . . .

Additional Protocol

At the moment of proceeding to the signature of the General Act of the Algeciras Conference, the Delegates of Great Britain, Germany, Austria-Hungary, Belgium, Spain, the United States of America, France, Italy, the Netherlands, Portugal, Russia, and Sweden, having regard to the declaration made by the Moorish Delegates that they are not in a position, for the moment, to affix their signatures thereto, the distance preventing them from obtaining an early reply from His Shereefian Majesty on the points which they considered themselves bound to refer to him, mutually engage, in virtue of their same full powers, to unite their efforts with a view to the ratification by His Shereefian Majesty of the said General Act in its entirety, and with a view to the simultaneous carrying out of the reforms therein contemplated, which are mutually interdependent.

They accordingly agree to charge His Excellency M. Malmusi, Italian Minister in Morocco and dean of the Diplomatic Body at Tangier, to take the necessary steps to this end, calling the attention of His Majesty the Sultan to the great advantages which must accrue to his Empire from the provisions unanimously adopted at the Conference by the Signatory Powers.

The accession of His Shereefian Majesty to the General Act of the Algeciras Conference shall be communicated through the intermediary of His Most Catholic Majesty's Government to the Governments of the other Signatory Powers. Such accession shall have the same effect as if the Moorish

Delegates had affixed their signatures to the General Act, and shall take the place of ratification by His Shereefian Majesty. . . .

(Declaration by the United States' Delegate, April 7, 1906)

The Government of the United States of America, having no political interests in Morocco, and having taken part in the present Conference with no other desires or intentions than to assist in assuring to all the nations in Morocco the most complete equality in matters of commerce, treatment, and privileges, and in facilitating the introduction into that Empire of reforms which should bring about a general state of well-being founded on the perfect cordiality of her foreign relations, and on a stable internal administration, declares: that in subscribing to the Regulations and Declarations of the Conference by the act of signing the General Act, subject to ratification according to constitutional procedure, and the Additional Protocol, and in consenting to their application to American citizens and interests in Morocco, it assumes no obligation or responsibility as to the measures which may be necessary for the enforcement of the said Regulations and Declarations.

169. EXCHANGE OF NOTES AND AGREEMENT ON AN ADMINISTRATIVE SEPARATING LINE (SINAI): ANGLO-EGYPT AND THE OTTOMAN EMPIRE
14 May–1 October 1906

[English translation of notes and English text of agreement, Hertslet, *Map of Africa by Treaty*, 3: 1199–1203]

The Sublime Porte did not surrender its claim to Egypt, even after Britain's occupation had clearly become permanent. The Porte, for example, insisted on keeping Muhtar Paşa in Cairo as its high commissioner, even after the failure to ratify the British-Ottoman convention on Egypt of 1887 (Doc. 147), and when Muhtar retired a few years before the outbreak of World War I, the Ottoman government sent another official to replace him. Britain itself, so long as its presence in Egypt bore the label of occupation, kept alive the legal fiction that the relation between the Ottoman sultan and the Egyptian khedive continued to be regulated by the *fermans* on Egypt that the Ottoman Imperial Government issued between 1841 and 1879. Under these fermans, it will be recalled, Ottoman suzerainty over Egypt was affirmed, and specific details were modified over the years in the khedive's favor in return for increases in annual tribute. Although the khedive therefore enjoyed a wide measure of autonomy, he was not fully sovereign (Doc. 127). In agreeing to the constitutional status quo in the Ottoman-Egyptian relationship, Britain accepted the practice of the Ottoman investiture of a new khedive by the formal issuance at the time of succession of a ferman that repeated the accepted rights of the khedive and his obligations to the sultan. On 27 March 1892 Sultan 'Abdülhamid II issued such a ferman investing 'Abbas Hilmi II (1892–1914) as khedive of Egypt. While the edict reaffirmed the rights listed in the last ferman of investiture in 1879, when Tawfiq, 'Abbas Hilmi's father, had ascended the viceregal throne, it also went on to modify the eastern boundary of Egypt by reassigning the major part of Sinai to direct Ottoman administration. In doing so, the Sublime Porte was clearly trying to shore up its legal claim by asserting that the Ottoman-Egyptian boundary was no more than an administrative separating line between the Sinai Peninsula in the province of Egypt and the *vilâyet* of Hijaz and the *sancak* of Jerusalem, and not a true or quasi-international boundary. The unilateral Ottoman act, which proposed to leave to the khedive only that fragment of Sinai west of a line from al-Arish to Suez, Britain refused to accept, for, as the earl of Cromer later candidly observed, "it was undesirable to bring Turkish soldiers down to the banks of the Suez Canal" (*Modern Egypt*, 2: 268). In the end, the Sublime Porte bowed to British demands. But the Ottoman government reopened the issue in 1905, when it made yet another, more determined attempt to redraw the eastern boundary of Egypt unilaterally. This time the dispute was settled by a formal agreement which fixed the boundary—called an "administrative separating line" as a sop to Ottoman sensitivities—on an almost straight line from al-Rafah on the Mediterranean to Ras Taba (six miles southwest of 'Aqabah) at the head of the Gulf of 'Aqabah. This line later became the boundary between Egypt and the Palestine Mandate. Cromer, op. cit., vol. 2, chap. 39; Holt. *Egypt and the Fertile Crescent*, chap. 15; Hirschzowicz, "The Sultan and the Khedive."

1. The Ottoman Minister of Foreign Affairs, Tevfik, to the British Ambassador (Istanbul), N. R. O'Conor, 14 May 1906

I have had the honour to receive the note which your Excellency was good enough to write to me on the 12th instant respecting the occupation of Taba.

Allow me to observe to you that it never entered the thought of the Imperial Government to ignore the contents of the telegram of the 8th April of the late Djevad Pasha to His Highness the Khedive. Besides, the communication which I had the honour to address to your Excellency on the 11th instant was quite explicit. The evacuation of Taba has been decided upon, and the orders have already been given in consequence.

It is agreed that the Staff officers at Akaba and the officials who shall be sent by His Highness the Khedive shall meet in order to effect on the spot, and in accordance with topographical data, a technical inquiry for marking on a map the points calculated to insure the maintenance, on the basis of the above-mentioned telegram of Djevad Pasha, of the *status quo* in the Sinaitic Peninsula, and in order to draw the line of demarcation starting at Rafeh, near El-Arish, and running towards the

south-east in an approximately straight line as far as a point on the Gulf of Akaba, at least 3 miles distant from Akaba.

The views expressed in the above-mentioned communication of your Excellency are thus fully realized.

In begging your Excellency to be so good as to communicate the above to London, we trust that the Government of His Majesty the King will see in it a fresh proof of our keen desire to maintain at all times our relations on a footing of the most complete cordiality. In conveying to us, on its side, an expression of its full satisfaction, it will itself have given proof of the value which it attaches to the preservation and to the strengthening of the good relations which so happily exist between the two States.

2. O'Conor to Tevfik, 15 May 1906

I lost no time in referring to my Government the note which your Excellency was so good as to address to me on the 14th instant in reply to my note of the 12th on the subject of the occupation of Taba and delimitation of the Peninsula of Sinai.

His Majesty's Government have received with pleasure your Excellency's declaration that the Sublime Porte does not question the contents of the telegram addressed by the deceased Grand Vizier, Djevad Pasha, to His Highness the Khedive on the 8th April, 1892; that the withdrawal of the Imperial troops from Taba has been decided upon; and that instructions have been sent to the Ottoman Staff Officers now at Akaba to delimit and record on a map, jointly with the officials to be appointed by His Highness the Khedive, the line of demarcation running approximately straight from Rafeh in a south-easterly direction to a point on the Gulf of Akaba not less than 3 miles from Akaba so as to insure the maintenance of the *status quo* in the Sinai Peninsula on the bases of the telegram above-mentioned of the 8th April, 1892.

On behalf of His Majesty's Government I have the honour to take act of the foregoing declarations, also of the declaration of his Highness the Grand Vizier that orders have been sent for the withdrawal of the Ottoman troops into Turkish territory to the east of Rafeh should any have crossed to the Egyptian side, and the restoration of the pillars said to have been lately destroyed there, and to express their satisfaction at the settlement of this question, which cannot fail to contribute to the maintenance and consolidation of those friendly relations which are so desirable in the interests of both countries, and which are no less appreciated by the Government of my august Sovereign than by that of His Imperial Majesty the Sultan.

3. British-Egyptian Agreement with the Sublime Porte, 1 October 1906

. . . ART. I. The Administrative Separating Line, as shown on map attached to this Agreement, begins at the point of Ras Taba, on the western shore of the Gulf of Akaba, and follows along the eastern ridge overlooking Wadi Taba to the top of Jebel Fort; from thence the Separating Line extends by straight lines as follows:

From Jebel Fort to a point not exceeding 200 metres to the east of the top of Jebel Fathi Pasha, thence to that point which is formed by the intersection of a prolongation of this line with a perpendicular line drawn from a point 200 metres measured from the top of Jebel Fathi Pasha along the line drawn from the centre of the top of that hill to Mofrak Point (the Mofrak is the junction of the Gaza-Akaba and Nekhl-Akaba roads). From this point of intersection to the hill east of and overlooking Thamilet-el-Radadi (place where there is water), so that the Thamila (or water) remains west of the line; thence to top of Ras Radadi, marked on the above-mentioned map as A 3; thence to top of Jebel Safra, marked as A 4; thence to top of eastern peak of Um Guf, marked as A 5; thence to that point marked as A 7, north of Thamilet Sueilma; thence to that point marked as A 8, on the west-north-west of Jebel Semaui; thence to top of hill west-north-west of Bir Maghara (which is the well in the northern branch of the Wadi Ma Yein, leaving that well east of the Separating Line); from thence to A 9; from thence to A 9 *bis* west of Jebel Megrah; from thence to Ras-el-Ain, marked as A 10 *bis*; from thence to a point on Jebel-um-Hawawit, marked as A 11; from thence to half distance between two pillars (which pillars are marked at A 13) under a tree 390 metres south-west of Bir Rafah; it then runs in a straight line at a bearing of 280° of the magnetic north (viz., 80° to the west) to a point on a sand-hill measured 420 metres in a straight line from the above-mentioned pillars; thence in a straight line at a bearing of 334° of the magnetic north (viz., 26° to the west) to the Mediterranean Sea, passing over hill of ruins on the sea-shore.

ART. II The Separating Line mentioned in Art. 1 has been indicated by a black broken line on duplicate maps (annexed to this Agreement), which shall be signed and exchanged simultaneously with the Agreement.

ART. III. Boundary pillars will be erected in the presence of the Joint Commission, at intervisible points along the Separating Line, from the point on the Mediterranean shore to the point on the shore of the Gulf of Akaba.

ART. IV. These boundary pillars will be under the protection of the Turkish Sultanate and Egyptian Khediviate.

ART. V. Should it be necessary in future to renew these pillars, or to increase them, each party shall send a Representative for this purpose. The positions of these new pillars shall be determined by the course of the Separating Line as laid down in the map.

ART. VI. All tribes living on both sides shall have the right of benefiting by the water as heretofore, viz., they shall retain their ancient and former rights in this respect.

Necessary guarantees will be given to Arab tribes respecting above.

Also Turkish soldiers, native individuals, and gendarmes shall benefit by the water which remained west of the Separating Line.

ART. VII. Armed Turkish soldiers and armed gendarmes will not be permitted to cross to the west of the Separating Line.

ART. VIII. Natives and Arabs of both sides shall continue to retain the same established and ancient rights of ownership of waters, fields, and lands on both sides as formerly. . . .

170. CONVENTION ON PERSIA AND AFGHANISTAN: GREAT BRITAIN AND RUSSIA
18/31 August 1907

(Ratifications exchanged, Saint Petersburg, 10/23 September 1907; denounced by Russia, 14 January 1918)
[Great Britain, *Treaty Series, 1907*, no. 34, Cd. 3753]

The Russian-Japanese War of 1904–05 interrupted exploratory negotiations between Britain and Russia aimed at settling their differences in Asia. Once the talks were resumed late in the spring of 1906, military defeat and internal unrest had rendered the tsarist regime's mood more pliant. Common fears of Germany's forward policies in Europe and the Middle East had served, moreover, to mitigate British-Russian hostility. Britain and Russia proceeded to accommodate their interests in Persia and Afghanistan without consulting either Middle East government, merely informing both and seeking their assent after the signature of the convention. Britain failed to obtain the insertion of a reference to Britain's exclusive position in the Persian Gulf into the preamble of the agreement on Persia, largely because the suggestion was introduced after the drafting of the Persian terms had been completed. Nevertheless, the two powers reached an accord on the division of Persia—without its consent—into spheres of influence. "To-day it is necessary that the Foreign Minister of Persia," noted one Tehrani newspaper, which reflected articulate nationalist opinion in the country, "should clearly inform the two Powers that no Agreement having reference to Persia and concluded without her knowledge is valid or entitled to the slightest consideration; and that any Power desiring to enter into relations with Persia must address itself directly to the Persians themselves, no one else having any right to intervene in any way" (*Habl al-Matin*, 11 September 1907, as cited in Browne, *Persian Revolution*, p. 187). In the convention on Afghanistan, Russia acknowledged that the amirate fell within the British sphere of influence in accordance with existing British-Afghan agreements which provided for Britain's exercise of Afghanistan's external sovereignty. In return, Russia received British assurances of equal commercial opportunity and the right to conduct local nonpolitical frontier relations directly with Afghanistan. At the time that British India's preclusive protectorate was established in 1880–83 (Doc. 140), Afghanistan had no fixed boundaries. These were demarcated in the south by the Durand agreement with 'Abd al-Rahman of 12 November 1893 (text in Aitchison, *Collection of Treaties . . . relating to India* [5th ed.], 13: 256–57) and in the north by an agreement signed in London on 11 March 1895 by Great Britain and Russia, describing their respective spheres of influence in the region of the Pamirs (text in Great Britain, *Treaty Series, 1895*, no. 8, C. 7643). It took a dozen years longer to procure Russia's recognition of the British-Indian protectorate. Although Amir Habib Allah (1901–19) never gave his formal consent, as laid down in article 5, the two signatories abided by the terms of the convention. Omitted below is the agreement on Tibet. R.P. Churchill, *Anglo-Russian Convention of 1907*; Kazemzadeh, *Russia and Britain in Persia*, chap. 7; Browne, op. cit., chaps. 6–11; Greaves, "Some aspects of the Anglo-Russian Convention"; Nicolson, *Portrait of a Diplomatist*, chaps. 8–9; Grey, *Twenty-five Years*, vol. 1, chap. 10; Korff, *Russia's Foreign Relations*, chap. 2; Fraser-Tytler, *Afghanistan*, pt. 2, chap. 9; Adamec, *Afghanistan*, chap. 4; Singhal, *India and Afghanistan*, chap. 11; Habberton, *Anglo-Russian Relations concerning Afghanistan*; Oncken, *Die sicherheit Indiens*, chap. 6; Lambton, "Secret Societies and the Persian Revolution"; Ramazani, *Foreign Policy of Iran*.

1. Agreement concerning Persia

The Governments of Great Britain and Russia having mutually engaged to respect the integrity and independence of Persia, and sincerely desiring the preservation of order throughout that country and its peaceful development, as well as the permanent establishment of equal advantages for the trade and industry of all other nations;

Considering that each of them has, for geographical and economic reasons, a special interest in the maintenance of peace and order in certain provinces of Persia adjoining, or in the neighbourhood of, the Russian frontier on the one hand, and the frontiers of Afghanistan and Baluchistan on the other hand; and being desirous of avoiding all cause of conflict between their respective interests in the above-mentioned provinces of Persia;

Have agreed on the following terms:—

I. Great Britain engages not to seek for herself, and not to support in favour of British subjects, or in favour of the subjects of third Powers, any Concessions of a political or commercial nature—such as Concession for railways, banks, telegraphs, roads, transport, insurance, &c.—beyond a line starting from Kasr-i-Shirin, passing through Isfahan, Yezd, Kakhk, and ending at a point on the Persian frontier at the intersection of the Russian and Afghan frontiers, and not to oppose, directly or indirectly, demands for similar Concessions in this region which are supported by the Russian Government. It is understood that the above mentioned places are included in the region in which Great Britain engages not to seek the Concessions referred to.

II. Russia, on her part, engages not to seek for herself and not to support, in favour of Russian subjects, or in favour of the subjects of third Powers, any Concessions of a political or commercial nature—such as Concessions for railways. banks, telegraphs, roads, transport, insurance, &c.—beyond a line going from the Afghan frontier by way of Gazik, Birjand, Kerman, and ending at Bunder Abbas, and not to oppose, directly or indirectly, demands for similar Concessions in this region which are supported by the British Government. It is understood that the above-mentioned places are included in the region in which Russia engages not to seek the Concessions referred to.

III. Russia, on her part, engages not to oppose, without previous arrangement with Great Britain, the grant of any Concessions whatever to British subjects in the regions of Persia situated between the lines mentioned in Articles I and II.

Great Britain undertakes a similar engagement as regards the grant of Concessions to Russian subjects in the same regions of Persia.

All Concessions existing at present in the regions indicated in Articles I and II are maintained.

IV. It is understood that the revenues of all the Persian customs, with the exception of those of Farsistan and of the Persian Gulf, revenues guaranteeing the amortization and the interst of the loans concluded by the Government of the Shah with the "Banque d'Escompte et des Prêts de Perse" up to the date of the signature of the present Agreement, shall be devoted to the same purpose as in the past.

It is equally understood that the revenues of the Persian customs of Farsistan and of the Persian Gulf, as well as those of the fisheries on the Persian shore of the Caspian Sea and those of the Posts and Telegraphs, shall be devoted, as in the past; to the service of the loans concluded by the Government of the Shah with the Imperial Bank of Persia up to the date of the signature of the present Agreement.

V. In the event of irregularities occuring in the amortization or the payment of the interest of the Persian loans concluded with the "Banque d'Escompte et des Prêts de Perse" and with the Imperial Bank of Persia up to the date of the signature of the present Agreement, and in the event of the necessity arising for Russia to establish control over the sources of revenue guaranteeing the regular service of the loans concluded with the first-named bank, and situated in the region mentioned in Article II of the present Agreement, or for Great Britain to establish control over the sources of revenue guaranteeing the regular service of the loans concluded with the second-named bank, and situated in the region mentioned in Article I of the present Agreement, the British and Russian Governments undertake to enter beforehand into a friendly exchange of ideas with a view to determine, in agreement with each other, the measures of control in question and to avoid all interference which would not be inconformity with the principles government the present Agreement.

2. Convention concerning Afghanistan

The High Contracting Parties, in order to ensure perfect security on their respective frontiers in Central Asia and to maintain in these regions a solid and lasting peace, have concluded the following Convention:—

ART. I His Britannic Majesty's Government declare that they have no intention of changing the political status of Afghanistan.

His Britannic Majesty's Government further engage to exercise their influence in Afghanistan only in a pacific sense, and they will not themselves take, nor encourage Afghanistan to take, any measures threatening Russia.

The Russian Government, on their part, declare that they recognize Afghanistan as outside the sphere of Russian influence, and they engage that all their political relations with Afghanistan shall be conducted through the intermediary of His Britannic Majesty's Government; they further engage not to send any Agents into Afghanistan.

ART. II. The Government of His Britannic Majesty having declared in the Treaty signed at Kabul on the 21st March, 1905, that they recognize the Agreement and the engagements concluded with the late Ameer Abdur Rahman, and that they have no intention of interfering in the internal government of Afghan territory, Great Britain engages neither to annex nor to occupy in contravention of that Treaty any portion of Afghanistan or to interfere in the internal administration of the country, provided that the Ameer fulfils the engagements already contracted by him towards His Britannic Majesty's Government under the above-mentioned Treaty.

ART. III. The Russian and Afghan authorities, specially designated for the purpose on the frontier or in the frontier provinces, may establish direct relations with each other for the settlement of local questions of a non-political character.

ART. IV. His Britannic Majesty's Government and the Russian Government affirm their adherence to the principle of equality of commercial opportunity in Afghanistan, and they agree that any facilities which may have been, or shall be hereafter, obtained for British and British-Indian trade and traders, shall be equally enjoyed by Russian trade and traders. Should the progress of trade establish the necessity for Commercial Agents, the two Governments will agree as to what measures shall be taken, due regard, of course, being had to the Ameer's sovereign rights.

ART. V. The present arrangements will only come into force when His Britannic Majesty's Government shall have notified to the Russian Government the consent of the Ameer to the terms stipulated above.

171. DECLARATION AND EXCHANGE OF NOTES ON MOROCCO: FRANCE AND GERMANY
9 February 1909

[Translated from the French texts in Lepsius, Mendelssohn-Bartholdy, and Thimme, *Die grosse Politik*, vol. 24, docs. 8490–92, pp. 489–91]

The conference at Algeciras turned out to be a nearly unmitigated failure for Germany, which in Morocco saved nothing of internationalism but its face, giving France (and Spain) freedom to "reorganize" and manage the police and the finances of that Islamic kingdom. The act produced by the conference (Doc. 168) could hardly have been expected to end French-German rivalry in Morocco, and even the slowdown of the French forward policy thereafter could be attributed more to domestic than to German opposition. Still, the French government did move forward cautiously, in the main by retrospective sanction of military initiatives. Minor incidents affecting French nationals in Morocco furnished pretexts for the military occupation of strategic localities. The murder in March 1907 of a French doctor who conducted a clinic in Marrakesh led to the seizure of Oudjda, near the Algerian border, by French forces under General Pierre Lyautey. About the same time a French company, under a proper franchise, started building modern port facilities at Casablanca. For the haulage of stone from a quarry to the site of the projected breakwater, the company constructed a railroad which when it passed the town wall ran between the waterfront and a Muslim cemetery, providing a focus for popular protest. On 30 July 1907 a band of tribesmen from the Shawiyya district collected in Casablanca where they were joined by local voluteers to attack the European workers, killing nine, among them three Frenchmen. Order was swiftly restored by the *qaid* , or Shawiyya leader, an uncle of Mawlay 'Abd al-'Aziz. Nevertheless, nearly a week later, a small French cruiser sent ashore a token force which, spoiling for action, responded to sporadic resistance by killing men, women, and children in their path of entry. Later, the cruiser bombarded Casablanca, wreaking heavy destruction of life and property in that coastal town of some 20,000 inhabitants. Over the next fortnight or so a French-Spanish force of more than 5,000—of whom about 400 were Spanish troops—landed at Casablanca, ostensibly as a police action under the act of Algeciras (Doc. 168). After installing themselves in Casablanca, the French troops proceeded to "pacify" the port's Shawiyya hinterlaind. The French military occupation of such widely separated spots as Oudjda and Casablanca stimulated the rapid growth among Moroccans of anti-European sentiment, swelling the ranks of an insurrectional movement against 'Abd al-'Aziz, who had come to personify capitulation to alien invaders and who in

September 1907 fled from the seat of government at Fez to Rabat, conveniently close to the French occupying forces. The rebels at Marrakesh proclaimed as their new ruler ʿAbd al-Hafiz, an older half-brother of the reigning monarch. With two rulers in the country, the domestic and international rivalries fused. ʿAbd al-ʿAziz abdicated in the summer of 1908, when he failed to rally popular support in an attempted campaign against the rebels. This solved the domestic contest but sharpened the international one. A French-German quarrel over the terms of European recognition of ʿAbd al-Hafiz as legal ruler of Morocco precipitated a major crisis on the Continent which was not resolved until Germany early in January 1909 acquiesced in the renewed endorsement of the conditions laid down at Algeciras, for which France had mustered overwhelming support among the signers of the act. This was followed by a French-German declaration and exchange of notes on 9 February, when Germany explicitly acknowledged the "special political interests of France" in Morocco in return for an explicit French assurance "not to obstruct German commercial and industrial interests" there. The mutual pledges were explicit, but their mode of expected application was not, so that French-German competition in Morocco persisted, giving rise in 1911 to a crisis more serious than any that had preceded it. Ashmead-Bartlett, *Passing of the Shereefian Empire*; Barlow, *Agadir Crisis*, chaps. 3–6; Edwards, "Franco-German Agreement on Morocco"; Abun-Nasr, *History of the Maghrib*, pp. 292–303; Tardieu, *Le mystère d'Agadir*, pp. 1–87; Usborne, *Conquest of Morocco*, chaps. 7–12; L. Maurice, *La politique marocaine de l'Allemagne*, chaps. 2–6.

1. Joint Declaration

The Government of the French Republic and the Imperial German Government, animated by an equal desire to facilitate the execution of the Act of Algeciras, have agreed to define the meaning that they attach to its clauses with a view to avoiding in the future every cause of misunderstanding between them.

Therefore,

The Government of the Republic of France, firmly attached to the maintenance of the integrity and the independence of the Sharifi Empire, resolved to safeguard the [principle of] economic equality and, accordingly, not to obstruct German commercial and industrial interests there;

And the Imperial German Government, pursuing only economic interests in Morocco, recognizing moreover that the special political interests of France there are tightly bound up with the consolidation of order and internal peace, and having decided not to obstruct those interests;

Declare that they will not pursue and will not encourage any measure of a nature to create in their favor or in that of any Power an economic privilege, and that they will seek to associate their nationals in affairs for which they are able to obtain the concession.

2. Jules Cambon, the French Ambassador (Berlin), to Wilhelm E. von Schoen, the Secretary of State at the Foreign Office

To avoid all misunderstanding on the meaning of our arrangement of today's date on Moroccan affairs, Your Excellency will permit me to specify that the political disinterest of Germany in no way prejudices the situations already acquired by its nationals but implies the noncandidacy of its subjects for the functions of directors or of technical counsellors of Moroccan public services having or likely to have a political character, or of instructors in these services.

On the other hand, it is agreed that in the affairs which may require an association of German and French interests, the fact will be taken into account, to the degree possible, that French interests in Morocco are more important than German interests.

3. Von Schoen to Cambon

I hasten to acknowledge receipt of the

letter that you sent me today in which you specify, to avoid all misunderstanding, the meaning of our arrangement of today's

date on Moroccan affairs.

I am pleased to inform you that I am entirely in agreement with you.

172. CONVENTION (POTSDAM) ON THE BAGHDAD RAILROAD AND RUSSIAN INTERESTS IN PERSIA: RUSSIA AND GERMANY
6/19 August 1911

[*American Journal of International Law*, 6 (1912): 120–22]

After October 1904 construction of the Baghdad railroad stalled for more than six years because of financial and political difficulties, which arose mostly from the strained relations of Germany with Britain, France, and Russia. Led by Britain, the Entente powers insisted (1907–10) on quadrilateral talks—or negotiations *à quatre*, as they were commonly known in the diplomatic parlance of the period. But Germany, determined to weaken Entente solidarity, sought bilateral agreements with each of the three governments. The first opportunity came early in November 1910 during Tsar Nicholas II's visit to Kaiser Wilhelm II at Postdam, where their foreign ministers reviewed Russian-German relations in Europe and in the Ottoman-Persian area. In the weeks that followed, the Wilhelmstrasse tried, without result, to detach Russia from the Entente in European affairs. Saint. Petersburg remained inflexible in limiting the discussions to issues bearing directly or indirectly on the prolongation of the Baghdad railroad from Anatolia into Syria and Mesopotamia. The Russian-German convention of 1911, which automatically went into force upon signature, addressed itself to these questions. Chapman, *Great Britain and the Bagdad Railway*, chap. 7; Wolf, *Diplomatic History of the Bagdad Railroad*, chap. 6; Earle, *Turkey, the Great Powers and the Bagdad Railway*, chap. 10; G. Gooch, *Before the War*, 2: 210–16, 289–301; Kazemzadeh, *Russia and Britain in Persia*, pp. 591–97; for repercussions in Persia, see Shuster, *Strangling of Persia*; Gooch and Temperley, *British Documents on the Origins of the War*, 10(i): 549–723.

ART. 1. The German Imperial Government declares that it has no intention to request for itself the construction of railways or the concession of navigation or telegraphic services or to support requests of that nature on the part of German or foreign citizens to the north of the line going from Casré to Chirine, passing by way of Ispahan, Yezd and Kakhk and reaching the Afghan frontier at the degree latitude of Gachik.

ART. 2. The Russian Government which intends to obtain from the Persian Government a concession with a view of creating a network of railways in northern Persia

engages itself on its part, among other things, to ask for the concession for the construction of railway which is to start from Teheran and to end at Khanikine, to connect this network of railways on the Turko-Persian frontier with the Sadijeh-Khanikine line as soon as the [Koniah-] Bagdad branch railway shall have been completed.

When this concession is obtained, the work of construction of the line indicated shall begin at the latest two years after the completion of the Sadijeh-Khanikine branch and [shall be] terminated within the space of four years.

The Russian Government reserves unto itself the right to establish at a proper time the definitive location of the line under consideration; but on this occasion it shall bear in mind the desiderata of the German Government. The two governments shall favor international traffic over the lines from Khanikine to Teheran and from Khanikine to Bagdad and avoid all measures that might interfere therewith, such, for instance, as the creation of transitory customs duties or the application of differential tariffs.

If at the end of a period of two years after the completion of the Sadijeh branch to Khanikine of the railway from Koniah to Bagdad, the construction of the line from Khanikine to Teheran is not commenced, then the Russian Government shall inform the German Government of its renunciation of the concession of this latter line. The German Government, in that case, shall have the right to solicit on its part the concession of said line.

ART. 3. In view of the general importance which the realization of the Bagdad railway has for international commerce, the Russian Government engages itself not to take any step that might prove an obstacle to the construction of the railway or prevent the participation of capital in this enterprise. Always, of course, with the understanding that no pecuniary or economic damage would accrue thereby to Russia.

ART. 4. The Russian Government reserves unto itself the right to entrust to a group of foreign financiers the construction of the projected junction between the network of railways in Persia and the Sadijeh to Khanikine line in place of undertaking itself this construction.

ART. 5. Independently of this, the Russian Government reserves unto itself the right to participate in the works in whatever form it may deem proper, whatever be the mode of construction of the line in question, and to reassume possession of the railway by reimbursing the actual amounts expended by the constructors.

The high contracting parties engage themselves besides to participate annually in the tariff or other privileges which one of the parties may obtain with regard to this line. All the other causes of the present agreement remain valid in all events.

173. CONVENTION ON MOROCCO SETTLING THE AGADIR CRISIS: FRANCE AND GERMANY
4 November 1911

(Ratifications exchanged, Paris, 12 March 1912)
[From the translated texts in Great Britain, *Parliamentary Papers, 1912*, Morocco no. 4 (1911), Cd. 6010, pp. 8–16]

The colonial party in France, with the enthusiastic support of military officers and the variable support of the politicians, kept French policy on Morocco more consistent than observers of the day may often have believed. After Algeciras, the French army officers on active assignment in Algeria and naval officers off Morocco's Atlantic coast appeared to force the hand of the politicians in Paris by the occupation of Oudjda and Casablanca and the creeping penetration into the hinterland of both. This was forward movement not by policy but by expediency. When France made such moves, Spain was not too far behind. Germany could not check the process, only its pace; and out of the crisis of 1908, contrived in Berlin, came the French-German reaffirmation in 1909 (Doc. 171) of the principle of economic equality, at the cost, however, of formal German acknowledgement of the special political position of France in Morocco. The vagueness of the 1909 exchange of pledges created friction, since every economic initiative had political overtones, just as every political initiative had economic implications. This was nowhere better exemplified than in French plans for railroad construction. By the end of 1910, France had drawn up blueprints for lines from Casablanca to Settat in the heart of Shawiyya territory and from Oudjda to Taourirt in the northeast, both intended for districts under French occupation. The Quai d'Orsay claimed that these lines were designed for security reasons only, but little imagination was demanded at the Wilhelmstrasse to see that they pointed toward each other, and when both were connected, as German officials were persuaded they would be, France would dominate Morocco south of the Rif by cutting the zone in half. The German resistance to French railroad plans rested on the 1906 international and the 1909 bilateral agreements, and on German participation in the Moroccan Society for Public Works—30 percent, if the Austrian subsidiary interest were included, as contrasted with the 50 percent French interest—which was guaranteed a monopoly of concessions for infrastructural development such as railroads. The dispute was complicated by rising unrest in Fez, stirred by European expansion but directed against Mawlay 'Abd al-Hafiz (1908–13), who was held responsible for Morocco's declining fortunes. 'Abd al-Hafiz appealed for help to France, which early in April 1911 notified the powers of possible military action, allegedly to rescue French and other European residents of the Moroccan coast, contending that such police action even in the interior was allowed under the act of Algeciras. That act would not be violated, the argument continued, since France had no intention of occupying Fez, damaging the mawlay's sovereignty, or ignoring the principle of economic equality. Before the end of April, the expedition was mounted, and in less than a month French troops entered Fez. They were still there on 1 July, when Germany notified the interested powers, just before taking action, that it was sending a warship to Agadir, a closed port on Morocco's south Atlantic coast, where it would remain "until the state of things in Morocco will have returned to its former calm " (as cited by Barlow, *Agadir Crisis*, p. 217). It seems clear now that Germany had hoped to isolate France by its gunboat diplomacy. Spain was losing sympathy for its partner in Morocco because of critical French press opinion, particularly early in June, after the Spanish occupation in its Moroccan sphere of Larache, al-Ksar, and Tetuan, an action it had been led to take by the earlier French expedition to Fez. The Wilhelmstrasse, however, had taken Whitehall too much for granted, by refusing even to respond to Foreign Secretary Sir Edward Grey's warning on 4 July that Britain could not "recognize any new agreements which might be come to without us" (as cited by Nicolson, *Sir Arthur Nicolson*, p. 345), until the then pro-German chancellor of the exchequer, David Lloyd George, speaking on behalf of the government, publicly declared on the twenty-first that peace at the German price was "intolerable." Thereafter, the British government suspended naval talks with Germany and placed the Admiralty on the alert. The crisis lingered through the rest of the summer, for not until 22 September did Alfred von Kiderlen-Wächter, the German foreign minister, finally induce the French to moderate their demands. By then, Germany had come to the realization that it would have to acquiesce in the French fait accompli in Morocco, but before doing so formally it was determined to use the Agadir crisis as a means of getting the largest return, first by demanding almost all of the French Congo. When Kiderlen finally reduced the terms to acceptable size late in September, the international crisis quickly subsided, and six weeks later France and Germany signed the accord, reproduced below, which liberated France to put the finishing touches on its policy of slow-motion annexation of southern Morocco. Barlow, op. cit.; Tardieu, *Le mystère d'Agadir*; Nicolson, op. cit., chap. 12; Usborne, *Conquest of Morocco*, chaps. 9–13; Mann, *Die Agadirkrisis des Jahres 1911*; Morel, *Morocco in Diplomacy*, pp. 125–218; Albin, *Le coup d'Agadir*; Bernard, *Le Maroc*, chap. 4; Touron, *Notre protectorat marocain*, chap. 8; Trout, *Morocco's Saharan Frontiers*, chap. 2; Woodward, *Great Britain and the German Navy*, chaps. 15–17.

1. Convention

In consequence of the troubles which have arisen in Morocco, and which have shown the necessity of carrying on, in that country, in the interests of all, the work of pacification and progress provided for by the Algeciras Act, the Government of the French Republic and the Imperial German Government have deemed it necessary to define more precisely and to complete the Franco-German Agreement of the 9th February, 1909.

Therefore, M. Jules Cambon, Ambassador Extraordinary of the French Republic accredited to His Majesty the German Emperor, and M. de Kiderlen-Waechter, Secretary of State for Foreign Affairs of the German Empire, having communicated to one another their full powers, found in good and due form, have agreed upon the following articles:—

ART. 1. The Imperial German Government declare that, having only economic interests in Morocco, they will not obstruct such action as may be taken by France with a view to assist[ing] the Moorish Government in the introduction of any administrative, judicial, economic, financial and military reforms of which they may stand in need for the good government of the Empire, as also of any new regulations and modifications in existing regulations which these reforms may entail. Consequently, the German Government adhere to the measures of reorganization, of control, and of financial guarantee, which the French Government, after obtaining the consent of the Moorish Government, may consider it necessary to take with this object in view, with the reservation that French action will ensure economic equality between the nations in Morocco.

In the event of France being led to strengthen and to extend her control and her protection, the Imperial German Government, recognizing France's full liberty of action, will raise no objection, subject to the reservation that the commercial liberty guaranteed by former treaties is respected.

It is agreed that the rights and proceedings of the Morocco State Bank, as defined in the Algeciras Act, shall not be in any way impeded.

ART. 2. With this view it is agreed that the Imperial Government will raise no objection to France, after obtaining the consent of the Moorish Government, proceeding with such military occupation of Moorish territory as she may consider necessary for the maintenance of order and the security of commercial transactions, and to her exercising all rights of police on land and in Moorish waters.

ART. 3. From now henceforward, if His Majesty the Sultan of Morocco should entrust to the diplomatic and consular agents of France the representation and protection of Moorish subjects abroad, the Imperial Government declare that they will raise no objection.

If, on the other hand, His Majesty the Sultan handed over to the French representative at the Moorish Court the duty of acting as intermediary with the other foreign representatives, the German Government would raise no objection.

ART. 4. The French Government declare that, firmly attached to the principle of commercial liberty in Morocco, they will not permit any inequality either as regards the establishment of customs duties, taxes, or other contributions, or as regards the establishment of tariffs for transport by rail, river, or other means, and especially as regards all questions of transit.

The French Government will also use their influence with the Moorish Government with a view to prevent any differential treatment of subjects of the different Powers; they will more particularly oppose any measure, the promulgation, for instance, of administrative decrees dealing with weights and measures, gauging, stamping, &c., which might place the merchandise of a Power in a position of inferiority.

The French Government engage to use their influence with the State Bank with a view to the posts of delegate which are in the gift of the bank, on the Commission of Customs Valuation and on the Standing Customs Committee being conferred in turn on the members of the management of the bank at Tangier.

ART. 5. The French Government will see that no export duty is levied in Morocco on iron ore exported from Moorish ports. Mines of iron ore will be subject to no special tax on their output or methods of working. They shall, apart from the general taxes, pay only a fixed charge, calculated by the hectare and yearly, and a charge in proportion to the gross output. These charges, which shall be fixed in accordance with articles 35 and 49 of the draft mining regulations attached to the protocol of the 7th June, 1910, of the Paris conference, shall be paid equally by all mining undertakings.

The French Government will see that the mining taxes are collected regularly, and that on no pretext whatever the whole or a part of these taxes shall be remitted.

ART. 6. The Government of the French Republic engage to see that the contracts for works and materials, which may be necessary in connection with any future concessions for roads, railways, harbours, telegraphs, &c., are allotted by the Moorish Government in accordance with the rules of adjudication.

They engage further to see that the conditions for tendering, more especially as regards the supply of materials and the limit of time within which tenders must be submitted, do not place the subjects of any Power in a position of inferiority.

The working of the great undertakings mentioned above shall be reserved to the Moorish State or entrusted, by a concession, to third parties, who may be asked to furnish the funds necessary for the pur-

pose. The French Government will see that as regards the working of railways and other means of transport, as also the application of the regulations which govern such working, no differential treatment is accorded to the subjects of the different Powers who use such means of transport.

The Government of the Republic will use their influence with the State Bank with a view to the post of delegate on the General Commission of Tenders and Contracts being conferred in turn on the members of the Management of the bank at Tangier.

Similarly, the French Government will use their influence with the Moorish Government in order that, so long as article 66 of the Algeciras Act remains in force, one of the three posts of Shereefian delegate on the Special Committee of Public Works is conferred on a subject of one of the Powers represented in Morocco.

ART. 7. The French Government will use their influence with the Moorish Government in order that the owners of mines and other industrial or agricultural undertakings, without distinction of nationality, and in accordance with the regulations which may be issued on the model of French legislation on the same subject, may be authorised to build light railways connecting their centres of production with the lines of general public utility and with the ports.

ART. 8. Each year a report on the working of the railways in Morocco shall be presented drawn up in the same form and under the same conditions as the reports which are laid before the meetings of shareholders in French railway companies.

The Government of the Republic shall entrust to one of the directors of the State Bank the duty of drawing up this report which, together with the materials on which it is based, shall be submitted to the Censors, and then published, with, if necessary, such observations as the latter may wish to append thereto, founded on their own information.

ART. 9. In order to avoid, as far as possible, diplomatic representations, the French Government will urge the Moorish Government to refer to an arbitrator, nominated *ad hoc* in each case by agreement between the French consul and the consul of the Power interested, or, failing them, by the two Governments, such complaints brought by foreign subjects against the Moorish authorities or agents acting in the capacity of Moorish authorities as shall not have been found capable of adjustment through the intermediary of the French consul and the consul of the Power interested.

This mode of procedure shall remain in force until such time as a judicial system, founded on the general principles embodied in the legislation of the Powers interested, shall have been introduced, which shall ultimately, by agreement between those Powers, replace the consular courts.

ART. 10. The French Government will see that foreign subjects continue to enjoy the right of fishing in Moorish waters and harbours.

ART. 11. The French Government will urge the Moorish Government to open to foreign commerce new ports from time to time in accordance with the growing requirements of trade.

ART. 12. In order to meet a request of the Moorish Government, the two Governments undertake to urge, in agreement with the other Powers and on the basis of the Madrid Convention, the revision of the lists and the reconsideration of the position of foreign-protected subjects and mokhalats ("associés agricoles"), which are dealt with in articles 8 and 16 of that convention.

They likewise agree to urge upon the signatory Powers any modifications of the Madrid Convention which may be made necessary, when the time comes, by the change in the status of foreign-protected persons and mokhalats ("associés agricoles").

ART. 13. Any clause of an agreement, convention, treaty, or regulation which may conflict with the foregoing stipulations is, and remains, abrogated.

ART. 14. The present agreement shall be communicated to the other signatory Powers of the Algeciras Act, and the two Governments engage to give their mutual support with a view to obtain the adhesion of those Powers.

ART. 15. The present convention shall be ratified, and the ratifications exchanged at Paris as soon as possible.

Done in duplicate at Berlin, the 4th November, 1911.

2. Alfred von Kiderlen-Wächter, German Foreign Secretary, to Jules Cambon, French Ambassador at Berlin

In order to make quite clear the agreement of the 4th November, 1911, respecting Morocco, and to define its meaning, I have the honour to inform your Excellency that, in the event of the French Government deeming it necessary to assume a protectorate over Morocco, the Imperial Government would place no obstacle in the way.

The adherence of the German Government, accorded in a general manner to the French Government in the first article of the said convention, applies of course to all questions as are provided for in the Algeciras Act, which require regulating.

You were good enough to inform me, on the other hand, that, should Germany wish to acquire from Spain Spanish Guinea, Corisco Island, and the Elobey Islands, France would be prepared to waive in Germany's favour the exercise of her preferential rights which she holds by virtue of the treaty of the 27th June, 1900, between France and Spain. I have pleasure in taking note of this assurance, and in adding that Germany will not intervene in any special agreements which France and Spain may think fit to conclude with each other on the subject of Morocco, it being understood that Morocco comprises all that part of Northern Africa which is situated between Algeria, French West Africa, and the Spanish colony of Rio de Oro.

The German Government, while they abstain from asking that the share to be granted to German industry in the construction of railways shall be fixed in advance, rely on the readiness of the French Government always to welcome the association of interests between nationals of both countries in schemes for which they may respectively obtain a concession.

They rely likewise on the construction of no other Moorish railway being put up to public tender before the railway from Tangier to Fez, in which all the nations are interested, is put up to public tender, and on the French Government proposing to the Moorish Government the opening of the port of Agadir to international commerce.

Finally, when the system of railways of general interest is planned, the German

Government request the French Government to see that the Moorish administration show a genuine regard for the economic interests of Morocco, and that, more particularly, the alignment of the lines of public interest is such as to facilitate, so far as may be possible, connections between the mining districts and the lines of public interest or the ports which form their natural outlet.

Your Excellency was good enough to assure me that as soon as the judicial system referred to in article 9 of the above-mentioned convention shall have been introduced, and the consular courts replaced, the French Government will ensure that German nationals are placed under the new jurisdiction in exactly the same conditions as French nationals. I have pleasure in taking note of this assurance, and at the same time in informing your Excellency that, when this judicial system is put into force, in agreement with the Powers, the German Government will consent to the abolition of their consular courts at the same time as those of the other Powers. I would add that, in my view, the expression "changes in the status of protected persons," which is used in article 12 of the convention of the 4th November, 1911, respecting Morocco, implies the abrogation, if it be thought necessary, of that part of the Madrid Convention which deals with protected persons and mokhalats ("associés agricoles").

Finally, being desirous of giving to the said convention the character of an act destined not only to remove every cause of conflict between our two countries, but also to strengthen their good relations, we unite in declaring that any disputes which may arise between the contracting parties on the subject of the interpretation and the application of the stipulations of the convention of the 4th November, and which shall not have been settled diplomatically, shall be submitted to a court of arbitration constituted in accordance with the terms of The Hague Convention of the 18th October, 1907. Terms of Reference shall be drawn up, and the procedure shall follow the rules laid down in the same convention so far as provision to the contrary has not been made by an agreement between the parties at the time of going to arbitration.

3. Cambon to Kiderlen-Wächter

I have the honour to take note of the declaration which your Excellency has been good enough to make to me that, in the event of the French Government deeming it necessary to assume a protectorate over Morocco, the Imperial Government would place no obstacle in the way, and that the adherence of the German Government, accorded in a general manner to the French Government in the first article of the agreement of the 4th November, 1911, respecting Morocco, applies as a matter of course to all questions which require regulating provided for in the Algeciras Act.

On the other hand, I have the honour to confirm the statement that, should the German Government wish to acquire from Spain Spanish Guinea, Corisco Island, and the Elobey Islands, France is prepared to waive in Germany's favour the exercise of her preferential rights which she holds by virtue of the treaty of the 27th June, 1900, between France and Spain. I am glad, on my part, to receive the assurance that Germany will not intervene in any special agreements which France and Spain may think fit to conclude with each other on the subject of Morocco, it being understood that Morocco comprises all that part of northern Africa which is situated between Algeria, French West Africa, and the Spanish Colony of Rio de Oro.

I have pleasure also in informing you that, while the German Government abstain from asking that the share to be granted to German industry in the construction of railways shall be fixed in advance, the French Government will welcome the association of interests between nationals of both countries in schemes for which they may respectively obtain a concession.

You may also rest assured that the construction of no other Moorish railway will be put up to public tender before the railway from Tangier to Fez, in which all nations are interested, is put up to public tender, and that the French Government will propose to the Moorish Government the opening of the port of Agadir to international commerce.

Finally, when the system of railways of public interest is planned, the French Government will see that the Moorish administration show a genuine regard for the economic interests of Morocco, and that, more particularly, the alignment of the lines of public interest is such as to facilitate, so far as may be possible, connections between the mining districts and the lines of public interest or the ports which form their natural outlet. Your Excellency may likewise rest assured that as soon as the judicial system referred to in article 9 of the convention of the 4th November, 1911, respecting Morocco is introduced, and the consular courts replaced, the French Government will ensure that German nationals are placed under the new jurisdiction in exactly the same conditions as French nationals.

I have, on the other hand, pleasure in taking note of the statement that when this judicial system is put into force, in agreement with the Powers, the German Government will consent to the abolition of their consular courts at the same time as those of the other Powers. I take note also of the statement that, in your Excellency's view, the expression "changes in the status of protected persons," which is used in article

12 of the above-mentioned convention, implies the abrogation, if it be thought necessary, of that part of the Madrid Convention which deals with protected persons and mokhalats ("associés agricoles").

Finally, being desirous of giving to the convention of the 4th November, 1911, respecting Morocco, the character of an act destined not only to remove every cause of conflict between our two countries, but also to strengthen their good relations, we are agreed in declaring that any disputes which may arise between the contracting parties on the subject of the interpretation and the application of the stipulations of the said convention, and which shall not have been settled diplomatically, shall be submitted to a court of arbitration constituted in accordance with the terms of The Hague Convention of the 18th October, 1907.

Terms of Reference shall be drawn up and the procedure shall follow the rules laid down in the same convention, so far as provision to the contrary has not been made, by an agreement between the parties at the time of going to arbitration.

174. CONVENTION (FEZ) FOR THE CREATION OF A PROTECTORATE: FRANCE AND MOROCCO
30 March 1912

(Approved by French law, 15 July 1912; ratified by French decree, 20 July 1912)
[Translated from the French text in Basdevant, *Traités et conventions*, 3: 69–70]

The convention with Germany of 4 November 1911 (Doc. 173) finally liberated France to fulfill its aspirations in its sphere of Morocco. Once the last of the European opponents of French expansion into Morocco had fallen into line, Mawlay ʿAbd al-Hafiz (1908–13) could no longer prevent France from assimilating his external—and a good deal of his internal—sovereignty. Still, considering that the process, begun under his predecessor's reign, of surrendering police and fiscal powers to France (and Spain) was accelerated after he came to undisputed power in August 1908, the mawlay nevertheless resisted to the bitter end "negotiation" with France of the protectorate convention reproduced below. France then had to clarify its position with Spain over the precise division of Moroccan spoils, which were stipulated in a separate convention signed in November 1912 (Doc. 176). France also approached each of the capitulatory powers asking for its voluntary surrender of the special privileges, including where pertinent the right to protect Moroccan subjects, on the ground that France was introducing European principles of law and justice that made continued extraterritoriality unnecessary. A majority of the capitulatory powers accepted the French invitation to bilateral agreements, mostly concluded between 1914 and 1916. Germany, Austria, and Hungary lost their rights in Morocco in the peace treaties after World War I. Invoking secret article 2 of the 1904 British-French Entente (Doc. 164), Britain did not surrender its capitulatory privileges or rights of protection in Morocco until after the capitulations were abolished in Egypt in 1937. The United States refused to give up its extraterritorial privileges in Morocco until France laid down its sovereignty in 1956. Stuart, *International City of Tangier*, chap. 2; Bernard, *Le Maroc*, pp. 332–420; A. Martin, *Le Maroc et l'Europe*, chap. 9; Touron, *Notre protectorat marocain*, p. 130 ff.; Usborne, *Conquest of Morocco*, chaps. 14–18; International Court of Justice, *Case concerning Rights of Nationals of the United States of America in Morocco*.

The Government of the French Republic and the Government of His Sharifi Majesty, anxious to establish in Morocco a stable regime, founded on internal order and general security, which will make the introduction of reforms possible and assure the economic development of the country, have agreed on the following clauses:

ART. 1. The Government of the French Republic and His Majesty the Sultan have agreed to institute in Morocco a new regime permitting the introduction on Moroccan territory [of such] administrative, judicial, educational, economic, financial, and military reforms as the French Government may judge useful.

This regime will safeguard the [prevailing] state of religious affairs, the traditional respect and prestige of the Sultan, the practice of the Muslin religion and [the operation of its] institutions, especially those of the *habus* [religious endowments]. It will allow the organization of a reformed Sharifi Makhzan [Moroccan Government].

The Government of the Republic will consult with the Spanish Government on the interests of that government deriving from its geographic position and its territorial possessions on the Moroccan coast.

Similarly, the city of Tangiers will preserve the special character that has been recognized and that will determine its municipal organization.

ART. 2. His Majesty the Sultan, as of now, permits the French Government, after notifying the Makhzan, to proceed with such military occupation of Moroccan territory as it may deem necessary for the maintenance of order and the security of commerce, and for the exercise of all police duties on Moroccan land and waters.

ART. 3. The Government of the Republic undertakes to give constant support to His Sharifi Majesty against any danger that might threaten his person or his throne or that might compromise the transquillity of his states. The same support will be given to the heir to the throne and to his successors.

ART. 4. The provisions required by the new regime of the protectorate will be decreed, on the proposal of the French Government, by His Sharifi Majesty or by those authorities to whom he might delegate such power. The same will hold true for new regulations or for the modification of existing regulations.

ART. 5. The French Government will be represented before His Sharifi Majesty by a Resident General Commissioner who, as guardian of the authority of the Republic in Morocco, will oversee the execution of the present agreement.

The Resident General Commissioner will be the Sultan's sole intermediary with foreign representatives and in the relations that these representatives maintain with the Moroccan Government. He will be responsible, in particular, for all matters concerning foreigners in the Sharifi Empire.

He will have the power to approve and

to promulgate, in the name of the French Government, all decrees issued by His Sharifi Majesty.

ART. 6. The diplomatic and consular agents of France will be responsible for representing and protecting Moroccan subjects and interests in foreign countries.

His Majesty the Sultan pledges to conclude no act of an international character without the prior consent of the Government of the French Republic.

ART. 7. The Government of the French Republic and the Government of His Sharifi Majesty intend to fix, by common accord, the principles of a financial reorganization which, while respecting the rights of creditors of the Moroccan public debt, will make it possible to guarantee the obligations of the Sharifi Treasury and to collect on a regular basis the revenues of the Empire.

ART. 8. His Sharifi Majesty agrees in the future not to contract, directly or indirectly, any public or private debt and not to grant any concession, in any form whatsoever, without authorization by the French Government.

ART. 9. The present convention will be submitted to the Government of the French Republic for ratification and the instrument of ratification will be delivered with the least possibly delay to His Majesty the Sultan. . . .

175. TREATY OF PEACE (OUCHY AND LAUSANNE) IN TRIPOLI AND THE DODECANESE ISLANDS: ITALY AND THE OTTOMAN EMPIRE
15–18 October 1912

(Ratifications exchanged, Lausanne, 18 October 1912; executed by Italian law no. 1312
of 16 December 1912)
[Translated from the French texts in Italy, Ministry of Foreign Affairs, *Trattati e convenzioni*, 22:
226–32, 243–48]

Ever since France in 1881 occupied Tunis, which had been Italy's first choice for expansion across the Mediterranean (Doc. 142), Tripoli (including Cyrenaica)—the last surviving Ottoman province in North Africa—became by the process of elimination the object of Italian imperial aspiration. Thirty years elapsed before its fulfillment, however. In the interval, Italy had anchored itself at Somaliland (1889) and Eritrea (1890) in East Africa, and from there it tried to penetrate Abyssinia (present-day Ethiopia). But the fiasco of the Abyssinian campaign in 1896 left Italy licking its wounds. As early as 1887, Germany had already given secret assurances of support to Italy's claim to Tripoli. Then in 1902 the Italian government lined up Austria, Britain, and France and seven years later Russia behind plans for the annexation of Tripoli. These diplomatic measures, like the accompanying promotion of Italian peaceful penetration into Tripoli, reflected only dimly the original French Moroccan models after which the Italian copies were patterned. After many false starts, the Italian government finally declared war on the Ottoman Empire on 29 September 1911, after years of contrived charges against the Sublime Porte of discrimination against Italian subjects and interests in Tripoli. The timing was hardly accidental. The German-French crisis over Agadir, which had passed its peak but was not yet formally settled, distracted Europe. Italian clumsiness, however, disturbed the other powers. If Italy triumphed, its seizure of Tripoli would create a new, and therefore unsettling, strategic reality in the Mediterranean, which had remained remarkably stable for nearly three decades, ever since France and Britain had installed themselves in Tunis and Egypt. Besides, war with the Ottoman Empire potentially entailed serious consequences in Europe itself, because that empire sprawled over three continents, and any threat to its territorial integrity also threatened the balance in Europe. At first, the anxiety was moderated by the lackluster Italian campaign. It is true that the Italian government announced on 5 November 1911 and legislated on 25 February 1912 the annexation of Tripoli and Cyrenaica, but those were empty gestures, since Italian troops had secured themselves only at intermittent points on the Mediterranean edge. Italy kept sending more and more troops, totaling about 115,000 by April 1912, and the latest weapons, including planes; yet they were hemmed in along the coast by poorly equipped Ottoman and local tribal forces less than a fifth their number. Italy quarreled with all the European powers except Russia, and, frustrated in Tripoli, it began to attack other parts of the Ottoman Empire. Italian ships bombarded Bayrut on 24 February 1912 and Ottoman forts at the mouth of the Dardanelles on 18 April; and between 28 April and 21 May Italian troops occupied the Dodecanese Islands along the southwest Anatolian littoral of the Ottoman Empire. These wide-ranging Italian feints shocked the major powers, which all along had sought to keep the war from spreading, especially into the Balkans; their response was a united mediatory effort which in March-April 1912 elicited from the Italian government and the Sublime Porte their respective terms for peace. However, all that that initiative yielded was the reaffirmation by both belligerents of their insistence on the acknowledged exercise of unconditional sovereignty in Tripoli. In the end, a settlement was reached in Switzerland by direct negotiations, which opened on 12 July, adjourned on 28 July pending a restructuring of the Ottoman government, and reopened on 13 August. In the following two treaties (the first one secret and provisional) and the three annexes, which together formed the Italian-Ottoman settlement the Sublime Porte did not formally surrender its sovereignty over Tripoli (annex 1), while the Italian king rested his claim to that sovereignty on Italian law (annex 2). Over the Dodecanese Islands, which Italy continued to occupy and administer, Ottoman sovereignty was recognized (annex 3). For de jure titles to the conquered territories, Italy had to wait until the ratification in 1924 of the peace settlement of the Allied and Associated Powers with Turkey. Ironically, Italy had to wait even longer for de facto possession, because the Arab resistance to Italian rule in Cyrenaica held out until 1931. Askew, *Europe and Italy's Acquisition of Libya*; Barclay, *Turco-Italian War and Its Problems*; Beehler, *History of the Italian-Turkish War*; Staley, *War and the Private Investor*, pp. 62–70; Woolf, *Empire and Commerce in Africa*, pt. 2, chap. 4; Enver Pasha, *Um Tripolis*; Abbott, "Tripolitan War from the Turkish Side"; Abun-Nasr, *History of the Maghrib*, pp. 303–12; Pinon, "L'Europe et la guerre italo-turque"; Tittoni, *Italy's Foreign and Colonial Policy*, pp. 19–27, 108–21; Piccioli, "La pace di Ouchy"; Solmi, *Making of Modern Italy*, chaps. 7–8; Volpe, *L'impresa di Tripoli*; Irace, *With the Italians in Tripoli*; Lémonon, "La Libye et l'opinion publique italienne"; McCullagh, *Italy's War for a Desert*; Meyer, *Die Neutralität Deutschlands und Österreich-Ungarns im italienisch-türkischen Krieg*; Allain, "Les débuts du conflit italo-turc"; Malgeri, *La guerra libica*; Polayan, "The Tripolitan War."

1. Secret and Provisional Treaty of Peace (Ouchy), 15 October 1912

His Majesty the King of Italy and His Majesty the Emperor of the Ottomans, prompted by a mutual desire to end the state of war existing between the two countries, in view of the difficulty of achieving it because of the inability of Italy to act contrary to the law of [25] Feburary 1912, which proclaimed its sovereignty over Tripolitania and over Cyrenaica, and in order that the Ottoman Empire might formally recognize this sovereignty, have named their Plenipotentiaries, who, after having exchanged their respective credentials, found in good and due form have agreed on the following secret *modus procedendi*:

ART. 1. The Imperial Government undertakes within three days to issue an imperial *ferman* addressed to the populations of Tripolitania and Cyrenaica, conforming to the attached text (Annex No. 1).

ART. 2. The representative of the Sultan and of the religious leaders must be approved in advance by the Royal Government.

The appointment of the above representative and of the *naibs* [agents] shall be fixed by agreement between the two Governments and paid from local revenues; those of the Qadi, however, shall be paid by the Imperial Government.

The number of the above religious leaders shall not exceed the number of those existing at the time of the declaration of war.

ART. 3. The Royal Government undertakes within three days following the promulgation of the imperial ferman mentioned in Article 1 to issue a royal decree, conforming to the attached text (Annex No. 2).

ART. 4. The Imperial Government undertakes within three days following the promulgation of the imperial *ferman* mentioned in Article 1 to issue an imperial *irade* [order], conforming to the attached text (Annex No. 3).

ART. 5. Immediately after the promulgation of the above three unilateral acts, the Plenipotentiaries of the two High Contracting Parties shall sign a public treaty conforming to the attached text (Annex No. 4).

ART. 6. It naturally remains understood and inviolate under the present accord that the Imperial Government undertakes not to send and not to permit the sending of arms, munitions, soldiers, and officers from Turkey to Tripolitania and Cyrenaica.

ART. 7. The expenses respectively incurred by the two Governments for the support of prisoners-of-war and hostages shall be considered as compensated.

ART. 8. The two High Contracting Parties undertake to keep the present accord secret.

However, the two Governments reserve time of the presentation of the public the right to make this accord public at the treaty (Annex No. 4) to the respective Parliaments.

The present accord shall enter into effect on the very day of its signature.

ART. 9. It is understood that the Annexes mentioned in the present accord form an integral part of it.

In witness whereof, the Plenipotentiaries have signed the present accord and have affixed to it their seals. . . .

ANNEX NO. 1

To the inhabitants of Tripolitania and Cyrenaica:

My Government finding it impossible to give you the effective help that you require to defend your country; anxious about your present and future happiness; wanting to escape the continuation of a war disastrous to you and your families and dangerous to Our Empire; for the purpose of restoring peace and prosperity to your country; [therefore] in the exercise of my sovereign rights I concede to you full and complete autonomy. Your country shall be governed by new laws and special regulations, to the preparation of which you will contribute your advice, so that [these laws and regulations] may correspond to your needs and your customs.

I name as my representative to you my faithful servant Şamseddin Bey, with the title of Naib al-Sultan [the Sultan's Agent], whom I charge with protecting Ottoman interests in your country. The mandate which I confer on him shall last for five years; after that, I reserve the right to renew his mandate or to provide for his succession.

Our intention being that the provisions of the sacred law of the Şeriat shall remain constantly enforced, we reserve to ourselves for this purpose the nomination of the Qadi, who in turn shall name the naibs among the local *ulema* in accordance with rule of the Şeriat. We shall pay the salary of this Qadi, while [the salaries] of the Naib al-Sultan and of the other officials of the Şeriat shall be deducted from local revenues.

ANNEX NO. 2

His Majesty the King of Italy

In view of Law No. 38 of 25 February 1912, by which Tripolitania and Cyrenaica have been placed under the full and complete sovereignty of the Kingdom of Italy;

For the purpose of hastening the pacification of the above provinces;

On the proposal of the Council of Ministers;

We have decreed and do decree:

ART. 1. Full and complete amnesty is accorded to those inhabitants of Tripolitania and Cyrenaica who took part in the hostilities or who might thus be compromised, with the exception of [those charged with] crimes of common law. Consequently, no individual of any class or station may be prosecuted or troubled in his person or property or in the exercise of his rights because of his political or military actions, or because of the opinions which he might have expressed during the hostilities. Persons detained or deported for this reason shall be set free immediately.

ART. 2. The inhabitants of Tripolitania and Cyrenaica shall continue to enjoy as in the past the greatest freedom in the practice of the Muslim religion. The name of His Imperial Majesty the Sultan, as Caliph, shall continue to be pronounced in the public prayers of the Muslims. His representative is recognized in the person that he names; his appointees shall be paid by local revenues.

The rights of the pious foundations [*evkaf*] shall be respected as in the past, and the relations of the Muslims with the religious leader called a Qadi, who shall be named by the Şeyhülislam [the head of the Ottoman religious establishment in Istanbul], shall in no way be impeded; nor will the relations with the naibs named by [the Qadi], whose salaries shall be paid by local revenues.

ART. 3. The above representative is also recognized for the protection of the interests of the Ottoman Empire and of Ottoman subjects insofar as they may continue to reside in the two provinces after [the enactment of] Law No. 38 of 25 February 1912.

ART. 4. A commission, named by royal decree and consisting in part of indigenous notables, shall propose the civil and administrative regulations for the two provinces under the inspiration of principles of liberty and of respect for local practices and customs.

ANNEX NO. 3

Administrative and judicial reform shall be instituted to assure the inhabitants of the islands in the Aegean Sea subject to Ottoman sovereignty equal distribution of justice, security, and well-being without distinction of cult and religion.

Officials and judges shall be named from among well-known persons familiar with the local language and having the desired ability.

Full and complete amnesty is accorded to the above inhabitants who have taken part in the hostilities or who might thus be compromised, with the exception of [those charged with] crimes of common law. Consequently no individual of any class or station may be prosecuted or troubled in his personal property or in the exercise of his rights because of his political or military actions, or because of the opinions which he might have expressed during the hostilities. Persons detained or deported for this reason shall be set free immediately.

2. Public and Definitive Treaty of Peace (Lausanne), 18 October 1912[1]

. . . ART. 1. The two Governments pledge that, immediately after the signature of the present Treaty, they will take the

---

1. Designated Annex No. 4 in the original.

necessary steps for the immediate and simultaneous cessation of hostilities. Special Commissioners shall be sent to the field to assure execution of the above measures.

ART. 2. The two Governments respectively pledge that, immediately after the signature of the present Treaty, they will order the recall of their officers, troops, and civil officials, the Ottoman Government from Tripolitania and Cyrenaica, and the Italian Government from the islands that it occupied in the Aegean Sea.

The actual evacuation of the above islands by Italian officers, troops, and civil officials shall take place immediately after Tripolitania and Cyrenaica have been evacuated by Ottoman officers, troops, and civil officials.

ART. 3. Prisoners-of-war and hostages shall be exchanged as soon as possible.

ART. 4. The two Governments pledge that they will declare a full and complete amnesty, the Royal Government to the inhabitants of Tripolitania and Cyrenaica and the Imperial Government to those inhabitants of the islands in the Aegean Sea subject to Ottoman sovereignty who may have taken part in the hostilities, or who may have compromised themselves, except [those charged with] crimes of common law. Consequently no individual of any class or station may be prosecuted or troubled in his person or his property or in the exercise of his rights because of his political or military actions, or because of the opinions that he might have expressed during the hostilities. Persons detained or deported for this reason shall be set free immediately.

ART. 5. All treaties, conventions, and engagements of every kind, sort, and nature concluded or in effect before the declaration of war between the two High Contracting Parties shall be reinstated immediately, and a situation between the two Governments and their respective subjects identical to that which prevailed before the hostilities shall be restored.

ART. 6. Italy pledges to conclude with Turkey at the same time that [the latter] may renew its treaties of commerce with the other Powers a treaty of commerce based on European public law, that is to say, it consents to leave to Turkey its full economic independence and the right to act in commercial and customs matters like all European Powers without being bound by the capitulations or other acts [already undertaken]. It is understood that the said treaty of commerce shall enter into force only to the extent that the treaties of commerce concluded by the Sublime Porte with other Powers on the same basis shall also enter into force.

Furthermore, Italy consents to the increase of the ad valorem duties in Turkey from 11 percent to 15 percent and the establishment of new monopolies or consumption surtax levies on the five following articles: petroleum, cigarette paper, matches, alcohol, and playing cards. All this rests on the condition that the same treatment shall be applied simultaneously and without distinction to imports from other countries.

Insofar as it may concern the import of articles that were the object of a monopoly, the administration of these monopolies must be furnished with articles of Italian origin according to the percentage established on the basis of the annual imports of the same articles, provided that the prices offered for the delivery of the monopoly articles conform to the condition of the market at the moment of purchase, taking into consideration the qualities of the furnished goods and the average price which prevailed in the three years preceding the declaration of war.

Moreover, if Turkey, instead of establishing new monopolies for the above-mentioned five articles, should decide to apply to them the consumption surtax, this surtax shall be imposed in the same measure on similar products from Turkey and from every other nation.

ART. 7. The Italian Government undertakes to abolish the Italian postal system in the Ottoman Empire at the same time that the other states having postal systems in Turkey abolish theirs.

ART. 8. The Sublime Porte proposing to start negotiations with the interested Great Powers in a European conference or otherwise for the purpose of ending the capitulatory regime in Turkey [and] replacing it by the regime of international law, Italy, recognizing the justice of these intentions of the Sublime Porte, declares as of now its desire to lend full and sincere support to this effort.

ART. 9. The Ottoman Government, wishing to attest to its satisfaction with the good and loyal services rendered to it by Italian subjects [formerly] employed in the bureaucracy but forcibly dismissed at the time of the hostilities, declares itself ready to reinstate them in the positions which they had quit.

A temporary unemployment salary shall be paid to them for the past months without work, and this interruption of service shall not prejudice any employee who may have a right to a retirement pension.

Moreover, the Ottoman Government undertakes to use its good offices in the institutions with which it is in communication (the Public Debt [Commission], railroad companies, banks, etc.), so that similar treatment may be given to Italian subjects who were in their service and who are similarly [unemployed].

ART. 10. The Italian Government undertakes to contribute annually to the account of the Ottoman Public Debt for the credit of the Imperial Government a sum corresponding to the average of the sums that had been appropriated to the service of the Public Debt by revenues from the two provinces in each of the three years preceding that of the declaration of war. The total amount of the above annuities shall be determined by agreement of two Commissioners, one named by the Royal Government, and the other by the Imperial Government. In case of disagreement, the decision shall be refered to an arbitration board named by agreement by the two Parties. If agreement is not reached on this subject, each Party shall designate a different Power and the choice of the final arbitrator shall be made by concert of the Powers thus designated.

The Royal Government and the administration of the Ottoman Public Debt may, by intervention of the Imperial Government, substitute for the above annuity by payment of a corresponding sum capitalized at the rate of 4 percent.

With reference to the preceding paragraph, the Royal Government acknowledges as of now that the annuity may not be less than the sum of two million Italian liras and that it is ready to contribute to the administration of the Public Debt the corresponding capitalized sum as soon as the demand for it is made.

ART. 11. The present Treaty shall come into effect the very day of its signature. . . .

176. CONVENTION AND EXCHANGE OF NOTES TO DEFINE THE STATUS OF THE PROTECTING POWERS IN MOROCCO: FRANCE AND SPAIN
27 November 1912

(Ratifications exchanged, Madrid, 2 April 1913)
[Translated from the French texts in France, *Journal Officiel*, 5 April 1913, pp. 3049–52]

The division of Morocco into French and Spanish protectorates took more than a dozen years to arrange. The involved negotiations illustrated multilateral diplomacy consummated through a succession of bilateral agreements that were designed to mesh with one another to form, as a group, a general settlement that satisfied all the interested European powers at the expense of Morocco. In one sense, the latest and final instrument, the French-Spanish convention reproduced below, was anticlimactic, for France had already established a formal protectorate by a special convention dictated at Fez to Mawlay 'Abd al-Hafiz eight months earlier (Doc. 174). In another sense, the French-Spanish convention of 1912 was indispensable, since it defined in explicit detail the allocation of territory between the protecting powers, and the jurisdictional relations to each other and of both to the Moroccan regime. The talks dragged on for more than a year because France insisted on enlarging its sphere, on the ground that it had made the major sacrifices and taken the major risks that led to the progressive subordination of Morocco. Spain in the end received less square mileage in the Rif and in the Ifni hinterland than had been agreed upon eight years earlier (Doc. 165), getting as compensation a large French-owned tract adjoining the Spanish colony of Rio de Oro. However, France failed to make good its starting claim to the Moroccan coast from Cape Spartel to Ceuta because of British opposition. Indeed, as an active participant in the French-Spanish negotiations of 1911–12, Britain upheld Spanish claims, as it had agreed to do in 1903, when Foreign Secretary Lansdowne persuaded the Spanish government to suspend its initial bilateral negotiations with France until after Britain and France had reached their own accommodation. This was hardly a case of altruism, but rather one of clever diplomacy, for by upholding Spanish claims Britain kept a major maritime power from annexing the Moroccan bank of the Strait of Gibraltar and procured a reaffirmation that "fortifications or strategic works" would be disallowed (except at Melilla) along that stretch of the Moroccan coast assigned to Spain, while at the same time assuring Britain itself a presence in Tangier through the promised special (international) regime. Such a plan had already been implied in articles 7–8 of the public declaration and in secret article 3 of the British-French entente of April 1904 (Doc. 164) and set forth explicitly in articles 2, 3, 6, and 9 of the French-Spanish agreement of the following October. Unlike France, Spain did not later conclude a special treaty with the mawlay of Morocco. Instead, Spain rested its protectorate on the 1912 convention with France and on a decree promulgated on 4 May 1913 by Mawlay Yusuf (1913–27). Barlow, *Agadir Crisis*, chap. 14; Stuart, *International City of Tangier*, chap. 3; Donnadieu, *Les relations diplomatiques de l'Espagne et du Maroc*, pt. 2; Vidal, *La politique de l'Espagne au Maroc*, pp. 184–287; Touron, *Notre protectorat marocain*, chaps. 9–10.

. . . ART. 1. The Government of the French Republic recognizes that, in the Spanish zone of influence, Spain shall look after the peace of said zone and lend its assistance to the Moroccan Government for the introduction of all administrative, economic, financial, judicial, and military reforms which it may require and of all new regulations and for the modification of existing regulations which these reforms may entail in conformity with the French-English declaration of 8 April 1904 and with the French-German agreement of 4 November 1911.

The districts included in the zone of influence determined in Article 2 shall remain under the civil and religious authority of the Sultan in accordance with the provisions of the present agreement.

These districts under the control of a Spanish High Commissioner shall be administered by a Khalifah [title given to the royal delegate] chosen by the Sultan from a list of two candidates presented by the Spanish Government. The duties of the Khalifah shall not be modified except by consent of the Spanish Government.

The Khalifah shall reside in the Spanish zone of influence and, as a rule, in Tetwan; the Sultan will provide him with a general delegation, with which [the Khalifah] will exercise his rights.

This delegation shall have a permanent character. In case of vacancy the duties of

the Khalifah shall be performed temporarily and officially by the Pasha of Tetwan.

The actions of the Moroccan authority
in the Spanish zone of influence shall be
controlled by the Spanish High Commissioner and his agents. The High Commissioner shall be the sole intermediary in
the relations that the Khalifah, in his role as
the delegate of the imperial authority in
the Spanish zone, must maintain with
foreign official representatives, undertaking not to act contrary to Article 5 of the
French-Sharifi treaty of 30 March 1912.

The Government of His Majesty the
King of Spain shall supervise the proper
execution of the treaties, especially the
economic and commercial clauses in the
French-German agreement of 4 November
1911.

The Sharifi Government shall not be
responsible for claims arising from actions
of the administration of the Khalifah in
the Spanish zone of influence.

ART. 2. In the north of Morocco, the
frontier separating the French and Spanish
zones of influence shall commence at the
mouth of the Muluya [River] and follow
the thalweg of that river until it reaches
one kilometer below Mechra Klila. From
this point, the demarcation shall follow the
sketch in Article 2 of the convention of 3
October 1904 to Mount Beni-Hasan.

If the mixed boundary commission,
outlined in Article 4, paragraph 1, below,
should determine that the Marabout of
Sidi-Maarouf depends on the fraction south
of the Beni-Buyahi, that point shall be
assigned to the French zone. Nevertheless,
the demarcation line between the two
zones, after having encircled the said
Marabout, shall not pass more than one
kilometer to the north and more than two
kilometers to the south, so as to rejoin the
demarcation line as fixed in the preceding
paragraph.

From Mount Beni-Hasan, the frontier
will rejoin the Wadi Wirgha north of the
Djemaa of Cheurfa Tafraut, upstream from
the bend formed by the river. From there,
moving west, it will follow the line of the
heights dominating the right bank of the
Wadi Wirgha until its interesection with
the north-south line defined by Article 2
of the 1904 convention. In this line, the
frontier will circumscribe in the straightest

way possible the limit north of the Wirgha
tributaries and the limit south of those
which are not water-rivers, in assuring
uninterrupted military communication
between the different districts of the
Spanish zone.

It will then rise toward the north, keeping at a distance of at least twenty-five
kilometers to the east of the road from
Fez to al-Qsar al-Kabir via Wazzan, until
its meeting with the Wadi Lukkos, where
it will follow the thalweg until the boundary
between the Sarsar and Tlig tribes. From
this point, it will skirt Mount Ghani,
leaving that mountain in the Spanish zone,
on condition that permanent fortifications
shall not be constructed there. Finally the
frontier will rejoin the 35° parallel of
north latitude between the *dawar* [beduin
encampment] Magaria and the Marya of
Sidi-Slama, and shall follow that parallel
to the sea.

In the south of Morocco, the frontier of
the French and Spanish zones shall be
defined by the thalweg of Wadi Dar'a,
which it will follow from the sea to its
meeting with the eleventh meridian west of
Paris; it will follow that meridian to the
south until it meets the parallel of north
latitude at 27° 40'. South of that parallel,
Articles 5 and 6 of the convention of 3
October 1904 shall remain applicable. The
Moroccan districts north and east of the
boundary line designated in the present
paragraph shall belong to the French zone.

ART. 3. The Moroccan Government
having conceded to Spain in Article 8 of
the treaty of 26 April 1860 a settlement in
Santa-Cruz-de-Mar-Pequeña (Ifni), it is
agreed that the territory of this settlement
shall have the following limits: on the
north, the Wadi Bu-Sedra from its mouth;
on the east, a line reaching approximately
twenty-five kilometers from the coast.

ART. 4. A technical commission, whose
members will be appointed in equal numbers by the French and Spanish Governments, shall determine the exact outline of
boundaries specified in the preceding articles. In its work, the commission shall keep
account of topographic accidents and of
local contingencies.

The reports of the commission shall not
have executive value until after ratification
by the two governments.

However, the work of the above commission shall not interfere with the immediate possession by Spain of its settlement in Ifni.

ART. 5. Spain undertakes neither to transfer nor to cede in any form, not even as a temporary title, its rights in all or part of the territory comprising its zone of influence.

ART. 6. To assure free passage through the Strait of Gibraltar, the two governments agree not to allow the construction of any fortifications or strategic works whatsoever in the part of the Moroccan coast designated in Article 7 of the French-English declaration of 8 April 1904 and in Article 14 of the French-Spanish convention of 3 October of the same year and included in the respective spheres of influence.

ART. 7. The city of Tangier and its suburb shall be endowed with a special regime to be determined later. They will form a zone within the limits here described.

From Punta-Altares, on the southern coast of the Strait of Gibraltar, the frontier shall follow a straight line on the crest of Jebel Beni Mayimel, leaving on the west a village called Dar al-Zaytun and will then follow the boundary line between Fahs on one side and the tribes of Anjera and the Wadi Ras on the other, until it meets with the Wadi al-Saghir. From there the frontier will follow the thalweg of the Wadi al-Saghir, then those of the Wadis M'harhar and Tzahadartz to the sea.

The whole shall conform to the outline indicated on the map (1906 edition) of the Spanish general staff, which is titled, "Croquis del Imperio de Marruecos," on a scale of 1/100,000.

ART. 8. The consulates, the schools, and all existing French and Spanish settlements in Morocco shall be maintained.

The two Governments pledge to respect the freedom and the customs of every religion in Morocco.

The Government of His Majesty the King of Spain, within his jurisdiction, shall see that the Spanish regular and secular clergy shall no longer exercise in the French zone the religious privileges they now enjoy. Nevertheless, the Spanish missions in that zone shall preserve their present institutions and properties, but the Government of His Majesty the King of Spain shall not oppose the assignment of clergy of French nationality [to the Spanish institutions]. The new institutions which these missions may found shall be entrusted to French clergy.

ART. 9. Until the construction of the railroad between Tangier and Fez, there shall be no interference with the passage either of supply convoys or of Sharifi or foreign functionaries between Fez and Tangier in either direction, or of their escorts, [or] of their arms and baggage, it being understood that the authorities of the zone of passage shall be notified in advance. No tax or special right of transit shall be charged for the passage.

After the construction of the railroad from Tangier to Fez, that line may be used for such traffic.

ART. 10. The duties and resources of every kind in the Spanish zone shall be allocated for the expenses of the said zone.

ART. 11. The Sharifi Government may not be asked to contribute to any expenses of the Spanish zone.

ART. 12. The Government of His Majesty the King of Spain in his zone of influence may not impair the rights, prerogatives, and privileges of the holders of the loan claims of 1904 and 1910.

To bring the exercise of these rights into harmony with the new situation, the Government of the Republic shall use its influence with the representative of the claimants, so that the guarantees in the said zone may comply with the following provisions:

The Spanish zone of influence shall contribute to the charges of the 1904 and 1910 loans in accordance with the allowance that the ports of the said zone, after the deduction of 500,000 Hasani pesetas of which more will be said later, shall furnish together with the customs receipts of the ports open to commerce.

This contribution is provisionally fixed at 7.95 percent, a figure based on the returns for the year 1911. It may be revised annually at the request of either party.

If such a revision should reduce French customs receipts at the Mediterranean ports, the Spanish contribution to the charges of the above-mentioned loans shall be suspended automatically.

The envisaged revision must be instituted before 15 May in accordance with the practice that is to serve as its basis. Account will be kept of the results involving the payment that the Spanish Government is to make on 1 June, in the following manner:

The Government of His Majesty the King of Spain shall deposit each year on 1 March for the service of the 1910 loan, and on 1 June for the service of the 1904 loan, with the representative of the holders of the claims to these loans, the amount of annuities fixed in the preceding paragraph. Accordingly, the collection for the loans shall be suspended in the Spanish zone by the application of Article 20 of the contract of 12 June 1904, and Article 19 of the contract of 17 May 1910.

The control of the title holders and the related rights whose exercise would have been suspended because of the Spanish Government payments shall be reestablished in their present form, if the representative of the title holders should have to resume direct collection in accordance with the contracts.

ART. 13. On the other hand, it is necessary to assure to the French zone and to the Spanish zone the share due to each from the customs duties collected at the time of import.

The two Governments agree:

1. That of the balance of the customs receipts, which each of the two administrative zones shall collect for the products admitted by their customs and destined for the other zone, the French zone should receive a sum of 500,000 Hasani pesetas, distributed in the following way:

(a) A forfeited sum of 300,000 Hasani pesetas applicable to the receipts of the western ports.

(b) A sum of 200,000 Hasani pesetas, applicable to the receipts of the Mediterranean coast, subject to revision when the functioning of the railroad shall furnish an exact basis for calculation. This eventual revision might be applicable to earlier payments, if the sum total should exceed the amount of payments later realized. However, these payments shall be made only on the capital, not on the interest.

If such a revision should reduce French customs receipts at the Mediterranean ports, the Spanish contribution to the charges of the above-mentioned loans shall automatically be suspended.

2. That the customs receipts collected by the Tangier office should be distributed between the internationalized zone and the two other zones on a proportional basis according to the destination of the goods. In expectation that the functioning of the railroad will allow an exact distribution of the sums due to the French zone and to the Spanish zone, the customs service shall deposit in the State Bank the excess of these receipts as payment made by Tangier.

The representatives of the customs administrations of the two zones shall meet periodically in Tangier to agree on the proper measures for ensuring a uniform application of the tariffs. For the common good, these representatives shall exchange all information that they can gather about smuggling and about possible irregularities in the customs offices.

The two Governments shall try to put into effect by 1 March 1913 the measures endorsed in the present Article.

ART. 14. The deposits assigned in the Spanish zone to French credit, by virtue of the French-Moroccan accord of 21 March 1910, shall be transferred to the credit of Spain, and reciprocally the deposits assigned in the French zone to the credit of Spain, by virtue of the Spanish-Moroccan treaty of 16 November 1910, shall be transferred to the credit of France. With a view to reserving to each zone the receipt of the mining rents which must naturally revert [to that zone], it is agreed that the proportional rents of extraction shall belong to the zone in which the mine is situated, even if they may be collected at the outset by the customs service of the other zone.

ART. 15. Regarding the advances made by the State Bank on the 5 percent duty, it has seemed equitable that the two zones should reimburse the said advances and, in a general way, the charges on the liquidation of the present liabilities of the Makhzan [the Moroccan Government].

If that liquidation should be effected by a long- or a short-term loan, each of the two zones shall contribute to the payment of the annuities of that loan (interest and amortization) in a proportion equal to that which has been fixed for each zone for the allotment of the charges of the 1904 and 1910 loans.

The rates of interest, the deferments of amortization and conversion, the conditions of issue and, if necessary, the guarantees of the loan shall be drawn up following agreement between the two Governments.

The debts contracted after the signing of the present accord shall be excluded from that settlement.

The total amount of the liabilities to be liquidated includes especially:

1. The advances of the State Bank pledged at 5 percent of the customs receipts; [and]

2. The debts settled by the commission, instituted by virtue of the ruling of the diplomatic corps of Tangier on 29 May 1910.

The two Governments reserve the right to examine jointly claims other than those endorsed above under numbers 1 and 2, to verify their legitimacy, and, if the total liabilities should perceptibly exceed the sum of 25 million frances, to include them in the evisaged liquidation or to exclude them.

ART. 16. Since the administrative autonomy of the French and Spanish zones of influence in the Sharifi Empire, in conformity with the Act of Algeciras, may not impair the rights, prerogatives, and privileges conceded by the Moroccan Government to the State Bank of Morocco for the entire territory of the Empire, the State Bank of Morocco shall continue to enjoy in each of the two zones all the rights which it holds by virtue of the deeds which govern it, without diminution or reserve. The autonomy of the two zones may not raise any obstacle to [the Bank's] action, and the two Governments shall facilitate the State Bank's free and complete exercise of its rights.

The State Bank of Morooc, in agreement with the two interested Powers, may modify the conditions of the territorial organization of each zone.

The two Governments shall recommend to the State Bank the study of an amendment of its statutes permitting:

1. The creation of a second Moroccan High Commissioner, who shall be no-

minated by the administration of the Spanish zone of influence, after agreement with the Administrative Council of the State Bank; [and]

2. The delegation to the second High Commissioner of powers identical to those exercised by the present High Commissioner, so as to safeguard the legitimate interests of the administration of the Spanish zone without impairing the normal functioning of the Bank.

All useful steps shall be undertaken by the two Governments to attain, in the sense indicated above, the regular revision of the statutes of the State Bank, and of the regulation of its relations with the Moroccan Government.

In order to specify and complete the agreement reached between the two Governments and verified by the letter addressed on 23 February 1907 by the Foreign Minister of the Republic to the Ambassador of His Majesty the King of Spain in Paris, the French Government, while reserving the rights of the Bank, pledges as regards the Spanish zone:

1. Not to support any candidacy besides that of the State Bank; [and]

2. To make known to the Bank its desire to see considered for the use of the said zone candidates of Spanish nationality.

Reciprocally, the Spanish Government, while reserving the rights of the Bank, pledges as regards the French zone:

1. Not to support any candidacy besides that of the State Bank; [and]

2. To make known to the Bank its desire to see considered for the use of the said zone candidates of French nationality.

Regarding:

1. The shares of the Bank which might belong to the Makhzan; [and]

2. The benefits due to the Makhzan from the operations of the striking and melting of coins and from all other monetary operations [described in Article 37 of the Act of Algeciras], it is agreed that the administration of the Spanish zone shall be entitled to one part calculated on the basis of the same percentage as that for the rents and the benefits of the tobacco monopolies.

ART. 17. Since the administrative autonomy of the French and Spanish zones of influence in the Sharifi Empire, in conformity with the Act of Algeciras, may not impair the rights, prerogatives, and privileges ceded by the Moroccan Government to the Société Internationale de Régie Co-intéressée des Tabacs au Maroc, the said Society shall continue to enjoy in each of the two zones all the rights, without diminution or reserve, which it holds by virtue of its acts of authorization. The autonomy of the two zones may not interfere with [the Régie's] actions, and the two Governments shall facilitate the free and complete exercise of its rights.

The present conditions of the exploitation of the monopoly and, in particular, the tariff on the sales prices may not be modified except by agreement between the two Governments.

The French Government shall not present any obstacle to the Royal Government and the Régie, acting in concert, either for the purpose of obtaining from that Society the retrocession to third parties of the entirety of its rights and privileges or in anticipation of buying back by private contract the said rights and privileges. If as a consequence of the anticipated repurchase the Spanish Government should desire to modify in its zone the general conditions of the exploitation of the monopoly and, for example, should seek to reduce the selling prices, an accord must be reached between the two Governments with the exclusive goal of safeguarding the interests of the French zone of influence.

The preceding stipulations shall be applied reciprocally, should the French Government desire to make use of the powers assigned above to the Spanish Government.

Since the Régie may object to a partial repurchase, the two Governments pledge in the future to carry out in the two zones as soon as possible (that is to say, by 1 January 1933, while notifying the Régie before 1 January 1931) the right of repurchase provided for in Article 24 of the specifications. Starting on 1 January 1933, each of the two zones shall become free to estbalish according to its convenience the duties that are to be levied on the monopoly.

While respecting the specifications, the two Governments shall agree to obtain:

(a) the appointment of a second Com-

missioner named by the administration of the Spanish zone of influence;

(b) the definition of the powers needed by the second Commissioner to safeguard the legitimate interests of the administration of the Spanish zone without impairing the normal functioning of the Régie; [and]

(c) the distribution in equal parts between the two Commissioners of the sum of 5,000 Makhzani rials provided annually by the Régie as the Commissioner's salary.

In order to maintain for the duration of the monopoly the identity of the tariff on sales prices in the two zones, the two Governments undertake not to subject the Régie or its allotted rights to new duties without prior agreement.

The receipt of fines levied against the Régie for not applying the specifications or for abuse (Article 31 of the specifications) shall be given to the Treasury of the zone in which the infractions or abuses are committed.

For the allotment of the fixed annual charge and of the benefits (Articles 20–23 of the specifications), there shall be applied a percentage determined by the volume of consumption of the Spanish zone in comparison of the total volume of consumption of the Empire. The volume of consumption shall be evaluated in accordance with the customs collection actually in the possession of the administration of the Spanish zone, account being taken of the payment provided for in Article 13 above.

ART. 18. Concerning the Committee of Tax Rates, the Special Committee of Public Works, and the General Commission of Adjudication in the period in which these Committees may continue in existence, the Khalifah of the Spanish zone shall designate one Sharifi delegate to each of the three Committees.

The two Governments agree to reserve to each zone and to assign to its public works the revenue from the special tax collected in its ports by virtue of Article 66 of the Act of Algeciras.

The respective services shall be autonomous.

Under terms of reciprocity, the delegates of the administration of the French zone shall vote with the delegates of the Khalifah in matters of interest to the Spanish zone, particularly for everything relating to the selection of works for execution with the funds of the special tax, their execution, and the designation of personnel that that execution entails.

ART. 19. The Government of the French Republic and the Government of His Catholic Majesty shall work in concert toward:

1. every modification of customs fees that may have to be made in the future; [and]

2. the standardization of postal and telegraph tariffs within the Empire.

ART. 20. The Tangier-Fez Railroad shall be constructed and developed according to the conditions stipulated in the Protocol annexed to the present Convention.

ART. 21. The Government of the French Republic and the Government of His Catholic Majesty pledge to bring about the revision, in agreement with the other Powers and on the basis of the convention of Madrid, of the lists and of the position of foreign protégés and of agricultural associates endorsed in Articles 8 and 16 of that convention.

They also agree to pursue together with the signatory Powers every modification of the Convention of Madrid which may involve at the proper time the changing of the regime of agricultural protégés and associates and eventually the abrogation of the part of the said Convention concerning the agricultural protégés and associates.

ART. 22. Moroccan subjects originating in the Spanish zone of influence shall be placed abroad under the protection of the diplomatic agents and Consuls of Spain.

ART. 23. In order to avoid as many diplomatic claims as possible, the French and Spanish Governments respectively shall place themselves in the service of the Sultan and his Khalifah so that those complaints brought by foreign subjects against the Moroccan authorities which cannot be settled by the mediation of the French or Spanish Consul or of the Consul of the interested Government shall be referred to an *ad hoc* arbitrator, designated in common agreement by the Consul of France or that of Spain and by the Consul of the interested Power or, upon their default, by the two Governments of the Consuls.

ART. 24. The Government of the French Republic and the Government of His Catholic Majesty reserve the power to proceed with the establishment in their respective zones of judicial organizations inspired by [French and Spanish] legislation. Once these organizations are established and the nationals and protégés in the zone submit to the jurisdiction of these tribunals, the Government of the French Republic in the Spanish zone of influence and the Government of His Majesty the King of Spain in the French zone of influence shall equally submit their respective nationals and protégés to this local jurisdiction.

As long as Article II, paragraph 3, of the convention of Madrid of 3 July 1880 shall remain in force, the right of His Sharifi Majesty's Foreign Minister to recognize by appeal matters of landed property belonging to foreigners shall be part of the powers delegated to the Khalifah for everything concerning the Spanish zone.

ART. 25. The signatory Powers undertake in the future to lend their entire cooperation in their African possessions to the Moroccan authorities for the surveillance and repression of the smuggling of arms and munitions of war.

The surveillance in territorial waters of the French and Spanish zones shall be exercised by forces organized by the local authority or of those of the protector government of the zone.

The two Governments shall act in concert to standardize the system of the right of visit.

ART. 26. The international accords concluded by His Sharifi Majesty in the future shall not extend to the Spanish zone of influence except with the prior consent of the Government of His Majesty the King of Spain.

ART. 27. The convention of 26 February 1904 renewed on 3 February 1909 and the general Hague convention of 18 October 1907 shall apply to disputes between the Contracting Parties over the interpretation and application of the provisions of the present Convention which are not settled by diplomacy. A compromise must be drawn up, and its procedures shall follow the rules of the same Convention, [unless another procedure is arranged] by explicit agreement at the time of litigation.

ART. 28. All clauses of treaties, conventions, and prior accords which may be contrary to the preceding stipulations are abrogated.

ART. 29. The present Convention shall be communicated to the signatory governments of the General Act of the International Conference at Algeciras.

ART. 30. The present Convention shall be ratified, and the ratifications shall be exchanged in Madrid as soon as possible. . . .

ANNEX 1. LEON MARCEL ISIDORE GEOFFRAY, THE AMBASSADOR OF FRANCE (MADRID), TO MANUEL GARCIA PRIETO, THE MINISTER OF STATE, MADRID

In order clearly to specify the scope of the provisions of the Convention signed today which refer to the nomination of the Khalifah and to his relations with foreign representatives, Your Excellency will permit me to remind him that he has kindly declared to me that:

Regarding the first of these points, the appointment of the Khalifah of the Spanish zone might be usefully arranged by confidential talks between the two Governments for the purpose of assuring that the Sultan shall choose that candidate of the two envisaged in Article 1 of the said Convention whom the Royal Government may prefer. However, it is agreed that, whatever may be the advantages of that procedure, each of the two Powers is free to renounce it in specific cases and to hold itself strictly to the clauses of the present Convention, which on the one hand oblige Spain to present a list of two candidates and on the other hand stipulate that His Sharifi Majesty shall have to choose one of these two candidates. It follows that these [candidates] must be personalities of stature.

Concerning the relations which the Khalifah, as delegate of the Imperial Authority in the Spanish zone, may have to conduct with official foreign representatives, it is agreed that the word "official" has been substituted since the drafting of the treaty for the word "consular," so as to avoid difficulties in practice, according to the expression of Your Excellency. These difficulties might arise from the fact that certain Powers, not having a career consular agent in Morocco except in the French zone, would not be able to deal directly with the administration of the Spanish zone in matters which relate to that zone and which the said zone alone can settle, in accordance with the terms of our Convention of today. As for the diplomatic relations of foreign governments with the Sultan, it is firmly agreed that the mention made in the present Convention of Article 5 of the French-Sharifi agreement of 30 March 1912 reserves the monopoly [of such relations] to France.

ANNEX 2. PRIETO TO GEOFFRAY

In order clearly to specify the scope of the provisions of the Convention signed today which refer to the nomination of the Khalifah and his relations with foreign representatives, I shall permit myself to remind Your Excellency that he has kindly declared to me that:

Regarding the first of these points, the appointment of the Khalifah of the Spanish zone might be usefully arranged by confidential conversations between the two Governments with a view to assuring that the Sultan shall choose that candidate of the two to which Article 1 of the said Convention refers whom the Government of His Majesty may prefer.

However, it is agreed that, whatever may be the advantages of that procedure, each of the two Powers shall be free to renounce it in specific cases and to hold itself strictly to the clauses of the future Convention, which on the one hand oblige Spain to present a list of two candidates and on the other stipulate that His Sharifi Majesty shall choose one of these two candidates. It is evident that these [candidates] must be persons of distinction.

Concerning the relations which the Khalifah, as delegate of the Imperial Authority in the Spanish zone, may have to conduct with foreign official representatives, it is agreed that the term "official" has been substituted since the drafting of the treaty for the word "consular," with a view to avoiding difficulties in practice in accordance with my expression. These difficulties might arise from the fact that certain Powers, not having in Morocco career consular agents except in the French zone, would not be able to deal directly with the administration of the Spanish zone in matters which relate to that zone and which can be resolved only by that administration, according to the terms of our Convention of today. As for diplomatic relations between foreign governments and the Sultan, it is firmly agreed that the mention made in the present Convention of Article 5 of the French-Sharifi Treaty of 30 March 1912 reserves the monopoly [of such relations] to France.

177. RESOLUTION OF THE ARAB-SYRIAN CONGRESS AT PARIS
21 June 1913

[Translated from the French text in Gooch and Temperley, *British Documents on the Origins of the War*, 10 (ii): 826]

The nationalist awakening in the Arab East originated in a cultural renaissance in the eighteen thirties and forties in Lebanon, where American and French missionaries opened schools with instruction in Arabic and presses for the printing of Arabic books. By the eve of World War I the movement had spread to Syria, Mesopotamia (present-day Iraq) and Egypt, becoming in transit increasingly political. Owing to resistance to the Dual Control and later to the British occupation, the movement in Egypt took the form primarily of Egyptian rather than Arab nationalism. In the decade before 1914, particularly after the Young Turk coup d'état of 1908, a number of Arab nationalist societies—a few of them secret—with avowed political objectives were founded. By and large these societies demanded, not independence, but political autonomy for the predominantly Arab districts and Arab representation in the imperial government at Istanbul on a basis of full equality with the Ottoman Turks. This emphasis is manifest in the following resolution, adopted by an Arab-Syrian Congress at Paris (18–24 June 1913), attended by twenty-four official delegates who, with the exception of three from the United States and two from Mesopotamia, came from Lebanon and Syria. Sharabi, *Arab Intellectuals and the West*; Antonius, *Arab Awakening*, chaps. 1–6; Khadduri, *Political Trends in the Arab World*, chap. 2; Hourani, *Arabic Thought in the Liberal Age*, chap. 11; Haim, *Arab Nationalism*, pp. 1–82; Holt, *Egypt and Fertile Crescent*, chap. 18; Rossi, *Documenti sull'origine e gli sviluppi della questione araba*; Kedourie, "Politics of Political Literature"; Jung, *Les puissances devant la révolte arabe*, and *La révolte arabe*, vol. 1, chaps. 1–5; Cataluccio, *Storia del nazionalismo arabo*, chap. 1.

1. Radical and urgent reforms are needed in the Ottoman Empire.

2. It is important to guarantee the Ottoman Arabs the exercise of their political rights by making effective their participation in the central administration of the Empire.

3. It is important to establish in each of the Syrian and Arab *vilâyets* a decentralized regime suitable to their needs and aptitudes.

4. The vilayet of Bayrut having formulated its claims in a special project adopted on 31 January 1913 by an ad hoc General Assembly and based on the double principle of the extension of the powers of the general council of the vilayet and the nomination of foreign councillors, the Congress requests the execution of the above project.

5. The Arabic language must be recognized in the Ottoman Parliament and con-

sidered as an official language in Syrian and Arab countries.

6. Military service shall be regional in Syrian and Arab vilayets, except in case of extreme necessity.

7. The Congress expresses the wish that the Ottoman Imperial Government provide the *mutasarriflık* (autonomous provincial district) of Lebanon with the means of improving its financial situation.

8. The Congress affirms that it favors the

reformist and decentralizing demands of the Armenian Ottomans.

9. The present resolution shall be communicated to the Ottoman Imperial Government.

10. These resolutions shall also be communicated to the Powers friendly to the Ottoman Empire.

11. The Congress conveys its grateful thanks to the Government of the [French] Republic for its generous hospitality.

178. BRITISH OTTOMAN DRAFT CONVENTION ON THE PERSIAN GULF AREA
29 July 1913

[Translated from the French text in Gooch and Temperley, *British Documents on the Origins of the War*, 10 (ii): 190–94]

As late as 1911–13 Germany and the Ottoman Empire still had to overcome British obstructive diplomacy before they could procede with the full execution of the Baghdad railroad scheme. "We have only got two objects as regards the Baghdad Railway," explained Foreign Secretary Sir Edward Grey to the British Committee of Imperial Defense on 26 May 1911; "one is to secure that when that railway is made British trade shall not be at a disadvantage," and the other "that the situation in the Persian Gulf . . . should not be altered in a way which would damage our . . . strategical position" (Gooch and Temperley, op. cit., 6: 786–87). Whitehall could afford to tarry, for the Sublime Porte depended on British consent to raise the tariff rates, the only likely source of funds with which to subsidize the concessionaires, as the Ottoman government had obligated itself to do. When England agreed at last to seek a settlement, the decision was taken to negotiate three bilateral agreements—British-Ottoman, British-German and Ottoman-German—which were to be articulated to one another. After more than two years of diplomatic exchanges, several instruments (texts in ibid., 10 [ii]: 183–98) forming part of a proposed comprehensive British-Ottoman settlement were signed on 29 July 1913, among them the draft convention reproduced below. Articles 1–3 of the draft understanding on Kuwayt included contradictory provisions, a British acknowledgment that the shaykhdom was an autonomous *kaza* (provincial subdistrict) of the Ottoman Empire and Ottoman recognition of the validity of the agreements under which Kuwayt was assimilated into the British quasi-protectorate system of the gulf. The potential conflict never came to the test, however, since the draft convention, designed to protect the British position and to satisty Ottoman claims in the Persian Gulf area, as well as the remaining instruments were never ratified. Chapman, *Great Britain and the Bagdad Railway*, chaps. 4–9; Wolf, *Diplomatic History of the Bagdad Railway*, chaps. 6–7;

Earle, *Turkey, the Great Powers and the Bagdad Railway*, chap. 10; Graves, *Life of Sir Percy Cox*, chaps. 9–13; Frischwasser-Ra'anan, *Frontiers of a Nation*, chap. 2; Busch, *Britain and the Persian Gulf*, chap. 10.

I. Kuwayt

ART. 1. The territory of Kuwayt, as delimited in Articles 5 and 7 of its convention, constitutes an autonomous kaza of the Ottoman Empire.

ART. 2. The Shaykh of Kuwayt will hoist, as in the past, the Ottoman flag, together with the word "Kuwayt" inscribed in the corner if he so wishes it, and he will enjoy complete administrative autonomy in the territorial zone defined in Article. 5 of this Convention. The Ottoman Imperial Government will refrain from interference in the affairs of Kuwayt, including the question of succession, and from any administrative act as well as any occupation or military act, in the territories belonging to it. In the event of vacancy, the Ottoman Imperial Government will appoint by Imperial *ferman* a *kaymakam* [governor of a kaza] to succeed the deceased Shaykh. It will also have the power to protect the Shaykh a Commissioner to protect the interests and the natives of other parts of the Empire.

ART. 3. The Ottoman Imperial Government recognizes the validity of the conventions which the Shaykh of Kuwayt previously concluded with the Government of His Britannic Majesty, dated 23 January 1899, 24 May 1900, and 28 February 1904, the texts of which are annexed (Annexes I, II, III) to the present Convention.* It also recognizes the validity of land concessions made by the said Shaykh to the Government of His Britannic Majesty and to British subjects, and the validity of the pledges included in the note of 24 October 1911, sent by H. M.'s Principal Secretary of State for Foreign Affairs to His Imperial Majesty the Sultan's Ambassador in London, the text of which is annexed (Annex IV).*

ART. 4. With a view to confirming the understanding already established between the two Governments following the exchange of assurances dated 6 September 1901, between the embassy of His Britannic Majesty at Constantinople and the Im-

perial Ministry of Foreign Affairs, the Government of His Britannic Majesty declares that, since no change will be effected by the Ottoman Imperial Government in the status quo of Kuwayt, as defined in the present Convention, it will not alter the nature of its relations with the Government of Kuwayt and will not establish a protectorate over the area ascribed to it. The Ottoman Imperial Government takes note of this declaration.

ART. 5. The autonomy of the Shaykh of Kuwayt is exercised by him in the territories the limit of which forms a semicircle with the town of Kuwayt in the center, the Khawr al-Zubayr at the northern extremity and al-Qurayyin at the southern extremity. This line is indicated in red on the map annexed to the present Convention (Annex V).* The islands of al-Warbah, Bubyan, Mashjan, Faylakah, 'Awahh, al-Kubr, Qaru, al-Maqta', and Umm-al-Maradim, together with the adjacent islets and waters, are included in this zone.

ART. 6. The tribes which are situated within the limits stipulated in the following Article are recognized as within the dependence of the Shaykh of Kuwayt, who will collect their tithes as in the past and will exercise the administrative rights belonging to him in his quality of Ottoman kaymakam. The Ottoman Imperial Government will not exercise in this region any administrative action independently of the Shaykh of Kuwayt and will refrain from establishing garrisons or undertaking any military action whatsoever without prior understanding with the Government of His Britannic Majesty.

ART. 7. The limits of the territory referred to in the preceding Article are fixed as follows:

The demarcation line begins on the coast at the mouth of Khawr al-Zubayr in the northwest and crosses immediately south of Umm-Qasr, Safwan, and Jabal Sanam, in such a way as to leave to the *vilâyet* of Basrah these locations and their

---

*Not reproduced here.

wells; arriving at the al-Batin, it follows it toward the southwest until Hafr-al-Batin which it leaves on the same side as Kuwayt; from that point on the line in question goes southeast leaving to the wells of al-Safah, al-Garaa, al-Haba, al-Warbah, and Antaa, reaching the sea near Jabal Munifa. This line is marked in green on the map annexed to the present convention (Annex V).*

ART. 8. In the event that the Ottoman Imperial Government agrees with the Government of His Britannic Majesty to prolong the Baghdad-Basrah railroad to the sea at the Kuwayt terminal or to any other terminal in the autonomous territory, the two Governments will agree on the measures to be taken concerning protection of the line and the stations as well as the establishment of customs offices, merchandise depots, and any other installation connected with the railroad.

ART. 9. The shaykh of Kuwayt will enjoy in full safety the rights of private property which he possesses in the territory of the vilayet of Basrah. These rights to private property will have to be exercised in accordance with Ottoman law, and the immovable properties will be subjected to duties and charges, to the rules of maintenance and transmission and to the jurisdiction established by Ottoman laws.

ART. 10. The criminals of neighboring provinces will not be received in the territory of Kuwayt and will be expelled if found; similarly, the criminals of Kuwayt will not be received in neighboring provinces and will be expelled if found.

It is understood that this provision will not be used by the Ottoman authorities as a pretext for interference in the affairs of Kuwayt; it will also not serve as a pretext to the shaykh of Kuwayt for interference in the affairs of the neighboring provinces.

II. Al-Qatar

ART. 11. The Ottoman *sancak* of Najd, the northern limit of which is indicated by the demarcation line defined in Article 7 of this Convention, ends in the south at the gulf facing the island of al-Zakhnuni-yah, which belongs to the said sancak. A line beginning at the extreme end of that gulf will go directly south up to the Rub'-al-Khali and will separate the Najd from

the peninsula of al-Qatar. The limits of the Najd are indicated by a blue line on the map annexed to the present convention (Annex Va).* The Ottoman Imperial Government having renounced all its claims to the peninsula of al-Qatar, it is understood by the two Governments that that the peninsula will be governed as in the past by the Shaykh Jasim bin Thani and his successors. The Government of His Britannic Majesty declares that it will not allow the interference of the Shaykh of Bahrayn in the internal affairs of al-Qatar, his endangering the autonomy of that area or his annexing it.

ART. 12. The inhabitants of Bahrayn will be allowed to visit the island of al-Zakhnuniyah for fishing purposes and to reside there in full freedom during the winter, as in the past, without the application of any new tax.

III. Bahrayn

ART. 13. The Ottoman Imperial Government renounces all its claims to the islands of Bahrayn, including the two islets Lubaynat al-Aliya and Lubaynat al-Safliya, and recognizes the independence of the country. For its part, the Government of His Britannic Majesty declares that it has no intention of annexing the islands of Bahrayn to its territories.

ART. 14. The Government of His Britannic Majesty pledges itself vis-à-vis the Ottoman Imperial Government to assure that the Shaykh of Bahrayn does not charge Ottoman subjects fishing dues for peral oysters exceeding the rate charged to the most favored [of the] other interested parties.

ART. 15. The subjects of the Shaykh of Bahrayn will be considered foreigners in Ottoman territories and will be protected by his Britannic Majesty's Consuls. This protection, however, will have to be exercised in conformity with the general principles of European international law, the subjects of Bahrayn not enjoying privileges granted subjects of certain Powers by the capitulations.

IV. The Persian Gulf

ART. 16. The Government of His Britannic Majesty having undertaken, for the pro-

---

*Not reproduced here.

tection of its special interests as well as for a higher purpose of humanity, maritime police measures at all times in the free waters of the Persian Gulf and on the borders belonging to the independent Shaykhs from the south of al-Qatar up to the Indian Ocean, the Ottoman Imperial Government is fully cognizant of the importance of these efforts already undertaken and declares that it will not be opposed to the Government of His Britannic Majesty exercising as in the past the following measures in the Persian Gulf:

(a) soundings, lighting of lighthouses, placement of buoys, piloting
(b) Maritime police
(c) quarantine measures

On this occasion, the Ottoman Imperial Government reserves all rights belonging to it as a territorial Power on the shores and in Ottoman territorial waters.

V. Commission for the Settlement of Boundaries

ART. 17. The two Governments agree to the establishment, in the shortest possible period of time, of a commission that shall apply to the territory the limits established by Articles 5, 7, and 10 of this Convention and shall draw up a detailed plan and explanatory report. The plan and the report, once drafted and duly signed by the respective commissioners, shall be considered an integral part of the present Convention.

179. THE KUWAYTI SHAYKH'S PLEDGE TO GREAT BRITAIN ON OIL
27 October 1913

[Aitchison, *Collection of Treaties . . . relating to India* (5th ed.), 11: 264–65]

"In the year 1907 the first flotilla of ocean-going destroyers wholly dependent upon oil was created," declared Winston Churchill, the First Lord of the Admiralty, in the House of Commons on 17 July 1913 (Great Britain, *Parliamentary Debates, Commons*, 5th ser., vol. 55, cols. 1465–66), "and since then, in each successive year, another flotilla of 'oil only' destroyers has been built. There are now built and building more than 100 destroyers—I purposely leave the number rather vague—including coastal destroyers, which are solely dependent upon oil fuel. Similarly, during the last five years, oil has been employed in coal-burning battle-ships and cruisers, to enable them to realise their full powers in an emergency." Churchill's speech was intended to prepare Parliament for the British government's purchase of a controlling interest in the Anglo-Persian Oil Company (Doc. 182). With the progressive substitution of oil for coal, it was clear, the Admiralty and the government were developing sensitivities to the liquid fuel. The following assurance from the Kuwayti shaykh paved the way for a comparable undertaking on 14 May 1914 by the Bahrayni shaykh (text in Aitchison, op. cit., p. 239). For references, see Doc. 182.

With the hand of friendship we received your esteemed letter dated the 26th Zu-al-Kada 1331 and in it you stated that with reference to the conversation which passed between us yesterday if we saw no objection therein it would be desirable for Your Honour to inform the British Government that we were agreeable to the arrival of

His Excellency the Admiral. We are agreeable to everything which you regard advantageous and if the Admiral honours our (side) country we will associate with him one of our sons to be in his service, to show the place of bitumen in Burgan and elsewhere and if in their view there seems hope of obtaining oil therefrom we shall never give a concession in this matter to any one except a person appoint from the British Government.

This is what was necessary and I pray for the continuance of your high regard and may you be preserved.

180. DRAFT AGREEMENT ON THE BAGHDAD RAILROAD: THE IMPERIAL OTTOMAN BANK AND THE DEUTSCHE BANK
15 February 1914

[Translated from the French text in Lepsius, Mendelssohn-Bartholdy, and Thimme, *Die grosse Politik*, 37(ii): 583–88]

On the eve of World War I France ranked second only to Germany in railroad investments in the Ottoman Empire. The French concessions were located chiefly in Syria (and Palestine) and Anatolia. The Russian-German agreement at Potsdam (Doc. 172) and the prospect of a British-German accord on Ottoman affairs stirred uneasiness in Paris by the spring of 1913 over the security of these investments and the special position of France in the zone where they were concentrated. The Sublime Porte, after suffering defeats in wars with Italy and the Balkan states (1911–13), was no less anxious to dissolve lingering French hesitations over the Baghdad railroad scheme, which remained for the Young Turks what it had represented to 'Abdülhamid—the most promising hope of economic development and improved communications and defenses. For an increase in the tariff rates, the approval of France was just as essential as that of Britain. The Sublime Porte accordingly prodded Germany to treat with France and, in the summer of 1913, sent its own economic adviser, Cavid Bey, to Paris to take part in the discussions. The Imperial Ottoman Bank and the Deutsche Bank initialed *ad referendum* the resulting agreement and its annexes at Berlin. The presence of representatives from the Wilhelmstrasse and the Quai d'Orsay and the provision for an exchange of notes between the two governments gave the instrument its official character. But the contract did not go into effect, for it was dependent on a final Ottoman-German understanding on the Baghdad railroad that was never concluded. Earle, *Turkey, the Great Powers and the Bagdad Railway*, pp. 244–52; Wolf, *Diplomatic History of the Bagdad Railroad*, chap. 7; Trumpener, *Germany and the Ottoman Empire*, chap. 1; Howard, *Partition of Turkey*, chap. 2; Frischwasser-Ra'anan, *Frontiers of a Nation*, chap. 2.

Between the Imperial Ottoman Bank, acting in its own name as well as, duly authorized, in the name and in behalf of the Ottoman Company of the Damascus-Hama and Extensions Railroad and the Company now in process of formation for the construction and operation of the Black Sea railroad system, these various establishments being designated here below under the name of the "French group," on the one hand; and the Deutsche Bank, acting in its own name as well as, duly authorized, in the name and in behalf of the Ottoman Railroad Company of Anatolia and the Imperial Ottoman Company of the Baghdad Railroad, these various establishments being designated here below under the name of the "German group," on the other hand; there have been agreed and declared the following:

ART. 1. The French group let it be known that it is presently seeking from the Imperial Ottoman Government a concession for an integrated railroad system extending from the Black Sea and comprising notably the principal line of Samsun-Sivas-Kharput [present-day Elâziğ] with extensions to Ergani Maden, Bitlis, and Van toward the east, to Kastamonu and Bolu toward the west, as well as a branch line leaving from the neighborhood of Suluseray and extending in the direction of Yozgat as far as the divide between the Yeşil Irmak and the Kizil Irmak.

The German group takes note of the declarations of the French group and declares, for its part, its intention to seek the concession for the lines intended to link the systems of the Anatolia and Baghdad Railroads with that of the Black Sea to Sivas by way of Kayseri and to Ergani Maden by way of Diyarbakır.

The French group takes note of these declarations.

ART. 2. As a result, the systems of the two groups will meet, to the west at Bolu in the station of the Anatolia Railroad, to the south at Sivas in the station of the Black Sea Railroad, to the east at Ergani Maden in the station of the Baghdad Railroad.

The technical conditions under which the junctions in joint railroad stations will be made and the exact conditions under which the junction at Bolu will be made shall form the subject of an equitable agreement between the companies concerned at a later date.

The two groups shall come to an understanding so that the construction and operation of the port of Heraclea [Ereğli] and of the railroads joining Heraclea with the rail networks of the interior might be accomplished, taking into just account French and German industrial interests in the Heraclea basin and the interests of the railroads of the two groups.

ART. 3. The two groups note that the respective positions of the Damascus-Hama and Extensions Railroad and of the Baghdad Railroad are fixed as of this date by the junction of the systems of these companies at Aleppo and by their access to the sea respectively at Alexandretta for the Baghdad Railroad and at Tripoli in Syria for the Damascus-Hama and Extensions Railroad.

With a view to strengthening their respective situations and pursuing the normal development of their railroad systems free from any rivalry or competition, the two groups are agreed on the announcement of the following arrangements (Articles 4–6):

ART. 4. The German group declares its intention eventually to seek the concession for a line intended to link Alexandretta directly with Aleppo, and Aleppo, by way of Maskanah, with a given point in the system already under concession to the Baghdad Railroad in Mesopotamia. The French group takes note of the declaration of the German group and, for its part, declares its intention eventually to seek the concession for a line intended to link Tripoli in Syria directly with the Euphrates by means of an extension from Homs to Dayr al-Zawr, where the Damascus-Hama and Extentions would join the Baghdad Railroad system. The German group takes note of this declaration.

ART. 5. With regard to the lines defined in the preceding article, the two groups recognize a protected zone for sixty kilometers to the south of the line of Alexandretta Aleppo-Maskanah and Extension, an equal zone to the north of the line Tripoli-Homs-Dayr-al-Zawr, and a protected zone of sixty kilometers on either side of the right of way of the existing line from Homs to Aleppo.

At the junction of the two systems, where they come into contact, the protected zones are delimited by a straight line drawn from the point of junction of the rails at Aleppo to the point of intersection of the outer limits of the two zones, following the markings which the parties have by mutual agreement made on the schematic map annexed to these presents.*

The protected zones are exclusively reserved to the action of the system to which they belong, each of the groups engaging itself neither to construct nor to operate railroads in the protected zone of the other group.

ART. 6. The two groups shall refrain from constructing or operating, without prior agreement, any new extension reach-

*Not reproduced here.

ing the sea in the free zone existing between the outer limits of the protected zones of the Alexandretta-Aleppo and Tripoli-Homs lines.

ART. 7. The points of junction defined above between the systems of the two groups (Articles 2, 3, and 4) are the only ones now foreseen; new junctions which may be decided upon at a later date by the Imperial Ottoman Government shall be the subject of a prior agreement between the two groups.

ART. 8. In order to give complete effect to the preceding stipulations, insofar as they tend to the formation of integral systems, the two groups mutually assure each other that they shall not seek the construction or operation of any railroad in the zone of action of a system of the other group, particularly taking into account the points of junction indicated above (Articles 2, 3, and 4).

In the same way, the two groups shall refrain from aiding or abetting either directly or indirectly any individual, or company, of whatever nationality, whose action would go counter to the provisions of the present agreement.

ART. 9. Traffic questions of interest to the systems of the two groups will be regulated by two special agreements entered into between the interested companies and annexed to these presents.*

ART. 10. The two groups, having been informed of the program of railroad construction with the execution of which the Imperial Ottoman Government intends to entrust them, recognize the necessity so to space the projects as to take account of the financial situation of Turkey.

To this end they express the desire and, for their part, intention to act in a way that the construction of the railroads for which the concessions have, or may be, granted and which are of the same importance to the economic development of the Empire shall be pursued insofar as possible pari passu, each group normally having recourse in an equal manner to the loans issued or guaranteed by the Ottoman Treasury.

The two groups consider that the interest of Turkey obliges her, in order to assure her credit and to facilitate her new issues, to restore the loans already advanced to the situation that existed before the Balkan War. Should the contribution assumed by

the Balkan states not fully suffice for the purpose, new guarantees equivalent to those guarantees lost must be earmarked for the service of the loans, subject to the following reservations:

The allocation shall be made only in the feasible amount, that is, the equivalent of the sums necessary for the service of the loan.

The new allocation shall have only a provisional character; it shall become void at a time when, after three consecutive years, the former pledges, owing to plus values, assure the service of the loans.

In general all excess from the earmarked pledges, the use of which the beneficiary enterprise shall no longer have, must revert to the Ottoman Treasury for its general needs and its free disposition.

With the end in mind of the maintenance and consolidation of Turkish credit, the two groups consider that their common interests suggest effective cooperation in the liquidation loans in their different markets.

ART. 11. All agreements and conventions entered into among the participants of the two groups previous to this date on the subject of the matters governed by these presents are declared specifically to be abrogated.

ART. 12. The present agreement being concluded in good faith, the two groups declare their intention to submit to arbitration the regulation of any difficulties which might arise from its application.

Each group shall choose an arbitrator. If necessary, the arbitrators shall designate a referee to reconcile them; in case of disagreement on the choice of a referee, the latter shall be designated, at the request of the parties, by the President of the Federal Tribunal of Lausanne.

ART. 13. The present agreement will be communicated to the French and German governments for their approval.

ART. 14. The final ratification of the present agreement is dependent upon:

1. the conclusion of an agreement between the French group and the Imperial Ottoman Government on the subject of the railroads for which the French group seeks the concession;

2. The conclusion of an agreement between the German group and the Imperial

---

*Not reproduced here.

Ottoman Government on the subject of the Baghdad and Anatolia Railroads;

3. the conclusion of a financial agreement between the two groups relative to the liquidation of the interest of the French group in the Baghdad Railroad enterprise.

ANNEX I. NOTE ADJOINED TO THE AGREEMENT OF THE GROUPS

1. In application of Article 2, paragraph 2, the Black Sea Company shall remain liable to the Anatolia Company for eventual loss of construction advantages which may result from the fixing of the point of juncture at Bolu.

2. The French negotiators have expressed the desire to insert in Article 8, paragraph 1, after the words "construction or operation," the words "nor control or direction." The definitive decision regarding this insertion remains in suspense.

3. The last paragraph of Article 10 does not refer to the Consolidation Loan now in process of negotiation at Paris.

4. The annexes mentioned in Article 9, which would regulate traffic questions, are reserved for study by the interested companies and for ultimate approval by the groups.

The drafts annexed *pro forma* to these presents, which (save for several modifications in form) were prepared September last [1913], have the value of general indications only.

5. A memorandum, annexed to these presents, indicates the general conditions under which the financial agreement mentioned in the third paragraph of Article 14 shall take place.

ANNEX II. MEMORANDUM

The liquidation of the interests of the French group in the Baghdad Railroad enterprise, mentioned in Article 14 (3), shall be accomplished by an exchange of these interests, comprising:

approximately 8,000 shares of the Baghdad Railroad Company frs.	4,000,000
approximately 3,900 shares of the Construction Company	1,950,000
approximately 55,500 bonds, Baghdad Series II	27,750,000
approximately 71,400 bonds, Baghdad Series III	35,700,000
or frs.	69,400,000

against the advance on the second installment of the Customs Loan of Constantinople, 1911, granted to the Ottoman Government by a German group, amounting to approximately frs. 66,000,000.

The conditions of the exchange shall be fixed by an agreement in common between the Imperial Ottoman Bank and the Deutsche Bank.

181. ARRANGEMENT FOR THE REORGANIZATION OF THE TURKISH PETROLEUM COMPANY: THE D'ARCY GROUP, THE DEUTSCHE BANK, AND THE ANGLO-SAXON PETROLEUM COMPANY
19 March 1914

[*Foreign Relations of the United States, 1927*, 2: 821;–22]

Three groups were competing for oil concessions in Mesopotamia (present-day Iraq) in 1913: the Deutsche Bank, the Anglo-Persian Oil Company, and the Anglo-Saxon Oil Company (a subsidiary of Royal Dutch-Shell, an Anglo-Dutch combine). The Deutsche Bank's claim derived from an option of 1904 that had been allowed to expire; that of the Anglo-Persian Oil Company from several petitions presented to the

Ottoman government by William Knox D'Arcy after 1906 and supported by the British ambassador at Istanbul; and that of the Royal Dutch-Shell from the friendly intervention of Calouste Sarkis Gulbenkian, "an Ottoman subject of considerable influence and ability, sometimes called the Talleyrand of oil diplomacy" (Earle, "Turkish Petroleum Company," 267). The British government insisted that the Anglo-Persian Oil Company, of which it was about to become the principal owner, should acquire the largest individual share. The accession of the two other groups to this condition led to the following arrangement, commonly known as the Foreign Office Agreement of 1914, for the negotiations took place in the British Foreign Office. Representatives of the British and German governments as well as of the companies signed the contract. The restrictive features of article 10—labeled in the oil trade "the self-denying ordinance"—were inherited from bilateral agreements between the earlier Turkish Petroleum Company (founded on 31 January 1911) and each of its three corporate constituents—the Deutsche Bank (agreement of 19 October 1912; text in *Foreign Relations of the United States, 1927*, 2: 820), the (British) National Bank of Turkey (22 October 1912), and the Anglo-Saxon Petroleum Company (23 October 1912) respectively—and were later enshrined in the Red Line Agreement of 1928. Earle, "Turkish Petroleum Company"; Longrigg, *Oil in the Middle East*, chap. 2; United States Senate, *International Petroleum Cartel*, chap. 4; Hoffman, *Ölpolitik*, chap. 4; Shwadran, *Middle East, Oil and the Great Powers*, chap. 7.

It is agreed that the interests shall be divided as follows:

Fifty per cent to the d'Arcy group,

Twenty-five per cent to the Deutsche Bank,

Twenty-five per cent to the Anglo-Saxon Petroleum Company,

and that, in order to carry out this division,

1. The shares in the Turkish Petroleum Company now held by The National Bank of Turkey shall be transferred in equal moieties to the Deutsche Bank and the Anglo-Saxon Petroleum Company.

2. The capital of the Turkish Petroleum Company shall be increased to £160,000 by the creation of 80,000 new shares of £1 each of the same class as those now existing.

3. These 80,000 new shares shall be allotted to the d'Arcy group on terms to be agreed upon between the parties.

4. The Board of the Company shall consist of eight members, of whom four will be nominated by the d'Arcy group, two by the Deutsche Bank, and two by the Anglo-Saxon Company.

5. The capital of the Turkish Petroleum Company shall be employed only in exploring, testing, and proving oil fields, a separate public company or companies being formed to work any field or fields the examination of which has proved satisfactory.

6. Such working company or companies shall issue to the Turkish Petroleum Company fully paid ordinary shares as consideration for the properties to be acquired; such ordinary shares shall carry full control of the working company or companies, which control shall in no circumstances be parted with by the Turkish Petroleum Company.

7. The working capital required by such working company or companies shall be raised by means of preference shares and (or) debentures which shall be offered to the public to such extent as the members of the Turkish Petroleum Company or any one of them shall elect not to subscribe for themselves.

8. The alterations in the memorandum and (or) article of association of the Turkish Petroleum Company necessary to carry out the above conditions shall be made forthwith.

9. Mr. C. S. Gulbenkian shall be entitled to a beneficiary five per cent interest without voting rights in the Turkish Petroleum Company, this five per cent being contributed equally by the d'Arcy group and the

Anglo-Saxon Company out of their respective holdings. The shares representing Mr. Gulbenkian's interest shall be registered in the names of nominees of the d'Arcy group and of the Anglo-Saxon Company, and shall be held by them, but undertakings shall be exchanged between these parties whereby
(1) Mr. Gulbenkian undertakes to pay the calls on the shares, and
(2) the d'Arcy group and the Anglo-Saxon Company undertake that Mr. Gulbenkian shall be entitled to all financial benefits of the shares.
(3) If Mr. Gulbenkian shall desire to dispose of this interest, and also in the event of his death, the d'Arcy group and the Anglo-Saxon Com-

pany shall have the option of purchasing the interests standing in their names as defined in Article 36 (b) of the article of association of the Turkish Petroleum Company.
10. The three groups participating in the Turkish Petroleum Company shall give undertaking on their own behalf and on behalf of the companies associated with them not to be interested directly or indirectly in the production or manufacture of crude oil in the Ottoman Empire in Europe and Asia, except in that part which is under the administration of the Egyptian Government or of the Sheikh of Koweit, or in the "transferred territories" on the Turco-Persian frontier, otherwise than through the Turkish Petroleum Company.

182. AGREEMENT OF THE BRITISH TREASURY AND ADMIRALTY WITH THE ANGLO-PERSIAN OIL COMPANY
20 May 1914

[Great Britain, *Parliamentary Papers, 1914*, vol. 54, Cd. 7419]

Once the British government opened negotiations with the Anglo-Persian Oil Company in 1913, the Admiralty set up a special commission to investigate the company's operations. The commission, which arrived in Persia on 23 October 1913 and returned to England on 25 January 1914, visited the company's fields in Kuwayt and Bahrayn. As part of the resulting agreement, the company statutes were amended. Article 91A, newly inserted, stipulated that either of the two ex officio directors of the company appointed by the British Treasury "shall have the right of negativing any resolution which may be proposed at any meeting of the Board or of any Committee of the Directors, provided always that in the event of the aforesaid right being exercised it shall be open to the other Directors, or a majority of them, to submit the proposed resolution to His Majesty's Government, who shall thereupon, after full consideration, determine in writing whether the same ought to be given effect to or not; and if His Majesty's Government shall determine that the proposed resolution ought to be given effect to, it shall be deemed to have been duly passed at the meeting at which it was proposed. For the purpose of this Article, His Majesty's Government shall mean the Treasury and the Admiralty acting jointly; and notice of any submission hereunder to His Majesty's Government shall be given both to the Treasury and the Admiralty." This clause, together with the government's acquisition of a majority interest in the enterprise, assured the Admiralty a substantial portion of its annual oil requirements, on reasonable terms, from a government-controlled company. Omitted below is the detailed schedule of amendments to the company's articles of association. Anglo-Iranian Oil Company, *Short History of the Anglo-Iranian Oil Company*; Longrigg, *Oil in the Middle East*, chap. 2; Hoffman, *Ölpolitik*, chap. 2; Caroe, *Wells of Power*, pt. 2, chap. 1; DeGolyer, "Some Aspects of Oil in the Middle East"; Hoskins, *Middle East*, chap. 10; Shwadran, *Middle East, Oil and the Great Powers*, chap. 2.

Whereas the Company has an authorised share Capital of £2,000,000 divided into (1) 1,000,000 Ordinary Shares of £1 each all of which have been issued and are fully paid up and (2) 1,000,000 Participating Preference Shares of £1 each of which 999,000 have been issued and are fully paid up.

And whereas the Company has issued £600,000 First Debenture Stock secured by a Trust Deed dated the 25th day of May 1909 and made between the Company of the one part and the Duke of Sutherland and the Earl of Lichfield of the other part.

And whereas the Company is interested in and is working various petroleum or oil bearing lands in Persia and is possessed of a refinery at Abadan Island and various pipe lines and other plant.

And whereas the oil products which the Company produces include oil fuel.

And whereas the Company is desirous of obtaining futher Capital for the development of its undertaking and more particularly in order that it may be enabled adequately to perform any Agreement which it may enter into with the Admiralty for the supply of oil fuel to the Admiralty.

And whereas the Company has proposed to the Treasury that such further Capital shall be provided by the Treasury upon the terms and subject to the conditions herein contained and the Treasury are willing to accede to such proposal.

Now it is hereby agreed between the parties hereto to follows:—

1. This Agreement is conditional upon:—

(*a*.) The Company's Ordinary Share Capital being increased as hereinafter mentioned.

(*b*.) The Company's Articles of Association being altered as hereinafter provided.

(*c*.) The necessary monies for enabling the Treasury to carry out the provisions of Clause 3 hereof being duly provided by Parliament.

(*d*.) An Agreement satisfactory to the Admiralty being entered into between the Company and the Admiralty for the supply of oil fuel by the Company to the Admiralty.

2. The Company shall forthwith obtain the necessary powers to increase it Ordinary Share Capital by the issue of 2,000,000 additional Ordinary Shares of £1 each ranking in all respects *pari passu* with the 1,000,000 Ordinary Shares already issued.

3. The Treasury shall upon the conditions mentioned in clause 1 hereof being duly fulfilled subscribe at par for 2,000,000 Ordinary Shares of the Company of £1 each and shall also subscribe at par for the 1,000 Preference Shares of the Company of £1 each which still remain unissued. The monies to be paid in respect of the said respective Shares shall be payable as follows:—

(1.) One-fourth on the date of the application for the same.

(2.) The remaining three-fourths as and when required by the Company (but subject always to not less than one calendar month's notice in writing of such requirement being given by the Company to the Treasury).

The said Shares shall be allotted to such persons as shall be appointed by the Treasury in such amounts as shall be directed by the instrument of appointment. The respective allottees shall upon payment in respect of the Shares allotted to them respectively of the monies mentioned under Heading (1) of this Clause be forthwith registered as the holders of such Shares and shall thereupon be entitled to full voting powers in respect thereof.

4. For the purpose of conferring on the Treasury the right of being at all times represented by two *ex officio* Directors on the Board of Directors of the Company and of defining the powers of such *ex officio* Directors and of making provision for other matters which it is hereby agreed shall be provided for, the Article of Association of the Company shall forthwith be altered by Special Resolution in the terms set forth in the Schedule hereto.

5. The Company shall in regard to the First Exploitation Company Limited, the Bakhtiari Oil Company Limited and any other subsidiary Company in which the Company (party hereto) shall have a sufficient controlling interest (each of which Companies is hereinafter called a subsidiary Company) forthwith

(*a.*) Procure the appointment on the Board of each subsidiary Company of two *ex officio* Director to represent the Treasury and to have the same powers and to be subject to the same provisions as to appointment, tenure of office and otherwise as will by the Article of Association of the Company (party hereto) when altered in accordance with the Special Resolution in the preceding Clause mentioned be conferred on and made applicable to the *ex officio* Directors of the Company (party hereto).

(*b.*) Procure such alterations to be made in the Articles of Association of each subsidiary Company as may be required for enabling such appointment powers and provisions to be respectively effected conferred and made applicable.

(*c.*) Procure [the necessary alterations so] that the Treasury and the Admiralty shall respectively have such other rights, powers and privileges in regard to each subsidiary Company as it is by Clause 7 hereof agreed that the Treasury and the Admiralty shall respectively have in regard to the Company (party hereto).

6. The Company shall not enter into or be party to any Trust or Combine but shall always be and remain an independent British Company.

7. The Treasury and the Admiralty shall respectively be at liberty from time to time to appoint such person or persons as the Appointing Department (which expression shall mean the Department—that is to say the Treasury or the Admiralty as the case may be—making the appointment) may think proper, with such powers as the Appointing Department may consider necessary or expedient, for the purpose of visiting and inspecting and of reporting to the Appointing Department upon the undertaking wells and works of the Company (including any wells or works which may be for the time being under construction) and the plant machinery and stores belonging thereto and/or for the purpose of investigating the accounts and affairs of the Company, whether in the United Kingdom or in Persia, and the Company shall afford every person so appointed all facilities (including such facilities as are given to the Accountants or Auditors of the Company) for the purpose of enabling him to perform the duties entrusted to him by the Appointing Department. Provided always that the powers and privileges which are by this Clause given to the Treasury and the Admiralty respectively are independent powers and privileges and are also independent of such powers as may from time to time be vested in or exercisable by the *ex officio* Directors of the Company or by the persons for the time being holding Shares as nominees of the Treasury or by any Department of His Majesty's Government through the medium of such last mentioned persons.

8. The Treasury shall as and when required by the Company (but subject always to not less than one calendar month's notice in writing of such requirement being given by the Company to the Treasury) take up at par Debenture Stock of the Company not exceeding in the aggregate the sum of £199,000 Debenture Stock which stock shall be issued to such nominee or nominees of the Treasury as the Treasury shall appoint. Such stock shall be part of and rank *pari passu* with the First Debenture Stock secured by the said Trust Deed of the 25th day of May 1909 and the Company shall from time to time do all such acts and things as may be necessary for the purpose of creating and issuing the same. Save as aforesaid no Debentures of Debenture Stock shall without the consent in writing of the Treasury be created or issued by the Company to rank *pari passu* with the First Debenture Stock secured by the said Trust Deed.

9. The Company (if required by the Treasury by notice in writing given to the Company not later than the 31st day of January 1920) shall on the 31st day of December 1920 redeem the whole of the present issue of £600,000 First Debenture Stock in accordance with the liberty in that behalf which is conferred on the Company under or by virtue of the said Trust Deed of the 25th day of May 1909 and shall reissue such stock when so redeemed to the

nominees of the Treasury at the redemption price of £105 per cent. and shall do all such acts and things as may be necessary for the above purposes.

10. In view of the provisions contained in the House of Commons (Disqualification) Acts 1782 and 1801 no member of the House of Commons shall be admitted to any share or part of this Agreement or to any benefit to arise therefrom.

11. The Company shall at all times carry on its business in a proper manner and shall comply with the terms of any concession of lands or rights in Persia which it may hold or in which it may be interested, and shall do all such acts and things as may from time to time be necessary to preserve each such concession or to prevent the same from being forfeited, and shall not do or suffer any act or thing or commit any default which may lead to a forfeiture of any such concession or which may render the security constituted by the said Trust Deed of the 25th day of May 1909 enforceable or which may give rise to any right on the part of the trustees of such deed to take possession or appoint a Receiver of the Company's undertaking or property or any part thereof.

12. The Company shall have at all times its registered and head office in England.

13. So soon as the Capital of the Company shall have been increased as aforesaid and the Special Resolution hereinbefore referred to shall have been confirmed, the Company shall forthwith execute and do all such instruments, acts and things as may be necessary or proper for giving full effect to this Agreement, and in particular if necessary or proper or if required so to do by the Treasury or the Admiralty shall cause the Seal of the Company to be reaffixed hereto or to be affixed to a supplementary document confirming this Agreement.

14. The Schedule to this Agreement shall be deemed to be part of this Agreement in all respects as if the same had been incorporated therein. . . .

183. BRITISH-GERMAN DRAFT CONVENTION ON THE BAGHDAD RAILROAD
15 June 1914

[Gooch and Temperley, *British Documents on the Origins of the War*, 10(ii): 398–408]

The reorganization of the Turkish Petroleum Company (Doc. 181) represented only one of many tightly interlocked problems in the Ottoman Empire that Britain and Germany were attempting to resolve. For the most part the issues centered on the Baghdad railroad project and, although economic in origin, they became in the aggregate political and strategic. A year of intense bargaining between English and German businessmen, financiers, and government officials ultimately produced the following draft convention, which British Foreign Secretary Sir Edward Grey and German Ambassador Prince Karl Mas Lichnowsky initialed in London. The ratification of the complex of bilateral instruments between the Entente powers, Germany and the Ottoman Empire awaited the conclusion of the Ottoman-German agreement. The Wilhelmstrasse transmitted its opening demands to the Sublime Porte in a memorandum of 14 November 1913 (French text in Lepsius, Mendelssohn-Bartholdy, and Thimme, *Die grosse Politik*, 37 (ii): 532–35). But the negotiations never reached their intended goal, for with the outbreak of World War I German-

Ottoman diplomacy sheered off in a new direction. Only the draft convention and the explanatory note appear below. Trumpener, *Germany and the Ottoman Empire*, chap. 1; Chapman, *Great Britain and the Bagdad Railway*, chaps. 10–11; Earle, *Turkey, the Great Powers and the Bargdad Railway*, chap. 10, and "Secret Anglo-German Convention of 1914"; Wolf, *Diplomatic History of the Bagdad Railroad*, chap. 7; Howard, *Partition of Turkey*, chap. 2; Frischwasser-Ra'anan, *Frontiers of a Nation*, chap. 2.

ART. 1. *Clause (a)*.—Recognising the general importance of the completion of the Bargdad Railway for international commerce, His Britannic Majesty's Government undertake not to take or encourage any measures likely to impede the construction or management by the Bagdad Railway Company of the Bagdad Railway system or to prevent the participation of capital in this undertaking.

Clause (b).—The Imperial German Government declare that they will use their best endeavours to secure that two British members, agreeable to His Britannic Majesty's Government, shall be admitted as representatives of British shareholders to the Board (Conseil d'Administration) of the Bagdad Railway Company.

ART. 2. *Clause (a)*.—The Bagdad Railway Company having concluded with the Imperial Ottoman Government an arrangement on the following basis, the Imperial German Government and His Britannic Majesty's Government declare, so far as concerns themselves, that they adhere to the said arrangement, and will use their best endeavours to secure its due execution:—

(i) The terminus of the Bagdad Railway Company's line shall be at Basra, and the Bagdad Railway Company has renounced all claims to construct a branch line from Basra (Zobeir) to the Persian Gulf referred to in article 1 of the Bagdad Railway Convention of the 5th March, 1903, and to build a port or railway terminus on the Persian Gulf, under article 23 of the said Bagdad Railway Convention.

(ii) As hitherto, no discrimination, direct or indirect, shall be permitted on the Bagdad Railway Company's system, either as regards facilities or rates of charge for the conveyance of like articles between the same points on account of ownership, origin, or destination of goods presented for transport, or in any other manner whatever.

(iii) The Bagdad Railway Company agrees that the periods fixed by article 21 of the "cahier des charges," relating to the notice to be given in case of any modification of the conditions of transport or rates of freight, shall uniformly be two months. The said notices shall be inserted in the Official Gazette of the Imperial Ottoman Government and in the Journal of the Ottoman Chamber of Commerce at Constantinople.

(iv) In the event of the construction of a branch line from Basra (Zobeir) to the Persian Gulf being undertaken, adequate arrangements shall be made to secure facilities for through traffic from and to the Bagdad Railway Company's system, and there shall be complete protection against discrimination, direct or indirect.

(v) The construction and exploitation of the proposed port of Basra and Bagdad, authorised by article 23 of the Bagdad Railway Convention of the 5th March, 1903, shall be carried out by a separate Ottoman Company.

No duties or charges of whatever nature or under whatever denomination shall be levied by the port company on any vessels or goods which shall not equally, under the same conditions, be imposed in like cases on all vessels or goods, whatever be the nationality of the vessels or their owners, or the ownership or country of origin or destination of the goods, and whatever be the places from which the vessels or goods arrive or to which they depart.

In all that relates to the stationing, loading and unloading of vessels in these ports, no privileges or facilities shall be granted to any vessel or vessels which shall not equally and under like conditions be granted to all other vessels.

In all that relates to the dues and charges

of whatever nature to be levied, and to the facilities to be accorded, in the ports of Basra and Bagdad, goods arriving or to be forwarded by water shall receive identic treatment to those arriving or to be forwarded by rail.

The Imperial Ottoman Government reserves to itself the right to confer upon the Commission, which it proposes to entrust with the improvement and maintenance of the navigability of the Shatt-el-Arab, its rights of control over the port of Basra.

No rights conferred upon the ports company shall prejudice or impair the right of the aforesaid Commission to perform any of the duties entrusted to it under the Anglo-Turkish Convention of the 29th July, 1913.

Clause (b).—The Imperial German Government declare that they will not oppose the acquisition by British interests of 40 per cent. of the share-capital of the separate Ottoman Company for the construction and exploitation of the ports of Barsa and Bagdad, mentioned in sub-clause (v) above, and their rateable representation on the Board (Conseil d'Administration) of the port company, and in the contracts, if any, for construction and maintenance.

ART. 3. *Clause (a).*—The Imperial German Government and His Britannic Majesty's Government declare that they will in no case support the construction of a branch from Basra (Zobeir) or from any point of the main line of the Bagdad Railway, to the Persian Gulf unless and until there is complete agreement on the subject between the Imperial Ottoman Government, the Imperial German Government, and His Britannic Majesty's Government.

Clause (b).—The Imperial German Government declare that they will in no case themselves establish, or support any claim by any persons or corporations whatsoever to establish, a port or railway terminus on the Persian Gulf unless and until there is complete agreement on the subject between the Imperial German Government and His Britannic Majesty's Government.

Clause (c).—His Britannic Majesty's Government declare that they will in no case themselves establish, or support any claim by any persons or corporations what-

soever to establish, in Ottoman territory, railway undertakings either in direct competition with the Bagdad Railway Company's lines, or in contradiction with that company's existing rights, unless and until ther is complete agreement on the subject between the Imperial German Government and His Britannic Majesty's Government. For the purposes of this article, the western terminus of the Bagdad Railway system shall be held to be at Konia and the eastern terminus at Basra.

ART. 4. *Clause (a).*—The Imperial German Government, having cognisance of the declaration signed on the 29th July, 1913, on behalf of the Imperial Ottoman Government, concerning navigation on the Rivers Tigris and Euphrates, declare that they will not oppose the execution, nor support any action directed against the execution, of such declaration, so long as the navigation on the said rivers is maintained in substantial accordance with the provisions thereof.

Clause (b).—His Britannic Majesty's Government declare that they will not oppose the acquisition by the Bagdad Railway interests of 40 per cent. of the share capital to be allotted to Turkish interests at the first allotment (*i.e.,* 20 per cent. of the whole share-capital) and the right in respect thereof to subscribe for a rateable proportion of further issues of capital of the Ottoman Company for river navigation, and their rateable participation (by directors agreeable to the Imperial German Government) in the board of the aforesaid Company out of the share of the directorate allotted to Turkish interests (*i.e.,* 20 per cent. of the whole directorate).

Clause (c).—It is, nevertheless, understood that nothing in this article shall be held to affect the rights conceded by article 9 of the Bagdad Railway Convention of the 5th March, 1903, except in so far that the Imperial German Government and His Britannic Majesty's Government agree, so far as concerns themselves, that the said rights shall cease on the completion of the construction of the Bagdad Railway to Basra, in accordance with the arrangement referred to in article 2 of the present Convention.

ART. 5.—The concessionnaire, nominated in pursuance of article 3 of the aforesaid declaration of the 29th July, 1913, having concluded with the Imperial Ottoman Government an arrangement on the following basis, the Imperial German Government and His Britannic Majesty's Government declare, so far as concerns themselves, that they adhere to the said arrangement and will use their best endeavours to secure its due execution:—

No discrimination, direct or indirect, shall be permitted by the Ottoman Company for river navigation, either as regards facilities or rates of charge for the conveyance of like articles between the same points on account of the ownership, origin, or destination of goods presented for transport, or in any other manner whatsoever. The Company shall grant no through bills of lading, rebates, or other privileges of any description in respect of goods carried by any ship between any place served by the Company's vessels, and any place oversea, unless the same privileges are accorded in respect of similar goods carried under the same conditions and in the same direction between the same places by all ships regularly trading between those places, irrespective of nationality.

ART. 6. The Imperial German Government and His Britannic Majesty's Government will join in using their good offices with the Imperial Ottoman Government to secure that the Shatt-el-Arab shall so far as practicable be brought into and permanently kept in a satisfactory state of conservancy in order that sea-going vessels may always be assured of free and easy access to the port of Basra, and to secure, further, that the navigation on the Shatt-el-Arab shall permanently be kept open for sea-going vessels, and be carried on under conditions of absolute equality for the vessels of all nations, without regard either to the nationality of the vessels or to their cargoes.

Dues shall be imposed, not for the mere fact of navigation, but only for administrative charges of the Commission referred to in article 7 and for repaying sums actually spent on improvements in the navigation of the Shatt-el-Arab and harbour facilities. They shall in no case exceed 1 fr. per registered ton (the dues to cover the coming in and going out of the same vessel) except

by agreement between the two Governments; any dues shall be levied on a basis of absolute equality without regard to the nationality of sea-going vessels or their cargoes.

ART. 7. (a) The Imperial German Government having taken note of the Anglo-Turkish Convention of the 29th July, 1913, under which the free navigation of the Shatt-el-Arab is assured on terms of absolute equality to the shipping of all nations and a Commission is established for the execution of such works as may be necessary for the improvement of its channel and for its maintenance and for other like purposes set out therein, and being of opinion that the provisions of the said Convention are conducive to the best interests of international commerce, will uphold it so long as it is not materially altered and so long as the duties imposed upon the Commission thereunder are satisfactorily carried out.

The Imperial German Government take note in this connection of the declaration, signed on the 21st October, 1913, and attached to the said Convention, to the effect that articles 7 and 8 thereof do not affect the rights enjoyed in the Ottoman Empire by the nationals of the Treaty Powers.

(b) His Britannic Majesty's Government, so far as they are concerned, agree:—

(i) That the German consul at Basra shall have the right to correspond with the Commission on matters within its competence;

(ii) That, if in any case the Commission fail to meet the reasonable requirements of the commerce of the river, and refuse to remove the causes of complaint raised by the German consul, the question at issue shall be referred to an impartial expert, to be nominated by agreement between the two members of the Commission and the German consul, provided that if a similar or analogous complaint is made by any other consul, he shall participate in the said nomination; and that, failing unanimous agreement, Her Majesty the Queen of the Netherlands shall be invited to designate the expert referee.

The Government of His Britannic Majesty will use their good offices with the Imperial Ottoman Government to ensure that effect is duly given to such recommendations as may be made by the expert referee.

ART. 8. The Imperial German Government and His Britannic Majesty's Government take note of the Heads of Agreement between the Smyrna-Aidin Railway Company on the one part and the Anatolian and Bagdad Railway Companies on the other part, initialled on the 28th March, 1914, and forming an annex[1] to the present Convention, and, so far as they are concerned, undertake to uphold the definitive agreement when signed.

ART. 9. Any difference of opinion arising out of this Convention or the explanatory note attached thereto shall be submitted to arbitration. If the two Governments fail to agree about a special Court or arbiter, the case shall be submitted to The Hague Tribunal.

Explanatory Note

SECTION I

In regard to article 1, clause (a), of the Convention, it is agreed as follows:—

The Bagdad Railway system is such as it is defined in the conventions concluded with the Imperial Ottoman Government on—

March 5, 1903.

March 21, 1911.

June, 1914.

A true copy of each of the said conventions has been communicated to His Britannic Majesty's Government by the Imperial German Government.

It is further agreed in regard to the said clause that no sacrifice of a pecuniary or economic character is to be incurred by Great Britain in consequence thereof; and that it does not involve the assent of His Britannic Majesty's Government to any levy of import dues, over 15 per cent *ad valorem*, in the Ottoman Empire. or to any other form of taxation not now in existence.

Nevertheless, His Britannic Majesty's Government will not oppose the Bagdad Railway Company in seucuring, from existing revenues or from proposed new revenues (to be derived from the increase of the customs duties to 15 per cent *ad valorem* or from the proposed monopolies or consumption taxes to be instituted in regard

to alcohol, petroleum, matches, tinder cigarette paper, playing cards and sugar), the requisite fresh guarantees to enable the Company to complete the line. This undertaking shall in no way prejudice prior rights of His Britannic Majesty's Government derived under the Anglo-Turkish Pecuniary Claims Convention of the June, 1914.

SECTION II

In regard to article 1, clause (b), the German group which controls the Bagdad Railway Company has given a written assurance to the Imperial German Government that it will always use its best endeavours and voting power to ensure the permanent presence on the Board of the Railway of two directors agreeable to His Britannic Majesty's Government; and the Imperial German Government undertake to His Britannic Majesty's Government that they will use their influence with the group concerned so that the said assurance may be always carried out.

SECTION III

In regard to article 3, clause (c), of the Convention, it is agreed as follows:—

1. No lines in that part of Asiatic Turkey which, west of the 36th meridian of east longitude, lies south of the 34th degree of latitude and/or in that part which, east of the said meridian, lies south of the 31st degree of latitude, shall be held to be in direct competition; but any line north of these limits shall be held to be in direct competition if it establishes direct railway communication between the Mediterranean and the Persian Gulf.

2. There shall be a protective zone extending for 60 kilom on either side of the lines of the Bagdad Railway system, and any line passing within the said zone shall be held to be in direct competition, provided that in the region between Museyib and Kurna the protective zone shall be bounded on the east by a line drawn midway between the Rivers Tigris and Euphrates from the latitude of Museyib to Kurna.

3. Local lines serving as feeders for the river navigation and not exceeding 100 kilom in length shall, provided they do not

---

1. Not reproduced here.

pass within the protective zone, not be held to be in direct competition.

4. The question of whether any other line is or is not in direct competition shall, in the event of failure to reach an agreement, be referred to arbitration in accordance with article 9 of the said Convention.

SECTION IV

In regard to articles 6 and 7 of the Convention, it is agreed that the following recommendations shall serve as a basis for the work of the Commission:—

1. The Commission to set to work as soon as possible.

2. The Commission to undertake a preliminary survey, during a period of at least twelve months, before recommending any large expenditure on permanent works.

3. The Commission to aim as a first step at a depth of 24 feet at high-water springs on the bar.

4. The channel of the river below Mohammerah to be buoyed as soon as possible

so as to indicate the position of a shoal in the river.

5. Fixed mooring buoys, allotted as far as possible to the several companies, to be provided at an early date at Basra.

6. The Commission might with advantage model its arrangements generally upon the analogy of the Danube Commission, so far as applicable.

SECTION V

In regard to article 7, clause (b), of the Convention, it is agreed as follows:—

The expert referce shall, unless it be otherwise agreed by the parties concerned, proceed to Basra for the purpose of his enquiry. He shall publish his report within four months after having received all the necessary materials from all the parties, including both Commissioners, or within four months of his arrival at Basra.

The expenses of the enquiry, including the remuneration of the referee, shall be borne in equal shares by the Governments concerned.

184. OTTOMAN PROMISE OF A CONCESSION TO THE TURKISH PETROLEUM COMPANY
28 June 1914

[United States, 68th Cong., 1st sess., Senate, doc. no. 97, "Oil Concessions in Foreign Countries," p. 49]

The British and German ambassadors at Istanbul on 19 June 1914 addressed a request to Grand Vezir Sa'id Halim Paşa that an oil concession embracing the *vilâyets* of Mosul and Baghdad be issued to the newly reorganized Turkish Petroleum Company (Doc. 181). Nine days later the Grand Vezir sent identic notes, reproduced below, to the European diplomats. The outbreak of war in midsummer prevented the completion of the negotiations, but on the strength of the 1914 promise the Turkish Petroleum Company obtained from the Iraqi government a decade later a definitive concession. For references, see Doc. 181.

In response to the note which Your Excellency had the kindness to address to me under date of the 19th instant, I have the honor to inform you as follows:

The Ministry of Finance being substi-

tuted for the Civil List with respect to petroleum resources discovered, and to be discovered, in the vilayets of Mossoul and Bagdad, consents to lease these to the Turkish Petroleum Company, and reserves to itself the right to determine hereafter its participation, as well as the general conditions of the contract.

It goes without saying that the Society must undertake to indemnify, in case of necessity, third persons who may be interested in the petroleum resources located in these two vilâyets.

Bibliography

Manuscript Collections

GREAT BRITAIN

India Office Library and Records, London.
Public Record Office, London.

IRAN

Archives of the Ministry of Foreign Affairs, Tehran.

TURKEY

State Archives, Istanbul.

Treaty Collections

FRANCE

Basdevant, Jules, comp. *Traités et conventions en vigeur entre la France et les puis-sances étrangères.* 4 vols. Paris: Imprimerie Nationale, 1918–22.

Clercq, Alexandre J. H. de, and Clercq, Jules de, comps. *Recueil des traités de la France.* 23 vols. Paris: Ministère des Affaires Etrangères, 1864–1907.

Hauterive, Count B. L. d', and Cussy, Baron F. de. *Recueil des traités de commerce de la France.* 10 vols. Paris: Rey et Gravier, 1834–44.

Rouard de Card, Edouard, comp. *Traités de la France avec les pays de l'Afrique du Nord.* Paris: Pedone, 1906.

GREAT BRITAIN

Foreign Office, Librarian and Keeper of the Records [Edward Hertslet]. *Treaties, etc., between Turkey and Foreign Powers, 1535–1855.* London: Harrison, for H. M. Stationery Office, 1855.

———. "Treaties between Great Britain and Algiers, subsisting between the two powers in 1814." *British and Foreign State Papers,* vol. 1, pt. 1 (1812–14), pp. 354–74.

———. "Treaties between Great Britain and Morocco, subsisting between the two powers in 1814." Ibid., pp. 428–62.

———. "Treaties between Great Britain and Tripoli, subsisting between the two powers in 1814." Ibid., pp. 710–33.

———. "Treaties between Great Britain and Tunis, subsisting between the two powers in 1814." Ibid., pp. 733–47.

———. *Treaty Series.*

Hertslet, Sir Edward, comp. *The Map of Africa by Treaty.* 3d ed. 3 vols. London: Harrison, for H. M. Stationery Office, 1909.

———. *The Map of Europe by Treaty.* 4 vols. London: Butterworth's, for H. M. Stationery Office, 1875–91.

———. *Treaties, etc., Concluded between Great Britain and Persia, and between Persia and Other Foreign Powers, Wholly or Partially in Force on 1st April, 1891.* London: Butterworth's, for H. M. Stationery Office, 1891.

Parliamentary Papers, 1854. "Treaties (Political and Territorial) between Russia and Turkey, 1744–1849." C. 88.

Parliamentary Papers, 1878. Turkey, no. 16. "Treaties and Other Documents relating to the Black Sea, the Dardanelles, and the Bosphorus, 1535–1877." C. 1953.

INDIA

Foreign and Political Department. *A Collection of Treaties, Engagements, and Sanads relating to India and Neighbouring Countries.* Compiled by C. U. Aitchison. 4th ed. 13 vols. Calcutta: Superintendent, Government Printing, 1909. 5th ed. 14 vols. Calcutta: Government of India, Central Publication Branch, 1929–33.

ITALY

Ministero degli Affari Esteri. *Trattati e convenzioni fra il regno d'Italia e gli altri stati.* 54 vols. Rome: Ministero degli Affari Esteri, 1861–1941.

MOROCCO

Rivière, P. Louis, comp. *Traités, codes, et lois du Maroc.* Paris: Sirey, 1924.

OTTOMAN EMPIRE

Noradounghian, Gabriel, comp. *Recueil d'actes internationaux de l'empire ottoman.* 4 vols. Paris: Pichon, 1897–1903.

Testa, Baron Ignaz de, ed. [continued by his sons and grandsons]. *Recueil des traités de la Porte Ottomane avec les puissances étrangères depuis le premier traité conclu en 1536 entre Suléyman I et François I jusqu'à nos jours.* 11 vols. Paris: 1864–1911.

PERSIA

Childs, James Rives, trans. and comp. *Perso-Russian Treaties and Notes of 1828–1931.* Translated from the Persian. Typescript. Tehran, 1935.

RUSSIA

Martens, Fedor Fedorovich, ed. *Recueil des traités et conventions conclus par la Russie avec les puissances étrangères.* 15 vols. in 13. Saint Petersburg: A. Böhnke, for Imprimerie du Ministère des Voies de Communications, 1874–1909.

UNITED STATES

Department of State. *Treaty Series.*

Malloy, William M. *Treaties, Conventions, International Acts, Protocols, and Agreements between the United States of America and other Powers, 1776–1909.* Washington, D.C.: Government Printing Offiice, 1910.

Miller, Hunter, comp. and ed. *Treaties and Other International Acts of the United States of America.* 8 vols. Washington: Government Printing Office, 1931.

GENERAL

Martens, George Frederic de. *Recueil des principaux traités . . . conclus par les puissances de l'Europe tant entre elles qu'avec les puissances et états dans d'autres parties du monde depuis 1761 jusqu'à présent.* 7 vols. Gottingue: Henri Dieterich, 1791–1801. Suppl., 4 vols. 1802–08.

Rousset de Missy, Jean. *Recueil historique d'actes, négotiations, mémoires et traités depuis la paix d'Utrecht jusqu'à présent.* 21 vols. in 23. The Hague: Scheurleer, 1728–56.

OFFICIAL PUBLICATIONS AND DIPLOMATIC PAPERS

FRANCE

Assemblée Nationale. *Annales.* Paris: Imprimerie et Librairie du Journal Officiel, 1870–71(?).

Gouvernement de la Défense Nationale. *Bulletin des Lois.* 12th Ser. Versailles: Imprimerie Nationale, 1871–72.

Ministère des Affaires Etrangères. *Documents diplomatiques, 1861–.* Paris: Imprimerie Nationale, 1862–.

————. *Documents diplomatiques: Question de la protection diplomatique et consulaire au Maroc.* Paris: Imprimerie Nationale, 1880.

————. Commission de la Publication des Documents Relatifs aux Origines de la Guerre de 1914. *Documents diplomatiques français, 1871–1914.* Ser. 1, 1871–1900, 16 vols.; ser. 2, 1901–11, 14 vols.; ser. 3, 1911–14, 11 vols.

Le Moniteur Universel, Journal Officiel de l'Empire Français. Paris, 1811–68.

Napoleon I, *Correspondance de Napoléon 1er. Paris:* Paris: Plon, 1858–70. 32 vols.

Parlement, *Journal Officiel.*

GERMANY

Lepsius, Johannes; Mendelssohn-Bartholdy, Albrecht; and Thimme, Friedrich, eds. *Die grosse Politik der Europäischen Kabinette, 1871–1914.* 40 vols. in 54. Berlin: Deutsche Verlagsgesellschaft für Politik und Geschichte, 1922–27.

GREAT BRITAIN

Foreign Office. *British and Foreign State Papers, 1812–.* London: H. M. Stationery Office, 1841–.

Gooch, George Peabody, and Temperley, Harold, eds. *British Documents on the Origins of the War, 1898–1914.* 11 vols. London: H. M. Stationery Office, 1926–38.

Journals of the House of Commons.

Parliamentary Debates.

Parliamentary Papers, 1879. Afghanistan, no. 6. "Despatch from the Government of India, No. 136 of 1879, Forwarding Treaty of Peace." C. 2362.

Parliamentary Papers, 1879. Egypt, no. 4. "Firmans Granted by the Sultans to the Viceroys of Egypt, 1841–73." C. 2395.

Parliamentary Papers, 1880. Morocco, no. 1. "Correspondence Relating to the Conference Held at Madrid in 1880, as to the Right of Protection of Moorish Subjects by the Diplomatic and Consular Representatives of Foreign Powers in Morocco." Cd. 2707.

INTERNATIONAL COURT OF JUSTICE

Report of Judgements, Advisory Opinions and Orders. *Case concerning Rights of Nationals of the United States of America in Morocco: France/United States of America.* Order of 22 November 1950.

LEAGUE OF NATIONS

Official Journal, vols. 1–21 (February 1920-March 1940). 21 vols. in 28. London: Harrison and Sons, 1920–40.

UNITED STATES

The Congressional Record.
Department of State. *Foreign Relations of the United States, 1861–.*
————. *The Suez Canal Problem, July 26-September 22, 1956.* Department of State Publication 6392. Washington: Government Printing Office, 1956.
Ravndal, Gabriel Bie. *The Origin of the Capitulations and of the Consular Institution.* 67th Congress, 1st sess. Senate Doc. no. 34. Washington: Government Printing Office, 1921.
Senate, Select Committee on Small Business, Subcommittee on Monopoly. *The International Petroleum Cartel.* Staff Report to the Federal Trade Commission. Washington: Government Printing Office, 1952.
Van Dyck, Edward A. *Report on the Capitulations of the Ottoman Empire.* 47th Congress, 1st sess., Senate Executive Doc. no. 3. Washington: Government Printing Office, 1881.

BOOKS AND ARTICLES

Abbas, Mekki. *The Sudan Question.* New York: Praeger, 1952.
Abbott, G. F. "The Tripolitan War from the Turkish Side." *Quarterly Review* 217 (July-October 1912): 249–64.
————. *Under the Turk in Constantinople: A Record of Sir John Finch's Embassy, 1674–1681.* London: Macmillan, 1920.
Abkarius, Iskander Ibn Yaq'ub. *The Lebanon in Turmoil. Syria and the Powers in 1860: Book of the Marvels of the Time concerning the Massacres in the Arab Country.* Translated from the Arabic and annotated, with an introduction and conclusion, by J. F. Scheltema. Yale Oriental Series: Researches, vol. 7. New Haven: Yale University Press, 1920.
Abu-Lughod, Ibrahim. "The Transformation of the Egyptian Elite: Prelude to the 'Urabi Revolt." *Middle East Journal* 21 (summer 1967): 325–44.
Abun-Nasr, Jamil M. *A History of the Maghrib.* Cambridge: Cambridge University Press, 1971.
Achoube-Amini, Rahmatollah. *Le conflit de frontière irako-iranien.* Paris: Delalain, 1936.
Adair, Sir Robert. *Negotiations for the Peace of the Dardanelles.* 2 vols. London: Longman, Brown, Green and Longmans, 1845.
Adamec, L. W. *Afghanistan, 1900–1923: A Diplomatic History.* Berkeley: University of California Press, 1967.
Adamiyat, Fereydun. *Bahrein Islands.* New York: Praeger, 1955.
Ageron, C. R. "Administration directe ou protectorate: Un conflit de méthode sur l'organisation de la province de Constantine." *Revue Française d'Outre-mer* 66 (January-February 1963): 5–40.
————. *Les algériens musulmans et la France, 1871–1919.* 2 vols. Paris: Presses Universitaires de France, 1968.

Ahmed, Jamal Mohammed. *The Intellectual Origins of Egyptian Nationalism*. London: Oxford University Press, 1960.

Albin, Pierre. *Le coup d'Agadir: Origines et dévelopement de la crise de 1911*. Paris: Alcan, 1912.

Alder, G. J. *British India's Northern Frontier, 1865–1895*. London: Longmans, 1963.

Allain, J. C. "Les débuts du conflit italo-turc: Octobre 1911–Janvier 1912, d'après les Archives françaises." *Revue d'Histoire Moderne et Contemporaine* 18 (January-March 1971): 106–15.

Allen, G. W. *Our Navy and the Barbary Corsairs*. Boston: Houghton, Mifflin, 1905.

Allen, William Edward David. *A History of the Georgian People*. London: Paul, 1932.

———. and Muratoff, Paul. *Caucasian Battlefields: A History of the Wars on the Turco-Caucasian Border, 1828–1921*. Cambridge: Cambridge University Press, 1953.

Anchieri, Ettore. *Constantinopoli e gli stretti nella politica russa ed europea dal trattato di Qüciük Kainjarji alla convenzione di Montreux*. Milan: Giuffre, 1948.

Anderson, Eugene N. *The First Moroccan Crisis, 1904–1906*. Chicago: University of Chicago Press, 1930. Reprint, Hamden, Conn.: Archon Books, 1966.

Anderson, M. S. *The Eastern Question, 1774–1923: A Study in International Relations*. London: Macmillan; New York: St. Martin's Press, 1966.

———. "Great Britain and the Russo-Turkish War of 1768–1774." *English Historical Review* 69 (1954): 39–58.

Anderson, R. C. *Naval Wars in the Levant, 1559–1853*. Princeton: Princeton University Press, 1952.

Andrew, Christopher. *Théophile Delcassé and the Making of the Entente Cordiale: A Reappraisal of French Foreign Policy, 1898–1905*. London: Macmillan, 1968.

Anthoine, Antoine Ignace, Baron de Saint-Joseph. *Essai historique sur le commerce et la navigation de la Mer-Noire*. 2d ed. Paris: n.p., 1920.

Antonius, George. *The Arab Awakening*. New York: Lippincott, 1939.

Apelt, Fritz. *Aden, eine kolonialgeographische und kolonialpolitische Studie*. Grossenhain: Weigel, 1929.

Archbold, W. A. J. "Afghanistan, Russia, and Persia." In *The Cambridge History of the British Empire*, vol. 4, edited by Henry Herbert Dodwell, pp. 483–521. Cambridge: Cambridge University Press, 1929.

Argyll, George Douglas Campbell, First Duke of. *The Afghan Question from 1841 to 1878*. London: Strahan, 1879.

Arnold, T. W. *The Caliphate*. Oxford: Clarendon Press, 1924.

Ashmead-Bartlett, E. *The Passing of the Shereefian Empire*. Edinburgh and London: William Blackwood and Sons, 1910.

Asian Circle, The. "A Note on the Abolition of Extraterritoriality in Persia." *Asiatic Review*, n.s. 23 (1927): 557–65.

Askew, William C. *Europe and Italy's Acquisition of Libya, 1911–1912*. Durham: Duke University Press, 1942.

Assad Efendi, Mohammed. *Précis historique de la destruction du corps des janissaires par le Sultan Mahmoud, en 1826*. Translated from the Turkish by Armand-Peirre Caussin de Perceval. Paris: Didot Frères, 1833.

Ault-Dumesnil, Edouard d'. *Relation d'expédition d'Afrique en 1830 et de la conquête d'Alger*. Paris: Delaunay, 1832. 2d ed. Paris: Palmé, 1868.

Auzoux, A. "La France et Muscate aux dix-huitième et dix-neuvième siècles." *Revue d'Histoire Diplomatique* 23–24 (1909–10): 518–40, 234–65.

Avery, P. *Modern Iran*. New York: Praeger, 1965.

Avram, Benno. *The Evolution of the Suez Canal Status from 1869 up to 1956: A Historical-Juridical Study*. Paris: Minard, 1958.

Azami-Zangueneh, 'Abd al-Hamid. *Le pétrole en Perse*. Paris: Editions Domat-Montchrestien, 1933.

Azan, Paul Jean Louis. *L'emir Abd el Kader, 1808–1883: Du fanatisme musulman au patriotisme français*. Paris: Hachette, 1925.

———. *L'expédition d'Alger*. Paris: Plon, 1929.

Baddeley, John Frederick. *The Russian Conquest of the Caucasus*. New York: Longmans, Green, 1908.

Bailey, Frank Edgar. *British Policy and the Turkish Reform Movement*. Cambridge: Harvard University Press, 1942.

Baldwin, George. *Political Recollections Relative to Egypt*. London: Cadell and Davies, 1801. 2d ed. London: The Author, 1802.

Balfour, Lady Betty. *The History of Lord Lytton's Indian Administration, 1876–1880*. London: Longmans, Green, 1890.

Bapst, Edmond. *Les origines de la guerre crimée: La France et la Russie de 1848 à 1854*. Paris: Delagrave, 1912.

Baratier, Albert Ernest Augustin. *Souvenirs de la mission Marchand*. 3 vols. Paris: Grasset, 1942.

———. *A travers l'Afrique*. Paris: A. Fayard, 1910.

Barbour, N., ed. *A Survey of North West Africa: The Maghrib*. London: Oxford University Press, for the Royal Institute of International Affairs, 1959.

Barclay, Sir Thomas. *The Turco-Italian War and Its Problems: With Appendices Containing the Chief State Papers Bearing on the Subject*. London: Constable, 1912.

Barlow, Ima Christian. *The Agadir Crisis*. Chapel Hill: University of North Carolina Press, 1940.

Barnby, H. G. *The Prisoners of Algiers: An Account of the Forgotten American-Algerian War of 1785–1797*. London: Oxford University Press, 1966.

Barrow, John. *The Life and Correspondence of Admiral Sir William Sidney Smith*. 2 vols. London: Richard Bentley, 1848.

Bayani, K. *Les relations de l'Iran avec l'Europe occidentale à l'époque safavide*. Paris: Presses Modernes, 1937.

Beatty, Charles Robert Longfield. *Charles De Lesseps of Suez: The Man and His Times*. London: Eyre and Spottiswoode. New York: Harper's, 1956.

Beehler, W. H. *History of the Italian-Turkish War*. Annapolis: U.S. Naval Institute, 1913.

Beer, Adolf. *Die orientalische Politik Österreichs seit 1774*. Prague: Tempsky, 1883.

Belgrave, Sir Charles. *The Pirate Coast*. London, G. Bell and Sons, 1966.

Bellew, Henry Walter. *Afghanistan and the Afghans. Being a Brief Review of the History of the Country and an Account of Its People, with a Special Reference to the*

Present Crisis and War with the Amir Shir Ali Khan. London: Sampson Low, Marston, Searle, and Rivington, 1879.

Bérard, Victor. *L'affaire marocaine.* Paris: Armand Colin, 1906.

Berkes, Niyazi. *The Development of Secularism in Turkey.* Montreal: McGill University Press, 1964.

Bernard, Augustin. *Les colonies françaises: L'Algerie.* Paris: Renouard, 1931.

———. *Le Maroc.* 4th ed., rev. Paris: Felix Alcan, 1916.

Berthezène, Baron Pierre. *Dix-huit mois à Alger ou récit des événements qui s'y ont passés depuis le 14 juin 1830 . . . jusqu'à la fin de décembre 1831.* Montpellier: Ricard, 1834.

Berthier, General Louis Alexander. *Relation des Campagnes du Général Bonaparte en Egypt et en Syrie.* Paris: Didot l'Aîné, 1800.

Bertrand, General Henri-Gratien, ed. *Napoléon 1er guerre d'orient. Campagnes d'Egypte et de Syrie, 1798–1799.* Dictated by Napoleon. 2 vols. Paris: The Editor, 1847.

Bertrand, Pierre Louis, comp. *Lettres inedités de Tallyrand à Napoléon, 1800–1809.* 2d ed. Paris: The Compiler, 1889.

Billot, A. *La France et l'Italie: Histoire des années troublées, 1881–1899.* 2 vols. Paris: Plon, 1905.

Biovès, Achille. *Français et anglais en Egypte, 1881–1882.* Paris: Roger et Chernoviz, 1910.

Blake, Robert. *Disraeli.* London: Oxford University Press, 1966.

Blunt, Wilfrid. *Desert Hawk: Abd el Kader and the French Conquest of Algeria.* London: Methuen, 1947.

———. *Secret History of the English Occupation of Egypt.* London: Unwin, 1907. New York: Knopf, 1922.

Bobichon, H. *Contribution à l'histoire de la mission Marchand.* Paris: n.p., 1936.

Böhm, Adolf. *Die zionistische Bewegung.* 2 vols. Berlin: Welt-Verlag, 1920–21. 2d ed., Berlin: Judischer Verlag, 1935–37.

Bompard, Louis Maurice. *La politique marocaine de l'Allemagne.* 4th ed. Paris: Plon-Nourrit, 1916.

Bonnassieux, P. *Les grandes compagnies de commerce, étude pour servir à l'histoire de la colonisation.* Paris: Plon, Nourrit, 1892.

Boulay de la Meurthe, A. *Le directoire et l'expédition d'Egypte.* Paris: V. Palmé, 1880.

Bréhier, Louis. *L'Egypte de 1798 à 1900.* Paris: Combet, 1901.

Bright, C. *Submarine Telegraphs: Their History, Construction, and Working.* London: C. Lockwood and Son, 1898.

Bright, Edward B., and Bright, Sir Charles. *The Life Story of the Late Sir Charles Tilston Bright.* 2 vols. Westminster: Constable, 1899.

Brignon, Jean; Amine, Abdelaziz; Boutaleb, Brahmim; Martinet, Guy; and Rosenberger, Bernard; with the collaboration of Terrasse, Michel. *Histoire du Maroc.* Paris: Haitier. Casablanca: Librarie Nationale, 1967.

Brinton, J. Y. "The Arabian Peninsula: The Protectorates and Sheikhdoms." *Revue égyptienne de droit international* 3 (1947): 5–38.

Broadley, A. M. *The Last Punic War: Tunis, Past and Present, with a Narrative of the French Conquest of the Regency*. 2 vols. London: William Blackwood and Sons, 1882.

Brockway, Thomas P. "Britain and the Persian Bubble." *Journal of Modern History* 13 (1941): 36–47.

Brown, Philip Marshall. *Foreigners in Turkey: Their Juridical Status*. Princeton: Princeton University Press, 1914.

Brown, Roger Glenn. *Fashoda Reconsidered: The Impact of Domestic Politics on French Policy in Africa, 1893–1898*. Baltimore: Johns Hopkins Press, 1970.

Browne, Edward Granville. *The Persian Revolution of 1905–1909*. Cambridge: Cambridge University Press, 1910.

Brydges, Sir Harford Jones. *An Account of the Transactions of His Majesty's Mission to the Court of Persia in the Years 1807–1811*. 2 vols. London: Bohn, 1834.

Buckingham, James Silk. *Travels in Assyria, Media, and Persia, Including a Journey from Bagdad by Mount Zagyos, to Hamadan, the Ancient Ecbatan, Researches in Ispahan and the Ruins of Persepolis, and Journey from thence by Shiraz and Shapoor to the Sea Shore. Description of Burrorah, Bushire, Bahrein, Ormuz, and Muscat, Narrative of an Expedition against the Pirates of the Persian Gulf, with Illustrations of the Voyage of Nearchus and Passage by the Arabian Sea to Bombay*. London: Colburn, 1829.

Burnes, Sir Alexander. *Cabool: Being a Personal Narrative*. London: Murray, 1842.

Bury, J. P. T. *Napoleon III and the Second Empire*. London: The English University Press, 1964.

Busch, Briton Cooper. *Britain and the Persian Gulf, 1894–1914*. Berkeley: University of California, 1967.

———. "Britain and the Status of Kuwayt, 1896–1899." *Middle East Journal* 21 (spring 1967): 187–98.

Cambon, Henri. *Histoire de la régence de Tunis*. Paris: Editions Berger-Levrault, 1948.

Caroe, Sir Olaf Kirkpatrick. *Wells of Power*. London: Macmillan, 1951.

Cataluccio, Francesco. *Italia e Francia in Tunisia, 1878–1939*. Rome: Istituto Nazionale di Cultura Fascista, 1939.

———. *Storia del nazionalizmo arabo*. Milan: Istituto per gli Studi di Politica Internazionale, 1939.

Cathcart, J. L. *The Captives*. La Porte, Ind.: Herald Print, 1899.

———. *Tripoli: Its First War with the United States*. La Porte, Ind.: Herald Print, 1901.

Cattaui, Joseph Edmond. *Histoire des rapports de l'Egypte avec la Sublime Porte*. Paris: Jouve, 1919.

Cawston, George, and Keane, A. H. *The Early Chartered Companies, 1296–1858*. London: n.p., 1896. Reprint, New York: Burt Franklin, 1968.

Cecil, Lady Gwendolen. *Life of Robert, Marquis of Salisbury*. 4 vols. London: Hodder and Stoughton, 1921–32.

Chandler, David G. *The Campaigns of Napoleon*. New York: Macmillan, 1966.

Chapman, Maybelle Rebecca Kennedy. *Great Britain and the Bagdad Railway, 1888–1914*. Northampton, Mass.: Smith College Studies in History, 1948.

Chardin, Sir J. *Travels in Persia*. London: Argonaut Press, 1927.

Charles-Roux, François. *L'Angleterre et l'expédition française en Egypte*. 2 vols. Cairo: L'Institut Français d'Archéologie Orientale pour la Société Royale de Géographie d'Egypte, 1925.

———. *Bonaparte, Gouverneur d'Egypte*. Paris: Plon, 1936. *Bonaparte: Governor of Egypt*. Translated from the French by E. W. Dickes. London: Methuen, 1937.

———. *Les échelles de Syrie et de Palestine au XVIIIᵉ siècle*. Paris: Geuthner, 1928.

———. *Les origines de l'expédition d'Egypte*. Paris: Plon-Nourrit, 1910.

———. *Thiers et Méhémet-Ali*. Paris: Plon, 1961.

Charles-Roux, F. J. "Une négociation pour l'évacuation de l'Egypte: La convention d'el-Arich (1800)." *Revue d'histoire diplomatique* 37 (1923): 48–88, 304–47.

Charrière, E. *Négociations de la France dans le Levant, ou correspondances, mémoires et actes diplomatiques des Ambassadeurs de France à Constantinople*. 4 vols. Paris: n.p., 1848–60.

Chénier, Louis de. *The Present State of the Empire of Morocco. Its Animals, Products, Climate, Soil, Cities, Ports, Provinces, Coins, Weights, and Measures. With the Language, Religion, Laws, Manners, Customs, and Character of the Moors; the History of the Dynasties since Edris; the Naval Force and Commerce of Morocco; and the Character, Conduct, and Views, Political and Commercial, of the Reigning Emperor*. Translated from the French. 2 vols. London: G. G. J. and J. Robinson, 1788.

Chesney, General Francis Rawdon. *Narrative of the Euphrates Expedition (1835–37)*. 2 vols. London: Longmans, Green, 1850.

Chew, Samuel Claggett. *The Crescent and the Rose*. New York: Oxford University Press, 1937. New York: Octagon Books, 1965.

Chirol, Sir Valentine. *The Middle Eastern Question*. London: Murray, 1903.

Churchill, Charles Henry Spencer. *The Druzes and the Maronites under the Turkish Rule, from 1840–1860*. London: Quaritch, 1862.

———. *The Life of Abdel Kader, Ex-Sultan of the Arabs of Algeria: Written from his own Dictation and Compiled from other Authentic Sources*. London: Chapman and Hall, 1867.

Churchill, Roger Platt. *The Anglo-Russian Convention of 1907*. Cedar Rapids, Iowa: Torch Press, 1939.

Churchill, Sir Winston Spencer. *The River War: An Historical Account of the Reconquest of the Soudan*. 2 vols. New York: Longmans, Green, 1899. 2d ed. New York: Longmans, Green, 1902.

Clauzel, B. *Observations du général Clauzel sur quelques actes de son commandement à Alger*. Paris: A. J. Déanin, 1821.

———. *Rapport du maréchal Clauzel à Monsieur le ministre de la Guerre sur l'expédition de Constantinople*. Lyon: Boursy Fils., n.d.

Cocheris, Jules. *Situation internationale de l'Egypte et du Soudan*. Paris: Plon-Nourrit, 1903.

Cohen, Israel. *Theodor Herzl, Founder of Political Zionism*. New York and London: Yoseloff, 1959.

———. *The Zionist Movement*. Edited and revised by Bernard G. Richards. New York: Zionist Organization of America, 1946.

Cohen, Jacques. *Les israélites de l'Algérie et le décret Crémieux*. Paris: 1900.

Coindreau, Roger. *Les corsaires de Salé.* Publications de l'Institut des Hautes Etudes Marocaines, vol. 47. Paris: Société d'Editions Géographiques, Maritimes, et Coloniales, 1948.

Compagnie Universelle du Canal Maritime de Suez. *Recueil chronologique des actes constitutifs de la Compagnie Universelle du Canal Maritime de Suez et des conventions conclues avec le gouvernement égyptien, 30 novembre 1854–1 janvier 1950.* 3d ed. Paris: Desfossés-Néogravure, 1950.

Conacher, J. B. *The Aberdeen Coalition, 1852–55: A Study in Mid-Nineteenth Century Politics.* Cambridge: Cambridge University Press, 1968.

———. "New Light on the Origins of the Crimean War." *Journal of Modern History* 3 (1931): 219–34.

Confer, Vincent. *France and Algeria: The Problem of Civil and Political Reform, 1870–1920.* Syracuse: Syracuse University Press, 1966.

Conker, Orhan. *Les chemins de fer en Turquie et la politique ferroviaire Turque.* Bibliothèque de l'Ecole Supérieure des Sciences Commerciales et Economiques de l'Université de Liège, vol. 10. Paris: Sirey, 1935.

Coquelle, P. "L'ambassade du maréchal Brune à Constantinople (1803–1805)." *Revue d'histoire diplomatique* 18 (1904): 53–73.

———. "Sébastiani, ambassadeur à Constantinople, 1806–1808." *Revue d'histoire diplomatique* 18 (1904): 574–611.

Cordier, Edouard-Henri. *Napoléon III et l'Algérie.* Algiers: V. Heintz, 1937.

Cossé-Brissac, P. de. *Les rapports de la France et du Maroc pendant la conquête de l'Algérie, 1830–1847.* Paris: Larose, 1931.

Coupland, Sir Reginald. *East Africa and Its Invaders.* Oxford: Clarendon Press, 1938.

Crabitès, Pierre. *Ismail: The Maligned Khedive.* London: Routledge and Sons, 1933.

Creasy, Edward Shepherd. *History of the Ottoman Turks.* 2d ed. New York: Henry Holt, 1878. Reprint, Bayrut: Khayats, 1961.

Cromer, Earl of [Evelyn Baring]. *Modern Egypt.* 2 vols. New York: Macmillan, 1908.

Cruickshank, Earl Fee. *Morocco at the Parting of the Ways.* Philadelphia: University of Pennsylvania Press, 1935.

Curzon, George Nathaniel. *Persia and the Persian Question.* 2 vols. London: Longmans, Green, 1892. Reprint, New York: Barnes and Noble, 1966.

Curzon, George Nathaniel. *Russia in Central Aisa.* London: Longmans, Green, 1899. New impression, London: Cass, 1967.

Daniel, Norman. *Islam, Europe, and Empire.* Edinburgh: Edinburgh University Press, 1966.

Davison, R. H. *Reform in the Ottoman Empire, 1856–1876.* Princeton: Princeton University Press, 1963.

———. "Turkish Attitudes concerning Christian-Muslim Equality in the Nineteenth Century." *American Historical Review* 59 (1954): 844–64.

Debbasch, Yvan. *La nation française en Tunisie (1577–1835).* Institut des Hautes Etudes de Tunis, Bibliothèque Juridique et Economique, vol. 4,. Paris: Sirey, 1957.

DeGolyer, Everette Lee. "Some Aspects of Oil in the Middle East." In *The Near East and the Great Powers,* edited by R. N. Frye, pp. 119–36. Cambridge: Harvard University Press, 1951.

Déhérain, Henri. *La vie de Pierre Ruffin.* 2 vols. Paris: Geuthner, 1929–30.

Dennis, Alfred Louis Pinneo. *Eastern Problems at the Close of the Eighteenth Century.* Cambridge: Harvard University Press, 1901.

Deschanel, Paul Eugène Louis. *Gambetta.* Translated from the French. London: Heinemann, 1920.

Dethan, G. "Le rapprochement franco-italien, 1896–1900." *Revue d'histoire diplomatique* 70 (October-December 1956): 323–39.

Dicey, Edward. *The Story of the Khedivate.* New York: Scribner's Sons, 1902.

Diercks, Gustav. *Die Marokkofräge und die Konferenz von Algeciras.* Berlin: Reimer, 1906.

Dodwell, Henry Herbert. *The Founder of Modern Egypt: A Study of Muhammad 'Ali.* Cambridge: Cambridge University Press, 1931.

Donnadieu, Marcel. *Les relations diplomatiques de l'Espagne et du Maroc de janvier 1592 à juillet 1926.* Montpellier: Languedoc Medical, 1931.

Douin, G. *Histoire du règne du khédive Ismail.* Cairo: Société Royale de Geographie d'Egypte, 1933.

Driault, Edouard, ed. *L'Egypte et l'Europe: La crise (orientale) de 1839–1941.* 5 vols. (documents). Cairo: L'Institut Français d'Archéologie Orientale du Caire, pour la Société de Géographie d'Egypte, 1930–34.

————. *La politique orientale de Napoléon.* Paris: Alcan, 1904.

————. *La question d'Orient.* 8th ed. Paris: Alcan, 1921.

Duflot, Georges. *La caisse de la dette et les finances égyptiennes.* Paris: Giard and Brière, 1904.

Du Mans, R. *Estat de la Perse en 1660.* Paris: n.p., 1890.

Dunlop, Hendrick., ed. *Bronen tot de Geschiedenis der Oostindische Compaagnie in Perzie.* The Hague: Nijhoff, 1930.

Dupyy, E. *Américains et Barbaresques, 1776–1824.* Paris: n.p., 1910.

Durand, Sir Henry Marion. *The First Afghan War and Its Causes.* Edited, with a memoir of the author, by Henry Mortimer Durand. London: Longmans, Green, 1879.

Earle, Edward Mead. "The Secret Anglo-German Convention of 1914 regarding Asiatic Turkey." *Political Science Quarterly* 38 (1923): 24–28.

————. *Turkey, the Great Powers and the Bagdad Railway.* New York: Macmillan, 1923.

————. "The Turkish Petroleum Company—A Study in Oleaginous Diplomacy." *Political Science Quarterly* 39 (1924): 265–79.

Edwards, E. W. "The Franco-German Agreement on Morocco, 1909." *English Historical Review* 78 (1963): 483–513.

Elliot, Arthur Ralph Douglas. *The Life of George Joachim Goschen.* 2 vols. New York: Longmans, Green, 1911.

Elphinstone, Mountstuart. *An Account of the Kingdom of Caubul and its Dependencies in Persia, Tartary and India: Comprising a View of the Afghan Nation, and a History of the Dooraunee Monarchy.* London: Longman, Hurst, and John Murray, 1815.

Emerit, Marcel. *L'Algérie à l'époque d'Abd el-Kader.* Paris: Larose, 1951.

Emily, J. *Mission Marchand.* Paris: Hachette, 1913.

Engelhardt, Edouard Philippe. *La Turquie et le Tanzimat.* 2 vols. Paris: Cotillon, 1882.

English, Barbara. *John Company's Last War.* London: Collins, 1971.

Enver, Pasha. *Um Tripolis.* Munich: H. Bruckmann, 1918.

Epstein, Mortimer. *The Early History of the Levant Company.* New York: Dutton, 1908.

Erian, Abdalla Ali el-. *Condominium and Related Situations in International Law.* Cairo: Fouad I University Press, 1952.

Esco Foundation for Palestine, Inc. *Palestine: A Study of Jewish, Arab and British Policies.* 2 vols. New Haven: Yale University Press, 1947.

Esmaili, Malek. *Le Golfe Persique et les Iles de Bahrein.* Paris: Loviton, 1936.

Esquer, Gabriel. *Les commencements d'un empire: La prise d'Alger, 1830.* Paris: Larose, 1929.

Estournelles de Constant, Paul Henri Benjamin d'. *La politique française en Tunisie: Le protectorat et ses origines, 1854–1891.* Paris: Plon, Nourrit, 1891.

Eubank, Keith. *Paul Cambon: Master Diplomatist.* Norman: University of Oklahoma Press, 1960.

Eversely, Lord George John S., and Chirol, Sir Valentine. *The Turkish Empire.* 2d. ed. London: Unwin, 1923.

Fanning, Leonard M. *Foreign Oil and the Free World.* New York: McGraw-Hill, 1954.

Farman Farmayan, Hafez. "The Forces of Modernization in Nineteenth-Century Iran: A Historical Survey." In *Beginnings of Modernization in the Middle East: The Nineteenth Century,* edited by William R. Polk and Richard L. Chambers, pp. 119–51. Chicago: University of Chicago Press, 1968.

Farnie, D. A. *East and West of Suez: The Suez Canal in History, 1854–1956.* Oxford: Clarendon Press, 1969.

Faroughy, Abbas. *The Bahrein Islands, 1750–1951.* New York: Verry, Fisher, 1951.

Ferah, C. "Lebanese Insurgence of 1840 and the Powers." *Journal of Asian History* 1 (1967): 105–32.

Ferrier, J. P. *Voyages en Perse, dans l'Afghanistan, le Beloutchistan et le Turkistan.* Paris: Dentu, 1860. *Caravan Journeys and Wanderings in Persia, Afghanistan, Turkistan, and Beloochistan.* Translated from the original unpublished French manuscript by William Jesse. London: n.p., 1856.

Feuvrier, Jean Baptiste. *Trois ans à la cour de Perse.* Paris: Juven, 1900.

Field, J. A. *America and the Mediterranean World, 1776–1882.* Princeton: Princeton University Press, 1969.

Fisher, A. W. *The Russian Annexation of the Crimea.* Cambridge: Cambridge University Press, 1970.

Fisher, Geoffrey. *Barbary Legend: War, Trade and Piracy in North Africa, 1415–1830.* Oxford: Clarendon Press, 1957.

Fitoussi, Elie, and Benazet, Aristide. *L'état tunisien et le protectorat français.* Paris: Arthur Rousseau, 1931.

Fitzgerald, Percy Hetherington. *The Great Canal at Suez.* 2 vols. London: Tinsley, 1876.

Fitzmaurice, Lord Edmond. *The Life of Granville*. 2d ed. 2 vols. New York: Long-mans, Green, 1905.

Florinsky, Michael T. *Russia: A History and an Interpretation*. 2 vols. New York: Macmillan, 1953.

Flournoy, Francis Rosebro. *British Policy towards Morocco in the Age of Palmerston, 1830–1865*. London: P. S. King and Son, 1935.

Forest, Louis. *La naturalisation des juifs algériens et l'insurrection de 1871*. Paris: Société Française d'Imprimerie et de Librairie, 1897.

Foster, Sir William. *England's Quest of Eastern Trade*. London: Black, 1933.

———. *Letters received by the East India Company from its Servants in the East*. London: Marston and Company, 1902.

———, ed. *The Travels of John Sanderson in the Levant, 1584–1602*. London: Printed for the Hakluyt Society, 1931.

Fraser, Lovat. *India under Lord Curzon and After.* London: Heinemann, 1911.

Fraser-Tytler, Sir W. Kerr. *Afghanistan: A Study of Political Developments in Central Asia*. London: Oxford University Press, 1950. 2d ed. 1953. 3d ed., retitled *Afghanistan: A Case Study in Political Development*. 1967.

Frechtling, Louis E. "The Reuter Concession in Persia." *Asiatic Review*, n.s. 34 (1938): 518–33.

Freycinet, Charles Louis de Saulces de. *La question d'Egypte*. Paris: Calmann-Lévy, 1905. 2d ed. Paris: Calmann-Lévy, 1906.

Frischwasser-Ra 'anan, Heinz Felix. *The Frontiers of a Nation*. London: Batchworth, 1955.

Ganiage, Jean. *Les origines du protectorat français en Tunisie, 1861–1881*. Paris: Presses Universitaires de France, 1959.

Gardane, Comte Alfred de. *Mission du général Gardane en Perse sous le premier empire*. Paris: Lainé, 1865.

Ghorbal, Shafik. *The Beginnings of the Egyptian Question and the Rise of Mehemet Ali: A Study in the Diplomacy of the Napoleonic Era Based on Researches in the British and French Archives*. London: Routledge, 1928.

Ghose, Dilip Kumar. *England and Afghanistan: A Phase in Their Relations*. Calcutta: World Press, 1960.

Giffen, Morrison Beall. *Fashoda: The Incident and Its Diplomatic Setting*. Chicago: University of Chicago Press, 1930.

Goldsmid, Sir Frederick John. *Telegraph and Travel*. London: Macmillan, 1874.

Gooch, B. D. "A Century of Historiography on the Origins of the Crimean War." *American Historical Review* 62 (1956): 33–58.

———. "The Crimean War in Selected Documents and Secondary Works." *Victorian Studies* 1 (1958): 271–79.

———. *The Reign of Napoleon III*. Chicago: Rand McNally, 1969.

Gooch, George Peabody. *Before the War*. 2 vols. New York: Longmans, Green, 1936–38.

Gordon, Leland James. *American Relations with Turkey, 1830–1930*. Philadelphia: University of Pennsylvania Press, 1932.

Goriainow, Sergiei M. *Le Bosphore et les Dardanelles: Etude historique sur la question des détroits d'après la correspondence diplomatique déposée aux Archives Centrales de Saint-Petersbourg et à celles de l'Empire.* Paris: Plon-Nourrit, 1910.

Goryainov, Sergius. "The Secret Agreement of 1844 between Russia and Great Britain." *Russian Review* (Liverpool, Eng.), vol. 1 (1912), no. 3, pp. 97–115; no. 4, pp. 76–91.

Gourdin, André. *La politique française au Maroc.* Paris: Arthur Rousseau, 1906.

Gramont, Henri Delmas de. *Histoire d'Alger sous la domination turque, 1515–1830.* Paris: Lerous, 1887.

Graves, Philip. *The Life of Sir Percy Cox.* London: Hutchinson, 1941.

Greaves, Rose Louise. "British Policy in Persia, 1892–1903." *Bulletin of the School of Oriental and African Studies* 28 (1965): 36–60, 284–307.

———. *Persia and the Defence of India, 1884–1892: A Study in the Foreign Policy of the Third Marquis of Salisbury.* London: Athlone Press, 1959.

———. "Some Aspects of the Anglo-Russian Convention and Its Working in Persia, 1907–14." *Bulletin of SOAS* 31 (1968): 69–91.

Gregorian, Vartan. *The Emergence of Modern Afghanistan: Politics of Reform and Modernization, 1880–1946.* Stanford: Stanford University Press, 1969.

Grey, Edward, Viscount of Falladon. *Twenty-Five Years, 1892–1916.* 2 vols. New York: Stokes, 1925.

Habberton, William. *Anglo-Russian Relations concerning Afghanistan, 1837–1907.* Illinois Studies in the Social Sciences, vol. 31, no. 4. Urbana: University of Illinois, 1937.

Haekal, Mohamed Hussein. *La dette publique égyptienne.* Paris: Rousseau, 1912.

Haim, Sylvia G., ed. *Arab Nationalism: An Anthology.* Berkeley: University of California Press, 1962.

Hajoui, Mohammed Omar el–. *Histoire diplomatique du Maroc, 1900–1912.* Paris: G.-P. Maisonneuve, 1937.

Hakluyt, Richard. *The Principal Navigations, Voyages, Traffiques and Discoveries of the English Nation.* 12 vols. Glasgow: J. MacLehose and Sons, 1903–05.

Hall, Luella J. *The United States and Morocco, 1776–1956.* Metuchen, N.J.: Scarecrow Press, 1971.

Hallberg, Charles William. *The Suez Canal: Its History and Diplomatic Importance.* New York: Columbia University Press, 1931.

Halpern, Ben. *The Idea of the Jewish State.* Cambridge: Harvard University Press, 1961.

Hammer, Joseph von. *Geschichte des osmanischen Reihes.* 4 vols. Pest: C.A. Hartlebens Verlage, 1832.

Hanway, Jonas. *An Historical Account of British Trade over the Caspian Sea; With a Journal of Travels from London through Russia into Persia . . . with the Particular History of the Great Usurper Nadir Kouli.* 4 vols. London: n.p., 1753.

Hanna, Colonel H. B. *The Second Afghan War, 1878–79–80: Its causes, its conduct and its consequences.* 2 vols. Westminster: Archibald Constable, 1899.

Hardinge, Sir Arthur Henry. *A Diplomatist in the East.* London: Cape, 1927.

Harik, Ilya. *Politics and Change in a Traditional Society: Lebanon, 1711–1845*. Princeton: Princeton University Press, 1968.

Hasenclever, Adolf. *Geschichte Ägyptens im 19. Jahrhundert, 1798–1914*. Halle: Niemeyer, 1917.

————. *Die orientalische Frage in den Jahren 1838–1841*. Leipzig: Koehler, 1914.

Hawley, Donald. *The Trucial States*. London: Allen and Unwin, 1970.

Hay, Miss Drummond, and Brooks, L. A. E., eds. *Memoir of Sir John Drummond Hay*. London: Murray, 1896.

Headlam-Morley, Sir James Wycliffe. *Studies in Diplomatic History*. London: Methuen, 1930.

Hekmat, M. A. *Essai sur l'histoire des relations politiques irano-ottomanes de 1722 à 1747*. Paris: Presses Modernes, 1937.

Helfferich, Karl Theodor. *Georg von Siemens*. 3 vols. Berlin: Springer, 1923.

Henderson, G. B. *Crimean War Diplomacy and Other Historical Essays*. Glasgow: Jackson, 1947.

Herbert, Thomas. *Some Years Travels into Divers Parts of Africa and Asia the Great*. London: Everingham, 1677.

Herbette, Maurice. *Une ambassade persane sous Louis XIV*. Paris: Perrin, 1907.

————. *Une ambassade turque sous le directoire*. Paris: Académique Didier, 1902.

Herold, J. Christopher. *Bonaparte in Egypt*. New York: Harper and Row, 1962.

Hertzberg, Arthur, ed. *The Zionist Idea*. New York: Doubleday, 1959.

Hill, Sir George Francis. *A History of Cyprus*. 4 vols. Cambridge: Cambridge University Press, 1940–52.

Hirschzowicz, Lukasz. "The Sultan and the Khedive, 1892–1908." *Middle Eastern Studies* 8 (October 1972): 287–312.

Hoffmann, Karl. *Ölpolitik und angelsächsischer Imperialismus*. Berlin: Ring-verlag, 1927.

Hofstetter, Balthasar. *Die Vorgeschichte des französischen Protektorats in Tunis bis zum Bardovertrag*. Bern: Francke, 1914.

Holborn, Hajo. *Deutschland und die Türkei, 1878–1890*. Berlin: Deutsche Verlagsgesellschaft für Politik und Geschichte, 1926.

Holland, Sir Thomas Erskine, comp. *The European Concert in the Eastern Question*. Oxford: Clarendon Press, 1885.

————. *A Lecture on the Treaty Relations of Russia and Turkey from 1774–1853*. London: Macmillan, 1877.

Holt, P. M. *Egypt and the Fertile Crescent, 1516–1922: A Political History*. London: Longmans, Green, 1966.

————. *The Mahdist State in the Sudan, 1881–1898: A Study of Its Origins, Development and Overthrow*. Oxford: Oxford University Press, 1958.

Hornik, M. F. "The Mission of Sir Henry Drummond-Wolff to Constantinople, 1885–87." *English Historical Review* 55 (1940): 598–623.

Horniker, A. L. "Anglo-French Rivalry in the Levant from 1583–1612." *Journal of Modern History* 18 (1946): 289–305.

————. "William Harborne and the Beginning of Anglo-Turkish Diplomatic and Commercial Relations." *Journal of Modern History* 14 (1942): 289–316.

Hösch, E. "Neuere Literatur über den Krimkrieg." *Jahrbücher für Geschichte Osteuropas*, n.s. 9 (1961): 399–433.

Hoskins, Halford Lancaster. "Background of the British Position in Arabia." *Middle East Journal* 1 (1947): 137–47.

———. *British Routes to India*. New York: Longmans, Green, 1928.

———. *The Middle East: Problem Area in World Politics*. New York: Macmillan, 1954.

Hourani, Albert. *Arabic Thought in the Liberal Age, 1798–1939*. London: Oxford University Press, for the Royal Institute of International Affairs, 1962.

———. *Syria and Lebanon: A Political Essay*. London: Oxford University Press, for the Royal Institute of International Affairs, 1946.

Howard, Harry Nicholas. *The Partition of Turkey: A Diplomatic History, 1913–1923*. Norman: University of Oklahoma Press, 1931. Reprint, New York: Fertig, 1966.

Huang, T. T. F. "Some International and Legal Aspects of the Suez Canal Question." *American Journal of International Law* 51 (1957): 277–307.

Hunt, George Henry. *Outram and Havelock's Persian Campaign*. London and New York: Routledge, 1858.

Hunter, Frederick Mercer. *An Account of the British Settlement of Aden in Arabia*. London: Trübner, 1877.

Hurewitz, J. C. "Lebanese Democracy in Its International Setting." *Middle East Journal* 17 (late autumn, 1963): 487–506. Also in *Politics in Lebanon*, edited by Leonard Binder, pp. 213–38. New York: John Wiley and Sons, 1966.

———. *Middle East Dilemmas :The Background of United States Policy*. New York: Harper Brothers, for the Council on Foreign Relations, 1953.

———. *Middle East Politics: The Military Dimension*. New York: Praeger, for the Council on Foreign Relations, 1969.

———. "Ottoman Diplomacy and the European State System." *Middle East Journal* 15 (spring 1961): 141–52. Also in *Belleten* (Ankara) 25 (Temmuz 1961): 455–66.

———. "Russia and the Turkish Straits: A Reevaluation of the Origins of the Problem." *World Politics* 14 (July 1962): 605–32. Also in *Belleten* (Ankara) 28 (Temmuz 1964): 459–503.

Ingram, Edward. "A Preview of the Great Game in Asia: The British Occupation of Perim and Aden in 1799." *Middle Eastern Studies* 9 (January 1973): 3–18.

Ingrams, William Harold. *Zanzibar: Its History and Its People*. London: Witherby, 1931.

Irace, Tullio. *With the Italians in Tripoli: The Authentic History of the Turco-Italian War*. London: John Murray, 1912.

Ireland, Philip Willard. *Iraq: A Study in Political Development*. London: Cape, 1937.

Irwin, Ray W. *The Diplomatic Relations of the United States with the Barbary Powers, 1776–1816*. Capel Hill: University of North Carolina Press, 1931.

Issawi, Charles, ed. *The Economic History of Iran, 1800–1914*. Chicago: University of Chicago Press, 1971.

————. *The Economic History of the Middle East*. Chicago: University of Chicago Press, 1966.

Jacob, Harold Fenton. *Kings of Arabia*. London: Mills and Boon, 1923.

Jaubert, Chevalier Pierre Amédée Emilien Probe. *Voyage en Arménie et en Perse, fait dans les années 1805 et 1806*. Paris: Pélicier et Neveu, 1821.

Jenks, Leland Hamilton. *The Migration of British Capital to 1875*. New York: Knopf, 1927; New York: Nelson, 1963.

[Jomini, Baron Alexandre de.] *Etude diplomatique sur la guerre de Crimée (1852–1856) par un ancien diplomate*. 2 vols. Paris: Tanera, 1874.

Jouplain, M. *La question du Liban: Etude d'histoire diplomatique et de droit international*. Paris: Rousseau, 1908.

Julien, C. A. *Histoire de l'Afrique du Nord: Tunisie, Algérie, Maroc de la conquête arabe à 1830*. 2d ed. Revised by Roger Le Tourneau. 2 vols. Paris: Payot, 1969.

————. *Histoire de l'Algérie contemporaine: La conquête et les débuts de la colonisation, 1827–1871*. Paris: Presses Universitaires de France, 1964.

————. *La question italienne en Tunisie, 1868–1938*. Paris: Jouve, 1939.

Julliany, Jules. *Essai sur le commerce de Marseille*. 2d ed. 3 vols. Paris: Renard, 1842.

Jung, Eugène. *La révolte arabe*. Paris: Colbert, 1925.

————. *Les puissances devant la révolte arabe: La crise mondiale de demain*. Paris: Hachette, 1906.

Kajare, Prince Firouz. *Le sultanat d'Omân*. Paris: Pedone, 1914.

Kamel, Sayed. *La conférence de Constantinople et la question égyptienne en 1882*. Paris: Alcan, 1913.

Kaye, Sir John William. *History of the War in Afghanistan*. 2 vols. London: Bentley, 1851, 2d ed. 3 vols. London: Bentley, 1858. 3d ed. 3 vols. London: Allen, 1874.

————. *The Life and Correspondence of Major-General Sir John Malcolm*. 2 vols. London: Smith Elder, 1856.

Kazemzadeh, Firuz. *Russia and Britain in Persia, 1864–1914: A Study in Imperialism*. New Haven: Yale University Press, 1968.

————. "Russian Imperialism and Persian Railways." In *Russian Thought and Politics*, edited by Hugh McLean, Martin E. Malia, and George Fischer, pp. 355–73. Cambridge: Harvard University Press, 1957.

Keddie, Nikki R. *Religion and Rebellion in Iran: The Tobacco Protest of 1891–1892*. London: Cass, 1966.

Kedourie, Elie. "The Politics of Political Literature: Kawakabi, Azoury, and Jung." *Middle Eastern Studies* 8 (May 1972): 227–40.

Kelly, J. B. *Britain and the Persian Gulf, 1795–1880*. Oxford: Oxford University Press, 1968.

————. "The Legal and Historical Basis of the British Position in the Persian Gulf." In *St. Antony's Papers, no. 4: Middle Eastern Affairs*, edited by Albert H. Hourani, pp. 119–40. New York: Praeger, 1959.

————. "The Persian Claim to Bahrayn." *International Affairs* 33 (January 1957): 51–70.

Kennedy, A. L. "Fashoda." *Quarterly Review* 286 (April 1948): 145–61.

Kerr, Malcolm H., ed. and trans. *Lebanon in the Last Years of Feudalism, 1840–60: A Contemporary Account by Antun Dahir al-'Aqiqi and Other Documents*. Beirut: American University of Beirut, 1959.

Khadduri, Majid. "Iran's Claims to the Sovereignty of Bahrayn." *American Journal of International Law* 45 (October 1951): 631–47.

———. *Political Trends in the Arab World: The Role of Ideas and Ideals in Politics*. Baltimore: Johns Hopkins University Press, 1970.

———, and Liebesny, Herbert J., eds. *Law in the Middle East*. Washington: Middle East Institute, 1955.

Kinross, Lord. *Between Two Seas: The Creation of the Suez Canal*. New York: William Morrow, 1969.

Kleine, Mathilde. *Deutschland und die ägyptische Frage, 1875–1890*. Greifswald: Abel, 1927.

Knox, Dudley Wright. *History of the United States Navy*. New York: G. P. Putnam's Sons, 1936.

Korff, Baron Sergiei Aleksandrovich. *Russia's Foreign Relations during the Last Half Century*. New York: Macmillan, 1922.

Krausse, Alexis Sidney. *Russia in Asia: A Record and a Study, 1558–1899*. London: Grant Richards, 1899.

Kumar, Ravinder. *India and the Persian Gulf Region, 1858–1907*. New York: Asia Publishing House, 1965.

Lacroix, Désiré. *Bonaparte en Egypte*. Paris, 1913.

La Jonquière, Clement Etienne de. *L'expédition d'Egypte*. 5 vols. Paris: Charles-Lavauzelle, 1899–1907.

Lal, Mohan. *Life of the Amir Dost Mohammed Khan, of Kabul: With his Political Proceedings towards the English, Russian, and Persian Governments, including the Victory and Disasters of the British Army in Afghanistan*. 2 vols. London: Longman, Brown, Green, and Longmans, 1846.

Laloy, Emile. *Les plans de Cathérine II pour la conquête de Constantinople*. Paris: Rahir, 1913.

La Mamye-Clairac, Louis André de. *Histoire de Perse depuis le commencement de ce siècle*. 3 vols. Paris: Jombert, 1750.

Lambton, A. K. S. "Secret Societies and the Persian Revolution of 1905–06." In *St. Antony's Papers no. 4: Middle Eastern Affairs, no. 1*, pp. 43–60. New York: Praeger, 1959.

———. "The Tobacco Regie: Prelude to Revolution." *Studia Islamica* 22 (1965): 119–57; 23 (1965): 71–90.

Landen, Robert Geran. *Oman since 1856: Disruptive Modernization in a Traditional Arab Society*. Princeton: Princeton University Press, 1967.

Landes, David S. *Bankers and Pashas: International Finance and Economic Imperialism in Egypt*. London: Heinemann, 1958.

Lane-Poole, Stanley. *The Life of the Right Honourable Stratford Canning, Viscount Stratford de Redcliffe: From His Memoirs and Private and Official Papers*. 2 vols. London: Longmans, Green, 1888.

Langer, William Leonard. *The Diplomacy of Imperialism, 1890–1902*. 2 vols. New York: Knopf, 1935. 2d ed. 1 vol. New York: Knopf, 1956.

————. *European Alliances and Alignments, 1871–1890.* New York: Knopf, 1931, 1960.

————. "The European Powers and the French Occupation of Tunis, 1878–1881." *American Historical Review* 31 (October 1925, January 1926): 55–78, 251–65.

————. "Russia, the Straits Question, and the European Powers." *English Historical Review* 44 (1929): 59–85.

Laqueur, Walter Z. *History of Zionism.* New York: Holt, Rinehart, and Winston, 1972.

Latreille, A. *La campagne de 1844 au Maroc: La bataille d'Isly.* Paris: n.p., 1912.

Laugier, Abbé Marc-Antoine. *Histoire des négociations pour la paix conclue à Belgrade le 18 septembre 1739.* 2 vols. Paris: Duchesne, 1768.

Laws, M. E. S. "The Capture of Aden." *Army Quarterly* (London) 38 (July 1939): 345–48.

Leaman, Bertha R. "The Influence of Domestic Policy on Foreign Affairs in France, 1898–1905." *Journal of Modern History* 14 (1942): 449–79.

Le Boeuf, Paul. *De la protection diplomatique et consulaire des indigénes au Maroc.* Bergerac: Imprimerie Générale du Sud-Ouest, 1905.

Lee, Dwight Erwin. *Great Britain and the Cyprus Convention Policy of 1878.* Cambridge: Harvard University Press, 1934.

Lémonon, E. "La Libye et l'opinion publique italienne." *Questions Diplomatiques et Coloniales* 36 (July-December 1913): 596–604.

Lesage, Charles. *L'invasion anglaise en Egypte.* Paris: Plon-Nourrit, 1906.

Lesseps, Ferdinand de. *Lettres, journals et documents pour servir à l'histoire du canal de Suez, 1854–69.* 5 vols. Paris: Didier, 1881.

Le Tourneau, Roger. *L'évolution politique de l'Afrique du Nord musulmane, 1920–1961.* Paris: Colin, 1962.

Lewis, Bernard. *The Emergence of Modern Turkey.* London: Oxford University Press, for the Royal Institute of International Affairs, 1961.

Liebesny, Herbert J. "International Relations of Arabia, the Dependent Areas." *Middle East Journal* 1 (April 1947): 148–68.

Litten, Wilhelm. *Persien von der "pénétration pacifique" zum "Protektorat."* Berlin: Gruyter, 1920.

Lockhart, Laurence. *The Fall of the Safavi Dynasty and the Afghan Occupation of Persia.* Cambridge: Cambridge University Press, 1958.

————. *Nadir Shah: A Critical Study Based Mainly upon Contemporary Sources.* London: Luzac, 1938.

Longrigg, Stephen Hemsley. *Four Centuries of Modern Iraq.* Oxford: Clarendon Press, 1925.

————. *'Iraq, 1900 to 1950: A Political, Social and Economic History.* New York: Oxford University Press, for the Royal Institute of International Affairs, 1953.

————. *Oil in the Middle East: Its Discovery and Development.* 2d ed. London: Oxford University Press, for the Royal Institute of International Affairs, 1961.

Loomie, A. J. "The Cyprus Convention of June 4, 1878." *Historical Bulletin* 26 (March 1948): 57–60.

Lord, Walter Frewen. *England and France in the Mediterranean, 1660–1830.* London: Sampson Low, Marston, 1901.

Lorimer, J. C. *Gazetteer of the Persian Gulf, Oman, and Central Arabia*. 2 vols. in 4. Calcutta: Superintendent Government Printing, 1908–15.

Lorini, Eteocle. *La Persia economica contemporanea e la sua questione monetaria*. Rome: Loescher, 1900.

Low, Charles Rathbone. *History of the Indian Navy*. 2 vols. London: Bentley, 1877.

McCoan, James Carlile. *Egypt as it is*. New York: Cassell, Petter and Galpin, 1877.

McCullagh, Francis. *Italy's War for a Desert: Being Some Experiences of a War-Correspondent with the Italians in Tripoli*. London: Herbert and Daniel, 1912.

Mackesy, Piers. *The War in the Mediterranean, 1803–1810*. London: Longmans, Green, 1957.

Macleod, Julia H. "Jefferson and the Navy: A Defense." *Huntington Library Quarterly* 8 (1944–45): 153–84.

MacMichael, Sir Harold Alfred. *The Sudan*. London: Benn, 1954.

Mahan, A. T. "The Persian Gulf and International Relations." *National Review* 40 (September 1902): 27–45.

Malcolm, Sir John. *The History of Persia from the Most Early Period to the Present Time: Containing an Account of the Religion, Government, Usages, and Character of the Inhabitants of that Kingdom*. 2d ed. 2 vols. London: John Murray, 1829.

Malgeri, Francesco. *La guerra libica, 1911–1912*. Rome: Edizioni di Storie e Letteratura, 1970.

Malleson, George Bruce. *History of Afghanistan: From the Earliest Period to the Outbreak of the War of 1878*. London: Allen, 1879.

Mange, Alyce Edythe. *The Near Eastern Policy of the Emperor Napoleon III*. Urbana: University of Illinois Press, 1940.

Manger, J. B. "Notes sur la crise marocaine de 1905." *Revue d'histoire de la guerre mondiale* 12 (1934): 311–40.

Mann, Walter. *Die Agadirkrisis des Jahres 1911*. Giessen: n.p., 1934.

Marlowe, John. *Cromer in Egypt*. New York: Praeger, 1970.

Marriott, Sir John Arthur Ransome. *The Eastern Question*. Oxford: Clarendon Press, 1917, 1918, 1924, 1940.

Martin, A. G. P. *Le Maroc et l'Europe*. Paris: Ernest Leroux, 1928.

Martin, Basil Kingsley. *The Triumph of Lord Palmerston*. London: Allen and Unwin, 1924.

Martin, Bradford G. *German-Persian Diplomatic Relations, 1873–1912*. The Hague: Mouton, 1959.

Martin, Claude. *L'histoire de l'Algérie française, 1830–1962*. Paris: Aymon, 1963.

———. *Les israélites algériens de 1830 à 1902*. Paris: Editions Herakles, 1936.

Martin, Montgomery, ed. *The Despatches, Minutes and Correspondence of the Marquess of Wellesley, K.G., during his Administration in India*. 5 vols. London: W. H. Allen, 1837.

Masson, Paul. *Histoire des établissements et du commerce français dans l'Afrique Barbaresque, 1560–1793*. Paris: Hachette, 1903.

———. *Histoire du commerce français dans le Levant au XVIIᵉ siècle*. Paris: Hachette, 1896.

———. *Histoire du commerce français dans le Levant au XVIIIᵉ siècle*. Paris: Hachette, 1911.

Mathews, J. J. *Egypt and the Formation of the Anglo-French Entente of 1904*. Philadelphia: University of Pennsylvania Press, 1939.

Matine-Daftary, Ahmad Khan. *La suppression des capitulations en Perse*. Paris: Les Presses Universitaires de France, 1930.

Maura y Gamazo, Gabriel. *La question du Maroc au point de vue espagnol*. Paris: A. Challamel, 1911.

Maurice, Sir Frederick Barton, and Arthur, Sir George. *The Life of Lord Wolseley*. London: Heinemann, 1924.

Maurrizi, Vincenzo [Shaikh Mansur]. *History of Seyd Said, Sultan of Muscat*. London: Booth, 1819.

Maxwell, Sir Herbert Eustace. *The Life and Letters of George William Frederick, Fourth Earl of Clarendon*. 2 vols. London: Arnold, 1913.

Meakin, Budgett. *The Moorish Empire: A Historical Epitome*. London: Swan Sonnenschien, 1899.

Mears, Eliot, ed. *Modern Turkey: A Politico-Economic Interpretation, 1908–1923 Inclusive, with Selected Chapters by Representative Authorities*. New York: Macmillan, 1924.

Medlicott, William Newton. *The Congress of Berlin and After*. London: Methuen, 1938.

————. "The Gladstone Government and the Cyprus Convention." *Journal of Modern History* 12 (1940): 186–208.

Meyer, Paul. *Die Neutralität Deutschlands und Österreich-Ungarns im italienisch-türkischen Krieg, 1911–1912*. Göttingen: Buchdruckerei Göttinger Tageblatts, 1932.

Miège, Jean Louis. *Le Maroc et l'Europe, 1830–1894*. 4 vols. Paris: Presses Universitaires de France, 1961–63.

Mignan, Robert. *A Winter Journey through Russia*. London: Colburn and Bentley, 1839.

Mikesell, Raymond F., and Chenery, Hollis B. *Arabian Oil*. Chapel Hill: University of North Carolina Press, 1949.

Mischef, P. H. *La Mer Noire et les détroits de Constantinople*. Paris: Rousseau, 1899.

Molden, Ernst. *Die Orientpolitik des Fürsten Metternich, 1829–1833*. Vienna: Hölzels, 1913.

Monger, George. *The End of Isolation: British Foreign Policy, 1900–1907*. London: Thomas Nelson, 1963.

Monypenny, William Flavelle, and Buckle, George E. *The Life of Benjamin Disraeli, Earl of Beaconsfield*. 6 vols. New York: Macmillan, 1911–20.

Morel, E. D. *Morocco in Diplomacy*. London: Smith, Elder, 1912.

Morgan, Edward Delmar, and Coote, C. H. eds. *Early Voyages and Travels to Russia and Persia by Anthony Jenkinson and other Englishmen with Some Account of the First Intercourse of the English with Russia and Central Asia by Way of the Caspian Sea*. London: Hakluyt Society, 1886.

Mosely, Philip E. *Russian Diplomacy and the Opening of the Eastern Question in 1838 and 1839*. Cambridge: Harvard University Press, 1934.

Mosse, W. E. "The End of the Crimean System: England, Russia and the Neutrality of the Black Sea, 1870–71." *Historical Journal* 4 (1961): 164–90.

————. *The Rise and Fall of the Crimean System, 1855–71: The Story of a Peace Settlement*. London: Macmillan, 1963.

Moyse-Bartlett, H. *The Pirates of Trucial Oman*. London: MacDonald, 1966.

Mühlmann, C. "Die deutschen Bahnunternehmungen in der asiatischen Türkei, 1889–1914." *Weltwirtschaftliches Archiv* 24 (1926): 121–37, 365–99.

Mulhall, Michael George. "Egyptian Finance." *Contemporary Review* 42 (October 1882): 525–35.

Muravieff, Boris. *L'alliance russo-turque au milieu des guerres napoléoniennes*. Neuchatel: Editions de la Baconniére, 1954.

Mustafa, Ahmed Abdel-Rahim. "The Breakdown of the Monopoly System in Egypt after 1840." In *Political and Social Change in Modern Egypt: Historical Studies from the Ottoman Conquest to the United Arab Republic*, edited by P. M. Holt, pp. 291–307. London: Oxford University Press, 1968.

Nahoum Efendi, Haim. *Recueil des firmans impériaux ottomans addressés aux khédives d'Egypte, 1597–1904*. Cairo: L'Institut Français d'Archéologie Orientale du Caire, pour la Société Royale de Géographie d'Egypte, 1934.

Newton, Lord Thomas Wodehouse Legh. *Lord Lansdowne*. London: Macmillan 1929.

Nicolson, Harold. *Sir Arthur Nicolson, Bart., First Lord Carnock. A Study in Old Diplomacy*. London: Constable, 1930. Amer. ed. *Portrait of a Diplomatist*. New York: Houghton, Mifflin, 1930.

Nolde, Boris. *La formation de l'empire russe: Études, notes et documents*. Paris: Institut d'Etudes Slaves, 1952.

Norris, J. A. *The First Afghan War, 1838–1842*. Cambridge: Cambridge University Press, 1967.

Oncken, Hermann. *Die sicherheit Indiens*. Berlin: Grote, 1937.

O'Rourke, Vernon Alfred. *The Juristic Status of Egypt and the Sudan*. Baltimore: Johns Hopkins Press, 1935.

Outram, Sir James. *Lieut.-General Sir James Outram's Persian Campaign in 1857: comprising General Orders and Despatches . . . also, Selections from his Correspondence, etc.* London: Privately printed, 1860.

Owen, R. J. *Cotton and the Egyptian Economy, 1820–1914: A Study in Trade and Development*. Oxford: Oxford University Press, 1969.

Parkes, James William. *A History of Palestine*. New York: Oxford University Press, 1949.

Paullian, Charles Oscar. *Diplomatic Negotiations of American Naval Officers, 1778–1883*. Baltimore: Johns Hopkins Press, 1912.

Pears, E. "The Spanish Armada and the Ottoman Porte." *English Historical Review* 8 (1893): 439–66.

Pélissié de Raussas, Gérard. *Le régime des capitulations dans l'empire ottoman*. 2 vols. Paris: Rousseau, 1902–05.

Penz, C., ed. *Journal du consulat-général de France à Maroc, 1767–1785*. Publications de l'Institut des Hautes Etudes Marocaines. Maroc: The Editor, 1943.

Peteani, Luigi. *La questione libica nella diplomazia europea*. Firenze: Carlo Cya, 1939.

Philby, Harry St. John Bridges. *Sa'udi Arabia*. New York: Praeger, 1955.

Phillipson, Coleman, and Buxton, Noel. *The Question of the Bosphorus and Dardanelles*. London: Stevens and Haynes, 1917.

Piccioli, A. "La pace di Ouchy." *Rassegna storica del risorgimento* 22 (1935): 651–83, 826–83.

Pinon, R. "L'Europe et la guerre italo-turque." *Revue des deux mondes* 9 (1912): 599–636.

Piquet, Victor. *La colonisation française dans l'Afrique du Nord*. Paris: Armand Colin, 1912.

Pisani, P. "L'expédition russo-turque aux iles ioniennes en 1798–1799." *Revue d'histoire diplomatique* 2 (1888): 190–222.

Plass, Jens B. *England zwischen Russland und Deutschland: Der Persische Golf in der britischen Vorkriegspolitik, 1899–1907: Dargestellt nach englischen Archivmaterial*. Hamburg: Gesellschaft für Völkerrecht und Auswärtige Politik, 1966.

Platt, Desmond Christopher St. Martin. *Finance, Trade, and Politics in British Foreign Policy, 1815–1914*. London: Oxford University Press, 1968.

Polayan, K. "The Tripolitan War: A Reconsideration of the Causes." *Africa* (Rome) 27 (March 1972): 613–26.

Polk, William R. *The Opening of South Lebanon, 1788–1840: A Study of the Impact of the West on the Middle East*. Cambridge: Harvard University Press, 1963.

Popowski, Josef. *The Rival Powers in Central Asia, or the Struggle between England and Russia in the East*. Translated from the German by Arthur Baring Brabant and edited by Charles E. D. Black. Westminster: Constable, 1893.

Posener, S. *Adolphe Crémieux, 1796–1880*. 2 vols. Paris: Félix, Alcan, 1933–34.

———. *Adolphe Crémieux: A Biography*. Translated from the French by Eugene Golob. Philadelphia: Jewish Publications Society, 1940.

Power, Thomas S., Jr. *Jules Ferry and the Renaissance of French Imperialism*. New York: King's Crown Press, 1944.

Pressel, Wilhelm von. *Les Chemins de fer en Turquie d'Asie*. 2d ed. Zurich: Füssli, 1902.

Priestley, Herbert Ingram. *France Overseas: A Study of Modern Imperialism*. New York: Appleton Century, 1938.

Purchas, Samuel. *His Pilgrimes, or Hakluytus Posthumus*. 20 vols. Glasgow: Maclehose and Sons, 1905–07.

Puryear, Vernon John. *England, Russia and the Straits Question, 1844–1856*. Berkeley: University of California Press, 1931.

———. *France and the Levant*. Berkeley: University of California Press, 1941.

———. *International Economics and Diplomacy in the Near East*. Stanford: Stanford University Press, 1935.

———. *Napoleon and the Dardanelles*. Berkeley: University of California Press, 1951.

Ragey, Louis. *La question du chemin de fer de Bagdad, 1893–1914*. Paris: Rieder, 1933.

Ramazani, Rouhollah K. *The Foreign Policy of Iran, 1500–1941*. Charlottesville: University of Virginia Press, 1938.

Rawlinson, H. F. "The Embassy of William Harborne to Constantinople, 1583–88." *Transactions of the Royal Historical Society* (London), 4th ser. 5 (1922): 1–27.

————. *England and Russia in the East: A Series of Papers on the Political and Geographical Condition of Central Asia.* London: John Murray, 1875.

Raymond, André. "Salisbury and the Tunisian Question, 1878–1800." In *St. Antony's Papers, no. 11: Middle East Affairs, no. 2,* edited by Albert Hourani, pp. 101–38. London: Chatto and Windus, 1961.

————. "Les tentatives anglaises de pénétration économiques en Tunisie, 1856–1877." *Revue historique* 214 (1955): 48–67.

Read, Convers. *Mr. Secretary Walsingham and the Policy of Queen Elizabeth.* 3 vols. Oxford: Clarendon Press, 1925.

Reading, Douglas Kugler. *The Anglo-Russian Commercial Treaty of 1734.* New Haven: Yale University Press, 1938.

Reid, Ruth R. "The Syrian Troubles and Mission, 1860–61." In *The Cambridge History of British Foreign Policy,* edited by Sir A. W. Ward and G. P. Gooch, n.s. 37 (1941): 65–80.

Rheindorf, Kurt. *Die Schwarze-Meer-(Pontus) Frage vom Pariser Frieden von 1856 bis zum Abschluss des Londoner Konferenz von 1871.* Berlin: Deutsche Verlagsgesellschaft für Politik und Geschichte, 1925.

Rivlin, Helen Anne B. "The Railway Question in the Ottoman-Egyptian Crisis of 1850–1852." *Middle East Journal* 15 (1961): 365–88.

Robbins, Robert R. "The Legal Status of Aden Colony and the Aden Protectorate." *American Journal of International Law* 33 (October 1939): 700–15.

Roberts, Edmund. *Embassy to the Eastern Courts of Cochin-China, Siam, and Muscat.* New York: Harper and Brothers, 1837.

Roberts, Lucien E. "Italy and the Egyptian Question, 1878–1882." *Journal of Modern History* 17 (1945): 314–32.

Roberts, Stephen H. *The History of French Colonial Policy, 1870–1925.* 2 vols. London: King, 1929.

Robinson, Gertrude. *David Urquhart.* Oxford: Blackwell, 1920.

Robinson, Ronald, and Gallagher, John, with Denny, Alice. *Africa and the Victorians: The Climax of Imperialism in the Dark Continent.* London: Macmillan, 1961.

Rodkey, Frederick Stanley. "Anglo-Russian Negotiations about a 'Permanent' Quadruple Alliance, 1840–1841." *American Historical Review* 36 (1930–31): 343–49.

————. *The Turco-Egyptian Question in the Relations of England, France, and Russia, 1832–1841.* 2 pts. Urbana: University of Illinois Press, 1924–25.

Ronaldshay, Earl of [Lawrence John Lumley Dundas Zetland). *The Life of Lord Curzon.* 3 vols. London: Benn, 1928.

Ronall, Joachim O. "The Beginnings of Modern Banking in Iran." In *Wissenschaft, Wirtschaft und Technik, Studien zur Geschichte: Wilhelm Treue zum 60. Geburtstag,* edited by Karl-Heinz Manegold. München: F. Bruckmann, 1969.

Rosedale, Honyel Gough, ed. *Queen Elizabeth and the Levant Company.* London: Frowde, 1904.

Ross, Sir E. Denison, ed. *Sir Anthony Sherley and His Persian Adventure, Including Some Contemporary Narratives Relating Thereto.* London: Routledge, 1933.

Ross, Frank E. "The Mission of Joseph Donaldson, Jr., to Algiers, 1795–97." *Journal of Modern History* 7 (December 1935): 422–33.

Rossi, Ettore. *Documenti sull'origine e gli sviluppi della questione araba, 1875–1944.* Rome: Istituto per l'Oriente, 1944.

Rouard de Card, E. *Accords secrets entre la France et l'Italie concernant le Maroc et la Lybie.* Paris: Pedone, 1921.

———. "La frontière franco-marocaine et le protocole du 20 juillet 1901." *Revue générale de droit international publique* 9 (1902): 263–79.

———. *La question marocaine et la négociation franco-espagnole de 1902.* Paris: Pedone, 1912.

———. *Les relations de l'Espagne et du Maroc pendant le XVIIIème et le XIXème siècles.* Paris: Pedone, 1905.

Rouire, Alphonse Marie Ferdinand. *La rivalité anglo-russe au XIXème siècle en Asie.* Paris: Colin, 1908.

Rousseau, *M. F. Kléber et Menou en Egypt depuis le départ de Bonaparte, août 1799–septembre 1801.* Paris: Picard, 1900.

Rowland, Albert Lindsay. *England and Turkey: The Rise of Diplomatic and Commercial Relations.* Studies in English Commerce and Exploration in the Reign of Elizabeth, no. 1. Philadelphia: University of Pennsylvania, 1924.

Rüdiger, Georg von. *Die Bedeutung der Algeciras-Konferenz.* München and Leipzig: Duncker und Humblot, 1920.

Ruete, Rudolph Said. *Said bin Sultan (1791–1856), Ruler of Oman and Zanzibar: His Place in the History of Arabia and East Africa.* London: Alexander Ouseley, 1929.

Ruschenberger, William Samuel Waithman. *Narrative of a Voyage Round the World.* 2 vols. London: Bentley, 1838.

Sabry, Mohammed. *L'empire égyptien sous Ismail, et l'ingérence anglo-française.* Paris: Paul Geuthner, 1933.

———. *L'empire égyptien sous Mohamed-Ali et la question d'Orient, 1811–1849.* Paris: Geuthner, 1930.

———. *La génèse de l'esprit national égyptien, 1863–1882.* Paris: Picart, 1924.

Sadre, M. K. *Relations de l'Iran avec l'Europe de l'antiquité, du moyen-age et la France des origines à la révolution de 1789.* Paris: Editions Internationales, 1938.

Safwat, Muhammad Mustafa. *Tunis and the Great Powers, 1878–1881.* Alexandria: Baganis, 1943.

Saint-Joseph, Antoine de. *Essai historique sur le commerce et la navigation de la Mer Noire.* Paris: Agasse, 1805.

Saint-Priest, Comte de. *Mémoires sur l'ambassade de France en Turquie.* Paris: Leroux, 1877.

Saint-René Taillandier, René Gaspard Ernest. *Les origines du Maroc français.* Paris: Plon, 1930.

Salibi, K. S. *The Modern History of Lebanon.* New York: Praeger, 1965.

Salil ibn Raziq. *The History of the Imâms and Seyyids of 'Omâm.* Translated by George Percy Badger. London: Printed for the Hakluyt Society. 1871.

Sammarco, Angelo. *Précis de l'histoire d'Egypte*, vol. 4, *Les Regnes de 'Abbas, de Sa'id et d'Isma'il, 1848–1879.* Rome: Stampato in Roma nell' Istituto Poligrafico dello Stato per la Reale Societádi Geografia d'Egitto, 1935.

Sanderson, G. N. *England, Europe, and the Upper Nile, 1882–1899*. Edinburgh: Edinburgh University Press, 1965.

Sanger, Richard Harlakenden. *The Arabian Peninsula*. Ithaca: Cornell University Press, 1954.

Schefer, C. *Mémoire historique sur l'ambassade de France à Constantinople par le Marquis de Bonnac*. Paris: Société d'Histoire Diplomatique, 1894.

Schiemann, Theodor. *Geschichte Russlands unter Kaiser Niklaus I.* 4 vols. Berlin: Reimer, 1904–19.

Schlechta-Wssehrd, O. von. "Die Kämpfe zwischen Persien und Russland in Transkaukasien seit 1804–1813." *Sitzungsberichte der Kaiserlichen Akademie der Wissenschaften, Philosophische-Historische Classe* 46 (1864): 4–67.

Schmitt, Bernadotte. "Diplomatic Preliminaries of the Crimean War." *American Historical Review* 25 (1919): 36–67.

Schonfield, Hugh J. *The Suez Canal*. Harmondsworth: Penguin Books, 1939.

Schuman, Frederick L. *War and Diplomacy in the French Republic: An Inquiry into Political Motivations and the Control of Foreign Policy*. New York: Whittlesey House, 1931.

Scott, William Robert. *The Constitution and Finance of English, Scottish and Irish Joint-Stock Companies to 1720*. 3 vols. Cambridge: Cambridge University Press, 1910–12.

Shaler, William. *Sketches of Algiers, Political, Historical, and Civil*. Boston: Cummings, Hilliard, 1826.

Sharabi, Hisham. *Arab Intellectuals and the West: The Formative Years, 1875–1914*. Baltimore and London: Johns Hopkins Press, in cooperation with the Middle East Institute, 1970.

Shaw, Stanford J. *Between Old and New: The Ottoman Empire under Sultan Selim III, 1789–1807*. Cambridge: Harvard University Press, 1971.

Shay, Mary Lucille. *The Ottoman Empire from 1720 to 1734, As Revealed in Despatches of the Venetian Baili*. Urbana: University of Illinois Press, 1944.

Shibeika, Mekki. *British Policy in the Sudan, 1882–1902*. New York: Oxford University Press, 1952.

Shirley, Evelyn Philip. *The Sherley Brothers*. Chiswick: Whittingham, 1848.

Shotwell, James Thomson, and Déak, Francis. *Turkey at the Straits*. New York: Macmillan, 1940.

Shupp, Paul Frederick. *The European Powers and the Near Eastern Question, 1806–1807*. New York: Columbia University Press, 1931.

Shuster, William Morgan. *The Strangling of Persia*. New York: Century, 1912.

Shwadran, Benjamin. *The Middle East, Oil and the Great Powers*. New York: Praeger, 1956.

Siassi, Ali-Akbar. *La Perse au contact de l'Occident*. Paris: Leroux, 1931.

Singhal, D. P. *India and Afghanistan, 1876–1907: A Study in Diplomatic Relations*. Saint Lucia: University of Queensland Press, 1963.

Sitki, B. *Das Bagdad-Bahn Problem, 1890–1903*. Freiburg im Breisgau: Gosdschagg, 1935.

Smelser, Marshall. *The Congress Founds the Navy, 1787–1798*. Notre Dame: University of Notre Dame Press, 1959.

Sokolow, Nahum. *History of Zionism, 1600–1918.* 2 vols. London: Longmans, Green, 1919.

Solmi, Arrigo. *The Making of Modern Italy.* New York: Macmillan, 1925.

Soloveytchik, George. *Potemkin: Soldier, Statesman, Lover and Consort of Catherine of Russia.* New York: Norton, 1947.

Sorel, Albert. *La Question d'Orient aux dix-huitième siècle.* Paris: Plon, 1878. English translation by F. C. Bramwell. *The Eastern Question in the Eighteenth Century: The Partition of Poland and the Treaty of Kainardji.* London: Methuen, 1898.

Sousa, N. *The Capitulatory Regime of Turkey.* Baltimore: Johns Hopkins Press, 1933.

Spagnolo, J. P. "Constitutional Change in Mount Lebanon, 1861–1864." *Middle Eastern Studies* 7 (January 1971): 25–48.

———. "Mount Lebanon, France and Daud Pasha: A Study of Some Aspects of Political Habituation." *International Journal of Middle East Studies* 2 (April 1971): 148–67.

Sprout, Harold and Margaret. *The Rise of American Naval Power, 1776–1918.* Princeton: Princeton University Press, 1946.

Staley, Eugene. "Business and Politics in the Persian Gulf: The Story of the Wönckhaus Firm." *Political Science Quarterly* 48 (September 1933): 367–85.

———. *War and the Private Investor: A Study in the Relations of International Politics and International Private Investment.* Chicago: Univesity of Chicago Press. Garden City: Doubleday, 1935.

Standish, J. F. "British Maritime Policy in the Persian Gulf." *Middle Eastern Studies* 3 (July 1967): 324–54.

———. "The Persian War of 1856–1857." *Middle Eastern Studies* 3 (October 1966): 18–45.

Stuart, Graham H. *The International City of Tangier.* 2d ed. Stanford: Stanford University Press, 1955.

Sumner, B. H. *Peter the Great and the Ottoman Empire.* Oxford: Blackwell, 1949.

———. "Tsardom and Imperialism in the Far East and the Middle East, 1880–1914." *Proceedings of the British Academy* 27 (1941): 25–65.

Swain, James Edgar. "The Occupation of Algiers in 1830: A Study in Anglo-French Diplomacy." *Political Science Quarterly* 48 (1933): 359–66.

———. *Struggle for the Control of the Mediterranean Prior to 1848: A Study in Anglo-French Relations.* Boston: Stratford, 1933.

Sykes, Sir Percey Molesworth. *A History of Afghanistan.* 2 vols. London: Macmillan, 1940.

———. *A History of Persia.* 3d ed. 2 vols. London: Macmillan, 1930.

Tadjbakhche, G. R. *La question des îles Bahrein.* Paris: Pedone, 1960.

Tardieu, André. *La conférence d'Algéciras: Histoire diplomatique de la crise marocaine.* 3d ed. Paris: Alcan, 1909.

———. *France and the Alliances.* New York: Macmillan, 1908.

———. "France et Espagne, 1902–1912." *Revue des deux mondes* 12 (1 December 1912): 633–62.

———. *Le mystère d'Agadir.* Paris: Calmann-Levy, 1912.

Taylor, A. J. P. "British Policy in Morocco, 1886–1902." *English Historical Review* 66 (1951): 342–74.

Taylor, Alan. *Prelude to Israel: An Analysis of Zionist Diplomacy, 1897–1947.* New York: Philosophical Library, 1959.

Temperley, Harold William Vazeille. "Disraeli and Cyprus." *English Historical Review* 46 (1931): 274–79, 457–60.

———. *England and the Near East: The Crimea.* New York: Longmans, Green. Reprint, Hamden, Conn.: Archon Books, 1964.

———. "Stratford de Redcliffe and the Origins of the Crimean War." *English Historical Review* 48 (1933): 601–21; 49 (1934): 265–98.

———. "The Treaty of Paris of 1856 and Its Execution." *The Journal of Modern History* 4 (1932): 387–414, 523–43.

Terent'ev, M. A. *Istoriia zavoevaniia Srednei Azii.* Saint Petersburg: Komarov, 1906.

Terenzio, Pio Carlo. *La rivalité anglo-russe en Perse et en Afghanistan jusqu'aux accords de 1907.* Paris: Rousseaux, 1947.

Terrasse, Henri. *Histoire du Maroc des origines à l'établissement du protectorat français.* 2 vols. Casablanca: Editions Atlantides, 1949–50.

Theobald, A. B. *The Mahdiya.* New York: Longmans, Green, 1951.

Thieury, Jules. *Documents pour servir à l'histoire des relations entre la France et la Perse.* Evreux: Hérissey, 1866.

Thompson, George Carslake. *Public Opinion and Lord Beaconsfield, 1875–1880.* 2 vols. London: Macmillan, 1886.

Thornton, A. P. "British Policy in Persia, 1858–1890." *English Historical Review* 69 (1954): 554–69; 70 (1955): 55–71.

Tignor, Robert L. *Modernization and British Colonial Rule in Egypt, 1882–1914.* Princeton: Princeton University Press, 1966.

Tittoni, Tommaso. *Italy's Foreign and Colonial Policy: A Selection from the Speeches Delivered in the Italian Parliament.* Translated by Bernardo Quaranta di San Severino. New York: Dutton, 1915.

Todd, C. B. *Life and Letters of Joel Barlow.* New York and London: Putnam, 1886.

Toscano, Mario. "Tunis." *Berliner Monatschefte* 17 (February 1939): 119–45.

Touron, Max. *Notre protectorat marocain.* Poitiers: Imprimerie Marc Texier, 1923.

Treue, W. "Russland und die persische Eisenbahnbauern vor dem Weltkriege." *Archiv für Eisenbahnwessen* 62 (1939): 471–94.

Trotter, Lionel James. *The Bayard of India: A Life of General Sir James Outram, Bart.* Edinburgh: Blackwood, 1903.

Trout, Frank E. *Morocco's Saharan Frontiers.* Geneva: Droz, 1969.

Trumpener, Ulrich. *Germany and the Ottoman Empire, 1914–1918.* Princeton: Princeton University Press, 1968.

Turki, Nikula ibn Yusuf al-[Nicholas Turc]. *Chroniques d'Egypte, 1798–1804,* edited and translated by Gaston Wiet. Cairo: n.p., 1950. Earlier translation by A. Cardin, *Journal d'Abderrahman Gabarti pendant l'occupation française en Egypte, suivi d'un précis de la même campagne par Moallem Nicholas El Turki, secrétaire du prince des Druses.* Paris: n.p., 1838.

Übersberger, Hans. *Russlands Orientpolitik in den letzten zwei Jahrhunderten.* Stuttgart: Deutsche Verlagsanstalt, 1913.

Ubicini, Jean Henri. *Letters on Turkey.* Translated from the French by Lady East-hope. 2 vols. London: Murray, 1856.

Usborne, Vice-Admiral C. V. *The Conquest of Morocco.* London: Stanley Paul. 1936.

Vadala, R. *Le Golfe Persique.* Paris: Rousseau, 1920.

Valentijn, François, *Oud en nieuw Oost Indiën.* 5 vols. in 9. Dordrecht and Amster-dam: J. van Braam, 1724–26.

Vandal, Albert. *Une ambassade française en orient sous Louis XV: La mission du marquis de Volleneuve, 1728–1741.* Paris: Plon, 1887.

———. *Napoléon et Alexandre Ier.* 3 vols. Paris: Plon, Nourrit, 1891–96.

Vatikiotis, P. J. *The Modern History of Egypt.* London: Weidenfeld and Nicolson, 1969.

Vaughn, E. V. "English Trading Expeditions in Asia under the authority of the Muscovy Company (1575–1581)." *Studies in the History of English Commerce in the Tudor Period,* pt. 2, pp. 127–214. Philadelphia: University of Pennsylvania Press. New York: Appleton, 1912.

Vidal, Emile. *La politique de l'Espagne au Maroc.* Montpellier: Firmin et Montane, 1913.

Volpe, Gioacchino. *L'impresa di Tripoli, 1911–12.* Rome: Leonardo, 1946.

Waddington, Francis. "Le rôle de la diplomatie française dans la question tuni-sienne." *Revue politique et parlementaire* 159 (April 1934): 92–116.

Walsh, Thomas. *Journal of the Late Campaign in Egypt.* London: Cadell and Davies, 1803.

Wansbrough, J. "The Safe Conduct in Muslim Chancery Practice." *Bulletin of The School of Oriental and African Studies* 34 (1971): 20–35.

———; Inalcik, Halil; Lambton, A.K.S.; and Baer, Gabriel. "Imtiyazat," EI², vol. 3: 1179–95.

Warburg, Gabriel. *The Sudan under Wingate: Administration in the Anglo-Egyptian Sudan, 1899–1916.* London: Cass, 1971.

Ward, Sir A. W., and Gooch, G. P., eds. *The Cambridge History of British Foreign Policy, 1783–1919.* 3 vols. Cambridge: Cambridge University Press, 1922–23.

Watson, Robert Grant. *A History of Persia from the Beginning of the Nineteenth Century to the Year 1858, with a View of the Principal Events that Led to the Estab-lishment of the Kajar Dynasty.* London: Smith, Elder, 1866.

Webster, Sir Charles Kingsley. *The Foreign Policy of Palmerston, 1830–1841: Britain, the Liberal Movement, and the Eastern Question.* 2 vols. London: Bell, 1951.

Wendel, Hugo C. M. "The Protégé System in Morocco." *Journal of Modern History* 2 (1930): 48–60.

Willan, T. S. *The Early History of the Russia Company, 1553–1603.* Manchester: University of Manchester Press, 1956.

Williamson, Francis Torrance. *Germany and Morocco before 1905.* Baltimore: Johns Hopkins Press, 1937.

Wilson, Arnold T. *The Persian Gulf: An Historical Sketch from the Earliest Times to the Beginning of the Twentieth Century.* Oxford: Clarendon Press, 1928. Reprint, London: George Allen and Unwin, 1954.

————. *The Suez Canal: Its Past, Present and Future.* 2d ed. London: Oxford University Press, 1939.

Wilson, Sir Charles Rivers. *Chapters from My Official Life.* London: Arnold, 1916.

Wilson, Sir Robert Thomas. *History of the British Expedition to Egypt.* London: Egerton; Philadelphia: Conrad, 1803.

Winder, Richard Bayly. *Saudi Arabia in the Nineteenth Century.* New York: St. Martin's Press, 1966.

Wolf, John B. *The Diplomatic History of the Bagdad Railroad.* Columbia: University of Missouri, 1936.

Wolff, Sir Henry Drummond. *Rambling Recollections.* 2 vols. London: Macmillan, 1908.

Wood, A. C. "The English Embassy at Constantinople, 1660–1762." *English Historical Review* 40 (1925): 533–61.

————. *A History of the Levant Company.* London: Oxford University Press, 1935.

Woodward, E. L. *Great Britain and the German Navy.* Oxford: Oxford University Press, 1935.

Woolf, Leonard Sidney. *Empire and Commerce in Africa: A Study in Economic Imperialism.* London: Allen and Unwin, 1919.

Wright, L. B., and Macleod, J. H. *The First Americans in North Africa.* Princeton: Princeton University Press, 1945.

Yapp, M. E. *British Policy in Central Asia, 1830–43.* Unpublished thesis, University of London.

Young, George, comp. *Corps de droit ottoman.* 7 vols. Oxford: Clarendon Press, 1905–06.

Zangueneh, Azami. *Le pétrole en Perse.* Paris: Domat-Montchrestien, 1933.

Zeller, Gaston. "Une légende qui a la vie dure: Les capitulations de 1535." *Revue d'histoire moderne et contemporaine* 2 (April-June 1955): 127–32.